Semantics

Semantics

A Reader

EDITED BY
STEVEN DAVIS AND BRENDAN S. GILLON

UNIVERSITY PRESS

2004

OXFORD
UNIVERSITY PRESS

Oxford   New York
Auckland   Bangkok   Buenos Aires   Cape Town   Chennai
Dar es Salaam   Delhi   Hong Kong   Istanbul   Karachi   Kolkata
Kuala Lumpur   Madrid   Melbourne   Mexico City   Mumbai   Nairobi
São Paulo   Shanghai   Taipei   Tokyo   Toronto

Copyright © 2004 by Oxford University Press, Inc.

Published by Oxford University Press, Inc.
198 Madison Avenue, New York, New York, 10016

www.oup.com

Oxford is a registered trademark of Oxford University Press

Library of Congress Cataloging-in-Publication Data
Semantics: a reader / edited by Steven Davis and Brendan S. Gillon.
p.   cm.
Includes bibliographical references and index.
ISBN 0-19-513697-7; 0-19-513698-5 (pbk.)
1. Semantics.   2. Semantics (Philosophy)   I. Davis, Steven, 1937–   II. Gillon, Brendan S.

P325.S3798 2004
401'.43—dc21   2003054940

9 8 7 6 5 4 3 2 1

Printed in the United States of America
on acid-free paper

To Lysiane Gagnon,
with love, SD

To Catherine Jenner,
with love, BSG

ACKNOWLEDGMENTS

There are many who we wish to thank for help with the volume and the introduction, Part I. We thank Robyn Carston, Ray Jennings, Jeff Pelletier, and Daniel Vanderveken, who have original papers in the collection, for their patience. We also thank Philippe Schlenker for his comments and Alan Bale, David Hunter, David Nicholas, Jeff Pelletier, and Rob Stainton for their detailed suggestions about the introduction. Their comments and suggestions helped us greatly improve this part. We are also very grateful to Brian van den Broek for assistance with the preparation of the index and to Michael Dascal for his unflagging aid with all aspects of the final version of the proofs. In addition we thank our editor, Peter Ohlin at Oxford University Press, and our copy editor, Cynthia Garver, for seeing the manuscript through to finished product. Most important, we thank our wives—one a lawyer, the other a journalist—both of whom have deadlines. As the years dragged on and the collection had not been sent to the publisher, we were often asked about whether we had a deadline. We tried to explain to them that academic life was different from other forms of life, a difference we are not sure they understand. And sometimes a form of life that we are not sure we understand ourselves.

CONTENTS

III. Approaches

IV. Topics

CONTRIBUTORS

†Jon Barwise
College Professor of Philosophy, Computer
Science, and Mathematics
Indiana University

Irena Bellert
Emeritus Professor of Linguistics
McGill University

Tyler Burge
Professor of Philosophy
University of California–Los Angeles

Robyn Carston
Reader in Linguistics
University College London

Robin Cooper
Professor of Computational Linguistics
Göteborg University

Max J. Cresswell
Emeritus Professor of Philosophy
Victoria University of Wellington

†Donald Davidson
Professor of Philosophy
University of California–Berkeley

Steven Davis
Professor of Philosophy
Carleton University

†Gareth Evans
Late Wilde Reader in Mental Philosophy
Oxford University

Gilles Fauconnier
Professor of Cognitive Science
University of California–San Diego

Gerald Gazdar
Professor of Computational Linguistics
University of Sussex

Brendan S. Gillon
Associate Professor of Linguistics
McGill University

Jeroen Groenendijk
Professor of Logic, Language and
Computation
University of Amsterdam

James Higginbotham
Professor of Philosophy and Linguistics
University of Southern California

†Deceased

Preliminaries

Some have taken *semantics* to apply to an internalized component of a speaker's linguistic competence in a particular language, as well as to the linguistic theory about this internal semantic competence.[1] Others have taken it to be a theory about the semantic facts of a language without any commitment to its being a theory of semantic competence.[2] Still others have taken it to be a part of a theory that would suffice for understanding a language.[3] There are even some, Wittgenstein (1953) and his followers, who think that it is impossible to have a theory of meaning. They argue that utterances and other things that have meaning vary their meanings from context to context and from user to user: since there is nothing constant across time and users, there is nothing for a theory to be about.[4] Moreover, Wittgenstein and his followers claim that it is impossible to give the meaning for some expressions. If we take necessary and sufficient conditions as our model for specifying the meaning of an expression, no meaning can be given, for example, for *game*, since there is nothing that all games have in common. Consider games of catch, chess, and solitaire. The first has no winners and losers and is a physical activity; the second has winners and losers but is not a physical activity; and the third does not have opposing sides but has a winner. To take another example, it is not clear what shared meaning can be assigned to the adjective *fast* so that it applies to such things as cars, tracks, runners, women, and sushi chefs. These applications are so diverse that it is difficult to see how *fast* could have a common meaning across all of them. These are genuine problems for a theory of meaning. We, however, reject the Wittgensteinian view that it is impossible to have a theory of meaning for natural languages, since a number of different semantic theories have produced interesting results. As we shall see, there are even some that have given what they regard to be an account of the meaning of *game* and *fast*.[5]

Another consideration that counts against Wittgensteinian skepticism is that our understanding of a complex expression generally results from our understanding of the constituent expressions that make it up. There is a difference in our understanding of the following:

1. (a) Dogs are animals.
   (b) Cows are animals.

We understand these two sentences differently; this difference in understanding is clearly to be attributed to the fact that we understand the words *dog* and *cow* differently. They make different contributions to our understanding of the two sentences. We return to this point and its relation to meaning later in this introduction.

1.1   What has meaning?

What then is a theory of meaning about? One way of understanding the question is to take it to be asking for a specification of the objects to which meanings are attributed. There are many things that are said to have meanings—for example, expressions, thoughts, actions, gestures, artifacts,[6] and even natural objects not connected to humans, such as tree rings or clouds. Some have attempted to give a unified theory of meaning that applies to all these objects. At first, the respect in which they have meaning does not seem to be uniform. Take expressions[7] and natural objects. Expressions, but not natural objects, can be analytic, contradictory, logically true, ambiguous, and anomalous, and they can be homonymous or synonymous and stand in logical relations with other expressions.[8] There is no sense in which nonhuman natural objects have any of these properties, properties that many theorists connect with meaning. It would seem, then, that if expressions and such natural objects have meanings, they do not have meanings in the same way. This does not mean that *mean* itself is ambiguous, any more than *wing* is ambiguous when it is applied to bats and birds,[9] even though many of the properties of bat and bird wings are different enough so that there is no unified biological theory of wings that covers both of them. For similar reasons, we think that there is no uniform theory of meaning that applies to expressions and to nonhuman natural objects and the other things that are said to have meaning. Our interest here is primarily in expressions. So, we shall take a theory of meaning, a semantics, to be a theory about expressions.[10]

1.2   What are the meanings that expressions and thoughts have?

Let us return to our question: What is a theory of meaning about? Another way to understand the question is to view it to be about what is attributed to expressions, when they are said to have meanings. One way to attempt to answer the question is to examine what *mean* means.[11] This is not our approach. At best, a theory of meaning based on the meaning of *mean* would be about what English speakers have meant by *mean*. It would be as if we tried to construct a theory of the physical world by appealing to what speakers mean by *solid, motion, energy, particle,* and so on (Chomsky 2000). Another approach is to begin, pretheoretically, with phenomena that we think are connected to meaning, to construct a theory, to explain the phenomena, and to take as meanings what the theory attributes to expressions. Our pretheoretical intuitions about meaning and our interests in constructing such a theory can help guide us in selecting data that such theories are supposed to explain. Such intuitions and interests, therefore, are only a starting point in our theorizing. The same holds for other theoretical activities: we want our physics to tell us why apples fall when we drop them, why the movement of the tides is connected to the moon, why there are eclipses, and so on.

1.3   Semantics, ontology, and the philosophy of language

We now consider a number of ontological issues that are of deep interest but are not central concerns of this volume and thus are not discussed at length here. The first is about the connection between an expression and its meaning. There is no logical or nomological connection between an expression and its meaning. It is compatible with the laws of nature and of logic for any expression to have had a different meaning than the one that it has. *Dog* could have meant the same as *cow* and be true of cows, for example. Indeed, it is a commonplace of historical linguistics that words change their meanings over time.[12] The English noun *bird* once meant any small fowl and now means any warm-blooded, feathered, egg-laying vertebrate animal having wings. Inversely, *fowl* once meant any bird, whereas now it means any of a rather narrow category of gallinaceous birds. So, there is no nomological or logical connection between an expression and its meaning. What then establishes the connection? A number of different theories attempt to account for the connection, but we do not discuss any of them here.[13] We simply assume that there is a connection between expressions and their meanings.

Some theorists, working within a certain conception of naturalism, are reluctant to admit into their ontology semantic entities (like meanings) and semantic relational properties (like meaning, naming, satisfaction, and referring).[14] Some see problems with these semantic entities and relations because they are not part of the physical world and, hence, semantics cannot be integrated into or reconciled with physical theories about the world. The reason for the desire for integration or reconciliation is the assumption of these theorists that the physical world exhausts what there is.[15] One way to quell this worry, it is argued, is to reduce the semantic properties and objects to nonsemantic properties and objects.[16] Reductionism is not an issue that we take up here, however.

Ontological concerns are at the center of some theorists' approaches to semantics. They choose one approach to semantics over another because of their views about the ontological questions raised here. It seems that those who undertake to theorize on the basis of antecedently given ontological concerns have their approach to semantics backward. Theoretical work in physics, mathematics, or biology is not determined antecedently by ontological concerns. One feels free to do mathematics, for example, without having a theory that shows what numbers really are, and to do biology without having a reduction of biological function to nonbiological properties. In general, work in the sciences is not led by ontology. Rather, ontological commitment flows from the existential commitments of the theories. What mathematical and biological objects and properties exist and what their natures are depend on mathematical and biological theories. This does not rule out reduction, but reduction is not from within a first philosophy that has precedence over the sciences and that is epistemologically and ontologically prior to scientific practice. Reduction, if it occurs, is part of scientific theorizing itself. Witness the discovery of the exact molecular structure of genes that showed that they are complex molecules with various chemical properties. It was a scientific discovery within biochemistry. The same considerations should apply to semantics.

Most of the papers in this volume take up various problems about the semantic properties of various types of linguistic expressions. The theories employed are not the same, and we discuss some of the differences in this introduction. The theories all draw on semantic properties and relations without considering the foundational questions about their ontological status. This is not to suggest that no issues falling within the philosophy of language are relevant to semantic theorizing. Questions have been raised about what counts as data for semantic theories and about the explanatory range that such theories should have. For example, some semantic theories draw on a distinction between analytic and synthetic sentences—that is, between a supposed analytic sentence such as *Bachelors are unmarried adult males* and a synthetic sentence such as *It is cold in Montreal in the winter*. If such a distinction exists, we can say that there is a range of facts that should be explained within a semantic theory. Other theorists deny that such a distinction can be drawn that is scientifically tenable. If no distinction can be drawn, we cannot have a semantic theory that presupposes the distinction or an account of the so-called facts.

The most famous attack on the scientific viability of these notions is Quine's (1953b). In addition, some theorists regard certain theoretical locutions that are used in the descriptive apparatus of some semantic theories, such as *means that*, as being scientifically intractable because they yield intensional contexts[17] (Davidson 1984g). For this reason, they opt for purely extensional locutions. We consider both this issue and Quine's worries later in Part I.

1.4   Research proposals and projects

We distinguish between research proposals and research projects in semantics. We take a *research proposal* to be a suggestion about the form of a theory, the explanatory range of the theory, what counts as evidence for a theory, and so on. For example, we can have a research proposal about what a semantic theory should be without its having been applied to a natural language or a fragment[18] of a natural language for which it provides a semantics. In contrast, a *research project* is an already developed theory that has been applied to a language or language fragment, producing results that show the viability of the theory. Viability, of course, is a relative notion; a theory's viability increases as the range of phenomena it explains increases in volume and in kind. So the viability of a semantic theory increases as it is successfully applied to different languages and to a variety of linguistic phenomena that have semantic import—for example, negation, quantified noun phrases, mass nouns, connectors, speech act constructions, propositional attitude reports, and questions. Our interest in this volume is in research projects: that is, in semantic theories that have been applied to linguistic data and have produced results. While research proposals do have theoretical interest and are crucial for the development of the field, they are not the focus of this volume.

There is a vast array of interesting research projects in semantic theory. We could not include them all and had to make a selection. Our criteria for selection are that the theories have produced a range of interesting results, that the theories are laid out precisely so that they can be evaluated, and that it is clear what counts as evidence for and against the theories.[19] For this reason, many of the chapters in this volume are drawn from formal semantics, but these are not the only kinds of theories that are represented here. We have also included work in lexical semantics and in relevance theory, two approaches to meaning that have produced interesting results. Even given our criteria for selection, we had to make choices among theories that meet them. Our choices here were dictated by trying to choose those theories that we thought representative of a particular theoretical approach to meaning and semantics.

To prepare readers for the selection of articles gathered in this volume, we provide a rather extensive introduction to the study of semantics. Semantics is one of the four central subdisciplines of linguistics, the other three being syntax, morphology, and phonology. Thus a proper perspective on semantics requires that one understand how it is situated in the larger discipline of which it is a part. In addition, linguistics itself is viewed by most working linguists as constituting part of the study of the human mind and, hence, as part of psychology. Thus, in Chapter 2, we present the field of linguistics and the location of semantics within it as it relates to psychology. This discussion is taken up again in Chapter 5.

Linguistics of the past fifty years also has been shaped by developments in logic. This is true not only of syntax but even more so of semantics. Indeed, no understanding of contemporary semantics is possible without some basic understanding of logic, in particular, recursion theory and model theory. Chapter 3 of our introduction gives the necessary background so that readers will have a basic appreciation of the field and will be in a better position to understand the articles collected in the volume. Since all formal fields of study today use the basic mathematics of set theory, we have incorporated Chapter 8 to explain all the set theoretic notions used in Part I. Almost all of the set theory required is covered in modern high school mathematical curricula.

Nonetheless, we thought it would be useful to have this material readily available for those who would like to make a quick review of the subject. The mathematically inexperienced reader should read through it once and then consult it again as the need arises.

After having discussed the basic concepts of semantic theory, we turn to a presentation of the various conceptions of meaning held by various theorists. We discuss some of the wide range of theories that fall under semantics in Chapter 4, dividing semantic theories into *theories of reference, theories of meaning*, and *mixed theories*. Under theories of reference we have placed Donald Davidson's satisfaction theory (section 4.1). In the section on theories of meaning, (4.2) we discuss what we call *atomic meaning theories* (section 4.2.1), a representative of which is Jerry Fodor's views about semantics. We then take up *molecular meaning theories* (section 4.2.2), which come in two forms: *analytic meaning theories* (section 4.2.2.1) and *encyclopedic meaning theories* (section 4.2.2.2). The former is represented by James Pustejovsky's *lexical semantics* and the latter by Ray Jackendoff's *conceptual semantics*, both of which we take up in section 4.4. In section 4.3 we turn to two-tiered semantic theories that are a combination of reference and meaning theories. In this section we consider Frege's semantic theory (section 4.3.1), and Kaplan's theory of character and content (section 4.3.2).

In addition to the categorization of semantic theories into theories of reference, theories of meaning, and mixed theories, theories can be characterized by their relation with the mind and the world. Those theories that are purely mental with no commitment to anything external to the mind we call *internalist theories*, and those theories that think that a word-world relationship is fundamental to semantics we call *externalist theories*. We take up the distinction between internalist and externalist semantic theories in Chapter 5, and we arrange the theories that we have discussed in Chapter 4 with respect to this distinction. Finally, in Chapter 6 we discuss the relationship between semantics and context. Chapter 7 provides a conclusion to Part I.

Notes

For background readings, we suggest John Lyons's *Linguistic Semantics* and Robert Stainton's *Philosophical Perspectives on Language*; for supplemental readings, Emmon Bach's *Informal Lectures on Formal Semantics*, James D. McCawley's *Everything That Linguists Have Always Wanted to Know about Logic but Were Ashamed to Ask*, and L. T. F. Gamut's *Logic, Language and Meaning*

1. See Chomsky (1965, 1976a, 1993, and 2000) and his followers.
2. Katz (1981) holds this view.
3. Davidson (1967: this volume, Chapter 12) has been associated with this view.
4. See Travis (1986).
5. Although we reject the Wittgensteinian view, we have included Ray Jennings's essay (this volume, Chapter 33), which shows that it is not a simple matter to give an account of the meanings of natural language connectives.
6. *Artifact* here includes works of art.
7. We include within "expressions" the signs of the deaf and conventional actions that express thoughts, such as hand gestures like a thumbs up.
8. It is a contentious issue that expressions have any of these properties.
9. Many philosophers, beginning with Paul Grice (1957), think that *mean* is ambiguous and applies to natural objects in one sense and to expressions in another. But see Horwich (1998) and Davis (1994) for problems with Grice's arguments about *mean*.
10. In what follows we distinguish various concepts that fall within semantics: meaning and reference (Chapter 4) and character and content (section 4.3.2).
11. See the work of Horwich (1998), Grice (1957), and Schiffer (1972) for this approach.
12. Chomsky (2000) would reject the possibility that a lexical item could change its meaning over time, since he identifies a lexical item with sets of phonetic and semantic features. Hence, a change in a semantic feature brings about a change in lexical item.

13. Among the theories that give an account of the relation between an expression and its meaning are use, conventionalist, informational, and teleological theories. For a use theory, see Horwich (1998); for a conventionalist theory, see Lewis (1969); for a teleological theory, see Millikan (1984); and for information theories, see Fodor (1987) and Dretske (1981).

14. See Field (1977) for a discussion of the physicalist reduction of truth and satisfaction in Tarski's (1944, 1956) theory of truth; see Chomsky (2000) for a criticism of reductionist conceptions of naturalism.

15. In effect, these theorists identify naturalism with physicalism. In addition, they have a certain view about what constitutes the physical universe. See Chomsky (2000) for a discussion of this view of physicalism.

16. The teleological and informational theorists in note 13 are concerned with this issue. Also, see Grice (1957), who can be interpreted as attempting to reduce semantic properties to psychological properties. For a further discussion of these issues, see McDowell (1998), especially on the relationship between Grice's communication intention theory of meaning and satisfaction theories of meaning.

17. A sentential context is intensional just in case there are grammatical expressions, terms, in the sentence for which coreferential expressions cannot be substituted *salva veritate*. For example, *the president of France* cannot be substituted for the second occurrence of *Jacques Chirac* in *It is necessary that Jacques Chirac is Jacques Chirac* and preserve the truth value of the sentence, since it is false that it is necessary that Jacques Chirac is the president of France. After all, someone other than Jacques Chirac could have won the election. An extensional context allows for such substitution.

18. *Fragment* is a technical notion for a part of language—relative clause constructions, for example—for which a theorist has given an account.

19. The requirement that theories be precise does not mean that they have to be formal theories. As well, preciseness of theory formulation does not exclude the possibility of accounting for the meanings of expressions that are not precise.

2

Linguistics and Psychology

The link between the study of language and psychology goes back to the beginning of modern psychology, when Wilhelm Wundt (1904) established psychology as an empirical science, independent of philosophy. It was the American linguist Leonard Bloomfield (1933) who first viewed the study of language, or linguistics as it had come to be known, as a special branch of psychology. The dominant view of psychology at the beginning of the twentieth century was behaviorism, whose central tenet is that only theoretical entities that can be directly observed may be admitted into theories about human behavior. Behaviorists took as the basic notions of their theories stimuli that impinge on the sensory organs of a subject, the subject's behavioral response to these stimuli, and schedules of reinforcement that induce in the subject tendencies or habits to respond in certain ways when confronted with specific stimuli. Most notably, behaviorists eschewed any appeal to internal states of organisms to explain behavior, including such things as beliefs, hopes, desires, capacities, and abilities. It might be thought that the behaviorist's appeal to habits is an appeal to internal states. But the behaviorist's tendencies or habits are not to be understood as internal states; they are merely the systematic matching of stimuli and responses that the organism exhibits. Thus, a particular organism's (o) tendency to respond (r) given a stimulus (s) is to be understood in terms of a conditional: if o were stimulated by stimuli of type s, then it would respond with behavior of type r. No appeal is made to internal states. Bloomfield (1933, ch. 2), adopting this approach and applying it to language, attempted to make linguistics fit the mold of this view of psychology.[1]

Many theorists studying language today still regard linguistics as a special domain within psychology, although their view about what kind of psychology is appropriate to linguistics is very different from that of Bloomfield. Currently, the fundamental idea for many theorists, including linguists, is to ascribe to organisms that behave in characteristic ways a capacity for such behavior. Thus, for example, it is characteristic of cats to hunt rodents and birds, of salmon to swim up river to spawn eggs, and of birds to build nests. It is clear that something about these animals enables them to behave in these ways. One might call this a capacity, which clearly differs across types of organisms. When mature, many organisms behave in ways in which they are not able to behave at birth. In such cases, it is natural to ask how such an organism comes to behave in the way it does. That is, how does the organism come to have its capacity for such behavior?

There are only two dimensions along which to search for pertinent facts: experience and innate endowment. It is clear that knowing the facts along either dimension alone is not sufficient for answering this question. Experience by itself is not sufficient, for an organism that is not disposed to develop a capacity can never develop it. Cats do not instinctively build nests; birds do not swim up stream to spawn eggs. Also, innate endowment by itself is not sufficient, for *ex hypothesi* the organism at inception cannot exercise the capacity. So, the question is, what balance is required between innate endowment and experience to bring about the organism's ability to exercise the capacity that it eventually acquires? To find an answer, two of three parameters must be fixed. Therefore, in order to ascertain what the innate endowment is, one has to fix what the capacity is which the organism comes to exercise and what kind of experience is pertinent to that capacity. If one pursues this line of inquiry, one might try to construct a device to simulate this process, which one might picture as follows:

EXPERIENCE ⇒ | INNATE ENDOWMENT | ⇒ CAPACITY

Here, experimental work done by Blakemore and Cooper (1970)[2] is illustrative. Mature cats have the capacity to detect horizontal and vertical lines. This is not a capacity they have at birth, for the visual capacity of cats, like that of many other kinds of mammals born with their eyes closed, develops gradually, with the most active point for kittens at about five weeks after birth. Now Blakemore and Cooper undertook the following: Newly born kittens were segregated into two groups. One group was placed in an environment set up in such a way that the kittens saw only vertical lines, while the other group was placed in an environment set up in such a way that they saw only horizontal lines. After some time, neurophysiologic recordings from their brains showed that the kittens raised in an environment with only vertical stripes possessed only vertically tuned striate neurons, while those raised in an environment with only horizontal stripes possessed only horizontally tuned striate neurons.[3] Kittens, then, pass through a period of exposure to vertical and horizontal stripes that permit them to come to be able to detect such stripes. Clearly, kittens have an innate endowment which, when properly stimulated, enables them to acquire a capacity to detect vertical and horizontal stripes.

Humans are incapable of linguistic behavior at birth, but their ability to speak a language is obviously a capacity they acquire. It is natural to conceive of this transformation in the following way:

EXPERIENCE ⇒ | INNATE ENDOWMENT | ⇒ LINGUISTIC CAPACITY

This picture suggests two immediate steps: to specify the nature of the relevant experience and to specify the nature of the capacity.

2.1 Grammatical competence

A little reflection on human linguistic capacity—the human capacity to use and understand language—suggests that it itself is composed of several subcapacities, including the capacity to remember, the capacity to form beliefs, and the capacity to focus attention on objects, among many others. Perhaps most important here is the capacity to form and recognize grammatical sentences.[4] A component of this capacity is information that speakers have that enables them to form and recognize grammatical sentences, information that is standardly divided into several sorts: phonological, morphological, syntactic, and semantic. This information, which Chomsky now calls the *I-language*, we shall call a speaker's *I-grammar*, or *grammar* for short. The internalized grammar then can be thought of as having three components: a phonology, a syntax, and a semantic. This grammar is part of a speaker's grammatical capacity. This capacity and the other capacities pertinent to speakers' using and understanding language constitute their linguistic capacity.[5] Of course, a grammar is not something that can be directly observed. Rather, it is manifested through the expressions of the language.[6] Thus, the first step in characterizing a grammar is to characterize the expressions of the language.

One of the early insights into the nature of language is that a language cannot be learned expression by expression, for there seems to be no upper bound to the number of expressions a language has. To learn a language, one must learn a (finite) set of rules, as noted by the great Sanskrit grammarian Patañjali (third century BC) in his commentary on Pāṇini's *Aṣṭādhyāyi* (fourth century BC), the earliest extant grammar of Sanskrit and, indeed, the earliest extant grammar of any language. A further insight, embodied in Pāṇini's grammar, is that linguistic expressions are complex: that they can be analyzed in terms of a finite number of basic expressions and that the rules of a grammar show how to construct complex expressions from less complex ones. Pāṇini's grammar also shows insight into the nature of the structure whereby complex expressions are built out of basic ones or other complex ones. The resulting complex expressions embody two structural properties: precedence and constituency.[7]

To see what these properties are, consider the following sentence:

1. The man saw the boy with the telescope.

When such a sentence is uttered, the speaker's mouth changes from configuration to configuration, thereby creating an acoustic signal. This sequence of changes imposes a linear order on the basic sounds, or phones. Linguists call this order *precedence*. This utterance also embodies another order, which linguists call *constituency*. This order is manifested when one considers the sentence in 1 in light of circumstances in which there is a man and a boy, the former sees the latter with the unaided eye, and the latter is carrying a telescope. With respect to these circumstances, the utterance in 1 may be judged alternately true and false. This alternation of judgment correlates with two distinct groupings of the elements in 1: one in which the prepositional phrase (PP) is taken as a modifier of *the boy*—as shown by the brackets in 2(a)—and one in which the prepositional phrase is taken as a modifier of *saw*—as shown by the brackets in 3(a).

2. (a) The man saw [the boy [$_{PP}$ with a telescope]].
    (b) The boy with a telescope was seen by the man.
3. (a) The man saw [the boy] [$_{PP}$ with a telescope].
    (b) The boy was seen through a telescope by a man.

One of the basic features of constituency is that a constituent of a certain type can have as a constituent another constituent of the same type. Thus, for example, a prepositional phrase may contain another prepositional phrase that, in turn, contains still another prepositional phrase:

4. (a) A man sat [$_{PP}$ in the first chair].
    (b) A man sat [$_{PP}$ in the first chair [$_{PP}$ behind the first chair]].
    (c) A man sat [$_{PP}$ in the first chair [$_{PP}$ behind the first chair [$_{PP}$ behind the first chair]]].
       etc.

Indeed, it is easy to show that many kinds of constituents in English, besides prepositional phrases, have this property. Coordinated independent clauses do, for example. Consider the English connector *and*. It can be put between two independent clauses—say the two in 5(a) and 5(b)—to form an independent, compound clause—the one is 5(c)—which itself can be joined to either of the initial clauses to form still another independent compound clause—the one in 5(d). The same thing can be done with the connector *or*.

5. (a) It is raining.
    (b) It is snowing.
    (c) It is raining and it is snowing.
    (d) It is raining and it is snowing and it is raining.
         etc.

Relative clauses furnish still another constituent having this property:

6. (a) Bill saw a man.
    (b) Bill saw a man who saw a man.
    (c) Bill saw a man who saw a man who saw a man.
    (d) Bill saw a man who saw a man who saw a man who saw a man.
         etc.

Indeed, this property, whereby a constituent of a certain type can contain as a constituent another of the same type, seems to be a property of every known human language. And it is by dint of this property, which mathematicians call *recursion*, that each human language comprises an infinite number of expressions. Put another way, the infinite set of expressions of a language can be obtained, or *generated*, by applying a finite set of recursive rules to a finite set of basic expressions, or minimal elements.[8] These rules and other rules are said to comprise the language's grammar and are thereby said to characterize the corresponding grammatical competence.

2.2   Autonomy

Just as the exercise of a speaker's linguistic capacity is thought to result from the exercise of several capacities together, including grammatical capacity, so the exercise of grammatical capacity is thought to comprise the utilization of the speaker's grammatical competence, his grammar, that involves the joint utilization of the phonological, morphological, syntactic, and semantic information that are components of the grammar. Moreover, while all these components are related, they are nonetheless distinguishable and not reducible one to the other. Another way this last point is made is to say that these components are autonomous from one another:

$$\boxed{\text{Phonology}} \Leftarrow \boxed{\begin{array}{c}\text{Syntax}\\ + \\ \text{Morphology}\end{array}} \Rightarrow \boxed{\text{Semantics}}$$

To understand better what is meant by autonomy, let us consider how various facts are explained. To begin, consider the expressions in 7:

7. (a) *Butted to when in did sorry he town.
    (b) *Bill called up me.

The unacceptability of these expressions is explained not by the rules of English phonology but by the rules of English syntax. The first fails to have any syntactic structure, while the second violates the English syntactic rule whereby a particle forming a unit with a verb must follow a pronoun that is the unit's direct object.

Similarly, the unacceptability of the next pair of expressions is explained, in the first case, by the rule of English that the noun of the subject noun phrase and the verb of the verb phrase agree in grammatical number and, in the second case, by the fact that the noun *mouse* is an exception to the rule of plural formation:

8. (a) *The boys is here.
   (b) *The mouses have escaped.

Notice that the sentences in 8 are interpretable. If uttered by either an adult for whom English is not a native language or a child, 8(a) would be interpreted as saying the same thing as either *The boys are here* or *The boy is here*. Sentence 8(b) would be interpreted as saying the same thing as *The mice have escaped*. Consequently, no linguist would suggest that such sentences are unacceptable for semantic reasons.

Consider finally another set of unacceptable expressions. They do not violate any recognized rules of English phonology or morphology. Moreover, each corresponds in syntactic structure to perfectly acceptable English sentences:

9. (a) *Sincerity admires Bill.
   (b) Mary admires Bill.
10. (a) *Quadruplicity drinks procrastination.
    (b) A cow drinks water.
11. (a) *Fred harvested a magnetic puff of amnesia. (Cruse 1986, 2)
    (b) Fred harvested a large bale of hay.

Such expressions, if interpretable at all, are interpretable only by reconstruing the meaning of one or another of their words. Such sentences are explained as unacceptable not for reasons of phonology, morphology, or syntax but for reasons of semantics—that is, because of a failure of the meanings of various expressions to cohere. Thus, we see how expressions, all judged to be unacceptable, have their unacceptability explained by different theoretical resources: some are explained by phonological rules, some by morphological rules, others by syntactic rules, and still others by semantic rules. Thus, phonology, syntax, morphology, and semantics are taken to be autonomous, though related, components of a grammar.

It is important to note that the mutual autonomy of these various components is not drawn into question by the fact that they may have overlapping domains of application. Here is one elementary example of how morphology and syntax on the one hand and phonology on the other can have overlapping domains of application. In French, the choice of the form of a word may be determined in some cases by purely morphosyntactic considerations and in other cases by phonological considerations:

12. (a) Son logement est beau.
        His dwelling is beautiful.
    (b) Sa demeure est belle.
        His dwelling is beautiful.
13. (a) Sa femme est belle.
        His wife is beautiful.
    (b) Son épouse est belle.
        His wife is beautiful.

In 12, the choice between the possessive adjectives *sa* and *son* is determined by the gender of the noun that follows: *logement* is masculine, so the form of the possessive adjective is the masculine form *son*, whereas since *demeure* is feminine, it receives the feminine possessive adjective *sa*. In 13(b), however, even though *épouse* is feminine, the appropriate form of the possessive adjective is the masculine form *son*, which is required by the fact that the immediately following word begins with a vowel.[9]

Not only have linguists held that the various components of grammar are autonomous with respect to one another, they have also held that grammatical competence and world knowledge are also autonomous from one another. Thus, the unacceptability of the next pair of sentences is ascribed to different sources: the first to a violation of a grammatical rule of syntax, the second to a conflict with our beliefs about the world.

14. (a) *I called up him.
     (b) *The man surrounded the town.
15. (a) *Sincerity admires Bill.
     (b) *Quadruplicity drinks procrastination.

Expressions such as those in 15, which seem to be in every respect like declarative sentences and yet seem to make no sense, are sometimes said to be *semantically anomalous* expressions. They are said to be anomalous, instead of false, since they do not seem to be expressions that are easily judged as true or false.[10] These contrast with the sentences in 16, which are inexorably judged false:

16. (a) I dislike everything I like. (Leech 1974, 6)
     (b) My uncle always sleeps awake. (Leech 1974, 7)
     (c) Achilles killed Hector, but Hector did not die.

Corresponding to sentences that are inexorably judged false are those that are inexorably judged true:

17. (a) I like everything I like.
     (b) My brother always sleeps asleep.
     (c) If Achilles killed Hector, then Hector died.

The inexorability of such judgments is thought to arise, not from a speaker's knowledge of the world, but from his knowledge of English. This inexorability contrasts with the lack of inexorable falsity of either of the sentences in 18, which we normally judge false because of our knowledge about the world:

18. (a) Some man is immortal.
     (b) My uncle always sleeps standing on one toe. (Leech 1974, 7)

After all, the truth of these sentences is conceivable, as is the falsity of the next two sentences:

19. (a) All men are mortal.
     (b) No cat is a robot.

However, it is not always clear whether a given sentence is inexorably true or inexorably false. Consider the sentence:

20. This man is pregnant.

Is this sentence necessarily false? And if so, is it necessarily false because of the meanings of the words in it? As Lyons puts it (1995, 122), it is not inconceivable that biotechnology will some day permit a fetus-bearing womb to be implanted in a man who can later deliver a child by cesarean section.

We can conclude, then, that some sentences are true, no matter what, by dint of the grammar of English, and others are false, no matter what, by dint of the grammar of English. Still other sentences are either true or false, depending on what the world is like. However, as we shall see later, distinguishing among these various classes of sentences is not always easy; indeed, some think that the distinction is impossible to draw (Quine 1953b).

2.3   Language faculty

In the preceding section, we set out the notion of a grammatical capacity that has a grammar as a constituent. This capacity, together with a number of other capacities, comprises linguistic competence. We now turn to that aspect of the innate human endowment by which humans come to have a grammar. As we noted earlier, the expressions of human languages are recursively generated, as a result of which the unbounded set of expressions are obtained from a finite subset of them. No other species has a set of signals that are recursively generated. Since these expressions arise from our grammatical competence, this competence and the innate endowment whereby we acquire it are also unique to humans.

Now, one capacity that humans have to a higher degree than any other species is the capacity to reason. It might be thought, then, that our grammars result from our general ability to reason. This is certainly an implicit commonsense view about language. However, it has been argued that this is not the case and that human grammars arise from a peculiar part of human innate endowment. Chomsky (1965) was the first modern theorist to propose the hypothesis of an innate language endowment unique to humans that enables the acquisition of a grammar. He has variously called this endowment, *language-acquisition device, universal grammar,* and *language faculty.* We might schematize its role in the following way:

EXPERIENCE ⇒ | LANGUAGE FACULTY | ⇒ GRAMMAR

Chomsky's argument to support this hypothesis is the so-called poverty of the stimulus argument.[11] The argument is based on a number of observations, which, when taken together, furnish presumptive evidence in favor of the hypothesis that humans have an innate predisposition to acquire grammars.

First, the structure of a language over which a child gains mastery is both complex and abstract from its acoustic signal. In particular, Chomsky has pointed out that, while precedence is manifest in the acoustic signal, constituency is not. Thus, the acoustic signal that gives rise to the expression in 1, *The man saw the boy with the telescope,* provides no information about the different constituent structures that the expression has. The very same acoustic signal can be understood as in 2(a), *The man saw [the boy [PP with a telescope]],* or as in 2(b), *The man saw [the boy] [PP with a telescope],* a difference that cannot be traced to the acoustic signal.

Second, in a short span of time children acquire a grammatical competence that enables them to produce and understand sentences, even though the structure of linguistic expressions to which they are exposed is both abstract from its acoustic signal and complex.

Third, this competence is acquired despite children having little exposure to signals carrying examples of the relevant structure, and despite the fact that many of the utterances exhibit these structures in a defective way—being interrupted or otherwise unfinished sentences.

Fourth, in spite of important differences in the sample of utterances to which children of the same linguistic community are exposed, they nonetheless converge on similar grammars.

Fifth, the rules that are characteristic of grammatical competence are not taught. Consider, for example, an anglophone child's mastery of the rule for plural noun formation in English. At most, anglophone children are taught in school that the letter -s is added to a noun (with the exception of such words as *man, foot,* etc.). But this is not the rule that they learn when they learn to speak English, for the simple reason that it is not the rule of English plural formation. The rule is, in fact, more complex. And no adult, native English speaker can state the rule, unless he has been linguistically trained. To be sure, there is a suffix. But, it is pronounced differently, depending on the sound immediately preceding it. Thus, the plural suffix, when attached to the word *cat*, yields one sound, namely /s/; when attached to the word *dog*, it yields another, namely /z/; and when attached to the word *bush*, it yields still another, namely, /iz/. Children discern and master the difference without instruction. Another example of anglophone speakers mastering an aspect of English without any instruction is illustrated in the following pair of sentences:

21. (a) John promised Mary to leave.
     (b) John persuaded Mary to leave.

Every native speaker of English knows that the agent of the leaving expressed in the sentence in 21(a) is the agent of the promising (that is, the person denoted by the subject of the main verb), whereas the agent of the leaving expressed in the sentence in 21(b) is the patient of the persuading (that is, the person denoted by the direct object). It cannot be due to any explicit instruction, for dictionary entries for the relevant verbs do not provide that kind of information about the verbs. And it cannot be due to left to right order of the words, for the two sentences differ from one another only in the choice of verb. Similarly, every native speaker of English knows when the third-person personal pronoun *it* can be used, as illustrated in 22–24, yet no speaker can state the rule governing its distribution:

22. (a) John threw out *the magazine* without reading *it*.
     (b) *John threw out *the magazine* without reading.
23. (a) *Which magazine* did John throw out without reading.
     (b) **Which magazine* did John throw out without reading *it*.
24. (a) I never saw *the magazine which* John threw out without reading.
     (b) *I never saw *the magazine which* John threw out without reading *it*.

Sixth, it is generally acknowledged that children's acquisition of their grammatical competence is independent of their intelligence, motivation, and emotional make-up.

Seventh, it is believed that no child is predisposed to learn one language rather than another. A child born to unilingual Korean speakers, if raised from birth by unilingual French speakers, will learn French as easily as a child learning French born to unilingual French speakers. And a child born to unilingual French speakers, if raised from birth by unilingual Korean speakers, will learn Korean as easily as a child learning Korean born to unilingual Korean speakers.

These seven observations give rise to the following limits on any hypothesis about the language-acquisition device. It cannot be so rich so as to predispose a child to acquire competence in the grammar of one language over that of another, for, as noted, no child is more disposed to learn one language rather than another. At the same time, the innate endowment cannot be so poor as to fail to account for a child's rapid acquisition of grammatical competence, in light of the abstract yet uniform nature of the competence, the quality of his exposure, the poverty of his exposure, and the independence of his acquisition from his intelligence, motivation, and emotional make-up (Chomsky 1967). In short, this innate endowment cannot be so rich as to preclude the acquisition of some attested language, but it must be rich enough to ensure that one can acquire any attested language within the limits of time, data, and access to data (Chomsky 1967).

This argument, though widely accepted by linguists, was greeted with skepticism by empirically minded philosophers such as Hilary Putnam (1967), who, disputing some of the observations just presented, argued for the conclusion that human linguistic competence is the result of the general human ability to learn. More recently, connectionists have presented computational models suggesting that it is indeed possible to abstract constituency structure from the acoustic signal (Elman et al. 1996). As stressed by Fodor (1981), the debate is not about whether there is an innate endowment to account for language learning—this no one disputes; rather, the debate is about the nature of the innate endowment, in particular, about whether the necessary innate endowment is specific to language learning or is an application of more general abilities to language.

The argument from the poverty of the stimulus is not the only basis used to support the hypothesis of a language-acquisition device. Another source of evidence adduced is the claim that human language acquisition passes through a critical period. In particular, investigators have tried to determine whether humans pass through a critical period in the acquisition of language similar to the critical period other mammals pass through in the acquisition of their capacities, as illustrated earlier in this discussion in the case of cats acquiring the capacity to see horizontal and vertical stripes. Specifically, one might wonder whether infants deprived of exposure to language during their childhood would ever fail to be natural speakers of a natural language. Of course, the experiment obviously required to test this hypothesis would never be carried out for evident moral reasons. It has been claimed, however, that such deprived children have been found. One case was that of a so-called wolf-child found in France in the nineteenth century in the wild, unable to speak, and reported never to have acquired a command of French despite rigorous training (Lane 1977). More recently, in Los Angeles, a young girl named Genie was discovered, who had been locked up in a room by herself from infancy; she also never became fully competent in English (Curtiss 1989).[12]

2.4   Mentalism theories of language: Internalism and externalism

Behaviorists, such as Skinner (1957), wished to study human behavior without positing any internal states to account for it. Accordingly, the only legitimate terms of analysis for the behaviorist are those referring to external stimulus, behavioral response, and schedules of reinforcement of the behavioral responses. This approach, which yielded no interesting results in the study of human language, was abandoned by the end of the 1950s. Since then, many researchers interested in language have replaced behaviorist with mentalist theories. Since mentalism is now the dominant view of the ontology of theories about grammatical competence, this is the approach that we take in the introduction to this volume.[13]

A mentalist theory about language is committed to the view that speakers' grammars are internally represented. Mentalist theories can be subdivided into two kinds: internalist and externalist. Externalist theories hold that theories of language must account for the relations between expressions and objects that are external to a subject. An example of such a theory is referential semantics in which the meaning of certain expressions—*water*, for example—is associated with a kind, in this case, water. We shall return to this. Internalist theories can be characterized as those that make no reference to anything external to individual subjects.[14] That is, internalism assumes what Putnam (1996) has dubbed "the principle of methodological solipsism": "This assumption is the assumption that no psychological state, properly so called, presupposes the existence of any individual[15] other than the subject to whom the state is ascribed" (Putnam 1996, 7).[16] This has consequences for our understanding of the nature of language. On this view, there is no language that is common to different speakers (Chomsky 1993, 18–19; 2000, 48–49). Each speaker has his own language that is identical to his internalized grammar, the grammar represented in his mind. A language is not to be identified with a set of "generated objects"— that is, well-formed expressions—but with the internalized grammar (Chomsky 2000, 73). The reason that language cannot be identified with a generated set, as we have seen, is that a grammar is able to generate an infinite set of strings that cannot be "in" a finite mind. Hence, if languages were such a generated set, they could not be internal. Let us call a speaker's internalized language, with Chomsky, a speaker's *I-language*, where "I" stands for internal, individual, and intensional (Chomsky 2000, 78).[17] On this view, a speaker's language, his I-language, is identified with his internalized grammar, his I-grammar.

Grammar has a dual role. It can be used for a speaker's I-grammar but also for a linguist's theory about an I-grammar.[18] We can say that for a theory of grammar to be mentalist it must be committed to there being for each speaker an internal mental representation of his grammar. For a theory to be internalist, it must hold that no relation between a speaker's grammatical states and anything external to these states plays a role in an account of a speaker's grammatical competence. For it to be an externalist theory, it must make the same commitment to mentalism but, within the range of the theory, must include relations between elements of the speaker's I-grammar and objects external to these elements. The difference between internalist and externalist theories comes out most vividly in the semantic component of grammars, something that we shall discuss later in this introduction.

We have taken a speaker's I-grammar, his internal grammar, to be an element of his grammatical competence. *Competence* is a bit misleading, since it can be taken to mean *ability* and, thus, grammatical competence might be thought to be similar to other sorts of abilities: the ability to ride a bicycle, to drive a car, or to catch a baseball. There is a double error here. First, on the assumption that grammatical competence is a capacity, it would be a mistake to assimilate it to these sorts of capacities. Rather, it has more in common with "intellectual abilities"—say, the ability to do mathematics or play chess. Second, these capacities can be viewed as having two components: knowing the subject matter (of mathematics, for example) and the content of the knowledge (that is, the mathematics itself). A speaker's grammatical competence is similar to knowing mathematics, and his grammar is similar to the mathematics that someone competent in mathematics knows. There is a difference, however, between the mathematics known and an internalized grammar. One's mathematical knowledge is either conscious or can be brought to consciousness, but our internalized grammar cannot be made conscious in the way in which our mathematical knowledge can be made conscious.[19] Thus, a speaker's grammatical competence is not merely knowing how to do something.[20] Rather, it involves structured linguistic information, mentally represented, that a speaker or hearer brings to bear in particular situations in understanding and using his language. A theory of grammar describes a speaker's internalized grammar—his information about his language—but does not say anything about how a speaker uses this linguistic information in speaking and understanding. The latter sort of theory is a theory of performance, a theory that accounts for the on-line processing of a speaker's language in speaking and understanding.

Chomsky's I-linguistics, because it is individualist, forces us to recast language learning, since, strictly speaking, there is no common language across a set of speakers for a child to learn. The way to think about language learning for an individual speaker, S, then, is to see it as successive changes in the structure of S's faculty of language (FL). S is born with a language faculty[21] and is then exposed to the utterances[22] of other speakers that are in part a product of their I-languages. In light of what S hears, there are changes in S's FL from the initial innate stage to subsequent stages. Since the changes happen over time, we can think of S's FL going through a series of state changes that, at one point in S's development, reach a steady state so that no further major changes occur. There can be changes in S's FL throughout his life, when for instance, a new item is added to his lexicon or his accent changes, but these changes are minor. Once all the major changes have occurred, we can say that the child has learned "a language." We can think of each person who has learned a language as having acquired an I-language where this is to be understood as his FL having moved from the initial state to a state of equilibrium.[23]

On Chomsky's view of I-linguistics, in using an individual speaker, S, as an informant and in constructing a theory of his internalized grammar, a linguist is not making a generalization about the internalized grammars of others who have I-grammars similar to S's. We might say that the linguist's grammar is a theory of S's individual grammar, a token, for which there is no general type that has any other token instances. It is probable that each I-grammar is unique, since it is more than likely that its lexicon, its set of words, is not identical to the lexicon of any other I-grammar. Let us call this view *radical I-linguistics*. Individualism in linguistics has theoretical and methodological consequences. Theoretical notions to which the theory appeals must be relativized to an individual speaker. I-linguistics that is individualistic cannot avail itself of truth; it must be *true for S*, *true in S's* idiolect, or, perhaps, *believed to be true by S* and similarly for other semantic notions (Jackendoff 1990).

A problem with this conception of linguistics is that by being limited to I-grammars, I-linguists appear to be constrained in the generalizations that they can make. There are two ways around this difficulty. First, although I-grammars may not be identical, they certainly may be similar. More than likely, a child's I-grammar will come to resemble quite closely the I-grammars the outputs of which he was exposed to that moved his FL through its various stages of development. Given the similarities, we could group I-grammars together to form resemblance classes and perhaps work up notions of dialect and language, which would be close to the traditional use of these notions. It should be understood that these would be constructions out of I-grammars. Another way around the problem is to idealize away from the differences among I-grammars in the way that theories about bat wings idealize away from the differences among individual bat wings to generalize about bat wings. The biologist is interested in bat wing types, not individual bat wings.

On this construal of I-linguistics we can take the I-linguist to be constructing a grammar not of an individual I-grammar token but of an I-grammar type, tokens of which are instantiated in different brains, but with minor variations. While types and resemblance classes are abstract objects, the I-linguist is still interested in cognitive states. An I-grammar type can be taken to be a cognitive state type that is about individual cognitive states in the same way that the biologists' theories about bat wing types is about the bat wings of individual bats. Hence, we can talk about two people having the same I-grammar where this is understood as their having the same grammar type, but their particular grammars are distinct grammar tokens that differ in minor ways. If the differences were major, they would not be tokens of the same type. Let us call the I-linguistics that is not about individual grammars, one at a time, but about grammar types or resemblance classes of grammars *moderate I-linguistics* (Higginbotham 1989). Although, strictly speaking, moderate I-linguistics is not about I-grammars that are internal to any particular individual, it does not make them externalist theories. Moderate I-linguistics is still committed to methodological solipsism and, thus, its theories are internalist.

Nevertheless, there is no necessary connection between linguistics being internalist and being individualist. It is possible for a semantics to be individualist without being internalist by being, for example, a theory of reference[24] relativized to an individual speaker. Also, we have just seen that it is possible for a linguistic theory to be internalist without being individualist.

Notes

1. See also Skinner (1957) for a further application of the behaviorist theory to language.
2. As reported in Frisby (1980, 95).
3. Striate neurons are neurons in the striate cortex, which is one of the centers of the brain responsible for visual awareness.

3

Linguistics and Logic

If the link between linguistics and psychology is strong, the link with logic is no less so.[1] Initially, logic sought to distinguish good arguments from bad ones. More particularly, it sought to identify which argument forms preserve truth and which do not. Since arguments are communicated, and to that extent, expressed in a language, it is natural to use the form of language to identify the forms of arguments. It is not surprising, then, that those interested in logic have been interested in language and, in their pursuit of logic, have made interesting observations about language and have developed important insights into language.

The intertwining of logical and linguistic concerns is evident from the beginning of the study of logic in Europe. In the course of developing his syllogistic, Aristotle introduced the distinction between subject and predicate, a distinction that has been with us ever since as both a grammatical and a logical one. This was not the only linguistic distinction drawn by Aristotle; he seems to have been the first European to have identified conjunctions as a lexical class, as well as to have identified tense as a feature of verbs, among many other things. The Stoics, too, had mixed concerns, leading to their identification of the truth-functionality of *and*, *or*, and *if* and to their distinguishing aspect from tense, among many other things. This mixture of logical and linguistic concerns appears again in the *logica nova* of the Middle Ages, especially with its treatment of syncategoremata.

The next major development to stimulate still further the intertwining of logical and linguistic concerns is the development of the formalization of mathematics. In particular, quantificational logic was developed as a means to represent mathematical reasoning. It does this by providing a notation in terms of which, it is generally agreed, all mathematical arguments can be framed. By focusing on mathematical arguments, or proofs, logic turned its attention to how all parts of a mathematical proof could be put into notation and how that notation could be rigorously specified. The study of how the notation could be rigorously specified led to recursion theory. The study of how the notation was to be interpreted led to model theory. We could think of model theory as providing a semantics for the notation. Both of these developments have had a fundamental influence on linguistics: the first made clear the nature of grammatical rules; the second how the meanings of constituent expressions contribute to the meaning of the expression of which they are constituents.

Let us begin with recursion. Recursion occurs when an infinite set is specified in terms of a proper subset. The set of numerals[2] used in arithmetic is an example of an infinite set that can be rigorously specified in terms of a smaller set—indeed, a finite set of ten elements—and two rules, one of which is recursive. The basic set comprises the following digits: '0', '1', '2', '3', '4', '5', '6', '7', '8', and '9'. Let us call this set of symbols D. The set of numerals (SN) is, then, defined by two rules: 1(a) every digit is a numeral; and 1(b) every numeral put together with a digit is a numeral. The first rule is not recursive, but the second is. This definition[3] can be stated more formally as follows:

DEFINITION 1. *Numerals (SN) of arithmetic.*
(1.1) if $x \in$ D, then $x \in$ SN;
(1.2) if $x \in$ SN and $y \in$ D, then $xy \in$ SN;
(1.3) nothing else is a member of SN.[4]

To understand the definition in 1, let us see how the numeral '235' is obtained. By the first rule 1(a), the digit '2' is a numeral and so is the digit '3'. So, by the second rule 1(b), '23' is a numeral. But, '5' is also a numeral (by the first rule). So, by the second rule, '235' is also a numeral. Notice that this numeral is three digits long and it is obtained by two applications of the second rule: the first application to obtain the left-most two digits '23', and then another application to obtain the left-most three digits '235', that is, the entire numeral. All numerals will be obtained in the same way. If a numeral contains n digits, then it will result from $n - 1$ applications of the second rule, starting from the left-most two digits and adding in $n - 2$ successive applications the remaining digits from left to right. It is through the second rule that the finite set of numerals specified in the first rule generates the infinite set of numerals. What is special about this latter rule is that it can apply to the result of any of its applications. Rules that can be applied to their own results are said to be *recursive*. These rules specify the set of numerals and are analogous to syntax rules in linguistic theory; they specify what a well-formed numeral is. They do not, however, tell us what the numerals mean.

Two ways of mathematically specifying the recursive structure of the expressions of a natural language have appeared in the study of language. One way arose out of the study of language itself, the other out of logic. The first way, popular among syntacticians, has its origins in Pāṇini's *Aṣṭādhyāyi*, for a great number of its phonological and morphological rules are, to a very close approximation, instances of what one calls today *context-sensitive rules* (Staal 1965a). Such rules were not used again in grammars for another 2,500 years, until Bloomfield (1933) rediscovered their utility, applying them not only in morphology and phonology, as Pāṇini had done, but also in syntax. Their use was subsequently greatly developed by Zellig Harris (1946), Rulon Wells (1947), Charles Hockett (1954), and others. Shortly thereafter, their formal structure was identified and studied by Chomsky (1957; 1963). He established, among other things, that context-sensitive rules were only one of the three types of recursive rules. In order of strength, these three are right-recursive, context-free, and context-sensitive recursive rules.[5]

Another way to specify the recursive nature of the expressions of natural language is to use what is known as *categorial grammar*. This has great currency among philosophers, logicians, and semanticists. Its basic idea goes back to Kazimierz Ajdukiewicz. He was interested in giving a mathematical characterization of the notation of the quantificational logic of Stanislaw Leśniewski. Drawing on ideas found in the *Fourth Logical Investigation* of Edmund Husserl, Ajdukiewicz devised the beginnings of categorial grammar. He explains some aspects of the mathematics of the notation by pointing out, in an anecdotal way, some of its possible applications in the study of natural language structure. But Ajdukiewicz's mention of natural language is completely opportunistic, for his concerns lay elsewhere. It is not until the 1950s, with the work of Yehoshua Bar-Hillel (1953) and Joachim Lambek (1958), that the ideas found in Ajdukiewicz's work were adapted for a serious study of natural language.

The other development in logic that has turned out to be of crucial importance to linguistics is model theory. Model theory is concerned with the relation of symbols of logical notation to sets. The basic idea, however, can be illustrated with the notation of modern arithmetic. Consider again the numeral '235'. Recall that it was obtained by putting together the digits '2' and '3' to form the numeral '23', and that numeral was put together with the digit '5' to form the numeral '235'. To assign a value to the numeral, we proceed as follows. First, assign to each digit its usual value. Thus, the digit '2' is assigned two, the digit '3' three, and the digit '5' five. Next, assign values to each numeral obtained in the construction of '235'. To assign a value to '23', one multiplies the value assigned to the digit '2', namely two, by ten and adds to that the value assigned to the digit '3', namely three, thereby obtaining a value of twenty-three. We can apply the same procedure to obtain the value of '235': namely, to multiply the value of the numeral '23' by ten, to obtain two hundred thirty, and to add to it the value of the digit '5', namely five, thereby obtaining two hundred thirty-five. The value of each numeral is obtained in the same way. If a numeral contains n digits, then a value is assigned to the numeral corresponding to the left-most two digits of the original numeral. This same procedure is applied $n - 2$ times to obtain values for each of the $n - 2$ numerals. The assignment of values is recursive, and it follows the recursive structure of the numerals.

Here is the formal definition of the recursive assignment of values to the numerals in SN:

DEFINITION 2. *Value assignment to the numerals (SN) of arithmetic.*
(1.1) if $x \in$ D, then $i(x) = \mathbf{x}$;
(1.2) if $xy \in$ SN and $y \in$ D, then $i(xy) = i(x)\cdot10 + i(y)$
(where bolded $\mathbf{x}$ is the natural number usually corresponding to the symbol x).[6]

The rules in Def. 2 show how a change in a digit in the numeral '235' leads to a change in value. The replacement of '3' in '235' by '4' results in '245', whose value is two hundred forty-five. The rules in Def. 2, applied to the numeral '245', yield precisely the value of two hundred forty-five. In short, the rules in Defs. 1 and 2 permit us to see how a change in our understanding of a complex numeral changes with a change in one of its constituents. These rules assign numbers to the numerals; they can be taken to be assigning meanings to the Arabic numerals and as being analogous to semantic rules in linguistic theory.

The observation that a change of a constituent expression within a larger expression may lead to a change in how one understands the larger expression goes back to Pāṇini. It is the observation that the meaning of each minimal constituent in a sentence contributes to the meaning of the entire sentence.[7] As repeatedly observed by Sanskrit grammarians, one understands differently the expressions *Dogs are animals* and *Cows are animals*. Moreover, it is clear that the difference in one's understanding of these expressions is due to the difference in one's understanding of the constituent expressions *dogs* and *cow*.

The analogy between the complex expressions of natural language and those of arithmetic is quite close. After all, both kinds of expressions have a recursive structure. Moreover, the values one associates with complex mathematical notation and the values one associates with the complex expressions of a natural language are determined, at least in part, by the values of their constituents. In particular, changes in the basic expressions can lead to a change in the interpretation of the complex expression. Thus, the difference in the values associated with the expressions '235' and '245' is attributable to the replacement of the digit '3' by the digit '4' and the difference in their values—namely, the number three and the number four. Similarly, the difference in the values of the expressions *Cows are animals* and *Dogs are animals* is attributable to the replacement of the word *cows* with the word *dogs* and the difference in their values—namely, the first word being true of cows and the second being true of dogs. It thus stands to reason that something like model theory can be used to make clear how the meaning of an expression is determined by the meaning of the expressions making it up.

The recognition of the pertinence of logic to the elucidation of this characteristic of meaning of natural language expressions is due to its founder, Alfred Tarski (1944 and 1956), though he himself doubted that a satisfactory formal account of this property of natural language expressions could be worked out. His student Richard Montague (1970a; 1970b), however, initiated just such an undertaking at the beginning of the 1970s. Montague was not alone. Max Cresswell (1973), David Lewis (1972: this volume, Chapter 11), and Edward Keenan (Keenan and Falz 1985) also took up the same challenge. All four used categorial grammar to characterize the recursive structure of natural language expressions, in particular English. These approaches make English look very much like a kind of logic.

Subsequent authors have made substantial departures. One innovation is the work of Jon Barwise and John Perry (1983), which has given rise to *situation theory* (1981: this volume, Chapter 15). Another is the work of Hans Kamp (1981: this volume, Chapter 13; Kamp and Reyle 1993), known as *discourse representation theory*. A third is known as *dynamic predicate logic*, devised by Jeroen Groenendijk and Martin Stokhof (1991: this volume, Chapter 14). Though each purports to provide a general framework in which to elucidate the compositional nature of the meaning of the expressions of natural language, each has had its own point of departure, situation theory in the problems raised by the contextual dependence of natural language expressions (Castañeda 1989; Kaplan 1977: this volume, Chapter 37; Perry 1979), discourse representation theory and dynamic predicate logic in problems of referential dependence of pronouns on their noun phrase antecedents (see section 3.4.4).

Semantics, then, addresses two central questions: What values are to be associated with the basic expressions of a language? How does the meaning of simpler expressions contribute to the meaning of the complex expressions the simpler ones make up? The utility of model theory is to enlighten us on how to proceed with answering the latter question. If a satisfactory answer is obtained, then it will explain not only how changes in our understanding of complex expressions change with changes in their constituents, but also how it is that humans are able to understand completely novel complex expressions. After all, one's understanding of complex expressions cannot be accounted for by appeal to memorization of a language's expressions[8] any more than an appeal to mere memorization can explain how it is that humans knowing elementary arithmetic can understand previously unencountered numerals. Rather, one is able to understand novel complex expressions since they are combinations of simple ones which are not novel and which are antecedently understood.

However, model theory will not enlighten us about how to answer the first question: What values are associated with the various expressions of a language? It might very well be thought that an answer to the question of how values are combined presupposes an answer to what the basic values are. The problem can be finessed by finding suitable values to serve as ersatz meanings. Once again, model theory furnishes help, for, as a first approximation, the very same kinds of values used in model theory can be used in semantics: namely, sets.

Next, we explore some of the ways in which the model theory of quantificational logic sheds light on the question of how the meaning of an expression is determined by the meaning of expressions making it up. We begin with a brief presentation of propositional logic and a short discussion of the analogy between propositional connectives and English connectors, in particular, the two coordinators *and* and *or* and the subordinator *if*. Then, we turn to a fragment of quantificational logic—the notation and logic of predicates—to see what light it can shed on the structure of simple English clauses. Finally, we present quantificational logic and discuss its use in helping us understand the antecedence relation, which pronouns bear to other expressions, and so-called quantified noun phrases.

3.1   Propositional connectives and English connectors

3.1.1   Propositional logic

The expressions of propositional logic (PL) are its formulae. Let us call this set of propositional formulae FM. Like the SN, FM is infinite. Now SN is defined recursively on the basis of the finite set D, but FM is defined on the basis of two sets: the set of propositional variables (PV) and the set of propositional connectives (PC). The former is infinite, typically being expressed by lowercase letters such as 'p', 'q', and 'r' with and without subscripts. The latter contains five elements: $\neg, \wedge, \vee, \rightarrow, \leftrightarrow$. Of these latter, the first is a unary connective, the sole member of the set UC, and the last four are binary connectives, comprising the set BC. The definition of FM states that all propositional variables are formulae. It also states that any formula prefixed with the unary connective ($\neg$) is a formula and that a pair of formulae, infixed with a binary connective and enclosed with parentheses, is a formula. Finally, it says that nothing else is a formula. Here is its formal definition:

> DEFINITION 3. *Formulae (FM) of PL*. FM, the formulae of PL, is the set defined as follows:[9]
> (1)   PV ⊆ FM;
> (2.1) if $\alpha \in$ FM and $* \in$ UC, then $*\alpha \in$ FM;
> (2.2) if $\alpha, \beta \in$ FM and $\bullet \in$ BC, then $(\alpha \bullet \beta) \in$ FM;
> (3)   nothing else is.

Given the definition of propositional formulae, one naturally wonders how one decides whether a string of symbols constitutes a propositional formula. If one considers any propositional formula, it must, according to the definition (Def. 3), either be a propositional variable or have one of the following forms: $\neg\alpha, (\alpha \wedge \beta), (\alpha \vee \beta), (\alpha \rightarrow \beta), (\alpha \leftrightarrow \beta)$. Consider the following list of strings of symbols: q, ¬p, (¬p), (¬p ∨ q), ((¬p) → (p ∧ q)). The first is a formula, since it is a propositional formula. This follows directly from the first clause of Def. 3, since all propositional variables are formulae. The remaining strings are not simple propositional variables. Hence, each of them must have one of the five forms listed: ¬p has the form $\neg\alpha$. By the second clause of Def. 3, $\neg\alpha$ is a formula just in case α is. Since α is p and p is a propositional variable, ¬p is a propositional formula. Next comes (¬p). It is neither a propositional variable nor has it any of the forms listed. Thus, it is not a propositional formula, since ¬p does not call for parentheses. In contrast, (¬p ∨ q) has the form $(\alpha \vee \beta)$. By the third clause of Def. 3, it is a formula just in case ¬p is a formula and q is a formula. Since it is a propositional variable, q is a formula. And, as we saw, ¬p is a formula. So, (¬p ∨ q) is a propositional formula.

There is a simple procedure permitting one to determine, in a finite number of steps, whether a string of symbols constitutes a propositional formula:

> STEP 1: Write down the string of symbols. Two possibilities arise: either the string comprises a single symbol, or the string comprises more than one symbol.
>> STEP 1.1: If the string comprises a single symbol, then the string is a formula if and only if (iff) it is a propositional variable.
>> STEP 1.2: If the string does not comprise a single symbol, proceed to the next step.
> STEP 2: The string comprises more than one symbol. Two possibilities arise: either the string has one of two forms—$*\alpha$ (where $* \in$ UC) or $(\alpha \bullet \beta)$ (where $\bullet \in$ BC)—or it does not.
>> STEP 2.1: If it does not have either of the two forms, then the string is not a formula.
>> STEP 2.2: If it does have one of the two forms, proceed to the next step.
> STEP 3: The string has one of two forms.
>> STEP 3.1: If the string has the form $*\alpha$ (where $* \in$ UC), draw two lines slanting

away from each other under the string and write down ∗ under the left line and α under the right. Return to STEP 1 for α.

STEP 3.2:   If the string has the form α•β, draw three lines under the string—the left-hand one slanting to the left, the middle one straight down, and the right-hand one slanting to the right—and write α under the left-hand line, β under the right-hand line, and • under the middle one. Return to STEP 1 for α and β.

STEP 4:   Continue the steps above until one can proceed no longer.

The resulting display is called a *categorematic construction tree*.[10] The string at the top of the categorematic construction tree is a propositional formula if, and only if, each branch terminates either in a propositional variable or a propositional connective and each propositional connective has an appropriate number of formulae as sisters:[11]

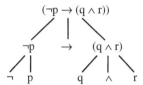

The various formulae in the construction tree are (¬p → (q ∧ r))'s subformulae. Note that (¬p → (q ∧ r)) is itself considered one of its subformulae. The main connective of a formula is the one that appears immediately under the formula itself.

Having described the structure of propositional logic's formulae, we now turn to the task of describing how the values of formulae are determined by an assignment of values to the propositional connectives and variables. That is, we turn to the task of providing a semantics for propositional logic. Just as each numeral in SN is assigned a natural number, so each formula in FM is assigned a truth value. For our purposes, we are concerned with only two truth values: the true (T) and the false (F).[12] As we saw, the assignment of natural numbers to the members of D and a rule that assigns a natural number to a complex expression on the basis of natural numbers assigned to its constituent parts guarantees that each expression of SN is assigned a unique natural number. Here, too, the assignment of truth values to the members of PV and a rule that assigns a truth value to a complex expression on the basis of truth values assigned to its constituent parts guarantees that each formula of FM is assigned a unique truth value. In other words, the values are assigned compositionally.

However, keep in mind that there are important differences between D (the set of digits) and PV (the set of propositional variables) in what these assignments are and how they are done. To begin, the members of D have a constant interpretation: each digit always stands for the same number. As a result, the members of SN have a constant interpretation, and the members of PV have a variable interpretation. Each propositional variable can be assigned either of the two truth values. Thus, the members of PV can be interpreted in a variety of ways. Each assignment of truth values to the set of propositional variables is called a *truth value assignment* (TVA). If there were only three propositional variables—say, p, q, and r—then there are eight possible truth value assignments (a's), or functions from {p,q,r} into {T,F}:

		a_1	a_2	a_3	a_4	a_5	a_6	a_7	a_8
p	↦	T	T	T	T	F	F	F	F
q	↦	T	T	F	F	T	T	F	F
r	↦	T	F	T	F	T	F	T	F

There are several points one should take note of in Def. 4. First, clause 1 requires that the truth value assignment a and the classical valuation v_a agree on the assignment of truth values to the atomic formulae, or propositional variables. In this way, the function v_a is said to be an extension of the function a. Since each a induces a unique function, v_a, it is common to indicate this by subscripting the symbol v with the symbol for the truth value assignment that it extends. Second, the clauses in (2) correspond to the truth functions assigned to each propositional connective. Third, each clause in (2) sets out that the value of a formula (given on the left-hand side of the equality) in terms of the values of its immediate subformulae (given on the right-hand side).

Another way to look at the definition of classical valuation for the formulae of PL is as a constraint on all possible bivalent functions for the formulae of PL. To see this, consider some partial specifications of bivalent valuations for formulae of PL.[16] Suppose again that PV contains only two propositional variables, p and q. Consider the following partial specification of bivalent valuations whose domain is the set of formula obtained from {p,q}:

		v_1	v_2	v_3	v_4
p	$\mapsto$	T	T	T	T
q	$\mapsto$	T	T	F	F
¬p	$\mapsto$	T	F	F	F
¬q	$\mapsto$	F	F	T	T
p ∧ q	$\mapsto$	T	T	T	F
p ∨ q	$\mapsto$	T	T	T	T
¬p ∨ q	$\mapsto$	F	T	T	T
q ∧ ¬p	$\mapsto$	T	T	T	F
.	.	.	.	.	.
.	.	.	.	.	.
.	.	.	.	.	.

If one were to complete the list of formulae and ensure that each position under one or other of the v's is filled in with precisely one of T or F, each v will provide a bivalent valuation. However, three of them certainly do not conform to Def. 4. For example, v_1 assigns T to both p and ¬p—contrary to clause 2.1. Moreover, v_3 assigns T to p ∧ q, though it also assigns F to q. This violates clause 2.2.1. Finally, v_4 assigns T to ¬p ∨ q, even though it assigns F to both ¬p and q— in violation of clause 2.2.2. Only v_2, at least to the extent it is specified, actually conforms to our earlier interpretation of the propositional connectives.

Classical valuations give rise to various ways to classify the formulae of FM. A formula that is assigned T regardless of the truth value assignment to its propositional variables is said to be a *tautology*. Examples are p ∨ ¬p, p → p, (p ∧ ¬p) → q, p → (q → p). A formula that is assigned F regardless of the truth value assignment to its propositional variables is called a *contradiction*: ∧ ¬p, (q ∨ ¬q) → (p ∧ ¬p), p ↔ ¬p are examples of these. Finally, a formula that may be assigned either T or F as a result of different truth value assignments to its propositional variables is known as a *contingency*. Three contingent formulae are p, p ∨ ¬q, and p → (p ∧ r). In addition, there is an important relation that a set of formulae bears to a single formula. This is the relation symbolized by ⊨ and called *entailment*. It is a relation of a set of propositions to a single proposition, and it holds just in case whenever every element in the set is true the single proposition is true too.

DEFINITION 5. *Entailment (for PL).* Let Γ be a set of formulae. Let α be a formula. Γ ⊨ α iff every truth value assignment that renders each formula in Γ true renders α true.

It is easy to check that {p, p → q} ⊨ q, but that {q, p → q} ⊭ p.

3.1.2   English connectors

Having laid out the essential ideas of classical propositional logic, let us see how these ideas might show how one's understanding of a complex expression results from one's understanding of its constituent expressions. When one judges a sentence to be true or false with respect to some situation, one does so on the basis of one's understanding of the sentence, on the one hand, and of the situation, on the other. Let us call what one understands when one understands an expression its *meaning*. It is the meaning of a sentence that determines whether it is true in a situation.[17] Truth and falsity are shadows that the meanings of sentences cast on situations. One way to track the meaning of a sentence is to track its truth conditions.

Now just as the propositional connectives in propositional logic are used to form complex expressions, or formulae, from simple expressions, or propositional variables, and other complex expressions, or formulae, so ordinary English connectors such as *and*, *or*, *if*, and *unless* are used to form complex, or compound, declarative sentences from simple ones or other compound ones. Moreover, it is natural to try to explain our judgments of the truth conditions of a compound declarative sentence in terms of the truth conditions of its constituent declarative clauses and a truth function hypothesized as characterizing at least part of the meaning of the connector, in the same way as the truth value of a formula is determined by the truth value of its constituent formulae and the truth function of its main connective.

By way of an example, consider the compound declarative sentence *it is raining and it is cold*. It seems to be that we judge the entire sentence to be true when and only when we judge each of its constituent declarative clauses to be true:

It is raining.	It is cold.	It is raining and it is cold.
T	T	T
T	F	F
F	T	F
F	F	F

Now, this is exactly the truth function $o_\wedge$ that interprets the propositional connective $\wedge$. It seems natural then to hypothesize that the truth function $o_\wedge$ characterizes at least part of the meaning of the English connector *and*.

Just as one cannot obtain a value for a complex piece of notation on the basis of an assignment of values to its basic symbols without knowing how the notation is structured, so one cannot obtain an interpretation of a compound declarative sentence of a natural language like English on the basis of interpretations of its constituent clauses without knowing how the constituent clauses combine. For this reason, we must ascertain how the connectors combine with other constituent clauses to form compound clauses or sentences. We start, then, with a review of the principal syntactic facts that pertain to English connectors and their clausal syntax.

English, like other languages, distinguishes between coordinated and subordinated clauses and between coordinators (for example, *and* and *or*) and subordinators (for example, *if* and *unless*). As we shall see, the syntactic structures in which they occur are quite different, and this difference has a direct bearing on whether or not the truth functions from propositional logic can be used to characterize the meaning of the corresponding English connector. Here are the principal differences. First, coordinators may connect verb phrases (VP), whereas subordinators may not:

1. (a) Dan [$_\text{VP}$ drank his coffee] *and* [$_\text{VP}$ left quickly].
   (b) *Dan [$_\text{VP}$ did not drink his coffee] *because* [$_\text{VP}$ left quickly].

Second, a difference manifests itself in verb ellipsis, or what is also known as *gapping*. Roughly, when two English clauses of parallel syntactic structure and sharing the same verb occur connected by a coordinator, the verb of the second clause may be omitted. This is not the case when the connector is a subordinator:

2. (a) Bill encouraged Mary and Dan encouraged Maggie.
   (b) Bill encouraged Mary and Dan __ Maggie.
3. (a) Bill encouraged Mary because Dan encouraged Maggie.
   (b) *Bill encouraged Mary because Dan __ Maggie.

Third, coordinators never occur one immediately after another, but subordinators may:

4. (a) *John is unhappy *and but* he does what he is told.
   (b) Bill left *because if* he hadn't, he would have been in trouble.
   (c) We don't need to worry about Carol *because if when* she arrives we are not home, she can let herself in with the key I lent her.

Moreover, a coordinator may immediately precede a subordinator:

5. Dan asked to be transferred *because* he was unhappy *and because* he saw no chance of promotion.

Finally, the English subordinator may occur at the beginning of the pair of connected clauses, but the English coordinator may not.

6. (a) [It is cold] *and* [it is raining].
   (b) [It is cold] *because* [it is raining].
7. (a) *And* [it is raining] [it is cold].
   (b) *Because* [it is raining] [it is cold].

It is clear from the preceding that coordinated clauses consist of two independent clauses, one on either side of a coordinator. This constituent structure is nicely depicted by the following diagram, called a *phrase marker*:

(where S is a clause and C_c is a coordinator). It is convenient to specify such a structure with a phrase structure rule: $S \Rightarrow S \ C_c \ S$. This rule says that two clauses flanking a coordinator form a clause.

The structure of the categorematic construction tree in which the propositional connective ∧ occurs is very similar to the structure of the phrase marker in which the coordinator *and* occurs. To see this, consider the following categorematic construction tree (left) for the formula schema α ∧ β. Replace each formula in it with the name of the set to which it belongs—namely, FM—and the propositional connective by the name of the set to which it belongs—namely, BC. This yields the middle tree. Next, replace the label FM with the label S and the label BC with the label C_c.

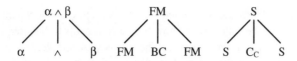

There is also a disanalogy, however. Nodes in a construction tree are labeled by formula, with the terminal nodes being labeled by atomic formulae. Nodes in a phrase marker are labeled by syntactic categories and its terminal nodes are labeled by expressions of English. This means that the phrase marker for a pair of coordinated English clauses contains more structure than given in the preceding diagram.

The English coordinator *and* bears other striking similarities to the propositional connective ∧. The truth of a clause which is formed from two independent clauses coordinated by *and* depends on the truth of its two constituent clauses in the same way that the truth of a complex formula formed from two formula connected by ∧ depends on its two constituent formulae. Consider, for example, two simple independent clauses: *it is raining* and *it is cold*. It is indisputable that the clause formed from these two independent clauses with the coordinator *and* is true under the circumstances in which both coordinated clauses are true, and not otherwise. And, as we saw, this is exactly the truth function that interprets ∧ of propositional logic. This truth function enjoys several logical properties which it seems to share with the coordinator *and*. To begin with, both are commutative:[18]

8. (a) It is raining *and* it is cold.
    (b) It is cold *and* it is raining.
9. (a) Mary studies at McGill *and* John studies at Concordia.
    (b) John studies at Concordia *and* Mary studies at McGill.

In addition, just as one can infer either of the immediate subformulae of a formula whose main connective is ∧, so one can infer either independent clause of a pair of independent clauses forming a clause connected by the coordinator *and*. Thus, in propositional logic, the following entailments hold:

10. (a) $p \wedge q \vDash p$
     (b) $p \wedge q \vDash q$
     (c) $p, q \vDash p \wedge q$

The analogue of these entailment relations holds in English as well:[19]

11. (a) it is raining *and* it is cold ENTAILS it is raining
     (b) it is raining *and* it is cold ENTAILS it is cold
     (c) it is raining, it is cold ENTAILS it is raining *and* it is cold

It should be evident that the same rule of interpretation which applies to the categorematic construction tree to assign a value to the mother node (namely, $o_{\wedge}(u_1, u_2)$) on the basis of values assigned to the daughter nodes (namely, u_1 and u_2) can apply to the phrase marker so that its mother node acquires a value determined by the values assigned to its daughter nodes:

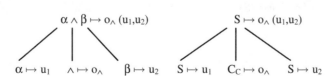

The phrase structure rule $S \Rightarrow S_1 \, C_C \, S_2$ characterizes the structure of the constituent. A corresponding interpretation rule must be stated to say how the constituent is to be interpreted on the basis of the interpretation of its immediate constituents. The rule is quite simple: $v(S) = v(C_C)(v(S_1), v(S_2))$. What this rule says is that the value of the S-node (v of S) is the value obtained by applying the value of the C_C (v of C_C) to the pair of values of the two daughter S-nodes.

However, the question remains: How are values assigned to the nodes C_C and *and*? As we saw, the English coordinator *and* includes in its meaning the truth function $o_\wedge$ Thus, *and* $\mapsto o_\wedge$ (that is, $v(and) = o_\wedge$). Finally, there must be a rule that states how the value of the node labeled with *and* is related to the value of the node labeled with C_c. Now, *and* is a lexical item and C_c is a lexical category. The rule is that the value of the lexical category X of a lexical item Y is the same as the value of the lexical item itself (that is, $Y \mapsto v$ iff $X \mapsto v$). The entire phrase marker fully interpreted is as follows:

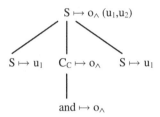

In addition, then, to the phrase structure rule $S \Rightarrow S_1 \, C_C \, S_2$ and the lexical rule $C_C \Rightarrow and$, there are two rules of interpretation (IR):

IR 0. Let [$_X$ Y] be the syntactic where Y is a lexical item. Let i be an interpretation function. Then, $v_i(X) = i(Y)$.

IR 1.1. Let [$_S$ S_1 C_C S_2] be a syntactic structure. Let i be an interpretation function. Then, $v_i(S) = v_i(C_C)(v_i(S_1), v_i(S_2))$.

But the adaptation of logic to language is not always quite so straightforward. Consider now the English subordinator *if* and the propositional connective →. Subordinated clauses have two structures, both of which differ from the structure of coordinated clauses:

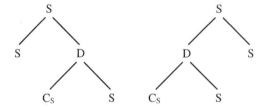

These phrase markers can be specified by three rules. The first—$D \Rightarrow C_s \, S$—states that a clause S preceded by a subordinator (C_s) constitutes a dependent clause (D). The second two—$S \Rightarrow D \, S$ and $S \Rightarrow S \, D$—state that a clause (S) either preceded or succeeded by a dependent clause (D) constitutes a clause (S). These are the phrase structure rules (PSR) given so far:

PSR 0: $X \Rightarrow Y$

(where Y is a lexical item, or word, and X is its lexical category)

PSR 1.1: $S \Rightarrow S \, C_c \, S$

PSR 1.2: $S \Rightarrow S \ D$

PSR 1.3: $S \Rightarrow D \ S$

PSR 1.4: $D \Rightarrow C_s \ S$

(where C_c is the lexical category of coordinators and C_s is the lexical category of subordinators).

Direct inspection of these phrase markers reveals that coordinated clauses and subordinated clauses have different structures. Moreover, we saw that the structure of the categorematic tree for a formula whose main connective is a binary one is the same as that of a coordinated clause. It follows, as we shall see, that a truth function that interprets a binary connective cannot be used to interpret a subordinator.

The truth function $o_\rightarrow$ simply cannot apply in either of the syntactic structures appropriate to subordinating conjunctions. The reason is clear. Whereas the coordinator has two sister clauses, the values of which provides a pair of values on which the binary truth function interpreting the coordinator can operate, the subordinator has only one sister clause, which provides but one value for the binary truth function to operate on. But the truth function $o_\rightarrow$ requires two truth values:

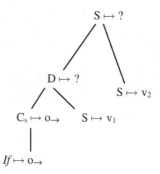

The solution is to find a truth function that is equivalent to $o_\rightarrow$ but can apply in the syntactic structures of subordinate clauses. The following shows how this might be done. Suppose that the apodosis is assigned T and the protasis is assigned T.[20] We know that the top node must be assigned T. The questions are: What is to be assigned to the node D, and what is to be assigned to the node C_S? D must be assigned a unary truth function. Moreover, since its sister node is assigned T and its mother node is assigned T, it must map T to T. Suppose, next, that D's sister node is assigned F. Then, the mother node must be assigned F, for any conditional sentence with a true apodosis and a false protasis is false. In short, then, if the apodosis clause is assigned T, then the D node must be assigned the unary truth function that maps T to T and F to F. This is known as an *identity function*. We shall designate it as o_I. Next, suppose that the apodosis node is assigned F. We know, then, that the top node must be assigned T, no matter what is assigned to the protasis. This implies that the D node must be assigned the constant unary truth function that maps both T and F to T. We shall call this function o_T. In short, then, *if* is to be interpreted by a function that maps T to the o_I function and F to the o_T function. The reader should check that this interpretation of *if* works, regardless of whether the subordinate clause precedes or follows the main clause.

The foregoing adaptation of the insights of propositional logic to expressions of language has a number of satisfying consequences. It can account for why it is that some sentences are judged true, no matter what the circumstances are:

12. (a) Either it is raining or it is not raining.
     (b) If it is raining, then it is raining.

It also accounts for why it is that some sentences are judged false, no matter what the circumstances are:

13.   It is raining and it is not raining.

Clauses are themselves complex expressions. So, one would like to know how their meanings emerge from the meanings of their constituents, or at least how their truth values emerge from the values associated with their parts. Again, logic provides the natural starting point.

The use of truth functions to elucidate the meaning of English connectors certainly has its limitations. Not all English connectors can be given a truth functional characterization. For example, the subordinator *because* escapes a truth functional interpretation. Consider the following situation. Bill attends a party with his wife. While there, he learns that his former wife is also in attendance. As a result, Bill leaves. Given the situation, the constituent clauses of the following two sentences are true:

14.   (a) Bill left the party *because* Bill's former wife was there.
        (b) Bill left the party *because* Bill's wife was there.

However, only the first sentence is true. It cannot be, then, that *because* has a truth functional interpretation, an interpretation that depends only on the truth values of clauses that *because* connects. In 14(a) and 14(b) all the constituent clauses are true, but 14(a) is true while 14(b) is false.

Not all uses of English connectors that have a truth functional characterization conform to what is implied by such an interpretation. For example, not all uses of the coordinator *and* are commutative. No one judges the following pair of sentences to be equivalent:

15.   (a) Bill died and he was buried.
        (b) Bill was buried and he died.

Problems of this kind are treated at length in Posner (1980: this volume, Chapter 31). Following Grice (1975), he argues that cases where the predicted construals do not arise are to be accounted for by independently motivated principles of conversational implicature. Reservations about the success of this approach are also developed in detail by Ray Jennings (1994: this volume, Chapter 33) and Robyn Carston (this volume, Chapter 40). Moreover, all the English coordinators and many of the subordinators can be used to connect subclausal constituents such as noun phrases, verb phrases, adjective phrases, and prepositional phrases, as well as nouns, verbs, adjectives, and prepositions. These coordinated structures clearly do not involve truth values. So what value is to be assigned to coordinators and subordinators in these uses?

16.   (a) Bill and Carl jog.
        (b) Allan jogs and swims.

This question is addressed by Gazdar (1980: this volume, Chapter 32).

3.2   Logical predicates and grammatical predicates

The tools of propositional logic are inadequate for a full analysis of the semantics of natural languages. We turn to predicate logic; it will give us greater resources for a description of the semantics of natural languages.

3.2.1   Predicate logic

Predicate logic (PDL) can be viewed as an enrichment of propositional logic (PL). In propositional logic, the atomic formulae, or propositional variables, have no internal structure. In predicate logic they are endowed with structure, since the atomic formulae are built up out of smaller units that are not themselves formulae. This structure is shown by the use of symbols drawn from two disjoint sets: CN, or the set of constants, and PD, or the set of predicates. The constants, like propositional variables, are an infinite, homogeneous set. Here, distinct lowercase letters from the beginning of the Roman alphabet serve as distinct constants. The predicates are an infinite, yet heterogeneous set. Distinct uppercase letters from the Roman alphabet serve as distinct predicates. The heterogeneous set PD can be partitioned into a set of homogeneous sets: one set comprising one-place predicates called PD_1 and another set comprising two-place predicates called PD_2, and so on. The number of places a predicate has is known as its *adicity*, or its *arity*. In general, when the adicity of a predicate is not determined by context, it will be indicated by the number of dashes placed after it. Thus, for example, in what follows, W is a one-place predicate, S a two-place predicate, and G is a three-place predicate.

We now define an atomic formula as any n-place predicate followed by n occurrences of any constants:

DEFINITION 6. *Atomic formulae (AF) of PDL.* $\alpha \in F$, the atomic formulae of PDL, iff, for some n, some $\Pi \in PD_n$ and some $c_1, \ldots, c_n \in CN$, $\alpha = \Pi c_1 \ldots c_n$.

Examples of how this rule distinguishes between atomic formulae and nonformulae are as follows:

Predicate	Atomic Formula	Nonformula
W_	W b̲, W a̲	W b̲ a , W_
S_ _	S a̲b̲, S a̲a̲	S a̲ _ , S b̲ a c
G _ _ _	G c̲b̲a̲, G a̲b̲a̲	G c̲ _ _ , G d̲b̲ _ , G c̲b̲a c

We use the definition of an atomic formula of PDL to define a formula of PDL:

DEFINITION 7. *Formulae (FM) of PDL.* FM, the formula of PDL,[21] is the set defined as follows (where UC is a unary connective, and BC is a binary connective):
(1)   AF $\subseteq$ FM;
(2.1) if $\alpha \in$ FM and $* \in$ UC, then $*\alpha \in$ FM;
(2.2) if $\alpha, \beta \in$ FM and $\bullet \in$ BC, then $(\alpha \bullet \beta) \in$ FM;
(3)   nothing else is.

Notice that this is just like the definition of formulae for PL, except that PV has been replaced by AF. It should not be surprising that categorematic construction trees can be used to analyze expressions of PDL:

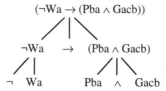

Once truth values are assigned to the atomic formulae, the truth values of the formulae of which they are constituents can be computed using the same rules as those used for propositional logic. However, the question remains of how atomic formulae of predicate logic acquire truth values.

A little reflection shows that the truth value of an atomic formula must arise from values assigned to the predicate and from constants that constitute the formula. The function that assigns values to the predicates and constants of PDL is an *interpretation* function. Its domain comprises the set of constants and the set of predicates (CN $\cup$ PD). Its codomain is built up from any nonempty set as follows: It comprises all the elements of some nonempty set—say $\{1,2\}$; together with all of its subsets—that is, together with $\varnothing$, $\{1\}$, $\{2\}$, and $\{1,2\}$; together with all the subsets of the set of its ordered pairs—$\{\langle 1,1\rangle,\langle 1,2\rangle,\langle 2,1\rangle,\langle 2,2\rangle\}$, $\{\langle 1,2\rangle,\langle 2,1\rangle,\langle 2,2\rangle\}$, $\{\langle 1,1\rangle,\langle 2,1\rangle,\langle 2,2\rangle\}$, $\{\langle 1,1\rangle,\langle 1,2\rangle,\langle 2,2\rangle\}$, $\{\langle 1,1\rangle,\langle 1,2\rangle,\langle 2,1\rangle\}$, . . . , $\{\langle 1,1\rangle\}$, $\{\langle 1,2\rangle\}$, $\{\langle 2,1\rangle\}$ and $\varnothing$; together with all the subsets of the set of its ordered triples, and so on.

Let us make this more precise. Let U, the *universe*, be a nonempty set. The set of all ordered pairs formed from elements of U is denoted by U^2, and the set of all ordered triples formed from the elements of U is denoted by U^3. In general, the set of all ordered n-tuples is denoted by U^n. Next, the set of all subsets of U is denoted by Pow(U), and the set of all subsets of the set of all ordered pairs formed from U is denoted by Pow(U^2). In general, the set of all subsets of the set of ordered n-tuples formed from elements of U is denoted by Pow(U^n). The codomain of an interpretation function, then, is U $\cup$ Pow(U) $\cup$Pow(U^2) $\cup$ . . . $\cup$ Pow(U^n) $\cup$. . . .

An interpretation function for predicate logic (PDL) is any function from CN $\cup$ PD to U $\cup$ Pow(U) $\cup$ Pow(U^2) $\cup$ . . . $\cup$ Pow(U^n) $\cup$ . . . , obeying the following limitations: when it is restricted to CN, its corresponding range is within U; when it is restricted to PD_1, its corresponding range is within Pow(U); when it is restricted to PD_2, its corresponding range is within Pow(U^2); in general, when it is restricted to PD_n, its corresponding range is within Pow(U^n).

DEFINITION 8. *Interpretation function for PDL.* Let U be a nonempty set. Let CN be a set of constants. Let PD be a set of predicates. Then, i is an interpretation function of CN and PD in U iff i satisfies the following:

CN $\rightarrow$ U
PD_1 $\rightarrow$ Pow(U) (i.e., subsets of U)
PD_2 $\rightarrow$ Pow(U^2) (i.e., subsets of U^2)
$\vdots$ $\rightarrow$ $\vdots$
PD_n $\rightarrow$ Pow(U^n) (i.e., subsets of U^n)
$\vdots$ $\rightarrow$ $\vdots$

In PDL, PD is infinite and so is CN. To illustrate our definition of an interpretation function, let us pretend, for the moment, that CN has only three elements—say, a, b, and c—while PD has just two—say P_ and R_ _. Let U be the set $\{1,2,3\}$. Both of the following are functions from CN $\cup$ PD to U $\cup$ Pow(U) $\cup$ Pow(U^2), but only the first, i, is an interpretation function:

i: a $\mapsto$ 1
    b $\mapsto$ 2
    c $\mapsto$ 3
    P _ $\mapsto$ $\{2,3\}$
    R _ _ $\mapsto$ $\{\langle 1,2\rangle,\langle 2,3\rangle,\langle 3,1\rangle\}$

j: a $\mapsto$ 1
    b $\mapsto$ 2
    c $\mapsto$ 3
    P _ $\mapsto$ $\{\langle 1,2\rangle,\langle 2,3\rangle,\langle 3,1\rangle\}$
    R _ _ $\mapsto$ $\{2,3\}$

On two counts, j fails to be an interpretation function: first, the one-place predicate P_ is not interpreted as a subset of U; second, R_ _ is not interpreted as a subset of the set of ordered pairs formed from U.

It is useful to have the idea of a model. A model has two ingredients: a universe U, which is nonempty, and an interpretation function i, whose domain is the constants and predicates of PDL and whose codomain is built from U in the way indicated above. Anything can constitute the set U. The only restriction is that it has to be nonempty. The elements can be physical objects, numbers, mental entities, and so on.

DEFINITION 9. *Model for PDL.* Let CN and PD be the constants and predicates of PDL. Then, $\langle U, i \rangle$ is a model for PDL iff U is a nonempty set and i is an interpretation function of CN and PD in U.

We now want to define a valuation for the atomic formulae of PDL. The valuation is defined in two stages. In the first stage, a bivalent truth value assignment to the atomic formulae is defined on the basis of an interpretation function. In the second stage, this truth value assignment is extended to all the formulae of PDL.[22]

DEFINITION 10. *A classical valuation for the formula of PDL.* Let $\langle U, i \rangle$ be a model for PDL.

Atomic formulae:
Let Π be a member of PD_1, and let c be a member CN. Then,
    (1.1) $v_i(\Pi c) = T$ iff $i(c) \in i(\Pi)$.
Let Π be a member of PD_n, and let $c_1, \ldots, c_n$ be occurrences of members of CN (where $n > 1$). Then,
    (1.2) $v_i(\Pi c_1 \ldots c_n) = T$ iff $\langle i(c_1), \ldots, i(c_n) \rangle \in i(\Pi)$.

Composite formulae:
Then, for each α and for each β in FM:
    (2.1) $v_i(\neg\alpha)$ $= o_\neg(v_i(\alpha))$;
    (2.2) $v_i(\alpha \wedge \beta)$ $= o_\wedge(v_i(\alpha), v_i(\beta))$;
    (2.3) $v_i(\alpha \vee \beta)$ $= o_\vee(v_i(\alpha), v_i(\beta))$;
    (2.4) $v_i(\alpha \to \beta)$ $= o_\to(v_i(\alpha), v_i(\beta))$;
    (2.5) $v_i(\alpha \leftrightarrow \beta)$ $= o_\leftrightarrow(v_i(\alpha), v_i(\beta))$.

Let us see how an atomic formula of PDL receives a truth value on the basis of a model and Def. 10. An atomic formula of predicate logic has a relatively simple structure. Consider, for example, the formula Rab. Its construction tree has exactly two generations: the generation of the mother Rab and the generation of her daughters R, a and b. The interpretation function i of the model $\langle U, i \rangle$ assigns values to each of the daughters, and clause 1.2 of Def. 10 determines the value of the mother node on the basis of the values of her daughter nodes:

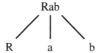

3.3 English verbs and simple clauses

We now turn to the problem of adapting the model theory of PDL to simple English clauses containing only a verb and proper names.

Consider the sentence *Allan runs.* It is the most minimal of simple English clauses. Its subject noun phrase is just the proper name *Allan*, and its verb is the intransitive verb *to run*. Indeed, it seems to have all the simplicity of a formula of PDL comprising a one-place predicate and a constant, although the order of the constituents is different:

As the reader can check from the interpreted construction tree and the interpreted phrase marker, both expressions are true in the models:

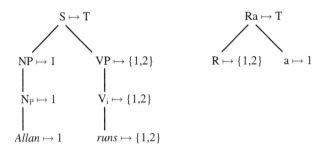

We have carried out here for a simple English sentence obtained from a proper noun and an intransitive verb precisely what we did earlier for an atomic formula from predicate logic comprising a one-place predicate and a single constant. Recall that predicate logic has a rule which states how an atomic formula is built from predicates and constants and a corresponding rule which states what truth value is assigned to an atomic formula, once values are assigned by an interpretation function to the predicate and the constants comprising it. Here, we have hypothesized several rules of English grammar which state how a simple sentence is built from a proper noun and an intransitive verb, and we have hypothesized the rules corresponding to them whose task is to transmit the values assigned to the lexical items to higher nodes in the phrase marker and, eventually, to assign to the top node a truth value.

We now turn to the case of a simple clause with a transitive verb:

19. (a) Allan admires Beth.
     (b) Aab

As always, an atomic formula of PDL has only two generations (i.e., levels); the English clause, however, has five. To see this, note that the sentence in 19(a) comprises a (subject) noun phrase *Allan* and a verb phrase *admires Beth*. The verb phrase, in turn, comprises a transitive verb (V_t) and a noun phrase. It is this structure, not found in the sentence in 17(a), which imparts to the phrase marker in sentence 19(a) its extra generation. The phrase structure rule required to characterize it is:

PSR 3.2: $VP \Rightarrow V_t\ NP$

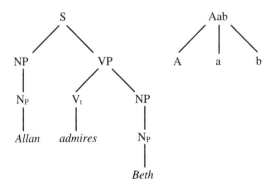

The complication in the English clause structure means that the interpretation rule for PDL does not straightforwardly adapt to the structure of the English clause. The situation is similar to the one we encountered when we wished to apply the interpretation for → in PL to the dependent clause structure. The interpretation rule for PDL requires a value from each of its two sisters to form an ordered pair whose membership in the value interpreting the two-place predicate determines whether the atomic formula is true. Since the V_t node has but one sister, the rule from the predicate calculus (Def. 10, 1.2) cannot apply. However, the rule can be adapted. Notice that the subphrase markers corresponding to the first two generations of the phrase markers for the sentences in 17 and 19 are exactly alike. (This is not a surprise. After all, they correspond to one and the same phrase structure rule.) Hence, we would expect the values associated with the NP and VP nodes to be the same kind of values regardless of which phrase marker we are considering. In the case of the phrase marker for the sentence in 17, the value associated with the NP is an individual in the domain, and the value associated with the VP is a subset of the members of the domain. Intuitively, associated with the NP is whatever the proper noun *Allan* denotes, and associated with the VP is the set of runners. By parity of reasoning, we should expect that associated with the NP of the phrase marker for the sentence in 19 is whatever the proper noun *Allan* denotes, and associated with the VP is the set of admirers of Beth. Now associated with *admires* is the set of ordered pairs whose first coordinates are admirers and whose second coordinates are those admired; in each pair, the first coordinate indeed admires the second. Thus, the set to be associated with the VP must be the set of those elements that are paired with the value of the object NP to form an ordered pair in the set associated with V. The generalization of this constitutes the next rule:

IR 3.2. Let $\langle D, i \rangle$ be a model. Let [$_{VP}$ V_t NP] be the syntactic structure. Then, $v_i(VP) = \{x: \langle x,y \rangle \in v_i(V_t)$ and $y = v_i(NP)\}$.

Using the models $\langle U, k \rangle$ and $\langle U, e \rangle$ and applying the rules of interpretation to the construction tree and phrase marker, respectively, one computes that the formula and sentence in 19 are true:

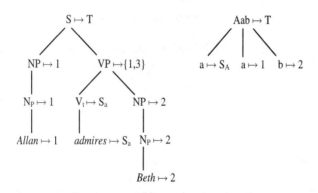

(where $S_a = \{\langle 1,2 \rangle, \langle 2,3 \rangle, \langle 1,3 \rangle, \langle 3,2 \rangle\}$ and $S_A = \{\langle 1,2 \rangle, \langle 2,3 \rangle, \langle 1,3 \rangle, \langle 3,2 \rangle\}$).

Notice that the value $\{1,3\}$ assigned to the VP node arises from IR 3.2. Associated with the node V_t is the set of ordered pairs S_a, and associated with its sister node NP is the value 2. The set $\{1,3\}$ is the set of elements that are paired with 2 in S_a.

Another mismatch between the structure of the formulae of PDL and the structure of English sentences arises with the English adverb *not*. At first, it appears that there is a close correspondence between *not* of English and the $\neg$ of PL. After all, just as one can prefix *it is not the case that* in front of a clause to obtain its negation, so one can prefix $\neg$ in front of a formula to obtain a formula:

20. (a) α: It is raining.
     (b) $\neg \alpha$: It is not the case that it is raining.

Moreover, it is indisputable that when the first is true, the second is false, and when the second is true, the first is false:

It is raining	*It is* not *the case that it is raining*
T	F
F	T

This is precisely the truth function o¬ of propositional logic.

Moreover, the subordinating clause *it is not the case* satisfies the law of double negation that is enjoyed by ¬:

21. (a) $\alpha \vDash \neg\neg\alpha$
     (b) $\neg\neg\alpha \vDash \alpha$
22. (a) It is raining ENTAILS it is *not* the case that it is *not* the case that it is raining.
     (b) It is *not* the case that it is *not* the case that it is raining ENTAILS it is raining.

Furthermore, on the assumption that the English coordinator *or* is accurately characterized by the truth function o$_\vee$, the subordinating clause *it is not the case* also satisfies the law of excluded middle:

23. $\vDash \alpha \vee \neg\alpha$

for it is impossible for it to be false that

24. Either it is raining or it is not the case that it is raining.

Similarly, on the assumption that the English coordinator *and* is accurately characterized by the truth function o$_\vee$, the subordinating clause *it is not the case* also satisfies the law of noncontradiction:

25. $\nvDash \alpha \wedge \neg\alpha$

for it is impossible for it to be true that

26. It is raining and it is not the case that it is raining.

However, while the truth function o¬ does seem to characterize the subordinating clause *it is not the case*, it is far from clear that it characterizes the adverb (AV) *not*. For, unlike the subordinating clause *it is not the case* that is prefixed to a clause to yield a clause, the adverb *not* is inserted in the middle of a clause:

27. (a) *It is not the case* that it is raining.
     (b) It is *not* raining.

And while the sentences in 27 are equivalent, we have not answered the question of what the semantic contribution of the English adverb *not* is. To do this, we must first determine its syntactic properties.

Close examination of the distribution of the adverb *not* shows that the syntactic structures in which it is found are quite disanalogous from the structure in which the propositional connective ¬ is found. In traditional grammar, *not* is classified as an adverb. Its pattern of distribution is virtually identical to that of the adverb *never*. In nonfinite clauses, they occur to the immediate left of the verb, if the verb is in a nonperiphrastic form; and they occur anywhere to the left of the verb up to the immediate left of the left most auxiliary, if the verb is in a periphrastic form.[26] In short, at least one verbal element must occur to their immediate right:

28.   (a) Joan regrets [*never/not* having attended parties].
      (b) Joan regrets [having *never/not* attended parties].
      (c) *Joan regrets [having attended *never/not* parties].

In finite clauses, the distribution of *not* and *never* obeys an additional constraint: they require at least one verbal element, an auxiliary verb, to their immediate left:[27]

29.   (a) Joan ?*never/*not* has attended parties.
      (b) Joan has *never/not* attended parties.
      (c) *Joan has attended *never/not* parties.

The one exception arises when the main verb is a nonperiphrastic form of the verb *to be*. Both adverbs give up the requirement, otherwise found, that some verbal element occur to their right:[28]

30.   (a) Joan ?*never/*not* is late.
      (b) Joan is *never/not* late.

Notice that this simple description accounts for the fact that the adverb *not* never occurs in main clauses without an auxiliary verb (AX), whereas *never* does.[29]

We summarize these observations in the following table:

Verb	Preceded by a verbal element	Followed by a verbal element
Nonfinite	Not required	Required
Finite	Required	Required
Simple copula	Required	Not required

As we can now see, the adverb *not* in English and the propositional connective ¬ occur in disanalogous syntactic structures. The propositional connective applies to a formula to yield a formula. A formula is assigned a truth value. Thus, the propositional connective is naturally interpreted as a truth function that yields a truth value, given truth value. The English adverb *not*, in contrast, occurs within a clause, the natural language counterpart of a formula. And, as we have seen, the constituents of clauses are noun phrases and verb phrases and these subsentential expressions do not have truth values. Thus, as the reader can easily check, the model $\langle U,e \rangle$, given here earlier, does not apply to the following sentence to yield a truth value:

31. Carl does not run.

The reason is that the phrase structure rule giving rise to this sentence is the following:

PSR 2.1n: $S \Rightarrow NP \; AX \; AV \; VP$

(where AX is the lexical category of auxiliary verbs such as *to do* and AV is the lexical category of the adverb *not*).

As a result, none of the sister constituents of AV has a truth value associated with it, and so the truth function o_¬, which interprets the adverb *not*, has nothing to which to apply:

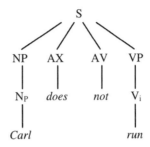

The problem is the same for copular sentences. Consider a copular sentence without *not*:

32. (a) Carl is courageous.
     (b) Carl is a runner.

The phrase structure rules for the verb phrases of these sentences are as follows:

PSR 3.3: $VP \Rightarrow V_c \ AP$

PSR 3.4: $VP \Rightarrow V_c \ NP$

PSR 3.5: $AP \Rightarrow A$

PSR 3.6: $NP \Rightarrow Dt \ N_c$

(where V_c is the lexical category of the copular verb *to be*, N_c is the lexical category of common nouns, and Dt is the lexical category of *a*, the indefinite article).

A view that dates back to the Middle Ages holds that adjectives and common nouns are assigned the sets of things of which they are true. Thus, for example, the adjective *courageous* is assigned the set of things that are courageous. Now surely the sentence in 32(a) is true just in case the thing denoted by the subject noun phrase is courageous. It follows, then, that the denotations of the adjective *courageous* and the verb phrase *is courageous* are the same. It follows further that the copula makes no semantic contribution: that is, the copula is semantically vacuous.

Generalizing with respect to this example, we formulate the following rule:

IR 3.3. Let $\langle D,i \rangle$ be a model. Let $[_{VP} \ V_c \ AP \ ]$ be the syntactic structure. Then, $v_i(VP) = v_i(AP)$.

On the basis of the model $\langle U,e \rangle$, we apply this interpretation rule and the others above to the phrase marker for the sentence in 34(a) to obtain the following:

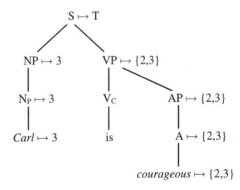

We now turn to the sentence in 32(b). Clearly, this sentence is nearly synonymous with the following sentence:

33. Carl runs.

Given that the sentences are nearly synonymous and that they have the same expression for a subject noun phrase, one concludes that here the verb phrases *runs* and *is a runner* make the same semantic contribution to their sentences and thus, have the same denotation associated with them. *Runner* has associated with it the set of runners, which is also what is associated with the verb *runs*. It follows, then, not only that the copula is semantically vacuous, but also that in this context the indefinite article is as well.[30]

Generalizing with respect to this example, we formulate the following two rules:

IR 3.4. Let $\langle D, i \rangle$ be a model. Let $[_{VP}\ V_c\ NP\ ]$ be the syntactic structure. Then, $v_i(VP) = v_i(NP)$.

IR 4.2. Let $\langle D, i \rangle$ be a model. Let $[_{NP}\ Dt\ N_c\ ]$ be the syntactic structure. Then, $v_i(NP) = v_i(N_c)$ (where N_c is a common noun).

These rules, applied to the phrase marker for the sentence in 34(b), yield the following interpreted phrase marker:

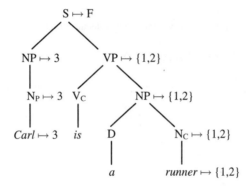

Let us return to the problem posed by the English adverb *not*. What the foregoing shows is that the prima facie syntactic structure of finite clauses containing the English adverb *not* fails to get assigned a truth value as long as the adverb is interpreted as the truth function $o_\_$. To overcome this problem, one must either alter the interpretation of the adverb or alter the structure of the finite clauses in which the adverb appears. We shall consider each alternative in turn.

To begin with the first alternative, consider again the sentence in 33, together with its unnegated counterpart:

34. (a) Carl does not run.
     (b) Carl runs.

It is certainly evident that the first sentence is true if and only if the person denoted by *Carl* fails to be in the set denoted by *runs*. But to fail to be in the set denoted by *runs* is to be in the complement of *runs*. Thus, an alternate way to characterize the truth of a sentence such as the one in 34(a) is this:

IR 2.1N. Let $\langle D,i \rangle$ be a model. Let $[_S\ NP\ AX\ AV\ VP\ ]$ be the syntactic structure. Then, $v_i(S) =$ T iff $v_i(NP) \in v_i(AV)v_i(VP)$ (where $i(not) = cp$, the complementation operator).[31]

Applied to the phrase marker for the sentence in 34(a), it yields the following:

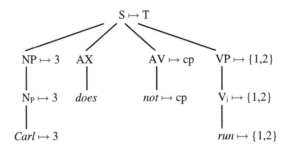

This interpretation of the adverb *not* works equally well for copular sentences. Consider the negated versions of the sentences in 32:

35. (a) Carl is not courageous.
    (b) Carl is not a runner.

Clearly, these sentences are true just in case the person denoted by *Carl* fails to be in the set denoted by *courageous* and the set denoted by *a runner*, respectively. The corresponding interpretation rules for PSR 3.4 and 3.5 can be formulated as follows:

IR 3.3N. Let $\langle D,i \rangle$ be a model. Let $[_{VP} V_c AV AP]$ be the syntactic structure. Then, $v_i(VP) = v_i(AV)v_i(AP)$.

IR 3.4N. Let $\langle D,i \rangle$ be a model. Let $[_{VP} V_c AV NP]$ be the syntactic structure. Then, $v_i(VP) = v_i(AV)v_i(NP)$.

We illustrate the first rule by showing its application to the phrase marker for the sentence in 35(a):

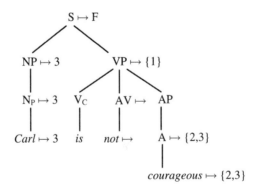

The semantic solution, as we just saw, retains the phrase structure rules given earlier and replaces the truth function $o_\neg$ with the complementation operation as the correct interpretation of *not*.[32] The syntactic solution, which we are about to see, retains the truth function $o_\neg$ as the correct interpretation of *not*. It postulates, instead, an additional syntactic rule, which we shall dub *not raising*, or NR for short.

The rule of NR is very different from the other syntactic rules we have encountered. All syntactic rules encountered so far are phrase structure rules. Mathematically speaking, they are all context-free rules. They specify constituent structure, or the local mother-daughter relation, within a phrase marker. NR is a transformational rule. Transformational rules operate on an entire phrase marker to yield a new phrase marker. The rule of NR, for example, applies to phrase markers with the adverb *not* and yields another phrase marker with the adverb *not*. Here is how it works. Divide the phrase marker for the sentence in 34(a) into two parts by removing from it the subphrase marker whose mother node is labeled AV. Next, reassemble these two parts—the removed subphrase marker and the phrase marker that results from the removal—by appending them to a single node labeled S with the first part first and the second part second:

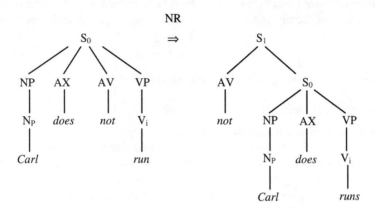

This operation is also described as the adjunction of AV to S. We shall abbreviate reference to the logical forms that are the result of NR as follows:

36. (a) Carl does not run.
          [$_S$ [$_{AV}$ not] [$_S$ Carl does run]]
     (b) Carl is not courageous.
          [$_S$ [$_{AV}$ not] [$_S$ Carl is courageous]]
     (c) Carl is not a runner.
          [$_S$ [$_{AV}$ not] [$_S$ Carl is a runner]]

Notice that the phrase markers that result from NR do not correspond to anything one hears. A phrase marker that corresponds to the sentence one hears is called by linguists its *surface form*, or its *s-structure*, and by philosophers its *grammatical form*, a term coined by Bertrand Russell. A phrase marker that does not correspond to what one hears yet provides a structure suitable for interpretation is called by linguists its *logical form*, or LF for short.[33]

An LF phrase marker is the phrase marker that yields to interpretation. As a result, an interpretation rule must be formulated for phrase markers such as those in 36:

IR FOR NR
Let $\langle D,i \rangle$ be a model. Let [$_S$ AV S] be the syntactic structure. Then, $v_i(S) = v_i(AV)v_i(S)$.

We illustrate this rule by applying it to the LF phrase marker for the sentence in 36(a):

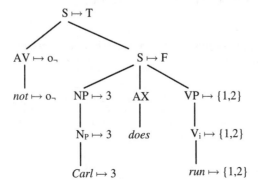

The reader may have noticed that all the noun phrases used in the illustrations so far have contained proper nouns and indefinite noun phrases containing the determiner *a*. We have said nothing about noun phrases such as *each man*, *some woman*, and *no child*. It has been recognized since the time of the Stoics that common nouns and proper nouns are different kinds of words, and their different semantic properties have been studied since the time of the Medieval logicians. The most satisfactory understanding of their semantic properties has been brought about by quantificational logic.

3. 4   Quantifier prefixes and noun phrases

3.4.1   Quantificational logic (QL)

Just as predicate logic is an enrichment of propositional logic, so quantificational logic is an enrichment of predicate logic. Its enrichment results from the addition of an infinite set of symbols known as *variables* (VR), typically referred to by lowercase letters from the end of the Roman alphabet, and a set containing two logical connectives known as *quantifiers* (QC, or $\{\exists, \forall\}$). To incorporate these new symbols into the notation, one must expand the definition of an atomic formula. This task is simplified by taking variables and constants together and calling them *terms* (TM). Thus, TM = CN $\cup$ VR.

> **DEFINITION 11.** *Atomic formulae (AF) of QL.* $\alpha \in$ AF, the atomic formulae of QL, iff, for some n and for some $\Pi \in PD_n$ and for some $t_1, \ldots, t_n \in$ TM, $\alpha = \Pi t_1 \ldots t_n$.

Here are some examples of atomic formulae, as well as sequences of symbols that may look like atomic formulae, but are not:

Predicate	Atomic formula	Nonformula
W _	W b, W x	W x a, W a x
S _ _	S z b, S x z, S z z	S z _, S x z y
G _ _ _	G x b z, G a x x	G z _, G z x, G c b a y

As in the case of predicate logic, we use the definition of an atomic formula of QL to define a formula of quantificational logic:

> **DEFINITION 12.** *Formulae (FM) of QL.* FM, the set of formulae of quantificational logic (QL), is defined as follows:
> (1)   AF $\subseteq$ FM;
> (2.1) if $\alpha \in$ FM and $* \in$ UC, then $*\alpha \in$ FM;
> (2.2) if $\alpha, \beta \in$ FM and $\bullet \in$ BC, then $(\alpha \bullet \beta)$ FM;
> (2.3) if $\alpha \in$ FM, $\nu \in$ VR and Q $\in$ QC, then $Q\nu\alpha \in$ FM;
> (3)   nothing else is.

To reinforce one's grasp of this definition, one might find it useful to compare the following formulae and nonformulae:

Formula	Nonformula
$\exists$x P x	$\exists$a P a
$\exists$x R x z	$\exists$xz R x z
$\forall$y R x z	$\forall$ R x z
$\neg\exists$z R a z	$\exists$z (R a z)

Not surprisingly, the procedure used to determine whether a string of symbols is a formula of propositional logic can be adapted to determine whether a string is a formula of quantificational logic:

STEP 1: Write down the string of symbols. Two possibilities arise: either the string comprises $n + 1$ symbol occurrences of which the first is an occurrence of an n-place predicate and the remainder are occurrences of terms, or it does not.

    STEP 1.1: If the string comprises $n + 1$ symbol occurrences of which the first is an occurrence of a n-place predicate and the remainder are occurrences of terms, then the string is a formula.

    STEP 1.2: If the string does not comprise such a sequence of symbols, proceed to the next step.

STEP 2: Two possibilities arise: either the string has one of three forms—$*\alpha$ (where $* \in$ UC), or $(\alpha \bullet \beta)$ (where $\bullet \in$ BC), or $Q\nu\alpha$ (where $Q \in$ QC and $\nu \in$ VR)—or it does not.

    STEP 2.1: If it does not have any of the three forms, then the string is not a formula.

    STEP 2.2: If it does have one of the three forms, proceed to the next step.

STEP 3: The string has one of three forms.

    STEP 3.1: If the string has the form $*\alpha$ (where $* \in$ UC), draw two lines slanting away from each other under the string and write down $*$ under the left line and α under the right. Return to STEP 1 for α.

    STEP 3.2: If it has the form $(\alpha \bullet \beta)$ (where $\bullet \in$ BC), draw three lines under the string—the left-hand one slanting to the left, the middle one straight down, and the right-hand one slanting to the right—and write α under the left-hand line, β under the right-hand line, and $\bullet$ under the middle one. Return to STEP 1 for α and β.

    STEP 3.3: If it has the form $Q\nu\alpha$ (where $Q \in$ QC and $\nu \in$ VR), draw two lines under the string—the left-hand one slanting to the left, and the right-hand one slanting to the right—and write $Q\nu$ under the left-hand line and α under the right-hand one. Return to STEP 1 for α.

STEP 4: Continue the steps above until one can proceed no longer.

Here is an example:

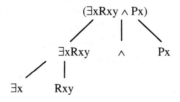

We now turn to a number of notions pertaining to the structure of formulae: the scope of a quantifier, free and bound variables, and, finally, open and closed formulae.

We have already encountered the notion of the scope of an occurrence of a logical connective: the scope of an occurrence of a logical connective within a formula is the smallest subformula containing the occurrence of the logical connective. We can broaden this notion to permit a quantifier occurrence to have scope: the scope of an occurrence of a quantifier within a formula is the smallest subformula containing the occurrence of the quantifier. Thus, in the formula $(\exists xRxy \wedge Px)$, the smallest subformula containing the only occurrence of the quantifier $\exists x$ is $\exists xRxy$. No formula contains an occurrence of a quantifier without an occurrence of a variable to its immediate right. Sometimes, it is useful to be able to refer to this sequence of a quantifier and a variable. We shall refer to it as a *quantifier prefix*. It should be clear that the scope of an occurrence of a quantifier and the scope of the occurrence of the quantifier prefix it helps to constitute are always the same.

Turning to the notion of free and bound variables, we have the following definition:

DEFINITION 13. *Binding for QL*. Let α be in FM. Let Qv_i be a quantifier prefix which occurs in α and let v_j be a variable in α. (An occurrence of) the quantifier prefix Qv_i binds an occurrence of the variable v_j iff
(1) $v_i = v_j$ (i.e., v_i and v_j are the same variable);
(2) the occurrence of v_j is within the scope of the occurrence of the quantifier prefix Qv_i; and
(3) no occurrence of either $\exists v_i$ or $\forall v_i$, distinct from the occurrence of the Qv_i, has the relevant occurrence of v_j within its scope and is itself within the scope of the relevant occurrence of Qv_i

The first two conditions stated in the definition are easier to grasp than the third. So, let us consider the definition, first in light of the first two conditions and then in light of the third. Consider again the formula $\exists xRxy \wedge Px$. The second occurrence of the variable x is bound by the only occurrence of the quantifier prefix $\exists x$, since the second occurrence of variable x is within the scope of the only occurrence of the quantifier prefix $\exists x$ and the occurrences of the variables are occurrences of the same variable x. In other words, the first two conditions in the definition are met. In contrast, the only occurrence of the variable y is not bound by the only occurrence of the quantifier prefix $\exists x$, for although the only occurrence of the variable y is within the scope of the only occurrence of the quantifier prefix $\exists x$, the occurrences of the variables are occurrences of distinct variables. In other words, though the second condition is met, the first is not. At the same time, the third occurrence of the variable x in the very same formula is not bound by the quantifier prefix $\exists x$, for although the occurrences of the variables are occurrences of the same variable, the third occurrence of the variable x is not within the scope of the only occurrence of the quantifier prefix $\exists x$.

Let us now turn to the third condition. It becomes operative only when a formula contains more than one occurrence of a quantifier prefix with the same variable occurring in each occurrence. Consider the formula $\forall x(Rxy \rightarrow \exists xPx)$. The last occurrence of the variable x satisfies the first two conditions of the definition, both with respect to the first quantifier prefix $\forall x$ and with respect to the second quantifier prefix $\exists x$. Now, it turns out to be undesirable to have any occurrence of a variable bound by two distinct occurrences of quantifier prefixes. To avoid such an undesirable consequence, one adopts condition 3, which will, so to speak, break any tie between competing occurrences of quantifier prefixes. Condition 3 requires that only the occurrence of a quantifier prefix with the smallest scope binds the occurrence of the variable. Thus, in the preceding example, the last occurrence of x is bound only by the quantifier prefix $\exists x$.

One question that naturally arises is: What is the status of the occurrence of the variable within an occurrence of a quantifier prefix? A careful reading of the definition of binding (Def. 13) reveals that the occurrence of the quantifier prefix binds the occurrence of the variable within it. Thus, for example, the occurrence of v in the quantifier prefix $\exists v$ is bound by that very occurrence of the quantifier prefix.

DEFINITION 14. *Bound variable*. (An occurrence of) a variable v_i is bound iff some quantifier prefix binds it.

DEFINITION 15. *Free variable*. (An occurrence of) a variable v_i is free iff no quantifier prefix binds it.

Consider the formula $Px \wedge \exists x \forall y(Rax \rightarrow Sxy)$. The first occurrence of x is free. The occurrence of x immediately following the only occurrence of "a" is bound by the only occurrence of the quantifier prefix $\exists x$, as is the occurrence of x immediately following the only occurrence of S. The last occurrence of "y" is bound by the only occurrence of the quantifier prefix ∀y.

The foregoing distinction between variables that are bound and variables that are free is used to distinguish two kinds of formulae: those that are closed and those that are open. A closed formula is one in which no free variables occur:

DEFINITION 16. *Closed formula.* A formula is closed iff it has no (occurrences of a) free variable.

Thus, each of the following formulae is closed: ∀zPz, ∃x∀yRxy, and ∃x∀y(Rax → Sxy).

An open formula is one in which at least one variable occurrence is free:

DEFINITION 17. *Open formula.* A formula is open iff it has at least one (occurrence of a) free variable.

Here are some examples: Pz, ∀yRxy, and ∃x∀y(Rax → Sxz).

We are now in a position to address the problem of how to define a classical valuation for the formulae of QL. A classical valuation is defined for propositional logic on the basis of a truth value assignment to the atomic formulae, or propositional variables, out of which are formed all the formulae of propositional logic, and five clauses, which extend the truth value assignment from the atomic formulae to all the formulae. Similarly, a classical valuation for predicate logic is defined on the basis of an assignment of truth values to the atomic formulae and five clauses, which extend the truth value assignment from the atomic formulae to all formulae. The difference between them is that the assignment of truth values to the atomic formulae in propositional logic is arbitrary, for the atomic formulae of propositional logic are just propositional variables, and they have no structure; in contrast, the assignment of truth values to the atomic formulae of predicate logic is not arbitrary. The atomic fomulae of predicate logic have structure: each formula comprises a predicate followed by a number of constants. In addition, a model's interpretation function assigns values to the predicates and constants, which induces a truth value assignment to each atomic formula.

The notation of quantificational logic is more elaborate than that of predicate logic. In addition to constants (CN), it has variables (VR); in addition to the unary and binary connectives, it has quantifiers. Variables and quantifiers pose a problem for defining a classical valuation. To see how, consider the formula ∀xPx. This formula comprises a quantifier prefix ∀x and a subformula Px. Should we proceed as before, we would expect that the truth value of ∀xPx would be determined on the basis of a truth value assigned to Px and some values assigned to ∀ and x. However, as we shall see, this is not how one usually proceeds. To begin with, it is not clear how to assign a truth value to Px; for, even given a model, one has no more of an idea whether Px is true or false in a model than whether or not $x \leq 5$ is true or false. Moreover, it is also very unclear what kinds of values to assign either to ∀ or to x.

Although the expression $x \leq 5$ cannot be determined to be true or false, it can be if we assign a value to x. Thus, if x is assigned 4, it is true; but if it is assigned 6, it is false. Similarly, the formula Px can be assigned a truth value in a model, provided that some element of the model's universe is assigned to x. The problem is that a truth value cannot be determined for a quantified formula such as ∀xPx or ∃xPx, at least in general, on the basis of a single value assigned to x.

Consider the formula ∀xPx. What should its truth value be in a model <U,i>, where U = {1,2,3} and where i(P) = {1,2}? Px, the subformula of ∀xPx, is true in this model if x is assigned 1, since 1 is a member of i(P). It is also true in the model if x is assigned 2, since 2 is a member of i(P). However, it is false in the model if x is assigned 3, since 3 is not in i(P). Since P is false of at least one thing, ∀xPx is false. In short, ∀xPx is true in a model just in case Px is true, no matter which member of the model's universe is assigned to x. Next, consider the formula ∃xPx. It is true just in case Px is true for some member of the model's universe assigned to x. As it happens, when x is assigned 1, Px is true. So, ∃xPx is true in the model. More generally, ∀vα is true in a model if and only if α is true in it for no matter which member of the model's universe is assigned to ν; and $\exists\nu\alpha$ is true in a model if and only if α is true in it for some member of the model's universe assigned to ν.

It is clear, then, that we need, in addition to a model, which provides an interpretation function, whereby values are assigned to predicates and constants, a way to assign values to variables. This can be done by a so-called variable assignment, a function from VR into the model's universe. The function defined next retains the clauses (1) and (2) found in Def. 10; however, two other sets of clauses have to be added: those in (0), which amalgamate the interpretation function of a model and a variable assignment, and those in (3), which assign truth values to formulae whose main connective is a quantifier prefix. The clauses in (1) through (3) ensure that every formula is assigned a truth value.

DEFINITION 18. *Truth in a model at a variable assignment.* Let M, $\langle U,i \rangle$, be a model for QL. Let g be a variable assignment from VR into U. Then [$]^{M,g}$ is a function from VR, CN, PD, and FM into {T,F}, satisfying the following conditions:

Symbols:
Let ν be a member of VR, let c be a member of CN, and let Π be a member of PD.
    (0.1) $[\nu]^{M,g} = g(\nu)$;
    (0.2) $[c]^{M,g} = i(c)$;
    (0.3) $[\Pi]^{M,g} = i(\Pi)$.

Atomic formulae:
Let Π be a member of PD_1, and let t be a member of TM. Then,
    (1.1) $[\Pi t]^{M,g} = T$ iff $\langle [t]^{M,g} \rangle \in [\Pi]^{M,g}$;
Let Π be a member of PD_n, and let $t_1, \ldots, t_n$ be occurrences of members of TM where $n > 1$.
   Then,
    (1.2) $[\Pi t_1 \ldots t_n]^{M,g} = T$ iff $\langle [t_1]^{M,g}, \ldots, [t_n]^{M,g} \rangle \in [\Pi]^{M,g}$.

Composite formulae:
Let α and β be members of FM.
    (2.1) $[\neg\alpha]^{M,g}$ $= o_\neg ([\alpha]^{M,g})$;
    (2.2.1) $[\alpha \wedge \beta]^{M,g}$ $= o_\wedge([\alpha]^{M,g}, [\beta]^{M,g})$;
    (2.2.2) $[\alpha \vee \beta]^{M,g}$ $= o_\vee([\alpha]^{M,g}, [\beta]^{M,g})$;
    (2.2.3) $[a \rightarrow b]^{M,g}$ $= o_\rightarrow ([\alpha]^{M,g}, [\beta]^{M,g})$;
    (2.2.4) $[a \leftrightarrow b]^{M,g}$ $= o_\leftrightarrow ([\alpha]^{M,g}, [\beta]^{M,g})$.

Composite formulae:
Let ν be a member of VR, and let α be a member of FM.
    (3.1) $[\forall\nu\,\alpha]^{M,g} = T$ iff for each e in U, $[\alpha]^{M,g}{}_{\nu \mapsto e} = T$;
    (3.2) $[\exists\nu\,\alpha]^{M,g} = T$ iff for some e in U, $[\alpha]^{M,g}{}_{\nu \mapsto e} = T$.

Up to this point, we have written functions with the function name on the left and parentheses enclosing the function's argument. In this definition, the function name appears on the right and is raised, and the argument is enclosed in square brackets. As an aid to memory, the function name contains the name of the underlying model and the underlying variable assignment. As stated, the clauses in (0) amalgamate the variable assignment and the interpretation function. In other words, if the function is applied to a variable, then the value of the function is the value which the underlying variable assignment would assign; and if function is applied to a predicate or a constant, then the value of the function is the value which the underlying interpretation function would assign. The clauses in (1) state how, in light of the clauses in (0), atomic formulae receive truth value assignments. Notice that even open formulae now receive a truth value assignment, since variables are assigned values. The clauses in (2) show how the truth value assignments to atomic formulae extend to composite formulae constructed with unary and binary connectives. Finally, the clauses in (3) state how truth value assignments are extended to composite formulae constructed with quantifier prefixes.

It is important to recognize that the clauses in (3) of the foregoing definition are of a different mathematical character from those in (0), (1), and (2). Consider the following formula:

37. $\forall x \exists y Rxy$.

This formula is true, for example, for any model whose universe is $\{1,2,3\}$ and whose interpretation function assigns $\{<1,2>, <2,3>, <3,1>\}$ to R. Let us see how.

According to clause 3.1, $[\forall x \exists y Rxy]^{M,g} = T$ if and only if, for each $e \in \{1,2,3\}$, $[\exists y Rxy]^{M,g_{x \to e}} = T$. Since the universe contains only three elements, the following three equalities must hold for the formula to be true:

38. (a) $[\exists y Rxy]^{M,g_{x \to 1}} = T$
     (b) $[\exists y Rxy]^{M,g_{x \to 2}} = T$
     (c) $[\exists y Rxy]^{M,g_{x \to 3}} = T$

The truth of these equalities is determined by clause 3.2. Again, since the universe contains only three elements, three more equalities arise for each preceding equality:

39. (a) $[Rxy]^{M,g_{x \to 1; y \to 1}} = F$
     (b) $[Rxy]^{M,g_{x \to 1; y \to 2}} = T$
     (c) $[Rxy]^{M,g_{x \to 1; y \to 3}} = F$

According to clause 3.2, if any one of these three hold, then 40(a) holds. As it happens, 39(b) holds, since $\langle 1,2 \rangle$ is in the set assigned to R. Thus, the equality in 38(a) holds.

Next, the equality in 38(b) holds, just in case one of the following equalities holds:

40. (a) $[Rxy]^{M,g_{x \to 2; y \to 1}} = F$
     (b) $[Rxy]^{M,g_{x \to 2; y \to 2}} = F$
     (c) $[Rxy]^{M,g_{x \to 2; y \to 3}} = T$

The equality in 40(c) holds, because $\langle 2,3 \rangle$ is in the set assigned to R. So again, by clause 3.2, the equality in 38(b) also holds.

Finally, we come to the equality in 38(c). It holds just in case one of the following holds:

41. (a) $[Rxy]^{M,g_{x \to 3; y \to 1}} = T$
     (b) $[Rxy]^{M,g_{x \to 3; y \to 2}} = F$
     (c) $[Rxy]^{M,g_{x \to 3; y \to 3}} = F$

The equality in 41(a) holds, since $\langle 3,1 \rangle$ is in the set assigned to R.

We have now seen that each of 38(a), 38(b), and 38(c) holds. So, by clause 3.1, $[\forall x \exists y Rxy]^{M,g} = T$—that is, the formula $\forall x \exists y Rxy$ in model M under the variable assignment g is true.

While the foregoing calculations assign a truth value to the formula in question, these calculations do not follow the structure of the formula in question. This can be seen in the following diagram where an attempt is made to apply the definition of truth in a model at a variable assignment (Def. 18) to the parts of the construction tree for $\forall x \exists y Rxy$:

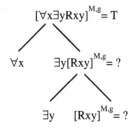

Notice that no value is assigned by the function $[\ ]^{M,g}$ to any node, except the one labeled by the formula $\forall x \exists y Rxy$. No functions are applied either to the node labeled $\forall x$ or to the one labeled $\exists y$. Three different functions are applied to the node labeled $\exists y Rxy$, and nine different functions are applied to the node labeled Rxy. Thus, the value of a mother node is not determined by a unique assignment of values to the daughter nodes; rather, the value of a mother node is determined by many values assigned to a daughter node.

This procedure stands in sharp distinction to the calculation of truth values for a formula in predicate logic (PDL) or in propositional logic (PL). In PDL and PL, the value of any mother node is determined solely on the basis of a single assignment to each of its immediate daughter nodes. Interpretation functions are said to be strongly compositional precisely if they behave like the valuations of PL and the models of PDL—namely, the value they assign to any mother node is completely determined by the values assigned to the daughter nodes.[34] The function defined in Def. 18 does not satisfy this condition, though it does assign a truth value to every formula.[35]

It is tempting to think that the function defined in Def.18 is a classical valuation for the closed formulae of QL. However, it does not state whether or not a closed formula is true in a model; it states whether or not it is true in a model under a variable assignment. Yet if one looks carefully at the illustrative calculation, one notices that the initial choice of variable assignment makes no difference to the outcome of the calculation. In other words, one would arrive at the very same result, no matter which variable assignment is chosen. This means that any closed formula true under one variable assignment is true under all variable assignments, and any closed formula false under one variable assignment is false under all variable assignments. The irrelevance of variable assignments to the truth or falsity of a closed formula permits one to speak of the truth or falsity of a closed formula in a model *simpliciter*. Here are the definitions:

DEFINITION 19. *Truth in a model*. Let M be a model for QL. For each $\alpha \in$ FM, $[\alpha]^M = T$ iff, for each variable assignment g from VR into U, $[\alpha]^{M,g} = T$.

DEFINITION 20. *Falsity in a model*. Let M be a model for QL. For each $\alpha \in$ FM, $[\alpha]^M = F$ iff, for each variable assignment g from VR into U, $[\alpha]^{M,g} = F$.

It is easy to show that these two definitions combined provide a classical valuation for the closed formula of QL. In other words, if M is a model for QL, then $[\ ]^M$ is a classical valuation for the closed formulae of QL:

FACT ABOUT CLASSICAL VALUATIONS FOR CLOSED FORMULA
Let M be a model for QL. Then, $[\ ]^M$ is a classical valuation for the closed formulae of QL.

One final remark is in order. The definition of truth in a model at a variable assignment (Def. 16) is not a categorematic definition, for the clauses in (3) assign no value to quantifier prefixes. The question that now arises is whether it is possible to provide categorematic versions of those in (3). The answer is yes. The idea is to assign to the quantifiers special sets. The quantifier $\forall$ is assigned the set whose sole member is the universe; the existential quantifier $\exists$ is assigned the set whose members are all the nonempty subsets of the universe. In other words, if the universe of the model is U, then $o_\forall = \{U\}$ and $o_\exists = \text{Pow}(U) - \{\varnothing\}$. Here are the clauses in (3) of Def. 18, reformulated in categorematic terms:

Composite formulae:
Let ν be a member of VR, and let α be a member of FM.
(3.1) $[\forall \nu \alpha]^{M,g} = T$ iff $\{e \in U : [\alpha]^{M,g_{\nu \mapsto e}} = T\} \in o_\forall$;
(3.2) $[\exists \nu \alpha]^{M,g} = T$ iff $\{e \in U : [\alpha]^{M,g_{\nu \mapsto e}} = T\} \in o_\exists$.

We can now use the classical valuations for the closed formulae of QL to classify them as either *tautologies* (also known as *logical truths*), *contingencies*, or *contradictions*.

DEFINITION 21. *Tautology.* A formula is a tautology iff every model renders it true (i.e., for each model M, $[\alpha]^M = T$).

Here are some examples: Pa $\vee$ $\neg$Pa, $\forall$x(Px $\vee$ $\neg$Px), and $\exists$y$\forall$xPxy $\rightarrow$ $\forall$x$\exists$yPxy.

DEFINITION 22. *Contradiction.* A formula is a contradiction iff every model renders it false (i.e., for each model M, $[\alpha]^M = F$).

Here are some examples: Pa $\wedge$ $\neg$Pa, $\exists$x(Px $\wedge\neg$Px), and $\exists$y$\forall$xRxy $\wedge$ $\exists$x$\forall$y$\neg$Rxy.

DEFINITION 23. *Contingency.* A formula is a contingency iff some model renders it true (i.e., for some model M, $[\alpha]^M = T$) and some model renders it false (i.e., for some model M, $[\alpha]^M = F$).

Here are some examples: Pa $\vee$ $\neg$Rab, $\exists$xPx, and $\forall$x$\exists$yRxy.

We can also use the notion of truth in a model to define entailment:

DEFINITION 24. *Entailment.* $\Gamma \vDash \alpha$ iff, for each model M, if $[\beta]^M = T$, for each $\beta \in \Gamma$, then $[\alpha]^M = T$.

For example, $\exists$x$\forall$yRxy $\vDash$ $\forall$y$\exists$xRxy, and $\neg\exists$x(Fx $\wedge$ Gx) $\vDash$ $\forall$x(Fx $\rightarrow$ $\neg$Gx).

3.4.2.   Quantified noun phrases

Having set out the basic concepts of quantificational logic, let us now see in what way these concepts can be used to elucidate how truth values associated with natural language clauses can be obtained from various other values associated with their constituents. In particular, let us see how variables can be used to elucidate the uses of third-person personal pronouns with antecedents and how the model theory of quantification might be used to elucidate the semantics of such quantified noun phrases as *every man* and *some woman*. We begin with quantified noun phrases.

Quantified noun phrases behave differently from other noun phrases, especially proper noun phrases. To see this, consider the following valid argument using proper nouns:

42.   (a) *Bill* has two cars.
      (b) *Fred* has one more car than *Bill*.
      (c) Therefore, *Fred* has three cars.

This argument remains valid for any substitution of proper names for *Bill* and *Fred*, respectively. Indeed, it remains true for substitutions by other kinds of noun phrases denoting a single individual:

43.   (a) *Your lawyer* has two cars.
      (b) *Your stockbroker* has one more car than *your lawyer*.
      (c) Therefore, *your stockbroker* has three cars.

However, as Lewis Carrol observed, this argument is no longer valid when the noun phrases are quantified:

44.   (a) *No dog* has two tails.
      (b) *Every dog* has one more tail than *no dog*.
      (c) Therefore, *every dog* has three tails.

The conclusion from puzzles such as this is that quantified noun phrases such as *no dog* and *every dog* do not have denotations, or at least they do not denote a single individual. How, then, are such noun phrases to be treated?

The model theory of quantification is widely thought to be of help here. It turns out, however, that the application is not trivial. The principal obstacle is that the English clauses and their corresponding formula have different ingredients and different structures. Consider, for example, the following two sentences and their logical renditions:

	ENGLISH	LOGIC
45.	(a) Some raven is black.	$\exists x(Rx \wedge Bx)$
	(b) Each raven is black.	$\forall x(Rx \to Bx)$

Both of the logical formulae have variables and a logical connective, whereas neither of the English sentences has anything corresponding to variables and neither has a connector, the English counterpart of a logical connective. For example, there is no *if* in the English sentence 45(b) corresponding to $\to$ in the logical formula. Moreover, the formulae have structures different from those of the English sentences, as shown:

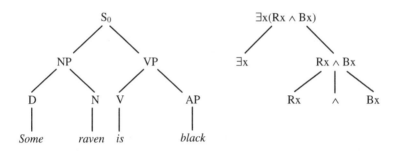

The model theory of quantificational logic cannot be applied to such sentences. However, the model theory of generalized quantification (GQL) can be. The theory of generalized quantification was pioneered by Andrzej Mostowski (1957) and developed by Per Lindstrom (1966). Its application to natural language, anticipated by Richard Montague (1974a; 1974b), Jens Fenstad (1978), and Christopher Peacocke (1979), was elaborated by Jon Barwise and Robin Cooper (1981: this volume, Chapter 23), James Higginbotham and Robert May (1981), and Edward Keenan and Jonathan Stavi (1986).[36] Although we do not have the space to go into detail, we shall present enough to make clear its utility to natural language semantics.[37]

We begin by defining the formulae of GQL. They are formed from the same atomic formulae from which the formulae of QL are formed:

DEFINITION 25. *Atomic formulae (AF) of GQL.* $\alpha \in AF$, the atomic formulae of GQL, iff, for some n and for some $\Pi \in PD_n$ and for some $t_1, \ldots, t_n \in TM$, $\alpha = \Pi t_1, \ldots, t_n$.

The difference comes in the definition of the formulae, in particular, in the clauses that introduce the quantificational connectives. In QL a formula preceded by a quantifier prefix, which comprises a quantificational connective and a variable, is a formula. In GQL, matters are more complex. A formula preceded by a quantifier prefix yields a restricted quantifier prefix (RQP); and RQP and a formula yield a formula:

DEFINITION 26. *Formulae of GQL.* FM, the set of formulae of generalized quantificational logic (GQL), is defined as follows:

(1)   AF ⊆ FM;
(2.1) if α ∈ FM and * ∈ UC, then *α ∈ FM;
(2.2) if α, β ∈ FM • ∈ BC, then (α•β) ∈ FM;
(3.1) if Q ∈ QC, ν ∈ VR, and α ∈ FM, then Qνα ∈ RQP;
(3.2) if γ ∈ RQP and β ∈ FM, then γ β ∈ FM;
(4)   nothing else is.

Thus, as the reader will have noticed, the clauses in (1) and (2) are just like the clauses in the definition of the formulae of QL (Def. 12). The difference comes in the clauses in (3). First, an intermediate unit is built, labeled RQP. Then, it, followed by a formula, yields a formula. Below are some examples of formulae and nonformulae of GQL:

Formula	Nonformula
∃xPxQx	∃xPx
∀xPx∃yQyRxy	∀xPx∃yRxy
∃xPx(Qx ∧ Rxy)	∃xPxQxRxy
∃x(Qx ∧ Px) ∀yRxy	∃x∀yRxy

Now the formula of GQL which, as we shall see, is equivalent to the formula ∃x(Rx ∧ Bx) of QL, is ∃xRxBx. Its construction tree is the following:

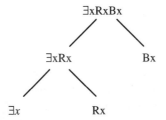

Let us now turn to the model theory for such formulae. As it happens, we can adopt all the clauses of Def. 18, except the clauses in (3). These clauses have to be modified as follows:

Composite formulae:
Let ν be a member of VR; let α and β be members of FM; and let γ be a member of RQP.
(3.1) $[\gamma \, \beta]^{M,g} = T$ iff $\{e \in U : [\beta]^{M,g_{\nu \to e}} = T\} \in [\,\gamma\,]^{M,g}$
(3.2) $[Q\nu\alpha]^{M,g} = o_Q(\{e \in U : [\alpha]^{M,g_{\nu \to e}} = T\})$.

To see how the clauses in (3) work, consider the formula ∃xRxBx with respect to the model <U, i>, where U = {1,2,3,4} and where i(R) = {1,2} and i(B) = {1,2,3}. In GQL, ∃ν is assigned the function whose domain is Pow(U), whose codomain is Pow(Pow(U)), and whose rule of association is $X \mapsto \{Y \subseteq U : X \cap Y \neq \varnothing\}$. Applying the clauses in (3) to the construction tree above yields the following:

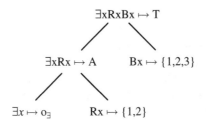

(where A is the set $\{Y \subseteq U: \{1,2\} \cap Y \neq \varnothing\}$). Members of A include $\{1,3,4\}$, $\{2,4\}$, and $\{1,2,3\}$, as well as other sets. Since $\{1,2,3\} \in A$, the formula $[\exists x R x B x]^{M,g} = T$.

Let us return, now, to 44(a) and see how to apply the model theory of generalized quantifier theory to simple English clauses containing noun phrases such as *some raven* or *each raven*:

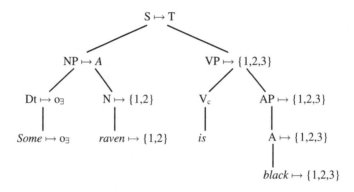

While generalized quantifier theory is easily adapted to the treatment of quantified noun phrases in the subject position, it does not apply to quantified noun phrases in other positions. Consider, for example, the following sentence:

46. Bill saw each raven.

The object noun phrase *each raven*, to which, according to generalized quantifier theory, is assigned the set of all supersets of the set of ravens in the universe, does not have a sister to which is assigned a subset of the universe. Rather, its only sister is assigned a set of ordered pairs—namely, the set of pairs of who in the universe saw what or whom in the universe. One way to circumvent this problem is to use a rule known as *quantifier raising*, or QR for short. This rule extracts a quantified noun phrase—in this case, *each raven*—and adjoins it to the clause:

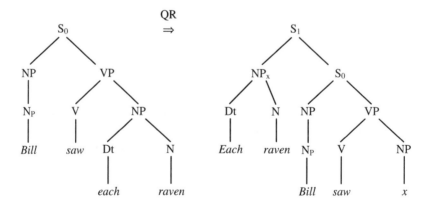

The result is a structure in which the quantifed noun phrase has a sister node whose value is suited to that of the quantified noun phrase. Here, for example, the sister of the quantified noun phrase *each raven* has for its sister the node S_0 whose value is the set of all things in the universe seen by Bill. The node S_1 is assigned T just in case the set assigned to S_0 is a member of the set of sets assigned to the quantified noun phrase.

3.4.3   Pronouns and variables

Let us now turn to third-person personal pronouns. It has been known since the Stoics that third-person personal pronouns have antecedents. Such pronouns, according to the Stoics, are substitutes for their antecedents. The prototypical cases involve pronouns whose antecedents are nouns. Hence the term *pronoun*, or *pro noun*, that which stands *for a noun*.

47.   (a)   John thinks that John is smart.

     (b)   *John* thinks that *he* is smart.[38]

Early generative grammar, recognizing that it is not nouns, but noun phrases that serve as antecedents, formalized the traditional view as a rule called *pronominalization*, a rule whereby a sentence containing a third-person personal pronoun and its antecedent is derived from one with two occurrences of the same noun phrase. Thus, the sentence in 47(b) is obtained from the one in 47(a) by the application of the rule of pronominalization, whereby the second occurrence of *John* in 47(a) is replaced by the third-person personal pronoun *he*.[39]

The inadequacy of this way of thinking about third-person personal pronouns was first recognized by Geach (1962) and Quine (1960), who observed that pronouns are not always mere substitutes for their antecedents. However, as they both made clear, an analysis of third-person personal pronouns as substitutes for their antecedents implies that a pair of sentences that differ from one another only insofar as one has a pronoun with an antecedent while the other has the pronoun's antecedent substituting for the pronoun should be synonymous. The pairs of sentences in 47 are synonymous, but the pair in 48 does not exhibit synonymy:

48.   (a)   Some man thinks that whiskey is good for some man.

     (b)   *Some man* thinks that whiskey is good for *him*.

Quine and Geach suggested that pronouns in sentences like those in 48 be viewed on an analogy with bound variables of logic.

Third-person personal pronouns are not the only pronouns that can be treated as are the variables of quantificational logic. So can reflexive pronouns:

49.   (a)   *John* is proud of *himself*.

     (b)   *Each boy* is proud of *himself*.

Linguists readily adopted this insight, extending it to other cases. In particular, they used it to account for many cases of identity of value, even those where no overt pronoun occurs (Higginbotham 1980: this volume, Chapter 22).

It has been known since Pāṇini that values of a valence, which is about to be explained, of one verb may be identical with that of another. Consider the following sentence:

50.   (a)   Devadattaḥ gantum icchati.

     (b)   Devadatta wishes to go.

The English sentence, like the Sanskrit one from which it is translated, contains two verbs: *wishes* (*icchati*) and *to go* (*gantum*). Moreover, associated with each verb is a valence or thematic role (*kāraka*): *wishes* has the valence of someone who wishes, the verb's agent (*kartā*); and *to go* has the valence of someone who goes, its agent. Now the valence of the verb *wishes* is overtly expressed by the subject noun phrase *Devadatta*. But there is no distinct overt expression of the agent of *to go*. However, as every English speaker and every Sanskrit speaker knows, if the wish expressed by the sentences in 50 is fulfilled, it is Devadatta who leaves. Thus, the agent of *wishes* and the agent of *to go* are the same—namely, Devadatta. Pāṇini captured this identity between valences of verbs by making the use of certain verb forms—in this case, the use of the infinitival form—conditional upon the identity of the agent of the verb with the infinitival form with the agent of the verb in the noninfinitival form.[40]

This is now known as the problem of control. It was rediscovered in Western grammar by generativists. Their initial treatment was to use a rule of deletion, which deleted, under certain circumstances, a noun phrase which was type identical with another noun phrase, and which made other necessary adjustments in the result. Thus, the second sentence below was obtained from the first by the deletion of the second noun phrase:

51. (a) Devadatta wishes that Devadatta leave.
     (b) Devadatta wishes to leave.

This rule was recognized to be inadequate for the same reason as the rule of pronominalization was so recognized. For it implies that pairs of sentences such as the following are synonymous, contrary to fact:

52. (a) Everyone wishes that everyone leave.
     (b) Everyone wishes to leave.

At the same time, it was recognized that the identity of valence could be handled by the posit of a phonetically null pronoun, called PRO, which can then be treated as a bound variable.

53. (a) Everyone wishes to leave.
     (b) *Everyone* wishes [$_S$ *PRO* to leave]

3.4.4   Quantified Noun Phrases and Pronouns

The view of quantified noun phrases and pronouns just sketched gives rise to a puzzle, first noted by Medieval logicians but brought to the attention of linguists and philosophers again only fifty years ago by Geach (1962). The puzzle is embodied in what has become to be known as donkey sentences, for reasons the two prototypical examples given below make clear:

54. (a) Every farmer who owns *a donkey* beats *it*.
     (b) If *a farmer* owns *a donkey, he* beats *it*.

These sentences show the inconsistency of three prima facie plausible assumptions: first, that the antecedent of the third-person personal pronoun *it* is the indefinite noun phrase *a donkey*; second, that indefinite noun phrases, such as *a donkey*, are restricted existential quantifiers; and third, that a third-person personal pronoun whose antecedent is a quantified noun phrase functions in natural language in a way analogous to the way a bound variable functions in QL.

To show the incompatibility, let us avail ourselves of the rule of QR, introduced earlier. The logical form of the sentence in 54(a), then, is this:

55. [$_S$ [$_{NP}$ a donkey]$_y$ [$_S$ [$_{NP}$ every farmer who owns y]$_x$ [$_S$ x beats y]]]

which corresponds to the familiar formula of quantificational logic:

56. $\exists y (Dy \wedge \forall x ((Fx \wedge Oxy) \rightarrow Bxy))$

(where D corresponds to 'donkey', F to 'farmer', O to 'own', and B to 'beat').

If no single donkey is beaten by every farmer, then the expressions in 55 and 56 are false. However, the sentence in 54(a) may still be true, provided that every farmer beats every donkey he owns.[41]

Three responses to the enigma of donkey anaphora have enjoyed varying currency. All three responses accept the assumption that the indefinite noun phrase is the antecedent of the pronoun. The most widely accepted response gives up the assumption that indefinite noun phrases are restricted existential quantifiers and maintains, instead, that indefinite noun phrases are restricted free variables. This approach was advocated independently by Kamp (1981: this volume, Chapter 13) and Heim (1982). A second response gives up the assumption that anaphoric third-person personal pronouns are functioning on the analogy with bound variables of quantificational logic. This second approach, due to Evans (1977),[42] has been recently elaborated in detail by Neale (1990, ch. 5). A third response, advocated by Groenendijk and Stokhof (1991: this volume, Chapter 14), gives up on two assumptions: that indefinite noun phrases are restricted existential quantifiers and that a third-person personal pronoun whose antecedent is a quantified noun phrase functions in a way analogous to the way a bound variable functions in quantificational logic.

We begin with Evans's view. Evans maintained that, while pronouns do sometimes function in the same way as the variables of quantificational logic, sometimes they function as what Neale (1990) has called descriptive pronouns.[43] As their name suggests, such pronouns are definite descriptions, albeit degenerate ones. What this proposal amounts to here is this: a grammatically singular, descriptive pronoun denotes the unique individual satisfying, on the one hand, the term of its antecedent and, on the other, the open clause obtained by deleting its antecedent from the clause in which it occurs.

To see how descriptive pronouns work, consider the following sentences:

57.   (a) Harry bought *a carpet* and John cleaned *it*.
      (b) Harry bought a carpet which John cleaned.

The first sentence implies that there is exactly one carpet relevant, while the second does not. The semantics for descriptive pronouns delivers this contrast. In 57(a), the antecedent of *it* is *a carpet*. The required open clause is *Harry bought____*. So, the denotation of *it* is the unique carpet such that Harry bought it. This rule of interpretation implies that the following is a good, though admittedly long-winded, paraphrase of the sentence in 57(a):

58.   Harry bought a carpet and John cleaned the carpet Harry bought.

This account, applied to the sentence in 54(a), makes it truth conditionally equivalent to:

59.   Every farmer who owns a donkey beats the donkey he owns.

However, the sentences in 54 and 59 do not seem equivalent. In particular, the one in 59 entails that each farmer owns a unique donkey, while the sentence in 54(a) does not.[44]

The approaches of Kamp (1981) and of Heim (1982) are more successful, at least at first sight. We shall sketch here the basic ideas of Kamp's *discourse representation theory* (1981: this volume, Chapter 13).[45] Recall that Kamp retains the assumption that anaphoric pronouns are well-modeled as bound variables of quantificational logic, but rejects the assumption that indefinite noun phrases are well-modeled as restricted existential quantifiers. This rejection requires that certain compensating assumptions be adopted. In discourse representation theory, the truth conditions of a sentence are determined, not with respect to the sentence's syntactic analysis but rather with respect to structures—so-called *discourse representation structures*—constructed from the sentence's syntactic analysis, where the construction proceeds top to bottom and left to right.

These structures comprise a list of free variables and a set of conditions. A discourse representation structure determines not only the truth conditions of the sentence from which it is constructed but also which noun phrases might serve as antecedents for which pronouns.

Now, treatment of the antecedence relation must specify the morphological and syntactic constraints on the relation and the semantic mechanism whereby appropriate values are assigned to the relata of the relation. Discourse representation theory does both. The antecedence relation obtains when an identity condition is created for the variables associated with the relevant noun phrases. Whether the appropriate identity condition is imposed depends on whether the variable corresponding to the antecedent is accessible to the variable corresponding to the pronoun. This, in turn, depends on two factors: the accessibility relation (defined over the structure of the discourse representation structure) and the positions in the discourse structure where the variables are introduced.

The sentence in 60(a), once syntactically analyzed, has the discourse representation structure in 60(d):

60.   (a) Some man arrived.
      (b) $[_S \ [_{NP} \ \text{Some man}] \ [_{VP} \ \text{arrived}]]$
      (c) $[_S \ [_{NP} \ \text{Some man}]_x \ [_S \ x \ \text{arrived}]]$
      (d) < x: x is a man, x arrived >

This structure comprises a list of variables (in this case, a list of one variable) and a set of conditions (in this case, two conditions).

To obtain an equivalence between the structure in 60(b) and the logical form in 60(c), Kamp avails himself of two facts of elementary model theory.[46] First, every formula in a finite set of formulae is true in a model if and only if the conjunction formed from the formulae in the set is true in it. Second,

61. $[\exists v \ \varphi \ (v)]^M = T$, iff, for some variable assignment g, $[\varphi \ (v)]^{M,g} = T$.

Let us turn to the sentence in 54(a). The basic idea is that it gives rise to the following discourse representation structure:

62.   <x y : <x is a farmer, y is a donkey, x owns y> $\Rightarrow$ <x beats y> >

The model theoretic interpretation of $\Rightarrow$, which is a connective between two structures, <x is a farmer, y is a donkey, x owns y> and <x beats y>, is that it is true, just in case every variable assignment which makes the first one true makes the second one true. It is easy to see that such a structure is true in all and only those situations in which every farmer beats every donkey he owns.

The third and the most recent approach is that of *dynamic predicate logic* (DPL). To see how it differs from the previous treatments, let us recall how the relation of antecedence is modeled in quantificational logic. Quantificational logic is very limited in its capacity to mimic the antecedence relation of natural language. To mimic the relation, the variable that corresponds to the pronoun must be the same as the variable that corresponds to the pronoun's antecedent, and both instances of the variable must be bound by one and the same quantifier. It is this syntactic configuration of quantificational logic alone that permits the values of the variable corresponding to the pronoun to depend on the values of the variable corresponding to the pronoun's antecedent. But it is common for a sentence containing a pronoun and its antecedent noun phrase to be rendered a formula in QL in such a way that the quantifier prefix corresponding to the antecedent noun phrase cannot bind the variable corresponding to the pronoun. The next sentence is an example:

63. *Some man* arrived and *he* was hungry.

The formula of quantificational logic that most closely corresponds to the sentence above is the following:

64. $\exists x$ (x is a man $\wedge$ x arrived) $\wedge$ x is hungry.

However, the fourth occurrence of the variable x is not within the scope of the quantifier that binds the third occurrence. As a result, the choice of value for the variable x in the formula 'x is hungry' is independent of the choice of value for the variable x in the formula 'x is a man' $\wedge$ 'x arrived'.

Let us first look at an important enrichment of the model theory of QL. We noted earlier that neither the function of truth in a model at a variable assignment (Def. 18) nor the function of truth in a model (Def. 19) yield functions which assign a value to a complex formula solely on the basis of a unique assignment of values to its immediate subformulae and logical connective. This, we noted, is in contrast to propositional logic and predicate logic. Using what they call *cylindrical algebras*, Henkin, Monk, and Tarski (1971) provided a model theory for quantificational logic in which a unique assignment of values to a formula's immediate subformulae and logical connective. On this approach, as before, a model M comprises a pair <U,i>, where U is a nonempty set, the universe, and i is a function, having as its domain the predicates,[47] where, if Π is an *n*-place predicate, then $i(\Pi) \in Pow(U^n)$. However, instead of assigning truth values to formulae, one assigns to each of them all the variable assignments that render them true. A formula is true if, and only if, it is assigned V, the set of all variable assignments; and it is false if and only if, it is assigned the empty set. The assignment of variable assignments is done by the function $[\ ]_M$ defined next:

DEFINITION 27. *Variable assignment in a cylindrical algebra.* Let Π be an *n*-place predicate. Let $v_1 \ldots v_n$ be variables. Let α and β be formulae. Let g and h be variable assignments. Let M be a model.

(1.1) $[\Pi v_1 \ldots v_n]_M = \{g: <g(v_1), \ldots g(v_n)> \in i(\Pi)\}$

(1.2) $[\neg\alpha]_M \quad = V - [\alpha]_M$

(1.3) $[\alpha \wedge \beta]_M \quad = [\alpha]_M \cap [\beta]_M$

(1.4) $[\alpha \vee \beta]_M \quad = [\alpha]_M \cup [\beta]_M$

(1.5) $[\alpha \to \beta]_M \quad = (V - [\alpha]_M) \cup [\beta]_M$

(2.1) $[\exists v\alpha]_M \quad = [\alpha]_M \cup \{g: g[v]h \text{ for some } h \in [\alpha]_M\}$

(2.2) $[\forall v\alpha]_M \quad = [\alpha]_M, \text{ if, for each } h \in [\alpha]_M, g \in [\alpha]_M \text{ where } h[v]g;$
$\quad\quad\quad\quad\quad \varnothing, \text{ otherwise}$

(where h[v]g means that, for some $e \in U$ $gv\mapsto e = h$). A formula α is true in a model M if and only if $[\alpha]_M = V$; and a formula is false in a model M if and only if $[\alpha]_M = \varnothing$.

Let us return to the sentence in 63. There are circumstances of evaluation which, intuitively speaking, render the sentence in 63 true, but whose model, together with the clauses in Def. 25, fails to render the formula in 64 true; inversely, there are circumstances of evaluation which, intuitively speaking, render the sentence in 63 false, but whose model, together with the clauses in Def. 25, fails to render the formula in 64 false.

Consider, on the one hand, the circumstances in which there are at least two people, one of whom is not hungry, the other of whom is a man, has arrived, and is hungry. Intuitively speaking, the sentence in 63 is true, but the formula in 64 fails to be true in the corresponding model, when evaluated in accordance to the clauses in Def. 27. Of course, in the model for these circumstances, there is a variable assignment which renders 'x is a man' $\wedge$ 'x arrived' true; and so, by Clause 2.1, $[\exists x (x \text{ is a man} \wedge x \text{ arrived})]_M = V$; that is, in this model, the first conjunct in 64 is true. At the same time, however, there is a variable assignment that renders the second conjunct, 'x is hungry', false. So, [x is hungry]$_M$ ≠ V. Thus, by Clause 1.3, [∃x (x is a man ∧ x arrived) ∧ x is hungry]$_M$ ≠ V. In other words, the formula in 64 is not true in the model, contrary to one's intuitions about the sentence in 63.

Consider, on the other hand, the circumstances in which there are at least two people, one of whom is hungry but is not a man, the other of whom is a man and has arrived but is not hungry. Intuitively speaking, the sentence in 63 is false, but the formula in 64 fails to be false in the corresponding model, when evaluated in accordance to the clauses in Def. 25. As before, there is a variable assignment which renders 'x is a man' ∧ 'x arrived' true, and so, by Clause 2.1, [∃x(x is a man ∧ x arrived)]$_M$ = V; that is, in this model, the first conjunct in 66 is true. At the same time, however, there is a variable assignment which renders the second conjunct, 'x is hungry', true. So, [x is hungry]$_M$ ≠ ∅. Thus, by Clause 1.3, [∃x(x is a man ∧ x arrived) ∧ x is hungry]$_M$ ≠ ∅. In other words, the formula in 64 is not false in the model, contrary to one's intuitions about the sentence in 63.

The problem is not only that open formulae that are not substitution instances of the tautologies and contradictions of classical propositional logic do not have a truth value (relative to a model) but also that such formulae never have the values of their free variables determined by the values of variables in closed formulae. The reason for the latter fact is simple: when a closed formula is true, the variable assignments that rendered it so are, as it were, washed out with the addition of new irrelevant variable assignments.

Groenendijk and Stokhof (1991: this volume, Chapter 14) have found a way to circumvent these problems. Their basic idea is to redo the clauses of Def. 27 so that not only is the truth of a formula reckoned but also the variable assignments whereby an open formula is rendered true are kept track of. This is how they do it. As before, a model is a pair <U,i>, where U is a nonempty set, the universe, and i is a function whose domain comprises the predicates,[48] where, if Π is an *n*-place predicate, then i(Π) ∈ Pow(U^n). Let V be the set of all variable assignments. Then one defines $\mid\mid_M$ as a function from formulae into Pow(V^2) as follows:

DEFINITION 28. *Model for DPL.*

(1.1) $\mid\Pi\upsilon_1 \ldots \upsilon_n\mid_M$ = {<g,g> : <g(υ_1), . . . , g(υ_n)> ∈ i(Π)}

(1.2) $\mid\neg\alpha\mid_M$ = {<g,g>: <g,h> ∈ $\mid\alpha\mid_M$, for no h}

(1.3) $\mid\alpha\wedge\beta\mid_M$ = {<g,h>: <g,k> ∈ $\mid\alpha\mid_M$ and <k,h> ∈ $\mid\beta\mid_M$, for some k}

(1.4) $\mid\alpha\vee\beta\mid_M$ = {<g,g>: either <g,h> ∈ $\mid\alpha\mid_M$ or <g,h> ∈ $\mid\beta\mid_M$, for some h}

(1.5) $\mid\alpha\rightarrow\beta\mid_M$ = {<g,g>: for each h such that <g,h> ∈ $\mid\alpha\mid_M$, there is a k such that <h,k> ∈ $\mid\beta\mid_M$}

(2.6) $\mid\exists\upsilon\alpha\mid_M$ = {<g,h>:g[υ]k and <k,h> ∈ $\mid\alpha\mid_M$}

(2.7) $\mid\forall\upsilon\alpha\mid_M$ = {<g,g>: for each h such that g[υ]h, there is a k such that <h,k> ∈ $\mid\alpha\mid_M$}

A formula α is true in a model M if and only if {g: for some h ∈ V, <g,h> ∈ $\mid\alpha\mid_M$} = V; and a formula α is false in a model M if and only if $\mid\alpha\mid_M$ = ∅. The first coordinates in the pairs of variable assignments which are assigned to formulae in DPL serve the same purpose as sets of simple variable assignments in QL—namely, to keep track of truth and falsity; while the second coordinates serve to furnish values to free variables in certain open formulae. As explained in their article, these clauses suffice to attribute to the sentences in 54 the same truth conditions as those that are thought to make these sentences true—namely, that each farmer beats every donkey he owns.

Notes

1. The appendix to Part I, Chapter 8, contains a brief review of the elementary set theory that is necessary to understand this discussion.

2. Numerals should be kept distinct from numbers. Numerals, sometimes called *Arabic numerals*, '1', '2', '3', . . . are contrasted with the English words *one, two, three,* . . . and with the Roman numerals

'I', 'II', 'III', ... The Arabic numerals, English words, and Roman numerals are expressions for the same numbers, 1, 2, 3, ... Arabic numerals are more accurately known as *Indian numerals*.

3. This definition permits SN to contain redundant numerals such as '00129'. We tolerate these superfluous numerals because to ban them would involve distracting complications and their presence does no harm.

4. These rules generate Arabic numerals, not numbers. Notice different rules would be necessary for generating Roman numerals.

5. Consult Partee, ter Meulen, and Wall (1990, ch. 16.5) for discussion of the nature of these rules and their differences.

6. i(x) means the value of 'x'.

7. The relevant rule is A 1.2.45—that is, rule 45 of Chapter 2 of Book I of his *Aṣṭādhyāyi*. See Bronkhorst (1998) for discussion.

8. This was explicitly noted by Patañjali some 2,300 years ago.

9. This is often called the syntax of propositional logic.

10. A *tree* is a mathematical structure. An example of such a structure is a genealogical tree of a family with no inbreeding that gives an individual and his or her descendants. The elements in the structure that correspond to people's names are its nodes, and the lines depict the relationship of one person as the descendant of another.

11. Two nodes are "sisters" when they are immediate descendants of one and the same node.

12. This need not be the case. There is an *n*-valued logic, for each $n > 1$, as well as infinite valued logics.

13. One should not confuse *truth value assignments* (which are functions from propositional variables to truth values) with *truth functions* (which are functions from truth values or pairs of truth values to truth values).

14. Technically, the two equalities should have been written: $o_\wedge (\langle F,T \rangle) = F$ and $o_\rightarrow (\langle F, T \rangle) = T$. However, it is customary to omit the angle brackets to enhance readability.

15. This is often considered the semantics for propositional logic.

16. Unlike truth value assignments to finite sets of propositional variables, valuations cannot be finitely specified, for even if PV contained only one propositional variable, the set FM would be infinite. For this reason, one cannot write down any valuation, since one cannot write down everything in a valuation's domain.

17. Because of the role that context plays, more than the meaning of a sentence must be included in what determines its truth conditions.

18. There appear to be counterexamples to this. *Alice got married and had a baby* does not have the same sense when it is commutated. We discuss this in Chapter 6, example 5.

19. "⊨" is a formally defined relation which holds between a set of formula of classical propositional logic and a single formula. It is not defined for sentences of English. The analogous relation for declarative sentences of English is referred to by ENTAILS.

20. The *apodosis* and *protasis* are the subordinate and superordinate clauses of a conditional sentence, what philosophers often call the *antecedent* and the *consequent*, respectively.

21. This can be taken to be the syntax of predicate logic.

22. Just as the truth value assignments induce a classical valuation for the formulae of PL through Def. 4, so models induce a classical valuation for the formulae of PDL through the next definition. It is common to use subscript for the model on the function symbol v to indicate the model that induces the classical valuation.

23. Notice that our universe of discourse, U, consists of a set of three numbers, sets of which are assigned as semantic values of the English expressions that follow. For the fragment of English that we consider here, the value assignments are able to provide truth conditions for the sentences formed from the expressions, but the sets of numbers cannot be taken to be the meanings of the expressions; they are only ersatz meanings. Despite this, what the model can show is how the "meaning(s)" of a complex expression, given the "meanings" of its parts, is a function of the meanings of the parts.

24. A variety of expressions are used to indicate the relation between an expression and the object or set of objects to which it applies: for example, *refers to*, *denotes*, *names*, *is true of*, and *applies to*. Here we use *denote*, but when we come to discuss Kaplan, we shall use *refers to*.

25. Here, we use *value* for the object that an expression denotes. Others use *referent*, *denotation*, or *extension*.

26. *Periphrasis* denotes forms of expression in which auxiliary words are used, instead of a suffix. For example, some English comparative adjectives, such as *tall*, are formed by the addition of the suffix *-er* —that is, nonperiphrastically; others, such as *admirable*, are formed periphrastically—that is, with the use of the word *more*. Periphrastic forms of verbs are those forms containing auxiliary verbs; nonperiphrastic ones are those which do not.

27. This additional restriction is relaxed if *never* is focused. Thus, the following sentence is perfectly acceptable, when *never* is emphasized: *Bill never left the house.*

28. Again, this additional restriction is relaxed if *never* is focused.

29. The description just given for the distribution of the adverbs *not* and *never* requires modification for interrogative clauses. See Baker (1989, ch. 11.3.5) for more details about the distribution of *not*.

30. This is not to say that the indefinite article is always semantically vacuous. Though it is here, we shall see later (section 3.4.2) that, in other contexts, it is not semantically vacuous.

31. In effect, $v_i(NP) \in v_i(AV)v_i(VP)$ means $v_i(NP) \in cp(v_i(VP))$, where $cp(v_i(VP))$ is the complement of the set assigned to VP.

32. A version of this solution is found in Keenan and Faltz (1985, 71).

33. This is what Chomsky and his followers call *logical form*, but it is not the same as the logician's notion of *logical form*.

34. For those familiar with algebra, a strongly compositional function is a homomorphism.

35. It is possible to define a strongly compositional function for classical quantificational logic. Tarski did so, using so-called cylindrical algebras. This definition is presented here in section 3.4.4. Further information is in Henkin, Monk, and Tarski (1971).

36. Since these seminal articles, many useful and interesting works on generalized quantification have appeared. See Westerståhl (1989) and Sher (1991).

37. See Westerståhl (2001) for a concise and lucid exposition.

38. Italics indicate that the expression is a term of the antecedence relation.

39. This rule should be understood to apply when both occurrences of *John* refer to the same person.

40. The phenomena are more complicated than the example suggests, and Pāṇini's treatment is accordingly more complicated. For details, see Deshpande (1980) and Gillon (2001).

41. As noted by Schubert and Pelletier (1987), not all *donkey* sentences of the form in 0(a) have a similar interpretation.

42. The insight seems to have been anticipated by Quine (1960, 23).

43. Evans (1977) called such pronouns *E-type pronouns*.

44. See Heim (1990) for further discussion.

45. For full details, see Kamp and Reyle (1993).

46. See Kamp and Reyle (1993, ch. 1.5) for details.

47. We omit individual constants from the notation of quantificational logic in order to simplify the presentation.

48. Again, individual constants are omitted in order to simplify the presentation.

4

Theories of Reference and Theories of Meaning

$\mathbf{I}$n discussing logic and its application to natural language, we have skirted around the central question of this volume: What is a semantic theory? One way of dividing semantic theories, due to Quine (1953b), is into theories of reference and theories of meaning, and one way of making this distinction is on the basis of the sorts of phenomena for which the theories attempt to give an account. The distinction is complicated by the fact that different theories of reference, for example, attempt to account for different but overlapping sets of phenomena. The same holds for theories of meaning. The set of phenomena that theories of reference attempt to account for include logical truth and falsity, necessary truth and falsity, contingent truth and falsity, entailment, presupposition, and truth conditions.[1] Moreover, theories of reference appeal to such notions as models, truth, satisfaction, possible worlds, denotation, and reference. Theories of meaning attempt to account for such things as intensional contexts, intentional discourse, analyticity, synonymy, entailment, anomaly, semantic redundancy, polysemy, antonomy, homonymy, and meaning inclusion; they appeal to such notions as sense, meaning, semantic marker, and lexical entry. As we shall see, there are mixed theories that try to give a unified account of phenomena that fall within the range of reference and meaning theories. There are different theories in each of the categories, differences that arise because of variations in the forms of the theories, in their ontological commitments, and in what they regard to be semantic phenomena. Some reference theories attempt to give an account of truth conditions, but not of necessary truth and falsity, and some theories of meaning attempt to give an account of certain intensional contexts, but not of synonymy and analyticity.

We begin with theories of reference and then turn to theories of meaning. We take Donald Davidson's satisfaction theory (1967: this volume, Chapter 12) to be an instance of a reference theory and Ray Jackendoff's (1989: this volume, Chapter 16) and James Pustejovsky's (1991: this volume, Chapter 18) theories to be instances of theories of meaning. We then consider theories that are a mix of reference and meaning theories within which we shall find Gottlob Frege's theory of sense and reference and David Kaplan's theory of character and content (1977: this volume, Chapter 37).

4.1   Theories of reference: Davidson's satisfaction theory

Davidson's semantic theory has given rise to a wide range of interpretations, because of its complexity and its having been presented over a number of years with a variety of changes and clarifications. Here we concentrate on the interpretation of Davidson's theory that we believe is most relevant to current work in semantics. Davidson's central insight is the application to natural languages of Tarski's (1944; 1956) satisfaction semantics, a semantics that was developed for formal languages. Using Tarski's framework, Davidson and others have generated various accounts for a range of semantic phenomena, work that belongs to the semantics of a particular natural language (this volume, Chapter 36). Davidson's work in semantics can be divided into three parts: his arguments against semantic theories that appeal to meanings, his proposal that a satisfaction semantics suffices as a theory of meaning for natural languages, and his application of satisfaction semantics to natural language. We consider each of these in turn.

4.1.1   Davidson's argument against meanings

Davidson's argument against theories that appeal to meanings is not against expressions being meaningful, since his theory is an account of the meaningfulness of expressions in terms of the notions of satisfaction and truth. Rather, his argument is against theories that appeal to notions beyond satisfaction and truth to provide theories of meaning.[2]

There is a close connection between meaning and understanding. Suppose that S says seriously and literally,

1. It is raining.

We understand what is said if we know that

2. In uttering 2, S meant that it is raining.

We know this if we know on this occasion that

3. 'It is raining' means that it is raining.

Let us call S's idiolect *S-ish*. We would understand S-ish, if for every sentence of S-ish, we were able to produce something of the form

4. 'X' means that *p*.

where 'X' is the name of a sentence and *p* its meaning. Let us call these M-sentences. All languages, including S-ish, have an infinite number of sentences. Hence, theories of meaning that take 4 to be the canonical form of meaning specifications must generate an infinite set of M-sentences. If we place as a condition on theories of meaning that they be learnable (a condition that is appropriate for theories that are part of an account of understanding), a theory that consists of a list of the M-sentences of a language would not be learnable. Since we have finite lives, we cannot learn an infinite set. Thus, theories of M-meaning, to be adequate, must be recursive. In addition, they must provide meanings for lexical items, as well as rules that combine the meanings of the lexical items and generate the meanings for the sentences that contain them.

Davidson objects to theories of meaning that have as their goal the generation of sentences of the form in 4. His objection is not the Quinean criticism that *mean* and related terms make no sense, since they constitute a small set, the definitions of which are circular (Quine 1953b;

Davidson 1984g). Rather, he claims that the reason for abandoning the appeal to meanings is that "they have no demonstrated use" (Davidson 1984a, 21). Consider the complex term,

5. The father of x.

Suppose we were to take the meaning of terms to be functions. Statement 5 and the terms that are the values of x have meanings associated with them, both of which serve to determine the reference of the respective terms. The meaning of 5 is supposedly a function that takes as arguments the references yielded by the meaning associated with x and yields as values the father of x. For example, in

6. The father of Sam,

the meaning associated with *Sam* yields Sam as its reference. In turn, Sam is the argument of the meaning of 5 that yields as value the reference of the father of Sam. We see then that we have a finite theory that determines the references for the infinite set of expressions that can be formed from 5.

Davidson's argument against this theory is to replace it with an alternative theory that yields the same results, references for the infinite set of complex terms formed from 5, but without appealing to meanings.[3] His theory is that

7. 'The father of t' refers to the father of t,

where t is a singular term. Hence, we have a semantic theory that provides the references of a complex term without appealing to its meaning or the meanings of its constituents and, thus, without appealing to meanings. In this way, Davidson's theory is superior to a theory of meaning that appeals to functions, since it yields the same results without invoking functions as meanings. That is, Davidson's theory is supposedly ontologically simpler than a meaning theory that invokes functions, but at the same time it is just as explanatorily adequate.

4.1.3   Satisfaction theory

The lesson that Davidson draws from his arguments against semantic theories that appeal to meanings is that it is possible to construct a semantic theory without appealing to them. A Davidsonian truth theory for a natural language is an empirical axiomatic theory that, if adequate, entails for every sentence of the language a truth sentence, a T-sentence, that gives the sentence's truth condition.[4]

The form of a T-sentence is

8. 'S' is true in L if and only if p.

For example,

9. 'La neige est blanche' is true in French if and only if snow is white.

Let us look more closely at 'S' and 'L' in 8.[5] In 8, 'S' denotes a syntactic description of a sentence of the language being described, the object language, which in 9 is French, that is being described in English, the meta-language. There are two reasons for requiring a sentence's syntactic description. First, the semantic rules of truth theories, the axioms of the theory, operate on the structure of sentences. Second, some sentences are structurally ambiguous. Consider

10. Old men and women got on the bus.

This can be understood in two different ways, depending on how the scope of the adjective *old* is interpreted.

11. (a) [NP [NP [AP Old] men] and women] got on the bus.
    (b) [NP [AP Old] [men and women]] got on the bus.

The ambiguity of 10 is brought out by a difference in the structures of 11(a) and 11(b). Hence, for 10, a satisfaction semantics must provide two T-sentences. To do this, the semantics must operate on the syntactic descriptions[6] of the sentence.

Let us consider L in 8. The reason for supplying a particular value for L is that without such a constraint, it would be possible to construct a theory that covered a range of languages. In such a case, there could be T-sentences for which the truth value would be difficult to determine. According to Davidson, satisfaction semantics is supposed to be an empirical theory, one element of which is that T-sentences are tested against the intuitions of speakers. Suppose that American and British English were blended together, but that the meta-language for the semantics for the blended language was British English. There would then be difficulties with the following T-sentence:

12. 'A bonnet is part of an automobile that covers the engine compartment' is true iff a bonnet is part of an automobile that covers the engine compartment.

The problem is that a speaker of British English would mark this as true, while a speaker of American English would mark it as false. Hence, the information contained in a truth theory must be relative to a particular language. A way around this problem that would fit into Chomsky's individualist conception of linguistics is to take semantic theories to be relative to individual speakers. The value of L, then, would be an individual speaker's idiolect.

4.1.4   Model theory and satisfaction theory

It is sometimes thought that Davidson's satisfaction theory and model theory are two different kinds of truth theoretic semantic theories. It is easy to show that for a given model theory, satisfaction theory is equivalent to model theory, something that we shall not prove here, but we shall indicate the direction in which the proof should go. Recall that the basic aim of model theory is to show how a recursively defined notation can be assigned values on the basis of an assignment of values to its primitive symbols and the notation's recursive structure. In the case of the notation of quantificational logic, the primitive symbols are the set of predicates (PD), the set of constants (CN), the variables (VR), and the logical constants (LC). A model consists of a nonempty set, a universe, and an interpretation function, whose domain is the set of predicates and constants and whose codomain comprises the members of the universe, the subsets of the universe, and the sets of n-tuples of the members of the universe. An atomic formula is built out of a predicate and an appropriate number of terms, a term being either a variable or a constant. Truth values are assigned to an atomic formula on the basis of a rule that assigns a value to the formula on the basis of the values assigned to its parts—the predicate and its terms—and their order. Thus, through an interpretation function and a variable assignment, each atomic formula can be guaranteed to have a truth value. Once the atomic formulae have truth values, the truth functions assigned to interpret the logical connectives guarantee that the composite formulae also receive a truth value. Unlike the logical connectives, the quantifiers are typically not assigned a constant value, though it is possible to do so, as is done in the paragraph above Def. 21 in Chapter 3.

Instead, the value of a formula over which a quantifier has immediate scope is determined indirectly, as is done in Def. 18 in Chapter 3.

Now, a satisfaction theory can also be used to show which formulae are true and which are false. It is called a *satisfaction theory*, since the relation of satisfaction (to be explained later in this chapter) plays a pivotal role in it. Satisfaction theory's approach minimizes the use of functions. In particular, the only functions used are term assignments, each of which is an amalgam of an interpretation function restricted to constants and a variable assignment. Thus, different term assignments may assign different values to the same variable, but each constant is always assigned the same value. In satisfaction theory, no function assigns values to predicates and no function assigns a truth value to formulae, whether atomic or composite. Instead, various relations are invoked. They are the relations of *being true of*,[7] of *satisfaction*, and of *being true*. Instead, then, of stating an interpretation function that gives the value of a predicate, one states what the predicate is true of. For example, rather than asserting that i(P_) = {a,b,c}, one asserts that P_ is true of *a*, P_ is true of *b*, and P_ is true of *c*; and instead of the asserting that i(R_ _) = {<a,b>, <b,c>, <a,c>}, one asserts that R_ _ is true of <a,b>, R_ _ is true of <b,c>, and R_ _ is true of <a,c>. Next, instead of a valuation (Def. 16) to give the truth value of a formula, one states what the term assignment function satisfies. So, instead of asserting that $[Rxy]^{M,f} = T$, one asserts that f satisfies Rxy, which holds just in case R is true of <f(x), f(y)>. Of course, the satisfaction relation must extend to all composite formulae.

The following definition states which variable assignment satisfies which formula. This is done in the usual way by taking advantage of the recursive structure of formula. Thus, the definition of which variable assignment satisfies which formula rests on which variable assignment satisfies which atomic formula. And which variable assignment satisfies which atomic formula rests on which predicate in the atomic formula is true of the object or the sequence of objects from the universe picked out by the constants in the atomic formula under the variable assignment.

DEFINITION 29. *Satisfaction.* Let α and β be formula of FM. Let τ be a term assignment. Let υ be a variable.

Atomic formulae:
Let Π be a member of PD_1; let t be a member of TM; and let τ be a term assignment. Then,
    (1.1) τ satisfies Πt iff Π is true of τ(t).
Let Π be a member of PD_n; let $t_1, \ldots, t_n$ be occurrences of members of TM (where $n > 1$);
    and let τ be a term assignment. Then,
    (1.2) τ satisfies $\Pi_n t_1, \ldots, t_n$ iff Π_n is true of $< \tau (t_1), \ldots, \tau (t_n) >$.

Composite formulae:
Let α and β be members of FM.
    (2.1)   τ satisfies ¬α iff τ does not satisfy α;
    (2.2.1) τ satisfies α ∧ β iff τ satisfies α and τ satisfies β;
    (2.2.2) τ satisfies α ∨ β iff τ satisfies α or τ satisfies β;
    (2.2.3) τ satisfies α → β iff if τ satisfies α then τ satisfies β;
    (2.2.4) τ satisfies α ↔ β iff τ satisfies α if and only if τ satisfies β.

Composite formulae:
Let υ be a member of VR, and let α be a member of FM.
    (3.1) τ satisfies ∀υ α iff for each u, $\tau_{\upsilon \mapsto u}$ satisfies α;
    (3.2) τ satisfies ∃υ α iff for some u, $\tau_{\upsilon \mapsto u}$ satisfies α.

Finally, we can define the truth of a formula by means of satisfaction:

DEFINITION 30. *Truth of a formula in satisfaction theory.* α is true in L iff, for each term assignment g, g satisfies α.

It is easy to show that, for any fixed model M, model theory and satisfaction theory will agree on which formulae are true and which are false. In particular, it is easy to prove that, for some fixed M, for all α in FM, α is true iff $[α]^M = T$.

4.1.5   Satisfaction theory and natural language

Davidson has been one of the most vigorous proponents of the use of satisfaction theory in providing a semantic theory for natural languages. His conception of a semantic theory has been advocated by Lepore, who, in collaboration with Ludwig (Lepore and Ludwig 2002), has provided an elaboration of the basic ideas. An extensive application of the ideas to the analysis of English has been set out by Larson and Segal (1995). As a result, here we illustrate only a few of the principal ideas.

Consider the simple Latin sentence in 13 and its phrase marker, given immediately below:

13. Carlus currit.

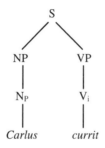

Turning to natural language, one must treat the lexical items *Carlus* and *currit*. The first is a proper name. Hence, treating it in the same way as one treats a constant in satisfaction theory for predicate logic, one assigns it a value. The second is an intransitive verb. So, treating it in the same way as a one-place predicate is treated in satisfaction theory (ST), one determines of which objects it is true. This is done by the following two biconditional statements:

14. (a) For each x, *currit* is true of x iff x runs.
     (b) For each x, $τ(Carlus) = x$ iff x = Carl.

Next, we require rules to treat the nodes, NP, N_p, VP, and V_i. This is done by the next two rules:

ST 0.1. Let $[_Z Y]$ be the syntactic structure where Y is a lexical item. Then, for each x, Z is true of x iff Y is true of x.

ST 0.2. Let $[_Z Y]$ be the syntactic structure where Y is not a lexical item. Then, for each term assignment τ, $τ(Z) = x$ iff $τ(Y) = x$.

Finally, we require a rule that allows treating the S node:

ST 1. Let $[_S NP VP]$ be the syntactic structure. Then, for each term assignment τ, τ satisfies S iff VP is true of τ(NP).

The biconditional statements in 0, together with the rules in ST 0.1 and ST 0.2, permit the following intermediate conclusions:

15. (a) For each x, $[_{Vi}\ currit]$ is true of x iff x runs.

  (b) For each x, $[_{VP}\ [_{Vi}\ currit]\ ]$ is true of x iff x runs.

  (c) For each x, $\tau\ ([_{Np}\ Carlus]) = x$ iff x = Carl.

  (d) For each x, $\tau\ ([_{NP}\ [_{Np}\ Carlus]\ ]) = x$ iff x = Carl.

Finally, on the basis of the biconditional statements in 15(b) and 15(d) and the rule in ST 1, one concludes 16(a); and since 16(a) contains no free variables, one further concludes 16(b):

16. (a) τ satisfies $[_S\ [_{NP}\ [_{Np}\ Carlus]]\ [_{VP}\ [_{Vi}\ currit]]]$ iff Carl runs.

  (b) $[_S\ [_{NP}\ [_{Np}\ Carlus]]\ [_{VP}\ [_{Vi}\ currit]]]$ is true iff Carl runs.

Sentence 16(b) is an instance of a T-sentence. A necessary condition for a satisfaction theory to be an adequate semantics for a natural language is that it generates for every sentence of the language, perhaps relative to an individual speaker, a T-sentence. That is, it generates T-sentences of the form in 8.

4.1.6   Objections to satisfaction theories

A possible objection to satisfaction theories is that there appear to be meaningful lexical items— *chimera*, for example—for which there is nothing for them to be true of. *Table* and *horse* are not problematic expressions for satisfaction theories, since they can be said to be true of tables and of horses. But spatial-temporal kinds like *tables* and *horses* are not the only things that can serve as the satisfiers of terms. There is nothing to exclude a satisfaction theory from taking abstract and mental objects and even fictional objects as serving this purpose.[8] Hence, this leaves open the possibility that a satisfaction theory could give a meaning to *chimera*.[9]

Another problem for satisfaction theories is that many sentences do not have truth conditions: interrogative and imperative sentences, and certain types of declarative sentences and performative sentences, for example. If in promising Alice to take her to the movies, Sam says to her, *I promise to take you to the movies*, he has performed a speech act, a promise, but he has not said something that is true or false. A number of authors in this volume take up this problem, including Vanderveken (this volume, Chapter 35) and Higginbotham (this volume, Chapter 34).

For some theorists, another problem arises because satisfaction theories are not able to account for a range of what these theorists regard to be semantic phenomena. Some expressions of natural language are ambiguous, some are synonymous with others, and some expressions contain redundancies. Such facts, it is thought, cannot be stated in a theory that tries to get by on such meager concepts as satisfaction, true of, and truth. To account for such phenomena, many theorists have felt it necessary to invoke meanings. Such theorists wish to associate a meaning with every elementary expression (or morpheme), and the meanings so associated play a part in a theory that accounts for such semantic properties as synonymy, semantic redundancy, ambiguity, and so on (Katz 1972).

4.2   Theories of meaning

Meanings have been taken to play a variety of roles in theories of linguistic understanding, of the determination of referents, of intentional states, and of a range of semantic phenomena—for example, analyticity, synonymy, entailment, anomaly, semantic redundancy, and polysemy. We consider these roles in what follows, but we begin by concentrating on the specification of the meanings of lexical items—a specification that provides a division into two sorts of semantic theories, atomic and molecular.

4.2.1   Atomic meaning theories

Atomic meaning theories treat meanings of simple expressions as nondecomposable elements that have no structure. Take *bachelor*. On this sort of theory, its meaning is not decomposable into *unmarried adult male*. Rather, an atomic meaning theory would connect *bachelor* with the concept [*bachelor*].[10] Thus, on an atomic meaning theory, lexical items are not definable. Another consequence is that there are no meaning entailment relations. Hence, someone who knows the meaning of 17(a) need not be able to draw the inference to 17(b) on the basis of the meaning of the lexical items in 17(a). That is, someone can know the meaning of *bachelor* without associating it with [*unmarried adult male*].

17.   (a)   S is a bachelor.
     (b)   S is an unmarried adult male.

Even if there were no meaning relation between 17(a) and 17(b), it would not rule out 17(a) entailing 17(b). It does, if the property of being a bachelor is necessarily the property of being an unmarried male adult. There being an entailment relation between 17(a) and 17(b), however, does not show that there is a meaning relation between *bachelor* and *unmarried adult male*. We can see this by considering another example. On the supposition that it is necessary that two is the even prime number, there is an entailment relation between

18.   (a)   Two is an even number.
     (b)   The even prime number is an even number.

But there is no lexical entailment relation. The reason is that necessity does not entail analyticity (Kripke 1980; Fodor 1998).[11]

One of the reasons that some have been attracted to atomic meaning theories is the difficulties that Quine (1953b) has raised about the possibility of constructing a viable theory of meaning that purports to provide analytical definitions for lexical items. Quine's worries turn on the difficulty in providing theoretically satisfying accounts of such notions as analyticity and synonymy that underpin theories that supposedly supply "definitions" for lexical items. Very briefly, Quine finds that when we attempt to provide criteria for analyticity and synonymy, we end up with a small set of circular definitions that give an account of one unclear notion, say analyticity, in terms of another, synonymy. Another reason some theorists have turned to atomic meaning theories is that there is a paucity of results in giving adequate theories that supply definitions for lexical items.

4.2.2   Molecular meaning theories

Molecular meaning theories decompose the meanings of lexical items into meaning constituents that give "definitions" for lexical items. Such theories are committed to there being inferential relations that sentences containing a lexical item enter into that are constitutive of the lexical item's meaning.[12] Lexical semantics is an example of this type of theory. In a lexical semantics, a lexical item is associated with a lexical entry that specifies the elements that constitute the meaning of the lexical item. There are two kinds of definitional molecular meaning theories, and, thus, two kinds of lexical semantics: analytic and encyclopedic.

4.2.2.1   Analytic meaning theories

Analytic meaning theories implicitly draw a distinction between two kinds of sentences: analytic and synthetic. The former are sentences the truth of which is determinable by their structure and the meanings of their words—for example, *Bachelors are unmarried adult males*; the latter are sentences the truth of which is determined by the way the world is—for instance, *Gold is an element*. In these theories, the analytic sentences are taken to contain information that should be part of semantics, since semantics is supposedly a theory about what words mean and not about the nature of the world. Analytic meaning theories are related not only to analyticity but also to other notions such as synonymy, antonymy, homonymy, and anomaly. We can relate analytic meaning theories to analyticity and synonymy in the following way:

19. 'X' means Y_1 &. . . . .& Y_n if and only if '(x)(x is X if and only if x is Y_1 &. . . . .& Y_n)' is analytic and 'X' is synonymous with 'Y_1 &. . . . .& Y_n'.[13]

An analytic meaning theory is committed to there being lexical meaning entailments: for example, 17(a) entailing 17(b) because of the meaning of *bachelor*. Hence, anyone who knows the meaning of *bachelor* must be able to draw the inference from 17(a) to 17(b). In fact, we can say that their ability to draw the inference is constitutive of their knowing the meaning of *bachelor*.

4.2.2.2   Encyclopedic meaning theories

Analytic meaning theories presuppose that there is a viable distinction between analytic and synthetic sentences and, hence, among different types of belief. There are molecular meaning theorists who think that no viable distinction can be drawn between these sentences and, thus, that it is impossible to specify something that would count as the analytic meaning of a lexical item.[14] Since it follows that all beliefs about X's are on an equal footing, it would appear that all information about X's must be included in the lexical entry for 'X'. Consequently, these theorists would include in the meaning of a lexical item, 'X', the substitutions instances for ϕ that occur in the form

20. It is believed that X's are ϕ's.

This can be relativized to individual speakers or to a group of speakers:

21. (a) It is believed by S that X's are ϕ's.
     (b) It is believed by speakers of L that X's are ϕ's.

We shall call such theories *encyclopedic meaning theories*; they dispense with analytic meanings of lexical items and replace them with encyclopedic entries for lexical items that include everything that is believed about X's. There must be some limitation on what encyclopedic meaning theories include in lexical entries, since on the preceding construal, it would have to include everything that a speaker or a group of speakers believes about X's. Perhaps it can be limited by including in lexical entries only what a speaker or a group of speakers consider to be their most central beliefs about X's. Encyclopedic meaning theories are also committed to meaning entailments. If Pierre believes that aristocrats are rich, and thus, *rich* is in his lexical entry for *aristocrat*, from 22(a), he will infer 22(b):

22. (a) Jones is an aristrocrat.
     (b) Jones is rich.

4.3   Lexical semantics

We wish to consider two views that we take to be exemplars of the two sorts of molecular meaning theories: Ray Jackendoff's *conceptual semantics* and James Pustejovsky's *generative lexicon*;

both of whom have essays in this volume (respectively, 1989: this volume, Chapter 16; and 1991: this volume, Chapter 18).[15] Jackendoff's and Pustejovsky's theories give for each lexical item a lexical entry that specifies semantic information about the lexical item, as well as information about its syntactic and phonological properties. In addition, both theories purport to be compositional, although they differ in the mechanisms that generate the meaning of a complex expression. Jackendoff treats lexical entries as fixed,[16] and the rules of composition that produce the meanings of complex expressions operate over the semantic content of the lexical entries. For Pustejovsky, when lexical items occur in the context of complex expressions, there are rules that operate on their lexical entries, producing new meanings that play a role in determining the meanings of the complex expressions of which the lexical items are a part (Pustejovsky 1995b, 55–60; 1998, 290–305).

On the surface, the two theories seem to share the same view about what a semantics for a particular language is supposed to explain. Jackendoff (1989: this volume, Chapter 16) takes a semantic theory to be a theory about the "form into which speakers encode their construal of the world"; it is a theory that "is concerned most directly with the form of the internal mental representations that constitute conceptual structure and with the formal relations between this level and other levels of representation." Pustejovsky (1991: this volume, Chapter 18) echoes this view: "The semantics of natural language should be the image of nonlinguistic conceptual organizing principles (whatever their structure)." These ways of characterizing semantics leave open what should be included within it.

There are two sorts of beliefs that fall under these characterizations: beliefs that are expressed by analytical sentences and beliefs that are expressed by synthetic sentences. The linguist's counterpart to this distinction is between linguistic or dictionary knowledge and world or encyclopedic knowledge. As we have seen, the former has been taken to contain information that should be part of semantics, since semantics is supposedly a theory about our beliefs about the meanings of words and not about our beliefs about the nature of the world. Both sorts of beliefs, however, belong to our "construal of the world." Which sorts of beliefs are to be incorporated, then, into semantics? Jackendoff and Pustejovsky seem to part company on this matter. Jackendoff (1996, 546; 1997, 64) claims that the concepts expressed by words "include all the richness and interconnections of human knowledge (sometimes called 'encyclopedic' knowledge and sometimes 'pragmatics')." He explicitly excludes from his theory a language-to-world connection, and, thus, his theory cannot be characterized as a reference theory or a combination of a reference theory and a theory of meaning. This means that his semantic theory is what we are calling a theory of meaning. Since it "include[s] all the richness and interconnections of human knowledge," it would appear that Jackendoff is committed to an encyclopedic theory of meaning.

It is more difficult to situate Pustejovsky. The main theoretical elements in Pustejovsky's theory (1995b, 1; this volume, Chapter 18) are lexical entries that specify the meanings of lexical items. At the same time, Pustejovsky tells us that "lexical semantics is the study of how and what the words of a language denote" (1995b: 1). Thus, it would seem that Pustejovsky's theory is both a theory of reference and a theory of meaning. For his theory to be a reference theory, however, the lexical entries in Pustejovsky's theory that give the meaning of a lexical item must also determine its referent, but it is not clear that they do. What Pustejovsky says is that what he calls "qualia structures"—part of the lexical entry of every lexical item—"contribute to (or, in fact, determine) our ability to name an object with a certain predication" (1995b, 85). That is, the semantic information encoded in lexical entries enables us to refer to or name objects, but this does not commit Pustejovsky to the view that the lexical entries, themselves, determine the referents of the associated lexical items. In addition, for a semantic theory to be a reference theory it must also provide rules of composition that yield referents of complex expressions using as input only the structural properties of the complex expressions and the referents of their parts. Pustejovsky's theory does not do this, and so it appears that Pustejovky's theory is not a theory of reference.

Pustejovsky (1995b, 38) wishes to account for the following relations among words: synonymy, antonymy, polysemy, and so on. In Pustejovsky's theory, two lexical items are synonymous if and only if they have the same lexical entry. An adequate treatment of synonymy would yield for every pair of synonymous expressions the same lexical entry and for no pairs of nonsynonymous expressions the same lexical entry. By having it that sameness of lexical entry yield synonymy, Pustejovsky excludes encyclopedic information from lexical entries. Suppose that we are constructing a semantics for the language of a speaker, S, who has *renate* and *cordate* in his lexicon and that his renate beliefs and cordate beliefs are the same. Let us suppose that these beliefs include such beliefs as "There are more renates in the Northern Hemisphere than in the Southern Hemisphere": that is, encyclopedic beliefs. If we allow these sorts of encyclopedic information to constitute the lexical entries for S's *renate* and *cordate*, it would turn out that *renate* and *cordate*, nonsynonymous expressions,[17] have the same lexical entries. But their having the same lexical entry would mark them as synonymous, given Pustejovsky's characterization of synonymy, and, consequently, would not adequately identify the synonym pairs in S's language. The moral of the story is that if a lexical semantics is to account for synonymy, it cannot allow encyclopedic information to be part of lexical entries. Thus, in Pustejovsky's semantic theory, a theory that wishes to account for synonymy, a distinction must be made between encyclopedic information that is not part of lexical entries and information that is analytically related to lexical items.[18] Hence, Pustejovsky's theory is an analytic meaning theory.

As we have seen, there are differences in what is contained in the lexical entries of Jackendoff's and Pustejovsky's theories. For the former theory, the content of our beliefs finds a place in the lexicon; for the latter, there is a distinction between beliefs that are "linguistic" and those that are about the world, and only the linguistic beliefs are encoded in the lexicon. The difference between the two theories can be brought out by the sorts of inference relations for which they purport to give an account. Notice that everyone judges that whenever the first member of the following pairs is true, the second is true:

23. (a) I took a taxi so that I would not be late.
    (b) So that I would not be late, I took a taxi.
24. (a) It is snowing, and it is cold.
    (b) It is cold.
25. (a) A tall woman entered the room.
    (b) A woman entered the room.

It is impossible for the first sentence in 23–25 to be true but the second to be false. What accounts for this is that on the assumption that the first member of 23–25 is true, its meaning and phrasal structure guarantees the truth of the second member of 23–25.

Now consider the following pairs of sentences:

26. (a) Bill killed Sam.
    (b) Sam is dead.
27. (a) Eddy forgot that the book is on the table.
    (b) The book is on the table.
28. (a) He is a member of the Hell's Angels.
    (b) He must be dangerous.
29. (a) She called him a fascist.
    (b) She insulted him.

The sentences in 26 and 27 are similar to those in 23–25. It is impossible for 26(a) or 27(a) to be true and, respectively, for 26(b) or 27(b) to be false. There is, however, this difference: there is nothing in the structure for 26(a) or 27(a) that guarantees the truth of 26(b) or 27(b). Rather, it is the meanings of *kill* and *forget* that guarantee the inference.

The pairs of sentences in 28 and 29 are different from those in 23–27. In the former, it is perfectly possible that 28(a) and 29(a) are true and 28(b) and 29(b) are false, but, given what we believe about Hell's Angels and being fascist, we can draw the inference from the first member of the pairs to the second member. Another way to see the difference is to take 28 and 29 to be missing premises. For 28 we have

30.   All Hell's Angels are dangerous.

For 29, we have

31.   Calling someone a fascist is to insult him.

No such missing premise is required for 26 and 27, since as we have seen, it is impossible pair wise for 26(a) and 27(a) to be true and 26(b) and 27(b) to be false; the first member of the pairs entails the second. No such relation holds between the pairs in 28 and 29. It is possible for the first member of the pairs to be true, but the second to be false. What warrants the inferences are the unarticulated premises in 30 and 31, both of which could be false.

One way to account for the difference is to ascribe meaning structures to *kill* and *forget* so that 26(a) entails 26(b) and 27(a) entails 27(b). By ascribing such structure to the lexical entries, we are committed to taking the inference relation to arise because of a speaker's linguistic knowledge. It is this sort of information that Pustejovsky's theory places in the lexical entries for lexical items. Jackendoff's theory not only includes this information in lexical entries, but also includes further information that constitutes knowledge about the world for example, in 30 and 31 in the lexical entries of, respectively, *Hell's Angels* and *fascist*.

Entailment is not the only property for which the two theories differ. A meaning theory marks the strings in 32 as anomalous:

32.   (a) She's a married bachelor.
        (b) He knows that it is raining, but doesn't believe it.

An encyclopedic theory for the semantics of the language of someone who knew some modern physics would mark the following as anomalous:

33.   (a) She walked faster than the speed of light.
        (b) Gold is lighter than helium.

In addition, what are marked as synonymous pairs would also come out differently on the two theories. An analytic theory marks the pairs in 34(a) to be synonymous, but not those in 34(b), while an encyclopedic theory marks the pairs in both as synonymous.

34.   (a) *sofa* and *couch, liar* and *prevaricator*
        (b) *renate* and *cordate, Yanks* and *Americans*.

In actual practice, there is a great deal of overlap in the sorts of data for which the two theories wish to give an account. The discussion of the particular data that Jackendoff and Pustejovsky claim are within the range of their theories is embedded in theoretical considerations about the structure of lexical entries, the general organization of the semantics, the interface between semantics and syntax, and so on. We cannot consider all of these phenomena here but concentrate on ambiguity.[19]

A lexical item is ambiguous if it has more than one meaning. There are two kinds of ambiguity. The first is homonymy in which a phonological form has associated with it several unrelated meanings. Thus, there would be different lexical entries in the lexicon for each of the associated meanings. The following contain examples of homonyms:

35. (a) The *bill* came to $50.
    (b) The *bill* of the eagle is hook-shaped.
36. (a) He wrote a *letter* to his father asking him for money.
    (b) The first *letter* of the English alphabet is *a*.
37. (a) The *mold* had spread throughout the refrigerator.
    (b) The *mold* was made of plastic.
38. (a) He put his *grip* [or suitcase] on the overhead rack.
    (b) He caught the *grip* [or *grippe*] and then passed it onto to his daughter.

The second kind of ambiguity, known as *polysemy*, is one in which the meanings are related:

39. (a) Harry *kept* the bird in the cage.
    (b) Susan *kept* the money.
    (c) Sam *kept* the crowd happy. (Jackendoff 1990, 25)
40. (a) He took the *fast* train from Calais.
    (b) I need a *fast* driver to get to the meeting on time.
    (c) He is a *fast* decision maker. (Pustejovsky 1995b, 44)
41. (a) He was a *good* person.
    (b) It was a *good* wine.
    (c) It was a *good* movie.
    (d) It is a *good* knife. (Pustejovsky 1995b, 43; Jackendoff 1997, 62)
42. (a) John's *book* has the same plot as Alice's.
    (b) John's *book* was used to hold the door open.

In each of 39–42, the occurrences of the same lexical item have different, although related, meanings. One way of handling these cases is to assimilate them to homonyms and have separate lexical entries for each of the different meanings. Another way of handling the problem is to have one lexical item but have the different meanings subscripted—meaning$_1$, meaning$_2$, et cetera. The problem with both of these, as Pustejovsky (1995b) points out, is that they would inflate the lexicon and, more important, miss generalizations about the relations among the meanings of the same lexical item.

Let us consider *keep* in 39. One proposal is Jackendoff's (1990, 26) in which he assigns a common element to the different subscripted meanings that are listed in the lexical entry for *keep*. He hypothesizes that it is

43. [$_{EVENT}$ STAY ([ ], [$_{PLACE}$])].

The difficulty with this as a general solution to the problem of related meanings is that it does not seem to work with adjectives like *good*. It does not appear that there is a common sense that unifies the different uses of *good* in 41. Contrary to Plato's view, it cannot be [*performing its function properly*] since people do not have a function the fulfilling of which makes them morally good. Pustejoveksy has a way around this problem. There is no fixed meaning for *good*; rather, there is a rule that operates on the lexical entry for *good* and the lexical entry of the nouns that *good* modifies in 41, selecting different elements of the lexical entries of the accompanying nouns.[20] Thus, Pustejovsky's theory is a generative theory of meaning. It generates meanings that are not contained in the lexical entries of single lexical items but are obtained by operating across the semantic information in the lexical entries of lexical items that occur in linguistic contexts. In this way, Pustejovsky's theory makes it possible to account for the meanings of new combinations of lexical items and, hence, might serve to quell some of the worries of the Wittgensteinians about the possibility of constructing semantic theories.

4.4   Two-tiered semantic theories

A range of two-tiered semantic theories may result from the combination of meaning and reference theories. The progenitor of two-tiered theories is Frege's, and we begin with a brief account of his theory. We then turn to a discussion of Kaplan's two-tiered theory.

4.4.1   Frege's semantic theory

Frege (1972) associates with all expressions *Sinn*, which has been translated as *sense*, and with certain expression *Bedeutung*, which has been translated as *reference*.[21] Senses play several roles in Frege's theory, including determining the reference of an expression, if it has one. To illustrate this, let us apply the distinction to declarative sentences. Frege holds that the references of declarative sentences that do not contain referenceless terms are truth values, the true and the false. Thus, all true sentences have the same references as well as all false sentences. If Frege's theory were only a reference theory, then all true sentences would turn out to have the same reference and, thus, the same content. To forestall this consequence, Frege (1977a) associates with declarative sentences senses, which he calls *thoughts*. Sentence pairs that are nonsynonymous would be associated with different senses. Since senses determine references, the senses of declarative sentences, the thoughts they express, determine, their references, if they have one. It follows from this that the thoughts expressed by declarative sentences give their truth conditions, while their reference gives their truth value. Two sentences, then, can have the same truth value, they can both be true, without it being the case that they have the same sense, the same truth conditions.

Frege's reason for introducing senses is to explain what has come to be called *Frege's puzzle*.[22] Consider 44(a) and 44(b), the constituent terms of which have the same reference:

44.   (a)   Mark Twain is Mark Twain.
      (b)   Mark Twain is Samuel Clemens.

If all that were available in Frege's theory were references, there would be no difference in content between 44(a) and 44(b). They have, however, a difference in cognitive value: a person can believe 44(a) without believing 44(b). Frege's account of this difference is that although the constituents of 44(a) and 44(b) have the same reference, they do not have the same sense.[23] Hence, the two sentences express different thoughts.[24]

Frege (1972) assigns other functions to senses besides being the determiners of reference. They serve as the objects of psychological attitudes like believing. Consider

45.   John believes that Mark Twain is Samuel Clemens.

Frege (1972) claims that the referent of the embedded sentence in 45 is the sense of the embedded sentence when it is unembedded. Since the referent of *John* is John, the referent of *believes* is a relation between John and the sense of 44(b). In addition, senses play a role in understanding expressions. A subject understands an expression by "grasping" its sense. Hence, a subject understands a declarative sentence by grasping the thought that it expresses—that is, its truth conditions.[25] Moreover, a sense is a way of thinking of the reference of an expression. As Frege (1972) puts it, the sense of an expression is a mode of presentation of an expression's reference, if it has one. Senses, then, have four roles: they determine the reference of an expression, if it has one; they are the objects of psychological attitudes; they provide an account for the understanding of an expression; and they are a way of thinking about the reference of an expression, if it has one.

Frege's theory offers an account of a range of phenomena that are taken to fall within semantic theory: intentional discourse, entailment, the relationship between language and the world, and truth conditions. Certain other semantic phenomena fall outside the scope of the theory, however: for example, synonymy, analyticity, meaning inclusion, and related notions. Let us call what synonyms have in common *linguistic meaning*. Thus, *two weeks* and *fortnight* have the same linguistic meaning. Do they have the same sense? Psychological attitudes, like believing, are sensitive to sameness of sense. We can say that two expressions have the same sense only if they can be substituted *salva veritate* in *p* in

46. S believes that *p*

It is possible for a speaker, S, to believe 47(a) without believing 47(b) (Burge 1979, 118 n.4):

47. (a) A fortnight is ten days.
     (b) Two weeks is ten days.

Hence, *two weeks* and *fortnight*, although synonymous, do not have the same sense in S's idiolect.[26] In addition, Frege (1956) regards 48(a) and 48(b) as having the same sense, but they do not have the same linguistic meaning, since *today* and *yesterday* are not synonymous:

48. (a) Today it rained.
     (b) Yesterday it rained.

Consequently, Frege's theory cannot be taken to be a semantic theory that gives an account of synonymy and related notions and, thus, cannot be an analytic meaning theory. The examples in 48 also show that Frege's theory cannot be an encyclopedic meaning theory. The encyclopedic information we could have about 48(a) might well be different from the encyclopedic information that we have about 48(b). Hence, the meaning that an encyclopedic theory assigns to the two sentences would be different, but, according to Frege, the two sentences have the same sense. This then adds another category to molecular meaning theories. In addition, to analytic and encyclopedic meaning theories we must add sense theories.

4.4.2   Kaplan's theory of character and content

Consider the sentence

49. I am a Canadian.

Let us suppose that Steven Davis and Brendan Gillon use tokens of 49 on May 30, 2003. Obviously, Davis and Gillon have said different things. A mark of the difference is that what Davis said is true, but what Gillon said is false. How can we account for this difference? The difference in what is said turns on a difference in the use of *I*. Davis's utterance of a token of *I* refers to him, while Gillon's utterance of a token of *I* refers to him.[27] The difference, then, is in the speakers who utter the tokens of 49. It is this difference that affects the semantic value of what Davis and Gillon say in uttering 49.

Other features of the situation in which a sentence is used—like time, place, and addressee—can affect the semantic value, the truth or falsity, of what is said. Consider the time at which a token of 49 is used. Had Davis used it in 1950, it would have been false, and he would have thereby said something different than what he said in using it on May 30, 2003. Consider a use of 50 in which the place of the use has a role in what is said:

50.   I am here.

Changes in the location of the speaker have an affect on what the speaker says in uttering 50. Kaplan calls the set of contextual parameters that include speaker, time, place, and addressee, which can play a role in fixing what is said in the use of sentence, the *context of use*.[28] Not only does the context of use of the tokens of 49 have a role in fixing what is said and thereby in determining the truth value of what is said, the truth values of these different tokens are also affected by the circumstances in which their truth values are evaluated. That is, given that the different tokens of the sentence are used in different contexts, we can go on to ask with respect to different circumstances, different ways the world could be, whether the sentence tokens as they are used in the different contexts are true at the different circumstances.

Let us consider some examples of different circumstances. Both Davis and Gillon moved to Canada, but only Davis became a naturalized Canadian. Davis might not have moved to Canada and thus would not have become a Canadian citizen. And Gillon could have become a Canadian citizen. Davis's not having moved to Canada and Gillon's becoming a Canadian citizen are not what actually happened, but they could have happened. There is, then, the circumstance of Davis's moving to Canada and the circumstance of his not moving to Canada, and there is the circumstance of Gillon's not becoming a Canadian citizen and the circumstance of his becoming a Canadian citizen. These are different ways that the world could be.[29] We can evaluate the truth value, then, of what Davis and Gillon said in uttering tokens of 49 with respect to these different circumstances. In the actual circumstance, they moved to Canada, and Davis, but not Gillon, became a Canadian citizen. Consequently, what Davis said is true, but what Gillon said is false. In the circumstances in which Davis does not move to Canada, what he said is false, and in the circumstance in which Gillon becomes a Canadian citizen, what he said is true. Notice that what is being evaluated with respect to these different circumstances is what Davis and Gillon actually said in uttering 49.

What about the referents of the tokens of *I* that occurred when Davis and Gillon used 49? Do they change their referents from circumstance to circumstance? Let us consider the following circumstances:

51.   (a) Davis and Gillon move to Canada, and Davis becomes a Canadian citizen but Gillon does not.
      (b) Davis and Gillon move to Canada, and neither becomes a Canadian citizen.
      (c) Davis and Gillon move to Canada, and Gillon becomes a Canadian citizen but Davis does not.
      (d) Gillon moves to Canada and becomes a Canadian citizen, but Davis does not move to Canada and does not become a Canadian citizen.[30]

When we ask whether 49 is true with respect to these different circumstances, we are asking about what is the case about Davis and Gillon in these different circumstances. Hence, the tokens of *I* in their uses of 49 have the same referents with respect to every circumstance. Hence, different tokens of *I* can have different referents from context to context, but once a person uses a token, the token does not change its referent from circumstance to circumstance.

Kaplan's account for the semantic properties of *I* is to associate with *I*, the type, a meaning that is represented by a function, its *character,* that takes as its arguments *contexts of use*, a fixed set of parameters including the time, place, and speaker of the utterance, and yields as its value another function, a *content* (all references to Kaplan are to this volume, Chapter 37). Kaplan takes the character of *I* to be represented by

52.   *I* refers to the speaker or writer.

The character of *I* can be thought of as a rule, a function, that given a context of use that includes the speaker, its argument, yields the content of *I* on the occasion of its use as its value.[31] Kaplan says that the content of *I* takes as its argument a *circumstance of evaluation*,[32] a possible world,[33] and yields as value the agent who used *I* in the particular context of use.[34] The character connected to *I* is context sensitive and changes its value, the content that it yields, with a change in context.

Let us consider two different uses of 49, Davis's and Gillon's. In Davis's use of 49, the context includes Davis who serves as the argument for the character of *I* that yields a content, content$_1$. In Gillon's use of 49, the results are similar, yielding another content, content$_2$. It is evident that content$_1$ is not the same as content$_2$ since Davis and Gillon are not the same person. In turn, Davis and Gillon express different thoughts in their utterances of 49, since what Davis says is true, but what Gillon says is false.[35] The difference in truth value can be traced to the only difference in what they said—namely, the difference in the content of the two occurrences of *I*.

Let us look more closely at content$_1$ and content$_2$, functions from possible worlds to the referents of *I*. Consider content$_1$ and the possible worlds in 51(a)–(d). For each of these possible worlds, the value of content$_1$ is Davis. We are asking with respect to him whether 49 would be true in these possible worlds. Not only is Davis the value of content$_1$ in these circumstances, but also he is the value of content$_1$ for every possible world. Similarly for content$_2$: it yields with respect to every possible world the same value, Gillon. Because of this, the two contents connected to the tokens of *I* in the utterances of 49 are constant functions, since they yield for every argument the same values (Kaplan, this volume, Chapter 37).[36] A constant function is what Kripke calls a *rigid designator*, a term that has the same referent in every possible world.[37] Let us call these values the *referents* of the respective tokens of *I* uttered by Davis and Gillon. Hence, the character attributed to the type, *I*, which represents its meaning, accounts for Davis's utterance of it in his use of 49 referring to himself and Gillon's utterance of it in his use of 49 referring to himself. The contents attributed to the different tokens of *I* account for the difference in truth values of 49 in the different circumstances in 51(a)–(d).

Let us look at the behavior of *Canadian* in 49.[38] It has connected with it a character that we can take to be the property of being Canadian, and it does not change its referent when Davis or Gillon, or anyone else, utters it in using 49. That is, it is context insensitive and does not change its referent from context to context. How can we represent this behavior of *Canadian* with respect to context? Kaplan's proposal is to connect with *Canadian* a fixed character that yields the same content for every context in which different speakers use *Canadian*. Thus, if time is held constant, the tokens of *Canadian* in Davis's and Gillon's uses of 49 have the same content.[39] Although the character of *Canadian* is fixed, its content is not a constant function. Imagine the possible world in 51(d) in which Davis did not come to Canada. If his utterance of 49 were evaluated with respect to this possible world, it would be false. The reason is that if he had not come to Canada, the set of Canadians would have been different. It would not have contained him. So, the difference between *I* and *Canadian* is that *I* does not have a fixed character, but the contents that are the values of the character are constant functions. In contrast, *Canadian* has a fixed character, but the content that is its value is not a constant function.

The distinction between character and content can also be brought out by considering 49 again and comparing its use to uses of

53.   You are Canadian.

Suppose that Davis utters 49 and Gillon utters 53 addressed to Davis. In one sense of *saying the same thing*, they have said the same thing. They have both said about Davis that he is Canadian. But in another sense of *saying the same thing*, they have not said the same thing, since *I* and *you* do not mean the same thing; they do not have the same characters. The distinction, then, between character and content can account for the different senses in which Davis and Gillon did and did not say the same thing in using, respectively, 49 and 53. The character of 49 and 53 are different, but their content is the same.[40]

The difference between character and content can also be brought out by considering Davis's and Gillon's uses of tokens of 49. The character associated with the sentence type they use is the same, but what they say, the content expressed, is not the same. Another way of putting this point is that the sentence tokens that Davis and Gillon uttered have the same linguistic meaning, but the statements that they make or the propositions that they express are not the same. The reason for this is that the truth conditions of what is said is different for the two utterances, because, as we have seen, the referents of *I* in the two cases are different. Davis's utterance is true with respect to a possible world just in case he is a Canadian in that world, or, equivalently, Davis's utterance is true with respect to a possible world just in case the content of *I* given in the context of utterance is in the set of Canadians in the possible world. Truth conditions for Gillon's use of 49 can be given in a similar manner.

The characters of *I* and *Canadian* play a different part in the contents of the occurrences of sentences. *I*, but not *Canadian*, is a device of *direct reference* (Kaplan, this volume, Chapter 37). That is, the character of *I* does not enter into the content of uses of 49. Kaplan's theory of direct reference, however, departs from his theory of character and content. In the latter theory, the content of *I* is a function from worlds to an individual, the same individual with respect to every possible world; the content of *Canadian* is a function from worlds to the set of Canadians at each world. In the former theory, the rule associated with *I* in 52 supplies an object to the content of 49, namely Davis, while the rule associated with *Canadian* supplies a property, the property of being Canadian. Let us then take 54, which is called a *singular proposition*,[41] to represent the content of the occurrence of 49 that results from Davis's use of it:

54.   <Davis, the property of being Canadian>

Davis and the property of being Canadian behave differently with respect to possible worlds. Suppose that we are evaluating the truth of 49 with respect to 51(d), the circumstance in which Davis does not come to Canada. At that possible world, it is Davis that matters for the truth value of 49, but the property of being Canadian yields the set of Canadians with respect to 51(d). Let us call this set {C}. Sentence 49 is true in 51(d), then, just in case Davis is in {C}. We can think of the property of being a Canadian as providing for each possible world the set of Canadians in that world. Since the property of being a Canadian has been identified as the character of *Canadian*, we can say that the character of *Canadian* becomes a constituent of the propositions that are expressed by sentences that contain *Canadian*. The character of *I* does not play the same role. It does not become part of the propositions expressed by the sentences of which it is a part. Rather it determines a content, the speaker, which becomes part of the proposition.[42]

We have identified the character of an expression with a function that represents its meaning. It is what a speaker of a language can be said to know by virtue of knowing his language. In contrast, what Davis and Gillon say, the statements that they make in uttering 49, are not part of linguistic knowledge. The reason is that knowledge of what content is expressed by a use of 49 involves knowledge of the context in which the sentence is used—in this case, knowledge of the speaker who uses the sentence. To know what statement Gillon makes in using the sentence, one must know that it was Gillon who used the sentence. Since this sort of knowledge depends on a particular use of an expression, it varies from context to context. Obviously, knowledge about the context of use of an expression cannot be part of a speaker's linguistic knowledge, since the latter does not vary from context to context.[43] Hence, the character of an expression is the same from context to context, but this does not exclude the value of the character changing from context to context. When Davis and Gillon use *I*, the character expressed is the same, although the value of the character is different. To mark the connection between character and content and meaning, we can say that an expression's character is its meaning in a language and its content is its meaning on an occasion of use. Characters are features of expression types and contents of expression tokens. In the uses of 49, character and content are not the same. The reason is that 49 contains an indexical, the character of which can have different values in different contexts.

4.4.2.1 Character, linguistic meaning, and sense

How does character and content match up with Fregean sense and linguistic meaning? Are either of the two Kaplan notions of character and content to be identified with either sense or linguistic meaning? The answer lies in the identity conditions for characters, contents, senses, and linguistic meanings. Characters are represented by functions from contexts to contents. Thus, two expressions have the same character if they express the same function. The functions will be the same if they yield as values the same contents for every context. Contents will be the same if they yield as values the same extensions in every possible world. Consider *the even prime number* and *the sum of 1 + 1*. These expressions express the same character, but they are not synonymous. Thus, they do not have the same linguistic meaning.[44] Moreover, someone can believe 55(a) without believing 55(b):

55. (a) The even prime number is the even prime number.
    (b) The sum of 1 and 1 is the even prime number.

Therefore, the two expressions do not express the same sense.[45] Consequently, character cannot be identified with Fregean sense. Moreover, content cannot be identified with Fregean sense or with linguistic meaning.

    Let us imagine that S looks in a mirror and sees someone that he thinks is fat, but does not realize that he is the person at whom he is looking (Perry 1979). Consider now S's uses of 56(a) and 56(b):

56. (a) I am fat.
    (b) He is fat.

These occurrences of the two sentences have the same content, since *I* and *he*, devices of direct reference, have the same content. The sentence occurrences, however, do not express the same sense, since S believes 56(a), but not 56(b). This example also shows that contents cannot be identified with linguistic meaning,[46] since the linguistic meanings of the two sentences are different, but as we have just seen, the Kaplanian contents they express are the same.

    Although character and content cannot be identified with Fregean sense, there are similarities. Both character and sense determine the referents of expressions, if they have referents. An important difference, however, is that some characters are context sensitive while senses are not. Another similarity between character and sense is that neither the verbal expression of the character nor the sense of an expression is synonymous with the expression. That is, neither gives the linguistic meaning, in the sense of analytic meaning, of an expression. For example, Kaplan gives *the speaker or writer in the context of use of 'I'* as the verbal expression of the character of *I*. But the former expression determines the referent of *I* in a context of use, but is not synonymous with it (Kaplan, this volume, Chapter 37). An additional similarity is that both senses and character play a role in understanding; it is by knowing the character or sense of an expression that a speaker understands the expression.[47] Content and sense are also similar. Both the contents and senses (thoughts) expressed by sentences are the bearers of truth value. A difference is that thoughts are timelessly true or timelessly false, but contents of some sentences can vary their truth values across times.

Although there are similarities between character and content on the one hand and senses on the other, there is a deep difference. They are ontologically distinct. Senses are entities that, among other roles, mediate the relation between expressions and their referents, if they have one. For Frege (1972) there are three kinds of referents: objects, concepts, and relations.[48] Characters and contents are types of functions. Since they are functions, they are sets of ordered pairs where the elements in the ordered pairs are limited to the sorts of entities that for Frege would be objects: that is, entities that serve as the referents of terms. But sets of ordered pairs of objects cannot play the role of Fregean senses. There is no sense in which they can be grasped or be a way that a speaker thinks about an object. Nor can they be rules that can be followed. They are of the wrong ontological type to have these roles. This does not prevent characters from being represented by rules, and we will have more to say about this in the next chapter.

Notes

1. Quine (1953b) does not think that a theory of reference can provide an account of necessity, since he thinks that no such account is possible.

2. We owe this point to Robert Stainton (personal communication).

3. The argument presented here is not given directly by Davidson but is one he suggests can be constructed analogously to an argument he presents against Frege's theory for the determination of the references of predicate expressions. See Lepore and Ludwig (2002) for a proposal.

4. It is an obvious criticism of Davidson to note that not all sentences have truth conditions, a criticism that Davidson recognizes (1984c). Hence, in the discussion of his theory in what follows, *sentence* should be understood as *declarative sentence*.

One of the principal divisions in views about semantics is between those who think and those who don't that central to providing a semantics for a language is the specification of truth conditions for its sentences. Lewis (1972: this volume, Chapter 11), for example, holds that "semantics with no treatment of truth conditions is not semantics." Lewis's conception of truth conditions is different from Davidson's, and so, too, is the theory that he develops to provide them for sentences. Davidson is not the first to suggest that an important task for a semantic theory is to provide truth conditions for sentences. The proposal is found in Frege (1972) and the early Wittgenstein. See Wiggins (1997) for a discussion of the history of the proposal.

5. We have left out a discussion of the value for *p* that is more problematic. It is not sufficient that substitution instances for *p* produce true T-sentences. For example, *'Snow is white' is true in English iff grass is green*, although true, cannot be part of an adequate semantics for English. What then is required for *p*? Davidson tells us that in a truth theory where the object language is not included in the meta-language, *p* must be a translation of the sentence denoted by "S". Translation, however, seems to be closely related to meaning, a notion that Davidson wishes to banish from his theory. Moreover, it would appear to let in synonymy, another notion to which Davidson (1984g, 26) does not wish to appeal.

6. See Gillon (this volume, Chapter 10) for further discussion.

7. Tarski (1944; 1956) does not use the relation of *being true of*. It is dispensable. We have used it for the sake of parallelism with model theory.

8. Some theorists seem to miss this point (Jackendoff 1996, 558).

9. See Parsons (1980) for a semantic theory that takes into account nonexistent objects.

10. We use square brackets to indicate a concept.

11. See Fodor (1998) and Fodor and Lepore (1992) for a discussion of the difference between atomic and molecular theories.

12. Fodor (1998) calls these kinds of theories *inferential role semantics*.

13. This is on the assumption that 'X' and 'Y' belong to the same language.

14. Atomic semantic theorists also think that no viable distinction can be drawn between analytic and synthetic sentences.

15. A number of other semantic theories fall within internalist semantics. See, for example, Gruber (1976), Langacker (1986), and Lakoff (1987).

16. This is in Jackendoff (1990). But in Jackendoff (1997) he changes his view and accepts Pustejovsky's rules that operate on lexical entries.

17. It might be wondered what would mark these expressions as being nonsynonymous for the speaker. We could suppose that the speaker has no current beliefs about nonactual situations involving renates and cordates, but if he were asked whether something could be a renate without being a cordate, he would answer in the affirmative. This would be sufficient for marking *renate* and *cordate* as being nonsynonymous for the speaker.

18. Pustejovsky seems to accept such a distinction (1995, 232–233; 1998, 296, 305–307). See Fodor and Lepore (1998) for a similar interpretation of Pustejovsky. However, certain remarks in Pustejovsky (1995) appear to raise doubts about whether his theory is an analytic meaning theory. In analyzing the meaning of *fast* he claims that it combines with *motorway* in *fastest motorway* to yield a new meaning for *fast*—that is, "the ability of vehicles on the motorway to sustain high speed" (Pustejovsky 1995, 45). As noticed by Jackendoff (1997), our knowledge that vehicles can move on a motorway at continuous high speed is part of "world knowledge" and not part of our knowledge of language.

19. Further discussion of ambiguity and synonymy is in Gillon (this volume, Chapter 10).

20. It is not clear that Pustejovsky's solution works for all occurrences of *good*. What is the lexical entry of *wine* that would yield a meaning for *good wine*? It cannot be the purpose of wine—namely, that it is to be drunk—because a drinkable wine is not necessarily a good wine.

21. On Frege's view (1972), expressions like *Santa Claus* have a sense, but no reference. *Sense* and *reference* are not the only translations that have been given of *Sinn* and *Bedeutung*. They have also been translated as *sense* and *meaning*, *sense* and *denotation*, and *meaning* and *reference*.

22. There is an extensive literature on the puzzle. See especially Salmon (1991).

23. Some have argued that there is tension between senses serving as the truth conditions of declarative sentences and their giving their cognitive significance. See Kaplan (1977: this volume, Chapter 37).

24. Fregean *Thoughts* are not mental entities.

25. The use of *grasping* here is of course metaphorical. Speakers understand an expression if they know what it means. They know what it means by knowing what its sense is. That they know the sense is manifested by their ability to use the expression in a wide range of contexts, including using it in a range of sentences and phrases and in a variety of speech situations.

26. It might be thought that *two weeks* and *fortnight* are not synonymous in S's idiolect. But Burge (1979) argues that they are synonymous, since S would defer to those he regards to be authoritative about the meaning of these words. *Two weeks* and *fortnight* cannot have the same sense in S's idiolect, since if they had the same sense, we could not account for the difference in belief expressed by 47(a) and 47(b).

27. There need not be two different tokens of 49. Imagine that the sentence is written on a chalkboard and, at the same time, Davis and Gillon point to it and say *That is true*.

28. There are cases in which contextual parameters do not play a role in determining what is said, for example, 2 + 2 = 4. The truth of an occurrence of this sentence is not affected by when, where, or by whom it is said.

29. We are leaving out of the discussion a range of other factors that have a role in specifying context and circumstance—for example, time, place, and addressee.

30. These, of course, do not exhaust the possible circumstances with respect to Davis and Gillon.

31. Kaplan (1977: this volume, Chapter 37) associates contents with "any meaningful part of speech taken in a context" and states that the content of a declarative sentence, given a context of use of the sentence, can be identified with what has been traditionally called *a proposition*.

32. More precisely, a circumstance of evaluation "usually includes a possible state or history of the world, a time, and perhaps other features as well" (Kaplan 1977: this volume, Chapter 37).

33. Kaplan's circumstances are the same as *possible worlds* (1977: this volume, Chapter 37). We shall use *possible world*, since this is what is current in the semantics literature.

34. This is not the only way to treat this case. We can take the value of the character expressed by *I* to be not the function but the agent of the context. That is, the content connected to Davis's use of *I* is Davis, himself. Hence, Davis would be part of the content of what is expressed by his use of 49. If contents of sentences used in a context are propositions, then Davis would be part of the proposition. Such propositions are called *singular propositions*. The two proposals are formally equivalent.

35. Content$_1$ and content$_2$ are not the contents of what Davis and Gillon express, since they are contents of their respective uses of *I*. However, these contents are constituents of the different contents that they express and account for the difference.

36. The character associated with *I*, a constant function, differs from the character associated with *the president of the United States*. The latter has associated with it, as its character, a function that yields, as its value, a function, or content, that at different possible worlds yields as its value different individuals.

37. As Kaplan points out, there are two notions of *rigid designation* at play in Kripke's work: a rigid designator is an expression that designates the same object in every possible world, or a rigid designator designates the same object in every possible world in which that object exists. The former seems to track better the semantic behavior of indexicals like *I*, since it can give a better account of the semantic properties of such sentences as *I do not exist*, a sentence that would be true at a world in which I do not exist (Kaplan 1977: this volume, Chapter 37).

38. We limit the discussion of *Canadian* to occurrences in extensional sentences. Its content would be affected if it were to occur within the scope of an intensional operator.

39. The content of *Canadian* can vary across times. The set of Canadians is different now than what it was ten years ago. This raises a problem about how to treat time with respect to predicates like *Canadian*. Is it part of the context so that at different times *Canadian* expresses a different content, or is it part of the circumstance of evaluation so that given a fixed time at which the expression is used, we can ask what its referent is at other times?

40. A similar account can be given for 48(a) and 48(b) that turns on uses of *today* and *yesterday* (Kaplan, this volume, Chapter 37).

41. Singular propositions are distinguished from general propositions. In the former, objects like Davis or Gillon, as well as properties such as being Canadian, are constituents; in the latter, only properties or universals such as the property of being Canadian are constituents. The distinction between singular and general propositions plays no part in Kaplan's theory of character and content in which these are represented by functions, however. There is no ontological difference between the content functions associated with *I* and *Canadian*. Both are functions from world to sets of individuals. The difference is that the former function is a constant function that yields for every world the same unary set, in which the member is the individual that used *I* in a particular context, whereas the latter function is not a constant function but yields different sets of individuals at different worlds. Both contents, then, are functions: that is, ordered pairs, of which the first members are worlds and the second members are sets of individuals. We should note that the difference between content and character, although not reflected directly in Kaplan's formal theory, can be defined within the theory. The difference between singular and general propositions, however, does not seem to have a place within Kaplan's formal semantics. Philippe Schlenker (personal communication) was helpful on these points.

42. All devices of direct reference are rigid designators, but not all rigid designators—for example, *the even prime number*—are devices of direct reference. *The even prime number* imports into the propositions expressed by sentences of which it is a part the property of being the unique number that is even and prime. This excludes the expression from the class of directly referential devices. This property picks out the same object in every possible world, the number 2, which makes *the even prime number* a rigid designator.

43. There can be variations in linguistic knowledge from context to context if a speaker adds new elements to his language—lexical items, for example. After a certain age, a speaker's linguistic knowledge is relatively fixed. For the sake of simplicity, we shall assume that it has reached a state of equilibrium.

44. There is a way around this problem by taking account of the internal structure and semantic properties of the expressions. The expressions consist of constituents that express different characters, and the characters of the complex expressions are functions of the characters of the constituents. We might say that two complex expressions have the same meaning, just in case their characters are a function of the characters of their constituents and their constituents express the same characters. This would work for the two expressions here but not for proper names like *Samuel Clemens* and *Mark Twain*.

45. We take it to be sufficient for 'p' and 'q' to differ in sense that someone can believe p without believing q. And we take it to be sufficient for 'a' and 'b', subsentential expressions, to differ in sense that 'p' and 'q' differ in sense and the only difference between them is that where one contains 'a' the other contains 'b'.

46. Kaplan appears to identify contents of sentences and Fregean thoughts (Kaplan, this volume, Chapter 37).

47. This is a view that Kaplan holds in "Demonstratives" (this volume, Chapter 37), but one he gives up in "Afterthoughts" (1989a).

48. When an expression occurs embedded within an intensional context such as *believes that* . . . , the referent of the expression is the sense of the expression when it is not embedded. Outside of such contexts, expressions have their direct referents.

5

Internalist and Externalist Semantic Theories

$\mathbf{F}$or a theory of language to be mentalist it must be committed to the view that grammars, including their semantic components, are represented in the mind. So for a semantic theory to be mentalist and externalist there must be some features of the internally represented lexical items that represent something that is external to the mind. This gives us two meanings of *represent*. A mentalist theory is committed to having the linguists' grammars *represented$_1$* in the mind—that is, instantiated in the mind. It does not follow that a grammar so represented$_1$ in the mind or any part of it *represents$_2$* or stands for anything (Chomsky 2000, 173). A grammar is representative$_2$ in the second sense if it or some part of it stands for something external to the grammar. For example, a lexical item, like *cow*, can be said to represent$_2$ or stand for its referent, the set of cows. Or the entry for a lexical item, a mental entity, can be taken to represent$_2$ the set of cows.

A theory about grammars can be representive$_1$ in the first sense without being representative$_2$ in the second sense. That is, it can be a mentalist internalist theory, mentalist in the sense that it is committed to the linguist's grammar being represented$_1$ in the mind of a speaker and internalist in the sense it holds that nothing in the grammar so represented$_1$ represents$_2$ or stands for anything external to the grammar. It is possible for a theory to be a representative$_2$ theory in the second sense without being representative$_1$ in the first sense. For example, a behaviorist theory that eschews mental representations$_1$ could hold that lexical items, actual inscriptions or utterances, represent$_2$ their referents. Moreover, a behaviorist theory is not even committed to having lexical items represented$_1$ in the mind, since on such a theory a lexical item is treated as a stimulus that triggers a response, and for the behaviorist stimuli are not represented$_1$ in the mind. An externalist mentalist theory is a representative theory in both senses, since it holds that lexical items and their lexical entries are internally represented$_1$ and that those mentally represented$_1$ lexical items and their entries that have a referent represent$_2$ something external to the grammar.[1]

We take semantic theories to be mentalist theories about the internal representations of speakers' semantic knowledge that characterizes their semantic competence. Speakers' internalized semantics are constituents of their internalized grammars that characterize their grammatical competence. *Semantics*, like *grammar*, does double duty, applying both to speakers' internalized semantics and to the linguists' theories of the internalized semantics. An internalist semantic theory is a mentalist theory, but, in addition, it is committed to there being no reference in the theory to anything beyond the grammatical and semantical elements that are internal to the grammar. That is, internalist semantic theories presuppose the principle of methodological solipsism that we described in Chapter 2. An externalist semantic theory is a mentalist theory as well, but it is committed to connecting some of the expressions in a language to objects that are external to the grammatical mental states of speakers. We consider internalist and externalist semantic theories in turn.

5.1   Internalist semantic theories

The difference between internalist and externalist semantic theories occurs at the level of lexical items.[2] An internalist semantic theory, an I-semantics, holds that in the description of the meaning of a lexical item there is no specification of a relationship between the lexical item and anything nonlinguistic. The meaning specification of lexical items is internal to the grammar; it is specified by appeal to meanings that are contained in the lexical items' lexical entries.[3] We have distinguished between atomic and molecular meaning theories and, in turn, within molecular meaning theories between analytic and encyclopedic meaning theories. Each of these can be construed as an internalist semantic theory.

5.1.1   Internalist atomic semantic theories

An atomic semantic theory associates lexical items with unanalyzable concepts that constitute their meanings. *Bachelor*, for example, is associated with the meaning [*bachelor*] and not with [*unmarried adult male*]. Some theorists who are committed to internalist atomic semantic theories take the atomic meanings that are associated with lexical items to be part of a language of thought.[4] Hence, an atomic semantic theory would provide an interface between a language and the thoughts that are expressed in using the language where the unanalyzed meanings like [*bachelor*] are constituents of the thoughts in the language of thought. In such internalist theories, however, there is no commitment to there being any connection between the concepts that are constituents of the language of thought and anything external to speakers. Rather, the language of thought is an internal representation over which various sorts of computations can take place, computations that involve relating one internal representation, a thought, to another internal representation, another thought. Such computations are involved in the use and understanding of the sentences of a language. The picture is that to understand a sentence a speaker attributes to it a syntactic structure and then, given the syntactic structure, provides a meaning specification of the sentence that in effect translates the sentence into the language of thought, albeit unconsciously.[5]

5.1.2   Internalist molecular theories of meaning

We have taken Jackendoff's encyclopedic semantics and Pustejovsky's analytic semantics, both examples of lexical semantics, to be instances of internalist semantic theories. In contrast, externalist theories require the semantics to specify for certain lexical items a relation between the lexical item and objects that are external to the grammar. For example, in an externalist semantics, we might have as part of the specification of the meaning of *gold* that it refers to gold; then, *refers to* relates *gold* to the element gold that is not part of speakers' mental furniture and, more important, not a part of their I-grammar. Such relations and objects are impossible in an I-semantics. What sorts of entities then can be included within I-semantics? We might think that they could include mental states such as anger or artifacts such as chairs, since in some sense they are mental. But this would be a mistake. Take the lexical entry for *anger*. Although anger is a mental entity, anger is not a constituent of speakers' I-grammars; hence, a lexical entry in an internalist theory cannot make reference to it. Similar considerations apply to chairs. In one sense chairs are mental entities, since they would not exist without humans having had a variety of mental states—that is, beliefs, intentions, and desires. This does not show, however, that chairs are part of the internal furniture of the mind. They are as much in the world, as opposed to being in the mind, as stars and quarks, and as such they cannot have any role in I-semantics.[6] More important, the intentions and desires that are necessary for the existence of chairs are not part of speakers' I-grammars.[7] Consequently, the kinds of entities that can serve in an I-semantics as meanings must not only be entities that would not have existed if humans had not existed but must be entities that exist internally to individual speakers' I-grammars, a condition that excludes chairs and other human artifacts as well as anger. So the entities that are available to the internalist for a semantic theory are those that are hypothesized to exist as part of a grammar, including such entities as syntactic categories, concepts in the language of thought, belief contents and their constituents, and so on.[8] This is not to suggest an ontological dualism between "objects in the world" and those entities to which I-semantics is committed. I-linguistics is open to the possibility of the eventual unification of internalist theories of the mind with neurophysiological theories of the brain (Chomsky 2000, 75–100).

5.2   Externalist semantic theories

We take an externalist semantic theory to be a semantic theory that relates lexical items to things that are external to the language system. This does not mean that the objects to which the lexical items are related must be outside the mind. It is compatible with externalism that the objects are mind dependent—Russellian sense data or Humean impressions, for example. Current versions of externalism reject sense data and impressions and opt for some of the objects to which lexical items are related being outside the mind.[9] In what follows, we assume that if a semantic theory relates lexical items to objects external to the language system, then it is committed to the latter sort of externalism.

It might seem that it is impossible that a semantic theory could be mentalist and externalist. Mentalism applied to semantics requires that the semantics be represented in the mind; externalism requires that the semantic theory relates some of its lexical items to objects that are external to the mind. It might be argued that since the objects to which an externalist theory relates some of its lexical items are external to the mind, they cannot be represented in the mind. So the conclusion is that mentalism and externalism are incompatible. But a moment's reflection shows that this is mistaken. Consider the following as a clause in an externalist semantic theory:

1.   *Apple* refers to apples.

The instance of the word *apples* in 1 that is used in this specification of the referential meaning of *apple* is a physical token that appears on the page of the copy of your book. Apples do not appear there, but 1 can represent the referential meaning of *apple* that relates this lexical item to apples. We can imagine that in a similar way an externalist semantics could have represented in the mind a specification of the meaning of a lexical item that relates the lexical item to something external to the mind.

There is a range of theories that are externalist and mentalist depending on what is taken to be the entities that are internally represented and that represent or stand for something. There are two possibilities: they can be either the lexical items themselves or the meanings of lexical items. If it is the first, then the theory is a mentalist reference theory of the sort we have in a

Davidsonian-style[10] satisfaction semantics; if the second, it is a meaning theory. Meaning theories divide into two kinds, atomic and molecular; and molecular theories divide into analytic and encyclopedic.

5.2.1   Atomic externalist theories

Atomic semantic theories that associate lexical items with unanalyzable meanings can also yield externalist semantic theories. Such theories are similar to Davidsonian satisfaction semantics, but with an extra step. A lexical item is first associated with a concept from the language of thought, and then concepts are connected with the objects of which they are concepts. The relation between a lexical item and the concept it expresses and that between a concept and the object of which it is a concept are not the same. The first is conventional. A lexical item might express any concept. *Gold* might have meant [*silver*], for example. That is, there is no necessary relation between a lexical item and its meaning. The relation between concepts and the objects of which they are concepts is logical. The concept [*gold*] must apply to gold. If it did not, it would not be the concept [*gold*].

External atomic meaning theories have one more step in their semantics than nonmentalist reference theories. That is, a lexical item is first associated with a meaning, and then the meaning is associated with an object or set of objects. Reference theories make do with the connection between lexical items and objects. It might be wondered what purpose this extra step serves. The reason is that by connecting lexical items to meanings the theory can provide an interface between language and thought. And, hence, an externalist atomic meaning theory provides a connection between language and our mental life on the one hand and with the world on the other.

5.2.2   Molecular externalist theories

Molecular internalist meaning theories can be easily transformed into externalist theories. What has to be added to make them externalist is the condition that the lexical entries associated with lexical items determine the lexical items' referents, if they have any. In this way we can turn Pustejovsky's and Jackendoff's internalist molecular semantic theories into externalist mentalist semantic theories. For Pustejovsky's semantic theory, this yields a semantic theory that is analytic, externalist, and mentalist; for Jackendoff's, a semantic theory that is encyclopedic, externalist, and mentalist. In both theories, the molecular meanings contained in the lexical entry associated with a lexical item determine the lexical item's referent, if it has one.

To illustrate the resulting molecular externalist theories, let us again consider *bachelor* and suppose that it is represented in an internal lexicon. An analytic meaning theory associates *bachelor* with its meaning [*unmarried male adult*], and an encyclopedic meaning theory with an encyclopedic entry that contains information that is believed to apply to bachelors by the speaker whose language is being described. We have then, respectively, the following lexical entries for analytic and encyclopedic externalist mentalist semantic theories. Note that '→' is to be read as *has as its lexical entry.*

2. (a) *Bachelor* → [*unmarried male adult*].
    (b) [*Unmarried male adult*] refers to bachelors.
3. (a) *Bachelor* → [*unmarried male adult who earns more on average than an unmarried female adult*].
    (b) [*Unmarried male adult who earns more on average than an unmarried female adult*] refers to bachelors.

In each case, the meaning of *bachelor* determines its referent. In the case of atomic and analytic theories the meanings represent properties that are necessary and sufficient for something's being a bachelor. With encyclopedic theories, the associated properties are properties that bachelors, in fact, have that are believed to distinguish them from nonbachelors, but not all of them are necessary for something to be a bachelor.

5.2.3 Fregean sense and externalism

It is clear that Frege's semantic theory (1956) is a theory of reference, since one of the functions of senses is to determine the referent of an expression if it has one. A question that remains is whether his theory is mentalist. Frege holds that senses are abstract objects that can be related to more than one person. If two people understand the same declarative sentence, then they grasp the same thought, the sense of the declarative sentence. It follows from this that senses are not mental objects in the minds of speakers. It would thus appear that Frege's theory should not be included within mentalist semantic theories. But there is a way in which his theory can be taken to fall into this category without doing much violence to it. Had Frege used the distinction be-tween type and token, there would be nothing to prevent thought types from being the same for different people, but for there to be different tokens of that type instantiated in their minds. Con-sider theories of perception. Suppose two people are looking at the same object, a cup. There is nothing to prevent a theory of perception from hypothesizing that each person has an internal representation of the object that serves in explaining the internal psychological processes that account for their visual experiences. Similarly, there is no reason not to take senses to be repre-sented in the minds of speakers and to appeal to these internal representations to explain the psychological processes that are involved in using and understanding a language. If we were to take this tack, a Fregean semantics would then be a version of what we have been calling an externalist meaning theory: a mentalist theory committed to the semantics being internally rep-resented in the minds of speakers, and an externalist theory committed to the internally repre-sented senses referring to entities that are external to the semantics.

5.2.4 Character and externalism

It is evident that Kaplan takes his theory to be externalist, since the value of a character is a con-tent and the value of a content is a referent that is not a constituent of an internally represented semantics. The question is what the relationship is between Kaplan's theory and mentalism. That is, the question is whether the character of an expression, which Kaplan takes to be established by convention and known by a competent speaker, can be in the mind of a speaker. Although Kaplan does not speak to this issue, this does not preclude his theory from having a mentalist interpretation.[11] The character of an expression is a function from possible contexts in which the expression can occur to contents. Let us consider I, the character of which is a function from contexts that include the speaker who uses sentences containing I to a content, another function from a possible world to the referent of I in that world. Could speakers have in their heads the character of I? It would seem not. Functions are sets of ordered pairs from the objects in a set that serve as arguments of the function, the function's *domain*, to the objects in a set that serve as values of the function, the function's *codomain*. The domain for the character of I is the set of possible contexts that have speakers—an infinite set—and the codomain is the set of contents that are themselves functions from a possible world to the speaker in that possible world. Since there are an infinite number of possible worlds, the codomain of the character of I is infinite. The problem is that speakers have finite minds and thus cannot have within them infinite sets. It would seem, then, that the character of I cannot be in the minds of speakers. There is another, even more obvious sense in which characters cannot be in the minds of speakers. Both the sets of contexts and the sets of ordered pairs of worlds and individuals that constitute the domain and codomain of the character of I are the wrong ontological types to be in the minds of speakers.

Speakers themselves are in the sets that constitute the codomain of the character of *I*, but it makes no sense to say that they are constituents of their own minds.

There is an advantage to think of the character of an expression as being a function. By so regarding it, characters can be given a formal treatment within model theory (Kaplan 1977: this volume, Chapter 37). The drawback, as we have seen, is that characters have infinite domains and codomains and thus cannot be psychologically instantiated. A solution to this problem would be to consider characters to be rules. Although the plus function has an infinite domain—the sets of pairs of numbers that are added together and an infinite codomain—the number that is the result of the addition, we are able to add a potentially infinite number of numbers and get the correct results. It is plausible to suppose that we must have a finite psychological representation of some rule that yields this result (Partee 1980, 11 n.2).

Similarly, we might take the character of *I* to be represented by the rule in 4, a rule that can be represented in a finite mind:

4. *I* refers to the speaker or writer. (Kaplan 1977: this volume, Chapter 37)[12]

A difficulty with this solution is that Kaplan's semantics is a model theory in which characters are functions.[13] Without the model theory, we have no precise idea how to assign contents to expressions and, thus, truth conditions to sentences. What is the relationship, then, between the rule in 4 and the function that serves as the character of *I*? For any given function there are an infinite number of rules that can stand proxy for it. One way to think of the relationship between formal semantics and internal psychological realizations is to take the set of theoretical objects in the model theory—for example, the functions that serve as characters—as providing constraints on what can serve as a rule. Even though there are an infinite number of rules that can represent the function, not any rule will do. For a rule to be a possible psychological realization of a function, its inputs and outputs must be the same as the domains and codomains of the related functions. We can take the function then to provide a structural constraint on the rule.

5.2.5   Model theory and externalism

It might seem that if we are committed to a model theory as our semantic theory, we have opted for an externalist semantic theory. Opting for model theory as the semantics for natural languages and supposing that there is a way that they can be represented in the minds of speakers, however, does not settle the issue as to whether the semantics is internalist or externalist. Some have argued that without a relationship between lexical items and objects in the world external to speakers' internalized grammars, it is impossible to provide a characterization of the truth conditions of declarative sentences. And without such a characterization we do not have a semantics, properly speaking. We think that it is a mistake to suppose that a model theoretic semantics requires a language to world relation where the world is taken to be external to an internalized grammar. A standard model theory contains among other elements a universe of discourse, a set of objects, and a function that associates these objects or sets of these objects with the lexical items in the lexicon of the language for which the model theory is providing a semantics. There is nothing in the notion of *universe of discourse* that limits what objects it contains. They could be concepts in the language of thought, numbers, mental proxies for numbers, and others. That is, it is possible for the entities in a universe of discourse to be mental elements in I-grammars and, thus, for a model theoretic semantics to be an internalized theory of meaning for a language. We wish to be clear about what we are suggesting. We are not claiming that it is possible to give an adequate model theoretic semantics that is psychologically plausible and that would have as the elements in its universe of discourse entities drawn from the I-grammars of speakers. What we are suggesting is that the impossibility does not follow from the semantics being a model theory. What is required to show that it is not possible are arguments that are extra-model theoretic.

It might be thought that model theories cannot be models of our mental semantic theories because their universes of discourse must be infinite sets. There are two points to be made against this criticism of model theoretic semantics construed as a mentalist theory. First, it is not a necessary feature of universes of discourse that they be infinite; it is perfectly possible to have a finite universe of discourse. Second, even if the universe of discourse were infinite, it would not follow that a model theory could not be a model of our internalized semantics. Rather than have an infinite set in the model theory, it would be possible to have a finitely axiomatizable specification that permits the interpretation of the linguistic expressions. The point here is no different than the proposal that many linguists make when they claim that the linguist's syntax for a language is a finite model of an internal structure that generates an infinite set—namely, the infinite set of the sentences of the language. Thus, it does not follow from a semantic theory's being a model theory that it cannot be a purely internalist and adequate semantic theory for a natural language.

5.2.6   Rules and mentalism

A possible solution to the problem of how to represent functions that serve as the meanings of lexical items as being psychologically real is to represent them by rules that speakers have as part of their internal and psychological semantic competence. The rules would serve to determine the semantic referents of the lexical items, if they had a referent. The problem with this is, as Hilary Putnam (1996) has shown, is that speakers can have competent mastery of a lexical item that has a semantic referent without its being the case that they know a rule either tacitly or consciously that determines the referent of the lexical item.

Putnam asks us to imagine a planet that is a twin of our planet on which for every item on our planet, save one, there is a molecule-for-molecule twin. Let us call this planet Twin Earth. Let us suppose that there are two people, Oscar on Earth and Boscar on Twin Earth, who are molecule-for-molecule identical,[14] who have had the same stimulus patterns that have impinged on their sensory organs, and who have behaved in the same way. That is, their internal physical status, stimulus inputs, and behavioral outputs are the same. The difference between Earth and Twin Earth is that where Earth has water Twin Earth has another substance, XYZ, that looks and acts like water under normal conditions. Both substances flow in rivers and streams, are found in lakes and oceans, and are good for washing and drinking. Further suppose that Oscar and Boscar are unaware of the chemical composition of water or XYZ. Moreover, they both use the same words for the respective substances, *water*. In fact, there is no difference in their languages, described purely syntactically and phonologically. In addition, they utter the same sentences at the same time and assent to the same sentences involving the term *water*. Their use of *water* passes muster on their respective planets so that they are regarded as competent users of the term. There is no reason to think they do not know the meaning of *water* in their respective languages and no reason to think that there is any difference between what they each have in their heads. The problem is that the semantic referents of their terms are different. When Oscar uses *water*, the semantic referent of his term is water; when Boscar uses the term, its semantic referent is XYZ. Hence, there cannot be rules that are part of their mental furniture that are internally individuated that determine the referents of their terms. As Putnam (1996, 13) puts it, "'Meanings' just ain't in the *head*!"[15]

The consequence this has for semantics is that a theory adequate for accounting for various sorts of semantic properties—entailment relations, for example—cannot thereby be an adequate theory that accounts for speakers' semantic competence. Let us return to our thought experiment. The problem arises because Oscar and Boscar are ignorant about the nature of the referent of *water* in their respective languages. Had they known this, the knowledge could be incorporated into their respective semantic theories. In Oscar's internalized semantic theory there would be a rule that connects *water* to H_2O, and in Boscar's semantic theory a rule that connects *water* to XYZ. It would no longer be the case, however, that they were twins, since they would have different rules in their I-semantics. To put the point another way, the thought experiment cannot be mounted for beings that are omniscient. Perhaps, then, we can take a semantic theory that is committed to there being rules that determine the referents of lexical items to be an idealization that applies to a being that is supercompetent. Such a theory, of course, would not apply to ordinary speakers, since they are all ignorant in some respect about the nature of the referents of certain of their lexical items. To have a theory that applies to ordinary speakers, we might relax some of the commitments of our theory to account for the difference in knowledge among speakers.[16] These theories, then, might be the ones that we could take to be plausible psychologically and that account for semantic competence.

Notes

1. Chomsky's theory (2000) is a representative theory in the first sense, and Fodor's (1998) is a representative theory in both senses. A word of caution is necessary here. When Chomsky talks about *semantic and phonetic representations*, he talks about the technical senses of the terms (2000, 173), where the contrast is with the representative theory of ideas, an externalist theory. It is not clear, however, that when Chomsky uses *represent* in his technical sense, he is using it in either of the ways that we are using the term.

2. The semantic level might not be the only place at which the distinction between internalist and externalist theories applies; it might apply as well at the phonological level.

3. This does not exclude the possibility that the meanings that are constituents of lexical entries are the conceptual building blocks of psychological states.

4. The theorist who has been most closely connected with an internalist atomic semantic theory is Fodor (1975; 1994). In more recent work, Fodor (1998) has given up on construing atomic semantic theories as internalist theories and opts to take them to be externalist theories. It is not at all evident that the meanings of expressions can be equated with concepts that are elements in a language of thought and thus are constituents of intentional states. See the discussion of the difference between Frege's senses, which are constituents of Thoughts, and linguistic meaning (see Chapter 4).

5. The language of thought has been invoked to account in part for language use and understanding; in addition, Fodor (1975) has appealed to it to account for language acquisition. He states that when children learn their first language, part of what they learn is to associate the lexical items of the language to which they are exposed with the concepts in their language of thought. This presupposes that children are born with a rich set of concepts—an innate language of thought—that enables them to make the association.

6. For an opposing view, see Jackendoff (1996, 557–558).

7. Perhaps some of the beliefs that we have about chairs make their way into the lexical entry for *chair* in encyclopedic meaning theories, but it is difficult to see how intentions and desires make their way into the lexical entry.

8. This is to accommodate encyclopedic theories of meaning in which the contents of beliefs are included in the lexical entries of lexical items. Internalism assumes that the criteria for individuation for the entities to which the internalist theories are committed are internal to I-grammars. Both Pustejovsky's and Jackendoff's semantic theories appeal to beliefs that supply the material for the entries for lexical items. It is not clear that beliefs can be individuated internally. See Burge (1979; 1982) for a discussion about beliefs.

9. Of course, some of the objects to which an externalist semantic theory relates some of its lexical items are in the mind. *Pain* is true of pain, and pains are in the mind.

10. It would be a mistake to take Davidson to be committed to mentalism, a view that he explicitly rejects. He claims that an adequate truth theory "[recovers] the structure of a complicated ability—the ability to speak and understand a language" (1984g, 25). Davidson further claims that "it does not add anything to this thesis to say that if the theory does correctly describe the competence of an interpreter, some mechanism in the interpreter must correspond to the theory" (1986, 438). Davidson also claims that "we may

maintain . . . that there is a mechanism in the interpreter that corresponds to the theory. If this means only that there is some mechanism or other that performs that task, it is hard to see how the claim can be false" (1984a, 141). This is compatible with a rejection of mentalism if the mechanism is not a representation of the theory. Correspondence is not the same as representation. There are others who have taken Davidson's theory to be a mentalist theory. See Larson and Segal (1995) for a theory of this sort.

11. It might be wondered why we are interested in examining the relationship between Kaplan's semantics and mentalism. The reason is that we think the most plausible theory about language is mentalist. Since semantics is part of a theory of language, there should be a way of construing semantic theories as mentalist theories.

12. It is psychologically implausible to take this to be the rule that speakers employ even tacitly to determine the semantic referent of their uses of *I*. It is difficult to see how to reformulate 4 to make it psychologically plausible without including within it *I* or one of its cognates.

13. When Kaplan introduces 4, he introduces it as the character of *I* and takes the related function to represent the character rather than taking the character to represent the function (1977: this volume, Chapter 37).

14. Of course, Oscar and Boscar cannot be molecule-for-molecule identical, since Oscar's body contains water and Boscar's does not. But this point is irrelevant for the thought experiment; it can always be changed using natural kinds that have no effect on Oscar's and Boscar's internal states.

15. Italics in the original. Putnam's criticism is directed against Carnap's semantics (1956) that appeals to intensions.

16. This suggestion is due to Partee (1980, 3). But Partee notes that semantic theories that appeal to model theory are still not unproblematic. She argues that they do not give an adequate account of the semantics of sentences that are reports of propositional attitudes. We do not pursue this issue here but note that an adequate treatment of the semantics of such sentences is still unresolved in semantic theory.

6

Semantics and Context

The theories that we have considered, except Kaplan's, assume the following picture of semantics. A semantics is a constituent of a grammar that operates on the output of a syntax, the sort provided by either linguists or logicians. The output of the syntax is a syntactic description of a sentence that contains as constituents individual lexical items for which the semantics provides semantic values. Internalist and externalist theories share this characterization of semantics; the difference between them is that internalist theories take the semantic values to be mental entities that are internal to an I-grammar, whereas externalist theories claim that the semantic values of some lexical items are entities that are external to I-grammars. Some externalist semantic theories—Kaplan's, for example—have it that context has a role in fixing the semantic values for lexical items that are context sensitive, the *indexicals*. Once the semantic values are fixed for the lexical items in a sentence, the semantics provides rules that take these semantic values and the structure of the sentence to yield a semantic value for the sentence.

Kaplan's theory does not adhere to this model, however. His theory allows certain values, the contextual parameters, to play a part in assigning semantic values to a sentence or a sentence token without assigning these values to lexical items that are constituents of the sentence or sentence token. It appears that certain sentences have a structure, semantic values for their lexical items, and rules of composition that are not sufficient for providing the sentence's semantic value. Some sentences that are the outputs of a linguistic or logical syntax have something missing that plays a semantic role. Consider the following argument:

1. (a) If it is raining now, we won't play tennis.
   (b) It is raining.
   _____
   (c) We won't play tennis.[1]

For the argument in 1 to be valid the time and place of the events in 1(b) and 1(c) must be the same. But there is nothing in the surface structure of the sentence tokens to mark this. There are two ways that an account could be provided to assign time and place to the two premises.

One proposal is syntactic; it proposes that there are placeholders for time and place specifications in the underlying syntactic structures of the two sentences that are then given semantic values by the context. Another proposal, provided by Kaplan's semantics, does not pass through the underlying syntactic structure of the sentences. In Kaplan's semantics, the context of the use of 1(b) and 1(c) provide the missing parameters; the truth conditions of an occurrence of a sentence token are assigned to it with respect to contextual parameters of time and place. In light of this, let us consider 1(b). Suppose that it is used at 5:00 pm on May 30, 1950, in Vancouver. The truth conditions for the sentence type are given in 2(a) and for the sentence token in 2(b) (Kaplan 1989a, 545):

2. (a) 'It is raining' is true at time t, place p, and world w iff it is raining at time t, place p, and world w.[2]

    (b) 'It is raining' is true at 5:00 pm at May 30, 1950, Vancouver, and the world w iff it is raining at 5:00 pm at May 30, 1950, Vancouver and world w.

In 2(b) the variable, w, is filled in by circumstances of evaluation, the possible worlds, at which what is said in using *It is raining* at 5:00 pm on May 30, 2003 is evaluated. Let us suppose that in the actual world, it was not raining in Vancouver on that date, so what was said in using *It is raining* was false. However, if w were a world in which it had been raining in Vancouver at that time and date, then what would be said in uttering *It is raining* on May 30, 1950, would be true.

In both the syntactic and Kaplan accounts, we might say that the sentence tokens in 1(b) and 1(c) contain unarticulated constituents—constituents that are necessary for fixing the semantic value of the sentences. In the first proposal the unarticulated constituents are syntactic, while in the second proposal they are constituents of the semantic representations of the sentences. The syntactic proposal for providing an account of the validity of 1 is similar to the claim that there are unarticulated constituents provided by the syntax, given in the square brackets, in the following cases of ellipsis:

3. (a) John is tall, and so too is Bill [tall].

    (b) John gave a book to Sally, and Bill [gave] a flower to Louise.

    (c) John went to Sam's house, and Bill [went] to Mary's [house].

There are other cases in which, it might be argued, it is not the syntax that provides the unarticulated constituents, but the lexicon:

4. (a) Sally is too tall. [for what?]

    (b) Sally is tall enough. [for what?]

    (c) That is Sally's book. [She owns, she wrote, she made?] (Carston, this volume, Chapter 40)

The lexical items *too* and *enough* and the genitive in 4(c) call for various sorts of completion that could then be provided by the context.

Let us look more closely at the syntactic account of the validity of 1. The proposal is that in 1(b) and 1(c) there are unarticulated variables for time and place in the underlying syntactic structures of the sentences on which the semantics operates, thereby providing semantic values for the variables by an appeal to the context and, thus, assigning meanings—that is, truth conditions—to the sentences.[3] The contextual information (time, place, speaker, and addressee) are properties of the actual occurrences of the tokens in 1(b) and 1(c). The tokenings occur at a particular time and place and are tokened by a particular speaker and addressed to a particular audience. A similar account cannot be given for the sentences in 4. Assuming that there are unarticulated variables in the underlying syntactic structure of these sentences, it is difficult to see how the semantics could operate on them to provide the missing constituents; at best the variables provide placeholders for information that must be added before it is possible to generate truth conditions for the sentences. This information, however, is not contextual and cannot be added by the semantics. Consider 4(c). The truth conditions of this sentence depend on whether *Sally's book* is to be interpreted as her owning the book, being the book's author, having the book in her possession, and so on. None of this information is connected to properties of the occurrence of the tokening of 4(c) and thus contained in the context of the tokening, nor is it semantic information that can be used to assign an interpretation to the sentence. Kaplan's semantic theory is no better than the syntactic proposal in providing an account of the truth conditions of 4(c); the only contextual information to which his theory can appeal is limited to speaker, time, place, and addressee and cannot fill in the information required by 4(c). So it seems that the grammar of a language does not contain all the information needed for providing semantic values for certain sentences.

This point can be driven home by considering other sentences that require completion where there does not seem to be any reason to suppose that there are unarticulated constituents or placeholders provided by the syntax, or that Kaplan's theory can give an account of their semantic value:

5. (a) Sally got married and [then] had a baby.[4]
    (b) Sam and Bill moved the piano [together].
    (c) Sam went to Chicago, and Bill to Paris [not together].
    (d) Sam has $78.12 [exactly].
    (e) Sam has a million dollars in the bank [not exactly].[5]

In these examples, what is understood are not the sentences without the brackets but the propositions expressed by the sentences with the brackets. There does not seem to be any reason for supposing that there are unarticulated constituents or variables in the underlying syntactic structure of these sentences or that Kaplan's theory gives the correct semantic value for the sentences. Could the information in brackets be added by lexical items in the sentences and thus be accounted for by the semantics? Take 5(a). It cannot be argued that *and* adds *then*, since it would have to be added with every occurrence of *and*, but there are clear cases in which this is not the case:

6. (a) 2 + 2 = 4, and 3 + 5 = 8.
    (b) Paris is the capital of France, and London is the capital of Great Britain.

It would make no sense to add *then* to these sentences. Is there a way to generate a *then* in 5(a), but not in 6(a)? It could be claimed that an encyclopedic meaning theory can account for the difference; there is information in the lexical entries for *married* that generates the *then*— namely, women usually have babies after they are married. This is an untenable proposal. It would require an unlimited amount of information in lexical items, since it does not seem that there is a limit to the beliefs we have that can play a part in interpretations of sentences containing *and*. But, more importantly, it does not account for the context sensitivity of the process that generates the *then*. Consider

7. It rained, and it snowed.

Suppose that there is a thin layer of ice on the streets with a light dusting of snow on top. In this situation, a speaker who utters 7 would be understood to have said

8. It rained, and then it snowed.

But if the context were different, if there were wet snow on the ground and puddles of water, a speaker who utters 7 in this situation would be interpreted as having said that it rained and snowed, but without there being any order to the events.

How, then, is an account of the interpretations of the sentences in 5, 6, and 7 to be given? Consider the following case made famous by H. P. Grice (1989). Suppose that Professor Kelconq has been asked to write a letter of recommendation for graduate studies in semantics for her student, Smith, and sends the following brief letter:

9. Smith has beautiful handwriting, comes to class on time, and is always neatly dressed.

Kelconq would be taken to be implying, although not saying, that

10. Smith is not very good at semantics.

In Grice's technical vocabulary, Kelconq has *implicated* the proposition expressed by 10, and this proposition is an *implicature* of what the speaker says in uttering 9.

Robyn Carston (this volume, Chapter 40) argues that exactly the same cognitive processes that account for the Grice example can be used to give explanations for the interpretations of 5, 6, and 7, but with an important difference. The proposition expressed by 5(a) with the material in the brackets is not something a speaker implicates in uttering 5(a) without the brackets, nor is it an implicature of the utterance of this sentence. Rather, the proposition expressed by 5(a) is an *explicature* of the utterance of the sentence without the brackets.[6] That is, it is what the speaker says in uttering the sentence, rather than what a speaker implies in uttering it.

The theory to which Carston appeals to explain the processes at play in capturing explicatures is not Grice's but, rather, the relevance theory developed by Dan Sperber and Deirdre Wilson (1995). They regard interpretation to be an on-line process that includes decoding and inference (Carston, this volume, Chapter 40). The decoding of the utterance involves assigning to the utterance grammatical information, including syntactic, semantic, and phonological information. The semantic information assigned to an utterance is conceptual information of the sort found in internalist molecular meaning theories. The representation that results as a consequence of grammatical processes is the input to pragmatic processes involving an inferential device that generates the final output, an interpretation of what the speaker has said. We can think of the process as being similar to hypothesis formation. The interpreter is confronted with a puzzle about what a speaker says in uttering a sentence. We can think of the output of the grammar, including its semantics, as providing evidence to the interpreter for an inference to the best explanation of the speaker's utterance. This evidence, together with contextual evidence and background assumptions, provides the material for the interpreter's inference. The inference is constrained, however, by a principle of relevance: maximize cognitive effects, and minimize processing effort. The cognitive effects are what is communicated in the context of the utterance. This can involve the strengthening of certain of the interpreter's assumptions (beliefs, presuppositions, theories, etc.), the weakening of certain of his assumptions by showing that they are false, or the adding of new assumptions to the set of assumptions that the interpreter already holds (Carston, this volume, Chapter 40).

The pragmatic processes in relevance theory are not only supposed to provide an account for implicatures and explicatures, but the same mechanisms are invoked in giving an account of the reference assignments to indexicals and the disambiguation of ambiguous lexical items. In discussing Kaplan, we concentrated on a subclass of indexicals that Kaplan calls *pure indexical*, which includes *I*, *you*, *today*, and *tomorrow*. Kaplan claims pure indexicals have connected with them a rule, a character, which determines their semantic value. Pure indexicals contrast with *demonstratives*, which include *that*, *this*, and *he*. One difference between them is that there is no rule similar to those for *I*, for example, which, given a context, determines their referents (Kaplan 1977: this volume, Chapter 37). For example, there is no rule connected to *that* in 11 that could determine its semantic value:

11. That's beautiful.

Anything could be the semantic value of *that*.[7]

It might be thought that demonstrations provide a rule for the reference determination of demonstratives—namely, the referent of an occurrence of *that* is the object to which the speaker is pointing. There are two problems with this. Pointing is always underdetermined. Point to a dog, for instance, and you have pointed to his coat, a part of his body, a flea on his body, or other aspect. This shows that pointing is not sufficient for reference determination. In addition, 11 can be used without a pointing gesture. Imagine that someone picks up a book and without pointing a speaker utters 11. Again, there is underdetermination. It could be the book, its cover, or the contents of the book that is the semantic value of the speaker's utterance of *that*. This shows that pointing is not necessary. How, then, does the interpreter, the person who picked up the book, figure out the semantic value of *that*? Kaplan claims that it is speakers' intentions that determine the semantic values of demonstratives (1989a, 582–583). But how are speakers' intentions to be determined? There is no employment of a rule that, given the context, can uncover what they are. Relevance theorists maintain that the same pragmatic processes that are involved in accounting for implicatures, explicatures, et cetera are applicable here as well. Suppose that it is mutually manifest to the interpreter and speaker that the copy of the book in the interpreter's hand is badly damaged and that the speaker is an avid reader. Given the context, background knowledge, and so on, it is plausible for the interpreter to take the speaker to be intending to refer to the content of the book in using *that* in 11 and, thereby, for the interpreter to assign the content of the book as the semantic value of the demonstrative.

An underlying assumption of relevance theory is that the interpreter is central in determining implicatures, explicatures, reference assignments, and so on. Reference theory, says Carston, is a theory of interpretation (this volume, Chapter 40). There are two different senses of *determine*, however: epistemological and metaphysical.[8] To say that the interpreter determines (epistemologically) the semantic value of *that* is to say that he finds out or comes to know what it is. But the interpreter does not determine (metaphysically), in the sense of fix, the semantic value of the speaker's use of *that*. That is up to the speaker and depends on his intention in using the expression.[9] Actual interpreters are not necessary for demonstratives to have semantic values. We can imagine that a speaker utters 11 without there being anyone there to hear him. He wishes to express his own aesthetic reaction to the book. Even without an interpreter present, the speaker's utterance of *that* would still have a semantic value.

A way around this criticism that interpreters are not necessary to determine (metaphysically) the semantic referent of *that* is to take it that it is not actual interpreters that are determiners (metaphysical) of the semantic values of demonstratives, et cetera, but possible interpreters. We might say that when there is no actual interpreter, the semantic value of *that* is determined, in the sense of fixed, by what an interpreter would assign as the semantic value to the speaker's utterance of 11. There is a problem with this strategy, however. Interpreters can be mistaken. The test of an interpreter's hypothesis, either actual or possible, about the semantic value of a demonstrative is the demonstrative's actual semantic value that is fixed by the intentions of the speaker. The upshot is that although the pragmatic processes that the relevance theorists invoke might well give an account of interpretation, they do not play any direct role in fixing explicatures, implicatures, or semantic values of indexicals. But they might play an indirect role in that when a speaker intends to communicate, he would do well to make his utterance open to interpretation. To fulfill his communicative intention, he is best served by making his utterance relevant in the context. That is, by making his utterance one that is open to interpretation by the cognitive processes that interpreters in fact employ in interpretation, processes for which relevance theory proposes an account. How this plays out in fixing what speakers say or imply is not something that we consider here.

Notes

1. This is a variation of the argument that Carston presents (this volume, Chapter 40). We have added *now* to the first premise to rule out the conditional being interpreted as *Whenever it is raining, we won't play tennis*. As Jeffrey Pelletier (personal communication) has pointed out to us, on this quantificational reading of the conditional the argument would be valid without any consideration of the time and place of the occurrences of the other premises of the argument.

2. This is a simplified presentation of the truth conditions of the sentence and the sentence token. For a complete specification of the truth conditions, an interpretation must be assigned to *raining*.

3. Stanley (2000) has been most closely associated with the view that there are unarticulated constituents in sentences that play a role in semantic interpretation. See Carston (this volume, Chapter 40) for criticisms of Stanley's arguments.

4. It might be argued that *then* is not part of the meaning of this sentence. If it is not, then this sentence should entail *Sally had a baby and got married*, but it does not.

5. Some of these examples are taken from Carston (this volume, Chapter 40).

6. Sperber and Wilson (1986, 182) were the first to introduce *explicature*. They take an explicature to be an explicitly communicated assumption, where an assumption is roughly a speaker's belief. And "an assumption communicated by an utterance U is explicit if and only if it is a development of a logical form encoded by U."

7. The semantic value cannot be provided by Kaplan's semantic theory, since it is not a property of the tokening of 11; it is not included of the set of Kaplan's contextual parameters.

8. We owe *metaphysical determination* to Rob Stainton (personal communication).

9. There is a long and complicated story to be told about what fixes the semantic values of demonstratives. See Reimer (1991; 1992).

7

Conclusion

To conclude Part I, we shall go over the main points that we have covered. We have made two assumptions that we think are worth repeating: the words *grammar* and *semantics* play a dual role applying to grammatical and semantical theories and to their cognitive realizations in the heads of speakers; a semantics in both senses is a component of a grammar, along with a phonology and a syntax, both of which operate on the information that is the output of the syntactic component of the grammar. The first assumption sees theories of grammar and semantics as psychological theories about speakers' internal cognitive states. It is an assumption about the ontological category of a grammar; it is a mental entity that is instantiated in the minds of speakers of the language. This assumption is what we have called *mentalism,* a view that is widely held among linguists but rejected by some philosophers and logicians. The second assumption regards the output of the syntactic component, the nature of which we leave open,[1] as the input to the semantic and phonological components. The output of the syntax is sentences of the language with their structural descriptions, labeled trees, which are the structured material on which the other two components operate, producing, respectively, semantic and phonological interpretations of the sentences of the language.[2]

Given these assumptions, we have divided semantic theories along two dimensions. The first distinguishes among semantic theories on the basis of the data that they are supposed to explain; the second on the basis of the relationship between semantic theories and the mind on the one hand and the world on the other. Let us begin with the first way of dividing up semantic theories. We have distinguished among theories of reference, theories of meaning, and theories that combine the two. Theories of reference include within the range of their data logical truth and falsity, necessary truth and falsity, contingent truth and falsity, entailment, presupposition, and truth conditions;[3] theories of meaning have within their range analyticity, synonymy, entailment, anomaly, semantic redundancy, polysemy, antonomy, homonymy, and meaning inclusion. Mixed theories of reference and meaning attempt to give a unified account of the phenomena that fall under the two sorts of theories.[4]

We have placed Davidson's semantic theory within reference theories. The goal of Davidson's theory is to provide the truth conditions for every declarative sentence of a language. Davidson proposed that this be done using Tarski's theory of satisfaction for formal notation. This theory uses a term assignment, an amalgamation of a variable assignment, and an interpretation function restricted to individual constants. Applied to English, it ensures that Manhattan is assigned to the proper noun *Manhattan*. The theory does not assign values to predicates; instead, it states for all the basic predicates what sorts of things they are true of.[5] Applied to English, it states of an intransitive verb (such as *run*) which things it is true of and of a transitive verb (such as *see*) which pairs of things it is true of. The term assignment and the relation of being true of, together with a specification of the syntax of the expressions of the language, lead to a statement of the truth conditions of each declarative sentence.

We have divided theories of meaning into atomic and molecular and, in turn, divided molecular theories into analytical and encyclopedic. An atomic meaning theory associates with a lexical item a meaning that has no structure—for example, with *bachelor* the meaning [*bachelor*]. But [*bachelor*] itself cannot be analyzed as [*unmarried adult male*]. The main reason given for rejecting such meaning structures is Quine's (1953b) worry. To assume that meanings have constituents is to hold that there is a distinction to be drawn between analytic and synthetic sentences. But Quine famously argues that no such distinction is to be had. Analytic meaning theorists are not moved by Quinean arguments and are committed to there being a viable criterion for identifying the analytic sentences of a language, or its meaning entailment relations, which comes to the same thing. In turn, these are supposed to give the analytic meaning theorist the material for constructing a lexicon for lexical items consisting of entries that contain such analyzed meanings. We have taken Pustejovsky's semantic theory to be an example of an analytic meaning theory. Encyclopedic meaning theorists can be said to bite the Quinean bullet and accept his arguments that no criteria are available for marking the distinction between analytic and synthetic sentences. Their move is to opt to include in the lexical entry for *bachelor*, for example, a speaker's beliefs about bachelors. As Jackendoff, who we take to be representative of this position, puts it, a semantic theory encapsulates how individual speakers conceptualize the world: that is, it includes their encyclopedic knowledge about the world.

Mixed semantic theories combine the explanatory goals of reference and meaning theories. They wish to explain data related to meanings, but as well to provide a connection between language and the world. They are committed to the lexical entry for a lexical item containing information that determines the lexical item's referent, if it has one. For example, a mixed atomic meaning theory would have it that *bachelor* applies to an individual just in case he has the property connected to [*bachelor*]. A mixed analytic theory would claim that the lexical item is true of an individual if he has the properties expressed by [*unmarried adult male*], and a mixed encyclopedic theory would claim that the lexical item is true of an individual just in case he has most of the properties that speakers believe apply to bachelors. The following table lays out the different theories of semantics that we have distinguished.[6]

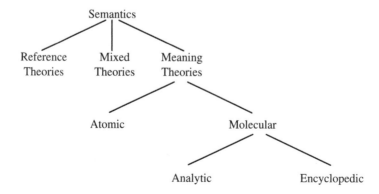

The subtree that appears under *Meaning Theories* should be repeated under *Mixed Theories*.

We have divided semantic theories into reference, mixed, and meaning theories, as well as into mentalist and nonmentalist theories. There are a number of different kinds of nonmentalist theories, the most prominent of which takes semantics to be a branch of mathematics (Montague 1974b). We have not discussed nonmentalist theories since the dominant view among linguists and most philosophers is that the theorist's grammar of a language and its component semantics is mentally represented, a commitment that distinguishes mentalist from nonmentalist theories. We have taken all the theories that we have considered in Part I of this volume to be mentalist theories.[7]

A commitment to the mental representation of the theorists' grammars is not a commitment to dualism. It is no part of mentalism that there are two substances, a mind and a body, and that internalized grammars are part of our mental, nonphysical minds. Rather, the proposal is that the theorists' grammars are psychological theories and, as such, are representations of cognitive capacities in the way in which any psychological theory is a representation of our internal states and capacities. On this view, then, the study of language, and with it the study of semantics, is a branch of psychology. The role that *mental* plays here is to indicate that the theory is not a neurophysiological theory, a theory that makes direct reference to the brain states of organisms. A commitment to psychological theorizing, however, does not preclude mentalist theories from being related in a systematic way to neurophysiologic theories and, in turn, for the entities hypothesized in psychological theories to be systematically related to brain states.

We have further subdivided mentalist semantic theories into externalist and internalist theories, a distinction that is played out at the level of the lexicon. Externalist theories are committed to there being a relation between some lexical items and entities external to the lexicon. Obviously, reference and mixed reference and meaning theories are externalist theories. For a theory to be externalist, the entities to which certain lexical items are related need not be external to the subject; externalist semantics does not want to prejudge idealism. For example, we could take *apple* to apply to sense data that are internal to subjects. All that is required for a theory to be externalist is that the entities to which such lexical items are related is external to the lexical item's lexical entry. Internalist theories, in contrast, take lexical items to be related to the meanings in their lexical entries without its being the case that the meanings are related to anything external to speakers. These meanings can be simple, as in atomic meaning theories, or complex, as in analytic and encyclopedic meaning theories. We have interpreted Jackendoff's and Pustejovsky's lexical semantic theories to be internalist theories.

Model theory is one of the most powerful theories that has been applied to natural languages to account for a range of linguistic data. There are many different ways in which it has been applied to natural language, however. Despite this variation, it would seem natural to suppose that the two distinctions that we have applied to semantic theories apply to them as well. Surely, it might be argued, a model theory for a particular language is at least a referential meaning theory, since it relates certain lexical items, singular terms like *France,* to objects and general terms like *bachelor,* to sets of objects in the model's universe of discourse. Moreover, there is also the question about whether applying model theory to natural languages precludes mentalism, since the objects to which some lexical items are associated are sets of objects and sets are abstract objects that are not part of our mental furniture. In addition, if we assume that model theoretic semantics can be construed as mentalist theories, it would seem that a model theoretic semantics is an externalist theory since it is a referential theory. Although these are natural conclusions to draw, they do not follow from the nature of model theory. What is basic to a model theory for a language is a model that includes a universe of discourse that contains a set of objects and an interpretation function that associates members of the set with expressions in the language. There is nothing in the specification of a universe of discourse that limits the sorts of objects that it can contain. It can contain anything, including numbers, fictional entities like Hamlet, physical and abstract objects, and even the sorts of entities that internalists like Jackendoff and Pustejovsky place in the lexical entries of lexical items. This can be seen by considering the model that we constructed in Chapter 3, section 3.3 ("English Verbs and Simple Clauses"), that provides a semantic value for *Allan runs*. We defined the universe of discourse to be {1,2,3} and the interpretation function for the model associated *Allan* with 1 and *run* with {1,2}. Given this, we were able to provide the truth conditions for *Allan runs*: namely, it is true just in case what *Allan* denotes in the model is in the set of objects denoted by *runs*. No one would take the number 1 or the set {1,2} to be the referents of, respectively, *Allan* and *runs* or to tell us anything about the meaning of these expressions, no matter how broadly *meaning* is construed. The point is that a theory insofar as it is a model theoretic semantics makes no commitment as to the sorts of objects with which lexical items can be associated.

That model theory makes no intrinsic commitment to the sorts of objects to which it relates lexical items does not mean that model theory is theoretically impotent and has no explanatory role to play in semantics. The model constructed for the language fragment we considered in section 3.3 does tell us something about semantics; it tells us how we can move up the construction tree for *Allan runs* so that given an interpretation for its constituents we are able to provide it with an interpretation; it gives ways, then, in which to specify the rules for semantic composition. It does not answer the basic questions about meaning, or semantics, by telling us what are the meanings, or semantic values, that should be associated with expressions of a language. Given a universe of discourse and an interpretation function, however, it provides us with a precise theory about how to construct complex meanings, or semantic values out of meanings, or semantic values associated with individual lexical items. In addition, it also gives us a way to explain a range of data, including accounting for entailment relations; identifying sentences as tautologies, contradictions, or contingencies; and explaining any other notions related to these.[8] What is important to note is that these explanations are neutral as to the specific kinds of objects that constitute the model's universe of discourse.

Notes

1. It could be a linguist's or a logician's syntax.

2. This is not meant to imply that the semantic component is merely an interpretative—that is, a nongenerative—component. Both Jackendoff and Pustejovsky attribute generative features to their semantics.

3. As we have noted, Quine (1960) who thinks that the only viable semantic theory is a theory of reference, would have no truck with necessity.

4. Frege's semantics (1972) is a mixed theory, but there is evidence that his theory does not include synonymy and related notions within the range of data that it is designed to explain.

5. See Chapter 4, note 7.

6. A more complete presentation of the range of views about semantic theories would distinguish among theories that claim that a semantics is to be given for an individual speaker's language and those who claim that it applies to the language of a community of speakers.

7. We are sure that Davidson would take issue with finding his theory in this category, but there are others, such as Larson and Segal (1995), who give a mentalist twist to satisfaction semantics. In addition, Frege (1977a) explicitly rejects mentalism, since Fregean senses are abstract objects that are not represented in the mind, but it does not do violence to Fregean semantics to view it as a mentalist semantics.

8. See Chapter 3, section 3.4.1, "Quantificational Logic."

Appendix

In this appendix, we shall review very briefly the basic notions of set theory used in Part I. Most of these notions are familiar from high school mathematics; however, as the reader may have forgotten them, we go over them briefly here.

8.1   Sets

Entities, be they abstract or concrete, can form sets, and the entities that form a set are members of the set they form. Thus, for example, all chairs with exactly four legs form a set, and any chair with exactly four legs is a member of that set. The natural numbers—0, 1, 2, 3, . . . —which are abstract entities, also form a set. Moreover, sets can contain both concrete and abstract entities. For example, all chairs with exactly four legs and all natural numbers together form a set.

8.1.1   Set membership

The most fundamental relation in set theory is the relation that obtains between a member of a set and the set itself. This relation is called the *set membership relation*, and it is denoted by the lowercase Greek letter epsilon, $\in$. Membership in a set is expressed by inserting the sign for set membership between a name for a member of a set and a name for the set. Thus, if A is a set and b is one of its members, then this fact can be expressed as follows: $b \in A$. Besides saying that b is a member of A, one may also say: b belongs to A, b is an element of A, or, simply, b is in A.

8.1.2   Notation for sets

Sometimes a set is denoted by listing its members within curly brackets. Such notation for a set is called *list notation*. Thus, for example, the set formed from the numbers 1, 2, and 3 is denoted by {1,2,3}. Sometimes a set is referred to by a description of its membership, as was done when we referred to the set of all chairs with exactly four legs. The notation for this way of denoting a set is called *abstraction notation* or *set builder notation*, and it has the following format: a description is placed within a pair of curly brackets; the description is preceded by a variable and either a vertical bar or a colon; and the description usually contains the same variable as the one that precedes the colon or vertical bar. Thus, abstraction notation can be used to denote the set of four-legged chairs as follows:

$\{x : x \text{ is a four-legged chair}\}$

There are two important facts about list notation to bear in mind. First, the order in which elements in the list within the curly brackets are given is irrelevant. In other words, no matter how the names of the members in the list are rearranged, the set denoted by the list within curly brackets is always the same. Thus, the very same set is denoted both by {a,b,c} and by {b,a,c}. Second, a redundant item in a list in list notation is irrelevant; that is, if two lists differ only in the repetition of names in the lists, the sets denoted by the two lists within curly brackets are the same. So, the very same set is denoted both by {a,b,c,a} and by {c,a,b,b}. In short, two names for the same set, both in list notation, can differ only in the order or the degree of redundancy of the names within the curly brackets.

Not only does list notation permit the very same set to be named in two different ways, but so does abstraction notation. Thus, the set of even (natural) numbers,

$\{x : x \text{ is an even natural number}\}$.

is the same as the set of natural numbers divisible by two,

$\{x : x \text{ is a natural number and } x \text{ is divisible by 2}\}$.

Finally, a name of a set in list notation and a name of a set in abstraction notation may denote one and the same set: for example,

$\{1,2,3\}$

can also be denoted by

$\{x : x \text{ is a natural number greater than 0 and less than 4}\}$.

8.1.3   Set size or cardinality

The size, or *cardinality*, of a set is the number of distinct members in it. A set may be either finite or infinite, depending on whether the number of distinct members it has is either finite or infinite, respectively. The size, or cardinality, of the set {2,3,5,7} is 4. The official way to write this is to put the name of the set between a pair of vertical lines and to write the resulting expression as equal to the appropriate number. Thus,

$|\{2,3,5,7\}| = 4$.

The same statement about the cardinality of this set can also be made using abstraction notation:

$|\{x : x \text{ is a prime number and } 1 < x < 10\}| = 4$.

8.1.4   Special sets

Some kinds of finite sets have special names. Sets with exactly two members are called *doubletons*. Sets with exactly one member are called *singletons*. There is exactly one special set with no members, and it is called the *empty set* or the *null set*. One very suggestive, though uncommon symbol, is { }. The symbol used here is the commonly used symbol $\varnothing$. The empty set is the set theoretic counterpart to the number zero. Zero and the empty set are not the same. They must never be confused: zero is a number, and the empty set is a set.

8.1.5   The subset relation

One important relation between sets is the subset relation. It is defined as follows:

DEFINITION 1. *The subset relation.* $X \subseteq Y$ iff every member of X is a member of Y.

The set {7,13,23}, for example, is a subset of the set {7,13,23,31}: that is,

$$\{7,13,23\} \subseteq \{7,13,23,3\},$$

since, as one can easily verify, every member of the first set is a member of the second. At the same time, {1,5,9} is not a subset of {5,9,10}: that is,

$$\{1,5,9\} \nsubseteq \{5,9,10\}^1$$

since 1 is a member of the first set but not of the second. From the discussion earlier, it should be evident that $\mathbf{N}$, the set of natural numbers, is a subset of $\mathbf{Z}$, the integers: that is,

$$\mathbf{N} \subseteq \mathbf{Z}.$$

An intuitively clear way to depict this relation is provided by Venn diagrams. In a Venn diagram, the position of closed figures representing sets does not depict anything about the relation between the sets. In such diagrams, two closed figures are drawn overlapping, as shown in Figure 8.1. Further notation is added to depict the relation obtaining between the sets represented by the closed figures. Notice that in this diagram (Figure 8.1) the rectangle is partitioned into four distinct regions, which are called *cells*. One cell, labeled 1, lies outside of both circles; another, labeled 2, is the crescent-shaped region that includes the left-hand circle but excludes the right-hand circle; another, labeled 4, is the crescent-shaped region that includes the right-hand circle and excludes the left-hand one; and the remaining one, labeled 3, is the lens-shaped region that is the overlap between the two circles.

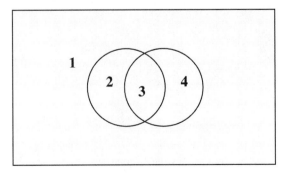

FIGURE 8.1 Venn diagram of two sets

To depict a relation between two sets in a Venn diagram, one annotates one or more of the cells with an appropriate symbol. The placement of a cross (x) within a region indicates that the set represented by the region is nonempty; and the shading of a region indicates that the set represented by the region is empty. To depict the set *A* as a subset of *B*, one shades in the left-hand crescent-shaped cell, as shown in Figure 8.2.

We shall now state three facts about the subset relation, two of which we shall elucidate with Venn diagrams. First, if one set is a subset of a second and the second of a third, then the first set is a subset of the third. Second, if one set is a subset of another and the other of the one, then the sets are identical. Third, every set is a subset of itself. We record these facts in notation:

FACTS ABOUT THE SUBSET RELATION
(1) If $X \subseteq Y$ and $Y \subseteq Z$, then $X \subseteq Z$.
(2) If $X \subseteq Y$ and $Y \subseteq X$, then $X = Y$.
(3) $X \subseteq X$.

While the third fact is not very clear from a Venn diagram, the first and second are, as shown in Figure 8.3. That set A is a subset of set B is depicted by shading in the crescent-shaped region of the circle representing A excluded from the circle representing B. That B is a subset of C is depicted by shading in the crescent-shaped region of the circle representing B excluded from the circle representing C. Once this is done, the crescent-shaped region of the circle representing A excluded from the circle representing C will have been shaded in, thereby depicting A as a subset of C.

It is important to stress that these diagrams are *not* proofs: they are simply aids to help one *see*, as it were, the fact which requires proof.

Let us turn to the second property, as shown in Figure 8.4. To depict A and B as the very same set, one must shade in the crescent-shaped region of the circle representing the set A, excluded from the circle representing the set B, as well as shade in the crescent-shaped region of the circle representing the set B, excluded from the circle representing the set A. That is, each of these crescent-shaped regions must be shaded in. Such a diagram not only depicts A as a subset of B but also B as a subset of A. Conversely, a diagram that depicts A as a subset of B and B as a subset of A does so by shading in the crescent-shaped region of the circle representing the set A, excluded from the circle representing the set B, as well as the crescent-shaped region of the circle representing the set B, excluded from the circle representing the set A. Of the region confined by the two circles depicting the sets A and B, only the lens-shaped region of their overlap is left unshaded, thereby depicting A and B as one and the same set.

8.2   Operations on sets

We now turn to four operations on sets: union, intersection, subtraction, and complementation.

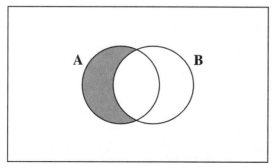

FIGURE 8.2 Venn diagram of A as a subset of B

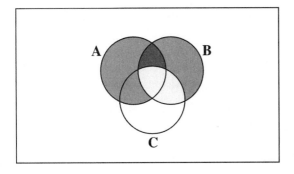

FIGURE 8.3 Venn diagram of subset relations between A, B, and C

8.2.1   Set union

We begin with the binary operation of *union*, symbolized by ∪:

DEFINITION 2. *Union.* x ∈ X ∪ Y iff x ∈ X or x ∈ Y.

The definition stipulates that the set formed from the union of two sets comprises precisely those elements that are found in *either* (and possibly both). Here are some examples:

$$\{1,2,5\} \cup \{3,6\} = \{1,2,3,5,6\},$$
$$\{1,2,5\} \cup \{1,3,4\} = \{1,2,3,4,5\},$$
$$\mathbf{N} \cup \mathbf{Z}^- = \mathbf{Z}.$$

($\mathbf{Z}^-$ or $\{-1,-2,-3, \ldots\}$, is the set of negative integers.) The same idea can be conveyed by a Venn diagram, as in Figure 8.5. In Figure 8.5, the area of the cells 2, 3, and 4 represents $A \cup B$.

Inspection of the Venn diagram reveals several interesting properties of this operation:

FACTS ABOUT UNION
(1) $X \cup Y = Y \cup X$.
(2) $X \subseteq X \cup Y$.
(3) $Y \subseteq X \cup Y$.
(4) $X \subseteq Z$ and $Y \subseteq Z$ iff $X \cup Y \subseteq Z$.
(5) $X \subseteq Y$ iff $Y = X \cup Y$.
(6) $X \cup X = X$.
(7) $X \cup \varnothing = X$.

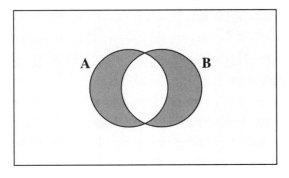

FIGURE 8.4 Venn diagram of A and B as the same set: A as a subset of B, and B as a subset of A

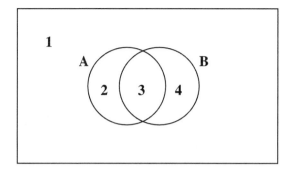

FIGURE 8.5 Venn diagram for set operations

8.2.2 Set intersection

We now turn to the binary operation, intersection, symbolized by ∩.

> DEFINITION 3. *Intersection.* $x \in X \cap Y$ iff $x \in X$ and $x \in Y$.

The definition stipulates that the set formed from the intersection of two sets comprises precisely those elements which are found in *both*. Below are a few examples:

$$\{1,2,6\} \cap \{2,3,6\} = \{2,6\},$$
$$\{1,2,5\} \cap \{1,2,4\} = \{1,2\},$$
$$\{1,2,3\} \cap \{6,5,4\} = \varnothing.$$

Again, a Venn diagram helps to convey how the operation works. In Figure 8.5, the area of cell 3 represents $A \cap B$.

Again, simple reflection on the diagram makes clear the following facts about intersection:

FACTS ABOUT INTERSECTION
(1) $X \cap Y = Y \cap X$.
(2) $X \cap Y \subseteq X$.
(3) $X \cap Y \subseteq Y$.
(4) $Z \subseteq X$ and $Z \subseteq Y$ iff $Z \subseteq X \cap Y$.
(5) $Y \subseteq X$ iff $Y = X \cap Y$.
(6) $X \cap X = X$.
(7) $X \cap \varnothing = \varnothing$.

8.2.3 Subtraction and set complementation

We now come to the last two operations: subtraction, a binary operation, and complementation, a unary operation.

> DEFINITION 4. *Subtraction.* $x \in X - Y$ iff $x \in X$ and $x \notin Y$.

The idea is this. The subtraction of one set from another amounts to the removal from the first of any member it has in common with the second. Thus

$$\{1,3,5\} - \{2,4,5\} = \{1,3\}$$

where 5, the member common to $\{1,3,5\}$ and $\{2,4,5\}$ is removed from $\{1,3,5\}$. In the Venn diagram in Figure 8.5, $A - B$ is cell 2.

DEFINITION 5. *Complementation.* $x \in -X$ iff $x \in U$ and $x \notin X$.

The definition stipulates that the complement of a set is formed from all the elements in the universe which are *not* in the set whose complement is being formed. Suppose that the universe $U = \{1,2,3,4,5\}$. Then,

$-\{1,2,5\} = \{3,4\}$,
$-\{5,4,1\} = \{3,2\}$.

The same idea can be conveyed by a Venn diagram. In the diagram in Figure 8.5, the area of cells 1 and 4 represents $-A$, while that of cells 1 and 2 represents $-B$.

Once again, reflection on Venn diagrams makes clear the following facts:

FACTS ABOUT COMPLEMENTATION
(1) $X \cap -X = \varnothing$.
(2) $--X = X$.
(3) $-X \cup -Y = -(X \cap Y)$.
(4) $-X \cap -Y = -(X \cup Y)$.
(5) $X \subseteq Y$ iff $-Y \subseteq -X$.
(6) $X–Y = X \cap -Y$.

8.3   Ordered sets

To explain the notion of an ordered set, let us begin by discussing the special case of an ordered pair.

8.3.1   Ordered pairs

An ordered pair is similar to, but quite distinct from, a doubleton. They are similar insofar as they are often named in similar ways. One usually names a doubleton by putting down two names, separated by a comma, and enclosing the whole thing in a pair of braces. For example, the doubleton comprising just one and two is denoted as follows: $\{1,2\}$. One usually names an ordered pair by putting down two names, separated by a comma, and enclosing the whole thing in a pair of angle brackets: for example, $<1,2>$.

As stated, sets are unordered; hence, the order in which the elements of a doubleton are listed does not matter. So, for example, $\{1,2\} = \{2,1\}$. Ordered sets are ordered; hence, the order in which its elements are listed does matter. Thus, $<1,2> \neq <2,1>$.

Since the order of the members of an ordered set matters, each position is given a name. In an ordered pair, the first member is said to be the *first coordinate* and the second the *second coordinate*. And, in general, the nth position in a sequence, or n-tuple, is the nth coordinate.

Another difference between an ordered set and an unordered one is that in an ordered set redundancy matters, whereas in an unordered set it does not. Thus, while $<1,1>$ is an ordered pair, $\{1,1\}$ is not a doubleton, since $\{1,1\} = \{1\}$ but $<1,1> \neq <1>$. Moreover, $<a,b>$ must be an ordered pair, regardless of whether or not a is identical with b; in contrast, $\{a,b\}$ may be a singleton, not a doubleton, depending on whether or not a is identical with b. Finally, every doubleton, but no ordered pair, is a set.

Two ordered pairs are identical just in case their first and second coordinates are identical. That is:

DEFINITION 5. *Equality of ordered pairs.*$<x,y> = <w,z>$ iff $x = w$ and $y = z$.

8.3.2   Cartesian product

We now come to an important binary operation, the *Cartesian product*, which is denoted by the symbol ×. This operation creates from two sets a set of ordered pairs where the first and second coordinates of each pair in the resulting set are taken from the first set and the second set, respectively. In spite of the symbol used, the Cartesian product should not be confused with the arithmetical operation of multiplication. The arithmetic operation of multiplication takes a pair of numbers and yields a number; the set theoretic operation of Cartesian product takes a pair of sets and yields a set. However, the two operations are connected, as we shall see, and it is the existence of this connection that justifies the choice of the very same symbol for the two distinct operations.

DEFINITION 6. *Cartesian product*. Let X and Y be sets. $<x,y> \in X \times Y$ iff $x \in X$ and $y \in Y$.

Logically equivalent to this definition is this equality:

$X \times Y = \{<x,y> :$ for some $x \in X$ and for some $y \in Y\}$

Here are some examples to clarify the definition:

$\{1,2\} \times \{2,3,4\} = \{<1,2>, <1,3>, <1,4>, <2,2>, <2,3>, <2,4>\}$
$\{1,2\} \times \{3,4\} = \{<1,3>, <1,4>, <2,3>, <2,4>\}$

There are two important points to bear in mind concerning this definition. First, the Cartesian product of two sets is a set, not an ordered pair. Second, each member of a Cartesian product is an ordered pair.

As stated and explained above, the operations of Cartesian product and arithmetic multiplication are distinct. Moreover, these operations are not trivially analogous, since arithmetic multiplication is commutative and associative, whereas the Cartesian product is neither. In other words, neither $X \times Y = Y \times X$, nor $X \times (Y \times Z) = (X \times Y) \times Z$ holds. The reader is invited to find specific cases to bear out the claim that the Cartesian product is not commutative. Following is an example to show that it is not associative. Let X be $\{1,2\}$, Y be $\{3,4\}$, and Z be $\{5,6\}$. Now,

$Y \times Z = \{<3,5>, <3,6>, <4,5>, <4,6>\}$

and, as we saw,

$X \times Y = \{<1,3>, <1,4>, <2,3>, <2,4>\}$.

Thus,

$(X \times Y) \times Z = \{<<1,3>,5>, <<1,4>,5>, <<2,3>,5>, <<2,4>,5>,$
$<<1,3>,6>, <<1,4>,6>, <<2,3>,6>, <<2,4>,6>\}$

and

$X \times (Y \times Z) = \{<1,<3,5>>, <1,<3,6>>, <1,<4,5>>, <1,<4,6>>,$
$<2,<3,5>>, <2,<3,6>>, <2,<4,5>>, <2,<4,6>>\}$.

As the reader can verify, $(X \times Y) \times Z$ and $X \times (Y \times Z)$ have different members and, hence, are distinct sets. In particular, $<<1,3>,5>$ is a member of $(X \times Y) \times Z$, but it is not a member of

X × (Y × Z). Relevant here is the fact that <<1,3>,5> and <1,<3,5>> are not equal. The first coordinate of the ordered pair <<1,3>,5> is itself an ordered pair—namely, <1,3>—while the first coordinate of <1,<3,5>> is 1, which is not an ordered pair.

The size of the set which is the Cartesian product of two sets is the multiplicative product of the size of the two sets—that is:

FACT ABOUT CARTESIAN PRODUCT
$|X \times Y| = |X| \times |Y|$.

This is the reason mathematicians use the same symbol both for arithmetic multiplication (used on the right side of the equation) and for the Cartesian product (used on the left side of the equation).

8.3.3   Sequences or *N*-tuples

The generalization of an ordered pair is an ordered set. An ordered pair has two coordinates. Alternatively, one says that an ordered pair is a sequence of length 2, or, somewhat awkwardly, a 2-tuple. Similarly, one has triples, or a sequence of length three, or a 3-tuple. Thus, <15,3,4> is a triple; 15 is in its first coordinate, 3 in its second, and 4 in its third. In general, one has sequences of length *n* or *n*-tuples. Not surprisingly, one also has sequences of length one, or a 1-tuple. So <π> is a sequence of length one and its only coordinate, its first coordinate, is π.

Only sequences of the same length can be equal, and they are equal precisely when both of their respective coordinates are equal, as defined next:

DEFINITION 7. *Equality of ordered sets.* $\langle x_1, \ldots, x_i, \ldots, x_n \rangle = \langle y_1, \ldots, y_i, \ldots, y_n \rangle$ iff $x_j = y_j$, for each j, $1 \leq j \leq n$.

Thus, for example, <1,2,3> is not equal to <1,3,2>, for even though they have the same members, some of the coordinates of one have members different from the corresponding coordinates of the other. Specifically, while the first coordinates of each of the triples are equal, the second coordinates are not, and neither are the third coordinates.

The operation that yields from the sets A_1 through A_n the set of all sequences of length *n* where the ith coordinate is a member of A_i is called the generalized Cartesian product. It is defined as follows:

DEFINITION 8. *Generalized Cartesian product.* Let X_1 through X_n be sets. Then, $\langle x_1, \ldots, x_n \rangle \in X_1 \times \ldots \times X_n$ iff, for each i (where $1 \leq i \leq n$), $x_i \in X_i$.

Logically equivalent to this definition is this equality:

$$X_1 \times \ldots \times X_n = \{\langle x_1, \ldots, x_n \rangle : x_i \in X_i \text{ where } 1 \leq i \leq n\}$$

8.4   Families of sets

A set can have sets as members. A set all of whose members are sets is often said to be a *family of sets*. Thus, for example, {{1,2}, {2,3}, {1,3}} is a set all of whose members are sets. It is, then, a family of sets. In this section, we discuss an operation that creates a family of sets from a set and two operations that create a set from a family of sets.

8.4.1   The power set operation

There is an operation that operates on a set to yield a family of sets. It is known as the *power set operation*, and it is denoted by the expression *Pow*. In particular, the power set operation collects into one set all the subsets of a given set. Consider, for example, the set {1,2}. Its power set is the set of all its subsets, namely,

{∅, {1},{2},{1,2}}

DEFINITION 9. *The power set operation.* X ∈ Pow(Y) iff X ⊆ Y.

This definition of the power set operation is in the form of a biconditional. Logically equivalent to this definition is the following equality:

Pow(Y) = {X : X ⊆ Y}.

Here are two more examples of applications of the power set operation.

Pow({1}) = {∅, {1}}
Pow({1,2,3}) = {∅, {1}, {2}, {3}, {1,2}, {2,3}, {1,3}, {1,2,3}}

The first two facts identify permanent members of any power set: the set from which the power set is formed and the empty set:

FACTS ABOUT THE POWER SET
(1) Every set is a member of its power set.
(2) ∅ ∈ Pow(X).
(3) |Pow(X)| = $2^{|X|}$

8.4.2   Generalized union and generalized intersection

In this section, we define two operations that are generalizations of the binary operations of union and intersection, introduced earlier. Those binary operations take pairs of sets and yield a set. Their generalizations take not just a pair of sets but a family of sets and yield a set. We begin with generalized union:

DEFINITION 10. *Generalized union.* x ∈ ⋃$\mathcal{Z}$ iff, for some Y ∈ $\mathcal{Z}$, x ∈> Y.

This definition leads to the following equality:

⋃$\mathcal{Z}$ = {x: x ∈ Y, for some Y ∈ $\mathcal{Z}$}

DEFINITION 11. *Generalized intersection.* x ∈ ⋂$\mathcal{Z}$ iff, for each Y ∈ $\mathcal{Z}$, x ∈ Y.

This definition leads to the following equality:

⋂$\mathcal{Z}$ = {x: x ∈ Y, for each Y ∈ $\mathcal{Z}$ }

To see how these operations apply, consider this family of sets:

$\mathcal{A}$ = {{1,2,3}, {2,3,4}, {3,4,5}}
⋃$\mathcal{A}$ = {1,2,3,4,5}
⋂$\mathcal{A}$ = {3}

Now, in all cases where the cardinality of the family of sets is finite, generalized union and generalized intersection reduce to a finite iteration of the binary operations of union and intersection, respectively. In other words, if $\mathcal{A} = \{A_1, \ldots, A_n\}$, then

$$\bigcup \mathcal{A} = A_1 \cup \ldots \cup A_n.$$
$$\bigcap \mathcal{A} = A_1 \cap \ldots \cap A_n.$$

8.5   Relations and functions

A *relation* is something that connects a number of entities. It is important to distinguish a relation from the instances that instantiate it. While this distinction may sound a bit arcane, it is not. After all, one easily distinguishes the color red from the instances that instantiate it. That is, one easily distinguishes the color red, on the one hand, from red fire trucks, red pencils, red hats, and so forth, on the other. The distinction between a relation and the instances that instantiate it is parallel. That is, the relation of being a father is distinct from any given pair comprising a father and the person of whom he is the father.

A relation that has pairs as instances is a binary relation. One that has triples as instances is a ternary relation. And one that has quadruples as instances is a quaternary relation. In general, a relation that has *n*-tuples as instances is an *n*-ary relation. An example of a binary relation is the relation of being a brother. This relation pairs a human male with any one of his siblings. Commonsense relations involving more than just pairs are unusual.

From a mathematical point of view, a relation comprises a set of sequences, and an instance of the relation is any one of these sequences. A binary relation comprises a set of ordered pairs, and each of its instances is an ordered pair in this set. A ternary relation comprises a set of triples, and each of its instances is a triplet in this set. We confine our attention to binary relations and their instances: that is, sets of ordered pairs and their members.

We just said that, from a mathematical point of view, a binary relation is a set of ordered pairs. Sometimes it is convenient to view a binary relation as comprising three sets: the set of candidates for the first coordinates of a set of ordered pairs, the set of candidates for the second coordinates of the same set of ordered pairs, and the set of ordered pairs itself. Consider, for example, the relation of being a city in a country. On the one hand, one can view it as comprising nothing more than a list of ordered pairs of city and the country in which the city is located. On the other hand, one might think of it as comprising three lists: the list of all cities, the list of all countries, and the list that pairs each city with the country in which it is located.

We use the term *graph* for the view that treats relations merely as a set of *n*-tuples (i.e., ordered sets of length *n*) and reserve the term *relation* for the view that treats relations as *n*-tuples together with the potential candidates for each coordinate of any *n*-tuple of the relation. In particular, we shall call a *binary relation* any specification comprising the set of things that may be related, the set of things that may be related to, and the actual pairing. In addition, we shall call a binary relation's set of ordered pairs its *graph*, the set of things that may serve as first coordinates in the graph its *domain*, and the set of things that may serve as second coordinates in the graph its *codomain*. Finally, we shall see that *functions* are just special binary relations.

8.5.1   Binary graphs

Let us first consider binary graphs. As stated, a binary graph is simply a set of ordered pairs. There are two reasons a set of ordered pairs is called a *graph*. First, in elementary algebra, a graph, or figure, depicted on a plane with Cartesian coordinates, itself corresponds to a set of ordered pairs—namely, the pairs of coordinates corresponding to each point in the graph or figure. Second, it is natural, then, to call a set of ordered pairs a graph. In graph theory, a graph comprises a set of *nodes*, depicted as points, and a set of edges, depicted as lines, where every edge connects a pair of nodes, depicted by every line, corresponding to an edge, linking the points corresponding to the nodes connected by the edge. A special kind of graph is called a *directed graph*. It is just like a graph, except that its edges are directed. Such edges are known as *directed edges* or *arcs* and are depicted by arrows. As we shall see, the graphs of graph theory are especially useful in displaying important properties of binary graphs.

Now suppose we have a set of ordered pairs. Each member of any ordered pair can be viewed as a node, and hence depicted by a point, and each ordered pair can be viewed as an arc, and hence depicted by an arrow. The point corresponding to the ordered pair's first coordinate is at the butt of the arrow, while the point corresponding to the very same ordered pair's second coordinate is at the tip of the arrow. An example will help make this clearer. Consider the following set of ordered pairs:

{<1,2>, <1,3>, <2,2>, <2,3>, <2,4>, <3,4>}

This set of ordered pairs can be depicted as the directed graph in Figure 8.6.

Binary graphs can also be viewed as what, in graph theory, is known as a *bipartite directed graph*. A bipartite directed graph is a kind of directed graph in which the points can be partitioned into two groups such that one group has nothing but points that coincide with the nocks of the graph's arrows, while the other group has nothing but points that coincide with the tips of the graph's arrows. Usually, such a graph is depicted as two vertical columns of points, with arrows (directed edges or arcs) connecting some or all of the points in the left column with all or some of the points in the right column.

One uses a bipartite directed graph to view a binary graph as follows: One makes two columns of nodes. The nodes in the first column correspond with the elements occurring in the first coordinates of the members of the binary graph, while the nodes in the second column correspond with the elements occurring in the second coordinates of the members of the binary graph. The arrows of the bipartite graph correspond with members of the binary graph. When a binary graph is viewed as a bipartite directed graph, one observes that from every point in the left-hand column emanates some arrow and into every point in the right-hand column terminates some arrow. The binary graph stated above is depicted in Figure 8.7 with a bipartite directed graph.

8.5.2   Binary relations

Recall that a *binary graph* is a set of ordered pairs and that a *binary relation* is any specification comprising the set of things that may be related, the set of things that may be related to, and the actual pairing. Here is the formal definition of a binary relation:

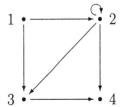

FIGURE 8.6 Directed graph of ordered pairs

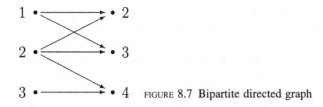

FIGURE 8.7 Bipartite directed graph

DEFINITION 12. *Binary relation.* Let R be <X, Y, G>. R is a binary relation iff X and Y are sets and G ⊆ X × Y.

Suppose that one has two sets A and B. How many binary relations are there from A to B? The answer is: there are as many binary relations from A to B as there are distinct sets of ordered pairs whose first coordinate is a member of A and whose second coordinate is a member of B. Thus, the number of binary relations from A to B is $2^{|A \times B|}$, or $2^{|A| \times |B|}$.

Two special relations among the set of all possible relations from A to B are the one whose graph is A × B and the one whose graph is the empty set. The former relation is known as the *universal relation* from A to B, and the latter is known as the *empty relation* or the *null relation* from A to B.

Binary relations can be depicted by either of these two kinds of diagrams used to depict binary graphs: namely, by diagrams for directed graphs and by diagrams for bipartite directed graphs. Next we discuss how each kind of diagram is used to depict a binary relation.

Recall that a directed graph comprises a set of *nodes*, depicted as points, and a set of directed edges, depicted as arrows, where every directed edge connects a pair of nodes. Notice that while it is required that every directed edge connect a pair of nodes, it is not required that every node be connected to some node. In contrast, a node of a binary graph may not be connected with any node. As an example, consider the binary relation

<A,B,G> where A = {1,2,3,4,6},
                B = {2,3,5},
                G = {<1,2>, <1,3>, <2,3>, <2,5>, <4,2>, <4,5>}

Its directed graph diagram is as in Figure 8.8

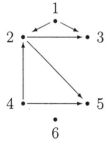

FIGURE 8.8 Directed graph of <A,B,G>

What distinguishes a binary graph from a binary relation is the fact that a relation's domain and codomain may be proper supersets of its graph's domain and range, respectively. For this reason, the diagrams of bipartite directed graphs are suited for depicting binary relations better than the diagrams of mere directed graphs. In such diagrams, the points in the left-hand column stand for the elements in the relation's domain, the points in the right-hand column stand for the elements in the relation's codomain, and the elements linked by arrows stand for the pairs of elements in the relation's graph. Under these conventions, the binary relation given above yields the bipartite directed graph diagram in Figure 8.9.

The last thing we wish to draw the reader's attention to in this initial discussion of binary relations is the following notational convention. We shall sometimes write "aRb" instead of the more cumbersome <a, b> ∈ G_R.

Left totality, right totality, left monogamy, and right monogamy are four important properties that binary relations may have. Each property has a role in determining functions and various kinds of functions, which is the subject of the next section.

A binary relation is left total precisely when each member of its domain bears the relation to some member of its codomain:

DEFINITION 13. *Left totality.* Let R = <X,Y,G> be a binary relation. R is left total iff, for each x ∈ X, there is a y ∈ Y, such that xRy.

The relation R_1 is left total,

R_1 = <A,B,G> where A = {a,b,c},
                      B = {2,4,6,8},
                      G = {<a,2>, <a,6>, <b,4>, <b,8>, <c,8>}

while the relation R_2 is not:

R_2 = <C,D,H> where C = {d,e,f},
                      D = {1,3,5,7},
                      H = {<d,1>, <d,5>, <f,5>, <f,7>}

Seen in terms of a diagram for a bipartite directed graph, a left total relation has at least one arrow emanating from each point in its left-hand column. R_1 satisfies this characterization, as one can see from an inspection of its bipartite directed graph diagram below; R_2 does not, since no arrow emanates from *e*.

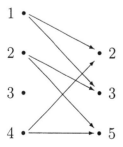

FIGURE 8.9 Bipartite directed graph of <A,B,G>

FIGURE 8.10 R_1 is left total; R_2 is not left total relation.

A binary relation is right total precisely when each member of its codomain has the relation borne to it by some member of its domain:

DEFINITION 14. *Right totality*. Let R = <X,Y,G> be a binary relation. R is right total iff, for each y ∈ Y, there is a x ∈ X, such that xRy.

The relation R_1, given above, is right total, but the relation R_2 is not. Characterizations fully parallel to those given for left totality apply here. Looking at the bipartite directed graph diagram for R_2, one sees that there is one element in its codomain into which no arrow terminates. Hence, R_2 is not right total. Looking at the diagram for R_1, however, one sees that each element in its codomain has at least one arrow terminating into it. For that reason, R_1 is right total. In general, a binary relation is right total just in case its bipartite directed graph diagram has the following property: each node in the codomain has at least one arrow terminating into it.

In the examples given, the very same relation is both left total and right total. This is a coincidence. Consider S_1, which is just like R_1, except that c is not related to 8. S_1 is right total but not left total. Moreover, consider S_2, which is just like R_2, except that e is related to 5. S_2 is left total but not right total (Figure 8.11).

A binary relation is left monogamous precisely when no member of its domain bears the relation to more than one member of its codomain. Neither R_1 nor R_2 above is left monogamous, since, on the one hand, aR_12 and aR_16, and, on the other hand, fR_25 and fR_27. The relation T_1 is left monogamous, however:

T_1 = <A,D,H> where A = {a,b,c},
D = {1,3,5,7},
H = {<a,1>, <b,7>, <c,7>}

Notice that, in the bipartite directed graph diagram of T_1, Figure 8.12, at most one arrow emanates from any point in its left-hand column. This is a defining characteristic of left monogamous relations.

FIGURE 8.11 S_1 is right total, but not left total; S_2 is left total, but not right total.

T_1:

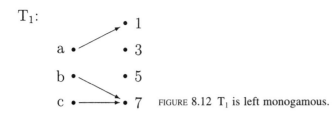

FIGURE 8.12 T_1 is left monogamous.

DEFINITION 15. *Left monogamy*[2]. Let R = <X,Y,G> be a binary relation. R is left monogamous iff, for each x ∈ X and each y, z ∈ Y, if xRy and xRz, then y = z.

Paired with the notion of left monogamy is the notion of right monogamy. A binary relation is right monogamous precisely when no member of its codomain has the relation borne to it by more than one member of its domain:

DEFINITION 16. *Right monogamy*. Let R = <X,Y,G> be a binary relation. R is right monogamous iff, for each x, z ∈ X and for each y ∈ Y, if xRy and zRy, then x = z.

None of the relations R_1, R_2, and T_1, is right monogamous. T_1, for example, is not right monogamous, since both bT_17 and cT_17. However, T_2 is right monogamous:

T_2 = <C,B,J> where C = {d,e,f},
                        B = {2,4,6,8},
                        J = {<d,2>, <d,4>, <f,6>}

In the bipartite directed graph of a right monogamous binary relation, at most one arrow terminates into any point in its right-hand column. This is illustrated in Figure 8.13.

8.5.3   Function

In high school algebra, everyone studies functions. Such functions are typically rather complex, hiding their rather simple nature. Functions involve three things: a domain, codomain, and a graph. The domain is a set of entities—entities of any sort, though in high school algebra, it is usually the set of real numbers. The codomain is also a set of entities—again, entities of any sort, though in high school algebra, it is usually the set of real numbers. To understand the graph of a function, imagine the domain and the codomain to have all of their elements exhaustively listed in their own respective lists, each list comprising a column of names. The graph of the function, then, is a pairing of members on the first list with members of the second list represented by an arrow going from *each* member on the first list to *exactly one* member on the second list. In other words, a function is a binary relation that is left total and left monogamous.

T_2:

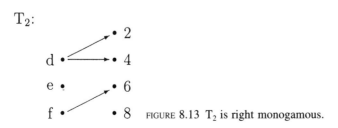

FIGURE 8.13 T_2 is right monogamous.

To see better what is involved, consider R and S: R is a function, while S is not. Observe that R comprises two lists, the list on the left being the domain and the list on the right being the codomain. Further, exactly one arrow connects each member of the domain with some member of the codomain. S fails to be a function for two reasons: first, there is no arrow connecting e to any member of the codomain; second, both d and f have more than one arrow connecting them to members of the codomain (Figure 8.14).

Since a function is a special kind of binary relation, the terminology and notation that apply to binary relations also apply to functions. However, since the mathematics of functions preceded the mathematics of binary relations, much of the mathematics of functions has notation and terminology peculiar to it. Thus, it is customary to denote a function, not as

$$f = <X,Y,G>,$$

but as

$$f : X \to Y,$$

specifying its graph separately. The graph's specification is not in the usual notation for a set of ordered pairsbut in the form of a vertical, irredundant list of pairs, where a butted arrow ($\mapsto$) between the elements of each pair replaces the angle brackets that would otherwise enclose them. For example, the following functional relation,

$$<\{1,2,3,4\}, \{a,b,c\}, \{<1,a>, <2,a>, <3,c>, <4,b>\}>,$$

whose graph can be expressed by the bipartite graph diagram in Figure 8.15, is displayed as follows:

$$f : \{1,2,3,4\} \to \{a,b,c\} \text{ where } \begin{array}{l} 1 \mapsto a \\ 2 \mapsto a \\ 3 \mapsto c \\ 4 \mapsto b \end{array}$$

This way of displaying a function's graph is in a form similar to that of a bipartite graph, except here, all arrows are parallel, and some members of the codomain may not appear, whereas in a proper bipartite graph, all arrows need not be parallel, and not only must each member from the domain appear exactly once, but also each member from the codomain must appear exactly once.

Thus, functions with finite graphs may be displayed in at least two forms: in the form of a bipartite graph and in the form of a vertical list. It might be helpful at this point to rehearse how the defining properties of a function, namely left totality and left monogamy, are reflected in these displays. In the bipartite graph display, each element in the left-hand column is connected

FIGURE 8.14 Bipartite directed graph of R and bipartite directed graph of S.

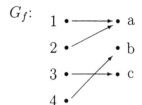

G_f:

FIGURE 8.15 Directed graph of functional relation G_f

by an arrow to exactly one element in the right-hand column: it is connected by at least one arrow, to satisfy the condition of left totality, and it is connected by at most one arrow, to satisfy the condition of left monogamy. In the vertical list display, each member of the domain appears exactly once: it appears at least once, to satisfy the condition of left totality, and it appears at most once, to satisfy the condition of left monogamy.

For most mathematical applications, the domain and codomain of a function are infinite, and so the function's graph cannot be enumerated. In such cases, it is customary to write down a rule from which any ordered pair in the function's graph can be calculated. I shall call such a rule *a rule of association*. For example, the function, part of whose graph is set out below,

$$f : \mathbf{Z}^+ \to \mathbf{Z}^- \text{ where } \begin{aligned} 1 &\mapsto -2 \\ 2 &\mapsto -4 \\ 3 &\mapsto -6 \\ \vdots &\mapsto \vdots \end{aligned}$$

can be precisely specified in any of several ways:

$f : \mathbf{Z}^+ \to \mathbf{Z}^-$ where $x \mapsto -2x$;
$f : \mathbf{Z}^+ \to \mathbf{Z}^-$ where $x \mapsto y$ such that $-2x = y$;
$f : \mathbf{Z}^+ \to \mathbf{Z}^-$ where $f(x) = -2x$.

Sometimes, the rule of association must be more complex: the domain of the function is partitioned and a distinct rule is given for the elements of each set in the partition. For example,

$$g : Z \to Z \text{ where} \begin{cases} x \mapsto x + 1 \text{ for } x < -1 \\ x \mapsto 2x \text{ for } -1 \leq x \leq 3 \\ x \mapsto 4x - 5 \text{ for } 3 < x \end{cases}$$

Thus, the enumeration of the elements of a function's graph is usually replaced by a rule of association. One cannot stipulate arbitrarily such rules of association and be assured that one has obtained a function—that is, a pairing that is both left total and left monogamous. This lack of assurance is a departure from what was encountered with sets and arbitrarily chosen binary relations. Within a fixed universe of discourse, one can use a property to define a set: the property may not have any possessors, in which case the set defined is empty, but there is a set nonetheless, the empty set. Similarly, one can use a rule of association to define a binary relation: the rule may not manage to pair anything in the domain with anything in the codomain, in which case the graph of the relation is empty, but there is a graph nonetheless. But one cannot set down any arbitrary rule of association and expect to obtain a relation that is both left total and left monogamous. Thus, to define a function, one defines the underlying relation and then establishes that the relation in question is both left total and left monogamous. It is this proof which guarantees that the definition given is truly a definition of a function and not of some nonfunctional, possibly empty, relation.

Mathematicians refer to the establishment of left totality as the establishment of *existence*. This is because left totality is defined as follows: for each member of the domain, there *exists* a member of the codomain such that the former is related to the latter. Mathematicians refer to the establishment of left monogamy as the establishment of *uniqueness*. This is because left monogamy requires that any member of the codomain associated with a member of the domain be *uniquely* associated with it.

The fact that functions are left total and left monogamous means that each member of the function's domain is related by the function's graph to a unique member of its codomain. This unique connection permits one to refer unambiguously to a member of the function's range by any member of its domain connected with it. In other words, if one knows which function one is talking about, once one specifies a member of the domain, one in effect uniquely specifies a member of its codomain.

According to the function displayed in Figure 8.15, 2 is uniquely related to a by f. Insofar as 2 is related to a by f, one writes in infix notation 2fa. However, in light of the fact that 2 is uniquely related to a by f, one can more perspicuously write in this traditional notation f(2) = a.

Functions have their own special vocabulary. Let us familiarize ourselves with it. Functions are often referred to as *maps* or *mappings*, on the one hand, or as *assignments*, on the other. Thus, one speaks of a map or mapping *from* a set, its domain, *to* a set, its codomain. A function, then, maps a member of its domain to a member of its codomain. According to the function in Figure 8.15, f maps 1 to a. One also speaks of a function as an assignment of members of its codomain to members of its domain. A function, then, assigns a member *of* its codomain *to* a member of its domain. When members of a function's domain and codomain are paired by the function, they are referred to as the function's *argument* and *value*, respectively. Thus, a is said to be the value of the argument 1 *under* the function f. It is also said to be the value of the function f *at* the argument 1. An argument and a value of a function are also referred to as its *preimage* and its *image*, respectively, in which case a is said to be the image of the 1, its preimage, under f:

f (_)   = _
   ↑   ↑
   argument;   value image
   preimage

Mathematicians have identified a number of different kinds of functions. Functions which are right total are said to be *surjections*. In other words, a surjection is a function, each element of whose codomain has a preimage. Functions that are right monogamous are said to be *injections*. In other words, an injection is a function where distinct images have distinct preimages. Functions that are both right total and right monogamous are *bijections*. Thus, bijections are functions that are both injections and subjections. In addition, mathematicians speak of *constant* functions. Constant functions are ones where the very same element of the codomain is the image of every element in the domain.

The following function is a constant function: every element of its domain is mapped to *a*:

<{1,2,3,4}, {a,b,c}, {<1,a>, <2,a>, <3,a>, <4,a>}>,

There are also so-called *partial* functions. The expression is somewhat unfortunate, since partial functions need not be functions. Recall that a function is, by definition, a binary relation that is both left total and left monogamous. A partial function is a binary relation that is left monogamous. It need not be left total, however. For example, the following binary relation is a partial function:

$$<\{1,2,3,4\}, \{a,b,c\}, \{<1,c>, <3,a>, <4,a>\}>,$$

It is not a function, however, since it is not left total. Nonetheless, since every function is both left total and left monogamous, it is left monogamous and hence a partial function. The idea behind the term *partial function* is that a partial function behaves like a function with respect to only part of its domain.

Two more notions pertaining to functions are useful: the notion that one function may be a near variant of another, and the notion that one function is an extension of another. One function is a near variant of another if, and only if, they have the same domain and codomain and their graphs differ at most with respect to one ordered pair. Consider the functions h and j:

$$h = <\{1,2,3,4\}, \{a,b,c\}, \{<1,c>, <2,b>, <3,a>, <4,b>\}>,$$
$$j = <\{1,2,3,4\}, \{a,b,c\}, \{<1,c>, <2,b>, <3,a>, <4,a>\}>,$$

They have the same domain and the same codomain. Moreover, their graphs are exactly the same, except for the ordered pair that has 4 as its first coordinate: that is, $<4,b> \in G_h$ but $<4,b> \notin G_j$, and $<4,a> \notin G_h$ but $<4,b> \in G_j$. In other words, for each member x of the $\{1,2,3,4\}$ except 4, $h(x) = j(x)$. When $x = 4$, $h(x) \neq j(x)$, since $h(x) = b$ and $j(x) = a$:

DEFINITION 17. *Near variant functions*. Let f and g be functions. Then f is a near variant of g iff $D_f = D = D_g$, $C_f = C = C_g$, and D has at most one element x such that $f(x) \neq g(x)$.

One immediate consequence of this definition is that each function is a near variant of itself.

It is convenient, when one function is a near variant of another, to name one function in terms of another. Thus, for example, h could be named by $j_{4 \mapsto b}$. The function $j_{4 \mapsto b}$ is just like the function j, except that it maps 4 to b. But this is just the function h. Equally, $h_{4 \mapsto a}$ is a function just like h except it maps 4 to a. But this is just the function j. Note finally that $h_{4 \mapsto b}$ is just h, and $j_{4 \mapsto b}$ is just j.

The other notion to be defined is that of one function being an *extension* of another. One function is an extension of another just in case the domain, codomain and graph of the second are subsets of the domain, codomain and graph of the first, respectively:

DEFINITION 18. *Extension*. Let f and g be functions. Then g is an extension of f iff $D_f \subseteq D_g$, $C_f \subseteq C_g$ and $G_f \subseteq G_g$.

Thus, for example, the function l is an extension of the function k:

$$k = <\{1,2,3\}, \{b,c\}, \{<1,c>, <2,b>, <3,b>\}>,$$
$$l = <\{1,2,3,4\}, \{a,b,c\}, \{<1,c>, <2,b>, <3,b>, <4,c>\}>,$$

Notes

1. A slash through a mathematical symbol turns that part of the statement involving the symbol with the slash into the negation of the very same part without the slash. For example, $1 \nsubseteq \{2,3\}$ is short for *it is not the case that* $1 \subseteq \{2,3\}$.

2. Left monogamy is also known as being single-valued.

BACKGROUND

FRANCIS JEFFRY PELLETIER

The Principle of Semantic Compositionality

1 Introduction: What is semantic compositionality?

The Principle of Semantic Compositionality is the principle that the meaning of an expression is a function of, and only of, the meanings of its parts together with the method by which those parts are combined.[1] As stated, the Principle is vague or underspecified at a number of points such as "what counts as a part," "what is a meaning," "what kind of function is allowed," and the like. But this hasn't stopped some people from treating it as an obviously true principle, true almost by definition, nor has it stopped some others from attacking it both on "empirical grounds" and on theoretico-methodological grounds. It seems to me that many of these discussions fail because of a lack of precision on the above-mentioned points and that other discussions are best described as "how compositionality can/cannot be accommodated within theory X" rather than whether the Principle is or is not true. In its most general form, for instance as stated above, the Principle makes no assumptions about what meaning is, nor does it say how one can tell whether two expressions have the same or different meanings. It makes no assumptions about what the parts of a complex expression are, nor does it put any restrictions on what is the function on the parts and the mode of combination.[2]

In general, the Principle has gotten good press. It is rather difficult to find anyone who has other than warm feelings towards the Principle, at least in the philosophical literature. However, many writers in the linguistic literature have pointed to certain types of sentences for which they think it is difficult to give a compositional account. Some of these sentences will be considered below. My own feeling is that although many of these sentences *can* be handled compositionally (indeed, perhaps all of the ones I'll mention), still, and nonetheless, the overall conclusion was right: compositionality is false. I shall not attempt to prove this here. Instead I will merely sketch what I take to be an alternative conception of semantics, one that relies on "groundedness" rather

Francis Jeffry Pelletier (1994) The principle of semantic compositionality. *Topoi* 13: 11–24. Reprinted by permission of Kluwer Academic Publishers.

than on "functionality." To this end I will survey some of the arguments both for and against the Principle of Compositionality and will argue that none of them achieves what they have set out to achieve; that is, none of them shows that compositionally either is or isn't false, and thus all we are left with is either the "warm fuzzy feeling" that arises when a theory claims to be compositional, or the "challenge for the establishment" feeling that arises when we claim our theory is non-compositional.

2   Some senses of "compositionality"

There have always been other notions of "compositionality" that are appealed to in scholarly work concerning whether the Principle is or isn't true. I mention here a few of them and try to give a feel for what is understood within the community by the notion of compositionality.

1. The only way to combine meanings is by function application.

The sentiment in (1) is attributed to Richard Montague (see Thomason 1974) by Brian Smith (1987), and has been called "the intuitive version of the Principle" by Theo Janssen (1983).

2. Meanings of complex symbols are systematically determined by their composition.

Example (2) is the understanding of 'compositionality' given in Haugeland (1987).

3. By 'compositionality' we mean that the meaning of the whole is a systematic function of the meaning of its parts.

Example (3) is taken from Graeme Hirst (1987). Together, (2) and (3) is what many people would understand by the notion of compositionality.

4. 'Compositionality' is taken to mean that with any piece you can associate something such that, given a whole made of parts, there is a way of systematically deriving the "meaning" of the whole from the "meanings" of the parts.

This is taken from Brian Smith (1987), who is giving a very general account of what the notion of compositionality means in terms of algebras for syntax and semantics. Together, these last three concepts of compositionality probably capture the popular notion that the functions which are used to combine meanings of parts into meanings of wholes have to in some sense always "work the same way." If they combine to form a given semantic category in one case where a noun phrase is combining with a verb phrase in a certain way, for example, then in all cases where a noun phrase is combining in that way with a verb phrase, it has to form an element of the same category. An extremely strong version of that very notion of compositionality is prevalent in the linguistics folklore. I have heard it on numerous occasions, and instead of citing anyone in particular, let me just attribute it to an anonymous participant in a recent Linguistic Society of America meeting.

5. 'Compositionality' means that the grammar obeys the "rule-to-rule hypothesis."

We see here that we're getting more and more specific understandings of what kinds of functions are going to be permitted in order for it to be considered a compositional function. The general thrust is that a compositional semantics has to be "systematic," in some or other sense of the term.

My own view is that one person's anarchy is another person's favorite form of systematic organization. What the above authors have just cited as being systematic (and by implication, the kinds of things they think are not systematic and hence not to be understood as falling under the Principle) might very well be exactly the sorts of things that I think are systematic. The Principle itself makes no claims *at all* about what sorts of functions there are. It would seem to me that it might be quite easy to argue against the notion of compositionality, if you insist that the functions have to be "systematic" in the senses that our authors have just given us.[3] However, it would be much more difficult to argue against the notion of semantic compositionality if you allowed *any* conceivable function whatsoever. Yet this is precisely what I intend to do later in the paper.

But before embarking on that task, I would like to turn to the topic of the *extent* to which the Principle applies. Our first quotation is taken from Allan (1986: 61–62). We'll see that Allan believes compositionality to be an extremely broad notion indeed:

> The meaning of S's Utterance delivered to H in context C is composed from:
> i.   The meaning of sentence Σ that S uses.
> ii. The meaning contributed by the prosody ϕ with which Σ is spoken.
> iii. The meaningful input to the interpretation of Σ spoken with ϕ in C and from background information of various kinds.
>
> Each of these components of U's meaning is itself compositional. . . . Although I have no more to say at this point about the compositionality of contextual or background meaning, it will be exemplified [later in book]. Sentence meaning is compositional; in fact it manifests a compositional hierarchy such that the meaning of a sentence is composed from the meanings of its constituent clauses (and their connectives), the meaning of a clause is composed from the meanings of its constituent phrases, the meaning of a phrase is composed from the meanings of its constituent words, and those in turn from the meanings of their constituent lexemes and morphemes (semantic primitives).

As we see from this quotation, Allan, a champion of the Principle, believes in compositionality "all the way up and all the way down." But it is not just champions of the Principle who have this view of the scope of compositionality. Some theorists who don't believe in the notion of semantic compositionality also have the view that the extent of the Principle is "compositionality all the way up and down." They just deny that it occurs. Here is a quotation taken from Hans Kamp (1990):

> The question here depends to a large extent on what we take the data that a semantic theory should account for. Thus, some people would question whether anaphora resolution . . . is something that a semantic theory should address. . . . I think that a theory of language should account for *all* linguistic data. . . . What are the facts that a comprehensive theory of language should explain? . . . My own answer is that linguistic meaning is to be understood in terms of the potential to modify states of information. . . . The theory should include an analysis of the inference mechanisms that create, modify and exploit the information states in terms of which linguistic meaning is defined. . . . To sum up, someone who takes seriously the idea that meaning is to be extricated in terms of information change potential, will find the chances for a compositional theory as extraordinarily slim.

We see here that Kamp and Allan agree about what a compositional theory would look like. It's a wide-ranging theory, starting with the individual lexemes and going all the way to the utterance in context. Allan believes that all of that is compositional. Kamp thinks that it's extraordinarily unlikely to be compositional.

3   A psychological argument against the Principle

Certain arguments that have been raised against the Principle of Semantic Compositionality seem to be less successful than others. A certain group of these arguments point out that human minds bring to bear a lot of in-built interpretations to things that they perceive. For example, Gestalt psychologists have long ago pointed out that people will tend to see many things which "aren't there" because their mind "fills in the gaps," or alternatively put, the mind makes certain inferences about the whole that is expected when only certain parts of the whole are seen. Since this can happen in ordinary situations, such as vision for example, some theorists conclude that the same thing might be happening in linguistic contexts. The mind might bring to bear many things that are not present in the actual linguistic input. So, having brought these things to bear, the meaning that is associated with the combination of these linguistic inputs might not be present in any of the parts, and so compositionality is false.

It seems to me that this sort of argumentation is not very good. One tactic to argue against it might be to say that, when the mind infers these kinds of things that "aren't there in the input," then in fact it is the action of "putting together" of these smaller parts which introduces "the things that the mind brings to bear." (Recall that the Principle did not only appeal to the meanings of the parts but also it appealed to the method by which the parts are composed; and one might say that it is here that these other aspects of the meaning of the whole are to be found). Another tactic, one that I am more in favor of, is to argue that many things which might be thought to fall under the rubric of "being brought to bear by the mind even though they aren't there in the parts" are not really in the meanings of the composed whole to begin with, so the whole argument structure is pointless. Let me approach this by means of an analogy. Gestalt psychologists have used examples such as the one in Figure 9.1.

According to Gestalt psychologists, we see a square in Figure 9.1, despite the fact that a careful examination reveals that the only things in the picture are emphasized corners. There is no square at all in Figure 9.1 despite what we "see." From this some theorists claim that the content of the entire picture in Figure 9.1 is something over and above the contents of the parts of the picture, since the contents of the parts are only the four corners.

One style of objection to such a claim was raised in the last paragraph: that the method of combining these four parts into a whole includes putting them in a certain relationship to one another, namely the specific relationship that would lead us to see a square. This is certainly a possible position for a compositionalist to take on the Gestalt figures, and so far as I can see there has never been an adequate rejoinder to this response-to-Gestalt-objections-to-compositionality. But I myself would prefer to use the second tactic to argue against the Gestaltist argument. I would like

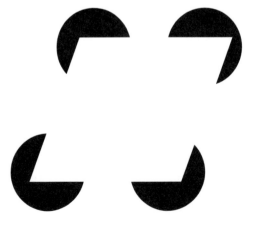

FIGURE 9.1 A Gestalt "square"

to say that the square is *not* really there *at all*. In this regard I'm reminded of a cartoon posted on the Psychology Department bulletin board which had the corners of a Gestalt square such as Figure 9.1, each being held by a fireman outside of a burning building in which a woman was trapped on the second floor. The firemen were shouting "Jump, Jump!" The title of the cartoon was "Gestalt firemen play a joke." The point is that even though the trapped person might *perceive* a square of safety netting being held by the Gestalt firemen, the fact of the matter is that there was *no* square there. Similarly one might say in Figure 9.1 that there simply is *no* square there regardless of what we seem to think. Figure 9.1 then represents no challenge to the Principle because there is nothing in it other than the four corners. And similarly, no Gestalt challenge to compositionality can work because we deny that the "inferred meanings" are there in the whole.

4   Some linguistic arguments against the Principle

In the linguistic literature there have been numerous attempts to show that compositionality is wrong, by actually presenting cases where the parts of a sentence have meanings that "just can't" be combined to form the correct meaning of the whole.[4]

One type of challenge might be said to come about because "there are things that we know are in the meaning of the whole that just are not in the parts." Consider the sentence:

6. A man is in this room.

and its representation:

7. $(\exists x) (Man(x) \& In(x, this\text{-}room))$

Note that in this representation, there are variables that are not in the original sentence. Furthermore note that there is no 'and' in the original sentence yet (7) asserts that there is an ampersand in the representation. Thus there are things in the representation that are not in the sentence. It is not clear to me whether this kind of an argument should be taken seriously, although it has been mounted by certain otherwise respected scholars who should remain nameless. In a way, this is similar to the "Gestaltist objection" canvassed earlier, and found wanting: the fact that there is "something in the representation" which is "not in the parts" is just irrelevant. There is no reason in the world that the composition function could not insert variables or &s.

Here is another type of example:

8. Jane isn't liked by many men.

Example (8) is ambiguous. It could mean either of

8. a. Most men do not like Jane.
    b. There is a specific group (of many men) who do not like Jane.

So the original sentence is ambiguous and can be understood in either one of those two ways. However, if you were to embed (8) into a larger context the ambiguity disappears. Consider

9. Jane isn't liked by many men and Sally isn't either.
10. Jane isn't liked by many men and Sally isn't liked by them either.

Each of these last two sentences is unambiguous; in each of those sentences the meaning of its first clause is unique. But this first clause is just the ambiguous (8)! In (9) the phrase "Jane isn't liked by many men" only has the meaning of (8a), whereas that very same phrase in (10) has only the (8b) meaning. At least that's the claim that some anti-compositional theorists make.

It seems to me that this is not a very successful argument against compositionality. For one thing, the meaning of the entire sentence in either of these latter two cases is conditioned in part by the second conjunct, and the Principle only predicts that the *entire* sentence should mean whatever it is that (9) and (10) mean. It does not say anything about the meanings of the component parts of those sentences. It neither has anything to say about *what* the meaning of the first clause will be as parts of (9) and (10), nor does it say what the meaning of these clauses will be in isolation, nor does it have anything to say about the relationship between the clause's meaning in isolation and its meaning in some context. So, clearly the component parts *could* be ambiguous in isolation, but in context they are not ambiguous; or rather, the entire sentence does not have an ambiguous first conjunct. So examples like (8)–(10) in no way defeat the Principle.

A similar sort of example that might be seen as more challenging is:

11. Dogs get fleas.

This sentence is a "generic" statement about the propensities or the dispositions (etc.) of dogs— namely that they are able to get fleas, or that they typically get fleas, or that they get fleas under usual or normal circumstances. However, if you embed (11) into a larger context, that portion of the sentence gets interpreted differently. Consider:

12. When dogs get fleas it is best to keep them away from children.

In this case the embedded sentence, "dogs get fleas," is interpreted as actual episodes or instances of dogs getting fleas, rather than about the propensities or the dispositions of dogs. From this, some have concluded (just as they have concluded from (8)–(10)) that there has been a change of meaning of (11), brought about by the embedding into a larger context; and thus it is not solely the meaning of the component parts that goes to making the meaning of the whole, as the Principle predicts, but rather something in addition. Once again however, this is a misunderstanding of what the Principle is committed to. The Principle says only that there is some meaning which can be attributed to the entire sentence based solely on the meanings of its parts. One relevant question, then, is: what are the parts of this sentence? Well, for sure, one of the parts is "dogs get fleas." But equally for sure, another part is that this sentence is embedded inside of a "when" clause. So it is open for one to say that if a generic statement gets embedded inside of such a clause, then the entire statement has as its meaning that actual episodes of the generic disposition are being manifested. This is all that the Principle is committed to; and certainly this is within the realm of compositional theories.

Another group of examples comes when the subject term is a superlative construction (or other construction that picks out an endpoint on some scale). For example, consider the following sentences:

13. a. *The first person* landed on the moon in 1969.
     b. *The person with the biggest grant* usually supports the rest of the department.
     c. *The tallest person* usually plays center for the team.
     d. *The first case of AIDS* was reported in 1975.

In these examples, whatever the meaning is of the italicized subject terms—whether you take it to be referential and hence it picks out the actual first person [Adam? Leakey's Lucy?] or the actual person with the biggest grant or the actual tallest person or the actual first case of AIDS, or whether you're more indirect and think that a phrase such as "the first person" designates a function on possible worlds which in each possible world picks out the first person of that world—nonetheless, in *none* of these sentences are *any* of these things being talked about. For, in each of these sentences there is something about the predicate which, in one way or another, gives an idiosyncratic understanding as to how the subject should be understood. It's *not* that the first person [Adam? Lucy?] landed on the moon in 1969 but rather the first person who landed on the moon did so in 1969. It's *not* that the tallest person, whoever that might be, has the property of usually playing center; but rather that, given a team, the tallest person in that team usually plays center for the team. Challenges such as these have formed the basis for a number of attacks on the Principle.

Another attack has come from such sentences as:

14.   a.º Every philosopher in the world can fit into this room.
       b. Every philosopher in New Zealand can fit into this room.

It seems quite clear, so the argument against compositionality goes, that in (14a) the meaning is "distributive"; that is, it says of each philosopher individually, that he or she could fit into this room. However, (14b) could have a collective meaning, in which case it would mean that all of the philosophers in New Zealand taken together could collectively fit into this room at the same time. Example (14a) seems to talk about the size (= fatness) of individual philosophers; (14b) seems to talk about the size (= number) of the group of philosophers in New Zealand. Once again this difference in the understanding of the sentence (whether distributive or collective) seems to be not traceable to either the verb phrase or the subject phrase, but rather is somehow dependent upon our knowledge of how many philosophers there are in the world and how many philosophers there are in New Zealand—that is to say, it relies on facts other than the meaning of the component parts.

Non-restrictive relative clauses also have been seen as forming challenges to the Principle of Semantic Compositionality. Consider, for example:

15.   Kim, whose paper was rejected from *Linguistics and Philosophy*, began to rant and rave.

It seems clear that the meaning of the non-restrictive relative clause construction is more than merely an *and*. In this case perhaps it means *because*. However, in other cases the non-restrictive relative clause construction might mean *despite* or sometimes *although*. We see that there is no one meaning for a non-restrictive relative clause construction, and this has been seen to be a challenge for compositional semantics.

Another challenge for compositionality has been seen to reside in adverbials which change the meaning of a given sentence in idiosyncratic ways. Consider the following four sentences:

16.   a. Laszlo has been reading Kim's diary *again*.
       b. Laszlo *even* suggested that Kim spend the weekend at his apartment.
       c. Laszlo hasn't *actually* made it with Kim *yet*.
       d. He hasn't touched her, *let alone* kissed her.

The meaning of any of those italicized adverbs is dependent on the discourse in which they are found and dependent upon world information that we each have about the kind of scenario that this discourse is likely to be describing; and it has been claimed that this has nothing to do with the lexical meaning of these individual words, and so compositionality is incorrect.

Another example along the same lines is provided by idioms and other tropes. Consider

17.   The symbolists are really *on the ropes* now!
18.   While I was holding Kim's baby, *the little sweetie* wet itself.

We see in these sentences that the literal meaning of the italicized phrases "on the ropes" and "the little sweetie" just are *not* what is relevant to the understanding of these sentences, and it seems that there is no compositional functional way to compute the meaning of the whole—or so the argument goes.

5   Gricean responses to challenges concerning compositionality: Some difficulties

I would like now to consider one kind of response that many compositionalists would give to such challenges as those of the last section. I only outline this response, I do not state it in any great detail. It is not, in any case, a response that I would care to give, although I think it will work in certain cases. After giving the response I will mention the reason why I think that the response cannot be used in full generality; why there seem to be cases not covered by this line of defense.

Compositionalists are tempted to use a "Grice-y" strategy when responding to such challenges. Consider the examples (14a,b). The phrases "Every philosopher in the world" and "Every philosopher in New Zealand" in fact are each able to carry both the distributive and the collective meanings, the Grice response would say, and therefore each of the sentences (14a,b) is, literally or really or underneath it all, ambiguous. But it is our world knowledge (our knowledge of empirical facts, not facts about language and meaning) which tells us that no *actual* room can hold all of the world's philosophers. Therefore, by Gricean mechanisms, we cannot be trying to communicate that meaning; so we must be trying to communicate the other meaning, the meaning that says of each philosopher, he or she can fit into the room—the distributive meaning. We get the *illusion* of non-ambiguity because we are not able to use one of the meanings for any reasonable communicative purpose. But the Grice position is that the sentence *does* have the meaning—it is just that it can't use it.

This is the kind of response that many compositionalists attempt to give to the previously mentioned sorts of challenges, especially the challenges concerning idioms, ambiguities, and the like. But there are some problems for Grice-y explanations. Consider a sentence like:

19. There are green ideas.

Such a sentence *never* gets used as a simple sentence with this literal meaning. Therefore, according to a Grice-y explanation, analyzing the meaning of a sentence like

20. Laszlo would never believe that there are green ideas.

will always fail. If you were faced with (20), then in accordance with the Grice-y explanation you would say that the sub-sentence "there are green ideas" can't possibly be used with its literal meaning. So, it must be used with some other meaning; and now it is our job to figure out this other meaning (using other Gricean mechanisms). And it is that other, discovered meaning which will turn out to be what Laszlo never believes—contrary to what our intuitions say about sentence (20).

Another reason to believe that there is something wrong with Gricean explanations in general is that we *do* understand outrageous and absurd tales. Consider the following (cited in Hirst 1987):

21. Go on, have your fun, it's always the children that suffer later: Los Angeles secretary Jannine Swift married a fifty pound rock in a formal ceremony in Layfette Park yesterday.

We understand this sentence entirely in its literal meaning despite the fact that it is never the case that the verb phrase "marries a fifty pound rock" can have its literal meaning. (Certainly in none of our lives have we encountered a sentence which truthfully and literally asserts that a person has married a rock; yet we, all of us, understood that sentence). If the Gricean mechanisms were right in their full generality we would never be able to understand a *National Enquirer* headline. But we do, and that's why the newspapers sell so well.

6   The argument from synonymy

The challenges to compositionality that we have so far been considering all have turned on expressions meaning something X_1 (which might be ambiguous, or even null) in context C_1 and meaning some other X_2 (perhaps a resolution of ambiguity or a creation of new meaning or a change to some related meaning etc.) in context C_2. I myself am not very taken with these arguments; I think all of them can be overcome one way or another and some of them are even downright silly. But I shall not myself attempt to refute the arguments; I'll leave it to the reader to determine what he or she thinks about the correctness of the Gricean response, or whether they can find some more sophisticated, but still compositional, functions that will do the job. For, I think, there are other arguments that show that compositionality is not a very attractive prospect. So let us now turn to a different strategy for arguing against compositionality. A fact about semantic compositionality that has not often been noticed is the following: If there are two different expressions which have the same meaning (i.e., if there is any synonymy in the language), then if there is any case where embedding one of these expressions into a context yields a different meaning than embedding the other expression into that same context, then semantic compositionality is false. (This would be a case where expressions X and Y mean the same but C(X) means something different from C(Y), where C is some linguistic context.) The reason that this shows that semantic compositionality would be false is that, *ex hypothesi*, the two expressions X and Y have the same meaning and therefore they contribute the same thing in whichever context they occur. If they occur in the same context, then the entire constructions must mean the same thing, according to semantic compositionality. So if there is ever a case where two different expressions mean the same thing, but when they are embedded the two wholes mean something different, then compositionality is false. Is there any such case? Consider the following argument.[5] Given these three assumptions:

A. If ϕ and ψ are sentences that have the same meaning, then they have the same truth value.
B. For a given syntactic theory, there is only one rule or sequence of rules which creates or analyzes sentences of the form
    Kim + believes + that + Sentence
C. If ϕ and ψ are syntactically distinct sentences then it is possible that exactly one of (i) and (ii) is true:
    (i)   Kim believes that ϕ.
    (ii) Kim believes that ψ.

Then, if there are any synonymous ϕ and ψ, the Principle has to be false. The argument for this conclusion is quite simple. Suppose that there are synonymous sentences S_1 and S_2. Then by assumption (B), it is the same rule or sequence of rules that analyzes both of

a. Kim believes that S_1
b. Kim believes that S_2

and therefore these two sentences, (a) and (b), mean the same thing—according to the Principle. But by assumption C, it is always possible that sentence (a) is true and sentence (b) is false; and hence by assumption A, sentences (a) and (b) do *not* mean the same thing. Therefore, given assumptions A–C, if there is any synonymy of sentences, the Principle of Semantic Compositionality is false.[6] If we believe in the existence of sentential synonymy and we believe these three assumptions, then we cannot believe the Principle of Semantic Compositionality. This strikes me as a rather powerful argument against the Principle, for surely these assumptions and the existence of synonymy are more plausible than the highly theoretical and methodologically motivated Principle.

7   Arguments in favor of semantic compositionality

So far as I have been able to tell, there are only four considerations that have been brought to bear in favor of compositionality in the literature. This is not to say, of course, that there are only a few people who believe in semantic compositionality. In fact, as I indicated earlier, almost everyone has a "warm and fuzzy feeling" towards compositionality. Almost everyone assumes it to be true. Almost everyone assumes that it is a desideratum of any adequate theory. Yet when one looks for arguments in favor of it, one finds very few. Here are the four that I have found.

> *Argument 1*: Compositionality is the only way to get an account of such semantic notions as truth, validity, and inference, etc.

> *Argument 2*: Semantics is a mirror of our cognitive states. Our cognitive states are compositional, and therefore, semantics must be compositional.

> *Argument 3*: If a language lacked compositionality it would be *unlearnable*.

> *Argument 4*: Compositionality is the only explanation of how a finite mechanism (such as the human brain/mind) can *understand* an infinite set of sentences.[7] (Without compositionality, novel utterances would be *non-understandable*).

These arguments seem to me to differ in their strength. The first argument merely asserts a falsehood: it is just not true that compositionality is the only way to get an account of these semantic notions. Indeed, the traditional Tarski notion defining validity and truth in terms of satisfiability is not compositional in *any* straightforward sense.[8] The second argument seems to me to beg the question. We have even less knowledge of the status of our cognitive states—whether they are compositional or not—than we do about semantics, and so it seems rather premature to assert that we can use facts about cognitive states to prove facts about semantics.

The third and fourth of these arguments seem to me to be strongest. If the meaning of the whole were not a function of the meaning of its parts, so these arguments say, then we would not be able to *learn* the language. We would not be able to *understand* all of the language. How else, so these arguments ask us, are we to be able to figure out the meaning of an arbitrary, new, novel sentence if it isn't by the fact that we've learned some finite number of parts and finite number of ways of putting them together. How is it that we can understand a novel sentence, except by predicting its meaning by our understanding of the meaning of its parts, so these arguments say. Towards the end of this paper I will try to sketch a different conception of semantics that allows languages to be learnable and understandable, even though they are not, strictly speaking, compositional.

8   Language and representation

Figure 9.2 gives us a picture of the organization of the semantic component of a linguistic theory. It is a picture that is very familiar in philosophy of language and also in many different linguistic theories.

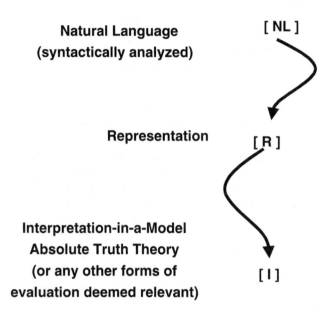

Natural Language
(syntactically analyzed)   [NL]

Representation   [R]

Interpretation-in-a-Model
Absolute Truth Theory
(or any other forms of   [I]
evaluation deemed relevant)

FIGURE 9.2 The structure of the semantic component of a theory of language, according to certain views

We see here a rather standard view, where the semantics is defined in two stages. One starts with a syntactically analyzed sentence (or other fragment of natural language) and one determines a representation of this piece of natural language, and from that one generates an interpretation of the representation. For example, one might take an individual sentence of English and represent this by means of a sentence of first order logic and then interpret first order logic in terms of Tarski-style truth conditions.

Some theorists prefer to take a short cut in this method. These are the Eliminativists depicted in Figure 9.3. Some Eliminativists start with the theory given in Figure 9.2, but then take each of f and g to be a function. Hence the representation [R] in the middle of Figure 9.2 is theoretically dispensable: one could just use function composition on the two functions and have a generated function of f∘g. So the level of representation [R] is dispensed with, and we are left with Figure 9.3. Montague, for example, took this view. In his (1974a), the level of representation was Intensional Logic but he held that this level was theoretically dispensable and that we could eliminate the representation by means of Intensional Logic. (This was laid out in his 1970b.)

Another way of eliminating one of the levels is illustrated in Figure 9.4. Here the theory might be called Straight Representationalism. The idea is that there is *no* interpretation of natural language over and above the level of representation. The kind of theorist that have this picture are cognitive grammarians, generally speaking, for instance Jackendoff (1987) and Langacker (1986), to name a few. These theorists deny the necessity of having *any* "external" interpretation of [R]; indeed, they view the translation (as we might call it) of natural language into some other representational language as itself sufficient for us to understand the meaning of natural language.

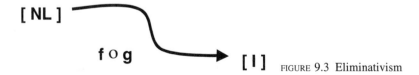

[NL]

f ∘ g   [I]   FIGURE 9.3 Eliminativism

[R]   FIGURE 9.4 Straight representationalism

In this belief these theorists reject the arguments in Lewis (1970) to the effect that translation into another language (the "Language of Thought" or into "Markerese") just isn't semantics in any real sense.

It should be noted that both Eliminativism and Straight Representationalism have exactly the same structure in that they are two-level theories wherein the levels are related by functions. Therefore they make the same sort of predictions for certain semantic data. In particular, for either one of these views to maintain compositionality (that is, for either one of these views to hold that the relationship between the natural language and whatever it gets mapped into—whether it's an interpretation as in Eliminativism or just into a representation as in Straight Representationalism—is a function), these theories must *deny* the existence of any "serious ambiguity." (A "serious ambiguity" occurs when a sentence of natural language has exactly one syntactic analysis but has two meanings, and this ambiguity is not traceable to a lexical ambiguity.) For, if the relationship between these two levels were a function, as compositionality demands, then there is no opportunity for "serious ambiguity" to arise. For compositionality to be true in these theories, all ambiguity must be "minor": either traceable to lexical ambiguity or else to differing syntactic analyses of the same English string.

Another view of the relationship between natural language and the interpretation is illustrated in Figure 9.5. In Crooked Representationalism, a syntactically analyzed sentence of natural language is associated with a level of representation, R_1, and then in some way or other, we are allowed to manipulate this representation and "do various things to it" until we reach a final representation, R_n, which is then interpreted. This "doing something" might be to bring in context, to resolve anaphora, to eliminate ambiguities, and to draw inferences (possibly from other sentences, possibly from the background theory, possibly from prototype theory and possibly from other areas). In general these "doings" will not be functional, for they will not be unique. If they were unique, then all of these intermediate levels between R_1 and R_n could be theoretically dispensed with; but most theorists believe that they are not theoretically dispensable, that they are essential to the inter-

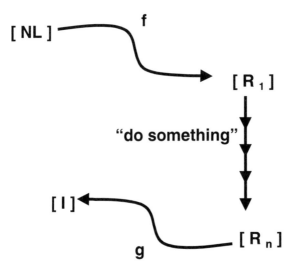

FIGURE 9.5 Crooked representationalism

pretation of the sentence. As examples of theorists who have held such views I might point to, for instance, Schubert and Pelletier (1982). In this theory the relationship between the natural language and R_1 was functional; that is, R_1 was compositionally determined on the basis of the syntactic features of a natural language sentence. However, then various "doings" were alleged to happen, such as scope ambiguity resolution and anaphora resolution, and various inferences were drawn. None of this was envisaged as being functional; that is to say, it was possible that one and the same level of representation might have different things happen to it at different times, and hence it was rather unpredictable as to what the outcome of a level R_i becoming R_{i+1} would be.

Having mentioned Crooked Representationalism we are in a position to give yet another version of Eliminativism, which, for definiteness, we call the GB Strategy [Figure 9.6]. Essentially what the GB Strategy does is take the Crooked Representationist point of view about everything, except for where the boundary is between analyzing a natural language utterance and doing the semantics on that utterance. In Crooked Representationalism, as we can see from Figure 9.5, the boundary is at the point where we have a syntactically analyzed surface structure of natural language. The rest of the diagram is viewed as part of the semantic theory for understanding the sentence. However the GB Strategy usurps all of the diagram up to R_n as part of the syntactic theory. After all of these "doing somethings" (in GB Theory this is applying the Quantifier Raising rules, for example), one arrives at a new syntactic level which is called LF. In some of the advanced versions of this theory, for example Higginbotham (1987) or Larson and Ludlow's (1993) "interpreted logical forms," it is possible to interpret these LF structures in a straightforwardly compositional way. So we see that the GB Strategy, at least as augmented by a real semantics, *a la* Higginbotham or Larson/Ludlow, is essentially the same as Eliminativism. This reveals a hitherto unnoticed close affinity between Montague and one time-slice of Chomsky in the formal features of their theories.

9   The argument from ambiguity

Once again let me emphasize a point that was made earlier: that any theory of either the Eliminativist type, the Straight Representationist type, or the GB Strategy type is committed to either denying the Principle of Semantic Compositionality or denying the existence of "serious ambiguity."[9] But can it really be true that there is *no* serious ambiguity? How about the following sentences?

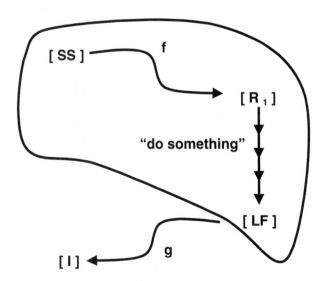

FIGURE 9.6 The GB strategy

22. Every linguist knows two languages.
23. John wondered when Alice said she would leave.
24. When Alice rode a bicycle, she went to school.
25. The philosophers lifted the piano.
26. The Canadian family used less water last year than the preceding year.

These sentences all are ambiguous and all ambiguous in the way that I mentioned before: namely, they have only one syntactic analysis but have at least two meanings. In (22) there is the obvious ambiguity between whether every linguist knows the same two languages or merely that every linguist knows two possibly different languages. This semantic ambiguity is plausibly analyzed as a "scope ambiguity"—that is to say, as having two different *semantic* analyses: one where *every* has wide scope, and one where *two* has wide scope. But doesn't it seem *really* implausible to say that (22) has two different *syntactic* analyses—in the way "Come alone or bring your spouse and have a good time" does? One would only say that if they were antecedently convinced of the truth of compositionality.

Example (23) clearly only has one syntactic analysis, but there are two different meanings. One meaning is that John wonders when Alice said something, and the other meaning is that John wonders when Alice is going to leave. Example (24) is ambiguous between stating (i) that on those occasions when Alice rode a bicycle, she rode it to school, and (ii) that back in the times when Alice had the disposition to be a bicycle rider, she also had the disposition or propensity to go to school (i.e., she was also a student). Example (25) manifests a familiar distributive/collective ambiguity about whether it was all of the philosophers together who lifted the piano, or whether they each did it separately. And (26) is ambiguous between whether it is the average Canadian family that used less water last year than the preceding year, or whether it's the total of Canadian family water usage that is less this year than the preceding year. (Contrast 'The Canadian family bought 9,500 BMWs last year' and 'The Canadian family owns 2.3 TV sets'). These two can have different truth conditions depending on how many Canadian families there are.

Besides the above-mentioned strategy of trying to attribute different syntactic analyses to account for the scope ambiguities, there are other syntactic strategies that have been used in trying to account for some of these ambiguities. For instance, Montague had "qualifying in" rules which would analyze the first of the sentences differently in the two meanings depending on which order the "quantifying in" rules were applied. And Cooper (1983) had a mechanism for storing quantified noun phrases so as to allow different analyses of their scopes. Other strategies for some of these sentences might involve "traces" and "gaps." Seems to me that all of these are rather desperate measures in that they try to invent a syntactic ambiguity when we know perfectly well that in reality there is no syntactic ambiguity. Admittedly there is a *semantic* ambiguity, but the only reason that this fact should call for a syntactic ambiguity is if you antecedently believe the Principle of Semantic Compositionality. The straightforward thing to do is to give up the Principle. I mentioned in the last section that compositionalists must find all ambiguities to be "minor." The syntactic strategies suggested in this paragraph take the route of saying that the type of minor ambiguity to be found is the one where the same string has differing syntactic analyses. But isn't that really silly for these examples? My recommendation is: don't force yourself to accept spurious syntactic ambiguities.

Another strategy that is often applied to some of the other sentences is to invent semantic features (as opposed to the syntactic features mentioned in the last paragraph) that are involved with some of the noun phrases. For example, one might have semantic Distributivity vs. Collectivity features and claim that the verb *lifted* is itself an ambiguous verb. One might similarly try to invent semantic Genericity features to account for the two different meanings of (24) and claim that *when* is ambiguous. The general methodology of this semantic strategy to defend compositionality is to describe the two different meanings by means of some semantic features, associating them with some phrase, and to claim that some lexical item in the sentence is ambiguous between a meaning using one vs. using the other of these features. I think this semantic strategy leaves a lot to be desired. True enough, these sentences are semantically ambiguous, and if you wish to use such features to describe what that ambiguity is, well and good. But there is no independent reason to say that these features are somehow inherent in the literal meanings of the lexical items themselves. It is unjustified and only motivated by a desire to maintain semantic compositionality. In fact, there is a hidden difficulty with the whole semantic enterprise. Consider the collective vs. distributive meanings of (25). It is not enough simply that *lifted* be viewed as ambiguous. In addition, the subject term, *the philosophers*, has to also be ambiguous. But where did that ambiguity come from? Are we to posit an underlying distributive/collective ambiguity in every lexical noun? (It has to be in the lexicon, for otherwise there would be a violation of compositionality in forming the meanings of the noun phrases.) Better to give up the semantic strategy.

10   Synonymy again

Recall from before that the Principle of Semantic Compositionality is incompatible with any form of synonymy. Can it really be true that there is no synonymy? Can it really be true that *attorney* and *lawyer* are not synonymous, or if you think that those are not quite synonymous then that there are *no* lexical items that are synonymous? What about phrases? Can you really deny that *a circle* and *a locus of all points on a plane equidistant from a given point* are synonymous? What about sentences? Can you really deny that *Dentists often need to hire an attorney* and *Tooth doctors commonly require the services of a lawyer* are synonymous? Isn't it better to give up the Principle of Semantic Compositionality? Isn't it better to just face the fact, that "warm and fuzzy" though it may be, semantic compositionality just is inconsistent with any reasonable interpretation of linguistic data?

But, I hear you say, if there really is synonymy, if there really is structural ambiguity, and therefore semantic compositionality is false, then how is it possible to learn language? How is it possible to understand an infinite (or hugely finite) number of these linguistic structures? This is the big question for non-compositional semantic theories. To answer this question will take a bit of a detour. I don't intend to answer it in great detail, but I do hope to give a feeling for why I think that these can be overcome.

11   The Principle of Semantic Groundedness

The Principle of Semantic Compositionality is closely related to inductive definitions, a general form of which is:

DEFINITION OF ϕ (*n*)

$\phi(n) =_{df}$ a,b,c . . . , if $n = 0, 1, 2 . . .$ }basis clauses
    $= \psi(\phi(n - 1))$, otherwise   }inductive clause

Some examples of inductive definitions are:

$n! =_{df} 1$, if $n = 0$
    $= (n - 1)!*n$, otherwise.

$n^m =_{df} 1$, if either $m = 0$ or $n = 0$
    $= n^{(m-1)}*n$, otherwise

The general feature of these inductive definitions in defining some operation ϕ is that after one has done some basic cases (the so-called basis clauses), one defines the operation ϕ on the arbitrary number n in terms of that very same operation on some lesser number(s). (It is the very same operation ϕ on the lesser number, but then we "do something" to this result. In the abstract definition of $\phi(n)$, this "doing something" was represented as ψ. In the examples of defining the factorial and exponentiation, the "doing something" was to multiply by n.) The reason that these are all called inductive definitions is that they apply the concept being defined to a number less than the number that is being defined. But in fact, there is no logical necessity for this clause to be an operation on the next smaller number $(n-1)$ or, indeed, on any number which is less than n. Think, for example, of programming a recursive procedure in some suitable programming language. There is no syntactic requirement that the recursive clause be a function of some number less than n. All that's required is that the function doing the evaluation ultimately be grounded for any value we wish to evaluate. For example,

$\phi(n) = 2$, if $n = 0$
$\quad\quad = 3$, if $n = 1$
else $= n*\phi(n - 2)$, if n is odd
$\quad\quad = n*\phi(2n + 1)$, if n is even

Note in this definition that the last clause defines $\phi(n)$ in terms of $\phi(2n + 1)$, and $(2n + 1)$ is of course larger than n. Therefore, this definition is not an inductive definition of the sort described above. We might instead call this type of definition by a different name; let's use "recursive definition."

A problem with these non-inductive, recursive definitions (which isn't a problem with just the pure inductive definitions) is that they are not always "grounded." For example:

$\phi(n) = _{df} 1$, if $n = 1$
else $= 1 + \phi(n/2)$, if n is even
$\quad\quad = 1 + \phi(3n - 1)$, if n is odd

(The last clause is a non-inductive form of definition, where ϕ is being applied to $3n - 1$.) I show here how this series evaluates n for values from 1 to 5.

$\phi(1) = 1$
$\phi(2) = 1 + \phi(1) = 1 + 1 = 2$
$\phi(3) = 1 + \phi(8) = 2 + \phi(4) = 3 + \phi(2) = 5$
$\phi(4) = 1 + \phi(2) = 1 + 2 = 3$
$\phi(5) = 1 + \phi(14) = 2 + \phi(7) = 3 + \phi(20) = 4 + \phi(10) = 5 + \phi(5)$

Note in the evaluation of $\phi(3)$, we needed to discover the value of $\phi(8)$; yet there was no problem here, this evaluated without any difficulties. Yet, when we did the same thing with $\phi(5)$, it called $\phi(14)$ which called $\phi(7)$ which called $\phi(20)$ which called $\phi(10)$, and this finally called $\phi(5)$ again and thus generated a circle, a "non-grounded" evaluation. Inductive definitions are always grounded because of the structure of the integers; however, these arbitrary recursive definitions are not always grounded. Sometimes, as before, this is a difficulty. But other times, there is no difficulty, as the following example shows:

$\phi(n) \quad\quad = _{df} 0$, if $n = 0$
else $\quad\quad = 0$, if n is even
$\quad\quad\quad = 1 + \phi(n + 1)$, otherwise
[Note: $\phi(0) = \phi(2) = \phi(4) = \ldots = 0$
$\phi(1) \quad\quad = \phi(3) = \phi(5) = \ldots = 1$]

This function is recursive but non-inductive, as can be seen from the last clause of the definition.

However, it can be seen from the evaluation that $\phi(n)$ is just a perfectly good alternative way of defining (n mod 2). There is no ungroundedness in this definition at all.

It is this notion of non-inductive but recursive definitions that I think lends a key to the understanding of how there might be a non-compositional semantics. Let's take a look at an example first put forward by Kaplan (1972) (in considerably different circumstances to make a considerably different point). The example is from elementary semantics of the sentence logic in which each of the connectives $\{\neg, \rightarrow, \leftrightarrow, \&, \vee\}$ are viewed as primitives and not defined by the others. We are going to construct an assignment of truth values function. The standard way of doing this, the way that you can always find in any textbook, is the following:

Let f be an assignment of truth values to atomic sentences.
$f^*(\phi) =_{df}$:
  $f^*(p) = f(p)$, if p is atomic
  $f^*(\neg\phi) = 1$, if $f^*(\phi) = 0$
          $= 0$, if $f^*(\phi) = 1$
  $f^*(\phi \rightarrow \psi) = 1$, if either $f^*(\phi) = 0$ or $f^*(\psi) = 1$
              $= 0$, if both $f^*(\phi) = 1$ and $f^*(\psi) = 0$
  $f^*(\phi \& \psi) = 1$, if both $f^*(\phi) = 1$ and $f^*(\psi) = 1$
           $= 0$, if either $f^*(\phi) = 0$ or $f^*(\psi) = 0$
  $f^*(\phi \vee \psi) = 1$, if either $f^*(\phi) = 1$ or $f^*(\psi) = 1$
           $= 0$, if both $f^*(\phi) = 0$ and $f^*(\psi) = 0$
  $f^*(\phi \leftrightarrow \psi) = 1$, if $f^*(\phi) = f^*(\psi)$
           $= 0$, if $f^*(\phi) \neq f^*(\psi)$

This definition of f* is completely compositional, in the intuitive sense of that notion; it is furthermore inductive in the sense currently under consideration. One defines f* applied to any formula in terms of how it is applied to the parts of that formula. Now, it seems completely clear that we could replace the very last clause of that definition by the following clause:

$$f^* (\phi \leftrightarrow \psi) = f^* ((\phi \rightarrow \psi) \& (\psi \rightarrow \phi))$$

Here we have defined the f* when applied to a certain category of formulas (the $\leftrightarrow$ formulas), in terms of something entirely different—in terms of an entirely different formula that has only a very tenuous relationship, syntactically speaking, to the $\leftrightarrow$ formula. (Recall that they were all primitive connectives). Still we all know that this is a correct definition, and that it will work. This new definition, as can be seen, is non-compositional. It defines the $\leftrightarrow$ in terms of things that are not part of the double arrow. Similarly, it is not inductive in the sense of defining things on the basis of parts.

It is this picture of semantics that I wish to urge upon the reader. A semantic evaluation, in general, can bring to play all kinds of facts, all kinds of information: it could bring in context, it could bring in inferences, it could bring in world knowledge to evaluate an expression, where these facts, etc. are not part of the meanings of the parts of the expression (and they are furthermore not dictated by the "method of combination" used to construct the expression). So long as this evaluation is always grounded, or perhaps more weakly, that it's grounded in the cases in which we actually employ it, then this will serve just as well as any compositional analysis. And as I have argued before, it is more in accord with the facts of language. It allows for ambiguity and it allows for synonymy, unlike semantic compositionality.

12   Why do people cling to compositionality?

In closing, I think that the apparent distaste that's manifested in the world of semantics for any denial of the Principle of Semantic Compositionality is due to a combination of father worship and disgust at certain theorists. The fact of the matter is that a certain group of us all admired the rigor, the clarity, and tough-mindedness that surrounded the initial appearance of Montague grammar. And didn't we all sneer at those who had logic anxiety. And, when we look at the loud voices of non-compositionality in the wider profession, we find a number of researchers who are opposed to doing anything with rigor, to doing anything tough-mindedly. And we say to ourselves that we would never want to be identified with them. And so we continue to hold on to the Principle of Semantic Compositionality. But these are not worthy reasons to adopt the Principle. Once it is recognized that what we really want is to avoid these other people's commitment to anti-formalism, and we recognize that this is separable from their opposition to compositionality, then I think that any fear of being mistaken for one of these anti-theoretical, flaky researchers will subside. That, together with giving up not our love but rather our blind adulation of Father Montague, will help us cheerfully embrace non-compositionality for the obvious truth that it is.

AFTERTHOUGHTS 2000

Afterthought on the warm and fuzzy feeling that compositionality gives us

In the years since this paper was completed (in 1993), I have come to appreciate that certain of the things I took for granted just were not true. One of these concerns is my presumption that the Principle of Compositionality gives everyone a "warm and fuzzy feeling," that it has gotten generally "good press," and that it is the methodological framework in which (almost) everyone works. Much of my then-belief had to do with the sort of framework within which I myself had done most of my work: I was simply unaware of the extent to which there were forces of non-compositionality in the profession.

Fodor and Lepore (1992: 7) put forward the claim that there are

> two great traditions in philosophy of language. The atomistic tradition proceeds from the likes of the British empiricists, via such of the pragmatists as Peirce and James. . . . The contemporary representatives of this tradition are mostly model theorists, behaviorists, and informational semanticists. Whereas people in this tradition think that the semantic properties of a symbol are determined solely by its relations to things in the nonlinguistic world, people in the second tradition think that the semantic properties of a symbol are determined, at least in part, by its role in a language. . . . This second tradition proceeds from the likes of the structuralists in linguistics and the Fregeans in philosophy. Its contemporary representatives are legion. They include Quine, Davidson, Lewis, Dennett, Block, Devitt, Putnam, Rorty, and Sellars among philosophers; *almost* everybody in AI and cognitive psychology; and it may be that they include absolutely everybody who writes literary criticism in French.

So apparently there are legions of writers on language who are in the second tradition. These theorists are characterized by Fodor and Lepore as "semantic holists." And according to the characterization given by Fodor and Lepore elsewhere in their book, this anti-atomism makes them be anti-compositionalists.

Well, though I confess to ignorance of the extent of holism in philosophy of language, I do not think the proposed oppositions are quite right. For, the version of "semantic grounding" that I advocated at the end of my paper seems to be completely non-holistic—indeed, it appears to be totally atomistic in any ordinary sense of the word. Yet it is not compositional in even the most basic sense of the word, much less in any of the more sophisticated senses, such as those requiring "systematicity" in addition to functionality of meaning composition.

It seems to me to be a better characterization of the "grand trends" in philosophy of language to say that the holists are committed to "contextuality"—the view that there is something importantly contributed *by context* to the meaning of a "whole" (e.g., to a sentence) which is not contributed by that context to the meanings of its "parts" (e.g., to the words). Specifically, these theorists commonly say, perhaps echoing a Wittgensteinian theme (or maybe a Fregean theme), that "words have meaning only in the context of a sentence."[10]

For sure, it is not at all clear what sort of semantic theory such theorists might have in mind. Could they really believe that the fundamental unit of meaning is the sentence? And therefore that the basic thing that is learned is a sentence? And that the meanings of component words are only learned afterwards, by considering *all* the sentences that the words occur in and determining what that word's contribution is to the meaning of *each* of these sentences? If this is what is meant, then certainly the "semantic groundedness" is not such a theory. It has been remarked many, many times (perhaps starting with Frege 1963[1923]) that such a theory could not really provide an account of how it is that people learn how to produce and understand infinitely many sentences. (The Arguments from Understanding and Learning mentioned in the paper above.)[11]

Afterthought on compositionality in other fields

In the preceding article, I concentrated on the concept of compositionality within the semantics of natural language and did not attend to the debate as it was carried out in other arenas, both other arenas within philosophy (such as philosophy of mind, epistemology, social/political philosophy, and philosophy of science) and other arenas that are manifested in different academic fields (such as the various social sciences, the medical sciences, education, and quantum mechanics). The two "grand trends" also manifest themselves in each of these fields. One gets the feeling, when reading the methodological dicta of authors in these fields, that the entire academic world can be divided into two types: "atomists" vs. "holists," although sometimes they use "individualism" vs. "collectivism" (or "socialism"). In this wider field of view, the debate can be seen as either methodological or as substantive. In its methodological guise the debate is over the "direction of explanation," while in its substantive guise the debate concerns whether there are complex entities that are not "reducible" to simple entities.

I did not intend to be talking about these other fields in the preceding text, and it is certainly difficult to see how the argument from synonymy or the argument from ambiguity might be applied to them. Nonetheless, there are certain morals that could perhaps be gleaned from the general discussion in my paper. It seems to me that many of the justifications given by holists in these other fields for their complex entities mirror the types of reasons I canvassed at the beginning of my paper for disbelieving compositionality. Arguments such as "you can't find '&' in any of the parts but it is in the whole" finds a cousin in "you can't find a commander-in-chief when you simply consider people as a group of individuals, but there is one when you have a nation" and in "no individual has a duty to pay corporate tax, yet the corporation has such a duty." Just as with the philosophy of language case, I think these theorists simply are not making use of the resources that are available in a compositional, atomistic, individualistic theory. But I will leave it to others to defend that view.

However, a variant on this type of argument about the power of compositional theories has become commonplace in the literature of philosophy of mind, thanks to Jerry Fodor and Zenon Pylyshyn (for example, see Fodor and Pylyshyn 1988; but it occurs in many of their other works also, both the jointly-authored ones and the singly-authored ones). One should imagine a holistic "connectionist" being asked to consider, for example, the complex thought of a brown cow and then asked to compare it to the complex thought of a brown hat. We might ask the connectionist: Is there anything at all that is common to these two thoughts? The natural answer is "yes," even if they aren't willing to say that it is brown-ness that is common, since they would like to hold that it is instead some complex vector of activation of neural units. But then, so the Fodor-Pylyshyn argument goes, the thought was compositionally structured after all. A non-compositional, "holistic" theory of thought holds that there are some properties of complex thoughts that are not present in the subparts of that complex thought. But the Fodor-Pylyshyn argument, constructed by considering similarities between different complex ideas, seems to show that there are no such properties.

I don't here want to pass a final judgment either on holistic theories of the mind or on this Fodor-Pylyshyn argument, but it does seem to me that the holists are not taking seriously enough the power of what a compositional theory can do. As far as I can see, their only way to evade the force of the Fodor-Pylyshyn argument is by making each complex idea independent of other complex ideas, so that there is "nothing in common" between any two ideas. There would be nothing in the brown cow idea that is common to the brown hat idea, and, indeed, nothing in common with either of them and the ideas of brown or of hat or of cow. Each idea is an independent and unanalyzable entity. Presumably, then, each idea would have to be learned independently, and whatever relations hold between two ideas is not a matter of how the ideas are structured. This seems as implausible here as the similar idea that each sentence was learned by itself and independently of separate knowledge of its parts. Something akin to the Arguments from Learning and Understandability ought to apply to such a conception.

Afterthoughts on Strong vs. Weak Compositionality

In works written by more linguistically sophisticated theorists, there is often a distinction drawn between saying that compositionality entails that the meaning of some whole is a function of its *immediate* components vs. is a function (possibly) of the parts of (the parts of . . .) these components. This second outlook on the topic of compositionality is clearest when one views sentences (and other syntactic elements) as being described by structural trees. A sentence S might be made from the components NP and VP; NP might itself be made from a DET and an N'; an N' might be made from an N and a RELS; a VP might be made from a V and an NP; and so on. In such a theory one might wonder whether compositionality should be a theory wherein the meaning of a whole (e.g., an S) is a function of the meanings of the NP and VP that "immediately" make it up (plus the mode of combination that was used) or a theory where the function that gives the meaning of S might also use the meaning of the N which partially made up the meaning of the N' which partially made up the meaning of the NP. This distinction was mentioned in Partee (1984) and expressed in Larson and Segal (1995) as saying that the compositionality is "strictly local" if the meaning function for a whole can appeal only to the meanings of that whole's immediate constituents. They also wish to make a restriction (called being "purely interpretive") on the type of function that can combine the meanings of these immediate constituents to form the meaning of the whole: such functions "interpret structure given by the syntax, and they interpret *only structure given by the syntax*. They never introduce structure of their own." Larson and Segal encapsulate the view that they argue for throughout their book as "Strong compositionality: $\mathcal{R}$ is a possible semantic rule for a human natural language only if $\mathcal{R}$ is strictly local and purely interpretive."

Unlike the challenges from holists that I mentioned in the previous sections, we have here a desire to strengthen compositionality.[12] Whereas before I charged that holists were not giving enough credit to compositional theories and incorrectly assumed that such theories could not accommodate &'s or commanders-in-chief as features of the whole, even though they were not features of any component, here we find the claim that compositional theories have too much descriptive power in the abstract and that we should restrict them in one way or another. In particular, we are urged to consider only some of the functions that put the simple parts together to form the whole.

There are two parts to the Larson/Segal recommendation: (a) that composition functions not be allowed to "see into" the meanings of the parts of immediate parts ("strictly local"), and (b) that the composition functions not be allowed to "introduce structure" that is not already in the parts ("purely interpretive"). Although they show in their book that many linguistic phenomena can be adequately described by strictly local and purely interpretive methods, I am not sure whether this really counts as evidence that "all possible human languages" have these features. But I don't wish to discuss that here. I will instead point out two apparent facts concerning their "strong compositionality," and leave it to others to discuss the topic further.

With regards to "strictly local" condition, it is not obvious to me that compositionality ever really did hold otherwise. In the general case, after all, if x is a part of y and y is a part of z, then there is surely a sense in which x is a part of z and that therefore the properties of z are perhaps best described by a function on x's. In the case of language, there is an independent notion of "part" given by the syntax, and therefore there may be a sense in which a real difference emerges between "local" and "arbitrarily deep" senses of compositionality. Consider, for example, the case of the sentence *Sheep are either brown or white*. If the meaning of *be brown* is something like a set of possible worlds in which something has the property of being brown, and similarly for *be white*, and so therefore the VP *are either brown or white* is the union of these two sets, then if the meaning of *sheep* is a name of a kind, the only meaning that is available under the "strictly local" interpretation is where either sheep are brown or sheep are white. The idea is that in a "strictly local" interpretation we are only given some set of possible worlds for the interpretation of the VP. We are not given the information that they came into existence as a union of two other sets. Yet it is that information that is needed in order to get the meaning that allows for the possibility that some sheep are brown and others white, but that they are of one or the other color.

Of course, it is not all that clear in detail how a "non-strictly-local" interpretation will handle such cases, either. But it does seem that some access is needed to the manner in which the meanings of the immediate parts were constructed. I believe, as do Larson and Segal, that the abstract conception of compositionality allows for this sort of access. But I am less sanguine than they as to whether it can be dispensed with.

The second manner in which Larson and Segal wish to strengthen the notion of compositionality is to make it "purely interpretive." It is easy to read more into this restriction than they are really calling for. Of course, it is absolutely necessary that the compositional function be able to refer to the "way the parts are put together" in addition to merely the parts themselves, for else there would be no difference in meaning between *Cats chase mice* and *Mice chase cats*. And it is because the compositional function can "add material" to the meaning of the parts in its construction of the meaning of the whole that allows it to assign a different meaning to these two wholes. So it is obvious that a compositional meaning function will need to have the ability to "add material." Larson and Segal claim that they want it to "interpret only structure given by the syntax and never introduce structure of its own," and apparently they would like it to be sensitive to the structure in the *cat-and-mouse* examples. But if so, it is very unclear just what is being ruled out. In the beginning it appeared as if we were being told that we could not introduce any structure. But now it merely seems that we cannot introduce any new *syntactic* structure. Whoever thought otherwise, since the compositional meaning function is a function from meanings (of parts) to *meanings* (of wholes)? (Answer: those in the GB framework where all this "semantic processing" really is happening in the syntax. The claim here is that when new [syntactic] structures in LF are produced from old [syntactic] structures by some LF-rules, these rules should not be allowed to create any syntactic structure that does not already appear in the old structures.) The fact that Larson and Segal can meaningfully make the "strong compositionality" claim in their theory shows just how removed this application is from more ordinary applications of semantic compositionality. They are talking about whether a certain subpart of syntax can be given a "compositional account" of a certain sort. Although their application of compositionality is interesting, it is not to be contrasted with semantic compositionality. It is, instead, a kind of syntactic compositionality.

Afterthoughts concerning compositionality as "merely a methodological matter"

A certain strand in discussions of semantic compositionality has concerned itself with the question of whether or not the Principle is "an empirical matter." The idea is this. If it can be proved that *any* non-compositional semantics of a language could be rewritten as an equivalent semantics which was compositional, then the constraint of compositionality would be vacuous: it could always be satisfied, and therefore there would be no empirical import to the constraint. Instead, the principle would be "methodological" and "not substantive." Over the years various theorists have announced formal proofs that are relevant in one way or another to this claim. Such a proof has been given by Janssen (1983), and this moral was drawn from it by certain other authors (although Janssen himself apparently does not agree with this moral in Janssen 1997), and other proofs with much the same import can be found in van Benthem (1984) and Zadrozny (1994).

There is not much to disagree with in these proofs themselves. What has been challenged is whether this conclusion about the lack of empirical import of compositionality really follows from the formal proofs. It is the current consensus of the literature that it does not follow. In the best discussion of the formal proofs,[13] Westerståhl (1998) argues that the proofs either (a) allow one to freely alter the syntactic structure of the language under construction so as to find a compositional semantics for the language given this new syntactic structure, or (b) allow one to vary the semantics of the lexical items freely, or (c) generate something that is not really a semantics. Pelletier (2000) follows up the "Argument from Ambiguity" mentioned in the current paper to show one presupposition that is made in certain of these formal proofs, and he argues that it is simply a question-begging assumption in favor of compositionality.

When one thinks about it, the question of what it might mean "to have the same semantics but in a compositional form" is not at all clear. Certainly not *every* item of the language can simultaneously be of the same syntactic type as before and have the same semantic value as before, or else the result would continue to be non-compositional. So obviously *some* changes will need to be made. But it would not be correct to change the syntactic description of the language (would it?), since then we would be giving a compositional semantics for some *different* language. If we decide to hold the syntax fixed, then the issue is which of the semantic values will be allowed to change. It seems to me that it simply wouldn't count as "the same semantics" if the values of the Sentences were allowed to change. Surely these must be the same values in both semantics for there to be any plausibility to the claim that one semantics has been "converted into" a compositional semantics (wouldn't it?). I have less confidence in requiring that the new semantics assign the same value to lexical items as the original semantics did, although this would seem quite plausible to many.

Given this understanding of what "the same semantics" means, the requirements for any relevant formal proof become more clear: without changing the syntax of the language (or perhaps, without changing any of the syntactic categories of the language), convert an arbitrary semantic theory for that language into an "equivalent" one which is compositional. To be equivalent, the two semantic theories must both assign the same values to the lexical items, and they must assign the same values to the Sentences. (In other words, they can differ only in the values that are assigned to non-terminal symbols other than Sentence).

This has not yet been proved. Indeed, I doubt if it has even been attempted. It seems on the surface very unlikely to be true; and therefore it seems very unlikely that the Principle of Semantic Compositionality is (merely) "a methodological principle with no empirical import."

AFTERTHOUGHTS 2004

In the time since the last afterthoughts were written (2000), I have become aware of a new direction in the formal study of compositionality. Wilfrid Hodges has written a series of papers that are relevant to this, but the two most cited ones are Hodges (1998, 2001). The outlook taken in these works has been adopted by many researchers, but as of this writing mostly unpublished (see, however, Werning 2003). I have seen unpublished work of Dag Westerståhl and Tim Fernando, to name but two. Hodges's work brings some new ideas into the discussion:

> A language is *Husserlian* if all synonymous expressions belong to the same grammatical categories. (That is, if α and β are synonymous expressions of the language, then in any linguistic context in which α occurs, one could substitute β for α and retain meaningfulness.)

> A language has *full abstraction* if for any two non-synonymous expressions α and β which are in the same semantic category, there are sentences that are identical except that one contains α where the other contains β and the two sentences differ in truth value.

The idea in the latter case is that every non-synonymous pair of (grammatically equivalent) terms have some pair of sentences that "witness" or "testify to" their non-synonymy. Hodges proves a number of results about the relationships that hold between languages that are Husserlian and certain conceptions of compositionality. And the following very interesting theorem is proved:

> HODGES'S THEOREM. Given a language with grammar G, let X be a cofinal subset of the set of all grammatical terms of G. Then, if μ is a compositional and Husserlian meaning function, there is (up to isomorphism) exactly one total Husserlian and compositional extension of μ.

For the details of the relevant background notions one should consult Hodges (2001) or Werning (2003). The upshot of the theorem, however, is that if one already has a meaning function for some subset of the expressions of the language (e.g., maybe the NPs and VPs) such that every basic expression of the language is a syntactic part of some member of this subset, then there is only one extension of this meaning function to the entire language. This is quite a challenging theorem for those who might argue against compositionality, for it puts much of the burden onto the property of being Husserlian and removes it from compositionality. Certainly much further work needs to be done to fully understand this new algebraic perspective.

Notes

1. The Principle is often stated incorrectly. Although their intent is to express what I've given in the text, many writers use the phrase "is a function of the meaning of its parts." They intend to say that the meanings of the parts actually take a role, indeed the *only* role, in determining the meaning of the whole. However, it is infelicitous to use the phrase "is a function of" to express this. Rather, what we should say

is "is *only* a function of." Otherwise we could allow the function to invoke other items than the meanings of the parts, and we might allow the meaning of the parts to appear vacuously as mere "dummy arguments" of the function. The intent of the Principle is that the meanings of the parts are *real arguments* of the function that determines the meaning of the whole. (Another question that arises as to whether the function is to be total; that is, whether *every* meaning of parts can give rise to a meaning of wholes. It seems pretty clear that this is implausible, and that it is intended that this function be partial. The issue of partiality will not concern us in this paper.)

2. The Principle is often said to trace back to Frege, and indeed many textbooks call the Principle of Semantic Compositionality "Frege's Principle." However, it is extraordinarily difficult to find the Principle in Frege. As Cresswell (1973: 75fn) says, "it is more of a tribute to the general tenor of his views on the analysis of language" that we attribute the Principle to him. It seems to me, though, that even this much is false; for what we find in Frege, rather than the Principle of Semantic Compositionality, is instead the *Principle of Contextuality*. This latter principle can be found in Frege's earlier writings (namely Frege 1950[1884]) and it says "it is only in the context of a sentence that a word has meaning." It is rather difficult to see how this sympathy can be combined with the Principle of Semantic Compositionality, although various writers (e.g., Dummett 1973) have attempted to do so. On a separate occasion I hope to trace the real history of the Principle of Semantic Compositionality, as well as Frege's role in this history. [See further comments in note 10 below.]

3. This is a point argued for by Zadrozny (1992).

4. I shall not attribute any of these arguments to anyone in particular. If I were to do so, I would have to be much more circumspect in my comments than I care to be. Careful research would find all of them in the literature however. (But I *am* pleased to acknowledge taking examples from Hirst 1987, and I agree with most of what he has to say about them.)

5. This argument is elaborated at more detail in Pelletier (1994b), and of course one should consult Mates (1952).

6. In Pelletier (1994b) I used similar arguments to show that the Principle of Semantic Compositionality is also inconsistent with phrasal synonymy and with lexical synonymy.

7. Actually, the argument need not be stated in terms of an infinite set of sentences, as Grandy (1990) has pointed out, the argument seems to work even if we just presume a hugely large but finite set of sentences.

8. In fact, Tarski's favorite way of defining these notions is not so well known—it depends on the notion of cylindrical algebras, and in these the notions *are* defined compositionally. (Thanks to David Israel for pointing this out to me.) But as I say, the traditional account attributed to Tarski, where 'satisfaction' is taken as the primitive notion, is not a compositional definition of 'truth.'

9. Once again, let me remark on what I mean by an ambiguous sentence here. It is where one and the same syntactic structure, using identical basic parts, can have two or more different meanings. This is different from sentences like *Visiting professors can be fun*, which arguably has two different syntactic analyses. With two different syntactic analyses, of course, a compositional theory can assign two different meanings. But what I mean here is a sentence that is *not* syntactically ambiguous but is nonetheless semantically ambiguous without the ambiguity being traceable to any lexical item.

10. In note 2 of this article I said that at some future date I hoped to trace the history of the notion of (semantic) compositionality. One central place to look, or so tradition says, is Frege. In Pelletier (2001) I examine the extent to which Frege is committed to semantic compositionality and to semantic contextuality, and I come to the conclusion that neither notion can be attributed to him in the sense that the terms are used today. Or if one of them (compositionality, especially) can be, then it is very much a background concept that is not at all central in his thinking. In this regard, one should also consult Janssen (2001).

11. On a yet further-in-the-future occasion, I hope to trace the origins of the Arguments from Understanding and Learning.

12. Or do I mean 'weaken'? The point is that fewer phenomena will be described as "features of the parts plus their mode of combination."

13. Other discussions, sometimes about different aspects of the proofs, can be found in Kazmi and Pelletier (1998), Dever (1999), and Pelletier (2000).

10

BRENDAN S. GILLON

Ambiguity, Indeterminacy, Deixis, and Vagueness

Evidence and Theory

1 Introduction

The concepts of ambiguity, indeterminacy, deixis, and vagueness are fundamental to linguistic theory in general and to semantic theory in particular. Yet linguists have made surprisingly little effort to understand them. And while philosophers have paid a great deal of attention to the concepts of deixis and vagueness, they have rather neglected those of ambiguity and indeterminacy. This essay takes a step in the direction of redressing this neglect. In particular, I seek not only to delineate each concept and to distinguish them clearly from one another but also to improve our understanding of what empirical evidence warrants their ascription to expressions of a language.

2 Ambiguity

Of the four concepts, certainly ambiguity is the one invoked most commonly in analyzing data pertaining to syntax and semantics. Yet it is not a concept for which either linguists or philosophers have a clear understanding. (See Gillon 1990b for discussion.) Aside from Kooij (1971), the little attention paid to this concept has been devoted almost exclusively to the task of devising tests for it. For example, tests have been proposed and critically discussed in Zwicky and Sadock (1975) and in Cruse (1986, pp. 54–68). However, neither of these two important works nor any other work discussing or using tests for ambiguity (e.g., Pustejovsky 1995b; Copestake and Briscoe 1995) have attempted to explain how the tests proposed or discussed in fact work. But what insight is gained from the declaration that something is a test, if no explanation is given of why the proposed test is indeed a test of what it purports to test.

A test, in essence, establishes a privileged prima facie link between observation, or evidence, on the one hand and theory on the other. Evidence in linguistics ultimately comprises speaker

This is an original chapter for this volume.

judgments. Thus, tests for ambiguity can be divided according to the kinds of judgments needed. Some use truth value judgments; others judgments of synonymy; still others judgments of antonymy; and others again judgments of acceptability. At the same time, these judgments, which are taken as prima facie evidence of ambiguity, are so taken on the basis of certain theoretical assumptions. In this section, I review the various tests found in the linguistic literature and render explicit the theoretical assumptions that underlie them.

2.1 Truth and ambiguity

To understand what ambiguity is and how to test for it, let us first understand in what the clearest case of ambiguity—namely, amphiboly, or structural ambiguity—consists and how it is tested for. Consider the sentence:

(1.0)   Bill saw a man with a telescope.

Next, contemplate the following state of affairs: Bill is a boy, and Fred is a man. Bill saw Fred. Fred possesses no telescope. Bill used a telescope to see Fred. With respect to such a state of affairs, the sentence in (1.0) can be judged to be true at one moment and judged to be otherwise at another.

The susceptibility of the sentence in (1.0) to give rise to alternate judgments of truth and of a lack thereof obtains for other states of affairs as well. Consider a state of affairs just like the one specified above, except Fred was in possession of a telescope and Bill saw Fred with his naked eyes.

It is important to stress that the sentence is not being judged both to be true and to be otherwise with respect to one and the same state of affairs at one and the same moment. Rather, there are distinct judgments, each evaluating the truth of the sentence differently. As noted almost fifty years ago by Hockett (1954, §3.1), the experience is similar to that of the perception of a Necker cube: one does not perceive it simultaneously from the perspective where its top forward corner is slightly tilted down and from the perspective of its bottom forward corner slightly tilted upward, rather one perceives it first from one perspective and then from the other (Figure 10.1). The same holds for the ambiguous sentence in (1.0). One does not judge it simultaneously to be true and to be otherwise with respect to the state of affairs specified, rather one judges it first to be true with respect to the state of affairs and then to be otherwise with respect to the very same state of affairs.

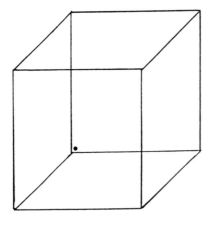

FIGURE 10.1 Necker cube: Look at the dot. Is it located in the lower left rear or in the lower left front?

What is the reason for these alternate acts of differing judgments of truth value? The sentence in (1.0) has two constituent structures: one in which the prepositional phrase *with a telescope* is a constituent of the noun phrase *a man with a telescope*, and another in which it is not. The difference in the constituent structures is made evident by labeled bracketings:

(1.1)   Bill [$_{VP}$ saw [$_{NP}$ a man] [$_{PP}$ with a telescope]]
(1.2)   Bill [$_{VP}$ saw [$_{NP}$ a man [$_{PP}$ with a telescope]]]

A *labeled bracketing*, or its notational equivalent, a *phrase marker*,[1] assigns to an expression a set of pairs of brackets, one of each pair of which is annotated with a (syntactic) label. Each pair of labeled brackets identifies a constituent of an expression, and the nesting among the pairs of labeled brackets reflects the relation of constituency that obtains among the expression's various constituents. This nesting forms what is known as a *partial order*. The partial order has a *greatest element*—namely, the constituent corresponding to the pair of labeled brackets enclosing the entire expression. It also has *minimal elements*—namely, those constituents that correspond to the expressions enclosed within a pair of brackets that enclose no other pairs of bracket: roughly, the words comprised in the entire expression.

The labeled brackets assigned to the sentence in (1.0) correlate with the difference in the truth value judgments reported above. With respect to the first state of affairs, the sentence in (1.0) is true relative to the labeled bracketing assigned in (1.1), and it is not true relative to the one assigned in (1.2). With respect to the second state of affairs, the sentence is not true relative to the labeled bracketing assigned in (1.1), and it is true relative to the one assigned in (1.2).

Of course, these constituent structures shown by the labeled bracketings are not made up ad hoc. Elementary English grammar recognizes that a prepositional phrase can serve as a modifier to a verb, thereby forming a constituent which is sister to the verb it modifies, as shown in (2.1), and that a prepositional phrase can serve as a modifier to a noun, thereby forming a constituent which is sister to the noun it modifies, as shown in (2.2):

(2.1)   Bill [$_{VP}$ watched [$_{PP}$ with a telescope]]
(2.2)   [$_{NP}$ A man [$_{PP}$ with a telescope]] [$_{VP}$ was watched]

What we have, then, is an observation on the one hand—namely that the sentence in (1.0) is judged both to be true and not to be true with respect to a specified state of affairs—and a specific theoretical fact on the other, which, together with a number of very general theoretical assumptions, explains the observation. One assumption, which can be traced back to the known inception of theoretical study of language—back to Pāṇini, the great Sanskrit grammarian of ancient India (c. 4th century BC)—is that each sentence can be analyzed into *minimal constituents* and that the sense of each minimal constituent contributes to the sense of the entire sentence.[2] It is understood that the senses of a sentence's minimal constituents contribute to the sentence's sense through the sentence's constituent structure. A second assumption, which fits with Hockett's observation of the analogy between Gestalt perception and ambiguity, is that a sentence is construed with respect to one assignment of one sense for each minimal constituent for each act of construal. A third assumption, due to Frege and based on his distinction between sense and reference, is that sense determines reference:

ASM 1: *Pāṇini's assumption.* Each sentence can be analyzed into minimal constituents, and the sense of each minimal constituent contributes to the sense of the entire sentence (where the sentence's minimal constituents contribute to the sentence's sense through the sentence's constituent structure).

ASM 2: *Hockett's assumption.* A sentence is construed with respect to one assignment of one sense for each minimal constituent for each act of construal.

ASM 3: *Frege's assumption.* Sense determines reference.

As noted, the sentence in (1.0) can be alternately judged to be true and judged not to be true with respect to one and the same state of affairs. Now the third assumption implies that, if two sentences have the same sense, their truth conditions are the same. Thus, if one sentence is true with respect to a state of affairs and another is not true, the sentences have different senses. So, the sentence in (1.0) must have two senses. According to the first assumption, the sense of the entire sentence is determined by the combination of the senses of its minimal parts through its constituent structure. Thus, either some minimal part of the sentence in (1.0) has more than one sense, or the sentence in (1.0) accommodates more than one constituent structure. As noted, a proper contiguous part of the sentence in (1.0)—namely, *saw a man with a telescope*—accommodates two labeled bracketings: [$_{VP}$ saw [$_{NP}$ a man] [$_{PP}$ with a telescope]] and [$_{VP}$ saw [$_{NP}$ a man [$_{PP}$ with a telescope]]].

These theoretical assumptions and the syntactic facts stated can be used to explain other observations. For example, one can use them to explain the fact that the following pair of sentences can be alternately judged consistent and judged inconsistent with respect to the first state of affairs specified:

(3.1)   Bill watched a man with a telescope.
(3.2)   Bill has never used a telescope.

Availing oneself of other obvious assumptions pertaining to the nature of questions and their answers, one can also explain the fact that one can truly answer yes and truly answer no to the following question asked with respect to the state of affairs specified earlier:

(4)   Did Bill watch a man with a telescope?

And, invoking still other obvious assumptions about commands, one can also explain the fact that Bill, in the state of affairs specified, can be alternately judged to have satisfied the command in (5) and judged to have failed to have satisfied it:

(5)   Watch a man with a telescope.

What is illustrated in (1.0) is amphiboly: the situation in which one form is liable to be assigned two constituent structures. With the right choice of state of affairs, amphibolous declarative sentences often give rise to differing judgments of truth value. Nonetheless, an expression's being susceptible of alternate judgments of truth value is not a necessary condition for its being amphibolous, for an expression may be amphibolous without giving rise to alternate truth value judgments. For example, the verb phrase *watch a man with a telescope* is amphibolous but gives rise to no truth value judgments at all. Even amphibolous declarative sentences that are liable to being either true or false can turn out to give rise to but one truth value judgment:

(6)   If Bill saw a man with a telescope, then Bill saw a man.

Here, the protasis entails the apodosis, no matter which of the two constituent structures the former has. Hence, the sentence is judged only to be true. Simple lexical replacements of the words in (1.0) give rise to other sentences which can be judged true one moment and not be judged true another with respect to one and the same state of affairs:

(7.1)   Mary struck a friend with a telescope.
(7.2)   Fred presented his guest with a cane.

Consider, however, another sentence obtained from the example in (1.0) by lexical replacement.

(8.0)   Bill struck a man with a beard.

This substitution yields the following distinct labeled bracketings corresponding to those found in (1.1) and (1.2), respectively:

(8.1)   Bill [$_{VP}$ struck [$_{NP}$ a man [$_{PP}$ with a beard]]]
(8.2)   Bill [$_{VP}$ struck [$_{NP}$ a man] [$_{PP}$ with a beard]]

Clearly, any state of affairs in which a man who has a beard is struck by someone named *Bill* renders the sentence in (8.0) true. Such a judgment is made relative to the sentence's being assigned the labeled bracketing in (8.1). However, the sentence in (8.0) need not be judged true in every such state of affairs, for it is possible to judge the sentence false relative to its being assigned the labeled bracketing in (8.2), provided that the person in the state of affairs named *Bill* does not use a beard as a weapon.

What is not so easy to do is to imagine a state of affairs in which the sentence in (8.0) is true relative to the constituent structure given in (8.2). After all, one does not typically use a beard as a weapon to strike someone else. Nonetheless, such a state of affairs is not impossible. Imagine that someone named *Bill* has a fake beard. In a fit of frustration, he strikes someone else with it. Clearly, the sentence in (8.0) is true with respect to such a state of affairs and it is so by dint of its being assigned the labeled bracketing in (8.2). Now, any state of affairs which is of the former kind but not of the latter kind renders the sentence in (8.0) true by dint of being assigned the labeled bracketing in (8.1) and false by dint of being assigned the one in (8.2).

Not only may the manifestation of amphiboly in sentences liable to being alternately judged to be true and judged not to be true be hampered by a speaker's beliefs about the world, be they implicit or explicit, it may also be inhibited by the grammar of the sentence. Consider this sentence:

(9)   The mother of the girl and the boy left.

This sentence is amphibolous:

(9.1)   [$_{NP}$ The mother [$_{PP}$ of [$_{NP}$ [$_{NP}$ the girl] and [$_{NP}$ the boy]]]] left.
(9.2)   [$_{NP}$ [$_{NP}$ The mother [$_{PP}$ of [$_{NP}$ the girl]]] and [$_{NP}$ the boy]] left.

and it can alternately be judged true and untrue with respect to one and the same state of affairs. The alternate truth value judgments correspond to whether the subject noun phrase is analyzed as singular or as plural.

However, once the verb in (9) is changed from the simple past tense to the present progressive, it is no longer possible to use the state of affairs adduced to show the amphiboly of (9) to obtain alternate truth value judgments with respect to either of the following sentences:

(10.1)   The mother of the girl and the boy are leaving.
(10.2)   The mother of the girl and the boy is leaving.

The reason is clear: only one of the two constituent structures assigned to the subject noun phrase in the sentence in (9) is compatible with the grammaticality of either sentence.

The attentive reader may have noticed the somewhat cumbersome phrasing of the test for ambiguity: namely, that a sentence can be alternately judged to be true and judged not to be true. Indeed, you may have wondered why the test was not formulated more simply as a sentence's being alternately judged true and judged false. The reason is that falsity is, in the mind of most speakers, a stronger notion than that of not being true. Consider the following sentences:

(11.1) Tokyo is the capital of Canada.
(11.2) Every circle is square.
(11.3) Truth is green.
(11.4) Sincerity admires Brutus.

No one would judge any of these sentences true. But many would judge the second not false but absurd. And many would judge the last two as nonsensical, rather than as either false or absurd. Moreover, speakers who do not judge these sentences as simply false often disagree among themselves as to which are false and which absurd, or which are absurd and which nonsensical. It is better, then, to have a test requiring of speakers a simpler judgment, and thereby having a better chance of reflecting any agreement which there might be among them, than to have a test requiring subtle judgment with respect to a possibly specious difference, and thereby risking introducing spurious disagreement.

So far, I have concentrated on amphiboly—the case in which an expression can be assigned more than one labeled bracketing. I now turn to so-called lexical ambiguity. The remainder of this section shows that lexical ambiguity is just a special case of amphiboly: it is the case where an expression can be assigned more than one labeled bracketing, where a labeled bracketing is the limiting one comprising a single node and its label.

To see how this is so, an important distinction is invoked: the one between labeled bracketings and expressions. An expression is a phonic or graphic form: the former has acoustic properties, and the latter spatial ones. (See Lyons 1977, vol. 1, ch. 3.3, for discussion.) A labeled bracketing is a mathematical structure: it has neither acoustic nor spatial properties, though the notation used to express it does. A labeled bracketing is an abstract syntactic entity, and so are, a fortiori, its terminal nodes and their associated labels. These labels cannot be identified with their corresponding expressions.

To see why such an identification is wrong, consider the expression *found*. As the following sentence, adapted from Lyons (1995, p. 56), shows, *found* is ambiguous for it is liable both to being judged true and to being judged untrue:

(12.0) They found hospitals.

These alternate truth value judgments provide evidence that the expression in (12.0) is ambiguous. By Frege's assumption (ASM 3), the sentence in (12.0) has two senses. Unlike the sentence in (1.0), the sentence in (12.0) is not to be assigned two constituent structures, since the nonminimal constituents are the same. Therefore, it must contain a minimal constituent that has two senses.

This conclusion is confirmed by independent morphological considerations which make clear that the word form *found* is both the perfect form of the verb *to find* and the present form of the verb *to found*. (See Lyons 1977, vol. 1, ch. 1.5, for discussion of word form.) Clearly, this morphosyntactic information must be encoded into the labeled bracketing. To see how this is done, we must understand something about the notation used to display labeled bracketings.

It is standard in the use of notation to use only as much as is necessary to make clear the relevant structure being shown. In the preceding examples, our attention was confined to some or other part of the constituent structure assigned to an expression. Thus, the lexical labels of the minimal constituents were not included in the annotation. In fact, the symbol used for the minimal constituent is just the symbol for the graphic expression of the word corresponding to it. While this practice is notationally convenient, it is theoretically misleading, for a labeled bracketing is an abstract syntactic entity; and while it is assigned to a phonic or graphic expression, it does not itself contain a phonic or graphic expression.

The terminal node of a labeled bracketing is assigned a specification of the minimal constituent's phonological value, syntactic category, morphosyntactic features (if any) and sense.[3] Turning to the sentence in (12.0), let us consider what its labeled bracketing must be. A first approximation appears in (12.1):

(12.1) $[_S [_{NP} \text{they}] [_{VP} \text{found} [_{NP} \text{hospitals}]]]$
(12.2) $[_S [_{NP} \text{they}] [_{VP} \text{find}_{perf} [_{NP} \text{hospitals}]]]$
(12.3) $[_S [_{NP} \text{they}] [_{VP} \text{found}_{pres} [_{NP} \text{hospitals}]]]$

They, then, is short-hand for a complex of symbols that must indicate the phonological value of *they*, its syntactic category (namely, that it is a pronoun), its morphosyntactic features (third-person plural), and some specification of its sense. *Hospitals* is shorthand for the phonological value, its syntactic category (count noun), its morphosyntactic features (plural), and its sense. *Found* in (12.1), however, is shorthand for two specifications; both specifications include the same phonological value and the same syntactic category (namely, a verb), but they specify different morphosyntactic features for different verbs: one is the third-person plural form of the present tense of the verb *to find*; the other is the third-person plural form of the past tense of the verb *to found*. This last difference can be signaled in the fashion displayed in (12.2) and (12.3), respectively, showing that the labeled bracketing displayed in (12.1) is, in fact, two labeled bracketings that differ precisely with respect to the label assigned to the minimal verbal constituent. Moreover, since these minimal constituents together with their labels constitute a minimal labeled bracketing, the expression, or word form, *found* is ambiguous in accordance with the definition of ambiguity proposed.

In the case of the word form *found*, the theory of morphology and syntax, on the one hand, and the observations of truth value judgments, on the other, are congruent. However, this is not always so. Lexical ambiguity may be posited on the basis of observation alone—say, for example, on the basis of truth value judgments—without any grounding for it in syntactic or morphological theory. Conversely, lexical ambiguity may be posited on the basis of morphological or syntactic theory without any simple confirmation from alternate truth value judgments.

Consider, for example, the noun *pen* in this sentence, where a man named *Bill* owns a ballpoint but owns no enclosures:

(13) Bill owns a pen.

The sentence in (13) can be alternately judged true and judged false with respect to the state of affairs specified. Yet, neither morphology nor syntax furnishes a theoretical basis for distinguishing two lexemes. Nonetheless, it is standard lexicographical practice to furnish the word form *pen* with two entries, one having the sense of a small enclosure for animals and the other having the sense of an instrument for writing or drawing with ink or similar fluid (sv. *Webster's Third International*). This lexicographic practice is uncontroversial when the word forms have distinct etymologies, for it can be given a clear historical basis. In an earlier stage of the language, such words had distinguishable phonological forms, which came to coincide as a result of the vagaries of phonological change.

Conversely, there are cases where the same word form is thought to belong to different lexical categories, yet in any sentence in which it occurs it fails to give rise to alternate truth value judgments. The word form *but* may be such an example. This word form serves not only as a coordinating conjunction but also as a preposition (in the sense of *except*) and an adverb (in the sense of *only*):

(14.1)   Bill stayed *but* Mary left.
(14.2)   Everyone stayed *but* Bill.
              Everyone stayed *except* Bill.
(14.3)   Bill was here *but* five minutes ago.
              Bill was here *only* five minutes ago.

Notice that the word form *but* is liable to three distinct specifications, which differ at least with respect to their lexical classification. This word form, too, is ambiguous.

But simple words are not the only minimal constituents to exhibit ambiguity; affixes of various kinds do so as well. Thus, the English suffix *-er* is ambiguous between one that applies to an adjective to yield the comparative form of the adjective (e.g., *tall-er*) and another that applies to a verb stem to yield an agentive noun (e.g., *sing-er*). Also, the English prefix *un-* is ambiguous between one that applies to an adjective to yield a privative adjective (e.g., *un-happy*) and another that applies to a verb denoting an action to yield a verb denoting the action done in reverse (e.g., *un-tie*). The positing of ambiguity in these cases is rarely, if ever, grounded in observations such as alternate truth value judgments. Again, the difference in their specification is necessary and sufficient for their being ambiguous.

Of course, not all words belonging to more than one word class fail to give rise to sentence forms liable to alternate truth value judgments. Consider, for example, the word *duck*, which is both a noun, denoting a kind of swimming bird, and a verb, denoting an abrupt lowering of the head. In fact, one can find a sentence form in which *duck* is used both as a noun and a verb and a state of affairs in which the sentence (15.0) can be alternately judged to be true and judged not to be true:

(15.0)   Bill saw her duck. (adapted from Zwicky and Sadock 1975, p. 3)

(15.1)   Bill saw Mary duck.

(15.2)   Bill saw Mary's duck.

As the sentences in (15.1) and (15.2) show, the amphiboly of the sentence (15.0) depends on the lexical ambiguity of both *duck* and *her*, which is the form both of the personal pronoun *she* (compare *him*) and the form of the possessive pronoun (compare *his*).

Perhaps an even more striking example of how several lexical ambiguities can induce an amphibolous sentence is this example from French (due to Riegel et al. 1994):

(16.0)   La petite brise la glace.
(16.1)   [NP la petite brise] [VP [NP la] glace]
              The light breeze chills her.
(16.2)   [NP la petite] [VP brise [NP la glace]]
              The little one breaks the ice.

The sentence in (16.0) has four lexical forms, each belonging to two lexical classes: *petite* is both an adjective and a noun; *brise* is both a noun and a verb; *la* is both a pronoun and a determiner; and *glace* is both a verb and a noun.

The fundamental idea underlying the definition of ambiguity proposed above, and restated here more formally, is not new. It has been the cornerstone of its treatment by both logically and linguistically minded semanticists.

DEFINITION 1. *Ambiguity*. An expression is ambiguous if and only if it can be assigned at least two distinct labeled bracketings.

On the one hand, linguistically minded semanticists, such as Katz (1972, chs. 1.5–1.6; 1977, p. 93), hold ambiguity to be a relation between many semantic representations and an expression corresponding to them in natural language. On the other hand, logically minded semanticists, such as Cresswell (1973, pp. 91–92; 1988, pp. 19–20) and Montague (1970a §7; 1970b §2), hold ambiguity to be a relation beween many syntactically unambiguous formulae of an intensional logic and an expression corresponding to them in natural language. The preceding DEF 1 shares with the view of each of these two kinds of semanticist the idea that ambiguity is a many-one relation; however, it differs from their views as to what sort of entity renders an expression ambiguous. According to DEF 1, the entities are neither semantic representations nor formulae in a canonical logic, but labeled bracketings.

The definition of ambiguity (DEF 1) has two assets. First, it is completely general, for it encompasses both amphiboly and lexical ambiguity. Indeed, lexical ambiguity is just the limiting case of amphiboly: for it is the case where the same word form can be assigned two distinct minimal labeled bracketings—that is, labeled bracketings comprised of one node and a label. Second, the definition obviates a problem that threatens the very possibility of providing an account of truth value judgments of those sentences of languages susceptible of them. The problem was first pointed out by Kathryn Parsons (1973) in connection with a proposal by Davidson (1967; 1970) to reduce a natural language's semantic theory to its truth definition, in the sense of Tarski (1956). Parsons argues that, contrary to the view initially espoused by Davidson (1967, p. 319), the lexical ambiguity of words such as *pen* cannot be ignored.

The argument, a version of which I have adapted from Lycan (1984, ch. 2.2), runs as follows. A Tarski-like truth definition for a language L will, among other things, entail, for every predicate P of the language L, a biconditional of the form:

(17)   For each x, R is true of x in L iff x Q

(where R is an expression in the metalanguage of L for the predicate P, and Q is its translation into the same metalanguage). Now, let L be English, let P designate the phonic expression *is a pen*, and let *is an enclosure* and *is a writing instrument* be translations of P into the metalanguage for English. The following are both instances of the schema in (17):

(18.1)   For each x, *is a pen* is true of x in L iff x is an enclosure.
(18.2)   For each x, *is a pen* is true of x in L iff x is a writing instrument.

It is an immediate, unwanted consequence of the biconditionals in (18) that

(19)   For each x, x is an enclosure iff x is a writing instrument.

This consequence is eliminated by letting P range, not over phonic expressions of L but over labeled bracketings for expressions of L, where, in accordance with DEF 1, the labeled bracketing to be used in (18.1) and the one to be used in (18.2) differ, inasmuch as the first contains the lexical entry for *pen* in the sense of an enclosure, while the second contains the lexical entry for *pen* in the sense of a writing instrument. This difference in labeled bracketing blocks the inference to (19), for no longer are the left-hand sides of the biconditionals in (18) the same.

Finally, amphiboly raises precisely the same problem for truth theoretic and model theoretic semantics as the one raised by lexical ambiguity. Its solution is exactly the same: to relativize the statement of truth conditions to labeled bracketings and not to expressions to which they are assigned.

In short, the definition of ambiguity (DEF 1), when coupled with the three theoretical assumptions—ASM 1, ASM 2 and ASM 3—permits one to establish a prima facie link of observation to ambiguity, for these assumptions provide an explanation of how an ambiguous expression can give rise to alternate truth value judgments used in the ambiguity test described above and more formally restated here:

ALTERNATE TRUTH VALUE JUDGMENT TEST. Let α be an expression. Let δ ( ) be an expression frame such that $\delta(\alpha)$ is a sentence liable to being judged with respect to a truth value. Let s be a state of affairs. If $\delta(\alpha)$ is alternately judged true and judged not true with respect to s, then α is prima facie ambiguous.

Moreover, the alternate truth value test furnishes merely a prima facie sufficient condition for the ambiguity of the expression being tested. The condition is merely prima facie sufficient, since, unless the expression frame used in the test is null or independently determined to be unambiguous, it is possible for the frame, and not the expression being tested, to be the source of the ambiguity and, hence, the source of the alternate truth value judgments. Put another way, the test provides a simple sufficient condition for the ambiguity of declarative sentences only. To determine what in the sentence is the source of the ambiguity requires additional theoretical assumptions about the morphosyntactic structure of the sentence and the ambiguity or nonambiguity of its minimal elements.

I turn now to other tests, or kinds of evidence, used to ascribe ambiguity to expressions of a language.

2.2   Synonymy and Ambiguity

There are five tests for ambiguity that rely on synonymy. The most common establishes that an expression is ambiguous by finding two other expressions that are synonymous with it but not with each other. For example, the verb *to put on* is judged synonymous with the verb *to don* and with the verb *to switch on*, but the latter two verbs are not judged synonymous with each other.

For ease of comparison with the other tests using synonymy, this test can be restated a little more formally, as follows:

NAIVE SYNONYMY TEST. Let α, β, and γ be expressions where α and β are judged synonymous, as well as α and γ. If β and γ are judged not to be synonymous, then α is prima facie ambiguous.

This test presumes, first, that there is such a relation as the synonymy relation and, second, that speakers are capable of judging whether or not it obtains between pairs of expressions. Only the second constitutes an assumption additional to those given in the previous section. The other follows trivially from the earlier assumption that acceptable expressions have senses and the definition of synonymy. Synonymy of expressions, as typically defined (see Carnap 1955, §5), is their having the same sense. Synonymy, then, is simply an equivalence relation over the expressions of a language. Its existence is guaranteed, since surely each expression is synonymous with itself. What is not guaranteed is that this relation is nontrivial: that is, that synonymy obtains between distinct expressions of a language:

DEFINITION 2. *Synonymy.* Expressions in a language are synonymous if and only if they have the same sense.

ASM 4. *Synonymy's nontriviality.* Expressions have distinct synonymous expressions.

ASM 5. *Synonymy's observability.* Speakers of a language can judge whether or not two of its expressions are synonymous.

I shall return to the question of whether or not the synonymy relation is nontrivial and to the assumption that speakers can judge whether or not this relation obtains later. First, however, I consider other tests for ambiguity that rely on judgments of synonymy.

A generalization of the previous test, also based on these assumptions, is anticipated by Aristotle in his *Topics* (bk. 1, ch. 15, 107a36–107b13; see also 107a3–17). It can be put into schematic form as follows:

CONTEXTUAL SYNONYMY TEST. Let α, β, and γ be three expressions. Let $\delta(\ )$ be a frame into which α, β, and γ can be grammatically substituted. Let $\delta(\alpha)$ and $\delta(\beta)$ be judged synonymous, and let $\delta(\alpha)$ and $\delta(\gamma)$ be judged synonymous. If $\delta(\beta)$ and $\delta(\gamma)$ are judged not to be synonymous, then α is prima facie ambiguous.

For example, consider the sentential frame *Bill ____ the headset* and the sentences that result from filling it with one of the three verbs mentioned in the discussion of the last test:

(20.0) Bill put on the headset. (adapted from Leech 1974, p. 78)

(20.1) Bill donned the headset.

(20.2) Bill switched on the headset.

While the first and second sentences and the first and third sentences are judged synonymous with each other, the second and third are not. One concludes, then, that the verb *put on* is ambiguous.

This test requires the nontriviality assumption and a weakened version of the synonymy observability assumption (ASM 5), for it does not require that speakers be able to judge the synonymy of constituents smaller than a sentence. However, should one decide to so restrict the assumption, it would be necessary to compensate for this weakening by invoking the three assumptions made in the previous section.

Let us see how this is so. If the sentences in (20.1) and (20.2) have different senses, yet they differ only in that one has in its constituent structure *don* where the other has *switch on*, then their difference in sense must be attributable to a difference in the senses of the two verbs. Yet the sentences in (20.1) and (20.2) are judged to have the same sense as the one in (20.0). Since all three sentences have the same constituent structure analysis, aside from which verb it contains, *switch on* and *don* must have the same sense as *put on*. Since the senses of the former two differ, the latter must have two senses.

It should be noted in passing that the ambiguity of *to put on* can be independently shown by the alternate truth value judgment test applied to the sentence in (20.0), as the reader can easily check. We now come to the third test relying on synonymy. It relies on another theoretical assumption, which dates back to Pāṇini. The assumption is that a word can impose requirements on what kinds of other expressions can occur with it. Pāṇini supplemented his grammar of Sanskrit, the *Aṣṭādhyāyi*, with a list of verbs (*dhātu-paṭha*), where are given various facts pertaining to each verb, including a specification not only of its conjugational class but also of its valency. This assumption is partially manifested by the practice of lexicographers to distinguish between transitive and intransitive verbs, and it appears in grammars based on constituent structure analysis in the practice of assigning so-called subcategorization frames to lexical items (Chomsky 1965, ch. 2 §2.3.4). A subcategorization frame is essentially a specification of a lexeme's local syntactic environment. A consequence of this is that individual lexemes carry some of the burden of accounting for syntactic ill-formedness. As a result, important simplification of the grammatical rules governing constituent structure can be achieved. Thus, for example, the unacceptability of sentences (21.1) and (21.2) is attributed, in the first instance, to the violation of the constituent formation rules of English, and in the second instance, to the violation of the subcategorization frame of the verb *to elapse*, which requires that it cannot be followed by a noun phrase:

(21.1)   *Mary may virtue the inspection.
(21.2)   *An hour may elapse the boy.

Lexemes have been thought not only to determine the syntactic categories of their neighboring constituents but also to impose values on those very same neighbors. For example, verbs impose so-called valences, or thematic roles, on some of their neighboring constituents. They are also thought to impose so-called selection restrictions. For example, they could require that a neighboring constituent denote something that is concrete or abstract, animate or inanimate. Evidence for such restrictions comes from what Gilbert Ryle (1949, p. 16) called category mistakes:

(22.1)   The boy admires Dan.
(22.2)   *The idea admires Dan.

The contrast in acceptability here is ascribed to a restriction of the verb *to admire*, which requires that the neighboring constituent (correlating with the subject position of the sentences above) denote something animate. Such restrictions are known as selection restrictions.

Underlying the foregoing is this assumption:

> ASM 6. *Lexeme's sense restriction on its neighbors.* A lexeme may require or exclude a sense otherwise associated with a neighboring expression.

This assumption, together with the assumptions of Pāṇini (ASM 1), Hockett (ASM 2), and Frege (ASM 3), gives rises to the fourth test using synonymy, which can also be traced back to Aristotle (*Topics*, bk. 1, ch. 15, 106b29–107a1).[4]

> CONTEXT-SENSITIVE SYNONYMY TEST. Let α, β, and γ be expressions. Let α and β be judged synonymous, and let α and γ be judged synonymous. Let $\delta(\ )$ be an expression frame into which α can be grammatically substituted, and let $\epsilon(\beta)$ be an expression frame into which β and γ can be grammatically substituted. If $\delta(\alpha)$ and $\epsilon(\beta)$ are judged synonymous but $\delta(\alpha)$ and $\epsilon(\gamma)$ are not, then α is prima facie ambiguous.

Consider the adjective *hard*, which has two near synonyms that are not synonyms of each other: *solid* (*Webster's Third International*: sv. 1a (1)) and *perplexing* (*Webster's Third International*: sv. 4a (1)). Consider further the expression frames *become* and the verb forming suffix *-en*. Only the sense of the first new synonym is retained when the adjective is turned into a verb by the suffixation of *-en* to yield *harden*.

		Synonym 1		Synonym 2
α:	hard	~ β:	solid	~ γ: perplexing
$\delta(\alpha)$:	hard-en	~ $\epsilon(\beta)$:	become solid	$\not\approx$ $\epsilon(\gamma)$: become perplexing

("~" is short for 'is synonymous with.') Thus, the fact that the suffix *-en*, when applied to *hard*, yields one of the two paraphrases of *hard* and not the other, is accounted for by assigning *hard* two senses and supposing that the suffix applies to the expression only under one of the senses.

Notice that, while this test provides a prima facie sufficient condition for the ascription of ambiguity to a word, it does not provide a necessary condition, for an affix may apply to a word in each of the different senses it has. Thus, for example, the English adjective *dull*, which has two senses—one sense in which it applies to minds (*Webster's Third International*: sv. 1) and

another in which it applies to blades (*Webster's Third International*: sv. 5)—can be suffixed by
-ness to yield the noun *dull-ness*, which is equally ambiguous (though *Webster's Third International* does not furnish separate entries):

		Synonym 1		Synonym 2
α:	dull	~ β:	stupid	~ γ:	blunt
$\delta(\alpha)$:	dull-ness	~ $\epsilon(\beta)$:	being stupid	~ $\epsilon(\gamma)$:	being blunt

A fourth test, similar to the second one, is one widely used in contemporary linguistics:

SYNONYMOUS FRAME TEST. Let α be an expression. Let $\delta_0(\ )$, $\delta_1(\ )$, and $\delta_2(\ )$ be expression
frames that are grammatically equivalent and which yield grammatical sentences when α is
substituted into them. Let $\delta_0(\alpha)$ and $\delta_1(\alpha)$ be judged synonymous, and let $\delta_0(\alpha)$ and $\delta_2(\alpha)$ be
judged synonymous. If $\delta_1(\alpha)$ and $\delta_2(\alpha)$ are judged not to be synonymous, then α is prima facie
ambiguous.

A crucial notion used in the statement of this test is that of grammatical equivalence. This is
intended to apply to expressions or expression frames which are related in a principled way by the
grammar and which are taken to be synonymous. In most applications of this test, the expression
frames that are grammatically equivalent are active sentence frames and their passive counterparts.

Here is an example of the use of this test taken from Chomsky (1957, ch. 7.6), where the
second two sentences below are passive counterparts of the first, yet the second two sentences
are nonsynonymous:

(23.0)   John found the boy studying in the library.
(23.1)   The boy studying in the library was found by John.
(23.2)   The boy was found studying in the library by John.

As always, it is prudent to corroborate the results of the application of a test with other evidence. Further evidence that the ambiguity lies with the verb *to find* arises from comparing the
sentence in (23.0) with other sentences just like it, except for the choice of verb. Such sentences
permit only one acceptable passive counterpart, as Chomsky notes:

(24.0)   John knew the boy studying in the library.
(24.1)   The boy studying in the library was known by John.
(24.2)   *The boy was known studying in the library by John.

We now come to the last test, which is a generalization of the previous one. It is used extensively in contemporary linguistics and it also relies on ASM 6:

CONTEXT-SENSITIVE SYNONYMOUS FRAME TEST. Let α, β, and γ be expressions. Let $\delta(\ )$ and $\epsilon(\ )$
be synonymous expression frames into which α can be grammatically substituted. Let $\delta(\alpha)$ be
judged synonymous with β and with γ. If $\epsilon(\alpha)$ is judged synonymous with β but is judged not
to be synonymous with γ, then α is prima facie ambiguous.

This test can be used to establish, for example, the ambiguity of the French verb *sentir*.

(25.1) $\delta(\alpha)$ Pierre sent la rose.
          ~ β Pierre hume la rose.

'Peter is smelling the rose.'

$\sim \gamma$ Pierre a la même odeur qu'une rose.

'Peter smells like a rose.'

(25.2) $\sim \epsilon(\alpha)$ La rose est sentie par Pierre.

$\sim \beta$ Pierre hume la rose.

$\dagger \gamma$ Pierre a la même odeur qu'une rose.

We see that the verb *sentir* is ambiguous between one sense corresponding to the verb that is liable to having both an active and a passive form, like the transitive English verb *to smell*, and another that has only an active form, like the intransitive English verb *to smell* (*like*).

All five tests set out in this section require the assumption that the synonymy relation is nontrivial (ASM 4) and that speakers are capable of judging the synonymy of distinct expressions (ASM 5).

It seems incontestable that at least some pairs of English sentences are synonymous and that speakers of English can and do so judge them; for example, the following two pairs:

(26.1)   Bill believes that Chisnau is the capital of Moldova.

(26.2)   Bill believes   Chisnau is the capital of Moldova.

(27.1)   Paul looked up the number

(27.2)   Paul looked   the number up.

Indeed, as shown, a frequent application of two of the tests requires only that active sentences and their passive counterparts be synonymous. And though this synonymy has been questioned (Ziff 1966), the evidence marshalled is unconvincing (Katz and Martin 1967).

Nonetheless, just how far one can go relying on speakers' judgments of synonymy is not clear. Consider the following pairs of sentences adapted from Leech (1974, p. 17):

(28.1)   Bill cast a stone at the police.

(28.2)   Bill chucked a stone at the cops.

Should the verbs *to chuck* and *to cast* be synonymous and the nouns *police* and *cops* also be synonymous, then the sentences in (28) should be synonymous, by Pāṇini's assumption (ASM 1). However, some have judged them not to be synonymous, claiming that the latter has an informal character which the former does not (see Nida 1949, ch. 6.1; White 1958).

While acknowledging, as one must, that the sentences in (28) evince a difference, theorists have urged that one distinguish between designative (Carnap 1956, p. 6), cognitive (Leech 1974, ch. 2), or descriptive (Lyons 1995, p. 44) sense, on the one hand, and emotive (Carnap 1956), associative (Leech 1974), or expressive (Lyons 1995, p. 44) sense on the other. As plausible as the distinction is, one is not told how this distinction is to be drawn and what kind of evidence can be used to apply it.

An alternative approach is to abandon the assumption that speakers can detect synonymy (ASM 5) and to find a test whereby the synonymy of expressions can be ascertained. An important idea contributing to this approach is one due to Mates, who suggested the following criterion:

MATES'S CRITERION OF SYNONYMY. Two expressions are synonymous in a language L if and only if they may be interchanged in each sentence in L without altering the truth value of the sentence. (Mates 1952, p. 119)

This criterion appears to be derivable from the definition of synonymy and the three theoretical assumptions mentioned in the previous section. By the definition of synonymy (DEF 2), two synonymous expressions have the same sense. By Frege's assumption (ASM 3), sense determines reference. Since interchanging expressions of the same syntactic category with the same sense preserves the constituent structure analyses and the senses of the proper constituents of the overall expression, the sense of the overall expression itself remains the same. By Pāṇini's (ASM 1) and Hockett's (ASM 2) assumptions, speakers' truth value judgments will remain the same for any two sentences that differ only by the relevant substitution.

However, this line of reasoning overlooks the fact that lexemes may impose restrictions on their neighboring constituents. Consider the two putatively synonymous English adjectives *likely* and *probable*. Even though these two adjectives belong to the same lexical category, they are not interchangeable, for although the first sentential frame permits their interchange, the second does not:

(29.1)   It is ____ that Bill will leave.
(29.2)   Bill is ____ to leave.

As the reader can observe, *likely*, and not *probable*, suits the second frame. The reason is that the former tolerates both finite clausal complements and infinite clausal complements, whereas *probable* tolerates only finite clausal complements. Put theoretically, the first adjective subcategorizes for either a finite clause or an infinite clause, whereas the second adjective subcategorizes only for a finite clause. This difference in subcategorization frames inhibits their intersubstitutability.

The obvious solution to the problem is to confine the substitution to expressions that are of the same syntactic category and impose the same kinds of syntactic categories on their neighboring constituents—that is, they must be of the same syntactic category and have the same subcategorization frames. However, once this is done, Mates's criterion can no longer be formulated as a biconditional. In general, tests cannot be formulated as biconditionals, for, as we have already seen, tests furnish only prima facie sufficient conditions of that for which they are a test.

The fact that context sensitivity curtails the scope of application of Mates's test has serious consequences for the alternative of using it, in lieu of speaker intuitions of synonymy, to enable one to use the synonymy tests for ambiguity. The problem is that some ambiguous words have one or another of their associated senses required or excluded by their co-text.

As Lyons (1995, ch. 2.3) has pointed out, the adjective *big* is ambiguous:

(30)   Teresa is Paul's big sister.

Consider this in light of the following state of affairs: Teresa is Paul's sister; she is younger than he; and Teresa is large for a woman. With respect to this state of affairs, the sentence in (30) is alternately judged to be true and judged to be not true.

Next consider the putatively synonymous English adjectives *big* and *large* (Lyons 1995, ch. 2.3). They are clearly interchangeable, preserving truth within the sentential frame *Bill has a ____ house*. There are, presumably, no circumstances under which one of the two sentences in (31) is true while the other is false:

(31.1)   Bill has a big house.
(31.2)   Bill has a large house.

Nonetheless, these adjectives are not interchangeable preserving truth in the sentence frame *Paul is my ____ brother*; that is, it is easy to specify a circumstance in which one of the following sentences is true while the other is false:

(32.1)   Paul is my big brother.
(32.2)   Paul is my large brother.

The problem is, of course, that the adjective *big* is ambiguous, having on the one hand a sense in common with the adjective *large* and on the other a sense paraphrasable by *older*, the latter occurring only when it modifies nouns denoting blood relations, as is borne out by the following pair of sentences:

(33.1)   My brother is big.
(33.2)   My brother is large.

Big and *little* are not the only adjectives in English one of whose senses requires a specific neighboring constituent. Other English adjectives include *old* and *poor* (see Bolinger 1967). Such adjectives are even more common in French. Thus, the adjectives *ancien, brave, certain, cher, dernier, different, drôle, grand, même, nouveau, pauvre, prochain, propre, sale,* and *seul*—to mention only a few—have one sense when placed in before a noun and another either when placed after or when used as in a predicate without modifying a noun (see Riegel et al. 1994, ch. 6 §4.2.2.2).

In short, Mates's test will not detect synonymy between pairs of expressions one of which is ambiguous and whose senses are either excluded or required by another expression in their co-text. In such cases, Mates's test will fail to detect synonymy and synonymy tests will thereby fail to detect ambiguity, unless, of course, one relies on the assumption that speakers can detect synonymy, in which case tests based on synonymy are only as good as the reliability of the judgments.

2.3   Antonymy and ambiguity

Antonymy is typically defined as an opposition of senses (Leech 1974, p. 90):

> DEFINITION 3. *Antonymy.* Two expressions in a language are antonymous if and only if they have opposite senses. In what, precisely, opposition consists is a question to be addressed later. For the moment, I turn to the tests based on antonymy.

Aristotle proposes several tests that rely on antonymy (*Topics*, bk. 1, ch. 15, 106a12–106b27). All of these tests require that speakers can detect antonymy:

> ASM 7. *Antonymy's observability.* Speakers of a language can judge whether or not two of its expressions are antonymous.

Only three tests using antonymy, two of which are taken directly from Aristotle, are discussed here.[5] The simplest one (*Topics*, bk. 1, ch. 15, 106a36–106b4) determines an expression to be ambiguous if some other expression can be judged to be and can be judged not to be its antonym:

> ANTONYMY GAP TEST. Let α and β be expressions. If α and β are judged antonymous and they are judged not to be antonymous, then α is prima facie ambiguous.

Thus, for example, the verb *to hate*, as Aristotle himself points out, is judged both to be an antonym of *to love*—in its sense of feeling affection (*Webster's Third International*: sv. *love* 1 vs. *hate* 1)—and is not judged to be an antonym—in its sense of copulation (*Webster's Third International*: sv. *love* 2c). Again, one can use alternate truth value judgment test to confirm this ambiguity. The sentence in (34) can be alternately judged impossible and judged true:

(34)   Bill loved Mary from a distance.

Aristotle used synonymy and antonymy to provide another test, analogous to the naive synonymy test. He observed that if a pair of antonyms for a word were not synonyms of each other, then the word in question is ambiguous in senses corresponding to the two antonyms (*Topics*, bk. 1, ch. 15, 106a9–22):

COMMONSENSE ANTONYMY TEST. Let α, β, and γ be expressions. Let α and β be judged antonymous, and let α and γ be judged antonymous. If β and γ are judged not to be synonymous, then α is prima facie ambiguous.

As Aristotle (*Topics*, bk. 1, ch. 15, 106a12–20) illustrates, the adjective *sharp*, when applied to a knife, has as its antonym *dull*, whereas when applied to a note, it has as its antonym *flat*. This test, like the naive synonymy test, naturally generalizes to a contextual test:[6]

CONTEXTUAL ANTONYMY TEST. Let α, β, and γ be expressions. Let δ( ) be a frame into which α, β, and γ can be grammatically substituted. Let δ(α) and δ(β) be judged antonymous, and let δ(α) and δ(γ) be judged antonymous. If δ(β) and δ(γ) are judged not to be synonymous, then α is prima facie ambiguous.

Consider, for example, the word *light*, which has as antonyms both *dark* and *heavy*:

(34.0)   The room was painted in a light color. (adapted from Cruse 1986, p. 55)
(34.1)   The room was painted in a dark color.
(34.2)   The room was painted in a heavy color.
(35.0)   Bill has a light teaching load this term. (adapted from Cruse 1986, p. 55)
(35.1)   *Bill has a dark teaching load this term.
(35.2)   Bill has a heavy teaching load this term.

Notice, however, that the substitution of *dark* and *heavy* for *light* in the sentence in (34.0) does not yield synonymous sentences, nor does the same substitution in the sentences in (35.0) yield synonymous sentences. (See *Webster's Third International*: sv. *light* 2 and 4.)

The reader is invited to apply this test to other adjectives—such as *fine* (*coarse* versus *large*) and *clear* (*opaque* versus *muffled*)—whose ambiguity can be revealed by it.

Notice that this ambiguity of the adjective *light* can be confirmed by the alternative truth value judgment test:

(35)   Bill's jacket is light.

After all, the preceding sentence can easily be imagined to express something true and to express something false.

Notice that, while a word's having such a contrasting pair of antonyms provides a prima facie sufficient condition for its being ambiguous, the existence of such a contrasting pair does not provide a necessary condition for ambiguity, for, as Aristotle (*Topics*, bk. 1, ch. 15, 106a23–36) points out, it is possible that an ambiguous word has an ambiguous antonym. Indeed, the English adjectives *sharp* and *dull*, like the ancient Greek words of which they are translations, are antonymic in each of two senses: not only are knives both sharp and dull, so are minds. (See *Webster's Third International*: sv. *sharp* 1a vs. 2a vs. *dull* 1 vs. 5.)

Cruse (1986, p. 56) rejects the contextual antonymy test. He correctly points out that *thin* has two antonyms, *fat* and *thick*, as shown by the following two pairs of sentences:

(36.1)   That person is a thin one.
(36.2)   That person is a fat one.

(37.1)   That tree is a thin one.
(37.2)   That tree is a thick one.

He also correctly points out that *fat* and *thick* are not synonyms. But he also denies that *thin* is ambiguous (in the pertinent respect), maintaining that "it is not illuminating to say either that *thin* is ambiguous or that its contexts restrict its meaning in mutually exclusive ways." Yet, at the same time, no less authorities than the *Webster's Third International Unabridged* (*W3*) and the *American Heritage* (*AH*) distinguish the sense of the adjective *thin* corresponding to an antonym of *fat* from a sense corresponding to an antonym of 'thick':

thin: not having a great diameter (*AH* sv. 2)

          having relatively little extent from one surface to its opposite (*W3* sv. 1a)

          measuring little in diameter (*W3* sv. 1b)

thin: being lean or slender of figure (*AH* sv. 3)

          not well fleshed: . . . not fat (*W3* sv. 3)

thick: relatively great in extent from one surface to the opposite: not thin (*AH* 1)

          being of relatively great extent from one surface to its opposite (*W3* sv. 1a)

fat: having too much fat (*AH* sv. 1)

          notable for having an unusual amount of fat (*W3* sv. 1)

Moreover, we note that *fat* is an antonym to *thin* in both of the relevant senses.

fat: being thick (*AH* sv. 7)

        well-filled out: . . . thick (*W3* sv. 2)

The preceding fits well with one's judgments that the preceding pairs of sentences are pairs of antonymous sentences.

Unlike synonymy, the existence of the relation of antonymy does not follow from the assumption of the existence of meaning. Moreover, it is not clear in what the opposition of antonymy consists. On the one hand, the opposition of antonymy is said to be exemplified by such pairs of words as *parent* and *child* or *to own* and *to belong to*. This kind of opposition is better known as *converseness*: "being a parent of" is the converse of "being a child of"; "owning" is the converse of "belonging to." However, this is not the kind of opposition that is appealed to in illustrative uses of the antonymy tests presented here. On the other hand, the opposition of antonymy is also said to be exemplified by such pairs of words as *man* and *boy*, *alive* and *dead*, and *open* and *shut*. The words in each of these pairs are not converses of one another, but contraries.

The contrariety of propositions is clear: two propositions are contrary if and only if they cannot both be true at the same time. This is not, however, what is meant by contrariety of words. One might think that two senses are contrary if and only if the expressions that carry those senses cannot both be true of the same thing at the same time. While this is true of the pairs "thick and thin" and "fat and thin," it is also true of such pairs of words as *man* and *table*, *boat* and *color*. However, the antonymy relation is thought to be stronger than the contrariety relation, for an expression's sense may have many contraries, but it is to have at most one antonym, an aspect of antonymy that is essential to the last two tests mentioned above.

The antonymy tests—in particular, the three antonymy tests set out above—are rather limited. First, they all rely on the notion of antonymy, which is not itself a very clear notion. While all three tests require the assumption that speakers can detect antonymy (ASM 6), two of them also require both the assumption that expressions have distinct synonymous expressions (ASM 4) and the assumption that speakers of a language can judge whether or not two of its expressions are synonymous (ASM 5). Finally, as with the synonymy tests, there is nothing that can be detected using the antonymy tests and cannot be detected using the alternate truth value judgment test.

2.4 Acceptability and ambiguity

Some tests for ambiguity rely on judgments of acceptability and depend on theoretical assumptions pertaining to coordination and to pronouns and ellipsis—expressions that I shall group under the heading *endophors*. I look at these tests based on the different assumptions that underlie them. First are those that make assumptions about coordination.

2.4.1 Coordination and ambiguity

As noted, lexemes may impose different subcategorization frame requirements on their neighboring constituents. Consider the verb *to load*. It has associated with it a direct object noun phrase followed by a prepositional phrase where the preposition is either *with* or *into*; however, to guarantee equivalence of acceptability, the order of the noun phrases in one subcategorization frame must be the opposite from the other, as illustrated by the fact that the complement noun phrases in the first sentences in (38) cannot be transposed nor can the ones in (39):

(38) Dan loaded a trunk with the luggage.
      *Dan loaded the luggage with a trunk.
(39) Dan loaded the luggage into a trunk.
      *Dan loaded a trunk into the luggage.

Notice that complements of the verb *to load* can be coordinated; but if they are, each coordinated sequence must have the same subcategorization frame as the other:

(40.1) Dan loaded a car with luggage and a truck with hay.
        Dan loaded luggage into a car and hay into a truck.
(40.2) ?Dan loaded a car with luggage and hay into a truck.
        ?Dan loaded luggage into a car and a truck with hay.

It is natural to assume, then, that if one sequence of constituents neighboring to a lexeme satisfies the lexeme's subcategorization frame, then all sequences coordinated with the lexeme satisfy the very same frame. Extending this idea to senses, one obtains the following assumption:

> ASM 8. *Distribution over coordinated arguments.* If one neighboring coordinated constituent satisfies a lexeme's selection restriction, then all the neighboring coordinated constituents do as well.

This, in turn, leads to the following test, which is sometimes called the *zeugma test* (e.g., Cruse 1986, p. 61):

> ARGUMENT COORDINATION TEST. Let α and β be grammatically congruent expressions. Let $\delta(\ )$ be an argument taking expression frame into which α and β can be grammatically substituted. Let $\delta(\alpha)$ and $\delta(\beta)$ be judged acceptable. If $\delta(\alpha$ and $\beta)$ is judged unacceptable, then α is prima facie ambiguous.

Here is an example of its application. Let *John* and *his driver's license* be α and β, respectively, and let *expired on Tuesday* be $\delta(\ )$. Clearly, both $\delta(\alpha)$ and $\delta(\beta)$, given in (41), are acceptable:

(41.1)   John expired on Tuesday.
(41.2)   His driver's license expired on Tuesday.

However, $\delta(\alpha$ and $\beta)$, as in (42), is unacceptable:

(42)   *John and his driver's license expired on Tuesday. (from Cruse 1986, p. 61)

The result of this test is borne out by *Webster's Third International*, which gives two senses for the verb *to expire*: one that means to breathe one's last breath, to die (sv. 1), and another that means to become void through the passage of time (sv. 2b).

The two senses of the verb *to expire* impose incompatible requirements on the denotation of the noun phrase serving as its subject. The former sense requires that whatever is denoted by the noun phrase serving as its subject be animate, and hence concrete, and the latter requires that it be nonconcrete. The analogy is clear: just as a lexeme imposes the same subcategorization frame on all its neighboring coordinated constituents, so it imposes the same selection restriction on all of its neighboring coordinated constituents.

It is useful to note that the results of the argument coordination test, illustrated with respect to the sentence in (42), are borne out by the test of alternate truth value judgments. Consider a state of affairs in which someone named *John* dies on a Tuesday. The sentence in (41.1) is judged true with respect to it. But it can also be judged as absurd or untrue. After all, how can a person become void through the passage of time?

As one might have guessed, ambiguous lexical forms with the same restrictions on their neighboring constituents escape detection by the argument coordination test. For example, the intransitive verb *to cry* is ambiguous between denoting shouting and weeping (see *Webster's Third International*: sv. 1 and 2, respectively). This is borne out by the fact that the first sentence can be alternately judged as true and as absurd or untrue (corresponding to the second and third sentences, respectively):

(43.0)   Mary cried silently in her room.
(43.1)   Mary wept silently in her room.
(43.2)   Mary shouted silently in her room.

Yet, as Lyons (1977, p. 408) points out, the following is impeccable:

(44)   Mary and Ruth cried: one was weeping profusely and the other was screaming blue murder.

Clearly, the predicate *cried* is not construed in the very same sense with respect to *Mary* and *Ruth* in (42).[7]

The inverse of the argument coordination test—which might be called the *predicate coordination test*—involves coordinated predicates. It is stated as follows:

> PREDICATE COORDINATION TEST. Let α be an expression. Let $\delta(\ )$ and $\epsilon(\ )$ be argument taking expressions, grammatically congruent frames into each of which α can be grammatically substituted. Let $\delta(\alpha)$ and $\epsilon(\alpha)$ be judged acceptable. If $(\delta$ and $\epsilon)$ (α) is judged unacceptable, then α is prima facie ambiguous.

This test is often illustrated with such common nouns as *newspaper* and *magazine*, which can denote physical objects, but also the company, or moral person, that is responsible for their production. To confirm that there is such an ambiguity, consider the following sentences:

(45.1) The newspaper fell on the floor.
(45.2) The newspaper fired the editor.

It is easy to see that each of the sentences is liable both to a plausible construal and to an absurd one.

To apply the predicate coordination test, one collapses the sentences so that there is but one subject noun phrase and one coordinated verb phrase. The resulting sentence strikes native speakers as humorous, if not odd:

(46) *The newspaper fell off the table and fired the editor.

The idea is that the verbs in the verb phrases in question impose incompatible selection restrictions on their shared subject noun phrase. The first verb phrase requires that the subject noun phrase's denotation be a physical object; the second requires that it have the capacity to make decisions. The basic sense of the noun phrase *the newspaper* satisfies the first requirement, but not the second, though the noun phrase may acquire through metonymy another sense that satisfies the second requirement. Because the noun phrase does not have one sense satisfying both requirements, the sentence in (46) is ungrammatical.

The assumption underlying the test is this:

ASM 9. *Distribution of coordinated predicates.* If two constituents are coordinated, then their corresponding sense restrictions must be simultaneously satisfied.

The subject position is not the only position with respect to which conjoined verbs may impose conflicting selection restrictions. The object can also furnish such a position:

(47) *Conrad Black established and carried the newspaper.

However, not all lexical ambiguities are detected by the predicate coordination test. Consider the noun *contract*. On the sense in which it refers to an agreement between two or more parties to do or not to do something (*Webster's Third International*: sv. 1a), what is denoted is not a physical object but a social artifact; on the sense in which it refers to a writing made by the parties to evidence the terms and conditions of a contract (*Webster's Third International*: sv. 3), it is a physical object. The first sense is pertinent to (48.1) and the second sense to (48.2). Both senses are pertinent to (48.3):

(48.1) The contract was annulled by the judge.
(48.2) The contract was torn up by Bill.
(48.3) The contract was annulled by the judge and torn up by Bill.

It is easy to check this ambiguity, for (48.1) is absurd in the sense of (48.2), and vice versa.

The example sentences given in (43) and (48) show that ASM 8 and ASM 9 are flawed. They also show that the tests based on them do not provide necessary conditions for the ascription of ambiguity. The tests, nonetheless, do seem to provide prima facie sufficient conditions for the ascription of ambiguity. Still again, however, it appears that any ambiguous expression whose ambiguity is detectable using either of the coordination tests is also detectable using the test of alternate truth value judgments.

2.4.2 Endophora and ambiguity

As stated, pronouns of various kinds and ellipsis—which go here under the heading of endophora— also have been used to test for ambiguity. Such an expression requires, for its correct construal, another expression, known as its *antecedent*, in its co-text. The idea is that the denotation of the endophoric expression is determined by its antecedent.

Endophoric expressions are construed with their antecedents roughly in two ways. The difference between the two kinds is well illustrated, to a first approximation, by the pronouns *one* and *it*. Consider this minimal pair:

(49.1)   Paul bought *a car* and Ed bought *it* too.
(49.2)   Paul bought *a car* and Ed bought *one* too.

(Endophoric expressions and their antecedents are put in italics.) The first sentence is not true in the state of affairs that Paul bought only one car and Ed bought only one car and the cars bought are different. The second sentence is true in that state of affairs. This difference can be reflected by the following paraphrases:

(50.1)   Paul bought a car and Ed too bought the car Paul bought.
(50.2)   Paul bought a car and Ed bought a car too.

The difference between these two kinds of endophora has sometimes been formulated, in Grinder and Postal (1971, pp. 269–272 and fn. 1). In the former case, the denotation of the antecedent determines the denotation of the endophor. Thus, in the first sentence, the denotation of the pronoun *it* is identical with the denotation of its antecedent *car*. In the latter case, the sense of the antecedent determines the sense of the endophor. Thus, in the second sentence, the sense of the pronoun *one* is the sense of its antecedent *car*. Let us state these two assumptions:

> ASM 10. *Identity of denotation.* The denotation of the endophoric expression is identical with the denotation of its antecedent.

> ASM 11. *Identity of sense.* The sense of the endophoric expression is identical with the sense of its antecedent.

Endophoric expressions whose mode of interpretation falls under the first assumption include the third-person personal pronouns *he*, *she*, and *it*, together with their plural and oblique case versions, as well as the relative pronouns; those whose mode of interpretation falls under the second assumption include the third-person personal pronoun *one*, the adverb *so*, the adjective *such*, and various forms of ellipsis. In the remainder of this section, I discuss how endophoric expressions of the former kind have been exploited to test for ambiguity.

Consider the ambiguous noun *ball*, which, insofar as it denotes a spherical object for play, may be something that can be burst and cannot be something that can be attended, but which, insofar as it denotes a social event, is something that can be attended and is not something that can be burst. The following sentences are odd:

(51.1)   *Reed attended *a ball which* Dan burst.
(51.2)   *Reed attended *a ball*. Dan burst *it*.

The reason is clear: the sense of the antecedent noun phrase, which is compatible with the sense of the verb *to attend*, determines a denotation none of whose members serve as second coordinates in the set of ordered pairs that constitute the denotation of the verb *to burst*; in other words, the set of things attended is disjoint from the set of things that burst.

Of course, this ambiguity can be equally well established by the alternate truth value judgments. After all, it is easy to imagine a situation with respect to which the following sentence can be judged alternately true and untrue:

(52)   Cinderella was given a ball.

The test underlying this illustration can be more generally stated as follows:

> IDENTICAL DENOTATION TEST. Let α be an expression and β be an endophoric expression satisfying ASM 10. Let δ( ) and ε( ) be grammatically congruent expression frames into which α and β can, respectively, be grammatically substituted. Let δ(α) ε(β) be a grammatical sentence or a grammatical sequence of sentences where α is the antecedent of β. If δ(α) ε(β) is judged unacceptable, then α is prima facie ambiguous.

Unfortunately, not all ambiguities are detected by this test. Consider again the ambiguous noun *contract*:

(53.1)   Paul signed *the contract which* Lee later broke.
(53.2)   Paul signed *the contract*. Lee later broke *it*.

It occurs perfectly felicitously in clauses linked by a pronoun where the things that satisfy the argument positions of the verbs linked by the endophora belong to disjoint sets. In this case, the set of things signed is disjoint from the set of things breached. Another long-recognized ambiguity that escapes detection by the identical denotation test is the ambiguity whereby a word can denote its own form:[8]

(54)   Bill did not know what *a platypus* is. So he looked *it* up in a dictionary.

Still another ambiguity that can evade detection by identical denotation test is sometimes referred to as the type token ambiguity. Consider the noun phrase *this car*. It can refer to the particular car in question, as well as to its make—the former being the token or instance, the latter the type or kind. Thus, the question in (55) is liable to two answers, depending on whether the noun phrase *this car* is taken to denote the make or the particular instance of the make:

(55)   A: Is this car the one you want?
        B: Yes. (It is the make I want.)
        B: No. (It is not the token I want.)

Notice that this ambiguity slips by unnoticed in the following sentences, where the noun phrase denotes a make of car and an instance of it, while the pronoun denotes an instance of the make and the make, respectively:

(56.1)   *This car* is the best-selling car on the lot. Take *it* for a drive.
(56.2)   Take *this car* for a drive. *It* is the best-selling car on the lot.

Several of the preceding sentences show a flaw in ASM 10 and, hence, show that the tests based on it are not necessary conditions for an expression's ambiguity. They do, nonetheless, appear to furnish prima facie sufficient conditions. As always, tests using alternate truth value judgments fill the lacunae.

To summarize, none of the tests discussed here provides a necessary condition for ambiguity, for it is always possible to find an ambiguous expression that fails one or other of the tests. At best, the tests canvassed provide prima facie sufficient conditions. Among the tests, the test using alternate truth value judgments seems to be broadest one, for we observed that all the ambiguous expressions that failed the tests relying on synonymy, antonymy, coordination, and endophora are nonetheless detectable by the test using alternate truth value judgments.

Moreover, the alternate truth value judgment test relies on the fewest assumptions, and the ones it does rely on are the least controversial.

3   Ambiguity versus indeterminacy

Indeterminacy is to be carefully distinguished from ambiguity. To see how they differ, I begin with an example of indeterminacy from outside of linguistics. Consider Hilbert's axiomatization of Euclidean geometry. Among its fifteen axioms is the so-called Playfair Axiom: for any straight line *m* and for any point *A* which is not on *m*, *A* is on at most one straight line that does not intersect *m*. Many propositions rendered determinately true or false under the fifteen axioms become indeterminate once the Playfair Axiom is removed. For example, under the Playfair Axiom, it is deducible that the sum of the interior angles of a triangle is two right angles. Once this axiom is dropped, it is indeterminate whether or not the sum of the interior angles is two right angles. It is compatible with these taken jointly, without the parallel postulate, for the sum of the angles of a triangle to be less than or greater than two right angles.

Turning to indeterminacy in linguistics, consider the following pair of sentences:

(57.1)   Sandy is a child.
(57.2)   Sandy is a girl.

The first sentence determines that the person referred to by *Sandy* is human, but it does not determine whether or not the person referred to is male or female. In other words, whether or not the person referred to by the first sentence is a non-adult human will determine its truth or falsity, but whether or not the person referred to is male or female will not. In contrast, whether or not the person referred to by the second sentence is male or female will determine its truth or falsity. The first sentence is indeterminate as to whether the person referred to by the subject noun phrase is male or female, the second sentence is not.

The question arises: how does indeterminacy differ from ambiguity? Consider the following sentence:

(58)   Sandy broke a nail.

This sentence is indeterminate with respect to whether or not what Sandy broke is long or short. If Sandy broke something that can be called a *nail*, then the sentence in (58) is true, regardless of whether the thing broken is long or short. And if Sandy did not break anything that can be called a *nail*, then the sentence is false, regardless of whether anything that can be called a nail is long or short. More particularly, the noun *nail* is indeterminate with respect to the longness or shortness of the things in its denotation.

It might be thought that the sentence in (58) is indeterminate with respect to whether what Sandy broke is an ungual or a fastener. If Sandy had broken an ungual, and not a fastener, the sentence in (58) can be alternately judged true and untrue. And if Sandy had broken a fastener, and not an ungual, the sentence in (58) can again be alternately judged true and untrue.

While alternate truth value judgments can distinguish ambiguity from indeterminacy, the most commonly used tests to distinguish them are those based on endophoric elements whose interpretation falls under ASM 11—that is, endophoric elements such as the third-person personal pronoun *one* and the adverb *so* used with the auxiliary verb *to do* (Lakoff 1970d), but all forms of ellipsis—verb phrasal, verbal (so-called gapping) and nominal. Recall that the assumption is that the sense of these endophoric elements is the sense of their antecedents. The test, then, can be stated as follows:

IDENTICAL SENSE TEST. Let α be an expression and β be an endophoric expression satisfying ASM 11. Let $\delta(\ )$ and $\epsilon(\ )$ be expression frames into which α and β, respectively, can be grammatically substituted. Let $\delta(\alpha)\,\epsilon(\beta)$ be a grammatical sentence or a grammatical sequence of sentences where α is the antecedent of β. If, in the expression $\delta(\alpha)\,\epsilon(\beta)$, α and β are judged synonymous, then α is prima facie ambiguous.

Let us illustrate the use of the test with a case of verb phrase ellipsis:

(59)   Sue *wore a light coat* and *so* did Mary.

According to ASM 11, the sense of *so* in the second clause must be the same as the sense of the antecedent verb phrase *wore a light coat* in the first. If *light* in the first clause is construed as light in weight, then the verb phrase of the first clause is construed as ascribing the wearing of a coat light in weight and the *so* in the second clause is also construed as ascribing the wearing of a coat light in weight. Alternatively, if *light* has the sense of light in color, both clauses are construed as ascribing the wearing of a coat light in color. Equivalently, what is not possible is that one clause ascribes the wearing of a coat light in color while the other ascribes the wearing of a coat light in weight.

These judgments contrast with those for sentences such as the following:

(60)   Sue *has a child* and *so* does Mary.

Here, it is perfectly possible to construe *a child* as being a boy in the one case and a girl in the other. The idea is that were *child* to have two senses, one synonymous with *boy* and another synonymous with *girl*, then the two clauses would have to be construed in a parallel fashion. But, they are not, so it is not the case that two senses are involved. The word *child* is indeterminate with respect to these two construals.

Similar tests can be performed with nominal and verbal ellipsis:

(61)   *Dan's *ball* was well attended and Reed's ____ was deflated.
(62)   *Julia *declined* a cocktail and Iris ____ an irregular Latin noun. (adapted from Zwicky and Sadock 1975, p. 20)

As carried out above, these tests require that one be able to judge that an endophoric expression and its antecedent have the same sense; that is to say, it requires the synonymy observability assumption (ASM 5). But as discussion of the examples given by Lakoff (1970d) show, this is not always an easy matter. Lakoff's claim is that certain English verbs, such as *to hit*, *to knock*, and *to cut*, are ambiguous between a sense in which the action denoted is purposely performed by the agent and a sense in which the action is accidentally performed. He supports this claim by appealing to the verb phrase ellipsis test:

(63)   John *hit the wall* and *so* did Pete.

According to Lakoff, either both clauses are understood with the hitting of the wall being a purposeful action carried out by whatever is denoted by the subject noun phrases, or both are understood with the hitting of the wall being an accidental action. What is not an available construal is that the hitting be purposeful in one case and accidental in the other.

These judgments are disputed by Catlin and Catlin (1972). They point out that the sentence in (63) could very well express a state of affairs in which John accidentally hits the wall, while Pete does so in purposeful imitation of John. Though these judgments are not questioned by

Zwicky and Sadock (1975, pp. 31–34), they do question the conclusion arrived at by Catlin and Catlin. It is worth noting, however, that the ambiguity which Lakoff alleges is not borne out by the test of alternate judgments of truth value. In particular, it seems that, with respect to a state of affairs in which the person denoted by *John* hits a wall, be it purposely or otherwise, the following sentence cannot be alternately judged to be true and judged not to be true, regardless of whether the action performed by the denotation of the subject was purposeful or accidental:

(64)   John hit the wall.

Perhaps it is possible to dispense with judgments of synonymity with respect to the verb phrase and the endophoric expression and to have recourse only to truth value judgments with respect to the two clauses. Consider, again, the sentence in (60). It is judged true with respect to any state of affairs in which Mary has a son or a daughter and Sue has a son or a daughter. Is the sentence in (59) judged true with respect to any state of affairs in which Mary wore a coat (be it light in color or light in weight) and Sue wore a coat (be it light in color or light in weight)? In particular, is the sentence judged false with respect to a state of affairs in which Sue wore a coat light in color but heavy in weight and Mary wore a coat light in weight but dark in color? Though some speakers might have some hesitation to judge the sentence true with respect to such a state of affairs, even they do not assert that it is false. However, it follows from ASM 11 that the endophor and its antecedent have the same sense; in turn this entails that the sentences in (57) should be judged false with respect to the state of affairs described.

As it happens, there are clear judgments to show that the assumption ASM 11 is wrong. It is well known that many English verbs—for example, the verb *to melt*—are ambiguous between an intransitive form with an inchoative sense and a transitive form with a causative sense. Yet Bouton (1969) noted that the first clause in the following sentences contains the verb used in its causative sense, while the second clause is construed as though the antecedent were used in its inchoative sense:

(65.1)   Sylvia tried to *melt* the iron, but it would not ____.
(65.2)   Though Sylvia tried to *melt* the iron, it did not ____.

Such sentences are clearly counterexamples to ASM 11.

Moreover, further evidence militating against ASM 11 comes from the following adaptation of the example due to Lyons given earlier:

(66)   Mary *cried* and *so* did Ruth: one was weeping profusely and the other was screaming blue murder.

Indeed, the same can be done for the sentence in (57):

(67)   Mary is *wearing a light coat* and *so* is Sue. However, Mary's is light in color, while Sue's is light in weight.

The correct assumption regarding the interpretation of the pronoun *one*, the adverb *so*, and the various forms of ellipsis is indeed the traditional assumption that was first set out by Dionysius of Thrax (c. 100 BC)—namely, that the endophoric element is a stand in, or *pro-noun*, for its antecedent:[9]

> ASM 12. *Stand-in*. The denotation of the endophoric expression is determined by whatever sense can be ascribed to its antecedent.

Still, the contrast remains: for all the states of affairs specified for the sentence in (60), it is un-equivocally judged true, whereas for some of the states of affairs specified for the sentence in (59), it is judged true only hesitatingly. Moreover, the contrasts in the judgments of synonymy between these sentences also remain. How, then, are these contrasts in judgments to be accounted for?

To begin, notice that sentence (68.1), which is obtained from the one in (59) by replacing its sole endophoric expression with a copy of its antecedent, gives rise, for each state of affairs speci-fied earlier, to the same truth value judgment. Similar observations apply to the sentences in (61) and (62) and their counterparts in (68.2) and (68.3):

(68.1)   Sue wore a light coat and Mary wore a light coat.
(68.2)   Dan's ball was well attended and Reed's ball was deflated.
(68.3)   Julia declined a cocktail and Iris declined an irregular Latin noun. (from Zwicky and Sadock 1975, p. 20)

It seems, then, that the same expressions are construed in the same way. Moreover, whatever principle underlies this is clearly a pragmatic one, since the sameness of construals can always be overridden without pain of contradiction, as illustrated by the sentences in (61) and (62).

The example sentences in (62) and (63) show that ASM 11 is false and, as well, that the tests based on it are not necessary conditions for an expression's ambiguity. Still, they do appear to provide prima facie sufficient conditions. Once again, tests using alternate truth value judgments detect cases of ambiguity which escape the detection by the tests discussed in this section.

Having distinguished ambiguity from indeterminacy, let us distinguish ambiguity from deixis.

4   Deixis and ambiguity

As Quine (1960, pp. 131–132 §27) once warned, one should not confuse a sentence's variation in truth value, resulting from ambiguity, with a sentence's variation in truth value, resulting from deixis. Consider, for example, the following sentence:

(69)   Brutus stabbed Julius Caesar.

If uttered anytime after 44 BC, it is true, while if uttered anytime before, it is false. But this varia-tion in truth value is not the same as the variation in truth value occasioned by ambiguity. In the case of ambiguity, a sentence is alternately judged as true and judged as untrue with respect to a fixed state of affairs and with respect to one and the same occasion of use. In the case of deixis, a sentence is alternately judged as true and judged as untrue with respect to a fixed state of af-fairs and with respect to different occasions of use.

It is useful, then, to distinguish the state of affairs with respect to which a sentence is judged true or false and the situation in which the sentence is used. Every sentence uttered is uttered by someone in a situation, or context. Let us call the situation in which a sentence is uttered its *setting*. An utterance's setting is centered about the person uttering the utterance. Its setting includes the time and location of not only the utterer but also other people in their relationship to him. Each language imposes a frame of reference on the setting to which various words or morphemes in the language are sensitive (see Lyons 1977, ch. 14.1 and ch. 15). The best known are the first- and second-person personal pronouns (*I, me, we, us, you*); the demonstrative adjectives and pronouns (*this, that, these, those*); and various temporal and locative adverbs, such as *yesterday, today, tomorrow, here*, and *there*. (See Fillmore 1997 and Levinson 1983, among many other works, for extensive discussion.)

In example (69), it is relatively easy to distinguish state of affairs by dint of which the sentence is either true or false from the setting in which it is uttered. Thus, the state of affairs that renders the sentence in (69) true is Brutus's assassination of Julius Caesar, which took place in 44 BC. Its setting might be a Roman history class or an English literature class taught at McGill University in 2000 AD.

However, the state of affairs expressed by a sentence and its setting need not always be distinct. Consider a person who has just finished exercising strenuously. He or she says:

(70)   I am hot.

The speaker is both in the setting of the utterance of the sentence in (70) and in the state of affairs it expresses. Nonetheless, even in this case, the two are distinguishable. Imagine a state of affairs in which Bill is hot. Imagine further that Bill utters the sentence in (70). Finally, imagine two people with exactly the same knowledge of this state of affairs, except one knows who uttered the sentence in (70) and the other does not. The former person is in a position to know that an utterance of the sentence in (70) is true, the latter person is not.

To see better how ambiguity and deixis can be distinguished, let us consider the notorious ambiguity of the directional nouns *left* and *right*. As we shall see, these nouns are ambiguous between a deictic sense and a nondeictic sense.

Suppose a speaker is looking at three people. Suppose, for the sake of easy exposition, these three people are in athletic jerseys and their names are printed on both the front and the back of their jerseys. Suppose further that the three people are aligned as follows:

BACK

Peter   Mary   John

FRONT

Now consider the sentence.

(71)   Peter is to the right of Mary.

And consider two different settings: one in which the speaker is facing the people (aligned as depicted) and one in which the speaker is looking at the backs of the people (aligned as depicted). In the first setting, the sentence in (71) can be judged alternately true and false; in the second setting, it can only be judged true. The contrast in truth value judgments with respect to the first setting shows that the sentence is ambiguous, while the contrast in truth value judgments arising from a change in setting shows that one of the senses contains a deictic element.

Let us see how this is so. The distinction between right and left is made to distinguish two sides of the human body. The word *right*, like the word *left*, designates a side of the body of the person denoted by the person named by the noun that is the object of the preposition *of*. This sense is nondeictic: that is, it does not depend on the setting for its interpretation. Indeed, it is invariant across settings. It is the sense whereby one judges the sentence in (71) true, whether the speaker is in front of the three people facing them or in back of them looking at their backs.

At the same time, the noun *right* also has a deictic sense—that is, a sense whose correct interpretation requires knowledge of the setting. On this sense, the word *right* is interpreted with respect to the orientation of the speaker with respect to the people being talked about. Under this sense, one must be able to identify the speaker in the setting in order to know which side of Mary is meant. A change in the orientation brings about a change in the truth value of the sentence. It is this sense that accounts for the judgment of false with respect to the first setting and true with respect to the second.

It is easy to garner further evidence for this explanation. Imagine that, in the picture, there appears, instead of Mary, a tree:

(72)   Peter is to the right of the tree.

This sentence can only be judged false with respect to the new state of affairs and the first setting and true with respect to new state of affairs and the second setting. With respect to this new state of affairs, only the deictic sense of the noun *right* remains salient, since trees fail to have a right and a left.

In sum, then, alternate truth value judgments to determine ambiguity rely on a fixed state of affairs and a fixed setting, whereas alternate truth value judgments to determine deixis rely on a change in setting.

Notice that this test does not provide a necessary condition for deixis. It is possible to construct sentences that are replete with indexical elements but whose truth value never changes, no matter how the setting is changed:

(73)   I am here now.

The deictic elements conspire, as it were, to guarantee that every utterance of the sentence in (73) is always a true one. (For a model theoretic treatment of various deictic lexemes, see Kaplan [1977: this volume, Chapter 37], among others.)

5   Ambiguity versus vagueness

A sentence is vague just in case it is a sentence for which there are states of affairs with respect to which one judges it clearly true and clearly false, but for which there are also states of affairs with respect to which one cannot judge it to be true or to be false, yet the failure of such a judgment is not attributable to ignorance on the part of the person judging. This definition of vagueness, which follows fairly closely one given by C. S. Peirce (1901), is nicely illustrated by terms that are featured in so-called *sōritēs* paradoxes.

Sōritēs paradoxes are so called by virtue of one of the paradoxes whose earliest known formulator is Eubulides of Miletus. The paradox features a heap, or *sōros*. Consider the following sequence of collections: the first comprises one grain; the second two grains adjacent to one another; the third three grains, one on top of two which are adjacent; etc. Now, consider the sentence

(74)   This is a heap.

Is this sentence true when *this* denotes the first collection? Surely the answer is no. Is it possible for the sentence to be false when *this* refers to a collection of n grains and to be true when it refers to a collection of $n + 1$? Surely again, the answer is no. It follows, paradoxically, that this sentence is false, even when *this* denotes a collection of a myriad of grains.

Eubulides of Miletus formulated another paradox of the same ilk using the word *bald*. Similar paradoxes can be formulated with countless other words. However, as observed by Alston (1964, pp. 87–93), vagueness is not limited to sentences with terms for which there is a linear ordering of their potential denotations. Alston illustrates such cases with the noun *religion*. (Compare *poem* as set out by Stevenson 1957.) Indeed, Wittgenstein's famous discussion of the word *game* (1953, art. 66–67) can be taken as a further illustration of this point (Hospers 1953, ch. 1.3.2). In fact, Waismann's (1945) discussion of the "open texture" of expressions can be understood as making attributing vagueness to a very large number of words, including scientifically used words. (Compare Alston 1964, pp. 93–95.)

Vagueness is distinct both from ambiguity (Black 1952, ch. 10.2; Quine 1960, §26–27) and from indeterminacy (Alston 1964, p. 85), though this is not always recognized (Pinkal 1983). There is, of course, a certain superficial similarity between ambiguity and vagueness, as well as between ambiguity and indeterminacy.

Ambiguous sentences and vague sentences are liable to giving rise to conflicting truth value judgments, but the reasons for these conflicting judgments are different. Vagueness, by its very definition, results from uncertainty, whereas ambiguity does not. A sentence is vague insofar as one is uncertain as to whether or not it is true with respect to a given state of affairs, and no further information about it will relieve the uncertainty. In contrast, ambiguity does not, by its very definition, result in uncertainty. To be sure, on hearing an ambiguous sentence, one may be uncertain with respect to what its utterer intends. But, once one judges an ambiguous sentence to be true and not to be true with respect to a given state of affairs, there need be no uncertainty with respect to these judgments.

Finally, indeterminacy should not be confused with vagueness. Though both indeterminate sentences and vague sentences give rise to uncertainty, what one is uncertain about is different. In the case of a vague sentence, one is uncertain of its truth relative to a specified state of affairs. No further knowledge of the state of affairs relieves the uncertainty. In the case of an indeterminate sentence, one need not be uncertain about the truth of the sentence relative to a specified state of affairs, though one may be uncertain of the truth of another sentence. Thus, told the first sentence in (75), one may be uncertain as to the truth or falsity of the second:

(75.1)   Mary has a child.
(75.2)   Mary has a boy.

6   Conclusion

In the foregoing, I have identified four fundamental semantic concepts: ambiguity, indeterminacy, deixis, and vagueness. I have distinguished each from the others. In addition, I have canvassed a number of tests, seeking on the one hand to ascertain the theoretical assumptions underlying them and on the other to set out their limits. It was shown that tests differ in the richness of the assumptions they rely on. Indeed, it was shown that some tests are without any theoretical foundation. It was also stressed that no test provides necessary conditions for the existence of that for which it is a test. At best, tests provide prima facie sufficient conditions.

Notes

The work reported in this essay was generously supported by a grant from the Social Sciences and Humanities Research Council (no. 410–98–0463). I am particularly grateful to Alan Bale, David Barner, Steven Davis, Eugene Joseph, David Nicolas, Gabriel Poliquin, and Benjamin Shaer for reading and discussing various drafts. Versions of this paper were presented to the McGill Cognitive Science Seminar, LACUS (Linguistic Association of Canada and the United States) at its 2001 meeting in Montreal, Canada, and the Conference on Ambiguity and Semantic Indeterminacy held August 22–25, 2001, at Florianopolis (Universidade Federal de Santa Catarina), Brazil. The paper has benefited as well from questions by members of these audiences.

1. Labeled bracketings and phrase markers are in one-to-one correspondence.

2. The relevant rule is A 1.2.45, that is, rule 45 of Chapter 2 of Book I of his *Aṣṭādhyāyi*. See Bronkhorst 1998 for discussion.

3. The precise content of this specification is a matter of controversy. Nonetheless, all agree that it contains at least what has been indicated above.

4. This test has been dubbed the *paronymy* test (Cruse 1986, p. 55).

5. Aristotle (*Topics*, bk. 1, ch. 15, 106a9–106b28) sets out six tests. I discuss only those two that are most relevant to the aim of this essay.

6. See Cruse (1986, p. 55) for a different formulation.

7. Notice that such sentences form an exception to Hockett's assumption.

8. This ambiguity was recognized by Pāṇini and exploited in his grammar of Sanskrit, *Aṣṭādhyāyi* (see Brough 1951; Staal 1965b). Medieval Europeans, like William of Sherwood, Peter of Spain, and Walter Burleigh, identified it with the distinction between *suppositio materialis* and *suppositio formalis*. See Lyons 1977, ch. 1.2 and 1.3, for a very careful discussion.

9. This is, in fact, the descriptive generalization captured by the device of deletion used by Grinder and Postal (1971), as well as other generative semanticists.

APPROACHES

11

DAVID LEWIS

General Semantics

I Introduction

On the hypothesis that all natural or artificial languages of interest to us can be given transformational grammars of a certain not-very-special sort, it becomes possible to give very simple general answers to the questions:

(1) What sort of thing is a meaning?
(2) What is the form of the semantic rules whereby meanings of compounds are built up from the meanings of their constituent parts?

It is not my plan to make any strong empirical claim about language. To the contrary: I want to propose a convenient format for semantics general enough to work for a great variety of logically possible languages. This paper therefore belongs not to empirical linguistic theory but to the philosophy thereof.

My proposals regarding the nature of meanings will not conform to the expectations of those linguists who conceive of semantic interpretation as the assignment to sentences and their constituents of compounds of 'semantic markers' or the like. (Katz and Postal 1964, for instance.) Semantic markers are *symbols*: items in the vocabulary of an artificial language we may call *Semantic Markerese*. Semantic interpretation by means of them amounts merely to a translation algorithm from the object language to the auxiliary language Markerese. But we can know the Markerese translation of an English sentence without knowing the first thing about the meaning of the English sentence: namely, the conditions under which it would be true. Semantics with no treatment of truth conditions is not semantics. Translation into Markerese is at best a substitute for real semantics, relying either on our tacit competence (at some future date) as speakers of

David Lewis (1972) General semantics. In Gilbert Harman and Donald Davidson (eds.), *Semantics of Natural Language*, 169–218. Reprinted by permission of Reidel Publishing.

Markerese or on our ability to do real semantics at least for the one language Markerese. Translation into Latin might serve as well, except insofar as the designers of Markerese may choose to build into it useful features—freedom from ambiguity, grammar based on symbolic logic—that might make it easier to do real semantics for Markerese than for Latin. (See Vermazen 1967, for similar criticisms).

The Markerese method is attractive in part just because it deals with nothing but symbols: finite combinations of entities of a familiar sort out of a finite set of elements by finitely many applications of finitely many rules. There is no risk of alarming the ontologically parsimonious. But it is just this pleasing finitude that prevents Markerese semantics from dealing with the relations between symbols and the world of non-symbols—that is, with genuinely semantic relations. Accordingly, we should be prepared to find that in a more adequate method, meanings may turn out to be complicated, infinite entities built up out of elements belonging to various ontological categories.

My proposals will also not conform to the expectations of those who, in analyzing meaning, turn immediately to the psychology and sociology of language users: to intentions, sense-experience, and mental ideas, or to social rules, conventions, and regularities. I distinguish two topics: first, the description of possible languages or grammars as abstract semantic systems whereby symbols are associated with aspects of the world; and second, the description of the psychological and sociological facts whereby a particular one of these abstract semantic systems is the one used by a person or population. Only confusion comes of mixing these two topics. This paper deals almost entirely with the first. (I discuss the second elsewhere: Lewis 1968b and 1969, ch. 5.)

My proposals are in the tradition of *referential*, or *model-theoretic*, semantics descended from Frege, Tarski, Carnap (in his later works), and recent work of Kripke and others on semantic foundations of intensional logic. (See Frege 1972; Tarski 1956; Carnap 1956 and 1963, §9; Kripke 1963 ; Kaplan 1964; Montague 1960, 1968, and 1970c; Scott 1970.) The project of transplanting referential semantics from artificial to natural languages has recently been undertaken, in various ways, by several philosophers and linguists (Davidson 1967; Parsons 1968; Montague 1969b, 1970a, and 1970b; Keenan 1969.) I have no quarrel with these efforts; indeed, I have here adapted features from several of them. I hope, however, that the system set forth in this paper offers a simpler way to do essentially the same thing. But simplicity is a matter of taste, and simplicity at one place trades off against simplicity elsewhere. It is in these trade-offs that my approach differs most from the others.

II Categorially based grammars

A *categorial grammar* in the sense of Ajdukiewicz (Ajdukiewicz 1967; Bar-Hillel 1964, Part II) is a context-free phrase structure grammar of the following sort.

First, we have a small number of *basic categories*. One of these is the category *sentence* (S). Others might be, for instance, the categories *name* (N) and *common noun* (C). Perhaps we can get by with these three and no more; indeed, Ajdukiewicz went so far as to do without the category *common noun*. Or perhaps we might do better to use different basic categories; we will consider dispensing with the category *name* in favor of an alternative basic category *verb phrase* (VP), or perhaps *noun phrase* (NP).

Second, we have infinitely many *derived categories*. Whenever $c, c_1, \ldots, c_n$ ($n \geq 1$) are any categories, either basic or derived, we have a derived category which we will write $(c/c_1 \ldots c_n)$. (However, we will usually omit the outermost parentheses.)

Third, we have context-free phrase-structure rules of the form

$$c \to (c/c_1 \ldots c_n) + c_1 + \ldots + c_n$$

corresponding to each derived category. That is to say: for any categories $c, c_1, \ldots, c_n$, the result of concatenating any expression of category $(c/c_1 \ldots c_n)$, then any expression of category c_1, then $\ldots$, and finally any expression of category c_n is an expression of category c. Accordingly, we will say that a $(c/c_1 \ldots c_n)$ *takes* a c_1 and $\ldots$ and a c_n and *makes* a c. The phrase-structure rules are implicit in the system of derived categories.

Finally, we have a lexicon wherein finitely many expressions—words or word-like morphemes—are assigned to categories. The categories of these lexical expressions may be either basic or derived; unless some lexical expressions belong to derived categories, no non-lexical compound expressions can be generated. Notice that although there are infinitely many derived categories and infinitely many phrase-structure rules, nevertheless with any given lexicon all but finitely many categories and rules will be unemployed. This is true even though many lexica will generate infinitely many compound expressions.

To specify a categorial grammar, we need only specify its lexicon. The rest is common to all categorial grammars. Consider this lexicon:

$$
\left[
\begin{array}{llll}
\langle a & (S/(S/N))/C\rangle & \langle pig & C\rangle \\
\langle believes & (S/N)/S\rangle & \langle piggishly & (S/N)/(S/N)\rangle \\
\langle every & (S/(S/N))/C\rangle & \langle Porky & N\rangle \\
\langle grunts & S/N\rangle & \langle something & S/(S/N)\rangle \\
\langle is & (S/N)/N\rangle & \langle the & (S/(S/N))/C\rangle \\
\langle loves & (S/N)/N\rangle & \langle which & (C/C)/(S/N)\rangle \\
\langle Petunia & N\rangle & \langle yellow & C/C\rangle
\end{array}
\right]
$$

It gives us a categorial grammar which is simply a notational variant of this rather commonplace context-free grammar:

$$
\begin{aligned}
S &\to \begin{cases} NP + VP \\ VP + Npr \end{cases} & Npr &\to \begin{cases} Porky \\ Petunia \end{cases} \\
& & NP &\to something \\
VP &\to \begin{cases} Adv + VP \\ Vt + Npr \\ Vs + S \end{cases} & Nco &\to pig \\
& & VP &\to grunts \\
NP &\to Art + Nco & Vt &\to \begin{cases} loves \\ is \end{cases} \\
Nco &\to Adj + Nco & & \\
Adj &\to Rel + VP & Vs &\to believes \\
& & Art &\to \begin{cases} a \\ every \\ the \end{cases} \\
& & Adj &\to yellow \\
& & Adv &\to piggishly \\
& & Rel &\to which
\end{aligned}
$$

There are three peculiarities about the grammar. First, proper nouns are distinguished from noun phrases. Proper nouns or noun phrases may be subjects (though with different word order) but only proper nouns may be objects. Second, there is nothing to prevent inappropriate iteration of modifiers. Third, the word order is sometimes odd. We will see later how these peculiarities may be overcome.

The employed rules in this example are the eight phrase-structure rules corresponding to the eight employed derived categories.

In this example, I have used only derived categories of the form (c/c_1) that take a single argument. I shall adopt this restriction for the most part in practice, but not in principle.

It is apparent that categorial grammars of this sort are not reasonable grammars for natural language. For that matter, they are not reasonable grammars for most artificial languages either—the exception being symbolic logic in Polish notation. Hence, despite their elegance, categorial grammars have largely been ignored since the early 1950s. Since then, however, we have become interested in the plan of using a simple phrase-structure grammar as a base for a transformational grammar. The time therefore seems ripe to explore *categorially based transformational grammars*, obtained by taking an Ajdukiewicz categorial grammar as base and adding a transformational component. So far as I know, this proposal has been made only once before (Lyons 1966), but it seems an obvious one.

It is obvious that by adding a transformational component to the categorial grammar of our example, we could rectify the word order and filter out inappropriate iterations of modifiers. Less obviously, we could provide for noun phrase objects by means of a transformational component together with a few additional lexical items—items that need never appear in the final generated sentences.

If reasonable categorially based transformational grammars can be given for all languages of interest to us, and if this can be done under the constraint that meanings are to be determined entirely by base structure, so that the transformational component is irrelevant to semantics, then it becomes extremely easy to give general answers to the questions: What is a meaning? What is the form of a semantic projection rule? Let us see how this can be done.

III   Intensions for basic categories

In order to say what a meaning *is*, we may first ask what a meaning *does*, and then find something that does that.

A meaning for a sentence is something that determines the conditions under which the sentence is true or false. It determines the truth-value of the sentence in various possible states of affairs, at various times, at various places, for various speakers, and so on. (I mean this to apply even to non-declarative sentences, but postpone consideration of them.) Similarly, a meaning for a name is something that determines what thing, if any, the name names in various possible states of affairs, at various times, and so on. Among "things" we include things that do not actually exist, but *might* exist in states of affairs different from the actual state of affairs. Similarly, a meaning for a common noun is something that determines which (possible or actual) things, if any, that common noun applies to in various possible states of affairs, at various times, and so on.

We call the truth-value of a sentence the *extension* of that sentence; we call the thing named by a name the *extension* of that name; we call the set of things to which a common noun applies the *extension* of that common noun. The extension of something in one of these three categories depends on its meaning and, in general, on other things as well: on facts about the world, on the time of utterance, on the place of utterance, on the speaker, on the surrounding discourse, et cetera. It is the meaning which determines how the extension depends upon the combination of other relevant factors. What sort of things determine how something depends on something else? *Functions*, of course; functions in the most general set-theoretic sense, in which the domain of arguments and the range of values may consist of entities of any sort whatever, and in which it is not required that the function be specifiable by any simple rule. We have now found something to do at least part of what a meaning for a sentence, name, or common noun does: a function which yields as output an appropriate extension when given as input a package of the various factors on which the extension may depend. We will call such an input package of relevant factors an *index*; and we will call any function from indices to appropriate extensions for a sentence, name, or common noun an *intension*.

Thus an *appropriate intension for* a sentence is any function from indices to truth-values; an *appropriate intension for* a name is any function from indices to things; an *appropriate intension for* a common noun is any function from indices to sets. The plan to construe intensions as extension-determining functions originated with Carnap (1956, §40; 1963). Accordingly, let us call such functions *Carnapian intensions.* But whereas Carnap's extension-determining functions take as their arguments models or state-descriptions representing possible worlds, I will adopt the suggestion (Montague 1968; Scott 1970) of letting the arguments be packages of miscellaneous factors relevant to determining extensions.

We may take indices as *n*-tuples (finite sequences) of the various items other than meaning that may enter into determining extensions. We call these various items *coordinates* of the index, and we shall assume that the coordinates are given some arbitrary fixed order.

First, we must have a *possible-world coordinate.* Contingent sentences depend for their truth-value on facts about the world, and so are true at some possible worlds and false at others. A possible world corresponds to a possible totality of facts, determinate in all respects. Common nouns also have different extensions at different possible worlds; and so do some names, at least if we adopt the position (defended in Lewis 1968a) that things are related to their counterparts in other worlds by ties of strong similarity rather than identity.

Second, we must have several *contextual coordinates* corresponding to familiar sorts of dependence on features of context. (The world coordinate itself might be regarded as a feature of context, since different possible utterances of a sentence are located in different possible worlds.) We must have a *time coordinate,* in view of tensed sentences and such sentences as 'Today is Tuesday'; a *place coordinate,* in view of such sentences as 'Here there are tigers'; a *speaker coordinate* in view of such sentences as 'I am Porky'; an *audience coordinate* in view of such sentences as 'You are Porky'; an *indicated-objects coordinate* in view of such sentences as 'That pig is Porky' or 'Those men are Communists'; and *previous discourse coordinate* in view of such sentences as 'The aforementioned pig is Porky'.

Third, it is convenient to have an *assignment coordinate*: an infinite sequence of things, regarded as giving the values of any variables that may occur free in such expressions as '*x* is tall' or 'son of *y*'. Each variable employed in the language will accordingly be a name having as its intension, for some number *n*, the *nth variable intension*: that function whose value, at any index *i*, is that thing which is the *n*th term of the assignment coordinate of *i*. That thing is the extension, or value, of the variable at *i*. (Note that because there is more than one possible thing, the variable intensions are distinct: nothing is both the n_1th and the n_2th variable intension for two different numbers n_1 and n_2.) The extensions of '*x* is tall' or 'son or *y*' depend on the assignment and world coordinates of indices, just as the extensions of 'I am tall' and 'son of mine' depend on the speaker and world coordinates. Yet the assignment coordinate cannot naturally be included among features of context. One might claim that variables do not appear in sentences of natural languages; but even if this is so, it may be useful to employ variables in a categorial base. In any case, I seek sufficient generality to accommodate languages that do employ variables.

Perhaps other coordinates would be useful. (See the appendix.) But let us stop here, even though the penalty for introducing a superfluous coordinate is mere clutter, while the penalty for omitting a needed one is inadequacy. Thus an *index* is tentatively any octuple of which the first coordinate is a possible world, the second coordinate is a moment of time, the third coordinate is a place, the fourth coordinate is a person (or other creature capable of being a speaker), the fifth coordinate is a set of persons (or other creatures capable of being an audience), the sixth coordinate is a set (possibly empty) of concrete things capable of being pointed at, the seventh coordinate is a segment of discourse, and the eighth coordinate is an infinite sequence of things.

Intensions, our functions from indices to extensions, are designed to do part of what meanings do. Yet they are not meanings; for there are differences in meaning unaccompanied by differences in intension. It would be absurd to say that all tautologies have the same meaning, but they have the same intension: the constant function having at every index the value *truth*. Intensions are part of the way to meanings, however, and they are of interest in their own right. We shall consider later what must be added to an intension to obtain something that can do *all* of what a meaning does.

We may permit Carnapian intensions to be partial functions from indices, undefined at some indices. A name may not denote anything at a given possible world. 'Pegasus', for instance, denotes nothing at our world, so its intension may be taken as undefined at any index having our world as its world coordinate. A sentence that suffers from failure of presupposition is often thought to lack a truth-value (for instance, in Strawson 1950; Keenan 1969; McCawley 1969). If we adopt this treatment of presupposition, sentences susceptible to lack of truth-value should have intensions that are undefined at some indices. They might even have intensions that are undefined at *all* indices; a sentence with inconsistent presuppositions should have as its intension the empty function, defined at no index.

Hitherto I have spoken uncritically of 'things'. Things are name extensions and values of name intensions; sets of things are common-noun extensions and values of common-noun intensions; sequences of things are assignment coordinates of indices. Change the underlying set of things and we change the sets of extensions, indices, and Carnapian intensions. What, then, are things? Of course I want to say, once and for all: *everything* is a thing. But I must not say that. Not all sets of things can be things; else the set of things would be larger than itself. No Carnapian intension can be a thing (unless it is undefined at certain indices); else it would be a member of . . . a member of itself. We must understand the above definitions of extensions, indices, and Carnapian intensions (and the coming definitions of compositional intensions, meanings, and lexica) as tacitly relativized to a chosen set of things. Can we choose the set of things once and for all? Not quite; no matter what set we choose as the set of things, the system of intensions defined over that set will not provide intensions for certain terms—'intension', for instance—of the semantic metalanguage corresponding to that choice. Consider the language of this paper (minus this paragraph) with the extension of 'thing' somehow fixed; it is an adequate semantic metalanguage for some languages but not for itself. To do semantics for it, we must move to a second language in which 'thing' is taken more inclusively; to do semantics for that language we must move to a third language in which 'thing' is taken more inclusively still; and so on. Any language can be treated in a metalanguage in which 'thing' is taken inclusively enough; but the generality of semantics is fundamentally limited by the fact that no language can be its own semantic metalanguage (cf. Tarski 1956) and hence there can be no universal semantic metalanguage. But we can approach generality as closely as we like by taking 'thing' inclusively enough. For the remainder of this paper, let us proceed on the assumption that the set of things has been chosen, almost once and for all, as some very inclusive set: at least as the universe of some intended model of standard set theory with all the non-sets we want, actual or possible, included as individuals. Let us ignore the sequence of semantic metalanguages that still escape treatment.

In that case there is overlap between things, sets of things, and truth-values. (Not all sets of things can be things, but some should be.) Moreover, there is overlap between sets and truth-values if we adopt the common conventions of identifying the truth-values *truth* and *falsity* with the numbers 1 and 0, respectively, and of identifying each natural number with the set of its predecessors. Thus the appropriate extensions and intensions for sentences, names, and common nouns overlap. The same function that is the intension of all contradictions is also the intension of the name 'zero' and of the common noun 'round square'. Such overlap, however, is harmless. Whenever we want to get rid of it, we can replace intensions by ordered pairs of a category and an intension appropriate for that category.

IV   Intensions for derived categories

Turning to derived categories, it is best to foresake extensions and Carnapian intensions in the interest of generality. Sometimes, for instance, a C/C—that is, an *adjective*—has an extension like that of a common noun: a set of things to which (at a given index) it applies. Probably 'married' is such an *extensional adjective*. But most adjectives do not have extensions. What is the set of things to which 'alleged' applies? An alleged Communist is not something which is, on the one hand, an alleged thing and, on the other hand, a Communist.

In general, an adjective takes a common noun to make a new, compound common noun; and the intension of the new common noun depends on the intension of the original common noun in a manner determined by the meaning of the adjective. A meaning for an adjective, therefore, is something that determines how one common-noun intension depends on another. Looking for an entity that does what a meaning does, we are led to say that an appropriate intension for an adjective is any function from common-noun intensions to common-noun intensions. In more detail: it is a function whose domain and range consist of functions from indices to sets. Thus the intension of 'alleged' is a function that, when given as argument the intension of 'Communist', 'windshield', or 'chipmunk' yields as value the intension of the compound common noun 'alleged Communist', 'alleged windshield', or 'alleged chipmunk', respectively. Note that it would not work to use instead a function from common-noun extensions (sets) to common-noun extensions; for at certain indices 'Communist' and 'Maoist' have the same extension but 'alleged Communist' and 'alleged Maoist' do not—or, at other indices, vice versa.

More generally, let us say that an *appropriate intension for* a $(c/c_1 \ldots c_n)$, where $c, c_1, \ldots,$ and c_n are any categories, basic or derived, is any n-place function from c_1-intensions, $\ldots$, and c_n-intensions to c-intensions. That is, it is any function (again in the most general set-theoretic sense) having as its range of values a set of c-intensions, having as its domain of first arguments the set of c_1-intensions, $\ldots$, and having as its domain of nth arguments the set of c_n-intensions. A $(c/c_1 \ldots c_n)$ takes a c_1 and $\ldots$ and a c_n and makes a c by concatenation; correspondingly, a $(c/c_1 \ldots c_n)$-intension takes a c_1-intension and $\ldots$ and a c_n-intension as arguments and makes a c-intension as function value. We will call these intensions for derived categories *compositional intensions*. (Intensions resembling some of my compositional intensions are discussed in Kaplan 1964; in Scott 1970; and—as appropriate intension for adjectives and other modifiers—in Parsons 1968 and Montague 1970a. The latter discussion is due in part to J. A. W. Kamp.) The general form of the semantic projection rules for an interpreted categorial grammar is implicit in the nature of compositional intensions, just as the general form of the phrase-structure rules is implicit in the nomenclature for derived categories. The result of concatenating a $(c/c_1 \ldots c_n)$ with intension ϕ_0, a c_1 with intension $\phi_1, \ldots c_n$ with intension ϕ_n is a c with intension $\phi_0(\phi_1 \ldots \phi_n)$.

We have considered already the derived category *adjective* C/C. For another example, take the derived category *verb phrase*, S/N.

A verb phrase takes a name to make a sentence. (We rely on the transformational component to change the word order if necesssary.) An appropriate intension for a verb phrase—an S/N-intension—is therefore a function from name intensions to sentence intensions. That is, it is a function from functions from indices to things to functions from indices to truth-values. The intension of 'grunts', for instance, is that function ϕ whose value, given as argument any function ϕ_1 from indices to things, is that function ϕ_2 from indices to truth-values such that, for any index i,

$$\phi_2(i) = \begin{cases} \textit{truth} \text{ if } \phi_1(i) \text{ is something which grunts at the} \\ \quad \text{world and time given by the appropriate} \\ \quad \text{coordinates of } i \\ \textit{falsity} \text{ otherwise.} \end{cases}$$

Applying the projection rule, we find that the sentence 'Porky grunts' is true at just those indices i such that the thing named by 'Porky' at i grunts at the possible world that is the world coordinate of i at the time which is the time coordinate of i. (The appearance of circularity in this account is spurious; it comes of the fact that I am using English to specify the intension of a word of English.)

For another example, take the derived category *adverb* (of one sort), (S/N)/(S/N). An adverb of this sort takes a verb phrase to make a verb phrase; so an appropriate intension for such an adverb—an (S/N)/(S/N)-intension—is a function from verb-phrase intensions to verb-phrase intensions; or, in more detail, a function from functions from functions from indices to things to functions from indices to truth-values to functions from functions from indices to things to functions from indices to truth-values.

I promised simplicity; I deliver functions from functions from functions to functions to functions from functions to functions. And worse is in store if we consider the sort of adverb that modifies ordinary adverbs: the category ((S/N)/(S/N))/((S/N)/(S/N)). Yet I think no apology is called for. Intensions are complicated constructs, but the principles of their construction are extremely simple. The situation is common: look at any account of the set-theoretic construction of real numbers, yet recall that children often understand the real numbers rather well.

In some cases, it would be possible to find simpler intensions, but at an exorbitant cost: we would have to give up the uniform function-and-arguments form for semantic projection rules. We have noted already that some adjectives are extensional, though most are not. The extensional adjectives could be given sets as extensions and functions from indices to sets as Carnapian intensions. Similarly for verb phrases: we may call a verb phrase *extensional* iff there is a function ϕ from indices to sets such that if ϕ_1 is the (compositional) intension of the verb phrase, ϕ_2 is any name intension, ϕ_3 is $\phi_1 (\phi_2)$, and i is any index, then

$$\phi_3 (i) = \begin{cases} \textit{truth if } \phi_2 (i) \text{ is a member of } \phi(i) \\ \textit{falsity otherwise.} \end{cases}$$

If there is any such function ϕ, there is exactly one; we can call it the Carnapian intension of the verb phrase and we can call its value at any index i the extension of the verb phrase at i. 'Grunts', for instance, is an extensional verb phrase; its extension at an index i is the set of things that grunt at the world and the time given by the world coordinate and the time coordinate of the index i. Verb phrases, unlike adjectives, are ordinarily extensional; but Barbara Partee has pointed out that the verb phrase in 'The price of milk is rising' seems to be non-extensional.

There is no harm in noting that extensional adjective and verb phrases have Carnapian intensions as well as compositional intensions. However, it is the compositional intension that should be used to determine the intension of an extensional-adjective-plus-common-noun or extensional-verb-phrase-plus-name combination. If we used the Carnapian intensions, we would have a miscellany of semantic projection rules rather than the uniform function-and-arguments rule. (Indeed, the best way to formulate projection rules using Carnapian intensions might be to combine a rule for reconstructing compositional intensions from Carnapian intensions with the function-and-arguments rule for compositional intensions.) Moreover, we would sacrifice generality: non-extensional adjectives and verb phrases would have to be treated separately from the extensional ones, or not at all. This loss of generality would be serious in the case of adjectives; but not in the case of verb phrases since there are few, if any, non-extensional verb phrases.

For the sake of generality, we might wish to take account of selection restrictions by allowing a compositional intension to be undefined for some arguments of appropriate type. If we thought that 'green idea' should lack an intension, for instance, we might conclude that the intension of 'green' ought to be a partial function from common-noun intensions to common-noun intensions, undefined for such arguments as the intension of 'idea'. It proves more convenient, however, never to let the intension be undefined but rather to let it take on a value called the *null intension* (for the appropriate category). The null intension for the basic categories will be the empty function; the null intension for any derived category $(c/c_1 \ldots c_n)$ will be that $(c/c_1 \ldots c_n)$-intension whose value for any combination of appropriate arguments is the null intension for c. Thus the intension of 'green', given as argument the intension of 'idea', yields as value the null intension for the category C. The intension of the adverb 'furiously', given as argument the intension of 'sleeps', yields as value the null intension for the category S/N, and that, in turn, given as value any name intension, yields as value the null intension for the category S. (I dislike this treatment of selection restrictions, but provide the option for those who want it.)

It is worth mentioning that my account of intensions for derived categories, and of the corresponding form for projection rules, is independent of my account of intensions for basic categories. Whatever S-intensions and N-intensions may be—even expressions of Markerese or ideas in someone's mind—it still is possible to take S/N-intensions as functions from N-intensions to S-intensions and to obtain the intension of 'Porky grunts' by applying the intension of 'grunts' as function to the intension of 'Porky' as argument.

V   Meanings

We have already observed that intensions for sentences cannot be identified with meanings since differences in meaning—for instance, between tautologies—may not carry with them any difference in intension. The same goes for other categories, basic or derived. Differences in intension, we may say, give us *coarse* differences in meaning. For *fine* differences in meaning we must look to the analysis of a compound into constituents and to the intensions of the several constituents. For instance 'Snow is white or it isn't' differs finely in meaning from 'Grass is green or it isn't' because of the difference in intension between the embedded sentences 'Snow is white' and 'Grass is green'. For still finer differences in meaning we must look in turn to the intensions of constituents of constituents, and so on. Only when we come to non-compound, lexical constituents can we take sameness of intension as a sufficient condition of synonymy. (See Carnap 1956, §14, on "intensional isomorphism"; C. I. Lewis 1944, on "analytic meaning.")

It is natural, therefore, to identify meanings with semantically interpreted phrase markers minus their terminal nodes: finite ordered trees having at each node a category and an appropriate intension. If we associate a meaning of this sort with an expression, we are given the category and intension of the expression; and if the expression is compound, we are given also the categories and intensions of its constituent parts, their constituent parts, and so on down.

Perhaps we would thereby cut meanings too finely. For instance, we will be unable to agree with someone who says that a double negation has the same meaning as the corresponding affirmative. But this difficulty does not worry me: we will have both intensions and what I call meanings, and sometimes one and sometimes the other will be preferable as an explication of our ordinary discourse about meanings. Perhaps some entities of intermediate fineness can also be found, but I doubt that there is any uniquely natural way to do so.

It may be disturbing that in our explication of meanings we have made arbitrary choices—for instance, of the order of coordinates in an index. Meanings are meanings—how can we *choose* to construct them in one way rather than another? The objection is a general objection to set-theoretic constructions (see Benacerraf 1965), so I will not reply to it here. But if it troubles you, you may prefer to say that *real* meanings are *sui generis* entities and that the constructs I call "meanings" do duty for real meanings because there is a natural one-to-one correspondence between them and the real meanings.

It might also be disturbing that I have spoken of categories without hitherto saying what they are. This again is a matter of arbitrary choice; we might, for instance, take them as sets of expressions in some language, or as sets of intensions, or even as arbitrarily chosen code numbers. It turns out to be most convenient, if slightly unnatural, to identify categories with their own names: expressions composed in the proper way out of the letters 'S', 'N', 'C' (and whatever others we may introduce later in considering revisions of the system) together with parentheses and diagonal slashes. This does not prevent our category-names from being names of categories: they name themselves. All definitions involving categories are to be understood in accordance with the identification of categories and category-names.

Some might even wish to know what a *tree* is. Very well: it is a function that assigns to each member of the set of nodes of the tree an object said to *occupy* or be *at* that node. The nodes themselves are finite sequences of positive numbers. A set of such sequences is the set of *nodes of* some tree iff, first, it is a finite set, and second, whenever it contains a sequence $\langle b_1 \ldots b_k \rangle$ then it also contains every sequence that is an initial segment of $\langle b_1 \ldots b_k \rangle$ and every sequence $\langle b_1 \ldots b_{k-1} b'_k \rangle$ with $b'_k < b_k$. We regard $\langle \ \rangle$, the sequence of zero length, as the topmost node; $\langle b_1 \rangle$ as the b_1th node from the left immediately beneath $\langle \ \rangle$; $\langle b_1 \ b_2 \rangle$ as the b_2th node from the left immediately beneath $\langle b_1 \rangle$; and so on. We can easily define all the requisite notions of tree theory in terms of this construction.

Once we have identified meanings with semantically interpreted phrase markers, it becomes natural to reconstrue the phrase-structure rules of categorial grammar, together with the corresponding projection rules, as conditions of well-formedness for meanings (cf. McCawley 1968a). Accordingly, we now define a *meaning* as a tree such that, first, each node is occupied by an ordered pair $\langle c \ \phi \rangle$ of a category and an appropriate intension for that category; and second, immediately beneath any nonterminal node occupied by such a pair $\langle c \ \phi \rangle$ are two or more nodes, and these are occupied by pairs $\langle c_0 \ \phi_0 \rangle, \langle c_1 \ \phi_1 \rangle, \ldots, \langle c_n \ \phi_n \rangle$ (in that order) such that c_0 is $(c/c_1 \ldots c_n)$ and ϕ is $\phi_0 (\phi_1 \ldots \phi_n)$.

A meaning may be a tree with a single node; call such meanings *simple* and other meanings *compound.* Compound meanings are, as it were, built up from simple meanings by steps in which several meanings (simple or compound) are combined as sub-trees under a new node, analogously to the way in which expressions are built up by concatenating shorter expressions. We may call a meaning *m'* a *constituent of* a meaning *m* iff *m'* is a sub-tree of *m*. We may say that a meaning *m* is *generated by* a set of simple meanings iff every simple constituent of *m* belongs to that set. More generally, *m* is *generated by* a set of meanings (simple or compound) iff every simple constituent of *m* is a constituent of some constituent of *m*, possibly itself, which belongs to that set.

We shall in many ways speak of meanings as though they were symbolic expressions generated by an interpreted categorial grammar, even though they are nothing of the sort. The *category of* a meaning is the category found as the first component of its topmost node. The *intension of* a meaning is the intension found as the second component of its topmost node. The *extension at* an index *i* of a sentence meaning, name meaning, or common-noun meaning is the value of the intension of the meaning for the argument *i*. A sentence meaning is *true* or *false at i* according as its extension at *i* is *truth* or *falsity*; a name meaning *names at i* that thing, if any, which is its extension at *i*; and a common-noun meaning *applies at i* to whatever things belong to its extension at *i*. As we have seen, extensions might also be provided for certain meanings in derived categories such as C/C or S/N, but this cannot be done in a non-artificial, general way.

Given as fundamental the definition of truth of a sentence meaning at an index, we can define many derivative truth relations. Coordinates of the index may be made explicit, or may be determined by a context of utterance, or may be generalized over. Generalizing over all coordinates, we can say that a sentence meaning is *analytic* (in one sense) iff it is true at every index. Generalizing over the world and assignment coordinates and letting the remaining coordinates be determined by context, we can say that a sentence meaning is *analytic* (in another sense) *on* a given occasion iff it is true at every index *i* having as its time, place, speaker, audience, indicated-objects and previous-discourse coordinates, respectively, the time, the place, the speaker, the audience, the set of objects pointed to, and the previous discourse on that occasion. Generalizing over the time and assignment coordinates and letting the others (including world) be determined by context, we define *eternal truth* of a sentence meaning *on* an occasion; generalizing over the assignment coordinate and letting all the rest be determined by context, we define simply *truth on* an occasion; and so on.

We also can define truth relations even stronger than truth at every index. Let us call a meaning m' a *semantic variant* of a meaning m iff m and m' have exactly the same nodes, with the same category but not necessarily the same intension at each node, and, whenever a common intension appears at two terminal nodes in m, a common intension also appears at those two nodes in m'. Let us call m' an *s-fixed semantic variant of* m, where s is a set of simple meanings, iff m and m' are semantic variants and every member of s which is a constituent of m is also a constituent, at the same place, of m'. Then we can call a sentence meaning *s-true* iff every *s*-fixed semantic variant of it (including itself) is true at every index. If s is the set of simple meanings whose bearers we would classify as logical vocabulary, then we may call *s*-true sentence meanings *logically true*; if s is the set of simple meanings whose bearers we would classify as mathematical (including logical) vocabulary, we may call *s*-true sentence meanings *mathematically true*. Analogously, we can define a relation of *s*-fixed semantic variance between sequences of meanings; and we can say that a sentence meaning m_0 is an *s-consequence* (for instance, a *logical consequence* or *mathematical consequence*) of sentence meanings $m_1, \ldots$ iff, for every *s*-fixed semantic variant $\langle m'_0 \, m'_1 \ldots \rangle$ of the sequence $\langle m_0 \, m_1 \ldots \rangle$ and every index i such that all of $m'_1, \ldots$ are true at i, m'_0 is true at i. (The premises $m_1, \ldots$ may be infinite in number. Their order is insignificant.) These definitions are adapted from definitions in terms of truth in all logically or mathematically standard interpretations of a given language. However, we have been able to avoid introducing the notion of alternative interpretations of a language, since so far we are dealing entirely with meanings.

VI   Grammars reconstructed

Our system of meanings may serve, in effect, as a universal base for categorially based transformational grammars. There is no need to repeat the phrase-structure rules of categorial well-formedness as a base component in each such grammar. Instead, we take the meanings as given, and regard a grammar as specifying a way to encode meanings: a relation between certain meanings and certain expressions (sequences of sound-types or of mark-types) which we will call the *representing relation* determined by the grammar. We might just identify grammars with representing relations; but I prefer to take grammars as systems which determine representing relations in a certain way.

If we were concerned with nothing but transformation-free categorial grammars, we could take a grammar to consist of nothing but a *lexicon*: a finite set of triples of the form $\langle e \, c \, \phi \rangle$ where e is an expression, c is a category, and ϕ is an intension appropriate for that category. We may say that an expression e *represents* or *has* a meaning m *relative to* a lexicon **L** iff **L** contains items $\langle e_1 \, c_1 \, \phi_1 \rangle, \ldots, \langle e_n \, c_n \, \phi_n \rangle$ such that, first, e is the result of concatenating $e_1, \ldots e_n$ (in that order), and, second, the terminal nodes of m are occupied by $\langle c_1 \, \phi_1 \rangle, \ldots, \langle c_n \, \phi_n \rangle$ (in that order).

We could instead have proceeded in two steps. Let us define a (*categorial*) *phrase marker* as a tree having categories at its non-terminal nodes and expressions at its terminal nodes. Then a phrase marker p represents or *has* a meaning m *relative to* a lexicon **L** iff p is obtained from m as follows: given any terminal node of the meaning m occupied by a pair $\langle c \, \phi \rangle$, place below it another node occupied by an expression e such that the item $\langle e \, c \, \phi \rangle$ is contained in the lexicon; then remove the intensions, replacing the $\langle c \, \phi \rangle$ pair at each non-terminal node by its unaccompanied category c.

Note that the set of meanings thus representable relative to a lexicon **L** comprises all and only those meanings that are generated by the set of simple meanings of the lexical items themselves; let us call it the set of meanings *generated by* the lexicon **L**.

Next, we define the *terminal string* of a phrase marker p as the expression obtained by concatenating, in order, the expressions at the terminal nodes of p. Thus we see that an expression e represents a meaning m relative to a lexicon **L**, according to the definition above, iff e is the terminal string of some phrase marker that represents m relative to **L**.

In the case of a categorially based transformational grammar, we have not two steps but three. Such a grammar consists of a lexicon **L** together with a *transformational component* **T**. The latter imposes finitely many constraints on finite sequences of phrase markers. A sequence $\langle p_1 \ldots p_n \rangle$ of phrase markers that satisfies the constraints imposed by **T** will be called a *(transformational) derivation of p_n from p_1 in* **T**. An expression e *represents* or *has* a meaning m in a grammar $\langle$ **L T** $\rangle$ iff there exists a derivation $\langle p_1 \ldots p_n \rangle$ in **T** such that e is the terminal string of p_n and p_1 represents m relative to the lexicon **L**. If so, we will also call e a *meaningful expression*, p_n a *surface structure of e*, p_{n-1} and ... and p_2 *intermediate structures of e*, p_1 a *base structure of e*, and m a *meaning of e* (all *relative to* the grammar $\langle$ **L T** $\rangle$). However, we will call any phrase marker p a *base structure* in $\langle$ **L T** $\rangle$ iff it represents a meaning relative to **L**, whether or not it is the base structure *of* any expression; thus we allow for base structures which are filtered out by not being the first term of any derivation in **T**.

The representing relation given by a grammar $\langle$ **L T** $\rangle$ is by no means a one-to-one correspondence between meanings and expressions. A given expression might be *ambiguous*, representing several different meanings. (If it represents several different but cointensive meanings, however, it might be inappropriate to call it ambiguous; for the common notion of meaning seems to hover between our technical notions of meaning and of intension.) On the other hand, several expressions might be *synonymous*, representing a single meaning. We might also call several expressions *completely synonymous* iff they share all their meanings; synonymy and complete synonymy coincide when we are dealing only with unambiguous expressions. If several expressions represent different but cointensive meanings, we may call them equivalent but not synonymous. If several expressions not only represent the same meaning but also have a single base structure, we may call them not only equivalent and synonymous but also *paraphrases* of one another.

Given a representing relation, all the semantic relations defined hitherto for meanings carry over to expressions having those meanings. (If we like, they may carry over also to the base, surface, and intermediate structures between the meanings and the expressions.) Thus we know what it means to speak, relative to a given grammar and qualified in cases of ambiguity by 'on a meaning' or 'on all meanings', of the category and intension of any meaningful expression; of the extension at a given index of any expression of appropriate category; of the thing named by a name; of the things to which a common noun applies; of the truth at an index, truth on an occasion, analyticity, logical truth, et cetera of a sentence; and so on.

We should note an oddity in our treatment of logical truth. A synonym of a logically true sentence is itself a logical truth, since it represents the same logically true meaning as the original. Hence a descendant by synonym-substitution of a logical truth is itself a logical truth if the synonym-substitution is confined to single lexical items in the base structure; but not otherwise. 'All woodchucks are groundhogs' comes out logically true, whereas 'All squares are equilateral rectangles' comes out merely analytic (in the strongest sense).

A transformational component may constrain sequences of phrase markers in two ways. There is the local constraint that any two adjacent phrase markers in a derivation must stand in one of finitely many relations; these permitted relations between adjacent phrase markers are the *transformations*. There may also be global derivational constraints specifying relations between nonadjacent phrase markers or properties of the derivation as a whole. An example is the constraint requiring transformations to apply in some specified cyclic (or partly cyclic) order.

A transformation-free categorial grammar is a special case of a categorially based transformational grammar. It has a transformational component with no transformations or global constraints, so that the derivations therein are all and only those sequences $\langle p_1 \rangle$ consisting of a single phrase marker.

I will not attempt to say more exactly what a transformation or a transformational component is. Mathematically precise definitions have been given (for instance, in Peters and Ritchie 1969), but to choose among these would involve taking sides on disputed questions in syntactic theory. I prefer to maintain my neutrality, and I have no present need for a precise delineation of the class of transformational grammars. I have foremost in mind a sort of simplified *Aspects*-model grammar (Chomsky 1965), but I have said nothing to eliminate various alternatives.

I have said nothing to eliminate generative semantics. What I have chosen to call the "lexicon" is the *initial* lexicon. Words not in that lexicon might be introduced transformationally on the way from base to surface, if that seems desirable. It might even be that none of the initial lexical items ever reach the surface, and that all surface lexical items (expressions found at terminal nodes of surface structures) are introduced transformationally within derivations. In that case it would be appropriate to use a standardized initial lexicon in all grammars, and to rechristen my base structures "semantic representation." In that case also there might or might not be a level between base and surface at which word-introducing transformations are done and other transformations have not yet begun.

I have also said nothing to eliminate surface semantics. This may seem strange, since I have indeed said that meanings are to be determined by base structures alone. However, I rely here on the observation (Lakoff 1970c, §3) that surface-structure interpretation rules are indistinguishable from global derivational constraints relating three levels: base structures (regarded as semantic representations), deep structures (an *intermediate* level), and surface structures. Deep structures might be ambiguous; a transformational grammar with base-deep-surface constraints might permit two derivations

$$\langle p_B^1 \ldots p_D \ldots p_S^1 \rangle$$
$$\langle p_B^2 \ldots p_D \ldots p_S^2 \rangle$$

differing at the base and surface but not at the deep level, but it might rule out other derivations of the forms

$$\langle p_B^2 \ldots p_D \ldots p_S^1 \rangle$$
$$\langle p_B^1 \ldots p_D \ldots p_S^2 \rangle.$$

In such a case base structure (and hence meaning) would be determined by deep and surface structure together, but not by deep structure alone. Similarly, we might have constraints relating base structure not only to deep and surface structure but also to structure at various other intermediate levels.

I have said nothing to eliminate a non-trivial phonological component; but I would relocate it as part of the transformational component. The last few steps of a transformational derivation might go from the usual pre-phonological surface structure to a post-phonological surface structure whence the output expression can be obtained simply by concatenation of terminal nodes.

I have said nothing to eliminate an elaborate system of selection restrictions; but these will appear not as restrictions on the lexical insertions between meanings and base structures but as transformational filtering later on. There will be base structures representing the meanings of such questionable sentences as 'Seventeen eats beans' and 'He sang a pregnant toothbrush'. But these base structures need not be the first terms of any derivations, so these meanings may be unrepresented by sentences. If we like selection restrictions, we might match the lexicon to the transformational component in such a way as to filter out just those meanings that have the null intension.

I have not stipulated that only sentential meanings may be represented; that stipulation could be added if there is reason for it.

In fact, the *only* restriction I place on syntax is that transformational grammars should be categorially based. In other words: a transformational component should operate on a set of categorial phrase markers representing a set of meanings generated by some lexicon. But categorial bases are varied enough that this restriction is not at all severe. I claim that whatever familiar sort of base component you may favor on syntactic grounds, you can find a categorial base (i.e., a suitable part of the system of meanings, generated by a suitable chosen lexicon) that resembles the base you favor closely enough to share its attractive properties. Indeed, with a few preliminary rearranging transformations you can go from my categorial base structures to (notational variants of) more familiar base structures; then you can proceed exactly as before. I shall not marshall evidence for this claim; but I think that the following exploration of alternative categorial treatments of quantification will exhibit the close similarities between these categorial treatments and several alternative familiar base components. If it were necessary to choose between a categorial base that was convenient for semantics and a non-categorial base that was convenient for transformational syntax, I might still choose the former. But I deny the need to choose.

This completes the exposition of my proposed system of categories, intensions, and meanings. Now I shall consider how this system—either as is or slightly revised—might be applied to two difficult areas: the semantics of quantification and the semantics of non-declaratives. The treatments following are intended only as illustrations, however; many further alternatives are possible, and might be more convenient for syntax.

VII   Treatment of quantification and noun phrases

Let us consider such expressions as 'a pig', 'most pigs', 'seventeen pigs', 'roughly seventeen pigs', 'some yellow pig', 'everything', 'nobody', and the like. We call these *quantifier phrases* (presupposing that they should belong to a common category). What category in our system is this? What sort of intensions do quantifier phrases have?

Quantifier phrases combine with verb phrases to make sentences: 'Some pig grunts', 'Nobody grunts', 'Roughly seventeen pigs grunt', and the like. Names do this, since the category *verb phrase* is the derived category S/N. But quantifier phrases cannot be names, under our semantic treatment of names, because they do not in general name anything. ('The pig' could be an exception at indices such that exactly one pig existed at the world and time given by the index.) The absurd consequences of treating 'nobody', as a name, for instance, are well known (Dodgson 1905). If a quantifier phrase combines with an S/N to make an S, and yet is not an N, it must therefore be an S/(S/N).

Except perhaps for one-word quantifier phrases—'nobody', 'everything', and such—quantifier phrases contain constituent common nouns. These may be either simple, as in 'some pig' or compound, as in 'every pink pig that wins a blue ribbon'. Indeed, we may regard common nouns simply as predicates used to restrict quantifiers. (This suggestion derives from Montague 1970a.) The expressions 'a', 'the', 'some', 'every', 'no', 'most', 'seventeen', 'roughly seventeen', and so on which combine with common nouns (simple or compound) to make quantifier phrases and which are variously called *quantifiers*, *determiners*, or *articles* must therefore belong to the category (S/(S/N))/C. And modifiers of quantifiers like 'roughly' which combine with certain quantifiers to make quantifiers, must belong to the category ((S/(S/N))/C)/((S/(S/N))/C). Selection restrictions by means of transformational filtering could be used to dispose of quantifiers like 'roughly the'.

The intension of 'some pig' may be taken as that function ϕ from S/N-intensions to S-intensions such that if ϕ_1 is any S/N-intension, ϕ_2 is the S-intension $\phi(\phi_1)$, and i is any index, then

$$\phi_2(i) = \begin{cases} \textit{truth} \text{ if, for some N-intension } \phi_3, \ \phi_3(i) \text{ is a pig and if } \phi_4 \text{ is } \phi_1(\phi_3) \text{ then } \phi_4(i) \text{ is } \textit{truth} \\ \textit{falsity} \text{ otherwise.} \end{cases}$$

The intension of 'some' may be taken as that function ϕ from C-intensions to S/(S/N)-intensions such that if ϕ_1 is any C-intension, ϕ_2 is the S/(S/N)-intension $\phi(\phi_1)$, ϕ_3 is any S/N-intension, ϕ_4 is the S-intension $\phi_2(\phi_3)$, and i is any index, then

$$\phi_4(i) = \begin{cases} \textit{truth} \text{ if, for some N-intension } \phi_5, \ \phi_5(i) \text{ is a member of } \phi_1(i) \text{ and if } \phi_6 \text{ is } \phi_3(\phi_5) \text{ then } \phi_6(i) \text{ is } \textit{truth} \\ \textit{falsity} \text{ otherwise.} \end{cases}$$

I spare you the intension of 'roughly'.

Other intensions might be specified for 'some pig' and 'some' that would differ from these only when a quantifier phrase was applied to a non-extensional verb phrase. If there are no non-extensional verb phrases in English, then the choice among these alternatives is arbitrary.

This treatment of quantifier phrases is motivated by a desire to handle simple sentences involving quantifier phrases as straightforwardly as possible, minimizing the use of transformations. But it raises problems. Quantifier phrases seemingly occur not only as subjects of sentences but also as objects of verbs or prepositions. And in all their roles—as subjects or as objects—they are interchangeable with names. That is why it is usual to have a category *noun phrase* comprising both quantifier phrases and names.

We might try the heroic course of doubling all our object-takers. We could have one word 'loves' which is an (S/N)/N and takes the object 'Petunia' to make the verb phrase 'loves Petunia'; and alongside it another 'loves' which is an (S/N)/(S/(S/N)) and takes the object 'some pig' to make the verb phrase 'loves some pig'. But we need not decide how much we mind such extravagant doubling, since it does not work anyway. It would give us one meaning for 'Every boy loves some girl': the weaker meaning, on which the sentence can be true even if each boy loves a different girl. But the sentence is ambiguous; where shall we get a stronger meaning, on which the sentence is true only if a certain girl—Zuleika, perhaps—is loved by all boys? (There are those who do not perceive this ambiguity; but we seek a treatment general enough to handle the idiolects of those who do.) The method of doubling object-takers is a blind alley; rather we must look to the method of variable binding, routinely used in the semantic analysis of standardly formulated symbolic logic.

The quantifiers of symbolic logic belong to the category S/NS, taking a name and a sentence to make a sentence. The name must be a variable; other combinations could be disposed of by transformational filtering. For instance, the logician's quantifier 'some' takes the variable 'x' and the sentence 'grunts x' to make a sentence translatable into English as 'something grunts'. The logician's 'some' has as its intension that function ϕ from N-intensions and S-intensions to S-intensions such that if ϕ_1 is the nth variable intension for any number n, ϕ_2 is any S-intension, ϕ_3 is $\phi(\phi_1\phi_2)$, and i is any index, then

$$\phi_3(i) = \begin{cases} \textit{truth} \text{ if, for some index } i' \text{ that is like} i \text{ expect perhaps at the } n \text{th term of the assignment} \\ \text{coordinate, } \phi_2(i') \text{ is } \textit{truth} \\ \textit{falsity} \text{ otherwise;} \end{cases}$$

and such that if ϕ_1 is any N-intension that is not a variable intension and ϕ_2 is any S-intension, then $\phi(\phi_1\phi_2)$ is the null intension. The intension of the logician's quantifier 'every' is specified similarly, with 'for every index i' . . .' replacing 'for some index i' . . .'.

It would be troublesome to employ logician's quantifiers in a grammar for English. In the first place, these quantifiers are unrestricted, ranging over everything. The base structure of 'Some pig grunts', for instance, would come out as

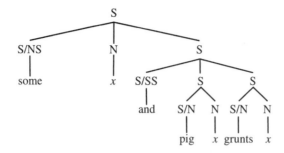

in which there is no constituent corresponding to 'some pig' and in which 'pig' and 'grunts' alike are put into the category S/N. (It was with structures like this in mind that Ajdukiewicz saw fit to omit the category C.) This attempt to dispense with quantifier phrases in favor of unrestricted quantifiers taking compound sentences is clumsy at best, and fails entirely for quantifiers such as 'most' (see Wallace 1965). In the second place, by having the quantifier itself do the binding of variables, we require there to be bound variables wherever there are quantifiers. We get the unnecessarily complicated base structure

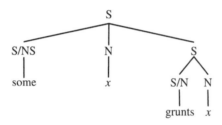

for 'Something grunts', whereas if we had employed quantifier phrases which take verb phrases and do not bind variables, we could have had

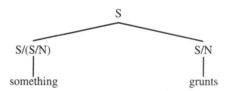

with three constituents instead of six and no work for the transformations to do.

It is not necessary, however, that the quantifier itself should bind variables. We can stick with verb-phrase-taking quantifier phrases of the category S/(S/N), restricted by constituent common nouns in most cases, and bind variables when necessary—but *only* when necessary—by means of a separate constituent called a *binder*: a certain sort of (S/N)/S that takes a sentence and makes an extensional verb phrase by binding a variable at all its free occurrences (if any) in the sentence. To every variable there corresponds a binder. Suppose 'x' is a variable; we may write its corresponding binder as '$\hat{x}$' and read it as 'is something x such that'. (But presumably binders may best be treated as base constituents that never reach the surface; so if the words 'is something x such that' ever appear in a meaningful expression, they will be derived not from an '$\hat{x}$' in base structure but in some other way.) For instance, the following base structure using a binder is equivalent to 'grunts' and might be read loosely as 'is something x such that x grunts':

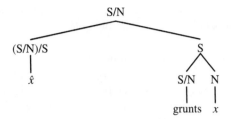

The following is a possible base structure for 'is loved by y':

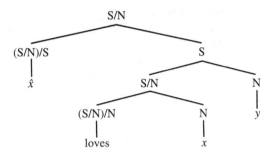

The following migbt be a base structure for 'Porky loves himself' (cf. McCawley 1969):

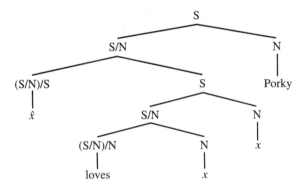

(Provided there is no ambiguity among our variables, we can use them in this way to keep track of coreferentiality, rather than subscripting the names in

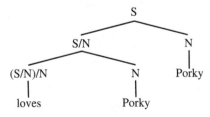

to indicate whether we are dealing with one Porky or two.)

If 'x' has the nth variable intension, then the corresponding binder '$\hat{x}$' has the nth *binder intension*: that function ϕ from S-intensions to S/N-intensions such that if ϕ_1 is any S-intension, ϕ_2 is the S/N-intension $\phi(\phi_1)$, ϕ_3 is any N-intension, ϕ_4 is the S-intension $\phi_2(\phi_3)$, i is any index, and i' is that index which has $\phi_3(i)$ as the nth term of its assignment coordinate and otherwise is like i, then $\phi_4(i) = \phi_1 (i')$. It can be verified that this intension justifies the reading of '$\hat{x}$' as 'is something x such that'.

A finite supply of variables and binders, however large, would lead to the mistaken omission of some sentences. To provide an infinite supply by means of a finite lexicon, we must allow our variables and binders to be generated as compounds. We need only three lexical items: one simple variable having the first variable intension; an N/N having as intension a function whose value, given as argument the nth variable intension for any $n \geq 1$, is the $(n + 1)$th variable intension; and an ((S/N)/S)/N having as intension a function whose value, given as argument the nth variable intension for any $n \geq 1$, is the nth binder intension. The first item gives us a starting variable; the second, iterated, manufactures the other variables; the third manufactures binders out of variables. However, we will continue to abbreviate base structures by writing variables and binders as if they were simple.

Variable-binding introduces a sort of spurious ambiguity called *alphabetic variance.* 'Porky loves himself' could have not only the structure shown but also others which 'x' and '$\hat{x}$' are replaced by 'y' and '$\hat{y}$', or 'z' and '$\hat{z}$', et cetera. Since different variables may have different intensions, these structures correspond to infinitely many different but cointensive meanings for 'Porky loves himself'. The simplest way to deal with this nuisance is to define an ordering of any such set of meanings and employ transformational filtering to dispose of all but the first meaning in the set (according to the ordering).

Binders have occasionally been discussed by logicians, under the name 'abstraction operators' or 'lambda operators'. (Church 1941; Carnap 1958, §33; Thomason and Stalnaker 1968.)

Now we are in a position to complete our account of the category S/(S/N) of verb-phrase-taking quantifier phrases, using binders as needed. The base structure for 'Every boy loves Zuleika' may be simply

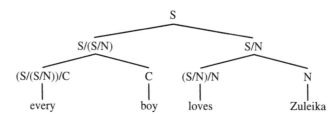

with no unnecessary variable-binding to make work for the transformational component. There is another base structure with variable-binding which we may read roughly as 'Every boy is something x such that x loves Zuleika'; it represents a different but equivalent meaning. We can either let these be another base structure and another (but equivalent) meaning for 'Every boy loves Zuleika' or get rid of them by transformational filtering. The base structure for 'Lothario loves some girl' is

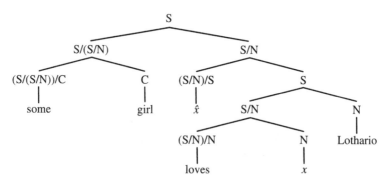

in which the quantifier phrase which is the surface object of 'loves' is treated as subject of a verb phrase obtained by binding the variable which is the base object of 'loves'. To reach an intermediate structure in which the quantifier phrase is relocated as the object of 'loves', we must have recourse to a transformation that moves the subject of a verb phrase made by variable binding into the place of one (the first?) occurrence of the bound variable and destroys the variable-binding apparatus. Note that, if desired, this transformation might apply *beneath* an intermediate level corresponding most closely to the ordinary level of deep structure. The two base structures for 'Every boy loves some girl' are

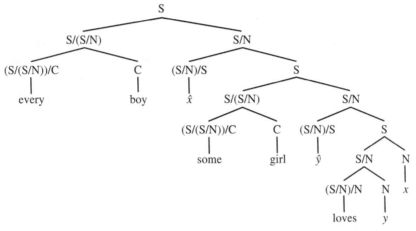

for the weak sense, and

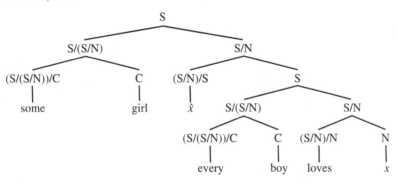

for the strong—Zuleika—sense.

It may be that quantifier-phrase objects should not be abandoned altogether. 'Lothario seeks a girl', in the sense in which it can be paraphrased as 'Lothario seeks a certain particular girl', can have the base structure

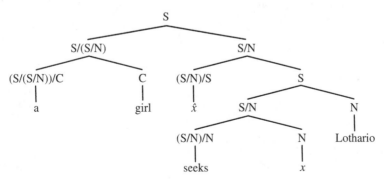

but what about the sense in which any old girl would do? We might give it the base structure

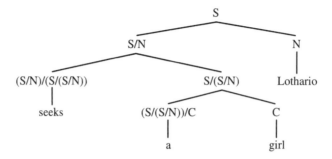

using a second 'seeks' that takes quantifier-phrase objects. The alternative is to let the word 'seeks' be introduced transformationally rather than lexically, as a transformational descendant of 'strives-to-find', so that the base structures would be

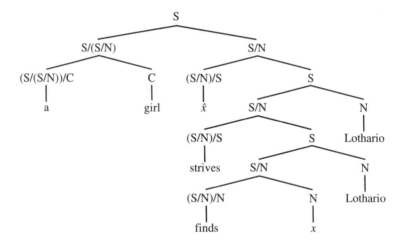

for the sense in which a certain particular girl is sought and

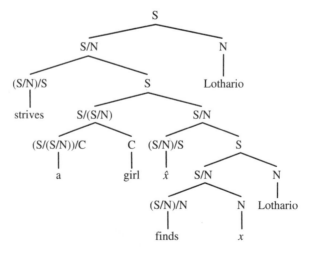

for the sense in which any old girl would do. But it is controversial whether we ought to let words be introduced transformationally in this way; and (as remarked in Montague 1969b) it is not clear how to apply this treatment to 'conceives of a tree'. Perhaps conceiving-of is imagining-to-exist, but perhaps not.

This completes one treatment of quantifier phrases, carried out with no modification of the system I originally presented. It is straightforward from the semantic point of view; however, it might result in excessive complications to transformational syntax. Ordinary bases have a category *noun phrase* which combines quantifier phrases and names; and transformations seem to work well on bases of that sort. By dividing the category of noun phrases, I may require some transformations to be doubled (or quadrupled, etc.). Moreover, my structures involving variable-binding are complicated and remote from the surface, so by doing away with quantifier-phrase objects I make lots of work for the transformational component. It might be, therefore, that this treatment is too costly to syntax. Therefore let us see how we might reinstate the combined category *noun phrase*. There are two methods: we might try to assimilate names to quantifier phrases, or we might try to assimilate quantifier phrases to names.

The method of assimilating names to quantifier phrases proceeds as follows. For every name in our lexicon, for instance 'Porky', we add to our lexicon a corresponding *pseudo-name* in the category S/(S/N). If the intension of the original name 'Porky' is the N-intension ϕ_1, then the intension of the corresponding pseudo-name 'Porky*' should be that function ϕ from S/N-intensions to S-intensions such that for any S/N-intension ϕ_2, $\phi(\phi_2) = \phi_2(\phi_1)$. As a result, a sentence such as 'Porky grunts' can be given either of the base structures

and will have the same intension either way. The category S/(S/N) may now be renamed *noun phrase*. It contains our former quantifier phrases together with our new pseudo-names. It does not contain names themselves. Names are now unnecessary as subjects, but still needed as objects; so the next step is to replace all name-takers except verb phrases by noun-phrase-takers. For instance, the category (S/N)/N of transitive verbs is to be replaced by the category (S/N)/(S/(S/N)) of pseudo-transitive verbs. The intensions of the replacements are related to the intensions of the originals in a systematic way which I shall not bother to specify. Names now serve no further purpose, having been supplanted both as subjects and as objects by pseudo-names; so the next step is to remove names from the lexicon. The category N is left vacant.

Since we have provided for noun-phrase objects for the sake of the pseudo-names, we can also have quantifier-phrase objects and so cut down on variable-binding. For instance, we have

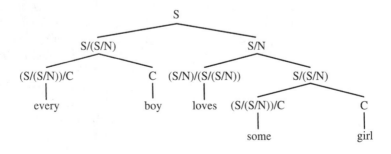

as the base structure for 'Every boy loves some girl' in the weak sense, leaving no work for the transformations. We cannot do away with variable-binding altogether, however. The base structure for 'Every boy loves some girl' in the strong—Zuleika—sense is now

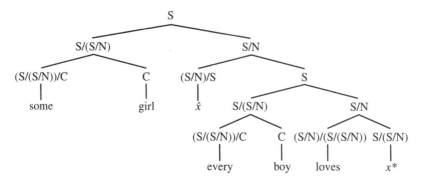

in which the seeming noun-phrase object 'some girl' is treated as subject of a verb phrase obtained by binding the pseudo-variable noun phrase 'x^*' which is the real object of 'loves'. Variables are names, of course, and therefore are replaced by pseudo-names just as any other names are; no change is made, however, in the corresponding binders.

So far we have not departed from the system I presented originally, and we *could* stop here. It is now advantageous, however, to take the step of eliminating the category N altogether and promoting the category *verb phrase* from a derived category S/N to a new basic category VP. Accordingly, the category of noun phrases becomes S/VP; the category of quantifiers becomes (S/VP)/C; the category of transitive verbs becomes VP/(S/VP); and the category which includes binders becomes VP/S.

We can also reopen the question of letting verb-phrase intensions be Carnapian rather than compositional. We rejected this simplification before, principally because it would require a projection rule which was not of our general function-and-arguments form; but that consideration no longer holds after names and verb-phrase-plus-name combinations are done away with. A lesser objection still applies: the simplification only works for extensional verb phrases. If any non-extensional verb phrases exist, they cannot go into our new basic category VP with Carnapian intensions. They will have to go into the category S/(S/VP) instead. The switch to Carnapian intensions for the now-basic verb phrases changes most other intensions in a systematic way which I need not stop to specify.

We turn last to the opposite method, in which quantifier phrases are assimilated to names to give an undivided category of noun phrases. This will require revising the extensions and intensions of names in a manner discussed by Mates (1968) and Montague (1969b; 1970b).

In the dark ages of logic, a story something like this was told. The phrase 'some pig' names a strange thing we may call the *existentially generic pig* which has just those properties that some pig has. Since some pig is male, some pig (a different one) is female, some pig is pink (all over), and some pig is grey (all over), the existentially generic pig is simultaneously male, female, pink, and grey. Accordingly, he (she?) is in the extensions both of 'is male' and of 'is female', both of 'is pink all over' and of 'is grey all over'. The phrase 'every pig' names a different strange thing called the *universally generic pig* which has just those properties that every pig has. Since not every pig is pink, grey, or any other color, the universally generic pig is not of any color. (Yet neither is he colorless, since not every—indeed, not any—pig is colorless). Nor is he(?) male or female (or neuter), since not every pig is any one of these. He is, however, a pig and an animal, and he grunts; for every pig is a pig and an animal, and grunts. There are also the *negative universally generic pig* which has just those properties that no pig has (he is not a pig, but he is both a stone and a number), the *majority generic pig* which has just those properties that more than half of all pigs have, and many more. A sentence formed from a name and an extensional verb phrase is true (we may add: at an index *i*) if and only if the thing named by the name (at *i*) belongs to the extension of the verb phrase (at *i*); and this is so regardless of whether the name happens to be a name like 'Porky' of an ordinary thing or a name like 'some pig' of a generic thing.

This story is preposterous since nothing, however recondite, can possibly have more or less than one of a set of incompatible and jointly exhaustive properties. At least, nothing can have more or less than one of them *as its properties*. But something, a set, can have *any* combination of them *as its members*; there is no contradiction in that.

Let us define the *character* of a thing as the set of its properties. Porky's character is that set which has as members just those properties that Porky has as properties. The various generic pigs do not, and could not possibly, exist; but their characters do. The character of the universally generic pig, for instance, is the set having as members just those properties that every pig has as properties.

A *character* is any set of properties. A character is *individual* iff it is a maximal compatible set of properties, so that something could possess all and only the properties contained in it; otherwise the character is *generic*.

Since no two things share all their properties (on a sufficiently inclusive conception of properties) things correspond one-to-one to their individual characters. We can exploit this correspondence to replace things by their characters whenever convenient. Some philosophers have even tried to eliminate things altogether in favor of their characters, saying that things are 'bundles of properties'. (Such a system is proposed as a formal reconstruction of Leibniz's doctrine of possible individuals in Mates 1968.) We need not go so far. We will replace things by individual characters as extensions of names, and as members of extensions of common nouns. However, we may keep the things themselves as well, taking them to be related to their names via their characters. Having made this substitution, we are ready to assimilate quantifier phrases to names by letting them also take characters—in most cases, generic characters—as extensions. 'Porky' has as extension Porky's individual character; 'every pig' has as extension the generic character of the universally generic pig. Even 'nobody' has an extension: the set of just those properties that nobody has.

We revise the system of meanings as follows. Our basic categories are *sentence* (S), *noun phrase* (NP), and *common noun* (C). Appropriate extensions for sentences are truth-values; appropriate extensions for noun phrases are characters, either individual or generic; appropriate extensions for common nouns are sets of individual characters. Intensions are as before: for basic categories, functions from some or all indices to appropriate extensions; for a derived category $(c/c_1 \ldots c_n)$, functions from c_1-intensions, . . . , and c_n-intensions to c-intensions. A *name* is an NP that never has a generic character as its extension at any index. The category of quantifiers becomes NP/C; the category of verb phrases becomes S/NP. Object-takers take NP objects which may or may not be names. Some variable-binding still is required; the two base structures for 'Every boy loves some girl' are

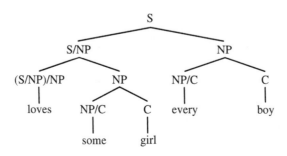

for the weak sense and

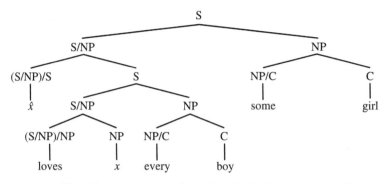

for the strong sense. Variables are names: the nth variable intension now becomes that NP-intension that assigns to every index i the character at the world coordinate of i of the thing that is the nth term of the assignment coordinate of i. The intensions of binders are revised to fit.

VIII   Treatment of non-declaratives

A meaning for a sentence, we said initially, was at least that which determines the conditions under which the sentence is true or false. But it is only declarative sentences that can be called true or false in any straightforward way. What of non-declarative sentences: commands, questions, and so on? If these do not have truth-values, as they are commonly supposed not to, we cannot very well say that their meanings determine their truth conditions.

One method of treating non-declaratives is to analyze all sentences, declarative or non-declarative, into two components: a *sentence radical* that specifies a state of affairs and a *mood* that determines whether the speaker is declaring that the state of affairs holds, commanding that it hold, asking whether it holds, or what. (I adopt the terminology of Stenius, 1967, one recent exposition of such a view.) We are to regard the sentences

> It is the case that you are late.
> Make it the case that you are late!
> Is it the case that you are late?

or more idiomatically

> You are late.
> Be late!
> Are you late?

as having a common sentence-radical specifying the state of affairs consisting of your being late, but differing in their moods: declarative, imperative, and interrogative. They might be given the base structures

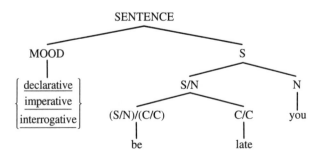

with S now understood as the category *sentence radical*. Different moods will induce different transformations of the sentence radical, leading to the different sentences above. The sentence radical is
not a declarative sentence. If it is represented on the surface at all, it should be represented as the
clause 'that you are late'. All that we have said about sentences should be taken as applying rather to
sentence radicals. It is sentence radicals that have truth-values as extensions, functions from indices
to truth-values as intensions, and meanings with the category S and an S-intension at the topmost
node. We may grant that a declarative sentence is called true iff its sentence radical has the value
truth; if we liked, we could also call an imperative or interrogative or other non-declarative sentence
true iff its sentence radical has the value *truth*, but we customarily do not. Fundamentally, however,
the entire apparatus of referential semantics (whether done on a categorial base as I propose, or otherwise) pertains to sentence radicals and constituents thereof. The semantics of mood is something
entirely different. It consists of rules of language use such as these (adapted from Stenius 1967):

> Utter a sentence representing the combination of the mood *declarative* with an S-meaning *m* only
> if *m* is true on the occasion in question.
>   React to a sentence representing the combination of the mood *imperative* with an S-meaning
> *m* (if adressed to you by a person in a suitable relation of authority over you) by acting in such
> a way as to make *m* true on the occasion in question.

In abstract semantics, as distinct from the theory of language use, a meaning for a sentence should
simply be a *pair* of a mood and an S-meaning (moods being identified with some arbitrarily chosen
entities).

The method of sentence radicals requires a substantial revision of my system. It works well
for declaratives, imperatives, and yes-no questions. It is hard to see how it could be applied to
other sorts of questions, or to sentences like 'Hurrah for Porky!'

I prefer an alternative method of treating non-declaratives that requires no revision whatever in my system of categories, intensions, and meanings. Let us once again regard S as the
category *sentence*, without discrimination of mood. But let us pay special attention to those
sentential meanings that are represented by base structures of roughly the following form:

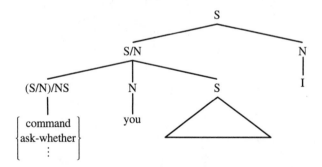

Such meanings can be represented by *performative sentences* such as these:

    I command you to be late.
    I ask you whether you are late.

(See Austin 1962, for the standard account of performatives; but, as will be seen, I reject part of
this account.) Such meanings might also be represented, after a more elaborate transformational
derivation, by non-declaratives:

    Be late!
    Are you late?

I propose that these non-declaratives ought to be treated as paraphrases of the corresponding performatives, having the same base structure, meaning, intension, and truth-value at an index or on an occasion. And I propose that there is no difference in kind between the meanings of these performatives and non-declaratives and the meanings of the ordinary declarative sentences considered previously.

It is not clear whether we would classify the performative sentences as declarative. If not, then we can divide sentential meanings into declarative sentential meanings and non-declarative sentential meanings, the latter being represented both by performatives and by imperatives, questions, et cetera. But if, as I would prefer, we classify performatives as declarative, then the distinction between declarative and non-declarative sentences becomes a purely syntactic, surface distinction. The only distinction among meanings is the distinction between those sentential meanings that can only be represented by declarative sentences and those that can be represented either by suitable declarative sentences (performatives) or by non-declarative paraphrases thereof. Let us call the latter *performative sentential meanings*. I need not delineate the class of performative sentential meanings precisely, since I am claiming that they do *not* need to be singled out for special semantic treatment.

The method of paraphrased performatives can easily be extended to those non-declaratives that resisted treatment by the method of sentence radicals. Not only yes-no questions but other questions as well correspond to performative sentences. The sentences below

I ask who Sylvia is.
Who is Sylvia?

for instance, might have a common meaning represented by a base structure something like this:

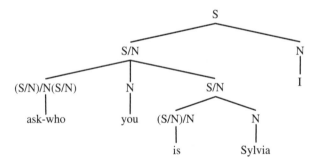

And the sentences

I cheer Porky.
Hurrah for Porky!

might have this base structure (thus the word 'Hurrah' would be introduced transformationally):

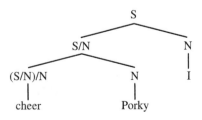

We may classify the sentential meanings represented by these base structures also as performative.

We noted at the outset that non-declaratives are commonly supposed to lack truth-values. The method of sentence radicals respects this common opinion by assigning truth-values fundamentally to sentence radicals rather than to whole sentences. We are under no compulsion to regard a non-declarative sentence as sharing the truth-value of its sentence radical, and we have chosen not to. The method of paraphrased performatives, on the other hand, does call for the assignment of truth-values to non-declarative sentences. The truth-value assigned is not that of the embedded sentence (corresponding to the sentence radical), however, but rather that of the paraphrased performative. If I say to you 'Be late!' and you are not late, the embedded sentence is false, but the paraphrased performative is true because I *do* command that you be late. I see no problem in letting non-declaratives have the truth-values of the performatives they paraphrase; after all, we need not ever mention their truth-values if we would rather not.

So far, I have assumed that performatives themselves do have truth-values, but that also has been denied. (Austin 1962, Lecture I.) I would wish to say that 'I bet you sixpence it will rain tomorrow' is true on an occasion of utterance iff the utterer *does* then bet his audience sixpence that it will rain on the following day; and, if the occasion is normal in certain respects, the utterer does so bet; therefore his utterance is true. Austin says it is obviously neither true nor false, apparently because to utter the sentence (in normal circumstances) is to bet. Granted; but why is that a reason to deny that the utterance is true? To utter 'I am speaking' is to speak, but it is also to speak the truth. This much can be said in Austin's defense: the truth-values (and truth conditions, that is intensions) of performatives and their paraphrases are easily ignored just because it is hard for a performative to be anything but true on an occasion of its utterance. Hard but possible: you can be play-acting, practicing elocution, or impersonating an officer and say 'I command that you be late' falsely, that is, say it without thereby commanding your audience to be late. I claim that those are the very circumstances in which you could falsely say 'Be late!'; otherwise it, like the performative, is truly uttered when and because it is uttered. It is no wonder if the truth-conditions of the sentences embedded in performatives and their non-declarative paraphrases tend to eclipse the truth conditions of the performatives and non-declaratives themselves.

This eclipsing is most visible in the case of performative sentences of the form 'I state that _____' or 'I declare that _____'. If someone says 'I declare that the Earth is flat' (sincerely, not play-acting, etc.) I claim that he has spoken truly: he does indeed so declare. I claim this not only for the sake of my theory but as a point of common sense. Yet one might be tempted to say that he has spoken falsely, because the sentence embedded in his performative—the content of his declaration, the belief he avows—is false. Hence I do not propose to take ordinary declaratives as paraphrased performatives (as proposed in Ross 1970) because that would get their truth conditions wrong. If there are strong syntactic reasons for adopting Ross's proposal, I would regard it as semantically a version of the method of sentence radicals, even if it employs base structures that look exactly like the base structures employed in the method of paraphrased performatives.

I provide only one meaning for the sentence 'I command you to be late'. Someone might well object that this sentence ought to come out ambiguous, because it can be used in two ways. It can be used to command; thus used, it can be paraphrased as 'Be late!', and it is true when uttered in normal circumstances just because it is uttered. It can be used instead to describe what I am doing; thus used, it cannot be paraphrased as an imperative, and it is likely to be false when uttered because it is difficult to issue a command and simultaneously say that I am doing so. (Difficult but possible: I might be doing the commanding by signing my name on a letter while describing what I am doing by talking.)

I agree that there are two alternative uses of this and other performative sentences: the genuinely performative use and the non-performative self-descriptive use. I agree also that the non-declarative paraphrase can occur only in the performative use. It still does not follow that there are two meanings. Compare the case of these two sentences:

> I am talking in trochaic hexameter.
> In hexameter trochaic am I talking.

The latter can be used to talk in trochaic hexameter and is true on any occasion of its correctly accented utterance. The former cannot be so used and is false on any occasion of its correctly accented utterance. Yet the two sentences are obviously paraphrases. Whether a sentence can be used to talk in trochaic hexameter is not a matter of its meaning. The distinction between using a sentence to talk in trochaic hexameter or not so using it is one sort of distinction; the distinction between using a performative sentence performatively and using it self-descriptively is quite another sort. Still I think the parallel is instructive. A distinction in uses need not involve a distinction in meanings of the sentences used. It can involve distinction in surface form; or distinction in conversational setting, intentions, and expectations; or distinction of some other sort. I see no decisive reason to insist that there is any distinction in meanings associated with the difference between performative and self-descriptive uses of performative sentences, if the contrary assumption is theoretically convenient.

We may ask to what extent the method of sentence radicals and the method of paraphrased performatives are compatible. In particular: given any sentence that can be analyzed into mood and sentence radical, can we recover the mood and the sentence-radical intension from the meaning of the sentence according to the method of paraphrased performatives?

We almost can do this, but not quite. On the method of sentence radicals, the difference between the performative and self-descriptive uses of performative sentences *must* be treated as a difference of meanings. So given a performative sentence meaning, we will get two pairs of a mood and a sentence-radical intension corresponding to the two uses. Suppose we are given a performative sentential meaning represented by a base structure like this, for instance:

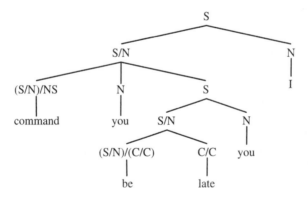

For the self-descriptive use, we do just what we would do for a non-performative sentence meaning: take the mood to be *declarative* and the sentence-radical intension to be the intension of the entire meaning. In this case, it would be the intension corresponding to the sentence radical 'that I command you to be late'. For the performative use, we take the mood to be determined by the (S/N)/NS-intension at node ⟨1 1⟩, and the sentence-radical intension to be the S-intension at node ⟨1 3⟩. In this case, these are respectively the intension of 'command', which determines that the mood is *imperative*, and the S-intension of the embedded sentence meaning, corresponding to the sentence radical 'that you are late'. Note here a second advantage, apart from fineness of individuation, of taking meanings as semantically interpreted phrase markers rather than as single intensions: we can recover the meanings of constituents from the meanings of their compounds.

Appendix: Indices expanded

Indices are supposed to be packages of everything but meaning that goes into determining extensions. Do we have everything? Let me speculate on several expansions of the indices that might prove useful.

First, consider the sentence *'This* is older than *this'*. I might say it pointing at a 1962 Volkswagen when I say the first 'this' and at a 1963 Volkswagen when I say the second 'this'. The sentence should be true on such an occasion; but how can it be? Using the intension of 'this', with its sensitivity to the indicated-objects coordinate, we obtain the intension of the whole sentence; then we take the value of that intension at an index with world and contextual coordinates determined by features of the occasion of utterance. (We generalize over indices alike except at the assignment coordinate; but we can consider any one of these, since the assignment coordinate is irrelevant to the sentence in question.) This procedure ignores the fact that the indicated object changes partway through the occasion of utterance. So the sentence comes out false, as it should on any occasion when the indicated object stays the same.

On a more extensional approach to semantics, a solution would be easy. We could take the two extensions of 'this' on the two occasions of its utterance and use these, rather than the fixed intension of 'this', to determine the truth-value of the sentence. The intension and the occasion of utterance of the sentence as a whole would drop out. But since the extensions of compounds are not in general determined by the extensions of their constituents, this extensional solution would preclude a uniform treatment of semantic projection rules.

An acceptable solution has been suggested to me by David Kaplan, as follows. Let the indicated-objects coordinate be not just one set of objects capable of being pointed at but an infinite sequence of such sets. Let the indicated-objects coordinate determined by a given occasion of utterance of a sentence have as its nth term the set of things pointed to at the nth utterance of 'this' during the utterance of the sentence so long as n does not exceed the number of such utterances, and let it be the empty set when n does exceed that number. Let there be an infinite sequence of constituents 'this$_1$', 'this$_2$', . . . with intensions such that 'this$_n$' depends for its extension at an index on the nth term of the assignment coordinate. So that the lexicon will remain finite, let all but 'this$_1$' be compounds generated by iterated application of a suitable N/N to 'this$_1$'. Let all members of the sequence appear as 'this' in surface structure. Use transformational filtering to dispose of all base structures except those employing an initial segment of the 'this'-sequence so arranged that if the subscripts were carried to the surface, they would appear in numerical order without repetition. Thus the only base structure for 'This is older than this' will be

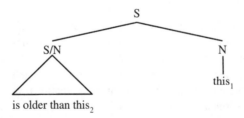

which will be true on occasions of the sort in question.

The solution must be modified to allow for the fact that 'this' is not the only demonstrative; I omit details. Similar difficulties arise, and similar solutions are possible, for other contextual coordinates: time, place, audience, and perhaps speaker.

Second, consider the sentence 'The door is open'. This does not mean that the one and only door that now exists is open; nor does it mean that the one and only door near the place of utterance, or pointed at, or mentioned in previous discourse, is open. Rather it means that the one and only door among the objects that are somehow prominent on the occasion is open. An object may be prominent because it is nearby, or pointed at, or mentioned; but none of these is a necessary condition of contextual prominence. So perhaps we need a *prominent-objects coordinate*, a new contextual coordinate independent of the others. It will be determined, on a given occasion of utterance of a sentence, by mental factors such as the speaker's expectations regarding the things he is likely to bring to the attention of his audience.

Third, consider the suggestion (Kaplan 1968; Donnellan 1970) that the extension of a personal name on a given occasion depends partly on the causal chain leading from the bestowal of that name on some person to the later use of that name by a speaker on the occasion in question. We might wish to accept this theory, and yet wish to deny that the intension or meaning of the name depends, on the occasion in question, upon the causal history of the speaker's use of it; for we might not wish to give up the common presumption that the meaning of an expression for a speaker depends only on mental factors within him. We might solve this dilemma (as proposed in Lewis 1968b) by including a *causal-history-of-acquisition-of-names coordinate* in our indices and letting the intensions of names for a speaker determine their extensions only relative to that coordinate.

Fourth, we have so far been ignoring the vagueness of natural language. Perhaps we are right to ignore it, or rather to deport it from semantics to the theory of language-use. We could say (as I did in Lewis 1969, ch. 5) that languages themselves are free of vagueness but that the linguistic conventions of a population, or the linguistic habits of a person, select not a point but a fuzzy region in the space of precise languages. However, it might prove better to treat vagueness within semantics, and we could do so as follows. (A related treatment, developed independently, is to be found in Goguen 1969.)

Pretend first that the only vagueness is the vagueness of 'cool' and 'warm'; and suppose for simplicity that these are extensional adjectives. Let the indices contain a *delineation coordinate*: a positive real number, regarded as the boundary temperature between cool and warm things. Thus at an index i the extension of 'cool' is the set of things at the world and time coordinates of i having temperatures (in degrees Kelvin) less than or equal to the delineation coordinate of i; the extension of 'warm' is the set of such things having temperatures greater than the delineation coordinate. A vague sentence such as 'This is cool' is true, on a given occasion, at some but not all delineations; that is, at some but not all indices that are alike except in delineation and have the world and contextual coordinates determined by the occasion of utterance. But sentences with vague constituents are not necessarily vague: 'This is cool or warm, but not both' is true at all delineations, on an occasion on which there is a unique indicated object, even if the indicated object is lukewarm.

The delineation coordinate is non-contextual. It resembles the assignment coordinate, in that we will ordinarily generalize over it rather than hold it fixed. We may say that a sentence is *true over* a set s of delineations at an index i, iff, for any index i' that is like i except perhaps at the delineation coordinate, the sentence is true at i' if and only if the delineation coordinate of i belongs to s. Given a normalized measure function over delineations, we can say that a sentence is *true to degree d* at i iff it is true at i over a set of delineations of measure d. Note that the degree of truth of a truth-functional compound of sentences is not a function of the degrees of truth of its constituent sentences: 'x is cool' and 'x is warm' may both be true to degree 0.5 at an index i, but 'x is cool or x is cool' is true at i to degree 0.5 whereas 'x is cool or x is warm' is true at i to degree 1.

Treating vagueness within semantics makes for simple specifications of the intensions of such expressions as 'in some sense', 'paradigmatic', '_____ish', and '_____er than'. The contemporary idiom 'in some sense', for instance, is an S/S related to the delineation coordinate just as the modal operator 'possibly' is related to the world coordinate. The intension of 'in some sense' is that function ϕ such that if ϕ_1 is any S-intension, ϕ_2 is $\phi(\phi_1)$, and i is any index, then

$$\phi_2(i) = \begin{cases} \textit{truth} \text{ if, for some index } i' \text{ that is like } i \text{ except perhaps at the delineation coordinate,} \\ \quad \phi_2(i') \text{ is } \textit{truth} \\ \textit{falsity} \text{ otherwise} \end{cases}$$

The comparative '_____er than' is a $((C/C)/N)/(C/C)$ having an intension such that, for instance, 'x is cooler than y' is true at an index i iff the set of delineations over which 'y is cool' is true at i is a proper subset of the set of delineations over which 'x is cool' is true at i. It follows that the sun is not cooler than Sirius unless in some sense the sun is cool; but that conclusion seems correct, although I do not know whether to deny that the sun is cooler than Sirius or to agree that in some sense the sun is cool. (This analysis of comparatives was suggested to me by David Kaplan.)

More generally, the delineation coordinate must be a sequence of boundary-specifying numbers. Different vague expressions will depend for their extensions (or, if they are not extensional, for the extensions of their extensional compounds) on different terms of the delineation. More than one term of the delineation coordinate might be involved for a single expression. For instance, the intension of 'green' might involve one term regarded as delineating the blue-green boundary and another regarded as delineating the green-yellow boundary. The former but not the latter would be one of the two terms involved in the intension of 'blue'; and so on around the circle of hues.

Notes

This paper is derived from a talk given at the Third La Jolla Conference on Linguistic Theory, March 1969. I am much indebted to Charles Chastain, Frank Heny, David Kaplan, George Lakoff, Richard Montague, and Barbara Partee for many valuable criticisms and suggestions.

12

DONALD DAVIDSON

Truth and Meaning

It is conceded by most philosophers of language, and recently even by some linguists, that a satisfactory theory of meaning must give an account of how the meanings of sentences depend upon the meanings of words. Unless such an account could be supplied for a particular language, it is argued, there would be no explaining the fact that we can learn the language: no explaining the fact that, on mastering a finite vocabulary and a finitely stated set of rules, we are prepared to produce and to understand any of a potential infinitude of sentences. I do not dispute these vague claims, in which I sense more than a kernel of truth.[1] Instead I want to ask what it is for a theory to give an account of the kind adumbrated.

One proposal is to begin by assigning some entity as meaning to each word (or other significant syntactical feature) of the sentence; thus we might assign Theaetetus to 'Theaetetus' and the property of flying to 'flies' in the sentence 'Theaetetus flies'. The problem then arises how the meaning of the sentence is generated from these meanings. Viewing concatenation as a significant piece of syntax, we may assign to it the relation of participating in or instantiating; however, it is obvious that we have here the start of an infinite regress. Frege sought to avoid the regress by saying that the entities corresponding to predicates (for example) are 'unsaturated' or 'incomplete' in contrast to the entities that correspond to names, but this doctrine seems to label a difficulty rather than solve it.

The point will emerge if we think for a moment of complex singular terms, to which Frege's theory applies along with sentences. Consider the expression 'the father of Annette'; how does the meaning of the whole depend on the meaning of the parts? The answer would seem to be that the meaning of 'the father of' is such that when this expression is prefixed to a singular term the result refers to the father of the person to whom the singular term refers. What part is played, in this account, by the unsaturated or incomplete entity for which 'the father of' stands? All we can think to say is that this entity 'yields' or 'gives' the father of x as value when the argument is x,

Donald Davidson (1967) Truth and meaning. *Synthèse* 17: 304–323. Reprinted by permission of Kluwer Academic Publishers.

or perhaps that this entity maps people onto their fathers. It may not be clear whether the entity for which 'the father of' is said to stand performs any genuine explanatory function as long as we stick to individual expressions; so think instead of the infinite class of expressions formed by writing 'the father of' zero or more times in front of 'Annette'. It is easy to supply a theory that tells, for an arbitrary one of these singular terms, what it refers to: if the term is 'Annette' it refers to Annette, while if the term is complex, consisting of 'the father of' prefixed to a singular term t, then it refers to the father of the person to whom t refers. It is obvious that no entity corresponding to 'the father of' is, or needs to be, mentioned in stating this theory.

It would be inappropriate to complain that this little theory *uses* the words 'the father of' in giving the reference of expressions containing those words. For the task was to give the meaning of all expressions in a certain infinite set on the basis of the meaning of the parts; it was not in the bargain also to give the meanings of the atomic parts. On the other hand, it is now evident that a satisfactory theory of the meanings of complex expressions may not require entities as meanings of all the parts. It behooves us then to rephrase our demand on a satisfactory theory of meaning so as not to suggest that individual words must have meanings at all, in any sense that transcends the fact that they have a systematic effect on the meanings of the sentences in which they occur. Actually, for the case at hand we can do better still in stating the criterion of success: what we wanted, and what we got, is a theory that entails every sentence of the form 't refers to x' where 't' is replaced by a structural description[2] of a singular term, and 'x' is replaced by that term itself. Further, our theory accomplishes this without appeal to any semantical concepts beyond the basic 'refers to'. Finally, the theory clearly suggests an effective procedure for determining, for any singular term in its universe, what that term refers to.

A theory with such evident merits deserves wider application. The device proposed by Frege to this end has a brilliant simplicity: count predicates as a special case of functional expressions, and sentences as a special case of complex singular terms. Now, however, a difficulty looms if we want to continue in our present (implicit) course of identifying the meaning of a singular term with its reference. The difficulty follows upon making two reasonable assumptions: that logically equivalent singular terms have the same reference; and that a singular term does not change its reference if a contained singular term is replaced by another with the same reference. But now suppose that 'R' and 'S' abbreviate any two sentences alike in truth value. Then the following four sentences have the same reference:

(1) R
(2) $\hat{x}(x = x.R) = \hat{x}(x = x)$
(3) $\hat{x}(x = x.S) = \hat{x}(x = x)$
(4) S

For (1) and (2) are logically equivalent, as are (3) and (4), while (3) differs from (2) only in containing the singular term '$\hat{x}(x = x.S)$' where (2) contains '$\hat{x}(x = x.R)$' and these refer to the same thing if S and R are alike in truth value. Hence any two sentences have the same reference if they have the same truth value.[3] And if the meaning of a sentence is what it refers to, all sentences alike in truth value must be synonymous—an intolerable result.

Apparently we must abandon the present approach as leading to a theory of meaning. This is the natural point at which to turn for help to the distinction between meaning and reference. The trouble, we are told, is that questions of reference are, in general, settled by extra-linguistic facts, questions of meaning not, and the facts can conflate the references of expressions that are not synonymous. If we want a theory that gives the meaning (as distinct from reference) of each sentence, we must start with the meaning (as distinct from reference) of the parts.

Up to here we have been following in Frege's footsteps; thanks to him, the path is well known and even well worn. But now, I would like to suggest, we have reached an impasse: the switch from reference to meaning leads to no useful account of how the meanings of sentences depend upon the meanings of the words (or other structural features) that compose them. Ask, for example, for the meaning of 'Theaetetus flies'. A Fregean answer might go something like this: given the meaning of 'Theaetetus' as argument, the meaning of 'flies' yields the meaning of 'Theaetetus flies' as value. The vacuity of this answer is obvious. We wanted to know what the meaning of 'Theaetetus flies' is; it is no progress to be told that it is the meaning of 'Theaetetus flies'. This much we knew before any theory was in sight. In the bogus account just given, talk of the structure of the sentence and of the meanings of words was idle, for it played no role in producing the given description of the meaning of the sentence.

The contrast here between a real and pretended account will be plainer still if we ask for a theory, analogous to the miniature theory of reference of singular terms just sketched, but different in dealing with meanings in place of references. What analogy demands is a theory that has as consequences all sentences of the form '*s* means *m*' where '*s*' is replaced by a structural description of a sentence and '*m*' is replaced by a singular term that refers to the meaning of that sentence; a theory, moreover, that provides an effective method for arriving at the meaning of an arbitrary sentence structurally described. Clearly some more articulate way of referring to meanings than any we have seen is essential if these criteria are to be met.[4] Meanings as entities, or the related concept of synonymy, allow us to formulate the following rule relating sentences and their parts: sentences are synonymous whose corresponding parts are synonymous ('corresponding' here needs spelling out of course). And meanings as entitles may, in theories such as Frege's, do duty, on occasion as references, thus losing their status as entities distinct from references. Paradoxically, the one thing meanings do not seem to do is oil the wheels of a theory of meaning—at least as long as we require of such a theory that it non-trivially give the meaning of every sentence in the language. My objection to meanings in the theory of meaning is not that they are abstract or that their identity conditions are obscure, but that they have no demonstrated use.

This is the place to scotch another hopeful thought. Suppose we have a satisfactory theory of syntax for our language, consisting of an effective method of telling, for an arbitrary expression, whether or not it is independently meaningful (i.e., a sentence), and assume as usual that this involves viewing each sentence as composed, in allowable ways, out of elements drawn from a fixed finite stock of atomic syntactical elements (roughly, words). The hopeful thought is that syntax, so conceived, will yield semantics when a dictionary giving the meaning of each syntactic atom is added. Hopes will be dashed, however, if semantics is to comprise a theory of meaning in our sense, for knowledge of the structural characteristics that make for meaningfulness in a sentence, plus knowledge of the meanings of the ultimate parts, does not add up to knowledge of what a sentence means. The point is easily illustrated by belief sentences. Their syntax is relatively unproblematic. Yet, adding a dictionary does not touch the standard semantic problem, which is that we cannot account for even as much as the truth conditions of such sentences on the basis of what we know of the meanings of the words in them. The situation is not radically altered by refining the dictionary to indicate which meaning or meanings an ambiguous expression bears in each of its possible contexts; the problem of belief sentences persists after ambiguities are resolved.

The fact that recursive syntax with dictionary added is not necessarily recursive semantics has been obscured in some recent writing on linguistics by the intrusion of semantic criteria into the discussion of purportedly syntactic theories. The matter would boil down to a harmless difference over terminology if the semantic criteria were clear; but they are not. While there is agreement that it is the central task of semantics to give the semantic interpretation (the meaning) of every sentence in the language, nowhere in the linguistic literature will one find, so far as I know, a straightforward account of how a theory performs this task, or how to tell when it has been accomplished. The contrast with syntax is striking. The main job of a modest syntax is to characterize *meaningfulness* (or sentencehood). We may have as much confidence in the correctness of such a characterization as we have in the representativeness of our sample and our ability to say when particular expressions are meaningful (sentences). What clear and analogous task and test exist for semantics?[5]

We decided a while back not to assume that parts of sentences have meanings except in the ontologically neutral sense of making a systematic contribution to the meaning of the sentences in which they occur. Since postulating meanings has netted nothing, let us return to that insight. One direction in which it points is a certain holistic view of meaning. If sentences depend for their meaning on their structure, and we understand the meaning of each item in the structure only as an abstraction from the totality of sentences in which it features, then we can give the meaning of any sentence (or word) only by giving the meaning of every sentence (and word) in the language. Frege said that only in the context of a sentence does a word have meaning; in the same vein he might have added that only in the context of the language does a sentence (and therefore a word) have meaning.

This degree of holism was already implicit in the suggestion that an adequate theory of meaning must entail *all* sentences of the form '*s* means *m*'. But now, having found no more help in meanings of sentences than in meanings of words, let us ask whether we can get rid of the troublesome singular terms supposed to replace '*m*' and to refer to meanings. In a way, nothing could be easier: just write '*s* means that *p*', and imagine '*p*' replaced by a sentence. Sentences, as we have seen, cannot name meanings, and sentences with 'that' prefixed are not names at all, unless we decide so. It looks as though we are in trouble on another count, however, for it is reasonable to expect that in wrestling with the logic of the apparently non-extensional 'means that' we will encounter problems as hard as, or perhaps identical with, the problems our theory is out to solve.

The only way I know to deal with this difficulty is simple, and radical. Anxiety that we are enmeshed in the intensional springs from using the words 'means that' as filling between description of sentence and sentence, but it may be that the success of our venture depends not on the filling but on what it fills. The theory will have done its work if it provides, for every sentence *s* in the language under study, a matching sentence (to replace '*p*') that, in some way yet to be made clear, 'gives the meaning' of *s*. One obvious candidate for matching sentence is just *s* itself, if the object language is contained in the metalanguage; otherwise a translation of *s* in the metalanguage. As a final bold step, let us try treating the position occupied by '*p*' extensionally: to implement this, sweep away the obscure 'means that', provide the sentence that replaces '*p*' with a proper sentential connective, and supply the description that replaces '*s*' with its own predicate. The plausible result is

(T)   *s* is *T* if and only if *p*.

What we require of a theory of meaning for a language *L* is that without appeal to any (further) semantical notions it place enough restrictions on the predicate 'is *T*' to entail all sentences got from schema *T* when '*s*' is replaced by a structural description of a sentence of *L* and '*p*' by that sentence.

Any two predicates satisfying this condition have the same extension[6], so if the metalanguage is rich enough, nothing stands in the way of putting what I am calling a theory of meaning into the form of an explicit definition of a predicate 'is *T*'. But whether explicitly defined or recursively characterized, it is clear that the sentences to which the predicate 'is *T*' applies will be just the true sentences of *L*, for the condition we have placed on satisfactory theories of meaning is in essence Tarski's Convention *T* that tests the adequacy of a formal semantical definition of truth.[7]

The path to this point has been tortuous, but the conclusion may be stated simply: a theory of meaning for a language *L* shows "how the meanings of sentences depend upon the meanings of words" if it contains a (recursive) definition of truth-in-*L*. And, so far at least, we have no

other idea how to turn the trick. It is worth emphasizing that the concept of truth played no os-
tensible role in stating our original problem. That problem, upon refinement, led to the view that
an adequate theory of meaning must characterize a predicate meeting certain conditions. It was
in the nature of a discovery that such a predicate would apply exactly to the true sentences. I hope
that what I am doing may be described in part as defending the philosophical importance of Tarski's
semantical concept of truth. But my defense is only distantly related, if at all, to the question whether
the concept Tarski has shown how to define is the (or a) philosophically interesting conception of
truth, or the question whether Tarski has cast any light on the ordinary use of such words as 'true'
and 'truth'. It is a misfortune that dust from futile and confused battles over these questions has
prevented those with a theoretical interest in language—philosophers, logicians, psychologists, and
linguists alike—from recognizing in the semantical concept of truth (under whatever name) the
sophisticated and powerful foundation of a competent theory of meaning.

There is no need to suppress, of course, the obvious connection between a definition of truth
of the kind Tarski has shown how to construct, and the concept of meaning. It is this: the definition works by giving necessary and sufficient conditions for the truth of every sentence, and to
give truth conditions is a way of giving the meaning of a sentence. To know the semantic concept of truth for a language is to know what it is for a sentence—any sentence—to be true, and
this amounts, in one good sense we can give to the phrase, to understanding the language. This
at any rate is my excuse for a feature of the present discussion that is apt to shock old hands: my
freewheeling use of the word 'meaning', for what I call a theory of meaning has after all turned
out to make no use of meanings, whether of sentences or of words. Indeed, since a Tarski-type
truth definition supplies all we have asked so far of a theory of meaning, it is clear that such a
theory falls comfortably within what Quine terms the 'theory of reference' as distinguished from
what he terms the 'theory of meaning'. So much to the good for what I call a theory of meaning,
and so much, perhaps, against my so calling it.[8]

A theory of meaning (in my mildly perverse sense) is an empirical theory, and its ambition
is to account for the workings of a natural language. Like any theory, it may be tested by comparing some of its consequences with the facts. In the present case this is easy, for the theory has
been characterized as issuing in an infinite flood of sentences each giving the truth conditions of
a sentence; we only need to ask, in selected cases, whether what the theory avers to be the truth
conditions for a sentence really are. A typical test case might involve deciding whether the sentence 'Snow is white' *is* true if and only if snow is white. Not all cases will be so simple (for
reasons to be sketched), but it is evident that this sort of test does not invite counting noses. A
sharp conception of what constitutes a theory in this domain furnishes an exciting context for
raising deep questions about when a theory of language is correct and how it is to be tried. But
the difficulties are theoretical, not practical. In application, the trouble is to get a theory that comes
close to working; anyone can tell whether it is right.[9] One can see why this is so. The theory
reveals nothing new about the conditions under which an individual sentence is true; it does not
make those conditions any clearer than the sentence itself does. The work of the theory is in relating the known truth conditions of each sentence to those aspects ('words') of the sentence that
recur in other sentences, and can be assigned identical roles in other sentences. Empirical power
in such a theory depends on success in recovering the structure of a very complicated ability—
the ability to speak and understand a language. We can tell easily enough when particular pro-
nouncements of the theory comport with our understanding of the language; this is consistent
with a feeble insight into the design of the machinery of our linguistic accomplishments.

The remarks of the last paragraph apply directly only to the special case where it is assumed
that the language for which truth is being characterized is part of the language used and understood by the characterizer. Under these circumstances, the framer of a theory will as a matter of
course avail himself when he can of the built-in convenience of a metalanguage with a sentence
guaranteed equivalent to each sentence in the object language. Still, this fact ought not to con us

into thinking a theory any more correct that entails "'Snow is white' is true if and only if snow is white" than one that entails instead:

(S)   'Snow is white' is true if and only if grass is green,

provided, of course, we are as sure of the truth of (S) as we are of that of its more celebrated predecessor. Yet (S) may not encourage the same confidence that a theory that entails it deserves to be called a theory of meaning.

The threatened failure of nerve may be counteracted as follows. The grotesqueness of (S) is in itself nothing against a theory of which it is a consequence, provided the theory gives the correct results for every sentence (on the basis of its structure, there being no other way). It is not easy to see how (S) could be party to such an enterprise, but if it were—if, that is, (S) followed from a characterization of the predicate 'is true' that led to the invariable pairing of truths with truths and falsehoods with falsehoods—then there would not, I think, be anything essential to the idea of meaning that remained to be captured.

What appears to the right of the biconditional in sentences of the form 's is true if and only if p' when such sentences are consequences of a theory of truth plays its role in determining the meaning of s not by pretending synonymy but by adding one more brush-stroke to the picture which, taken as a whole, tells what there is to know of the meaning of s; this stroke is added by virtue of the fact that the sentence that replaces 'p' is true if and only if s is.

It may help to reflect that (S) is acceptable, if it is, because we are independently sure of the truth of 'Snow is white' and 'Grass is green'; but in cases where we are unsure of the truth of a sentence, we can have confidence in a characterization of the truth predicate only if it pairs that sentence with one we have good reason to believe equivalent. It would be ill advised for someone who had any doubts about the color of snow or grass to accept a theory that yielded (S), even if his doubts were of equal degree, unless he thought the color of the one was tied to the color of the other. Omniscience can obviously afford more bizarre theories of meaning than ignorance; but then, omniscience has less need of communication.

It must be possible, of course, for the speaker of one language to construct a theory of meaning for the speaker of another, though in this case the empirical test of the correctness of the theory will no longer be trivial. As before, the aim of theory will he an infinite correlation of sentences alike in truth. But this time the theory-builder must not be assumed to have direct insight into likely equivalences between his own tongue and the alien. What he must do is find out, however he can, what sentences the alien holds true in his own tongue (or better, to what degree he holds them true). The linguist then will attempt to construct a characterization of truth-for-the-alien which yields, so far as possible, a mapping of sentences held true (or false) by the alien onto sentences held true (or false) by the linguist. Supposing no perfect fit is found, the residue of sentences held true translated by sentences held false (and vice versa) is the margin for error (foreign or domestic). Charity in interpreting the words and thoughts of others is unavoidable in another direction as well: just as we must maximize agreement, or risk not making sense of what the alien is talking about, so we must maximize the self-consistency we attribute to him, on pain of not understanding *him*. No single principle of optimum charity emerges; the constraints therefore determine no single theory. In a theory of radical translation (as Quine calls it) there is no completely disentangling questions of what the alien means from questions of what he believes. We do not know what someone means unless we know what he believes; we do not know what someone believes unless we know what he means. In radical translation we are able to break into this circle, if only incompletely, because we can sometimes tell that a person accedes to a sentence we do not understand.[10]

In the past few pages I have been asking how a theory of meaning that takes the form of a truth definition can be empirically tested, and have blithely ignored the prior question whether there is any serious chance such a theory can be given for a natural language. What are the prospects for a formal semantical theory of a natural language? Very poor, according to Tarski; and I believe most logicians, philosophers of language and linguists agree.[11] Let me do what I can to dispel the pessimism. What I can in a general and programmatic way, of course; for here the proof of the pudding will certainly be in the proof of the right theorems.

Tarski concludes the first section of his classic essay on the concept of truth in formalized languages with the following remarks, which he italicizes:

> *The very possibility of a consistent use of the expression 'true sentence' which is in harmony with the laws of logic and the spirit of everyday language seems to be very questionable, and consequently the same doubt attaches to the possibility of constructing a correct definition of this expression.*[12]

Late in the same essay, he returns to the subject:

> The concept of truth (as well as other semantic concepts) when applied to colloquial language in conjunction with the normal laws of logic leads inevitably to confusions and contradictions. Whoever wishes, in spite of all difficulties, to pursue the semantics of colloquial language with the help of exact methods will be driven first to undertake the thankless task of a reform of this language. He will find it necessary to define its structure, to overcome the ambiguity of the terms which occur in it, and finally to split the language into a series of languages of greater and greater extent, each of which stands in the same relation to the next in which a formalized language stands to its metalanguage. It may, however be doubted whether the language of everyday life, after being 'rationalized' in this way, would still preserve its naturalness and whether it would not rather take on the characteristic features of the formalized languages.[13]

Two themes emerge: that the universal character of natural languages leads to contradiction (the semantic paradoxes), and that natural languages are too confused and amorphous to permit the direct application of formal methods. The first point deserves a serious answer, and I wish I had one. As it is, I will say only why I think we are justified in carrying on without having disinfected this particular source of conceptual anxiety. The semantic paradoxes arise when the range of the quantifiers in the object language is too generous in certain ways. But it is not really clear how unfair to Urdu or to Hindi it would be to view the range of their quantifiers as insufficient to yield an explicit definition of 'true-in-Urdu' or 'true-in-Hindi'. Or, to put the matter in another, if not more serious way, there may in the nature of the case always be something we grasp in understanding the language of another (the concept of truth) that we cannot communicate to him. In any case, most of the problems of general philosophical interest arise within a fragment of the relevant natural language that may be conceived as containing very little set theory. Of course, these comments do not meet the claim that natural languages are universal. But it seems to me this claim, now that we know such universality leads to paradox, is suspect.

Tarski's second point is that we would have to reform a natural language out of all recognition before we could apply formal semantical methods. If this is true, it is fatal to my project, for the task of a theory of meaning as I conceive it is not to change, improve or reform a language, but to describe and understand it. Let us look at the positive side. Tarski has shown the way to giving a theory for interpreted formal languages of various kinds; pick one as much like English as possible. Since this new language has been explained in English and contains much English we not only may, but I think must, view it as part of English for those who understand it. For this fragment of English we have, ex hypothesi, a theory of the required sort. Not only that, but in interpreting this adjunct of English in old English we necessarily gave hints connecting old and new. Wherever there are sentences of old English with the same truth conditions as sentences in the adjunct we may extend the theory to cover them. Much of what is called for is just to mechanize as far as possible what we now do by art when we put ordinary English into one or another canonical notation. The point is not that canonical notation is better than the rough original idiom, but rather that if we know what idiom the canonical notation is canonical *for*, we have as good a theory for the idiom as for its kept companion.

Philosophers have long been at the hard work of applying theory to ordinary language by the device of matching sentences in the vernacular with sentences for which they have a theory. Frege's massive contribution was to show how 'all', 'some', 'every', 'each', 'none', and associated pronouns, in some of their uses, could be tamed; for the first time, it was possible to dream of a formal semantics for a significant part of a natural language. This dream came true in a sharp way with the work of Tarski. It would be a shame to miss the fact that as a result of these two magnificent achievements, Frege's and Tarski's, we have gained a deep insight into the structure of our mother tongues. Philosophers of a logical bent have tended to start where the theory was and work out toward the complications of natural language. Contemporary linguists, with an aim that cannot easily be seen to be different, start with the ordinary and work toward a general theory. If either party is successful, there must be a meeting. Recent work by Chomsky and others is doing much to bring the complexities of natural languages within the scope of serious semantic theory. To give an example: suppose success in giving the truth conditions for some significant range of sentences in the active voice. Then with a formal procedure for transforming each such sentence into a corresponding sentence in the passive voice, the theory of truth could be extended in an obvious way to this new set of sentences.[14]

One problem touched on in passing by Tarski does not, at least in all its manifestations, have to be solved to get ahead with theory: the existence in natural languages of 'ambiguous terms'. As long as ambiguity does not affect grammatical form, and can be translated, ambiguity for ambiguity, into the metalanguage, a truth definition will not tell us any lies. The trouble, for systematic semantics, with the phrase 'believes that' in English is not its vagueness, ambiguity, or unsuitability for incorporation in a serious science: let our metalanguage be English, and all *these* problems will be translated without loss or gain into the metalanguage. But the central problem of the logical grammar of 'believes that' will remain to haunt us.

The example is suited to illustrating another, and related, point, for the discussion of belief sentences has been plagued by failure to observe a fundamental distinction between tasks: uncovering the logical grammar or form of sentences (which is in the province of a theory of meaning as I construe it), and the analysis of individual words or expressions (which are treated as primitive by the theory). Thus Carnap, in the first edition of *Meaning and Necessity*, suggested we render 'John believes that the earth is round' as 'John responds affirmatively to "the earth is round" as an English sentence'. He gave this up when Mates pointed out that John might respond affirmatively to one sentence and not to another, no matter how close in meaning. But there is a confusion here from the start. The semantic structure of a belief sentence, according to this idea of Carnap's, is given by a three-place predicate with places reserved for expressions referring to a person, a sentence, and a language. It is a different sort of problem entirely to attempt an analysis of this predicate, perhaps along behavioristic lines. Not least among the merits of Tarski's conception of a theory of truth is that the purity of method it demands of us follows from the formulation of the problem itself, not from the self-imposed restraint of some adventitious philosophical puritanism.

I think it is hard to exaggerate the advantages to philosophy of language of bearing in mind this distinction between questions of logical form or grammar, and the analysis of individual concepts. Another example may help advertise the point.

If we suppose questions of logical grammar settled, sentences like 'Bardot is good' raise no special problems for a truth definition. The deep differences between descriptive and evaluative (emotive, expressive, etc.) terms do not show here. Even if we hold there is some important sense in which moral or evaluative sentences do not have a truth value (for example, because they cannot

be 'verified'), we ought not to boggle at " 'Bardot is good' is true if and only if Bardot is good";
in a theory of truth, this consequence should follow with the rest, keeping track, as must be done,
of the semantic location of such sentences in the language as a whole—of their relation to generalizations, their role in such compound sentences as 'Bardot is good and Bardot is foolish',
and so on. What is special to evaluative words is simply not touched: the mystery is transferred
from the word 'good' in the object language to its translation in the metalanguage.

But 'good' as it features in 'Bardot is a good actress' is another matter. The problem is not
that the translation of this sentence is not in the metalanguage—let us suppose it is. The problem
is to frame a truth definition such that " 'Bardot is a good actress' is true if and only if Bardot is
a good actress"—and all other sentences like it—are consequences. Obviously 'good actress'
does not mean 'good and an actress'. We might think of taking 'is a good actress' as an unanalyzed
predicate. This would obliterate all connection between 'is a good actress' and 'is a good mother',
and it would give us no excuse to think of 'good', in these uses, as a word or semantic element.
But worse, it would bar us from framing a truth definition at all, for there is no end to the predicates we would have to treat as logically simple (and hence accommodate in separate clauses in
the definition of satisfaction): 'is a good companion to dogs', 'is a good twenty-eight-year-old
conversationalist', and so forth. The problem is not peculiar to the case: it is the problem of attributive adjectives generally.

It is consistent with the attitude taken here to deem it usually a strategic error to undertake
philosophical analysis of words or expressions which is not preceded by or at any rate accompanied by the attempt to get the logical grammar straight. For how can we have any confidence in
our analyses of words like 'right', 'ought', 'can', and 'obliged', or the phrases we use to talk of
actions, events, and causes, when we do not know what (logical, semantical) parts of speech we
have to deal with? I would say much the same about studies of the "logic" of these and other
words, and the sentences containing them. Whether the effort and ingenuity that has gone into
the study of deontic logics, modal logics, imperative and erotetic logics has been largely futile or
not cannot be known until we have acceptable semantic analyses of the sentences such systems
purport to treat. Philosophers and logicians sometimes talk or work as if they were free to choose
between, say, the truth-functional conditional and others, or free to introduce non-truth-functional
sentential operators like 'Let it be the case that' or 'It ought to be the case that'. But in fact the
decision is crucial. When we depart from idioms we can accomodate in a truth definition, we
lapse into (or create) language for which we have no coherent semantical account—that is, no
account at all of how such talk can be integrated into the language as a whole.

To return to our main theme: we have recognized that a theory of the kind proposed leaves
the whole matter of what individual words mean exactly where it was. Even when the metalanguage is different from the object language, the theory exerts no pressure for improvement,
clarification or analysis of individual words, except when, by accident of vocabulary, straightforward translation fails. Just as synomy, as between expressions, goes generally untreated,
so also synomy of sentences, and analyticity. Even such sentences as 'A vixen is a female fox'
bear no special tag unless it is our pleasure to provide it. A truth definition does not distinguish
between analytic sentences and others, except for sentences that owe their truth to the presence
alone of the constants that give the theory its grip on structure: the theory entails not only that
these sentences are true but that they will remain true under all significant rewritings of their
non-logical parts. A notion of logical truth thus given limited application, related notions of logical
equivalence and entailment will tag along. It is hard to imagine how a theory of meaning could
fail to read a logic into its object language to this degree; and to the extent that it does, our intuitions of logical truth, equivalence and entailment may he called upon in constructing and testing
the theory.

I turn now to one more, and very large, fly in the ointment: the fact that the same sentence
may at one time or in one mouth be true and at another time or in another mouth be false. Both

logicians and those critical of formal methods here seem largely (though by no means universally) agreed that formal semantics and logic are incompetent to deal with the disturbances caused by demonstratives. Logicians have often reacted by downgrading natural language and trying to show how to get along without demonstratives; their critics react by downgrading logic and formal semantics. None of this can make me happy: clearly demonstratives cannot be eliminated from a natural language without loss or radical change, so there is no choice but to accommodate theory to them.

No logical errors result if we simply treat demonstratives as constants;[15] neither do any problems arise for giving a semantic truth definition. "'I am wise' is true if and only if I am wise," with its bland ignoring of the demonstrative element in 'I' comes off the assembly line along with "'Socrates is wise' is true if and only if Socrates is wise" with *its* bland indifference to the demonstrative element in 'is wise' (the tense).

What suffers in this treatment of demonstratives is not the definition of a truth predicate but the plausibility of the claim that what has been defined is truth. For this claim is acceptable only if the speaker and circumstances of utterance of each sentence mentioned in the definition is matched by the speaker and circumstances of utterance of the truth definition itself. It could also be fairly pointed out that part of understanding demonstratives is knowing the rules by which they adjust their reference to circumstance; assimilating demonstratives to constant terms obliterates this feature. These complaints can be met, I think, though only by a fairly far-reaching revision in the theory of truth. I shall barely suggest how this could be done, but bare suggestion is all that is needed: the idea is technically trivial, and quite in line with work being done on the logic of the tenses.[16]

We could take truth to be a property, not of sentences, but of utterances, or speech acts, or ordered triples of sentences, times and persons; but it is simplest just to view truth as a relation between a sentence, a person, and a time. Under such treatment, ordinary logic as now read applies as usual, but only to sets of sentences relativized to the same speaker and time; further logical relations between sentences spoken at different times and by different speakers may be articulated by new axioms. Such is not my concern. The theory of meaning undergoes a systematic but not puzzling change: corresponding to each expression with a demonstrative element there must in the theory be a phrase that relates the truth conditions of sentences in which the expression occurs to changing times and speakers. Thus the theory will entail sentences like the following:

'I am tired' is true as (potentially) spoken by p at t if and only if p is tired at t.
'That book was stolen' is true as (potentially) spoken by p at t if and only if the book demonstrated by p at t is stolen prior to t.[17]

Plainly, this course does not show how to eliminate demonstratives; for example, there is no suggestion that 'the book demonstrated by the speaker' can be substituted ubiquitously for 'that book' *salva veritate*. The fact that demonstratives are amenable to formal treatment ought greatly to improve hopes for a serious semantics of natural language, for it is likely that many outstanding puzzles, such as the analysis of quotations or sentences about propositional attitudes, can be solved if we recognize a concealed demonstrative construction.

Now that we have relativized truth to times and speakers, it is appropriate to glance back at the problem of empirically testing a theory of meaning for an alien tongue. The essence of the method was, it will be remembered, to correlate held-true sentences with held-true sentences by way of a truth definition, and within the bounds of intelligible error. Now the picture must be elaborated to allow for the fact that sentences are true, and held true, only relative to a speaker and a time. The real task is therefore to translate each sentence by another that is true for the same speakers at the same times. Sentences with demonstratives obviously yield a very sensitive test of the correctness of a theory of meaning, and constitute the most direct link between language and the recurrent macroscopic objects of human interest and attention.[18]

In this paper I have assumed that the speakers of a language can effectively determine the meaning or meanings of an arbitrary expression (if it has a meaning), and that it is the central task of a theory of meaning to show how this is possible. I have argued that a characterization of a truth predicate describes the required kind of structure, and provides a clear and testable criterion of an adequate semantics for a natural language. No doubt there are other reasonable demands that may be put on a theory of meaning. But a theory that does no more than define truth for a language comes far closer to constituting a complete theory of meaning than superficial analysis might suggest; so, at least, I have urged.

Since I think there is no alternative, I have taken an optimistic and programmatic view of the possibilities for a formal characterization of a truth predicate for a natural language. But it must be allowed that a staggering list of difficulties and conundrums remains. To name a few: we do not know the logical form of counterfactual or subjunctive sentences, nor of sentences about probabilities and about causal relations; we have no good idea what the logical role of adverbs is, nor the role of attributive adjectives; we have no theory for mass terms like 'fire', 'water', and 'snow', nor for sentences about belief, perception, and intention, nor for verbs of action that imply purpose. And finally, there are all the sentences that seem not to have truth values at all: the imperatives, optatives, interrogatives, and a host more. A comprehensive theory of meaning for a natural language must cope successfully with each of these problems.

Notes

An earlier version of this paper was read at the Eastern Division meeting of the American Philosophical Association in December, 1966; the main theme traces back to an unpublished paper delivered to the Pacific Division of the American Philosophical Association in 1953. Present formulations owe much to John Wallace, with whom I have discussed these matters since 1962. My research was supported by the National Science Foundation.

1. Elsewhere I have urged that it is a necessary condition, if a language is to be learnable, that it have only a finite number of semanticat primitives: see "Theories of Meaning and Learnable Languages," in *Proceeding of the 1964 International Congress for Logic, Methodology and Philosophy of Science* (North-Holland Publishing Company, Amsterdam, 1965), pp. 383–394.

2. A 'structural description' of an expression describes the expression as a concatenation of elements drawn from a fixed finite list (for example of words or letters).

3. The argument is essentially Frege's. See A. Church, *Introduction to Mathematical Logic*, Vol. 1 (Princeton 1956), pp. 24–25. It is perhaps worth mentioning that the argument does not depend on any particular identification of the entities to which sentences are supposed to refer.

4. It may be thought that Church, in "A Formulation of the Logic of Sense and Denotation," in *Structure, Method and Meaning: Essays in Honor of H. M. Sheffer*, ed. Henle, Kallen and Langer (Liberal Arts Press, New York, 1951), pp. 3–24, has given a theory of meaning that makes essential use of meanings as entities. But this is not the case: Church's logics of sense and denotation are interpreted as being about meanings, but they do not mention expressions and so cannot of course be theories of meaning in the sense now under discussion.

5. For a recent and instructive statement of the role of semantics in linguistics, see Noam Chomsky, "Topics in the Theory of Generative Grammar," in *Current Trends in Linguistics*, ed. Thomas A. Sebeok, Vol. 3 (The Hague, 1966). In this article, Chomsky (1) emphasizes the central importance of semantics in linguistic theory, (2) argues for the superiority of transformational grammars over phrase structure grammars largely on the grounds that, although phrase structure grammars may be adequate to define sentence-hood for (at least) some natural languages, they are inadequate as a foundation for semantics, and (3) comments repeatedly on the "rather primitive state" of the concepts of semantics and remarks that the notion of semantic interpretation "still resists any deep analysis."

6. Assuming, of course, that the extension of these predicates is limited to the sentences of *L*.

7. Alfred Tarski, "The Concept of Truth in Formalized Language," in *Logic, Semantics, Metamathematics* (Oxford, 1956), pp. 152–278.

8. But Quine may be quoted in support of my usage: "in point of *meaning* . . . a word may be said to be determined to whatever extent the truth or falsehood of its contexts is determined." "Truth by Convention," first published in 1936; now in *The Ways of Paradox* (New York, 1966), p. 82. Since a truth definition determines the truth value of every sentence in the object language (relative to a sentence in the metalanguage), it determines the meaning of every word and sentence. This would seem to justify the title "Theory of Meaning."

9. To give a single example: it is clearly a count in favor of a theory that it entails " 'Snow is white' is true if and only if snow is white." But to contrive a theory that entails this (and works for all related sentences) is not trivial. I do not know a theory that succeeds with this very case (the problem of "mass terms").

10. This sketch of how a theory of meaning for an alien tongue can be tested obviously owes its inspiration to Quine's account of radical translation in chapter 2 of *Word and Object* (New York, 1960). In suggesting that an acceptable theory of radical translation take the form of a recursive characterization of truth, I go beyond anything explicit in Quine. Toward the end of this paper, in the discussion of demonstratives, another strong point of agreement will turn up.

11. So far as I am aware, there has been very little discussion of whether a formal truth definition can be given for a natural language. But in a more general vein, several people have urged that the concepts of formal semantics be applied to natural language. See, for example, the contributions of Yehoshua Bar-Hillel and Evert Beth to *The Philosophy of Rudolph Carnap* (ed. by Paul A. Schilpp), La Salle, Ill., 1963, and Bar-Hillel's (1964) "Logical Syntax and Semantics," *Language* 30: 230–237.

12. Tarski, ibid., p. 165.

13. Ibid., p. 267.

14. The rapprochement I prospectively imagine between transformational grammar and a sound theory of meaning has been much advanced by a recent change in the conception of transformational grammar described in Chomsky in (1966). The structures generated by the phrase-structure part of the grammar, it has been realized for some time, are those suited to semantic interpretation; but this view is inconsistent with the idea, held by Chomsky until recently, that recursive operations are introduced only by the transformation rules. Chomsky now believes the phrase-structure rules are recursive. Since languages to which formal semantic methods directly and naturally apply are ones for which a (recursive) phrase-structure grammar is appropriate, it is clear that Chomsky's present picture of the relation between the structures generated by the phrase-structure part of the grammar, and the sentences of the language, is very much like the picture many logicians and philosophers have had of the relation between the richer formalized languages and ordinary language. (In these remarks I am indebted to Bruce Vermazen.)

15. Quine has good things to say about this in *Methods of Logic* (New York, 1950), §8.

16. For an up-to-date bibliography, and discussion, see A. N. Prior, *Past, Present, and Future* (Oxford, 1967).

17. There is more than an intimation of this approach to demonstratives and truth in Austin's 1950 article "Truth", reprinted in *Philosophical Papers* (Oxford, 1961). See pp. 89–90.

18. These remarks clearly derive from Quine's idea that "occasion sentences" (those with a demonstrative element) must play a central role in constructing a translation manual.

13

HANS KAMP

A Theory of Truth
and Semantic Representation

1   Introduction

Two conceptions of meaning have dominated formal semantics of natural language. The first of these sees meaning principally as that which determines conditions of truth. This notion, whose advocates are found mostly among philosophers and logicians, has inspired the disciplines of truth-theoretic and model-theoretic semantics. According to the second conception meaning is, first and foremost, that which a language user grasps when he understands the words he hears or reads. This second conception is implicit in many studies by computer scientists (especially those involved with artificial intelligence), psychologists and linguists—studies which have been concerned to articulate the structure of the representations which speakers construct in response to verbal inputs.

It appears that these two conceptions, and with them the theoretical concerns that derive from them, have remained largely separated for a considerable period of time. This separation has become an obstacle to the development of semantic theory, impeding progress on either side of the line of division it has created.

The theory presented here is an attempt to remove this obstacle. It combines a definition of truth with a systematic account of semantic representations. These two components are linked in the following manner. The representations postulated here are (like those proposed by others; see, e.g., Hendrix 1975 or Karttunen 1976) similar in structure to the models familiar from model-theoretic semantics. In fact, formally they are nothing other than partial models, typically with small finite domains. Such similarity should not surprise; for the representation of, say, an indicative sentence ought to embody those conditions which the world must satisfy in order that the sentence be true; and a particularly natural representation of those conditions is provided by a partial model with which the (model describing the) real world will be compatible just in case the conditions are fulfilled.

Hans Kamp (1981) A theory of truth and semantic representation. In *Formal Methods in the Study of Language*, part 1, 277–322. MC Tract 135. Stichting Mathematisch Centrum, Amsterdam. Reprinted by permission of CWI Tracts.

Interpreting the truth-conditional significance of representations in this way we are led to the following characterization of truth: A sentence S, or discourse D, with representation m is true in a model M if and only if M is compatible with m; and compatibility of M with m, we shall see, can be defined as the existence of a proper embedding of m into M, where a *proper embedding* is a map from the universe of m into that of M which, roughly speaking, preserves all the properties and relations which m specifies of the elements of its domain.

A theory of this form differs fundamentally from those familiar from the truth-theoretical and model-theoretical literature, and thus a substantial argument will be wanted that such a radical departure from existing frameworks is really necessary. The particular analysis carried out in the main part of this paper should be seen as a first attempt to provide such an argument. The analysis deals with only a small number of linguistic problems, but careful reflection upon just those problems already reveals, I suggest, that a major revision of semantic theory is called for.

The English fragment with which the analysis deals contains sentences built up from these constituents: common nouns, certain transitive and intransitive verbs (all in the third-person singular present tense), personal and relative pronouns, proper names, and the particles *a*, *every*, and *if . . . (then)*. These can be combined to yield the following sorts of compounds:

(i)   Complex singular terms such as *a man, every woman, a man who loves every woman, every woman whom a man who owns a donkey loves*, etc. (We can embed relative clauses inside others, and there is no upper bound to the depth of embedding.)
(ii) Singular terms—i.e., complex terms of the kind just exemplified, proper names and personal pronouns—can be combined with verbs to yield sentences.
(iii) Sentences may be joined with the help of *if* to form larger sentences of conditional form; sentences serve moreover as the sources of relative clauses.

The choice of this fragment is motivated by two central concerns: (a) to study the anaphoric behaviour of personal pronouns; and (b) to formulate a plausible account of the truth conditions of the so-called donkey-sentences (which owe their name to the particular examples in Geach 1962, the work that kindled contemporary interest in sentences of this type). As these donkey-sentences will play a prominent role in the theory developed below, let me briefly review the problem that they have been taken to present. We shall concentrate on the following two instances:

(1)   If Pedro owns a donkey he beats it
(2)   Every farmer who owns a donkey beats it.

For what needs to be said at this point it will suffice to focus on (1). For many speakers, including the author of this paper, the truth conditions of (1) are those determined by the first-order formula

(3) $\forall x$ (Donkey (x) $\wedge$ Owns (Pedro,x) $\rightarrow$ Beats (Pedro,x)).

(As a matter of fact not all English speakers seem to agree that (3) correctly states the truth conditions of (1). Unfortunately, an adequate discussion of diverging intuitions is not possible within the confines of the present contribution.)

The problem with (1) and (3) is that the indefinite description *a donkey* of (1) reemerges in (3) as a universal quantifier. How does an expression of a type which standardly (or so it always seemed) conveys existence manage to express universality in a sentence such as (1)? One way in which one might hope to explain this is by refering to the familiar equivalence between universal quantifiers with wide and existential quantifiers with narrow scope. Sentence (4), for instance, can be symbolized not only as (5) but also as (6):

(4)   If Pedro owns a donkey he is rich
(5) $\forall x$ (Donkey (x) $\wedge$ Owns (Pedro,x) $\rightarrow$ Rich (Pedro))
(6) $\exists x$ (Donkey (x) $\wedge$ Owns (Pedro,x)) $\rightarrow$ Rich (Pedro).

Out of these two, (6) would appear to be the "natural" symbolization of (4) as it renders the indefinite *a donkey* as an existential quantifier. [Example] (5), we might be inclined to say, is adequate only for indirect reasons, viz. in virtue of its logical equivalence to (6). Note, however, that (1) cannot be captured by an analogue of (6). For in such a formula the scope of the existential quantifier would have to be restricted, just as it is in (6), to the antecedent alone; but then the quantifier would be incapable of binding the position corresponding to that occupied by *it* in the main clause of (1).

   No one of the solutions to this problem that can be found in the existing literature strikes me as fully satisfactory. As I see the problem a proper solution should provide: (i) a general account of the conditional; (ii) a general account of the meaning of indefinite descriptions; and (iii) a general account of pronominal anaphora; which, when jointly applied to (1), i–iii assign to it those truth conditions which our intuitions attribute to it. These requirements are met, I wish to claim, by the theory stated in the next two sections.

   As earlier remarks implied, there are three main parts to that theory:

1. A generative syntax for the mentioned fragment of English (I have cast the syntax in a form reminiscent of the syntactic descriptions which are used by Montague; the reader may verify, however, that many other syntactic descriptions would be equally compatible with the remaining components of the theory.)
2. A set of rules which from the syntactic analysis of a sentence, or sequence of sentences, derives one of a small finite set of possible non-equivalent representations.
3. A definition of what it is for a map from the universe of a representation into that of a model to be a proper embedding, and, with that definition, a definition of truth.

The analysis thus obtained not only yields an account of the truth conditions of the donkey sentences (as well as of certain other notoriously problematic sentences which the fragment admits, such as, e.g., some types of Bach-Peters sentences), it also reveals two more general insights concerning, respectively, personal pronouns and indefinite descriptions.

   1) Personal pronouns, it has been pointed out, have a number of apparently distinct functions. Sometimes they seem to behave as genuinely referential terms, as, for example, the *he* in *Pedro owns a donkey. He beats it.* Sometimes, as the *him* of *Every man who loves a woman who loves him is happy*, they appear to do precisely what is done by the bound variables of formal logic. Yet another occurrence—noted in particular by Evans (1977; 1980), who coined the term "E-type pronoun" for it—cannot be understood, or so it has been claimed, either on the model of a simple referential expression or on that of a bound variable. An example is the occurrence of *it* in *If Pedro owns a donkey he beats it*. The present theory brings out what these three different types have in common in that it offers, at the level of representation-formation a single rule which equally applies to each of them. This rule may interact in various ways with other rules, which are associated with different syntactic constructions, and this gives rise to the seeming multiplicity of functions which the recent philosophical and linguistic literature has noted. (There are several pronoun uses, such as "pronouns of laziness" and deictic pronouns, which have no instances within the fragment of English studied in this paper and which, therefore, cannot be discussed here. Such occurrences, however, can also be accommodated along the lines sketched in this paper.)

   2) Indefinite descriptions are, on the account given here, referential terms, not existential quantifiers. When an indefinite has existential force, it has that force in virtue of the particular

role played by the clause containing it within the sentence or discourse of which it is part. It is true that the clausal roles which impose an existential, rather than a universal, reading upon indefinites are the more prominent; and this, I take it, has been responsible for the familiar identification of the indefinite article as a device of existential quantification. But these are not the only roles. The antecedent of a conditional, for instance, plays a role which is not of this kind; a simple clause which occurs in this role confers a universal interpretation on the indefinite descriptions it contains.

There is much that ought to be said about the conceptual implications of the present theory and about the range of its possible applications. But, as space is limited, I shall confine myself to a couple of brief remarks.

1. It should be stressed that truth as it is defined here applies not only to single sentences but also to multi-sentence discourse. This is of special importance where intersentential relations within the discourse (such as intersentential anaphoric links) contribute to its meaning. As will be seen below, the links between anaphoric pronouns and their antecedents invariably have their impact on the discourse representation (irrespective of whether pronoun and antecedent occur in the same or in different sentences) and thus on the truth conditions of the discourse, which the discourse representation embodies. Other intersentential relations, such as the relation which obtains between the sentences of past tense narratives on account of their sequential order—which is typically understood to convey the temporal relations between the events which the sentences report—can be encoded into the discourse representation with equal ease.

2. The role representations are made to play within the theory developed in this paper places substantial constraints on their internal structure. (Careful reading of the subsequent sections will, I hope, confirm this assessment.) This is of particular significance if, as I have already more or less implied, discourse representations can be regarded as the mental representations which speakers form in response to the verbal inputs they receive. I should point out that the specific theory that is presented below does not render such identification essential. Even if the representations it posits are thought of as purely theoretical devices whose raison d'être is to be found solely in the contribution they make to an effective account of certain semantic properties of sentences and sentence complexes, the theory may merit comparison with other schemes of linguistic description which have been applied to the same phenomena. But this is not how I would like to see the proposal of this paper myself. I conjecture that the structures which speakers of a language can be non-trivially described as forming to represent verbal contents are, if not formally identical, then at least very similar to the representations here defined.

If this identification is legitimate, then a theory of the sort I have tried to develop brings to bear on the nature of mental representation and the structure of thought, a large and intricate array of data relating to our (comparatively firm and consistent) intuitions about the truth-conditions of the sentences and sentence sequences we employ. I very much hope that along these lines it may prove possible to gain insights into the objects of cognitive operations, as well as into these operations themselves which are unattainable if these data are ignored, and which have thus far been inaccessible to psychology and the philosophy of mind precisely because those disciplines were in no position to exploit the wealth of linguistic evidence in any systematic fashion.

2   The theory: Informal preliminaries

2.1   Anaphoric pronouns

The analysis of pronominal anaphora I shall sketch is informed by the conviction that the mechanisms which govern deictic and anaphoric occurrences of pronouns are basically the same. This is an intuition that has guided many recent theories of pronominal reference; inevitably the account given here will resemble some of these in various respects.[1]

Our point of departure will be the hypothesis that both deictic and anaphoric pronouns select their referents from certain sets of antecedently available entities. The two pronoun uses differ
with regard to the nature of these sets. In the case of a deictic pronoun the set contains entities
that belong to the real world, whereas the selection set for an anaphoric pronoun is made up of
constituents of the representation that has been constructed in response to antecedent discourse.

About deixis I shall have no more to say in this paper. But a little more needs to be said
about anaphoric pronouns before we can proceed to the detailed analysis of some particular pieces
of discourse.

The strategies used in selecting the referents of anaphoric pronouns are notoriously complex; they usually employ background assumptions about the real world, "grammatical" clues,
such as the requirement of number and gender agreement between the anaphor and its antecedent, and the order in which the potential referents were introduced by the preceding discourse.[2]

The integration of these various factors often involves, moreover, what seem to be quite
intricate patterns of inference. Efforts to understand these strategies have claimed much thought
and hard work, but, in its general form at least, the problem appears to be far too complex to
permit solution with the limited analytic tools that are available at the present time.[3]

About the strategies I shall have nothing more to say. Our concern will be, rather, with the sets
of referential candidates from which they select. These entities will constitute the universes of the
representations of which I spoke in section 1. I have already said that these discourse representations, or DR's as I will call them for short, are formed in response to the discourses they represent
and that their formation is governed by certain rules. These rules—and this is a new, and crucial,
assumption of the theory—operate on the syntactic structures of the sentences of the discourse, and
it is via them that syntactic form determines what the resulting DR will be like. This determination
is not complete however. The syntactic structure does not, for instance, determine the anaphoric
links between pronouns and their antecedents, which the DR makes explicit.

Most of the real work that the present theory will require us to do concerns the exact formulation of the rules of DR-formation. The exact formulation of these rules will be rather compact,
and will betray, I suspect, little of either motivation or empirical implications to any but the initiated. I have decided therefore to first present a number of applications of the theory. I hope that
if we proceed in this manner its formal features will reveal themselves more naturally and that
the subsequent reading of the exact definitions in section 3 will thus be less disagreeable than it
would be without such preparation.

Let us begin by considering the two-sentence discourse

(7)   Pedro owns Chiquita. He beats her.

The DR for the first sentence of (7) will contain two elements, call them u and v, which represent, respectively, Pedro and Chiquita, and furthermore the information that the first of these,
u, owns the second, v. Schematically we shall represent this information as follows:

$m_1(7)$

u   v
.   .
Pedro owns Chiquita
u = Pedro
v = Chiquita
u owns v

To incorporate the information contained in the second sentence of (7) we must extend structure $m_1(7)$. But to do that we must make two decisions, regarding the reference of, respectively,

he and *her*. It is natural to understand *he* as referring back to *Pedro* and *her* as referring back to *Chiquita*. Let us agree to interpret the pronouns in this way and to expand $m_1(7)$ accordingly. What we get is:

m(7)

u   v
.   .
Pedro owns Chiquita
u = Pedro
v = Chiquita
u owns v
He beats her
u beats her
u beats v

I said that linking *he* with *Pedro* and *her* with *Chiquita* yields what seems the most natural reading of (7). "But," you might ask, "what *other* readings could (7) have?" The answer to that question depends on the setting, or context, in which (7) is supposed to be used. If (7) were uttered by a speaker who points at some individual other than Pedro while saying *he*, or at some being distinct from Chiquita when he says *her*, the gesture would recruit this demonstrated individual as referent for the pronoun. Similarly, if (7) were part of a larger discourse *he* or *her* could conceivably refer back to some other individual introduced by an earlier part of that discourse; and this could result in a genuine referential ambiguity. However, if (7) is used by itself (that is, without preceding verbal introduction) and also in the absence of any act of demonstration, then—and this is another important hypothesis of our theory—there are no other potential referents for *he* and *her* than the discourse referents which have been introduced in response to *Pedro* and *Chiquita*. Let us agree that henceforth (except where the contrary is indicated explicitly) all our examples of simple and multi-sentence discourses shall be understood in the last of these three ways: that is, as used without accompanying deictic gestures and not preceded by any related discourse.

Even when we understand (7) in this third way its anaphoric links are not fully determined by what we have said. For why cannot *he* and *her* both refer to *u*, say, or *he* to *v* and *her* to *u*? The reason is of course obvious: *he* must refer to a male individual, and *her* to a female one. But, obvious as the determining principle may be, it is not quite so easy to state it in a form that is both general and accurate. For what is it that determines an antecedently introduced discourse referent as male, rather than female, or neither male nor female? [Example] (7) allows us to infer that *u* is male because we know that *Pedro*, typically, refers to male individuals. But often the antecedent term which led to the introduction of a discourse item is not quite so explicit about the gender of its referent. Consider, for example, such terms as *Robin, Hilary, the surgeon, the president, an officer in the Air Force, the professor, the professor's secretary, the first inhabitant of this cave*. Often we can do no better than guess whether the referent is male or female, or human or non-human. Some of these guesses are more educated than others. And not infrequently where the anaphoric link between the antecedent and some particular pronoun is clear on independent grounds it is, in fact, the gender of the pronoun which resolves the uncertainty.[4]

Applying the principle of gender agreement will thus often involve drawing various inferences from the information that is given explicitly; and as in all other processes where inference can be involved, there appears to be no clear upper bound to its potential complexity.

There is a further complication that an exact statement of the principle must take into account. The gender of the pronoun that is used to refer to a certain object is not exclusively determined by the nature of that object, but, to some extent, also by the actual *form* of the anaphoric antecedent which made it available as a referent. Thus let us suppose that the name *Chiquita* in (7) actually refers to a donkey. In most situations we refer, or at any rate may refer, to a donkey by means of *it*. But in a discourse such as (7) this would be inappropriate. The name *Chiquita* highlights, one might wish to say, the fact that its referent is female, and this makes *she* the correct resumptive pronoun. But nonetheless the task of giving even an approximate formulation of the principle appears to be well beyond our present means. In what follows we shall ignore the principle of gender agreement, just as we ignore all other factors that help to disambiguate the reference of anaphoric pronouns. But where, in subsequent examples, the need for gender agreement clearly excludes certain anaphoric links I shall not bother to mention those without referring to the principle explicitly.

Clearly (7) is true, on the reading of it that is given by m(7) if and only if the real Pedro stands to the real Chiquita in a relation of ownership and also in the relation expressed by the verb *beat*. Put differently, if M is a model, representing the world—consisting of a domain U_M and an interpretation function F_M, which assigns to the names *Pedro* and *Chiquita* members of U_M and to the transitive verbs *own* and *beat* sets of pairs of such members—then (7) is *true in* M iff the pair $<F_M$ (*Pedro*), F_M (*Chiquita*)$>$ belongs both to F_M (*own*) and to F_M (*beat*). Moreover, the righthand side of this last biconditional is fulfilled if there is a map f of the universe of m(7); that is, the set $\{u,v\}$, into U_M so that all specifications of m(7) are satisfied in M—f(u) is the individual denoted in M by *Pedro*, f(v) is the individual F_M (*Chiquita*), and it is true in M that f(u) both owns and beats f(v), in other words, that $<f(u), f(v)>$ belongs to both F_M (*own*) and F_M (*beat*).

Let us now consider

(8)   Pedro owns a donkey. He beats it.

The first sentence of (8) induces a DR that can be represented thus:

m_1 (8)

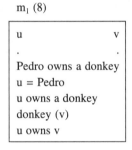

u   v

Pedro owns a donkey
u = Pedro
u owns a donkey
donkey (v)
u owns v

Once again there is no choice for the anaphoric antecedent of either *he* or *it* in the second sentence of (8). So the complete DR of (8) becomes:

m(8)

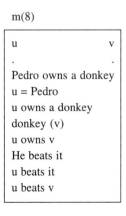

u   v

Pedro owns a donkey
u = Pedro
u owns a donkey
donkey (v)
u owns v
He beats it
u beats it
u beats v

[Example] (8) is true in the model M, provided there is an element d of U_M such that $\langle F_M$ *(Pedro)*, d$\rangle$ belongs to both F_M *(own)* and F_M *(beat)*; and furthermore d is a donkey in M—formally, d $\in F_M$ *(donkey)*, if we assume that common nouns are interpreted in the model by their extensions. This condition is fulfilled if there is a map g from $U_{m(8)}$ (= {u,v}) into U_M, which preserves all conditions specified in m(8). Note that g(v) is not required to be the bearer in M of some particular name, but only to belong to the extension of the noun *donkey*.

Before turning to the donkey sentences (1) and (2) of section 1.2, let us take stock of some principles applied in the construction of the DR's which we have encountered so far:

1. Certain singular terms, among them proper nouns and indefinite descriptions, provoke the introduction of items into the DR that function as the "references" of these terms. We shall later address the question which singular terms give rise to such introductions and whether these introductions are obligatory or optional.
2. Other singular terms, viz. personal pronouns, do not introduce elements into the DR; instead, they can only refer to items which the DR already contains.[5]

2.2   Conditionals

Our next aim is to construct a representation for the "donkey sentence" (1), which for convenience we repeat here:

(1)   If Pedro owns a donkey he beats it.

Before we can deal with (1) however, we must say something about conditionals in general.

The semantic analysis of natural language conditionals is a notoriously complicated matter, and it seems unlikely that any formally precise theory will do justice to our intuitions about all possible uses of sentences of this form. The literature on conditionals now comprises a number of sophisticated formal theories, each of which captures some of the factors that determine the meaning of conditionals in actual use.[6] Although these theories differ considerably from each other they all seem to agree on one principle, namely that a conditional

(9)   If A then B

is true if and only if

(10)   Every one of a number of ways in which A can be true constitutes, or carries with it, a way of B's being true.

Up to now this principle has generally been interpreted as meaning that B is true in, or is implied by, every one of a certain set of *relevant possible situations* in which A is true. (This is true in particular of each of the theories mentioned in note 6.) The analysis of truth in terms of DR-imbeddability, however, creates room for a slightly different implementation of (10).

Where M is a model and m a DR for the antecedent A, there may be various proper embeddings of m into M—various ways, we might say, of showing that A is true in M. This suggests another interpretation of (10), viz. that each such way of verifying A carries with it a verification of B. In what sense, however, could such a way of verifying A—that is, such a proper embedding of m—entail a verification of B? To verify B, in that sense of the term in which we have just been using it, we need a representation of B; but as a rule the content of B will not be represented in the DR m of A. To verify B in a manner consistent with some particular verification of A we must therefore extend the DR m involved in that verification to a DR m' in which

B is represented as well. Thus we are led to an implementation of (10) according to which the conditional (9) is *true*, *given* a pair (m,m'), consisting of a DR m of A and an extension m' of m which represents B as well, iff

(11)   every proper embedding of m can be extended to a proper embedding of m'.[7]

This is not yet an explicit statement of the truth conditions of (9), for it fails to tell us anything about the target structures of the verifying embeddings, and about their relation to the situation, or model, with respect to which (9) is evaluated. Here we face all the options that have confronted earlier investigators. We may elaborate (11) by stipulating that (9) is true in a model M iff every proper embedding of m into M is, or is extendable to, a proper embedding of m' on M. Or we may insist that (9) is true in the possible world w iff every proper embedding of m into any of the (models representing the) nearest A-worlds induces some proper embedding m' into that world. Indeed, any one of the existing theories could be combined with the principle conveyed by (11).

Here we shall, primarily for expository simplicity, adopt the first of the options mentioned:

Let m be a DR of A and m' an extension of m which incorporates the content of B. Let M be a model. Then *if* A *then* B is true in M, given (m,m'), iff

(12)   every proper embedding of m into M can be extended to a proper embedding of m' into M.

For conditionals in which there are no anaphoric links between antecedent and consequent, (12) boils down to the truth conditions for the material conditional. But where such a link exists its implications are somewhat different. To see this, let us apply the condition to (1). We have already constructed DRs of the kind needed in the application of (12) to (1)—namely m_1 (8) and m(8). According to (12), (1) is true in M given (m_1(8),m(8)), iff every function f from $U_{m_1(8)}$ (= {u,v}) into U_M such that (i) f(u) = F_M (*Pedro*), (ii) f(v) ∈ F_M (*donkey*), and (iii) <f(u),f(v)> ∈ F_M (*own*), can be extended to a function g from $U_{m(8)}$ into U_M such that <g(u),g(v)> ∈ F_M (*beat*). Of course, in the present case $U_{m(8)}$ = $U_{m_1(8)}$ and, consequently, there is no question of *extending* f to g. So the above condition reduces to the stipulation that every f as described has the additional property that <f(u),f(v)> ∈ F_M (*beat*). Clearly this condition is equivalent to the truth in M of the formula (3), which we adopted in section 1.2 as giving the truth conditions of (1).

It is easy enough, however, to come up with examples which do involve the extension of embeddings, for example:

(13)   If Pedro owns a donkey he lent it to a merchant.

If we extend m_1 (8) to a DR which incorporates the content of the consequent of (13), we get something like:

m(13)

u   v   w
.   .   .
Pedro owns a donkey
u = Pedro
u owns a donkey
donkey (v)
u owns v
he lent it to a merchant
u lent it to a merchant
u lent v to a merchant
merchant (w)

In relation to $m_1(8)$ and $m(13)$, (12) requires that every mapping f of the kind described in the preceding analysis of (1) can be extended to a function g from {u,v,w} into U_M such that— if we assume for simplicity that *lent to* is interpreted in M as a set of ordered triples of members of U_M—(i) g(w) $\in$ F_M (*merchant*); and (ii) <g(u),g(v),g(w)> $\in$ F_M (*lent to*).

2.3   Universals

One of the important insights that went into Frege's discovery of the predicate calculus was that the restricted quantification typical of natural language is expressible in terms of unrestricted quantifiers and truth functions. Our handling of indefinite descriptions, which formal logic treats as expressions of existential quantification, harmonizes with this insight. For, as can be seen for instance from $m_1(8)$, the introduction of a discourse referent u for an indefinite term is accompanied by two conditions, one to the effect that u has the property expressed by the common noun phrase of the term, and the other resulting from substituting u for the term in the sentence in which it occurs.

I wish to propose a treatment of terms of the form *every* α that is in similar accord with Frege's analysis of restricted universal quantification. Again it will be easier to illustrate the proposal before I state it. Consider:

(14)   Every widow admires Pedro.

A representation for (14), like those for conditional sentences, involves a pair of DR's. The first of these states that some "arbitrary" item x satisfies the common noun *widow*; the second extends this DR by incorporating the content of the condition *x admires Pedro*. Thus we obtain:

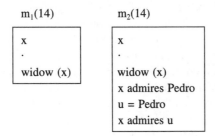

The truth value of (14) in M is to be determined by $(m_1(14),m_2(14))$ in precisely the same way as that of (1) is determined by $(m_1(8),m(8))$. Thus (14) is true iff every correlation of x with an element a of U_M such that a $\in$ F_M (*widow*) can be extended to a proper embedding of $m_2(14)$— that is, to a function g such that g(u) = F_M (*Pedro*) and <g(x),g(u)> = <a,g(u)> $\in$ F_M (*admires*). Clearly this confers on (14) the intuitively correct truth conditions.

In the same way

(15)   Every widow admires a farmer

licenses the construction of the following pair of DR's:

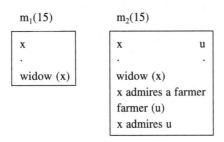

Again the condition that every association of x with an object a that is a widow in the sense of M can be extended to a proper embedding of $m_2(15)$ gives the correct truth conditions of (15); or, to be precise, the truth conditions it has on what is generally considered its most natural reading.

Consider now the second donkey sentence of section 1.2:

(2)   Every farmer who owns a donkey beats it.

Sentence (2) gives rise to the following pair of DR's:

$m_1(2)$	$m_2(2)$
x	x v
.	. .
farmer (x)	farmer (x)
x owns a donkey	x owns a donkey
donkey (v)	donkey (v)
x owns v	x owns v
	x beats it
	x beats v

So (2) is true in M iff every f such that $f(x) \in F_M$ (*farmer*), $f(v) \in F_M$ (*donkey*), and $<f(x),f(v)> \in F_M$ (*own*) has the additional property that $<f(x),f(v)> \in F_M$ (*beat*). This is exactly as it should be.

Our treatment of conditionals and universal sentences gives—for the cases, at any rate, that we have thus far considered—intuitively correct conditions of truth. But it seems at odds with the *general* definition of truth which I put forward earlier, according to which a discourse is true in M, given some representation m of it, iff *there is some* proper embedding of m into M. The semantic analyses of the sentences we have considered in this section refer to pairs of DRs rather than to single DRs and involve conditions on *all* proper embeddings of a certain kind, instead of demanding the existence of at least one proper embedding.

To resolve this apparent conflict I must say a little more about the intuitive ideas behind the DR constructions of which we have now seen a few instances. Essential to the analysis of the majority of our examples was the way in which we have treated indefinite descriptions. It would be quite unsatisfactory if there were no other justification for that treatment than the observation that, combined with additional principles for DR-construction they give the truth conditions that speakers in fact associate with the sentences we have sampled. There is, however, a reason why we should *expect* a construction principle for indefinites such as we have applied, but no direct analogue of it for phrases of the form *every* α. Let us go back to the first sentence of (8). What justifies us in adding to the partial DR of (8) the element v as a "referent" for *a donkey* is this: as I already argued, the DR of a sentence functions as a partial description of how the world ought to be if the sentence is true. To fulfill that role, the DR must represent whatever information has been encoded into it in such a way that the significance of that representation is unaffected when one extends it to incorporate further information—or, what comes in this connection to much the same, when the DR is identified as a certain substructure of a larger "real world" model via some proper embedding. The conditions *u = Pedro, donkey* (*v*) and *u owns v* which make up $m_1(8)$ clearly satisfy this requirement. They convey precisely same information in any extension of $m_1(8)$ as they do in $m_1(8)$ itself.[8] The content of an existential sentence has been exhausted once an individual has been established which satisfies the conditions expressed by the indefinite description's common noun phrase and by the remainder of the sentence.

But a universal sentence cannot be dealt with in such a once-and-for-all manner. It acts, rather, as a standing instruction: of each individual check whether it satisfies the conditions expressed by the common noun phrase of the universal term; if it does, you may infer that the individual also satisfies the conditions expressed by the remainder of the sentence. This is a message that simply *cannot* be expressed in a form more primitive than the universal sentence itself. The universal is thus, at the level of the DR to which it belongs, *irreducible.* The same is true of conditionals. *If* A *then* B functions as an instruction to check, and keep checking, whether the antecedent A has been satisfied, and to infer, when this is found to be so, that the consequent B must also hold. This, too, is a piece of information that cannot be represented in any more elementary form.

This means that when we form the DR of a universal sentence, such as (14), or of a conditional, such as (1), we cannot decompose the sentence in some such fashion as we were able to decompose, say, the first sentence of (8) when constructing $m_1(8)$. So the DR for (14) cannot itself be elaborated beyond the trivial initial stage:

$$m_0(14)$$

Every widow admires Pedro

in which the sentence (14) occurs as a condition, but nothing else does.

There is, however, another way in which we can represent the internal structure of (14)—namely, by constructing separate DRs for its components, and by integrating these DRs into a structure in which their connection reflects the syntactic construction by means of which these different components are amalgamated into the complex sentence. This is, in fact, essentially what I did when constructing the DR-pairs I earlier presented for (1), (14), (15), and (2).

But these pairs do not provide, by themselves, the structural representations to which we can apply our general definition of truth. To obtain such a representation for, say, (14) we must combine the pair $(m_1(14), m_2(14))$ with the DR $m_0(14)$. This gives us the following structure:

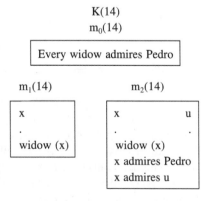

Similarly, the complete representation for (1) will now look thus:

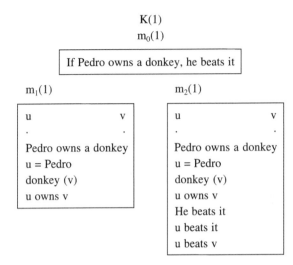

It may appear as if something is still missing from these structures. For what tells us that the subordinate DRs $m_1(1)$ and $m_2(1)$ represent the antecedent and consequent of a conditional, while $m_1(14)$ and $m_2(14)$ represent the components of a universal? The answer to this is simple: the necessary information is provided by the sentences in $m_0(1)$ and $m_0(14)$ whose components are represented by the subordinate DRs $m_1(1)$, $m_2(1)$, and $m_1(14)$, $m_2(14)$. In fact, we shall assume that with each syntactically well-formed sentence is given a particular syntactic analysis of it, which specifies unambiguously its immediate components and the construction which forms the sentence out of these. (For the fragments we shall study in section 3, this condition will be automatically fulfilled as each of its well-formed expressions has a unique syntactic analysis.) The role which, say, $m_1(1)$ and $m_2(1)$ play in the representation of (1) can thus be recognized by comparing their relevant entries, viz., *Pedro owns a donkey* and *he beats it*, with the syntactic analysis of the sentence (1) to be found in $m_0(1)$. All this will be discussed in detail in section 3.

A representation of the sort just displayed, which involves structured families of DRs, will be called a *Discourse Representation Structure* or, for short, DRS. Each sentence or discourse induces the construction of such a DRS, and only where the sentence or discourse is comparatively simple will the DRS consist of a single DR only. Among the DRs that constitute a DRS there will always be one which represents the discourse as a whole. (In the two DRS's we displayed these are, respectively, $m_0(14)$ and $m_0(1)$.) This DR will be called *the principal* DR of the DRS.

Once we assign to (1) the DRS $K(1)$ the earlier conflict between the general definition of truth and our particular account of the truth value of a conditional can be resolved. We slightly modify the truth definition to read:

(16)   D *is true in* M, *given* the DRS K iff there is a proper embedding into M of the principal DR of K.

Let us try to apply (16) to (1) and its DRS $K(1)$. [Example] (1) is true given $K(1)$ iff there is a proper embedding of $m_0(1)$ into M. Since the universe of $m_0(1)$ is the empty set, there is only one embedding from $m_0(1)$ into M, viz. the empty function, $\wedge$. What is it for $\wedge$ to be proper? $\wedge$ is proper iff the conditions of $m_0(1)$ are true in M of the corresponding elements of U_M. In the present case, however, there are no elements in $U_{m_0(1)}$, thus no corresponding elements of U_M; and there is only one condition in $m_0(1)$—namely, (1) itself. Thus $\wedge$ is proper iff (1) is true in M.

It might seem at this point that we are trapped in a circle. But in fact we are not. To see that we are not, it is necessary to appreciate the difference between (i) asking for the truth value in M of (1), given $K(1)$; and (ii) asking for the truth value in M of some condition that belongs to some member of K(1). This second question has, as we saw earlier, a straightforward answer when the condition has the form of an atomic sentence. For in that case it is directly decided by the embedding and the function F_M. But when the condition is a complex sentence—for example, a conditional or a universal, which permits no further analysis *within the very DR to which it belongs*—the answer involves an appeal to certain members of the DRS that are *subordinate* to that DR. Thus the condition (1) of $m_1(1)$ is to be taken as true in M iff it is true, in the sense defined earlier, *given* the pair $(m_1(1), m_2(1))$ of DRs subordinate to $m_0(1)$; and in *that* sense (1) is true in M, we saw already, iff M verifies the first-order formula (3).

To see more clearly how the various components of our theory are to be fitted together, we should look at a few more examples.

The next example shows why it is that certain anaphoric connections are impossible. In

(17)   If Pedro owns every donkey then he beats it.

it cannot have *every donkey* for its antecedent. The reason for this becomes transparent when we try to construct a DRS which gives such a reading to (17):

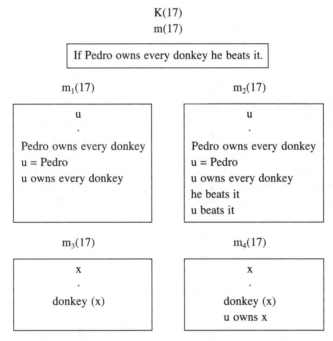

We cannot complete this DRS as intended, for the discourse referent x, which we want to assign to the pronoun *it* of $m_2(17)$, is not available, as it occurs only at the level of $m_3(17)$, which is below that of $m_2(17)$. A similar explanation shows why *it* cannot be anaphorically linked to *every donkey* in

(18)   Every farmer who owns every donkey beats it

and also why in

(19)   If Pedro likes every woman who owns a donkey he feeds it

it cannot be co-referential with a *donkey*, whereas such a link does seem possible in

(20)   If Pedro likes a woman who owns a donkey he feeds it.[9]

These last examples give, I hope, an inkling of the predictive powers of what in particular linguists might think constitutes the most unusual feature of the theory I have so far sketched: the fact that it handles singular terms of the forms a β and *every* β in entirely different ways. I hope that these and subsequent illustrations will help to persuade them that the conception of a perfect rule-by-rule parallelism between syntax and semantics is one that must be proved rather than taken for granted.[10] In fact, the data here presented point toward the conclusion that this conception is ultimately untenable.

Another feature that distinguishes the present account from many, albeit not all, existing theories of reference and quantification is its entirely uniform treatment of third-person personal pronouns. This has already been apparent from the examples at which we have looked. It is further illustrated by such sentences as

(21)   Every farmer courts a widow who admires him.

Occurrences such as that of *him* in (21) have been put forward as paradigms of the use of pronouns as bound variables—an identification that is natural, and in fact well-nigh inescapable, when one believes that the logical forms of natural language sentences are expressions of the predicate calculus. Indeed, several earlier theorists have perceived a real chasm separating these pronoun uses from those which we find exemplified by, say, *her* in (7) and *he* in (7) and (8); and, looking at pronouns from this perspective, they have often felt helpless vis-à-vis the pronoun occurrences that have been of particular concern to us in this section, viz. those exemplified by (1) and (2). Forcing these either into the mold that had been designed for uses such as that in (7), or into that measured to fit occurrences such as that of *him* in (21), turned out to be hopeless enterprises. Evans (1977; 1980: this volume, chapter 21), gives conclusive evidence against the latter of these two; but his own suggestions, which go some way toward assimilating the problematic pronouns to definite descriptions, do not appear to be fully satisfactory either.[11]

Note that the more unified treatment of these pronoun uses given here is possible partly because the same construction rule for pronouns operates both at the level of the principal DR's and at subordinate levels. Thus the DRS for (21) is constructed as follows (the numbers in parentheses which precede discourse referents and conditions indicate the order in which the operations are carried out; we shall often use this notational device):

$m_0(21)$

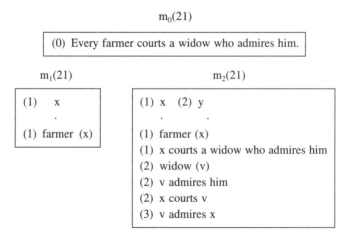

The rule for pronouns applies here in just the same way to the *him* of *v admires him* in $m_2(21)$ as it does, for example, to the *he* and *it* in the DRS construction of (8) or the *it* of (1) in the construction of the DR of (1).

3   The formal theory

3.1   Syntax

The time has come for a more formal and systematic presentation. We shall consider a fragment of English for which I shall give an explicit syntax and explicit formal rules for DRS construction. Our fragment will be exceedingly simple to start with, much simpler even than that of Montague (1973).[12] The syntax adopted resembles Montague's, but the resemblance is rather superficial; for the syntactic analysis of a sentence will play a much more modest role in the determination of its interpretation than it does in Montague grammar. In presenting the syntax I shall presume some familiarity with Montague grammar, specifically with Montague (1970a) and (1973). Our fragment, to which I shall refer as L_0, contains expressions of the following categories with the following basic members:

1) T   (Term)   : *Pedro, Chiquita, John, Mary, Bill, . . . , he, she, it*
2) CN (Common Noun phrase)   : *farmer, donkey, widow, man, woman, . . .*
3) IV (Intransitive Verb phrase)   : *thrives, . . .*
4) TV (Transitive Verb)   : *owns, beats, loves, admires, courts, likes, feeds, loathes, . . .*
5) S   (Sentence)   : —
6) RC (Relative Clause)   : —

Formation rules

FR1.   If $\alpha \in$ TV and $\beta \in$ T, then $\alpha\beta \in$ IV, where $\beta' = $ *him* if $\beta = $ *he* and $\beta' = $ *her* if $\beta = $ *she* and $\beta' = \beta$ otherwise.

FR2.   If $\alpha \in$ IV and $\beta \in$ T, then $\beta\alpha \in$ S.

FR3.   If $\alpha \in$ CN, then (i) *a(n)* α, and (ii) *every* α is in T.

FR4.k If $\phi \in$ S and the kth word of ϕ is a pronoun, then $\beta\phi' \in$ RC, where ϕ' is the result of eliminating the kth word from ϕ and β is *who, whom,* or *which,* according to whether the pronoun is *he* or *she, him* or *her,* or *it,* respectively.

FR5.   If α is a basic CN and $\beta \in$ RC, then $\alpha\beta \in$ CN.

FR6.   If $\phi, \psi \in$ S, then *if* ϕ, ψ and *if* ϕ *then* $\psi \in$ S.

Some comments

1. The rule schema FR4.k is defective inasmuch as it allows for wh-movement out of forbidden positions. Within the present fragment there are only two sorts of noun phrase positions to which wh-movement may not apply—those inside relative clauses and those inside the antecedents of conditionals. It is not difficult to modify the syntax in such a way that these restrictions are observed. For instance, we could stipulate that each time a relative clause is formed, all pronouns it contains are marked, and that the same is done to those occurring in the antecedent of a conditional at the time when antecedent and consequent are joined together. The rule of relative clause formation can then be altered so that it applies to unmarked pronouns only. Such a solution is rather ad hoc, and because it would moreover complicate the syntax as a whole, I have refrained from incorporating it. I must beg the reader to keep in mind that the syntax of this section is intended as no more than a convenient basis for the definition of DRS-construction rules, and that it has no pretensions of capturing important syntactic generalizations.[13]

2. The present fragment differs from most familiar versions of Montague grammar in that it contains neither variables nor indexed pronouns.[14] Consequently, the syntactic analysis of a sentence of the present fragment tells us nothing about anaphoric relations.

3. Every well-formed expression of L_0 has a unique syntactic analysis. This is a feature that is bound to be lost at some point as we extend the present fragment. It allows us, however, to

omit, while uniqueness of syntactic analysis obtains, all explicit reference to syntactic analyses in discussions and, particularly, in definitions where such reference becomes essential as soon as well-formed strings do not unambiguously determine their analyses.

4. When defining the process of DRS construction, we shall have to specify the order in which various parts, of a given sentence are to be treated. What we need here is, in essence, a specification of scope order. I shall assume in this paper that the scope relations within a sentence are directly determined by its syntactic construction. Thus the subject term of a simple clause will always have wide scope over the object term; the *if* of a conditional sentence will always have wide scope over the terms occurring in antecedent and consequent, etc. Let us call the formation rule which is applied last in the construction of an expression γ the *outermost rule of* γ. Where γ is a sentence and the outermost rule is FR6, γ is called a *conditional* (*sentence*). If the outermost rule of γ is FR1 or FR2, and this rule forms γ by combining some IV or TV with the term α, α is said to *have*, or to *be the term with*, *maximal scope in* γ. If the outermost rule is FR1 and begins with *every*, γ is called a *universal IV*; similarly, if the outermost rule of γ is FR2 and α begins with *every*, then γ is called a *universal sentence*.

By eliminating Montague's rule of substitution and quantification we have dispensed with one natural way of distinguishing between alternative scope relations—such as, for instance, the two possible relations between *a widow* and *every farmer* in

(22)   A widow admires every farmer.

Sentence (22) can be generated in only one way, and according to that generation the subject has wide scope over the direct object as it enters the construction of the sentence at a later stage. No syntactic analysis would thus appear to convey upon (22) the reading given by

(23) $(\forall x) (\text{farmer}(x) \rightarrow (\exists y) (\text{widow}(y) \land \text{admires}(x,y)))$.

It might be thought that the construction of a DRS which imposes this latter reading upon (22) involves an order of application of the construction rules which contravenes the scope relations implied by the syntax. This problem too must be left for another paper.

5. We shall refer to the basic terms *Pedro, Chiquita, John, Mary,* . . . as the *proper names* of L_0 and to *he, she, it* as the *pronouns* of L_0. Terms of the form *every* β will be called *universal terms*.

6. I have admitted only compound common noun phrases consisting of a common noun and *one* relative clause. It would, of course, be possible to relax FR6 so that it can attach several relative clauses to the same head noun. Many of the resulting expressions, however, seem marginal at best. I have decided to cut the knot and keep such complex common nouns out of the fragment altogether.

3.2   Models and discourse representation

By a *model for* L_0 we shall understand a structure of the form $<U,F>$ where (i) U is a non-empty set and (ii) F is an interpretation function which assigns an element of U to each of the proper names of L, a subset of U to each of its basic CN's and basic IV's, and a set of pairs of elements of U to each of the basic TV's.

We must now address ourselves to the main tasks of this section, the formulation of the rules of DRS-construction and of the definition of truth for L_0. To state the rules, we shall have to decide on a format for DR's and DRS's. In choosing such a format I have been partly guided by considerations of notational convenience. In particular, it is just a matter of convenience to specify (as I have already done in the examples discussed in the preceding section) that one or more discourse referents satisfy a certain predicate by adding to the relevant DR a sentence which is obtained by combining that predicate with, in the appropriate positions, these referents themselves—using them, that is, autonymously (a policy against which there can be no objection, given the symbolic nature which must be attributed to the discourse referents in any case). Almost all other features, however, of the DR-format I have chosen are determined by empirically significant aspects of the rules of DRS-construction.

Let V be a denumerable set of entities none of which is a basic expression of L_0 or a string of such expressions. V is the set from which the elements are drawn that make up the universes of the DRs. We shall often refer to the members of V as *discourse referents*. For any subset X of V let L_0 (X) be the result of adding the members of X to the set of basic terms of L_0. Where M is a model for L_0 and $X \subseteq V$, there is a canonical way of expanding M to a model M' of $L_0(X)$, viz. by adding to the interpretation function F_m the pairs <u,u> for all $u \in X$. In the sequel we shall not bother to differentiate notationally between these two models and thus write "M" where strictly speaking we ought to have put "M'."[15]

As all our earlier examples showed, the introduction of a discourse referent is always accompanied either by a condition which identifies it as the referent of a proper name or else by one which stipulates that it satisfies some common noun. These conditions cannot be expressed in L_0 (X); so we must slightly extend the notation which that language provides. We shall allow in addition to what $L_0(X)$ contains already, sentences of the form $u = \alpha$ where α is a proper name and $u \in X$, to express the former, and sentences of the form β (u) where, again, $u \in X$ and $\beta \in CN$, to express the latter type of condition. We shall refer to the language obtained from $L_0(X)$ through these additions as L_0' (X).

We shall limit ourselves here to the simplest type of discourse, that of a discourse constituted by a finite sequence of declarative statements, made by one and the same speaker. Formally we shall identify—as in fact we already did implicitly in section 1.2—such a discourse with the sequence of the uttered sentences. So let us, where L is any language, define an L-*discourse* to be any finite string of sentences of L.

The examples we considered in the preceding section were carefully chosen so that the same singular term would never occur more than once. This made it unnecessary to distinguish between different occurrences of the same expression. In general, however, different occurrences must be kept apart. The need for this is most obvious in connection with pronouns—it is only too common a phenomenon that the very same pronoun occurs twice in a bit of discourse, but each time refers to a different individual, as, for example, might be intended by someone using the sentence

(24)   If Bill courts a widow who admires him then Pedro courts a widow who admires him.

But in longer stretches of discourse other expressions are liable to recur as well. Although the DRS construction rules defined below only require us to keep track of the individual occurrences of certain expressions, little if anything would be gained by introducing a mechanism for distinguishing just *those* individual occurrences. In fact, probably the simplest way to distinguish the individual expression occurrences is this: Let $D = <\phi_1, \ldots, \phi_n>$ be an L_0 discourse, and let $<\tau_1, \ldots, \tau_n>$ be the sequence of the (uniquely determined) syntactic analyses of the sentences of D. It is easy to formulate an algorithm which assigns a unique index—say, a positive integer— to each of the nodes of these analyses and, by proxy, also to the expressions formed at any such node. For instance, we enumerate first all the nodes of τ_1, in some order fixed by its structure, then those of τ_2, and so on, until we have dealt with the entire discourse. There is no point to go into greater detail here. We shall simply assume that one such algorithm has been fixed. By an *occurrence* of an expression α *in* D we shall understand a pair $<\alpha,n>$ where n is the index of a node of the syntactic analysis of one of the sentences of D to which α is attached.

The relation which holds between two expressions α and β if α is a subexpression of β has an obvious counterpart between expression occurrences: $<\alpha,n>$ is a "suboccurrence" of $<\beta,m>$ if $<\alpha,n>$ occurs as part of the syntactic analysis of $<\beta,m>$. I shall often speak, by a minor slight of hand, of one expression occurrence being a *subexpression* (*subformula*, etc.) of some other occurrence. No confusion should arise from this.

The construction of a DRS for D does not only require the separate identification of particular occurrences of expressions of L_0; we must also be able to keep track of different occurrences of the same expressions of $L'_0(X)$. However, as our examples have already indicated (and we shall soon make this fully explicit) the expressions from $L'_0(X)\backslash L_0$ which enter into DR's are always derived from corresponding expressions of L_0. To be specific, they result either (i) through one or more substitutions of members of X for singular terms in some sentence of L_0; or (ii) from placing a member of X in parentheses behind a CN of L_0; or (iii) from combining a member of X with = and a proper name of L_0. In the first case, we can label the $L'_0(X)$-sentence occurrence unambiguously with the index of the occurrence of the L_0-sentence from which it is obtained through successive substitutions; in the second case, we assign the index of the relevant occurrence of the common noun; and in the third, we assign the index of the relevant occurrence of the proper name. In each of the cases (i), (ii), and (iii), we shall say that the sentence of $L'_0(X)$ is a *descendant of* the relevant expression of L_0, and, similarly, that the occurrence of the $L'_0(X)$-sentence is a *descendant of* the corresponding occurrence of an expression of L_0. Formally we shall represent any occurrence of such an expression also as a pair consisting of the expression together with the appropriate index.

There is one other notion which we have already defined for L_0 but which must also be extended to cover certain expressions of L'_0 (X) as well. This is the notion of the *outermost rule of* an expression. We shall need to refer to the outermost rule only of those sentences of $L'_0(X)\backslash L_0$ which result from making in sentences of L_0 one or more substitutions of members of V for occurrences of singular terms of $L_0(X)$. Any such substitution leaves the syntactic structure of the sentence in which it takes place essentially inviolate: it can only lead to some "pruning" of the syntactic tree, viz. where the replaced singular term occurrence is itself complex. In that case the subtree dominated by the node to which the singular term (α) is attached is deleted and replaced by a single node to which is attached the inserted (basic) term (u). The outermost rule FRi of the resulting sentence should *not* count as the outermost rule of the syntactic analysis of the substitution result. For FRi is the rule which combines u with the remainder γ of the sentence, and this is a syntactic operation which, unlike the analogous operation that combines the replaced singular term with γ, should give rise to no further step in the DRS construction (the singular term α has after all just been dealt with!). Thus we should identify as the *outermost rule of* the substitution result, rather the outermost rule of γ. Since, as we already observed, each of the $L'_0(X)$-sentences in question results from a finite sequence of such substitutions, the above stipulation defines the outermost rule of each such sentence.

Having extended the concept of the outermost rule of an expression to certain sentences of $L_0(X)$ we can now also apply the notions *conditional* and *universal sentence* to those sentences. Moreover, we shall call *atomic* those sentences of $L'_0(X)$ which consist either (i) of a discourse referent followed by an IV; or (ii) a TV flanked by two discourse referents; or (iii) a CN followed by a discourse referent in parentheses; or (iv) a discourse referent followed by = and a proper name of L_0.

Here is the definition of the "format" of Discourse Representations I have chosen, as well as of some related notions which we shall need in later definitions:

DEFINITION 1. Let D be an L_0-discourse.
1. A *possible DR* (*Discourse Representation*) *of* D is a pair $<U,Con>$, where
   (i) U is a subset of V; and
   (ii) Con is a set of occurrences in D of sentence of L'_0 (U).

2. Where m and m' are possible DRs for D, we say that m' *extends* m if $U_m \subseteq U_{m'}$ and $Con_m \subseteq Con_{m'}$.

3. Let m be a possible DR for D. A sentence $\phi \in Con_m$ is called *unreduced in* m iff Con_m contains no descendant of ϕ. And m is called *maximal* if each unreduced member of Con_m is either (i) an atomic sentence, (ii) a conditional, or (iii) a universal sentence.

We have seen in section 2 that in general we must associate with a given discourse a Discourse Representation *Structure*—that is, a partially ordered family of DRs, rather than a single DR. As it turns out the partial orders of those DRS's which our rules enable us to construct can always be defined in terms of the internal structure of their members. This makes it possible to define a DRS simply as a set of DRs.

To show how the partial order can be defined in terms of the structure of the DRs that make up the DRS, we have to make explicit the structural relationship that holds between a DR m which contains a conditional or universal sentence ϕ and the pair of DRs which must be constructed to represent the content of ϕ. But before we can do that we must first discuss, and introduce, a slight modification of the schema for representing conditionals and universals that we have used in our examples. So far we have represented a conditional *if* A (*then*) B by a DR m_1 of A, together with an extension m_2 of m_1 which incorporates into it the information contained in B. There can be no objection to this schema as long as the information contained in A can be fully processed in m_1 before one extends it by processing B. It is not always possible, however, to proceed in this way, as is illustrated by (25):

(25)   If a woman loves him Pedro courts her.

The order in which the construction rules must be applied to yield a DRS which links *him* with *Pedro* and *her* with *a woman* is indicated in the following diagram:

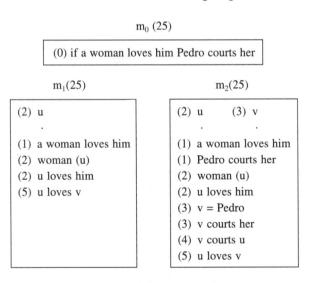

Not only is there duplication here of the conditions which occur both in $m_1(25)$ and $m_2(25)$, but some of the operations have to be performed simultaneously *and in the same way*, on the identical entries of these two DRs. It would be possible to characterize DRS-construction so that such entries are treated simultaneously in all the DRs in which they occur and give rise in each of these DRs to the same descendants. But this is awkward, particularly where the treatment produces new subordinate DRs. It is easier to introduce into the second DR of the pair representing a conditional only the information conveyed by the consequent. In the case of (25), this will lead to a DRS of the form:

m_0 (25)

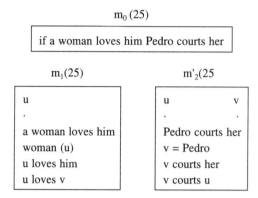

Similarly, we shall represent a universal sentence by a pair of DRs into the second of which we enter the information that the remainder of the sentence is true of the discourse referent which stands in for the singular term *every β* in question. For example the DRS K(15) for

(15)   Every widow admires a farmer

now becomes

K(15)

m_0 (15)

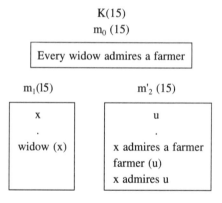

Evidently the second members of the representing pairs about which we have been speaking up to now can be reconstructed from these new pairs: where (m_1,m_2) is the old pair and (m_1,m'_2) the pair which replaces it according to the present stipulation, m_2 is the union of m_1 and m'_2, where the *union* of two DRs $<U_1,Con_1>$, $<U_2,Con_2>$ is the DR $<U_1 \cup U_2, Con_1 \cup Con_2>$—thus, in particular, $m_2(15)$ is the union of $m_1(15)$ and $m'_2(15)$, and $m_2(25)$ that of $m_1(25)$ and $m'_2(25)$. Note that the truth clause (12) for conditionals and its analogue for universal sentences are not affected by this change.

Let us now describe how we can recognize two DRs m_1 and m_2 as representing a conditional or universal sentence that occurs among the conditions of the DR m. We first assume that m contains the occurrence $<\phi,k>$, that ϕ is a conditional, and that its antecedent and consequent are, respectively, $<\psi,r>$ and $<\chi,s>$.[16] We say that the pair of DRs $<m_1, m_2>$ *represents* $<\phi,k>$ iff:

(i) $<\psi,r> \in Con_{m_1}$ and every member of Con_{m_1} is a descendant of a subexpression of $<\psi,r>$;
(ii) $<\chi,s> \in Con_{m_2}$ and every member of Con_{m_2} is a descendant of a subexpression of $<\chi,s>$.

Now suppose $<\phi,k>$ is a universal sentence. Here it is convenient to distinguish between the case where the term with maximal scope is of the form *every β*, where β is a basic CN and that where it has the form *every* $\beta\gamma$ with β a CN and γ a RC. Let us begin by considering the first of these. We say the pair $<m_1,m_2>$ *represents* $<\phi,k>$ iff for some $x \in$ V (i) $x \in U_{m_1}$; (ii) $Con_{m_1} = \{<\beta (x),i>\}$; (iii) $<\phi',k> \in Con_{m_2}$ and each member of Con_{m_2} is a descendant of a subexpression of $<\phi',k>$, where i is the index of the occurrence of β in the term (occurrence) *every* β in question and ϕ' is the result of replacing that term occurrence in ϕ by x.

Now consider the case where the term with maximal scope has the form *every* $\beta\gamma$, where β is common noun and γ a relative clause. In this case $<m_1,m_2>$ *represents* $<\phi,k>$ iff for some $x \in$ V (i) $x \in U_{m_1}$; (ii) $<\beta(x),i>$, $<\delta,r> \in Con_{m'_1}$ and every member of Con_{m_1} other than $<\beta(x),i>$ is a descendant of an occurrence of a subexpression of $<\delta,r>$; and (iii) $<\phi',k> \in Con_{m_2}$ and every member of Con_{m_2} is a descendant of an occurrence of a subexpression of $<\phi',k>$. Here i and ϕ' are as above, r is the index of the occurrence of γ in the relevant occurrence of *every* $\beta\gamma$, and δ is determined as follows: let ζ be the sentence from which the relative clause has been formed through "wh-movement"; δ is obtained by substituting x in ζ for the pronoun occurrence which was eliminated in the transition from ζ to γ.

Next we must give the definition of *partial Discourse Representation Structures*.

DEFINITION 2. A *partial DRS (Discourse Representation Structure)* for D is a set k of possible DR's for D such that whenever m is a member of K and Con_m contains a conditional or universal sentence $<\phi,k>$, then there is at most one pair of members m_1 and m_2 of K which represents $<\phi,k>$.

We say that a member m' of K is *immediately subordinate to* m iff either (i) there is a conditional or universal sentence occurrence $<\phi,k> \in Con_m$ such that m' is the first member of a pair which represents $<\phi,k>$; or (ii) m is itself the first member of such a pair and m' is the second member of that pair. And m' is *subordinate to* m iff there exists a finite chain of immediate subordinates connecting m and m'.

The rules for constructing DRS's will guarantee that they will always have a principal member. If the partial DRS K contains such a member, it will be denoted as m_0 (K). Where K and K' are partial DRS's, we say that K' *extends* K iff there is a one-to-one map f from K into K' such that for each $m \in$ K f(m) extends m. For $m \in$ K we denote as $K^{\geq}$ (m) the set consisting of m and all the members of K that are superordinate to m. We shall also write "U_K" for "$\bigcup_{m \in K} U_m$" and "$U_K^{\geq}$ (m)" for "$U_M \cup \bigcup\{U_{m'} : m' \in$ K and m' is superordinate to m$\}$".We say that a partial DRS K is *complete* iff (i) every member of K is maximal and (ii) whenever m is a member of K and Con_m contains an occurrence of $<\phi,k>$ of a conditional or universal sentence K contains a pair which represents $<\phi,k>$.

We can now proceed to give a precise statement of the rules for DRS-construction. It is they, I must repeat here, that carry virtually all the empirical import of the theory. Their exact formulation is therefore of the greatest importance. Instead of trying to do justice to all relevant linguistic facts at once, I shall begin by stating the rules in a fairly simple manner. This will then serve as a basis for further exploration.

For the fragment L_0 there are five rules: one for proper names, one for indefinite descriptions, one for pronouns, one for conditionals, and one for universal terms. The effect of applying a rule to a particular condition in some member of a DRS is always an extension of that DRS.

Only the rules for conditionals and universals lead to the introduction of new DR's. But this does not mean that the effect of each of the other rules is confined to the particular DR m which contains the condition to which the rule is applied. Thus, for instance—and this is a point we have so far neglected in our examples—the application of the rule for proper names will always result in the introduction of a new discourse referent into the principal DR of the DRS, even if the condition to which the rule is being applied belongs itself to some other member of the structure. (I shall argue below that the rule for proper names *must* operate in this fashion.) Directly connected with this is the need to refer, in the statement of the rule for pronouns, not just to the universe of the DR m that contains the relevant condition, but also to the universes of certain other members of the DRS—in fact, as it turns out, of all those members which are superordinate to m.

To state the first three rules, let us assume that K is a partial DRS, that $m \in K$, that $\langle\phi,k\rangle \in Con_m$ is an unreduced member of m, and that $\langle a,i\rangle$ is an occurrence of a term in $\langle\phi,k\rangle$ which has maximal scope in $\langle\phi,k\rangle$:

CR1. Suppose a is a proper name. We add to $U_{m_0}(K)$ an element u from $V\backslash U_K$. Furthermore, we add to $Con_{m_0}(K)$ the occurrence $\langle u=a,i\rangle$ and to Con_m the occurrence $\langle\phi,k\rangle$, where ϕ' is the result of replacing the occurrence of a in $\langle\phi,k\rangle$ with index i by u.

CR2. Assume a is an indefinite singular term. (a) a is of the form $a(n)\beta$, where β is a common noun. We add to U_m an element u from $V\backslash U_K$ and to Con_m the occurrences $\langle\beta(u),r\rangle$ (where r is the index of the occurrence of β in $\langle a,i\rangle$) and $\langle\phi',k\rangle$, where ϕ' is as under CR1. The other members of K remain unchanged. (b) a is of the form $a(n)\beta\gamma$, where β is a basic common noun and γ a relative clause. We add $u \in V\backslash U_K$ to U_m and expand Con_m with $\langle\beta(u),r\rangle$, $\langle\phi',k\rangle$ and the pair $\langle\delta,s\rangle$ where δ is determined as in the definition of *represents* given above, and s is the index of the occurrence of γ in $\langle a,i\rangle$.

CR3. Assume a is a pronoun. Choose a "suitable" member u from $U_K^\geq (m)$. Add $\langle a=u,i\rangle$ and $\langle\phi',k\rangle$ to Con_m.

NB: I have given a deliberately "fudgey" formulation of this rule by inserting the word "suitable." To state what, in any particular application of the rule, the set of suitable referents is, we would have to make explicit what the strategies are that speakers follow when they select the antecedents of anaphoric pronouns. In the applications we shall consider below, the restriction to "suitable" referents that I have built into CR3 will never play an overt role (although I will occasionally ignore, without comment, readings of the sampled sentences which would impose anaphoric links that are ruled out by various factors that enter into these strategies, such as, for example, the principle of gender agreement). Nonetheless, I have included "suitable" in the formulation of CR3, as a reminder that the rule is incomplete as it stands.

To state the last two rules, let us assume that K and m are as above, that $\langle\phi,k\rangle$ is an unreduced member of Con_m and that ϕ is either a universal sentence or a conditional:

CR4. Assume $\langle\phi,k\rangle$ is a conditional with antecedent $\langle\psi,r\rangle$ and consequent $\langle\chi,s\rangle$. We add to K the member $\langle\phi,\{\langle\chi,r\rangle\}\rangle$ and $\langle\phi,\{\langle\chi,s\rangle\}\rangle\rangle$.

CR5. Assume $\langle\phi,k\rangle$ is a universal sentence and the term with maximal scope is $\langle every\ \beta,i\rangle$, with β a basic CN. We add, for some $u \in V\backslash U_K$ $\langle\{u\},\{\langle\beta (u),r\rangle\}\rangle$, and $\langle\phi,\{\langle\phi',k\rangle\}\rangle$, where r and ϕ' are as just above Definition 2. Similarly, where the term with maximal scope is $\langle every\ \beta\gamma,r\rangle$ where $\beta \in CN$ and $\gamma \in RC$, the DRs that must be added are $\langle\{u\},\{\langle\beta(u),r\rangle,$ $\langle\delta,s\rangle\}\rangle$ and $\langle\phi,\langle\phi',k\rangle\}\rangle$, where, again, $u \in V\backslash V_K$ and s,δ,ϕ' are as in the statement of CR2.

Note that if K is a finite DRS—that is, a finite set of finite DR's—then a finite number of applications of the rules CR1–CR5 will convert it into a complete DRS. Any complete DRS obtained from K by a series of rule applications is called a *completion* of K. Clearly, if K has a principal member, then so does every completion of K.

We can at last define the notion of a *complete DRS for* a discourse D. The definition proceeds by recursion on the length of D:

DEFINITION 3. (i) Suppose D is a discourse consisting of one sentence ϕ. Let k be the index of ϕ in D. A *complete DRS (Discourse Representation Structure)* for D is any completion of the DRS $\{\langle\phi,\{\langle\phi,k\rangle\}\rangle\}$.

(ii) Suppose that D has the form $\langle\phi_1, \ldots, \phi_n, \phi_{n+1}\rangle$ and that the set of complete DRS's for the discourse $D' = \langle\phi_1, \ldots, \phi_n\rangle$ has already been defined. Let k be the index of the occurrence of ϕ_{n+1} as last sentence of D. Then K is a *complete DRS for* D iff K is a completion of a DRS of the form $(K' - \{m_0(K')\}) \cup \{m\}$, where K' is some complete DRS for D' and m is the DR $<U_{m_0}(K'),Con_{m_0}(K') \cup \{<\phi,k>\}>$.

NB: It follows from this definition, together with earlier remarks, that every set of possible DRs which is a complete DRS for some discourse D contains a principal DR.

3.3 Truth

Our next task is to define truth. Much has already been said about this in the preceding chapters. So we can proceed with the formal definition almost at once.

There is just one feature of the definition that might be puzzling without a brief preliminary discussion. The evaluation of conditionals and universals as a rule involves only embeddings that respect certain previously assigned values to some of the discourse referents in superordinate positions. In other words, we keep, in the course of such evaluations, certain functions fixed and consider only embeddings compatible with these functions. This means that the recursive definition underlying the characterization of the truth in M must be of a concept which is sensitive not only to the information encoded in the DRS but also to some partial function from the discourse referents of that DRS into U_M. If a sentence contains several nested embeddings of conditionals or universals, the maps considered in the evaluation of deeply embedded constructions may have to agree with several functions that have been stored, so to speak, along the way down to the conditional or universal concerned. However, as these stored functions must also be compatible with each other, we need consider only single functions in this connection; intuitively these are the unions of the sets of different functions accumulated along the path toward the embedded construction.

Let K be a complete DRS for D and M a model of D. We shall give the definition of the *truth value of D in M given* K in two steps. The first stage will give a characterization, by simultaneous recursion, of two relations: (i) the relation which holds between a member m of K, a function f from U_m into U_M, and a partial function g from U_K into U_M iff, as we shall express it, f *verifies* m *in* M *given* K, *relative to* g; and (ii) the relation which holds between m, an unreduced member $<\phi,k>$ of Con_m, a function f from U_m into U_M, and a function g from U_K into U_M iff, as we shall say, $<\phi,k>$ *is true in* M *under* f, *given* K, *relative to* g. The second stage uses the first of these two relations to define truth:

DEFINITION 4. Let D be an L_0-discourse, K a complete DRS of D, and M a model for L_0. D *is true in* M *on* K iff there is a function f from $U_{m_0}(K)$ into U_M which verifies $m_0(K)$ in M, given K, relative to $\wedge$. ($\wedge$ is the empty function!)

The recursive part of the definition is inevitably somewhat more involved:

DEFINITION 5. Let D, K, M be as in Definition 4; let $m \in K$, and let g be a partial function from U_K into U_M.
(i) f *verifies* m *in* M *given* K, *relative to* g iff each unreduced member $<\phi,k>$ of Con_m is true in M under f, given K, relative to g.
(ii) Suppose $<\phi,k>$ is an occurrence of an atomic sentence in Con_m. Then ϕ has one of the following four forms:
(a) $u\alpha$, where $u \in V$ and $\alpha \in IV$;
(b) $u\alpha v$, where $u,v \in V$ and $\alpha \in TV$;
(c) $u=\alpha$, where $u \in V$ and α is a proper name;
(d) $\alpha(u)$, where $u \in V$ and α is a basic common noun.
The question whether $<\phi,k>$ *is true in* M *under* f *given* K, *relative to* g splits up into the corresponding four clauses below (we omit the qualification 'in M under f, given K relative to g'):
(a) $<\phi,k>$ *is true* iff $f(u) \in F_M(\alpha)$;
(b) $<\phi,k>$ *is true* iff $<f(u),f(v)> \in F_M(\alpha)$;

(c) $<\phi,k>$ *is true* iff $f(u) = F_M(\alpha)$;

(d) $<\phi,k>$ *is true* iff $f(u) \in F_M(\alpha)$.

(iii) Suppose $<\phi,k>$ is an occurrence of a conditional or universal sentence in Con_m. Then K will contain a unique pair $<m_1,m_2>$, which represents $<\phi,k>$. $<\phi,k>$ *is true in M under* f *given K, relative to* g iff every map h from U_{M_1} into U_M which is compatible with $g \cup f$ and which verifies m_1 in M given K relative to $g \cup f$ can be extended to a function k from U_{m_2} into U_M and verifies m_2 in M given K relative to $g \cup f$.

We shall call a function which verifies $m_0(K)$ in M, given K, relative to $\wedge$ a *verifying*, or *truthful, embedding of K into M*. We shall also say of such a map that it *verifies* D *in M on* (*the reading provided by*) K.

Many of the DRS's we have earlier displayed fail to be in complete agreement with the construction procedure as we have now formally described it. This is true, in particular, of the second representation I gave in section 2.3 for (14). The DRS K(14) violates the rule CR1 in that the item u, which is introduced as the referent of the proper name *Pedro* should have been entered into the universe of $m_0(14)$ rather than into that of m(14). Let us give the DRS for (14) once more, this time in its proper form:

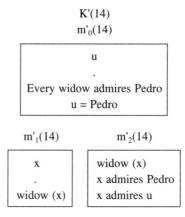

The need to place the discourse referent introduced by a proper name into the principal DR is illustrated by (25) for which I gave a DRS in section 3.2. This DRS is unacceptable by our rules as the referent u in $m_2(25)$ is not accessible from the position of *him* in $m_1(25)$, to which, at step (5) it was nonetheless assigned. This difficulty would not have arisen had CR1 been properly applied in the first place. The correct DRS for (25) looks as follows:

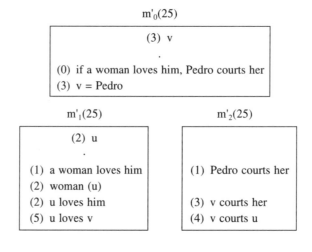

Let us, for good measure, also give a corrected version of the DRS for (1), as the analysis of that sentence motivated so much of what I have been saying, and yet its earlier representation also contains a violation of CR1:

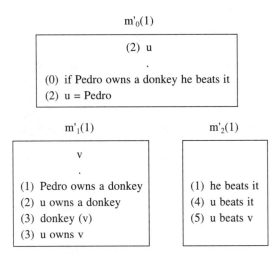

We already saw in section 2 how important it is that the discourse referents available to a given pronoun must all occur in the same, or else in some superordinate, DR. This, we saw, accounts for the fact that *it* cannot have *every donkey* as its antecedent in a sentence such as (17) or (18), or be anaphorically linked to *a donkey* in (19). The reader will inevitably ask, however, why subordination is defined in the precise way it has been. Why, for instance is, where (m_1, m_2) represents a conditional or universal, m_2 subordinate to m_1 but not m_1 subordinate to m_2; or, to put it more directly, why may the elements of m_2 not serve as referents for pronouns in sentences belonging to Con_{m_1} while the members of U_{m_1} are admitted as referents for pronouns occurring in m_2?

That the elements of m_1 must be available for the pronouns of m_2 is too central an assumption of our theory to permit tampering: our analysis of the crucial sentences (1) and (2) depended essentially on that hypothesis. But what about referents in m_2 for pronouns in m_1? Here is an example which shows that the sets of possible referents must be as we have specified them:

(26)   Every farmer who admires her courts a widow.

It is my intuitive judgment that in (26) *her* can be coreferential with *a widow*, but only if *a widow* has wide scope over *every farmer*. Such "wide scope" readings for indefinites that occupy positions which correspond to narrow scope according to our syntax are not discussed in this paper. A reading which (26) *cannot* have is, according to my intuitions, the one given by (27):

(27) $\forall x \, (farmer(x) \rightarrow \exists y \, (widow(y) \land admires(x,y) \land courts(x,y)))$.

To block this reading we must stipulate that the element v of $m_2(26)$ is not available to the pronoun in $m_1(26)$:

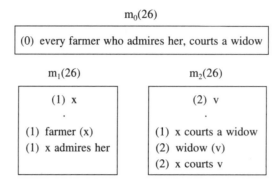

Our theory seems to rule out a parallel reading for the conditional

(28)   If a farmer admires her, he courts a widow.

It predicts, that is, that (28) cannot mean what is expressed by (27). Again, *her* in (28) can be understood as coreferential with *a widow* if the latter is taken to have wide scope—as it normally would in, say,

(29)   If a farmer admires her he courts a certain widow I have dated and therefore know quite well.

(28) appears to have still another reading, in which *a widow* is taken as generic, a reading that is approximated by

(30) $\forall x \forall y [\text{farmer}(x) \land \text{widow}(y) \land \text{admires}(x,y) \rightarrow \text{courts}(x,y)]$.

Generics, however, are among the most recalcitrant constructions known to me. They will not be treated in this paper. Note also that

(31)   If Pedro admires her he courts a widow,

though understandable, on the assumption that *her* refers to *a widow*, does not sound natural— barely more natural, in fact, than (26) and (28) on their wide scope reading, given by

(32) $\exists y [\text{widow}(y) \land \forall x [\text{farmer}(x) \land \text{admires}(x,y) \rightarrow \text{courts }(x,y)]]$.

The reason is that in order to get a reading of (31) in which *her* and *a widow* are coreferential, we have to suppose—just as we must in connection with (26) and (28)—that *a widow* has wide scope over the subject Pedro. In another paper we shall have more to say about why such readings tend to be somewhat unnatural.

Notes

This paper was written while I held a post-doctoral fellowship at the Center for Cognitive Science of the University of Texas at Austin. Anybody who has the faintest acquaintance with my personality will realize that it would not have been written had the directors of the center not given me this opportunity, and thus understand the depth of my indebtedness to them. I would also like to thank, among the many who helped me during my stay in Austin, Kate Ehrlich, Alan Garnham, Lauri Karttunen, and Stanley Peters for their comments and suggestions.
    1. Theories that to a greater or lesser degree accord with this intuition have emerged within artificial intelligence and computer science, as well as within linguistics. A significant contribution of this kind that

comes from the first field is Webber (1978). Examples of such theories that have been proposed by linguists are the theories outlined in Bartsch (1976; 1979), Cooper (1975; 1979), Hausser (1974; 1979), and Karttunen (1976).

By no means is every recent account of pronouns predicated on the assumption that all cases of pronominal reference can be brought under one unifying principle. Compare, for instance, Evans (1977; 1980: Chapter 21 in this volume), Lasnik (1976), and Partee (1978).

2. There seems to be a rough preference for referents introduced by terms that appear in the discourse *before* the anaphoric pronoun over those that are introduced by subsequent terms, as well as a preference for referents that are introduced by terms that occur *near* the anaphor. (Thus the referent introduced by the last referential term preceding the anaphoric pronoun is, other factors permitting, a strong referential candidate.)

3. A large part of the research that has been done on anaphora by computer scientists and people working in artificial intelligence has been concerned with this problem—understandably enough, as the lack of effective routines for the detection of anaphoric antecedents has for many years been one of the main obstacles to producing satisfactory computer systems for question answering and translation. However useful some of this work may have been, I have the impression that its theoretical significance is rather limited. Indeed, I much incline to the opinion expressed, for example, in Partee (1978, p. 80) that all we can reasonably expect to achieve in this area is to articulate orders of preference among the potential referents of an anaphoric pronoun, without implying that the item that receives the highest rating is in each and every case the referent of the anaphor.

4. We are much assisted in our making of such guesses by the spectrum of our social prejudices. Sometimes, however, these may lead us astray, and embarrassingly so, as in the following riddle which advocates of women's liberation have on occasion used to expose members of the chauvinistic rearguard: In a head-on collision, both father and son are critically wounded. They are rushed into a hospital where the chief surgeon performs an emergency operation on the son. But it is too late, and the boy dies on the operating table. When an assistant asks the surgeon, "Could you have a look at the other victim?", the surgeon replies "I could not bear it. I have already lost my son." Someone who has the built-in conception that chief surgeons are men will find it substantially more difficult to make sense of this story than those who hold no such view.

5. As we have already observed, this is not quite correct, since a pronoun can be used deictically, in which case the referent need not belong to the DR; we shall, however, ignore the deictic use of pronouns in the course of this paper.

6. See for example Lewis (1973), Turner (1981), Veltman (1976), and Kratzer (1979).

7. [Example] (11) is akin in spirit to the game theoretical analysis of *if . . . then . . .* sentences proposed in Hintikka and Carlson (1978), according to which a winning strategy for the defender of *if A then B* is a function which maps every winning strategy for the defender of A onto a winning strategy for the defender of B.

8. The fact that "existential" quantifier phrases can be represented in this manner is closely related to the familiar model theoretic proposition that purely existential sentences are preserved under model extensions.

9. I have found at least one speaker for whom (20) is distinctly less acceptable than for instance (1).

10. See for example Carlson (1977a, ch. 1), which warns against this prejudice in similar terms.

11. Proposals similar to that of Evans can be found, for example, in Cooper (1979) and Hausser (1974). These suffer in my view from similar shortcomings.

12. The two fragments have roughly the same quantificational powers. But the present fragment lacks adjectives, prepositional phrases, and intensional contexts.

13. One might have hoped that a theory of semantic processing such as the one attempted here could provide an explanation of why island-constraints exist and why they operate in precisely those linguistic contexts that are subject to them. I have not succeeded, however, in finding such an explanation.

14. See e.g. Montague (1970a,b; 1974a), Partee (1975a), Thomason (1976), Cooper and Parsons (1976), and Cooper (1979).

15. The expansion of M to M' is part of a convenient, and familiar, model-theoretic device that serves as an alternative to the notion of satisfaction: If M is a model for a first-order language L and $\phi(x_1, \ldots, x_n)$ is a formula of L with free occurrence of the variables $x_1, \ldots, x_n$ and no others, and $u_1, \ldots, u_n \in U$, then

clearly $u_1, \ldots, u_n$ satisfy $\phi(x_1, \ldots, x_n)$ in M if M makes true the L(U)-sentence ϕ ($u_1, \ldots, u_n$). Thus by passing from L to L(U) we can define *truth in* M without any need of the concept of satisfaction as such. It is in this spirit that I shall use here the sentences of L(V). Where m is a DR which contains the discourse referents ($u_1, \ldots, u_n$), a sentence $\phi(u_1, \ldots, u_n)$ of L($\{u_1, \ldots, u_n\}$) is to express that in m $u_1, \ldots, u_n$ satisfy the condition expressed by the λ-abstract $\lambda x_1, \ldots, \lambda x_n \, \phi(x_1, \ldots, x_n)$.

16. With the *occurrence* $\langle\phi, k\rangle$ are associated, of course, particular *occurrences* of antecedent and consequent.

14

JEROEN GROENENDIJK AND MARTIN STOKHOF

Dynamic Predicate Logic

1 Introduction

This paper is devoted to the formulation and investigation of a dynamic semantic interpretation of the language of first-order predicate logic. The resulting system, which will be referred to as "dynamic predicate logic," is intended as a first step toward a compositional, non-representational theory of discourse semantics.

In the last decade, various theories of discourse semantics have emerged within the paradigm of model-theoretic semantics. A common feature of these theories is a tendency to do away with the principle of compositionality, a principle which, implicitly or explicitly, has dominated semantics since the days of Frege. Therefore the question naturally arises whether non-compositionality is in any way a necessary feature of discourse semantics.

Since we subscribe to the interpretation of compositionality as constituting primarily a methodological principle, we consider this to be a methodological rather than an empirical question. As a consequence, the emphasis in the present paper lies on developing an alternative compositional semantics of discourse, which is empirically equivalent to its non-compositional brethren, but which differs from them in a principled methodological way. Hence, no attempts are made to improve on existing theories empirically.

Nevertheless, as we indicate in section 5, the development of a compositional alternative may in the end have empirical consequences, too. First of all, it can be argued that the dynamic view on interpretation developed in this paper suggests natural and relatively easy to formulate extensions which enable one to deal with a wider range of phenomena than can be dealt with in existing theories.

Moreover, the various approaches to the model-theoretic semantics of discourse that have been developed during the last decade have constituted a "fresh start" in the sense that much of

Jeroen Groenendijk and Martin Stokhof (1991 Dynamic predicate logic. *Linguistics and Philosophy* 14: 39–100. Reprinted by permission of Kluwer Academic Publishers.

what had been accomplished before was ignored, at least for a start. Of course, this is a justified strategy if one feels one is trying to develop a radically different approach to recalcitrant problems. However, there comes a time when such new approaches have to be compared with the older one, and when an assessment of the pros and cons of each has to be made.

One of the main problems in semantics today, we feel, is that a semantic theory such as Montague grammar and an approach like Kamp's discourse representation theory are hard to compare, let alone that it is possible to unify their insights and results. One of the main obstacles is that the latter lacks, or has abolished, the principle of compositionality which is so central a feature of the former. Hence, the development of a compositional alternative to the semantics of discourse may very well have empirical import on this score as well: in the end, it may contribute to a unification of these two approaches which have largely complementary descriptive domains.

In the extension of model-theoretic semantics from the sentential to the discourse level, various theories have emerged: beside discourse representation theory (Kamp 1981: chapter 13 in this volume; 1983), we should mention Heim's file card semantics (Heim 1982; 1983), and, in a different framework, the work of Seuren (1986). None of these theories makes compositionality its starting point. (However, it seems that Heim (1982, ch. 3) does attach some value to compositionality.) Since the aim of this paper is restricted to showing that a compositional alternative can be developed, and since Kamp's discourse representation theory is both self-consciously non-compositional and formally most explicit, we feel justified in restricting comparison to just the latter theory.

The paper is organized as follows. In section 2, we introduce the elements of dynamic interpretation in a heuristic fashion, discussing a small number of well-known problematic cases. In section 3, we recapitulate our findings, formulate the dynamic semantics of predicate logic systematically, and study its logical properties. The resulting system is compared with ordinary predicate logic, discourse representation theory, and quantificational dynamic logic in section 4. In section 5, we indicate prospects for further developments and, in retrospect, we present our philosophical and methodological motives.

To end this introductory section, we remark that Barwise's 1987 proposal for the interpretation of anaphoric relations within the framework of situation semantics, which in Rooth (1987) is compared with Heim's file card semantics and with Montague grammar, are akin in spirit and content to our approach. So is Schubert and Pelletier (1989). Equally akin in spirit, but less in content, is Zeevat (1989).

2   Elements of dynamic interpretation

2.1   Cross-sentential and donkey-anaphora

We begin this section with a brief discussion of two well-known problems: cross-sentential anaphora and anaphoric relations in donkey-sentences. We state them anew, because we want to make clear what, we feel, is the real challenge they offer.

If we use standard first-order predicate logic (henceforth, PL) in translating a natural language sentence or discourse, anaphoric pronouns will turn up as bound variables. In many cases, this means that in order to arrive at formulas which are good translations—that is, which express the right meaning—we have to be pretty inventive and should not pay too much attention to the way in which the natural language sentence or discourse is built up. Let us illustrate this with three simple examples, which nevertheless are representative for the kind of problems we meet:

(1)   A man walks in the park. He whistles
(2)   If a farmer owns a donkey, he beats it
(3)   Every farmer who owns a donkey, beats it

In order for the pronoun *he* in the second sentence of (1) to be anaphorically linked to *a man* in the first sentence, we have to give an existential quantifier wide scope over the conjunction of the two sentences involved. Doing so, we arrive at (1a):

(1a) $\exists x[\text{man}(x) \wedge \text{walk-in-the-park}(x) \wedge \text{whistle}(x)]$

Now, notice that the translation of the first sentence in (1), which would be $\exists x[\text{man}(x) \wedge \text{walk-in-the-park}(x)]$, does not occur as a subformula in (1a). Apparently, we do not get from (1) to (1a) in a step-by-step—compositional—way. If we did, we would rather translate (1) as (1b):

(1b) $\exists x[\text{man}(x) \wedge \text{walk-in-the-park}(x)] \wedge \text{whistle}(x)$

But this is not a proper translation of (1), at least not in standard predicate logic, since in (1b) the last occurrence of the variable x is not bound by the existential quantifier, and hence the anaphoric link in (1) is not accounted for. However, suppose we could interpret (1b) in such a way that it *is* equivalent with (1). Evidently, (1b) would be preferred to (1a) as a translation of (1), since it could be the result of a compositional procedure.

Turning to examples (2) and (3), we observe that a proper translation in PL for both of them is (2a):

(2a) $\forall x \forall y[[\text{farmer}(x) \wedge \text{donkey}(y) \wedge \text{own}(x, y)] \to \text{beat}(x, y)]$

These cases are more dramatic than the previous one. Although (2) and (3) contain indefinite terms, which normally translate as existentially quantified phrases, we need universal quantification to account for their meaning in these kinds of examples. And notice, moreover, that the corresponding universal quantifiers $\forall x$ and $\forall y$ have to be given wide scope over the entire formula, whereas the indefinite terms in (2) and (3) to which they correspond, appear inside the antecedent of an implication in the case of (2) and way inside the relative clause attached to the subject term *every farmer* in the case of (3). If we use PL as our means to represent meaning, these kinds of examples prevent us from uniformly translating indefinite terms as existentially quantified phrases. Again, this constitutes a breach of the principle of compositionality, a principle which is not only intuitively appealing but also theoretically parsimonious and computationally plausible.

From a compositional point of view, translations like (2b) for sentence (2) and (3b) for sentence (3) are to be preferred:

(2b) $\exists x[\text{farmer}(x) \wedge \exists y[\text{donkey}(y) \wedge \text{own}(x, y)]] \to \text{beat}(x, y)$
(3b) $\forall x[[\text{farmer}(x) \wedge \exists y[\text{donkey}(y) \wedge \text{own}(x, y)]] \to \text{beat}(x, y)]$

But then again, (2b) and (3b) do not have the proper meaning in PL. For one thing, the occurrences of the variable y in the case of (3b) and of the variables x and y in the case of (2b), in the respective consequents, are not bound by the existential quantifiers in the antecedents. Hence, (2b) and (3b) are not equivalent with (2a), at least not in PL.

Examples like (1)–(3) have been treated successfully in discourse representation theory (henceforth DRT), but at a cost: the problem of providing a compositional translation is not really solved, and DRT uses a rather non-orthodox logical language. In DRT, (1) would be represented as (1c); (2) and (3) as (2c):

(1c) $[x][\text{man}(x), \text{walk-in-the-park}(x), \text{whistle}(x)]$
(2c) $[\ ][[x, y][\text{farmer}(x), \text{donkey}(y), \text{own}(x, y)] \to [\ ][\text{beat}(x, y)]]$

We will not go into the semantics of these discourse representation structures here (cf. section 4.2); for the moment it suffices to note that (1c) and (2c) have essentially the same truth conditions as (1a) and (2a), respectively. The important thing, however, is that these representations differ in structure from the corresponding sentences in much the same way as the PL-translations. In fact, the structure of (1c) is essentially that of (1a) and not that of (1b). And in (2c), no representation of the relative clause *who owns a donkey* or of the intransitive verb phrase *own a donkey*—which form a constituent in (2) and (3), respectively—can be isolated as a substructure of (2c). So, from a compositional point of view, they are hardly a change for the better. For the moment we leave it at this observation, but we return to the issue in some detail in section 4.2.

In this paper we give an alternative account of the phenomena exemplified by (1)–(3): we do so by replacing the standard semantics of the language of first-order predicate logic by a dynamic semantics, which is inspired by systems of dynamic logic as they are used in the denotational semantics of programming languages. (See Harel 1984 for an overview.) The resulting system of dynamic predicate logic (henceforth DPL) constitutes an improvement over DRT in the following sense: to the extent that this is possible in a first-order language at all, it gives a compositional semantic treatment of the relevant phenomena, while the syntax of the language used, being that of standard predicate logic, is an orthodox one. More specifically, using DPL it becomes possible to represent the meanings of the sentences (1), (2), and (3) by means of the formulas (1b), (2b), and (3b). As we remarked above, such representations are to be preferred from a compositional and a computational point of view. The dynamic semantics of DPL makes sure that (1b) comes out with the same truth conditions as (1a) is assigned in PL, and that (2b) and (3b) come out with the same truth conditions as (1a) and (2a) have in PL.

2.2   The dynamic view on meaning

The general starting point of the kind of semantics that DPL is an instance of is that the meaning of a sentence does not lie in its truth conditions but, rather, in the way it changes (the representation of) the information of the interpreter. The utterance of a sentence brings us from a certain state of information to another one. The meaning of a sentence lies in the way it brings about such a transition. Although this "procedural" dynamic view on meaning as such is not particular to semantic theories of discourse (it can also be found in theories about sentence meaning, e.g., in the work of Stalnaker), it is a view which is endorsed by all approaches to discourse semantics which we referred to above.

It should he noted, though, that in most cases one really studies only one particular aspect of the information change potential that makes up the meaning of a sentence at a time. For example, in the standard version of DRT, information change is narrowed down to the (im)possibilities of subsequent anaphoric reference that sentences determine. All other information that a sentence conveys is treated in a static, rather than in dynamic, fashion. DPL is like DRT in this respect. It, too, restricts the dynamics of interpretation to that aspect of the meaning of sentences that concerns their potential to "pass on" possible antecedents for subsequent anaphors, within and across sentence boundaries. (See Groenendijk and Stokhof 1988 for some more discussion of this point.)

As has been observed by several authors, there is a strong correspondence between the dynamic view on meaning, and a basic idea underlying the denotational approach to the semantics of programming languages, viz. that the meaning of a program can be captured in terms of a relation between machine states. Given the restriction to antecedent-anaphor relations, the observed correspondence comes down to the following. A machine state may be identified with an assignment of objects to variables. The interpretation of a program can then be regarded as a set of ordered pairs of assignments, as the set of all its possible "input–output" pairs. A pair $\langle g, h \rangle$ is in the interpretation of a program π, if when π is executed in state g, a possible resulting state is h.

For example, the execution of an atomic program consisting of a simple assignment statement '$x := a$' transforms a state (assignment) g into a state (assignment) h which differs from g at most with respect to the value d assigns to x and in which the object denoted by the constant a is assigned to x.

Another simple illustration is provided by sequences of programs. The interpretation of a sequence of programs '$\pi_1 : \pi_2$' is as follows. It can take us from state g to h, if there is some state k such that the program π_1 can take us from g to k, and π_2 from k to h. Or, to put it differently, the second program is executed in a state which is (partly) created by the first.

As we intend to show in this paper, the basic idea that (certain aspects of) meaning can be described in terms of relations between states, can be applied fruitfully in natural language semantics as well. It should be remarked, though, that the aims and perspectives of systems of dynamic logic as they are used in the semantics of programming languages, are rather different from the purpose for which we want to use the system to be developed below. And consequently, there are differences between these systems as such. Some discussion of these matters can be found in section 4.3.

2.3   Dynamic conjunction and existential quantification

In the present and the next two sections, we introduce a dynamic interpretation for the language of extensional first-order predicate logic in a step-by-step fashion, deferring an explicit statement and a formal investigation of DPL to section 3. In the present section we introduce dynamic conjunction and existential quantification, which will enable us to deal with the first of the three examples discussed above, which concerned cross-sentential anaphora. In section 2.4, we discuss implication and existential quantification. Their dynamic treatment will give us the means to treat simple donkey-sentences, such as exemplified by the second example. And finally in section 2.5, we turn to universal quantification and negation in order to be able to deal with the more complicated donkey-sentences as exemplified by the last example.

The vocabulary of DPL consists of n-place predicates, individual constants, and variables. They are interpreted in the usual fashion. The models that we use are ordinary extensional first-order models, consisting of a domain D of individuals and an interpretation function F, assigning individuals to the individual constants, and sets of n-tuples of individuals to the n-place predicates. Further, we use assignments as usual—that is, as total functions from the set of variables to the domain. They are denoted by 'g', 'h', and so on. By '$h[x]g$' we mean that assignment h differs from g at most with respect to the value it assigns to x. When in what follows we speak of the interpretation of an expression, we mean its semantic value in a suitable model. The function assigning semantic values is denoted by [ ].

In the standard semantics of predicate logic, the interpretation of a formula is a set of assignment, viz. those assignments which verify the formula. In the dynamic semantics of DPL, the semantic object expressed by a formula is a set of ordered pairs of assignments. Trading on the analogy with programming languages, such pairs can be regarded as possible 'input–output' pairs: a pair $\langle g, h \rangle$ is in the interpretation of a formula ϕ iff when ϕ is evaluated with respect to g, h is a possible outcome of the evaluation procedure. Since g and h are assignments of objects to variables, the difference between an input assignment g and an output assignment h can only be that a different object is assigned to one or more variables. This is precisely what happens when an existentially quantified formula is interpreted dynamically. Consider the formula $\exists x Px$. In the standard semantics, an assignment g is in the interpretation of $\exists x Px$ iff there is some assignment h which differs from g at most with respect to the value it assigns to x, and which is in the interpretation of Px—that is, which assigns an object $h(x)$ to x such that $h(x) \in F(P)$. When $\exists x Px$ is treated dynamically, all assignments h such that $h[x]g$ & $h(x) \in F(P)$, are taken to be possible outputs with respect to input g. In other words:

$$[\exists xPx] = \{\langle g,h \rangle \mid h[x]g \ \& \ h(x) \in F(P)\}$$

This will not yet do for the general case of $\exists x \phi$. We have to reckon with the possibility that the interpretation of ϕ, too, has dynamic effects. (For example, ϕ itself might be an existentially quantified formula.) Taking this into account, the dynamic interpretation of $\exists x \phi$ will consist of those pairs of assignments $\langle g,h \rangle$ such that there is some assignment k which differs from g at most in x and which together with h forms a possible input–output pair for ϕ. The interpretation clause for existentially quantified formulas then reads as follows:

$$[\exists x \phi] = \{\langle g,h \rangle \mid \exists k: k[x]g \ \& \ \langle k, h \rangle \in [\phi]\}$$

In order to show that this interpretation of $\exists x \phi$ squares with the one given above for $\exists xPx$, we first have to state the interpretation of atomic formulas.

Unlike existentially quantified formulas, atomic formulas do not have dynamic effects of their own. Rather, they function as a kind of 'test' on incoming assignments. An atomic formula tests whether an input assignment satisfies the condition it embodies. If so, the assignment is passed on as output; if not, it is rejected. So the dynamics of an atomic formula consists in letting pass the assignments which satisfy it and blocking those that don't. This is captured in the following definition:

$$[\,Rt_1 \ldots t_n] = \{\langle g,h \rangle \mid h = g \ \& \ \langle [t_1]_h, \ldots, [t_n]_h \rangle \in F(R)\}$$

Here, as usual, $[t]_h = F(t)$ if t is an individual constant, and $[t]_h = h(t)$ if t is a variable.

We first work out our simple example of an existentially quantified formula $\exists xPx$:

$$[\exists xPx] = \{\langle g, h \rangle \mid \exists k: k[x]g \ \& \ \langle k, h \rangle \in [Px]\} = \{\langle g,h \rangle \mid \exists k: k[x]g \ \& \ k = h \ \& \ h(x) \in F(P)\}\} = \{\langle g,h \rangle \mid h[x]g \ \& \ h(x) \in F(P)\}$$

This example illustrates the interpretation of the existential quantifier and that of atomic formulas. The meaning of $\exists xPx$ determines that for a given input assignment g, we get as possible outputs those assignments h which differ from g at most in x and which satisfy the condition that the individual $h(x)$ has the property $F(P)$.

The dynamic interpretation of existential quantification presented here is only one ingredient of a treatment of cross-sentential anaphoric binding as it was illustrated by the first example discussed in section 2.1. The example consists of a sequence of two sentences, the first of which contains an indefinite term which functions as the antecedent of an anaphoric pronoun occurring in the second sentence. Although this obviously is not all there is to it, within the framework at hand, simple sentence sequencing is best represented as *conjunction*. Going about compositionally, what we get in this case is a conjunction consisting of an existentially quantified formula and a formula containing a free occurrence of the variable corresponding to the quantifier. The simplest example of a formula that is of this form is $\exists xPx \land Qx$.

To get the required interpretation for this kind of formula, a dynamic interpretation of existential quantification alone does not suffice; we need a dynamic treatment of conjunction as well. For example, in order to get the required anaphoric reading we have to interpret $\exists xPx \land Qx$ in such a way that the second occurrence of x, which is outside the scope of the quantifier, is bound by that quantifier with the same force as the first occurrence of x, which is inside its scope.

So the first thing we require of the dynamic interpretation of conjunction is that it passes on values of variables from the first conjunct to the second. Moreover, we note that values assigned to variables in a conjunction should remain available for further conjuncts that are added. If we continue the discourse 'A man walks in the park. He meets a woman' with 'He kisses her', we must view this as adding another conjunct. And this newly added conjunct may contain "free" occurrences of variables (pronouns) which nevertheless are bound by existential quantifiers (indefinite terms) which have occurred earlier on.

In fact, this is exactly what the interpretation of a sequence of programs as described above amounts to. Hence, our definition of dynamic conjunction is the following:

$$[\phi \wedge \psi] = \{\langle g, h \rangle \mid \exists k \colon \langle g, k \rangle \in [\phi] \ \& \ \langle k, h \rangle \in [\psi]\}$$

According to this definition, the interpretation of $\phi \wedge \psi$ with input g may result in output h iff there is some k such that interpreting ϕ in g may lead to k, and interpreting ψ in k enables us to reach h.

We are now fully equipped to deal with the first of the three examples discussed above, which concerned cross-sentential anaphora. Calculating the interpretation of $\exists x P x \wedge Q x$ shows that, indeed, the binding effects of an existential quantifier may reach further than its scope, more in particular they reach over further conjuncts:

$$[\exists x P x \wedge Q x] = \{\langle g,h \rangle \mid \exists k \colon \langle g,k \rangle \in [\exists x P x] \ \& \ \langle k,h \rangle \in [Q x]\} = \{\langle g,h \rangle \mid \exists k \colon k[x]g \ \& \ k(x) \in F(P) \ \&$$
$$h = k \ \& \ h(x) \in F(Q)\} = \{\langle g,h \rangle \mid h[x]g \ \& \ h(x) \in F(P) \ \& \ h(x) \in F(Q)\}$$

Here, we see that the occurrence of x in the second conjunct $Q x$, although it is not in the scope of the quantifier $\exists x$ in the ordinary sense, is nevertheless bound by it with the same force as the occurrence of x in $P x$ in the first conjunct, which obviously is in the scope of $\exists x$. This means that in DPL there is no difference in meaning between the formula $\exists x P x \wedge Q x$ and the formula $\exists x [P x \wedge Q x]$. From the latter fact it is also clear that if we continue a conjunction $\phi \wedge \psi$ with a further conjunct χ, the binding force of quantifiers in either one of the conjuncts ϕ and ψ will remain active.

Because of its power to pass on variable bindings from its left conjunct to the right one, we call conjunction an *internally dynamic* connective. And because of its capacity to keep passing on bindings to conjuncts yet to come, we call it an *externally dynamic* connective as well. For similar reasons, the existential quantifier is called both internally and externally dynamic: it can bind variables to the right, both inside and outside its scope.

It is precisely this feature of DPL—that it allows for existential quantifiers to bind variables yet to come which are outside their scope—that lends it the power to solve the problem of getting a compositional treatment of antecedent-anaphor relations which go across sentence boundaries. It allows us to translate the sentence containing the antecedent indefinite term, without having to look ahead at what is still to come, treating it as an ordinary existentially quantified phrase. Then we can translate a sentence which follows and which contains an anaphor without having to re-analyze the translation so-far, regarding the anaphoric pronoun as an ordinary variable. The dynamic semantics takes care of the rest. It makes sure that the pronoun is treated as a variable bound by the quantifier which corresponds to the indefinite term.

2.4   Dynamic existential quantification and implication

The second kind of example which we introduced in section 2.1 concerns simple donkey-sentences. The main problem of donkey-sentences is the occurrence of an indefinite term in the antecedent of an implication which is anaphorically linked to a pronoun in the consequent. As we indicated above, if we are to represent the meaning of such sentences in ordinary predicate logic, which allows quantifiers to bind only those variables which occur in their syntactic scope, then we are forced to regard the indefinite term as a universal quantifier and to give it wide scope over the implication as a whole. This goes against compositionality in two ways: first of all, we cannot use the ordinary, lexically determined meaning of indefinite terms; and secondly, we must deviate from the syntactic structure by "raising" these terms from their position in the antecedent to a position outside the implication. In order to show that this kind of example can be treated in DPL in a more compositional, and hence more satisfactory way, we have to say what the dynamic interpretation of implication is.

The simplest example of a formula corresponding to a donkey-sentence is $\exists xPx \to Qx$. In order for this formula to get the required interpretation, the dynamic interpretation of implication has to allow for an existential quantifier in its antecedent to bind a variable in its consequent. This means that implication is like conjunction in the following respect: it passes on values assigned to variables in its antecedent to its consequent. In other words, implication is an internally dynamic connective.

But that is not all. We also observe that the existential quantifier in the antecedent has universal force. This can be accounted for as follows. With respect to an input assignment, the antecedent of an implication results in a set of possible output assignments. For the implication as a whole, it seems reasonable to require that *every* assignment that is a possible output of the antecedent be a possible input for the consequent. By this we mean that an output assignment h of the antecedent, when taken as input to the consequent, should result in at least one output assignment k. In other words, the interpretation of an implication $\phi \to \psi$ should be such that for every pair $\langle g,h \rangle$ in the interpretation of ϕ there is some assignment k such that $\langle h,k \rangle$ is in the interpretation of ψ. This feature of the interpretation of implication results in universal force of an existential quantifier occurring in the antecedent. Consider $\exists xPx \to Qx$. With respect to an input assignment g, the antecedent $\exists xPx$ results in the set of assignments h such that $h[x]g$ and $h(x) \in F(P)$. If we require, as we do, that every such h should be a proper input of the consequent Qx, the result is that every h such that $h(x) \in F(P)$ also satisfies $h(x) \in F(Q)$.

This does not yet determine which pairs of assignments constitute the interpretation of $\phi \to \psi$; it only tells us with respect to which assignments $\phi \to \psi$ can be "successfully executed." To get at the full interpretation of $\phi \to \psi$ we need yet another observation, which is that normally an implication as a whole does not pass on values assigned to variables by quantifiers in the implication itself, to sentences yet to come. Consider the following example:

(4)   If a farmer owns a donkey, he beats it.* He hates it.

In this example, the pronouns *he* and *it* in the second sentence cannot be anaphorically linked to the indefinite terms in the preceding implication. And quite generally it is concluded on the basis of examples such as these that a quantifier which occurs inside an implication, be it in the antecedent or in the consequent, cannot bind variables outside the implication. (A lot more needs to be said about this, and for some of it we refer to section 5.1.) In this respect implication is unlike conjunction: it is not externally dynamic; like an atomic formula, an implication as a whole has the character of a test.

What we thus end up with as the dynamic interpretation of implication is the following:

$$\llbracket \phi \to \psi \rrbracket = \{\langle g,h \rangle \mid h = g \ \& \ \forall k: \langle h,k \rangle \in \llbracket \phi \rrbracket \Rightarrow \exists j: \langle k,j \rangle \in \llbracket \psi \rrbracket\}$$

The interpretation of $\phi \to \psi$ accepts an assignment g iff every possible output of ϕ with respect to g leads to a successful interpretation of ψ, and it rejects g otherwise. Armed with this definition, we can now proceed to show that DPL assigns the required interpretation to formulas which correspond to the kind of donkey-sentences exemplified by our second example. By way of illustration, we work out the interpretation of the formula $\exists xPx \to Qx$:

$$\begin{aligned}
\llbracket \exists xPx \to Qx \rrbracket &= \{\langle g, h \rangle \mid h = g \ \& \ \forall k: \langle h, k \rangle \in \llbracket \exists xPx \rrbracket \Rightarrow \exists j: \langle k, j \rangle \in \llbracket Qx \rrbracket\} \\
&= \{\langle g, g \rangle \mid \forall k: \langle g,k \rangle \in \llbracket \exists xPx \rrbracket \Rightarrow \exists j: \langle k, j \rangle \in \llbracket Qx \rrbracket\} \\
&= \{\langle g, g \rangle \mid \forall k: k[x]g \ \& \ k(x) \in F(P) \Rightarrow k(x) \in F(Q)\}
\end{aligned}$$

This example shows that the binding effects of an existential quantifier occurring in the antecedent of an implication extend to occurrences of the corresponding variable in the consequent and that such a quantifier occurrence has universal force. It also shows that dynamic effects are restricted to the implication as such and are not passed on to any formulas which might follow it. In effect, as we shall see below, $\exists x Px \rightarrow Qx$ is equivalent in DPL to $\forall x[Px \rightarrow Qx]$.

2.5   Universal quantification, negation, and disjunction

For a treatment of the second, more complicated kind of donkey-sentences, exemplified by our third example, we need to state the interpretation of the universal quantifier. One aspect of this interpretation is illustrated by the following two examples:

(5)   Every man walks in the park. *He whistles.
(6)   Every farmer who owns a donkey beats it. *He hates it.

The pronoun *he* occurring in the second sentence of (5) cannot be interpreted as being anaphorically linked to the universal term in the sentence preceding it. Nor can the pronouns *he* and *it* in the second sentence of (6) be anaphorically linked to the terms *every farmer* and *a donkey* in the first sentence of (6). Generally, from examples such as these it is concluded that the universal quantifier shares with implication the characteristic of being externally static. Neither a universal quantifier itself nor any existential quantifier inside its scope can bind variables outside the scope of that universal quantifier. (Again, we refer to section 5.1 for some discussion of this point.) But, of course, inside the scope of a universal quantifier dynamic effects may very well occur, as the donkey-sentence (3) shows. This leads to the following definition of the interpretation of universal quantification:

$$[\![\forall x\phi]\!] = \{\langle g,h\rangle \mid h = g \ \& \ \forall k: k[x]h \Rightarrow \exists m: \langle k,m\rangle \in [\![\phi]\!]\}$$

So, a universally quantified formula $\forall x\phi$, too, functions as a test. An input assignment g is passed on iff every assignment that differs at most from g in x is a proper input for ϕ; otherwise it is blocked. An output assignment is always identical to the corresponding input.

That the dynamic interpretation of the universal quantifier, together with that of the existential quantifier and implication, allows us to deal with the donkey-sentence (3) in the manner discussed at the beginning of this section is shown by working out the interpretation of a formula that exhibits the relevant structure:

$$[\![\forall x[[Px \wedge \exists y[Qy \wedge Rxy]] \rightarrow Sxy]\!] = \{\langle g, h\rangle \mid h = g \ \& \ \forall k: k[x]h \Rightarrow \exists m: \langle k, m\rangle \in [\![Px \wedge \exists y[Qy \wedge$$
$$Rxy]] \rightarrow Sxy]\!]\}$$
$$= \{\langle g, g\rangle \mid \forall k: k[x]g \Rightarrow (\forall j: \langle k, j\rangle \in [\![Px \wedge \exists y[Qy \wedge Rxy]\!] \Rightarrow$$
$$\exists z: \langle j, z\rangle \in [\![Sxy]\!])\}$$
$$= \{\langle g, g\rangle \mid \forall k: k[x]g \ \& \ k(x) \in F(P) \Rightarrow (\forall j: j[y]k \ \& \ j(y) \in$$
$$F(Q) \ \& \ \langle j(x), j(y)\rangle \in F(R) \Rightarrow \langle j(x), j(y)\rangle \in F(S))\}$$
$$= \{\langle g, g\rangle \mid \forall h: h[x,y]g \ \& \ h(x) \in F(P) \ \& \ h(y) \in F(Q) \ \& \ \langle h(x),$$
$$h(y)\rangle \in F(R) \Rightarrow \langle h(x), h(y)\rangle \in F(S)\}$$

This example illustrates that the dynamic semantics of DPL enables us to treat the more complicated type of donkey-sentences, too, in a straightforward, intuitive, and compositional manner. DPL allows us to translate an indefinite term uniformly as an existentially quantified phrase in situ—that is, when and where we encounter it in a structure—without any need of reanalysis. We can treat a pronoun which is anaphorically linked to such a term simply as a variable corresponding to the quantifier. The dynamic interpretation of the existential quantifier and of the implication ensures that the proper bindings result and that the indefinite term has the required universal force.

Within the limits set by a first-order language, the account we have given above of cross-sentential anaphora and donkey-sentences is as compositional as can be. Using DPL as our semantic representation language, we can proceed to obtain representations of the meanings of simple natural language discourses in an on-line, more or less left-to-right manner, guided by the ordinary syntactic structures and the usual lexical meanings of the phrases we encounter.

We conclude this section by stating the interpretation of negation and disjunction. Negation is like implication and universal quantification in that it, too, normally blocks anaphoric links between a term that occurs in its scope and a pronoun outside of it—that is, negation is static. (More on this in section 5.1.) The following two examples illustrate this:

(7)   It is not the case that a man walks in the park. *He whistles.
(8)   No man walks in the park. *He whistles.

Hence, the interpretation of a negation $\neg\phi$ will be of the type of a test: it returns an input assignment g iff ϕ cannot be successfully processed. If ϕ can be successfully processed with respect to g as input, g is blocked by $\neg\phi$:

$$[\neg\,\phi] = \{\langle g,h\rangle\,|\,h = g\ \&\ \neg\ \exists k\colon \langle h,k\rangle \in\ [\phi]\}$$

The following example, which has the structure of such sequences of sentences as (7) and (8), illustrates how negation works:

$$
\begin{aligned}
[\neg\exists xPx \wedge Qx] &= \{\langle g, h\rangle \mid \exists k\colon \langle g, k\rangle \in\ [\neg\,\exists xPx]\ \&\ \langle k, h\rangle \in\ [Qx]\} \\
&= \{\langle g, h\rangle \mid \exists k\colon \langle g, k\rangle \in\ [\neg\,\exists xPx]\ \&\ h = k\ \&\ h(x) \in F(Q)\} \\
&= \{\langle g, h\rangle \mid \langle g, h\rangle \in\ [\neg\,\exists xPx]\ \&\ h(x) \in F(Q)\} \\
&= \{\langle g, h\rangle \mid h = g\ \&\ \neg\ \exists k\colon \langle h, k\rangle \in\ \{\langle g, h\rangle\ h[x]g\ \&\ h(x) \in F(P)\}\ \&\ h(x) \in F(Q)\} \\
&= \{\langle g, h\rangle \mid h = g\ \&\ \neg\ \exists k\colon k[x]h\ \&\ k(x) \in F(P)\ \&\ h(x) \in F(Q)\} \\
&= \{\langle g, g\rangle \mid \neg\ \exists k\colon k[x]g\ \&\ k(x) \in F(P)\ \&\ g(x) \in F(Q)\}
\end{aligned}
$$

As we can see, the first conjunct, being a negation, does not change the assignment with respect to which the second conjunct is interpreted. The test-like character of a negation leaves the occurrence of x in the second conjunct unbound by the existential quantifier which occurs within its scope in the first conjunct. This means that, whereas $\exists xPx \wedge Qx$ and $Qx \wedge \exists xPx$ differ in meaning, $\neg\,\exists xPx \wedge Qx$ is equivalent to $Qx \wedge \neg\,\exists xPx$.

As for disjunction, it shares the feature of being externally static with implication, negation, and the universal quantifier. It, too, tests an input assignment g, and the condition it embodies is that at least one of its disjuncts be interpretable successfully with g as input. Only if this condition is met is g returned as output:

$$[\phi \vee \psi] = \{\langle g, h\rangle \mid h = g\ \&\ \exists k\colon \langle h, k\rangle \in\ [\phi] \vee \langle h, k\rangle \in\ [\psi]\}$$

According to this interpretation of disjunction, no antecedent-anaphor relations are possible between the disjuncts: that is, disjunction is not only externally but also internally static. We will come back to this in sections 4.3 and 5.1.

This concludes our introduction of the ingredients of DPL. In the next section, we will present DPL more systematically and investigate some of the logical facts touched upon above in somewhat more detail.

3   DPL: A system of dynamic predicate logic

This section is devoted to a formal study of the DPL-system. In section 3.1, we present its syntax and semantics systematically. Section 3.2 contains definitions of some basic semantic notions, such as truth and equivalence. In section 3.3, we turn to the subject of scope and binding, and in section 3.4, we state some logical facts. Section 3.5 is concerned with the notion of entailment.

3.1   Syntax and semantics

The non-logical vocabulary of DPL consists of n-place predicates, individual constants, and variables. Logical constants are negation $\neg$, conjunction $\wedge$, disjunction $\vee$, implication $\rightarrow$, the existential and universal quantifiers $\exists$ and $\forall$, and identity $=$.

DEFINITION 1. *Syntax*
1. If $t_1, \ldots, t_n$ are individual constants or variables, R is an n-place predicate, then $Rt_1 \ldots t_n$ is a formula.
2. If t_1 and t_2 are individual constants or variables, then $t_1 = t_2$ is a formula.
3. If ϕ is a formula, then $\neg\phi$, is a formula.
4. If ϕ and ψ are formulas, then $[\phi \wedge \psi]$ is a formula.
5. If ϕ and ψ are formulas, then $[\phi \vee \psi]$ is a formula.
6. If ϕ and ψ are formulas, then $[\phi \rightarrow \psi]$ is a formula.
7. If ϕ is a formula and x is a variable, then $\exists x\phi$ is a formula.
8. If ϕ is a formula and x is a variable, then $\forall x\phi$ is a formula.
9. Nothing is a formula except on the basis of 1–8.

So, the syntax of DPL is that of ordinary predicate logic.

A model M is a pair $\langle D, F \rangle$, where D is a non-empty set of individuals and F is an interpretation function having as its domain the individual constants and predicates. If α is an individual constant, then $F(\alpha) \in D$; if α is an n-place predicate, then $F(\alpha) \subseteq D''$. An assignment g is a function assigning an individual to each variable: $g(x) \in D$. G is the set of all assignment functions. Next, we define $[t]_g = g(t)$ if t is a variable and $[t]_g = F(t)$ if t is an individual constant. Finally, we define the interpretation function $[\ ]\ _M^{\mathrm{DPL}} \subseteq G \times G$ as follows. (As usual, we suppress subscripts and superscripts whenever this does not give rise to confusion.)

DEFINITION 2. *Semantics*
1. $[Rt_1 \ldots t_n] = \{\langle g, h\rangle \mid h = g\ \&\ \langle [t_1]_h, \ldots, [t_n]_h\rangle \in F(R)\}$.
2. $[t_1 = t_2] = \{\langle g, h\rangle \mid h = g\ \&\ [t_1]_h = [t_2]_h\}$.
3. $[\neg \phi] = \{\langle g, h\rangle \mid h = g\ \&\ \neg\exists k: \langle h, k\rangle \in [\phi]\}$.
4. $[\phi \wedge \psi] = \{\langle g, h\rangle \mid \exists k: \langle g, k\rangle \in [\phi]\ \&\ \langle k, h\rangle \in [\psi]\}$.
5. $[\phi \vee \psi] = \{\langle g, h\rangle \mid h = g\ \&\ \exists k: \langle h, k\rangle \in [\phi] \vee \langle h, k\rangle \in [\psi]\}$.
6. $[\phi \rightarrow \psi] = \{\langle g, h\rangle \mid h = g\ \&\ \forall k: \langle h, k\rangle \in [\phi] \Rightarrow \exists j: \langle k, j\rangle \in [\psi]\}$.
7. $[\exists x\phi] = \{\langle g, h\rangle \mid \exists k: k[x]g\ \&\ \langle k, h\rangle \in [\phi]\}$.
8. $[\forall x\phi] = \{\langle g, h\rangle \mid h = g\ \&\ \forall k: k[x]h \Rightarrow \exists j: \langle k, j\rangle \in [\phi]\}$.

Besides the clauses that were discussed in the previous section, Definition 2 also contains a clause which gives the interpretation of identity statements. It will come as no surprise that such statements are interpreted as tests.

3.2   Meaning, truth, and equivalence

The notion of the interpretation of a formula that the semantics of DPL specifies differs from the one we are familiar with from PL. The latter can be given in the form of a recursive specification of a set of assignments, those which satisfy a formula, whereas the semantics stated above defines a recursive notion of a set of pairs of assignments, those which are proper input–output pairs.

The notion of interpretation of PL brings along a notion of truth with respect to an assignment which is defined as follows: ϕ is true with respect to g iff g is an element of the set denoted by ϕ. In the present, essentially richer scheme, a similar notion can be defined. We call a formula true with respect to an assignment g in a model M iff with g as input, it has an output:

DEFINITION 3. *Truth.* ϕ is *true with respect to g in M* iff $\exists h{:}\langle g,h \rangle \in [\![\phi]\!]_M$.

In terms of this notion, we define when a formula is *valid* and when it is a *contradiction*:

DEFINITION 4. *Validity.* ϕ is *valid* iff $\forall M \forall g$: ϕ is true with respect to g in M.

DEFINITION 5. *Contradictoriness.* ϕ is a *contradiction* iff $\forall M \forall g$: ϕ is false with respect to g in M.

Notice that the interpretation of any contradiction is always the empty set. For valid formulas things are different: no unique semantic object serves as their interpretation. They either denote the identity relation on G, or a certain extension of this. For example, $Px \lor \neg Px$ always denotes the set of all pairs $\langle g,g \rangle$, but $\exists x[Px \lor \neg Px]$ denotes the set of all pairs $\langle g,h \rangle$ such that h differs at most with respect to x from g. Both formulas are valid according to Definition 4, since both are true with respect to any g in any M. So, whereas semantically there is only one contradiction, there are many different tautologies. What distinguishes these can be expressed in terms of the variables they bind.

The set of all assignments with respect to which a formula is true in M, we call its *satisfaction set in M*, and we denote it by '\ \$_M$':

DEFINITION 6. *Satisfaction set.* $\backslash\phi\backslash_M = \{g \mid \exists h: \langle g,h \rangle \in [\![\phi]\!]_M\}$.

So, truth with respect to g in M can also be defined as $g \in \backslash\phi\backslash_M$, validity as $\backslash\phi\backslash_M = G$ for every M, and contradictoriness as $\backslash\phi\backslash_M = \emptyset$ for every M.

The notion of a satisfaction set is of the same type as the notion of interpretation in PL. But truth conditions do not exhaust dynamic meaning. The satisfaction set of a compound formula cannot always be defined in terms of the satisfaction sets of its compounds, it is determined by its compositional interpretation in terms of the notion $[\ ]$. The latter gives the building blocks of meaning. And meaning in its turn determines, globally but not locally, what the truth conditions of compound expressions are.

These considerations make clear that the notion of equivalence of standard logic, that of two formulas having the same truth conditions, although definable in DPL in terms of the notion of a satisfaction set, has only a marginal role to play. We call it *s-equivalence* and denote it by '$\simeq_s$':

DEFINITION 7. *s-equivalence.* $\phi \simeq_s \psi \Leftrightarrow \forall M: \backslash\phi\backslash_M = \backslash\psi\backslash_M$.

Full equivalence of two formulas requires that their interpretations be the same in every model. We call it *equivalence* simpliciter, and denote it by $\simeq$:

DEFINITION 8. *Equivalence.* $\phi \simeq \psi \Leftrightarrow \forall M: [\![\phi]\!]_M = [\![\psi]\!]_M$.

Of course, if two formulas are equivalent, they will also have the same satisfaction set: that is, they will be s-equivalent:

FACT 1. $\phi \simeq \psi \Rightarrow \phi \simeq_s \psi$.

The reverse does not hold. For example, $\exists x Px$ and $\exists y Py$ have the same satisfaction sets, G or $\emptyset$, but they differ in meaning since they produce different output assignments, viz. $\{h \mid h(x) \in F(P)\}$ and $\{h \mid h(y) \in F(P)\}$, respectively. The first formula has the potential to bind free occurrences of x in formulas to come, and the second has the potential to bind occurrences of y. We can formulate this in terms of the notion of the *production set* of a formula, the set consisting of those assignments which are its possible outputs, which we write as '/ $/_M$':

DEFINITION 9. *Production set.* $/\phi/_M = \{h \mid \exists g: \langle g,h \rangle \in [\![\phi]\!]_M\}$.

Whereas the satisfaction sets of $\exists x Px$ and $\exists y Py$ are the same, their production sets are different. If two formulas always have the same production set, we call them *p-equivalent*, denoted by '$\simeq_p$':

DEFINITION 10. *p-equivalence.* $\phi \simeq_p \psi \Leftrightarrow \forall M: /\phi/_M = /\psi/_M$.

Of course, analogous to the previous fact. we have:

FACT 2. $\phi \simeq \psi \Rightarrow \phi \simeq_p \psi$.

So, if two formulas have the same meaning, they always have the same satisfaction set and the same production set. However, the reverse does not hold:

FACT 3. $\phi \simeq_s \psi \,\&\, \phi \simeq_p \psi \nRightarrow \phi \simeq \psi$.

If two formulas always have the same satisfaction set and always the same production set, this does not imply that they have the same meaning. So meaning cannot be defined in terms of satisfaction and production sets. Consider the following simple example. The two tautologies $Px \vee \neg Px$ and $\exists x[Px \vee \neg Px]$ both have the total set of assignments G as their satisfaction set and as their production set. But, as we have seen above, their meanings are different. The interpretation of the former is $\{\langle g,h \rangle \mid g = h\}$, and that of the latter is $\{\langle g,h \rangle \mid h[x]g\}$.

We end this section with the definitions of two other notions that will prove useful for what is to come.

As we have seen in the previous section, various kinds of DPL-formulas have the characteristic that they do not pass on bindings created by expressions which occur in them. They function as a kind of "test" in this sense that they examine whether an input assignment meets a certain condition, return it as output if it does, and reject it otherwise. Semantically, they can be characterized as follows:

DEFINITION 11. *Test.* ϕ is a *test* iff $\forall M \forall g \forall h: \langle g,h \rangle \in [\![\phi]\!]_M \Rightarrow g = h$.

Notice that for a test ϕ the definition of truth with respect to g given above boils down to $\langle g,g \rangle \in [\![\phi]\!]$. Also, we observe that for tests equivalence, s-equivalence and p-equivalence coincide.

FACT 4. If ϕ and ψ are tests, then $\phi \simeq_s \psi \Leftrightarrow \phi \simeq \psi \Leftrightarrow \phi \simeq_p \psi$.

The notion of a test is a semantic one. A partial syntactic characterization can be given as follows. In view of their semantic interpretation, atomic formulas, negations, implications, disjunctions, and universally quantified formulas are tests. Further, it holds that a conjunction of tests is a test. We will refer to this syntactically delineated class of formulas as *conditions*:

DEFINITION 12. *Conditions*.
1. If ϕ is an atomic formula, a negation, a disjunction, or an implication, then ϕ is a condition;
2. If ϕ and ψ are conditions, then $[\phi \wedge \psi]$ is a condition;
3. Nothing is a condition except on the basis of 1 or 2.

And we note the following fact:

FACT 5. If ϕ is a condition, then ϕ is a test.

With the exception of contradictions, which have the empty set as their interpretation, and hence are tests, the syntactic notion of a condition characterizes the semantic notion of a test:

FACT 6. ϕ is a test iff ϕ is a condition or a contradiction.

3.3   Scope and binding

A distinctive feature of DPL is that it allows for existential quantifiers to bind variables which are outside their syntactic scope. In this section we give a syntactic characterization of when an occurrence of a variable is bound by an occurrence of a quantifier. This characterization will consist of a simultaneous recursive definition of three notions:

- bp (ϕ), the set of *binding pairs* in ϕ;
- aq (ϕ), the set of *active quantifer occurences* in ϕ;
- fv (ϕ), the set of *free occurrences of variables* in ϕ.

A binding pair consist of a quantifier occurrence and a variable occurrence such that the first binds the second. An active quantifier occurrence is one which has the potential to bind occurrences of the corresponding variable further on. A free occurrence of a variable is one which is not in any binding pair. The definition, which is a bit sloppy since we have refrained from explicitly introducing a notation for occurrences, is as follows:

DEFINITION 13. *Scope and binding*.
1. $\text{bp}(Rt_1 \ldots t_n) = \varnothing$
   $\text{aq}(Rt_1 \ldots t_n) = \varnothing$
   $\text{fv}(Rt_1 \ldots t_n) = \{t_1 \mid t_1 \text{ a variable}\}$.
2. $\text{bp}(\neg\phi) = \text{bp}(\phi)$
   $\text{aq}(\neg\phi) = \varnothing$
   $\text{fv}(\neg\phi) = fv(\phi)$.
3. $\text{bp}(\phi \wedge \psi) = \text{bp}(\phi) \cup \text{bp}(\psi) \cup \{\langle \exists x, x \rangle \mid \exists x \in \text{aq}(\phi) \ \& \ x \in \text{fv}(\psi)\}$
   $\text{aq}(\phi \wedge \psi) = \text{aq}(\psi) \cup \{\exists x \in \text{aq}(\phi) \mid \exists x \notin \text{aq}(\psi)\}$
   $\text{fv}(\phi \wedge \psi) = \text{fv}(\phi) \cup \{x \in \text{fv}(\psi) \mid \exists x \notin \text{aq}(\phi)\}$.
4. $\text{bp}(\phi \vee \psi) = \text{bp}(\phi) \cup \text{bp}(\psi)$
   $\text{aq}(\phi \vee \psi) = \varnothing$
   $\text{fv}(\phi \vee \psi) = \text{fv}(\phi) \cup \text{fv}(\psi)$.
5. $\text{bp}(\phi \rightarrow \psi) = \text{bp}(\phi) \cup \text{bp}(\psi) \cup \{\langle \exists x, x \rangle \mid \exists x \in \text{aq}(\phi) \ \& \ x \in \text{fv}(\psi)\}$
   $\text{aq}(\phi \rightarrow \psi) = \varnothing$
   $\text{fv}(\phi \rightarrow \psi) = \text{fv}(\phi) \cup \{x \in \text{fv}(\psi) \mid \exists x \notin \text{aq}(\phi)\}$.
6. $\text{bp}(\exists x\phi) \ \text{bp}(\phi) \cup \{\langle \exists x, x \rangle \mid x \in fv(\phi)\}$.

aq($\exists x\phi$) = aq(ϕ) $\cup$ {$\exists x$}, if $\exists x \notin$ aq(ϕ), = aq(ϕ) otherwise
fv($\exists x\phi$) = fv(ϕ) minus the occurences of x in ϕ.
7. bp($\forall x\phi$) = bp (ϕ) $\cup$ {$\langle \forall x,x \rangle \mid x \in$ fv(ϕ)}
    aq($\forall x\phi$) = $\emptyset$
    fv($\forall x\phi$) = fv(ϕ) minus the occurrences of x in ϕ.

The "test"-like character of atomic formulas, negations, disjunctions, implications, and universally quantified formulas is reflected in the above definition by the fact that for such formulas ϕ, aq(ϕ) = $\emptyset$—that is, no quantifier occurring in such a formula is able to bind occurrences of the corresponding variable further on. Notice that if we conjoin two formulas which each have an empty set of active quantifier occurrences, the resulting conjunction has no active occurrences either. This reminds us of the notion of a condition defined above. In fact, the requirement that aq(ϕ) = $\emptyset$ characterizes those ϕ which are conditions and hence it also characterizes those ϕ which are tests, with the exception of contradictions.

The extra(-ordinary) binding power of the existential quantifier, the fact that it is externally dynamic, is reflected in Clause 6. The occurrence of $\exists x$ in $\exists x\phi$ is added to the active occurrences of ϕ, unless, of course, there is already an active occurrence of that same quantifier in ϕ, in which case the latter remains the active occurrence. It is precisely in this respect that the binding properties of existential and universal quantification differ. Only existential quantifiers can have active occurrences, and for any formula, only one occurrence of a quantifier in that formula can be active.

That disjunction is internally static is reflected in the first line of Clause 4. The set of binding pairs of a disjunction is simply the union of the binding pairs of its disjuncts. So no binding relations are possible across the disjuncts of a disjunction. In contrast to this, the binding pairs of a conjunction or an implication are not simply obtained by putting together the binding pairs of the constituent formulas; what is further added are pairs consisting of active occurrences of quantifiers in the first conjunct or in the antecedent, together with free occurrences of the corresponding variables in the second conjunct or in the consequent.

In addition to the three notions just introduced, we define a fourth one, which will turn out to be convenient when we compare DPL and PL in section 4.1. It is the set of *scope pairs*, sp(ϕ), of a formula ϕ:

DEFINITION 14. *Scope pairs.*
1. sp($Rt_1, \ldots, t_n$) = $\emptyset$.
2. sp($\neg\phi$) = sp(ϕ).
3. sp($\phi \wedge \psi$) = sp(ϕ) $\cup$ sp(ψ).
4. sp($\phi \vee \psi$) = sp(ϕ) $\cup$ sp(ψ).
5. sp($\phi \rightarrow \psi$) = sp(ϕ) $\cup$ sp(ψ).
6. sp($\exists x\phi$) = sp(ϕ) $\cup$ {$\langle \exists x, x \rangle \mid x \in$ fv(ϕ)}.
7. sp($\forall x\phi$) = sp(ϕ) $\cup$ {$\langle \forall x, x \rangle \mid x \in$ fv(ϕ)}.

We note two things about this definition. First, if we replace the notion fv(ϕ), the notion of a free variable in DPL as defined above, by the notion $\text{fv}_{PL}(\phi)$, the notion of a free variable in PL, we end up with the notion of binding in PL. Secondly, concerning DPL itself again, the following fact can be proved by simple induction:

FACT 7. sp(ϕ) $\subseteq$ bp(ϕ).

So it is sufficient but not necessary for a variable to be bound by a quantifier that it occurs in its scope. Of course, in some cases, all variables bound by a quantifier are also inside its scope. This holds, for example, for $\exists x[Px \wedge Qx]$: bp($\exists x[Px \wedge Qx]$) = sp($\exists x[Px \wedge Qx]$). In section 3.6, we will show that for any formula ϕ there is a formula ϕ' which is equivalent in DPL to ϕ, such that $bp(\phi') = sp(\phi')$.

For some purposes it is convenient to talk about the free variables of a formula rather than about their occurrences. We will write the set of free variables in ϕ as 'FV (ϕ)':

DEFINITION 15. $x \in FV(\phi)$ iff there is an occurrence of x in $fv(\phi)$.

For similar reasons, we introduce the notion of the set of variables x such that there is an active occurrence of $\exists x$ in ϕ and denote it as 'AQV(ϕ)':

DEFINITION 16. $x \in AQV(\phi)$ iff $\exists x \in aq(\phi)$.

It is useful to point out the following two facts, which both can be proven by simple induction on the complexity of ϕ (by $g =_{FV(\phi)} h$ we mean that for all $x \in FV(\phi)$: $g(x) = h(x)$):

FACT 8. If $g =_{FV(\phi)} h$, then $\forall M$: $g \in \backslash\phi\backslash_M \Leftrightarrow h \in \backslash\phi\backslash_M$.

FACT 9. If $\exists M$: $\langle g, h \rangle \in [\![\phi]\!]_M$ & $g(x) \neq h(x)$, then $x \in AQV(\phi)$.

Fact 8 says that if two assignments differ in that the one is in the satisfaction set of a formula ϕ, whereas the other is not, they should also differ in the value they assign to at least one of the free variables of ϕ. And Fact 9 says that if two assignments which assign a different value to a certain variable x form an input–output pair in the interpretation of a formula ϕ, then there is an active occurrence of the quantifier $\exists x$ in ϕ.

3.4   Some logical facts

Let us now turn to an exposition of some basic logical facts, which will illustrate various properties of DPL.

We start with the interdefinability of the logical constants. A simple calculation with the relevant clauses of Definition 2 shows that negation, conjunction, and existential quantification can be used as our basic logical constants, the others being definable in terms of them in the usual way:

$$\phi \rightarrow \psi \simeq \neg[\phi \wedge \neg\psi]$$
$$\phi \vee \psi \simeq \neg[\neg\phi \wedge \neg\psi]$$
$$\forall x\phi \simeq \neg\exists x\neg\phi$$

It should be noted, though, that contrary to what is the case in ordinary predicate logic, a different choice of basic constants is not possible. The following facts show that we cannot do with the universal quantifier and disjunction, nor with the universal quantifier and implication:

$$\phi \wedge \psi \not\simeq \neg[\phi \rightarrow \neg\psi]$$
$$\phi \wedge \psi \not\simeq \neg[\neg\phi \vee \neg\psi]$$
$$\exists x\phi \not\simeq \neg\forall x\neg\phi$$

The reason for this is, of course, that the expressions on the right are tests, which lack the dynamic binding properties of the expressions on the left. In the first and in the last case, the satisfaction sets—the truth conditions—of the expressions on the right and of those on the left indeed are the same: they are *s*-equivalent. This does not hold in the second case because of the fact that disjunction is not only externally but also internally static:

$$\phi \wedge \psi \simeq_s \neg [\phi \to \neg \psi]$$
$$\phi \wedge \psi \not\simeq_s \neg [\neg \phi \vee \neg \psi]$$
$$\exists x \phi \simeq_s \neg \forall x \neg \phi$$

Furthermore, we may note that, whereas disjunction can be defined in terms of implication, the reverse does not hold:

$$\phi \vee \psi \simeq \neg \phi \to \psi$$
$$\phi \to \psi \not\simeq \neg \phi \vee \psi$$

Disjunctions and implications are both tests—they are externally static. However, an implication is internally dynamic; that is, an existential quantifier in the antecedent can bind variables in the consequent. But no such binding relations are possible between the disjuncts of a disjunction, the latter being also internally static. This is also the reason why in the last case not even the truth conditions of the expressions on the right and on the left are the same: no s-equivalence obtains in this case:

$$\phi \to \psi \not\simeq_s \neg \phi \vee \psi$$

In some special cases, some of these non-equivalences do hold. For example, if (and only if) $\phi \wedge \psi$ is a test, it is equivalent with $\neg [\phi \to \neg \psi]$. And if ϕ is a test, or more generally if no binding relations exist between ϕ and ψ—if $AQV(\phi) \cap FV(\psi) = \emptyset$—then $\phi \to \psi$ is equivalent with $\neg \phi \vee \psi$. Similarly, $\exists x \phi$ is equivalent with $\neg \forall x \neg \phi$ iff $\exists x \phi$ is a test, which it is only if ϕ is a contradiction.

A relationship between the existential and the universal quantifier that does hold unconditionally is:

$$\neg \exists x \phi \simeq \forall x \neg \phi$$

Of course, this follows from the fact that negation turns anything into a test.

From the latter observation, we may conclude that the law of double negation will not hold unconditionally. Consider a formula ϕ that is not a test. Negating ϕ results in the test $\neg \phi$, and a second negation, which gives $\neg \neg \phi$, does not reverse this effect. And this seems correct, since a doubly negated sentence in general does not allow subsequent pronouns to refer back to elements in the scope of the negations. (But see section 5.1 for some further discussion.) Precisely in this respect, ϕ and $\neg \neg \phi$ may differ in meaning. However, as far as their truth conditions are concerned, the two coincide, so ϕ and $\neg \neg \phi$ are s-equivalent. We can formulate the following restricted versions of the law of double negation:

$$\phi \simeq_s \neg \neg \phi$$
$$\neg \neg \phi \simeq \phi \text{ iff } \phi \text{ is a test.}$$

Hence, double negation is not in general eliminable. The effect of applying double negation is that the meaning of a formula is restricted, so to speak, to its truth conditions. It is useful to introduce an operator, $\diamond$, which performs this function:

DEFINITION 17. *Closure.* $[\diamond \phi] = \{ \langle g, h \rangle \mid g = h \ \& \ \exists k : \langle h, k \rangle \in [\phi] \}$.

One can look upon $\diamond$ as a kind of assertion or closure operator. It can be used to close off a piece of discourse, blocking any further anaphoric reference, stating: this is how things stand.

We notice that the following hold:

$\diamond\phi \simeq \neg\neg\phi \simeq \phi$ iff ϕ is a test
$\diamond\phi \simeq \diamond\psi \Leftrightarrow \phi \simeq_s \psi$
$\diamond\diamond\phi \simeq \diamond\phi \simeq \neg\neg\phi$
$\diamond\neg\phi \simeq \neg\phi \simeq \neg\diamond\phi$

In terms of the operator $\diamond$ we can also state the restricted versions of the interdefinability of the logical constants discussed above:

$\diamond[\phi \wedge \psi] \simeq \neg[\phi \rightarrow \neg\psi]$
$\diamond\phi \wedge \diamond\psi \simeq \neg[\neg\phi \vee \neg\psi]$
$\diamond\exists x\phi \simeq \neg\forall x\neg\phi$
$\diamond\phi \rightarrow \psi \simeq \neg\phi \vee \psi$

Let us now turn to some properties of conjunction. First of all, it can be noticed that conjunction is associative:

$[\phi \wedge \psi] \wedge \chi \simeq \phi \wedge [\psi \wedge \chi]$

Notice that associativity holds despite the increased binding power of the existential quantifier. This is so because if two conjuncts each contain an active occurrence of the same quantifier, it is the rightmost one which is active in the conjunction as a whole, the left one being "deactivated." Compare $[\exists xPx \wedge \psi] \wedge \exists xQx$ with $\exists xPx \wedge [\psi \wedge \exists xQx]$. The last occurrence of $\exists x$ is the active one. Hence, it is this occurrence that binds the x in Hx, both in $[[\exists xPx \wedge \psi] \wedge \exists xQx] \wedge Hx$ and in $[\exists xPx \wedge [\psi \wedge \exists xQx]] \wedge Hx$. The structure of the respective conjunctions is irrelevant in this respect.

Conjunction is not unconditionally commutative, however, as the simple example of $\exists xPx \wedge Qx$ and $Qx \wedge \exists xPx$ shows. In fact, the latter of these two formulas is a counterexample against idempotency of conjunction as well:

$\phi \wedge \psi \not\simeq \psi \wedge \phi$
$\phi \not\simeq \phi \wedge \phi$

Of course, if both ϕ and ψ are tests, commutativity holds, and if ϕ is a test idempotency holds:

$\diamond\phi \wedge \diamond\psi \simeq \diamond\psi \wedge \diamond\phi$
$\diamond\phi \simeq \diamond\phi \wedge \diamond\phi$

That ϕ is a test is not a necessary condition for idempotency of conjunction to hold. It is sufficient that active occurrences of a quantifier in ϕ are unable to bind free variables in ϕ:

$AQV(\phi) \cap FV(\phi) = \emptyset \Rightarrow \phi \simeq \phi \wedge \phi$

This condition isn't a necessary one, either—for example, $Px \wedge \exists xPx \simeq [Px \wedge \exists xPx] \wedge [Px \wedge \exists xPx]$.

Similarly, ϕ and ψ need not necessarily be both tests for commutativity of conjunction to hold. An example of a conjunction which does not consist of tests, but which nevertheless is commutative, is $\exists xPx \wedge Qy$, which has the same meaning as $Qy \wedge \exists xPx$. Commuting this conjunction does not interfere with its binding pattern. In general, if commuting the conjuncts does not change the binding pairs, nor the active occurrences of quantifiers in the conjunction, commutativity holds:

$$\left. \begin{array}{l} AQV(\phi) \cap FV(\psi) = \emptyset \\ AQV(\psi) \cap FV(\phi) = \emptyset \\ AQV(\phi) \cap AQV(\psi) = \emptyset \end{array} \right\} \Rightarrow \phi \wedge \psi \simeq \psi \wedge \phi$$

In this case, too, the conditions are sufficient but not necessary. A case in point is the contradiction $[Px \wedge \neg Px] \wedge \exists x Qx$.

As is to be expected, disjunction, being both internally and externally static, is unconditionally idempotent, commutative, and associative:

$$\phi \simeq \phi \vee \phi$$
$$\phi \vee \psi \simeq \psi \vee \phi$$
$$\phi \vee [\psi \vee \chi] \simeq [\phi \vee \psi] \vee \chi$$

Idempotency and commutativity of disjunction reflect that there cannot be any anaphoric relations across disjuncts. (But see sections 4.3 and 5.1 for some discussion.)

As for the classical de Morgan laws, DPL validates the following:

$$\diamond[\phi \wedge [\psi \vee \chi]] \simeq [\phi \wedge \psi] \vee [\phi \wedge \chi]$$
$$\phi \vee [\diamond\psi \wedge \chi] \simeq [\phi \vee \psi] \wedge [\phi \vee \chi]$$

The latter is a special instance of:

$$AQ(\psi) \cap FV(\chi) = \emptyset \Rightarrow \phi \vee [\psi \wedge \chi] \simeq [\phi \vee \psi] \wedge [\phi \vee \chi]$$

Turning to implication, we may observe that the following form of contraposition goes through unconditionally:

$$[\neg\phi \rightarrow \psi] \simeq [\neg\psi \rightarrow \phi]$$

But for the general case we need, again, the condition that no binding pairs are distorted:

$$[\diamond\phi \rightarrow \psi] \simeq [\neg\psi \rightarrow \neg\phi]$$
$$AQV(\phi) \cap FV(\psi) = \emptyset \Rightarrow [\phi \rightarrow \psi] \simeq [\neg\psi \rightarrow \neg\phi]$$

The reason that we need a condition here is that quantifiers in the antecedent of an implication may bind variables in the consequent. Implications, as we noted repeatedly, are internally dynamic. But no outside binding effects are permitted, they are externally static, and this is reflected in the following two equivalences:

$$[\phi \rightarrow \psi] \simeq \diamond [\phi \rightarrow \psi]$$
$$[\phi \rightarrow \psi] \simeq [\phi \rightarrow \diamond\psi]$$

The first equivalence is another way of saying that an implication is a test, the second expresses that an implication turns its consequent into a test.

A last fact concerning implication that we want to note the following:

$$\phi \rightarrow [\psi \rightarrow \chi] \simeq [\phi \wedge \psi] \rightarrow \chi$$

Finally, we notice some facts concerning the interplay of quantifiers and connectives:

$$\exists x\phi \wedge \psi \simeq \exists x[\phi \wedge \psi]$$
$$x \notin (FV(\phi) \cup AQV(\phi)) \Rightarrow \phi \wedge \exists x\psi \simeq \exists x[\phi \wedge \psi]$$

The first fact illustrates the dynamics of the existential quantifier: its binding power extends indefinitely to the right. This is what makes DPL a suitable instrument for the representation of antecendent-anaphor relations across sentence boundaries. The second fact states under which condition the scope of an existential quantifier may be extended to the left in a conjunction: under the usual condition that the left conjunct has no free occurrences of x, and further that the active occurrence of $\exists x$ is not "deactivated" by an occurrence of that same quantifier in the first conjunct.

The following equivalence is important for the analysis of "donkey"-like cases of anaphora:

$$\exists x \phi \rightarrow \psi \simeq \forall x [\phi \rightarrow \psi]$$

Existential quantifiers in the antecedent of an implication may bind occurrences of variables in the consequent, and they have "universal" force.

One final observation:

$$\exists x \phi \not\simeq \exists y [y/x] \, \phi$$

Here, $[y/x] \, \phi$ denotes, as usual, the result of replacing all free occurrences of x in ϕ by y. This non-equivalence illustrates the fact that bound variables in DPL are "more meaningful" expressions than in PL. Notice that $\exists x \phi$ and $\exists y [y/x] \, \phi$ are s-equivalent if no occurrence of y that is free in $\exists x \phi$ is bound in $\exists y [y/x] \, \phi$:

$$y \notin FV(\phi) \Rightarrow \exists x \phi \simeq_s \exists y [y/x] \, \phi$$

The above observations mark some of the ways in which the dynamic semantics of DPL differs from the ordinary, static interpretation of PL. A more detailed comparison can be found in section 4.1.

3.5   Entailment

In standard logic, ϕ entails ψ iff whenever ϕ is true, ψ is true as well. Since we have defined a notion of truth in DPL, we can also define an analogue of this notion of entailment for DPL. We will refer to it as *s-entailment*, and write it as ' $\vDash_s$ ':

> DEFINITION 18. *s-entailment.* $\phi \vDash_s \psi$ iff $\forall M \forall g$: if ϕ is true with respect to g in M, then ψ is true with respect to g in M.

In other words, ϕ s-entails ψ iff $\forall M$: $\backslash \phi \backslash_M \subseteq \backslash \psi \backslash_M$. Obviously, s-equivalence as it was defined above is mutual s-entailment.

Unlike the notion of entailment in PL, in DPL the notion of s-entailment does not coincide with that of meaning inclusion, which is denoted '$\preccurlyeq$':

> DEFINITION 19. *Meaning inclusion.* $\phi \preccurlyeq \psi$ iff $\forall M$: $[\![\phi]\!]_M \subseteq [\![\psi]\!]_M$.

In DPL, meaning is a richer notion than in PL, where interpretation and satisfaction coincide. Meaning inclusion implies s-entailment, but not the other way around:

> FACT 10. $\phi \preccurlyeq \psi \Rightarrow \phi \vDash_s \psi$.

The notion of equivalence $\simeq$ defined in section 3.2 is nothing but mutual meaning inclusion.

In an important sense, the notion of s-entailment is not a truly dynamic notion of entailment. One way to illustrate this is to point out the fact that the notion of s-entailment does not correspond in the usual way to implication. For example, although it holds that $\vDash_s \exists x Px \rightarrow Px$, we have $\exists Px \vDash_s Px$. Whereas in an implication an existential quantifier in the antecedent can bind variables in the consequent, the notion of s-entailment does not account for similar binding relations between premise and conclusion. However, in natural language, such relations do occur. From *A man came in wearing a hat*, we may conclude *So, he wore a hat*, where the pronoun in the conclusion is anaphorically linked to the indefinite term in the premise. As we have just seen, if we want to account for this, the notion of *s*-entailment is not the one we are after. For similar reasons, meaning inclusion is not what we are looking for either. It is too strict: $\exists x P x \not\preccurlyeq P x$. And it is also not strict enough. For $\preccurlyeq$ is reflexive, but, as is argued below, dynamic entailment is not: $P x \wedge \exists x Q x$ does not entail $P x \wedge \exists x Q x$.

Hence, we have to find another, an inherently dynamic notion of entailment. Taking up our processing metaphor once more, which means looking at sentences as a kind of program, a reasonably intuitive notion is the following. We say that ϕ entails ψ if every successful execution of ϕ guarantees a successful execution of ψ. Or, to put it slightly differently, ϕ entails ψ iff every assignment that is a possible output of ϕ is a possible input for ψ. This is captured in the following definition of dynamic entailment:

DEFINITION 20. *Entailment.* $\phi \vDash \psi$ iff $\forall M \forall g \forall h: \langle g, h \rangle \in [\![\phi]\!]_M \Rightarrow \exists k: \langle h, k \rangle \in [\![\psi]\!]_M$.

Using the notions of satisfaction set and production set, we can write this more economically as:

$\phi \vDash \psi$ iff $\forall M: /\phi/_M \subseteq \backslash\!\backslash\psi\backslash\!\backslash_M$

As requested, the notion of dynamic entailment corresponds in the usual way to the interpretation of implication:

FACT 11. *Deduction theorem.* $\phi \vDash \psi$ iff $\vDash \phi \rightarrow \psi$.

Entailment is related to *s*-entailment in the following way:

FACT 12. $\phi \vDash_s \psi$ iff $\diamond \phi \vDash \psi$.

More generally, entailment and *s*-entailment coincide if no binding relations exist between premise and conclusion:

FACT 13. If $\mathrm{AQV}(\phi) \cap \mathrm{FV}(\psi) = \emptyset$, then: $\phi \vDash_s \psi \Leftrightarrow \phi \vDash \psi$.

We note further that mutual entailment of ϕ and ψ does not mean that ϕ and ψ are equivalent. For example, $\exists x P x$ and $P x$ do entail each other, but they are not equivalent. The same pair of formulas illustrates that entailment does not imply meaning inclusion. And the reverse does not hold in general, either. For example, the meaning of $Q x \wedge \exists x P x$ includes the meaning of $Q x \wedge \exists x P x$, but the latter does not entail the former. Meaning inclusion does imply entailment if there are no binding relations between premise and conclusion:

FACT 14. If $\mathrm{AQV}(\phi) \cap \mathrm{FV}(\psi) = \emptyset$, then: $\phi \preccurlyeq \psi \Rightarrow \phi \vDash \psi$.

In the proof of this fact, the two Facts 8 and 9 stated in section 3.3 play a central role. Suppose $\mathrm{AQV}(\phi) \cap \mathrm{FV}(\psi) = \emptyset$ and $\phi \preccurlyeq \psi$. Let $h \in /\phi/_M$—that is $\exists g: \langle g, h \rangle \in [\![\phi]\!]_M$. Since, if $\langle g, h \rangle \in [\![\phi]\!]_M$, then $h[\mathrm{AQV}(\phi)]g$ (Fact 9), and $\mathrm{AQV}(\phi) \cap \mathrm{FV}(\psi) = \emptyset$, it holds for all $x \in \mathrm{FV}(\psi)$ that $g(x) = h(x)$. Since $\phi \preccurlyeq \psi$, it also holds that $\langle g, h \rangle \in [\![\psi]\!]_M$ and hence that $g \in \backslash\!\backslash\psi\backslash\!\backslash_M$. From $g(x) = h(x)$ for all $x \in \mathrm{FV}(\psi)$, and $g \in \backslash\!\backslash\psi\backslash\!\backslash_M$, we may conclude on the basis of Fact 8 that $h \in \backslash\!\backslash\psi\backslash\!\backslash_M$ as well.

Precisely because the notion of entailment is truly dynamic in the sense that it allows active quantifiers in a premise to bind variables in the conclusion, it lacks some properties which more orthodox notions, such as *s*-entailment, do have, notably the properties of reflexivity and transitivity.

We already encountered a typical counterexample to reflexivity of dynamic entailment in the formula $Px \wedge \exists x Qx$, which does not entail itself. The reason is that in the occurrence of this formula as a conclusion, the variable x in the first conjunct gets bound by the quantifier in the occurrence of the formula as a premise, whereas in the occurrence of the formula as a premise it is free. The following restricted fact about reflexivity, however, does hold as an immediate consequence of Fact 14 and the reflexivity of $\preccurlyeq$:

FACT 15. *Reflexivity.* If $AQV(\phi) \cap FV(\phi) = \emptyset$, then $\phi \vDash \phi$.

The condition on reflexivity given here is a sufficient, but not a necessary, one. For example, the formulas $Px \wedge \exists x Px$ and $Px \wedge \exists x Px \wedge Qx$ both entail themselves. Conditions similar to the one on reflexivity can be laid upon other facts about entailment known from ordinary predicate logic, in order to accommodate them to DPL. An example is the following:

If $AQV(\psi) \cap FV(\psi) = \emptyset$, then $\phi \wedge \psi \vDash \psi$.

We mention in passing that if one would use DPL for practical purposes, one would certainly choose active quantifiers and free variables in such a way that these troublesome cases are avoided.

Not only reflexivity but transitivity, too, may fail when free occurrences of variables in a conclusion are bound a premise. If we arrive at a conclusion χ in several steps $\psi_1 \ldots \psi_n$ from an initial premise ϕ, we cannot simply omit these intermediary steps and conclude immediately from ϕ to χ. Roughly speaking, we first have to make sure that there are no antecedent–anaphor relations between one of the intermediate steps and the conclusion which are not due to a similar relation between premise and conclusion. For example, although $\neg\neg\exists x Px \vDash \exists x Px$, and $\exists x Px \vDash Px$, we notice that $\neg\neg\exists x Px \nvDash Px$.

The cases which present problems for transitivity can be characterized as follows. Suppose $\phi \vDash \psi$ and $\psi \vDash \chi$. If we want to conclude from this that $\phi \vDash \chi$, then problems may arise if $x \in FV(\chi)$ and $x \in AQV(\psi)$. Consider again $\neg\neg\exists x Px$, $\exists x Px$, and Px. Clearly, the first entails the second, and the second entails the third, without the first entailing the third. On the other hand, consider $\exists x Px$, $\exists x Px$, and Px or $\exists x Px \wedge Qx$, $\exists x Px$, and Px. These are two cases where nothing goes wrong. So, not all cases where χ contains a free occurrence of x, and ψ contains an active occurrence of $\exists x$, are to be excluded. Evidently, what also matters is what ϕ "says" about x, in the dynamic sense of what constraint it puts on whatever free occurrences of x that are still to come. Roughly speaking, what ϕ says about variables which occur freely in χ and which are bound by ψ should be at least as strong as what ψ says about them. So what is needed is a stronger version of the notion of entailment that covers the condition that the premise puts at least as strong a condition on certain variables as the conclusion does. This notion can be defined as follows, where by '$h =_{x_1 \ldots x_n} g$' we mean '$h(x_1) = g(x_1)$ & $\ldots$ & $h(x_n) = g(x_n)$':

DEFINITION 21. $x_1 \ldots x_n = Entailment.$ $\phi \vDash_{x_1 \ldots x_n} \psi$ iff $\forall M \forall g: g \in /\phi/_M \Rightarrow \exists h: \langle g, h \rangle \in [\![\psi]\!]_M$ &
$h =_{x_1 \ldots x_n} g$.

Notice that $\phi \vDash_{x_1 \ldots x_n} \psi$ implies that $\phi \vDash \psi$ and that if $n = 0$, then $\phi \vDash_{x_1 \ldots x_n} \psi$ collapses into $\phi \vDash \psi$.

Now we are ready to state the following fact:

FACT 16. *Transitivity.* $\phi \vDash_{AQV(\psi) \cap FV(\chi)} \psi$ & $\psi \vDash \chi \Rightarrow \phi \vDash \chi$.

The proof of this fact runs as follows. Suppose $g \in /\phi/_M$. Then $\exists h: \langle g, h \rangle \in [\![\psi]\!]_M$, and for all $x \in AQV(\chi) \cap FV(\psi)$, it holds that $g(x) = h(x)$. Since $\psi \vDash \chi$, it holds that $h \in \backslash\chi\backslash_M$. For any variable

$x \in FV(\chi)$, if $x \in AQV(\psi)$ then $g(x) = h(x)$ by assumption: but if $x \notin AQV(\psi)$, then also $g(x) = h(x)$, since $\langle g, h \rangle \in [\![\psi]\!]_M$ (use Fact 9). Hence, we have $g(x) = h(x)$ for all variables $x \in FV(\chi)$, and hence $g \in \backslash\chi\backslash_M$ (Fact 8).

The above shows that there are some complications inherent in the notion of dynamic entailment. These do pay off, however. We can translate "natural language" reasonings in which pronouns are introduced in intermediary steps directly into DPL. Consider the following, admittedly stylized, example and its translation into DPL:

1. It is not the case that nobody walks and talks ($\neg\neg\exists x[Px \wedge Qx]$).
2. So, somebody walks and talks ($\exists x[Px \wedge Qx]$).
3. So, he walks (Px).
4. So, somebody walks ($\exists xPx$).
5. So, it is not the case that nobody walks ($\neg\neg\exists xPx$).

The interesting bit is the step from 2 to 3. The pronoun *he* occurring in 3 is bound by *somebody* in 2. So, although 1 implies 2, and 2 implies 3, 1 does not imply 3, precisely because 1 cannot, and should not, bind the pronoun in 3. But in the transition from 2 via 3 to 4, 3 can be omitted. And the same holds for all other intermediate steps. So, in the end, 5 is a consequence of 1.

Up to now, we have only discussed entailment with respect to a single premise. It makes sense to generalize the definition of entailment given above in the following way:

DEFINITION 22. *Entailment, general form.* $\phi_1, \ldots, \phi_n \vDash \psi$ iff $\forall M \forall h \forall g_1 \ldots g_n$: $\langle g_1, g_2 \rangle \in [\![\phi_1]\!]_M$ & $\ldots$ & $\langle g_n, h \rangle \in [\![\phi_n]\!]_M \Rightarrow \exists k$: $\langle h, k \rangle \in [\![\psi]\!]_M$

Notice that it is not a set, but a sequence of formulas, a *discourse*, that can be said to entail a formula. In view of the above, this is not surprising. What holds, of course, is:

$$\phi_1, \ldots, \phi_n \vDash \psi \text{ iff } \phi_1 \wedge \ldots \wedge \phi_n \vDash \psi \text{ iff } \vDash [\phi_1 \wedge \ldots \wedge \phi_n] \rightarrow \psi$$

Since the order of the conjuncts matters for the interpretation of a conjunction, so will the order of the premises matter for entailment. For example, although $\exists xPx, \exists xQx \vDash Qx$, we have $\exists xQx, \exists xPx \nvDash Qx$. Further, we note that in a certain sense dynamic entailment is not monotonic. Whereas it holds unconditionally that if $\phi \vDash \psi$, then $\chi, \phi \vDash \psi$, we may not always conclude from $\phi \vDash \psi$ that $\phi, \chi \vDash \psi$. The reason for this being, again, that χ may interfere with bindings between ϕ and ψ, for example, it does hold that $\exists xPx \vDash Px$, but we have $\exists xPx, \exists xQx \nvDash Px$.

Again, for practical purposes, these complications can be evaded by a suitable choice of active quantifiers and free variables. For example, in adding a premise which contains an active quantifier, we better choose one which does not already occur actively in one of the other premises.

Such practical considerations are particularly important in designing a proof system. In cooperation with Roel de Vrijer, a sound and complete system of natural deduction for DPL is being developed, which we hope to present in a separate paper.

4   Comparisons

In section 4.1, we compare DPL with ordinary predicate logic. In section 4.2, the relation between DPL and DRT is discussed. And in section 4.3, we turn to a comparison of DPL with quantificational dynamic logic.

4.1   DPL and PL

In discussing some basic logical facts concerning DPL, we have noticed a number of differences between DPL and PL, all arising from the essentially richer notion of binding of the former. In this section we show that this is indeed exactly the point at which the two systems differ. First we show that for any formula ϕ there is a formula ϕ' which is DPL-equivalent to ϕ, in which all variables bound by a quantifier are brought under its scope—that is, for which it holds that $bp(\phi')$ = $sp(\phi')$. Then we show that for any formula ϕ such that $bp(\phi) = sp(\phi)$, the truth conditions of ϕ in DPL and in PL coincide. If we put these two facts together, it follows that for any formula ϕ there is a formula ϕ' which is equivalent to it and for which it holds that its truth conditions in DPL and PL are the same.

We already noticed above that the satisfaction set of a DPL-formula, the set of assignments with respect to which it is true, is the same type of semantic object as the PL-interpretation of a formula. Because PL and DPL have the same syntax, we may speak of the PL- and the DPL-interpretation of one and the same formula.

We first define the semantics of PL in the same kind of format we used for the semantics of DPL. PL-models are the same as DPL-models, as are assignments and the interpretation of terms. The definition of the interpretation function $[\ ]_M^{PL} \subseteq G$ is as follows. (We drop subscripts whenever this does not lead to confusion, and we continue to use '$[\ ]$' without a superscript to denote interpretation in DPL.)

DEFINITION 23. *PL-semantics.*
1. $[Rt_1 \ldots t_n]^{PL} = \{g \mid \langle [t_1]_g \ldots [t_n]_g \rangle \in F(R)\}$.
2. $[t_1 = t_2]^{PL} = \{g \mid [t_1]_g = [t_2]_g\}$.
3. $[\neg \phi]^{PL} = \{g \mid g \notin [\phi]^{PL}\}$.
4. $[\phi \vee \psi]^{PL} = \{g \mid g \in [\phi]^{PL} \vee g \in [\psi]^{PL}\}$.
5. $[\phi \rightarrow \psi]^{PL} = \{g \mid g \in [\phi]^{PL} \Rightarrow g \in [\psi]^{PL}\}$.
6. $[\phi \wedge \psi]^{PL} = \{g \mid g \in [\phi]^{PL} \& g \in [\psi]^{PL}\}$.
7. $[\exists x\phi]^{PL} = \{g \mid \exists k: k[x]g \& k \in [\phi]^{PL}\}$.
8. $[\forall x\phi]^{PL} = \{g \mid \forall k: k[x]g \Rightarrow k \in [\phi]^{PL}\}$.

The set of assignments which is the interpretation of a formula, consists of those assignments which satisfy the formula: we call ϕ *true with respect to g in M* iff $g \in [\phi]_M^{PL}$.

The satisfaction set $\backslash\phi\backslash$ of a formula in *DPL* and its interpretation $[\phi]^{PL}$ in PL are both sets of assignments. But the satisfaction set of a formula need not be the same as its PL-interpretation. For example, the satisfaction set of $\exists xPx \wedge Qx$ is not identical to its PL-interpretation. However, for the formula $\exists x[Px \wedge Qx]$, which is equivalent to $\exists xPx \wedge Qx$ in DPL, it does hold that its satisfaction set and its PL-interpretation are the same. The difference between the two is that in the latter all occurrences of x which are bound by the existential quantifier are also brought in its scope. Similarly, the satisfaction set and the PL-interpretation of $\exists xPx \rightarrow Qx$ are different, whereas the satisfaction set and the PL-interpretation of $\forall x[Px \rightarrow Qx]$, which is equivalent in DPL to $\exists xPx \rightarrow Qx$, are the same. Again, the difference between the two is that in the latter case all bound variables are brought under the scope of a quantifier.

In fact, for every formula ϕ there is a formula ϕ' which is equivalent to ϕ in DPL such that in ϕ' all variables which are bound by a quantifier occur in its scope. We define a recipe b which provides us with such a variant for every formula. We will call $b\phi$ the *normal binding form* of ϕ:

DEFINITION 24. *DPL normal binding form*
1. $bRt_1 \ldots t_n = Rt_1 \ldots t_n$.
2. $b(t_1 = t_n) = (t_1 = t_n)$.
3. $b \neg \psi = \neg b\psi$.
4. $b[\psi_1 \vee \psi_2] = [b\psi_1 \vee b\psi_2]$.

5. $b\exists x\psi = \exists x b\psi$.
6. $b\forall x\psi = \forall x b\psi$.
7. $b[\psi_1 \wedge \psi_2] =$
   (a) $b[\chi_1 \wedge [\chi_2 \wedge \psi_2]]$ if $\psi_1 = [\chi_1 \wedge \chi_2]$.
   (b) $[\exists x b [\chi \wedge \psi_2]]$ if $\psi 1 = \exists x\chi$.
   (c) $[b\psi_1 \wedge b\psi_2]$ otherwise.
8. $b[\psi_1 \rightarrow \psi_2] =$
   (a) $b[\chi_1 \rightarrow [\chi_2 \rightarrow \psi_2]]$ if $\psi_1 = [\chi_1 \wedge \chi_2]$.
   (b) $[\forall x b[\chi \rightarrow \psi_2]]$ if $\psi_1 = \exists x\chi$.
   (c) $[b\psi_1 \rightarrow b\psi_2]$ otherwise.

The interesting bit in this definition are Clauses 7 and 8. Clause 7(a) rebrackets complex conjunctions in such a way that all closing brackets are moved to the right end side. For example, $[[Px \wedge Qx] \wedge Rx]$ is turned into $[Px \wedge [Qx \wedge Rx]]$, and $[[[Px \wedge Qx] \wedge Rx] \wedge Sx]$ is first turned into $[[Px \wedge Qx] \wedge [Rx \wedge Sx]]$ and then into $[Px \wedge [Qx \wedge [Rx \wedge Sx]]]$. Clause 7(b) moves existential quantifiers (which are inside the first conjunct of a conjunction) outside that conjunction. For example:

$$b[[\exists xPx \wedge \exists yQy] \wedge Rxy] = b[\exists xPx \wedge [\exists yQy \wedge Rxy]]$$
$$= \exists x b[Px \wedge [\exists yQy \wedge Rxy]]$$
$$= \exists x[bPx \wedge b[\exists yQy \wedge Rxy]]$$
$$= \exists y\exists x[Px \wedge [Qy \wedge Rxy]].$$

The workings of 7(a) and 7(b) make sure that after repeated application, one will always end up with a conjunction of which the first conjunct is neither a conjunction nor an existentially quantified formula: that is, it will be a condition. That is when Clause 7(c) applies. Clause 8 defines an analogous procedure for implications. Notice that all clauses leave the length of the formula unchanged. A proof that the recipe will always terminate can easily be given.

Now, we prove the following fact:

FACT 17. For all formulas ϕ: $\phi \simeq b\,\phi$.

The proof is by induction on the length of ϕ. For the cases which concern the Clauses 1–6, 7(c), and 8(c), the proof is trivial. For the Clauses 7(a) and (b), and 8(a) and (b), it suffices to point out the following four DPL-equivalences:

$$[\phi \wedge \psi] \wedge \chi \simeq \phi \wedge [\psi \wedge \chi]$$
$$\exists x\phi \wedge \psi \simeq \exists x[\phi \wedge \psi]$$
$$[\phi \wedge \psi] \rightarrow \chi \simeq \phi \rightarrow [\psi \rightarrow \chi]$$
$$\exists x\phi \rightarrow \psi \simeq \forall x[\phi \rightarrow \psi]$$

Next, we show that when a formula is brought in normal binding form, all variables bound by a quantifier are in its scope:

FACT 18. $bp(b\phi) = sp(b\phi)$.

The proof is by induction on the length of ϕ.

Clauses 1–6 are simple. For 7(a) we only need to remark that $bp([\chi_1 \wedge \chi_2] \wedge \psi_2) = bp\,(\chi_1 \wedge [\chi_2 \wedge \psi_2])$, as can be seen from Definition 13. Similar observations can be made for 7(b), 8(a), and 8(b).

The crucial clauses are 7(c) and 8(c). Consider Case 7(c): $\phi = \psi_1 \wedge \psi_2$ and $b\phi = b\psi_1 \wedge b\psi_2$. We have $bp(b\psi_1 \wedge b\psi_2) = bp(b\psi_1) \cup bp(b\psi_2) \cup \{\langle\exists x, x\rangle \mid \exists x \in aq(b\psi_1) \,\&\, x \in fv(b\psi_2)\}$. Since in this case $b\psi_1$ cannot be a conjunction or an existentially quantified formula, it holds that $aq(b\psi_1) = \varnothing$. This means that in this case $bp(b\psi_1 \wedge b\psi_2) = bp(b\psi_1) \cup bp(b\psi_2)$. By induction, $bp(b\psi_1) =$

$sp(b\psi_1)$ and $bp(b\psi_2) = sp(b\psi_2)$. Hence, $bp(b\psi_1 \wedge b\psi_2) = sp(b\psi_1) \cup sp(b\psi_2)$. And according to the definition of sp, the latter is the same as $sp(b\psi_1 \wedge b\psi_2)$. For 8(c) similar reasoning can be given.

Now we show that for any formula in which all variables which are bound by a quantifier are inside its scope, it holds that its satisfaction set and its PL-interpretation coincide:

FACT 19. If $bp(\phi) = sp(\phi)$, then $\forall M$: $\backslash\phi\backslash_M = [\![\phi]\!]_M^{PL}$.

The proof proceeds by induction on the length of ϕ.

Obviously, it holds for atomic formulas. And for all but the internally dynamic connectives $\rightarrow$ and $\wedge$, the result follows by a straightforward induction. For example: let $\phi = \exists x\psi$, and suppose $bp(\exists x\psi) = sp(\exists x\psi)$. This is the case iff $bp(\psi) = sp(\psi)$. Now,

$$\backslash\exists x\psi\backslash = \{g \mid \exists k: k[x]g \,\&\, \exists h: \langle k, h \rangle \in [\![\psi]\!]\} = \{g \mid \exists k: k[x]g \,\&\, k \in \backslash\psi\backslash\}$$

By induction the latter is the same as:

$$\{g \mid \exists k: k[x]g \,\&\, k \in [\![\psi]\!]^{PL}\}$$

which in turn equals:

$$[\![\exists x\psi]\!]^{PL}$$

The case of $\rightarrow$ is slightly more complex. Let $\phi = \psi \rightarrow \chi$. Suppose $bp(\psi \rightarrow \chi) = sp(\psi \rightarrow \chi)$. In other words, $bp(\psi) = sp(\psi) = bp(\chi), sp(\chi)$, and if $\exists x \in aq(\psi)$, then $x \notin fv(\chi)$. We also know that:

$$\backslash\psi \rightarrow \chi\backslash = \{g \mid \forall h: \langle g,h \rangle \in [\![\psi]\!] \rightarrow h \in \backslash\chi\backslash\}$$

It follows by Facts 8 and 9 from section 3.3 that this is equal to:

$$\{g \mid \forall h: \langle g, h \rangle \in [\![\psi]\!] \rightarrow g \in \backslash\chi\backslash\}$$

For, by Fact 9, g and h differ only in variables which have a corresponding active occurrence in ψ. By our assumption that $bp(\psi \rightarrow \chi) = sp(\psi \rightarrow \chi)$, these variables do not occur freely in χ, whence it follows by Fact 8 that if $h \in \backslash\chi\backslash$, then $g \in \backslash\chi\backslash$.

The above, in its turn, is equal to:

$$\{g \mid g \in \backslash\psi\backslash \rightarrow g \in \backslash\chi\backslash\}$$

Applying induction, we see that this is the same as:

$$\{g \mid g \in [\![\psi]\!]^{PL} \Rightarrow g \in [\![\chi]\!]^{PL}\}$$

which equals:

$$[\![\psi \rightarrow \chi]\!]^{PL}$$

We end the proof by noting that for the remaining case of $\phi = \psi \wedge \chi$, the proof proceeds in a similar fashion.

From Facts 18 and 19 it now follows that:

FACT 20. $\forall M$: $\backslash b\phi\backslash = [\![b\phi]\!]^{PL}$.

And putting the latter fact together with Fact 17 we get:

FACT 21. For any formula ϕ there is a formula ϕ' such that $\forall M$: $[\phi]_M = [\phi']_M$, and $\backslash\phi'\backslash_M = [\phi']^{PL}_M$.

Moreover, we also have that:

FACT 22. For any formula ϕ there is a formula ϕ' such that $\forall M$: $[\phi]^{PL}_M = [\phi']^{PL}_M$, and $[\phi']^{PL}_M = \backslash\phi'\backslash_M$.

It is easy to see that this holds. In PL any formula ϕ is equivalent to a formula $\#\phi$ in which all occurrences of $\wedge$, $\rightarrow$, and $\exists x$ are eliminated in favour of $\vee$, $\neg$, and $\forall$. Clearly, bp($\#\phi$)=sp($\#\phi$). Hence, by Fact 19, $\backslash\#\phi\backslash_M = [\#\phi]^{PL}_M$, for all M.

Finally, we note the following:

FACT 23. If bp(ϕ) = sp(ϕ), then $\vDash_{PL} \phi$ iff $\vDash_{DPL} \phi$.

This follows directly from Fact 19.

Summing up:

FACT 24. For any formula ϕ:
1. There is a formula ϕ' such that $\vDash_{DPL} \phi$ iff $\vDash_{DPL} \phi'$ iff $\vDash_{PL} \phi'$.
2. There is a formula ϕ'' such that $\vDash_{PL} \phi$ iff $\vDash_{PL} \phi''$ iff $\vDash_{DPL} \phi''$.

4.2   DPL and DRT

In this section we compare the language of DPL with what corresponds to it in Kamp's DRT, viz. the language in which the discourse representation structures (DRS's) are formulated. DPL is intended to be "empirically equivalent" to DRT: it was designed to deal with roughly the same range of natural language facts. The difference between the two approaches is primarily of a methodological nature, and compositionality is the watershed between the two. Therefore, besides giving a formal comparison of the logical languages of the two systems in the present section, we shall also discuss the matter of compositionality in somewhat more detail in section 5.2.

The DRS-language and the language of DPL differ in several respects. First of all, in the DRS-language, a syntactic distinction is made between *conditions* and DRS's. It is by means of the latter that natural language sentences and discourses are represented; conditions are elements out of which DRS's are constructed. In other words, conditions occur as subexpressions of DRS's. Corresponding to this syntactic disinction, there is a semantic one: conditions are interpreted in terms of their truth conditions; DRS's are interpreted in terms of their *verifying embeddings*.

A second difference between the DRS-language and the language of DPL is that the former contains negation, implication, and disjunction, but not conjunction and no quantifiers. The basis of the DRS-language is formed by a set of atomic conditions. Further, there is a single, noniterative rule which has DRS's as output: DRS's are formed by prefixing a number of variables to a number of conditions. This rule is to compensate DRT's lack of conjunction and quantifiers. The prefixed variables function as DRT's quantification mechanism, and the conditions to which they are prefixed can be viewed as the conjunction of those conditions. These conditions can be either atomic or complex. Complex conditions are in turn built from DRS's by means of the connectives. Negation turns a DRS into a condition; implication and disjunction take two DRS's and deliver a condition.

Choosing a format that resembles as closely as possible that of DPL, the syntax and semantics of DRT can be defined as follows. The non-logical vocabulary consists of n-place predicates, individual constants, and variables. Logical constants are negation $\neg$, disjunction $\vee$, implication $\rightarrow$, and identity $=$. The syntactic rules are as follows:

DEFINITION 25. *DRT-syntax*

1. If $t_1 \ldots t_n$ are individual constants or variables, and R is an n-place predicate, then $Rt_1 \ldots t_n$ is a condition.
2. If t_1 and t_2 are individual constants or variables, then $t_1 = t_2$ is a condition.
3. If ϕ is a DRS, then $\neg\phi$ is a condition.
4. If ϕ and ψ are DRS, then $[\phi \vee \psi]$ is a condition.
5. If ϕ and ψ are DRS's, then $[\phi \rightarrow \psi]$ is a condition.
6. If $\phi_1 \ldots \phi_n$ ($n \geq 0$) are conditions, and $x_1 \ldots x_k$ are variables ($k \geq 0$), then $[x_1 \ldots x_k]$ $[\phi_1 \ldots \phi_n]$ is a DRS.
7. Nothing is a condition or a DRS except on the basis of 1–6.

Models for the DRS-language are the same as those for DPL, as are assignments and the interpretation of terms. Parallel to the syntactic distinction between conditions and DRS's, the semantics defines two notions of interpretation. First of all, we define an interpretation function $[\![\ ]\!]_M^{DRS} \subseteq G \times G$, for DRS's. Here, '$\langle g,h \rangle \in [\![\phi]\!]^{DRS}$' corresponds to the DRT-notion 'h is a verifying embedding of ϕ with respect to g'. Since DRS's are built up from conditions, we also need to define a notion of interpretation of conditions: $[\![\ ]\!]_M^{Cond} \subseteq G$, where '$g \in [\![\phi]\!]^{Cond}$' corresponds to the DRT-notion 'ϕ is true with respect to g'. So, DRS's receive the same type of interpretation as DPL-formulas. In one respect our definition of these notions differs from the one given in DRT: we prefer assignments to be total functions rather than partial ones. This is no matter of principle. Just as is usually done in DRT, we could rephrase the semantics of DPL in terms of partial assignments.

The simultaneous recursive definition of the notions $[\![\ ]\!]_M^{Cond}$ and $[\![\ ]\!]_M^{DRS}$ runs as follows (where we drop subscripts again, whenever this does not lead to confusion):

DEFINITION 26. *DRT-semantics*

1. $[\![Rt_1 \ldots t_1]\!]^{Cond} = \{g \mid \langle [\![t_1]\!]_g , \ldots , [\![t_n]\!]_g \rangle \in F(R)\}$.
2. $[\![t_1 = t_2]\!]^{Cond} = \{g \mid [\![t_1]\!]_g = [\![t_2]\!]_g\}$.
3. $[\![\neg\phi]\!]^{Cond} = \{g \mid \neg\exists h: \langle g, h \rangle \in [\![\phi]\!]^{DRS}\}$.
4. $[\![\phi \vee \psi]\!]^{Cond} = \{g \mid \exists h: \langle g, h \rangle \in [\![\phi]\!]^{DRS} \vee \langle g, h \rangle \in [\![\psi]\!]^{DRS}\}$.
5. $[\![\phi \rightarrow \psi]\!]^{Cond} = \{g \mid \forall h: \langle g, h \rangle \in [\![\phi]\!]^{DRS} \Rightarrow \exists k: \langle h, k \rangle \in [\![\psi]\!]^{DRS}\}$.
6. $[\![[x_1 \ldots x_k][\phi_1 \ldots \phi_n]]\!]^{DRS} = \{\langle g, h \rangle \mid h[x_1 \ldots x_k]g \ \& \ h \in [\![\phi_1]\!]^{Cond} \ \& \ \ldots \ \& \ h \in [\![\phi_n]\!]^{Cond}\}$.

In order to make clear in what sense the set of variables introduced in Clause 6 functions as DRT's quantification mechanism, we first define the notion of a DRS being true with respect to an assignment in a model:

DEFINITION 27. *Truth in DRT.* A DRS ϕ is *true with respect to g in M* iff $\exists h: \langle g,h \rangle \in [\![\phi]\!]_M^{DRS}$.

So, the notion of truth for DRS's is the same as the notion of truth in DPL. And from Definition 27 we see that the variable set in a DRS behaves like existential quantification over these variables. A simple DRS like $[x][Px,Qx]$ has the same truth conditions as the formula $\exists x[Px \wedge Qx]$ in PL and DPL. Moreover, the interpretations of this DRS and of the DPL-formula are also the same. To give another example, the DRS $[x, y][Px,Qx,Rxy]$ has the same meaning as the DPL-formula $\exists x\exists y[Px \wedge Qy \wedge Rxy]$.

Notice that DRS's can also be built from conditions by means of empty DRS-quantification. For example, $[\ ][Px]$ is a DRS, and its interpretation according to Definition 26 is $\{\langle g, h \rangle \mid h[\ ]g$

& $h(x) \in F(P)$}. Now, $h[\ ]g$ means the same as $h = g$, so the "atomic DRS" $[\ ][Px]$ and the atomic DPL-formula Px have the same interpretation. In fact, this procedure can be applied to turn any DRT-condition into a DRS, giving it structurally the same interpretation as the corresponding DPL-condition.

The interpretation of a DRS, being the same kind of object as the interpretation of formulas in DPL, is of a dynamic nature. The dynamics of DRS's is put to use in the interpretation of implications (and nowhere else, by the way). For example, the DRT-condition $[x][Px] \to [\ ][Qx]$ has the same truth conditions as the DPL-formula $\exists x Px \to Qx$. This, of course, is the key to DRT's successful treatment of donkey-sentences.

Having made these observations, we now turn to the definition of a translation from the DRS-language into that of DPL. We translate both DRS's and DRT-conditions into DPL-formulas. Blurring the syntactic and semantic distinction between DRS's and conditions in this way is justified, since DRT-conditions will translate into DPL-conditions, and the latter are tests: that is, their meaning and truth conditions in DPL are one-to-one related. The translation $\dagger\phi$ of a DRS or a condition ϕ is defined as follows:

DEFINITION 28. *DRT-to-DPL translation*
1. $\dagger Rt_1 \ldots t_n = Rt_1 \ldots t_n$.
2. $\dagger(t_1 = t_n) = (t_1 = t_n)$.
3. $\dagger\neg\psi = \neg \dagger \psi$.
4. $\dagger[\psi_1 \vee \psi_2] = [\dagger\psi_1 \vee \dagger\psi_2]$.
5. $\dagger[\psi_1 \to \psi_2] = [\dagger\psi_1 \to \dagger\psi_2]$.
6. $\dagger[x_1 \ldots x_k][\psi_1 \ldots \psi_n] = \exists x_1 \ldots \exists x_k[\dagger\psi_1 \wedge \ldots \wedge \dagger\psi_n]$.

We prove that our translation is meaning-preserving in the following sense:

FACT 25
1. If ϕ is a condition, then $\forall M$: $[\phi]_M^{\text{Cond}} = \backslash\dagger\phi\backslash_M$.
2. If ϕ is a DRS, then $\forall M$: $[\phi]_M^{\text{DRS}} = [\dagger\phi]_M$.

This fact is proven by induction on the complexity of ϕ. For the Clauses 1–5 of Definition 25, which build DRT-conditions, the proof is trivial. So what remains to be shown is that:

$$[[x_1 \ldots x_k][\psi_1 \ldots \psi_n]]^{\text{DRS}} = [\exists x_1 \ldots \exists x_k[\dagger\psi_1 \wedge \ldots \wedge \dagger\psi_n]]$$

By definition it holds that:

$$[[x_1 \ldots x_k][\psi_1 \ldots \psi_n]]^{\text{DRS}} = \{\langle g, h \rangle \mid h[x_1 \ldots x_k]g \ \& \ h \in [\psi_1]^{\text{Cond}} \ \& \ldots \& \ h \in [\psi_n]^{\text{Cond}}\}$$

By induction: $[\psi_i]^{\text{Cond}} = \backslash\dagger\psi_i\backslash$, for $1 \leqslant i \leqslant n$. So we may continue our equation as follows:

$$= \{\langle g, h \rangle \mid h[x_1 \ldots x_k]g \ \& \ h \in \backslash\dagger\psi_1\backslash \ \& \ldots \& \ h \in \backslash\dagger\psi_n\backslash\}.$$

Next we note two auxiliary facts:

FACT 26. If ϕ and ψ are DRT-conditions, then $\dagger\phi \wedge \dagger\psi$ is a condition in DPL as well.

From Definition 28 it is easy to see that if ϕ and ψ are DRT-conditions, then $\dagger\phi$ and $\dagger\psi$ are conditions in DPL as well. By Definition 12 it then follows that $\dagger\phi \wedge \dagger\psi$ is also a DPL-condition.

FACT 27. If ϕ and ψ are DPL-conditions, then $\backslash\phi \wedge \psi\backslash = \backslash\phi\backslash \bigcap \backslash\psi\backslash$.

This can be proven by a simple calculation.

Now we return to our proof of Fact 25. On the basis of our auxiliary facts, we arrive at the following continuation of our equation:

$$= \{\langle g, h \rangle \mid h[x_1 \ldots x_k]g \ \& \ h \in \setminus\dagger\psi_1 \wedge \ldots \wedge \dagger\psi_n\setminus\}$$

Since $\dagger\psi_1 \wedge \ldots \wedge \dagger\psi_n$ is a DPL-condition, it holds that $h \in \setminus\dagger\psi_1 \wedge \ldots \wedge \dagger\psi_n\setminus$ iff $\langle h, h \rangle \in [\dagger\psi_1 \wedge \ldots \wedge \dagger\psi_n]$. This implies that we can continue as follows:

$$= \{\langle g, h \rangle \mid \exists k \ k[x_1 \ldots x_k]g \ \& \ \langle k, h \rangle \in [\dagger\psi_1 \wedge \ldots \wedge \dagger\psi_n]\}$$
$$= [\exists x_1 \ldots \exists x_k[\dagger\psi_1 \wedge \ldots \wedge \dagger\psi_n]]$$

By which the proof of Fact 25 is completed.

Before turning to the less urgent, but more difficult problem of translating DPL-formulas into DRS's, we return, by way of a short intermezzo, to two of the examples discussed in section 2.1 and compare, once again, the corresponding DPL-formulas and DRS's. By †DRT we mean the translation of the DRT-representation in DPL.

(1) A man walks in the park. He whistles.
(1a) $\exists x[man(x) \wedge walk\text{-}in\text{-}the\text{-}park(x) \wedge whistle(x)]$ PL/†DRT
(1b) $\exists x[man(x) \wedge walk\text{-}in\text{-}the\text{-}park(x)] \wedge whistle(x)$ DPL
(1c) $[x][man(x), walk\text{-}in\text{-}the\text{-}park(x), whistle(x)]$ DRT
(3) Every farmer who owns a donkey beats it.
(3a) $\forall x \forall y[[farmer(x) \wedge donkey(y) \wedge own(x,y)] \rightarrow beat(x,y)]$ PL
(3b) $\forall x[[farmer(x) \wedge \exists y[donkey(y) \wedge own(x,y)]] \rightarrow beat(x,y)]$ DPL
(3c) $[\ ][[x,y][farmer(x), donkey(y), own(x,y)] \rightarrow [\ ][beat(x,y)]]$ DRT
(3d) $\exists x \exists y[farmer(x) \wedge donkey(y) \wedge own(x,y)] \rightarrow beat(x,y)$ †DRT

Consider the first example. If our diagnosis of the problem that such a sequence poses—viz. that the real problem is to provide a compositional translation of such sequences of sentences into a logical representation language—is correct, then the DRT-representation has as little to offer as the PL-translation. The two component sentences cannot be retrieved from (1c), neither can they be isolated from (1a) as subformulas. The DPL-representation differs precisely at this point.

As for the second example, it is not possible to retrieve the component parts of the sentence from either the PL- or the DRT-representation, nor from the †DRT-translation. But in the DPL-formula, we do find an open formula which corresponds to the complex noun *farmer who owns a donkey*, viz. $farmer(x) \wedge \exists y[donkey(y) \wedge own(x, y)]$. But no such subexpression is to be found in the DRT-representation or in the corresponding †DRT-formula.

In fact, each of the two examples can be used to make a point in favor of DPL. The preferable DPL-translation of the first example is available precisely because DPL has dynamic conjunction, whereas such a concept is lacking in DRT. As for the second example, here DPL fares better because, unlike DRT-quantification, DPL-quantification is iterative. It is precisely these two concepts of DPL which enable us to give a compositional treatment of the cases at hand. In fact, if both conjunction of DRS's and iterative quantification were added to DRT, it would simply collapse into DPL.

This is a rather surprising result, since one of the trademarks of theories such as those of Kamp and Heim is the *non-quantificational* analysis of indefinite terms, whereas it is characteristic of DPL that it does allow us to treat such terms as existentially quantified expressions.

A host of arguments have been presented against a quantificational analysis of indefinites, see in particular Heim (1982). However, these arguments now appear to be directed not against a quantificational analysis as such but only against the traditional quantificational analysis, which is *static*. The dynamic DPL-approach is not affected by these.

We do not discuss the various arguments here, with one exception. This argument concerns what Heim calls the "chameleontic" nature of the quantificational force of indefinites. What follows is in essence, but not in all details, taken from Heim (1982).

Consider the following variants of our example (2):

(9)   If a farmer owns a donkey, he always/usually/sometimes/never beats it.

These variants of the donkey-example (2) have readings which can be paraphrased as in (10):

(10)   In all/most/some/no cases in which a farmer owns a donkey, he beats it.

Examples such as those in (9) are taken to support the view that what appears to be the quantificational force of an indefinite term is, in fact, either due to a different expression, a so-called adverb of quantification, as in (9), or is implicit in the construction, as for example in the original donkey-sentence (2). Following Lewis (1970: this volume, Chapter 30), it is assumed that the sentences in (9) are to be analyzed along the following lines. The main operator is the adverb of quantification, which takes two arguments—the antecedent and the consequent. The indefinite terms are treated as free variables, which are unselectively bound by the main operator, which determines the quantificational force. The antecedent serves as a restriction on the unselective quantification. For the original donkey-sentence, which lacks an overt adverb of quantification, it is assumed that the construction itself acts as a universal adverb of quantification.

At first sight, this argument seems not to be restricted to the traditional, static quantificational analysis, but seems to apply to any quantificational approach which associates a specific quantificational force with indefinite terms. However, in view of our observations concerning the relationship between DPL and DRT, this cannot really be correct. In fact, it is not difficult to incorporate the "adverbs-of-quantification" analysis of sentences such as (9) in DPL, thus showing its compatibility with a quantificational treatment of indefinites.

Recall that in the interpretation clause of implication, there is universal quantification over the output assignments of the antecedent:

$$[\![\phi \to \psi]\!] = \{\langle g, h \rangle \mid h = g \ \& \ \text{for } all \ k: \langle h, k \rangle \in [\![\phi]\!], \exists j: \langle k, j \rangle \in [\![\psi]\!]\}$$

What we can do is simply generalize this to other quantificational forces and index the implication accordingly:

$$[\![\phi \to_Q \psi]\!] = \{\langle g, h \rangle \mid h = g \ \& \ \text{for } Qk: \langle h, k \rangle \in [\![\phi]\!], \exists j: \langle k, j \rangle \in [\![\psi]\!]\}$$

This has the required effects. Consider the following example:

(11)   If a farmer owns a donkey, he never beats it.

If we translate this using $\to_{no}$, the result is:

$$\exists x[\text{farmer}(x) \land \exists y[\text{donkey}(y) \land \text{own}(x,y)]] \to_{no} \text{beat}(x,y)$$

This denotes the following set of pairs of assignments:

$$\{\langle g, g \rangle \mid \neg \exists h: h[x,y]g \ \& \ h(x) \in F(\text{farmer}) \ \& \ h(y) \in F(\text{donkey}) \ \& \ \langle h(x), h(y) \rangle \in F(own) \ \& \\ \langle h(x), h(y) \rangle \in F(\text{beat})\}$$

Notice that this analysis works precisely because indefinite terms are analyzed as dynamically existentially quantified expressions. For this has the effect that the quantification in the general scheme is restricted to the variables which correspond to indefinite terms.

We do not intend this as a final analysis of adverbs of quantification, since, for one thing, such an analysis has to be higher-order and intensional, and DPL is only first-order and extensional. But we do take the above to show that an "adverbs-of-quantification" analysis is perfectly compatible with a quantificational analysis of indefinite terms, provided this is a dynamic one.

After this intermezzo, we return to the formal comparison of DPL and DRT. As we already remarked above, the formulation of a translation from the DPL-language to the DRS-language, is more difficult than the other way around. In fact, no strict interpretation-preserving translation is possible, though one which preserves truth conditions is. We point out the main features of such a translation, written as §, without, however, going into details.

Notice that the fact that DRT distinguishes between conditions and DRS's presents no problem. Defining a translation from DPL-formulas into DRS's is sufficient, for as we saw above, any DRT-condition can easily be turned into a DRS by means of empty DRT-quantification.

Now there are three complications. The first concerns universal quantification, which is lacking in DRT. We can either use the definition of $\forall x\phi$ in terms of $\neg\exists x\neg\phi$ or turn $\S\forall x\phi$ directly into the condition $[x][\ ] \rightarrow \S\phi$.

The remaining two complications, not surprisingly, stem from the two essential differences between DRT and DPL which we noticed above. Because DRT lacks a notion of DRS-conjunction, we cannot compositionally translate a DPL-conjunction. Something like $\S[\phi \wedge \psi] = [\ ][\S\phi, \S\psi]$ would work only if both conjuncts are DPL-conditions, which, of course, they need not be.

Similarly, no compositional translation of existentially quantified formulas is possible either. Again, $\S\exists x\phi = [x]\S\phi$ works only if ϕ is a DPL-condition. Suppose that ϕ in its turn is $\exists yRxy$. Then the resulting translation would be $[x][y]Rxy$. But this is not a well-formed DRS, since $[y]Rxy$ is not a DRT-condition.

To get things to work, we first need to define a special format for DPL-formulas which enables us to translate them in a non-compositional, global manner into DRS's. In order to arrive at the required format, any DPL-formula ϕ should be turned into a formula ϕ', such that any subformula of ϕ' is of the form $\exists x_1 \ldots \exists x_n\psi$ ($n \geq 0$), where ψ is a DPL-condition.

It is possible to give an algorithm that has the required effect, but it is not strictly meaning-preserving. The following two examples may serve to illustrate this. Consider the formula $Px \wedge \exists xQx$. In order to give it the right format, the existential quantifier in the second conjunct has to be moved outside of the conjunction. But this can't be done, since there is a free occurrence of x in the first conjunct. So we have to resort to an alphabetic variant: $\exists y[Px \wedge Qy]$. As a second example, consider $\exists xPx \wedge \exists xQx$. In this case, too, both quantifiers have to be moved outside the conjunction, and then, again, we need an alphabetic variant: $\exists x\exists y[Px \wedge Qy]$. The use of alphabetic variants implies that the algorithm is not meaning preserving, for in DPL such variants have different meanings: $\exists x\phi \not\equiv \exists y[y/x]\phi$.

These features of DPL-to-DRT-translation illustrate once more, we think, what exactly makes DPL a more suitable instrument for semantic analysis. Its dynamic notion of conjunction, and its dynamic and iterative concept of existential quantification, allow us to deal with various phenomena in a simple, intuitive, and compositional manner.

4.3   DPL and quantificational dynamic logic

Although there are important resemblances between DPL and certain systems of dynamic logic, as they are discussed in Harel (1984), there are also major differences. To begin with, there is an important difference in perspective and overall aims. Dynamic logic is meant to be used in the formalization of reasoning about computer programs, about the effects of their execution, their soundness and correctness, and so on. Typically, the formulas of a system of dynamic logic are interpreted as assertions about programs. And the semantic interpretation of these formulas is an ordinary static interpretation. However, in order to be able to talk about programs in a logical language, one also needs expressions that refer to these programs. And that is where dynamic interpretation comes in. The expressions, which are the logical stand-in's for programs, do receive a dynamic interpretation. However, they only appear as sub-expressions in the formulas that make up the logical system; they are not themselves formulas of the logic.

We note in passing that in this respect we find precisely the opposite situation in DRT. There as well we have a distinction between statically interpreted expressions, DRT's conditions, and dynamically interpreted ones, the DRS's. But in DRT it is the dynamic expressions that play first fiddle, and the static conditions only occur as subexpressions in these.

In DPL, it is the formulas themselves that receive a dynamic interpretation, the kind of interpretation that programs receive in ordinary dynamic logic. DPL is a system in which certain kinds of "programs" can be expressed, but we cannot formulate assertions about these programs in DPL itself. Since it is a logical language which is designed to represent meanings of natural language sentences, one could say that it embodies the view that the meaning of a sentence is a program, an instruction to the interpreter. So one could view DPL as a kind of "programming language" rather than as a language to reason about such programs. Of course, one can reason about it in a metalanguage. And, in fact, one could use ordinary dynamic logic as a means to formalize reasoning about DPL.

Of course, this difference in what the systems are meant to be able to do is reflected in various aspects of their organization. We illustrate this by presenting the syntax and semantics of a particular system of quantificational dynamic logic, referred to as "QDL," which proves to be intimately related to DPL.

Dynamic logic is related to modal logic. The models contain a set S of possible (execution) states. The formulas are interpreted as sets of states, the set of states in which a formula is true. Programs are conceived of as transformations of possible states—that is, as relations between possible states. In this respect, the interpretation of a program is like an accessibility relation in modal logic. Each program π corresponds to an accessibility relation $[\pi]_M \subseteq S \times S$. A pair $\langle s,s' \rangle$ is an element of $[\pi]_M$ if when executed in s, π may lead to s'. (If the program is deterministic, $[\pi]_M$ would be a (partial) function.)

In view of their association with accessibility, relations, we can build modal operators $\langle \pi \rangle$ and $[\pi]$ around a program π. Like their counterparts in modal logic, these operators can be prefixed to a formula ϕ to form another formula, $\langle \pi \rangle \phi$ or $[\pi]\phi$. A formula $\langle \pi \rangle \phi$ is true in a state s iff execution of π in s may lead to a state s' such that ϕ is true in s'. In other words, $\langle \pi \rangle \phi$ expresses that it is possible that ϕ is true after π has been executed. Similarly, $[\pi]\phi$ is true in s iff all executions of π in s will lead to a state s' in which ϕ is true. So $[\pi]\phi$ means that ϕ must be true after π has been executed, $[\pi]\phi$ is equivalent to $\neg\langle \pi \rangle \neg\phi$, where $\neg$ is interpreted as ordinary static negation.

In systems of quantificational dynamic logic, the set of possible states is not just a set of primitive objects but is identified with the set of assignment functions G. The interpretation of a formula ϕ is $[\phi]_M \subseteq G$. And the interpretation of a program π is $[\pi]_M \subseteq G \times G$.

We now present a particular version of QDL that has precisely the features we need to compare it with DPL. We start out from the language of PL and add the following features. Basic programs are random assignments to variables, written as '$x := \text{random}$'. (This is a feature not present in standard QDL, where ordinary deterministic assignments '$x := a$' figure in the language.) Further, we add an operator '?' which turns a formula ϕ into a program ?ϕ. Such a program is called a "test," and its interpretation is indeed like that of a test in DPL: it is the set of identity pairs $\langle g,g \rangle$ such that ϕ is true with respect to g. Next, we add the operator ':' to form sequences of programs. (Ordinary deterministic assignments can be defined in terms of these notions as $x := $ random; $?x = a$.) Finally, we add the "modal operators" discussed above. So QDL has the following syntax:

DEFINITION 29. *Syntax of QDL*

1. T is a formula.
2. If $t_1 \ldots t_n$ are individual constants or variables and R is an n-place predicate, then $Rt_1 \ldots t_n$ is a formula.
3. If t_1 and t_2 are individual constants or variables, then $t_1 = t_2$ is a formula.
4. If ϕ is a formula, then $\neg\phi$ is a formula.
5. If ϕ and ψ are formulas, then $[\phi \rightarrow \psi]$, $[\phi \wedge \psi]$, and $[\phi \vee \psi]$ are formulas.
6. If ϕ is a formula, then $\exists x\phi$ is a formula.
7. If ϕ is a formula, then $\forall x\phi$ is a formula.
8. If ϕ is a formula, then $?\phi$ is a program.
9. If x is a variable, then $x := $ random is a program.
10. If π_1 and π_2 are programs, then $[\pi_1 : \pi_2]$ is a program.
11. If π is a program and ϕ is a formula, then $\langle\pi\rangle\,\phi$ is a formula.
12. If π is a program and ϕ is a formula, then $[\pi]\phi$ is a formula.
13. Nothing is a formula or a program except on the basis of 1–12.

Models for QDL are like those for (D)PL. Like in DRT, we simultaneously define two interpretation functions: one for formulas—$[\![\ ]\!]_M^{QDL} \subseteq G$—and one for programs—$[\![\ ]\!]_M^{Prog} \subseteq G \times G$—as follows (as usual, we suppress subscripts whenever this does not give rise to confusion):

DEFINITION 30. *Semantics of QDL*

1. $[\![T]\!]^{QDL} = G$.
2. $[\![Rt_1 \ldots t_n]\!]^{QDL} = \{g \mid \langle [t_1]_g , \ldots , [t_n]_g \rangle \in F(R)\}$.
3. $[\![\, t_1 = t_2]\!]^{QDL} = \{g \mid [t_1]_g = [t_2]_g\}$.
4. $[\![\neg\,\phi]\!]^{QDL} = \{g \mid g \notin [\![\phi]\!]^{QDL}\}$.
5. $[\![\phi \rightarrow \psi]\!]^{QDL} = \{g \mid g \in [\![\phi]\!]^{QDL} \Rightarrow g \in [\![\psi]\!]^{QDL}\}$, and similarly for $\wedge$, $\vee$.
6. $[\![\exists x\phi]\!]^{QDL} = \{g \mid \exists k: k[x]g \And k \in [\![\phi]\!]^{QDL}\}$.
7. $[\![\forall x\phi]\!]^{QDL} = \{g \mid \forall k: k[x]g \Rightarrow k \in [\![\phi]\!]^{QDL}\}$.
8. $[\![?\phi]\!]^{Prog} = \{\langle g, h \rangle \mid h = g \And h \in [\![\phi]\!]^{QDL}\}$.
9. $[\![x := \text{random}]\!]^{Prog} = \{\langle g, h \rangle \mid h[x]g\}$.
10. $[\![\pi_1; \pi_2]\!]^{Prog} = \{\langle g, h \rangle \mid \exists k: \langle g, k \rangle \in [\![\pi_1]\!]^{Prog} \And \langle k, h \rangle \in [\![\pi_2]\!]^{Prog}\}$.
11. $[\![\langle\pi\rangle\phi]\!]^{QDL} = \{g \mid \exists h: \langle g, h \rangle \in [\![\pi]\!]^{Prog} \And h \in [\![\phi]\!]^{QDL}\}$.
12. $[\![[\pi]\phi]\!]^{QDL} = \{g \mid \forall h: \langle g, h \rangle \in [\![\pi]\!]^{Prog} \Rightarrow h \in [\![\phi]\!]^{QDL}\}$.

First, we note that the language defined above can be economized rather drastically. Of course, the interdefinability of the connectives and quantifiers in PL carries over to QDL. But, moreover, as appears from the following two equivalences, we can conclude that all that is characteristic of PL can be eliminated altogether:

$$\phi \rightarrow \psi \simeq [?\phi]\psi$$
$$\exists x\phi \simeq \langle x := \text{random}\rangle\phi$$

So, in terms of negation, the test-operator, random assignments, and one of the two modal operators, all other logical constants can be defined.

As we noted above, DPL-formulas can be conceived of as a kind of program. The following definition presents a translation '$\triangleright$' of DPL-formulas into QDL-programs:

DEFINITION 31. *DPL-to-QDL translation*

1. $\triangleright Rt_1 \ldots t_n = ?Rt_1 \ldots t_n$.
2. $\triangleright \neg \phi = ?\neg\langle\triangleright \phi\rangle T$.

3. $\triangleright [\phi \wedge \psi] = [\triangleright \phi: \triangleright \psi]$.
4. $\triangleright [\phi \mid \psi] = ?[\langle \triangleright \phi \rangle T \vee \langle \triangleright \psi \rangle T]$.
5. $\triangleright [\phi \rightarrow \psi] = ?[\triangleright \phi]\langle \triangleright \psi \rangle T$.
6. $\triangleright \exists x\phi = [x := \text{random}: \triangleright \phi]$.
7. $\triangleright \forall x\phi = ?[x := \text{random}]\langle \triangleright \phi \rangle T$.

The last but one of these clauses illustrates that in DPL we need not introduce the existential quantifier syncategorematically: we could take $\exists x$ itself to be a formula of DPL, with the same interpretation as a random assignment statement, and we could write $\exists x \wedge \phi$ instead of $\exists x\phi$.

The following fact can be proven by induction the complexity of ϕ:

FACT 28. $\forall M$: $[\phi]_M = [\triangleright \phi]_M^{\text{Prog}}$.

Unlike in the case of DRT, we can equally easily define a translation in the opposite direction. Like in our translation from DRT to DPL, we don't pay attention to the distinction between formulas and programs in QDL. No problems can arise from this, since QDL-formulas will be translated into DPL-conditions. We make only one small addition to DPL: we add T as a basic formula and interpret it as the identity relation on G. We denote the translation function by '$\triangleleft$':

DEFINITION 32. *QDL-to-DPL translation*
1. $\triangleleft T = T$.
2. $\triangleleft Rt_1 \ldots t_n = Rt_1 \ldots t_n$.
3. $\triangleleft \neg\phi = \neg\triangleleft \phi$.
4. $\triangleleft [\phi \rightarrow \psi] = [\triangleleft \phi \rightarrow \triangleleft \psi]$, and similarly for $\vee$ and $\wedge$.
5. $\triangleleft \exists x\phi = \Diamond \exists x \triangleleft \phi$.
6. $\triangleleft \forall x\phi = \forall x \triangleleft \phi$.
7. $\triangleleft ?\phi = \triangleleft \phi$.
8. $\triangleleft x := \text{random} = \exists x T$.
9. $\triangleleft [\pi_1; \pi_2] = [\triangleleft \pi_1 \wedge \triangleleft \pi_1]$.
10. $\triangleleft \langle \pi \rangle \phi = \Diamond[\triangleleft \pi \wedge \triangleleft \psi]$.
11. $\triangleleft [\pi]\phi = [\triangleleft \pi \rightarrow \triangleleft \psi]$.

By simultaneous induction on the complexity of the programs π and formulas ϕ of QDL, it can he shown that the translation is meaning-preserving in the following sense:

FACT 29
1. $\forall M$: $[\phi]_M^{\text{QDL}} = \backslash\triangleleft \phi\backslash_M$.
2. $\forall M$: $[\phi]_M^{\text{Prog}} = [\triangleleft \phi]_M$.

The redundancy of QDL is reflected illuminatingly in the translation. Most DPL-operators can be found twice on the right-hand side. In some cases, they occur once in a dynamic and once in a static variant, the latter being obtained by prefixing the closure operator. Notice that since PL forms a fragment of QDL, the translation presented above is also a translation of PL into DPL.

We end this section by discussing two standard features of quantificational dynamic logics that we have left out so far. The one is program disjunction; the other is program repetition. We also discuss briefly their possible use in natural language semantics.

The syntax and semantics of program-disjunction are defined as follows:

DEFINITION 33. *Program disjunction*
1. If π_1 and π_2 are programs, then $[\pi_1 \cup \pi_2]$ is a program.
2. $[\pi_1 \cup \pi_2]^{\text{Prog}} = [\pi_1]^{\text{Prog}} \cup [\pi_2]^{\text{Prog}}$.

Of course, the same definition could be used to introduce a second notion of disjunction $\cup$ besides $\vee$ in DPL. Unlike the latter, $\cup$ is a dynamic notion, but it differs in an interesting way from dynamic implication and conjunction. Whereas implication is only internally dynamic, and conjunction is both internally and externally dynamic, $\cup$ is only externally dynamic. An existential quantifier $\exists x$ in the first disjunct cannot bind free occurrences of x in the second disjunct (nor vice versa), but an existential quantifier in either disjunct can bind variables in a further conjunct. In the formula $[\exists x Px \cup \exists x Qx] \wedge Hx$, both occurrences of $\exists x$ in the first conjunct bind the occurrence of x in the second conjunct. In fact, the formula in question is equivalent to $[\exists x Px \wedge Hx] \cup [\exists x Qx \wedge Hx]$. More generally the following holds:

$$[\phi \cup \psi] \wedge \chi = [\phi \wedge \chi] \cup [\psi \wedge \chi]$$
$$[\phi \cup \psi] \to \chi = [\phi \to \chi] \wedge [\psi \to \chi]$$

Adding this kind of disjunction to our dynamic repertoire would enable us to treat the anaphoric links in examples like (12) and (13) in a completely straightforward way:

(12)   A professor or an assistant professor will attend the meeting of the university board. He will report to the faculty.

(13)   If a professor or an assistant professor attends the meeting of the university board, then he reports to the faculty.

However, as we shall see in the next section, adding this new kind of dynamic disjunction still leaves certain dynamic features of natural language disjunction unexplained.

We now turn to program repetition. This concept is important in the semantic analysis of program constructions like '*while ... do ...*' and *repeat ... until ...*'. The syntax and semantics of program repetition is defined as follows:

DEFINITION 34. *Program repetition*
1. If π is a program, then π^* is a program.
2. $[\pi^*]^{\text{Prog}} = \{\langle g, h\rangle \mid \exists n \exists g_0. g_1, \ldots, g_n: g_0 = g \ \& \ g_n = h \ \& \ \forall i: 1 \leqslant i \leqslant n: \langle g_{i-1}, g_i\rangle \in [\pi]_M^{\text{Prog}}\}$.

According to this definition, a pair $\langle g, h\rangle$ is in the interpretation of π^* iff h can be reached from g by a repeating π a finite but non-deterministically determined number of times.

At first sight, this kind of concept seems of no use in natural language semantics. However, consider the following example (due to Schubert and Pelletier 1989):

(14)   If I've got a quarter in my pocket, I'll put it in the parking meter.

Notice first of all that, unlike a DRT/DPL-analysis would have it, one who utters (14) probably does not intend to spend all the quarters in his pocket on the parking meter. Now notice that a procedural meaning of (14) could informally be paraphrased as "Repeat getting coins out of your pocket until it is a quarter; then put it in the parking meter." So maybe, after all, adding repetition to DPL could add to its use as a tool in natural language semantics.

As one of the referees pointed out, the Schubert and Pelletier analysis can be dealt with in DPL in a more straightforward way, too. It would suffice to define another notion of implication as follows:

$$\phi \mapsto \psi =_{\text{def}} \neg\phi \vee [\phi \wedge \psi]$$

See also Chierchia (1988; 1990), where this conservative notion of implication is argued for.

5   Prospect and retrospect

5.1   Problems and prospects

As we have pointed out in the introduction of this paper, we are interested in developing a compositional, non-representational semantics of discourse, one which will enable us to marry the compositional framework of Montague grammar to a dynamic outlook on meaning such as can be found in DRT and its kin. The development of DPL is only a first step in achieving this overall aim. At the empirical level, DPL matches DRT, and from a methodological point of view, it is in line with MG. At least at the following two points, DPL needs to be extended. First of all, like DRT, DPL is restricted to the resources of an extensional first-order system, whereas MG essentially makes use of intensional higher order logic. And secondly, DPL shares several empirical characteristics with DRT which have been disputed in the literature.

As for the first point, DPL offers as compositional a treatment of natural language expressions as a first-order system permits: nothing more, nothing less. However, to match MG—and, more in particular, to be able to cope with compositionality below the sentential level in the way familiar from MG—we do need more. In fact, we need a higher-order, intensional language with λ-abstraction, or something else that is able to do what that does. In Groenendijk and Stokhof (1990) one way to go about is presented, which uses a version of dynamic intensional logic (DIL) as it was developed in Janssen (1986) with the aim of providing a Montague-style semantics for programming languages. The resulting system of "dynamic Montague grammar" (DMG) is able to cope with the phenomena DPL deals with in a completely compositional fashion—below, on, and beyond the sentential level.

The second issue we want to touch upon here concerns certain empirical predictions that DPL shares with DRT.

As we remarked several times in the above, only conjunction and the existential quantifier are treated in a fully dynamic fashion. They are both internally and externally dynamic. All other logical constants are externally static. In this respect, DPL is like DRT. In our informal introduction to DPL in section 2, we motivated the interpretation clauses for the various logical constants by pointing out that they behave differently with regard to possible anaphoric relations. (Cf. examples (4)–(8).) Thus it was argued, for example, that conjunction and implication should be internally dynamic because both allow an antecedent in their first argument to bind an anaphor in their second argument. However, it was concluded that only conjunction is also externally dynamic, since it also passes on bindings to sentences to come, whereas implication, in view of the fact that it lacks this feature, should be treated as externally static. The interpretation of the universal quantifier, negation, and disjunction was motivated in a similar fashion.

Several authors have provided examples which seem to indicate that the predictions that DRT and DPL make here, are not borne out by the facts. (See, e.g., Roberts 1987; 1989 and Kadmon 1987.) Consider the following examples (which are (variants of) examples that can be found in the literature):

(15)   If a client turns up, you treat him politely. You offer him a cup of coffee and ask him to wait.
(16)   Every player chooses a pawn. He puts it on square one.
(17)   It is not true that John doesn't own a car. It is red, and it is parked in front of his house.
(18)   Either there is no bathroom here, or it is in a funny place. In any case, it is not on the first floor.

Different conclusions may be drawn from these observations, some of which are compatible with the way in which the logical constants are interpreted in DRT and DPL. However, one might also take these examples to show that, at least in certain contexts, the universal quantifier, implication, disjunction, and negation are both internally and externally dynamic. Without wanting to commit ourselves to the latter position, we want to explore its consequences a little here.

As for the first of the examples, it can then be observed that the second sentence is interpreted as an additional conjunct of the consequent of the implication in the first sentence, as the following paraphrase of (15) shows:

(19)   If a client turns up, you treat him politely, you offer him a cup of coffee, and ask him to wait.

So what we need is an interpretation of implication which will make (20) equivalent to (21):

(20) $[\exists x[\text{client}(x) \wedge \text{turn up}(x)] \rightarrow \text{treat politely}(y, x) \wedge \text{offer coffee}(y, x) \wedge \text{ask to wait}(y, x)$
(21) $\exists x\text{client}(x) \wedge \text{turn up}(x)] \rightarrow [\text{treat politely}(y, x) \wedge \text{offer coffee}(y, x) \wedge \text{ask to wait}(y, x)$

More generally, an externally dynamic interpretation of implication will make $[\phi \rightarrow \psi] \wedge \chi$ equivalent with $\phi \rightarrow [\psi \wedge \chi]$.

As for the second example, similar observations can he made. It can be paraphrased as (22), which indicates that an externally dynamic treatment of universal quantification will make (23) equivalent with (24):

(22)   Every player chooses a pawn, and (he) puts it on square one.
(23) $\forall x[\text{player}(x) \rightarrow \exists y[\text{pawn}(y) \wedge \text{choose}(x, y)]] \wedge \text{put on (square one}(x, y)$
(24) $\forall x[\text{player}(x) \rightarrow \exists y[\text{pawn}(y) \wedge \text{choose}(x, y) \wedge \text{put on square one}(x, y)]]$

So, on this approach, $\forall x\phi \wedge \psi$ turns out to be equivalent with $\forall x[\phi \wedge \psi]$. And if this is combined with a dynamic interpretation of implication, $\forall x[\phi \rightarrow \psi] \wedge \chi$ will be equivalent with $\forall x[\phi \rightarrow[\psi \wedge \chi]]$.

In a similar fashion, the third example may be taken to indicate that a dynamic version of negation is needed for which the law of double negation holds.

The last example indicates that disjunction, too, can sometimes be interpreted dynamically. This interpretation should make $[\phi \vee \psi] \wedge \chi$ equivalent with $\phi \vee [\psi \wedge \chi]$. Notice that the dynamic interpretation of disjunction that is at stake here differs from the one discussed in section 4.3. The latter, as we have seen, is essentially internally static and only externally dynamic, whereas the present notion is both internally and externally dynamic. Also, their external dynamic behavior is different: $[\phi \cup \psi] \wedge \chi$ is equivalent with $[\phi \wedge \chi] \cup [\psi \wedge \chi]$.

These observations characterize one way of dealing with such examples as (15)–(18). We end our discussion of them with three remarks. First of all, saying what the desired effect of the dynamic interpretations of the logical constants involved are, is, of course, not the same as actually giving the interpretations themselves. And secondly, the availability of suitable dynamic interpretations would leave unanswered the question why it is that the logical constants involved act dynamically in certain contexts but not in others. Finally, in view of the latter fact, one would not want to postulate two independent interpretations. Rather, the static interpretation should be available from the dynamic one by a general operation of closure.

The first and the last issue are discussed at length in Groenendijk and Stokhof (1990). There it is shown that by using the richer framework of DMG, the required dynamic interpretations can indeed be obtained, and in such a fashion that the static interpretations are the closures of the dynamic ones. As for the second point, this seems to be more an empirical than a formal question, to which DMG as such does not provide an answer.

From this, we conclude that the kind of dynamic approach to natural language meaning that is advocated in this paper is not restricted to the particular form it has taken here—that is, that of the DPL-system—but is sufficiently rich to allow for alternative analyses and extensions (see, e.g., Chierchia 1988 and 1990; Dekker 1990; van den Berg 1990).

5.2   Meaning and compositionality

The primary motivation for the DPL-undertaking was that we were interested in the development of a compositional and non-representational theory of meaning for discourses. Compositionality is the cornerstone of all semantic theories in the logical tradition. As a consequence, it has also been of prime importance in those approaches to natural language semantics which use tools developed in the logical paradigm. However, compositionality has been challenged as a property of natural language semantics. Especially when dealing with the meaning of discourses people have felt, and sometimes argued, that a compositional approach fails.

In the context of natural language semantics, we interpret compositionality as primarily a methodological principle, which gets empirical, computational, or philosophical import only when additional and independently motivated constraints are put on the syntactic or the semantic part of the grammar that one uses. In other words, it being a methodological starting point, it is always possible to satisfy compositionality by simply adjusting the syntactic and/or semantic tools one uses, unless, that is, the latter are constrained on independent grounds. In view of this interpretation of compositionality, our interest in the possibility of a compositional semantics of discourse is also primarily of a methodological nature. Faced with non-compositional theories that give an account of interesting phenomena in the semantics of natural language discourses, we wanted to investigate the properties of a theory that is compositional and accounts for the same facts. We knew in advance that such a theory should exist; what we wanted to know is what it would look like: it might have been that being compositional was the only thing that speaks in favor of such a theory, in which case there would have been good reasons to abandon it.

As we already remarked in the introduction, beside these methodological considerations, there may also be practical reasons to be interested in trying to keep to compositionality. One such reason can be found in computational requirements on the semantics of discourses, or texts. For example, in a translation program one would like to be able to interpret a text in an on-line manner—that is, incrementally, processing and interpreting each basic unit as it comes along, in the context created by the interpretation of the text so far. Although certainly not the only way to meet this requirement, compositionality is a most intuitive way to do so. As such, on-line interpretation does not preclude that in the interpretation of a unit of text, other things than the interpretation of the text so far play a role. But it does require that at any point in the processing of a text we are able to say what the interpretation thus far is. In other words, it does rule out approaches (such as DRT) in which the interpretation of a text is a two-stage process, in which we first build a representation, which only afterward—at the end of the text, or a certain segment of it—mediates interpretation of the text as such. So, from the viewpoint of a computational semantics, there is ample reason to try and keep to compositionality.

Yet another reason is provided by certain philosophical considerations. These concern the fact that non-compositional semantic theories usually postulate a level of semantic representation, or "logical form," in between syntactic form and meaning proper, which is supposed to be a necessary ingredient of a descriptively and explanatorily adequate theory. Consider the following two sequences of sentences (the examples are due to Partee; they are cited from Heim 1982):

(25)   I dropped ten marbles and found all of them, except for one. It is probably under the sofa.
(26)   I dropped ten marbles and found only nine of them. It is probably under the sofa.

There is a marked contrast between these two sequences of sentences. The first one is all right, and the pronoun *it* refers to the missing marble. The second sequence, however, is out. Even though it may be perfectly clear to us that the speaker is trying to refer to the missing marble with the pronoun *it*, evidently this is not the way to do this. Like most authors, we start from the assumption that co-reference and anaphora are, by and large semantic phenomena. ("By and large" in view of the fact that sometimes certain syntactic features are involved in pronoun resolution as well. A case in point is syntactic gender in languages like German and Dutch.) Therefore, we may take the following for granted: the contrast between (25) and (26) marks a difference between the respective opening sentences, and this difference is one of meaning, in the broad, intuitive sense of the word. But what does this difference consist in? For notice that the first sentences of (25) and (26) do characterize the same situation. There is no difference in their truth conditions; therefore it seems that they are semantically equivalent. Indeed, they are equivalent in any standard semantic system that explicates meaning solely in terms of truth (or more generally, denotation) conditions. And we speculate that it is for this reason that many semanticists have taken the view that the difference in question is one of (logical) form, of (semantic) representation, rather than one of content.

For various reasons, we think that one should not adopt this point of view too hastily. For it means that one has to postulate an intermediate level of representation in between natural language and its interpretation. True, most semantic frameworks interpret natural language via translation into a logical language, but the general methodological strategy here has always been to make sure that the translation procedure is compositional and, hence, in view of the compositional nature of the interpretation of the logical language, in principle dispensable. As the logical translation serves practical purposes only, in principle it can be discarded. But notice that the level of representation that is assumed if one views the difference between (25) and (26) as one of form is not of this (optional) nature. The two sentences involved will be mapped onto different logical forms, or semantic representations, which in their turn will receive an equivalent interpretation. Accounting for the difference between (25) and (26) in this way makes the existence of this level of representation imperative rather than useful. It would be a necessary go-between natural language and its meaning. So it seems that, perhaps without being aware of it, many have put a constraint on the semantics: meaning *is* truth (denotation) conditions. Then, indeed, compositionality becomes a contentfull, rather than a methodological principle, and one which is falsified: the facts force the existence of a level of semantic representation on us.

There are several reasons why we think that the move to a semantic theory which assumes such an independent level of semantic representation—distinct both from syntactic structure and from meaning proper—should be looked upon with reserve. First of all, there is the familiar, almost commonplace reason of theoretical parsimony. Levels of representation, too, should not be multiplied beyond necessity, and although this is perhaps not too exciting a comment to make, we feel that from a methodological point of view it is still a sound one. Of course, its relevance in the present context does presuppose that we are not really forced to introduce such a level of semantic representation, that we can do without it. Such a claim cannot be substantiated in general, but it can be shown to be correct in particular cases. And the development of the DPL-system shows that, in the case at hand, the principle of compositionality not only has negative implications but also points positively toward a satisfactory treatment of the issues involved. For the phenomena in question, no level of representation is needed, for compositionality clearly guides toward a notion of meaning which allows us to do without.

Be that as it may, our appeal to this methodological principle will be waived by those who claim that there is empirical evidence for the existence of a level of semantic representation. In fact, quite often when such a level of representation is postulated, this is accompanied by the claim that it is somehow psychologically "real." We must be careful in our evaluation here, for one might be making a weaker and a stronger claim. The weaker one is that in producing and understanding language, people somehow represent meaning, extract them from linguistic structures, manipulate them, "put them into words," and so on. This claim is, in fact, subsidiary to the view of the mind as a calculating machine. Notice, however, that this weaker claim is not necessarily at odds with our parsimonious starting point. For as such, there may very well be a separate level of semantic representation, without it being a necessary ingredient of a descriptively and explanatorily adequate semantic theory. The stronger claim adds exactly this to the weaker one: it claims not just the cognitive reality of representation of meaning but the existence of a level of representation which carries information that goes beyond that what is represented there, viz. meaning. In effect, this view splits the intuitive notion of meaning in two: those aspects which are covered by the technical notion of meaning (or interpretation) that the theory provides (or borrows from other frameworks), and those which are accounted for by properties of the particular kind of representation of the former.

Thus, we call "a mentalist" someone who claims that a level of representation is *necessary*, not someone who merely claims that it exists. Should we include among the mentalists the latter kind of person, too, we would be forced to consider the Wittgenstein of the *Tractatus* as a mentalist, for he claimed that there exists a level of thoughts and thought-elements which is isomorphic to language and, hence, to the world. However, he did consider this level completely irrelevant for an account of the nature of meaning and the way in which it is established. Thus Wittgenstein apparently accepted the *existence* of a level of "semantic representation" but considered its existence of no interest for semantics proper. In connection with this, it may be worthwhile to point out the close correspondence between the isomorphic "picturing" relation between language and the world of the *Tractatus*, and the modern-day, algebraic explication of compositionality, as it can be found, for example, in Janssen (1986). Of course, the later Wittgenstein would have discarded even any talk of a "cognitive" sub-stratum of our linguistic behavior, which may help to remind us that even the weaker claim is not as philosophically neutral as some apparently think it is.

To return to the main point, we think that the stronger claim is unwarranted and that it certainly cannot be justified simply by an appeal to the linguistic facts of the matter. As for the weaker claim, the view on the mind and its operations that it stems from, when taken literally, is, of course, not philosophically neutral. Those who really subscribe to it face the burden of showing that there are such things as "mental" representations and the like, a task which is not without philosophical pitfalls. Notoriously, these issues are as interesting as they are undecidable. Our own opinion, for whatever it is worth, is that the calculating mind is a metaphor rather than a model. It is a powerful metaphor, no doubt, on which many branches of "cognitive" science are based, and sometimes it can be helpful, even insightful. But it remains a way of speaking, rather than a true description of the way we are. However, whatever stand one would like to take here, it does not affect the point we want to make, which is that it is better to try to keep one's semantic theory, like every theory, as ontologically parsimonious and as philosophically neutral as possible. The stronger claim goes against this and, hence, has to be rejected, unless, somehow, proven.

As for the weaker claim, subscribing to it or not makes no real difference, but one has to be careful not to let it interfere with the way one sets up one's semantic framework. The best way to go about it, then, is to carry on semantics as really a discipline of its own, not to consider it a priori a branch of cognitive science, and to enter into the discussion of the reality of mental representations in a "modular" frame of mind.

It may be the case, though, that for some the acceptance of a level of logical representation springs forth from a positive philosophical conviction, viz. a belief in the deficiencies of natural language as a means to convey meaning. Now such there may be (or not) when we consider very specialized kinds of theoretical discourse, such as mathematics, or philosophy, or particle physics. And again, natural language may be deficient (or not) when we consider a special task that we want to be performed in a certain way, such as running a theorem prover based on natural deduction on natural language sentences or such a thing. In such cases, clearly there is room for extension and revision, for regimentation and confinement. But that is not what is at stake here. Here, it turns on the question whether natural language structures themselves, as we encounter them in spoken and written language, then and there are in need of further clarification in order to convey what they are meant to convey. In this matter, semantics, we feel, should start from the premise that natural language is all right. If anything is a perfect means to express natural language meaning, natural language is. It can very well take care of itself and is in no need of (psycho)logical reconstruction and improvement in this respect. To be sure, that means taking a philosophical stand, too, but one that is neutral with respect to the question whether there is such a thing as an indispensable level of logical representation in semantics. As we said above, if such there is, this has to be shown, not taken for granted.

Our ideological point of view concerning the status of mental representations is in line with the methodological interpretation of the principle of compositionality. As was already remarked above, this interpretation not only forces us to reject certain approaches to the problems we started out with, it also positively suggests to us a proper solution. Compositionality dictates that the meanings of (23) and (24) should be functions of the meanings of their parts. We take it to be an obvious fact that the immediate components of the sequences of sentences (23) and (24) are the two sentences of which they consist. Because of the difference in acceptability we cannot but conclude that the first sentence of (23) and the first sentence of (24) differ in meaning. Accepting the fact that their truth conditions are the same, this leads to the inevitable conclusion that truth conditions do not exhaust meaning. ("Do not exhaust meaning" because we do want to stick to the idea that truth conditions are an essential ingredient of meaning.) What compositionality strongly suggests, then, is that we look for an essentially richer notion of meaning of which the truth conditional one is a special case. Our claim is that the kind of dynamic semantics that DPL is an instance of, naturally suggests itself as a first step on the right track.

Notes

The first version of this paper was presented in June 1987 at the ASL/LSA-meeting in Stanford, and on several other occasions. A pre-final version was prepared for the First European Summerschool on Natural Language Processing, Logic and Knowledge Representation, held in Groningen in July 1989.

At these and other meetings, and in correspondence, many friends and colleagues have prompted even more questions and comments, which have helped and stimulated us. We thank them, and the two anonymous referees of *Linguistics and Philosophy*.

Since the summer of 1988, our ITLI–colleague Roel de Vrijer has joined in with our work on DPL. More in particular, he has dedicated himself to the development of a complete and sound proof theory for DPL. We hope to report on the results in a separate, joined paper. Some of the results of this cooperative work have already penetrated the present paper. More in particular, this holds for the sections on scope and binding and on entailment. And at many other points as well, we have greatly benefitted from Roel's acute comments and criticisms.

The paper partly originates from a research project carried out by the first author from September 1986 to September 1988, commissioned by Philips Research Laboratories, Eindhoven, the Netherlands. At the final stage of this research, both authors were engaged on the *Dyana*-project (EBRA-3715) commissioned by the European Community.

15

JON BARWISE AND JOHN PERRY

Situations and Attitudes

Reading the early work in logic by Frege and Russell, one can hardly fail to be struck by the extent to which their thinking was shaped by a concern to understand the verbs of cognitive attitudes, verbs like *wonder*, *believe*, and *know*. In spite of this concern, and all the subsequent progress in logic, there is still no satisfactory systematic account of the logic of the attitudes.

In this paper we outline an approach which we believe will lead to a satisfactory and systematic account. For our sample of verbs we take *see*, *know*, *believe*, and *say*. We call our theory *situation semantics*; it is closer in spirit to Russell than it is to Frege in some fundamental ways. We begin with some key features of situation semantics, and then move to a discussion of philosophical and semantical issues surrounding the attitudes. A rigorous semantics for a fragment of English incorporating these verbs, as well as tense, indexicals, demonstratives, and definite descriptions, proper names, pronouns, and conditionals, is in preparation.

Situations

Situations are basic an ubiquitous. We are always in some situation or other. Human cognitive activity categorizes these situations in terms of objects having attributes and standing in relations to one another at locations—connected regions of space-time. Human languages reflect (and enhance) this cognitive activity by giving us a way of communicating information about situations, both those we find ourselves in and those removed from us in space and time.

In attempting to develop a theory of linguistic meaning that concentrates on situations, we recognize the epistemological primacy of situations, but follow the lead of language and take objects, relations, and locations as the primitives of our theory, reconstructing situations from them. Thus we have as primitives:

Jon Barwise and John Perry (1981) Situations and attitudes. *Journal of Philosophy* 78: 668–691. Reprinted by permission of The Journal of Philosophy.

1. A set A of individuals $a, b, c \ldots$;
2. A set R of relations, $R = R_0 \cup R_1 \cup \ldots R_n \cup \ldots$, where R_n consists of the n-ary relations; and
3. A set L of space-time locations $l, l_1, \ldots$

A *situation* **s** is characterized by its *location* l and its *type* s, $\mathbf{s} = \langle l, s \rangle$. The type represents which objects stand in which relations at the location. We represent these types by means of partial functions from relations $r \in R_n$ and sequences $\langle a_1, \ldots, a_n \rangle$ of objects to 1 (true) and 0 (false).[1] The partial function s_0 defined by

$$s_0 \text{ (awake, Jackie)} = 1$$
$$s_0 \text{ (awake, Molly)} = 0$$

will be realized in those situations s where the first author's dog is awake, the second's asleep, regardless of what the reader's dog is doing, if she or he has one (s_0 is realized in $\mathbf{s} = \langle l, s \rangle$ if $s_0 \subseteq s$). We use S for the set of situation types $s, s_0, s_1, \ldots$ and $\mathbf{S}$ ($= L \times S$) for the set of situations $\mathbf{s}, \mathbf{s}_0, \mathbf{s}_1 \ldots$.

A *course of events* σ is a partial function from the set L of locations into S. Thus every course of events is also a set of situations, at most one at any given location l. If $l \in \text{domain}(\sigma)$ we write σ_l for the situation type $\sigma(l)$. We use Σ for the set of all courses of events. A *total course of events* is a course of events defined for all locations. We distinguish one among these as the *actual course of* events σ^*. A situation $\mathbf{s} = \langle l, s \rangle$ is *actual* if $s \subseteq \sigma_l^*$; that is, if the type of s is part or all of what is actually the case at l.

A (realistic) *proposition* is a set $P \subseteq \Sigma$ satisfying:

(Monotonicity) $\sigma \in P$ and $\sigma \subseteq \sigma'$ implies $\sigma' \in P$.

The adjective "realistic" here is used to emphasize that these are constructs of real objects, properties, and locations, not things in someone's head. [A (realistic) unlocated proposition is a set $P \subseteq S$ satisfying a similar monotonicity constraint: $s \in P$ and $s \subseteq s'$ implies $s' \in P$.]

There are three basic relations on space-time locations that are represented in English:

$l_1 \circ l_2$ l_1 temporally overlaps l_2
$l_1 < l_2$ l_1 temporally and wholly precedes l_2
$l_1 \, @ \, l_2$ l_1 spatially overlaps l_2

We take these to be extensional relations on L, relations out of which one can construct "instants" of time and "points" of space in the manner of Whitehead and Russell.

The starting point of situation semantics is that untensed indicative statements describe or designate situation types and that tensed indicative statements designate propositions, sets of courses of events. We use the term *statement* advisedly here, for a sentence like *I am sitting* can be used to make as many different statements as there are speakers and times to utter it. The sentence has a fixed "meaning," but the different statements will describe different events. That is, the different statements will have different "interpretations." This distinction between meaning and interpretation is the subject of the next section.

Meaning and interpretation

A number of important themes in situation semantics can be developed by discussing the following simple sentences:

(1)   I am sitting.
(2)   Sandy is sitting.
(3)   She was sitting.

Let us begin with the word *I*. A reasonable thing to say about this expression is that, whenever it is used by a speaker of English, it stands for, or designates, that person. We think that this is all there is to know about the meaning of *I* in English and that it serves as a paradigm rule for meaning.

Consider the relation:

The expression α (of the language L) as used by x, stands for y.

which we write as $[\alpha]\,(x,y)$. A theory that tells us every condition under which $[\alpha]\,(x,y)$ holds is our candidate for a theory of meaning for the language L. What we were told about *I* gives us one condition:

$[\,I\,]\,(a,y)$ iff $a = y$

This relation view of meaning demands that systematic attention be paid to the appropriate values of each coordinate. Our starting point in situation semantics is that, when the first coordinate α is a tensed indicative sentence, then courses of events are the appropriate third coordinate y.

This decision has ramifications for the second coordinate x. It shows that speakers are too simple a choice for this coordinate. Sentence (1) can be used by a single person at different places in space-time to describe different events. Similarly, the designation of *you, now, she, this, was* varies from utterance to utterance, depending on who the speaker is talking to when, and about whom, what, and when. We represent the utterance-specific facts with reference to *discourse situations* and *connections*.

A *discourse situation d* represents the situation in which the speaker and addressee find themselves. It consists of a situation $s_d = \langle l_d, s_d \rangle$ with a designated individual a_d such that s_d (speaks a_d) $= 1$. We modify the rule for *I* given above to

$[I]\,(d,y)$ iff $y = a_d$.

Similarly, *now* constrains the time being referred to overlap the time of utterance: so we can define

$[now]\,(d,y)$ iff $y \in L$ and $y \circ l_d$.

Similarly,

$[here]\,\,(d,y)$ iff $y \in L$ and $y \,@\, l_d$.

However, there are often utterance-specific facts that have constituents not present to the actual discourse situation. Consider sentences (2) and (3) above, for example. It is reasonable to suppose that in an interpretable utterance of (2) [or (3)] *Sandy* stands for Sandy (or that *she* stands for some female). But which Sandy—Sandy Koufax, Sandy Dennis, or Little Orphan Annie's dog? What is unaccounted for here is that a meaningful use of (2) is about some specific individual Sandy [and that a meaningful use of (3) is about some specific female]. Since these individuals need not be present in the actual discourse situation, we have no choice but to recognize another component of our second coordinate, a component representing the connections c between certain words and things in the world implicit in any meaningful use of those words. Thus an utterance of (2) where the speaker was talking about Sandy Koufax would be represented by the expression (2), a particular discourse d, and a partial function c with $c(Sandy) =$ Sandy Koufax. We can then represent the meanings of *Sandy* and *she* by

[*Sandy*] (d,c,y) iff $c(Sandy) = y$ and y is named *Sandy*.
[*She*] (d,c,y) iff $c(she) = y$ and y is a female.

(Even this is overly simple, but it is good enough for now.)

We have now disposed of the noun phrases in (1) to (3) and have the tools at hand for disposing of the verb phrases *am sitting*, *is sitting*, and *was sitting*. These are all various progressive forms of the verb *sit*. Like most verbs, its interpretation is d.s.i.—insensitive to the discourse situation in which it is uttered. However, *sit* can be used to designate either an activity $sit_a \in R_1$, the activity of sitting down, or a state $sit_s \in R_1$, the state of being seated. It's up to the speaker. Thus connections come up again:

[*sit*](d,c,y) iff $c(sit) = y$ and $y = sit_a$ or $y = sit_s$.

Now we turn to the tense of (1) to (3). Like *now*, the present-tense forms of (1) and (2) indicate that the sitting is taking place at a time that temporally overlaps the time of the utterance. The past-tense forms are used to indicate that the sitting took place in the past. But, just as part of the meaning of *she was sitting* is that it must be used of a particular female to make a statement, so, too, to make a statement it must be used of a particular past space-time location. To interpret correctly my claim that she was sitting, you must correctly interpret my uses of *she* and *was* as being about a female and a past space-time location. To represent the connections between tense markers and space-time locations, we allow our connections to assign space-time locations to tense markers. Thus:

If α is *am/are/is*, then [α](d,c,y) iff $c(\alpha) = y \in L$ and $y \circ l_d$.
If α is *was/were/was*, then [α](d,c,y) iff $c(\alpha) = y \in L$ and $y < l_s$.

When we fix all that is specific to a particular utterance of an expression α, we obtain what we call the *interpretations* of the utterance. Thus if we fix a particular expression α, discourse situation d, and connection c, we obtain those y such that [α](d,c,y) holds, which we write alternatively as $y \in {}_{d,c}[\alpha]$. If there is a unique such y, we call y *the* interpretation of the utterance α,d,c and write ${}_{d,c}[\alpha] = y$. Thus, for example, ${}_{d,c}[I] = a_d$ and ${}_{d,c}[was] = c(was)$, a certain location $l < l_d$.

We can now assign meanings to all sentences α of the form

NP PROG VP

where NP $\in \{I, Sandy, she\}$, PROG $\in \{am, are, is, was, were\}$, and VP $= sit$, namely:

[α](d,c,σ) iff $\sigma_l(P,a) = 1$

where ${}_{d,c}[PROG] = l$, ${}_{d,c}[VP] = P$, and [NP] $= a$. An utterance of α describes a course of events σ just in case a is sitting (in the appropriate sense) at the intended location l in the course of events σ. Notice that ${}_{d,c}[\alpha]$ is a proposition, a monotone set of courses of events.

The importance of the meaning interpretation distinction for an understanding of the attitudes cannot be overemphasized. It rests in part on the following two related facts—(1) efficiency and (2) perspective-relativity:

Efficiency: A given expression α with a single meaning [α] can be used in different circumstances with different interpretations.

A word like *I*, for instance, can be used to designate any of us, Although this makes language efficient, allowing a given expression to be used over and over to different ends, it also has a corollary. A sentence that describes a given situation from one person's perspective won't in general describe the same situation from some other perspective. In order that we may get at the same situations, a human language will satisfy the second principle.

Relativity: Different expressions with different meanings can be used in different circumstances with a single interpretation.

Thus, for you, the future reader, to express the fact that I am sitting (now), you could say "He was sitting."[2]

One might say that meaning is a function from discourse situation and connections to interpretation. Thus the proposition $_{d,c}[\alpha]$ is the unique set of courses of events σ such that $[\alpha](d,c,\sigma)$ holds. This isn't wrong, but it can be very misleading. The interpretation—the set we get when we fix expression, discourse situation, and connections—is very important. It amounts to one sort of uniformity over utterances, and it is a very important uniformity; recognition of its importance is built right into language. But by remembering that meaning is a relation, we are reminded of a number of other important uniformities, and these are crucial in understanding the attitudes.

Besides the interpretation, we can construct a number of "inverse interpretations," fixing the last coordinate of meaning and allowing the others to vary. Such inverse interpretations are used in daily life and are often implicitly involved in talk of "truth conditions" and "when a sentence is true." Suppose, for example, that we say that a child b understands *this is milk*, because she says it only when it is true. What we mean is that she says it only when attending to a glass of milk. We are appealing to

$$\{\langle d, c\rangle\} \mid [this\ is\ milk](d,c,\sigma^*)\ \text{and}\ a_d = b.$$

And when we think that this is a good test for understanding this sort of sentence, it is because we think there is some uniformity, perceptually discoverable by a_d, across this set or a significant subset of it. The uniformity is not interpretation, assuming that she interacts with different bottles of milk at different times.[3]

Some philosophers hold that the true vehicles of meaning can be neither relative nor efficient; this view leads to logical atomism. Others think the true vehicles can be relative, but not efficient. This leads to the view that the efficient sentences of natural language must be backed by senses or mental representations that take up the slack—that are "complete in every respect." We think that sentences of natural language are true vehicles of meaning, and that the slack is taken up by other factors in the utterance. Language learning requires coordination of language with the more and less remote parts of the environment, not with senses or mental representations.

Innocent attitudes

Statements made with sentences of the following sort we call *attitude reports*:

(4) Agnes saw me jump in the fountain.
(5) Agnes saw that I was sitting in the fountain.
(6) Agnes knew that I was hot and tired.
(7) Agnes said that I was drunk.
(8) The policeman believed what Agnes said.

Attitude verbs combine with sentences to produce verb phrases which are used to classify individuals. Notice, however, that the interpretation of a particular report involving any of (4) to (8) features the interpretation of the embedded sentence, *not* its meaning. A rather straightforward semantic approach, and a first approximation of our own, is to take the attitude verbs as expressing a relation between an individual and the interpretation of the embedded statement. An utterance of (6), for example, would express a relation between Agnes and the fact that I was hot and tired, a complex involving me, two properties, and a location.

This approach to the attitudes exemplifies what Donald Davidson calls "semantic innocence":

> If we could but recover our pre-Fregean semantic innocence. I think it would be plainly incredible that the words "the earth moves," uttered after the words "Galileo said that," mean anything different, or refer to anything else, than is their wont when they come in other environments.[4]

On the approach just sketched, the embedded statements and their constituents have exactly the same meaning and interpretation as when they are not embedded.

Traditional objections to the innocent approach have been based on the belief that the only plausible interpretation (reference) of a sentence is its truth value, which obliterates the subject matter of the sentence. The belief that a truth value is the only plausible interpretation for a sentence has been supported by a formal argument which we call "the slingshot." We have shown elsewhere that this argument depends on ignoring from the start the possibility of a situation-based semantics.[5]

Once this objection has been removed, the innocent approach seems quite natural. By focusing on the interpretation (not meaning) of the embedded sentence, it allows us to account for the perspectival relativity of the embedded sentence in a straightforward way.

In the case of first-person, present-tense reports of attitudes, an expressive sentence is used as the embedded sentence in the report. I report the belief I would express with *I am sitting* with *I believe that I am sitting*. But, in general, the sentences we use to report another's attitudes, or they themselves use to report their own past attitudes, are not the sentences they would use or would have used to express those attitudes. Thus you will report my belief with *He believed that he was sitting*, not *He believed that I am sitting*. The same point carries over to the other attitude verbs (AV's). Attitudes are attitudes toward propositions. An attitude report NP AVα gets at a proposition P by using an embedded sentence α whose interpretation from the *speaker's* perspective (d,c) is P. The agent a $(= {}_{d,c}[\text{NP}])$ would have to use some expressive sentence α' whose interpretation relative to his own perspective (d',c') would also be P:

$$P = {}_{d,c}[\alpha] = {}_{d',c'}[\alpha']$$

What might be called the "received theory" of the attitudes (setting aside *see* and other perception verbs) goes like this. Attitudes are relations toward sentences, sentence meanings, senses of sentences, or mental representations which are taken to be something like sentence meanings. An attitude report NP AVα reports the agent's attitude toward the sentence α or toward a mental representation somehow associated with α. This is a "*de dicto*" attitude report. The sentence is not used innocently to refer to what it usually refers to, but to refer to itself, its meaning or sense, or to a mental representation.

To account for the phenomenon we have been discussing—the disparity between the speaker's embedded sentence and the agent's expressive sentence, the received theory admits that attitudes are sometimes *reported* in a different way, but maintains that the attitude itself is an attitude toward the received sort of object. Thus, in so-called *de re* reports, some parts of the embedded sentence are used not to contribute their meaning (sense, etc.) but to identify, say, an individual *b*. Such a *de re* report, it is claimed, means that the agent has the attitude toward a sentence or meaning that has *b* as the reference of one of its parts. Problems with tense are usually ignored but would presumably be handled in a similar manner.

There are serious problems with all versions of the received theory—these problems being our impetus for working out an innocent semantics. In the first place, what seems to us to be a straightforward phenomenon gets, on the received theory, an extremely complicated explanation that has never been worked out in detail [consider (8), for example].

The idea that attitudes are relations toward sentences is plausible in the case of saying, scarcely plausible in the cases of belief and knowledge, and just wild in the case of perception. And, even in the case of saying, the theory does not run at all smoothly—as Davidson makes clear.

When we turn from sentences to meanings, senses, or mental representations different problems beset us. Frege's notion of sense is often appealed to as if it were a well-developed technical tool. But it is not. Attempts to work out a full-fledged theory of senses meet with serious technical problems, problems that reflect philosophical objections to the very notion of sense.

The index or "possible worlds" semantics developed for modal logic, as adapted for the attitudes, offers us yet another alternative designation for the embedded sentence—its "intension," the set of possible worlds where the sentence is true. Even if one thinks that the primitive idea of a possible world makes sense, the problem of logical equivalence arises. Consider for example,

(9)   Fred sees Betty enter.
(10)   Fred sees Betty enter and (Sally smoke or Sally not smoke).

We certainly cannot go from (9) to (10), however logically gifted Fred may be. If we did, we should have to admit that Fred either saw Sally smoke or saw Sally not smoke, even though he has never laid eyes on Sally. The admission would be forced by the principles:

If Fred sees P and Q, then Fred sees Q.
If Fred sees P or Q, then Fred sees P or Fred sees Q.

(We wouldn't expect omnipercipience, even among the logically omniscient.[6])

Situation semantics, and semantic innocence, resolve the problem of logical equivalence. Logically equivalent sentences, even in the same discourse situation, are not assigned the same proposition; different subject matters give different sets of situation types. This is the dividend of using partial functions freely in the development of situation semantics. Indeed, from the point of view of situation semantics, the phrase *logically equivalent* should be used for sentences true in the same situation types or courses of events, not for those which satisfy the weaker condition of being true in the same total types or courses of events. The phrase *logical equivalence* having an entrenched use, however, we refer to this stricter relation as *strong equivalence*.

Our innocent approach, then, is straightforward, natural, solves some problems, and avoids others. There are, however, some difficulties.

Innocence threatened

In this section we list four problems that threaten our account of the attitudes, problems that point to a missing constituent in our theory.

The logic of the attitudes

There are a number of facts involving the attitudes which seem to require a semantic explanation. These are especially clear in the case of epistemically neutral perception reports [*sees* versus *sees that* as in (4) above].[7] We have stated two of them earlier:

1. If a sees ϕ and ψ, then a sees ϕ and a sees ψ.
2. If a sees ϕ or ψ, then a sees ϕ or a sees ψ.

3. If a sees ϕ, then ϕ.
4. If a sees $\phi(t_1)$ and $t_1 = t_2$, then a sees $\phi(t_2)$.

Our account so far provides an explanation only for (item 4).[8]

Opacity

The astute reader will have noticed that our account violates Frege's and Russell's beginning wisdom on the attitudes—the claim that substitution of co-referential expressions does not preserve truth value in attitude reports. After all, if our account predicts (item 4) above, it is going to make a similar claim for all the attitudes. By taking the attitudes to be relations to real objects, properties, and relations, we are committed to the claim that they are, in some sense, transparent.

Missing objects of the attitudes

Our account has taken the objects of the attitudes to be propositions. In connection with seeing and saying, this is philosophically unsatisfactory. With seeing it misses the connection with what was actually seen, and with saying it misses the connection with what was actually uttered. Suppose that speaker a, in a discourse situation d and with connections c, says

(11) b said that ϕ

We have seen that ϕ itself cannot in general serve as b's actual utterance. But surely it follows from the truth of (11) that b actually uttered *something*, that there is some sentence ψ uttered by b such that, from b's discourse location d' and with b's connections c', $_{d,c}[\phi] = _{d',c'}[\psi]$ and $c(\text{said}) = l_d$. Similarly, if a truly said

(12) b saw ϕ.

then what b actually saw was a scene where $_{d,c}[\phi]$ was realized, not a proposition.

Cognitive content of the attitudes

Missing in our account is the fact that the attitudes have something to do with minds (or brains) and cognition. Just as saying requires the agent to utter something meaningful, and seeing requires the agent to see something with his eyes (a part of the brain), so too believing and knowing require the agent to be in a meaningful cognitive state. Part of what attitude reports give us is information about the agent's cognitive state. That's what makes attitude reports useful in explaining and predicting what people will do. People with similar perceptions, beliefs, and desires behave similarly.

Concentrating on this aspect of the problem makes Fregean senses seem attractive. By interpreting an attitude as a relation to a sense, or "mental representation," as some versions of the theory would have it, one can see the object of the attitude as classifying cognitive states. On this theory, similarity of attitudes points to similarity of states, apparently explaining similarity of actions. On our theory, however, different people could believe exactly the same thing in countless different ways. The theory so far does not reflect any cognitive similarity at all.

These four problems are interrelated, and all require us to ponder just what it is we are doing when we attempt a semantic theory of the attitude verbs, or of any other "nonlogical" words for that matter. And it is there our defense rests.

Innocence defended

If simple statements describe situations, then attitude reports must describe situations involving the attitudes, perceptual situations **p** in the cases of *sees* and *sees that*, epistemic situations **k** in the case of *knows that*, doxastic situations **b** with *believes that*, and utterances **u** in the case of *says that*. But just what is it that we are saying about a situation when we say that in it *a sees that* ϕ or *b says that* ψ? Just what is it about the agent that is missing in our earlier account? And what is it about these attitude situations that makes them classifiable with embedded sentences and, hence, according to innocent semantics, with realistic propositions, propositions not in general true of the attitude situation? To answer these questions, we must make a slight digression.

Structural constraints

Things cannot fall out just any old way. There are all kinds of constraints on the types of situation that can actually arise and on the course events can actually take. Some constraints arise from rather obvious properties of and relations between relations. (Kissing involves touching: being a grandfather involves being a father.) Others arise from natural laws. Still others are rather temporary and somewhat accidental (typing used to involve making keys move). A native speaker of a language normally understands many of these constraints and uses this knowledge in discourse. The felicity of exchanges like the following can only be explained relative to such constraints:

"Did you kiss me?" "I didn't touch you."
"Is it hot out?" "Well, it's snowing."
"Why aren't you typing?" "The keys are stuck."

Traditional semantic theories, recognizing the importance of such constraints, attempt to impose them via "meaning postulates" on expressions of language. This strikes us as just backward. We believe these constraints on courses of events are (except in the most singular cases) independent of which natural-language expressions (if any) designate the constituent objects, relations, and locations.

When the relevant constituents are clearly individuated, it is possible to represent the constraints fairly clearly:

If $\sigma_l(\text{kiss}, a, b) = 1$ then $\sigma_l(\text{touch}, a, b) = 1$
If $\sigma_l(\text{bachelor}, a) = 1$ then $\sigma_l(\text{married}, a) = 0$
If $\sigma_l(\text{kick}, a, b) = 1$ and $l \circ l'$ then $\sigma_{l'}(\text{kick}, a, b) \neq 0$
If $\sigma_l(\text{snowing}) = 1$ then $\sigma_l(\text{hot}) \neq 1$

In other cases, it may be rather difficult. For example, it would be impossible to spell out all the constraints on σ^* imposed by $\sigma_1^*(\text{walk}, a) = 1$.

Systems of constraints can be used for a variety of purposes. A course of events σ is *structurally complete* relative to a set C of such constraints if σ satisfies each constraint in C. A course of events σ is *structurally coherent* with respect to C if σ is part of some complete σ'.[10] If it is not coherent, it is *incoherent*.

A constraint is *correct* if σ^*, the actual course of events, satisfies the constraint. A set C of constraints is correct if each constraint in C is correct, that is, if C correctly captures constraints on the way things can actually happen so that σ^* is complete with respect to C. If C is correct, then every part of σ^* is coherent with respect to C. No part of the actual course of events can be structurally incoherent, though it might be structurally incomplete.

If a_d is an organism in the world, its biological endowment and, what it has learned from past experience will lead it to act in accord with certain correct constraints—to be *attuned* to these constraints. As we have seen above, people are attuned to all kinds of constraints they cannot actually state—like all the things that are involved in walking. This is not surprising, since fish are attuned to certain natural laws of water and swimming, and they can't say a word.

But when we are doing the semantics of some word like *kiss* or *walk*, we are forced to reflect on the constraints on kissing and walking with which native speakers of English are attuned and which are reflected and exploited in their use of English.

The same applies to the attitude verbs we have been considering here. Structural constraints come in with attitude reports in two ways. First, there are all kinds of correct structural constraints on attitude situations, just as there are on kissings and walks. Secondly, though, there are also correct structural constraints with which the agent of an attitude situation is attuned and which effect his attitudes. We are interested primarily in spelling out constraints of the first type, leaving the second to other parts of science.

When we concentrate on the constraints of the first sort which are clearly reflected in language, we find a striking difference between factives (*sees, sees that, knows that*) and nonfactives (*believes that, says that*). The difference shows up most clearly at the extremes with the epistemically neutral *sees* (*Bill saw June win*) and with *says that* (*Bill said that Jane won*); so we begin by discussing and then comparing these two.

Seeing

There is a variety of uniformities across visual perception situations. One sort is built directly into the structure of perceptual reports, but other uniformities are needed to explain the uses we can make of perceptual reports. With epistemically neutral *see* statements, we treated "sees" as a relation between an agent a and an unlocated proposition P. This is the way language works: a *sees* ϕ focuses on a, on seeing, and on *what is true* of what a sees, $P = {}_{d,c}[\![\phi]\!]$. But the semantic properties of such sentences listed in the first problem reflect a different uniformity—namely, the scene that a visually apprehends. Seeing involves a visually apprehended scene. A scene is an actual situation $\langle l,s \rangle$, but its type does not include everything that happens at l, only that part which is visible under the relevant conditions. These conditions include the direction and distance of the agent from l, the lighting conditions, and much besides. In terms of scenes, we can state the following constraint:

$\sigma_l(\text{sees}, a, P) = 1$
iff there is a scene $\mathbf{s} = \langle l, s \rangle$ such that $\sigma_l(\text{sees}, a, s) = 1$ and $s \in P$.

All the semantic principles involving *sees* listed in the previous section fall out of this structural constraint. The constraint draws out another uniformity in visual situations, the visually apprehended scene. In doing so, it gives us an alternative indirect way of classifying individuals, by what they saw. That is why we can say

Mary saw a truck stop in front of her. Bill saw it too.

It seems that epistemically neutral reports of visual situations report primarily on what is true of a visually apprehended scene. It is not hard to imagine why language should give us a mechanism for such reports. One need only think of scouts, whose job is to scan the horizons for signs of hostile pioneers. Here we use the perceptual report as evidence, about what the inspected world is like, because the inspected world, not the agent, is what we are really interested in.

But we also use perceptual reports to *explain* the activities of agents as, for example, when we say that Mary hit the brakes because she saw a truck stop in front of her.

To explain and predict activities of agents, we need to find principles of classification which are projectible onto activities, that is, similarities among agents which lead to similar actions.

Given the complexity of the causes of action, these connections will not be simple. But the idea is that any adequate or near-adequate theory—as the theory that supports our explanation of why Mary hit the brakes surely is—must work with a supply of states of the agent which are systematically related to other states and ultimately to activities.

Now we can see the impact of relativity and efficiency. *The chosen uniformities do not by themselves supply all the states or principles of classification we use.* Let us consider our explanation of Mary's hitting the brakes. Consider the class of perceptual situations determined by *saw a truck stopping in front of her.* Clearly, there are many relevant differences. One who sees a truck stopping a mile away will not hit the brakes, nor one who sees a truck stopping in the far lane.

In these last two examples, we have narrowed the classification, in two different ways. In the second case, we augmented the embedded sentence; in the first we considered the distance between the agent and parts of the scene. The general picture that emerges is this. The chosen uniformity—truth of a given proposition in the visually apprehended scene—is not a principle of classification which supports explanation by itself. But it is a part of such a system. The chosen uniformity, together with other factors, gives us a system of (abstract) states useful in prediction and explanation of the agent's activities. Even when we explain by reporting an attitude, we rely on an understanding of the other factors. Thus, in the above explanation of Mary hitting the brakes, the listener limits the other factors in such a way as to make the explanation work—that is, assumes that the truck was in front of Mary, and not very far ahead.

Says

In seeing, the visually apprehended actual situation plays a crucial role in the classificatory scheme. With a nonfactive, like *says*, there need be no actual situation to support the classification. When we say, *Bill said that Jane won*, *Jane won* is not serving to classify some actual situation to which George has some relation, say "assertive apprehension." How then does the classification work?

The answer is easy to see or hear. We use *says* to classify utterances. The uniformities across utterances are the very uniformities that we have developed an account of above. Utterances involve discourse situations, connections, and expressions. The chosen uniformity is the interpretation of the utterance.

Indeed, we use the word *says* in two different ways, one that concentrates on what is said in the sense of interpretation, the other in terms of the words uttered. For the latter we use *says* with quotation marks around the embedded sentence. These two uses of *says* focus on two ways of classifying utterance situations. One focuses on the uniformity of interpretation, the other on the uniformity of the meaningful sentence.

> Mary said that I was in danger.
> Mary said "You are in danger."
> Mary said "He is in danger."
> Mary said "Watch out!"

Notice that neither of these uniformities can be uniquely determined by the other. The proposition that is stated is absolute:

$$\{\sigma \mid \sigma_l(\text{in danger}, a_d) = 1\}$$

The expressions *You are in danger* and *He is in danger* are not. The efficiency and relativity of language make it impossible to get from either of these to the other in a unique way.

Note that the two different ways of classifying agents, provided by the two different senses of *say*, provide very different classes of agents, classes that are relevant to different sorts of generalizations. Suppose Hugh says *I am a killer*. Then he belongs to two different but overlapping classes, those who say *I am a killer* and those who say that Hugh is a killer.

Even though these uniformities do not uniquely determine one another, given additional information one sort of classification can lead us, more or less smoothly, to the other. To say *Hugh said that he was a killer* does not *automatically* classify him as an utterer of *I am a killer*, but it suggests it very strongly, since this is the normal way for Hugh to say that he is.

These implications are involved in the explanations of actions by reference to "what was said." Consider for example,

Bill jumped out of the way because he heard Mary say that he was in danger.

As an explanation this makes sense only if Mary said that Bill was in danger in a way that conveyed to him a sense of danger—if she used some expression that is uniform across situations where the addressee is in danger. *Watch out!* and *You're in danger* are such expressions. *He is in danger* won't, in general, do. What explains Bill's behavior is the existence of a way of saying that he is in danger that is systematically related to situations where the addressee is in danger. It is not just the relativity of language that matters, the fact that there are lots of ways of saying the same thing, but the efficiency of language. An expression like *Watch out!* can be used in many situations to warn of danger.

To complete our theory of saying, then, we need merely to exploit situation semantics (and the other use of *says*) in stating a structural constraint:

If $\sigma_i(\text{says that}, b, P) = 1$, then there is an utterance $u = \langle \psi, d', c' \rangle$ such that $\sigma_i(\text{says}, d', c', \psi) = 1$, where $b = a_{d'}$, $l = l_{d'}$, and $_{d',c'} [\![\psi]\!] = P$.

Now let us compare seeing and saying. The rationale behind the chosen uniformity is quite different. In seeing, the realistic proposition directly classifies an actual situation, and so indirectly classifies the agent who visually apprehends the situation. (Note that we have a theory of *direct* perception, and indirect classification of perceivers.) But, in *saying*, the proposition cannot work their way, for there may be no actual situation that the proposition fits.

For this second scheme to work, there must be something that "fills the gap" left by the absence of any classifiable actual situation. This something is the uttered sentence, or, more plausibly, the utterance of a meaningful sentence with a certain set of intentions. Instead of a relation to an actual situation that the proposition characterizes, we have a relation to a meaningful entity which, in the utterance, has the proposition as its interpretation.

However, there is an important difference between the relation to the actual situation and the role of the uttered sentence.

In seeing, the proposition connects to the agent "through" the apprehended scene. In saying, the proposition connects to the agent through the produced sentence. But the proposition is true in the situation of which the scene is a part, quite independent of the agent's location, connections, history, et cetera. The situation, we might say, gives us a pool of propositions; the other factors merely influence the way the agent can apprehend the scene of which it is true.

But, in saying, the proposition does not in general (if ever) connect to the isolated meaningful sentence, but only to the entire utterance. The proposition does not serve to classify *one* of the factors, and thereby the whole, but characterizes the whole by the relationship among the factors. (A special case would be the utterance of a sentence whose meaning uniquely determined its interpretation, if there are any.)

When we move to the question of the interest in the chosen uniformity across utterances, we find a similarity with seeing. *Says that* is designed to tell us what the world is like if what the agent says is true. But, as with seeing, other uniformities are crucial when we use *says* to explain and predict activities of the agent, or of those who hear or read the utterance.

Sees that, knows that

Suppose the identical twins June and Jane entered the marathon and Bill saw that one of them won. In fact, it was June, but Bill can't tell them apart. If asked which one, he couldn't say. Cases like this bring out the difference between nonepistemic *sees* and *sees that* and *knows that*. If Bill saw one of the twins win, and June won, then Bill saw June win. But even though he saw that one of them won, and knows that one of them won, he doesn't see that June won, or know that June won.

Seeing that involves scenes (or, more generally, courses of events), but the relation is less direct than in the case of *sees*. The structural constraints are (roughly):

> σ_l(sees that, a, P) = 1
> iff there is an event σ_0 (possibly a scene s) such that
> (i) σ_l(sees, a, σ_0) = 1
> (ii) there is a system C of correct structural constraints with which a is visually attuned such that every σ containing σ_0 which is complete with respect to C is in P.

In the above example there is a certain visual property p such that Bill is attuned to:

> If $\sigma_l(p, x) = 1$, then $\sigma_l(p_{\text{June}}, x) = 1$ or $\sigma_l(p_{\text{Jane}}, x) = 1$.

where p_{June} is the property of being named June. Any structurally complete σ containing the event Bill saw will have $\sigma_l(p, x) = 1$ and $\sigma_l(p_{\text{June}}, x) = 1$, but this σ_0 was not complete.

The difference between reports using *sees* and reports using *sees that* lies partly in these constraints, but also on different interpretation strategies for noun phrases and verb phrases in the embedded sentences. We discuss this briefly as "value loading" in the next section.

One can give a similar structural constraint for *knows*. The basic idea is that to know is to be attuned. We will be simple-minded and pretend that vision is the only form of perception, for expository purposes. Then one could say

> σ_l(knows that, a, P) = 1
> iff there is a course of events σ_0 such that
> (i) σ_l(sees, a, σ_0) = 1
> (ii) if C' is the set of all correct structural constraints with which a is attuned, then every σ containing σ_0 which is complete with respect to C' is in P.

The reader will notice that the only difference here between *sees that* and *knows that* lies in the fact that a wider set C' of correct constraints is admitted for *knows that*. This presumably has something to do with the tendency to say we see that something is the case when we mean we know it.

As with seeing, the treatment of *sees that* and *knows that* explains the many sorts of uniformities, other than the "chosen ones," across epistemic situations. In particular, the structure of knowledge allows for knowing the same thing on the basis of different sets of past experiences, a difference that might be relevant to how the knowledge affects one.

Believing

It is usually thought that knowing that P implies believing that P. And in language we usually assume that, if the speaker says that P, he believes that P. In this regard, believing seems more or less intermediate between knowing and saying. But, from a realist perspective, belief is by far the most puzzling of our four attitudes. For where or what is the real invariant in various actual doxastic situations which supports their classification together as situations in which an agent believes that P (where P is a realistic proposition)?

With seeing, seeing that, and knowing that, there is an actual course of events of which P is true. With belief, there need be no such; so believing seems more like saying that. But in the case of saying that, there is the expression actually uttered, something real, which, together with the discourse situation and speaker connections, gave rise to the proposition. What is analogous is the case of belief.

It seems that the realist, if he believes in belief, is forced either into a metaphysics that includes real but not actual situations (an outlandish move that surely no one would advocate) or into a metaphysics that countenances real "belief states," some kind of abstract but real invariants across actual doxastic situations, invariants that support their classification by realistic propositions the way sentences support propositions in the case of saying.

This is where one might think that something akin to Fregean senses comes in, "complete and eternal thoughts" grasped by minds. We could modify the Fregean account so that the reference of a thought T was a realistic proposition $P = \text{ref}(T)$ and use the structural constraint:

$\sigma_l(\text{believes } a, P) = 1$
iff there is a thought T such that $\sigma_l(\text{doxastically grasps}, a, T)$ and $\text{ref}(T) = P$.

This would allow us to capture the relativity of belief, the fact that different people can believe the same thing in different ways, by having different thoughts. But this would be a serious mistake! It is just as important for belief states to be both efficient and relative as it is for sentences. There are other factors that play a role in going from the state S_i to the proposition: $P = F(S_i, \ldots ?)$. What are these other factors?

The agent, of course, is one such factor. When it is in what we might call the "I'm in danger" belief-state, its beliefs are about itself and its present location in time and space. And there is no reason to suppose that other properties of the agent, say his height or education, might not play a role in the interpretation of his belief state. We lump all this into an agent situation $d = \langle s_d, a_d \rangle$ where $s_d = \langle l_d, s_d \rangle$, a_d being the agent, l_d its location, and s_d the facts about a which are needed for interpretation. This d is analogous to the discourse situation in the case of saying.

But of course we can have beliefs about things other than ourselves and our present location. We have connections with objects, relations, and locations which arise through perception, and these connections help determine what our beliefs are about.

Thus talk about belief presupposes an abstract classification system $S_1, S_2, \ldots$ of *states* and a relation bel that holds between states, agent situations, connections, and courses of events:

$\text{bel}(S_i, d, c, \sigma)$

Then we impose the constraint that $\sigma_l(\text{believes that}, a, P) = 1$ iff there is a d, c, and S_i such that $l = l_d$, $a = a_d$, $\sigma_l(S_i, d, c) = 1$, and $P = \{\sigma | \text{bel}(S_i, d, c, \sigma)\}$.

The relation bel is analogous to [ ]. Just as [ ] identifies a proposition relative to an expression, discourse situation, and connections, bel identifies a proposition relative to a belief state, doxastic situation, and connections: the proposition that a person in that state, in such a doxastic situation, with such connections, believes. The postulation of such a relation and such a system of "meaningful" states is presupposed by the way we use *believes*. This approach to belief seems to us to fit well with a number of approaches to the philosophy of mind, which emphasize how attributions of mental states are connected with activities of species and of individuals.

In the case of agents that speak a language L, it is very tempting to assume that the meaningful sentences of L can be embedded in the structure of the belief states, that there is a function $S(\phi)$ from sentences of L into the system of belief states. This suggests that belief states have a certain "syntax" analogous to the syntax of L and that this "syntax" is important in the analysis of bel, just as language syntax is important in the analysis of $_{d,c}[\phi] = P$. This temptation should be distinguished from something we do not find very tempting: the view that believing consists in having some relation to some sentences of some language.

Opacity

The interaction of attitude verbs with singular terms (proper names and definite descriptions, for example) was a driving force behind the theories of Russell and Frege—different as these theories were. It is certainly possible for George IV to wonder whether Scott is the author of Waverly without wondering whether Scott is Scott, and it is possible for one to believe that the morning star is a planet without believing that the evening star is a planet. These facts caused Frege to say that, within the scope of an attitude verb, an expression refers to its usual "sense," not to its ordinary reference. Russell introduced "logical form" and argued that definite descriptions do not denote but rather contribute the defining properties to the proposition properly understood. (Many contemporary theories appeal to both sense and logical form.)

We do not appeal to either sense or logical form, but handle these problems basically with the resources already at hand. There is not space to explain our treatment of names, although the reader can probably guess how such notions as inverse interpretations and connections allow us to replace such old questions as "Do proper names have sense?" and "What are the truth conditions of a sentence with proper names?" with more tractable questions. We shall explain the basic ideas behind our treatment of descriptions, a treatment that has many Russellian features but does not threaten us with atomism or require appeal to logical form.

To simplify discussion, we ignore issues of time and place, so that we can deal with situation types rather than courses of events. We also restrict ourselves to descriptions α that are not sensitive to discourse situation d or connection c, so that we can write $[\alpha]$ for the interpretation $_{d,c}[\alpha]$, again just to simplify discussion.

The interpretation of a definite description is a relation between situation types s and individuals a:

$$[The\ \beta](s, a) \text{ iff } \{a\} = \{x|[\beta](s,x)\}$$

This relation can also be viewed as a *partial* function from situation types s to individuals a. Using standard function-argument notation, we can write $a = [the\ \beta](s)$. This function sets up a mutual constraint between s and a. Given an s in its domain, we can use *the* β to refer to $a = [the\ \beta](s)$. Or, given an a, we can use *the* β to claim that the situation s is one where $[the\ \beta](s) = a$. Or it can be used simply to say that, whatever s and a are, $[the\ \beta](s) = a$.

EXAMPLES
1. I walk into Alfred's study where he sits with his dog Clarissa. He says "Be careful. The dog has fleas." The situation s_0 we are in makes it clear that he is referring to Clarissa ($= [the\ dog](s_o)$).
   He has asserted the realistic proposition:

   $$\{s_1|s_1(\text{has fleas, Clarissa}) = 1\}$$

   Notice that, if I believe him, then what I believe is not that there exists a unique dog that has fleas but, rather, that this particular dog has fleas.
2. Now there are several dogs in the room. Pointing at Clarissa, Alfred says *This is the dog that bites*. Here the definite description *the dog that bites* is not being used to pick out Clarissa but, rather, to attribute to her the property of being the unique dog that bites. The proposition is

$\{s_1 \mid \text{Clarissa} = [\textit{the dog that bites}](s_1)\}$

3. Now we are in a situation where Agnes once told me of a certain individual a, *She is a fool*. Agnes is a shrewd judge of character. Accordingly, I counsel you against investing in a's bank by warning you, *Agnes believes the president of First Federal is a fool*. Here the interpretation of my utterance is, essentially,

$$\{s_1 \mid s_1(\text{believes, Agnes, } P_{s_1}) = 1\}$$

where

$$P_{s_1} = \{s_2 \mid s_2(\text{fool, } [\textit{the president of First Federal}](s_1)) = 1\}$$

The definite description constrains s_1 to contain a unique president of First Federal, a_{s_1}, and asserts that Agnes believes that a_{s_1} is a fool (P_{s_1}).

We use the notation: *a says(believes/knows/sees)that(—(the)$_j$ . . .)* with $j = 0$, 1, or 2 to indicate the readings where $[\textit{the } \beta]$ is evaluated at an accessible situation type s_0, as in (i); to constrain the situation type s_1 designated by the whole (as in iii); or to constrain the situation types s_2 described by the embedded sentence, respectively. For $j = 0$ this corresponds to Donnellan's referential use. For $j = 2$ it is his attributive use. The case $j = 1$ is somewhere in between.

These various readings might appear to coincide with different scope readings. But they really reflect a different phenomenon, one that is widely confused with scope. The distinction is most easily seen with indefinite descriptions, like *member of the family*. The interpretation of an indefinite description *a* β (e.g., *a dog, an elephant*) is also a relation between situations and individuals:

$[a \; \beta](s,b)$ iff $[\beta](s,b)$

Consider the case where Jack has been murdered. Holmes has assembled all the members of the family and said, "One of you has murdered Jack." "What did he say?" asks deaf old Aunt Agnes. "He said that a member of the family murdered Jack," yells Jack's widow Jill.

Now there is certainly nothing wrong with Jill's report, but it cannot be accounted for with only the wide scope≠arrow scope distinction. Holmes didn't say of any particular member in the family that he was the murderer, so it is not wide scope. But he didn't say anything at all about family membership, so it is not narrow scope. It is what we would write as *He said that (a member of the family)$_1$ murdered Jack*. The interpretation is:

$$\{s_1 \mid s_1(\text{says, Holmes, } P_{s_1}) = 1\}$$

where

$$P_{s_1} = \{s_1 \mid \text{for some } a \text{ such that } [a \textit{ member of the family}](s_1, a), s_2(\text{murdered, } a, \text{Jack}) = 1\}$$

Foundational issues

Certain foundational issues confront anyone who tries to work out a careful semantic theory of the attitudes. We cannot here discuss the exact guise in which these appear for situation semantics, or the details of our solution. The basic idea is to restrict ourselves to the hereditarily finite set-theoretical objects built out of the objects, relations, and locations at our disposal. Ultimately, this requires us to be more realistic about the sentences, states, and other factors involved in the attitudes. For example, ultimately, we define

$$\sigma_l(\text{says}, a, P) = 1$$

by

$$\exists d, e, \psi[\sigma_l(\text{says}, d, c, \psi) = 1 \;\&\; {}_{d,c}[\![\psi]\!] = P]$$
(with $\sigma_l(\text{says}, a, p) = 0$, otherwise).

This allows us to avoid having propositions as arguments of situation types. At this point, our theory has led us up a spiral. We started from a realism toward situations in the world and were forced to be realists about objects, properties, relations, and locations. This forced upon us a philosophical realism toward cognitive states and activities. In the end, this allows a slight abandonment of pure innocence in favor of a sort of worldly innocence, which we hope that some readers may find attractive.

Notes

This paper represents joint work of the authors; the order of names is merely alphabetic. J. B. is grateful to the National Science Foundation. The paper was completed while J. E. was a fellow at the Center for Advanced Study in the Behavioral Science, and he is grateful for support from the center, the National Endowment for the Humanities, the Andrew Mellon Foundation, and Stanford University. Both authors are grateful to the center for gracefully accommodating the needs of collaborators.

We owe much to discussions with John Etchemendy, Michael Turvey and others at the center and at Stanford. Our point of view was profoundly influenced by Turvey and others working in the tradition of ecological realism. For an introduction to this point of view, readers may consult Claire Michaels and Claudia Carello, *Direct Perception* (Englewood Cliffs, N.J.: Prentice Hall, 1980).

1. We regard truth values as slipping into the universe in the process of abstraction from situations to objects standing or not standing in various relations.

2. The astute reader will realize that in describing my situation, his or her connections are

$c(he) = \text{me}$ $c(was) = \text{here and now}$

These are objectively determined by which of the authors wrote this part of the paper, where and when, and are independent of the reader's ability to specify them in some more complete fashion. On the other hand, the reader's reading is connected, causally, with the writing.

3. For a discussion of some of these issues, see John Perry (1986a) "Perception, Action and the Structure of Believing," in Richard Grandy and Richard Warner (Eds.), *Philosophical Grounds of Rationality: Intentions, Categories, Ends.* New York: Oxford University Press.

4. D. Davidson, "On Saying That," 1984d; reprinted in Donald Davidson and Gilbert Harman, eds., *The Logic of Grammar* (Encino, Calif.: Dickenson, 1975), p. 152. Originally published in Synthèse 19 (1968–69): 130–146.

5. J. Perry and J. Barwise, "Semantic Innocence and Uncompromising Situations," *Midwest Studies in Philosophy* 6 (1981): 387–403.

6. See J. Barwise "Scenes and Other Situations," *Journal of Philosophy*, 78(7) (July 1981): 369–397.

7. See Barwise, ibid., for more detail on these points.

8. Space precludes a discussion of logical relationships between the attitudes, such as the claim that knowing involves believing. We hope readers will be able to see more or less what we would say, from our discussion of the individual attitudes.

9. But see Perry (1986a), where it is shown that this theory doesn't work.

10. σ_1 is *part* of σ_2 if $\text{dom}(\sigma_1) \subseteq \text{dom}(\sigma_2)$ and, for each $l \in \text{dom}(\sigma_1)$, $\sigma_1(l) \subseteq \sigma_2(l)$.

16

RAY JACKENDOFF

What Is a Concept, That a Person May Grasp It?

1 Prologue

Asking a psychologist, philosopher, or a linguist what a concept is is much like asking a physicist what mass is. An answer cannot be given in isolation. Rather, the term plays a certain role in a larger worldview that includes the nature of language, of meaning, and of mind. Hence, the notion of a concept cannot be explicated without at the same time sketching the background against which it is set, and the "correctness" of a particular notion of concept cannot be evaluated without at the same time evaluating the worldview in which it plays a role.

In turn, the evaluation of a worldview is at least in part dependent on one's purposes. A worldview incorporating a geocentric universe evidently was well-suited for the purposes of the Church of the sixteenth century; a worldview incorporating the Newtonian notions of mass and energy is perfectly adequate for building bridges. On the other hand, a worldview incorporating a heliocentric planetary system is more suitable for unifying the theories of terrestrial and celestial motion; a worldview incorporating relativistic notions of mass and energy is more suitable if our purpose is building nuclear weapons.

My purpose is to better understand human nature. My method is to attempt to characterize the mental resources that make possible the articulation of humans' knowledge and experience of the world.

2 E-concepts and I-concepts

There is a fundamental tension in the ordinary language term *concept*. On one hand, it is something out there in the world: "the Newtonian concept of mass" is something that is spoken of as

Ray Jackendoff (1989) What is a concept, that a person may grasp it? *Mind and Language* 4.1–2: 68–102. Reprinted by permission of Blackwell Publishers.

though it exists independently of who actually knows or grasps it. Likewise, "grasping a concept" evokes comparison to grasping a physical object, except that one somehow does it with one's mind instead of one's hand. On the other hand, a concept is spoken of as an entity within one's head, a private entity, a product of the imagination that can be conveyed to others only by means of language, gesture, drawing, or some other imperfect means of communication.

Precisely the same tension has been discussed by Chomsky 1986b with respect to the term *language*. He differentiates the two poles as "E-language" (external language, the language seen as external artifact) versus "I-language" (internal language, the language as a body of internally encoded information). I will adopt Chomsky's terminology and speak of E-concepts versus I-concepts.

For Chomsky's purpose—the characterization of the mental resources that make possible human knowledge of language—the notion of I-language rather than E-language is the appropriate focus of inquiry. Chomsky argues this point at length in Chomsky 1986b, and he has in fact been quite explicit about it at least since Chomsky 1965. The new terminology only helps make clearer an old and forceful position.

However, the choice of I-language as the focus of Chomsky's linguistic theory does not rest on a priori argumentation alone. It rests primarily on the suitability of this notion to support scientific investigation into the issues that flow from the overarching goals of the inquiry. To the extent that generative linguistics has indeed been successful in increasing our understanding of the human language capacity, the choice of I-language as the object of inquiry has been vindicated. (And notice that disagreement—even violent disagreement—among its practitioners does not diminish the fact that progress has been made. It stands to reason that, at any particular moment, the most time and energy is being spent at the frontiers of understanding, not in the areas that have been settled. As any linguist will acknowledge, these frontiers have expanded considerably over the past three decades.)

My purpose—the characterization of the mental resources that make possible human knowledge and experience of the world—is conceived as an extension of Chomsky's goals. Accordingly, an important boundary condition on my enterprise is that it be in all respects compatible with the worldview of generative linguistics.

In particular, if we think very roughly of language as a vehicle for expressing concepts, an integrated theory of language and the mind must include a way for linguistic expressions to be related to concepts. If, for my purposes and Chomsky's, the notion of I-language rather than E-language is the suitable focus of inquiry, then on the face of it one should also choose I-concepts rather than E-concepts as the focus for a compatible theory of knowledge.

In this paper I hope to accomplish two things. First, I will ground a theory of I-concepts called Conceptual Semantics in first principles parallel to those of generative syntax and phonology and show how other approaches are incompatible with this outlook. Second, since I have stressed that a worldview is evaluated by how well it suits one's purposes, I will demonstrate some actual empirical results that flow from adopting my approach. (Most of the arguments are elaborated in much greater detail in Jackendoff 1983, 1987, 1990.)

3   First principles of conceptual knowledge

The fundamental motivation behind generative syntax is of course the creativity of language—the fact that a speaker of a language can understand and create an indefinitely large number of sentences that he or she has never heard before. It follows from this observation that a speaker's repertoire of syntactic structures cannot be characterized just as a finite list of sentences. Nor, of course, can it be characterized as an infinite set of possible sentences of the language, because it must be instantiated in a finite (albeit large) brain. Rather, one's potential repertoire of syntactic structures must be mentally encoded in terms of a finite set of primitives and a finite set of principles of combination that collectively describe (or generate) the class of possible sentences. In speaking or understanding a sentence, then, a language user is taken to be creating or invoking a mental information structure, the syntactic structure of the sentence, which is organized in conformance with the principles of syntactic structure.

Parallel arguments obtain for conceptual knowledge, in two different ways. First, a language user presumably is not gratuitously producing and parsing syntactic structures for their own sake: a syntactic structure expresses a concept. On the basis of this concept, the language user can perform any number of tasks, for instance checking the sentence's consistency with other linguistic or extralinguistic knowledge, performing inferences, formulating a response, or translating the sentence into another language. Corresponding to the indefinitely large variety of syntactic structures, then, there must be an indefinitely large variety of concepts that can be invoked in the production and comprehension of sentences. It follows that the repertoire of concepts expressible by sentences cannot be mentally encoded as a list, but must be characterized in terms of a finite set of mental primitives and a finite set of principles of mental combination that collectively describe the set of possible concepts expressed by sentences. For convenience, I will refer to these two sets together as the "grammar of sentential concepts."

It is widely assumed, and I will take for granted, that the basic units out of which a sentential concept is constructed are the concepts expressed by the words in the sentence—that is, *lexical* concepts. It is easy to see that lexical concepts too, are subject to the argument from creativity. For instance, consider the concept expressed by the word *dog*. Someone who knows this concept, upon encountering an indefinitely large variety of objects, will be able to judge whether they are dogs or not. Thus the concept cannot be encoded as a list of the dogs one has previously encountered; nor, because the brain is finite, can it be a list of all dogs there ever have been and will be, or of all possible dogs. Rather, it must be some sort of finite schema that can be compared with the mental representations of arbitrary new objects to produce a judgment of conformance or nonconformance.

Two immediate qualifications. First, there may well be objects for which people's judgments disagree. This does not entail that there is no concept *dog* or that people do not know the meaning of the word. Rather, since our concern is with people's internalized schemas, we simply conclude that people may have schemas for *dog* that differ in various details and that these differences too may bear examination.

Second, there may be novel objects such that one cannot judge clearly whether they are dogs or not. ("It's sort of a dog and sort of a wolf.") Again, this does not necessarily challenge the idea that one has an internalized schema. Rather, from such examples we may conclude that there is a potential degree of indeterminacy, either in the lexical concept itself or in the procedure for comparing it with mental representations of novel objects, or in both. Such indeterminacies are in fact rampant in lexical concepts; section 7 will discuss some characteristics of conceptual knowlege that give rise to them.

To sum up so far: paralleling the argument from syntactic creativity to the necessity for principles or rules in syntactic knowledge, we have argued (1) that sentential concepts cannot be listed but must be mentally generated on the basis of a finite set of primitives and principles of combination; (2) that lexical concepts cannot consist of a list of instances but must consist of finite schemas that can be creatively compared (i.e., in rule-governed fashion) to novel inputs.

The second major issue in the foundation of syntactic theory flows from the problem of acquisition: how can a child acquire the rules of syntax on the basis of the fragmentary evidence available? In particular, how does the child induce *rules* from *instances* of well-formed sentences? This question is rendered especially pointed by the fact that the community of generative linguists, with all their collective intelligence, have not been able to fully determine the syntactic rules of English in over thirty years of research, supported by many centuries of traditional grammatical description; yet, of course, every normal child exposed to English masters the grammar by the age of ten or so. This apparent paradox of language acquisition motivates the central hypothesis of generative linguistics: that the child comes to the task of language learning equipped with an innate Universal Grammar that narrowly restricts the options available for the grammar he or she is trying to acquire. The driving issue in generative linguistics, then, is to determine the form of Universal Grammar, consonant both with the variety of human languages and also with their learnability.

The parallel argument can be made for the logical problem of concept acquisition, in both the sentential and lexical domains. For the former case, consider that the language learner must acquire not only the principles for constructing syntactically well-formed sentences but also the principles for constructing the corresponding sentential concepts. Like the rules of syntax, these principles must be acquired on the basis of some combination of linguistic experience, nonlinguistic experience, and innate constraints on possible principles. As in syntax, then, an important part of our task is to determine what aspects of the grammar of sentential concepts are learned and what aspects are innate; the innate parts must be sufficiently rich to make it possible to acquire the rest.

Turning to lexical concepts, consider that one is capable of acquiring during one's life an indefinitely large number of concepts, each of them on the basis of rather fragmentary evidence. (What evidence might be involved in learning the concepts expressed by such words as *bevel*, *prosaic*, *phonology*, *justice*, or *belief*?) Again, since lexical concepts must be encoded as unconscious schemas rather than lists of instances (and in the case of the words above, it is not even clear what *could* be presented as instances), lexical concept acquisition too presents a problem parallel to the acquisition of syntax. As in syntax, we adopt the hypothesis that one's stock of lexical concepts is constructed from an innate basis of possible concepts, modulated by the contribution of linguistic and nonlinguistic experience.

But now the argument from creativity applies in a new way. If there is an indefinitely large stock of possible lexical concepts, and the innate basis for acquiring them must be encoded in a finite brain, we are forced to conclude that the innate basis must consist of a set of generative principles—a group of primitives and principles of combination that collectively determine the set of lexical concepts. This implies, in turn, that most if not all lexical concepts are composite—that is, that they can be decomposed in terms of the primitives and principles of combination of the innate "grammar of lexical concepts." Learning a lexical concept, then, is to be thought of as constructing a composite expression within the grammar of lexical concepts, associating it with phonological and syntactic structures, and storing them together in long-term memory as a usable unit. (This contrasts sharply with Jerry Fodor's view that lexical concepts are cognitively primitive monads linked with each other by meaning postulates. Section 8 compares the two positions.)

Given the parallelism in first principles, I therefore believe that the central issue of the theory of conceptual knowledge ought to parallel that of the theory of syntax: What are the innate units and principles of organization that make human lexical and sentential concepts both possible in all their variety and also learnable on the basis of some realistic combination of linguistic and nonlinguistic experience?

4   Three models for the description of meaning

The preceding section has used the expression "concept" operationally to mean essentially "a mental representation that can serve as the meaning of a linguistic expression." In the present framework, then, the act of understanding a sentence S—recovering its meaning—is to be regarded as placing S in correspondence with a concept C, which has internal structure derivable from the syntactic structure and lexical items of S. On the basis of C, one can draw inferences—that is, construct further concepts that are logical entailments of C. One can also compare C with other concepts retrieved from memory ("Do I know this already?"; "Is this consistent with what I believe?") and with conceptual structures derived from sensory modalities ("Is this what's going on?"; "Is that what I should be looking for?"). That is, the meaning of the sentence can be evaluated with respect to what one believes and perceives.

The idea that a meaning is a sort of mental representation is, of course, not universally accepted. Perhaps the most prestigious tradition in the study of meaning grows out of Frege's "Sense and Reference" (1972 [1892]), where he very carefully disassociates the "sense" of an expression—what he takes to be an objective, publicly available entity—from the "idea" that a user of the expression carries in his head, which is subjective and variable. Frege's notion of sense underpins the approach to meaning in model-theoretic semantics. This is seen clearly, for instance, in the following quote from David Lewis's foundational paper "General Semantics":

> I distinguish two topics: first, the description of possible languages or grammars as abstract semantic systems whereby symbols are associated with aspects of the world; and second, the description of the psychological and sociological facts whereby a particular one of these abstract semantic systems is the one used by a person or population. Only confusion comes of mixing these two topics. This paper deals almost entirely with the first. (Lewis 1972 [1970], p. 170: Chapter 11)

It is hard to find a clearer statement that the purposes of model-theoretic semantics are different from those of generative linguistics, and that their worldviews are incompatible. To be sure, both generative grammar and model-theoretic semantics treat language as a formal system. But they differ radically in the goals they wish to accomplish through such treatment. The avowed purpose of model-theoretic semantics is to explicate Truth, a relation between language and reality, independent of language users. In turn, the truth-conditions of sentences can be treated as speaker-independent only if both reality *and* the language that describes it are speaker-independent as well. Hence, a truth-conditional semantics in the Tarskian or Davidsonian sense requires a theory of E-language, of language as an abstract artifact extrinsic to speakers.

As stressed in section 2, the purpose of generative grammar has always been to explicate I-language, the principles internalized by speakers that constitute knowledge of a language. A typical statement of generative linguistic theory, say 'Sentence S is grammatical in Language L because of Principle P', is taken to be shorthand for a psychological claim, roughly 'A speaker of Language L treats Sentence S as grammatical because his knowledge of Language L includes Principle P', subject to the usual caveats about attentional and processing limitations. A compatible theory of meaning must therefore concern the principles internalized in the speaker that permit him or her to understand sentences, draw inferences from them, and judge their truth: it must be a theory of I-semantics, not E-semantics. Within a theory of I-semantics, a statement in the Tarskian vein like 'Sentence S in Language L is true if and only if condition C is met' is taken as shorthand for something like 'A speaker of Language L treats Sentence S as true if and only if his construal (or mental representation) of the world meets condition C', and it is subject to similar caveats about attentional and processing limitations. This is the basis of the approach of Conceptual Semantics, in which a level of mental representation called conceptual structure is seen as the form in which speakers encode their construal of the world.

It is sometimes proposed that there is no inherent conflict between the two approaches to semantics. One is about the way the world *is*, and the other is about the way we *grasp* the world. They might lead to altogether different insights—hopefully complementary ones. I see nothing wrong with this conclusion in principle: you go your way, I'll go mine. The difficulty is one of terminological imperialism, as exemplified by Lewis's widely quoted slogan to the effect that the study of "Mentalese"—in effect I-semantics—isn't *really* semantics. Similar difficulties arise in the Introduction to the Forum, in which the philosopher asserts that the study of concepts has nothing to do with psychology. Along with this goes the implication that what the I-semanticist and the psychologist are doing isn't really *anything* worth doing. As I have stressed in section 1, whether it's worth doing cannot be determined until the results are in; as promised, I will present some. I don't care what you call the enterprise; but notice for example that relativistic physics *is* treated as a way of doing physics, not some curious non-enterprise, and it legitimately took over most of the basic terminology of Newtonian physics despite a radical conceptual restructuring. Such, I suggest, is the case in the contrast of E-semantics and I-semantics.

It is also sometimes suggested that my characterization of model-theoretical semantics is unfair. In principle, model-theoretic semantics is neutral between E-semantics and I-semantics; even if Davidson and Lewis designed the theory with E-semantics in mind, we are always free to choose a model that conforms to psychological constraints and thereby to produce a model-theoretic I-semantics. Again I agree—in principle. But to my knowledge, all model-theoretic semantics, other than a few exceptions such as Bach 1986a, has in practice been E-semantics. And, of course, the project of determining a psychologically defensible model theory is pretty much equivalent to the enterprise of Conceptual Semantics—that is, finding out how human beings actually encode their construal of the world. So again, I don't want to make heavy weather of the terminology. If some readers are more comfortable thinking of Conceptual Semantics as a very particular and eccentric brand of model-theoretic semantics, I have no objection. It is the *psychological* claim, not the name of the theory, that is crucial. (See Jackendoff 1983, Chapters 2, 3, 5, and Jackendoff 1987, Chapter 7 for amplifications of these points.)

It is next necessary to differentiate Conceptual Semantics from Fodor's 1975 "Language of Thought" Hypothesis. On the face of it Fodor's position seems closer to mine: his purpose is to understand the character of mind. Unlike the model theorists, he is committed to a combinatorial mental representation in terms of which language users make inferences and formulate responses. Moreover, Fodor stresses that the performance of these tasks must be explained purely by virtue of the form of the representations. There can be no appeal to what the representations "mean." His argument is that the buck has to stop somewhere: if one is to characterize the brain as a computational device, driven by the syntax of internal representations, an appeal to "meaning in the outside world" amounts to an invocation of magic.

So far Fodor's story is altogether compatible with Conceptual Semantics. But now it splits in two directions. On one hand, Fodor 1980 argues for "methodological solipsism"—the idea that the only causal determinants of behavior (including inference) are the formal properties of internal representations. This is again consistent with Conceptual Semantics, in which rules of inference do not reach out from conceptual structures to the "world" but are rather confined to examining conceptual structures themselves.

However, another thread in Fodor's work (seen especially in Fodor 1987) is his insistence on *Intentional Realism*, the idea that the mental representations over which these computations take place still *do* nonetheless have further semantic content—that they are representations of propositions with real-world reference and truth-value. This view allegedly makes contact with Chomsky's notion of Universal Grammar in the following way:

> It is, however, important to the Neocartesian [i.e., Chomskian] story that what is innately represented should constitute a bona fide object of propositional attitudes. . . . Now, the notion of computation is intrinsically connected to such semantic concepts as implication, confirmation, and logical consequence. Specifically, a computation is a transformation of representations which respects these sorts of semantic relations. . . . So, Chomsky's account of language learning is the story of how innate endowment and perceptual experience interact *in virtue of their respective contents.* (Fodor 1983, pp. 4–5; Fodor's italics)

But let us look at the representations of, say, generative phonology. It makes little sense to think of the rules of phonology as propositional; for instance it is strange to say that English speakers know the proposition, *true in the world independent of speakers of English*, that in English syllable-initial voiceless consonants aspirate before stress. This amounts to an appeal to the properties of E-language. In generative phonology as it is conducted by its practitioners, the rule of aspiration is regarded as a principle of internal computation, not a fact about the world. "Such semantical concepts as implication, confirmation, and logical consequence" seem curiously irrelevant. In short, the notion of computation need not have anything to do with "respecting semantic relations," at least in the domains of phonology and syntax.

If one has hesitations about this argument with respect to phonology, we may also consider a slightly more exotic cognitive domain, the understanding of music. As shown in Lerdahl and Jackendoff 1983, the factors that make a piece of music cohere for a listener into something beyond a mere sequence of notes involve complex internal computations over abstract mental representations of the piece. Fodor's insistence on respecting semantic relations seems totally out of place here: these abstract structures are part of mental life, but one would hardly want to make a metaphysical claim about there being something "real" in the world, propositional or otherwise, which they are representations of.

The question at issue, then, is whether conceptual structure is somehow different from phonology, syntax, and music—whether, when we enter the domain of meaning, the rules of the game should be changed, so that propositional content rather than computational form ought to be the focus of inquiry. Fodor's position, as I understand it, is that the generalizations (or laws) of psychology are intentional (that is, concern the propositional content of representations, outside the head), but that the mental mechanisms that instantiate these generalizations are merely formal computations that have no access to propositional content. For Fodor, the fact that these mental computations preserve semantic properties comes from the fact that the formal structures mimic the structure of the (non-mental) content in considerable detail. In fact, Fodor argues for the combinatorial character of mental representations precisely on the grounds that they must mimic what he takes to be the undeniable combinatoriality of propositional content. Put in present terms, his position is that we *grasp* the world the way we do precisely because that is the way the world *is*. (This argument is perhaps clearest in the appendix to Fodor 1987.) What Fodor appears to require, then, is a marriage between the Realism of truth-conditional semantics and the mentalism of generative grammar—that is, a unified theory of E-semantics and I-semantics, mediated by the relation of intentionality, which even to Fodor is mysterious.[1]

Conceptual Semantics, on the other hand, is concerned most directly with the form of the internal mental representations that constitute conceptual structure and with the formal relations between this level and other levels of representation. The theory of conceptual structure is thus taken to be entirely parallel to the theory of syntactic or phonological structure. The computation of inference, like for instance the computation of rhyme in phonology, is a matter internal to the organism.

For Fodor, as for the model theorists, such an inquiry does not count as semantics: he requires a theory of semantics to include a Realist account of truth-conditions and inference. Once again, I don't care too much about terminology. I would prefer that the enterprise be judged on its merits rather than being summarily dismissed because it doesn't address issues that someone calls the True Issues of Semantics. If one would rather call the enterprise logical or conceptual syntax, or the "Syntax of Thought" Hypothesis, that's fine with me. We should be clear, though, that it is in principle as different from "straight" syntax (the grammar of NPs, VPs, etc.) as straight syntax is from phonology.

Given the meager positive empirical results of Fodor's approach, which has been largely devoted to showing what else won't work, I submit that the merits of the Language of Thought Hypothesis over the Syntax of Thought Hypothesis have yet to be demonstrated.

How do the two approaches differ empirically? The difference is that Fodor insists that all combinatorial properties of I-concepts must be mirrored in Reality, while a theory of pure I-semantics is not necessarily subject to that constraint. As will be shown below, there are many structural properties of Conceptual Semantics that make little sense as properties of Reality, but a great deal of sense as properties of mind. I will therefore conclude that Fodor's insistence on Intentional Realism is misguided for the purpose of doing scientific psychology.

(Note that this conclusion is not inconsistent with Fodor's observation, seconded by Dennett 1987, that Intentional Realism is an extremely useful stance for dealing with people in ordinary life. But "folk physics" is a good stance for ordinary life, too. That does not make it a productive constraint for doing scientific physics. So why get mired in "folk psychology" when studying the mind?)

To conclude this section, I should mention the relation of Conceptual Semantics to a program of research called Cognitive Grammar or Cognitive Semantics (e.g., Fauconnier 1984; Langacker 1986; Herskovits 1986; Lakoff 1987). This work, like Conceptual Semantics, is concerned with the mental representation of the world and its relation to language. It shares with Conceptual Semantics a concern with the encoding of spatial concepts and their extension to other conceptual fields (see section 6). Some work in this tradition, especially that of Talmy (1985; 1983; 1988), has provided important insights and analyses to the present framework. Conceptual Semantics differs from Cognitive Grammar, however, in that (1) it is committed to an autonomous level of syntactic representation rather than its abandonment; (2) it is committed to rigorous formalism, insofar as possible, on the grounds that formal treatment is the best way of rendering a theory testable; (3) it makes contact with relevant results in perceptual psychology rather than leaving such relationships tacit; (4) it is committed to exploring issues of learnability and hence to the possibility of a strong innate formal basis for concept acquisition.

5   Organization of language

Next I must spend a little time sketching the relation of the putative level of conceptual structure to language. For concreteness, I will assume an overall organization of the mental information structure involved in language, as diagrammed in (1).

(1)

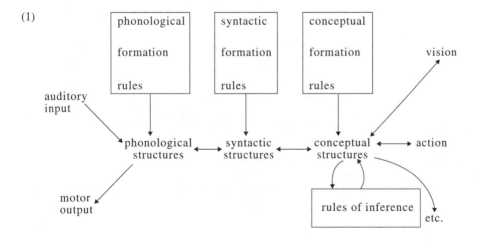

This organization includes three autonomous levels of structure: phonological, syntactic, and conceptual. Each of these has its own characteristic primitives and principles of combination and its own organization into subcomponents, such as segmental phonology, intonation contour, and metrical grid in phonology, and D-structure, S-structure, Phonetic Form (PF), and Logical Form (LF) (or counterparts in other theories) in syntax. Each of the levels is described by a set of *formation rules* that generates the well-formed structures of the level.

The grammar also contains sets of *correspondence rules* that link the levels. The correspondence of phonological structure to syntactic structure is specified by one such set. This is, for instance, the locus of "readjustment rules" such as cliticization. The correspondence of syntactic and conceptual structures is specified by what used to be called "projection rules" (Katz and Fodor 1963), which determine the relation of syntactic structure to meaning.

Example (1) also includes correspondence rules between the linguistic levels and nonlinguistic domains. On one end, there must be a mapping from the acoustic analysis provided by the auditory system into phonological structure; this mapping is the subject matter of acoustic phonetics. There must also be a mapping from phonological structure into motor commands to the vocal tract, the domain of articulatory phonetics. On the other end, there must be mappings between conceptual structure and other forms of mental representation that encode, for instance, the output of the visual faculty and the input to the formulation of action. One such representation will be mentioned briefly in section 7.

Since conceptual structure is the domain of mental representation over which inference can be defined, example (1) also includes a component called "rules of inference," which maps conceptual structures into conceptual structures. As argued in Jackendoff 1983, chapters 5 and 6, I include in this component not only rules of logical inference but also rules of invited inference, pragmatics, and heuristics: whatever differences there may be among these categories of principles, they are all defined over the same level of mental representation. That is, there is no proprietary level of "semantic representation" at which only logical properties of sentences are encoded, with other "pragmatic" properties reserved for a different level.

It should be pointed out that, under the view being laid out here, the level of conceptual structure is not completely language-dependent, since it serves as an interface between linguistic information and information germane to other capacities such as vision and action. I assume, on grounds of evolutionary conservatism, that nonlinguistic organisms—both higher animals and babies—also possess a level of conceptual structure in their mental repertoire, perhaps not as rich as ours, but formally similar in many respects. The difference between us and the beasts is that we have evolved a capacity to process syntactic and phonological structures, as well as the mappings from them to conceptual structure and to the auditory and motor peripheries. These mappings are what permit us a relatively overt realization of conceptual structure—language—that is unavailable to other organisms.

Example (1) as it stands contains no explicit lexical component. Where is the lexicon in this picture? Under the standard view of the lexicon, a lexical item establishes a correspondence between well-formed fragments of phonological, syntactic, and conceptual structure; that is, the lexicon is a part of the correspondence rule component. Thus we can regard each component in example (1) as divided into lexical principles (those that apply within words) and supralexical principles (those that apply to domains larger than the word level). However, the basic alphabet of primitives and principles of combination is shared by the two subcomponents. For instance, Selkirk 1982 has argued that the syntactic part of morphology, or word formation, consists essentially of an extension of the principles of syntax down below the word level. Similarly, in phonology, the lexical and supralexical principles of stress assignment, though different in details, deal in exactly the same kinds of formal entities.

In parallel fashion, we can ask about the relation between the grammar of sentential concepts and the grammar of lexical concepts, both of which are subsumed under the rubric "conceptual formation rules" in example (1). Gruber 1965, Jackendoff 1983, and indeed the generative semanticists (McCawley 1968b; Postal 1970; Lakoff 1970c) argue that the semantic combinations that can be expressed through syntactic phrases can in many cases also be incorporated into lexical conceptual structures. For instance, to the extent that *two times* paraphrases *twice*, or *cause to die* paraphrases *kill*, or *break violently* paraphrases *smash*, or *give away in exchange for money* paraphrases *sell*, the supralexical conceptual structures expressed by the paraphrases must be reproduced internal to unitary lexical items.[2] That is, the grammars of sentential concepts and of lexical concepts interpenetrate in much the same way as do the grammars of, say sentential and lexical stress: they share many of the same primitives and principles of combination, even if they differ in details. In short, the division of the overall grammar into three independent levels linked by correspondence rules is crosscut by a subsidiary division in each component into lexical versus supralexical principles.

6   Feature-based aspects of conceptual structure

Section 3 argued that the central issue of a theory of I-conceptual knowledge ought to be the innate units and principles of organization that underlie human lexical and sentential concepts. I have now presented enough background to be able to sketch out three major subsystems within conceptual structure. The first involves the major category system and argument structure; the second involves the organization of semantic fields; the third involves the conceptualization of boundedness and aggregation.

6.1   Ontological categories and argument structure

Jackendoff 1983, chapters 3 and 4, proposes a basic organization of major conceptual categories. Instead of a division of formal entities into such familiar logical types as constants, variables, predicates, and quantifiers, each of which has nothing in common with the others, it is argued that the major units of conceptual structure are *conceptual constituents*, each of which belongs to one of a small set of major ontological categories (or conceptual "parts of speech") such as Thing, Event, State, Place, Path, Property, and Amount. These are obviously all quite different in the kind of reference they pick out, but formally (algebraically) they have a great deal in common. Here are six points of similarity.

(a) Each major syntactic constituent of a sentence (excluding contentless constituents such as epenthetic *it* and *there*) corresponds to a conceptual constituent in the meaning of the sentence. For example, in *John ran toward the house*, the NPs *John* and *the house* correspond to Thing-constituents, the PP *toward the house* corresponds to a Path-constituent, and the entire sentence corresponds to an Event-constituent.

Note that this correspondence is stated very carefully. As will be seen presently, the converse mapping does not hold. That is, not every conceptual constituent in the meaning of a sentence corresponds to a syntactic constituent, because (for one thing) many conceptual constituents of a sentence's meaning are completely contained within lexical items. In addition, note that the matching is by *constituents*, not by *categories*, because the mapping between conceptual and syntactic categories is many-to-many. For instance, an NP can express a Thing (e.g., the *dog*), an Event (*the war*), or a Property (*redness*); a PP can express a Place (*in the house*), a Path (*to the kitchen*), or a Property (*in luck*); an S can express a State (*Bill is here*) or an Event (*Bill ran away*).

(b) Each conceptual category supports the encoding of units not only on the basis of linguistic input but also on the basis of the visual (or other sensory) environment. For example, (2a) points out a Thing in the environment; (2b) points out a Place; (2c) accompanies the demonstration of an Action; (2d) accompanies the demonstration of a Distance, independent of the object whose length it is:

(2)   a. *That* is a robin.
      b. *There* is your hat.

    c. Can you do *this*?

    d. The fish was *this* long.

    (c) Many of the categories support a type-token distinction. For example, just as there are many individual tokens of the Thing-type expressed by *a hat*, there may be many tokens of the Event-type expressed by *John ate his hat*, and there may be many different individual Places of the Place-type expressed by *over your head*. (Properties and Amounts, however, do not so clearly differentiate tokens and types.)

    (d) Many of the categories support quantification, as seen in (3):

(3)   a. Every dinosaur had a brain. (Things)

      b. Everything you can do, I can do better. (Actions).

      c. Any place you can go, I can go too. (Places)

    (e) Each conceptual category has some realizations in which it is decomposed into a function-argument structure; each argument is, in turn, a conceptual constituent of some major category. The standard notion of 'predicate' is a special case of this, where the superordinate category is a State or Event. For instance, in (4a), which expresses a State, the arguments are *John* (Thing) and *tall* (Property); in (4b), also a State, both arguments are Things; and in (4c), an Event, the arguments are *John* (Thing) and *<PRO> to leave* (Event or Action):[3]

(4)   a. John is tall.

      b. John loves Mary.

      c. John tried to leave.

But in addition a Thing also may have a Thing as argument, as in (5a) or (5b); a Path may have a Thing as argument, as in (6a), or a Place, as in (6b); a Property may have a Thing (7a) or an Event/Action (7b) as argument:

(5)   a. father of the bride

      b. president of the republic

(6)   a. to the house

      b. from under the table

(7)   a. afraid of Harry

      b. ready to leave

    (f) The conceptual structure of a lexical item is an entity with zero or more open argument places. The meanings of the syntactic complements of the lexical item fill in the values of the item's argument places in the meaning of the sentence. For instance, the verb *be* in (4a) expresses a State function whose arguments are found in the subject and predicate adjective positions; *love* in (4b) expresses a State-function whose arguments are found in subject and object positions; *try* in (4c) expresses an Event-function whose arguments are the subject and the complement clause; *father* and *president* in (5) express Thing-functions whose arguments are in the NP complement; *from* in (6b) expresses a Path-function whose argument is a complement PP; *afraid* in (7a) expresses a Property-function whose argument is the complement NP.

    These observations, though slightly tedious, should convey the general picture: though none of the major conceptual categories can be insightfully reduced to the others, they share important formal properties. Thus a basic formation rule for conceptual categories can be stated along the lines in (8):

(8)

$$\text{Entity} \rightarrow \begin{bmatrix} \text{Event}/\text{Thing}/\text{Place}/\ldots \\ \text{Token}/\text{Type} \\ F(<\text{Entity}_1,<\text{Entity}_2,<\text{Entity}_3 >>>) \end{bmatrix}$$

Example (8) decomposes each conceptual constituent into three basic feature complexes, one of which, the argument structure feature, allows for recursion of conceptual structure and hence an infinite class of possible concepts.

In addition, observation (a) above—the fact that major syntactic phrases correspond to major conceptual constituents—can be formalized as a general correspondence rule of the form (9); and observation (f)—the basic correspondence of syntactic and conceptual argument structure— can be formalized as a general correspondence rule of the form (10). (XP stands for any major syntactic constituent; X° stands for any lexical item that occurs with (optional) complements YP and ZP.)

(9)   XP corresponds to Entity

(10) $$\begin{bmatrix} X^\circ \\ \underline{\quad} <\text{YP} <\text{ZP}>> \end{bmatrix} \text{corresponds to} \begin{bmatrix} \text{Entity} \\ F(<\text{E}_1,<\text{E}_2,<\text{E}_3>>) \end{bmatrix}$$

where YP corresponds to E_2, ZP corresponds to E_3, and the subject (if there is one) corresponds to E_1.

The examples in (a)–(f) above show that the syntactic category and the value of the conceptual n–ary feature Thing/Event/Place ... are irrelevant to the general form of these rules. The algebra of conceptual structure and its relation to syntax are best stated cross-categorially.

6.2   Organization of Semantic Fields

A second cross-categorial property of conceptual structure forms a central concern of the "localistic" theory of Gruber 1965 and others. The basic insight of this theory is that the formalism for encoding concepts of spatial location and motion, suitably abstracted, can be generalized to many other semantic fields. The standard evidence for this claim is the fact that many verbs and prepositions appear in two or more semantic fields, forming intuitively related paradigms. Example (11) illustrates some basic cases:

(11)   a. Spatial location and motion
        i. The bird went from the ground to the tree.
        ii. The bird is in the tree.
        iii. Harry kept the bird in the cage.
    b. Possession
        i. The inheritance went to Philip.
        ii. The money is Philip's.
        iii. Susan kept the money.
    c. Ascription of properties
        i. The light went/changed from green to red.
            Harry went from elated to depressed.
        ii. The light is red.
            Harry is depressed.
        iii. Sam kept the crowd happy.

    d. Scheduling of activities
        i. The meeting was changed from Tuesday to Monday.
       ii. The meeting is on Monday.
      iii. Let's keep the trip on Saturday.

Each of these sets contains a verb *go* or *change* (connected with the prepositions *from* and/or *to*), the verb *be*, and the verb *keep*. The *go* sentences each express a change of some sort, and their respective terminal states are described by the corresponding *be* sentences. The *keep* sentences all denote the causation of a state that endures over a period of time. One has the sense, then, that this variety of uses is not accidental.

On the other hand, the generalization of lexical items across semantic fields is by no means totally free. Each word is quite particular about what fields it appears in. For instance, *go* cannot be substituted for *change* in (11d), and *change* cannot be substituted for *go* in (11a). *Travel* occurs as a verb of change only in the spatial field; *donate* only in possessional; *become* only in ascriptional; and *schedule* only in scheduling.

Gruber's Thematic Relations Hypothesis, as adapted in Jackendoff (1972; 1976; 1983, ch. 10), accounts for the paradigms in (11) by claiming that they are each realizations of the basic conceptual paradigm given in (12). (The ontological category variable is notated as a subscript on the brackets; nothing except convenience hangs on this notational choice as opposed to that in (8).)

(12)

    i. $\left[_{\text{Event}}\text{GO}\,([\quad],\ \left[_{\text{Path}}\begin{array}{c}\text{FROM}\,([\quad])\\\text{TO}\,([\quad])\end{array}\right])\right]$

    ii. $\left[_{\text{State}}\text{BE}\,([\quad],[_{\text{Place}}\quad])\right]$

    iii. $\left[_{\text{Event}}\text{STAY}\,([\quad],[_{\text{Place}}\quad])\right]$

The paradigms are distinguished from one another by a *semantic field feature* that designates the field in which the Event or State is defined. In the works cited above, the field feature is notated as a subscript on the function: $\text{GO}_{\text{Spatial}}$ (or, more often, plain GO) vs. GO_{Pass} vs. GO_{Ident} (using Gruber's term Identificational) vs. GO_{Temp}. Again, not much hangs on this particular notation. The point is that at this grain of analysis the four semantic fields have parallel conceptual structure. They differ only in what counts as an entity being in a Place. In the spatial field, a Thing is located spatially; in possessional, a Thing belongs to someone; in ascriptional, a Thing has a property; in scheduling, an Event is located in a time period.

This notation captures the lexical parallelisms in (11) neatly: the different uses of the words *go, change, be, keep, from,* and *to* in (11) are distinguished only by the semantic field feature, despite the radically different sorts of real-world events and states they pick out. On the other hand, the exact values of the field feature that a particular verb or preposition may carry is a lexical fact that must be learned. Thus *be* and *keep* are unrestricted; *go* is marked for spatial, possessional, or ascriptional, and *change* is marked for ascriptional or scheduling. By contrast, *travel, donate, become,* and *schedule* are listed with only a single value of the field feature. Similarly, *from* and *to* are unrestricted, but *across* is only spatial and *during* is only temporal.

Recall that in each paradigm in (11), the *be* sentence expresses the endstate of the *go* sentence. This can be captured in the informally stated inference rule (13), which is independent of semantic field.

(13) At the termination of $[_{\text{Event}}\text{GO}\,([X],\quad [_{\text{Path}}\text{TO}\,([Y])])]$,
     it is the case that $[_{\text{State}}\text{BE}\,([X],\quad [_{\text{Place}}\text{AT}\,([Y])])]$.

A variety of such inference rules appear, in slightly different formalism, in Jackendoff 1976. In particular, it is shown that many so-called implicative properties of verbs follow from generalized forms of inference rules developed to account for verbs of spatial motion and location. Thus inferential properties such as "factive," "implicative," and "semi-factive" need not be stated as arbitrary meaning postulates. This is exactly the sort of explanatory power one wants from a theory of lexical decomposition into conceptual features.

Each semantic field has its own particular inference patterns as well. For instance, in the spatial field, one fundamental principle stipulates that an object cannot be in two disjoint places at once. From this principle plus rule (13), it follows that an object that travels from one place to another is not still in its original position. But in the field of information transfer, this inference does not hold. If Bill transfers information to Harry, by (13) we can infer that Harry ends up having the information. But since information, unlike objects, can be in more than one place at a time, Bill still may have the information, too. Hence rule (13) generalizes from the spatial field to information transfer, but the principle of exclusive location does not. Thus inference rules as well as lexical entries benefit from a featural decomposition of concepts: the Thematic Relations Hypothesis and the use of the semantic field feature permit us to generalize just those aspects that are general, while retaining necessary distinctions.[4]

Notice how this treatment of the paradigms in (11) addresses the issues of learnability discussed in section 3. The claim is that the different concepts expressed by *keep*, for example, are not unrelated: they share the same functional structure and differ only in the semantic field variable. This being the case, it is easier for a child learning English to extend *keep* to a new field than to learn an entirely new word. In addition, the words that cross fields can serve as scaffolding upon which a child can organize new semantic fields of abstract character (for instance scheduling), in turn providing a framework for learning the words in that field that are peculiar to it. Thus the Thematic Relations Hypothesis, motivated by numerous paradigms like (11) in English and many other languages, forms an important component of a mentalistic theory of concepts and how humans can grasp them.

6.3   Aggregation and boundedness

The phenomena discussed so far in this section involve areas where the syntactic category system and the conceptual category system match up fairly well. In a way, the relation between the two systems serves as a partial explication of the categorial and functional properties of syntax: syntax presumably evolved as a means to express conceptual structure, so it is natural to expect that some of the structural properties of concepts would be mirrored in the organization of syntax.

On the other hand, there are other aspects of conceptual structure that display a strong featural character but which are not expressed in so regular a fashion in syntax (at least in English). One such aspect (discussed in Vendler 1967a; Verkuyl 1972; Mourelatos 1981; Talmy 1978; Platzack 1979; Declerck 1979; Dowty 1979; Hinrichs 1985; and Bach 1986b, among others) can be illustrated by the examples in (14):

(14) $\begin{cases} \text{For hours,} \\ \text{Until noon,} \end{cases}$

    a. Bill slept.
    b. the light flashed. [repetition only]
    c. lights flashed.
    d. *Bill ate the hot dog.
    e. Bill ate hot dogs.
    f. *Bill ate some hot dogs.
    g. Bill was eating the hot dog.

h. ?Bill ran into the house. [repetition only]

i. people ran into the house.

j. ?some people ran into the house. [repetition only]

k. Bill ran toward the house.

l. Bill ran into houses.

m. Bill ran into some houses. [repetition only]

n. Bill ran down the road.

o. *Bill ran 5 miles down the road.

   [ok only on reading where 5 miles down the road is where Bill was, not where 5 miles
   down the road is how far he got.]

The question raised by these examples is why prefixing *for hours* or *until noon* should have
such effects: sometimes it leaves a sentence acceptable, sometimes it renders it ungrammatical,
and sometimes it adds a sense of repetition. The essential insight is that *for hours* places a measure on an otherwise temporally unbounded process, and that *until noon* places a temporal boundary on an otherwise temporally unbounded process. *Bill slept*, for instance, inherently expresses
an unbounded process, so it can be felicitously prefixed with these expressions. On the other
hand, *Bill ate the hot dog* expresses a temporally bounded event, so it cannot be further measured or bounded.

In turn, there are two ways in which a sentence can be interpreted as a temporally unbounded
process. One is for the sentence to inherently express a temporally unbounded process, as is the
case in (14a, c, e, g, i, k, l, n). We will return to these cases shortly. The other is for the sentence
to be interpreted as an indefinite repetition of an inherently bounded process, as in (14b, h, j, m).
(*Bill ate the hot dog*, like *Bill died*, is bounded but unrepeatable, so it cannot be interpreted in
this fashion.) This sense of repetition has no syntactic reflex in English, though some languages
such as Hungarian and Finnish have an iterative aspect that does express it.

How should this sense of iteration be encoded in conceptual structure? It would appear most
natural to conceive of it as an operator that maps a single Event into a repeated sequence of individual Events of the same type. Brief consideration suggests that in fact this operator has exactly the same semantic value as the plural marker, which maps individual Things into collections
of Things of the same type. That is, this operator is not formulated specifically in terms of Events,
but should be applicable in cross-categorial fashion to any conceptual entity that admits of individuation. The fact that this operator does not receive consistent expression across syntactic categories should not obscure the essential semantic generalization.

Returning to the inherently unbounded cases, it has often been observed that the bounded/
unbounded (event/process, telic/atelic) distinction is strongly parallel to the count/mass distinction in NPs. An important criterion for the count/mass distinction has to do with the description
of parts of an entity. For instance, a part of *an apple* (count) cannot itself be described as *an
apple*; but any part of a body of *water* (mass) can itself be described as *water* (unless the part
gets too small with respect to its molecular structure). This same criterion applies to the event/
process distinction: a part of *John ate the sandwich* (event) cannot itself be described as *John ate
the sandwich*. By contrast, any part of *John ran toward the house* (process) can itself be described
as *John ran toward the house* (unless the part gets smaller than a single stride). These similarities
suggest that conceptual structure should encode this distinction cross-categorially too, so that
the relevant inference rules do not care whether they are dealing with Things vs. Substances or
Events vs. Processes.

It has also been often observed that plurals behave in many respects like mass nouns, and
that repeated events behave like processes. (Talmy 1978 suggests the term "medium" to encom-
pass them both.) The difference is only that plural nouns and repeated events fix the "grain size"
in terms of the singular individuals making up the unbounded medium, so that decomposition of

the medium into parts is not as arbitrary as it is with substances and processes. Thus the structure of the desired feature system is organized as in (15):

(15)

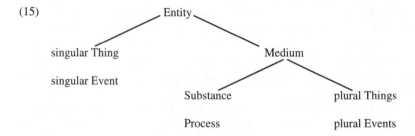

That is, the features that distinguish Things from Events are orthogonal to the features differentiating individuals from media, and within media, homogeneous media from aggregates of individuals.

The examples in (14) provide evidence that Paths also participate in the system shown in (15). For instance, *to the house* is a bounded Path; no parts of it except those including the terminus can be described as *to the house*. By contrast, *toward the house* and *down the road* are unbounded Paths, any part of which can also be described as *toward the house* or *down the road*. *Into houses* describes multiple bounded Paths, one per house. Thus the cross-categorial feature system in (15) extends to yet another major ontological category.

Here is an example that illustrates some of the explanatory power achieved through the system of features in (15): the meaning of the word *end*. For a first approximation, an *end* is a zero-dimensional boundary of an entity conceived of as one-dimensional. So, for the simplest case, the end of a line is a point. A beam is conceived of (as in Marr 1982) as a long axis elaborated by a cross-section. The end of a beam is a point bounding the long axis, elaborated by the same cross-section; this makes it two-dimensional. A table can be said to have an end just in case it can be seen as having a long axis (e.g., it is rectangular or oval but not square or circular); the end is then just the boundary of the long axis elaborated by the short axis. However, in the expected cross-categorial fashion, we can speak of the end of a week (a point bounding a one-dimensional period of time) and the end of a talk (a zero-dimensional State bounding an Event that extends over time).

However, there is an apparent difficulty in this account of *end*. If the end of a talk is a point in time, how can one felicitously say, "I am now giving the end of my talk" or "I am now finishing my talk"? The progressive aspect in these sentences implies the existence of a process taking place over time and therefore seems to attribute a temporal extent to the end.

The answer is provided by looking at the treatment of the boundaries of Things. Consider what is meant by *Bill cut off the end of the ribbon*. Bill cannot have cut off just the geometrical boundary of the ribbon. Rather, the sense of this sentence shows that the notion of end permits an optional elaboration: the end may consist of a part of the object it bounds, extending from the actual boundary into the object some small distance ϵ.

There are other boundary words that *obligatorily* include this sort of elaboration. For instance, a *crust* is a two-dimensional boundary of a three-dimensional volume, elaborated by extending it some distance ϵ into the volume. *Border* carries a stronger implication of such elaboration than does *edge*: consider that the *border of the rug* is liable to include a pattern in the body of the rug, while the *edge of the rug* is more liable to include only the binding.

The claim, then, is that *end* includes such an elaboration as an optional part of its meaning. Going back to the case of Events, I can therefore felicitously say "I am giving the end of my talk" or "I am finishing my talk" if I am within the region that extends backward the permissible distance ϵ from the actual cessation of speech. In other words, the featural machinery of dimensionality and boundaries, with which we characterize Things and the regions of space they occupy, extends over to Events as well. That's why the word *end* is so natural in either context. The main difference in the systems is that Things have a maximum dimensionality of three, while Events have a maximum dimensionality of only one, so that certain distinctions in the Thing system are leveled out or unavailable in the Event system. Only in a theory of conceptual structure that permits this sort of cross-categorial generalization can even the existence of a word like *end* be explained, much less the peculiarities of its use in so many different contexts—and the fact that these peculiarities are evidently learnable. (This subsystem of conceptual structure will be treated in detail in Jackendoff 1991.)

A general conclusion emerges from these three brief case studies. Beneath the surface complexity of natural language concepts lies a highly abstract formal algebraic system that lays out the major parameters of thought. The distinctions in this system are quite sharp and do not appear to be based on experience. Rather, I would claim, they are the machinery available to the human mind to channel the ways in which all experience can be mentally encoded—elements of the Universal Grammar for conceptual structure.

Significantly, the primitives of this system cannot appear in isolation. Rather, they are like phonological features or the quarks of particle physics: they can only be observed in combination, built up into conceptual constituents, and their existence must be inferred from their effects on language and cognition as a whole. This result militates against Fodor's Intentional Realism, in that one should not expect constant counterparts in reality for every aspect of the conceptual system. Roughly speaking, concepthood is a property of conceptual *constituents*, not conceptual *features*.

7   Where traditional features fail

One of the abiding reasons for skepticism about feature-based semantics, even among those who believe in semantic decomposition, is that simple categorical features are clearly inadequate to the full task of conceptual description. These suspicions have been voiced since the earliest days of semantics in generative grammar (Bolinger 1965; Weinreich 1966) and continue to the present day (e.g., Lakoff 1987). This section will briefly mention three of the problems and the forms of enrichment proposed within Conceptual Semantics to deal with them.

7.1   Spatial structure of objects

The first problem has to do with specifying the shapes of objects. For instance, consider the lexical entries for *duck* and *goose*. Both of these presumably carry features to the effect that they are animate, nonhuman, categories of Things, that they are types of birds, perhaps types of waterfowl. But what comes next?—how are they distinguished from one another? One possible factor, which clearly enters into learning the words in the first place, is how ducks and geese *look*, how they differ in appearance. But to encode this difference in binary features, say [± long neck], is patently ridiculous. Similarly, how is a *chair* to be distinguished from a *stool*? Do they differ in a feature [± has-a-back]? What sort of feature is this? It is surely not a primitive. But, if composite, how far down does one have to go to reach primitives—if one can at all? To put a ± sign and a pair of brackets around any old expression simply doesn't make it into a legitimate conceptual feature.

This problem is addressed in Jackendoff 1987 chapter 10, in the context of the connection between the linguistic and visual faculties. In order for an organism to accomplish visual identification and categorization, independent of language, there must be a form of visual representation that encodes geometric and topological properties of physical objects. The most plausible proposal I have encountered for such a representation is the *3D model structure* of Marr 1982. In turn, this structure can be interfaced with conceptual structure via a set of correspondence rules, as suggested in example (1) above. This correspondence effects a translation of visual information into linguistic format, enabling us to talk about what we see.

Marr's approach is interesting because of the way it goes beyond a simple template theory of visual recognition. The 3D model is much more than a "statue in the head." It is an articulated structure that encodes the decomposition of objects into parts, the geometric systems of spatial axes around which objects are organized, and the relations among the parts. Within this framework, it is possible to represent not just single objects in single positions, but ranges of sizes, ranges of angles of attachment of parts, and ranges of detail from coarse- to fine-grained. Thus it is admirably suited to encoding just those geometric aspects of an object's appearance that are an embarrassment to any reasonable feature system.

Jackendoff 1987 suggests, therefore, that the lexical entry for a physical object word includes a 3D model representation in addition to its phonological, syntactic, and conceptual structures. The 3D model, in fact, plays the role sometimes assigned to an "image of a stereotypical instance," except that it is much more highly structured, along the lines suggested by Marr, and it includes parameters of variation among instances. The distinctions between *duck* and *goose* and between *chair* and *stool*, then, can appear in the 3D model instead of conceptual structure. We thereby eliminate the need for a plethora of objectionable conceptual features in favor of a geometric representation with entirely different primitives and principles of combination. It is shown that this natural division of labor is of benefit not only to the theory of the lexicon but also to the theory of visual categorization; I will not repeat the arguments here.

I should add, however, that the use of the 3D model need not pertain just to objects and the nouns that denote them. Marr and Vaina 1982 propose a natural extension of the 3D model to encode action patterns such as throwing and saluting. This can be used to address a parallel problem in the verbal system: how is one to distinguish, say, *running* from *jogging* from *loping*, or *throwing* from *tossing* from *lobbing?* If the lexical entries for these verbs contain a 3D model representation of the action in question, no distinction at all need be made in conceptual structure. The first set of verbs will all simply be treated in conceptual structure as verbs of locomotion, the second set as verbs of propulsion. Thus again we are relieved of the need for otiose feature analyses of such fine-scale distinctions.

7.2   Focal values in a continuous domain

A second area in which a simple feature analysis fails concerns domains with a continuous rather than a discrete range of values. Consider the domain expressed by temperature words (*hot*, *warm*, *tepid*, *cool*, *cold*, etc.) or the domain of color words. One cannot decompose *hot* or *red* exhaustively into discrete features that distinguish them from *cold* and *yellow*, respectively. The proper analysis seems to be that these words have a semantic field feature (Temperature or Color) that picks out a "cognitive space" consisting of a continuous range of values. In the case of Temperature, the space is essentially linear; in the case of Color, it is the familiar three-dimensional color solid (Miller and Johnson-Laird 1976). For a first approximation, each temperature or color word picks out a point in its space, which serves as a focal value for the word.

According to this analysis, a percept is categorized in terms of its relative distance from available focal values. So, for example, a percept whose value in color space is close to focal red is easily categorized as red; a percept whose value lies midway between focal red and focal orange is categorized with less certainty and with more contextual dependence. Thus color categorization is a result of the interaction between the intrinsic structure of the color space—including physiologically determined salient values—and the number and position of color values for which the language has words (Berlin and Kay 1969).

Refinements can be imagined in the structure of such spaces. For example, the field of temperature has both positive and negative directions, so one can ask either *how hot?* or *how cold?* By contrast, the field of size words has only a positive direction from the zero point, so that *how big?* asks a neutral question about size but *how small?* is intended in relation to some contextually understood small standard. I will not pursue such refinements here. The point is that the introduction of continuous "cognitive spaces" in which words pick out focal values is an important enrichment of the expressive power of conceptual structure beyond simple categorical feature systems.

7.3 Preference rule systems

A different challenge to feature systems arises in the treatment of so-called cluster concepts. Consider the following examples:

(16)   a. Bill climbed (up) the mountain.
       b. Bill climbed down the mountain.
       c. The snake climbed (up) the tree.
       d. ?*The snake climbed down the tree.

Climbing appears to involve two independent conceptual conditions: (1) an individual is traveling upward; and (2) the individual is moving with characteristic effortful grasping motions, for which a convenient term is *clambering*. On the most likely interpretation of (16a), both these conditions are met. However, (16b) violates the first condition, and, since snakes can't clamber, (16c) violates the second. If *both* conditions are violated, as in (16d), the action cannot at all be characterized as climbing. Thus neither of the two conditions is necessary, but either is sufficient.

However, the meaning of the word *climb* is not just the disjunction of these two conditions. That would be in effect equivalent to saying that there are two unrelated senses of the word, one having to do with going up, and one having to do with clambering. If this were the correct analysis, we would have the intuition that (16a) is as ambiguous as *Bill went down to the bank*, which may refer equally to a river bank or a savings bank. But in fact we do not. Rather, (16a), which satisfies both conditions at once, is more "stereotypical" climbing. Actions that satisfy only one of the conditions, such as (16b, c), are somewhat more marginal but still perfectly legitimate instances of climbing. In other words, the two conditions combine in the meaning of a single lexical item *climb*, but not according to a standard Boolean conjunction or disjunction. Jackendoff 1983, chapter 8, calls a set of conditions combined in this way a *preference rule system*, and the conditions in the set *preference rules* or *preference conditions*.[5]

A similar paradigm can be displayed for the verb *see*:

(17)   a. Bill saw Harry.
       b. Bill saw a vision of dancing devils.
       c. Bill saw the tree, but he didn't notice it at the time.
       d. *Bill saw a vision of dancing devils, but he didn't notice it at the time.

The two preference conditions for *x sees y* are roughly that (1) x's gaze makes contact with y, and (2) x has a visual experience of y. Stereotypical seeing—that is, veridical seeing—satisfies both these conditions: x makes visual contact with some object and thereby has a visual experience of it. Example (17b) violates condition (1), and (17c) violates condition (2), yet both felicitously use the word *see*. But if both are violated at once, as in (17d), the sentence is extremely odd. Again, we don't want to say that there are two homonymous verbs *see* and hence that (17a) is ambiguous. The solution is to claim that these two conditions form a preference rule system, in which stereotypical seeing satisfies both conditions and less central cases satisfy only one—but either one.[6]

Similar phenomena arise in the lexical entries for nouns that denote functional categories: form and function often are combined in a preference rule system. For instance, a stereotypical *chair* has a stereotypical form (specified by a 3D model) and a standard function (roughly "portable thing for one person to sit on"). Objects with the proper function but the wrong form—say beanbag chairs—are more marginal instances of the category; and so are objects that have the right form but which cannot fulfill the function—say chairs made of newspaper or giant chairs. An object that violates both conditions, say a pile of crumpled newspaper, is by no stretch of imagination a chair. This is precisely the behavior we saw in *climb* and *see*.

A further aspect of preference rule systems is that when one lacks information about the satisfaction of the condition, they are invariably assumed to be satisfied as *default values*. Thus, the reason (16a) and (17a) are interpreted as stereotypical climbing and seeing is that the sentences give no information to the contrary. It is only in the b and c sentences, which *do* give information to the contrary, that a condition is relinquished.

The examples of preference rule systems given here have all involved only a pair of conditions. Systems with a larger number of conditions are likely to exist, but are harder to ferret out and articulate without detailed analysis. A preference rule system with only one condition degenerates to a standard default value. More generally, preference rule systems are capable of accounting for "family resemblance" categories such as Wittgenstein's 1953 well-known example *game*, for Rosch's 1978 "prototypes," and for other cases in which systems of necessary and sufficient conditions have failed because all putative conditions have counterexamples (but not all at once).

Still more broadly, Jackendoff 1983 shows that preference rule systems are an appropriate formalism for a vast range of psychological phenomena, from low-level visual and phonetic perception to high-level operations such as conscious decision-making. The formalism was in fact developed originally to deal with phenomena of musical cognition (Lerdahl and Jackendoff 1983) and was anticipated by the gestalt psychologists in their study of visual perception (Wertheimer 1923). There seems every reason, then, to believe that preference rule systems are a pervasive element of mental computation; we should therefore have no hesitation in adopting them as a legitimate element in a theory of I-concepts. (See Jackendoff 1983 chapters 7 and 8, for extended discussion of preference rule systems, including comparison with systems of necessary and sufficient conditions, prototype theory, and fuzzy set theory.)

To sum up, this section has suggested three ways in which the decomposition of lexical concepts goes beyond simple categorical feature oppositions. These mechanisms conspire to make word meanings far richer than classical categories. Each of them creates a continuum between stereotypical and marginal instances, and each can create fuzziness or vagueness at category boundaries. Moreover, each of them can be motivated on more general cognitive grounds, so we are not multiplying artifices just to save the theory of lexical decomposition. And indeed, they appear collectively to go a long way toward making a suitably expressive theory of word meaning attainable.

8   Lexical composition versus meaning postulates

Section 3 argued from the creativity of lexical concept formation to the position that lexical conceptual structures must be compositional, and that one has an innate "universal grammar of concepts" that enables one to construct new lexical concepts as needed. An important aspect of Fodor's work on the Language of Thought Hypothesis has been to deny lexical compositionality. Not that Fodor has offered any alternative analysis of lexical concepts that deals with any of the problems discussed in the last two sections; indeed his arguments are almost exclusively negative. Nevertheless, for completeness I had better address his concerns.

Fodor's first set of arguments (Fodor 1970; Fodor, Garrett, Walker, and Parkes 1980) builds on the virtual impossibility of giving precise definitions for most words. If definitions are impossible, Fodor argues, there is no reason to believe that words have internal structure. But, in fact, all this observation shows is that if there are principles of lexical conceptual composition, they are not entirely identical with the principles of phrasal conceptual composition. If the principles are not identical, it will often be impossible to build up an expression of conceptual structure phrasally that completely duplicates a lexical concept. In particular, it appears that the nondiscrete elements discussed in section 7 play a role only in lexical semantics and never appear as a result of phrasal combination. Hence phrasal expansions of these aspects of lexical meaning cannot be constructed. Yet they are indubitably compositional. So this argument of Fodor's does not go through; it is founded on a false assumption of complete uniformity of lexical and phrasal composition.

The second set of arguments concerns processing. Fodor's supposition is that if lexical concepts are composite, a more complex word ought to induce a greater processing load and/or take more time to access or process than a less complex word. Finding no experimental evidence for such effects (Fodor, Fodor, and Garrett 1975), Fodor concludes again that lexical items cannot have compositional structure.[7] I see no reason to accept the premise of this argument. As is well known, the acquisition of motor concepts (such as playing a scale on the piano) *speeds up* performance over sequential performance of the constituent parts. Nevertheless, such motor concepts must still be compositional, since in the end the same complex motor patterns must be evoked. It stands to reason, then, that acquisition of a lexical concept might also speed up processing over a syntactically complex paraphrase, without in any way reducing conceptual complexity: a lexical item is "chunked," whereas a phrasal equivalent is not.

Because Fodor can find no system of lexical composition that satisfies his criteria of intentionality and of decomposition into necessary and sufficient conditions (both of which are abandoned in Conceptual Semantics), he decides that the enterprise is impossible and that lexical concepts must in fact be indissoluble monads. He recognizes two difficulties in this position having to do with inference and acquisition, and he offers answers. Let me take these up in turn.

The first issue is how inference can be driven by lexical concepts with no internal structure. If one is dealing with inferences such as $(P \& Q) \rightarrow P$, as Fodor does in most of his discussion, there is little problem, assuming principles of standard logic. But for inferences that involve nonlogical lexical items, such as *John forced Harry to leave* → *Harry left* or *Sue approached the house* → *Sue got closer to the house*, there can be no general principles. Rather, each lexical item must be accompanied by its own specific meaning postulates that determine the entailments of sentences it occurs in. This is the solution Fodor advocates, though he does not propose how it is to be accomplished except perhaps in the most trivial of cases, such as *Rover is a dog* → *Rover is an animal.*

The trouble with such an approach, even if it can succeed observationally, is that it denies the possibility of generalizing among the inferential properties of different lexical items. Each item is a world unto itself. Thus, for instance, consider the entailment relationship between the members of causative-noncausative pairs such as those in (18):

(18)   a. x killed y → y died

     b. x lifted y → y rose

     c. x gave z to y → y received z

     d. x persuaded y that P → y came to believe that P

In a meaning-postulate theory, these inferences are totally unrelated. Intuitively, though, they are all instances of a schema stated roughly as (19), where E is an Event:

(19)   x cause E to occur $\rightarrow$ E occur

In order to invoke a general schema like (19), the left-hand verbs in (18) must have meaning postulates like (20), in which the bracketed expressions are Events:

(20)   a. x kill y $\rightarrow$ x cause [y die]
       b. x lift y $\rightarrow$ x cause [y rise]
       c. x give z to y $\rightarrow$ x cause [y receive z]
       d. x persuade y that P $\rightarrow$ x cause [y come to believe that P]

But this is a notational variant of the analysis of causatives in a lexical decomposition theory: it claims that there is an element *cause* which (1) is mentioned in the analysis (here, the lexical meaning postulates) of many lexical items and (2) gives access to more general-purpose rules of inference.

I suggest that, for fans of meaning postulates, lexical decomposition can be regarded systematically in this light: each element in a lexical decomposition can be regarded as that item's access to more general-purpose rules of inference. The problem of lexical decomposition, then, is to find a vocabulary for decomposition that permits the linguistically significant generalizations of inference patterns to be captured formally in terms of schemas like (19) and rule (13) in section 6.2. (See Jackendoff 1976 for a range of such rules of inference.)

I conclude therefore that a meaning postulate approach to inference either misses all generalizations across inferential properties of lexical items or else is essentially equivalent to a decomposition theory. Thus Fodor has correctly identified a problem for his approach but has proposed a nonsolution.

The second difficulty Fodor sees for noncompositional lexical concepts is how one could possibly acquire them. In any computational theory, "learning" can consist only of creating novel combinations of primitives already innately available. This is one of the fundamental arguments of Fodor 1975, and one that I accept unconditionally. However, since for Fodor all lexical concepts are primitive, they cannot be learned as combinations of primitive vocabulary. It follows that all lexical concepts must be innate, including such exotica as *telephone, spumoni, funicular,* and *soffit,* a conclusion that strains credulity but which Fodor evidently embraces.

Notice how Fodor's position is different from saying that all lexical concepts must be within the innate expressive power of the grammar of conceptual structure, as advocated here. The difference is that in the present approach it is the *potential* of an infinite number of lexical concepts that is inherent in the grammar of conceptual structure—just as the potential for the syntactic structures of all human languages is inherent in Universal Grammar; lexical acquisition then requires constructing a particular lexical concept and associating it with a syntactic and phonological structure.

Fodor notes, of course, that not every speaker has a phonological realization of every lexical concept. Since his notion of "realization" cannot include learning, he advocates that somehow the attachment of an innate lexical concept to a phonological structure is "triggered" by relevant experience, perhaps by analogy with the way parameter settings in syntax are said to be triggered. However, the analogy is less than convincing. The setting of syntactic parameters is determined within a highly articulated theory of syntactic structure, where there is a limited number of choices for the setting. Fodor's proposed triggering of lexical concepts takes place in a domain where there is by hypothesis *no* relevant structure, and where the choices are grossly underdetermined. As far as I know, then, Fodor has offered no account of lexical concept realization other than a suggestive name. By contrast, real studies of language acquisition have benefited from decompositional theories of lexical concepts (e.g., Landau and Gleitman 1985; Pinker 1989), so the decomposition theory has empirical results on its side in this area as well.

An especially unpleasant consequence of Fodor's position is that, given the finiteness of the brain, there can be only a finite number of possible lexical concepts. This seems highly implausible, since one can coin new names for arbitrary new types of objects and actions ("This is a glarf; now watch me snarf it"), and we have no sense that we will someday run out of names for things. More pointedly, the number of potential category concepts is at least as large as the number of concepts for individuals (tokens), since for every individual X one can form a category of 'things just like X' and give it a monomorphemic name. It is hard to believe that nature has equipped us with an ability to recognize individual things in the world that is limited to a finite number. So far as I know, Fodor has not addressed this objection. (See Jackendoff 1983, sec. 5.2, for a stronger version of this argument.)

From these considerations I conclude that Fodor's theory of lexical concepts cannot deal at all with the creativity of concept formation and with concept acquisition. Nor can any other theory that relies on monadic predicates linked by meaning postulates. By contrast, a compositional theory in principle offers solutions parallel to those for the creativity and acquisition of syntax.

9   Ending

So what is a concept? I have shown here that for the purpose of understanding the mind, the apposite focus of inquiry is the notion of I-concept, a species of mental information structure. The program of Conceptual Semantics provides a theoretical realization of this notion that unifies it in many ways with a mentalistic theory of the language faculty and with the theories of perception, cognition, and learning. In particular, I have identified the notion of *I-concept* with the formal notion of *conceptual constituent* as developed in Conceptual Semantics. Furthermore, I have sketched a number of the major elements of the internal structure of concepts, showing how the approach accounts for various basic phenomena in the semantics of natural language, and how the approach meets various well-known objections to theories of lexical decomposition.

In evaluating this approach, I think two things must be borne in mind. First, It does not address what are taken to be some of the standard hurdles for a theory of concepts—for example, Putnam's Twin Earth problem. What must be asked with respect to such problems, though, is whether they are relevant at all to a theory of I-concepts, or whether they are germane only to the theory of E-concepts, as I believe is the case with the Twin Earth problem. If they are problems only for E-conceptual theory, they play no role in evaluating the present approach.

Second, what I find appealing about the present approach is that it leads one into problems of richer and richer articulation: What are the ontological categories, and do they themselves have internal structure? What sorts of fundamental functions are there that create Events, States, Places, and Paths? How are various semantic fields alike in structure, and how do they diverge? How do nondiscrete features interact with each other in phrasal combination? What are the conceptual primitives underlying social cognition and "folk psychology"? How are conceptual systems learnable? And so forth. The fact that Conceptual Semantics begins to provide a formal vocabulary in which such questions can be couched suggests to me that, despite its being at odds with most of the recent philosophical tradition, it is a fruitful framework in which to conduct scientific inquiry.

Notes

Much of this paper is excerpted from my monograph *Semantic Structures* (1990). The title was selected with apologies to Warren McCulloch. I am grateful to Noam Chomsky, John Macnamara, and Jerry Fodor for comments on an earlier version of the paper. I do not, however, intend to imply by this that they endorse my approach; in particular, Fodor doesn't believe a word of it. This research was supported in part by National Science Foundation Grant IST 84-20073 to Brandeis University.

1. My interpretation here is confirmed by Dennett's (1987, p. 288) revealing remarks on Fodor.

2. Generative Semantics used this observation as motivation for assimilating semantics to syntactic principles. The central program of the theory was to reduce all semantic compositionality to syntax. As more and more was discovered about semantic structure, it became clear that this program was not feasible. For at least some Generative Semanticists, the conclusion was that syntax should be abandoned altogether. As seen in example (1), the approach here is to retain syntax for its proper traditional purposes, but to invest semantic expressivity in a different component with appropriate expressive power: conceptual structure.

3. A point of notation: I will use angle brackets < > to enclose an optional constituent in a formal expression, the traditional parentheses being reserved to notate arguments of a function.

4. See Jackendoff (1983), *Semantics and Cognition*, sections 10.3–5 for further discussion of the Thematic Relations Hypothesis, in particular how it is different from a theory of "metaphor" à la Lakoff and Johnson 1980, and why it is justification for the approach of Conceptual Semantics as opposed to model-theoretic (E-)semantics. These sections also implicitly answer Dowty's 1989 charge that the "metaphorical extension" of thematic relations to nonspatial fields is incoherent; basically, Dowty is looking for an explication of thematic relations based on E-semantics, and the generalization of thematic relations probably only makes sense in terms of I-semantics.

5. This analysis of *climb* was to my knowledge first proposed by Fillmore 1982; a formal treatment in terms of preference rules appears in Jackendoff 1985.

6. This analysis of *see* is adapted from Miller and Johnson-Laird 1976 and appears in more detail in Jackendoff 1983, chapter 8.

7. Actually, he finds evidence but disregards it: see Jackendoff 1983, pp. 125–127 and p. 256, note 8.

17

GILLES FAUCONNIER

Mental Spaces, Language Modalities, and Conceptual Integration

In working on matters related to language over the years, my greatest surprise has been to find out how little of the rich meanings we construct is explicitly contained in the forms of language itself. I had taken it for granted, at first, that languages were essentially coding systems for semantic relations, and that sentences, when appropriately associated with "natural" pragmatic specifications, would yield full meanings. Quite interestingly, this is not the way language works, nor is it the way that meaning is constructed. Rather, language, along with other aspects of expression and contextual framing, serves as a powerful means of prompting dynamic on-line constructions of meaning that go far beyond anything explicitly provided by the lexical and grammatical forms. This is not a matter of vagueness or ambiguity; it is in the very nature of our systems of thought. But grammar, in this scheme, is not to be disdained, for although it does not provide the landscape or the means of moving through it, it does show us the way. It guides our elaborate conceptual work with an admirable economy of overt indications, and an impressive reliability in moving us along conceptual paths.

Mental spaces are part of this story. They organize the processes that take place behind the scenes as we think and talk. They proliferate in the unfolding of discourse, map onto each other in intricate ways, and provide abstract mental structure for shifting of anchoring, viewpoint, and focus, allowing us to direct our attention at any time onto very partial and simple structures, while maintaining an elaborate web of connections in working memory, and in long-term memory. We are not conscious of these processes. What we are conscious of, to a high degree, is language form on the one hand and experiencing "meaning" on the other. The effect is magical; as soon as we have form, we also have meaning, with no awareness of the intervening cognition. Introspectively, our experience in this regard is analogous to perception—we see an object because it is there, we understand a sentence instantly because it "has" that meaning. This remarkable and invisible efficiency of our meaning-assigning capacities drives our folk theories about language, which conflate form and meaning, just as folk theories about the world conflate existence and perception.

Gilles Fauconnier (1998) Mental spaces, language modalities, and conceptual integration. In Michael Tomasello (ed.), *The New Psychology of Language*, 251–277. Reprinted by permission of Lawrence Erlbaum Publishers.

The technical description of mental space phenomena is developed in a number of publications.[1] I would like to attempt, in this chapter, to give a more informal view of the phenomena, their complexity, and their importance for psychologists interested in language and thought.

An example: Connectors and access paths

Consider the simple statement *Max thought the winner received $100*. Perhaps the most obvious way to understand this is to assume that there was a contest, that prizes were given out, that one person won the contest and received a prize, and that Max, who was aware of all this, believed that prize to have been $100. But the statement by itself contains none of this. It just fits a plausible scenario, which our background knowledge makes available. We shall see that it also fits many other scenarios, some of which might be more appropriate in some contexts, and some of which are extremely implausible. What exactly then is the sentence telling us?

An important part of what the language form is doing is prompting us to set up mental spaces, elements, and connections between them. The form provides key indications about the mental process in which we need to engage, but it is also deeply underspecified, which accounts for the multiplicity of scenarios that it may successfully fit. An interesting challenge for cognitive science at large is to understand how this underspecification can be resolved, how and why in certain situations certain mental space configurations are unconsciously chosen over others, and how the understander converges on specific appropriate scenarios and connection patterns.

Mental spaces are small conceptual packets constructed as we think and talk, for purposes of local understanding and action. They are very partial assemblies containing elements, and structured by frames and cognitive models. They are interconnected and can be modified as thought and discourse unfold.

In our example, two mental spaces are set up.[2] One is the base space, B, the initial space with partial structure corresponding to what has already been introduced at that point in the discourse, or what may be introduced freely because it is pragmatically available in the situation. Another mental space, M, subordinate to this one will contain partial structure corresponding to 'what Max thinks'. It is structured by the form "_____*received $100*" (the subordinate complement clause of *thought*). That form evokes a general frame <x receive y>, of which we may know a great number of more specific instances (receive money, a shock, a letter, guests, etc.). The expression *Max thought* is called a space builder, because it explicitly sets up the second mental space. *Max* and *the winner* are noun phrases and will provide access to elements in the spaces. This happens as follows: The noun phrase is a name or description that either fits some already established element in some space, or introduces a new element in some space. That element, in turn, may provide access to another element, through a cognitive connection (called a connector), as we shall illustrate and explain. Elements are conceived of as high-order mental entities (like nodes in Shastri's models[3]). They may or may not refer to objects in the world. In our example, the name *Max* accesses an element *a* in B, the base space (which intuitively might correspond to a real or fictive person called Max). The description *the winner* accesses an element *w* that we call a role, and is assumed to belong to a general frame of winning (*w* wins), and also to a more specific instance of that frame appropriate for the given context (winning a particular race, lottery, game, etc.). Roles can have values, and a role element can always access another element that is the value of that role. So we can say *The winner will get $100*, without pointing to any particular individual. This is the role interpretation. Or we can say *The winner is bald*, where being bald is a property of the individual who happened to win, not a condition for getting the prize. This is the value interpretation. Roles, then, are linked cognitively to their values by a role-value connector.

The two mental spaces B and M are connected. There can be counterparts of elements of B in M. For example, if we said *Max thinks _he_ will win*, intending the pronoun *he* to refer back to Max, then space B would contain *a* (for Max) and space M (*Max thinks_____*) would contain a counterpart *a'* of *a*. In space M, a relation equivalent to '*a*' wins' would be satisfied, whereas the same relation would not necessarily be satisfied in the base B for *a* (the counterpart of *a'*). It is convenient to use mental space diagrams such as that shown in Fig. 17.1 to represent this evolving structure.

An important principle defines a general procedure for accessing elements:

ACCESS PRINCIPLE

If two elements *a* and *a'* are linked by a connector *F* [*a'* = *F*(*a*)] then element *a'* can be identified by naming, describing, or pointing to, its counterpart *a*.

This very general principle applies to all types of connectors across and within mental spaces (identity, analogy, metaphor, metonymy, role/value). A simple example of its application would be *Max thinks Harry's name is Joe*. An element *e* associated with the name *Harry* is set up in the base. Its counterpart *e'* in M satisfies <*e'* named *Joe*>. And *e'* is accessed by means of its counterpart *e* in the base, using the name *Harry* associated with *e*. In other words, even though *Harry* is the appropriate name in one space, it can be used to access the corresponding element in another space, where another name is appropriate.

Returning now to the original example, let's see what the accessing possibilities might be. Suppose first that the access principle does not apply at all. Then the description *the winner* must identify a role *w* directly in space M. The structure added to M by the sentence is <*w* receive $100>. This is a pure role interpretation within space M. It does not access any corresponding value for that role. Therefore, the interpretation is that Max thought there was a contest, and that he thought it was a feature of that contest to award $100 to whoever wins. This accessing strategy is noncommittal as to whether the speaker also assumes there was such a contest, and as to whether an actual winner was ever selected, or as to whether Max thinks that a winner was selected. The sentence under this strategy would be appropriate in a variety of contexts. For example, minidiscourses like the following could include the above strategy:

The Boston marathon will take place next week. Max thought the winner received $100, but it turns out there won't be any prize money.

My friends were under the impression that I was running a lottery in my garage. Max thought the winner received $100. But they were all wrong, there was no lottery.

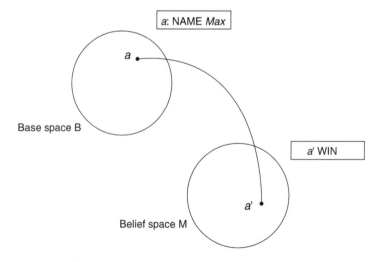

FIGURE 17.1 Mental space diagram

Suppose now that the accessing principle operates, but only within the subordinate space M, linking the role "winner" to a value of that role, b. As before, Max believes that there was a contest, and moreover that somebody won and he has additional beliefs about the person whom he assumes won. The structure in M is now $<b$ receive $100>$. Although a likely default is that the $100 was prize money, this is no longer imposed. Max may believe that something else happened, causing the person who won to receive $100 independently. In plain English, this is illustrated most distinctly by a situation in which (according to the speaker) Max believes (perhaps incorrectly) that Susan won a race, and that she also independently got $100 for the used car that she was selling.

In the two accessing possibilities just considered, a word (*winner*) simply evokes a script within a single space. But the access principle may also operate across spaces. The speaker may have a particular contest in mind, for which there is a role *winner*, set up as an element w in the base B. That role can have a value a (for example, Harry) with a counterpart a' in M. The access principle allows *the winner* to access w, and then its value a, and finally the counterpart of a, element a' in the subordinate space M. The structure set up in M is $<a'$ receive $100>$. The interpretation is that the speaker presents Harry as the winner, and says that Max thought Harry received $100. This is compatible with Max knowing nothing about the contest, or believing that someone other than Harry won, and that Harry got the $100 for selling the used car, or as a consolation prize in the contest.

Other accessing paths are available for this simple sentence, if counterpart roles are considered, or if the extra space introduced by the past tense is taken into account, or if other spaces are accessible at that point in the discourse to provide counterparts. Typically, an understander does not have to consider all possibilities. The intended path will be favored by the space configuration in the discourse at the point when the statement is made. We might already have the role *winner* in space B, or in space M but not B. We might already have different values in M and B for the "same" role (w and its counterpart w'), and so on. In other cases, of course, the understander will lack sufficient information, and may have to revise a space configuration, or may simply misunderstand a speaker's intent.

Our example had a subordinate space corresponding to "belief." There are many other kinds of spaces, but they all share these complex accessing possibilities. For instance, time expressions are space builders and set up new spaces in discourse. Consider (as part of a larger discourse) *In 1968, the winner received $100.* As before, we have a base B and a subordinate space M, corresponding to 1968, set up by the space builder *In 1968.* And as before, the noun phrase *the winner* can access a role in M, or the counterpart role in M of a role in B, or the counterpart in M of a value in B, or a value of a role in M. Situations that fit these respective strategies might be:

- There was a certain type of game in 1968 (no longer played today) in which you got $100 for winning.
- There is a certain sports competition, say the Boston marathon, which exists today (role w in space B) and also existed in 1968 (counterpart role w' in space M). In 1968 (as opposed to today), whoever won got $100.
- The winner of the chess championship held today is Susan; back in 1968, in unrelated circumstances (e.g., selling her used car), Susan received $100.
- The winner back in 1968 of the contest we are talking about was Harry, and that year, Harry received $100 (perhaps for selling his used car).

The access paths available in this example involving time (1968) are exactly the same as the access paths in the previous example involving belief. Even though time and belief are conceptually quite different, they give rise, at the level of discourse management considered here, to the same mental space configurations. More generally, we find that mental spaces are set up for a wide variety of conceptual domains that include time, belief, wishes, plays, movies, pictures, possibility, necessity, hypotheticals and counterfactuals, locatives, and reality. The connectors, the access principle, the role/value distinctions work uniformly across this broad range of cases.

The choice of an access path and of particular connectors is underspecified (or sometimes not specified at all) by the language forms. This is not vagueness, however. A speaker has a particular path in mind, and it must be recovered by the understander. Paths can be forced by elaboration. For instance, in our previous example case, one might have said:

> In 1968, the winner received $100, but Harry, although he won, only got $50, because he was fined for yelling at the umpire.

This will force the role reading inside space M: The rules of the game at the time were that the winner got $100. The rest of the statement is about the particular individual who won, and the fact that *he* only got $50. This could also have been expressed using a role/value link: *That year, the winner only got $50, because he was fined for yelling at the umpire.*

Such examples illustrate (very partially) the kinds of accessing strategies that may be available and that may have to be reconstructed in understanding what is meant. An important feature of such constructions from a psychological and processing point of view is that in many cases, the access paths will collapse, because counterparts in the relevant spaces do not differ from each other. This is in fact the default assumption that we typically make in the absence of explicit information to the contrary. We call this default principle "optimization" of spaces. So, for example, using our *winner* example once more, *Max thought the winner received $100*, if spaces B and M are identically structured in terms of background assumptions and connections (existence and nature of the contest, identity of the winner, focus on the nature of the prize), there will no longer be any difference between the interpretations provided by the connecting paths. The role *winner* and its value (say Harry) will be the same in both spaces, and the import of the statement, with any connecting path, will be the same. It will be about the prize amount that Harry, qua winner, received in the contest. Notice that this is in fact the interpretation that first came to mind when we saw the sentence presented as a statement in isolation. Because there had been no prior discourse structure set up, we directly made the most simple (i.e., optimized) default assumptions and obtained a sensible interpretation. The hidden assumption we made was that the two spaces (base and belief) had matching structure. In addition, we completed the resulting configuration by means of the most obvious available background scenario (contest with prize money) that would fit <winner> and <____receive $100>.

However, as soon as a sentence is part of extended discourse, it will be prompting strategies *within* the mental space configuration already set up at the time when that sentence comes into the discourse. Explicit links and structures present *at that time* in the meaning-building process will constrain the construction of accessing paths and the imposition of scenarios. In particular, such existing discourse connections may prevent optimization, default strategies, or the adoption of default scenarios.

Crucially, then, the apparently simple or prototypical cases are only special (default) instances of the general space-building operations. The drawback of studying sentences in isolation (as a linguist or as a psycholinguist) is that only the defaults will emerge. Those defaults, far from helping us understand the general strategies, actually occlude them from the observer by effectively conflating them.

Modality: The case of ASL

Spoken languages offer considerable evidence for mental space organization. But interestingly, independent evidence is also available from sign languages such as ASL, which operate in a different modality, visual-gestural rather than oral-auditory. Van Hoek (1996), Liddell (1995; 1996), and Poulin (1996) are among those who very successfully pursued an approach initiated by Richard Lacy in unpublished work in the late 1970s. Their research provided extensive evidence for mental space constructions in ASL. As Liddell demonstrated, sign languages additionally make use of grounded mental spaces in their grammars by taking advantage of the spatial modality.

The clearest example of this is the signing space set up by signers in order to perform various referential and conceptual operations. As Scott Liddell (1996) wrote:

> Sign languages are well known for their ability to create, as part of the most ordinary discourse, elaborate conceptual representations in the space in front of the signer. Because of the importance of space in ordinary signed discourse, signed languages have come to be structured in ways which take advantage of those spatial representations. Pronouns and some types of verbs can be produced at specific locations in space or directed toward specific areas of space to produce distinctive meanings. Signs of this type can also be directed toward things that are physically present, including the signer, the addressee, other participants, and other entities. . . . The linguistic uniqueness of the ability to make semantic distinctions by producing signs toward an apparently unlimited number of locations is beyond question. (p. 145)

The physical signing space with referential loci that one can point to serves to ground a corresponding mental space in which elements are being introduced and structured. Subspaces can then be set up with overt counterpart structure analogous to the mental space connections described earlier for our English example. Strikingly, the access principle operates transparently in such cases. As Karen Van Hoek showed, one can point to loci in order to access the counterparts in some space of the elements corresponding to those loci. The choice of accessing strategies is particularly interesting, because it depends on subtle distinctions having to do with focus, viewpoint, and the ultimate goals of the conversational exchange. Figure 17.2 is an example from Van Hoek's work. The notation is explained below the transcription.

In this short piece of discourse, two different loci are set up in the signing space for the same individual (the beautiful friend). One locus is to the left of the signer—

and corresponds to present time and to the Paris location. The other locus, to the right of the speaker—

corresponds to past time, with location in Texas. In almost all of the discourse, the present/Paris locus is used to access "the friend," except in the part corresponding to "I knew that she would be ugly all her life," where the point of view shifts to the past, and the other locus (past/Texas) is used. Then it shifts back to present time, and the present locus ("I see, she's beautiful, . . ."). Immediately after this passage, the signer was asked more about his memories and went on with the discourse shown in Figure 17.3, which shifted viewpoint and focus back to the past, and now accessed the same individual (the beautiful friend) from the past locus (to the right of the signer).

With examples like these and many others, Van Hoek showed that, just like in our 1968 example, the elements in one mental space may be accessed from the referential locus in the signing space appropriate for that particular mental space (e.g., past), or from a locus for its counterpart in some higher space (e.g., present/Base). The spatial modality allows the spaces to be grounded: One can actually point or direct other signs toward one or the other referential locus, as one would in

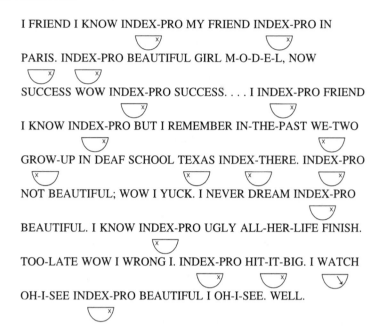

I FRIEND I KNOW INDEX-PRO MY FRIEND INDEX-PRO IN

PARIS. INDEX-PRO BEAUTIFUL GIRL M-O-D-E-L, NOW

SUCCESS WOW INDEX-PRO SUCCESS. . . . I INDEX-PRO FRIEND

I KNOW INDEX-PRO BUT I REMEMBER IN-THE-PAST WE-TWO

GROW-UP IN DEAF SCHOOL TEXAS INDEX-THERE. INDEX-PRO

NOT BEAUTIFUL; WOW I YUCK. I NEVER DREAM INDEX-PRO

BEAUTIFUL. I KNOW INDEX-PRO UGLY ALL-HER-LIFE FINISH.

TOO-LATE WOW I WRONG I. INDEX-PRO HIT-IT-BIG. I WATCH

OH-I-SEE INDEX-PRO BEAUTIFUL I OH-I-SEE. WELL.

'My friend, I know her—my friend, she's in Paris. She's a beautiful
girl, a model now, and wow is she successful. . . . I—she's a friend, I
know her, but I remember in the past, we grew up together in the deaf
school in Texas. She wasn't beautiful; I would think, "Yuck." I never
dreamed she would become beautiful. I knew she would be ugly all her
life. Too late I realized I was wrong. She hit it big. I look at her and I
think, "Oh, I see, she's beautiful, I see. . . . Well . . ."

The notation used for ASL examples is as follows: ASL signs are represented
by Enlgish glosses; where more than one word is needed to gloss a single
sign, the glosses are joined by hyphens. Some of the glosses have small
semicircles under them, representing the space in front of the signer. Arrows
represent the direction of movement for a sign which is articulated with a
path movement; Xs represent the space in which a stationary sign is articulated. The third-person pronoun and the sign meaning 'there' are articulated
almost identically, as both consist of a pointing gesture. They are frequently
distinguished by differences in palm orientation, but in some contexts they
are phonologically identical.

FIGURE 17.2 ASL discourse

pointing deictically at relevant objects, physically present in the context. Liddell (1995; 1996) showed
how the manipulation of such grounded spaces (token space, surrogate space, and real space) is
incorporated into the grammar of ASL to yield intricate reference mechanisms. Poulin (1996) showed
how such spaces can be shifted to reflect changes in viewpoint or epistemic stance. This is typically accomplished physically by body shifts, and repositioning, as shown in Fig. 17.4. In A, the
two referents *i* and *j* are set up as loci in the signing space in front of the signer. In B, there is a body
shift to the right, and the signer identifies with referent *i* (taking the viewpoint of *i* so to speak). In
C, there is a body shift to the left, and the signer now identifies with the other referent, *j*.

I REMEMBER IN-THE-PAST WE-TWO IN SCHOOL INDEX-THERE

TEXAS. I AWFUL I PICK-ON INDEX-PRO THROW M-U-D WOW

TEND CALL INDEX-PRO P-I-Z-Z-A FACE AWFUL WOW TRUE.

INDEX-PRO CRY. I LOOK, FRIEND, BUT I QUOTE WE-TWO

FRIEND YES BUT I NEVER THINK INDEX-PRO BEAUTIFUL. I

LOOK QUOTE TOO-LATE INDEX-PRO NEVER MARRY, ETC.

NOW TRANSFORM. I LOOK WOW INDEX-PRO BEAUTIFUL

WOW.

'I remember in the past, we were in school in Texas. I was awful, I
picked on her, I threw mud at her, wow, I used to call her pizza-face,
really awful. She would cry. I would look at her—we were kind of
friends, but I never thought she would be beautiful. I would always look
at her like "It's too late for her, she'll never marry," and so on. Now
she's transformed. I look at her and wow, she's beautiful.'

FIGURE 17.3 ASL discourse

Liddell (1996) showed in great detail the link between such referential processes incorporated into ASL grammar, and general linguistic and nonlinguistic mental space building and
grounding.

The relevant language universals here are the modality-independent principles of connections and access across mental spaces. The modality-specific universals are the ways in which
these mental configurations can be indicated through language (spoken or signed). In both spoken
and signed languages, we find grammatical devices for building spaces (adverbials, subject-verb
combinations, conjunctions, etc.); in spoken language pronominal systems and other anaphoric
devices code linearly the construction or reactivation of mental space elements. In sign language,
the same effect is achieved by constructing grounded spaces, which take advantage of the spatial
modality.

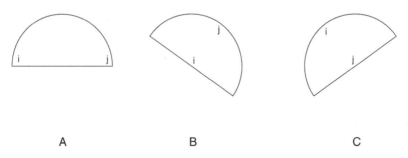

A   B   C

FIGURE 17.4 Use of space and referential shift

Tense and mood

The spaces we have been talking about are set up dynamically throughout an ongoing discourse, on the basis of linguistic and nonlinguistic clues and information. The general scheme is one of new spaces built relative to existing ones, as shown in Fig. 17.5.

A piece of discourse will start with a base B. Space M_1 is then set up subordinate to B, then space M_{11}, subordinate to M_1, and so on. Returning to the base B, one can open space M_2, then M_{21}, and so forth, then return to B a number of times, opening spaces M_i, and daughter spaces M_{ij}, M_{ijk}, and so on.

At any given stage of the discourse, one of the spaces is a *base* for the system, and one of the spaces (possibly the same one) is in *focus*. Construction at the next stage will be relative either to the base space or to the focus space.[4] The discourse moves through the lattice of spaces; viewpoint and focus shift as we go from one space to the next. But at any point, the base space remains accessible as a possible starting point for another construction.

Dinsmore (1991) and Cutrer (1994) showed that a major function of tense in language is to establish local time-ordering relations between neighboring mental spaces, and to keep track of viewpoint and focus shifts. Cutrer (1994) developed a sophisticated set of principles for mental space connections guided by tense, and explained thereby many mysterious features of the ways in which we construct time and viewpoint organization with language. We cannot, here, go into the mechanics of tense and time, but the following example, borrowed from Fauconnier (1997) helps to give an informal idea of what is going on.

The example is a very short piece of discourse:

> Max is 23. He has lived abroad. In 1990, he lived in Rome. In 1991 he would move to
> Venice. He would then have lived a year in Rome. (p. 73)

The space-building dynamics associated with the production and/or understanding of this ministory run as follows:

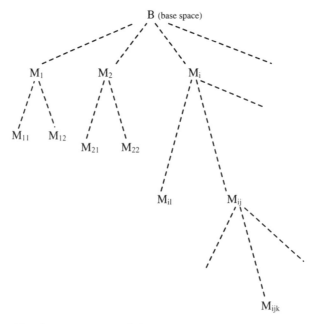

FIGURE 17.5 Relationship of new spaces to existing ones

1. We start with a single space, which is the base, and also the initial viewpoint and focus. We structure that space with the information that Max is 23 years old.
2. Keeping that space in focus, we add the (present) information that Max has lived abroad. This information is presented via a past event space ("Max live abroad").
3. In the next sentence, *in 1990* is a space builder. It sets up a new focus space, in which we build the content "Max live in Rome." This is also the new event space, because we are considering the event/state of Max living in Rome.
4. This focus space now becomes a viewpoint from which to consider Max's next move. Intuitively, when we say *In 1991, he would move . . .* , we are presenting 1991 as a future with respect to 1990. The 1990 space ("Max in Rome") becomes a viewpoint from which to set up the next focus (and event) space, 1991, with the content "Max move to Venice." We could have said the same thing differently by using the base (present time) as a viewpoint: *In 1991, Max moved to Venice.*
5. The last sentence, *He would then have lived a year in Rome*, keeps 1990 as the viewpoint, and 1991 as the focus, while using an event space ("live a year in Rome") that is past time relative to the focus 1991.

Schematically, the space configuration develops with successive shifts of event, focus, and viewpoint, as shown in Fig. 17.6.

The virtue of this type of cognitive organization is to allow local manipulation of the spaces with losing sight of the entire configuration. Because time is the relevant dimension here, we need some indication of the time relationship between spaces. Typically, tense will provide us with indications of *relative* time relationship. Cutrer (1994) proposed putatively universal semantic tense-aspect categories, with language-specific means of expressing some of their combinations. She also introduced a crucial distinction: New structure introduced into spaces may be marked as FACT or as PREDICTION, depending on the semantic tense aspect. Much of Cutrer's work is devoted to establishing the constraints on the space configurations that are set up in this way. The (putatively universal) categories constrain the configuration in specific ways. For instance, in the case of PAST, we have:

PAST applied to space N indicates that:
    i. N is in FOCUS.
    ii. N's parent is VIEWPOINT.
    iii. N's time is prior to VIEWPOINT (i.e., prior to N's parent).
    iv. Events or properties represented in N are FACT (in relation to the parent VIEWPOINT space).

These general constraints are coded grammatically by languages in different ways. So what we call the grammatical "simple past," "past participle," and so on, are distinguished from the semantic PAST, which specifics mental space relationships. English has the following coding system:

PAST is coded by the simple past (*lived, went, brought*) or by *have + past participle* if the verb is in infinitival position ("*will have forgotten,*" "*may have left,*" "*claims to have forgotten*"). Code: Verb + past or *have +* (Verb + past participle).
FUTURE is coded by *will +* Verb.

The construction of connected spaces, with viewpoint and focus shifts is reflected in the language code by retracing the path from the base to the focus space, using grammatical tenses.

In our example, when the sentence *In 1991, he would move to Venice* comes into the discourse, K is the FOCUS/EVENT space, N (1990) is the VIEWPOINT space, and M is the BASE. The grammatical coding reflects the path followed from the BASE to the FOCUS:

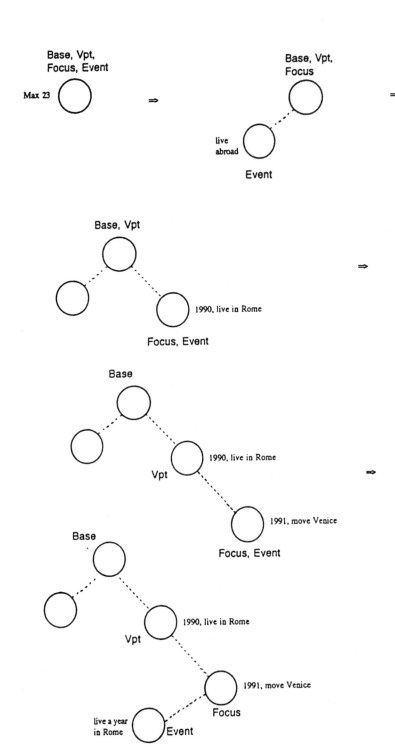

FIGURE 17.6 Space configuration showing shift of viewpoint, even, and focus

Base Space M —PAST→ Viewpoint Space N —FUTURE → Focus Space K

The coding will appear on the verb *move*, because the verb is introducing new structure into the current focus space. The FUTURE connection of K to N will be coded in English by (*will* + Verb *move*). The PAST connection of N to M will be coded by the simple past. The full coding from base to focus is compositional:

> simple past + (*will* + Verb *move*)
> ⇒ (past + *will*) + *move*
> ⇒ *would move*

Languages have different ways of coding the time path, and grammar may highlight some aspects of the path, while underspecifying others. What seems to be universally available is the construction of paths and the shifts of focus and viewpoint within the dynamic evolving mental space configuration.

General principles govern the ways in which focus and viewpoint (and even base) are allowed to shift. Cutrer (1994) proposed detailed principles of discourse organization, which include constraints like the following:

- Only one FOCUS, one BASE at any given moment of the discourse interpretation.
- New spaces are built from BASE or FOCUS.
- FOCUS can shift to EVENT, BASE, or previous FOCUS.
- VIEWPOINT can shift to FOCUS or BASE.

The account of tense developed by Dinsmore and Cutrer explains why tense does not directly reflect conceptual time as one might think (and as many semantic accounts suggest). Instead, the grammar of tense specifies partial constraints on time and fact/prediction status that hold locally between mental spaces within a discourse configuration. We may obtain actual information about time by combining this with other pragmatic information made available. Accordingly, the same tense may end up indicating very different objective time relations relative to the speech event:

> The boat leaves next week.
> When he comes tomorrow, I'll tell him about the party.
> If I see him next week, I'll ask him to call you.

[The "present" tense in this example corresponds to a "future" time.]

> I'm walking down the street one day when suddenly this guy walks up to me . . .
> He catches the ball. He runs. He makes a touchdown. (morning-after sports report)

[The "present" tense in this example corresponds to a "past" event.]

> Do you have a minute? I wanted to ask you a question.
> I wish I lived closer to my family, now.
> 1f I had time now, I would help you.

[The "past" tense corresponds to a "present" time.]

> If I had the time next week, I would go to your party.
> I can't go to the concert tonight. You'll have to tell me how it was.

[The "past" tense corresponds to a "future" time.]

> That will be all for now.
> He's not on the train. He will have missed it.

[The "future" tense corresponds to a "present" time.]

More generally, tenses are used not just to reflect local time relations between neighboring spaces but also to reflect epistemic distance—that is, whether a space is hypothetical or counterfactual with respect to its parent space. The coding system remains the same, and a particular tense sequence may reflect both time and epistemic distance. Here are some examples offered by Sweetser (1996):

> If you have Triple-A, then if you go to a telephone, you can solve your problem.
> If you had Triple-A, then if you went to a telephone, you could solve your problem.
> If you had had Triple-A, then if you'd gone to a telephone, you could have solved your problem.
> (p. 323)

We can interpret all three as referring to present time, but with different epistemic stances. The first is neutral as to the chances that you have Triple-A. The second suggests that maybe you don't have it. And the third is counterfactual—"you don't have Triple-A, but if you did . . . " Alternatively, one could interpret the second sentence as referring to a past event and being neutral as to what happened, and as to whether you had Triple-A, and the third sentence as referring to a past event, and being counterfactual. The embedded tenses (*go*, *went*, *had gone*, and *can solve*, *could solve*, *could have solved*) reflect the full epistemic and time path from the base, regardless of the corresponding objective time.

Mood (subjunctive vs. indicative) can serve to indicate distinctions in space accessibility. So, for example, a sentence like *Diogenes is looking for a man who is honest* opens a space in which "Diogenes finds an honest man." Because of the access principle that was discussed earlier, the description *a man who is honest* can either access a new element directly in that space or can identify a new element in the base and access its counterpart in the "look for" space. The first accessing path corresponds to a nonspecific interpretation: any honest man will do. The second accessing path corresponds to a specific reading: there is a particular honest man that Diogenes is looking for. In French, the equivalent of the verb copula *is* can be marked as either indicative or subjunctive:

> Diogène cherche un homme qui est honnête. [Indicative]
> Diogène cherche un homme qui soit honnête. [Subjunctive]

The first sentence with the indicative allows both accessing paths, as in English, with perhaps a preference for access from the base (the specific interpretation). The second sentence, on the other hand, allows only direct access to an element in the *look for* space—that is, the nonspecific reading. This is because the subjunctive forces the description to be satisfied in the embedded *look for* space.

A range of intricate space accessibility phenomena linked to grammatical mood was studied by Mejías-Bikandi (1993; 1996). Rich aspectual phenomena, involving spaces and viewpoint are discussed in Doiz-Bienzobas (1995).

Mappings and conceptual integration

Language, on the surface, seems to have its own very special principles, structures, and formal constraints. It has been studied extensively as an autonomous product of the human mind, and claims have even been made that this autonomy is reflected at the biological level in the form of specialized, innately based, genetically transmitted, neurobiological structures. In contrast, cognitive linguistics has repeatedly uncovered, behind the idiosyncrasies of language, evidence for the operation of more general cognitive processes. Mappings between mental spaces are part of this general organization of thought. Although language provides considerable data for studying such mappings, they are not in themselves specifically linguistic. They show up generally in conceptualization, and there is no reason to think that they are limited to humans. A striking case of a general cognitive operation on mental spaces, that is reflected in many language phenomena, but not restricted to such phenomena, is conceptual integration. There has been a good deal of recent research on conceptual integration and blending.[5] In this section, I give a quick overview of some of the results Mark Turner and I have obtained in our joint work on this topic.

Conceptual integration consists in setting up networks of mental spaces that map onto each other and blend into new spaces in various ways. In everyday thinking and talking, we use conceptual integration networks systematically in the on-line construction of meaning. Some of the integrations are novel, others are more entrenched, and we rarely pay conscious attention to the process because it is so pervasive.

A basic conceptual integration network contains four mental spaces. Two of these are called the *input spaces*, and a *cross-space mapping* is established between them. The cross-space mapping creates, or reflects, more schematic structure common to the inputs. This structure is constructed in a third space, called the *generic*. A fourth space, called the *blend*, arises by selective projection from the inputs. It develops emergent structure in various ways and can project structure back to the rest of the network.

There are simple everyday nonlinguistic examples of this around us all the time. For instance, we can create new activities by blending known activities with new environments. Coulson (1997) considered the case of children in a dormitory inventing a game, based on basketball, in which you must throw a crumpled-up sheet of paper into a wastepaper basket. This new game is a blend. One input is partial knowledge of basketball, the other input is the trash disposal situation with crumpled paper, a wastepaper basket, and so on. The partial mental mapping relates a ball to crumpled paper, a basketball basket to a wastepaper basket, players to children. In the new game, as defined by the blend, some properties are projected from the "basketball" input (scoring points when the ball falls into the basket, opponents in a game, winning and losing, etc.), some properties are projected from the "trash disposal" input (the basket is on the floor, not high up in the air, the ball has specific properties of crumpled paper, etc.), and some properties are shared by the two inputs (throwing a projectile into a receptacle). Many other properties of the game will emerge from affordances of the context (particular ways of throwing, conventions for scoring, fouls, etc.). The generic space linked to the cross-space mapping in this case is the more schematic situation of throwing some object into a container. This very simple example illustrates central properties of integration, in particular the fact that it is creative (a new activity, different from basketball, and different from throwing away paper, is produced) and underspecified (there is more than one way to project from the inputs, and more than one possible emergent structure).

The overall result of this dynamic process is a network of the type shown in Fig. 17.7. In the example, input I_1 is partial structure from basketball, input I_2 is partial structure from trash disposal, the generic space is the highly schematic throwing of an object into a container, and the blend is the emergent game of trashcan basketball.

Cognitive work on such a network consists in aligning the input spaces and developing a corresponding generic space, projecting selectively into the novel blended space, and structuring the blended space through pattern completion and elaboration (by mental simulation or actual action). Integration of this type occurs in many cases of action and design, such as computer interfaces or automatic bank tellers. The Macintosh desktop interface integrates two previously known inputs (computer commands and office work) by mapping them onto each

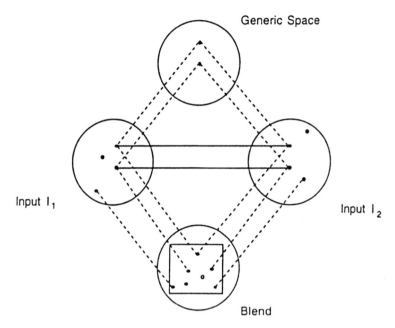

FIGURE 17.7 Diagram of the basic conceptual integration network. *Solid lines*, cross-space mapping; *dotted lines*, selective projection from inputs; *top three circles*, composition, completion, elaboration; *bottom circle*, blend; *square*, emergent structure and integration

other metaphorically, and by integrating them into a novel integrated conceptual and physical space (the interface, with its specific properties). Fauconnier and Turner (1998) showed in some detail how blending operates here, and how it conforms to a general set of optimality principles. In the same vein, Barbara Holder (1997) discussed the nice example of ATMs, where a cross-space mapping connects the inputs of computer manipulation and banking activity, and the ATM itself integrates aspects of both inputs in a physically and conceptually novel design.

Many linguistic constructions originate in conceptual blends and reflect them formally in systematic ways. The most transparent case is perhaps noun compounding, where an integration is reflected by a compound consisting of two nouns linked respectively to an element in each of the inputs. For example, Coulson's game with the crumpled paper in the dorm could be called *trashcan basketball*. One noun is the name of the game in one input, the other noun is linked to a salient element in the other input. By picking other elements, the same game might get called, more or less felicitously, *dorm basketball, basketball paperthrowing, wastepaper ball*, and so on. Almost all cases of noun-noun or adjective-noun compounding involve some degree of conceptual integration. It is only in the simplest possible default cases (and perhaps not even in those cases) that such compounds reduce to Boolean union of properties. So, for example (Turner and Fauconnier 1995), if we call a big American car a *land yacht*, we will be mapping two inputs (travel on land, travel on sea) with counterparts such as 'vehicle/boat', 'driver/skipper', 'road/ ocean', and selectively projecting into a blend, where some features of yachts now apply to certain automobiles (see Fig. 17.8).

We can see the access principle at work here, because the term *yacht* is being used to access its counterparts in the other spaces. We also see that the compound is formed by using names of elements that are not counterparts in the cross-space mapping (land and yacht).

Adjectives typically trigger integration processes. When we are concerned with a child playing at the beach with a shovel, and say things like *The child is safe, The beach is safe, The shovel is*

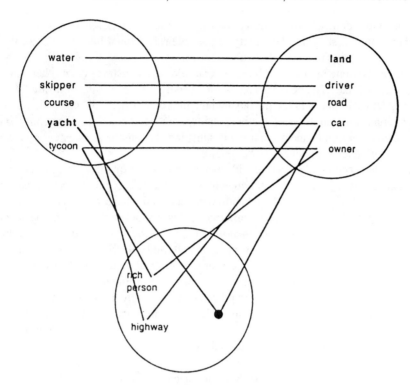

FIGURE 17.8 Diagram for the conceptual blend *land yacht*

safe, there is no fixed property that "safe" assigns to *child*, *beach*, and *shovel*. The first means that the child will not be harmed, but so do the second and the third—they do not mean that the beach will not be harmed or that the shovel will not be harmed. *Safe* does not assign a property; it prompts us to evoke scenarios of danger appropriate for the noun and the context. We worry about whether the child will be harmed by being on the beach or by using the shovel. Technically, the word *safe* evokes an abstract frame of *danger* with roles like victim, location, and instrument. Modifying the noun with the adjective prompts us to integrate that abstract frame of *danger* and the specific situation of the child on the beach into a counterfactual event of *harm* to the child. We build a specific counterfactual scenario of *harm* in which *child*, *beach*, and *shovel* are assigned to roles in the *danger* frame. Instead of assigning a simple property, the adjective is prompting us to set up a conceptual integration network where the inputs are, on the one hand, a frame of danger, and on the other, the specific situation of the child on the beach with a shovel. The output of the integration (the blend) is the counterfactual scenario in which the child is harmed. The word *safe* implies a disanalogy between the counterfactual blend and the specific input, with respect to the entity designated by the noun. If the shovel is safe, it is because in the counterfactual blend, it is too sharp, but in the specific situation, it is too dull to cut.

This process is general, and underspecified, as we see by assigning the same values to different frame roles in the relevant scenario. In *The shovel is safe*, the child is the victim in the blend if we are concerned about the shovel's injuring the child, but the shovel is the victim in the blend if we are concerned about the child's breaking the shovel. Furthermore, any number of roles can be recruited for the *danger* frame. In the counterfactual blend for "the jewels are safe," the jewels are neither victim nor instrument; they have the role *possession* and the *owner* is the victim. If we ship the jewels in packaging, then the counterfactual blend for "the packaging is safe" has *jewels* as victim, external forces as *cause of harm*, and *packaging* as *barrier to external forces*. Other examples showing the variety of possible roles would be "Drive at a safe speed," "Have a safe trip," and "This is a safe bet."

Even more elaborate blends, involving several roles, are constructed for other syntactically simple expressions, like "The beach is shark-safe" versus "The beach is child-safe." In the context of buying fish at a supermarket, the label on the tuna can read, "This tuna is dolphin-safe" to mean that the tuna was caught using methods that prevent accidents from happening to the dolphins. This blend looks more spectacular but is constructed using the same integration principles as in the unremarkable "safe beach" or "safe trip."

Safe is not an exceptional adjective with special semantic properties. The principles of integration are needed quite generally. Color adjectives, for instance, require noncompositional conceptual integration. *Red pencil* can be taken to mean a pencil whose wood has been painted red on the outside, a pencil that leaves a red mark (the lead is red, or the chemical in the pencil reacts with the paper to produce red, etc.), a pencil used to record the activities of the team dressed in red, a pencil smeared with lipstick, not to mention pencils used only for recording deficits. Theories of semantics typically prefer to work with examples like "black bird" or "brown cow" because these examples are supposed to be the prototypes of compositionality of meaning, but in fact, even these examples illustrate complicated processes of conceptual integration. From a psychological perspective, the key point in all this is the uniformity and availability of the cognitive operation (conceptual integration) in the full array of cases—those that look unexceptional and those that are more evidently noncompositional, such as:

> "The political war over the future of Medicare, a cannonade of oratory and *statistical rotten tomatoes* that has already thoroughly spattered both parties, is about to resume."[6]

The example of *safe* shows how an apparently simple expression can covertly introduce counterfactual scenarios and mappings. In fact, counterfactuals, which play a key role in our reasoning capacities, are themselves very good examples of conceptual integration. The meaning of expressions like *If I were you, I would hire me* involve a mapping from a reality space, where *you is* doing the hiring, to a counterfactual space in which the speaker's dispositions, but not her or his situation have been transferred to the addressee *you*. The space connection between speaker in reality, and the addressee in the counterfactual, allows the counterfactual employer to be identified as *I* by virtue of the access principle. Such counterfactuals are also clearly analogical. They invite an analogical interpretation in an intuitively obvious way: Compare the present situation in which *you* are doing the hiring to one in which *I* am in your place, confronted with the same decisions to make, and the same candidates. Then export some features (like "who I would hire") from one situation to the other. However, what we find in the linguistic expression, "*I would hire me*," cannot be a reflection of either one of these situations. It is not being suggested that the employer should hire herself, or that the employee should take power and hire himself. The linguistic expression signals a blend, which has been set up by the cross-space analogical mapping between the two situations. In the blend, we find partial projection of input 1, the employer and the employee (*me*) being hired, and partial projection of input 2, the speaker's dispositions and decisions. The projections, underspecifications, and optimality constraints that govern them, are studied in some detail in Fauconnier (1997), and in Turner and Fauconnier (1998). It turns out that all counterfactuals are analogical and require some degree of blending. Just like the cases of the compounds, some cases of counterfactuals are more visible than others. Eve Sweetser came across the following comment on Dostoevsky:

> "If Dostoevsky had lived in America, and had had a sunnier disposition, he might have been Emerson."

And the following appeared in the *Los Angeles Times*:

[A woman who had already been in a coma for 10 years was raped by a hospital employee, and gave birth to a child. A debate ensued concerning whether the pregnancy should have been terminated. The article reporting the case ended with a comment by law professor Goldberg.]

"Even if everyone agrees she [the comatose woman] was pro-life at 19, she is now 29 and has lived in PVS [persistent vegetative state] for 10 years. Do we ask: 'Was she pro-life?' Or do we ask more appropriately: 'Would she be pro-life as a rape victim in a persistent vegetative state at 29 years of life?'"

The inputs are, respectively, the one in which the young woman falls into a coma at nineteen, is raped and becomes pregnant at twenty-nine, and the one in which she leads a normal life, her opinions may change, and she is now twenty-nine years old. This second input space is of course fictive (counterfactual). Selective projection operates from these two inputs into the blend. From the first, we project recent events—the rape, the pregnancy, and also the coma without its consequences. From the second, we project the typical evolution of a young woman in command of her faculties, capable of understanding the situation, including the aspects of the situation that pertain to a person in a coma. In the blend, the young woman is a rape victim, is in a coma, and has all the faculties and judgment of an ordinary person—namely herself—if things had gone otherwise. Clearly, the blend is not constructing a "possible world." Its function is to allow the operation of certain analogies and lines of reasoning, because it remains linked within the integration network to the other spaces and to the applicable cultural models.

Metaphor is another area where integration networks are routinely constructed. Take the stock example *This surgeon is a butcher*. The statement underscores the clumsiness of the surgeon and its undesirable effects. But such inferences are not simply transferred from the domain of butchers to the domain of surgery. Butchers are in fact typically quite deft in their own domain of meat cutting, and their actions in that domain (producing roasts, steaks, and so on) are considered desirable. In an integration network, two input spaces with very partial structures from meat carving and surgery are mapped onto each other, on the basis of shared generic properties (cutting flesh, sharp instruments, white coat, professional activity, etc.). But neither the clumsiness nor its catastrophic consequences appear in those input spaces. They emerge in the blend. In the blend, there is projection on one hand of the operating room, the patient, and the surgeon, and on the other of the butcher's tools, the butcher's methods and manner of carving, and so forth. Emergent structure ensues from simulation of this unusual situation, and we are able to grasp instantly the nefarious effects of the procedure. The resulting failings of the surgeon, represented with considerable hyperbole in the blend, are projected back to the input space of surgery, where they yield an inference of gross incompetence.

Mark Turner (personal communication) offered the following simple example to illustrate this very general process. The reference is to the stock market, a bull market until recently. Investors in such a market are commonly called "bulls." When the market showed signs of weakness, a financier, Arnie Owen, was quoted in the *Wall Street Journal* as saying "Everybody has their horns pulled in." In the input space of cattle behavior, bulls can't pull in their horns. In the input space of finance, investors don't have horns, but they can pull back on their investing. In the blend, the investors end up as bulls with retractable horns. This emergent and inferentially efficient structure in the blend is not available through direct source/target metaphorical mapping.

In Fauconnier and Turner (1998, 2002), we showed how integration allows basic metaphors and metonymies to operate very generally in conceptual integration networks to produce complex, and often multiple, blends. This is the case for instance in the well-known ANGER as HEAT and FAILING as DYING metaphors. Interestingly, blending allows mapping between inputs that may clash in certain relevant respects such as intentional, causal, or temporal structure.

When we examine the full range of conceptual integration networks, we find that there is no sharp distinction of kind between simple framing, nontypical framing, analogy, source-target metaphor, and multiple metaphor. Rather, we have a continuum within the range of networks, with simple Fregean semantics at one end and elaborate metaphor at the other, with the same integration principles in all cases applying to a variety of topological configurations. On this continuum, we find points that are prototypical in certain respects, and it is those prototypical points that we associate with the notions, familiar and superficially different in appearance, of predicate-calculus, framing, analogy, simple metaphor, and abstract metaphor. We have been able to show (Fauconnier and Turner 2002) that the mapping schemes in all these cases were the same, and that they were compositional in an interesting cognitive, but not truth-conditional, sense. One may get an intuitive sense of this continuum by looking at a set of examples like the following, ordered along a dimension of complexity of integration networks: *Paul is the father of Sally. He is my genetic father but not my real father. Zeus is the father of Athena. I am your father for today* (friend of the family taking care of a child for a short time). *George Washington is the father of our country. Newton is the father of modern physics. Fear, father of cruelty* (Ezra Pound). *The child is the father of the man* (Wordsworth).

Conclusion

I have tried to give an idea of the elaborate backstage cognition that operates behind everyday utterances through spoken or signed modalities. This brief and informal overview does not do justice to other extensive work in this area. In particular, the construction of richer discourse and narrative has not been described here. Sanders and Redeker (1996), Cutrer (1994), and Mushin (1998) provided fascinating case studies and elaborations of the mental space model to deal with them. Rubba (1996) showed how multiple spaces are constructed on the basis of sparse linguistic information and elaborate, but covert, cultural and cognitive models. Fridman-Mintz and Liddell (1998) also found that multiple and successive connected spaces are constructed in short narratives in ASL. Work by Hutchins (1995) showed how conceptual blending can use material anchors to produce situated behavior, such as navigation of ships and planes. Coulson (1997) developed integration accounts of rhetorical strategies, noun and adjective compounding, and argumentative counterfactuals. Turner (1996), Oakley (1995), and Freeman (1997) developed elaborate analyses of mental space construction and integration in literary narratives, poetry, and general rhetoric. Zbikowski (1997) showed how similar processes operate in music. Lakoff and Nunez (1998) found many cases of conceptual blends in mathematics in addition to the ones pointed out in Fauconnier and Turner (1998a).

The role of conceptual blending in grammar was demonstrated in Mandelblit (1997) and Fauconnier and Turner (1996). Mandelblit and Zachar (1998) explore some consequences of these findings for the epistemology of cognitive science.

Two central points stand out in all of this work and are particularly relevant for cognitive psychology:

1. Backstage cognition: Language works in concert with "behind the scenes" understandings and cognitive processes. Language is neither a representation of such processes nor a representation of meaning. Rather, it serves as a powerful and directed, but vastly underspecified, set of prompts for triggering the dynamic processing itself and the corresponding construction of meaning. Backstage cognition has not received the attention it deserves from linguists because it is largely unconscious, immediate, and structurally invisible.

2. An especially important set of such processes (that are especially well hidden from conscious view) concerns mental spaces and their associated cognitive operations.

There is little doubt that mental space constructions permeate much of our thought, our use of language, and other forms of expression. The study of such general cognitive operations should be a fertile ground for experimental psychology. The findings in this area converge nicely with those of Bloom (1974; 1991), Barsalou (1996), and Mandler (1997).

Notes

1. Fauconnier (1994; 1997), Cutrer (1994), Fauconnier and Sweetser (1996), Fauconnier and Turner (1998), Huumo (1996).

2. I simplify the account here for expository purposes, by leaving out additional spaces set up by the past tense operators.

3. Shastri and Grannes (1996).

4. This is the scheme developed in Dinsmore (1991).

5. Fauconnier and Turner (1994; 1996; 2002), Coulson (1995; 1997), Oakley (1995), Robert (1998), Mandelblit (1997), Mandelblit and Zachar (1998), Turner (1996).

6. Michael Wines, "Political Stakes Increase in Fight to Save Medicare," *New York Times*, Monday, 3 June 1996.

IV

TOPICS

18

JAMES PUSTEJOVSKY

The Generative Lexicon

In this paper, I will discuss four major topics relating to current research in lexical semantics: methodology, descriptive coverage, adequacy of the representation, and the computational usefulness of representations. In addressing these issues, I will discuss what I think are some of the central problems facing the lexical semantics community, and suggest ways of best approaching these issues. Then, I will provide a method for the decomposition of lexical categories and outline a theory of lexical semantics embodying a notion of *cocompositionality* and *type coercion*, as well as several levels of semantic description, where the semantic load is spread more evenly throughout the lexicon. I argue that lexical decomposition is possible if it is performed *generatively*. Rather than assuming a fixed set of primitives, I will assume a fixed number of generative devices that can be seen as constructing semantic expressions. I develop a theory of *qualia structure*, a representation language for lexical items, which renders much lexical ambiguity in the lexicon unnecessary, while still explaining the systematic polysemy that words carry. Finally, I discuss how individual lexical structures can be integrated into the larger lexical knowledge base through a theory of *lexical inheritance*. This provides us with the necessary principles of global organization for the lexicon, enabling us to fully integrate our natural language lexicon into a conceptual whole.

1   Introduction

I believe we have reached an interesting turning point in research, where linguistic studies can be informed by computational tools for lexicology as well as an appreciation of the computational complexity of large lexical databases. Likewise, computational research can profit from an awareness of the grammatical and syntactic distinctions of lexical items; natural language processing systems must account for these differences in their lexicons and grammars. The

James Pustejovsky (1991) The generative lexicon. *Computational Linguistics* 17: 409–441. Reprinted by permission of MIT Press Journals.

wedding of these disciplines is so important, in fact, that I believe it will soon be difficult to carry out serious computational research in the fields of linguistics and NLP [natural language processing] without the help of electronic dictionaries and computational lexicographic resources (cf. Walker et al. 1995, and Boguraev and Briscoe 1988). Positioned at the center of this synthesis is the study of word meaning, lexical semantics, which is currently witnessing a revival.

In order to achieve a synthesis of lexical semantics and NLP, I believe that the lexical semantics community should address the following questions:

1. Has recent work in lexical semantics been methodologically sounder than the previous work in the field?
2. Do theories being developed today have broader coverage than the earlier descriptive work?
3. Do current theories provide any new insights into the representation of knowledge for the global structure of the lexicon?
4. Finally, has recent work provided the computational community with useful resources for parsing, generation, and translation research?

Before addressing these questions, I would like to establish two basic assumptions that will figure prominently in my suggestions for a lexical semantics framework. The first is that, without an appreciation of the syntactic structure of a language, the study of lexical semantics is bound to fail. There is no way in which meaning can be completely divorced from the structure that carries it. This is an important methodological point, since grammatical distinctions are a useful metric in evaluating competing semantic theories.

The second point is that the meanings of words should somehow reflect the deeper, conceptual structures in the system and the domain it operates in. This is tantamount to stating that the semantics of natural language should be the image of nonlinguistic conceptual organizing principles (whatever their structure).

Computational lexical semantics should be guided by the following principles. First, a clear notion of semantic well-formedness will be necessary to characterize a theory of possible word meaning. This may entail abstracting the notion of lexical meaning away from other semantic influences. For instance, this might suggest that discourse and pragmatic factors should be handled differently or separately from the semantic contributions of lexical items in composition.[1] Although this is not a necessary assumption and may in fact be wrong, it may help narrow our focus on what is important for lexical semantic descriptions.

Secondly, lexical semantics must look for representations that are richer than thematic role descriptions (Gruber 1965; Fillmore 1968). As argued in Levin and Rappaport (1986), named roles are useful at best for establishing fairly general mapping strategies to the syntactic structures in language. The distinctions possible with *theta*-roles are much too coarse-grained to provide a useful semantic interpretation of a sentence. What is needed, I will argue, is a principled method of lexical decomposition. This presupposes, if it is to work at all, (1) a rich, recursive theory of semantic composition, (2) the notion of semantic well-formedness mentioned above, and (3) an appeal to several levels of interpretation in the semantics (Scha 1983).

Thirdly, and related to the point above, **the lexicon is not just verbs**. Recent work has done much to clarify the nature of verb classes and the syntactic constructions that each allows (Levin 1985; 1993). Yet it is not clear whether we are any closer to understanding the underlying nature of verb meaning, why the classes develop as they do, and what consequences these distinctions have for the rest of the lexicon and grammar. The curious thing is that there has been little attention paid to other lexical categories (but see Miller and Johnson-Laird 1976; Miller and Fellbaum 1991; and Fass 1988). That is, we have little insight into the semantic nature of adjectival predication, and even less into the semantics of nominals. Not until all major categories have been studied can we hope to arrive at a balanced understanding of the lexicon and the methods of composition.

Stepping back from the lexicon for a moment, let me say briefly what I think the position of lexical research should be within the larger semantic picture. Ever since the earliest attempts at real text understanding, a major problem has been that of controlling the inferences associated with the interpretation process. In other words, how deep or shallow is the understanding of a text? What is the unit of well-formedness when doing natural language understanding; the sentence, utterance, paragraph, or discourse? There is no easy answer to this question because, except for the sentence, these terms are not even formalizable in a way that most researchers would agree on.

It is my opinion that the representation of the context of an utterance should be viewed as involving many different *generative factors* that account for the way that language users create and manipulate the context under constraints, in order to be understood. Within such a theory, where many separate semantic levels (e.g., lexical semantics, compositional semantics, discourse structure, temporal structure) have independent interpretations, the global interpretation of a "discourse" is a highly flexible and malleable structure that has no single interpretation. The individual sources of semantic knowledge compute local inferences with a high degree of certainty (cf. Hobbs et al. 1988; Charniak and Goldman 1988). When integrated together, these inferences must be globally coherent, a state that is accomplished by processes of cooperation among separate semantic modules. The basic result of such a view is that semantic interpretation proceeds in a principled fashion, always aware of what the source of a particular inference is, and what the certainty of its value is. Such an approach allows the reasoning process to be both tractable and computationally efficient. The representation of lexical semantics, therefore, should be seen as just one of many levels in a richer characterization of contextual structure.

2   Methods in lexical semantics

Given what I have said, let us examine the questions presented above in more detail. First, let us turn to the issue of methodology. How can we determine the soundness of our method? Are new techniques available now that have not been adequately explored? Very briefly, one can summarize the most essential techniques assumed by the field, in some way, as follows (see, for example Cruse 1986):

- On the basis of categorial distinctions, establish the fundamental differences between the grammatical classes; the typical semantic behavior of a word of category X. For example, verbs typically behave as predicators, nouns as arguments.
- Find distinctions between elements of the same word class on the basis of collocation and cooccurrence tests. For example, the nouns *dog* and *book* partition into different selectional classes because of contexts involving *animacy*, while the nouns *book* and *literature* partition into different selectional classes because of a mass/count distinction.
- Test for distinctions of a grammatical nature on the basis of diathesis—that is, alternations that are realized in the syntax. For example, *break* vs. *cut* in (1) and (2) below (Fillmore 1968; Lakoff 1970a; Hale and Keyser 1986):

(1) a. The glass **broke**.
     b. John **broke** the glass.
(2) a. *The bread **cut**.
     b. John **cut** the bread.

Such alternations reveal subtle distinctions in the semantic and syntactic behavior of such verbs. The lexical semantic representations of these verbs are distinguishable on the basis of such tests.

- Test for entailments in the word senses of a lexical item, in different grammatical contexts. One can distinguish, for example, between *context-free* and *context-sensitive* entailments. When the use of a word always entails a certain proposition, we say that the resulting entailment is not dependent on the syntactic context (cf. Katz and Fodor 1963; Karttunen 1971, 1974; Seuren 1986). This is illustrated in example (3), where a *killing* always entails a *dying*:

(3) a. John **killed** Bill.
     b. Bill **died**.

When the same lexical item may carry different entailments in different contexts, we say that the entailments are sensitive to the syntactic contexts—for example, *forget* in example (4):

(4) a. John **forgot** that he locked the door.
     b. John **forgot** to lock the door.

Example (4a) has a factive interpretation of *forget* that (4b) does not carry: in fact, (4b) is counterfactive. Other cases of contextual specification involve aspectual verbs such as *begin* and *finish*, as shown in example (5):

(5) a. Mary **finished** the cigarette.
     b. Mary **finished** her beer.

The exact meaning of the verb *finish* varies depending on the object it selects, assuming for these examples the meanings *finish smoking* or *finish drinking*.

- Test for the ambiguity of a word. Distinguish between homonymy and polysemy, (cf. Hirst 1987; Wilks 1975b); that is, from the accidental and logical aspects of ambiguity. For example, the homonymy between the two senses of *bank* in example (6) is accidental.[2]

(6) a. the **bank** of the river
     b. the richest **bank** in the city

In contrast, the senses in example (7) exhibit a polysemy (cf. Weinreich 1972; Lakoff 1987):

(7) a. The **bank** raised its interest rates yesterday (i.e., the *institution*).
     b. The store is next to the new **bank** (i.e., the *building*).

- Establish what the compositional nature of a lexical item is when applied to other words. For example, *alleged* vs. *female* in example (8):

(8) a. the **alleged** suspect
     b. the **female** suspect

While *female* behaves as a simple intersective modifier in (8b), certain modifiers such as *alleged* in (8a) cannot be treated as simple attributes; rather, they create an intensional context for the head they modify. An even more difficult problem for compositionality arises from phrases containing frequency adjectives (cf. Stump 1981), as shown in (8c) and (8d):

(8)   c. An **occasional** sailor walks by on the weekend.
      d. Caution: may contain an **occasional** pit (notice on a box of prunes).

The challenge here is that the adjective doesn't modify the nominal head, but the entire proposition containing it (cf. Partee 1992 for discussion). A similar difficulty arises with the interpretation of scalar predicates such as *fast* in example (9). Both the scale and the relative interpretation being selected for depends on the noun that the predicate is modifying:

(9)   a. a **fast** typist: one who types quickly
      b. a **fast** car: one which can move quickly
      c. a **fast** waltz: one with a fast tempo

Such data raise serious questions about the principles of compositionality and how ambiguity should be accounted for by a theory of semantics.

This just briefly characterizes some of the techniques that have been useful for arriving at pre-theoretic notions of word meaning. What has changed over the years are not so much the methods themselves as the descriptive details provided by each test. One thing that has changed, however—and this is significant—is the way computational lexicography has provided stronger techniques and even new tools for lexical semantics research: see Atkins (1987) for sense discrimination tasks; Amsler (1989), Atkins et al. (forthcoming) for constructing concept taxonomies; Wilks et al. (1988) for establishing semantic relatedness among word senses; and Boguraev and Pustejovsky (1996) for testing new ideas about semantic representations.

3   Descriptive adequacy of existing representations

Turning now to the question of how current theories compare with the coverage of lexical semantic data, there are two generalizations that should be made. First, the taxonomic descriptions that have recently been made of verb classes are far superior to the classifications available twenty years ago (see Levin 1985 for review). Using mainly the descriptive vocabulary of Talmy (1975; 1985) and Jackendoff (1983), fine and subtle distinctions are drawn that were not captured in the earlier, primitives-based approach of Schank (1972, 1975) or the frame semantics of Fillmore (1968).

As an example of the verb classifications developed by various researchers (and compiled by the MIT Lexicon Project; see Levin 1985; 1993), consider the grammatical alternations in the example sentences below (cf. Dowty 1991):

(10) a. John **met** Mary.
      b. John and Mary **met**.
(11) a. A car **ran** into a truck.
      b. A car and a truck **ran** into each other.
(12) a. A car **ran** into a tree.
      b. *A car and a tree **ran** into each other.

These three pairs show how the semantics of transitive motion verbs (e.g., *run into*) is similar in some respects to reciprocal verbs such as *meet*. The important difference, however, is that the reciprocal interpretation requires that both subject and object be animate or moving; hence (12b) is ill-formed (cf. Levin 1993; Dowty 1991).

Another example of how diathesis reveals the underlying semantic differences between verbs is illustrated in examples (13) and (14) below. A construction called *the conative* (see Hale and Keyser 1986 and Levin 1985) involves adding the preposition *at* to the verb, changing the verb meaning to *an action directed toward an object*:

(13) a. Mary **cut** the bread.
      b. Mary **cut** at the bread.
(14) a. Mary **broke** the bread:
      b. *Mary **broke** at the bread.

What these data indicate is that the conative is possible only with verbs of a particular semantic class—namely, verbs that *specify the manner of an action that results in a change of state of an object.*

As useful and informative as the research on verb classification is, there is a major short-coming with this approach. Unlike the theories of Katz and Fodor (1963), Wilks (1975a), and Quillian (1968), there is no general coherent view on what the entire lexicon will look like when semantic structures for other major categories are studied. This can be essential for establishing a globally coherent theory of semantic representation. On the other hand, the semantic distinctions captured by these older theories were often too coarse-grained. It is clear, therefore, that the classifications made by Levin and her colleagues are an important starting point for a serious theory of knowledge representation. I claim that lexical semantics must build upon this research toward constructing a theory of word meaning that is integrated into a linguistic theory, as well as interpreted in a real knowledge representation system.

4   Explanatory adequacy of existing representations

In this section I turn to the question of whether current theories have changed the way we look at representation and lexicon design. The question here is whether the representations assumed by current theories are adequate to account for the richness of natural language semantics. It should be pointed out here that a theory of lexical meaning will affect the general design of our semantic theory in several ways. If we view the goal of a semantic theory as being able to recursively assign meanings to expressions, accounting for phenomena such as synonymy, antonymy, polysemy, metonymy, et cetera, then our view of compositionality depends ultimately on what the basic lexical categories of the language denote. Conventional wisdom on this point paints a picture of words behaving as either active functors or passive arguments (Montague 1974b). But we will see that if we change the way in which categories can denote, then the form of compositionality itself changes. Therefore, if done correctly, lexical semantics can be a means to reevaluate the very nature of semantic composition in language.

In what ways could lexical semantics affect the larger methods of composition in semantics? I mentioned above that most of the careful representation work has been done on verb classes. In fact, the semantic weight in both lexical and compositional terms usually falls on the verb. This has obvious consequences for how to treat lexical ambiguity. For example, consider the verb *bake* in the two sentences below:

(15) a. John **baked** the potato.
      b. John **baked** the cake.

Atkins, Kegl, and Levin (1988) demonstrate that verbs such as *bake* are systematically ambiguous, with both a *change-of-state* senses (15a) and a *create* sense (15b).

A similar ambiguity exists with verbs that allow the resultative construction, shown in examples (16) and (17), and discussed in Dowty (1979), Jackendoff (1983), and Levin and Rappoport (1988):

(16)   a. Mary **hammered** the metal.
       b. Mary **hammered** the metal flat.
(17)   a. John **wiped** the table.
       b. John **wiped** the table clean.

On many views, the verbs in examples (16) and (17) are ambiguous, related by either a lexical transformation (Levin and Rappoport 1988) or a meaning postulate (Dowty 1979). In fact, given strict requirements on the way that a verb can project its lexical information, the verb *run* in example (18) will also have two lexical entries, depending on the syntactic environment it selects (Talmy 1985; Levin and Rappaport 1988):

(18)   a. Mary **ran** to the store yesterday.
       b. Mary **ran** yesterday.

These two verbs differ in their semantic representations, where *run* in (18a) means *go-to-by-means-of-running*, while in (18b) it means simply *move-by-running* (cf. Jackendoff 1983).

The methodology described above for distinguishing word senses is also assumed by those working in more formal frameworks. For example, Dowty (1985) proposes multiple entries for control and raising verbs and establishes their semantic equivalence with the use of meaning postulates. That is, the verbs in examples (19) and (20) are lexically distinct but semantically related by rules:[3]

(19)   a. It **seems** that John likes Mary.
       b. John **seems** to like Mary.
(20)   a. Mary **prefers** that she come.
       b. Mary **prefers** to come.

Given the conventional notions of function application and composition, there is little choice but to treat all of the above cases as polysemous verbs. Yet, something about the systematicity of such ambiguity suggests that a more general and simpler explanation should be possible. By relaxing the conditions on how the meaning of a complex expression is derived from its parts, I will, in fact, propose a very straightforward explanation for these cases of *logical polysemy*.

5   A framework for computational semantics

In this section, I will outline what I think are the basic requirements for a theory of computational semantics. I will present a conservative approach to decomposition, where lexical items are minimally decomposed into structured forms (or templates) rather than sets of features. This will provide us with a generative framework for the *composition* of lexical meanings, thereby defining the well-formedness conditions for semantic expressions in a language.

We can distinguish between two distinct approaches to the study of word meaning: *primitive-based* theories and *relation-based* theories. Those advocating primitives assume that word meaning can be exhaustively defined in terms of a fixed set of primitive elements (e.g., Wilks 1975a; Katz 1972; Lakoff 1970c; Schank 1975). Inferences are made through the primitives into which a word is decomposed. In contrast to this view, a relation-based theory of word meaning claims that there is no need for decomposition into primitives if words (and their concepts) are associated through a network of explicitly defined links (e.g., Quillian 1968; Collins and Quillian 1969; Fodor 1975; Carnap 1956; Brachman 1979). Sometimes referred to as *meaning postulates*, these links establish any inference between words as an explicit part of a network of word concepts.[4] What I would like to do is to propose a new way of viewing primitives, looking more at the generative or *compositional* aspects of lexical semantics rather than the decomposition into a specified *number* of primitives.

Most approaches to lexical semantics making use of primitives can be characterized as using some form of *feature-based* semantics, since the meaning of a word is essentially decomposable into a set of features (e.g., Katz and Fodor 1963; Katz 1972; Wilks 1975; Schank 1975). Even those theories that rely on some internal structure for word meaning (e.g., Dowty 1979; Fillmore 1985) do not provide a complete characterization for all of the well-formed expressions in the language. Jackendoff (1983) comes closest but falls short of a comprehensive semantics for *all* categories in language. No existing framework, in my view, provides a *method for the decomposition of lexical categories*.

What exactly would a method for lexical decomposition give us? Instead of a taxonomy of the concepts in a language, categorized by sets of features, such a method would tell us the minimal semantic configuration of a lexical item. Furthermore, it should tell us the compositional properties of a word, just as a grammar informs us of the specific syntactic behavior of a certain category. What we are led to, therefore, is a *generative* theory of word meaning, but one very different from the generative semantics of the 1970s.

To explain why I am suggesting that lexical decomposition proceed in a *generative* fashion rather than the traditional *exhaustive* approach, let me take as a classic example, the word *closed* as used in example (21) (see Lakoff 1970a).

(21)   a. The door is **closed**.
       b. The door **closed**.
       c. John **closed** the door.

Lakoff (1970a), Jackendoff (1972), and others have suggested that the sense in (21c) must incorporate something like *cause-to-become-not-open* for its meaning. Similarly, a verb such as *give* specifies a transfer from one person to another—for example, *cause-to-have*. Most decomposition theories assume a set of primitives and then operate within this set to capture the meanings of all the words in the language. These approaches can be called *exhaustive* since they assume that with a fixed number of primitives, complete definitions of lexical meaning can be given. In the sentences in (21), for example, *close* is defined in terms of the negation of a primitive, *open*. Any method assuming a fixed number of primitives, however, runs into some well-known problems with being able to capture the full expressiveness of natural language.

These problems are not, however, endemic to all decomposition approaches. I would like to suggest that lexical (and conceptual) decomposition is possible if it is performed *generatively*. Rather than assuming a fixed set of *primitives*, let us assume a fixed number of *generative devices* that can be seen as constructing semantic expressions.[5] Just as a formal language is described more in terms of the productions in the grammar than its accompanying vocabulary, a semantic language is definable by the rules generating the structures for expressions rather than the vocabulary of primitives itself.[6]

How might this be done? Consider the sentences in example (21) again. A minimal decomposition on the word *closed* is that it introduces an *opposition* of terms: *closed* and *not-closed*. For the verbal forms in (21b) and (21c), both terms in this opposition are predicated of different subevents denoted by the sentences. In (21a), this opposition is left implicit, since the sentence refers to a single state. Any minimal analysis of the semantics of a lexical item can be termed a *generative* operation, since it operates on the predicate(s) already literally provided by the word.

This type of analysis is essentially Aristotle's *principle of opposition* (cf. Lloyd 1968), and it will form the basis of one level of representation for a lexical item. The essential opposition denoted by a predicate forms part of what I will call the *qualia structure* of that lexical item. Briefly, the qualia structure of a word specifies four *aspects* of its meaning:

- The relation between it and its constituent parts
- That which distinguishes it within a larger domain (its physical characteristics)
- Its purpose and function
- Whatever brings it about

I will call these aspects of a word's meaning its *Constitutive Role*, *Formal Role*, *Telic Role*, and its *Agentive Role*, respectively.[7]

This minimal semantic distinction is given expressive force when combined with a theory of event types. For example, the predicate in (21a) denotes the *state* of the door being closed. No opposition is expressed by this predicate. In (21b) and (21c), however, the opposition is explicitly part of the meaning of the predicate. Both these predicates denote what I will call *transitions*. The intransitive use of *close* in (21b) makes no mention of the causer, yet the transition from *not-closed* to *closed* is still entailed. In (21c), the event that brings about the *closed* state of the door is made more explicit by specifying the actor involved. These differences constitute what I call the *event structure* of a lexical item. Both the opposition of predicates and the specification of causation are part of a verb's semantics and are structurally associated with slots in the event template for the word. As we will see in the next section, there are different inferences associated with each event type, as well as different syntactic behaviors (cf. Grimshaw 1990 and Pustejovsky 1991b).

Because the lexical semantic representation of a word is not an isolated expression, but is in fact linked to the rest of the lexicon, in section 7 I suggest how the global integration of the semantics for a lexical item is achieved by structured inheritance through the different *qualia* associated with a word. I call this the *lexical inheritance structure* for the word.

Finally, we must realize that part of the meaning of a word is how it translates the underlying semantic representations into expressions that are utilized by the syntax. This is what many have called the *argument structure* for a lexical item. I will build on Grimshaw's recent proposals (Grimshaw 1990) for how to define the mapping from the lexicon to syntax.

This provides us with an answer to the question of what levels of semantic representation are necessary for a computational lexical semantics. In sum, I will argue that lexical meaning can best be captured by assuming the following levels of representation:

1. *Argument Structure*: The behavior of a word as a function, with its arity specified. This is the predicate argument structure for a word, which indicates how it maps to syntactic expressions.
2. *Event Structure*: Identification of the particular event type (in the sense of Vendler 1967a) for a word or phrase: e.g., as state, process, or transition.
3. *Qualia Structure*: The essential attributes of an object as defined by the lexical item.
4. *Inheritance Structure*: How the word is globally related to other concepts in the lexicon.

These four structures essentially constitute the different levels of semantic expressiveness and representation that are needed for a computational theory of lexical semantics. Each level contributes a different kind of information to the meaning of a word. The important difference between this highly configurational approach to lexical semantics and feature-based approaches is that the recursive calculus defined for word meaning here also provides the foundation for a fully compositional semantics for natural language and its interpretation into a knowledge representation model.

5.1   Argument structure

A logical starting point for our investigations into the meaning of words is what has been called the functional structure or argument structure associated with verbs. What originally began as the simple listing of the parameters or arguments associated with a predicate has developed into a sophisticated view of the way arguments are mapped onto syntactic expressions (for example, the *f-structure* in Lexical Functional Grammar [Bresnan 1982] and the *Projection Principle* in Government-Binding Theory [Chomsky 1981]).

One of the most important contributions has been the view that argument structure is highly structured independent of the syntax. Williams's (1981) distinction between external and internal arguments and Grimshaw's (1990) proposal for a hierarchically structured representation provide us with the basic syntax for one aspect of a word's meaning.

The argument structure for a word can be seen as a minimal specification of its lexical semantics. By itself, it is certainly inadequate for capturing the semantic characterization of a lexical item, but it is a necessary component.

5.2   Event structure

As mentioned above, the theory of decomposition being outlined here is based on the central idea that word meaning is highly structured, and not simply a set of semantic features. Let us assume this is the case. Then the lexical items in a language will essentially be generated by the recursive principles of our semantic theory. One level of semantic description involves an event-based interpretation of a word or phrase. I will call this level the *event structure* of a word (cf. Pustejovsky 1991b; Moens and Steedman 1988). The event structure of a word is one level of the semantic specification for a lexical item, along with its argument structure, qualia structure, and inheritance structure. Because it is recursively defined on the syntax, it is also a property of phrases and sentences.[8]

I will assume a sortal distinction between three classes of events: states (e^S), processes (e^P), and transitions (e^T). Unlike most previous sortal classifications for events I will adopt a *subeventual* analysis or predicates, as argued in Pustejovsky (1991b) and independently proposed in Croft (1991). In this view, an event sort such as e^T may be decomposed into two sequentially structured subevents, (e^P, e^S). Aspects of the proposal will be introduced as needed in the following discussion.

6   A theory of qualia

In section 5, I demonstrated how most of the lexical semantics research has concentrated on verbal semantics. This bias influences our analyses of how to handle ambiguity and certain noncompositional structures. Therefore, the only way to relate the different senses for the verbs in the examples below was to posit separate entries:

(22) a. John **baked** the potato.
       ($bake_1$ = *change* (x, *State*(y)))
    b. John **baked** the cake.
       ($bake_2$ = *create* (x,y))
(23) a. Mary **hammered** the metal.
       ($hammer_1$ = *change* (x, *State*(y)))
    b. Mary **hammered** the metal flat.
       ($hammer_2$ = *cause*(x, *Become* (*flat*(y))))
(24) a. John **wiped** the table.
       ($wipe_1$ = *change* (x,*State*(y)))

    b. John **wiped** the table clean.

      ($wipe_2 = cause\ (x,\ Become(clean(y))))$

(25) a. Mary **ran** yesterday.

      ($run_1 = move\ (x))$

    b. Mary **ran** to the store yesterday.

      ($run_2 = go\text{-}to\ (x,\ y))$

Although the complement types selected by *bake* in (22), for example, are semantically related, the two word senses are clearly distinct and therefore must be lexically distinguished. According to the sense enumeration view, the same argument holds for the verbs in (23)–(25) as well.

    A similar philosophy has lead linguists to multiply word senses in constructions involving Control and Equi-verbs, where different syntactic contexts necessitate different semantic type:[9]

(26) a. It **seems** that John likes Mary.

    b. John **seems** to like Mary.

(27) a. Mary **prefers** that she come.

    b. Mary **prefers** to come.

Normally, compositionality in such structures simply refers to the application of the functional element, the verb, to its arguments. Yet, such examples indicate that in order to capture the systematicity of such ambiguity, something else is at play, where a richer notion of composition is operative. What then accounts for the polysemy of the verbs in the examples above?

    The basic idea I will pursue is the following. Rather than treating the expressions that behave as arguments to a function as simple, passive objects, imagine that they are as active in the semantics as the verb itself. The product of function application would be sensitive to both the function and its active argument. Something like this is suggested in Keenan and Faltz (1985), as the *Meaning–Form Correlation Principle*. I will refer to such behavior as *cocompositionality* (see below). What I have in mind can best be illustrated by returning to the examples in (28):

(28) a. John **baked** the potato.

    b. John **baked** the cake.

Rather than having two separate word senses for a verb such as *bake*, suppose there is simply one, a *change-of-state* reading. Without going into the details of the analysis, let us assume that *bake* can be lexically specified as denoting a *process* verb, and is minimally represented as example (29):[10]

(29) Lexical Semantics for *bake*:[11]

    $\lambda y \lambda x \lambda e^P[bake(e^P) \wedge agent(e^P, x) \wedge object(e^P, y)]$

In order to explain the shift in meaning of the verb, we need to specify more clearly what the lexical semantics of a noun is. I have argued above that lexical semantic theory must make a logical distinction between the following qualia roles: the *constitutive*, *formal*, *telic*, and *agentive* roles. Now let us examine these roles in more detail. One can distinguish between *potato* and *cake* in terms of how they come about; the former is a natural kind, while the latter is an artifact. Knowledge of an object includes not just being able to identify or refer, but more specifically, being able to explain how an artifact comes into being, as well as what it is used for; the denotation of an object must identify these roles. Thus, any artifact can be identified with the state of being that object, relative to certain predicates.

As is well known from work on event semantics and *Aktionsarten*, it is a general property of *processes* that they can shift their event type to become a *transition* event (cf. Hinrichs 1985; Moens and Steedman 1988; and Krifka 1987). This particular fact about event structures, together with the semantic distinction made above between the two object types, provides us with an explanation for what I will refer to as the *logical polysemy* of verbs such as *bake*.

As illustrated in example (30a), when the verb takes as its complement a natural kind such as *potato*, the resulting semantic interpretation is unchanged—that is, a process reading of a state-change. This is because the noun does not "project" an event structure of its own. That is, relative to the process of *baking*, *potato* does not denote an event-type:[12]

(30)   a. bake as *Process*:
$\exists e^P [bake(e^P) \wedge agent(e^P, j) \wedge object(e^P, a\text{-}potato)]$

   b.

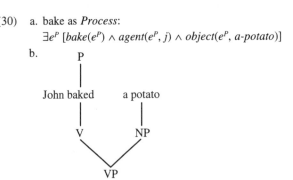

What is it, then, about the semantics of *cake* that shifts this core meaning of *bake* from a state-change predicate to its creation sense? As just suggested, this additional meaning is contributed by specific lexical knowledge we have about artifacts, and *cake* in particular; namely, there is an event associated with that object's "coming into being," in this case the process of baking. Thus, just as a verb can select for an argument-type, we can imagine that an argument is itself able to select the predicates that govern it. I will refer to such constructions as *cospecifications*. Informally, relative to the process *bake*, the noun *cake* carries the selectional information that it is a process of "baking" that brings it about.[13]

We can illustrate this schematically in example (31), where the complement effectively acts like a "stage-level" event predicate (cf. Carlson 1977a) relative to the process event-type of the verb (i.e., a function from processes to transitions, <P,T>).[14] The change in meaning in (31) comes not from the semantics of *bake* but, rather, in composition with the complement of the verb, at the level of the entire verb phrase. The "creation" sense arises from the semantic role of *cake* that specifies it is an artifact (see below for discussion):

(31)   a. bake as a derived *Transition*:[15]
$\exists e^P, e^S [create(e^P, e^S) \wedge bake(e^P) \wedge agent(e^P, j) \wedge object(e^P, x) \wedge cake(x) \wedge object(e^S, x)]$

   b.

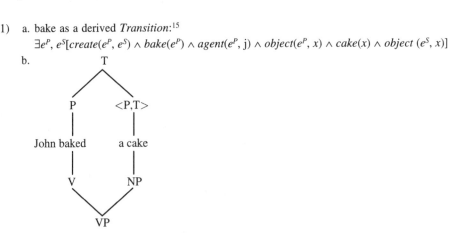

Thus, we can derive both word senses of verbs like *bake* by putting some of the semantic weight on the NP. This view suggests that, in such cases, the verb itself is not polysemous. Rather, the sense of "create" is part of the meaning of *cake* by virtue of it being an artifact. The verb appears polysemous because certain complements add to the basic meaning by virtue of what they denote. We return to this topic below, and provide a formal treatment for how the nominal semantics is expressed in these examples.

Similar principles seem to be operating in the resultative constructions in examples (23) and (24); namely, a systematic ambiguity is the result of principles of semantic composition rather than lexical ambiguity of the verbs. For example, the resultative interpretations for the verbs *hammer* in (23b) and *wipe* in (24b) arise from a similar operation, where both verbs are underlyingly specified with an event type of *process*. The adjectival phrases *flat* and *clean*, although clearly *stative* in nature, can also be interpreted as stage-level event predicates (cf. Dowty 1979). Notice, then, how the resultative construction requires no additional word sense for the verb, nor any special semantic machinery for the resultative interpretation to be available. Schematically, this is shown in example (32):

(32)

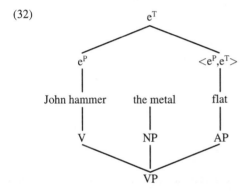

In fact, this analysis explains why it is that only process verbs participate in the resultative construction, and why the resultant phrase (the adjectival phrase) must be a subset of the states, namely, stage-level event predicates. Because the meaning of the sentence in (32) is determined by both function application of *hammer* to its arguments and function application of *flat* to the event-type of the verb, this is an example of *cocompositionality* (cf. Pustejovsky 1995b for discussion).

Having discussed some of the behavior of logical polysemy in verbs, let us continue our discussion of lexical ambiguity with the issue of *metonymy*. Metonymy, where a subpart or related part of an object "stands for" the object itself, also poses a problem for standard denotational theories of semantics. To see why, imagine how our semantics could account for the "reference shifts" of the complements shown in example (33):[16]

(33)   a. Mary enjoyed the book.
        b. Thatcher vetoed the channel tunnel. (cf. Hobbs 1987)
        c. John began a novel.

The complements of *enjoy* in (33a) and *begin* in (33c) are not what these verbs normally select for semantically—namely, a property or action. Similarly, the verb *veto* normally selects for an object that is a legislative bill or a suggestion. Syntactically, these may simply be additional subcategorizations, but how are these examples related semantically to the normal interpretations?

I suggest that these are cases of semantic *type coercion* (cf. Pustejovsky 1989a), where the verb has coerced the meaning of a term phrase into a different semantic type. Briefly, type coercion can be defined as follows:[17]

DEFINITION. *Type Coercion* A semantic operation that converts an argument to the type that is expected by a function, where it would otherwise result in a type error.

In the case of (33b), it is obvious that what is vetoed is some proposal relating to the object denoted by *the tunnel*. In (33a), the book is enjoyed only by virtue of some event or process that involves the book, performed by Mary. It might furthermore be reasonable to assume that the semantic structure of *book* specifies what the artifact is used for—reading. Such a coercion results in a word sense for the NP that I will call *logical metonymy*. Roughly, logical metonymy occurs when a logical argument (i.e., subpart) of a semantic type that is selected by some function denotes the semantic type itself.

Another interesting set of examples involves the possible subjects of causative verbs.[18] Consider the sentences in examples (34) and (35):

(34)   a. Driving a car in Boston **frightens** me.
      b. To drive a car in Boston **frightens** me.
      c. Driving **frightens** me.
      d. John's driving **frightens** me.
      e. Cars **frighten** me.
      f. Listening to this music **upsets** me.
      g. This music **upsets** me.
      h. To listen to this music would **upset** me.

(35)   a. John **killed** Mary.
      b. The gun **killed** Mary.
      c. John's stupidity **killed** Mary.
      d. The war **killed** Mary.
      e. John's pulling the trigger **killed** Mary.

As these examples illustrate, the syntactic argument to a verb is not always the same logical argument in the semantic relation. Although superficially similar to cases of general metonymy (cf. Lakoff and Johnson 1980; Nunberg 1978), there is an interesting systematicity to such shifts in meaning that we will try to characterize below as logical metonymy.

The sentences in (34) illustrate the various syntactic consequences of metonymy and coercion involving experiencer verbs, while those in (35) show the different *metonymic extensions* possible from the causing event in a killing. The generalization here is that when a verb selects an *event* as one of its arguments, type coercion to an event will permit a limited range of logical metonymies. For example, in sentences (34a, b, c, d, f, h), the entire event is directly referred to, while in (34e, g) only a participant from the coerced event reading is directly expressed. Other examples of coercion include "concealed questions" (36) and "concealed exclamations" (37) (cf. Grimshaw 1979; Elliott 1974):

(36)   a. John knows *the plane's arrival time.*
         (= what time the plane will arrive)
      b. Bill figured out *the answer.*
         (= what the answer is)
(37)   a. John shocked me with *his bad behavior.*
         (= how bad his behavior is)
      b. You'd be surprised at *the big cars he buys.*
         (= how big the cars he buys are)

That is, although the italicized phrases syntactically appear as NPs, their semantics is the same as if the verbs had selected an overt question or exclamation.

In explaining the behavior of the systematic ambiguity above, I made reference to properties of the noun phrase that are not typical semantic properties for nouns in linguistics: for example, artifact, natural kind. In Pustejovsky (1989b) and Pustejovsky and Anick (1988), I suggest that there is a system of relations that characterizes the semantics of nominals, very much like the argument structure of a verb. I called this the *qualia structure*, inspired by Aristotle's theory of explanation and ideas from Moravcsik (1975). Essentially, the qualia structure of a noun determines its meaning as much as the list of arguments determines a verb's meaning. The elements that make up a qualia structure include notions such as container, space, surface, figure, artifact, and so on.[19]

As stated earlier, there are four basic roles that constitute the qualia structure for a lexical item. Here I will elaborate on what these roles are and why they are useful. They are given in example (38), where each role is defined, along with the possible values that these roles may assume.

(38) **The Structure of Qualia:**
    1. *Constitutive Role*: the relation between an object and its constituents, or proper parts
- Material
- Weight
- Parts and component elements

    2. *Formal Role*: that which distinguishes the object within a larger domain
- Orientation
- Magnitude
- Shape
- Dimensionality
- Color
- Position

    3. *Telic Role*: purpose and function of the object
- Purpose that an agent has in performing an act
- Built-in function or aim that specifies certain activities

    4. *Agentive Role*: factors involved in the origin or "bringing about" of an object
- Creator
- Artifact
- Natural kind
- Causal chain

When we combine the qualia structure of a NP with the argument structure of a verb, we begin to see a richer notion of compositionality emerging, one that looks very much like object-oriented approaches to programming (cf. Ingria and Pustejovsky 1990).

To illustrate these structures at play, let us consider a few examples. Assume that the decompositional semantics of a nominal includes a specification of its qualia structure:

(39) *Object(Const, Form, Telic, Agent)*

For example, a minimal semantic description for the noun *novel* will include values for each of these roles, as shown in example (40), where x can be seen as a distinguished variable, representing the object itself:

(40) novel(x)
        Const: narrative(x)
        Form: book(x), disk(x)
        Telic: read(e^T,y,x)
        Agentive: artifact(x), write(e^T,z,x)

This structures our basic knowledge about the object: it is a narrative; typically in the form of a book; for the purpose of reading (whose event type is a *transition*); and is an artifact created by a *transition* event of writing. Observe how this structure differs minimally, but significantly, from the qualia structure for the noun *dictionary* in example (41):

(41)   dictionary (x)
        Const: alphabetized-listing (x)
        Form: book(x), disk(x)
        Telic: reference(e^P, y, x)
        Agentive: artifact (x), compile (e^T, z, x)

Notice the differences in the values for the *constitutive* and *telic* roles. The purpose of a dictionary is an activity of referencing, which has an event structure of a *process*.

    I will now demonstrate that such structured information is not only useful for nouns, but necessary to account for their semantic behavior. I suggested earlier, that for cases such as (33), repeated below, there was no need to posit a separate lexical entry for each verb, where the syntactic and semantic types had to be represented explicitly:

(42)   a. Mary enjoyed the book.
      b. Thatcher vetoed the channel tunnel.
      c. John began a novel.

Rather, the verb was analyzed as *coercing* its complement to the semantic type it expected. To illustrate this, consider (42c). The type for *begin* within a standard typed intensional logic is <VP,<NP,S>>, and its lexical semantics is similar to that of other subject control verbs (cf. Klein and Sag 1985 for discussion).

(43) $\lambda P \lambda PP \lambda x[begin(P(x))(x)]$

    Assuming an event structure such as that of Krifka (1987) or Pustejovsky (1991b), we can convert this lexical entry into a representation consistent with a logic making use of event-types (or sorts) by means of the following meaning postulate:[20]

(44) $\forall P \forall x_1 \ldots x_n \square [P_\sigma(x_1) \ldots (x_n) \leftrightarrow \exists e^\sigma [P(x_1) \ldots (x_n)(e^\sigma)]]$

This allows us to type the verb *begin* as taking a transition event as its first argument, represented in example (45):

(45) $\lambda P_T \lambda PP \lambda x[begin(P_T(x))(x)]$

Because the verb requires that its first argument be of type *transition* the complement in (33c) will not match without some sort of shift. It is just this kind of context where the complement (in this case *a novel*) is *coerced* to another type. The coercion dictates to the complement that it must conform to its type specification and the qualia roles may in fact have values matching the correct type. For purposes of illustration, the qualia structure for *novel* from (40) can be represented as the logical expression in example (46):

(46)   **novel** translates into:
        $\lambda x[novel(x) \wedge Const(x) = narrative(x) \wedge$
        $Form(x) = book(x) \wedge$

$Telic(x) = \lambda y,\, e^T[read(x)(y)(e^T)] \wedge$
$Agent(x) = \lambda y,\, e^T[write(x)(y)(e^T)]]$

The coercion operation on the complement in the above examples can be seen as a request to find any transition event associated with the noun. As we saw above, the qualia structure contains just this kind of information.

We can imagine the qualia roles as partial functions from a noun denotation into its sub-constituent denotations. For our present purposes, we abbreviate these functions as Q_F, Q_C, Q_T, Q_A. When applied, they return the value of a particular qualia role. For example, the purpose of a novel is for reading it, shown in (47a), while the mode of creating a novel is by writing it, represented in (47b):

(47)   a. Q_T (**novel**) $= \lambda y,\, e^T[read(x)(y)(e^T)]$
       b. Q_A (**novel**) $= \lambda y,\, e^T[write(x)(y)(e^T)]$

As the expressions in (47) suggest, there are, in fact, two obvious interpretations for this sentence in (42c):

(48)   a. John began to **read** a novel.
       b. John began to **write** a novel.

One of these is selected by the coercing verb, resulting in a complement that has a event-predicate interpretation, without any syntactic transformations (cf. Pustejovsky 1989a for details).[21] The derivation in (49a) and the structure in (49b) show the effects of this coercion on the verb's complement, using the *telic* value of *novel*:[22]

(49)   a. John began a novel.
       b. **begin** $(Q_T(\textbf{a novel}))(\textbf{John}) \Rightarrow$
       c. **begin** $(\lambda x,\, e^T[read(\textbf{a novel})(x)(e^T)])(\textbf{John}) \Rightarrow$
       d. **John** $\{\lambda x[\textbf{begin}(\lambda x,\, e^T\,[read(\textbf{a novel})(x)(e^T)](x))(x)]\} \Rightarrow$
       e. **John** $\{\lambda x[\textbf{begin}(\lambda e^T\,[read(\textbf{a novel})(x)(e^T)])(x)]\} \Rightarrow$
       f. **begin** $(\lambda e^T[read(\textbf{a novel})(\textbf{John})(e^T)])(\textbf{John})$
       g.

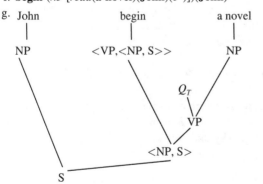

The fact that this is not a unique interpretation of the elliptical event predicate is in some ways irrelevant to the notion of type coercion. That there is *some* event involving the complement is required by the lexical semantics of the governing verb and the rules of type well-formedness, and although there are many ways to act on a novel, I argue that certain relations are "privileged" in the lexical semantics of the noun. It is not the role of a lexical semantic theory to say what readings are preferred but, rather, which are available.[23]

Assuming the semantic selection given above for *begin* is correct, we would predict that, because of the process event-type associated with the telic role for *dictionary*, there is only one default interpretation for the sentence in (50): namely, the *agentive* event of "compiling":

(50) a. Mary began a dictionary. (Agentive)
      b. ?? Mary began a dictionary. (Telic)

Not surprisingly, when the noun in complement position has no default interpretation within an event predicate—as given by its qualia structure—the resulting sentence is extremely odd:

(51) a. *Mary began a rock.
      b. ?? John finished the flower.

The semantic distinctions that are possible once we give semantic weight to lexical items other than verbs are quite wide-ranging. The next example I will consider concerns scalar modifiers, such as *fast*, that modify different predicates depending on the head they modify. If we think of certain modifiers as modifying only a subset of the qualia for a noun, then we can view *fast* as modifying only the telic role of an object. This allows us to go beyond treating adjectives such as *fast* as intersective modifiers—for example, as $\lambda x[car(x) \wedge fast(x)]$. Let us assume that an adjective such as *fast* is a member of the general type $\langle N, N \rangle$, but can be subtyped as applying to the Telic role of the noun being modified. That is, it has as its type, $\langle [N\ \text{Telic}], N \rangle$. This gives rise directly to the different interpretations in example (52):

(52) a. **a fast car**: driving
         $Q_T(\textbf{car}) = \lambda x \lambda y \lambda e^P [drive(x)(y)(e^P)]$
      b. **a fast typist**: typing
         $Q_T(\textbf{typist}) = \lambda x \lambda e^P [type(x)(e^P)]$
      c. **a fast motorway**: traveling
         $Q_T(\textbf{motorway}) = \lambda x \lambda e^P [travel(cars)(e^P) \wedge on(x)(cars)(e^P)]$

These interpretations are all derived from a single word sense for *fast*. Because the lexical semantics for this adjective indicates that it modifies the telic role of the noun, it effectively acts as an event predicate rather than an attribute over the entire noun denotation, as illustrated in example (53) for *fast motorway* (cf. Pustejovsky and Boguraev 1991 for discussion):

(53) $\lambda x[motorway(x) \ldots [Telic(x) = \lambda e^P [travel(cars)(e^P) \wedge on(x)(cars)(e^P) \wedge fast(e^P)\ ]]]$

As our final example of how the qualia structure contributes to the semantic interpretation of a sentence, observe how the nominals *window* and *door* in examples (54) and (55) carry two interpretations (cf. Lakoff 1987 and Pustejovsky and Anick 1988):

(54) a. John crawled through *the window*.
      b. *The window* is closed.
(55) a. Mary painted *the door*.
      b. Mary walked through *the door*.

Each noun appears to have two word senses: a physical object denotation and an aperture denotation. Pustejovsky and Anick (1988) characterize the meaning of such "Double Figure-Ground" nominals as inherently relational, where both parameters are logically part of the meaning of the noun. In terms of the qualia structure for this class of nouns, the formal role takes as its value the *Figure* of a physical object, while the constitutive role assumes the *Invert-Figure* value of an aperture:[24]

(56)   Lexical Semantics for **door**:
      door(x,y)
            Const: aperture(y)
            Form: phys-obj(x)
            Telic: pass-through(e^T,z,y)
            Agentive: artifact(x)

The foregrounding or backgrounding of a nominal's qualia is very similar to argument structure-changing operations for verbs. That is, in (55a), *paint* applies to the formal role of *the door*, while in (55b), *through* will apply to the constitutive interpretation of the same NP. The ambiguity with such nouns is a logical one, one that is intimately linked to the semantic representation of the object itself. The qualia structure, then, is a way of capturing this logical polysemy.

In conclusion, it should be pointed out that the entire lexicon is organized around such logical ambiguities, which Pustejovsky and Anick (1988) call *Lexical Conceptual Paradigms*. Pustejovsky (1995b) distinguishes the following systems and the paradigms that lexical items fall into:

(57)   a. Count/Mass Alternations
       b. Container/Containee Alternations
       c. Figure/Ground Reversals
       d. Product/Producer Diathesis
       e. Plant/Fruit Alternations
       f. Process/Result Diathesis
       g. Object/Place Reversals
       h. State/Thing Alternations
       i. Place/People

Such paradigms provide a means for accounting for the systematic ambiguity that may exist for a lexical item. For example, a noun behaving according to paradigm (57a) exhibits a logical polysemy involving packaging or grinding operators—for example, *haddock* or *lamb* (cf. Copestake and Briscoe 1991 for details).

7   Lexical inheritance theory

In previous sections, I discussed lexical ambiguity and showed how a richer view of lexical semantics allows us to view a word's meaning as being flexible, where word senses could arise generatively by composition with other words. The final aspect of this flexibility deals with the logical associations a word has in a given context: that is, how this semantic information is organized as a global knowledge base. This involves capturing both the inheritance relations between concepts and, just as importantly, how the concepts are integrated into a coherent expression in a given sentence.

I will assume that there are two inheritance mechanisms at work for representing the conceptual relations in the lexicon: *fixed* inheritance and *protective* inheritance. The first includes the methods of inheritance traditionally assumed in AI and lexical research (e.g., Roberts and Goldstein 1977; Brachman and Schmolze 1985; Bobrow and Winograd 1977); that is, a *fixed* network of relations, which is traversed to discover existing related and associated concepts (e.g., hyponyms and hypernyms). In order to arrive at a comprehensive theory of the lexicon, we need to address the issue of global organization, and this involves looking at the various modes of inheritance that exist in language and conceptualization. Some of the best work addressing the issue of how the lexical semantics of a word ties into its deeper conceptual structure includes that of Hobbs et al. (1987) and Wilks (1975a; 1975b), while interesting work on shared information structures in NLP domains is that of Flickinger et al. (1985) and Evans and Gazdar (1989; 1990).

In addition to this static representation, I will introduce another mechanism for structuring lexical knowledge, the *projective* inheritance, which operates *generatively* from the qualia structure of a lexical item to create a relational structure for ad hoc categories. Both are necessary for projecting the semantic representations of individual lexical items onto a sentence level interpretation. The discussion here, however, will be limited to a description of projective inheritance and the notion of "degrees of prototypicality" of predication. I will argue that such degrees of salience or coherence relations can be explained in structural terms by examining a network of related lexical items.[25]

I will illustrate the distinction between these mechanisms by considering the two sentences in example (58) and their relative prototypicality

(58)   a. The prisoner *escaped* last night.
        b. The prisoner *ate* dinner last night.

Both of these sentences are obviously well-formed syntactically, but there is a definite sense that the predication in (58a) is "tighter" or more prototypical than that in (58b). What would account for such a difference? Intuitively, we associate prisoner with an *escaping* event more strongly than an *eating* event. Yet this is not information that comes from a fixed inheritance structure, but is rather usually assumed to be commonsense knowledge. In what follows, however, I will show that such distinctions can be captured within a theory of lexical semantics by means of generating ad hoc categories.

First, we give a definition for the *fixed inheritance* structure of a lexical item (cf. Touretzky 1986). Let Q and P be concepts in our model of lexical organization. Then:

DEFINITION. A sequence $\langle Q_1, P_1, \ldots, P_n \rangle$ is an *inheritance path*, which can be read as the conjunction of ordered pairs $\{\langle x_1, y_i \rangle \mid 1 \leq i \leq n\}$.

Furthermore, following Touretzky, from this we can define the set of concepts that lie on an inheritance path, the *conclusion space*:

DEFINITION. The *conclusion space* of a set of sequences ϕ is the set of all pairs $\langle Q, P \rangle$ such that a sequence $\langle Q, \ldots, P \rangle$ appears in ϕ.

From these two definitions we can define the traditional is-a relation, relating the above pairs by a *generalization* operator, $\leq_G$,[26] as well as other relations that I will not discuss.[27]

Let us suppose that, in addition to these fixed relational structures, our semantics allows us to dynamically create arbitrary concepts through the application of certain transformations to lexical meanings. For example, for any predicate, Q—for example, the value of a qualia role—we can generate its opposition, $\neg Q$ (cf. Pustejovsky 1991b). By relating these two predicates temporally, we can generate the arbitrary transition events for this opposition (cf. von Wright 1963):

(59)   a. $\neg Q(x) \leq Q(x)$
        b. $Q(x) \leq \neg Q(x)$
        c. $Q(x) \leq Q(x)$
        d. $\neg Q(x) \leq \neg Q(x)$

Similarly, by operating over other qualia role values we can generate semantically related concepts. I will call any operator that performs such an operation a *projective transformation*, and define them below:

> DEFINITION. A *projective transformation*, π, on a predicate Q_1 generates a predicate, Q_2, such that $\pi(Q_1) = Q_2$, where $Q_2 \notin \phi$. The set of transformations includes: $\neg$, negation: $\leq$, temporal precedence; $\geq$, temporal succession; $=$, temporal equivalence; and *act*, an operator adding agency to an argument.

Intuitively, the space of concepts traversed by the application of such operators will be related expressions in the neighborhood of the original lexical item. This space can be characterized by the following two definitions:

> DEFINITION. A series of applications of transformations, $\pi_1, \ldots, \pi_n$, generates a sequence of predicates, $\langle Q_1, \ldots, Q_n \rangle$, called the *projective expansion* of Q_1, $P(Q_1)$.

> DEFINITION. The *projective conclusion space*, $P(\phi_R)$, is the set of projective expansions generated from all elements of the conclusion space, ϕ, on role R of predicate Q: as: $P(\phi_R) = \{\langle P(Q_1), P(Q_n) \rangle \mid \langle Q_1, \ldots, Q_n \rangle \in \phi_R\}$.

From this resulting representation, we can generate a relational structure that can be considered the set of ad hoc categories and relations associated with a lexical item (cf. Barselou 1983).

Using these definitions, let us return to the sentences in example (58). I will assume that the noun *prisoner* has a qualia structure such as that shown in (60):

(60)   Qualia Structure of **prisoner**:

   prisoner(x)

   Form: human(x)

   Telic: [confine(y,x) & location(x, prison)]

Furthermore, I assume the following lexical structure for *escape*:

(61)   Lexical Semantics for *escape*:

   $\lambda x \lambda e^T \exists e^P, e^S[escape(e^T) \wedge act(e^P) \wedge confined(e^P) \wedge agent(e^P, x) \wedge \neg confined(e^S) \wedge object(e^S,x)]$

Using the representation in (60) above, I now trace part of the derivation of the projective conclusion space for *prisoner*. Inheritance structures are defined for each qualia role of an element. In the case above, values are specified for only two roles.

For each role, R, we apply a projective transformation π onto the predicate Q that is the value of that role. For example, from the telic role of *prisoner* we can generalize (e.g., drop the conjunct) to the concept of *being confined*. From this concept, we can apply the negation operator, generating the predicate opposition of *not-confined* and *confined*. To this, we apply the two temporal operators, $\leq$ and $\geq$, generating two states: *free before capture* and *free after capture*. Finally, to these concepts, if we apply the operator *act*, varying who is responsible for the resulting transition event, we generate the concepts: *turn in*, *capture*, *escape*, and *release*:

(62)   Projecting on *Telic* Role of *prisoner*:

   a. $\leq_G$: $[confine(y, x) \wedge loc(x, prison)] \Rightarrow confine(y, x)$

   b. $\neg$: $\exists e_1[\neg confine(e_1, y, x)]$

   c. $\exists e_2[confine(e_2, y, x)]$

   d. $\leq$: $e_1 \leq e_2 = e_1^T$

e. $\leq:e_2 \leq e_1 = e_2^T$

f. act: $act(x, e_1^T)$ = "turn in"

g. act: $act\ (y, e_1^T)$ = "capture"

h. act: $act(x, e_2^T)$ = "escape"

i. act: $act(y, e_2^S)$ = "release"

These relations constitute the *projective conclusion space* for the telic role of *prisoner* relative to the application of the transformations mentioned above. Similar operations on the formal role will generate concepts such as *die* and *kill*. Generating such structures for all items in a sentence during analysis, we can take those graphs that result in no contradictions to be the legitimate semantic interpretations of the entire sentence.

Let us now return to the sentences in example (58). It is now clear why these two sentences differ in their prototypicality (or the relevance conditions on their predication). The predicate *eat* is not within the space of related concepts generated from the semantics of the NP *the prisoner*; *escape*, however, did fall within the projective conclusion space for the Telic role of *prisoner*, as shown in example (63):

(63)   Conclusion Space for (58):

$escape \in P(\phi_T(prisoner))$

$eat \notin P(\phi_T(prisoner))$

This is illustrated in example (64):

(64) $release(e^T, y, x)$ $escape(e^T, x)$ $capture(e^T, y, x)$ $turn\text{-}in(e^T, x)$

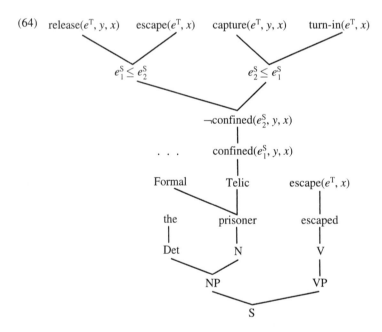

We can therefore use such a procedure as one metric for evaluating the "proximity" of a predication (Quillian 1968; Hobbs 1982). In the examples above, the difference in semanticality can now be seen as a structural distinction between the semantic representations for the elements in the sentence.

In this section, I have shown how the lexical inheritance structure of an item relates, in a generative fashion, the decompositional structure of a word to a much larger set of concepts that are related in obvious ways. What we have not addressed, however, is how the fixed inheritance information of a lexical item is formally derivable during composition. This issue is explicitly addressed in Briscoe et al. (1990), as well as Pustejovsky and Briscoe (1991).

8   Conclusion

In this paper I have outlined a framework for lexical semantic research that I believe can be useful for both computational linguists and theoretical linguists alike. I argued against the view that word meanings are fixed and inflexible, where lexical ambiguity must be treated by multiple word entries in the lexicon. Rather, the lexicon can be seen as a generative system, where word senses are related by logical operations defined by the well-formedness rules of the semantics. In this view, much of the lexical ambiguity of verbs and prepositions is eliminated because the semantic load is spread more evenly throughout the lexicon to the other lexical categories. I described a language for structuring the semantic information carried by nouns and adjectives, termed *qualia structure*, as well as the rules of composition that allow this information to be incorporated into the semantic interpretation of larger expressions, including explicit methods for type coercion. Finally, I discussed how these richer lexical representations can be used to generate projective inheritance structures that connect the conceptual information associated with lexical items to the global conceptual lexicon. This suggests a way of accounting for relations such as coherence and the prototypicality of a predication. Although much of what I have presented here is incomplete and perhaps somewhat programmatic, I firmly believe this approach can help clarify the nature of word meaning and compositionality in natural language, and at the same time bring us closer to understanding the creative use of word senses.

Notes

I would like to thank the following for comments on earlier drafts of this paper: Peter Anick, Sabine Bergler, Bran Boguraev, Ted Briscoe, Noam Chomsky, Bob Ingria, George Miller, Sergei Nirenburg, and Rich Thomason.

1. This is still a contentious point and is an issue that is not at all resolved in the community. Hobbs (1987) and Wilensky (1991), for example, argue that there should be no distinction between commonsense knowledge and lexical knowledge. Nevertheless, I will suggest below that there are good reasons, both methodological and empirical, for establishing just such a division. Pustejovsky and Bergler (1991) contains a good survey on how this issue is addressed by the community.

2. Weinreich (1972) distinguishes between contrastive and complementary polysemy, essentially covering this same distinction. See section 4 for discussion.

3. Both Klein and Sag (1985) and Chomsky (1981) assume, however, that there are reasons for relating these two forms structurally. See below and Pustejovsky (1989a) for details.

4. For further discussion on the advantages and disadvantages to both approaches, see Jackendoff (1983).

5. See Goodman (1951) and Chomsky (1955) for explanations of the method assumed here.

6. This approach is also better suited to the way people write systems in computational linguistics. Different people have distinct primitives for their own domains, and rather than committing a designer to a particular vocabulary of primitives, a lexical semantics should provide a method for the decomposition and composition of lexical items.

7. Some of these roles are reminiscent of descriptors used by various computational researchers, such as Wilks (1975b), Hayes (1979), and Hobbs et al. (1987). Within the theory outlined here, these roles determine a minimal semantic description of a word that has both semantic and grammatical consequences.

8. This proposal is an extension of ideas explored by Bach (1986b), Higginbotham (1985), and Allen (1984). For a full discussion, see Pustejovsky (1988, 1991b). See Tenny (1987) for a proposal on how aspectual distinctions are mapped to the syntax.

9. For example, Dowty (1985) proposes multiple entries for verbs taking different subcategorizations. Gazdar et al. (1985), adopting the analysis in Klein and Sag (1985), propose a set of lexical type-shifting operations to capture sense relatedness. We return to this topic below.

10. I will be assuming a Davidsonian-style representation for the discussion below. Predicates in the language are typed for a particular event-sort, and thematic roles are treated as partial functions over the event (cf. Dowty 1989 and Chierchia 1989).

11. More precisely, the process e^P should reflect that it is the substance contained in the object x that is affected. See note 20 for explanation.

12. However, relative to the process of *growing*, the noun *potato* does denote an event:

> (i) Mary grew the potato.

13. Other examples of cospecifications are (a) *read a book*, (b) *smoke a cigarette*, (c) *mail a letter*, (d) *deliver a lecture*, and (e) *take a bath*.

There are several interesting things about such collocations. First, because the complement "selects" the verb that governs it (by virtue of knowledge of what is done to the object), the semantics of the phrase is changed. The semantic "connectedness," as it were, is tighter when cospecification obtains. In such cases, the verb is able to successfully drop the dative PP argument, as shown below in (1). When the complement does not select the verb governing it, dative-drop is ungrammatical as seen in (2) (although there are predicates selected by these nouns—for example, *keep a secret*, *read a book*, and *play a record*):

> (i)   a. Romeo gave the lecture.
>   b. Hamlet mailed a letter.
>   c. Cordelia told a story.
>   d. Gertrude showed a movie.
>   e. Mary asked a question.
> (ii) a. *Bill told the secret.
>   b. *Mary gave a book.
>   c. *Cordelia showed the record.

For discussion see Pustejovsky (1993).

14. See Pustejovsky (1998) for details.

15. As mentioned in note 11, this representation is incomplete. See note 20 for semantics of *bake*.

16. See Nunberg (1978) and Fauconnier (1985) for very clear discussions of the semantics of metonymy and the nature of reference shifts. See Wilks (1975a) and Fass (1988) for computational models of metonymic resolution.

17. I am following Cardelli and Wegner (1985) and their characterization of polymorphismic behavior.

18. See Verma and Mohanan (1991) for an extensive survey of experiencer subject constructions in different languages.

19. These components of an object's denotation have long been considered crucial for our commonsense understanding of how things interact in the world. Cf. Hayes (1979), Hobbs et al. (1987), and Croft (1991) for discussion of these qualitative aspects of meaning.

20. It should be pointed out that the lexical structure for the verb *bake* given in the text in (30) and (31) can more properly be characterized as a process acting on various qualia of the arguments.

> (i) $\lambda y \lambda x \exists e^P \exists e^S [bake\ (e^P) \wedge agent\ (e_P, x) \wedge (object(e^P, Q_c\ (y)) \wedge cake\ (e^S) \wedge object\ (e^S, Q_F\ (x))]$

21. There are, of course, an indefinite number of interpretations, depending on pragmatic factors and various contextual influences. But I maintain that there are only a finite number of default interpretations available in such constructions. These form part of the lexical semantics of the noun. Additional evidence for this distinction is given in Pustejovsky and Anick (1988) and Briscoe et al. (1990).

22. Partee and Rooth (1983) suggest that all expressions in the language can be assigned a base type while also being associated with a type ladder. Pustejovsky (1989a) extends this proposal and argues that each expression α may have available to it, a set of shifting operators, which we call Σ_α, which operate over an expression, changing its type and denotation. By making reference to these operators directly in the rule of function application, we can treat the functor polymorphically, as illustrated below:

(i) Function Application with Coercion (FA$_c$):
If α is of type $<b,a>$, and β is of type c, then
  (a) if type $c = b$, the $\alpha(\beta)$ is of type a.
  (b) if there is a $\sigma \in \Sigma_\beta$ such that $\sigma(\beta)$ results in an expression of type b, then $\alpha(\sigma(\beta))$ is of type a.
  (c) otherwise a type error is produced.

23. There are interesting differences in complement types between *finish* and *complete*. The former takes both NP and a gerundive VP, while the latter takes only an NP (cf. for example, Freed 1979 for discussion).

(i)   a. John finished the book.
      b. John finished writing the book.
(ii) a. John completed the book.
      b. *John completed writing the book.

The difference would indicate that, contrary to some views (e.g., Wierzbicka 1988 and Dixon 1991), lexical items need to carry both syntactic and semantic selectional information to determine the range of complement and not the telic role. The scope of semantic selection is explored at length in Pustejovsky (1993).

24. There are many such classes of nominals both two-dimensional such as those mentioned in the text, and three-dimensional, such as "room," "fireplace," and "pipe." They are interesting semantically, because they are logically ambiguous, referring to either the object or the aperture, but not both. Boguraev and Pustejovsky (1995b) show how these logical polysemies are in fact encoded in dictionary definitions for these words.

25. Anick and Pustejovsky (1990) explore how metrics such as *association ratios* can be used to statistically measure the notions of prototypicality mentioned here.

26. See, for example, Michalski (1983) and Smolka (1988) for a treatment making use of subsorts.

27. Such relations include not only hypernymy and hyponymy but also troponymy, which relates verbs by manner relations (cf. Miller 1985; Beckwith et al. 1989; Miller and Fellbaum 1991).

19

BRENDAN S. GILLON

Towards a Common Semantics
for English Count and Mass Nouns

The distinction between mass nouns and count nouns, first remarked upon by Jespersen (1909, vol. 2, ch. 5.2) in connection with English, is found in a number of the world's languages, including Chinese, Tamil, German, and French. In English, the most common way to distinguish these two classes of words is syntactic. Cardinal numerals and quasi-cardinal numerals (e.g., "several") modify count nouns, never mass nouns. Moreover, "little" and "much" modify mass nouns, never count nouns, whereas "few" and "many" modify count nouns, never mass nouns. Count nouns admit a morphological contrast between singular and plural; mass nouns do not, being almost always singular. The pronoun "one" may have as its antecedent a count noun, not a mass noun (Baker 1978. ch. 10.1). Mass nouns with singular morphology do not tolerate the indefinite article, whereas singular count nouns do. Finally, mass nouns occur only with the plural form of those quantifiers whose singular and plural forms differ.

It has also been thought that mass nouns and count nouns can be distinguished by what they denote. The two criteria most commonly proposed are cumulativity and divisivity of reference. Quine (1960, p. 91) observed that if a mass term such as "water" is true of each of two items then it is true of the two items taken together; he dubbed this semantical property of mass terms "cumulative reference." This characterization, while apt, does not, however, distinguish mass nouns from count nouns; for, as Link (1991) has pointed out, cumulativity of reference also holds of plural count nouns: just as it is the case that "If the animals in this camp are horses and the animals in that camp are horses, then the animals in the two camps are horses," so it is the case that "if a is water and b is water then a and b together are water" (see also Bunt 1985, p. 19).

The second criterion, that of the divisivity of reference, suggested by Cheng (1973, pp. 286–287), states that any part of something denoted by a mass noun is denoted by the same mass noun. However, this criterion is belied by two facts pointed out by Quine (1960, p. 99):

Brendan S. Gillon (1992) Towards a common semantics for English count and mass nouns. *Linguistics and Philosophy* 15: 597–639. Reprinted by permission of Kluwer Academic Publishers.

There are parts of water, sugar and furniture too small to count as water, sugar, furniture. More-over, what is too small to count as furniture is not too small to count as water or sugar; so the limitation needed cannot be worked into any general adaptation of 'is' or 'is a part of', but must be left rather as the separate reference-dividing business of the several mass terms.

While some semanticists retain the divisivity of reference as a criterion to distinguish mass nouns from count nouns, in spite of the facts given above, only Bunt (1979; 1985) has attempted to justify the retention. Bunt (1985, p. 45) restates Quine's point as follows: "For each mass noun 'M' there is a specific minimal size that parts of its referent may have in order to count as 'M'." Bunt calls this "the Minimal Parts Hypothesis" and questions its relevance to the problem of formulating the semantics of mass nouns (see also Bunt 1979, p. 255). As he sees it, this hypoth-esis could be either about natural language or about the world. He maintains that insofar as it is a hypothesis about the world, it is true but irrelevant; and insofar as it is a hypothesis about natu-ral language, it is false.

Bunt (1985, pp. 45–46) goes on to claim that "mass nouns provide the possibility of talking about things *as if if they do not consist of discrete parts*" and that "a linguistic semantic theory should take into account that the use of a mass noun is a way of talking about things as if they were homogeneous masses, i.e., as having some part-whole structure but without singling out any particular parts and without any commitments concerning the existence of minimal parts." He calls this the homogeneous reference hypothesis and restates it as follows: "Mass nouns refer to entities as having a part-whole structure without singling out any particular parts and without making any commitments concerning the existence of minimal parts" (Bunt 1985, p. 46; see also Bunt 1979, pp. 255–256).

There are, it seems, two claims which go under the heading of the homogeneous reference hypothesis. On the one hand, Bunt seems to claim that the minimal parts hypothesis has no sys-tematic role to play in the grammar of the language: the grammar is simply mute on the question of whether or not there are minimal parts. This is how I understand the last citation in the previ-ous paragraph and the portion of the preceding citation following the "i.e." I shall call this "the weak version of the homogeneous reference hypothesis." On the other hand, Bunt claims that the divisivity of reference is a grammatical principle for the interpretation of mass nouns. This is how I understand the first citation of the previous paragraph and the part of the succeeding cita-tion preceding the "i.e." I shall call this "the strong version of the homogeneous reference hy-pothesis." These versions of the hypothesis are incompatible. That Bunt intends the strong version is borne out by the fact that he adopts the divisivity criterion as an axiom of the formal semantics of mass nouns. (See (34) in Bunt 1979, p. 262, and (14.13) and (14.15) in Bunt 1981, p. 165.) In more recent work, the strong version of the homogeneous reference hypothesis has also been adopted by ter Meulen (1981, p. 123), Roeper (1983, pp. 256–257), and Lønning (1987, sec. 1).

However, the strong version of the homogeneous reference hypothesis is certainly to be rejected, for reasons set out by Parsons (1970a, sec. VI.A). Under the standard and plausible mereological assumption that two wholes are identical if and only if they have the same proper parts, it turns out that, in a world in which all furniture is made of wood and all wood has been made into furniture, the whole of wood would be identical with the whole of furniture—an im-plausible consequence. (However, see Bunt 1985, pp. 47–48, for a reply.)

The view adopted here is that the grammar is mute on whether or not a mass term which is true of a thing is also true of any of its proper parts. More specifically, I shall argue that the syn-tactic and semantic differences between mass noun phrases and count noun phrases are deriv-able from general syntactic and semantic principles and the two pairs of contrasting syntactic features ±CT and ±PL. That is to say, it is these two pairs of syntactic features and the constraints imposed by their semantic interpretation that determine the differences between mass noun phrases and count noun phrases.

1   Syntax

In light of the basic role played by syntax in the proposal being propounded here, the natural place to begin its elaboration is with the underlying syntax. The task is to delineate a syntactic taxonomy of English nouns and noun phrases, which makes clear not only the domain in terms of which the proposal is to be elaborated but also certain distributional regularities which the proposal successfully captures.

For the sake of exposition, I wish to confine my account of the grammar of English common nouns to their syntactic and semantic roles in simple sentences. By the term "simple sentence" I mean a sentence of the form

(1)   a. NP V
      b. NP V NP,

where NP is simple; and by the term "simple noun phrase," I mean a noun phrase containing neither an S node nor any other phrasal nodes.[1]

How one sees the syntactic structure of English noun phrases depends, in part at least, upon antecedent assumptions about the organization of the syntax. I shall assume, following Selkirk (1982) as well as Di Sciullo and Williams (1987), that word formation rules and phrase formation rules operate at different levels of English grammar. One advantage of this assumption is that it permits the formulation of a rather nice generalization pertaining to the syntactic structure of those elements in an English noun phrase which precede its head noun. This can be expressed in terms of the following phrase structure rule:[2]

(2)   NP → (NP's/DET) (AP) N.

Further dividends are paid, once one observes that, by and large, determiners in English do not iterate. Indeed the generalization is perfect, if one sets aside as idiomatic the iterations found in expressions such as "every which way" and "what a man" and if one posits that expressions such as "all the men" and "both the women" are contractions of their partitive counterparts, "all of the men" and "both of the women," where the partitive preposition is elided. This generalization, together with the rule in (2), implies that quasi-cardinal numerals such as "several" and cardinal numerals are adjectives. It also permits a tripartite division of English determiners, depending on whether they trigger WH movement, QR movement, or no movement. These classes are in-terrogatives (e.g., "which" and "what"), quantifiers (e.g., "a", "some", "each", "all," and "no"), and demonstratives (e.g., "the", "this," and "that").[3]

Nouns, too, form syntactic classes, which are distinguished by two characteristics: whether or not they occur with determiners and whether or not they admit of the contrast between singular and plural. On the one hand, it is generally recognized that pronouns and count nouns admit the contrast between singular and plural, even if the morphological realization is sometimes the same (e.g., "sheep"). It is also generally recognized that proper names and mass nouns do not admit of such a contrast, being either singular alone or plural alone. On the other hand, proper names and pronouns do not admit determiners, though sometimes the definite article has come to be part of a proper name, while mass nouns and count nouns do, though need not. (See Vendler 1967a, ch. 2.5–2.7, for discussion.) In short, there are four kinds of nouns (see Table 19.1), depending on which characteristic applies from each contrasting pair: proper names, pronouns, mass nouns, and count nouns (the last two taken together comprise common nouns).

This classification does not preclude the attested fact that the same phonological shape can occur in more than one class. This is widely acknowledged in the case of nouns and verbs: "ham-mer" and "truck," for example, are classified both as nouns and as verbs. (See Clark and Clark

TABLE 19.1

A determiner	Occurs with singular and plural	Admits to contrast of
Proper name	–	–
Pronoun	–	+
Mass noun	+	–
Count noun	+	+

1979 for discussion.) The same situation obtains among the subclassifications of nouns. Thus, the same phonological shape can be associated with both a proper name and a count noun:

(3) a. Tom is a friend.
     b. Every Tom I know is away on vacation.

And similarly, the same phonological shape can be associated with both a mass noun and a count noun:

(4) a. How many chickens are in the yard?
     b. How much chicken should be served to each guest?

In some cases, the dual occurrence is the result of either of two productive rules, one mapping count nouns into mass nouns, sometimes referred to colorfully as the "universal grinder" (Pelletier 1975, pp. 5–6), another mapping mass nouns into count nouns, dubbed by Bunt (1985, p. 11) as the "universal sorter." In other cases, the dual occurrence is a lexicographical legacy of the application of such rules at an earlier point in the history of the language.[4]

Above, I adopted the view that word formation and phrase formation take place at different levels of grammar. One kind of word formation is compounding; one kind of compounding is where a pair of words come together to form one word. This is a very productive process in English, one of the commonest forms of compounding being a word composed of two nouns. Count nouns and mass nouns can come together to form compounds. When they do, if the head of the compound is a mass noun, then the compound is a mass noun; and if the head is a count noun, then the compound is a count noun. Thus, while "ocean" is a count noun and "water" is a mass noun, the compound "ocean water," in which "water" is the head, is a mass noun. Similarly, while "water" is a mass noun and "wheel" is a count noun, the compound "water wheel," in which "wheel" is the head, is a count noun. A common hypothesis to handle this inheritance of syntactic characteristics of a head noun by the compound of which it is a head, is to postulate a feature possessed by the head which is passed onto the whole compound, so-called percolation. (For further details pertaining to either the headedness of compounds or the percolation of features, see Selkirk 1982, ch. 2.2; Di Sciullo and Williams 1987, ch. 2; and Lieber 1992, ch. 3.) Following such an approach here, let us assume that the features +CT and –CT distinguish count nouns from mass nouns.

The syntactic principles pertaining to grammatical number in English are fairly straightforward. To begin with, a count noun in any acceptable sentence has either singular or plural morphology. It is natural to see this morphological fact as a phonological reflex of a syntactic requirement that each count noun be assigned exactly one of the two features, +PL and –PL. It is not so obvious that the noun phrase node immediately containing a count noun inherits the feature assigned to the count noun it contains. However, three generalizations pertaining to agreement in grammatical number, which are true of Indo-European languages in general and which are virtually universally thought to be true of English in particular, in spite of its morphological poverty, suggests that this is so.

The first generalization, a paradigmatic instance of what is called in current syntactic jargon "specifier-head agreement," is the agreement between the grammatical number of determiners and the grammatical number of the nouns they modify. Table 19.2 provides some routine examples.

A second generalization, which current syntactic theory also maintains to be an instance of specifier-head agreement, is that inflected verbs agree in grammatical number with their subjects:

(5) a. This person is always punctual.
     b. *This person are always punctual.

These two generalizations are respected, if one assumes that the features of a count noun are assigned to its first dominating noun phrase node (i.e., its maximal projection) and that the features assigned to a determiner must be consistent with the features of its first dominating noun phrase node.

English also conforms to a third generalization, namely, that pronouns agree in number with their antecedents:[5]

(6) a. [The critic]$_i$ admires [himself]$_i$.
     b. *[The critic]$_i$ admires [themselves]$_i$.
     c. [The critics]$_i$ think that [they]$_i$ are great.
     d. *[The critics]$_i$ think that [he]$_i$ is great.

Moreover, the antecedence relation is defined over noun phrase nodes. Again, this generalization is respected, if one assumes that the features of a count noun (or a pronoun) are assigned to its first dominating noun phrase node and that the features of two noun phrase nodes, one of which bears the relation of antecedence to the other, must be consistent.

Two more details must be attended to. First, pronouns with split antecedents are plural:

(7) a. John told Mary that they should meet.
     b. *John told Mary that he/she should meet.

Second, conjoined noun phrases are plural, even if its conjuncts are singular:[6]

(8) a. John and Mary are leaving.
     b. *John and Mary is leaving.

This can be handled by a simple rule: the feature of a pronoun with an antecedent is the sum of the features of its antecedent noun phrases and the feature of a conjoined noun phrase is the sum of the features of the conjuncts, where the sum of xPL$_i$ is –PL if $i = 1$ and + PL otherwise (where x ranges over + and – and i enumerates the ith conjunct in the conjunction).

TABLE 19.2

Singular	Plural
this table	*this tables
*these table	these tables
that dart	*that darts
*those dart	those darts
each friend	*each friends
*all friend	all friends

Usages appearing to resist these generalizations are well known, being thoroughly documented in the more complete descriptive grammars of English. (See, for example, either Jespersen 1909, vol. 2, ch. 3, or Quirk et al. 1985, ch. 10.34ff.) Since limitations of space preclude my addressing each of them, I shall confine my attention to only those usages which have been suggested by referees as counterexamples to one or more of the three generalizations just discussed.

Let me begin with a usage which challenges the third generalization. It is well known that many speakers of English prefer the second sentence below to the first:

(9)   a. Every child loves his mother.
      b. Every child loves their mother.

The first sentence conforms to the third generalization, whereas the second does not. That is to say, while the antecedent of the third-person personal pronoun is, in each case, the subject noun phrase, which is singular in grammatical number; the pronoun in the first case is singular, in conformity with the generalization, whereas the pronoun in the second is plural, contrary to the generalization.

What can be concluded from this usage? Before answering this question, let us recall some well known facts about gender in Indo-European languages. Gender, in many Indo-European languages, is a set of morphosyntactic features, typically including masculine, feminine, and neuter, which is associated with every noun and adjective. Common nouns differ from adjectives insofar as the gender of a common noun is intrinsic to the noun, whereas the gender of an adjective depends on its syntactic relation to some noun, usually that of modification or predication. Pronouns, unlike common nouns, but like adjectives, do not have intrinsic gender. Like adjectives, they depend for their gender on syntactic relations with other noun phrases; but unlike adjectives, if they bear no relevant syntactic relation to other nouns, they depend for their gender assignment on certain criteria being met by their intended denotation. In the case of the third-person personal pronoun, the determination of its grammatical gender correlates with the two distinct, but related, functions it serves: deixis and anaphora. When used in the latter function, its gender is determined by the gender of its antecedent; but when used in its former function, its gender is determined by the kind of object being demonstrated. Finally, when, in its deictic use, there is insufficient information to determine which criteria for gender are satisfied by the intended object, a default gender is selected, typically, the masculine gender, if the object is human.

In English, gender has no morphosyntactic role to play: except for pronouns, there is no distinction of gender in English. And even in the case of pronouns, gender distinguishes only the singular forms of the third-person personal pronouns. Their selection is not syntactically but notionally determined. Roughly, "it" is used primarily with respect to entities which are not human; "she" with respect to entities which are female, typically human; and "he" with respect to human males. This notional determination gives rise to a dilemma when the third-person personal pronoun is required for an anaphoric role. In conformity with the general Indo-European pattern, its morphosyntactic features, case and grammatical number, are determined syntactially: case is determined by what governs it and grammatical number by its antecedent. But, as was said, its gender is determined notionally. What is to be done, then, when the antecedent of the third-person personal pronoun is a grammatically singular quantified noun phrase whose domain of quantification contains entities some of which satisfy the condition for the selection of one version of the third-person singular personal pronoun, say the masculine form, and others satisfy the condition for the selection of another version, say the feminine form.

As is well known, there are three ways of making the selection. The one which is historically first is the one which patterns with many Indo-European languages—namely, the one where the masculine form of the pronoun is autohyponomous between a sense in which the relevant objects in the domain are considered masculine and human and a sense in which they are considered merely human.

For many speakers of English, the masculine form of the third-person singular personal pronoun is not autohyponomous: it has but one sense, the narrower one. For these speakers, the sentence in (9a) entails that all the children are boys. The question arises: how can such speakers assert, in one sentence, using the word "child" in the singular, what is expressed by the following two sentences?

(10)   a. Every boy loves his mother.
       b. Every girl loves her mother.

One possibility is to conform to the requirement that a pronoun agree with its antecedent in grammatical number and to use a disjunction of singular pronouns, as exemplified below:

(11)   Every child loves his or her mother.

Many speakers, however, find such disjunctions cumbersome, especially in protracted discourse. The other possibility, then, is to use the "nearest" pronoun which neutralizes the difference in gender. The "nearest" such pronoun is the third-person plural personal pronoun.

It is important to observe that those speakers who resort to the third-person plural personal pronoun have not abandoned the requirement pertaining to grammatical number of pronouns with antecedents entirely. None of these speakers tolerates a singular pronoun with a plural antecedent:

(12)   a. All chairs are in their place.
       b. *All chairs are in its place.

Moreover, I have found that speakers who not only use the third-person plural personal pronoun with a singular antecedent but also find (9b) acceptable to the exclusion of (9a), nonetheless conform to the generalization when notional considerations are not relevant, preferring the sentences in (a) below to the ones in (b):

(13)   a. Each cat licks its whiskers.
       b. Each cat licks their whiskers.
(14)   a. Every chair is in its place.
       b. *Every chair is in their place.

Let me now turn to the first generalization—namely, that the features of determiners and of the nouns they modify be consistent with one another. A usage which might be thought to counterexemplify it is found in some dialects of English, though not in mine. It appears that, in noun phrases such as "those kind of people," the determiner "those" has plural grammatical number, while the head "kind" has singular.

This usage, observed by Jespersen (1909, vol. 2, ch. 3.8) for example, has, I believe, a simple account which preserves the requirement in question: for speakers who accept such expressions, the head noun is not "kind" but "people." In other words, "kind of" is an adjectival modifier of "people".

This account might seem implausible, since one does not usually think of a sequence of words comprising a noun and a preposition, in that order, as a single word. Yet, this very same sequence is known to have an adverbial function, illustrated below:

(15)   a. Bill kind of liked the book.
       b. Bill liked the book, kind of.

Thus, if "kind of" is a word, why not an ambiguous one, one being an adverb, the other an adjective? (Compare words like "fast" which are both adverbs and adjectives.)

Further corroboration of the view that "people" and not "kind" is the head of the noun phrase "those kind of people" comes from the fact that those who countenance such usage make the verb plural and not singular, when the noun phrase serves as a subject to a non-finite clause:[7]

(16)   a. Those kind of people are a nuisance.
      b. *Those kind of people is a nuisance.

A challenge to the second generalization—that inflected verbs agree with their subjects—comes from sentences such as the following:

(17)   Twenty-five cents does not buy a cup of coffee anymore.

It appears here that the head noun of the subject noun phrase, "cents," has plural grammatical number, while the verb, "does buy," has singular grammatical number.

In my view, better theoretical results are obtained, if one retains the generalization in the face of the usage. This implies that either the subject noun phrase has singular grammatical number or the verb has plural grammatical number. As it happens, there is good independent evidence supporting the former alternative.

To begin with, the usage in question has nothing to do with the choice of verb. It depends entirely on the choice of lexical item for the head of the subject noun phrase: the head noun must denote a unit of measurement. The two sentences below differ only in the grammatical number of the verb. At the same time, the head noun of the subject noun phrase is treated as a unit of measure. Yet, they differ in acceptability:

(18)   a. *Twenty-five marbles is on the floor.
      b. Twenty-five marbles are on the floor.

In addition, noun phrases of this kind, when they occur without overt determiners, have different interpretations. The difference correlates with whether they are the subjects of verbs with singular or plural grammatical numbers:

(19)   a. Twenty-five cents is on the floor.
      b. Twenty-five cents are on the floor.

The former sentence can be truly used in any situation where the monetary total of the coins on the floor adds up to twenty-five cents, whether there are twenty-five coins, three coins, or just one, whereas the latter sentence can be truly used only in situations where there are twenty-five pennies on the floor.

Moreover, the very same kind of noun phrases, when outfitted with determiners, tolerate only verbs whose grammatical number matches that of the noun phrase's determiner:

(20)   a. That twenty-five cents was on the floor.
      b. *That twenty-five cents were on the floor.
(21)   a. *These five dollars is now worth ten.
      b. These five dollars are now worth ten.

If, as the evidence suggests, the noun phrase in (17) has singular grammatical number, what is the syntactic status of the "s" suffix? It is, I suggest, a phonological reflex, not of the morphosyntactic feature +PL, but of a derivational suffix of limited productivity:[8] it creates an invariably singular noun (compare "news").

It has been suggested that the usage discussed here goes beyond nouns denoting units of measurement. One finds, for examples, sentences such as this:

(22)   Twenty-five marbles is a lot to lose in one game.

It may well be that the lexical rule I hypothesize has greater lexical scope than what I have posited. But I am inclined to see such examples as instances of another challenge to the generalization that inflected verbs agree with their subject noun phrases in grammatical number.

This challenge comes from copular sentences whose copulas are flanked by noun phrases of different grammatical number. In such cases, there is often a toleration, and sometimes even a requirement, that the copula agree with the grammatical number of the predicate noun phrase:[9]

(23)   a. The only thing George respects is money and power.
        b. The only thing George respects are money and power.

It is this usage, I suspect, which is evinced in the sentence in (22). For just as the difference in the grammatical number of the copula in the sentences in (23) makes no difference in their meaning or acceptability, neither does the difference in the grammatical number of the copula in the sentences in (22) and (24) make any difference in theirs:

(24)   Twenty-five marbles are a lot to lose in one game.

However, a difference in the grammatical number of the copula in the sentences in (21) does make a difference in their acceptability.

Another challenge to the second generalization is thought to arise from partitive noun phrases. A partitive noun phrase—for example, "a majority of voters"—is one containing a prepositional phrase, whose head is the preposition "of" and in which the denotation of the head of the noun phrase, in this case "majority," is delimited by the denotation of the head of the preposition's noun phrase complement, here "voters." It is not unusual to find that the grammatical number of the verb is that of the noun contained in the complement of the prepositional phrase and not that of the subject noun phrase's head noun:

(25)   A majority of eligible voters prefer not to vote.

While there is no question that such usage is relevant to the generalization that an inflected verb agrees with its subject in grammatical number, the exact nature of its relevance is not obvious. To begin with, such usage is a counterexample to this generalization, only under the additional assumptions that the sentence has the syntactic structure it appears to have and the feature of the head's grammatical number is the same as that of its projection. In other words, this usage is a counterexample to the generalization that an inflected verb agrees in grammatical number not with the subject noun phrase but with the head noun of the subject noun phrase—under the syntactic analysis assumed in the description of the example. Thus, if it turns out that expressions such as "majority of" are to be reanalyzed along the lines of the expression "kind of,"[10] or if it turns out that grammatical number can percolate to the subject noun phrase from one of its complement noun phrases, then this usage would not challenge but, rather, would conform to the generalization about subject verb agreement.

Second, the usage evinces idiosyncrasies. For example, whether or not an inflected verb agrees in grammatical number with the head noun of the subject noun phrase is sensitive to the choice of determiner preceding the head noun. This sensitivity is especially evident in the case of "a number of":

(26) a. A number of candidates have withdrawn.
      b. *A number of candidates has withdrawn.
(27) a. The number of candidates exceeds the number of voters.
      b. *The number of candidates exceed the number of voters.

Moreover, such usage clearly falls within the ambit of proximity effects, a phenomenon widely remarked upon by traditional grammarians with regard to many different Indo-European languages. Usage which is problematic to the generalization that inflected verbs agree with their subjects in grammatical number is not confined to partitive noun phrases. Surely, for example, the following usage (taken from Follett 1966, p. 231) is equally problematic:

(28) a. Among those attending were George M. Humphrey, former Secretary of the Treasury.
      b. What purpose has all his objections served?

What seems to be relevant here, and what is equally true of partitive noun phrases in the configuration exemplified above, is that the inflected verb seems to be agreeing with the smallest immediately preceding noun phrase. At the same time, it cannot be an accident that the exact analog of the determination of agreement in grammatical number found in the usages under discussion surface in the determination of overt case for pronouns. Thus, in addition to the unproblematic usage found in (29), there is also the commonly attested problematic usage found in (30):

(29) a. Janet accompanied me to the opera.
      b. *Janet accompanied I to the opera.
(30) a. Janet accompanied Bill and I to the opera.
      b. Janet accompanied me and Bill to the opera.
      c. *Janet accompanied I and Bill to the opera.

What seems to be true here is that oblique case is being assigned only to the smallest noun phrase immediately following the case assigner.

The fact of the matter is that none of the usages discussed in the foregoing digression warrants that any of the three generalizations pertaining to agreement in grammatical number be abandoned. For these usages turn out, on closer scrutiny, either to conform to the generalizations or to have no known satisfactory analysis. Ill-understood English usage is not a sound source of counterexamples for generalizations recognized to hold otherwise not only of English but also of most Indo-European languages and even of many non-Indo-European languages.

The generalizations just discussed are true, not just of count nouns but also of mass nouns. Thus, a verb whose subject contains only one (morphologically singular) mass noun is singular:

(31) a. This gold is heavy.
      b. *This gold are heavy.

However, a verb whose subject is a conjoined noun phrase, each conjunct of which contains at least one mass noun, is plural:

(32) a. The wiring and the piping are in the storeroom.
      b. *The wiring and the piping is in the storeroom.

Moreover, if the antecedent of a pronoun is a non-conjunctional mass noun phrase, the pronoun is singular, not plural:

(33)   a. This equipment here maintains itself.
   b. *This equipment maintains themselves.

But if the antecedent is split, the pronoun is plural:

(34)   a. The livestock told the poultry that they should meet.
   b. *The livestock told the poultry that it should meet.

(English seems to lack mass nouns which denote paradigmatic cognitive agents; the sentences above should be considered in the context of something like Orwell's *Animal Farm*, say.)

  Though the preponderance of mass nouns in English have invariable singular grammatical number, some do have invariable plural grammatical number: for example, "annals," "bowels," "brains," "dues," "earnings," "effects," "goods," and "spirits." Not only do they have plural morphology, but so do the determiners which modify them, the verbs of which they are subjects and the pronouns of which they are antecedents:

(35)   a. The club requires these dues to be paid immediately.
   b. *The club requires this dues to be paid immediately.
(36)   a. Dues are to be paid upon joining.
   b. *Dues is to be paid upon joining.
(37)   a. The person who collects dues knows how much they are.
   b. *The person who collects dues knows how much it is.

Yet, like their singular brothers, they resist contrast between singular and plural grammatical number,[11] and they do not tolerate modification by cardinal numerals.[12]

  In light of the foregoing, the two pairs of features, ±CT and ±PL, are interrelated as follows: Any noun associated with the feature +CT must be assigned exactly one of the features, ±PL, modulo the constraints on agreement outlined above; and any noun with the feature −CT must be assigned the feature −PL, unless it is marked in its lexical entry as taking the feature +PL − which, presumably, each plural mass noun is. Finally, nouns assigned +PL require plural morphology, while nouns assigned − PL require singular morphology.

2   The semantics of English common noun phrases

Above, attention has been confined to the morphosyntactic consequences of the pair of syntactic features, ±CT and ±PL. It is now time to advert to their semantic import and consequences. The best expository strategy to be followed here is that of divide and conquer. A division is provided by the syntactic classification of determiners and nouns discussed above. Earlier, it was observed that one characteristic which distinguishes pronouns and proper names on the one hand from common nouns on the other is that the former do not admit determiners whereas the latter do. The fact that common nouns admit determiners does not mean they require them. Indeed, mass nouns and plural count nouns are known for being able to occur without determiners. Common noun phrases can be bifurcated into those without determiners, bare (common) noun phrases (BNPs), and those with determiners. Since determiners are of three kinds, common noun phrases with determiners can be divided into three kinds: interrogative (common) noun phrases (INPs), quantifier (common) noun phrases (QNPs), and demonstrative (common) noun phrases (DNPs).

Below, I shall treat the semantics of DNPs, QNPs, and BNPs, alternating between the case of the count noun phrase and the case of the mass noun phrase. The treatment of INPs must be postponed to another occasion.

3 The semantics of demonstrative noun phrases

Michael Bennett (1979, p. 264) once conjectured that the key to the semantics of mass nouns is the semantics of plural count nouns. The key to the semantics of plural count nouns is, in my view, demonstrative plural count nouns. For these reasons, I shall dwell first and longest on the semantics of demonstrative count noun phrases.

3.1 Demonstrative count noun phrases

It has long been thought that plural DCNPs (demonstrative count noun phrases) introduce ambiguity into the sentences in which they occur. Such a noun phrase can accommodate a collective reading, as well as a distributive one.[13] Consider this sentence:

(38)   These men wrote operas.

If "these men" denotes Mozart and Handel, then the only reading on which it is true is the distributive one: Mozart wrote operas, Handel wrote operas, but they never collaborated to write even one opera. If "these men" denotes Gilbert and Sullivan, then the only reading on which it is true is the collective one: Gilbert and Sullivan collaborated to write operas, but it is not the case that each wrote an opera on his own.

The collectivity and distributivity of collective and distributive readings should not be identified with collaboration or a lack thereof, respectively. While the notion of collaboration helps to highlight the difference between collective and distributive readings of plural noun phrases, it does not characterize the difference between them. For plural DCNPs retain this ambiguity even in cases where no sense can be made of collaboration and failure to collaborate. These examples from Copi (1982 [1953], p. 125) make the point.

(39)   a. The buses in this town consume more gasoline than the cars.
       b. The conventional bombs dropped in World War II did more damage than the nuclear bombs
          dropped.

The first sentence is true when "the buses in this town" and "the cars (in this town)" are each read distributively, but false when each is read collectively; conversely, the second sentence is false when "the conventional bombs dropped in World War II" and "the nuclear bombs dropped (in World War II)" are each read distributively, but true when each is read collectively.

How, then, are collective and distributive readings to be understood? In general, the collective reading of a plural noun phrase is one where the objects in the set associated with the noun phrase (i.e., the denotation of the noun phrase) are treated as a unit, or an aggregate object: the distributive is one where it is not the case that any two distinct members of the denotation of the noun phrase are treated as a unit, or an aggregate object. So, consider a (simple) sentence of this form: $[_S \text{ NP}_{+PL}\text{VP}]$. Such a sentence is true on the collective reading of the subject noun phrase just in case the verb phrase is true of the aggregate object made up of all the members of the denotation of the subject noun phrase; otherwise, it is false (on the collective reading). It is true on the distributive reading just in case the verb phrase is true of each member of the denotation of the subject noun phrase.

Moreover, it should not be thought that collective and distributive readings are occasioned only by plural DCNP in subject position. Such ambiguities surface in other argument positions as well. Consider a variant of the sentence in (39a), where an ambiguity analogous to the one there surfaces for the same noun phrases, now objects of prepositions:

(40)   The attendant put more gasoline in the buses than into the cars.

At the same time, the existence of these readings for DCNPs in nonsubject argument positions may not always be evident. Consider this sentence:

(41)   Bill drove through the trees.

One might be inclined to think that no distributive reading is available here: after all, how can one drive a car through a tree? But, in fact, in California one can drive a car through a tree: some Californian redwood trees have tunnels through them.

In addition, a moment's reflection shows that the collective and distributive readings are not the only readings to which a plural noun phrase is susceptible. For suppose that "the men" denotes Mozart and Handel, as well as Gilbert and Sullivan. Surely (38) is true then as well. However, it is not true on the collective reading, since the four did not collaborate on any opera; and it is not true on the distributive reading, since neither Gilbert nor Sullivan ever wrote an opera on his own. So, there must be other readings; but what are they? Consider again the denotation of "the men" and the division imparted to the denotation by the situation verifying (38):

(42)   a.   {Mozart, Handel, Gilbert, Sullivan}
        b.   {{Mozart}, {Handel}, {Gilbert, Sullivan}}

The latter is a partition of the former.[14] Note that the collective and distributive readings of a plural noun phrase correspond to two partitions of the noun phrase's denotation—namely, the greatest and least partition of the denotation, respectively. So, there are at least as many readings of a plural noun phrase as there are partitions of its denotation.

This conclusion is supported by the syntax and semantics of sentences with reciprocal pronouns. There are two desiderata on such sentences: first, that these sentences be special cases of sentences which have plural noun phrases in lieu of reciprocal pronouns; second, that the reciprocal relation be symmetric and connected over distinct pairs. Now Langendoen (1978) has shown that no analysis can both respect the second desideratum and define the reciprocal relation over individual objects in the denotation of the antecedent noun phrase to the reciprocal pronoun. Higginbotham (1981) has shown that both can be respected, if the reciprocal relation is defined over some partition of the denotation of the reciprocal pronoun's antecedent. These points are illustrated by this sentence:

(43)   [Those grandparents]$_i$ hate [each other]$_i$.

As has been pointed out by Lauri Carlson (1980, Part I, sec. 12), this sentence is true even if the reciprocal hatred is only between the maternal grandparents on the one hand and the paternal grandparents on the other. In this case, there is no symmetric, connected relation of hatred definable over the four grandparents, but there is one definable over a partition of the grandparents into the paternal ones and the maternal ones.

Although the partitions of the denotation of a plural DCNPs provide many of the readings to which the plural noun phrase is susceptible, they do not provide all of them. This is shown by a variant of the sentence in (38):

(44)   These men wrote musicals.

Let "these men" denote Rodgers, Hammerstein, and Hart. This sentence is true when these men are the denotation of its subject noun phrase. Yet there is no partition of the set containing these three men in which the verb phrase "wrote musicals" is true of the unit corresponding to each element of the partition. Rather, the sentence is true because Rodgers and Hammerstein collaborated to write musicals and Rodgers and Hart collaborated to write musicals. Thus, the number of readings to which a plural noun phrase is liable is not the number of partitions, but the number of basic covers, to which its denotation is liable.[15] In the case just considered, the set consisting of Rodgers and Hammerstein plus the set consisting of Rodgers and Hart together form a set which basically covers the set consisting in Rodgers, Hammerstein, and Hart. I shall assume henceforth that the minimal covers correctly characterize the range of readings to which subject plural noun phrases are liable.

In light of the foregoing remarks on the range of readings for plural noun phrases, it will prove convenient to introduce some terms to simplify discussion. Let an object formed from one or more members of a given background set be an aggregate. For example, let the background set have exactly three distinct elements: **a**, **b**, and **c**. Then, exactly seven aggregates can be formed from its elements: a, b, c, ab, ac, bc, and abc.

If a, b, and c are concrete particulars, then so are ab, ac, bc, and abc. Moreover, if a, b, and c are concrete individuals, then ab, ac, bc, and abc are what Russell (1936 [1903]) called "classes as many," Leśniewski called "distributive classes," and Simons calls "plural classes" or, more simply, "pluralities."[16] Moreover, the concrete individuals **a**, **b**, and **c** can be seen as a, b, and c, the limiting cases of the aggregates formed from a, b, and c. In general, a concrete individual is a concrete aggregate comprising just one individual. Russell (1936 [1903], pp. 43, 55n) called such aggregates "classes as one," and Simons (1987, ch. 4.3–4.4) calls them "singular classes."[17]

A plurality is not the same as a collective, or a group: a plurality is nothing more than the sum of its atomic parts, whereas a collective is more than the sum of its atomic parts.[18] The constituency of a collective can change without the collective changing. As is well known, not only can the members of a collective come and go with the collective remaining intact, but, the very same people may make up two distinct collectives.[19] What is crucial to collectives is that they are subject to constituting conditions which determine how the members of the collective constitute the collective of which they are members; whereas pluralities do not have such constituting conditions. Indeed, as Simons (1987, ch. 4.4) has pointed out, a plurality can be seen as the limiting case of a collective: a plurality is a collective without conditions governing its constitution. (For further insightful discussion, see Simons 1982a; 1982b; and 1987, ch. 4.4.)

The set of aggregates accruing to the formation of aggregates from elements of a background set has the algebraic structure of a complete join semi-lattice with a unit and without a zero.[20] The relation of being a sub-aggregate is a partial ordering on the set of all aggregates formed from the background set. The elements of the background set are the minimal aggregates in the set of all aggregates, while the aggregate formed from all of the background set's elements is the unique maximal aggregate—that is, the greatest aggregate or unit aggregate.

In addition, an aggregation is defined to be a set of aggregates with the requirement that their join yields the greatest aggregate (that is, the unit aggregate) and that it is minimal, in the sense that no aggregate in the set is a proper sub-aggregate of any other aggregate in the set.[21] In Figure 19.1 are given all the aggregations which can be formed from the background set: {**a,b,c**}. Notice that the collective reading of a plural noun phrase whose denotation is {**a,b,c**} corresponds to the aggregation {abc} and its distributive reading corresponds to the aggregation {a,b,c}.[22]

The main idea is that a predicate whose argument is a DCNP is evaluated not with respect to the DCNP's denotation but with respect to the elements in an aggregation constructed from its denotation,

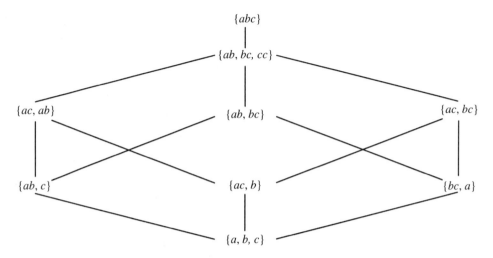

FIGURE 19.1 Aggregations possible from {**a,b,c**}

where the choice of aggregation is determined pragmatically. The denotation associated with the DCNP is the extension of its constituent N which satisfies the constraints imposed by the demonstrative adjective. This extension consists only of individuals. Indeed, this is the semantic import of the feature +CT—namely, that denotations associated with such nouns and their projections consist only of individuals in the domain of interpretation, I shall call such denotations atomic.

In addition to the feature +CT, DCNPs also have one of the features ±PL. The semantic import of the features +PL and –PL assigned to a noun phrase node is to constrain the size, or cardinality, of the denotation of the noun phrase. The feature –PL requires the size of the denotation to be one, whereas the feature +PL permits the size of the denotation to be greater than one. In other words, if the noun phrase node, NP, is assigned the feature –PL, then $| [NP]^D | = 1$; if the noun phrase node, NP, is assigned +PL, then $| [NP]^D | \geq 1$.[23] Next, the denotation of the noun phrase makes available to the predicate of which it is an argument aggregations any of which the predicate can be evaluated with respect to.

To get a better idea of how these semantic principles apply, let us consider a simple sentence, whose subject noun phrase denotes, say, Tom, Dick, and Jerry:

(45)   These men rowed.

The denotation of the subject noun phrase certainly satisfies the constraint placed on it by the +PL feature assigned to the noun phrase node. Moreover, there are exactly eight aggregations which can be constituted from this denotation of three elements. (See Fig. 19.1.) Now consider these situations:

(46)   a. Tom, Dick, and Jerry were in one boat, each pulling an oar.
      b. Tom and Jerry were in one boat, at some point, each pulling an oar; and Tom and Dick were in one boat, at some other time, each pulling an oar.
      c. Tom and Dick were in one boat, each pulling an oar, while Jerry was in another boat rowing.
      d. Tom was in one boat rowing; Dick was in another boat rowing; Jerry was in still another boat rowing.

These situations render the sentence in (45) true on the readings of its plural noun phrase subject corresponding to the following aggregations of the noun phrase's denotation:

(47) a. {*Tom–Dick–Jerry*}
      b. {*Tom–Jerry, Tom–Dick*}
      c. {*Tom–Dick, Jerry*}
      d. {*Tom, Dick, Jerry*}

where the first and the last aggregations correspond to the collective and the distributive readings, respectively.

The principles outlined and illustrated above apply equally as well to sentences with transitive verbs and with plural demonstrative noun phrases for subject and object. In the sentence,

(48) Those men endorsed these women,

suppose "those men" denotes Rick and Randy and "these women" denotes Diane and Lillian. Certainly the sentence in (48) would be true if Rick and Randy collectively endorsed Diane and Lillian taken collectively; that is, Rick and Randy make up a committee and decide as a committee to endorse the slate made up of Diane and Lillian. The sentence would also be true if Rick endorsed the slate of Diane and Lillian, and Randy endorsed the same slate. If Rick and Randy as a committee endorsed Diane and also endorsed Lillian, the sentence would still be true. And finally, if Rick endorsed Diane and Randy endorsed Lillian, or if Rick endorsed Lillian and Randy endorsed Diane, the sentence would be true. In other words, there are two choices of aggregations for each of the noun phrases.

(49) M_1: {*Rick–Randy*} W_1: {*Diane–Lillian*}
      M_2: {*Rick, Randy*} W_2: {*Diane, Lillian*}

The sentence in (48) is true on any given choice, just in case, on that choice each aggregate in the subject's aggregation bears the relation expressed by the verb to some aggregate in the object's aggregation and each aggregate of the object's aggregation has the same relation borne to it by some aggregate in the subject's aggregation. Such situations are depicted in Figure 19.2 by means of directed bipartite graphs.

Notice that each graph is complete. The first three choices of aggregations admit of only one complete directed bipartite graph each: the last choice admits of five of which only two, which are shown above, are minimal. The point is that non-minimal ones are superfluous. If Rick's endorsing of Diane and Randy's endorsing of Lillian are together sufficient for the sentence in (48) to be true, then it is still sufficient even if, in addition, either Rick endorses Lillian or Randy endorses Diane.

Let the previously adduced principles governing grammatical number be supplemented with the following principle governing the interpretation of a noun phrase which contains only a pronoun and has an antecedent within the sentence:[24]

(50) If NP_1 is the antecedent of NP_2, then the denotation of NP_2 is the denotation of NP_1 (i.e., $[NP_1]^D$ = $[NP_2]^D$).

So, the semantic import of the relation of antecedence is merely to guarantee identity of denotation in the interpretation of the relata of the relation of antecedence; it places no restriction on the aggregations with respect to which the predicates having the noun phrases related by antecedence for arguments are to be evaluated. This is exemplified by the following variant of (48):

(51) [These candidates]$_i$ endorsed [themselves]$_i$.

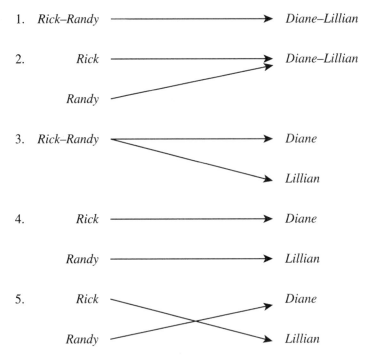

FIGURE 19.2 Bipartite directed graph of the relation for (48)

Suppose that "these candidates" denotes Rick and Randy. The available readings of (51) are essentially those of (18), except that Rick and Randy have replaced Diane and Lillian as the denotation of the object noun phrase. (See Fig. 19.3).

The reciprocal pronoun differs from the third-person personal pronouns which are not used deictically and the reflexive pronouns in two ways. First, the reciprocal pronoun requires an antecedent which has plural grammatical numbers:

(52)   a. *[Eliza]$_i$ saw [each other]$_i$.
       b. [The women]$_i$ saw [each other]$_i$.

Nor should this distribution be viewed as a matter of common sense, that is an extra-grammatical matter, for collective nouns which denote collections of objects, are never acceptable antecedents of reciprocal pronouns, unless they have plural grammatical number.

(53)   a. *[The army]$_i$ shot at [each other]$_i$.
       b. [The armies]$_i$ shot at [each other]$_i$.

Second, the reciprocal pronoun requires that the predicate to which it and its antecedent are arguments express a relation which is symmetric and connected over distinct pairs. Adapting a proposal put forth by Higginbotham (1981),[25] one can capture the intuition as follows:

(54)   Let NP$_2$ be the first noun phrase node dominating the reciprocal pronoun. Let NP$_1$ be the antecedent of NP$_2$. Let NP$_1$ be a demonstrative noun phrase. The predicate which has NP$_1$ and NP$_2$ for arguments is to be evaluated with respect to every pair of distinct elements in an aggregation corresponding to a partition of the denotation of the antecedent NP$_1$.

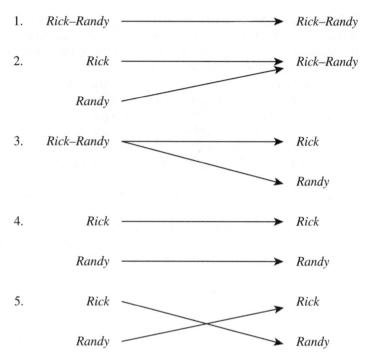

FIGURE 19.3 Bipartite directed graph of the relations for (51)

This[26] and earlier semantic principles also serve to capture readings pointed out by Lauri Carlson (1980, Part I, sec. 9) in connection with this pair of sentences:

(55) a. [These men]$_i$ pulled [themselves]$_i$ up.
      b. [These men]$_i$ pulled [each other]$_i$ up.

He observed that, in circumstances in which two window washers, who are standing on a window-washing platform, pull on ropes on opposite sides of the platform thereby raising the platform, both sentences in the pair above are true when "these men" denotes the two window washers. The first sentence is true on the reading in which the aggregation selected for the subject noun phrase and object noun phrase is the one whose sole member is the aggregate made up of both men. The second sentence is true on its only available reading in which the aggregation selected for the subject noun phrase is the one which contains the two minimal aggregates, each made up of one of the window washers.

In closing this section on the semantics of plural DCNPs, let me advert to a broader range of sentences which, though falling outside the stated purview of the paper, nonetheless warrant attention since not only do they yield to fairly evident additions to the syntax and semantic principles already stated but, in doing so, they illustrate important differences between the approach adopted here and the approaches adopted by others.

The first kind of sentence is what Link (1984) has dubbed a hydra sentence. A hydra sentence is one which has a conjoined noun phrase and hence is, as it were, multiply headed. Here is one such sentence:

(56) [The maternal grandparents and the paternal grandparents]$_i$ hate [each other]$_i$.

This sentence is liable to all of the readings the sentence in (43) is liable to, though of course certain ones are more salient than others as a result of the subject noun phrase containing two noun phrases, instead of just one. Among the salient readings are (i) the one where each grandparent hates every other grandparent, (ii) the one where the maternal grandparents hate the paternal grandparents and the paternal grandparents hate the maternal ones, and (iii) the one where the maternal grandparents hate each other and the paternal grandparents hate each other. Each of these correspond to a reciprocal relation defined over the aggregates obtained from a partition of the noun phrase's denotation.[27] These interpretations result, provided that the preceding syntactic and semantic principles are supplemented with the further, self-evident semantic principle that the denotation of a conjoined noun phrase is the union of the denotations of its conjuncts:

(57)   Let NP be a conjunction of NPs, NP_1 through NP_j. Then, $[NP]^D = U[NP_i]^D$ (where $1 \leq i \leq j$).

A second kind of sentence is any sentence involving inter-clausal and inter-sentential anaphora. Such sentences can easily be cases where a referentially dependent pronoun has one reading, say a collective one, while its antecedent has another, say a distributive one:

(58)   [The men]$_i$ each believe that[they]$_i$ should meet.

The adverb "each" forces the distributive reading with respect to the matrix predicate "believe," but such a reading is impossible for the referentially dependent third-person plural pronoun, since "meet" is predicated of it. Any theory which must assess the two predicates with respect to one and the same value founders on such sentences. The theory advocated here does not: though the denotation of "the men" and "they" is the same, the predicates can be assessed with respect to different aggregations. A similar point holds for sentences where the anaphoric element is a relative pronoun: the predicate of the relative clause can be taken collectively, say, with respect to a relative pronoun, while the predicate of the principal clause may be taken distributively with respect to the relative pronoun's antecedent:[28]

(59)   [The men]$_i$[who]$_i$ met this morning weigh less than fifty kilograms.

3.2   Demonstrative mass noun phrases

Mass nouns have the feature –CT. According to the syntactic rule connecting the features –CT and ±PL, mass nouns must be assigned the feature –PL, unless its lexical entry requires that it have the feature +PL. When applied to count nouns, the semantic import of this feature is to confine the cardinality of the denotation to one. Assuming a uniform interpretation of the feature, one must conclude that the denotation associated with the DMNP has a cardinality of one. The obvious candidate is the greatest aggregate of which its constituent N is true, while satisfying the constraints imposed by the demonstrative adjective.

Predicates of DMNPs, like those of DCNPs, are evaluated not with respect to their denotations but with respect to the elements of an aggregation, which is a set of sub-aggregates of the DMNP's denotation, with the requirement that their join yields the greatest aggregate, or the unit aggregate (that is, the DMNP's denotation) and that it is minimal, in the sense that, no aggregate in the set is a proper sub-aggregate of any other aggregate in the set. This principle of evaluation permits the capturing of a range of interpretations, associated usually with DCNPs, but clearly also true of DMNPs. Consider the range illustrated by the following examples. On the one hand, there are collective readings. Suppose that there is a pile of leaves and a bundle of wires. As remarked by Lauri Carlson (1980), even if only one leaf is touching one wire, both of the following sentences can be construed as true in the situation:

(60)   a. This foliage is touching that wiring.

      b. These leaves are touching those wires.

On the other hand, there are distributive readings. Suppose that there are five oranges, each of which had been wrapped in a paper wrapper. Both of the following sentences can be construed as true in the situation:

(61)   a. This fruit was wrapped in that paper.

      b. These oranges were enclosed in those wrappers.

Note that, in the context, "this fruit" denotes the greatest aggregate which comprises the denotation of "those oranges"; similarly, in the context, "that paper" denotes the greatest aggregate which comprises the denotation of "those wrappers."

     Moreover, even if general world knowledge does not provide the nonlinguistic information whereby atomic sub-aggregates can be associated with mass nouns such as "foliage" and "wiring," nonetheless context can provide sufficient non-linguistic information whereby appropriate sub-aggregates can be associated with a mass term so that a distributive reading can be found. Suppose that there is a jewelry store which displays and sells its jewelry according to the quantities of precious metal in it. Suppose further that a certain customer, aware of the store's arrangement and practice, is in the store shopping for jewelry. Suppose finally that the salesman has shown the customer a display containing jewelry with an ounce and a half of gold, but that the customer, finding the price of such jewelry too high, asks to see gold jewelry which is less expensive. It seems that the salesman might say, turning around and pointing to a display case,

(62)   This jewelry contains just one ounce of gold,

where the pieces of jewelry in the display have just one ounce of gold each. Now, if the pieces of jewelry were rings, then it would be that each ring has just one ounce of gold; but if the pieces of jewelry were earrings, then it would be that each pair of earrings has one ounce of gold.[29]

     This approach circumvents problems which plague the other standard approaches to mass nouns. If the subject NP is assigned the set of quantities of jewelry in the display, there are quantities for which the predicate fails, as a result of which the sentence must be false. If the subject NP is assigned the mereological whole, the sentence will again be false. (For discussion of this problem in connection with the definite article, see Bunt 1981, pp. 41–43; Pelletier and Schubert 1989; and Lønning 1987.)

     In light of the earlier discussion of hydra sentences, it is important to note that nothing special needs to be said to provide for the semantics of such sentences where the heads of the conjoined noun phrases are mass nouns. Under the assumption that a DMNP has a denotation comprising a single entity—namely, the greatest aggregate of things of which it is true and under the assumption that the reciprocal pronoun requires the predicate to be true of all pairs of distinct collectives corresponding to a partition of the denotation of the antecedent—then it follows that a non-conjunctional DMNP cannot be the antecedent of a reciprocal pronoun, though a conjunctional one can be:

(63)   a. *[The drapery]$_i$ resembles[each other]$_i$.

      b. *[The carpeting]$_i$ resembles[each other]$_i$.

      c. [The drapery and the carpeting]$_i$ resemble[each other]$_i$.

Moreover, these very same principles imply that the sentence in (63c) and (64) form a minimal pair:

(64)   The drapes and the carpets resemble each other.

The sentence in (63c) has only one reading—namely, the one in which the drapery resembles the carpeting and the carpeting resembles the drapery—whereas the one in (64) has additional ones, including the one in which the carpets resemble each other and the drapes resemble each other. In particular, consider a situation in which there are two drapes and two carpets. Suppose further that neither drape resembles either carpet but the drapes resemble each other and the carpets resemble each other. The sentence in (63c) is false in such a situation, whereas the sentence in (64) has a reading in which it is true.

4   The semantics of quantified noun phrases

4.1   Count noun phrases

Having stated and illustrated the principles governing plural demonstrative noun phrases, I turn to those governing plural quantified noun phrases. As always, a denotation is associated with a count noun, namely, the set of individuals in the domain of discourse of which the noun is true. But the quantifier is restricted not to the count noun's denotation but to an aggregation built from that denotation. The choice of aggregation is partially constrained by the features +PL. If the feature assigned to the noun phrase node of the quantified noun phrase is +PL, then the choice of aggregation is unconstrained; but if it is –PL, then the choice is constrained to the least aggregation, that is, the set of all the minimal aggregates of the count noun's denotation—which is, of course, just the count noun's denotation. Notice that this is analogous to the constraint imposed by these features on the denotation of demonstrative noun phrases. Next, if the quantifier is universal, then the predicate must be true of each aggregate in the aggregation to which the quantifier is restricted; and, if it is existential, then the predicate must be true of at least one aggregate in the aggregation to which the quantifier is restricted.[30]

To see how the principles work, consider this sentence with plural quantified noun phrases:

(65)   All men endorsed some women.

Suppose the denotation of "men" is m_1, m_2, m_3, m_4, m_5, m_6, m_7 and the denotation of "women" is, w_1, w_2, w_3, w_4, w_5. Suppose further that the men form committees of various sizes (including committees of one)—say, m_7, $m_1m_2m_3$, $m_1m_2m_4$, and $m_4m_5m_6$—and that the women, too, form committees: say, w_1w_2, w_1w_3, and w_4w_5. Finally, suppose that there is an endorsement of the female committees by the male committees, as depicted in Fig. 19.4.

The situation certainly renders the sentence in (65) true, and that it is so can be derived by any rule which assigns clausal scope to quantified noun phrases. First, the quantified noun phrases in the sentence in (65) can be assigned the scopal configuration shown in (66):

(66) $[_s[_{NP}$ All men$]_x[_s[_{NP}$ some women$]_y[_s[_{NP}$ x$][_{NP}$ endorsed $[_{NP}$ y$]]]]]$.

Next, the following two sets are aggregations formed from the denotation of "men" and "women," respectively:

(67)   a. m_7, $m_1m_2m_3$, $m_1m_2m_4$, and $m_4m_5m_6$
        b. w_1w_2, w_1w_3, and w_4w_5

Finally, each aggregate in (67a) bears the relation of endorsing to some aggregate in (67b).

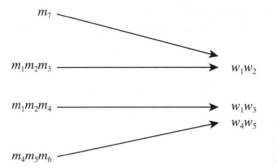

FIGURE 19.4 Bipartite directed graph for a relation for (65)

No illustration of sentences with singular quantified noun phrases is required, since the semantic principles adduced here reduce to those for restricted quantifiers ranging over the denotation of the noun of the quantified noun phrase. For the quantifier ranges over the aggregation of minimal aggregates: that is, the count noun's denotation.

4.2   Mass noun phrases

Before spelling out the semantic principles governing QMNPs, it may be worthwhile seeing that QMNPs are every bit as much quantified noun phrases as QCNPs. To begin with, they exhibit weak cross-over effects:

(68)   a. [All fruit]$_i$ is hidden by[its]$_i$ foliage.
      b. [Some fruit]$_i$ is hidden by[its]$_i$ foliage.
      c. [Each orange]$_i$ is hidden by[its]$_i$ foliage.
(69)   a. *[Its]$_i$ foliage hides[all fruit]$_i$.
      b. *[Its]$_i$ foliage hides[some fruit]$_i$.
      c. *[Its]$_i$ foliage hides[each orange]$_i$.

Second, as observed by Roeper (1983, pp. 252–253, 263), QMNPs interact with one another scopally:

(70)   a. All fruit is enclosed in some paper.
      b. Each orange is enclosed in some wrapper.
(71)   a. Some foliage grows on all shrubbery.
      b. Some leaf grows on each tree.

Third, QMNPs typically have their scope confined to the clauses in which they occur:

(72)   a. Some inspector made the statement that all fruit was destroyed.
      b. Some inspector made the statement that each pear was destroyed.
(73)   a. Some inspector thinks that for all fruit to be destroyed is absurd.
      b. Some inspector thinks that for each pear to be destroyed is absurd.

If QMNPs are truly quantified noun phrases, then what do the quantifiers range over? In the case of QCNPs, they range over elements in the aggregation formed from elements in the denotation of the noun phrase's count noun. In the case of QMNPs, they also range over elements in the aggregation formed from the denotation of the noun phrase's mass noun, which is the greatest aggregate in the domain of discourse of which the mass noun is true. In many cases, the choice of aggregation is virtually arbitrary:

(74) a. All water is wet.
      b. All information is valuable.

In other cases, the choice is constrained by common knowledge:

(75) a. All regular mail in Canada is 38 cents.
      b. Some footwear in this store is size 13.
      c. No furniture on this floor has four legs.
      d. All phosphorus is either red or black.

(This last sentence is from Roeper 1983.)

One other facet of QMNPs and QCNPs should be noted: they interact scopally: that is, a QMNP can be assigned scope wider than QCNP, and vice versa:

(76) a. All fruit is enclosed in some wrapper.
      b. Each orange is enclosed in some paper.
(77) a. Some foliage grows on each tree.
      b. Some leaf grows on all shrubbery.

On the view urged here, nothing special needs to be said to handle such facts.

5   Bare common noun phrases

Bare common noun phrases exhibit a remarkable similarity not only to one another but also to the indefinite singular noun phrases. First, they occur in free variation in the NP position of a "there existential":

(78) a. There is a shoe behind the door.
      b. There are shoes behind the door.
      c. There is footwear behind the door.

Second, they occur in free variation in the subject position of copular sentences, uniformly carrying a universal-like construal,

(79) a. A dog is a mammal.
      b. Dogs are mammals.
      c. Gold is a metal.

or uniformly carrying an existential-like construal:

(80) a. A dog is on the lawn.
      b. Dogs are on the lawn.
      c. Gold is on the lawn.

Third, they occur in free variation in the predicate position of a copular sentence,

(81) a. This is a shoe.
      b. These are shoes.
      c. This is footwear.

carrying uniformly no existential import, as is shown by the infelicity of following up any of the preceding sentences with the following respective questions:

(82) a. *Which shoe is it?
      b. *Which shoes are they?
      c. *Which footwear is it?

Fourth, all three admit of both appositive and restrictive relative clauses:

(83) a. A pot which had belonged to China's last emperor was auctioned off.
      b. A pot, whose value I do not know, was sold for ten dollars.
(84) a. Pots which had belonged to China's last emperor were auctioned off.
      b. Pots, whose value I do not know, were sold for ten dollars.
(85) a. Pottery which had belonged to China's last emperor was auctioned off.
      b. Pottery, whose value I do not know, was sold for twenty dollars.

Fifth, each licenses so-called donkey-anaphora:

(86) a. Every man who owns[a donkey]$_i$ beats[it]$_i$.
      b. Every man who owns{donkeys]$_i$ beats[them]$_i$.
      c. Every man who owns[livestock]$_i$ beats[it]$_i$.

In addition to these parallels in syntactic distribution, there are also ones in semantic interpretation, remarked on by Cartwright (1975a) and documented by G. Carlson (1980, ch. 7.6.0). As Carlson (1980, p. 295) points out with respect to the latter parallels: "Any analysis which fails to account for these overwhelming distributional parallelisms in some principled way is not adequate." In fact, there is a simple analysis for both types of parallels.

To see what this analysis is, first consider these facts about the syntactic distribution and morphology of English determiners. Every English determiner has a plural form, be it the same form as the singular form or a special plural counterpart, except the English indefinite article, which has no plural counterpart (see Table 19.3).

The supposition that the indefinite article has a plural form which is phonetically null yields two generalizations. The first is that every English determiner has both a singular and plural form, though in some cases, the forms do not differ phonetically. The second is that mass nouns, for some unknown reason, tolerate only the plural form of quantifiers: mass nouns do not tolerate either "every" or "each" as determiners, nor do they tolerate the (singular) indefinite article. This very same supposition provides a syntactic and lexical basis, when coupled with the semantic theory of mass nouns and count nouns given above, for the interpretational parallels between bare singular MNPs and bare plural CNP, remarked on by Carlson and Cartwright.

Militating against this simple hypothesis is an argument by Carlson against the view that bare plural CNPs are plural indefinite noun phrases. In his pioneering work on bare plural CNPs, Carlson (1976, 1977, 1980) argued that if bare plurals are in fact plural indefinite noun phrases, then any difference between two sentences which differ only insofar as one has a (singular) indefinite noun phrase where the other has its bare plural version is merely the difference in grammatical number (Carlson 1977, pp. 415–416). He proceeded to adduce pairs of sentences in which

TABLE 19.3

	Singular	Plural
Interrogatives	which	which
	what	what
Demonstratives	the	the
	this	these
	that	those
Quantifiers	some	some
	any	any
	no	no
	every	all
	each	all
	a	—

the difference between the construals of the sentences appears to exceed any difference ascribable to their difference in grammatical number. To show such a discrepancy, Carlson introduced two auxiliary hypotheses. First, he supposed that the grammatically available interpretation of the indefinite article is that of the existential quantifier; second, he supposed that the semantic import of grammatical number is to determine whether a noun phrase denotes one object or more than one object (Carlson 1977, p. 416).

Recently, I have argued that the analysis of bare plurals which Carlson rejects does not suffer from the inadequacy which he ascribes to it. I pointed out that work subsequent to Carlson's has shown that, independently of any considerations of the facts pertaining to bare plurals, both of the auxiliary hypotheses he adopts are empirically inadequate: the indefinite article does not have simply the semantics of the existential quantifier (see Fodor and Sag 1982, among others), and the semantic import of grammatical number is not simply to determine whether or not a noun phrase denotes one or more than one object (see Langendoen 1978 and Higginbotham 1981, which have served as a starting point for the view developed above). Modifying his auxiliary hypotheses along the lines of this subsequent work, I showed the analysis of bare plurals which Carlson rejects does not entail the discrepancies in construal which he ascribes to it. (See Gillon 1989, for details.)

6   Conclusion

In the foregoing, I have argued, in effect, that MNPs and CNPs differ only minimally grammatically. The basis for this minimal difference has been ascribed to a difference in the features ±CT. On the syntactic side of the grammatical coin, these features determine the available options for the assignment of grammatical number, itself determined by the features ±PL: +CT places no restriction on the available options, while –CT, in the unmarked case, restricts the available options to –PL. On the semantic side of the same coin, these features of ±CT determine the sort of denotation which can be associated with DNPs and QNPs. The feature –CT requires that the associated denotation be the set whose sole member is the greatest aggregate of which the noun phrase (in the case of DNPs), or noun (in the case of QNPs), is true; while the feature +CT requires that the associated denotation be the set whose members are all and only those minimal aggregates of which the noun phrase (in the case of DNPs), or noun (in the case of QNPs), is true. At the same time, neither MNPs nor CNPs which are arguments of a predicate have their predicate evaluated with respect to their denotations. Rather, the predicate is evaluated with respect to an aggregation, a set of aggregates constructed from the denotation of the noun phrase which is an argument of the predicate.

As we have seen above, not only do demonstrative and quantified noun phrases fall within the purview of this approach to the grammar of English mass and count noun phrases, but so do determinerless noun phrases, so-called bare plurals and bare singulars.

The single most important implication of this approach is that two sentences which differ only in that one has a plural count noun where the other has a synonymous mass noun should have the same construals, modulo differences in the implicatures attributable either to the grammaticalization of the atomicity of the denotation, in the former case, or to the lack of it, in the latter case. Indeed, this synonymity has been exploited in the discussion above of demonstrative, quantified, and bare noun phrases. Interestingly, this same synonymity occurs in the case of interrogative noun phrases, as is illustrated by the examples below:

(87) a. Which drapery did you buy?
      b. Which drapes did you buy?
(88) a. Which drapery goes with which carpeting?
      b. Which drapery goes with which carpets?
      c. Which drapes go with which carpeting?
      d. Which drapes go with which carpets?

This fact bodes well for the prospect of the syntactic and semantic principles stated above encompassing interrogative noun phrases and thereby encompassing all simple common noun phrases.

Notes

This paper was presented to McGill University's Department of Linguistics (5 March 1990), the University of Toronto's Department of Linguistics (28 February 1990), and at the Workshop on the Semantic Issues of Mass Nouns, Plurals and Events, held at the University of Tübingen's Seminar für Naturlichsprachliche Systeme (17–18 June 1989). I thank the audiences in attendance at these presentations for their comments and criticisms. I also thank Peter Simons for written comments on an earlier draft of this paper.

1. X' theory and its recent developments, in which S is identified with IP and S^1 with CP, permits an even more succinct definition: a simple NP is one which contains no other maximal projections.

2. For reasons of expository simplicity, I have collapsed the distinction between N and N' in this rule. This distinction is relevant only with respect to the syntactic structure of elements *following* the head noun of a noun phrase: here, I am interested in the syntactic structure only of elements *preceding* the head noun of a noun phrase.

3. Many lexical items fall into more than one syntactic category. There is no reason to think that determiners are any exception. One clear candidate for dual status is the indefinite article, being both a quantifier and a demonstrative (Fodor and Sag 1982). Another candidate might very well be the definite article.

4. This dual classification has led some to call into question the distinction between mass nouns and count nouns. (See Pelletier and Schubert 1989 for further discussion.)

5. The generalization is intended, both as it is found in the traditional grammatical literature and in contemporary syntactic theory, as having for its purview sentences and sentences which have at most one unsubordinated clause. I adhere to that intention here.

Thus, this generalization is not to be construed as taking in the antecedence relation exhibited by the kind of usage of third-person personal pronouns, first identified and discussed by Evans (1977; 1980: chapter 21 in this volume). Such usage is found in the following sentence:

(i) Every student in the class attended the party. They had a good time.

There is a sense in which the noun phrase "every student in the class" is the antecedent of the pronoun "they"; yet the noun phrase has singular grammatical number, whereas the pronoun has plural grammatical number.

6. Hoeksema (1983) has drawn attention to other forms of conjunction, including what he calls "intersective conjunction" and "appositive conjunction," whose syntax, I believe, does not so much constitute part of phrase formation, as supervene upon it, being a kind of parenthetical, in the sense of McCawley (1982).

7. I owe the sentence in (16a) and its judgment to an anonymous referee; I owe the judgment of the sentence in (16b) to a non-linguistic colleague who finds the sentence in (16a) acceptable.

8. It is worth remarking in this connection that, according to Jespersen (1924, p. 208), the counterpart of these noun phrases show up in German and Danish as singular noun phrases: "drei mark" (two marks) and "fem daler" (five dollars).

9. In some cases, agreement with the apparent predicate is to the exclusion of agreement with the apparent subject:

    (i)   The majority are men.
    (ii) *The majority is men.

But notice:

    (iii) Men are the majority.
    (iv) *Men is the majority.

10. Indeed, Akmajian and Lehrer (1976) have made just such a proposal, citing as their evidence facts pertaining to PP extraposition. For further discussion of the syntactic facts relevant to partitive noun phrases, see Jackendoff (1977; ch. 5.3) and Selkirk (1977).

11. Clearly, some plural mass nouns have singular counterparts, but these counterparts have a sense different from that of the plural. Thus, there are the words "brain" and "brains." But "brains" is ambiguous between the plural of the singular count noun "brain" and the plural mass noun, an ambiguity found in the following sentence:

    (i)   These animals have brains.

12. It seems as though neither "many" (or "few") nor "much" (or "little") fare well with plural mass nouns. Informants I have asked find either selection awkward. My judgments with respect to modification of plural by either "many" (or "few") or "much" (or "little") vary. In some instances, I prefer "much" (or "little") to "many" (or "few"):

    (i) a. *How many brains does Bill have?
        b. How much brains does Bill have?
    (ii) a. *How few brains does Bill have?
        b. How little brains does Bill have?

In others, I prefer "many" (or "few") to "much" (or "little"):

    (iii) a. How many effects did Mary bring with her?
         b. *How much effects did Mary bring with her?
    (iv) a. How few effects did Mary bring with her?
         b. *How little effects did Mary bring with her?

13. This section is essentially section 2 of Gillon (1989), modified only slightly to bring the grammar of MNPs within the purview of the grammar of plural CNPs, as developed there. The views presented here and in Gillon (1989) make more precise those found in Gillon (1987). For a criticism of Gillon (1987), see Lasersohn (1990). A reply to these criticisms is found in Gillon (1990a).

14. A partition is a family of sets, each of which is a non-empty subset of a given set, distinct sets in which family are disjoint and the union of which family is the given set. This can be put more formally as follows:

    (i) X partitions Y iff $X \subseteq P(Y)$ and $\emptyset \notin X$ and $\bigcup X = Y$ and $\forall x,y \in X(x \cap y \neq \emptyset \rightarrow x = y)$
        (where "$P(Y)$" means "the power set of X").

15. A cover is just like a partition except it is not restricted to disjoint sets.

    (i) X covers Y iff $X \subseteq P(Y)$ and $\emptyset \notin X$ and $\bigcup X = Y$.

A basic cover of a set is a family of the set's non-empty subsets whose distinct members are not subsets one of the other:

(ii) X basically covers Y iff X covers Y and $(\forall Z, W \in X)$ if $W \neq Z$ then $W \nsubseteq Z$.

16. In earlier work, Simons (1982a, 1982b) refers to pluralities as manifolds.

17. "Class," as used by these authors, is to be distinguished from "set," as used in set theory. For a careful discussion of the difference between these two concepts and their role in the development of set theory, see Simons (1982a).

18. I am using the terms "collective" and "group" as synonyms here.

19. Simons (1982b, sec. 2) reports that it once happened that the same musicians made up the Chapel Orchestra, the Court Opera Orchestra, and the Vienna Philharmonic. A point similar to the one made by Simons is ascribed by Bennett (1979, p. 275) to David Kaplan.

20. Aggregates are more general than classes. In the case where the background set is determined by the extension of a count noun, the set of aggregates accruing to that background set forms an atomic complete join semi-lattice with a unit and without a zero. The canonical, isomorphic representative for the lattice in question is the set of non-empty subsets of the background set, where the join operation is set theoretic union and the unit is the background set.

21. Under the canonical isomorphism with the canonical set theoretic representative of the join semi-lattice with a unit, an aggregation is a minimal cover.

22. The terms "collective" and "plurality," used in Gillon (1989), are replaced by the terms "aggregate" and "aggregation," respectively, since the latter are connotatively more congenial to the intended generalization here than the former.

A referee has wondered "whether shifting to talk of aggregates and aggregation instead of sets and covers is a mere terminological change or plays a substantive role." To begin with, misgivings about the appropriateness of sets as the interpretations of plural count nouns go back to Russell (1936 [1903]) and Leśniewski, among others. (See Simons 1982a, for discussion.) Simons (1982a) himself develops these misgivings into very convincing arguments, some of which are echoed by Link (1984). Now recently, Link's arguments have come under criticism from Landman (1989a, 1989b), who uses sets to interpret plural count nouns. But even Landman, who has no proposal concerning the semantics of mass nouns, concedes that "the analogies between mass terms and count terms form a forceful argument" (1989a, p. 568) for such a shift.

In my view, it is not the analogies between the two kinds of nouns that is important, but the fact that they interact and overlap in so many ways that it seems manifestly wrong to give these nouns semantic interpretations which are not, in some fundamental way, the same. Thus, quantified mass noun phrases are liable to the same relativity of construal of scope as their count noun counterparts. Moreover, quantified mass and count noun phrases interact scopally. And indeed, within a fixed context of use, a mass noun and a count noun can be synonymous. Suppose, for example, I have a pair of curtains hanging in my window: it seems clear that in the context of use "this drapery" (a mass noun phrase) and "these drapes" (a count noun phrase) refer to the very same thing. It is not clear to me how this is going to be captured, unless the interpretational domains are unified; and while it is clear how it can be done with mereological concepts such as aggregates, it is not at all clear how it is to be done with set theoretic concepts, as Landman (1989a, p. 568) himself points out.

23. It might seem odd that feature +PL permits, rather than requires, the denotation of the noun phrase to which it is assigned to be greater than or equal to one. After all, the supposition one usually makes when a plural noun phrase is used is that more than one individual in the domain of discourse is involved. This supposition, however, cannot be based in grammar, for there are just too many unimpeachable sentences where a plural noun phrase has a singleton for a denotation:

(i)   Although it was the ancient Babylonians who first observed [the Morning Star and the Evening Star], nonetheless, it was the ancient Greeks who first discovered [them] to be the same planet.

(ii) These men, Mark Twain and Samuel Clemens, are the same man. Rather, the supposition is based on extra-grammatical considerations, like conversational implicature.

24. For the sake of ease of exposition, attention is confined to simple cases of sentences containing referentially dependent pronouns. The treatment is based on Higginbotham (1983).

25. Heim et al. (1988) have criticized this approach, maintaining that it cannot properly distinguish some readings which arise in sentences such as

(i)   [John and Mary]ᵢ told [each other]ᵢ that [they]ᵢ should leave.

I believe that this criticism cannot be sustained, though I do not have the space to show it here. In any event, the analysis of reciprocal pronouns presented by Heim et al. (1988) cannot, by their own admission, capture well-known readings of reciprocal pronouns such as the one mentioned in connection with the sentence in (43).

26. A referee has suggested that an observation due to Fiengo and Lasnik (1973, p. 455) undermines this principle. He observes that, in a situation where there are, say, four trays and the first one is on the top of the second, the second on the third and the third on the fourth, the sentence,

(i)   The trays are stacked on top of each other

is true, though no reciprocal (i.e., symmetric and connected) relation of stacking can be defined over any aggregation corresponding to a partition of the subject noun phrase's denotation.

Langendoen (1978, sec. 7) has pointed out that such usage of the reciprocal pronoun is confined to predicates expressing strict, immediate precedence and, moreover, expressing it from a particular point of view. If the non-reciprocal interpretation were a generally available interpretation, one would expect that the following sentence would be equally acceptable vis-à-vis the circumstances stipulated above:

(ii)   The trays are stacked under each other.

But, according to Langendoen's judgment and mine, it is not.

In fact, there is independent evidence that the problem lies not with the reciprocal pronoun but with the expression "on top of," as the following attested sentence makes clear (Lobel 1981, p. 49):

(iii) Uncle Elephant was wearing everything on top of everything.

Here there is neither a reciprocal pronoun nor an intended reciprocal reading of the expression "wear x on top of y," yet the expression is presumably to be interpreted as a case of strict immediate precedence, which cannot be a universal relation over a finite set, contra what the universally quantified noun phrases require.

27. Hydra sentences lead Link (1984) to countenance the semantic association with plural noun phrases, not only of pluralities but also of groups (or collectives). This admission of groups to the semantics of plural noun phrases has the effect of re-insinuating into the semantics, types of groups parallel to the types of sets which Link had hoped to eliminate in the first place by elimination of sets in favor of pluralities in his earlier work (Link 1983). This point is made by Landman (1989a, sec. 1.4). Unconvinced by the considerations adduced by Link (1983) to replace sets with pluralities, Landman (1989a) reverts to sets and avails himself of both types and type-lifting.

28. Lasersohn (1990), objecting to earlier work of mine, has asserted that my approach to the semantics of plural common nouns founders on an analogous kind of sentence:

(i)   John and Mary met in a bar and had a beer.

But, as I pointed out in my rejoinder (Gillon 1990, p. 482), there are at least two ways to accommodate such a sentence on my view. On the one hand, one might hypothesize that the second conjunct of a conjoined verb phrase is, in fact, a clause with a phonetically null pronoun whose antecedent is the phonetically overt subject noun phrase. In other words, this sentence would yield to the same analysis as

(ii)   [John and Mary]ᵢ met in a bar; and [they]ᵢ had a beer

which is subject to the same semantic principles as the sentence in (58).

On the other hand, one might hypothesize the different conjuncts of a conjoined verb phrase are evaluated separately, thereby permitting different aggregations of the relevant subject noun phrase to be invoked on each evaluation.

29. It has been asked by a referee how this reading is to be distinguished from the readings which Greg Carlson (1977a, 1977b) calls a generic reading. I have urged elsewhere (Gillon 1989, sec. 3.3) that one needs to distinguish generic readings where characteristics of varying degrees of intrinsicness, in-

cluding tendencies, dispositions, and habits, are ascribed to something and generic readings in which a property is attributed to a kind of object through reference to an instance of it. The situation satisfying the sentence in question need not be envisaged as involving either the ascription of a characteristic of some degree of intrinsicness or the ascription of a property to a kind of object through reference to an instance of it.

30. Under this account, it is, in principle, possible for the plural universal quantifier and the plural existential quantifier to share a reading—namely, where the aggregation to which each is restricted is the aggregation containing the greatest aggregate, since that aggregation has only one aggregate. But "all" and "some" do not share a reading. I assume that this is a peculiarity of the plural existential quantifier "some," which is handled in its lexical entry by a stipulation to the effect that, say, its domain of quantification does not contain the greatest aggregate (unless, of course, it is the least aggregate as well).

20

TYLER BURGE

Reference and Proper Names

It is perhaps surprising that one needs to theorize about proper names.[1] They seem to present a straightforward, uncomplicated example of how language relates to the world. During the last eighty years, however, there has been considerable disagreement on issues surrounding them. The disagreement has centered on three broad questions: (a) the question of how to explicate the conditions under which a proper name designates an object; (b) the question of how best to speak (semantically and pragmatically) about nondesignating proper names; and (c) the question of the logical role of proper names in a formal theory of language.

In this paper I will be primarily concerned with the third of these questions, although I shall touch briefly on the other two. In particular, I will be concerned with the logical role of proper names in a semantical account of natural languages. The semantical framework within which I shall be working is Tarskian truth theory as applied to the sentences of a person at a time. But most of what I have to say will hold for other semantical approaches.

At the outset I want to place a condition of adequacy on our approach. This is the condition that the theory of truth be *fully formalized*—that is, that the sense and reference (if any) of every expression of the theory should be unambiguously determinable from its form.[2] Interpretation of the truth theory should depend on no contextual parameter other than the inescapable one: the symbols of theory are to be construed as symbols in the language of the theorist. So much context must be presupposed. But natural languages intuitively exhibit two further sorts of context-dependence: dependence on context for determination of the intended reference of token-reflexive constructions, and dependence on context for determination of the intended reading of ambiguous words and grammatical constructions. An effect of the condition is to rule out use of demonstratives or ambiguous constructions in a truth theory to account for use of demonstratives or ambiguous constructions by the person whose sentences are being studied. The motivation for the condition is simply that theories of language should be no less general and precise (where feasible) than mathematical or physical theories.

Tyler Burge (1973) Reference and proper names. *Journal of Philosophy* 70: 425–439. Reprinted by permission of The Journal of Philosophy.

It is possible to distinguish two major positions on the question of the role that proper names play in a formal semantical theory. One is the view that proper names play the role of constant, noncomplex singular terms. The other is the view of Russell, elaborated by Quine, that they play the role of predicates.[3]

To my knowledge there are no arguments in the literature for thinking that proper names are individual constants. But the intuitive considerations that seem to support this position lie right on the surface: in their most ordinary uses proper names are singular terms, purporting to pick out a unique object; they appear to lack internal semantical structure; they do not seem to describe the objects they purportedly designate, as definite discriptions do; and in some sense they specify the objects thus purportedly designated, as demonstratives do not. It is probably true to say that most philosophers, linguists, and logicians have on these grounds accepted an individual-constants view of proper names.

The traditional predicate view has been prompted by a sense of the clarity and simplicity that results in one's theory of reference if one treats proper names as abbreviated or manufactured descriptions. Whatever its philosophical virtues, this view has been widely regarded as having the vice of artificiality, at least insofar as it is supposed to give analyses of sentences in natural languages.

The view I shall maintain is, roughly speaking, a modified predicate view. The main body of the paper will be devoted to setting out my view with explicit reference to the predicate approach of Russell and Quine. In sections II and III I shall relate that view briefly to the questions about application conditions and about failures of designation. I shall conclude in section IV by criticizing the treatment of proper names as individual constants.

I

I remarked that the traditional predicate view was widely thought to have the disadvantage of artificiality. In fact, there are three points at which the Russellian approach has been held to do violence to ordinary preconceptions. The first is its treatment of proper names as abbreviated or manufactured descriptions. The violated preconception here is simply the notion that names do not describe. Appeals to abbreviation or manufacture are transparently ad hoc. The second point at which Russell's approach has seemed artificial is its elimination of definite descriptions (including proper names) as incomplete symbols. In this case, the violated preconception is the notion that names play the semantical and grammatical role of singular terms. The third alleged element of artificiality is the closing of apparent truth-value gaps. And the violated preconception here is that some sentences that involve failures of designation are neither true nor false.

These points are, of course, recognized by Russell and Quine. Russell tends to regard the cited preconceptions as indefensible confusions. Quine sees them as relevant evidence for understanding natural language, but irrelevant to, or dispensable in the face of, his purpose of constructing a smooth logical theory suitable for the general use of natural science. Since we are concerned with understanding natural languages, we need not take exception to Quine's view of the matter here. Our grammatical and semantical preconceptions are evidence for a theory of natural language; their bearing on the development of logical theory for general scientific use is a further question.

I intend to postpone the issues regarding the elimination of definite descriptions and the closing of so-called truth-value gaps, and concentrate on the first source of artificiality in the traditional predicate view: the claim that proper names are abbreviated or manufactured descriptions.

There are two ways in which a proper name has been seen to function as an abbreviation. One is that it abbreviates a string of descriptive general terms that the language-user would employ—or abbreviates an artificial predicate like 'Aristotelizes'. The other is that a proper name abbreviates into one symbol the semantical roles of operator and predicate which, in definite descriptions, are usually represented separately by at least two symbols: the 'the' (or an analogous construction) and the general term. In explaining my view I shall deal consecutively with these two senses of abbreviation. I shall argue first that proper names do not abbreviate predicates but are predicates in their own right. Then I shall argue that they do not abbreviate the roles of predicate and operator, but that in some of their uses they play the roles of predicate and demonstrative.

Russell sometimes holds that a proper name abbreviates the descriptions the speaker associates with the putative designation of the name. Since this view has been criticized in detail elsewhere,[4] I will not take the time to discuss the difficulties with it here. Suffice it to say that proper names ordinarily have at best a tenuous logical relation to the descriptions that language users associate with them, certainly not the relation of abbreviation.[5]

In one passage, Russell suggests that a proper name abbreviates the description "the object called 'PN'," where 'PN' stands for the proper name.[6] I think that there is something to be said for this suggestion, and we shall return to it later. But one may say against it that it is needlessly counterintuitive and that it leads to unnecessary theoretical complications. Intuitively, proper names simply do not describe. Theoretically, it is undesirable to postulate abbreviation rules if they can be avoided. I think that they can be.

A proper name is a predicate true of an object if and only if the object is given that name in an appropriate way. There is and need be no claim that a proper name abbreviates *another* predicate, even a roughly coextensive predicate such as "is an entity called 'PN'." A proper name is a predicate in its own right.[7]

Failure to appreciate this point has stemmed largely from concentrating on singular, unmodified uses of proper names:

Alfred studies in Princeton.

But proper names take the plural:

There are relatively few Alfreds in Princeton.

They also take indefinite and definite articles:

An Alfred Russell joined the club today.
The Alfred who joined the club today was a baboon.

And quantifiers:

Some Alfreds are crazy; some are sane.

Proper names are usually used in singular and unmodified form. But there is nothing ungrammatical about the above sentences.[8] Moreover, the occurrences of proper names in them are literal and not metaphoric or ironic. Contrast these uses with the metaphoric use in

George Wallace is a Napoleon.

George Wallace is not literally one of the Napoleons—he has not been given the name 'Napoleon' in a socially accepted way. Rather, he is like the most famous Napoleon in significant respects.

The modified proper names in the examples just given have the same conditions for literal application to an object that singular, unmodified proper names have. This point is confirmed by such sentences as

(1)   Jones is a Jones.

which is an obvious truth under normal conditions of use.

Now one might claim that the uses I have cited are "special" uses of proper names, and that they should not be taken as throwing light on the usual uses. Vendler, for example, notes that there is "something unusual" about noun phrases like 'the Joe in our house':

> Such phrases do occur and we understand them. It is clear, however, that such a context is fatal to the name as proper name, at least for the discourse in which it occurs. The full context, explicit or implicit, will be of the following sort:
>
> The Joe in our house is not the one you are talking about. . . . As the noun replacer, *one*, makes abundantly clear, the name here simulates the status of a count noun. There are two Joe's presupposed in the discourse, and this is, of course, inconsistent with the idea of a logically proper name. *Joe* is here really equivalent to something like *person called Joe*, and because this phrase fits many individuals, it should be treated as a general term by the logician.[9]

We may agree with Vendler that modified occurrences of ordinary names are in a sense not "proper" to any one object. But it would be a mistake to think that the passage provides any reason to hold that modified and unmodified occurrences of ordinary proper names are semantically independent of each other. For no reason is given to believe that ordinary names are ever "logically proper names" (presumably individual constants). In a limited context, proper names may be—and often are—assumed to apply to a unique object. But a semantical theory (like ours), which is applicable to a language without restrictions on the context in which sentences of the language may be used, cannot commit itself to such an assumption.

Postulation of special uses of a term, semantically unrelated to what are taken to be its paradigmatic uses, is theoretically undesirable—particularly if a straightforward semantical relation between these different uses can be found. We have already indicated what this relation is: a proper name is (literally) true of an object just in case that object is given that name in an appropriate way.

In holding that a name applies to an object just in case the object bears a certain pragmatic relation to that name, I am suggesting that the name itself enters into the conditions under which it is applicable. In this respect, proper names differ from many other predicates. Take, for example, the predicate 'is a dog'. An object could be a dog even if the word 'dog' were never used as a symbol. But an object could not be a Jones unless someone used 'Jones' as a name. This mild self-referential element in the application conditions of proper names can be further illustrated by comparing

(2)   Jones is necessarily a Jones.

with

(3)   This entity called 'Jones' is necessarily an entity called 'Jones'.

To obtain (3) we have substituted for 'Jones' in (2) the roughly co-extensive predicate expression "entity called 'Jones'." Not surprisingly, both sentences come out false on any occasion of use. Thus, proper names are like ordinary predicates containing quotation marks in their intuitively clear failure to be necessarily true of objects to which they apply.

Our predicate view of proper names avoids one source of artificiality in the views of Russell and Quine. It does not involve the claim that proper names abbreviate any descriptive predicates, nor does it involve the manufacture of predicates that are not present in ordinary natural languages. Our account also seems to meet the charge, often raised against the abbreviated-description view, that proper names do not convey information about, or attribute characteristics to, the named object. I do claim that, when a speaker uses the name 'Aristotle' (taken literally), he purports to convey the information that the object of which he speaks, if any, is called 'Aristotle'. But this does not seem to be something anyone would want to deny.

So far I have held that although in surface grammar proper names function sometimes as singular terms and sometimes as general terms, they play the semantical role of predicates—usually true of numerous objects—on all occurrences. How then are we to represent unmodified occurrences, where proper names function as singular terms? This question brings us to the second sense in which proper names may be said to be abbreviations on the Russell-Quine view—abbreviations in one symbol of the semantical roles of a uniqueness operator and a predicate.

Consider the sentence 'Aristotle is human'. On the Russell-Quine view, this sentence would be analyzed as

(4) $(\exists x)((y) (\text{Aristotle}(y) \leftrightarrow y = x) \, \& \, \text{Is-Human}(x))$

or in unexpanded form:

(5) $\text{Is-Human} \, (\imath x) \, (\text{Aristotle}(x))$

It has frequently been pointed out that, in order for the Russell-Quine analysis to be strictly correct, the predicate 'Aristotle' must be uniquely true of the designated object (if any). But it is not: there are many Aristotles. The usual answer to this point is that we ordinarily rely on context to resolve the ambiguities of ordinary language.[10] But although it is perfectly in order for natural-language *users* to rely on context to clarify intended reference, the condition that we placed on our discussion at the outset prevents the *theorist* from relying on context in a like manner to clarify intended references in his analyses of truth conditions. Most of the proper names that a person is capable of using at a given time will be true of more than one object. We should therefore reject the claim that proper names in singular unmodified form abbreviate the roles of the uniqueness operator and a predicate.

They play instead the roles of a demonstrative and a predicate. Roughly, singular unmodified proper names, functioning as singular terms, have the same semantical structure as the phrase 'that book'. Unlike other predicates, proper names are usually (though, as we have seen, not always) used, with the help of speaker-reference and context, to pick out a particular. For this reason demonstratives are not ordinarily attached to proper names, although, of course, they may be so attached. In general, modifications of proper names occur when the speaker is not relying on them, unsupplemented, to pick out a particular. But whether or not the speaker's act of reference is explicitly supplemented with a demonstrative like 'this' is semantically irrelevant.

Evidence for the view that proper names in singular unmodified form involve a demonstrative element emerges when one compares sentences involving such names with sentences involving demonstratives. Apart from speaker-reference or special context, both *Jim is 6 feet tall* and *That book is green* are incompletely interpreted—they lack truth value. The user of the sentences must pick out a particular (e.g., a particular Jim or book) if the sentences are to be judged true or false. It is this conventional reliance on extrasentential action or context to pick out a particular which signals the demonstrative element in both sentences.

Further evidence for the view that proper names functioning as singular terms involve a demonstrative element derives from the fact that such proper names usually take widest possible scope. In this respect they are like demonstratives and descriptions governed by demonstratives.[11] Note, for example, that it is hard to hear a reading of either (2) or (3) under which the scope of the singular term is small and the sentence comes out true.

Object-language formalizations of sentences containing proper names that function as singular terms are open sentences. 'Aristotle is human', for example, receives the analysis

(6)   Is-Human $([x_i]\text{Aristotle}(x_i))$

Our logic includes the uniqueness operator, and we adjust our formation rules to allow open singular terms of the form

(i) $[x_i]A_j^n(x_1 \ldots x_i \ldots x_n)$

The bracketed 'x_i' marks the free variable in the term which represents the demonstrative governing the whole scope of the term. '$[x_i]$' is *not* an operator for binding the variable 'x_i'. (i) is to be understood as equivalent to

(ii) $[\imath y]A_j^n(x_1 \ldots y \ldots x_n) \& y = x_i)$

I prefer the form (i) to the more usual form (ii) because it seems to me to represent better the syntax of English. Since 'x_i' is a *free* variable as it occurs in (i), it may be quantified from outside the term—just as 'x_i' can in (ii).

An open sentence like (6) takes on truth value only if the user of the sentence carries out an act of reference in the process of using the sentence, and thereby performs extrasententially a task analogous to that which the iota operator performs in classical logical theory.

Whereas the language user himself relies on extrasentential action or context to designate the object, the truth-theorist is barred by our initial condition from doing the same in his metalanguage. The object referred to by the language user (if any) is specified in the truth theory by means of a set of reference clauses:

(7) $(x)(y)$(Reference(x), & By(x,p) & At(x,t) & With$(x$, 'Aristotle$_1$', 'Aristotle is human') & To(x,y) →
       ('Aristotle is human' is true with respect to p at $t \leftrightarrow$ Human$([y]$ Aristotle$(y))))$

Read: For all x and y, if x is an act of reference by person p at time t to y with the first occurrence of 'Aristotle' in 'Aristotle is human', then 'Aristotle is human' is true with respect to p at t just in case the object which is y and is an Aristotle is human. Here is not the place to expand on the analysis.[12] For our purposes what is important is the contrast between the context-dependence of the object-language representation (6) and the *analysis of context* that occurs in the account of truth conditions (7).

So far I have argued (a) that proper names do not abbreviate other predicates but are themselves predicates, and (b) that in their most common uses proper names involve a demonstrative element. Before arguing against the individual-constants approach to the semantical role of proper names, I want in sections II and III to place our predicate approach in the context of the two other traditional issues regarding proper names: the question of the conditions under which they designate an object, and the question of how to account for them when they fail to designate.

II

I have suggested that a proper name functioning as a singular term designates an object only if the object is given that name in an appropriate way. Despite its intended vagueness, this suggestion provides an explication for the fact that we talk of the normal or literal use of proper names.

Literal use contrasts with metaphorical use. Unlike metaphorical uses ('George Wallace is a Napoleon'), literal uses of proper names—whether or not in singular unmodified form—involve application only to objects that bear them.

It is not always desirable to identify the designation of a proper name functioning as a singular term with the reference a speaker makes in using the name. Unlike the object that a speaker designates the object that the proper name itself designates can only be an object that bears that name. The point is perhaps most evident in the case of misidentifications.[13] Suppose a novice is fooled into thinking that he is speaking to Hilbert at the Convention for Aggregative Psychology. Afterward he reports, "Hilbert spoke more about mental mechanisms than about syntax." Now if the man at the convention to whom he speaks is not called "Hilbert," the name does not designate that man, although the novice does. This is because 'Hilbert' is not true of the aggregative psychologist: he is not a Hilbert (literally, as well as metaphorically). The novice thinks that he is, but the novice is wrong. Intuitively, one might want to say that what the novice reported was true of what the novice designated, but false of what the name designated.

Of course, one might hold that, since the novice used the name to designate the psychologist, it *did* designate the psychologist. Speakers often use singular terms in ways other than their normal or literal uses—whether by mistake or by design (lying, irony)—in order to designate an object other than an object that the terms would normally be expected to designate. Having noted this special sense in which names "designate" objects, I propose to ignore it. It seems entirely parasitic on the use of 'designate' to signify a relation between a person and an object, and so can be passed over without loss. When we use 'designate' to signify a relation between a proper name and an object, we shall be concerned with a relation between names and those objects which the names normally or literally apply to.

The relation of designation between proper name (functioning as singular term) and object is definable by means of 'refers to' (speaker-designation) and 'is-true-of': a proper name occurring in a sentence used by a person at a time designates an object if and only if the person refers to that object at that time with that proper name, and the proper name is true of that object. On this usage, when the language user (e.g., the novice) refers to an object (e.g., the psychologist) and mistakenly calls the object by a proper name ('Hilbert') which not it but some other (intended) object bears, we shall not say that the proper name designates that other object at that time. But the proper name *is* true of the intended object. And the language user will normally refer to objects of which the name is true when he uses sentences containing the name. The element of predication in singular unmodified proper names accounts for the intuition that one can speak of normal or literal applications of a proper name and contrast them, in some cases, with the object designated or referred to by the speaker.

I have held that a proper name designates an object only if the object is given that name in an appropriate way. I do not intend to define 'given' or 'appropriate way'. It is not incumbent on us (as truth theorists) to define the conditions under which proper names, or any other predicates, are true of objects. The vague necessary and sufficient application condition for proper names which I have offered may be regarded as a mere stand-in for a full-fledged empirical account of how objects get proper names attached to them. Baptism, inheritance, nicknaming, brand-naming, labeling may all be expected to enter into such an account. Semantics, however, need not await the full returns of sociology. Rules like the following are sufficient: 'O'Hara' is true of any object *y* just in case *y* is an O'Hara.

The demonstrative-references that occur with the use of singular, unmodified proper names seem often to occur when there is some causal-like relation between named object and language user. But this point does not go very far. At most, it is the bare beginning of a sociological account of the designation conditions of proper names. Moreover, even in this vague form, the point is not fully generalizable. Sometimes names lack designations. Either the proper name is true of nothing or the language user refers to nothing that it is true of. Sometimes names are introduced as surrogates for definite descriptions even when the introducer is not causally related to the named object. Here the demonstrative in our analysis, which is usually represented by a free variable, is not a device for referring to an extra-linguistic object, but is a pronominal place marker whose antecedent is the definite description. (Cf. note 11.) Thus: "The shortest spy in the 21st century will be Caucasian. Call him 'Bertrand'. (That) Bertrand will also be bald." There are other cases in which the demonstrative acts as a bound variable—as when we say, "Someone cast the first stone. Whoever he was, call him 'Alfred'. (That) Alfred was a hypocrite." In neither of these cases need there be a causal relation between language user and named object.

III

A full account of the semantics and pragmatics of nondesignating proper names is beyond the scope of this paper. But it may help illuminate our treatment of proper names as predicates to make some brief remarks on the subject. Let us consider the sentence

(8)   It is not the case that Pegasus exists.

as uttered at a particular time by me, where the utterance is to be construed as a denial of what believers in the existence of an ancient winged horse might assert. The proper name is functioning as a singular term. So the logical form of (8) is the same as

(9)   It is not the case that that Pegasus exists.

where the second occurrence of 'that' is read as a demonstrative. The truth-theoretic biconditional for (8) is roughly

(10) $(x)(y)$(Reference(x) & By$(x,$TB*$)$ & At$(x,$4/23/1970/11 AM EST$)$ & With$(x,$ 'Pegasus$_1$', 'Pegasus does not exist'$)$ & To(x,y) $\rightarrow$ ('Pegasus does not exist' is true with respect to TB* at 4/23/1970/ 11 AM EST $\leftrightarrow$ $\sim(\exists z)$ $(z = [y]$Pegasus$(y))))$

('TB*' represents a complete canonical specification of me.)

In the case of proper names that designate an object, the person's act of reference provides the open singular term representing the proper name with an interpretation and the containing sentence with a truth value. The effect of such an act on the truth condition of the sentence is specified metalinguistically in sentences like (10). But what of the case in which the proper name designates nothing—as in (8)? According to our definition of designation in the previous section, this case will be realized if and only if either the proper name is true of nothing or the language user refers to nothing that it is true of.

Now the failure of 'Pegasus' to designate in my utterance of (8) does not follow from a failure of 'Pegasus' to be true of anything. There are plenty of Pegasi; Richard Gale, for example, has a dog by that name. Hence the failure of 'Pegasus' to designate in my utterance of (8) follows from the fact that I referred to nothing that this proper name is true of. We are assuming that there was an act of reference by me at 4/23/1970/11 AM EST with 'Pegasus'. So I could refer to nothing that the proper name is true of only if one of two cases holds. On the one hand, it might be that 'Pegasus' in (8) failed to designate because I referred to something that is not a Pegasus:

(11) $(\exists x)$ $(\exists z)$(Reference(x) & By$(x,$ TB*$)$ & With$(x,$ 'Pegasus$_1$', 'Pegasus does not exist'$)$ & At$(x,$ 4/23/1970/11 AM EST$)$ & To(x, z) & $\sim$ Pegasus $(z))$

On the other hand, it might be that I *referred* but referred to nothing at all, so a fortiori to no Pegasus:

(12) $(\exists x)$(Reference(x), & By$(x$, TB*) & With$(x$, 'Pegasus$_1$', 'Pegasus does not exist') & At$(x$, 4/23/ 1970/11 AM EST) & $\sim (\exists z)$(To(x, z)))

In the first case, I might be referring to the events that began the Pegasus myth. In the second case, my reference would have spatio-temporal direction toward the ur-events of the myth. But it would have no referred-to object. It is clear that sentences like (11) sometimes hold. Such sentences are useful in explaining misidentifications of the sort the novice made. Whether sentences like (12) ever hold is perhaps debatable, though I am inclined to think that they probably do. Fortunately, our formalization in (10) does not force us to take a stand on the issue. The failure of 'Pegasus' to designate in my utterance of (8)—and the truth of the utterance itself—may be explicated by either (11) or (12).[14]

IV

I want to close by making some derogatory remarks about the individual-constants view of the semantical role of proper names. One disadvantage of the view has already been brought out. Our account covers plural and modified occurrences, as well as singular, unmodified ones. A constants view not only is more complicated in that it must give a different semantics for these different occurrences (and fail to account as neatly for the obviousness of (1)). But it is also faced with the task of justifying its disunification. Appeal to "special" uses whenever proper names clearly do not play the role of individual constants is flimsy and theoretically deficient.

A second disadvantage of the individual-constants view emerges from reflecting on the respective accounts of the "ambiguity" of proper names. If proper names are treated as ambiguous individual constants, then occurrences designating different objects will have to be differentiated (indexed) in the truth theory for a person at a time. Otherwise, the truth conditions of sentences treated by the theory would be ambiguous, and our initial condition would be violated. But such differentiation poses a problem. There is no evident limit on the number of objects that bear a given name. So there is no way to know how many indexes to provide, much less what denotations to provide them with.

A proponent of the constants view may wish to avoid this problem by claiming that the number of objects that a person at a given time knows to correlate with any given name is probably delimitable and manageable. Thus, the claim would be that one need only provide a denotation for each indexed name for which a person has a denotation in his ken.

This position is not as simple as it may seem. In the first place, a name like 'John' would complicate the semantical theory considerably. Whereas the individual-constants approach would have to provide a large number of denotation rules for the name (say, four hundred), our predicate approach provides a single satisfaction rule for it, plus the set of primitive reference clauses applicable to all occurrences of demonstratives (implicit or explicit) in sentences. In the second place, the truth theorist for the idiolect of a person at a time would be presented with the awesome task of actually tracking down and specifying each of the Johns that a person has in his ken in order to complete his theory. Quite apart from the practical difficulties involved—difficulties that would have no analog in any other part of the theory—there are unpleasant theoretical problems in deciding what objects fall within a person's ken at a given time. None of these problems arises on the predicate approach.

A sophisticated variant of the multi-indexed individual-constants treatment of proper names would be to parse them as fully interpreted constants only when they are being used and as dummy constants otherwise.[15] Such a view would allow for the fact that unmodified occurrences of proper names receive their semantical interpretation in and through a person's actually using them. If it were to avoid the previously mentioned problems in specifying the denotations of (used) proper names, the view would have to invoke something like the apparatus that we utilized in our analysis (7). The "denotation" of the proper name would be determined in the context of use by the reference of the language user. Such an approach would treat proper names as very like free variables—a treatment with which I would have considerable sympathy. The disadvantage of the approach is that it would ignore the conventional predicative element, the element of literalness or factuality, in the application conditions of proper names. For example, it would fail to give a semantical representation to the fact that a given name—whether used or unused (at a given time) applies to some objects and not others. As a result, the approach would fail to give a unified account of modified and unmodified occurrences of proper names (cf. (1)).

Our account's handling of the foregoing problems is simple. Proper names are predicates. One need not distinguish truth-theoretically the objects of which they are true. When a proper name occurs in singular-term position, the object designated by the name (if any) is picked out by the language user's reference. And the truth theory specifies that object in a context-independent manner. The designative indefiniteness or "ambiguity" of proper names is reflected by the variable in formal representations. Insofar as proper names exemplify a fundamental way in which language relates to the world, they provide reason to focus not on individual constants, but on variables—and not the variables of quantification, but free variables which represent demonstratives and which receive their interpretation extralinguistically, through the referential actions of language users.

Notes

I am indebted to Keith Donnellan, Richard Grandy, Gilbert Harman, Edwin Martin, and John Wallace for comments on earlier versions of this paper. An abbreviated version was presented at the meetings of the American Philosophical Association, Eastern Division, in December 1971.

1. In what follows I shall use "proper name" in an intuitive way. Intuitively, proper names are nouns that do not describe the objects, if any, to which they apply, and which may in natural language function without modification as singular terms. I exclude from present considerations certain names—"canonical names" such as 'O'—which are perhaps best represented as individual constants. Roughly, such names carry a uniqueness presupposition at all their occurrences that is sufficiently global for them to figure in our most comprehensive, context-free theories. Like "proper name," the term *designate* is to be construed intuitively—until it is defined.

2. For expressions of this notion of a formal system, see Gottlob Frege, "On Sense and Reference," in P. Geach and M. Black, eds., *Translations from the Philosophical Writings of Gottlob Frege* (Oxford: Blackwell's, 1966), p. 58; and Alfred Tarski, "The Concept of Truth in Formalized Languages," in J. H. Woodger (ed. and trans.), *Logic, Semantics, Metamathematics* (Oxford: Oxford, 1956), pp. 165–166.

3. For an example of the constants view, see H. P. Grice, "Vacuous Names," in Donald Davidson and Jaakko Hintikka (eds.), *Words and Objections* (Dordrecht: Reidel, 1969). Chief sources of the predicate view are Bertrand Russell, "Knowledge by Acquaintance and by Description," *Proceedings of the Aristotelian Society* 11 (1911): 108–128; Russell, "The Philosophy of Logical Atomism" (1918) in Robert Charles Marsh (ed.), *Logic and Knowledge* (London: Macmillan 1956b), esp. pp. 241–254; W. V. O. Quine, "On What There Is" (1948) in *From a Logical Point of View* (New York: Harper, 1953a), p. 6; and Quine, *Methods of Logic* (New York: Holt, 1950), pp. 218–219 (in 3rd ed., 1972, pp. 228–230).

4. Keith S. Donnellan, "Proper Names and Identifying Descriptions," *Synthèse* 21 3/4: 335–358; Saul Kripke, "Naming and Necessity," in Donald Davidson and Gilbert Harman (eds.), *Semantics of Natural Languages* (Dordrecht: Reidel, 1972), pp. 253–355.

5. Some philosophers have held that a proper name does not abbreviate but, rather, presupposes a set of descriptions uniquely true of the designated object (if any). Cf. John Searle, "Proper Names," *Mind* 67 (1958): 166–173; P. F. Strawson, *Individuals* (New York: Doubleday, 1959), p. 20. This view faces a number

of difficulties, but it is compatible with various positions on the semantic role of proper names, so there is no pressing reason to discuss it here.

6. Russell "The Philosophy of Logical Atomism."

7. Calling proper names "predicates" slurs a distinction which for present purposes is unimportant but which is worth bearing in mind. Strictly speaking proper names are general terms which, together with a copula and an indefinite article on some occurrences, are parsed as predicates in a formal semantical theory.

8. Worth mentioning here is the syntactic theory of Clarence Sloat, "Proper Nouns in English," *Language*, 45 (1969): 26–30, which Edwin Martin and Barbara Partee called to my attention. Sloat gives a neat account of proper names which treats them on a close analogy to common nouns. Clearly, such a syntactical account is congenial with our predicate view of the semantical role of proper names—and uncongenial with an individual-constants view.

9. Z. Vendler, "Singular Terms," in *Linguistics in Philosophy* (Ithaca, N.Y.: Cornell University Press, 1967b), pp. 40–41. I have eliminated one of Vendler's examples and adjusted the grammar to accommodate the elimination.

10. Cf. Quine, *Methods of Logic*, p. 216 (3rd ed., p. 227).

11. There are pronominal occurrences of demonstratives and demonstrative-governed singular terms which do not take widest scope if their antecedents do not. These occurrences will be ignored for present purposes. It should be mentioned, however, that in such occurrences proper names sometimes play an abbreviative rather than an independently predicative role.

12. Fuller discussion occurs in my dissertation "Truth and Some Referential Devices" (Princeton University, 1971). As a result of a suggestion by David Kaplan, the bracket notation replaced a less perspicuous predecessor. Note that the quantifier 'y' binds the variable 'y' both as it occurs in 'To (x,y)' and as it occurs in '$[y]$Aristotle(y)'. The subscript on 'Aristotle' marks a particular occurrence of the term in the sentence. (One might use the term more than once in a given sentence to refer to more than one object.) All positions in sentence (7) are fully extensional. The formulation of the antecedent owes something to Donald Davidson's treatment of action verbs; cf. his "The Logical Form of Action Sentences," in Nicholas Rescher, ed., *The Logic of Action and Decision* (Pittsburgh: University of Pittsburgh Press, 1968), pp. 81–95.

13. Other aspects of misidentifications are given valuable discussion by Donnellan in "Proper Names and Identifying Descriptions," and "Reference and Definite Descriptions," *Philosophical Review*, 75 (1966): 281–304.

14. It should be noted that, if (12) is chosen as the explication, an additional axiom is needed to prevent (10) from being uninformative because the condition laid down by the antecedent is unfulfilled. But supplying such an axiom is not difficult.

15. Dummy constants are discussed in Rudolf Carnap, *The Logical Syntax of Language* (London: Routledge and Kegan Paul, 1937), pp. 189–195. (Carnap does not propose the view of proper names I am here constructing.) It should be noted that in some free logics Carnap's way of distinguishing dummy constants and free variables breaks down.

21

GARETH EVANS

Pronouns

Introduction

A very natural, preliminary classification of the uses of pronouns would include the following three categories:

> (*i*) Pronouns used to make a reference to an object (or objects) present in the shared perceptual environment, or rendered salient in some other way. The sentence (1),

(1) He's up early.

said of a man passing in the street, or (2),

(2) I'm glad he's left.

said of a man who has just walked out of the room, exemplify this use.

> (*ii*) Pronouns intended to be understood as being coreferential with a referring expression occurring elsewhere in the sentence. One of the readings of the sentence (3) results from such a use of the pronoun *his*:

(3) John loves his mother.

> (*iii*) Pronouns which have quantifier expressions as antecedents and are used in such a way as to be strictly analogous to the bound variables of the logician. The pronoun in the sentence (4) appears to be used in this way:

Gareth Evans (1980) Pronouns. *Linguistic Inquiry* 11: 337–362. Reprinted by permission of MIT Press Journals.

(4)   Every man loves his mother.

I have two main points which I want to make about pronouns. First, there is a fourth category, which I call "E-type pronouns", the members of which are very frequently confused with the members of category (*iii*), but which, in fact, are semantically quite different. E-type pronouns also have quantifier expressions as antecedents, but they are not bound by those quantifiers. For example, the pronoun in the sentence (5)

(5)   Few M.P.s came to the party but they had a good time.

is an E-type and not a bound pronoun. I shall discuss these pronouns in section 2.

My second main point concerns the semantics of pronouns in category (*iii*)—"bound pronouns," as I shall call them. Linguists tend to regard the semantics of bound pronouns (or of bound variables) as a mystery clearly understood by logicians, and to leave matters there. But we cannot afford to be so incurious. It is a very striking fact about pronouns in natural languages that they have this use, in addition to their other uses, and we must wonder whether this is an accident or whether there is some underlying semantic principle which accounts for these apparently disparate uses in a unified way. In fact, there is this very striking connection between pronouns in categories (*ii*) and (*iii*): whenever we substitute a singular term for a quantifier binding a pronoun, we arrive at a sentence in which the pronoun can be interpreted as coreferential with that singular term. This surely suggests that some common principle underlies the use of pronouns in categories (*ii*) and (*iii*)—that the capacity we have to understand sentences like (3) is, at the very least, *connected with* the capacity we have to understand sentences like (4). If we look at matters in this way, we see that the relationship between pronouns in categories (*ii*) and (*iii*) is a version of a problem which is frequently encountered in semantics, for there are many devices which occur, apparently univocally, in both singular and quantified sentences. The semantic problem posed by those dual occurrences can be solved quite generally if we provide a semantic account of quantified sentences which proceeds by way of a semantic account of their singular instances. If we adopt such an account, which is motivated quite independently of any consideration of pronouns, we have only to explain the semantic significance of pronouns in category (*ii*) and nothing whatever has to be said, in addition, about pronouns in category (*iii*)—they simply look after themselves. I shall attempt to show this in section 3.

The ideas which I shall advance in section 3 place me in direct opposition to an approach to pronouns originally advanced by Lasnik (1976) and received with favor by some other linguists.[1] One way of explaining Lasnik's main idea is to say that he proposes an incorporation of pronouns in category (*ii*) into category (*i*). If we regard an object's having been mentioned in a previous conversation, or having been mentioned previously in the conversation, as a way of its being salient for purposes of reference, as we must, why should we not regard being mentioned elsewhere in the same sentence as a limiting case of this mode of salience? If we do so, there is no good reason for distinguishing pronouns in category (*ii*) from those in category (*i*). (Since the reference of pronouns in category (*i*) is determined by what may loosely be called "pragmatic" factors, I shall call Lasnik's theory "the pragmatic theory of coreference.") At first sight, Lasnik's proposal has the appeal of simplicity, but on further reflection, we can see that its price is too high. For to assimilate pronouns in category (*ii*) to those in category (*i*) is to preclude the recognition of any connection whatever between pronouns in the unified category (*i*) + (*ii*) and those in category (*iii*)—that is, it forces us to regard as a complete accident that the same expression shows up in both (3) and (4). I shall attempt to explain this point, and the distinction between pragmatics and grammar which it forces upon us, in section 4. In the remaining section I shall advance some other criticisms of Lasnik's approach to pronouns.

2   The existence of E-type pronouns

I shall begin my attempt to demonstrate the existence of a fourth category of pronouns by considering sentences containing plural quantifiers, since the distinction between a bound and an E-type interpretation of a pronoun comes out most clearly when the pronoun has a plural quantifier as antecedent. Consider the two sentences (6) and (7):

(6)   Few congressmen admire only the people they know.
(7)   Few congressmen admire Kennedy, and they are very junior.

At first sight the relationship between the quantifier phrase *few congressmen* and the pronoun *they* in these two sentences appears to be the same, but on closer inspection we can see that it is really quite different. In (6) the pronoun is bound by the quantifier phrase, while in (7) it cannot be. If the pronoun in (7) is to be bound by the quantifier phrase, *few congressmen*, then its scope must extend to the second conjunct, and the sentence would be interpreted as meaning that few congressmen both admire Kennedy and are very junior. But this is not the interpretation naturally placed upon (7). First, (7) entails, as its supposed paraphrase does not, that few congressmen admire Kennedy, period. Second, (7) entails, as its supposed paraphrase does not, that *all* the congressmen who admire Kennedy are very junior.

Similarly, in the sentence (8), the quantifier phrase *some sheep* does not bind the pronoun *them*:

(8)   John owns some sheep and Harry vaccinates them in the spring.

If it did bind the pronoun, the sentence would be equivalent to (9), in which both pronouns are bound:

(9)   Some sheep are such that John owns them and Harry vaccinates them in the spring.

But (9) is not equivalent to (8); (8) entails, as (9) does not, that Harry vaccinates *all* the sheep which John owns.

A useful test of whether or not a pronoun is bound by an antecedent quantifier is to replace the antecedent with the quantifier expression *No*, and see whether the result makes sense. Where a pronoun is bound by a quantifier, as in (10),

(10)   Few men despise those who stand up to them.

it is part of a complex predicate (e.g. ( ) *despise those who stand up to them*), which is affirmed to be satisfied in the case of many girls, some sheep, or, in the example, few men, and which can be affirmed to be satisfied in the case of no girls, no sheep, or no men. Thus we have:

(11)   No men despise those who stand up to them.

When we apply this test to the pairs of examples we have considered, we find confirmation of the semantic difference which we have noticed:

(12)   No congressmen admire only the people they know.
(13)   *No congressmen admire Kennedy, and they are very junior.
(14)   No sheep are such that John owns them and Harry vaccinates them in the spring.
(15)   *John owns no sheep, and Harry vaccinates them in the spring.

When a pronoun is bound by a quantifier expression, it does not make sense to ask to what it refers (on that occasion of use). If you have any doubt of this, you should be able to convince yourself of its truth by attempting to answer the question in the case of sentences like (4), (6), (11), (12), and (14). You will get into hopeless muddles, which have been analyzed in detail by Geach (1962) in his book *Reference and Generality*. How the semantic functioning of bound pronouns is to be accounted for is something I shall discuss in section 3, but it ought to be clear at even this early stage that a pronoun bound by a quantifier does not refer to anything. However, just looking at the examples we have so far considered, it appears that the pronouns we have shown not to be bound by their quantifier antecedents *are* interpreted as referring to something. If someone asked, about (8), "Harry vaccinates *them*? Which sheep?," the natural (and, in my view, rule-governed) answer is: "The sheep which John owns, of course." Equally, the question *"They* are junior? Who do you mean?" would be answered "Why, the congressmen that admire Kennedy." It looks as though the role of the pronoun in these sentences is that of referring to the object(s), if any, which *verify* the antecedent quantifier-containing clause.[2] If this is the role of these E-type pronouns, we explain why the truth of the clause containing them requires that *all* the relevant objects satisfy the predicate, and we explain why these pronouns cannot have a *No* quantifier as antecedent.

It is clear from the examples I have given that whether or not a pronoun is interpreted as bound by a quantifier phrase depends upon the grammatical relation in which it stands to that quantifier phrase. All the examples so far have involved coordinate structures, but consideration of a wide range of examples containing plural quantifiers supports the generalization that a pronoun will be interpreted as bound by a quantifier phrase only if it precedes and c-commands the pronoun.[3] Using this rule, one can construct endless examples of E-type pronouns:

(16)   After Harry bought some sheep, Harry vaccinated them.
(17)   *After Harry bought no sheep, Harry vaccinated them.
(18)   If many men come to the ball, Mary will dance with them.
(19)   *If no men come to the ball, Mary will dance with them.

When we come to consider *singular* quantifiers, it appears that the precede and c-command relationship marks a similar semantic distinction. For example, it is clear that the scope of the quantifier in sentence (20)

(20)   Just one man drank champagne and he was ill.

can extend only to the end of the first clause; if it is interpreted as extending to the whole sentence, to bind the pronoun *he*, we get the quite different proposition: *Just one man both drank champagne and was ill.* The point also shows up very clearly with *every*-sentences. When the quantifier *every* precedes and c-commands a singular pronoun, as in (4), the pronoun is interpreted as bound, but when it does not stand in this relation to the pronoun, the result is unacceptable:

(21)   *Every congressman came to the party, and he had a marvelous time.[4]

If it is the role of pronouns not c-commanded by their quantifier antecedents to refer to the object(s) which verify the antecedent clause, the deviance of (21) is explained, since in the antecedent clause there are asserted to be a plurality of such objects. (21) is certainly improved by pluralizing the pronoun:

(22)   ?Every congressman came to the party, and they had a marvelous time.

It is also possible to show that the precede and *c*-command configuration determines the difference between bound and E-type pronouns in the case of the simple existential quantifiers, *some man, a boy, there is a girl,* et cetera. If we look back on the arguments which we have used to show that a given pronoun is not bound by a quantifier antecedent, we shall see that they are basically of two kinds. One kind of argument is scope argument; we show that in order to give a certain sentence the correct interpretation, the scope of the quantifier cannot extend to the clause containing the pronoun—we show that the quantifier must have "narrow scope." If we use "Q + CN" to represent a given quantifier plus common noun, "A( )" to represent the context of the quantifier expression in the first clause, and "B( )" to represent the context of the pronoun in the second clause, then the conjunctive sentences on which we have been concentrating can be represented schematically as follows:

A(Q + CN) and B(it/them, etc.)

To represent the pronoun in the second clause as bound requires understanding the whole sentence as having the form

$Q_{CN}x(A(x) \& B(x))$

in which the quantifier phrase, $Q_{CN}x$—for example, "For some man x" and "For all girls y"—has "wide scope." And in the case of certain quantifiers (*few, most, just one, three,* etc.), we are able to show that this interpretation is incorrect, since the original sentence entails, as the "wide scope" interpretation does not, the simple

$Q_{CN}x(A(x))$

The second kind of argument that a pronoun is not bound depends upon its being interpreted in such a way that the truth of the clause containing it requires that *all* of the objects of a certain class satisfy the predicate of that clause. This again is a feature of the interpretation of the sentence which does not obtain if the pronoun is taken to be bound by the quantifier. I explained this feature by suggesting that the pronoun has a referential role, similar to that of the phrase *the congressmen who came.*

With slight modification, both of these kinds of argument can be constructed for the case of the simple existential quantifiers. A scope argument cannot focus upon conjunctive sentences, since the wide scope

Some man x (A(x) and B(x))

does entail

Some man x (A(x))

However, a clear difference between wide and narrow scope interpretations of the existential quantifiers shows up in conditional sentences. Thus, in sentence (23)

(23)   If a man enters this room, he will trip the switch.

we must give the *a man* quantifier narrow scope (leaving *he* unbound); we are not saying that there is a man such that if *he* comes, he will trip the switch. Equally, in sentence (24)

(24)   If there is a man in the garden, John will tell him to leave.

the *there is a man* quantifier must have narrow scope; we are not saying that there is a man such that, if *he* is in the garden, John will tell him to leave.

The second kind of argument can apply even in cases in which the scope argument cannot apply, but we must first ask what is the feature of the use of a *singular* pronoun which corresponds to the requirement made by a plural pronoun that *all* the members of a certain class satisfy the predicate. If it is the role of E-type pronouns in general to refer to the object or objects which verify the antecedent clause, and if an E-type pronoun is singular, then we would predict that the use of that pronoun will convey the implication that there is *just one* object verifying the antecedent clause—an implication which is not carried by the use of the existential quantifiers themselves. It seems to me that this is exactly what we find. When a pronoun is in a clause coordinate with the clause containing the quantifier, as in (25),

(25)   Socrates owned a dog and it bit Socrates.

there is a clear implication that Socrates owned just one dog. It is precisely because of the implication carried by such pronouns that it is not acceptable to report the non-emptiness of the class of Welsh doctors in London by saying (26):

(26)   There is a doctor in London and he is Welsh.

Notice that no such implication is carried by the use of a pronoun which is *c*-commanded by its antecedent:

(27)   Socrates owns a dog which bites its tail.

This point about uniqueness may be felt to be slender evidence, though the counterexamples that have been suggested to me normally ignore the temporal parameter implicit in the tense of the verb.[5] In a great many cases the implication is clear, and since the presence or absence of this implication appears to depend upon the precede and *c*-command configuration presumed to be relevant on quite independent grounds, the hypothesis that that configuration determines the difference between bound and E-type pronouns seems to be sustained even in the case of simple existential quantifiers.

The principle I have stated effectively restricts the scope of a quantifier to those elements which it precedes and *c*-commands. However, there are quantifiers in English which are almost always given wide scope, and the principle must be qualified to exclude them. The two most important examples are *a certain* and *any*. Thus, in the sentences (28) and (29), the quantifiers are given wide scope, and the pronouns are bound and not E-type:

(28)   If a certain friend of mine comes, he will tell the police.
(29)   If any man loves Mozart, he admires Bach.

I mention these exceptions not only for the sake of accuracy but also as a partial explanation of why it has taken so long for the important *grammatical* distinction between bound and E-type pronouns to be noticed. If these "wide-scope-seeking" quantifiers are not excluded, it is very difficult to see a pattern in the jumble of examples.

Finally, what is the importance of the distinction between bound and E-type pronouns—of the addition of another category of pronouns to the list? Not, it must be admitted, very great. Pronouns are often used as referring expressions, and it is not particularly surprising that some of them should have their reference fixed by a description recoverable from the antecedent, quantifier-containing, clause. The point only assumes importance in the context of certain current views. Certain logically-minded philosophers have been so impressed by the undoubted analogies which exist between some pronouns and the bound variables of quantification theory that they have enthusiastically adopted the hypothesis that *all* natural language pronouns with quantifier antecedents are bound by those antecedents.[6] Other researchers, concentrating upon sentences containing E-type pronouns, have naturally been impressed by the idea that such pronouns are referring expressions, and have, in a contrary excess of enthusiasm, attempted to regard bound pronouns as referring expressions, but without any success. There has therefore arisen the idea that there are two approaches to the unified subject of "anaphora"—the bound variable, and the referential—between which we have to choose.[7] The one merit of taking seriously the argument of this section is that this profitless debate should end. There is not a single class of pronouns for which we must find a unitary explanation. There are two kinds of pronouns, which are sharply distinguished by their grammatical position, and which function in quite different ways.[8]

3   The semantics of bound pronouns

With E-type pronouns out of the way, we can raise the question of the proper treatment of bound pronouns. Any such treatment must take account of two fundamental points. The first point is very well known. We cannot give the same account of the pronoun in the sentence (4)

(4)   Every man loves his mother.

as we might be inclined to give to the pronoun in the sentence (3),

(3)   John loves his mother.

namely that of referring to whatever its antecedent refers to, since the antecedent expression *every man* is not an expression referring to anything.[9] I mentioned the second point in my introduction; it is equally important but it has not received the attention it deserves. We cannot give utterly unconnected explanations of the roles of the pronouns in the sentences (3) and (4); it is simply not credible that the speaker's capacity to understand the sentences *John loves his mother, Harry loves himself, Susan admires those who are nice to her*, et cetera, is in no way connected with his understanding of the sentences *No man loves his mother, Every man loves himself, Just one girl admires those who are nice to her*, and so on. Putting these points together, we are confronted with the following problem: we must provide an account which is adequate to deal with pronouns in both our categories (*ii*) and (*iii*), but we cannot *directly* apply the most obvious account of pronouns in category (*ii*) to pronouns in category (*iii*).

This may seem to be an insoluble problem: in fact, it is a version of a problem with which the semantics of quantified sentences make us very familiar. For there are many devices which appear in both singular and quantified sentences in such a way that, though the two uses are clearly connected, the most obvious account of their occurrence in singular sentences does not immediately apply to their occurrence in quantified sentences. The most familiar examples are provided by the sentential operators, *and, or, if*, et cetera. When these expressions join singular sentences, as in (30),

(30)   If John is in love, John is happy.

they can be regarded as truth-functions—that is to say, expressions which map pairs of truth values onto truth values. If they joined only singular sentences—expressions which have a truth value—then all we would need to say about them is that they yield a true sentence when the constituent sentences have such and such a combination of truth values. But, in the sentence (31)

(31)   If any man is in love, he is happy.

the constituents which *if* joins are not sentences with a truth value at all. [Example] (31) is true iff[10] any man satisfies *if ( ) is in love he is happy*, but here *if* joins the parts of a complex predicate, and since the parts do not have a truth value, we do not yet appear to have any account of this role. A position parallel to the one which certain contemporary linguists adopt in the case of pronouns would then be to cast around for another account to deal with the connective *if* in this role—a position on which *if* (and all the other connectives) are deemed to be ambiguous. But Frege, and subsequent logicians, were not content with this approach; they searched for a way to unify the two roles.

One very natural, though not the only, way of doing this was adopted by Frege. Frege's approach involves no modification whatever of the truth-functional account of the role of the connectives; this is left to stand as the single account of their semantic contribution. The novelty comes in the account which Frege offered of the notion of *satisfaction*. When a predicate is complex, a Fregean explains the notion of an object's satisfying it in terms of the *truth* of a sentence which results when a singular term referring to that object is substituted in, or coupled with, the predicate. Thus, a Fregean does not define the conditions under which an object satisfies the predicate (32)

(32)   If ( ) is in love, he is happy

directly, in terms of the satisfaction conditions of the two parts, but rather says this: an object x satisfies the predicate (32), iff the *sentence* (33)

(33)   If (β) is in love, he is happy

is true when we interpret "β" as referring to x. Now, relative to that interpretation of "β," once again joins expressions which may be assigned a truth value, and its role as a truth-function can be invoked.

I do not say that this is the only way to provide a unitary account of the role of the sentential operators, but it is certainly a very natural way. And it is completely general. If we adopt this Fregean explanation of what it is for an object to satisfy a complex predicate, we have only to explain the significance of a device as it occurs in singular sentences, and its occurrence in quantified sentences simply takes care of itself. In particular, this observation applies to pronouns; if we adopt a Fregean account of satisfaction, we have only to give an account of the pronoun-antecedent construction as it occurs in singular sentences—no further explanation need be given of pronouns with quantifier antecedents.

As we have seen, a natural explanation of the role of pronouns with singular antecedents is in terms of *coreference*—the pronoun refers to whatever the antecedent refers to. This account will secure the result that there is a reading of the sentence *John loves his mother* on which the reference of *his* is the same as that of *John*, and hence that the whole sentence is true iff John loves John's mother. If we put this obvious account together with the general Fregean explanation of satisfaction—an explanation which is independently needed to provide a unification of the roles of other devices which occur in both singular and quantified sentences—then we have an explanation of the role of the bound pronoun in (4):

(4)   Every man loves his mother.

Such a sentence is true if every man satisfies the complex predicate ( ) *loves his mother*. By the Fregean explanation, we know that an arbitrary object, x, satisfies that predicate iff, taking "β" as referring to x, the sentence (β) *loves his mother* is true. Now we can apply the coreference rule quite properly, and learn that such a sentence is true iff the referent of "β" loves the mother of the referent of "β," and hence iff x loves the mother of x. Hence, x satisfies the complex predicate iff x loves x's mother, and so the whole sentence is true iff for every man x, x loves x's mother.

This explanation of the functioning of bound pronouns presupposes the following: that whenever we replace a quantifier which binds a pronoun with a singular term, in order to form a relevant substitution instance, the resulting sentence will be one which admits of a reading on which the pronoun is coreferential with that singular term. (I am ignoring the problem of number-agreement.) But this is exactly what we find. We remarked earlier that a quantifier can bind a pronoun only if it precedes and c-commands that pronoun, and it is sufficient (though not neces-sary) for a pronoun to be interpretable as coreferential with a singular antecedent that it be pre-ceded and c-commanded by that antecedent. The fact that this is so constitutes a powerful argument, not for the need to unify the two roles, which I take to be indisputable, but for a uni-fication along Fregean lines. The fact that there is this correspondence between sentences con-taining bound pronouns and singular sentences containing pronouns admitting of a coreferential interpretation can no more be regarded as an accident than the fact that pronouns are used in both singular and quantified sentences in the first place.

When we come to evaluate substitution instances of the form (β) *is A* we must use informa-tion about the context in which the original quantified sentence (e.g., *Everything is A*) is uttered in order to evaluate any ambiguous or context-dependent words which occur in A. In particular, we presume that anyone who utters a token of the sentence type (4)

(4)   Every man loves his mother.

intends to use *his* either as a device making an independent reference to some salient object or as a device for registering coreference. In the first case, we evaluate the truth of instances of the form (β) *loves his mother* by taking the reference of *his* to be constant and determined by the appropriate contextual factors. In the second case, we evaluate it as before.

To summarize: while it is quite correct to observe that one cannot deal with bound pronouns by directly applying a coreference rule, this point should not lead us to the desperate conclusion that pronouns with singular and quantified antecedents are semantically unrelated. If we employ a Fregean explanation of the notion of satisfaction of a complex predicate (and some such expla-nation is independently needed to deal with other devices which show up in both singular and quantified sentences), we find that a coreferential explanation of pronouns is all the explanation we need.

With these considerations in mind, let us look at the main ideas behind a theory of pronouns which is currently popular among linguists. I think that we can show that it is incompatible with this, or any other, attempt to see a unitary semantical phenomenon in pronouns with singular and quantified antecedents and, hence, must be wrong.

4   Consequences for bound pronouns of the pragmatic theory of coreference

Lasnik (1976) begins his article by taking account of the existence of pronouns in category (i), and then goes on to question whether any additional account needs to be given of pronouns in the supposed category (ii). Pronouns in category (i) involve a reference to an object which is salient in some way. Since one of the ways in which an object can be salient is by having been mentioned in a previous conversation, it would appear to be possible to regard reference to an object mentioned elsewhere in the same sentence or clause as a limiting case of the exploitation of this kind of salience. What we might rather loosely call "pragmatic" factors would seem to ensure that one of the uses of the sentence *John loves his mother* is to say that John loves the mother of John.

The flavor of this, at first sight very plausible, approach can be gathered from Lasnik's discussion of the sentence (34):

(34)   After John talked to Mary, they left the room.

> Within the system I have proposed . . . (34) is not problematic . . . that is, no co-reference rule is needed to explain (34) because there is nothing to explain. *They* in (34) can be used to refer to any group of entities; under many discourse situations, however, John and Mary are only likely candidates.[11]

Lasnik's main thesis is that "even sentence-internal cases of coreference are not produced by any rule" (p. 9). According to Lasnik, the only rule of the language which concerns the interpretation of pronouns is a rule of *Non*coreference which, for example, prohibits any two noun phrases related as *he* and *John* are related in (35) from being coreferential, unless the second is a pronoun:

(35)   He is happy when John is in love.

I will not discuss Lasnik's, Noncoreference rule until the next section; what concerns me here is the view that all the rules of the language tell us about a sentence like (3)

(3)   John loves his mother.

is that the pronoun *can be* referential with *John*; there is no special rule which secures an interpretation on which it is.

Implicit in this statement of Lasnik's position, and throughout his paper, is the distinction between those facts about the interpretation of an utterance which are explained by reference to *the rules of the language*, and those facts which are explained by "pragmatic" factors. Although the distinction is difficult to make precise, it is impossible to deny, since one must admit that there are facts about the interpretation of a sentence which are in no way determined by a linguistic rule. For example, there is no linguistic rule which determines that a *he* or a *that man* refers to x rather than y in the vicinity, or that it refers to someone who has just left rather than someone who has recently been mentioned.

Chomsky has built this distinction into his current framework:

> Let us say that the grammar contains a system of rules that associate a derivation with a representation of LF (read 'logical form' but for the present without assuming additional properties of this concept). I will understand LF to incorporate whatever features of sentence structure (1) enter directly into the semantic interpretation of sentences and (2) are strictly determined by properties of sentence grammar. The extension of this concept remains to be determined. Assume further that there is a system of rules that associates logical form and the products of other cognitive faculties with another system of representation SR (read 'semantic representation'). Representations in SR, which may involve beliefs, expectations and so on, in addition to properties of LF determined by grammatical rule, should suffice to determine role in inference, conditions of appropriate use etc. (Some would argue that LF alone should suffice, but I leave that an open empirical question.) (1976b, 305–306)

For his part, Chomsky has stated elsewhere his viewpoint on this empirical issue:

Given the logical forms generated by sentence grammar, further rules may apply. Pronouns not yet assigned antecedents may be taken to refer to entities designated elsewhere in the sentence, though this is never necessary, and is not permitted under certain conditions. . . . These further rules of reference determination may involve discourse properties as well, in some manner; and they interact with considerations relating to situation, communicative intention and the like. (1976a, 104)

One important, and traditional, constraint upon the domain of grammar proper is that it should deal only with matters that are "sentence-internal." Chomsky considers the discourse (36)

(36)   Some of the men left today. The others will leave later.

and argues, using this constraint: "The rule assigning an interpretation to *the others* however is not a rule of sentence grammar at all, as (36) indicates" (1976b, 323). He continues:

Returning to the basic theory outlined earlier, the rule of reciprocal interpretation, and DR [Chomsky's rule of Disjoint Reference/GE] relate derivations . . . to LF, while the rule assigning an interpretation to *the others* belongs to an entirely different component of the system of cognitive structures relating LF and other factors to a full semantic representation. It might be quite appropriate to assign this rule to a theory of performance (pragmatics) rather than to the theory of grammar.

Chomsky then goes on to apply this point in the case of anaphoric pronouns:

In [15] I pointed out that the rules of anaphora associating *he* with *John* in such sentences as (37) appear to violate otherwise valid conditions, a problem for the theory presented there:

(37)   a. John thought that he would win.
       b. John thought that Bill liked him.

Others have reiterated this point, arguing that it undermines the theory outlined. But my observation was simply an error. The rule of anaphora involved in the (normal but not obligatory) interpretation of (37) should in principle be exempt from the conditions of sentence-grammar, since it is no rule of sentence grammar at all. Cf. Lasnik.[12]

Chomsky's notion of *rule of sentence grammar* comprises both syntactic and semantic (or interpretive) rules, and it is clear from his paper that when Lasnik maintains that "even sentence internal cases of coreference are not produced by any rule," he is using "rule" in pretty much this sense. As his criticism of Jackendoff's interpretive rule of coreference makes clear, Lasnik's thesis is not simply that there is no *syntactic* rule (e.g., a pronominalization transformation) underlying cases of coreference. I stress this, because I do not wish to be taken to be committed to the existence of a pronominalization transformation by opposing Lasnik's basic thesis.

Although some line must be drawn between matters belonging to grammar (widely understood) and matters belonging to pragmatics, it is not at all clear where the line should be regarded as falling. For example, while it may be clear that *syntactic* processes are "sentence-internal," it is not at all clear to me why *semantic* rules (rules mapping surface structures onto their logical forms, in Chomsky's current framework) can concern only single sentences taken one by one, rather than sequences of such sentences. The thesis that semantic rules are sentence-internal constitutes a substantial empirical hypothesis for which empirical reasons should be given. In the light of these and other similar questions, one might despair of being able to assess Lasnik's treatment of pronouns without a tremendous amount of preliminary, and fundamental, work.

However, the argument I wish to advance against Lasnik's position will exploit only the most unchallengeable property of the distinction between what belongs to grammar and what belongs to pragmatics. For it seems indisputable that if certain truth-relevant features of the interpretation of any utterance of a sentence type are held to depend upon the context in which that utterance is made, then it will not make any sense to inquire into the truth value of the sentence type, considered independently of a particular context of utterance. Since Lasnik holds that the reference of all (nonbound) pronouns is determined by pragmatic factors—"considerations relating to situation, communicative intention and the like"—he must hold that it does not make any sense to inquire into the truth value of the sentence *John loves his mother* considered independently of any particular context of utterance; this is so even when the interpretations of the expressions "John," "loves," and "mother" are given. This is the only property of a pragmatic explanation of coreference on which I need to rely. Relying on it, I want to show that Lasnik's pragmatic theory of coreference precludes any explanation of the connection between pronouns in his unified category (*i*) + (*ii*) and pronouns in category (*iii*), and thus treats it as an accident that the same expression is used in sentences like (3) and (4).

The best way to see the difficulty for the pragmatic theory of coreference is to attempt to apply the natural, and perfectly general, method of unification which I have ascribed to Frege. We know that *Every man loves his mother* is true iff every man satisfies ( ) *loves his mother*, and, using the Fregean notion of satisfaction, we know that an arbitrary object x satisfies this predicate iff, interpreting "β" as referring to x, the sentence (β) *loves his mother* is true. But at this point we are stopped, for it does not make sense, on Lasnik's view, to inquire into the truth value of a sentence of the form (β) *loves his mother* independently of information about a particular context of utterance, and this is so even when the interpretation of the name "β" is fixed. It is, of course, true that the original quantified sentence will be uttered in a context, and facts about that context can be used to determine the interpretation of context-dependent or ambiguous expressions in the substitution instances. But these facts will enable us to settle upon a preferred interpretation of a given expression which is constant in all the substitution instances; there is no way these facts can determine a different referent for the pronoun in each substitution instance. We could attempt to say that x satisfies the predicate iff there is *some* possible context of utterance in which the sentence type (β) *loves his mother* could be truly uttered, but then we will certainly get the truth conditions of the quantified sentence wrong. For if there is a context of utterance in which Harry is salient, and in which I can refer by the pronoun *his* to Harry, then, if John loves Harry's mother, but not his own, I can truly utter the sentence *John loves his mother*, so that John will satisfy the complex predicate despite the fact that he is a counterexample to the claim made by the quantified sentence.

Lasnik himself makes no attempt to explain the connection between the pronouns in his unified category (*i*) + (*ii*) and bound pronouns; he reserves bound pronouns for an appendix to the main article in which he states that "the relationship [between antecedent quantifier and bound pronoun/GE] should be characterized as that holding between a quantifier and the variable it binds" (1976, 18), and he leaves matters there. It should now be clear that this feature of Lasnik's treatment is not an accidental defect of the presentation of his ideas, but an immediate consequence of those ideas themselves. Strictly, I have only considered the unavailability of the Fregean way of discerning a connection to one who holds a pragmatic theory of coreference, but the point holds quite generally, since the alternative (Tarskian) mode of discerning the connection between devices in singular and quantified sentences is even less compatible with Lasnik's views.[13] The point should be obvious. For it seems clear that there is no common semantic principle explaining the behavior of pronouns in categories (*i*) and (*iii*), and this is obviously unaffected by the inclusion of members of category (*ii*) in category (*i*).

It is the price of being able to recognize the obvious semantic connection between pronouns with singular and quantified antecedents that we distinguish semantically between pronouns used as devices of coreference, and pronouns whose reference is secured in some other way—for example, deictically. But this is not a complication of the same kind as we have just pointed to in Lasnik's treatment, and which therefore must be thrown into the balance and weighed against it. In Lasnik's case, the complexity results from a failure to discern a connection between two obviously connected capacities. The connection can be shown empirically by demonstrating the speakers' capacity to understand new sentences—those which contain, as bound pronouns, expressions which had not explicitly figured in that role before—a capacity which presumably relies upon their familiarity with sentences in which the expression has a singular term as antecedent. But to distinguish between the functioning of pronouns in categories (*i*) and (*ii*) is not to bifurcate a single capacity in the same way. Let us agree that to understand a pronoun as referring to an object mentioned in a previous conversation is to interpret the pronoun in a way which is not specifically secured by any rule of the language—it is simply a manifestation of one speaker's general capacity to *make sense of* the acts (including the linguistic acts) of others. Now, I am suggesting that when the previous reference is within the same sentence as the pronoun (and subject to certain further conditions) the coreferential interpretation of the pronoun is secured, as one interpretation of the sentence, by a linguistic rule. Is this to fail to see a connection between connected capacities? Not at all; we are not obliged to postulate a different mechanism of understanding in the two cases, as though in one case a book labeled *Rules of the English Language* is consulted, while in the other case, it is the book labeled *How to Make Sense of One's Fellow Men*. It is just that we *describe* a propensity to interpret what speakers say as being in accordance with a rule of the language only under certain conditions; one of these conditions is when the interpretation of *other* utterances obliges us to ascribe semantic properties to sentence types considered independently of context.

Here we touch upon a point of general interest, for it becomes clear that we can use the interpretation of quantified sentences as a general guide in drawing the line between grammar and pragmatics. In order to illustrate this, let me go back to E-type pronouns. Given what I said in section 2, it might be tempting to hold that E-type pronouns are referring expressions whose reference is fixed by pragmatic factors. On this view, all that the grammar of the language tells us about the pronoun in the sentence (38)

(38)   John owns some donkeys and feeds them at night.

is that it can refer to any group of entities salient in the context; one very likely (but, from the point of view of the semantics of the language, in no way privileged) group will be the donkeys which John owns.[14] However, an objection can be made to this pragmatic theory which is exactly parallel to the objection I have just made to Lasnik's pragmatic theory of coreference. For we also have to consider E-type pronouns in sentences like (39):

(39)   Every villager owns some donkeys and feeds them at night.

Now, it plainly does not make sense to ask which group of donkeys the pronoun in (39) refers to. Once the proper name *John* has been supplanted by the quantifier *Every villager*, there is no determinate answer to such a question. Hence, since it is not referring to anything in (39), a pragmatic account of E-type pronouns in sentences like (38) would leave this pronoun unaccounted for. But, once again, it is obviously wrong to see no connection between the use of the pronouns in (38) and (39), and to cast around for a new account of the pronoun in (39)—whatever that could be. Here is yet another facet of the general problem presented by devices showing up in both singular and quantified sentences, and it is susceptible of the same, Fregean, solution. Provided we give an account of the E-type pronoun in a sentence like (38), the pronoun in (39)—of which (38) is a substitution instance—will take care of itself. However, once again, the Fregean treatment presupposes that there is an interpretation of the pronoun in (38) on which its reference is determined by linguistic rule, and not by "considerations relating to situation, communicative intention, and the like." As in the previous case, the intention of the person who utters the quantified sentences is germane to the interpretation of that utterance, for we must know whether or not he uttered the pronoun as governed by the hypothesized rule rather than with the intention of referring to some salient group of donkeys. But if he did so, it is the rule which determines the reference of the pronoun in the relevant substitution instances; *their* reference cannot be determined by pragmatic factors, since pragmatic factors cannot determine the reference of a pronoun in a sentence whose interpretation we are considering independently of any particular context of utterance.

5   Other difficulties in the pragmatic theory of coreference

Lasnik's thesis is that the grammar of English does not oblige us to draw any distinction between the uses of pronouns in categories (*i*) and (*ii*). Clearly we can make the objection to such a thesis that there appear to be quite delicate syntactic restrictions upon when a pronoun can be used with the intention that it be understood to be coreferential with a given singular term—restrictions which have no parallel in the case of pronouns which are intended to be understood as making an independent reference. The restrictions concern the case in which the pronoun precedes the term with which it is intended to be coreferential; in general, such a use is felicitous only if the pronoun does not *c*-command the term.[15] For example, the pronoun in the sentence (40)

(40)   He is happy when Oscar is in love.

cannot felicitously be used with the intention that it be understood as coreferential with the term *Oscar*. The restriction is not pragmatic; (40) confronts the hearer with the same task of deciding upon a referent for the pronoun, and one highly salient candidate is Oscar. Examples like this make it appear that there are grammatical rules of the language which specifically regulate the occurrence of pronouns in category (*ii*), and hence that the grammar of the language obliges us to distinguish between pronouns in categories (*i*) and (*ii*). In this final section, I want to see whether this impression is correct, and thus to see whether the very general argument of section 4 can be reinforced by an argument resting upon details of English grammar. (Simply to have some notation, let me use the symbols *he*→, ←*she*, ←*them*, et cetera, to represent occurrences of pronouns which are intended to be understood as being coreferential with some succeeding or preceding singular term, and *he*↗, *them*↗, etc., to represent occurrences of pronouns which are intended to be understood as making references of all other kinds.)

Of course, Lasnik is aware of the apparent distinction the grammar of language draws between ←*he* and *he*↗, and he attempts to render the facts consistent with his unification of the categories to which ←*he* and *he*↗ belong in the following way. It is true, he says, that on the coreferential interpretation, (40) infringes a rule of grammar, but the rule is not one which is specifically concerned with the possibilities of pronominal coreference. The rule which (40) infringes is more general, since it prohibits coreference between *any* two noun phrases occupying the positions which *he* and *John*, respectively, occupy in (40), unless the latter position is occupied by a pronoun. Lasnik observes that we are inclined to take the two *Oscar*'s in the sentence (41)

(41)   Oscar is happy when Oscar is in love.

as referring to different people, and his idea is to bring this observation under the same rule which explains the infelicity of (40). The final formulation which he offers of the relevant rule of *Noncoreference* is (42):

(42) If NP$_1$ precedes and *c*-commands NP$_2$ and NP$_2$ is not a pronoun, then NP$_1$ and NP$_2$ are disjoint in reference.[16]

Now if the infelicity of (40) is indeed explained by this rule, then no argument against Lasnik's position can be based upon it. [Example] (42) is a rule of grammar which, insofar as it mentions pronouns at all, can be regarded as dealing with a unitary category, to which ←*he* and *he*↗ both belong.

Before proceeding, we must take note of an extraordinary feature of the rule which Lasnik formulates and defends: the notion of *disjoint reference* which it uses is a purely extensional one. Two NPs are coreferential in the sense of the rule (i.e., are not disjoint in reference) iff, as a matter of fact, they refer to the same thing. Hence, the rule predicts that a simple sentence of the form *NP$_1$–Verb–NP$_2$* is *ungrammatical* if it so happens that NP$_1$ and NP$_2$ refer to the same thing. (When I use the term *ungrammatical* in the context of Lasnik's views, I mean simply "infringes a rule of sentence grammar." The rule may of course be a semantic one.) This is not an error in formulation; Lasnik explicitly considers the objection that his rule makes all true identity statements ungrammatical and responds to it not by holding it to be based upon misunderstanding but by espousing an indefensible metalinguistic theory of identity statements (1976, fn. 7). But the absurdities to which a purely extensional rule of Noncoreference gives rise are not limited to identity statements, and so no theory of identity statements, however eccentric, can repair the damage. For example, Lasnik must hold that the simple sentence (43)

(43) This man is the same height as Stalin.

(said, perhaps, as part of an investigation into the man's identity) is not true, but rather *ungrammatical* if *this man* does in fact refer to Stalin. But even beyond this, Lasnik's theory predicts a difference in our reactions to the sentences (44) and (45) when *his*↗ and *this man* are both being used to refer deictically to Stalin:

(44) Stalin signed this man's papers.
(45) Stalin signed *his*↗ papers.

According to Lasnik's rule, (44) is ungrammatical while (45) is not.

It is not necessary for Lasnik to embrace these views. It *is* necessary that his Noncoreference rule should not be specifically concerned with the coreference possibilities of pronouns, and hence that it include *Oscar–Oscar* pairs in addition to *Oscar–his* pairs. But it is *not* necessary that it embrace *Cicero–Tully* pairs as well. Lasnik does say at one point (1976, 6 fn. 5) that "it is possible that the notion of coreference in this rule and elsewhere in this discussion should be replaced with that of intended coreference," and such a change certainly seems indicated. Actually formulating the required notion is not easy, since one who sincerely utters an identity statement does intend that the two terms be coreferential. However, I shall suppose that it can be done— that there is some notion which can apply both to a pair of expressions one of which is a proper name and the other of which is a pronoun which has that name as antecedent, and also to two occurrences of the same proper name. For I want to challenge the heart of Lasnik's position that there is a common source to the unacceptability of (40) and (41) when this relation of "intended coreference" holds between the two NPs in both sentences.

Consider a very simple example of a sentence which, when the two names are intended to be taken as coreferential, infringes Lasnik's rule:

(46) Oscar loves Oscar's mother.

It seems to me doubtful that this sentence is ungrammatical at all. Here, oddly enough, Chomsky seems to agree. Considering the two sentences *John is here, but will he shoot* and *If John is here then he will shoot*, he writes:

> In the latter case, and perhaps the former as well, substitution of *John* for *he* seems to me to impose disjoint reference. It seems that the rule applying here is not a rule of sentence-grammar, but is rather a rule assigning a higher degree of preference to disjoint interpretation the closer the grammatical connexion. (Chomsky 1976b, fn. 37)

One reason for maintaining that the principle is not one of sentence grammar is that it also appears to apply to sequences of sentences; as Chomsky notes, substitution of *John* for *he* in (47) is difficult, if coreference is intended:

(47)   John is here. Will he shoot?

Another, perhaps better, reason is the fact that it is easy enough to find contexts in which repetition of the name has some point, and in which the implication of disjointness of reference is canceled. For example, a logic teacher might say to a student:

(48)   Look, fathead. If everyone loves Oscar's mother, then certainly Oscar must love Oscar's mother.

Or again, someone might reasonably say:

(49)   I know what John and Bill have in common. John thinks that Bill is terrific and Bill thinks that Bill is terrific.[17]

Or again:

(50) Who loves Oscar's mother? I know Oscar loves Oscar's mother, but does anyone else?

When the conversational concern is with those who satisfy the predicate ( ) *loves Oscar's mother*, there is some point in abandoning the familiar and less prolix way of saying that Oscar loves his mother which pronouns make possible, and uttering (46) instead. Whether or not we go all the way with Chomsky and deny that the infelicity of (46) is grammatical in origin, it cannot be denied that the appropriate conversational setting vastly increases the acceptability of such sentences. However, we will find that nothing can be done to increase the acceptability of sentences which infringe the conditions upon when a pronoun can pick up its reference from an NP elsewhere in the sentence, and this constitutes fairly strong evidence that the explanation of the unacceptability of the sentences (40) and (41) is different.

It might appear that the right way to test the hypothesis that there is a single phenomenon underlying the deviance of (40) and (41) is to compare the discourses (51) and (52):

(51)   Everyone has finally realized that Oscar is incompetent.
       Even Oscar has realized that Oscar is incompetent.
(52)   Everyone has finally realized that Oscar is incompetent.
       Even he has finally realized that Oscar is incompetent.

However, the sentence which is supposed to provide the appropriate conversational setting unfortunately also provides an alternative antecedent for the pronoun, and the result is quite tolerable. (I shall return to this kind of discourse below.) To test the hypothesis, we need a suitable conversational setting which does not provide an antecedent for the pronoun. For example:

(53) Everyone here admires someone on the committee. Joan admires Susan, Mary admires Jane, and Oscar admires Oscar.

(54) Everyone here admires someone on the committee. Joan admires Susan, Mary admires Jane, and he admires Oscar.

Although to my ear (53) is tolerable, (54) is quite impossible, yet Lasnik's grammar cannot distinguish between them. Again, consider:

(55) Everyone eventually realizes that someone dear to them is incompetent. For example, Mary has realized that Fred is incompetent, Susan has realized that her daughter is incompetent, and Oscar has realized that Oscar is incompetent.

(56) Everyone eventually realizes that someone dear to them is incompetent. For example, Mary has realized that Fred is incompetent, Susan has realized that her daughter is incompetent, and he has realized that Oscar is incompetent.

These examples show that the unacceptability of a sentence like (40) is not due to its infringing a general rule prohibiting "intended coreference" between any two NPs related as the NPs are in (40). We get no closer to the truth by restricting Lasnik's Noncoreference rule to pronominal coreference, though that would undermine Lasnik's position. For a discourse like (52) shows that a pronoun can both precede and *c*-command an NP with which it is intended to be coreferential—*so long as it does not pick up its reference from that NP*. To formulate the rule correctly, we need this idea of one term's *picking up its reference from* another. So far, we have considered rules which use a *symmetrical* relation between NPs, whether it is the purely extensional notion of "referring to the same thing" or the notion of "intended to be understood as referring to the same thing," which we supposed Lasnik could formulate.[18] But it seems that (40) infringes a rule which states when a term, normally a pronoun, can pick up its reference from another term—and this is an asymmetrical relation between the terms. To avoid confusion with the symmetrical relations, let us use the expression *t is referentially dependent on t'* to mean that *t* is to be understood by being taken to have the same reference as *t'*. Now, this relation of referential dependence is quite different from, though it entails, that of intended coreference; while two occurrences of the proper name *Oscar* or two occurrences of the pronoun *you* may be intended to be coreferential, neither occurrence is referentially dependent on the other. In our discourse (52), while the pronoun is intended to be coreferential with the second occurrence of the name *Oscar* (since it is referentially dependent upon the first occurrence, which is itself intended to be coreferential with the second), it is referentially dependent upon the first occurrence of the name, and not the second.[19]

Using this notion, we can formulate the rule which (40) infringes as follows:

(57) A term can be referentially dependent upon an NP iff it does not precede and *c*-command that NP.

The precise formulation of the rule does not matter.[20] The important point is that a principle of grammar must be explicitly concerned with the relation of referential dependence between pronouns and antecedents. The grammar to which (57) belongs will have to provide a list of expressions which can be referentially dependent upon other expressions—it will include third-person pronouns as well as pronominal epithets, but will exclude first- and second-person pronouns as well as proper names. It will have to explain the semantic significance of the relation of referential dependence, and it will therefore have to recognize as one among other interpretations of a sentence like (3), that it is true iff John loves John's mother. Since it will also have to recognize that pronouns can be used to make independent reference to salient objects, the grammar must itself distinguish between ←*he* and *he*↗, and will treat a sentence like (3) as ambiguous—in the sense that interpretations can be provided for it which exploit different rules of the grammar.

So far, I have been concerned to show that Lasnik's grammar, which combines a pragmatic theory of the reference of all pronouns with a Noncoreference rule, is not adequate. I have not yet examined the main argument he offers for his position. The structure of his argument is this: any grammar which incorporates such a rule as (57) must also incorporate a Noncoreference rule like (42), but the latter rule will suffice, on its own, to reject all the ungrammatical sentences. Lasnik states his argument succinctly in response to a suggestion of Wasow. He considers the sentence (58),

(58)   I told him that John was a jerk.

which he claims is ungrammatical when *him* is coreferential with *John*, and says:

> True, his [Wasow's] anaphora rule will not apply in (58). But Wasow explicitly stipulates that "the failure of two NP's to be related anaphorically does not entail that they have distinct referents." Here again, no provision is made for disallowing "accidental" coreference. I argued earlier that regardless of whether there is a pronominalization transformation or an interpretive coreference rule, a noncoreference rule is required to account for the ungrammaticality of such examples as (58). In fact, I concluded that both types of coreference devices can be dispensed with . . . and that the noncoreference rule cannot be dispensed with. (Lasnik 1976, 13)

We have already seen considerable deficiency in Lasnik's claim that a Noncoreference rule *suffices* to account for the grammatical sentences, but we are now in a position to see what is wrong with the argument that is supposed to establish the *need* for a Noncoreference rule.

I understand Lasnik's idea to be this. Any grammar with a coreference rule like (57) will have to acknowledge the existence of pronouns used to make an independent reference, and hence will have to allow that a sentence like (58) might involve such a use of the pronoun. And such a pronoun can be used to refer to anything. Thus, unless it is explicitly prohibited by a Noncoreference rule, one possible interpretation of (58) will be that on which *him* refers to John— that is, is coreferential with *John*. (This is what Lasnik means by "accidental coreference.") But, according to Lasnik, such a use of the pronoun will result in an ungrammatical sentence.

This argument seems to me to rest upon a confusion between the three notions associated with the term *coreference* which we have been at pains to distinguish. The sentence (58) is ungrammatical if, *and only if*, the pronoun is intended to be *referentially dependent* upon the later occurrence of the name *John*. Since our rule (57), and Wasow's parallel principle, expressly prohibit such dependence, there is no possibility of such an interpretation of the sentence being declared acceptable. Now, alternatively, the pronoun in (58) may be used to make a reference to John, but one which is independent of the occurrence of *John* in (58). There are two cases to consider, but neither of them results in an ungrammatical sentence, which must then be excluded by a Noncoreference rule. In the first case, suggested by the notion of "accidental coreference," the pronoun is used to make a reference, possibly deictic, to a salient individual who turns out to be John. In this case, *him* and *John* in (58) are coreferential in merely the extensional sense, and the resulting utterance is in no way deviant. Another possibility is that the pronoun stands in the relation of intended-coreference with *John*, although not referentially dependent upon it. This would be the result if the pronoun was referentially dependent upon some prior occurrence of the name *John* which itself stands in the relation of intended-coreference with the occurrence of the name *John* in the sentence. Here again, strict ungrammaticality does not result, as can be seen from the discourse (similar to (52)):

(59)   What do you mean John loves no one? He loves John.

Strict ungrammaticality is produced when and only when the pronoun is intended to be referentially dependent upon that occurrence of the name which it precedes and *c*-commands. And (57) blocks any such sentence.

I have discussed Lasnik's argument in order to illustrate the importance of keeping in mind the difference between the three notions of *coreference* that we have distinguished. To give one final example of the necessity for clarity on this matter, let me show how a major problem in the literature on anaphora dissolves when one attempts to formulate it in the vocabulary I have proposed. I shall let Lasnik introduce the subject (1976, 11):

> I turn now to a complex phenomenon hinted at in Jackendoff and Postal and discussed at length in Wasow. Wasow points out that there is no reading of (60) on which the three italicized NP's can all be understood as co-referential.
>
> (60)   The woman *he* loved told *him* that *John* was a jerk.
>
> However, it appears that independently, *he* can be coreferential to *him* and *he* can be coreferential to *John*:
>
> (61)   a. The woman *he* loved told us that *John* was a jerk.
>   b. The woman *he* loved told *him* that we were all jerks.

Lasnik goes on to say that a grammar needs a Noncoreference rule to exclude the impossible reading of (60); without it, the reading would be allowed "because of the transitivity of coreference" (1976, 12).

Let us formulate this supposed problem using the notion of referential dependence. We start from the fact that there is no reading of (60) on which both *he* and *him* are referentially dependent upon *John*—presumably because there is no reading at all on which *him* is referentially dependent on *John*, as is predicted by (57). [Example] (61a) shows us that the first pronoun can be referentially dependent on *John*, and (61b) shows us that the second pronoun can be referentially dependent upon the first pronoun, or, indeed, conversely. Construed in the first way, (61b) can be represented as (62):

(62)   The woman he↗ loved told ←him that we were all jerks.

Construed in the other way, it can be represented as (63):

(63)   The woman he→ loved told him↗ that we were all jerks.

Presumably what matters for the supposed conundrum is that there exists the reading we have represented as (62), for then we have it that the first pronoun in (60) can be referentially dependent upon *John*, and that the second pronoun can be referentially dependent upon the first pronoun. Does it follow that the second pronoun can be referentially dependent upon *John*? Certainly not. Examples (61a,b) did not establish the possibility of the *simultaneous* dependence of the first pronoun on *John*, and the second pronoun upon the first. On the contrary, when we suppose the second pronoun to be referentially dependent upon the first, we suppose that the first pronoun is making an independent reference, and, thus construed, it cannot be referentially dependent upon anything. Therefore, when we formulate the problem with the notion of referential dependence, and when we make the natural assumption that if *t* is referentially dependent upon *t'*, then *t'* cannot be referentially dependent upon anything, the problem simply disappears.[21]

Notes

About the origin of this article. A couple of years ago I published in the *Canadian Journal of Philosophy* (Evans 1977) a long paper, addressed to a philosophical audience, on the semantics of pronouns. Since my ideas bore upon recent work by linguists, it was suggested to me that it might be of interest if I presented them in a form and place more accessible to linguists, and "Pronouns" is an attempt to do this. Although it is intended to be self-contained, and includes much that is not in the original paper (especially sections 4 and 5, which are devoted to a discussion of Lasnik's views on coreference), I hope that those who are interested will be encouraged to consult the original paper, where many matters merely raised here are dealt with in detail. I am very grateful to Deirdre Wilson and Andrew Radford for helpful comments.

1. See, for example, Bresnan (1978, 11–13) and Chomsky (1976b). Lyons puts forward a doctrine similar to Lasnik's in Lyons (1977, sec. 15.3).

2. By "objects, if any, which verify the antecedent quantifier-containing clause" I mean those objects, if any, which satisfy the predicate in the antecedent clause and thereby make that clause true.

3. A constituent A *c*-commands a constituent B if and only if B is dominated by the first branching node which dominates A. In Evans (1977) I used Klima's term "in construction with" for the converse of this relation.

4. (21) is similar to an example noticed by Chomsky in Chomsky (1976b, 336):

(i)   Every soldier is armed, but will he shoot?

5. For example, the sentence (i) has been given to me by Geach as a counterexample to my claim that such pronouns carry an implication of uniqueness:

(i)   Socrates kicked a dog and it bit him and then Socrates kicked another dog and it did not bite him.

However, the tense in the verb effectively introduces an initial existential quantifier *There was a time such that* . . . , and my claim is that the truth of the sentence requires that there be a time such that Socrates kicked only one dog *at that time*, not that Socrates only kicked one dog *ever*. However, the interpretation of a-expression is unclear, and we may be forced to recognize that they are sometimes used as equivalent to *any* and sometimes to *a certain*. (See below.) This affects only the scope, and not the substance, of my claim.

6. The most prominent example is Geach; see especially the papers collected in section 3 of Geach (1972a).

7. See, for example, Stenning (1978).

8. I am by no means the first to have noticed that some pronouns with quantifier antecedents are not bound by them. Apart from the paper of Chomsky's cited in n. 4, reference should be made to Karttunen (1969) and Jackendoff (1972, 283). However, these works contain isolated examples rather than theory, and give no clue of the extent of the phenomenon. In reply to an example of Jackendoff's, Janet D. Fodor (1977) suggests that the thesis that all pronouns with quantifier antecedents are bound might be sustained by "relaxing the usual constraints on the binding of variables" (p. 192)—an intriguing proposal which I wish I could understand.

9. Even if you can persuade yourself that *every man* refers to every man, *his* still cannot be coreferential with its antecedent, on pain of generating the incorrect reading: Every man loves the mother of every man.

10. That is, "if and only if."

11. In this and subsequent quotations, I have altered the numbering of examples to conform to the ordering in this article.

12. Here "15" refers to Chomsky (1973), and "Lasnik" to Lasnik (1976).

13. I give an account of the Tarskian approach to quantified sentences in Evans (1977, 471–475). If Frege can be said to take the role of a device in singular *sentences* as primitive, Tarski does the opposite by taking the role of devices in forming complex *predicates* as primitive. The Tarskian account of the role of pronouns would then be in terms of the impact they have upon whether or not a sequence of objects satisfies the predicate in which they occur; the same element of the sequence would have to be assigned to the pronoun as is assigned to this or that other position in the predicate. I say that this is not compatible with Lasnik's views because the Tarskian cannot prevent the complex predicate ( ) *loves his mother* from being attached to a referring expression (like *John*), thus providing a source of a kind not recognized by Lasnik for the sentence *John loves his mother*.

14. I think that this is the proposal which B. H. Partee has in mind when she suggests (Partee 1978, 3) that E-type pronouns involve "pragmatic" uses of pronouns. However, the reasoning in her section 2 is another argument to the same conclusion as I try to establish in the present section.

15. Actually, Lasnik uses the notion *kommand* defined as follows: "A kommands B if the minimal cyclic node dominating A also dominates B." Whether we should formulate the relevant restrictions using the notion of *c*-command or of kommand is not a matter on which I am competent to pronounce, and is anyway not relevant to the disagreement I go on to express. I have retained the notion of *c*-command to avoid irrelevant complication.

16. See note 15.

17. To deem sentences like *John thinks that John is ill* ungrammatical is to claim the existence of a significant limitation upon the expressive power of English. How are we to state John's possession of a "non-self-conscious" belief that he may have about someone who is in fact himself, but whom he does not know to be himself?

18. A relation R is symmetrical iff, whenever *a* is R to *b*, *b* must also be R to *a*.

19. It seems clear that we must be able to speak of a pronoun's being referentially dependent upon one rather than another occurrence of a term. Compare the discourses (i) and (ii):

  (i) What do you mean, Oscar loves no one? He loves Oscar.
  (ii) What do you mean, no one loves Oscar? He loves Oscar.

It seems clear that the second is less acceptable than the first, which can only be explained by allowing that the pronoun is picking up its reference from the previous rather than the subsequent occurrence of the name, and that (as is well known) it is easier for a pronoun in subject position to pick up its reference from a term in subject position than from one in object position.

20. In particular, I make no allowances for the fact that a pronoun which is to be referentially dependent upon a prior occurrence of a term which stands in a certain grammatical relation to it must be a reflexive rather than an ordinary pronoun, and I have consistently ignored the need for number and gender agreement.

21. It has been suggested by a reader that my notion "*t* is referentially dependent upon *t′*" is equivalent to Chomsky's notion "*t* is an anaphor whose antecedent is *t′*." This cannot be so for two reasons. First, Chomsky endorses Lasnik's pragmatic theory of the reference of (supposedly coreferential) pronouns, and, on that theory, it is not clear that it makes sense to speak of a pronoun's picking up its reference from one rather than another occurrence of a singular term, both of which serve to render their referent salient. Second, and more importantly, Chomsky speaks of quantifiers as antecedents of bound variables, when the relation of referential dependence is out of the question.

22

JAMES HIGGINBOTHAM

Pronouns and Bound Variables

1   The problem

Suppose that Σ is a surface structure, A is an occurrence of a quantificational NP in Σ, and B is an occurrence of a pronoun in Σ. Under what circumstances can the pronoun be interpreted as a variable, bound to the quantificational NP? Our analysis has for its target sentences such as (1):

(1)   Everyone here thinks he's a nice fellow.

Example (1) admits both a *deictic* interpretation, in which the pronoun *he* functions as purporting to refer to some individual, and a *bound* interpretation, in which it functions as a variable controlled by the quantificational subject, *everyone here*.[1]

In (1) and in the other examples given in this article, the bound interpretation of the pronoun is optional. We exclude, for reasons given below, the case in which B is reflexive or reciprocal. We also exclude the case of ordinary pronouns which must be interpreted as bound anaphora in certain constructions; for instance, the *him* of (2):

(2)   Someone brought a knife with him.

In (2), *him* must be interpreted as a bound variable. Similarly, it must be interpreted as coreferential with *John* in (3):

(3)   John brought a knife with him.

An appropriate account of (3) will imply as a special case the necessity of the bound interpretation of *him* in (2).

James Higginbotham (1980) Pronouns and bound variables. *Linguistic Inquiry* 11: 679–708. Reprinted by permission of MIT Press Journals.

Presupposed here will be the general form of the theory of Chomsky (1980), and the rule QR of quantifier construal given in May (1977). In the next section and the remainder of this one, we will consider in light of these works, and others to be cited, some preliminary suggestions toward solving the central problem of this article; these suggestions will be modified and extended as we proceed. In conclusion, the extended analysis will be applied to a number of special cases.

The general organization of syntax is taken to be (4),

(4)   DS _____ SS _____ LF

where DS is deep structure, SS is surface structure, and LF is logical form; see Chomsky (1976b). May's QR is among the rules of grammar mapping from SS to LF. QR assigns scopes to quantificational NPs by Chomsky-adjoining them to the node S, leaving trace.[2] The notion of *scope* is so defined that the scope of an NP adjoined by QR is the S to which adjunction takes place. The trace of QR is interpreted as a variable; it is bound to the quantifier if within its scope.

The effect of QR on the surface structure (5) is (6),

(5) $[_s[_{NP}$ someone here] is nice]
(6) $[_s[_{NP}$ someone here]$_i$ $[_s$ e_i is nice]]

where e_i is the trace, coindexed with the moved element. The *scope* of a constituent is what it *c*-commands.[3] In (6), e_i is within the scope of the quantifier and is therefore properly bound by it.

Suppose that the status of *him* in (3) above is expressed by some rule of bound anaphora, obligatorily coindexing this pronoun with its antecedent, the subject *John*. Suppose further that the bound anaphora rule coindexes *someone* and *him* in (2). Then after QR applies we shall obtain from (2) the structure (7):

(7) $[_s[_{NP}$ someone]$_i$ $[_s$ e_i brought a knife with him$_i$]]

Making the natural assumption that a pronoun coindexed with a variable is itself a variable, we can let (7) be the proper LF representation of the surface structure of (2). Note that both the pronoun and the trace of QR are within the scope of the quantifier.

Proceeding by analogy with (2) to the target cases of this article, we might propose that an occurrence B of a pronoun will be interpreted as a variable bound to $A = NP_i$, A quantificational, iff (i) B can be coindexed with A at LF, and (ii) at LF, B is within the scope of A. For the bound interpretation of (1) we would propose the representation (8):

(8) $[_s[_{NP}$ everyone here]$_i$ $[_s$ e_i thinks he$_i$'s a nice fellow]]

For the deictic interpretation we would propose (9), with $i \neq j$:

(9) $[_s[_{NP}$ everyone here]$_i$ $[_s$ e_i thinks he$_j$'s a nice fellow]]

Following Chomsky (1980), we will assume a condition on surface structures that we will express informally as (10):

(10)   Every *anaphor* (i.e., element requiring an antecedent) must be coindexed at SS with an element that *c*-commands it.

With QR as the rule of quantifier construal, (10) already solves the problem of this article for the case where the pronoun B is an anaphor; for if B is an anaphor, it may already be coindexed at SS with any quantificational antecedent that it may have.

2   Indexing

In this section we will outline the relevant parts of the analysis of Chomsky (1980), and consider further the hypothesis that (1) may have at LF both representations like (8) and representations like (9). In Chomsky (1980), there are two *distinct* mechanisms of NP indexing. The first is *coindexing*, which relates anaphoric elements to their antecedents. The other might be called *contraindexing*; this mechanism relates pairs of elements at least one of which is not anaphoric.

Considering for the moment only the simplest case, that of singular referential NPs, we may bring out the intended interpretations of the application of these two mechanisms as follows. If A, B can be coindexed in a surface structure Σ, then they can be purported to be coreferential; if they must be coindexed, then they must be so purported. If A, B are contraindexed in Σ, then they cannot be purported to be coreferential; otherwise, they can.[4] In the simplest examples, (11) and (12),

(11)   John saw himself.
(12)   John saw him.

the coindexing mechanism will ensure that *John* and *himself* bear the same index, and the contraindexing mechanism will ensure that *John* and *him* in (12) are contraindexed.

In Chomsky (1980), it is assumed that every NP will be assigned some index or other, called its *referential index*.[5] Coindexing A and B then means assigning them the same referential index. Contraindexing works by assigning to nonanaphoric NPs (i.e., those not requiring antecedents) *anaphoric indices*. An anaphoric index is a set of referential indices. The intended interpretation of this device for the simplest case is (13):

(13) NP_i, NP_j cannot be purported to be coreferential if the referential index of either is an element of the anaphoric index of the other.

In the case of plurals, "coreferential" in (13) may be replaced by "overlapping in reference."

Every nonanaphor is doubly indexed, bearing both a referential and an anaphoric index. The initial principle governing the assignment of anaphoric indices is (14):

(14)   Assign the anaphoric index of NP_i the set of all referential indices of NPs that c-command NP_i, if NP_i is not an anaphor.

Consider again the simple example (12), repeated here,

(12)   John saw him.

and assume that the subject NP *John* c-commands the pronoun *him*, though not conversely. Indexing will yield (15):

(15)   John$_{i,\phi}$ saw him$_{j,\{i\}}$.

The anaphoric index of *John* is empty, since nothing c-commands it. But the anaphoric index of *him* = $\{i\}$ contains the referential index of the c-commanding *John*. Applying (13) we have, correctly, that (12) cannot constitute an assertion that John saw himself.

Now consider (16):

(16)   John thinks he's a nice fellow.

The items *John, he* should not be contraindexed, for purported coreference between them is possible. Applying (14), we shall index (16) in the pertinent respects as (17), with $i \neq j$:

(17)   John$_i$ thinks he$_{j,\ \{i\}}$'s a nice fellow.

For this and similar cases, Chomsky in (1980) has proposed that rules of grammar may delete some referential indices from the anaphoric indices of pronouns, thus permitting purported coreference. To state the rule, we require a few definitions. A pronoun *B* is *free(i)* in *X* iff it occurs in *X* and there is nothing in *X* with referential index *i* that c-commands *B*. *B* is *nominative* if governed by tense, and *in the domain of the subject of X* if *X* has a subject *Y* that c-commands *B*. If $X = \bar{S}$ or NP, *X* is *minimal* if it contains *B* and every $Y = \bar{S}$ or NP that contains *B* contains *X*. Now we may state (18):

(18)   If *B* is a pronoun that is free(*i*) in the minimal $X = \bar{S}$ or NP containing *B*, and *B* is either:
    (a) nominative; or,
    (b) in the domain of the subject of *X*,
    then *i* deletes from its anaphoric index.[6]

The clause (a) in (18) is the *Nominative Island Condition* (NIC); the clause (b) is the *Opacity Condition* (OC). Now, (17) will have the structure (19):

(19)   [$_{\bar{s}}$ John$_i$ thinks [$_{\bar{s}}$ he$_{j,\ \{i\}}$'s a nice fellow]]

Hence the NIC applies, and *i* deletes from the anaphoric index of the pronoun. For an example of OC, consider (20):

(20)   John$_i$ wants [$_{\bar{s}}$ Mary to visit him]

The pronoun *him* will be free(*i*) in $\bar{S}$, and in the domain of the subject *Mary*. So the OC applies, and purported coreference between *him* and *John* is permitted. In the simple case (12) above, repeated with indices in place as (21),

(21)   [$_{\bar{s}}$ John$_i$ saw him$_{j,\ \{i\}}$]

the pronoun is not free(*i*) in $\bar{S}$, and neither the NIC nor the OC applies. In (22),

(22)   John$_i$ wants [$_{\bar{s}}$ him$_{j,\ \{i\}}$ to win]]

him$_j$ is free(*i*) in $\bar{S}$; but it is not nominative, since $\bar{S}$ is infinitival, nor in the domain of the subject, since it is the subject. So again neither the NIC nor the OC applies; a correct result in this case, because (22) cannot be used as purporting coreference between *John* and *him*.

This concludes our brief outline of the principles governing the algorithm presented in the appendix to Chomsky (1980) (hereafter: the Indexing Algorithm) and the relevant details of its operation. We return now to the problem of pronominal binding. Consider again the example (1):

(1)   Everyone here thinks he's a nice fellow.

Example (1) will be indexed in the relevant respects as (23):

(23)   [$_{\bar{s}}$[$_{NP}$ everyone here]$_2$ thinks [$_{\bar{s}}$ he$_{3,\{2\}}$'s a nice fellow]]

By the NIC, 2 deletes from the anaphoric index of he_3. But the pronoun cannot share a referential index with the subject NP *everyone here*. Suppose, however, that there were some reindexing rule, optionally changing the indices of nonanaphoric pronouns, where this rule, like QR, relates SS to LF. If this rule affects he_3 in (23), changing it to he_2, then following the application of QR we will obtain from (23) the structure (24):

(24) $[_s[_{NP}$ everyone here$]_2$ $[_s$ e_2 thinks he_2's a nice fellow]]

In (24), he_2 will be interpreted as a bound variable.

In the next two sections, we will make more precise the form of the reindexing opperation just suggested.[7]

3   Coreference and binding

As we have seen, the Indexing Algorithm provides a partial answer to the question of when referential overlap between referential NPs is permitted by the rules of sentence grammar. But referential overlap will be permitted between positions A and B where binding of B by A will not be possible, because binding must take quantifier scope into account. Contrast (25) and (26):

(25)   Somebody who liked *John* lent *him* money.
(26)   *Somebody who liked *everybody* lent *him* money.

(Above and hereafter, the italicization invites the reader to consider the coreferential interpretation (as in (25)) or the bound interpretation (as in (26)); a * expresses the judgment that the indicated interpretation is not available.) The Indexing Algorithm predicts that purported coreference should be possible between *John* and *him* in (25), because neither of these NPs *c*-commands the other. But binding is impossible in (26) because the embedded quantifier cannot escape its surface clause and so will fail at LF to *c*-command the pronoun.

A general observation, which any adequate theory of pronominal binding must imply, is that a pronoun can be bound to a quantificational NP only if it could overlap in reference with a referential NP occupying the same position as the quantifier. Possibilities for binding form a subset of possibilities for overlapping reference—a proper subset, as (25)–(26) show. For some simple examples, consider (27)–(30):

(27)   He expected to see him.
(28)   He expected Bill to see him.
(29)   Someone expected to see him.
(30)   Someone expected Bill to see him.

Example (27) cannot be used as purporting coreference between *he* and *him*; but (28) can. Similarly, *him* cannot be bound to the subject *someone* in (29), but is bindable in (30). Suppose for this exposition that the Equi in (27) and (29) is *self*-deletion; then to the surface structure of (27) the Indexing Algorithm assigns indices as shown in (31):

(31) he_2 expected $[_s$ for e_2 self to see $him_{3,\{2\}}]$

Indexing of (28) gives (32):

(32) he_2 expected $[_s$ $Bill_{3,\{2\}}$ to see $him_{4,\{2,3\}}]$

By the OC, 2 deletes from the anaphoric index of him_4 in (32). But in (31), him_3 is not free(2) in $\bar{S}$, and so 2 does not delete from its anaphoric index. Since 2 is the referential index of he_2, these positions cannot purport to be coreferential. By exactly the same reasoning, in (29) but not in (30) the referential index of the quantifier *someone* will be an element of the anaphoric index of the pronoun *him*, presumably making binding impossible in (29). Generalizing, we might say that we cannot bind a pronoun B to quantificational NP A if the referential index of either is an element of the anaphoric index of the other; that is, if A, B are contraindexed.

Now consider (33):

(33)   Everyone told someone he expected to see him.

On the class of interpretations with *everyone* taking wide scope, (33) is seven ways ambiguous: we can bind either pronoun to either quantifier, or bind neither, et cetera. But we cannot bind both pronouns to the same quantifier. For instance, (33) cannot be interpreted as meaning that everyone is an x such that x told someone that x expected to see x. We see, therefore, that the generalization of the last paragraph requires supplementation.

Suppose now that the reindexing rule for pronouns were subject to the condition (34):

(34)   For all i, j, if pronoun$_j$ reindexes as pronoun$_i$, then every occurrence of j in the structure to which reindexing applies is to be replaced by an occurrence of i.

The principle (34) ensures that when a pronoun is bound to a quantificational NP, then every anaphor of which it is the antecedent is bound as well. Thus, in (35),

(35)   Someone forgot he brought a knife with him.

either both or neither of *he, him* are bound variables. By (34), it is impossible to reindex either without reindexing the other.

To see the effect of (34) in conjunction with the Indexing Algorithm, first consider (36):

(36)   Someone saw him.

Assignment of indices to the surface structure of (36) gives (37),

(37)   someone$_2$ saw $him_{3,\{2\}}$

with him_3 not free(2) in S (and so not free(2) in $\bar{S}$). If him_3 reindexes to him_2, either before or after QR has applied in (37), we shall obtain at LF (38):

38     $[_s$ someone$_2$ $[_s$ e$_2$ saw $him_{2,\{2\}}]]$

The pronoun then has its own referential index contained in its anaphoric index. But, as Robert May first pointed out in (1979), in conjunction with his analysis of certain cases of misgeneration due to movement, we have good reason for regarding (38) as semantically absurd. Recalling the understood significance of assignments of referential and anaphoric indices, it is natural to interpret the position marked by $him_{2,\{2\}}$ as instantiatable only to objects that are distinct from themselves; therefore, to no objects at all.

We return to the case of (33), repeated here:

(33)   Everyone told someone he expected to see him.

Initial assignment of indices to (33) gives (39):

(39)   everyone$_2$ told someone$_{3,\{2\}}$ [$_\bar{s}$ he$_{4,\{2,3\}}$ expected [$_\bar{s}$ for e$_4$ self to see him$_{5,\{2,3,4\}}$]]

The NIC and OC now apply, deleting 2 and 3 from the anaphoric indices of both pronouns. But 4 will not delete from the anaphoric index of *him$_5$*, because this pronoun is *c*-commanded in the minimal $\bar{S}$ by an anaphor controlled by *e$_4$*. Given the result (40) of carrying out the indicated deletions in (39),

(40)   everyone$_2$ told someone$_{3,\{2\}}$ [$_\bar{s}$ he$_4$ expected [$_\bar{s}$ for e$_4$ self to see him$_{5,\{4\}}$]]

consider what will happen if we attempt through reindexing, subject to (34), to bind both pronouns to the same quantifier—say, *everyone$_2$*—he$_4$ and *him$_5$* must both reindex to 2, and so by (34) the anaphoric index of the latter will contain 2. Since further reindexing cannot change this situation, the only possible derived structures will have the form (41):

(41)   ... he$_2$ expected ... him$_{2,\{2\}}$

These structures will be "strange" at LF, just as (38) is. Henceforth, we assume (34) as a condition on reindexing.[8]

4   Directional asymmetries

We have seen that if reindexing is coupled with the convention (34), then we have the correct consequence that possibilities for binding are constrained by possibilities for coreference, or overlapping reference. We turn now to cases where binding is impossible due to "crossover." Consider (42)–(44):

(42)   His father hates John.
(43)   His father hates someone.
(44)   Who does his father hate?

Purported coreference between *his* and *John* is possible in (42), but pronominal binding is impossible in both (43) and (44). Example (43) cannot be interpreted as asserting that someone is an *x* such that *x*'s father hates *x*; neither can (44) be interpreted as a general question, asking which person is an *x* such that *x*'s father hates *x*. We saw earlier that the possibility of coreference did not always imply the possibility of binding, because of considerations on scope; but these considerations are of no avail above. Why, then, is binding impossible?

Chomsky (1976) proposed a distinction between possibilities for binding and possibilities for coreference which he expressed initially as (45):

(45)   A variable cannot be the antecedent of a pronoun to its left.

I will call (45) the *Leftness Condition*. Applied to (46), derived from (43), or to (47), derived from (44), the Leftness Condition correctly predicts that the pronoun cannot be bound, since its "antecedent"—the variable *x*—occurs to its right at LF:

(46)   [for some *x*: *x* is a person] his father hates *x*
(47)   [for which *x*: *x* is a person] his father hates *x*

Now consider (48):

(48)   Some musician will play every piece you want him to.

Him can be bound to *some musician*. The bound interpretation of (48) would be given at LF by (49):

(49)   [some x: x is a musician] [every y: y is a piece you want him (= x) to play]
       x will play y

But in (49), *him* is to the left of x.

Example (48) is an obstacle in the path of any attempt to interpret the Leftness Condition as a filter (or well-formedness condition) on representations at LF. Simply put, leftness is a phenomenon of surface structure order, and the operation QR (or, it seems, any other quantifier-adjunction rule) will have the effect of rearranging the order of constituents.[9]

We turn now to a somewhat more subtle set of examples, of which the following are representative:

(50)   a. Mary's seeing his father pleased every boy.
       b. Seeing his father pleased every boy.
(51)   a. Their getting letters from their sweethearts is important for many of the soldiers.
       b. Getting letters from their sweethearts is important for many of the soldiers.
(52)   a. For his wife to visit his old neighborhood would embarrass someone I know.
       b. To visit his old neighborhood would embarrass someone I know.

The (b) examples above all freely allow binding of the pronoun in the subject sentence to the quantifier to its right. The (a) examples are much less acceptable in this respect.[10] The latter fact is a consequence of the Leftness Condition. But the Leftness Condition would likewise rule out binding in (50b), which clearly admits the interpretation (53):

(53)   [every x: x is a boy] x's seeing x's father pleased x

The other (b) examples are similar. The difference between the (a) and (b) examples, I believe, is that in the (b) examples each subject sentence has a PRO subject, controlled by the quantifier, whereas in the (a) examples the subject position is lexically filled. PRO acts as a "gate" through which the genitive pronouns in the (b) examples can reindex, but the (a) examples have no gates. The phenomenon also occurs with WH:

(54)   a. Who did her forgetting what he said to him annoy?
       b. Who did forgetting what he said to him annoy?

In (54a), and again in accordance with the Leftness Condition, none of the pronouns can be bound to *who*. But in (54b), either pronoun can be bound to *who* (but not both, because the anaphoric index of *him* contains the referential index of *he*).

Suppose now that we assume that a pronoun reindexes to the index of a source trace which is to its left at the point of application of the Reindexing rule. The principle involved might be stated in various ways, depending on the notation adopted for this sort of rule. Informally, we may present it thus:

(55)   *The Reindexing Rule*
       In a configuration:

$$\ldots e_i \ldots \text{Pronoun}_j \ldots$$
reindex j to i.

Example (55) thus permits us to coindex a pronoun with the index of an empty category to its left, regardless of whether this category is trace or PRO, and therefore regardless of whether PRO is formally assimilated to trace in the syntax or not.

We assume that (55) is optional, that it may reapply to the same pronoun, and that it is unordered with respect to the rule QR of quantifier construal.

Consider how the cases that we have discussed so far will fare under the proposal that (55) is the rule of Reindexing, subject to the convention (34). In typical crossover situations, binding will be impossible because the structure for the application of (55) will not exist. Thus, from (56) one derives (57) by QR:

(56)   [his$_3$ father]$_2$ hates someone$_{4,\{2\}}$
(57)   [someone]$_{4,\{2\}}$ [his$_3$ father]$_2$ hates e_4

No empty category with index 4 occurs to the left of *his*$_3$, so (55) cannot apply.

In cases such as (48), the bound interpretation is derived as follows. Given the indexed surface structure (58) (with irrelevant indices omitted), adjunction of the subject to S gives (59):

(58)   [some musician]$_2$ will play [every piece you want him$_3$ to (play)]$_4$
(59)   [$_s$[Some musician]$_2$ [$_s$ e_2 will play [every piece you want him$_3$ to (play)]$_4$]]

The rule (55) may apply in (59), allowing 3 to become 2. QR then adjoins the object NP to the interior S, giving (60):

(60)   [$_s$[some musician]$_2$ [$_s$[every piece you want him$_2$ to (play)]$_4$ [$_s$ e_2 will play e_4]]]

Example (60) represents the bound interpretation of (48).

After the first two steps of the above derivation, we could have adjoined the object NP to the exterior S. We would then derive (61):

(61)   [$_s$[every piece you want him$_2$ to (play)]$_4$ [$_s$[some musician]$_2$ [$_s$ e_2 will play e_4]]]

In (61), *him*$_2$ will not be interpreted as a bound variable, because although coindexed with the quantifier *some musician* it is not within the scope of that phrase.

The rule (55) makes the correct predictions with respect to each of the examples in (50)–(52). In each of the (a) sentences, (55) is inapplicable; but in each of the (b) sentences, the controlled PRO may serve as a reindexing source. We turn now to the question of whether the purported directional asymmetries in pronominal binding are to be taken as primitive.[11]

5   Leftness and *c*-command

In all of the cases that we have considered so far, the empty category that served as a source for pronominal reindexing not only has been to the left of the pronoun to be reindexed but also has *c*-commanded it. But analysis of two sorts of examples shows, I believe, that *c*-command of the pronoun by the empty category is not in general necessary for reindexing. The first kind of example involves "inversely linked" quantification in the sense of May (1977). Consider (62):

(62)   Every daughter of every professor in some small college town wishes she could leave it.

The scopes of the quantified NPs in (62) are inverse to their surface order. Both *she* and *it* admit binding. Using QR and (55), we can derive from the surface structure of (62) the logical form (63):

(63)   [$_s$[some small college town]$_2$ [$_s$[every professor in e$_2$]$_3$ [$_s$[every daughter of e$_3$]$_4$ [$_s$ e$_4$ wishes [$_s$ she$_4$ could leave it$_2$]]]]]

Both at the point of application of Reindexing, and in the derived structure (63), e$_2$ fails to c-command *it*.

Say that the *depth* of an empty category e$_i$ = [$_{NP}$ e]$_i$ is the number of NPs dominating e$_i$. In all the "inversely linked" cases with PPs, such as (62), the depth of the empty category e$_i$ will be at most 1 at the point where it serves as a source for the reindexing of a pronoun. Depth 1 can also be obtained in the rare cases of quantification into a relative clause, as in (64):

(64)   Nobody who despises *anybody* lends *him* money.

On the other hand, QR traces in Determiner position can have arbitrary depth. Assume that QR applies in sentences like (65) to produce logical forms like (66):

(65)   Every boy's mother was amused.
(66)   [every boy]$_2$ e$_2$'s mother was amused

Then e$_2$ has depth 1. In (67), the trace of *every boy* will have depth 2; and so on:

(67)   [[[every boy]'s mother]'s best friend] likes tea

We can then consider the possibilities of binding in (68)–(72), for example:

(68)   *Whose* mother loves *him*?
(69)   *Every boy*'s father thinks *he*'s a genius.
(70)   *Which man*'s dog do you think might bite *him*?
(71)   *Some boy*'s father's best friend's daughter wants *him* to marry her.
(72)   The teacher gave *every child*'s parents a report on *his* progress.

These seem acceptable to me; others may find them marginal (see, for instance, Lasnik 1976, 18). In (72), the depth of the trace of *some boy* will be 3; deeper embeddings seem possible. The rules that we have stated so far will derive the bound interpretations of (68)–(72). We will assume in what follows that (55) is not subject to structural conditions in English.[12]

6   Lowering from COMP

Consider examples such as (73):

(73)   *Whose* mother does *he* love?

In the theory of syntax assumed in this article, the indexed surface structure of (73) will be represented by (74):

(74)   [who$_2$se mother]$_3$ does he$_4$ love e$_3$

Neither of *who, he* c-commands the other, so these items will not be contraindexed. Following the treatment of genitive quantifiers used in the last section, we would expect to obtain from (74) a logical form such as (75):

(75)   [who]$_2$ [e$_2$'s mother]$_3$ does he$_4$ love e$_3$

In (75), the empty category e_2 is to the left of he_4; so, applying the Reindexing rule (55), we should be able to obtain the bound interpretation indicated in (73). But this interpretation is not possible.

In Chomsky (1976), examples such as (73) were brought under the Leftness Condition through an operation which displaced from the COMP position everything except the *wh*-phrase itself. We call this operation *lowering*. Appeal to lowering resolves the problem of (73) within the assumptions of Chomsky (1976b, because the position e_2—to be construed as a variable position—comes to be rightward of the pronoun. Lowering would also take care of (73) assuming the Reindexing rule (55), because its effect is to destroy the environment within which Reindexing is constrained to take place. Nevertheless, it seems to me that lowering is inadequate to account for all cases of the nature of (73).

There are two reasons for skepticism about the efficacy of lowering. One is in part semantic in nature, and I will sketch it below, without going at length into details. The other arises from matters which are endemic to the reindexing system in general, whether it is expressed as suggested in Chomsky (1976) or along the lines of this article. We consider the semantic objection first; the other is postponed until the next section.

Consider the following examples:

(76)   Which driver of which millionaire's car was hired by his father?
(77)   Which driver of which millionaire's car did his father hire?

It seems to me that (76), but not (77), can be interpreted as a general question; that is, *his* can be bound to *which millionaire* in (76) only. An answer to (76) as a general question might be (78):

(78)   This driver of Ford's car and that driver of Rockefeller's car.

The impossibility of binding in (77) does not follow from constraints on purported coreference; (79) is acceptable:

(79)   Which driver of *Rockefeller*'s car did *his* father hire?

Examples (76) and (77) exhibit inversely linked quantification in COMP. Suppose that from (77) we were to obtain the logical form (80):

(80)   [which millionaire]$_2$ [which driver of e$_2$'s car]$_3$ did his$_4$ father hire e$_3$

Then (77) would pose the same problem for our analysis as (73) does. If the lowering operation were a general solution to the problems posed by (73) and the like, then it could be expected to apply at some point in the derivation of the logical form of (77). Could lowering produce (81)?

(81)   [which millionaire]$_2$ did his$_4$ father hire [which driver of e$_2$'s car]$_3$

From a purely formal point of view, the hypothesis that (77) has logical form (81) might indeed prevent pronominal binding in (77); but the suggestion is not yet even intelligible semantically. For what has been lowered in the case of (77) is not a referring expression, but rather an expression of generality, to which QR is supposed to apply. To make sense of (81), we would have to propose a semantics in which such expressions were interpreted in place. Although there is no reason to suppose that such a semantics could not be produced, this price of the recourse to lowering in the case of (77) seems to me very high.

7   Constraints on crossing

We now present a further problem for the analysis given to this point; suggest a mechanism for its solution; and show that this mechanism, if adequate, will obviate the need for a lowering rule for the examples discussed in the last section.

Consider (82) and (83):

(82)   Everybody in some city hates its climate.
(83)   Its climate is hated by everybody in some city.

Despite the obviously intended meaning, binding of *it* to *some city* is far less acceptable in (83) than in (82). But from the principles given so far, bound interpretations of either are obtained. In the case of (83), with relevant indices as in (84), we derive after two applications of QR the structure (85):

(84) it_2s climate is hated by [everybody in [some city]$_4$]$_3$
(85)   [some city]$_4$ [everybody in e_4]$_3$ it_2s climate is hated by e_3

The rule (55) may now apply, reindexing *it* $_2$ as *it* $_4$. Since the pronoun is *c*-commanded by [*some city*]$_4$ at LF, it will be a bound variable.

In (83), we have repeated the problem posed by (73) and (77), this time using ordinary quantifiers. A bound interpretation of (83) could be derived because the variable which the quantifier *some city* binds can occur to the left of the pronoun at LF, even though the quantifier is to the right of the pronoun at surface structure. Suppose, however, that the Reindexing rule (55) were subject to the constraint that, at the point of its application, the configuration (C) could not be created:

(C)   ... [$_{NP}$ ... e_i ...]$_j$ ... pronoun$_i$ ... e_j ...

I will call (C) the *Crossover Configuration*. It is exemplified by the result of reindexing the pronoun in (85), giving (86):

(86)   [some city]$_4$ [everybody in e_4]$_3$ it_4s climate is hated by e_3

By the constraint just proposed, the bound interpretation of (83) is underivable (the bound interpretation of (82) is derived without hindrance from the proposed constraint). The restriction that (C) not be created by (55) will be referred to as the *C-Constraint*.

Assuming the C-Constraint, we can distinguish (76) from (77) above. In (76), binding is possible just as it is in (82); in (77), binding is blocked in the same way as for (83).

Given the C-Constraint, the lowering rule sketched in Chomsky (1976b) and elaborated further in Guéron (1978) becomes superfluous, so far as the analysis of pronominal binding is concerned, for these cases (though that is not to say that lowering cannot be independently motivated).[13] Suppose, for instance, that from (73) one derives (87):

(87) $[who]_2$ $[e_2$'s mother$]_3$ does he love e_3

Then, by the C-Constraint, *he* cannot reindex to 2.

The C-Constraint states a condition on the application of the rule (55), and does not state a condition on structures derivable by (55) in conjunction with QR. For all the cases that we have considered up to now, however, the C-Constraint need not have been stated in this way; instead, we could just have prohibited the configuration (C) at LF. But an analysis of more complicated cases appears to show that (C) can appear in derived structures. Consider (88):

(88)   Every friend of someone here knows someone who hates him.

Example (88) admits an interpretation in which *him* is bound to *someone here*. The derived structure is (89):

(89) $[someone here]_2$ [every friend of $e_2]_3$ [someone who hates $him_2]_4$ e_3 knows e_4

The Crossover Configuration is realized in (89). But there is a derivation of (89) (in fact, there are two) in which the C-Constraint is observed. Thus, the C-Constraint, like the condition on direction of reindexing, cannot (on the assumptions that we have made) be stated as an LF filter.

With the above cases, our preliminary analysis of pronouns as bound variables is completed. In brief review, the principles employed have been the following:

(90)   The rule QR of quantifier construal, subject to constraints given in May (1977).
(91)   The Reindexing rule (55) for pronouns; the rule is optional, and is unordered with respect to QR.
(92)   The convention (34) on the Reindexing rule; this ensures, via May's (1979) device of "contradictory indices," that binding is constrained by coreference.
(93)   The C-Constraint.

The principles given above do not reduce the directional asymmetries associated with pronominal binding to any more fundamental facts. What these principles do provide, to the degree that they are materially adequate, is an expression of what the asymmetry consists in, within the framework of Chomsky (1980). The convention (34) writes into binding conditions the conditions on purported coreference; and the C-Constraint serves to "encode" the fact that an empty category e_i, otherwise available via (55) as a source for reindexing, cannot serve as such a source in cases where the phrase that binds it "originated" in an embedded position to the right of the pronoun. *Origin* is not immediately determined by surface structure position, as the examples with *wh* illustrate. The ad hoc appearance of the C-Constraint in particular might be remedied somewhat if it could be seen as a special case of some other conditions. In concluding the main exposition of this article, I will report briefly on some research of mine into Chinese, which perhaps gives some hope that the C-Constraint has just such status.

8   The case of Chinese

In Mandarin Chinese, it is not difficult to verify the existence of conditions on purported coreference, directly comparable to English conditions in simple cases. Binding is constrained by coreference in Chinese, as in English. Despite the absence of morphological Tense, the assumption that Tense is in fact present, and that verbs are marked for whether or not they can take tensed complements, leads to systematic and correct predictions, for instance, in the case of verbs of propositional attitude. The question-words corresponding to *who*, *what*, et cetera, do not move in Chinese. When one turns to pronominal binding, the Leftness Condition holds:

(94)   Shéi kanjyàn tā mŭchin?
        who see   he mother
(95)   Tā mŭchin kanjyàn shéi?
        'Who did his mother see?'

Here (94), but not (95), can be interpreted as a general question. (In the above and in subsequent examples, I employ the Yale system of transliteration—the characters are not included, since these are easily recoverable from the English translations.) As in English, there are "gates" which allow pronouns to be bound to quantifiers occurring on their right at surface structure:

(96)   Kanjyàn tāde mŭchin ràng shéi dōu hěn gāūsying.
        see   his mother make everyone very happy
        'Seeing his mother made everyone very happy.'

In (96), *tā* can be bound, presumably through the PRO subject of *kanjyàn* (one informant said that on the bound interpretation of (96) her image was of prisoners in a jail, whose mothers were being allowed to visit them).

When one turns to *shéi* embedded in NPs, however, a distinction between English and Chinese emerges:

(97)   Shéi de mŭchin kanjyàn tā?
        who   mother see   him
        'Whose mother saw him?'

Example (97) is unambiguous: the pronoun can only be deictic. Example (98) is a similar case:

(98)   Shéi de mŭchin dōu kanjyàn tā.
        'Everyone's mother saw him.'

(Wyn Chao informs me that the analogues of (97) and (98) are likewise unambiguous in her dialect, Cantonese.) On the assumption that (97) has surface structure (99) and that QR applies to yield (100),

(99) $[_S[_{NP}[_{NP}$ shéi$]$ de $[_N$ mŭchin$]]$ $[_{VP}$ kanjyàn tā$]]$
(100) $[_{NP}$ shéi$]_2$ $[_S[_{NP}$ e_2 de mŭchin$]$ kanjyàn tā$]$

the hypothesis suggests itself that the depth of the trace e_2 may be responsible, for (94) is ambiguous. The most powerful generalization would be that the Reindexing rule in Chinese is subject to the constraint that the source trace must c-command the pronoun to be reindexed; this constraint might be expressed by the principle that the Reindexing rule cannot apply so as to create the configuration (CC):

(CC) $\ldots [_{NP} \ldots e_i \ldots]_j \ldots$ pronoun$_i \ldots$

The configuration (C) is then a special case of (CC), and the binding possibilities in Chinese, therefore, a proper subset of the binding possibilities for English. Roughly speaking,

English permits violations of (CC) in the "uncrossed" cases, but not the "crossed" cases. We may be able to motivate (C), therefore, by showing that it is the constraint which results when (CC) is weakened.[14]

9   Special constructions

Supposing some degree of adequacy for the analysis presented above, it may be possible to use this analysis as a tool for understanding more complex constructions than those considered up to now. In concluding this article, I will consider some cases that seem relatively clear. These are: (i) partitives and *only*; (ii) the dative passive, and some questions on argument positions; and (iii) relative clauses and clefts.

Before we proceed, it will be well to recall a respect in which the Indexing Algorithm is incomplete; namely, that algorithm fails to allow overlapping reference between a genitive pronoun and an NP which *c*-commands it, except when the Opacity Condition applies. Defining *genitive* as *domain of* $\bar{N}$, the problem is to explain why construal, bound anaphora, and overlapping reference are all possible in this domain. We will not undertake an examination of this problem here, but it will be assumed in what follows that referential indices of *c*-commanding NPs delete from the anaphoric indices of genitive, nonanaphoric pronouns. Then binding is possible in sentences such as (101):

(101)   *Every boy* loves *his* mother.

Because the exposition of the matters following will be less involved and the examples in general much clearer with the assumption, we will use it freely.[15]

9.1   Partitives and *only*

Consider (102)–(104):

(102)   Only John expects to win.
(103)   Only John expects him to win.
(104)   Only John expects that he will win.

(Cases of this sort are discussed in Partee 1975b.)

Example (102) is unambiguous: what is asserted is that John and John alone has expectations of winning. Example (103) admits two interpretations, neither of which is equivalent to (102). On the first, John and John alone expects that he, John, will win; the others expect someone other than John to win, if they have any expectations at all as to the winner. On the second, *him* refers to some individual *a* given outside the sentential context, and what is asserted is that John alone expects *a* to win. Example (104) admits an interpretation in which *he* refers to *a* similarly; on this interpretation, it is equivalent to the second interpretation of (103). Besides this interpretation, (104) is ambiguous between an interpretation equivalent to (102), and an interpretation equivalent to the first interpretation of (103). Now, all these facts follow from the Indexing Algorithm, and the analysis of pronominal binding given here, on the assumption that QR applies to phrases such as *only John*.[16]

Example (102) is a case of control. From the indexed surface structure (105),

(105)   [only John$_3$]$_2$ expects [$_S$ for e$_2$ self to win]

in which the anaphor has been coindexed, not with *John₃*, but with the *c*-commanding [only John₃]₂, in accordance with the general requirement on anaphors ((10) in section 1 above), we obtain (106) by QR:

(106)   [only John₃]₂ e₂ expects [ₛ for e₂ self to win]

The interpretation of (106) might be represented more transparently by (107):

(107)   [only x_2: x_2 = John₃] x_2 expects x_2 to win

(See note 7.) Example (106) is the only well-formed logical form that can be derived from (102) (up to alphabetic variance on indices), and it has uniquely the single interpretation of that sentence.

Turning to (103), it follows from the Indexing Algorithm that *him*, being the subject of an infinitive, will be contraindexed with the subject NP *only John*. Therefore, it cannot be bound to this expression, and a logical form with the interpretation of (106) cannot be derived. On the other hand, since *John* does *not* *c*-command *him* in (103), these expressions can be purported to be coreferential. If they are taken to be so purported, then one obtains the first interpretation given above of (103), and if they are not one obtains the second.

In (104), finally, the embedded pronoun is the subject of a tensed clause; hence, the NIC applies, and binding of the pronoun to *only John* is possible, giving an interpretation corresponding to that of (102). Since *he* may be purported to be coreferential with *John*, (104) has in addition both the interpretations of (103).

The above analysis of *only*-phrases accounts for the distinction between (108) and (109), discussed at length by Fodor (1975, 133–145):

(108)   Only Churchill remembers giving the speech.
(109)   Only Churchill remembers his giving the speech.

Example (108), like (102), is a case of control, but (109) is three ways ambiguous, just as (104) is.

We turn now to quantificational partitive NPs. These pattern with respect to pronominal binding in the same way as *only*-phrases. Consider (110)–(112):

(110)   Several of the men expect to work past midnight.
(111)   Several of the men expect them to work past midnight.
(112)   Several of the men expect that they will work past midnight.

Example (110) asserts unambiguously that there are several x, x among the men, such that x expects x to work past midnight. Example (111) does not have this interpretation but does admit an interpretation with *them = the men*; in this case, the meaning is that for several x, x among the men, x expects the men to work past midnight. Last, (112) is ambiguous between the above.

At first sight, the following use of partitives may seem to be a counterexample to the above analysis of pronominal binding:

(113)   Their fathers hate all the men.

Assuming the antecedent of *their* to be given within the sentence, (113) is still ambiguous between the following two interpretations, where S is the plurality denoted by *the men*: (i) every father of a member of S hates each member of S; (ii) every member x of S is hated by x's father. The logically stronger interpretation (i) of (113) is available within the analysis given here. Because *their* does not *c*-command *the men*, the pluralities denoted by these expressions can be identical; if they are, then (i) results. The interpretation (ii) is logically equivalent to the indicated reading of (114):

(114)   *All the men* are hated by *their* fathers.

In (114), the interpretation (ii) is available through the reindexing of *their* to the index of *all the men*, whose trace will be to the left of the pronoun. But no source for reindexing is made available in (113).
     But consider (115):

(115)   Their fathers hate the men.

It seems that (115) by itself admits the interpretation (ii) of (113), although in this case no quantifier is present. If so, then the availability of (ii) for (113) might be ascribed to the presence of the plural definite *the men*, rather than to "backwards binding." The article must be present, as (116) shows:

(116)   Their fathers hate all men.

In (116), binding is impossible; the sentence can mean only that the fathers of a certain collection of men are misanthropes. The ambiguity of (113) is not, then, a counterexample to the analysis given here; but its description and explanation fall outside the domain of pronominal binding by quantificational NPs, so it would seem.[17]

9.2   Argument positions

The Reindexing rule (55) is blind to the status at LF of the empty category e_i to whose referential index pronoun$_j$ reindexes. In particular, then, j may reindex to i, NP$_i$ not quantificational, when e_i is the trace of NP Movement, or a controlled PRO. In both (117) and (118), the reindexing $3 \rightarrow 2$ is permitted.

(117)   John$_2$ was seen e_2 with his$_3$ mother.
(118)   PRO$_2$ watching his$_3$ father fall upset John$_2$.

Our analysis implies that some, but not all, possibilities of coreference will be directly representable at LF.[18]
     Consider dative passives with inversely linked *wh*-phrases, as in (119)–(121):

(119)   Which book about *which naturalist* was given to *his* father?
(120)   Which book about *which naturalist* was given *his* father?
(121)   *Which book about *which naturalist* was *his* father given?

Assuming the judgments above, (119) and (121) are as predicted; it is the acceptability of (120) that raises questions. On an analysis in which the indexed surface structure of (120) is, for example, (122),

(122)   [which book about [which naturalist]$_3$]$_2$ [$_s$ e_2 was given [his$_4$ father]e_2]

in which the indirect object is to the left of the trace of the direct object, the reindexing $4 \rightarrow 3$ cannot apply, because of the C-Constraint. One might remark that, of the two occurrences of e in the matrix S of (122), the second does not represent an argument position and so exempts the reindexing from the C-Constraint, in this case. However, this complication is unnecessary if, after Fiengo (1980), one assumes that direct and indirect objects can occur in either order following V. For then, besides (122), the surface structure (123) also underlies (120):

(123)   [which book about [which naturalist]$_3$]$_2$ [$_s$ e$_2$ was given e$_2$ [his$_4$ father]]

In this case, $4 \rightarrow 3$ will not violate the C-Constraint.

There are further data involving binding that support Fiengo's "free ordering" hypothesis:

(124)   Into *which child*'s hands shall I put *his* candy?
(125)   **Which child*'s hands shall I put *his* candy into?

In (125), the stranded preposition forces violation of the C-Constraint, assuming no lowering (see section 6). Furthermore, any lowering in (125) must be to the vacated object-position of *into*, and so will yield no source for reindexing. But in (124), using Fiengo's hypothesis that the source of *into which child's hands* can be immediately after the V *put*, the pronoun can reindex freely. The examples below are similar:

(126)   *Which person* did you talk about with *his* wife?
(127)   **Which person* did you talk with *his* wife about?
(128)   To *whom* did you send *his* books?
(129)   **Who* did you send *his* books to?

It seems, then, that accounting for the data presented in this section need not force any complications in the statement of the Reindexing rule. We turn now to the cases of relative clauses and clefts.

9.3   Relatives

We consider first the contrast between pairs such as (130) and (131):

(130)   The singer of his song-knows Fred.
(131)   The person who sang his song-knows Fred.

In (131), binding is permitted: the subject NP can be interpreted as referring to the x, x a person, such that x sang x's song. For (130), this interpretation of the subject NP is impossible.

Of course, where the reference of *his* = a, it might turn out that *the singer of a's song* = a. Moreover, such coreference might even be purported, viz. (132):

(132)   John is the best singer of his song.

In general, a description may overlap in reference with an NP properly contained within it.

The distinction between the descriptions in (130) and (131) is therefore not a matter of conditions on purported coreference but, rather, a matter of binding. Semantically—and speaking loosely—the descriptions differ in that only the description *the person who sang his song* can be used to establish the identity of an object without fixing the reference of the pronoun *his* from outside. This difference is what is represented by the possibility of binding in (131), but not in (130).[19]

The source of binding in (131) is of course the trace of *Wh*-movement in the relative clause. Pronominal binding in this situation continues to be subject to directional asymmetries:

(133)   I know every boy *who* loves *his* mother.
(134)   *I know every boy *whom his* mother loves.

It is straightforward to verify that the other conditions that we have discussed also hold in the domain of a relative S̄.

There is an intuitive semantic distinction between the restrictive and the nonrestrictive relatives. Roughly speaking, the head NP of a restrictive relative [$_{NP}$ NP S̄] is *incomplete*; it has no reference at all in such occurrences. But the head of a nonrestrictive relative has a determinate reference. Compare (135) and (136):

(135)   The man, who I know his wife loves, admires Mozart.
(136)   The man who I know his wife loves admires Mozart.

In (136), the pronoun cannot be interpreted as a bound variable. As in other examples, coreference between the pronoun and the containing NP is possible:

(137)   The man who I know his wife loves is Fred.

Example (137) can be true with *his = Fred = the man who I know his wife loves*. But coreference between *his* and *the man* is out of the question in (136) or (137); the expression *the man*, as it there occurs, is not to be taken as referring to anything at all, so I would maintain. But in (135), a nonrestrictive relative, the head NP *the man* is semantically complete and has a reference. Notice that coreference between *his* and *the man* is entirely possible, although binding is impossible.

But coreference between the head of a nonrestrictive relative and a pronoun contained in the relative clause is nevertheless subject to restrictions, viz. (138):

(138)   *John, who *he* hates, knows Fred.

To analyze this phenomenon within the framework assumed here, we first advert to a discussion of the role of anaphoric indices for other cases than the contraindexing of referential NPs.

Recall that if NP_i contains j as an element of its anaphoric index, then this is to have the following interpretation: the reference of NP_i does not purportedly overlap with the reference of any NP with referential index j. This statement, however, is significant only if NP_i, NP_j are both referential. If either is interpreted as a variable, or is quantificational, then the question of reference does not arise. On the other hand, we can associate with a quantificational NP a *universe of discourse*, and correspondingly with each occurrence of a variable a set of *admissible values* of that variable. In many cases, restrictions on values of variables appear to be influenced by the same factors that determine failure of purported coreference. Thus, compare (139) and (140):

(139)   John hates him.
(140)   Someone hates him.

Example (139) cannot be interpreted as an assertion that John hates himself. Similarly, it seems to be a necessary condition for the truth of (140) in ordinary discourse that b hate a be true for some $b \neq a$. In the dual situation of (141),

(141)   Everyone hates him.

if *him* refers to a, it is not necessary for the truth of (141) that a hate a. Finally, in cases of multiple quantification such as (142),

(142)   Everyone wants someone to be rich.

the favored interpretation is that each person is an x such that for some $y \neq x$, x wants y to be rich.

Suppose that NP_i, NP_j are quantificational NPs, contraindexed in a surface structure Σ. Then they are also contraindexed at LF, and one must be within the scope of the other (otherwise they would not have been contraindexed at SS). If NP_j is within the scope of NP_i, then the favored interpretation results by including the clause "$x_i \neq x_j$" within the restriction on NP_j. Thus, (142) will be interpreted as shown in (143):

(143)   [every x: x is a person] x wants [[some y: y is a person & $y \neq x$] y to be rich]

Such is the interpretation of "disjoint reference" applied to quantificational NPs.[20]

For the simpler case, suppose that NP_i is quantificational, NP_j is referential, and they are contraindexed. Then the favored interpretation includes the clause "$x_i \neq NP_j$" or "$x_i \notin NP_j$", depending on whether NP; is singular or plural.

Consider again (138), repeated here:

(138)   *John, who *he* hates, knows Fred.

The referential index of *who* in (138) will be an element of the anaphoric index of *he*; in short, these items will be contraindexed. Then it follows from the interpretation of contraindexing just suggested that in the structure (144)

(144) $[_s[who]_3\ he_{4,\{3\}}\ hates\ e_3]$

the reference of the pronoun is excluded as a possible value of the variable bound by *who*. But since the nonrestrictive relative as a whole refers to John, it is proper to assume that John is among the admissible values of this variable. Then the reference of the pronoun cannot be to John.

The analysis just given extends to pronouns occupying other positions in nonrestrictive relatives:

(145)   *John, who hates *him*, . . .
(146)   John, who hates *his* father, . . .
(147)   John, who *his* father hates, . . .
(148)   John, whose father hates *him*, . . .
(149)   (?)John, whose father *he* hates, . . .

The slight oddity of (149) calls for explanation, particularly since there are nonrestrictives on this pattern that are clearly unacceptable:

(150)   *The shah, through whose father's usurpation *he* became king, . . .
(151)   ??John, whose face *he* shaves regularly, . . .

What the explanation may be is not clear.[21]

With the exception just noted, the appropriate generalizations, which follow from the analysis given here, are (152) and (153):

(152)   In a nonrestrictive relative, a pronoun not contraindexed with the relative *wh* can be co-referential with the head.
(153)   In a restrictive relative, pronominal binding follows the pattern of direct and indirect questions.

In (1979), Chomsky suggests that the data discussed above, on "disjoint reference" and quantification, arise not from the rules of grammar, but from independent considerations on commonsense belief and principles of language use. Certainly, there is nothing absurd in, say, the inference (154), despite the favored interpretation of the conclusion:

(154)   Everyone wants himself to be rich; therefore, everyone wants someone to be rich.

Likewise, if (155) is true,

(155)   Carter voted for everyone on the Democratic ticket.

then we naturally assume that it is asserted in particular that Carter voted for himself. In the text, I have suggested that it is (154), (155), and the like that call for special explanation in terms of commonsense belief and conditions on language use, rather than the presumptions of disjointness in the quantificational cases. The issue is not over the data, but over their explanation.

However, a weakness for the analysis given here appears to emerge no matter how the data are explained. For suppose that we wish to extend the analysis to account for (154), (155), and the like, while retaining the proposition that a pronoun cannot be bound to a quantificational NP with which it is contraindexed. How would this be done? A natural suggestion is that there are principles of some sort, perhaps "pragmatic" in nature, that remove restrictions that the grammar would otherwise impose. These principles could be expressed by the optional deletion of elements of anaphoric indices, under certain circumstances. So in, say, (156),

(156)   [someone]$_i$ e$_i$ hates him$_{j,\{i\}}$

we might permit i to delete from the anaphoric index of him_j, thereby allowing inclusion of its reference in the domain over which the quantifier ranges. Call these principles *relaxation rules*. Still, however relaxation rules are formulated, we must *not* be able to delete i from the anaphoric index of an element with referential index i. To do so would be to permit the impossible cases of binding. Hence, so far as can be seen, one would have to incorporate a special principle barring as inputs to the relaxation rules structures that contained indices of the form (157):

(157) $i, \{\ldots i \ldots\}$

In short, the impossibility of binding in cases like (156) would no longer follow automatically from the interpretation of contraindexing. With this change, the analysis given here would lose a good deal of its explanatory force, although its material adequacy would be unaffected. I hope to take up these issues elsewhere.

In concluding this article, we turn to cleft sentences. It turns out that they exhibit the pattern of restrictives rather than nonrestrictives. The critical examples are (158) and (159):

(158)   *It was *John* whose friend *he* betrayed.
(159)   *It was *John* who *his* friend betrayed.

The contrast between (159) and (160) is especially striking:

(160)   *John*, who *his* friend betrayed, is a nice fellow.

Assuming the analysis of clefts given in Chomsky (1977b, 94–95), (159) will have the surface structure (161), in which *John* is Topic of S̄:

(161)   it was [$_{\bar{s}}$[$_{TOP}$ John] [$_{\bar{s}}$[who]$_i$ [$_s$ his friend betrayed e$_i$]]]

From our earlier analysis, it follows that *his* cannot be a bound variable in (161), but one must explain further why it cannot be coreferential with the semantically complete Topic. At the moment, I see no solution to this problem that goes much beyond stipulation. There are some suggestive data, however, which may indicate that the solution resides in a more accurate analysis of conditions on purported coreference in equative constructions, of which clefts are an instance. Thus, consider (162)–(165):

(162)   *Mary* is *her* cook.
(163)   *We* are *our* friends.
(164)   *His* friend denied being *Bill*.
(165)   *Fred* wanted to become *his* housekeeper.

These are in contrast to (166)–(169):

(166)   *Mary* likes *her* cook.
(167)   *We* look after *our* friends.
(168)   *His* friends denied knowing *Bill*.
(169)   *Fred* wanted to see *his* housekeeper.

In equative constructions, then, one cannot have coreference between the genitive NP which is determiner of NP to one side of the copula and NP on the other side. This property of equatives is preserved in negation:

(170)   *Mary* isn't *her* cook.
(171)   *We* aren't *our* friends.
(172)   *His* friend didn't deny being *Bill*.
(173)   *Fred* didn't want to become *his* housekeeper.

Furthermore, it is not semantic; compare (174) to (175):

(174)   *That number* is *its* square.
(175)   *That number* is identical to *its* square.

Notice that when the genitive is embedded further down, then coreference becomes possible:

(176)   *Mary* is *her* cook's best friend.

We might conjecture, then, that equative constructions are marked exceptions to the principles which allow purported coreference in (for example) (166)–(169). If so, it might follow that *who* in (159) cannot include the reference of *his* among the values of its variables; in this way, the data concerning clefts would be accounted for. Then coreference should be possible in (177):

(177)   It was *John* who *his* friend's mother betrayed.

This conclusion seems to me correct, but it remains to spell out the principles governing (162)–(165) and (170)–(174).[22]

Notes

Research for this article, an abbreviated version of which has appeared as Higginbotham (1979), was carried out during the author's tenure as Fellow in the Humanities, Columbia University. For their criticism, and for their encouragement, I am indebted especially to Noam Chomsky, Robert Fiengo, Alexander George, Zellig Harris, and Robert May. Comments by Jacqueline Guéron and by anonymous reviewers have also been very helpful. As noted below, the analysis in this article is carried out within the framework of Chomsky (1980). For a different point of view on the matters considered here, see Higginbotham (1980).

1. The distinction between deictic and bound interpretation may be drawn independently of the question of quantification into opaque contexts. Merely for the sake of expository brevity and uniformity of notation, I will speak in this article as though quantification past the opacity-making verb *thinks* and the like were possible. But the analysis can be translated into other frameworks—for example, those of Quine (1956) or Kaplan (1969).

2. See Fiengo and Higginbotham (1979) for proposed extensions of QR.

3. By definition, X c-commands Y iff neither of X, Y dominates the other, and the first branching node dominating X dominates Y; see Reinhart (1979). It should be noted that the definition of scope in terms of c-command is, by means of some auxiliary apparatus, interdefinable with the more traditional conception of Russell.

4. The contraindexing in Chomsky (1980) is a further development of ideas suggested in Lasnik (1976), who in turn notes their affinity to Lakoff (1968). My interpretation of contraindexing differs from Lasnik's, for reasons given in Higginbotham (1980), note 1.

5. The term "referential" here must not be taken literally, because referential indices attach to all NPs indiscriminately, regardless of their semantic role. The precise interpretation of coindexing will vary, depending on the constructions involved.

6. Example (18) is a special case of the more general rule of Chomsky (1980).

7. No bound variables are actually visible in (24), which is assumed to yield eventually what we may represent by (i),

    (i)   [every x: x is a person here] x thinks x is a nice fellow

where [*every x*: *x is a person here*] is a restricted quantifier. In general, representations such as (i) are eschewed here, because their derivation requires further elaboration of rules, on which no issues in the present discussion appear to depend. These representations are used occasionally below, where it seemed that intended interpretations could be given more transparently thereby.

8. An anonymous reviewer has suggested that the reindexing operation given here is made necessary by the assumption of Chomsky (1980) that nonanaphoric NPs are at most contraindexed and never coindexed. This suggestion is mistaken. Suppose that the answer to the problem with which we began could be formulated as (H):

    (H)   Pronoun B can be bound to quantificational NP A in surface structure Σ iff:
        (i) A, B are not contraindexed; and
        (ii) There is a representation Σ^* of Σ at LF in which B is within the scope of A.

Then no reindexing would be necessary. We can even generalize (H) to cover cases such as (33) of the text, as follows. If S is a set of occurrences of NPs in Σ, we say that S is *maximal* iff S contains everything in Σ that is coindexed with anything in S. We say that S is *harmonious* if no two elements of S are contraindexed. Then we can propose (H'):

    (H')   A set T of occurrences of pronouns can be bound to quantificational NP A in Σ iff there is a maximal, harmonious S such that:
        (i) S contains A, and everything in T;
        (ii) S-{A} is composed wholly of occurrences of pronouns and anaphors; and
        (iii) There is an LF representation Σ^* of Σ such that every element of S-{A} is within the scope of A.

(H') is inadequate because of "crossover," discussed below. Crossover aside, however, (H') would be a solution to the general problem considered in this article, with no mention of reindexing.

9. This is perhaps recognized in the more explicit formulation of the Leftness Condition given in Chomsky (1976b, 343), as follows: "Let us take [the Leftness Condition] to assert that a pronoun *P* within the scope of a quantifier may be rewritten as a variable bound by this quantifier unless *P* is to the left of an occurrence of a variable already bound by this quantifier." That is, in our terminology, the reindexing rule is subject to a constraint on application, rather than an LF filter.

10. If the context is properly rigged, then the (a)-type examples can become fully acceptable on the bound interpretation. For instance, Jacqueline Guéron gives (i):

(i)   The teacher's writing to his father annoyed every child in the class.

Virtually this same example was suggested by Bonnie Gildin and others at Columbia. The view taken here is that (i) and the like are deviant structures on the bound interpretation, but that contextual factors including the meanings of the various quantifiers, et cetera, can combine to make some relatively accessible. But the (b) examples are readily interpretable as containing bound pronouns, independently of contextual factors, the meanings of the quantifiers, and other matters.

11. The central idea behind (55), that pronouns become bound variables through the mediation of empty categories appropriately related to them, may also account for the possibility of binding in examples like (i), first brought to my attention by Robert Fiengo:

(i)   Devotion to *his* country is expected of *every soldier*.

Observe that purported coreference is not possible in (ii):

(ii)   *Devotion to *Jack*'s country is expected of *him*.

The status of (ii) would follow at once from the Indexing Algorithm if we supposed that the subject NP had a PRO subject, coindexed with *him* (for analyses along these lines, see Lasnik 1976). Then we have support for the idea that binding is possible in (i) because we may have the surface structure (iii):

(iii)   [PRO$_i$ devotion to his$_i$ country] is expected of [every soldier]$_i$.

The reindexing $j \rightarrow i$ is then possible through (55). We then predict that a bound interpretation should be less accessible in (iv) than in (i):

(iv)   The Queen's devotion to *his* country inspires *every soldier*.

This prediction is borne out, I believe.

12. When the analysis presented in this article was first worked out, the research of Reinhart (1979) was unknown to me. I do not examine here the idea that pronominal binding is not in fact subject to conditions traceable to linear order, but only to structural conditions; but see Higginbotham (1980).

13. It appears that some lowering operations might have to be performed before indexing, for instance to account for (i):

(i)   *Which picture of *Fred* did *he* see?

There is at least one sort of case in which movement prior to indexing may affect possibilities for binding, but not for purported coreference, namely extraposition. The following example is noted in Partee (1975b):

(ii)   *It would be advisable for *everyone* for *him* to get a job.

Coreference in the italicized positions in (ii) is permitted:

(iii)   It would be advisable for *him* for *John* to get a job.

The case (ii) would follow if we supposed that the structure to which indexing applies is that of the "intraposed" (iv):

(iv)   *For *him* to get a job would be advisable for *everyone*.

However, if the pronoun to be bound in the extraposed clause is not a subject, then the sentences appear more acceptable than (ii):

(v)   (?)It would be good for *everyone* for Harry to meet *him*.

Contrast (vi):

(vi) *For Harry to meet *him* would be good for *everyone*.

So matters are not so clear.

14. See Higginbotham (1980) for a conjecture. The configuration (CC) is realizable from my informants in the case of the quantifier *yǒu*, whose force is existential:

(i) *Yǒude nyǔhádidze* de péngyou dōu kànjyàn *tā*
  a girl's friend all see her
 'Every friend of *a girl* saw *her.*'

The force of this example is small, however, because *yǒu* occurs other than as a determiner. When one turns to quantifiers that only appear in determiner position, then binding appears to obey the constraint (CC). Thus, we find (ii):

(ii) * *Měi yīge nyǔháidze* de péngyǒu dōu kàniyàn *tā*
  every girl's friend all see her
 'Every *girl*'s friend saw *her.*'

It has proved very difficult to obtain relevant data on the "inversely linked" cases, because the constructions themselves are felt as marginal unless topicalized.

I would like to thank Chung-Keng Ch'ou, Jim Huang, Irene Lyou, and others for their assistance.

15. See Fiengo and Higginbotham (1979) for an analysis of the genitive in the context of the theory of Chomsky (1980).

16. Here I am indebted to Robert May.

17. Similar remarks hold for generics.

18. We might speculate further that the Reindexing rule is insensitive to whether the source empty category plays any semantic role at all. Many people, myself included, find binding in (i) more acceptable than in (ii):

(i) Who do you think his father hates?
(ii) Who does his father hate?

Suppose that, as in Chomsky (1977b), we assume the successive cyclicity of *Wh*-movement. Then the indexed surface structure of (i) will be as shown in (iii):

(iii) who$_2$ do you think [$_s$ e$_2$[$_s$ his$_3$ father hates e$_2$]]

Then the Reindexing rule, applying blindly, could recognize the semantically inert empty category in COMP as a source. This would yield a bound interpretation of (i).

That some possibilities for coreference are now given by rules of grammar, as in (117) and (118), does not contradict the general point of view of Chomsky (1980) or Lasnik (1976), that optional coindexing is superfluous for referential expressions. Rather, these possibilities obtain on the present analysis, just because there is no reason to complicate the Reindexing rule so as to prevent them.

19. Turning to idioms, the contrast between pairs of NPs of the sorts displayed in the examples above is still more striking. Thus, we can have (i) but not (ii):

(i) the person who blew his cool
(ii) *the blower of his cool

For further remarks, see Higginbotham and May (1979).

20. Thanks to the reviewer who forced me to make this interpretation explicit.

21. Milner (1979) observes that the analogue of (148) is quite unacceptable in French:

(i) *Jean*, dont le père *le* haït, . . .

Milner also mounts an argument for the successive cyclicity of Qu-movement in French, based on facts involving disjoint reference. The relevant data hold also in English. We cannot have (ii):

(ii) *John* who you know *he* said would attend, . . .

The explanation assuming successive cyclicity would be that the trace of *Wh*-movement in the COMP of [$_s$ COMP [$_s$ *he said would attend*]] implies that the anaphoric index of *he* contains the referential index of the moved element.

The discussion in the text assumes that the *wh* of every relative is quantificational; that is, that it binds variables. Milner (1979) shows in detail that conditions on disjoint reference are reflected in relatives, concluding therefrom that relative pronouns are "referential." But it appears that Milner's data (from French) are accounted for on the analysis suggested here, which assumes that relative pronouns are quantificational but constrained in admissible values of variables by the conditions on disjoint reference. In the text, I have refrained from assuming with Chomsky (1976b) that variables have the status of names at LF. Suppose that this assumption were added to the rules and principles employed above, in the form (A):

(A) Variables are assigned anaphoric indices.

Then (A) predicts the status of (iii),

(iii) **John*, who *he* hates, . . .

on the assumption that *John* and *who* are coindexed at LF. We will have (iv):

(iv) John$_2$, who$_2$ he$_{3,(2)}$ hates e$_{2,(3)}$

So that construal of *he*$_3$ as *John*$_2$ will assign the index 2,{2} to the trace *e*$_2$, an LF variable. But application of (A) is inessential for (iii), because under the construal $3 \rightarrow 2$ *he* will also bear this index. So (A) is redundant in this and other cases discussed in the text, as the reader may verify.

Notice now that (A) predicts the status of (ii) and the like independently of the question of successive cyclicity of *Wh*-movement, because *he* will *c*-command the trace of *who*. A powerful case for (A) appears to follow from examples such as (v), first brought to my attention by Robert Fiengo:

(v)   **John*, who I saw *his* picture of, . . .

In (v), the referential index of *who* will delete from the anaphoric index of *his*, by whatever principle allows coreference between genitive NPs and NPs that *c*-command them. Yet, *his* and *John* cannot be coreferential. If (A) were assumed, however, then the trace of *who* would have the referential index of *his* as part of its anaphoric index. The status of (v) then follows at once.

Acceptance of (A) in the light of (ii), (v), and similar examples will not alter the analysis in the text at all, it appears.

22. Jan Edwards, employing in part suggestions of Robert Fiengo and Higginbotham, has examined this topic in unpublished work; she suggests that principles of case assignment are intimately involved.

23

JON BARWISE AND ROBIN COOPER

Generalized Quantifiers and Natural Language

In 1957, the Polish logician Andrzej Mostowski pointed out that there are many mathematically interesting quantifiers that are not definable in terms of the first-order $\forall$, $\exists$ and initiated study of so-called generalized quantifiers (cf. Mostowski 1957). Since then logicians have discovered and studied a large number of generalized quantifiers. At last count there were well over 200 research papers in this area. Most of this work has been directed toward cardinality quantifiers (e.g., Keisler 1969) and topological quantifiers (e.g., Sgro 1977) which are not particularly relevant to natural language, but even so, it has forced logicians to rethink the traditional theory of quantification.

The quantifiers of standard first-order logic (as presented in elementary logic textbooks) are inadequate to treat the quantified sentences of natural languages in at least two respects. First, there are sentences which simply cannot be symbolized in a logic which is restricted to the first-order quantifiers $\forall$ and $\exists$. Second, the syntactic structure of quantified sentences in predicate calculus is completely different from the syntactic structure of quantified sentences in natural language. The work on generalized quantifiers referred to above has led to new insights into the nature of quantifiers, insights which permit logical syntax to correspond more closely to natural language syntax. These insights, we argue, may also make a significant contribution to linguistic theory.

Section 1 discusses the nature of generalized quantifiers and their relationship to the syntax of English in general terms. Section 2 develops a logic containing generalized quantifiers. Section 3 shows how this logic may be formally related to a fragment of a syntax for English.

Section 4 is the main section of the paper. In it we discuss some of the general implications of the notion of generalized quantifier for a theory of natural language of the kind that is interesting to linguists.

Our conclusion, in section 5, attempts to draw some general conclusions about the relationship between syntax, semantics and logic.

Jon Barwise and Robin Cooper (1981) Generalized quantifiers and natural language. *Linguistics and Philosophy* 4: 159–219. Reprinted by permission of Kluwer Academic Publishers.

The paper has four appendices. Appendix A contains additions to the fragment in section 3 which are suggested by the results in section 4. Appendix B contains some possible semantic postulates on the meaning of nonlogical determiners. Appendix C contains the proofs of the facts about quantifiers asserted in the body of the paper. Appendix D consists of a chart classifying English determiners according to the semantic categories introduced in section 4.

Some (but not all) of the points made in sections 1 to 3 of this paper are implicit or explicit in Montague (1974), especially in PTQ, "The Proper Treatment of Quantification in Ordinary English." (Some of the suggestions in 1–3 are also similar to suggestions in other papers: for example, Fenstad 1978; Peacocke 1979). Our hope is to develop Montague's treatment of noun phrases further in a straightforward way (without lambdas), and to show some of its implications for a theory of natural language.

1   Generalized quantifiers and noun phrases

1.1   Some examples of generalized quantifiers

Viewed from a modern perspective, the familiar $\forall$ and $\exists$ are extremely atypical quantifiers. They have special properties which are entirely misleading when one is concerned with quantifiers in general. We begin this paper by discussing some simple examples of generalized quantifiers from mathematics to draw out some of the general features of quantifiers. Consider the following examples:

(1)   (a)   There are only a finite number of stars.
        (b)   No one's heart will beat an infinite number of times.
(2)   (a)   More than half of John's arrows hit the target.
        (b)   More than half the people voted for Carter.
(3)   (a)   Most of John's arrows hit the target.
        (b)   Most people voted for Carter.

1.2   Many quantifiers are not definable using first-order $\forall$ and $\exists$

There is no doubt that in any human language in which modern science can be formulated, sentences like (1) and (2) can be expressed. We suspect that sentences with quantifiers like those in (2) and (3) can be expressed in any human language. But the quantifiers in (1)–(3) cannot be expressed in terms of the first-order quantifiers $\forall x(\ldots x \ldots)$ and $\exists x(\ldots x \ldots)$. It is not just that we do not see how to express them in terms of $\forall$ and $\exists$; it simply cannot be done. Thus, a semantic theory for natural language cannot be based on the predicate calculus alone.

First, before seeing just what the problems are, let us abstract out the quantifiers at work in (1)–(3) as follows.

(1')   Finitely many things x satisfy $\varphi(x)$, *or, more symbolically*, Finite $x[\varphi(x)]$.
(2')   More than half the x such that $\psi(x)$ satisfy $\varphi(x)$, *or*, (more than $\frac{1}{2}\psi)x[\varphi(x)]$.
(3')   Most x such that $\psi(x)$ satisfy $\varphi(x)$, *or* (most $\psi)x[\varphi(x)]$.

Let E be an arbitrary non-empty set of things (individuals, entities, call them what you will) over which our variables range. First-order logic only allows quantification over objects in E, not over arbitrary sets of things, functions from things to things or other sorts of abstract objects not in E. Within this framework, it is easy to prove that none of the quantifiers used in (1)–(3) is definable in terms of the ordinary $\forall$ and $\exists$.

Consider the case of "more than half." It is a routine application of familiar techniques in first-order logic to prove that this cannot be defined from $\forall$ and $\exists$; that is, that there is no fixed definition that works even in all finite domains. This is proved in Appendix C (C12). One has to leave traditional first-order logic in one of two ways. One possibility is to expand the domain E of quantification to a bigger domain $E \cup A$, where A includes numbers and functions from sub-sets of E to numbers. That is, one might mirror the high-order set-theoretic definition of "more than half" in the semantics by forcing every domain E to contain all of the abstract apparatus of modern set-theory.

A different approach, one that model-theorists have found more profitable, is to keep the formal definition as part of the metalanguage, and treat generalized quantifiers without bringing all the problems of set theory into the syntax and semantics of the logic per se. We'll see just how this is done in a moment. The point to make here is that, once we make this move, it also gives us a way to treat determiners like "most," "many," "few," and others.

1.3   Quantifiers correspond to noun-phrases, not to determiners

We have been at some pains *not* to call "most" and "more than half" quantifiers. To see why, note for example that there is no way to define "more than half of John's arrows" from "more than half of all things"—that is, it cannot be formalized as something like

"More than half $x(\ldots x \ldots)$."[1]

This is why, in (2'), we symbolized the quantifier with ψ built into the quantifier prefix. What this means, semantically, is that "more than half" is not acting like a quantifier but like a deter-miner.[2] It combines with a set expression to produce a quantifier. On this view, the structure of the quantifier may be represented as below:

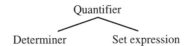

If we compare this structure with the syntactically simple sentence (3b), we can see that the struc-ture of the logical quantifier corresponds in a precise way to the structure of the English noun-phrase (NP) as represented in:

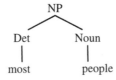

For exactly the same reason, "most" must be treated as a determiner, not as a quantifier. It is the NP "most people" that is the quantifier. There is no way to paraphrase a sentence like (3b) that begins "most things are such that if they are people then . . ." This can be proved, given reasonable assumptions about the meaning of "most," in the same way as for "more than half."

1.4   Quantifiers are not necessarily logical symbols

There is a mistaken notion that the meaning of the quantifiers must be built into the logic, and hence that it cannot vary from one model to another. This is mistaken on several counts even for mathematical examples. Unfortunately, the most convincing examples of this are outside the scope of this paper. For example, the meaning of the quantifier $Qx\varphi(x)$ which asserts that $\{x|\varphi(x)\}$ contains a non-empty open set (studied by Sgro 1971) is determined not by logic but by some underlying notion of distance, or, more precisely, by an underlying "topology." To interpret such a quantifier, we need not just an ordinary model but also a topology to make the quantifier precise. The same idea can be applied to the determiner "more than half" when one turns to infinite sets. Measures have been developed in which (4) and (5) make perfectly good sense.

(4)   More than half the integers are not prime.
(5)   More than half the real numbers between 0 and 1, expressed in decimal notation, do not begin with 7.

However, the truth or falsity of (4), (5) will depend not on a priori logic but on which underlying measure of infinite sets one is using.[3] This measure must be included as part of the model before the sentences have any truth value whatsoever.

One of the simplifying assumptions often made in the model theory is that one has a fixed context which determines the meaning of the basic expressions. We can think of this context as providing an interpretation for non-logical determiners in the above examples. In this paper we shall assume throughout that there is a rich context held fixed that determines the precise meaning for basic expressions, even those like "most," "many," and "few." We refer to this as the *fixed context assumption*. It should be pointed out, however, that even with this assumption the interpretation of quantifiers, even those like "every man," will vary from model to model since the interpretations of "man" is determined by the model. The difference between "every man" and "most men" is this. The interpretation of both "most" and "man" depend on the model, whereas the interpretation of "every" is the same for every model. "Every," unlike "open," "more than half," and "most," is a logical quantifier.

The fixed context assumption is our way of finessing the vagueness of non-logical determiners. We think that a theory of vagueness like that given by Kamp (1975: chapter 26 in this volume) for other kinds of basic expressions could be superimposed on our theory.[4] We do not do this here, to keep things manageable.

1.5   Quantifiers denote families of sets

Quantifiers are used to assert that a set has some property. $\exists x \varphi(x)$ asserts that the set of things which satisfy $\varphi(x)$ (informally $\{x \mid \varphi(x)\}$ or, in our formal notation $\hat{x}[\varphi(x)]$) is a nonempty set. That is, the set of individuals having property φ contains at least one member. $\forall x \varphi(x)$ asserts that the set contains all individuals. Finite $x \varphi(x)$ asserts that the set is finite. It is clear that a quantifier may be seen as dividing up or partitioning the family of sets provided by the model. When combined with some sets it will produce the value "true" and when combined with others it will produce the value "false." In order to capture this idea formally, quantifiers are taken to denote the family of sets for which they yield the value "true." The truth of a sentence $Qx[\varphi(x)]$ is then determined by whether or not the set $\hat{x}[\varphi(x)]$ is a member of the quantifier denotation. The denotation $\|Q\|$, of a quantifier symbol Q, can be specified informally as follows for some of the quantifiers we have discussed. (We let E represent the set of entities provided by the model.)

$\|\exists\| = \{X \subseteq E \mid X \neq \phi\}$
$\|\forall\| = \{E\}$
$\|\text{Finite}\| \{X \subseteq E \mid X \text{ is finite}\}$
$\|\text{More than half of } N\| = \{X \subseteq E \mid X \text{ contains more than half of the Ns}\}$
$\|\text{Most } N\| = \{X \subseteq E \mid X \text{ contains most Ns}\}$

To emphasize the role of the set, we will write $Q\hat{x}[\varphi(x)]$ rather than just $Qx[\varphi(x)]$ in the logic developed in section 2. If φ is a simple set expression we may write $Q\varphi$.

1.6   Proper names and other noun-phrases are natural
        language quantifiers

We are now in a position to examine the notorious mismatch between the syntax of noun phrases in a natural language like English and their usual representations in traditional predicate logic. To review the mismatch, notice that the sentences in (6) are all to be analyzed as consisting of a noun phrase followed by a verb-phrase as represented by the labeled brackets:

(6)   a. [Harry]$_{NP}$[sneezed]$_{VP}$
       b. [Some person]$_{NP}$[sneezed]$_{VP}$
       c. [Every man]$_{NP}$[sneezed]$_{VP}$
       d. [Most babies]$_{NP}$[sneeze]$_{VP}$

There is strong evidence that the phrases labeled as NP's here belong to a single syntactic category. For example, they may occur not only as the subjects of intransitive verbs (as in (6)) but also as the objects of transitive verbs (7) and of prepositions (8):

(7)
$$\text{Susan kissed} \begin{cases} \text{Harry} \\ \text{some person} \\ \text{every man} \\ \text{most babies} \end{cases}$$

(8)
$$\text{I saw Susan with} \begin{cases} \text{Harry} \\ \text{some person} \\ \text{every man} \\ \text{most babies} \end{cases}$$

This constituent structure is not reflected in the translation of sentences containing NP's into predicate calculus. (6a–c) might be represented, ignoring tense, as (9a–c), respectively.

(9)   a. **sneeze (h)**
       b. $\exists x[\textbf{person}(x) \wedge \textbf{sneeze}(x)]$
       c. $\forall x[\textbf{man}(x) \rightarrow \textbf{sneeze}(x)]$
       d. (There is no predicate calculus representation for (6d))

While (9a) contains a representation of the English NP *Harry*, (9b) and (9c) do not contain constituents representing the NP's *some person* and *every man*. Furthermore, these two expressions contain open sentences joined by two place connectives which do not correspond to constituents of the English sentences. The correct choice of the connective depends on the quantifier which is to be prefixed to the open sentence.

    From our discussion of generalized quantifiers we can see that the mismatch between (6a–d) and (9a–d) is not necessary. (9b) is not really a translation of (6b), but of the logically equivalent, but linguistically quite different, sentence:

(10)   Something was a person and sneezed.

What is wanted, to translate (6b)–(6d), is (in our notation):

(11)   b. **(Some person)** $\hat{x}[\textbf{sneeze}\ (x)]$
        c. **(Every man)** $\hat{x}[\textbf{sneeze}(x)]$
        d. **(Most babies)** $\hat{x}[\textbf{sneeze}\ (x)]$.

Or, more simply,

(12)   b. **(Some person) (sneeze)**
     c. **(Every man) (sneeze)**
     d. **(Most babies) (sneeze)**.

These sentences will be true just in case the set of sneezers (represented either by $\hat{x}[\textbf{sneeze}\ (x)]$ or by **sneeze**) contains some person, every man, or most babies, respectively.

All that is left to make the treatment of NP's as quantifiers uniform is the observation that even proper names can be treated as quantifiers. In our logic, (13) may be translated as (14), or rather, something like (14) in structure:

(13)   Harry knew he had a cold.
(14)   Harry $\hat{x}[x$ knew x had a cold].

[Example] (14) must be true just in case Harry is a member of the set. Hence the quantifier represented by the NP *Harry* can be taken as denoting the family of sets which contain Harry. To have our cake and eat it too (preserving the intuition that proper names denote individuals, rather than sets of sets) we will let the lexical item or word *Harry* denote an individual. However, the NP containing just this word, represented by [Harry]$_{NP}$, will denote the family of sets containing Harry.

1.7   Quantifiers can degenerate in some models

As mentioned above, we can think of a noun phrase as dividing the sets corresponding to verb phrases into two classes—corresponding to those which make it true and those which make it false. As a denotation of the noun phrase, we choose the set of those which make it true. It seems the most natural way to formalize the intuitions. Thus noun phrases act, semantically, like the logician's generalized quantifiers.

In some interpretations (models), however, these NP denotations may degenerate in one of three ways. They may denote the empty set, denote the set of all sets, or, the worst case, fail to denote any set at all. The first two types of degeneracies are discussed in section 4.5.

To see how a noun phrase can fail to denote, notice that determiners will be interpreted as functions from common noun denotations (sets of things) to noun phrase denotations (sets of sets). However, functions have domains, and a set may fail to be in the domain of function which serves as the denotation of a given determiner. In particular, the determiners *the*, *both*, and *neither* have domains which are special. *The blond man*, for example, does not denote anything at all unless there is a unique blond man in the state of affairs represented by the model. Any attempt to assign it an ad hoc denotation is bound to give rise to some incorrect inferences. Thus, we treat the determiner ‖**the**‖ as a function with domain the set of sets with exactly one element. ‖**both**‖ and ‖**neither**‖ are defined on those sets with exactly two elements. (This treatment is similar to some presuppositional treatments that have been proposed in the literature.)

We now turn to spelling out the ideas of section 1 formally. Some readers might prefer to turn directly to section 4 to see the kind of applications we have in mind.

2   A logic with generalized guantifiers: **L(GQ)**

The logic developed here has no basic quantifier symbols. All quantifiers are built up by applying some basic determiner symbol **D** to some set term η.

2.1 Logical symbols

The logical symbols of **L(GQ)** include the following:

  a. Propositional connectives: ∧, ∨, ~
  b. Variables: $x, y, z, x_0, \ldots$
  c. A distinguished *set term*: **thing**
  d. Parentheses: (,); brackets: [,]; and a *cap symbol:* ^ . . .
  e. An equality symbol: =
  f. Some of the following *logical determiners*: **some, every, no, both, neither, 1, 2, 3, . . . , !1, !2, !3, . . . , the 1, the 2, the 3, . . .**

The semantics of **L(GQ)** will be defined so that **thing** always denotes the set E of things in our model—that is, the set of individuals or objects. The semantics of the numerical determiners will be defined so that **3 men run** will mean that at least three men run; **!3 men run** will mean that exactly three men run; **the 3 men run**, following 1.7, will only have a meaning in those models where there are exactly three men. In such models it will be true if they all run.

2.2 Nonlogical symbols

The nonlogical symbols include the following:

  a. Some set (possibly empty) of *constant symbols*, say **c, d,** . . . .
  b. For each $n = 1, 2, \ldots$, some set (possibly empty) of *n-ary relation symbols*, say **R, S,** . . . . The 1-ary relation symbols are also called *predicate symbols*.
  c. Some set (possibly empty) of *nonlogical determiners*, say $\mathbf{D}_1, \mathbf{D}_2, \ldots$. These may include **most, many, few, a few**, etc.

Thus **L(GQ)** is not just one language but is, rather, a whole family of languages, depending on the choices made in 2.lf and 2.2.

2.3 Syntactic formation rules

There are six syntactic formation rules which, together, provide an inductive definition of the three kinds of expressions of **L(GQ)**—namely, *set terms, quantifiers,* and *formulas.* These rules are given in (R1)–(R6) below:

  R1. Any predicate symbol is a set term.
  R2. If φ is a formula and u is a variable, then $\hat{u}[\varphi]$ is a set term.
  R3. If **D** is a determiner and η is a set term, then **D**(η) is a quantifier.
  R4. If **R** is an *n*-ary relation symbol and $t_1, \ldots, t_n$ are constants or variables, then $\mathbf{R}(t_1, \ldots, t_n)$ is a formula. Similarly, if η is a set term and t is a variable or constant, then η(t) is a formula.
  R5. If Q is a quantifier and η is a set term Q(η) is a formula. *We leave off the parentheses if no confusion is likely.*
  R6. The formulas are closed under the propositional connectives ∧ (*and*), ∨ (*or*), and ~ (*not*).

Some remarks and then some examples. Formulas are built up by R4–R6. Set terms are built up by R1 and R2. Quantiflers are built by R3. In particular, R3 gives us the quantifiers: **every(thing)** (denoted in accordance with tradition by ∀), **some(thing)** (denoted by ∃), and

no(thing). Given a set term η, we write **the**(η) for the quantifier **the 1**(η). In R4, $\eta(t)$ is used rather than the more customary $(t \in \eta)$, just because it makes the formulas neater. We will abbreviate the formula $= (t_1, t_2)$ (given by R4) by $(t_1 = t_2)$.

2.4   Some examples

In the examples below we assume that our language **L(GQ)** has the determiners displayed in addition to the obvious stock of relation symbols. Below each sentence of **L(GQ)** we write an appropriate rendering in English and, where possible, a predicate calculus equivalent:

(15) a. **Some(thing) run**.
      b. Something runs.
      c. $\exists x[\mathbf{run}(x)]$.
(16) a. **Every(man) sneeze**.
      b. Every man sneezes.
      c. $\forall x[\mathbf{man}(x) \rightarrow \mathbf{sneeze}\ (x)]$.
(17) a. **5(woman)** $\hat{x}$ [**the(man)** $\hat{y}$ [**kiss** (x, y)]].
      b. Five (or more) women kiss the man.
      c. $\exists x_1 \exists x_2 \exists x_3 \exists x_4 \exists x_5[x_1 \neq x_2 \wedge x_1 \neq x_3 \wedge \ldots \wedge \mathbf{woman}(x_1)$
         $\wedge \mathbf{woman}(x_2) \wedge \ldots$
         $\wedge\ \exists y[\mathbf{man}(y) \wedge \forall z[\mathbf{man}(z) \rightarrow y = z] \wedge$
         $\mathbf{kiss}(x_1, y) \wedge \mathbf{kiss}(x_2, y) \wedge \ldots \wedge \mathbf{kiss}(x_5, y)]]$.
(18) a. **No(woman)** $\hat{x}$ [**run** $(x) \wedge$ **sneeze** (x)].
      b. No woman runs and sneezes.
      c. $\sim\exists x[\mathbf{woman}\ (x) \wedge \mathbf{run}\ (x) \wedge \mathbf{sneeze}\ (x)]$.
(19) a. **Some(woman)** $\hat{y}$ [**most(men)** $\hat{x}$ [**kiss** (x, y)]].
      b. Most men kiss a (particular) woman.
      c. (No predicate calculus equivalent for *most*.)
(20) a. **Many(men)** $\hat{x}$ [$\sim$ **see** $(x, \mathbf{h})$].
      b. Many men don't see Harry.
      c. (No predicate calculus equivalent for *many*.)

2.5   The semantics of **L(GQ)**

A model for **L(GQ)** is a function M which assigns interpretations to expressions of the language that need interpretations. It assigns to **thing** some non-empty set E, and it assigns to each basic symbol **S** an interpretation $\|\mathbf{S}\|$ satisfying (S1)–(S6) below. (To exhibit the important parts of M separately, we sometimes identify M with the ordered pair $\langle E, \|\ \|\rangle$.)

S1. If t is a constant or variable, then $\|t\| \in E$.
S2. $\|\mathbf{thing}\| = E$.
S3. $\| = \| = \{\langle a, a\rangle \mid a \in E\}$ (i.e., the equality relation on E).
S4. If **R** is an n-ary relation symbol, then $\|\mathbf{R}\| \subseteq E \times \ldots \times E$ (n-times). Similarly, if **U** is a basic set term (2.2b), then $\|\mathbf{U}\| \subseteq E$.
S5. a. $\|\mathbf{Some}\|$ is the function which assigns to each $A \subseteq E$ the family
          $\|\mathbf{Some}\|(A) = \{X \subseteq E \mid X \cap A \neq 0\}$.
        b. $\|\mathbf{Every}\|$ is the function which assigns to each $A \subseteq E$ the family
          $\|\mathbf{Every}\|(A) = \{X \subseteq E \mid A \subseteq X\}$.
        c. $\|\mathbf{no}\|$ is the function which assigns to each $A \subseteq E$ the family
          $\|\mathbf{no}\|(A) = \{X \subseteq E \mid A \subseteq X = \phi\}$.

d. For each natural number n, $\|n\|$, $\|!n\|$, and $\|$the n$\|$ are functions on sets defined by:

$\|n\|(A) = \{X \subseteq E \mid |X \cap A| \geq n\}$

$\|n!\|(A) = \{X \subseteq E \mid |X \cap A| = n\}$

$\|\textbf{the n}\|(A) = \begin{cases} \|\text{every}\|(A) & \text{if} \quad |A| = n \\ \text{undefined} & \text{otherwise} \end{cases}$

$\|\textbf{both}\|(A) = \|\text{the 2}\|(A)$

$\|\textbf{neither}\|(A) = \begin{cases} \|\text{no}\|(A) & \text{if } |A| = 2 \\ \text{undefined} & \text{otherwise} \end{cases}$

where $|Y|$ is the cardinality of the set Y.

Note that for each of these determiners $\mathbf{D}$, $\|\mathbf{D}\|(A)$ is a family of sets Q with the property that $X \in Q$ if and only if $(X \cap A) \in Q$. That is, whether or not X is a member of $\|\mathbf{D}\|(A)$ depends only on $X \cap A$. This property is described by saying that the quantifier $\|\mathbf{D}\|(A)$ *lives on A*. It is a universal semantic feature of determiners that they assign to any set A a quantifier (i.e., family of sets) that lives on A. When we turn to nonlogical determiners, it is the only condition we impose as part of the *logic*. The other properties will be determined by the meaning of the determiner in question in a given context, just like with other nonlogical symbols. Just as with other nonlogical symbols, we may place nonlogical semantic constraints on their interpretations. We will discuss some of their constraints in Appendix A.

S6. If $\mathbf{D}$ is a nonlogical determiner symbol then $\|\mathbf{D}\|$ assigns to each set A some family of sets that lives on A.

If more than one model is around, we can keep track of the model M by writing $\|\mathbf{S}\|^M$ for the denotation of $\mathbf{S}$ with respect to M. Given a model $M = \langle E, \| \ \| \rangle$, a variable u and an $a \in E$, we let $M(^a_u) = \langle E, \| \ \|' \rangle$, be the model which is just like M except that $\|u\|' = a$. We use this notation below to assign interpretations to all expressions of our logic by extending the function $\| \ \|$. We use 1 for "true," 0 for "false." (Formally speaking, rules S7–S10 constitute a definition of $\|\mathbf{S}\|^M$ by recursion on expressions $\mathbf{S}$ of $\mathbf{L(GQ)}$, simultaneously for all models M.)

S7. If $\mathbf{R}$ is an n-ary relation symbol then

$\|\mathbf{R}(t_1, \ldots, t_n)\| = \begin{cases} 1 & \text{if } \langle \|t_1\|, \ldots, \|t_n\| \rangle \in \|\mathbf{R}\| \\ 0 & \text{if } \langle \|t_1\|, \ldots, \|t_n\| \rangle \notin \|\mathbf{R}\|. \end{cases}$

Similarly, if η is a set term, then

$\|\eta(t)\| = \begin{cases} 1 & \text{if } \|t\| \in \|\eta\| \\ 0 & \text{if } \|t\| \notin \|\eta\|. \end{cases}$

S8. If $\mathbf{D}$ is a determiner and η a set term then the quantifier $D(\eta)$ denotes the result of applying the denotation of D to the denotation of η—i.e.:

$\|\mathbf{D}(\eta)\| = \|\mathbf{D}\|(\|\eta\|)$.

It is a family of sets that lives on $\|\eta\|$.

S9. If Q is a quantifier and ψ is a set term, then $Q\psi$ denotes true or false depending on whether or not the denotation of ψ is one of the sets in the denotation of Q—i.e.:

$\|Q\psi\| = \begin{cases} 1 & \text{if } \|\psi\| \in \|Q\| \\ 0 & \text{if } \|\psi\| \notin \|Q\|. \end{cases}$

S10. The usual truth table rules for $\wedge$, $\vee$, $\sim$. E.g.:

$$\|\varphi \wedge \psi\| = \begin{cases} 1 & \text{if } \|\varphi\| = \|\psi\| = 1 \\ 0 & \text{otherwise.} \end{cases}$$

We are only interested in models where our quantifiers turn out to be defined. However, to make things definite, we might use the conventions of Kleene (1952)—his logic of "true", "false" and "undefined" on p. 344, extended in the usual ways. A formula φ is said to be *true in M if* $\|\varphi\|^M = 1$.

3   Application to English syntax

The similarity of the structure of the logical expression in the examples (15)–(20) at the end of 2.4 to the structure of their corresponding English expressions should be evident. To make this relationship explicit, we characterize a small fragment of English and define a translation relation between the English fragment and **L(GQ)**, thereby inducing a semantics onto the fragment. The fragment will be extended in Appendix A.

FRAGMENT 1

3.1   Lexicon

NP – {John, Harry, Susan, something, everything, he_0, he_1, . . .}
 N – {person, man, woman, book, thing}
VP – {sneeze, run}
 V – {kiss, see, read}
Det – {a, some, every, each, all, the, both, no, neither, many, few, most, a few, one, two, . . .}

3.2   Syntactic rules

We define the set SD of *structural descriptions* (phrase structure trees) by means of an inductive (i.e., recursive) definition. We say α is an SD rather than the more accurate α is a member of SD.

3.2.1   Lexical insertion

SD0. If α is a word listed in the lexicon under A (where A is NP, N, etc.) then $[\alpha]_A$ is an SD. $[\alpha]_A$ may be identified with the tree $\overset{A}{\underset{\alpha}{|}}$.

3.2.2   Phrase structure rules

SD1. NP $\rightarrow$ Det N.

(In words, if α, β are SDs of forms $[\delta]_{\text{Det}}$, $[\eta]_N$, respectively, then $[\alpha\beta]_{\text{NP}}$ is an SD. $[\alpha\beta]_{\text{NP}}$ may be identified with the tree NP.)

$$\overset{\displaystyle\bigwedge}{\alpha \quad\quad \beta}$$

SD2. $\text{VP} \rightarrow \begin{cases} \text{VP } and \text{ VP} \\ \text{V } \text{NP} \end{cases}$

SD3.
$$S \rightarrow \begin{cases} \text{NP} \quad \text{VP} \\ \text{NP } \textit{do not } \text{VP} \\ \text{S } \textit{and } \text{S} \\ \text{S } \textit{or } \text{S} \end{cases}$$

SD4. N → NR
SD5. R → *that* VP

SD4 and SD5 are used to generate rudimentary relative clauses, as in *every man that runs*. Of course, these two rules do not present anything like a complete treatment of English relative clauses.

3.2.3 Quantification rule

SD6.

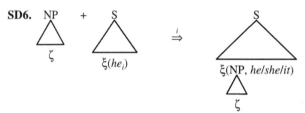

SD6 is shorthand for the following: If $[\zeta]_{NP}$ and $[\xi]_s$ are SDs, and if ξ contains at least one occurrence of he_i, then the result of replacing the first $[he_i]_{NP}$ in ξ by $[\zeta]_{NP}$ and subsequent occurrences of he_i by *he*, *she*, or *it* (depending on the gender of $[\zeta]_{NP}$) is an SD.

3.3 Morphological rules

We need additional morphological rules to obtain the correct forms of pronouns and verbs. We shall not specify these here. See Cooper (1978) for details.

3.4 Examples

We give structural descriptions of the English examples in 2.4.

(15')   a.   [[Something]$_{NP}$ [run]$_{VP}$]$_S$.
      b.   [[Some]$_{Det}$ [thing]$_N$]$_{NP}$ [run]$_{VP}$]$_S$.

The two SDs obtained for *something* may be regarded as alternatives for the analysis of this word or as making the claim that English contains a word *something* with stress on the first syllable in addition to the phrase *some thing* with stress on the second syllable. The truth conditional semantics of the two are shown to be the same by our translation procedure. Similar remarks can be made about *everything* and *every thing*:

(16')   [[[Every]$_{Det}$ [man]$_N$]$_{NP}$ [sneeze]$_{VP}$]$_S$
(17')   [[[Five]$_{Det}$ [woman]$_N$]$_{NP}$ [[kiss]$_V$ [[the]$_{Det}$ [man]$_N$]$_{NP}$]$_{VP}$]$_S$
(18')   [[[no]$_{Det}$ [woman]$_N$]$_{NP}$ [[run]$_{VP}$ and [sneeze]$_{VP}$]$_{VP}$]$_S$.

To get the SDs for 2.4 (19) and (20) whose derivation reflects the desired scope dependencies, we must use the quantification rule.[5]

(19') $[[a]_{Det} [woman]_N]_{NP} + [[[most]_{Det} [man]_N]_{NP} [[kiss]_V [he_0]_{NP}]_{VP}]_S$
$\overset{0}{\Rightarrow} [[most]_{Det} [man]_N]_{NP} [[kiss]_V [[a]_{Det} [[woman_N]_{NP}]_{VP}]_S$

(20') $[[many]_{Det} [man]_N]_{NP} + [[he_1]_{NP} \text{ do not } [[see]_V [Harry]_{NP}]_{VP}]_S$
$\overset{1}{\Rightarrow} [[many]_{Det} [man]_N]_{NP} \text{ do not } [[see]_V [Harry]_{NP}]_{VP}]_S$

3.5   The translation of fragment 1 into **L(GQ)**

We define a relation α' *as a translation of* α by induction on derivations of structural descriptions α by means of rules T0–T4 below. We will use α' to vary over translations of α, keeping in mind that α' is not necessarily uniquely determined by α (due to rule SD6) α' is uniquely determined by a derivation of α.

On the left we list lexical items α of Fragment 1, on the right their translation α' in **L(GQ)**:

NP	John, Harry, Susan	**j, h, s** (constant symbols)
	something, everything	**some(thing), every(thing)**
	he$_i$	x_i
N	person, man, woman, book, thing	**person, man, woman, book, thing** (predicate symbols)
VP	sneeze, run	**sneeze, run** (predicate symbols)
V	kiss, see, read	**kiss, see, read** (relation symbols)
Det	a, some	**some**
	every, each, all	**every**
	the	**the** (i.e. **the 1**)
	no, neither	**no, neither**
	one, two, three	**1, 2, 3**
	both	**both**
	most, many, few, a few	**most, many, few, a few**

T0. If α is an SD of the form $[\eta]x$, where η is in the lexicon, then α' is η' as given in the above list *unless* X is NP and η is a proper name or pronoun, in which case α' is the quantifier **the** $\hat{y}[y = \eta']$.

Let us explain the exception in the above rule. The denotation (in a model $M = \langle E, \| \ \| \rangle$) of the lexical item *Harry* is the denotation of its translation **h**—namely, $\|\mathbf{h}\|$ or Harry. However, the noun phrase $[Harry]_{NP}$ denotes $\{X \subseteq E \mid \|\mathbf{h}\| \in X\}$. To see this we simply compute:

$$
\begin{aligned}
\|\textbf{the } \hat{y}[y = \mathbf{h}]\| &= \|\textbf{the}\|(\|\hat{y}[y = \mathbf{h}]\|) \\
&= \|\textbf{the}\|(\{\|\mathbf{h}\|\}) \\
&= \{X \subseteq E \mid \{\|\mathbf{h}\|\} \subseteq X\} \quad \text{since} \quad |\{\|\mathbf{h}\|\}| = 1 \\
&= \{X \subseteq E \mid \|\mathbf{h}\| \in X\}.
\end{aligned}
$$

This set of sets is called the *principal ultrafilter* generated by $\|\mathbf{h}\|$. The computation shows the logical validity of the following:

$$\textbf{the } (\hat{y}[y = t])\hat{x}[\varphi (x)] \leftrightarrow \varphi (t)$$

(as long as t is not a bound variable of $\varphi(x)$). We could have used a special notation, say **h***, for such quantifiers in our logic. The present treatment has the virtue of pointing out the relationship of proper names to definite descriptions. Many languages employ definite determiners with proper names (e.g., German *der Hans*, Spanish *el Juan*). Pronouns are translated similarly: he_i and $[he_i]_{NP}$ are translated as x_i and as **the** $\hat{y}[y = x_i]$, respectively.

T1.

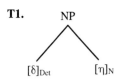

NP

[δ]_Det   [η]_N

translates as $\delta'(\eta')$, a quantifier.
(We suppress the labeled brackets in translations
for ease of reading.)

T2.

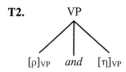

VP

[ρ]_VP   *and*   [η]_VP

translates as $\hat{x}[\rho'(x) \wedge \eta'(x)]$

If the quantifier Q is a translation of $[\rho]_{NP}$, then

VP

[ν]_V   [ρ]_NP

translates as $\hat{x}[Q(\hat{y}[\nu'(x,y)])]$.

There would be a closer correspondence between the structure of this kind of phrase and its translation if we were to adopt Montague's treatment in PTQ, of intensional verbs like *seek*. Under his treatment the translation would be $v'("^\wedge"Q)$ where "$^\wedge$" is an intensional operator). We avoid this here because we are not presently concerned with the semantics of intensional contexts. The translation we have provided corresponds to Montague's rule of VP-quantification.

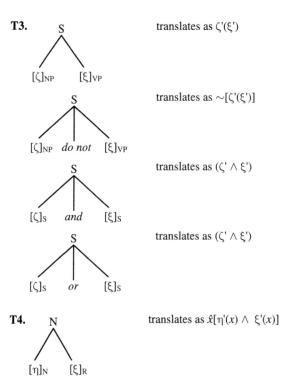

T3.

S

[ζ]_NP   [ξ]_VP

translates as $\zeta'(\xi')$

S

[ζ]_NP   *do not*   [ξ]_VP

translates as $\sim[\zeta'(\xi')]$

S

[ζ]_S   *and*   [ξ]_S

translates as $(\zeta' \wedge \xi')$

S

[ζ]_S   *or*   [ξ]_S

translates as $(\zeta' \wedge \xi')$

T4.

N

[η]_N   [ξ]_R

translates as $\hat{x}[\eta'(x) \wedge \xi'(x)]$

T5.

translates as ζ'

T6. Suppose α is an SD that comes via the quantification rule

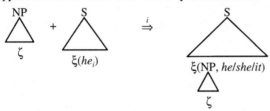

Then α' is $(\zeta'\hat{x}_i[\xi'])$.

We leave it to the reader to check that if α is any of (15')–(20') above, then α' is the corresponding formula of 2.4. This is true except in the cases of (19') and (20'), where the quantifier rule is used. The actual translation of (20'), for example, turns out to be

many(men) $\hat{x}[\sim \textbf{the } (\hat{y}[y = h])\hat{y} \ [\textbf{see}(x, y)]]$.

To get the formula (20), you need to use the logical validity of the scheme

the $(\hat{y}[y = t])\hat{y}[\varphi \ (y)] \leftrightarrow \varphi(t)$

pointed out in the discussion of translation rule T0.

4   Generalized quantifiers and linguistic theory

Linguistic theory is concerned, in part, with *natural language universals*, facts which hold for all naturally occurring human languages and which distinguish them from other logically possible languages. In this section we suggest some potential universals which relate to the theory of generalized quantifiers. In discussing these universals we shall restrict ourselves largely to *simple NP's* of English: proper nouns, a single determiner element followed by a common count noun and basic count words like *men* and *everybody*.[6]

4.1   The universality of noun phrases

There is a strong intuition that every natural language has a syntactic category which should be labeled NP. This category includes proper names and is also the locus of determiners such as *every, most*, and *one*. If the language has pronouns and definite or indefinite articles (*the* or *a*), they also occur inside NPs. However, there is no simple way to give a universal syntactic definition of NP. NPs in the world's languages having varying internal structure and the positions in which they can occur in a sentence vary from language to language.

This is just the sort of situation where semantics can contribute to syntactic theory. The kind of semantics we are suggesting allows us to propose the following universal for consideration:

> **U1.** *NP-quantifier universal.* Every natural language has syntactic constituents (called noun phrases) whose semantic function is to express generalized quantifiers over the domain of discourse.

It would probably be wrong to claim that NPs are the only quantifiers in natural language. (It seems possible, for example, that temporal adverbs should express quantifiers over moments or intervals of time as has been suggested by Partee (1973): Chapter 25 in this volume; Dowty (1979); and others). It does seem reasonable, however, to claim that the noun phrases of a language are all and only the quantifiers over the domain of discourse—that is, the set E of things provided by the model.

The quantifier universal not only allows us to consider something which may be true of all natural languages but also serves to distinguish natural languages from some other languages— like the standard formulation of first-order predicate calculus.

4.2   Scope involves whole NPs, not just determiners

In readings for natural language sentences, it is always the interpretations associated with whole NPs that enter into scope relationships, *not* simply the determiner interpretation. This is one of the mismatches between standard predicate calculus and natural languages. On a generalized quantifier analysis, where NPs function as generalized quantifiers, this fact about natural language would follow from the universal fact that quantifiers may be given different scope interpretations.

4.3   Dislocated phrases

It has been proposed recently (e.g., Karttunen 1977; Cooper 1978; Gazdar 1979; Chomsky 1980) that some phenomena (which in a traditional transformational grammar would be accounted for by means of movement rules) are associated with semantic rules having to do with the binding of variables by quantifiers. An example is the rule of *wh*-movement, which would be involved in deriving the sentence *who did John see*. On the traditional analysis, *who* has been moved from its deep structure position after *see*. It seems significant that many such rules involve the movement of NPs. In order not to prejudice the issue of whether such sentences are to be accounted for by a movement rule, we will adopt the term *phrase in dislocated position* (due to Stanley Peters) and propose the following as a candidate for a universal:

> **U2.** *Dislocated phrase universal.* If a language allows phrases to occur in a dislocated position associated with a rule of variable binding, then at least NPs (i.e., the syntactic category corresponding to quantifiers over the domain of discourse) will occur in this position.

We would not expect to find a natural language in which adjectives or prepositional phrases, but *not* noun phrases, occur in dislocated positions associated with variable binding. In particular, we would not expect a language to allow dislocated determiners if it did not also allow dislocated NPs. If determiners were regarded as quantifiers, one might expect the opposite to be true.

4.4   The property "lives on"

Quantifiers denote families of subsets of the domain E of discourse. In this and future sections we will often refer to the families as *quantifiers*, rather than as quantifier or NP *denotations*, and use Q as a variable over such quantifiers. It should always be clear from the context what is meant by the term *quantifier*.

In a model $M = \langle E, \| \ \| \rangle$, a quantifier Q *lives on* a set $A \subseteq E$ if Q is a set of subsets of E with the property that, for any $X \subseteq E$,

$$X \in Q \text{ iff } (X \cap A) \in Q.$$

English examples which illustrate this notion are the following equivalences

> Many men run ↔ Many men are men who run.
> Few women sneeze ↔ Few women are women who sneeze.
> John loves Mary ↔ John is John and loves Mary.

The quantifiers represented by the subjects of the sentences live on the set of men, women and the singleton set containing John, respectively. The peculiarity of the sentences on the righthand side of the biconditionals is presumably due to the fact that they are obviously redundant. We know of no counterexamples in the world's languages to the following requirement:

> **U3.** *Determiner universal.* Every natural language contains basic expressions (called determiners) whose semantic function is to assign to common count noun denotations (i.e., sets) A a quantifier that lives on A.

4.5   Proper quantifiers as "sieves"

We think of a quantifier Q on a model $M = \langle E, \| \ \| \rangle$ as separating ("sifting") the VP denotations into those that do and those that do not combine with it to make a true sentence. There are situations, however, where this sifting process is degenerate: when it lets *every* set through (i.e., $Q = \{X \mid X \subseteq E\}$, called Pow($E$)), and when Q doesn't let *any* set through (i.e, $Q = \phi$). We call Q *a proper quantifier denotation* or *sieve* if neither of these happen—that is, if Q is a non-empty proper subset of Pow(E). Notice that this is a property that applies to quantifiers as NP denotations, not to NPs themselves. That is, it is a semantic property. For example, ‖**many men**‖ = ϕ in exactly those models where there aren't many men. ‖**Every man**‖ = Pow(E) in exactly those models where there aren't any men.

Table 23.1 shows conditions under which various NPs can fail to denote proper quantifiers. We work in a fixed model $M = \langle E, \| \ \| \rangle$. The first column indicates by "yes" or "no" whether the quantifier can ever be ϕ. The second column indicates whether it can ever be Pow(E). The next two columns give equivalent conditions for the quantifier to be proper; column 3 a formal description, column 4 an informal description.

It is often assumed in normal conversation that noun phrases denote sieves. For example, given the utterance (21) we could naturally assume the truth of (22). However, this assumption may be explicitly contradicted as in (23):

(21)   No boy at the party kissed Mary.
(22)   There were boys at the party.
(23)   No boy at the party kissed Mary since there weren't any boys at the party.

With some NPs it is harder to contradict the assumption that the denotation is a sieve. For example, (24a) invites the assumption (24b), and the explicit denial in (24c) sounds quite odd.

(24)   a. Every man at the party kissed Mary.
      b. There were men at the party.
      c. ?Every man at the party kissed Mary, but only because there weren't any men at the party.

In column 5 of our chart we indicate our judgment as to whether it is easy or hard to interpret the NP as denoting an improper quantifier (i.e., a non-sieve). In the next section we find an independent semantic characterization of these classes. Column 6 has to do with that characterization.

TABLE 23.1

	(1) Can NP denote φ?	(2) Can NP denote Pow(E)?	(3) When does it denote a sieve?	(4) Informal description of ℨ	(5) Easy or hard to interpret as a non-sieve?	(6) Strong or weak determiner
1. Every η	No	Yes	$\|\eta\| \neq \phi$	There is some η	Hard	Strong
2. Some η	Yes	No	$\|\eta\| \in \|$some $\eta\|$	There is some η	Easy	Weak
3. Most η	No	Yes	$\|\eta\| \neq \phi$	There is some η	Hard	Strong
4. Many η	Yes	No	$\|\eta\| \in \|$many $\eta\|$	There are many η's	Easy	Weak
5. Few η	No	Yes	$\|\eta\| \notin \|$few $\eta\|$	~ (There are few η's)	Easy	Weak
6. No η	No	Yes	$\|\eta\| \notin \|$no $\eta\|$	There is an η, i.e. ~ (There are no η's)	Easy	Weak
7. 3η	Yes	No	$\text{Card}(\|\eta\|) \geq 3$	There are 3 η's	Easy	Weak
8. !3η	Yes	No	$\text{Card}(\|\eta\|) \geq 3$	There are 3 η's	Easy	Weak
9. The 1η	No	No	$\text{Card}(\|\eta\|) = 1$	Undefined unless there is exactly one η	Impossible	Strong
10. Both η	No	No	$\text{Card}(\|\eta\|) = 2$	Undefined unless there are exactly two η's	Impossible	Strong
11. Neither η	No	No	$\text{Card}(\|\eta\|) = 2$	Undefined unless there are exactly two η's	Impossible	Strong (–)
12. John	No	No	Always	Always	Impossible	Strong (the y [y = j])

Note that, according to our analysis, **the n** η, **both** η, and **neither** η will always denote a proper quantifier when they denote anything at all. We suggest that these are special cases of a general phenomenon which we attempt to capture with U4:

> **U4.** *Constraint on determiners that can create undefined NPs.* Let D represent a simple determiner such that $\|D\|(A)$ is sometimes undefined.
> 1. Whenever $\|D\|(A)$ is defined it is a sieve.
> 2. There is a simple determiner D^+ such that $\|D^+\|(A)$ is always defined and whenever $\|D\|(A)$ is defined, $\|D\|(A) = \|D^+\|(A)$.

This suggests that the partial determiners D function semantically just like their completions D^+ with the added import that they denote sieves. A completion of *the n* and *both* is *every*. The completion of *neither* is *no*. By U4, we would not expect to find a language with a word for *neither* without one for *no*. Similarly, we predict that no natural language has a simple NP D *men* with the same meaning as *every man*, except that it would be undefined only if there were more than 2 men. D *men* would be defined but improper if there were no men. This contrasts with *The 2 men* which is undefined unless there are exactly two men.

Finally, note that no determiner has a "yes" in both column (1) and column (2). It would be logically possible to have a determiner D which sometimes failed to be a sieve by having $D(\eta)$ denote ϕ for some η and $\text{Pow}(E)$ for other η. It appears to be a rather trivial universal that *no natural language determiner will have this property*. An even more trivial universal is that *no determiner is always trivial*.

4.6   Weak, strong, and definite determiners

In this section we define, semantically, a division of the determiners into "weak" and "strong." We then make a further division by defining the definite determiners as a subset of the strong determiners.

> PROPOSITION. If a quantifier Q on $M = \langle E, \| \ \| \rangle$ lives on A, then $A \in Q$ iff $E \in Q$. (Cf. Appendix C, C1 for the proof.)

> DEFINITION. A determiner D is *positive strong* (or *negative strong*, respectively) if for every model $M = \langle E, \| \ \| \rangle$ and every $A \subseteq E$, if the quantifier $\|D\|(A)$ is defined, then $A \in \|D\|(A)$. (Or $A \notin \|D\|(A)$, respectively.) If D is not (positive or negative) strong, then D is *weak*.

To classify a determiner D as (1) positive strong, (2) negative strong, or (3) weak, you form a simple sentence of the form

D N is a N/are Ns

and see if it is judged (1) automatically valid, (2) contradictory, or (3) contingent on the interpretation. For examples, *every gnu is a gnu* is true in every model, *neither gnu is a gnu* is false in every model in which it is defined, and *many gnus are gnus* will be true just in case there are many gnus. These judgements classify *every*, *neither*, and *many* as positive strong, negative strong, and weak, respectively. Table 23.2 presents our classification of the determiners we are considering.

The terms "weak" and "strong" (though not the definitions) are borrowed from Milsark (1977). Weak determiners for Milsark are those which create noun phrases which sound good after *there is* or *there are*. (Such NPs are called indefinite in earlier literature.)

Note that a theory of demonstratives (*this, that, these, those*) should work out so that they are strong determiners, since they sound odd in *there is* contexts. Note also that the weak determiners are exactly the ones marked "easy" in column 5 of Table 23.1.

TABLE 23.2

Weak	Strong
a	the 1, the 2, . . .
some	both
one, two, three	all
many	every
a few	each
few	most
no	neither (negtive strong)

We can use our definition to explain *why* noun-phrases with strong determiners sound strange in *there*-sentences:

A sentence of the form *there is/are* NP can be interpreted as meaning that the set of individuals in the model (E) is a member of the quantifier denoted by the NP.

For any positive strong determiner the result will be a tautology, since to say that E is in the quantifier is the same as to say that A is in the quantifier (4.6.1). For negative strong determiners, the result will be a contradiction. While tautologies and contradictions are not ungrammatical, they are not very informative and are normally restricted to use in special situations construed as set phrases. For example, to say *there's John* (in the existential, not the locative sense) is to say something that could not possibly be false since our semantics will require that *John* has a denotation, whatever the model.[7] The sentence is therefore used in a special kind of situation with special intonation, as in the following dialogue:

Who could possibly play Hamlet?
Well, there's John.

The speaker is using a tautology here to avoid making the direct assertion that John could play Hamlet but nevertheless implicating that this is a possibility.

We can also gain some insight into the dichotomy observed in the previous section. NPs constructed with strong determiners sound much more peculiar than those with weak determiners when they do not denote a proper quantifier (sieve). For an NP $D\eta$ where D is weak, the "sievehood" of $\|D\eta\|$ is contingent on whether $\|\eta\| \in \|D\eta\|$ or not. On the other hand, with strong determiners, $\|\eta\| \in \|D\eta\|$ is always true (except for the negative strong, where it is always false). Thus in the case of weak determiners we are able to cancel the implicature that $D\eta$ is a sieve by saying something like *there is(n't)/are(n't)* $D\eta$, whereas this is not possible in the case of strong determiners. This hardly constitutes an explanation of the dichotomy, but the weak/strong distinction is clearly relevant to any explanation of this phenomenon. The exact match between columns 5 and 6 of Table 23.1 can hardly be an accident.

We now turn to *definite determiners*. Of the determiners we are considering, the definite ones are *the n* and *both*.

DEFINITION. A determiner D is definite if for every model $M = \langle E, \| \ \| \rangle$ and every A for which $\|D\|(A)$ is defined, there is a non-empty set B, so that $\|D\|(A)$ is the sieve $\{X \subseteq E \mid B \subseteq X\}$. (Hence, $\|D\|(A)$ is what is usually called the principal filter generated by B.)

PROPOSITION. If D is definite, then D is positive strong. (See C3 for a proof.)

NPs of the form $D\eta$, where D is definite, will be called definite NPs. When the cardinality of the set B of generators is greater than 2, these NPs can occur in frames like: *all of——*, *most of——, some of——, many of——*. None of the weak determiners fit here. For example, one cannot say **all of many men*. It seems that a proper treatment of demonstratives like *that, these, those* would treat them as definite determiners. If a is a definite NP and if $Q = \|a\|$ is its denotation, then $\cap\, Q$, the intersection of all sets in Q, is the generator of Q. In the case of *the n*, we have $\cap\, \|the\ n\ \eta\| = \|\eta\|$. (We suppose that in the case of demonstratives, one would have only $\cap\, \|D\eta\| \subseteq \|\eta\|$.) We suspect that it is this ability to uniquely determine the generator from the NP that allows the NP to play the role of a common noun and recombine with a determiner. The additional information being supplied by the definite determiner is just that the set being quantified over is non-null. We shall interpret *of NP* in the above construction as the intersection of the quantifier denoted by the NP and apply certain determiners to the result.

An implementation of these suggestions for the treatment of *there* sentences and definite determiners can be found in Fragment 2 in Appendix A. Note that we have no explanation of the contrast between *one of the two men* and **one of both men* since we are treating *the two* and *both* as equivalent.

4.7   Monotone quantifiers

In this section we discuss two subclasses of quantifiers suggested by work in model theory and recursion theory. The classes seem equally important for linguistic theory.

DEFINITION. A quantifier Q is *monotone increasing* (mon ↑) if $X \in Q$ and $X \subseteq Y \subseteq E$ implies $Y \in Q$ (i.e., for any set $X \in Q$, Q also contains all the supersets of X).

Q is *monotone decreasing* (mon ↓) if $X \in Q$ and $Y \subseteq X \subseteq E$ implies $Y \in Q$ (i.e., for any set $X \in Q$, Q also contains all the subsets of X). A determiner D is *monotone* increasing (or decreasing) if it always gives rise to monotone increasing (or decreasing) quantifiers $\|D\|$ (A). To test an NP for monotonicity we take two verb phrases, VP_1 and VP_2, such that the denotation of VP_1 is a subset of the denotation of VP_2, and then check whether either of the following seem logically valid:[8]

If NP VP_1, then NP VP_2. (NP is mon ↑)
If NP VP_2, then NP VP_1. (NP is mon ↓)

EXAMPLES. Take VP_1 to be *entered the race early* and VP_2 to be *entered the race*. The following are valid:

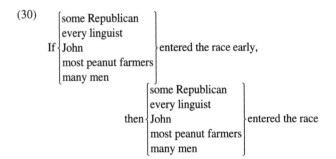

(30)

If { some Republican / every linguist / John / most peanut farmers / many men } entered the race early,

then { some Republican / every linguist / John / most peanut farmers / many men } entered the race

Notice that the reverse implications do not hold, since there clearly could be people who entered the race but did not enter early. The validity of these implications follow from the fact that the NPs are mon ↑. To exhibit some mon ↓ NPs, we note the validity of:

(31)

$$\text{If } \begin{Bmatrix} \text{no plumber} \\ \text{few linguists} \\ \text{neither Democrat} \end{Bmatrix} \text{ entered the race,}$$

$$\text{then } \begin{Bmatrix} \text{no plumber} \\ \text{few linguists} \\ \text{neither Democrat} \end{Bmatrix} \text{ entered the race early.}$$

By considering such examples, one comes to the following fairly clear judgements of monotonicity:

Monotone increasing: he, John, men, a man, some man, some men, somebody, the man/men, these/those men, most men,[9] many men, several men, either man, at least two men

Monotone decreasing: no man/men, few men, neither man, nobody, none, nothing, at most two men

Not monotone: exactly two men, exactly half the men

There are some NPs which could arguably be regarded as being able to denote both monotone and non monotone quantifiers. If *a few* is used to mean *some but not many*, then *a few men* is not monotone. If it is used to mean *at least a few*, it is mon ↑. It is likely that the mon ↑ reading is the only one that should be accounted for by the semantics, conversational implicature explaining the illusion of a non-monotone reading. (Cf. Grice 1975 and Horn 1976.) Similar remarks apply to *several*, *quite a few*, and *two*.

The first thing that strikes one about the above list is that there are far fewer mon ↓ NPs than mon ↑. What decreasing ones there are have traditionally been treated as negations of increasing quantifiers (*no man* of *a man*, *few men* of *many men* or perhaps of *several men*). We can state a general relationship between mon ↑ and mon ↓ quantifiers, once we define ~ Q and Q ~:

DEFINITION. Given a quantifier Q on E, define new quantifiers
$$\sim Q = \{X \subseteq E \mid X \notin Q\}$$
$$Q \sim = \{X \subseteq E \mid (E - X) \in Q\}$$

Note that $\sim Q$ and $Q \sim$ are sieves just in case Q is a sieve and that if Q is not a sieve, then $Q = Q\sim$. $\sim Q$ corresponds to negating a sentence beginning with Q, (e.g. *not one man ran*). $Q\sim$ corresponds to negating the VP following Q (e.g., *one man didn't run*).

PROPOSITION. *Negation reverses monotonicity.*
1. If Q is mon ↑, then $\sim Q$ and $Q\sim$ are mon ↓.
2. If Q is mon ↓, then $\sim Q$ and $Q\sim$ are mon ↑. Further, $\sim \sim Q = Q = Q\sim \sim$. (See C9 in Appendix C.)

It follows that we can think of any monotone decreasing quantifier as $\sim Q$ for some mon ↑ Q. This, together with our discussion of weak determiners in section 4.6, allows us to consider the following potential language universal:

U5. *Monotonicity correspondence universal.* There is a simple MP which expresses the mon ↓ quantifier $\sim Q$ if and only if there is a simple NP with a weak non-cardinal determiner which expresses the mon ↑ quantifier Q.

This potential universal suggests the following relationship between English determiners:

mon $\downarrow$ Q	Corresponding mon $\uparrow$ Q
no man / men ⎫ neither man ⎭	some man(men) a man
few men	many men several men
nobody	some person, etc.

This proposal would predict that no language would have basic determiners meaning *not most*, *not every*, or *not the* since *most*, *every*, and *the* are strong. It would also predict that no language would have a basic determiner meaning *not (at least) two* since *two* is a cardinal determiner. Thus, such a proposal, if correct, puts real constraints on the set of basic determiners in a human language. Another significant aspect of this kind of universal is that we can talk in semantic (i.e., model theoretic) terms. We do not have to assume, for example, that *few* is the same as *not many* at any syntactic level.

4.8   A monotonicity constraint on simple NPs

There do not seem to be any simple NPs in English which could not conceivably be analyzed as monotone quantifiers or as a conjunction of monotone quantifiers. For example, if we claim that *a few men* has a non-monotone reading, we could say that it expresses the same quantifier as the conjunction *some men but not many men*. Similarly, a non-monotone reading of *two men* could be the same as *at least two men but at most two men*. (Semantically, conjoining NPs is simply intersection of quantifiers and will be taken up in section 4.) These observations suggest the following candidate for a universal:

> **U6.** *Monotonicty constraint*. The simple NPs of any natural language express monotone quantifiers or conjunctions of monotone quantifiers.

This proposed universal has the effect of ruling out many logically possible quantifiers as simple NP denotations. Examples are the denotations of *an even number of men*, *exactly three or exactly five men*, *all but one man*. It seems unlikely that any natural language would have a basic determiner meaning *an even number of*, *exactly three* or *exactly five*, or *all but one*.

If the monotonicity constraint is true, it seems to be more than an arbitrary restriction on the quantifiers found in human languages. Rather, it seems to be related to the way people understand quantified sentences. We take this up in the next section.

Recall our discussion of strong and weak determiners from section 4.6. **D** is positive strong just in case $A \in \|\mathbf{D}\|(A)$ is always true. It does not follow from this that **D** is monotone increasing. For example, we could define an artificial determiner D which was strong but not mon $\uparrow$ by

$$\|D\|(A) \; \{X \mid \text{Card } (X - A) \text{ is finite and even}\}.$$

Then $A \in \|D\|(A)$ and if $a, b \in A$, $a \neq b$ then $A - \{a, b\} \in \|D\|(A)$ but $(A - \{a\}) \notin \|D\|(A)$. However, there do not seem to be any such determiners that arise in natural language. This leads us to propose another possible universal:

> **U7.** *Strong determiner constraint*. In natural languages, positive strong determiners are monotone increasing. Negative strong determiners are monotone decreasing.

This proposal makes some predictions as to the logical behavior of strong determiners. To see just what they are, we note the following proposition:

PROPOSITION. If D is positive strong and monotone increasing, then for any model $M = \langle E, \| \; \| \rangle$ and any sets A, B in M: $B \in \|D\|(A \cap B)$.

If D is negative strong and monotone decreasing, then we have $B \notin \|D\|(A \cap B)$. (Cf. C8 in Appendix C.)

Thus, U7 predicts that if D is a (natural language) positive strong determiner, then any sentence of the form

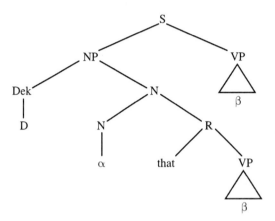

should be judged valid (since its translation is true in M just in case $\|\beta'\| \in \|D (\alpha' \wedge \beta')\|$, which is equivalent to $\|\beta'\| \in \|D\|(\|\alpha'\| \cap \|\beta'\|)$.) This prediction is borne out by the following examples:

(32) $\begin{bmatrix} \text{Most} \\ \text{Both} \\ \text{The three} \end{bmatrix}$ men that love Mary, love Mary.

(33) $\begin{Bmatrix} \text{Every} \\ \text{The} \end{Bmatrix}$ man that loves Mary, loves Mary.

The corresponding prediction for negative strong determiners is that such sentences are judged contradictory, as in (34):

(34) Neither man that loves Mary, loves Mary.

When one carries out the same test with weak determiners, the results are odd and certainly not universally valid, as the examples in (35) and (36) show:

(35) $\begin{bmatrix} \text{(a) No man} \\ \text{(b) Some man} \\ \text{(c) (At least) three men} \\ \text{(d) Exactly three men} \end{bmatrix}$ that love(s) Mary, love(s) Mary.

(36) $\begin{bmatrix} \text{(a) Many men} \\ \text{(b) Few men} \\ \text{(c) A few men} \end{bmatrix}$ that love Mary, love Mary.

We judge the examples in (35) to be logically equivalent to those in (37), but it is not clear that the same holds for (36) and (38):

(37) $\begin{cases} \text{(a) No man} \\ \text{(b) Some man} \\ \text{(c) At least three men} \\ \text{(d) Exactly three men} \end{cases}$ love(s) Mary.

(38) $\begin{cases} \text{(a) Many men} \\ \text{(b) Few men} \\ \text{(c) A few men} \end{cases}$ love Mary.

Accepting these equivalences amounts to asserting that weak determiners satisfy the *intersection condition*.

DEFINITION. D satisfies the intersection condition if for all models $M = \langle E, \| \ \| \rangle$ and all X, $A \subseteq E$, $X \in \|D\|(A)$ iff $X \in \|D\|(A \cap X)$.

PROPOSITION. Strong determiners do not satisfy the intersection condition. (Cf. C6.)

The second author is inclined to think that weak determiners *all* satisfy the intersection condition, but it violates the first author's intuitions for *many* and *few*. It would say, for example, that *many* could not mean something approximately like the following in a model M containing 1,000 men:

$$\|D\|(A) = \{X \subseteq E \mid |X \cap A| \ge \tfrac{3}{10}|A| \quad \text{and} \quad |X \cap A| \ge 30\}.$$

Here the number that counts as "many" gets smaller the smaller A is, but nothing smaller than thirty ever counting as "many" men. If *many* is interpreted in this way in some model, and if thirty-five men love Mary in the model, *then Many men love Mary* is false, but *Many men that love Mary, love Mary* is true.

The issue hangs on the one's interpretation of the fixed context constraint in relation to relative clause constructions. It can probably only be resolved by working out a (Kamp-like?) theory of the vagueness to superimpose on our treatment, and seeing which interpretation of the constraint provides the smoother theory. (This same issue comes up in deciding whether *many* is persistent, as defined in the next section.)

Sentences involving determiners that satisfy the intersection condition can be expressed, up to logical equivalence, in a number of ways, due to the following facts.

PROPOSITION. If D is a determiner satisfying the intersection condition, then for any $A, B \subseteq E$,
(1) $B \in \|D\|(A)$ *iff* $E \in \|D\|(A \cap B)$
(2) $B \in \|D\|(A)$ *iff* $A \in \|D\|(B)$

(Cf. Appendix C, C4, and C5 for proofs.)

The right hand of the first biconditional corresponds to the semantics for the there is/are sentences, as in (37'). The righthand side of (2) corresponds to switching the verb and noun as in (37"):

(37')
    There is/are $\begin{cases} \text{(a) no man} \\ \text{(b) some man} \\ \text{(c) at least three men} \\ \text{(d) exactly three men} \end{cases}$ that love(s) Mary.

(37")   (a) No one that loves Mary ⎫ is a man.
        (b) Someone that loves Mary ⎭

        (c) At least three people that love Mary ⎫ are men.
        (d) Exactly three people that love Mary ⎭

The proposition predicts that corresponding sentences in (37), (37'), and (37") are equivalent. And, as above, the equivalence of the sentences in (38), (38'), and (38") is much less clear:

(38')
                    ⎧(a) many men ⎫
        There are ⎨(b) few men   ⎬ that love Mary.
                    ⎩(c) a few men ⎭

(38")
        ⎧(a) Many people that love Mary ⎫
        ⎨(b) Few people that love Mary   ⎬ are men.
        ⎩(c) A few people that love Mary ⎭

4.9   Processing quantified statements

An objection that could be leveled against Montague's treatment of NPs is that it would seem to make checking the truth of a simple sentence like *John runs* well nigh impossible. For, the argument might go, one would first have to "calculate" the denotation of $[John]_{NP}$—namely, the family of all sets X to which John belongs—and then see if the set of runners is one of these sets. But this clearly corresponds in no way to the reasoning process actually used by a native speaker of English.

Using the monotonicity constraint, we wish to show that something very much like an intuitive checking procedure is always possible for simple NPs. The procedure rests on the notion of *witness sets*:

DEFINITION. A *witness set* for a quantifier $D(A)$ living on A is any subset w of A such that $w \in D(A)$.

EXAMPLES. The only witness set for ‖*John*‖ is {John}. A witness set for ‖*a woman*‖ is any nonempty set of women. A witness set for ‖*most women*‖ is any set of women which contains most women. A witness set for ‖*few women*‖ consists of any set of women which contains only a few women. A witness set for ‖*(exactly) two women*‖ is any set of exactly two women.

PROPOSITION. Let w range over witness sets for the quantifier $D(A)$ living on A.
   (i) If $D(A)$ is mon $\uparrow$, then for any X, $X \in D(A)$ iff $\exists w[w \subseteq X]$.
   (ii) If $D(A)$ is mon $\downarrow$, then for any X, $X \in D(A)$ iff $\exists w[(X \cap A) \subseteq w]$.

(Cf. C11 in Appendix C for the proof.)
We can paraphrase this proposition as follows:

To evaluate $X \in D(A)$ do the following:
1. Take some subset w of A which you know to be in $D(A)$.
2. (i) For mon $\uparrow$ $D(A)$, check $w \subseteq X$.
   (ii) For mon $\downarrow$ $D(A)$, check $(X \cap A) \subseteq w$.
3. If there is such a w, the sentence is true. Otherwise it is false.

These procedures are not totally unlike some computational models for the verification of quantified sentences which have been suggested in the psychological literature. (See Clark 1976.)

We imagine it might be possible to design experiments which check the predictions of a psychological theory based on witness sets. For example, we predict that response latencies for verification tasks involving decreasing quantifiers would be somewhat greater than for increasing quantifiers, and that for the non-monotone it would be still greater. These predictions are based on the complexity of the checking procedure we have suggested above.

> EXAMPLE. Imagine a yard full of animals, including some dogs. Let us imagine a dog Fido that looks like a spaniel, but we're not sure if it is a spaniel. Imagine deciding which of the following are true:
> a. Fido is in the yard.
> b. Some spaniels are in the yard.
> c. No spaniel is in the yard.
> d. Exactly one spaniel is in the yard.
> e. An even number of spaniels are in the yard.

In all of these, the set $X = \{y \mid y$ is in the yard$\}$ is the set X denoted by the VP. For (a), the only witness set is $\{$Fido$\}$. We check to see if Fido $\in X$. For (b), we need to find some non-empty set w of spaniels, $w \subseteq X$. For (c), the only witness set is ϕ. We must see if $X \cap \|$spaniels$\| = \phi$. This will cause us no problems if there is a clearcut spaniel in the yard, for then clearly $X \cap \|$spaniels$\| \neq \phi$, so (c) is false whether Fido is in the yard or not. If Fido $\in X$ but no clearcut spaniel is in X, then we won't be able to compute the truth or falsity of (c) without deciding whether Fido is a spaniel. For (d), we must do two things to see that it is true: find some spaniel in X and show that there is at most one spaniel in X. This corresponds to breaking down *exactly one spaniel* into *some spaniel* and *at most one spaniel*. For (e), we must decide whether $X \cap \|$spaniels$\|$ contains an even number of things. We will not be able to do this without deciding whether Fido is a spaniel.

There is another distinction, related to monotonicity, that seems to affect processing of quantifiers and is bound to interact with processing requirements by montonicity:

> DEFINITION. A determiner D is *persistent* if for all $M = \langle E, \| \ \| \rangle$, and all $A \subseteq B \subseteq E$, if $X \in \|D\|(A)$, then $X \in \|D\|(B)$. (On the other hand, D is *anti-persistent* if $A \subseteq B \subseteq E$ and $X \in \|D\|(B)$ implies $X \in \|D\|(A)$.)

The idea here is that if D is persistent, then once you see that $X \in \|D\|(A)$ you know that $X \in \|D\|(B)$ for any set B that contains A. For example, if $B = \{x \mid x$ is a man that left the party before 10 PM$\}$ and $A = \{x \mid x$ a man that left the party before 9 PM$\}$, then $A \subseteq B$ so that a persistent determiner D:

(39) D men that left the party before 9 PM went home

will imply

(40) D men that left the party before 10 PM went home.

Logical (and mathematical) examples of persistent determiners are *some*, *at least n*, (*infinitely many*, *uncountably many*). Other determiners that seem to function as persistent determiners are *several* and *many*(??). For anti-persistent determiners D, the implication goes the other way, from (40) to (39). These include *every*, *no*, *few*(?), *at most n*, and *finitely many*. Other determiners are neither persistent nor anti-persistent.

A glance at the table in appendix D suggests another proposition for consideration as a universal. (See also C7 in Appendix C.)

U8. *Persistent determiner universal.* Every persistent determiner of human language is mon ↑ and weak.

Since it is not difficult to construct artificial determiners which fail U8 (Cf. Appendix C), this would, if true, provide another constraint on the class of human languages among the class of all possible languages.

In terms of witness sets, persistence works as follows. If D is persistent and if w is a witness set for $D(A)$, then w will be a witness set for any B that contains A ($A \subseteq B$). It seems clear that between monotone quantifiers D_1, D_2, which are otherwise comparable, if D_1 is persistent and D_2 isn't, then D_1 should be easier to process, especially when the universe is too large to perceive all at once, since a witness set for $D_1(B)$ maybe able to be found on the basis of some manageable $A \subseteq B$. Continuing the above examples, it should be easier to verify (f) than (g), since any witness set for (g) must contain most dogs in the yard, whereas for (f) it might suffice to have a witness set for *several dogs in the yard which are close enough to see.*

    f. Several dogs in the yard are spaniels.
    g. Most dogs in the yard are spaniels.

Persistent determiners were introduced in Barwise (1978). Ladusaw (1979) has put them to excellent use in his discussions of polarity items. They turn out to be important for the logic of perception (Barwise 1981).

4.10   Monotonicity and NP-conjunction

An advantage of treating natural language NPs as generalized quantifiers is that we can treat NP-conjunction (instances of NP *and* NP, NP *or* NP, NP *but* NP, etc.) directly. "NP$_1$ *and* NP$_2$" denotes the intersection of ||NP$_1$|| and ||NP$_2$||; "NP$_1$ *or* NP$_2$" denotes the union of the two quantifiers. We may similarly extend the logic **L(GQ)** to **L(GQ$_2$)** by adding a formation rule R8:

R8. If Q_1 and Q_2 are quantifiers, so are $(Q_1 \wedge Q_2)$, $(Q_1 \vee Q_2)$.

The corresponding semantic rule S13:

S11. $\|Q_1 \wedge Q_2\| = \|Q_1\| \cap \|Q_2\|$, $\|Q_1 \vee Q_2\| = \|Q_1\| \cup \|Q_2\|$.

This logic allows us to represent new quantifiers but provides no real strengthening of the logic, since

$$(Q_1 \wedge Q_2)\hat{x}[\varphi\,(x)] \leftrightarrow Q_1\hat{x}[\varphi(x)] \wedge Q_2\hat{x}[\varphi(x)]$$
$$(Q_1 \vee Q_2)\hat{x}[\varphi\,(x)] \leftrightarrow Q_2\hat{x}[\varphi(x)] \vee Q_2\hat{x}[\varphi(x)]$$

are logically valid. That is, we cannot express any sentences that were not already represented, up to *logical* equivalence.

Not all instances of NP-conjunction are acceptable in English. In general, it seems to be difficult to use *and* or *or* between two NPs if they represent quantifiers of different monotonicity. Examples are given in(32):

(32)   a. *increasing + increasing*: a man and three women, several men and a few women, the professor or some student, most men and any woman (could lift this piano)
      b. *decreasing + decreasing*: no man and few women (could lift this piano), no violas or few violins (are playing in tune)

c. *mixed*: *John and no woman, *few women and a few men (could lift this piano), *two violas and few violins (are playing in tune).[10]

The unacceptability of the mixed conjunctions is not simply due to the peculiarity of the message which would be expressed by sentences containing them. There are acceptable sentential conjunctions which would express the same proposition:

(33) a. John was invited and no woman was, so he went home alone again.
     *John and no woman was invited, so he went home alone again.

    b. Few mathematicians have worked on natural language conjunction and a few linguists have—so I don't think you have the right to make these unfounded statements.
     *Few mathematicians and a few linguists have worked on natural language conjunction . . .

    c. When two violas are playing in tune and few violins are, Berlioz begins to sound like Penderecki.
     *When two violas and few violins are playing in tune, . . .

This restriction on NP-conjunction could be related to the preservation of properties of monotonicity. The conjunction or disjunction of two increasing quantifiers will be another increasing quantifier and similarly for the decreasing quantifiers. The conjunction or disjunction of an increasing and decreasing quantifier will normally not be a monotone quantifier. For example, the putative conjunction *John and no woman* would have the denotation represented in (34):

(34) $\{X \mid \text{John} \in X \text{ and } X \cap \{\text{woman}\} = \phi\}$.

This would, for example, contain the set {John} but not all of its supersets or subsets.

Not all instances of NP-conjunction demand monotonicity in the way we have suggested. It is possible to conjoin an increasing and a decreasing quantifier with *but*, as illustrated in (35):

(35) a. John but no woman was invited.

    b. Few mathematicians but $\begin{Bmatrix} \text{a few} \\ \text{many} \end{Bmatrix}$ linguists have worked on natural language conjunction.

    c. Two violas but $\begin{Bmatrix} \text{few} \\ \text{no} \end{Bmatrix}$ violins are playing in tune.

In fact, in order to use *but* in this way, it seems necessary or at least preferable to mix increasing and decreasing quantifiers. Compare the sentences in (36):

(36) a. *John but a woman $\begin{Bmatrix} \text{was} \\ \text{were} \end{Bmatrix}$ invited.

    b. *Few mathematicians but no linguists have worked on natural language conjunction.

    c. ?Two violas but three violins are playing in tune.

We assume that the interpretation of *but* is the same as that of *and* for the purpose of truth conditional semantics. However, there are important ways in which it behaves differently from *and*. Conjunction with *and* can be repeated indefinitely many times. This is not possible with *but*, no matter how one mixes the quantifiers:

(37) a. John and a woman and three children were invited.

    b. *John but no woman but three children were invited.

    c. *Few mathematicians but many linguists but no physicists have worked on natural language conjunction.

This lack of iteration might be related to the fact that monotonicity is not guaranteed for a mixed conjunction and, hence, that the verification procedure we have discussed might apply separately to each conjunct. It is interesting to note that similar peculiarities are true of more complex conjunctions that might be considered as mixed conjunctions.

(38)   a.   John and not Mary is invited to the party.[11]

b.   John and $\left\{ \begin{array}{l} \text{nobody else} \\ \text{no other man} \end{array} \right\}$ can keep the party going.

As with *but*, these kinds of NPs cannot be further conjoined with other NPs:

(39).   a.   *John and not Mary and not Helen is invited to the party.

b.   *John and no other man and Helen can keep the party going.

An extension of Fragment 1 to include the basic cases of conjunction of simple NPs can be found in Appendix A.

4.11   Negation of noun phrases and duals

Certain NPs in English may be preceeded by *not* when they occur in subject position, while others can't. Here are some data:

(40)   a.   Not every man left.
       b.   Not all men left.
       c.   Not a (single) man left.
       d.   Not one man left.
       e.   Not many men left.
(41)   a.   *Not each man left.
       b.   *Not some man left.
       c.   *Not John left.
       d.   *Not the man left.
       e.   (*) Not few men left.
       f.   *Not no man left.
       g.   ?*Not most men left.

Notice that this distribution cannot be explained *purely* in terms of the semantics of quantifiers, as comparison of (40a,b) with (41a) and of (40c) with (41b) shows. (One might try to explain the unacceptability of (41a,b) as having something to do with the preference of *some* and *each* for wide scope reading.) There are some semantic generalizations to be captured, however.

The first observation is that only mon $\uparrow$ quantifiers can be negated in this way. Recall our universal that to every mon $\downarrow$ simple NP α denoting a quantifier $\sim Q$, there corresponds a mon $\uparrow$ simple NP α' denoting the mon $\uparrow$ Q. Thus, to negate $[[\alpha]_{NP}[\beta]_{VP}]_S$ one could simply use $[[\alpha'][\beta]]_S$. For example, instead of saying (41e) or (41f), one could say *many men left* or *some men left*.

To see what is going on in (41c,d), we use the model-theoretic notion of the dual of a quantifier:

DEFINITION. The *dual* of a quantifier Q on E is the quantifier $\check{Q}$ defined by $\check{Q} = \{X \subseteq E \mid (E - X) \notin Q\}$—that is, $\check{Q} = \sim (Q\sim) = (\sim Q)\sim$. If $Q = \check{Q}$, then Q is called *self-dual*.

EXAMPLES. The dual of ‖some man‖ is ‖every man‖, and vice versa. On a finite set $A \subseteq E$ of odd cardinality, $\{X \subseteq E \mid X$ contains more than half $A\}$ is self-dual. For any $a \in E$, $\{X \subseteq E \mid a$

$\in X$} is self-dual. Hence, $\|\textbf{the 1 } \eta\|$ is always self-dual, when defined. For any Q, the dual of $\breve{Q}$ is the original Q. Also, if Q is mon $\uparrow$, so is $\breve{Q}$ (since $\breve{Q} = \sim Q\sim$ and two minuses make a plus, so to speak).

The following is clearly valid:

$\sim Q\hat{x}[\varphi(x)] \leftrightarrow \breve{Q}\hat{x}[\sim\varphi(x)]$.

As special cases of this we have the usual

$\sim \forall x\varphi \leftrightarrow \exists x \sim \varphi$

$\sim \exists x\varphi \leftrightarrow \forall x \sim \varphi$.

If Q is self-dual, then the above simplifies to

$\sim Q\hat{x}[\varphi(x)] \leftrightarrow Q\hat{x}[\sim \varphi(x)]$.

That is, we can push negations back and forth across self-dual quantifiers. Hence, there is no need to use any syntactic construction to show that negation has wide scope over quantification when the quantifier is self-dual.

These observations lead us to propose the following as a candidate for a language universal:

U9. *Constraint on negating self-dual and mon $\downarrow$ quantifiers.* If a language has a syntactic construction whose semantic function is to negate a quantifier, then this construction will not be used with NPs expressing mon $\downarrow$ or self-dual quantifiers.

Of the unacceptable determiners in (41), aside from (a) and (h) which we have already discussed, this constraint leaves only (g) unexplained:

(41)   g. ?*Not most men left.

The odd thing here is that there just isn't any way to express the intended sentence without using sentence negation:

(42)   It is not true that most men left.

(If *most* meant exactly the same as *more than half,* then (42) could be paraphrased by

(43)   At least half the men didn't leave

since the dual of $\|$More than half the η's$\|$ is $\|$At least half the η's$\|$.)

If $\|D\|$ is a determiner interpretation, we can define $\|\breve{D}\|(A) = \|D\|(A)$. For example, $\|\widecheck{some}\|$ = $\|$every$\|$ and $\|\widecheck{every}\|$ = $\|$some$\|$. We do not know exactly why the following should be true, but we can find no counterexamples to it, so propose it for consideration:

U10. *Dual quantifier universal.* If a natural language has a basic determiner for each of D and $\breve{D}$ then these are semantically equivalent to "some" and "every."

An apparent exception to U10 as stated is the pair *the 1, the 1.* In other words, *the 1* is self-dual when defined. But then this is not really an exception, since when *the 1* is defined it is semantically equivalent to both *some* and *every.*

In connection with U10 we would point out the following simple fact. It may have something to do with the reason U10 is true (if it is true):

PROPOSITION. If Q is monotone increasing, then $Q\hat{x}[\varphi(x)] \wedge \check{Q}\hat{x}[\psi(x)]$ implies $\exists\hat{x}[\varphi(x) \wedge \psi(x)]$. (Cf. C10 in Appendix C.)

An example of a pair of dual determiners from mathematics is "more than half" and "at least half." Some people consider "most" as synonomous with "more than half," but there is no basic determiner in English synonomous with "at least half." Another dual pair is "more than 75%" and "at least 25%." U10 would predict that no human language would have basic determiners for each element of such pairs. The proposed universal also predicts that of the sentences below, only (44a,b) could be paraphrased as D *men left* for some basic determiner D:

(44)   a. It is not true that some man didn't leave. (I.e., every man left.)
       b. It is not true that every man didn't leave. (I.e., some man left.)
       c. It is not true that most men didn't leave.
       d. It is not true that two men didn't leave.
       e. Not many men didn't leave.

Some people are tempted to express (44e) by (45)—

(45)   Quite a few men left—

which amounts to using "quite a few" as the dual of "many." However, faced with (46), they are not usually willing to paraphrase it by (47), which suggests that they are not consistent in treating "quite a few" and "many" as dual:

(46)   Not many men left.
(47)   Quite a few men didn't leave.

Also, faced with the following argument, which would be valid if "many" and "quite a few" were dual (by the above proposition), they judge it highly dubious:

> Many men voted for Carter.
> Quite a few men voted for Ford.
> _____
> Therefore some man voted for both Ford and Carter.

Thus, we see that "quite a few" and "many" are not consistently used as duals of each other. And, even if they were, it is unlikely that "quite a few" should be considered a basic determiner element.

5   Conclusion

In this paper we have focused attention on the semantics of English determiners and noun phrases, defined and illustrated a number of semantic properties of them, and proposed a number of possible universals. Ultimately, however, we are less concerned with the fate of these proposals, or even of the details of our semantic treatment of noun phrases and determiners, than with illustrating some general points about the analysis of natural language—points not always fully appreciated by linguists or logicians.

5.1 Semantics is part of a linguistic theory

Linguists often feel that a model-theoretic semantics is an appendage to a linguistic theory and that it will not further the linguist's aim of characterizing the class of possible human languages. Such a view suggests that the relationship between languages and models of the world has more to do with the world than with the structure of language. It might even claim that facts elucidated by a model-theoretic semantics are logically necessary facts and thus cannot possibly serve to separate the class of natural languages from the class of logically possible languages.

We believe that the results of section 4 show some ways in which this is mistaken. The confirmation of any of the universals presented there (or more refined versions of them) would invalidate such a view. None of the proposed universals is logically necessary, and several of them effect sharp reductions in the class of possible human languages.

Furthermore, it seems that such universals could be related to a psychological theory of language. The drastic reduction in the available interpretations of natural language determiners suggested by our proposed universals, hints at a theory of acquisition following Chomsky, in that children faced with the task of learning language need only consider a restricted set of possible determiner interpretations. Another relationship to a psychological theory is discussed in section 4.9, where it is suggested that the nature of determiner interpretations guarantees the availability of certain verification procedures.

We should emphasize that the psychological considerations have emerged from examination of certain formal set-theoretic properties of the interpretations of natural language determiners. We feel that this illustrates the possibility of basing psychological theories on research in model-theoretic semantics. It is a mistake to reject such research as irrelevant to psychological theories just because its relationship to a theory of language learning or use is not apparent on the surface. For example, it has been suggested that taking NP-denotations to be families of sets runs counter to any reasonable psychological theory. We believe that our further investigations of the structure of these families suggests otherwise.

Our discussion has concentrated on purely semantic distinctions among various kinds of determiners and noun phrases. While these semantic distinctions are often reflected in the syntax of sentences, there are no syntactic correlates to these distinctions in the structure of the noun phrases themselves. For example, the semantic weak/strong distinction is closely reflected in the acceptability of the "There is _____ " construction, but it is not reflected in the syntactic structure of the associated NPs "many men," "most men," et cetera. Similarly, the fact that an NP corresponds to a monotone increasing or decreasing quantifier is not reflected in the syntactic structure of "many men" or "few men" (although it is reflected in the arbitrary choice of basic lexical items).

The importance of this type of semantic analysis for a linguistic theory has rarely been emphasized—even in the literature which has adopted a model-theoretic approach toward semantics, such as Montague Grammar. Previous work, for example, has shown that the use of model-theoretic semantics allows us to capture semantic relationships between sentences without making the relationships explicit in the syntax. It is clear that, in the long run, understanding the relationship between syntax and semantics will be at least as important as, say, that between syntax and phonology. However, important as this is, we believe it is only a part of the role that semantics can play in linguistic theory, and we suggest that the study of semantics in its own right will be as important as the study of phonology or syntax.

5.2 Semantic intuitions

While it is seldom made explicit, it is sometimes assumed that there is some system of axioms and rules of logic engraved on stone tablets—that an inference in natural language is valid only if it can be formalized by means of these axioms and rules. In actuality, the situation is quite the reverse. The native speaker's judgments as to whether a certain inference is correct, whether the truth of the hypothesis implies the truth of the conclusion, is the primary evidence for a semantic theory in just the way that grammaticality judgments are used as primary evidence for a syntactic theory. We have used such judgments concerning inference in order to determine many aspects of the model-theoretic treatment we have provided. In particular, all of the properties of determiners and NPs we have used rest on such evidence.

Just as a syntactic theory must draw the boundaries around grammaticality in some way, so too with semantic theory and inference. For example, just which inferences involving "most" count as "logical" depends on just where one draws the lines. The raw data of speaker judgments may be represented differently within different theories. Nevertheless, our clues to the meaning of the string of sounds represented by "most," and the inferential uses to which it may be put, are not determined by any logic writ in stone but come only from the intuitions of native speakers. We have built one semantic intuition about determiners (the one captured by the determiner universal) directly into the semantics. Thus, "Most men run" is *logically equivalent* to "Most men are men and run" in our semantics. And, of course, just as with grammaticality judgments, there are some very clear cases and some for which it is difficult to get a definitive answer—as we saw at the end of section 4.8.

5.3   The role of translation and complexity of fragments

Like Montague in PTQ, we have used translation into a logic to induce a semantics on our formalization of a fragment of English. It has been pointed out many times in the literature, initially by Montague himself, that the intermediate language is a convenience, not a necessary stage in the interpretation of English. It would be easy enough to define the semantics directly on the syntactic component of the English fragment.

In studying Montague's fragment in PTQ and subsequent work in the same tradition, however, it is easy to get the impression that the model-theory per se is essentially trivial. It often appears from this work that the translation procedure must be more contentful since it is so complex. There are two reasons for this impression.

A theory may be trivial because it says so little that it is easy to understand it completely, or because it is so complicated that there is little known to say about it. The model theory that goes along with Montague's logic IL is trivial for the second reason. Montague packed so much into the semantics of his logic that it is extremely difficult to discover any very general facts about it. His reasons for doing this were, presumably, twofold. In the first place, he wanted his logic to be sufficiently expressive to use as a tool for showing that very large portions of English could be given a model-theoretic semantics. Secondly, Montague had an unflinching Platonistic attitude toward set theory which is deeply imprinted on his logic.

The reason Montague's translation procedure is more complex than necessary is that the syntax of his logic IL very directly reflects the semantic interpretation. Once one has mastered his symbolism, the model-theoretic interpretation can be read directly off the formulas of the logic in a straightforward manner. The situation can be visualized as a scale of 1 to 10, with the syntax of Montague's English fragment at 1, the model theory at 10. One could imagine interpolating a formal language anywhere in between. Montague chose to put his IL at about 9.5.

His decision has allowed researchers extending his work to concentrate their efforts on the translation relation of larger English fragments into IL, leaving the model theory largely untouched. This has been a fruitful approach, but it has had the unfortunate side effect of diverting attention away from the properties of the model theory.

A major lesson learned from over sixty years of work in model theory is that there are great insights to be gained by (temporarily) limiting the expressive power of your formal language (as with first-order logic) so that one has tools for studying the resultant models. By making the language less expressive, one obtains a non-trivial model theory with applications to those areas which happen to lie within the realm of the logic. Now that we have learned that it is possible to give a model-theoretic semantics for large portions of English, the time seems ripe to apply this lesson as a research strategy for natural language semantics.

The strategy has guided us in the work reported here. We have deliberately restricted ourselves to a very simple fragment of extensional English, concentrating on determiners and NPs. We have set up our logic so that the translation procedure is essentially trivial, concentrating our efforts on genuinely semantic issues. The potential contributions to the linguistic theory of determiners and noun phrases suggested in section 4 result from this attention to model-theoretic semantics. They would certainly not have been apparent had we studied translation—either ours or Montague's.

5.4   Logic as a part of linguistics

If our claims in sections 5.1 and 5.2 are correct, then the traditional logical notions of validity and inference are a part of linguistics—a conclusion not likely to comfort many logicians or linguists. The phenomenal success of first-order logic within mathematics has obscured—indeed, nearly severed—its ties with its origins in language. Except for tense and modal logic, research in model theory in the past twenty-five years has taken its problems almost entirely from pure mathematics, becoming ever more specialized and remote from language. Even the work in generalized quantifiers mentioned in the introduction is devoted almost exclusively to mathematical quantifiers, going out of its way to avoid mentioning possible applications to natural language. This same success of first-order logic within mathematics also fostered the mistaken idea, discussed in section 5.2, that the "laws of logic" are autonomous, perhaps part of mathematics, but not a property of language and language use.

It is here that Montague made his biggest contribution. To most logicians (like the first author) trained in model-theoretic semantics, natural language was an anathema—impossibly vague and incoherent. To us, *the* revolutionary idea in Montague's paper PTQ (and earlier papers) is the claim that natural language is not impossibly incoherent, as his teacher Tarski had led us to believe, but that large portions of its semantics can be treated by combining known tools from logic, tools like functions of finite type, the λ-calculus, generalized quantifiers, tense and modal logic, and all the rest.

Montague had a certain job that he wanted to do and used whatever tools he had at hand to do it. If the product he built looks a bit like a Rube Goldberg machine, well, at least it works pretty well. It proved its point and should lead others to explore natural language semantics further, while at the same time paying rigorous attention to its syntax. It is an exciting possibility, one that could lead to a revitalization of model theory and open up new domains for the construction of linguistic theories.

Appendix A. Additions to fragment 1

Fragment 2 incorporates *there* sentences and definite determiners following the ideas in section 4.6.

FRAGMENT 2. *Incorporation of there-sentences.*

The syntactic analysis we present is culled from Gazdar (1979) and Jenkins (1975). Add to the rules of Fragment 1:

SD 1.1   NP   → there
              [there]
SD 2.1   VP   → be NP
              [there]
SD 3.1 S→ NP   VP
              [there]   [there]

To the translation rules we add:

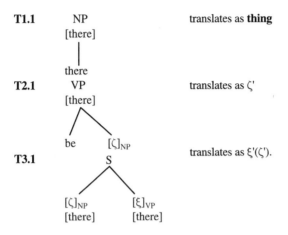

T1.1   NP   translates as **thing**
                [there]

                |

                there
T2.1   VP   translates as ζ'
                [there]

            be $[\zeta]_{NP}$
T3.1   S   translates as $\xi'(\zeta')$.

        $[\zeta]_{NP}$ $[\xi]_{VP}$
        [there]   [there]

It is important for our semantic analysis that only an NP follow *be* in the *there*-VP, and it is hoped that this feature of the analysis could be maintained in larger fragments that include such sentences as *there is a man in the garden* and *there are four people standing by the fountain*. The plausibility of such an analysis is argued for with a large number of examples by Jenkins (1975). Even Jenkins, however, does not consider the italicized strings in (1) to be NPs:

(1)   a. There are *two people sick/drunk*.
       b. There are *five cookies left*.

Indeed, they do not occur in all the places where one would expect NPs to be, as shown in the ungrammatical sentences in (2):

(2)   a. *Two people sick/drunk entered the room.
       b. ?*The cookies left were moldy.

However, they do show up in grammatical sentences after prepositions where the only reasonable analysis would show them to be NPs:

(3)   a. Among the people sick/drunk, were Bob and his wife.
       b. Of the cookies left, two were moldy.

While we do not understand the distribution of these strings, it does not seem unlikely that they are NPs which are somehow restricted in their distribution to *there*-sentences and certain other contexts.

Other problematic examples involve phrases such as *standing on the corner* (often referred to in the transformational literature as "reduced relative clauses") when they occur after a full relative clause. It is not normally possible to have such a sequence occurring within a single NP. This is shown by the ungrammatical example (4a), which is contrasted with the grammatical example (4b) with the same string in a *there*-sentence:

(4) a. *A girl [*who knows you*] [*standing on the corner*] waved to me as I went by in the bus.
     b. There is a girl who knows you standing on the corner.

A possible way out of this problem is to say that *standing on the corner* is a sentential modifier and hence not within the VP at all. This is supported by the fact that *standing on the corner* can also occur at the beginning of the sentence: *Standing on the corner there is a girl who knows you.* However, not all such "reduced relatives" may be explained away in this fashion. [Example] (5a) suggests that *a girl who knows you interested in this problem* is not an NP; (5b) shows that the string may occur in a *there*-sentence; (5c) shows that the reduced relative cannot occur at the beginning of the sentence:

(5) a. *I met a girl who knows you interested in this problem.
     b. There is a girl who knows you interested in this problem.
     c. *Interested in this problem, there is a girl who knows you.

It is not clear, however, whether there may not be other special NP positions in which these strings may nevertheless occur as NPs. Consider: *Of the girls who we know interested in this problem, Mary is by far the most likely to find a solution.*

Finally, we would expect that in a larger fragment the feature *there* on the VP would percolate up to higher VP-nodes in the manner suggested by Gazdar (1979) in order to account for sentences such as *there appear to be five men in the park.*

INCORPORATION OF DET OF NP
Add to the lexicon:
Det
[of] :*all, each, most, some, one, two, . . . , many, a few, few*

Add to the syntactic rules:
SD1.2 If ζ is a NP constructed with a definite determiner, then [of ζ]$_N$ is an SD.
SD1.3 NP → DetN   [of]
             [of] [of]

In order to translate this extended fragment, we must slightly enlarge the logic (thereby creating **L(GQ)**$_1$) by adding the following syntactic and semantic rules:

Syntax: if Q is a quantifier, then $\wedge$ Q is a set term.

Semantics: $\|\wedge Q\|$ is $\cap\|Q\|$.

The translation of the syntactically special determiners in the lexicon is the same as their translation in Fragment 1.

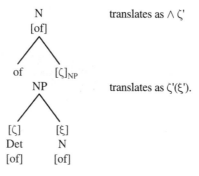

N   translates as $\wedge \zeta'$
[of]

of   [ζ]$_{NP}$
       NP   translates as $\zeta'(\xi')$.

[ζ]   [ξ]
Det   N
[of]   [of]

FRAGMENT 3. *NP-conjunction*

Add to the syntax of Fragment 1:

NP-conjunction
   (a) If α, β are of the form [ζ]_{NP} and [ξ]_{NP} where neither ζ or ξ is of the form [η]_{NP} *but*
       [χ]_{NP}, and the denotations of α, β induced by translation are monotone quantifiers of
       the same kind, then [α *and* β]_{NP} and [α *or* β]_{NP} are members of SD.
   (b) If α, β are of the form specified and denote monotone quantifiers of different kinds,
       then [α *but* β]_{NP} is a member of SD.[12]

We specify that the translation is into the language $\mathbf{L}(\mathbf{GQ_2})$ defined at the beginning of 4.10 and
add the following translation rule:

NP-conjunction

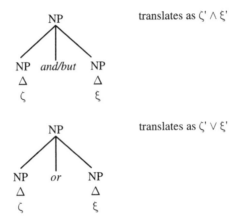

NP translates as $\zeta' \wedge \xi'$

NP translates as $\zeta' \vee \xi'$

Appendix B: Semantic postulates for few, most, and many

In the course of section 4 we discussed various semantic properties of the non-logical determiners *few*, *most*, and *many*, properties which are not insured by our definition of model in section 1.5. To guarantee that the formal semantics reflects the intuitions from English, we must restrict the class of all models to those which satisfy these properties. We refer to the formal versions as semantic postulates. They are not quite of the same character as the restrictions on models introduced by Montague in PTQ, for they are not expressed as sentences in our formal language but, rather, as set-theoretic conditions on the models themselves. The extent to which such semantic postulates can be captured syntactically may be discussed in a later paper.

Let $M = \langle E, \| \quad \| \rangle$. From section 4.2 we have the following:

SP1. **Most** is a positive strong determiner. That is, for every $A \subseteq E$, $A \in \|\mathbf{most}\|(A)$.

From 4.3 we have

SP2. **Most** and **many** are mon ↑, **few** is mon ↓. That is, for all $X, Y, A \subseteq E$:
   $X \subseteq Y, X \in \|\mathbf{most}\|(A)$ implies $Y \in \|\mathbf{most}\|(A)$
   $X \subseteq Y, X \in \|\mathbf{many}\|(A)$ implies $Y \in \|\mathbf{many}\|(A)$
   $Y \subseteq X, X \in \|\mathbf{few}\|(A)$ implies $Y \in \|\mathbf{few}\|(A)$.

If most people do X and most people do Y, then someone does both. This much seems clear from the meaning of "most." We can express this by:

SP3. If $A \neq 0$ then $\|\textbf{most}\|(A)$ is a sieve and, for, $X, Y \in \|\textbf{most}\|(A)$, $X \cap Y \neq \phi$.

If one wants to demand that *few men* be equivalent to *not many men* (or *not several men*), one can postulate one of:

SP4. (*optional*): $\|\textbf{Few}\| = \sim \|\textbf{many}\|$. I.e. for any A,
$$\|\textbf{few}\|(A) \sim = (\|\textbf{many}\|(A))$$
$$= \{X \subseteq E \mid X \notin \|\textbf{many}\|(A)\}$$
or: $\|\textbf{few}\|(A) = \sim \|\textbf{several}\|(A)$.

The persistence of *many* and anti-persistence of *few* discussed in section 4.7 was less clear than most of the above.

SP5. (*optional*): **few** is persistent **many** is anti-persistent. That is, for all $A \subseteq B \subseteq E$,
$$\|\textbf{few}\|(A) \subseteq \|\textbf{few}\|(B)$$
$$\|\textbf{many}\|(B) \subseteq \|\textbf{many}\|(A).$$
SP6. If $X \in \|\textbf{many}\|(A)$, then $X \neq \varnothing$.

This guarantees that if many men do something, then some man does it.

These are by no means all of the semantic properties that seem to be enjoyed by the determiners *most*, *many*, and *few*, but they are the ones that seem most clearly reflected in the semantic judgments of native English speakers.

Appendix C.   Some simple results about quantifiers and determiners

Until C12, we let $M = \langle E, \| \ \| \rangle$ be a fixed model. A *quantifier Q* on M is any set of subsets of E. Q is a *proper quantifier* or *sieve* if Q is non-empty and is not the set of all subsets of E. Q *lives on A*, where A is some subset of E, if for every $X \subseteq E$, $X \in Q$ iff $(X \cap A) \in Q$. ("iff" is an abbreviation for "if and only if.")

C1. PROPOSITION. If Q is a quantifier on M, and Q lives on A, then $A \in Q$ iff $E \in Q$.
PROOF. Since Q lives on A, $E \in Q$ iff $(E \cap A) \in Q$ but $E \cap A = A$. $\square$ ($\square$ marks the end of a proof.)

A quantifier Q is called the *principal filter* generated by B if

$$Q = \{X \subseteq E \mid B \subseteq X\}.$$

Note that the principal filter generated by B is a sieve unless $B = \varnothing$.

C2. PROPOSITION. If Q is the principal filter generated by B, then Q lives on A iff $B \subseteq A$.
PROOF. If $B \subseteq A$, then for any X the following are equivalent:
$X \in Q$
$B \subseteq X$
$B \subseteq (X \cap A)$ (since $B \subseteq A$)
$X \cap A \in Q$.
Thus Q lives on A. Now suppose Q lives on A and let us show $B \subseteq A$. Since $B \subseteq E$, $E \in Q$ so
$A \in Q$ by Cl. Thus $B \subseteq A$ by the definition of principal filter. $\square$

A determiner D is a *definite* determiner if for all $A \subseteq E$, $D(A)$ is such that, for any $A \in$ domain(D), $D(A)$ is a quantifier that lives on A. A determiner D is *proper* if $D(A)$ is defned for all

$A \subseteq E$ and, for some $A \subseteq E$, $D(A)$ is proper. Universal U.4 in section 4.4 implies that every natural language determiner is the restriction of a proper natural language determiner.

A determiner D is a *definite* determiner if for all $A \subseteq E$, $D(A)$ is a principal filter. D is *positive strong* if for every A, $A \in D(A)$.

C3. COROLLARY. Every definite determiner is positive strong.
PROOF. Since D is definite, $D(A)$ is the filter generated by some B. Since $D(A)$ lives on A, $B \subseteq A$ by C2. But then $A \in D(A)$ by the definition of principal filter. $\square$

A determiner D is *symmetric* if for all $A, B, B \in D(A)$ iff $A \in D(B)$. D satisfies the *intersection condition* if for all $A, B, B \in D(A)$ iff $B \in D(A \cap B)$. We will show that these two conditions are equivalent in C5.

PROPOSITION. If D satisfies the intersection condition, then for every $A, B \subseteq E$:
$B \in D(A)$ iff $E \in D(A \cap B)$.
PROOF. The following are equivalent:

$B \in D(A)$	
$(A \cap B) \in D(A)$	(since $D(A)$ lives on A)
$(A \cap B) \in D(A \cap (A \cap B))$	(the intersection condition)
$(A \cap B) \in D(A \cap B)$	$(A \cap B = A \cap (A \cap B))$
$E \in D(A \cap B)$	(C1 applied to $A \cap B$). $\square$

C5. COROLLARY. *D satisfies the intersection condition iff D is symmetric.*
PROOF. Assume D satisfies the intersection condition. Then $A \in D(B)$ iff $E \in D(A \cap B)$ by C4 but $B \in D(A)$ iff $E \in D(A \cap B)$ also by C4. Thus $A \in D(B)$ iff $B \in D(A)$. For the converse, assume D is symmetric. The following are then equivalent:

$B \in D(A)$	
$A \in D(B)$	(by symmetry)
$(A \cap B) \in D(B)$	(since $D(B)$ lives on B)
$B \in D(A \cap B)$	(by symmetry). $\square$

C6. THEOREM. Let D be a proper strong determiner. Then D does not satisfy the intersection condition and hence is not symmetric.
PROOF. To recall the definition of strong, D is *positive strong* if for all A, $A \in D(A)$. D is *negative strong* if for all A, $A \notin D(A)$. D is *strong* if D is positive strong or negative strong. Assume that D satisfies the intersection condition. We claim that if D is positive strong then for every A, $D(A)$ is the set of all subsets of E whereas if D is negative strong then for every A, $D(A)$ is empty. Thus if D is either positive or negative strong, then D is not proper. To prove our claim, note the following equivalences:

$B \in D(A)$ iff	$B \in D(A \cap B)$	(the $\cap$-condition)
iff	$(A \cap B) \in D(B)$	(symmetry, C5)
iff	$(A \cap B) \in D(A \cap B)$	(the $\cap$-condition again).

Thus if D is positive strong, $B \in D(A)$, for all A, B whereas if D is negative strong then $B \notin D(A)$, *for all A, B.* $\square$

A quantifier Q on M is *monotone increasing* (mon $\uparrow$) if for all $X, Y \subseteq E$, $X \in Q$, and $X \subseteq Y$ implies $Y \in Q$. A determiner D is mon $\uparrow$ if for all A; if $D(A)$ is defined, then $D(A)$ is mon $\uparrow$. This should not be confused with the notion of a *persistent* determiner, one such that for all $A, B \subseteq E$, if $A \subseteq B$, then $D(A) \subseteq D(B)$.

Here is an example of a determiner which is persistent but not mon $\uparrow$ or symmetric. Let E have at least two elements and define D by

$$D(A) = \{X \subseteq E \mid A \cap X \neq 0 \quad \text{and} \quad A - X \neq \emptyset\}.$$

That is, $D(A)$ means "some but not all of the things in A." It is easy to see that $A \subseteq B$ implies $D(A)$ $\subseteq D(B)$, so that D is persistent. However, D is not mon $\uparrow$ since $E \notin D(A)$ for all A. Since, for $0 \neq A \neq E$, $A \in D(E)$, this also shows that D is not symmetric.

In our persistent determiner universal U.8 in section 4.9 we proposed that all simple persistent determiners of human languages are mon $\uparrow$ and weak. In view of the following proposition (and C6), a stronger universal would be to assert that the simple persistent determiners of human languages are all symmetric—that is, satisfy the intersection condition. Our lack of clear-cut intuitions about which non-logical weak determiners satisfy the intersection condition prevents us from making this proposal.

C7. PROPOSITION. If D is persistent and symmetric, then D is mon $\uparrow$.
PROOF. Suppose $X \in D(A)$ and $X \subseteq Y$. We need to show $Y \in D(A)$. But $X \in D(A)$ implies $A \in D(X)$ by symmetry, so $A \in D(Y)$ by persistence and, hence, $Y \in D(A)$ by symmetry. $\square$

C8. PROPOSITION. (1) If D is positive strong and mon $\uparrow$, then for all A, $B \subseteq E$, $B \in D(A \cap B)$.
    (2) If D is negative strong and mon $\downarrow$, then $B \notin D(A \cap B)$.
PROOF. (1) $(A \cap B) \in D(A \cap B)$ since D is positive strong so $B \in D(A \cap B)$ since $A \cap B \subseteq B$. (2) is similar. $\square$

Recall the definitions of $Q\sim$ and $\sim Q$ from section 4.7 and $\breve{Q}$ from 4.11.

C9. PROPOSITION. (1) If Q is mon $\uparrow$, then $Q\sim$ and $\sim Q$ are mon $\downarrow$.
    (2) If Q is mon $\downarrow$, then $Q\sim$ and $\sim Q$ are mon $\uparrow$.
    (3) If Q is mon $\uparrow$, so is $\breve{Q}$.
PROOF. (1) Assume Q is mon $\uparrow$. First, suppose $Y \in (Q\sim)$ and $X \subseteq Y$. Then $(E - Y) \in Q$ and $(E - Y) \subseteq (E - X)$, so $(E - X) \in Q$, so $X \in (Q\sim)$. Now suppose $Y \in (\sim Q)$ and $X \subseteq Y$. But then $Y \notin Q$, so $X \notin Q$, so $X \in (\sim Q)$. (2) This is similar to (1). (3) This follows from (1) and (2) since $\breve{Q} = \sim(Q\sim)$. $\square$

C10. PROPOSITION. If Q is mon $\uparrow$, $A \in Q$ and $B \in \breve{Q}$, then $A \cap B \neq \emptyset$.
PROOF. Suppose $A \cap B = \emptyset$. Then $A \subseteq (E - B)$ so, by monotonicity, $(E - B) \in Q$. But then $B \in (Q\sim)$, so $B \notin \sim(Q\sim)$, a contradiction. $\square$

A *witness set* for a quantifier Q living on A is any subset w of A that is an element of Q.

C11. PROPOSITION. Let w range over witness sets for the quantifier Q that lives on A.
    (i) If Q is monotone increasing, then for any X, $X \in Q$ iff some w is a subset of X.
    (ii) If Q is monotone decreasing, then for any X, $X \in Q$ iff $X \cap A$ is contained in some w.
PROOF. (i) Assume that $X \in Q$. Then $X \cap A$ is in Q since Q lives on A, so we may take $X \cap A$ for w. Conversely, if $w \subseteq X$, then since $w \in Q$ and since Q is monotone increasing, $X \in Q$. (ii) If $X \in Q$, then $X \cap A$ is suitable. Conversely, if $(X \cap A) \subseteq w$, then since $w \in Q$ and Q is monotone decreasing, $X \cap A$ is in Q and hence $X \in Q$, since Q lives on A. $\square$

To conclude this appendix we return to some of the points made in section 1, especially in 1.2 and 1.3. We want to prove that, in our terminology, "most" and "more than half" must be treated as determiners, not as quantifiers. In other words, we want to prove that there is no way to define *most V's are U's* in terms of *most things x(... U ... V ... x ...).* To avoid problems of vagueness, we treat "more than half." For the proof, it will be convenient to first prove a weaker result—namely, that *more than half the V's are U's* cannot be defined in first-order logic. This result is probably somewhere in the literature, but we haven't been able to find it so present a proof. It is a routine application of the "Fraïssé method." To motivate the complexity of the proof, note that for any fixed upper bound K on the size of the universe E, there is a sentence φ_K that "works" for models of size $\leq K$, a giant disjunction of K formulas.

C12. THEOREM. Consider a first-order language L with equality and two unary predicate symbols **U**, **V**. There is no sentence φ of L so that in every finite model $M = \langle E, U, V \rangle$,

$$M \vDash \varphi \quad \text{iff} \quad \text{Card}(U \cap V) > \tfrac{1}{2}\text{Card}(V).$$

PROOF. We will prove more for the purposes of the next proof. Namely, for all natural numbers m and k with $k > 3m$, we construct two models $M_1 = \langle E, U_1, V \rangle$ and $M_2 = \langle E_2, V \rangle$ with the same domain E and same interpretation V of **V**, such that

(1) $U_1 \subseteq U_2 \subseteq V$.
(2) $2 \cdot \text{Card}(U_2) > \text{Card}(V) = 2m$, hence, $M_2 \vDash$ "More than half the V's are U's."
(3) $\text{Card}(V) = 2 \cdot \text{Card}(U_1)$, hence, $M_1 \nvDash$ "More than half the V's are U's."
(4) $\text{Card}(E) = k$.
(5) For any sentence φ of L with less than m quantifiers, $M_1 \vDash \varphi$ iff $M_2 \vDash \varphi$.

Ignoring condition (4), this will prove the theorem, for given a purported definition φ of "More than half the V's are U's," we apply this to some m greater than the number of quantifiers in φ and some $k \geq 3m$.

To construct M_1 and M_2 satisfying (1)–(5) we let E be any set of k objects, V a subset of E of size $2m$, U_2 a subset of V of size $m+1$, and U_1 a subset of U_2 of size m. Only (5) needs to be proved. Notice that if $n < m$, then $\text{Card}(E - V) \geq n$, $\text{Card}(V - U_1) \geq n$, and $\text{Card}(V - U_2) \geq n$, as well as $\text{Card}(U_1) \geq n$ and $\text{Card}(U_2) \geq n$. This fact allows us to prove (5) by proving the following stronger (6). Define for any formula φ, $c(\varphi) =$ number of quantifiers in $\varphi +$ number of free variables in φ.

(6) If $\varphi(x_1 \ldots x_l)$ is a formula with $c(\varphi) < m$, and if we have any one-one correspondence.

$$a_1 \leftrightarrow b_1$$
$$\cdot$$
$$\cdot$$
$$\cdot$$
$$a_e \leftrightarrow b_l$$

between elements of E satisfying $a_i \in U_1$ iff $b_i \in U_2$, and $a_i \in V$ iff $b_i \in V$, for all $i = 1, \ldots, \ell$, then $M_1 \vDash \varphi(a_1 \ldots a_l)$ if $M_2 \vDash \varphi(b_1 \ldots b_l)$. ((5) is the special case of (6) where $\ell = 0$.)

Stated this explicitly, the proof of (6) is quite easy—by induction on $c(\varphi)$. The point is that there is always enough room to extend the one–one correspondence one more step when you come to a quantifier. (Draw a picture.) □

C13. THEOREM. There is no way to define "More than half the V's" in terms of "More than half of all things" and the operations of first-order logic, even if one restricts attention to finite models.

PROOF. More explicitly, what we prove is the following. Let L be the first-order monadic language of C12 and introduce a new quantifier symbol Q. Let $L(Q)$ be the language which allows all the syntactic constructions of L plus, for each formula $\varphi(x)$ of $L(Q)$, $Qx[\varphi(x)]$ is a new formula of $L(Q)$. The semantics for Q is defined on finite models M by $M \vDash Qx[\varphi(x)]$ iff $\text{Card}\{a \mid M \vDash \varphi(a)\} > \tfrac{1}{2}\text{Card}(E)$.
What we prove is that there is no sentence φ of $L(Q)$ so that $M \vDash \varphi$ iff more than half the V's are U's. The intuitive idea is that if E is very large compared to U and V, then it will swamp out U and V in the language $L(Q)$. To make it precise, we will define a function $*$ from formulas ψ of $L(Q)$ to formulas ψ^* of L so that ψ is equivalent to ψ^* on models M where the gap between the size of V and that of E is great enough. Namely:

(P) For any formula $\psi(x_1 \ldots x_k)$ of $L(Q)$ and any model $M = \langle E, U, V \rangle$ where $U \subseteq V \subseteq E$ and $\text{Card}(E) \geq 2 \cdot (\text{Card}(V) + c(\psi))$

$$M \vDash \forall x_1 \ldots x_k[\psi(x_1 \ldots x_k) \leftrightarrow \psi^*(x_1 \ldots x_k)].$$

From (P) and the proof of C12 we can easily conclude the proof of C13. For suppose that φ is a sentence of $L(Q)$ which is true in a model M just in case more than half the V's are U's. Let

$m > c(\varphi)$ and let $k > 2(2m + c(\varphi))$. For this m and k let M_1, M_2 be models satisfying conditions (1)–(5) in the proof of C12. Thus $M_2 \vDash \sim \varphi$ but $M_1 \vDash \varphi$, by (2) and (3). But since Card $(E) = k > 2(2m + c(\varphi)) = 2(\text{Card }(V) + c(\varphi))$, Condition (P) implies that $M_1 \vDash$ $(\varphi \leftrightarrow \varphi^*)$, $M_2 \vDash (\varphi \leftrightarrow \varphi^*)$. But by (5), $M_1 \vDash \varphi^*$ iff $M_2 \vDash \varphi^*$, since φ^* is a first-order sentence with $c(\varphi^*) < m$. This is a contradiction (since $M_1 \vDash \varphi$ implies $M_1 \vDash \varphi^*$ implies $M_2 \vDash \varphi^*$ implies $M_2 \vDash \varphi$ but $M_2 \vDash \sim\varphi$).

Thus we need only define ψ^*, show that $c(\psi)$ $c(\psi^*)$, and prove (P). The definition of ψ^* is by recursion on ψ and only does things to the quantifier Q. Thus:

If ψ is atomic, then ψ^* is ψ.

If ψ is $\neg\theta$, $(\theta_1 \wedge \theta_2)$ or $\forall x[\theta]$, respectively, then ψ^* is $\neg(\theta^*)$, $(\theta^*_1 \wedge \theta^*_2)$ or $\forall x[\theta^*]$, respectively.

If ψ is $Qx\theta$ $(x, y_1 \ldots y_k)$, then ψ^* is $\forall x[V(x) \vee x = y_1 \vee \ldots \vee x = y_k \vee \theta^*(x, y_1 \ldots y_k)]$.

(I.e., ψ^* says that *every* $x \notin V \cup \{y_1 \ldots y_k\}$ satisfies $\theta^*(x, y_1 \ldots y_k)$.) To prove (P), one argues by induction on the length of ψ. The only nontrivial case is where ψ is of the form $Qx\theta(x, y_1 \ldots y_k)$. So suppose that (P) holds for θ, by induction, and let $M = \langle E,U,V \rangle$ be a model with Card $(E) \geq 2(\text{Card }(V) + c(\psi)) > 2(\text{Card }(V) + c(\theta))$.

First assume $\psi(a_1 \ldots a_k)$ holds in M—that is, more than half the b's in E satisfy $\theta(b, a_1 \ldots a_k)$. Since $k \leq c(\theta)$, and since $\frac{1}{2}$ Card $(E) >$ Card $(V) + c(\theta)$, at least one such b is not in $V \cup \{a, \ldots a_k\}$. But a trivial automorphism argument then shows that any $b' \notin V \cup \{a_1 \ldots a_k\}$ satisfies $\theta(b', a_1 \ldots a_k)$. By our inductive assumption, $\theta^*(b', a_1 \ldots a_k)$ holds for any such b'. In other words, $\psi^*(a_1 \ldots a_k)$ holds in M. The other half of the equivalence is easier. This proves (P) and hence the theorem. $\square$

After finishing this paper, we learned that a theorem related to Theorem C13 was proved by David Kaplan in 1965 but was never published. Extend the quantifier "More than half of all things" into the infinite following Rescher (1962) by defining $M \vDash Qx\phi$ to mean that the set of a such that $M \vDash \phi(a)$ has greater cardinality than its compliment. Kaplan showed that the relativized notion could not be defined from the unrelativized. This follows from C13. Kaplan's proof makes essential use of infinite structures. His proof is unpublished, but some other interesting results for this quantifier are contained in his abstracts Kaplan (1966).

Monotone quantifiers have been studied in model theory and generalized recursion theory for some time. See Barwise (1979) for references. The notion of persistence was introduced in Barwise (1978). The other notions are new here. We have included a few of the classic papers on generalized quantifiers in the references: Mostowski (1957), Lindstrom (1966), Keisler (1969). Other references can be found in Barwise (1978, 1979).

APPENDIX D

	Logical?	Always defined?	Always sieve when defined?	± Strong (s) or weak (w)	Definite?	Mon ↑, ↓ or neither	Simple dual?	Self-dual?	Persistent?	Anti-persistent?	Intersection condition (= symmetric)
NP's containing simple Det's											
1. Some/a	Yes	Yes	No	w	No	↑	(2)	No	Yes	No	Yes
2. Every/each/all	Yes	Yes	No	+s	No	↓	(1)	No	No	Yes	No
3. No	Yes	Yes	No	w	No	↓	No	No	No	Yes	Yes
4. (At least) 1, 2, 3, . . .	Yes	Yes	No	w	No	↑	No	No	Yes	No	Yes
5. The 1, 2, 3, . . .	Yes	No	Yes	+s	Yes	↑	The 1	The 1	No	No	No
6. Both	Yes	No	Yes	+s	Yes	↑	(1)	No	No	No	No
7. Neither	Yes	No	Yes	−s	No	↓	No	No	No	No	No
8. Most	No	Yes	No	+s	No	↑	No	No	?	No	No
9. Many/several	No	Yes	No	w	No	↑	No	No	No	No	?
10. Few	No	Yes	No	w	No	↓	No	No	No	Yes(?)	?
11. This/that	No	?	Yes	+s	Yes	↑	(11)	Yes	No	No	No
Other Det's											
12. A few	No	Yes	No	w	No	−?	No	No	?	No	?
13. Exactly 1, 2, 3, . . .	Yes	Yes	No	w	No	neither	No	No	No	No	Yes
14. At most 1, 2, 3, . . .	Yes	Yes	No	w	No	↓	No	No	No	Yes	Yes
15. More than half	No	Yes	No	+s	No	↑	(16)	No	No	No	No
16. At least half	No	Yes	No	+s	No	↑	(15)	No	No	No	No
17. Finitely many	Yes(?)	Yes	No	w	No	↓	No	No	No	Yes	Yes
18. Infinitely many	Yes(?)	Yes	No	w	No	↑	No	No	Yes	No	Yes
19. Open	No	Yes	No	w	No	↑	No	No	—	—	—
Proper names and pronouns											
20. John, he	—	Yes	Yes	+s	Yes	↑	(20)	Yes	—	—	—

Notes

1. This is proved formally in Theorem C13 of Appendix C.

2. Throughout this paper we use "determiner" to refer to a wide class of syntactic elements which also include what are sometimes called predeterminers, postdeterminers, numerals, and so on. A more detailed investigation may well show that some of these finer distinctions are necessary.

3. For example, a number theorist interested in prime numbers will use a measure that "lives on" the set of primes so that (4) would be false. More common measures which do not give special weight to primes will make (4) true. The notion of "lives on" will be defined below.

4. Kamp's proposal is basically to evaluate a sentence with respect to a class of models, rather than a single model.

5. For each of (19) and (20) there are alternate derivations of the same SD which do not use the quantification rule. In the translation defined below, these alternate derivations will translate, respectively, as:

most (**men**)$\hat{x}$[**some**(**woman**)$\hat{y}$[**kiss** (x, y)]]

~ [**many**(**men**)$\hat{x}$[**see** $(x, \mathbf{h})$]]].

The unlikelyhood of interpreting (6) with this particular scope relation between *not* and *many* is discussed in section 4.11.

6. The notion of simple NP is well defined only within the context of a given syntactic analysis. For example, not every analysis will treat *a few* as a single determiner element.

7. Note that this is different from claiming that John exists. We might assume that the model includes some things which do not actually exist. The set of things that exist is a subset of the set of things that there are (in the model).

8. In applying this test, we must make sure that we do not violate our assumption of fixed context.

9. It might be objected that *most Republicans entered the race early* does not entail *most Republicans entered the race* since the former is often used in context to mean *most Republicans who entered the race entered it early*. This is an example of the violation of the fixed context assumption. Clearly the NP *most Republicans* corresponds to different quantifiers in different contexts. We are interested at present in isolating the properties of the quantifiers themselves rather than the complex relationship between NPs, quantifiers and context.

10. Some speakers seem to feel that not all mixed conjunctions with *and* deserve a full star, particularly if the conjuncts are not simple NPs: *John has invited at least five women and at most four men to the party, many of the men and at most six of the women have failed the exam.* We have no explanation for why there should be variation on the judgments in these cases.

11. Apparently *not Mary* should not be considered as an NP since it cannot occur alone in an NP position:

*Not Mary is invited to the party.

12. These rules do not meet the requirements of autonomous syntax—that is, they use information about the semantic interpretation of constituents in order to define syntactic well-formedness. There are, of course, equivalent formulations in which the category NP is subdivided in the syntax according to the kind of quantiifier denoted (a species of autonomy-preserving treatment often found in Montague grammar). We believe that it might also be possible to allow free generation of conjoined NPs and design a semantic filter (cf. Chomsky) which would rule out certain of the conjunctions as semantically unacceptable.

24

HANS REICHENBACH

The Tenses of Verbs

A particularly important form of token-reflexive symbol is found in the tenses of verbs. The tenses determine time with reference to the time point of the act of speech—that is, of the token uttered. A closer analysis reveals that the time indication given by the tenses is of a rather complex structure.

Let us call the time point of the token the *point of speech*. Then the three indications—"before the point of speech," "simultaneous with the point of speech," and "after the point of speech"—furnish only three tenses; since the number of verb tenses is obviously greater, we need a more complex interpretation. From a sentence like 'Peter had gone' we see that the time order expressed in the tense does not concern one event, but two events, whose positions are determined with respect to the point of speech. We shall call these time points the *point of the event* and the *point of reference*. In the example, the point of the event is the time when Peter went; the point of reference is a time between this point and the point of speech. In an individual sentence like the one given, it is not clear which time point is used as the point of reference. This determination is rather given by the context of speech. In a story, for instance, the series of events recounted determines the point of reference which in this case is in the past, seen from the point of speech; some individual events lying outside this point are then referred, not directly to the point of speech, but to this point of reference determined by the story. The following example, taken from W. Somerset Maugham's *Of Human Bondage*, may make these time relations clear:

> But Philip ceased to think of her a moment after he had settled down in his carriage. He thought only of the future. He had written to Mrs. Otter, the *massière* to whom Hayward had given him an introduction, and had in his pocket an invitation to tea on the following day.

The series of events recounted here in the simple past determine the point of reference as lying before the point of speech. Some individual events, like the settling down in the carriage,

Hans Reichenbach (1947) The tenses of verbs, *The Elements of Symbolic Logic*, section 51: 287–298. Reprinted by permission of Maria Reichenbach.

the writing of the letter, and the giving of the introduction, precede the point of reference and are therefore related in the past perfect.

Another illustration for these time relations may be given by a historical narrative, a quotation from Macaulay:

> In 1678 the whole face of things had changed . . . eighteen years of misgovernment had made the . . . majority desirous to obtain security for their liberties at any risk. The fury of their returning loyalty had spent itself in its first outbreak. In a very few months they had hanged and half-hanged, quartered and emboweled, enough to satisfy them. The Roundhead party seemed to be not merely overcome, but too much broken and scattered ever to rally again. Then commenced the reflux of public opinion. The nation began to find out to what a man it had intrusted without conditions all its dearest interests, on what a man it had lavished all its fondest affection.

The point of reference is here the year 1678. Events of this year are related in the simple past, such as the commencing of the reflux of public opinion, and the beginning of the discovery concerning the character of the king. The events preceding this time point are given in the past perfect, such as the change in the face of things, the outbreaks of cruelty, the nation's trust in the king.

In some tenses, two of the three points are simultaneous. Thus, in the simple past, the point of the event and the point of reference are simultaneous, and both are before the point of speech; the use of the simple past in the above quotation shows this clearly. This distinguishes the simple past from the present perfect. In the statement 'I have seen Charles' the event is also before the point of speech, but it is referred to a point simultaneous with the point of speech; that is, the points of speech and reference coincide. This meaning of the present perfect may be illustrated by the following quotation from Keats:

> Much have I traveled in the realms of gold,
> And many goodly states and kingdoms seen;
> Round many western islands have I been
> Which bards in fealty to Apollo hold.

Comparing this with the above quotations we notice that here obviously the past events are seen not from a reference point situated also in the past, but from a point of reference which coincides with the point of speech. This is the reason that the words of Keats are not of a narrative type but affect us with the immediacy of a direct report to the reader. We see that we need three time points even for the distinction of tenses which, in a superficial consideration, seem to concern only two time points. The difficulties which grammar books have in explaining the meanings of the different tenses originate from the fact that they do not recognize the three-place structure of the time determination given in the tenses.[1]

We thus come to the following tables, in which the initials 'E', 'R', and 'S' stand, respectively, for "point of the event," "point of reference," and "point of speech," and in which the direction of time is represented as the direction of the line from left to right:

Past Perfect	*Simple Past*	*Present Perfect*
I had seen John	I saw John	I have seen John
$E \quad R \quad S$	$R,E \quad S$	$E \qquad S,R$
Present	*Simple Future*	*Future Perfect*
I see John	I shall see John	I shall have seen John
S,R,E	$S,R \qquad E$	$S \qquad E \qquad R$

In some tenses, an additional indication is given concerning the time extension of the event. The English language uses the present participle to indicate that the event covers a certain stretch of time. We thus arrive at the following tables:

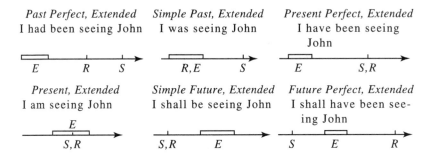

The extended tenses are sometimes used to indicate, not duration of the event, but repetition. Thus we say 'women are wearing larger hats this year' and mean that this is true for a great many instances. Whereas English expresses the extended tense by the use of the present participle, other languages have developed special suffixes for this tense. Thus the Turkish language possesses a tense of this kind, called *muzari*, which indicates repetition or duration, with the emphasis on repetition, including past and future cases. This tense is represented by the diagram

Turkish Muzari
görürüm

$$\underset{S,R}{\underline{E\quad E\quad E\quad E\quad E\quad E}} \longrightarrow$$

An example of this tense is the Turkish word "görürüm," translatable as 'I usually see'. The syllable "gör" is the root meaning 'see', "ür" is the suffix expressing the muzari, and "üm" is the suffix expressing the first person 'I'.[2] The sentence 'I see' would be in Turkish "görüyorum"; the only difference from the preceding example is given by the inflection "üyor" in the middle of the word, expressing the present tense. The Greek language uses the *aorist* to express repetition or customary occurrence in the present tense. The aorist, however, is originally a nonextended past tense and has assumed the second usage by a shift of meaning; in the sense of the extended tense, it is called *gnomic aorist*.[3]

German and French do not possess extended tenses but express such meanings by special words, such as the equivalents of 'always', 'habitually', and so on. An exception is the French simple past. The French language possesses here two different tenses, the *imparfait* and the *passé défini*. They differ insofar as the *imparfait* is an extended tense, whereas the *passé défini* is not. Thus we have

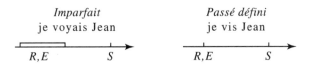

We find the same distinction in Greek, the Greek imperfect corresponding to the French imparfait, and the Greek aorist, in its original meaning as a past tense, corresponding to the French passé défini. Languages which do not have a passé défini sometimes use another tense in this meaning; thus Latin uses the present perfect in this sense (historical perfect).

We may add here the remark that the adjective is of the same logical nature as the present participle of a verb. It indicates an extended tense. If we put the word 'hungry', for instance, in the place of the word 'seeing' in our tables of extended tenses, we obtain the same extended tenses.

A slight difference in the usage is that adjectives are preferred if the duration of the event is long; therefore adjectives can often be interpreted as describing permanent properties of things. The transition to the extended tense, and from there to the permanent tense, is seen in the examples 'he produces', 'he is producing', 'he is productive'.

When we wish to express not repetition or duration but validity at all times, we use the present tense. Thus we say 'two times two is four'. There the present tense expressed in the copula 'is' indicates that the time argument is used as a free variable; that is, the sentence has the meaning 'two times two is four at any time'. This usage represents a second temporal function of the present tense.

Actual language does not always keep to the schemas given in our tables. Thus the English language sometimes uses the simple past where our schema would demand the present perfect. The English present perfect is often used in the sense of the corresponding extended tense, with the additional qualification that the duration of the event reaches up to the point of speech. Thus we have here the schema

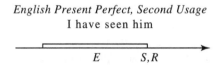

English Present Perfect, Second Usage
I have seen him

In the sense of this schema we say, for instance, 'I have known him for ten years'. If duration of the event is not meant, the English language then uses the simple past instead of the present perfect, as in 'I saw him ten years ago'. German and French would use the present perfect here.

When several sentences are combined to form a compound sentence, the tenses of the various clauses are adjusted to one another by certain rules which the grammarians call the rules for the *sequence of tenses*. We can interpret these rules as the principle that, although the events referred to in the clauses may occupy different time points, the reference point should be the same for all clauses—a principle which, we shall say, demands *the permanence of the reference point*. Thus, the tenses of the sentence, 'I had mailed the letter when John came and told me the news', may be diagramed as follows:

(1)   1st clause: $E_1 - R_1 \quad - S$
      2nd clause: $\quad\quad R_2, E_2 - S$
      3rd clause: $\quad\quad R_3, E_3 - S$

Here the three reference points coincide. It would be incorrect to say, 'I had mailed the letter when John has come'; in such a combination, the reference point would have been changed. As another example, consider the compound sentence, 'I have not decided which train I shall take'. That this sentence satisfies the rule of the permanence of the reference point is seen from the following diagram:

(2)   1st clause: $E_1 - S, R_1$
      2nd clause: $\quad\quad S, R_2 - E_2$

Here it would be incorrect to say, 'I did not decide which train I shall take'.

When the reference point is in the past, but the event coincides with the point of speech, a tense $R - S, E$ is required. In this sense, the form 'he would do' is used, which can be regarded as derived from the simple future 'he will do' by a backshift of the two points R and E. We say, for instance, 'I did not know that you would be here'; this sentence represents the diagram:

(3)   1st clause: $R_1, E_1 - S$
      2nd clause: $R_2 \quad - S, E_2$

The form 'I did not know that you were here' has a somewhat different meaning; it is used correctly only if the event of the man's being here extends to include the past time for which the 'I did not know' is stated—that is, if the man was already here when I did not know it. Incidentally, in these sentences the forms 'would be' and 'were' do not have a modal function expressing irreality (cf. Reichenbach 1947, §57); that is, they do not represent a conditional or a subjunctive, since the event referred to is not questioned. The nonmodal function is illustrated by the sentence 'I did not know that he was here', for which the form 'that he were here' appears incorrect.

When a time determination is added, such as is given by words like 'now' or 'yesterday', or by a nonreflexive symbol like 'November 7, 1944', it is referred not to the event but to the reference point of the sentence. We say, 'I met him yesterday'; that the word 'yesterday' refers here to the event obtains only because the points of reference and of event coincide. When we say, 'I had met him yesterday', what was yesterday is the reference point, and the meeting may have occurred the day before yesterday. We shall speak, therefore, of the *positional use of the reference point*; the reference point is used here as the carrier of the time position. Such usage, at least, is followed by the English language. Similarly, when time points are compared by means of words like 'when', 'before', or 'after', it is the reference points to which the comparison refers directly, not the events. Thus in example (1), the time points stated as identical by the word 'when' are the reference points of the three clauses, whereas the event of the first clause precedes that of the second and the third. Or consider the sentence, 'How unfortunate! Now that John tells me this I have mailed the letter'. The time stated here as identical with the time of John's telling the news is not the mailing of the letter but the reference point of the second clause, which is identical with the point of speech; and we have here the schema:

(4)   1st clause: S, R_1, E_1
      2nd clause: $E_2 — S, R_2$

For this reason it would be incorrect to say, 'Now that John tells me this I mailed the letter'.

If the time relation of the reference points compared is not identity, but time sequence—if one is said to be before the other—the rule of the permanence of the reference point can thus no longer be maintained. In 'he telephoned before he came' R_1 is said to be before R_2; but, at least, the tenses used have the same structure. It is different with the example, 'he was healthier when I saw him than he is now'. Here we have the structure:

(5)   1st clause: $R_1, E_1 — S$
      2nd clause: $R_2, E_2 — S$
      3rd clause: S, R_3, E_3

In such cases, the rule of the permanence of the reference point is replaced by the more general rule of the *positional use of the reference point*. The first rule, therefore, must be regarded as representing the special case where the time relation between the reference points compared is identity.

Incidentally, the English usage of the simple past where other languages use the present perfect may be a result of the strict adherence to the principle of the positional use of the reference point. When we say, 'this is the man who drove the car', we use the simple past in the second clause because the positional principle would compel us to do so as soon as we add a time determination, as in 'this is the man who drove the car at the time of the accident'. The German here uses the present perfect, and the above sentence would be translated into *dies ist der Mann, der den Wagen gefahren hat*. Though this appears more satisfactory than the English version, it leads to a disadvantage when a time determination is added. The German is then compelled to refer the time determination, not to the reference point, but to the event, as in *dies ist der Mann, der den Wagen zur Zeit des Unglücksfalles gefahren hat*. In such cases, a language can satisfy either the principle of the permanence of the reference point or that of the positional use of the reference point, but not both.

The use of the future tenses is sometimes combined with certain deviations from the original meaning of the tenses. In the sentence 'Now I shall go' the simple future has the meaning S, $R — E$; this follows from the principle of the positional use of the reference point. However, in the sentence 'I shall go tomorrow' the same principle compels us to interpret the future tense in the form $S — R, E$. The simple future, then, is capable of two interpretations, and since there is no prevalent usage of the one or the other we cannot regard one interpretation as the correct one.[4] Further deviations occur in tense sequences. Consider the sentence, 'I shall take your photograph when you come'. The form 'when you will come' would be more correct, but we prefer to use here the present tense instead of the future. This usage may be interpreted as follows. First, the future tense is used in the first clause in the meaning $S — R, E$; second, in the second clause the point of speech is neglected. The neglect is possible because the word 'when' refers the reference point of the second clause clearly to a future event. A similar anomaly is found in the sentence, 'We shall hear the record when we have dined', where the present perfect is used instead of the future perfect 'when we shall have dined'.[5]

Turning to the general problem of the time order of the three points, we see from our tables that the possibilities of ordering the three time points are not exhausted. There are on the whole thirteen possibilities, but the number of recognized grammatical tenses in English is only six. If we wish to systematize the possible tenses, we can proceed as follows. We choose the point of speech as the starting point; relative to it the point of reference can be in the past, at the same time, or in the future. This furnishes three possibilities. Next we consider the point of the event; it can be before, simultaneous with, or after the reference point. We thus arrive at $3 \cdot 3 = 9$ possible forms, which we call *fundamental forms*. Further differences of form result only when the position of the event relative to the point of speech is considered; this position, however, is usually irrelevant. Thus the form $S — E — R$ can be distinguished from the form $S, E — R$; with respect to relations between S and R on the one hand and between R and E on the other hand; however, these two forms do not differ, and we therefore regard them as representing the same fundamental form. Consequently, we need not deal with all the thirteen possible forms and may restrict ourselves to the nine fundamental forms.

For the nine fundamental forms we suggest the following terminology. The position of R relative to S is indicated by the words 'past', 'present', and 'future'. The position of E relative to R is indicated by the words 'anterior', 'simple', and 'posterior', the word 'simple' being used for the coincidence of R and E. We thus arrive at the following names:

Structure	New Name	Traditional Name
$E — R — S$	Anterior past	Past perfect
$E, R — S$	Simple past	Simple past
$R — E — S$		
$R — S, E$	Posterior past	—
$R — S — E$		
$E — S, R$	Anterior present	Present perfect
S, R, E	Simple present	Present
$S, R — E$	Posterior present	Simple future
$S — E — R$		
$S, E — R$	Anterior future	Future perfect
$E — S — R$		
$S — R, E$	Simple future	Simple future
$S — R — E$	Posterior future	—

We see that more than one structure obtains only for the two *retrogressive* tenses, the posterior past and the anterior future, in which the direction $S — R$ is opposite to the direction $R — E$. If we wish to distinguish among the individual structures, we refer to them as the first, second, and third posterior past or anterior future.

The tenses for which a language has no established forms are expressed by transcriptions. We say, for instance, 'I shall be going to see him' and thus express the posterior future $S — R — E$ by speaking not directly of the event E but of the act of preparation for it; in this way we can at least express the time order for events which closely succeed the point of reference. Languages which have a future participle have direct forms for the posterior future. Thus the Latin *abiturus ero* represents this tense, meaning verbally 'I shall be one of those who will leave'. For the posterior past $R — E —S$, the form 'he would do' is used—for instance, in 'I did not expect that he would win the race'. We met with this form in an above example where we interpreted it as the structure $R — S, E$; but this structure belongs to the same fundamental form as $R — E — S$ and may therefore be denoted by the same name. Instead of the form 'he would do', which grammar does not officially recognize as a tense,[6] transcriptions are frequently used. Thus we say, 'I did not expect that he was going to win the race', or, in formal writing, 'the king lavished his favor on the man who was to kill him'. In the last example, the order $R — E — S$ is expressed by the form 'was to kill', which conceives the event E, at the time R, as not yet realized, but as a destination.

Incidentally, the historical origin of many tenses is to be found in similar transcriptions. Thus 'I shall go' meant originally 'I am obliged to go'; the future tense meaning developed because what I am obliged to do will be done by me at a later time.[7] The French future tense is of the same origin; thus the form *je donnerai*, meaning 'I shall give', is derived from *je donner ai'*, which means 'I have to give'. This form of writing was actually used in Old French.[8] The double function of 'have', as expressing possession and a past tense, is derived from the idea that what I possess is acquired in the past; thus 'I have seen' meant originally 'I possess now the results of seeing', and then was interpreted as a reference to a past event.[9] The history of language shows that logical categories were not clearly seen in the beginnings of language but were the results of long developments; we therefore should not be astonished if actual language does not always fit the schema which we try to construct in symbolic logic. A mathematical language can be coordinated to actual language only in the sense of an approximation.

Notes

1. In J. O. H. Jespersen's excellent analysis of grammar (*The Philosophy of Grammar*, H. Holt, New York, 1924) I find the three-point structure indicated for such tenses as the past perfect and the future perfect (p. 256), but not applied to the interpretation of the other tenses. This explains the difficulties which even Jespersen has in distinguishing the present perfect from the simple past (p. 269). He sees correctly the close connection between the present tense and the present perfect, recognizable in such sentences as 'now I have eaten enough'. But he gives a rather vague definition of the present perfect and calls it "a retrospective variety of the present."

2. Turkish vowels with two dots are pronounced like the German vowels "ö" and "ü."

3. This shift of meaning is explainable as follows: One typical case of the past is stated, and to the listener is left the inductive inference that under similar conditions the same will be repeated in the future. A similar shift of meaning is given in the English "Faint heart never won fair lady." Cf. W. W. Goodwin, *Greek Grammar*, Ginn, Boston, 1930, p. 275.

4. The distinction between the French future forms *je vais voir* and *je verrai* may perhaps be regarded as representing the distinction between the order $S, R — E$ and the order $S — R, E$.

5. In some books on grammar we find the remark that the transition from direct to indirect discourse is accompanied by a shift of the tense from the present to the past. This shift, however, must not be regarded as a change in the meaning of the tense; it follows from the change in the point of speech. Thus 'I *am* cold' has a point of speech lying before that of 'I said that I *was* cold'.

6. It is sometimes classified as a tense of the conditional mood, corresponding to the French conditional. In the examples considered above, however, it is not a conditional but a tense in the indicative mood.

7. In Old English no future tense existed and the present tense was used for both the expression of the present and the future. The word 'shall' was used only in the meaning of obligation. In Middle English the word 'shall' gradually assumed the function of expressing the future tense. Cf. *The New English Dictionary*, Oxford, Vol. 8, Pt. 2, S—Sh, 1914, p. 609, col. 3.

8. This mode of expressing the future tense was preceded by a similar development of the Latin language, originating in vulgar Latin. Thus instead of the form *dabo*, meaning the future tense 'I shall give', the form *dare habeo* was used, which means 'I have to give'. Cf. Ferdinand Brunot, *Précis de grammaire historique de Ia langue française*, Masson et Cie., Paris, 1899, p. 434.

9. This is even more apparent when a two-place function is used. Thus 'I have finished my work' means originally 'I have my work finished', or 'I possess my work as a finished one'. Cf. *The New English Dictionary*, Oxford, 1901, Vol. V, Pt. I, H, p. 127, col. 1–2. The German still uses the original word order, as in *Ich habe meine Arbeit beendet*.

25

BARBARA HALL PARTEE

Some Structural Analogies between Tenses and Pronouns in English

$\mathbf{T}$he area of tense logic and its relation to English covers a wide range of problems, but I want to narrow my attention here to certain aspects of the uses of the two English tense morphemes *Past* and *Present*,[1] and compare them with related uses of the personal pronouns (*he, she, it*, etc.). I will argue that the tenses have a range of uses which parallels that of the pronouns, including a contrast between deictic (demonstrative) and anaphoric use, and that this range of uses argues in favor of representing the tenses in terms of variables and not exclusively as sentence operators.

In restricting my attention to the two tenses *Past* and *Present*, I am following the syntactic analysis of the English auxiliary system first set out by Noam Chomsky:[2]

(1)   Aux $\rightarrow$ Tns(Modal)(have + en)(be + ing)

$$\text{Tns} \rightarrow \begin{Bmatrix} \text{Present} \\ \text{Past} \end{Bmatrix}$$

$$\text{Modal} \rightarrow \begin{Bmatrix} \text{will} \\ \text{may} \\ \text{can} \end{Bmatrix}$$

In this system, the affixes *Present, Past, en*, and *ing* are subsequently attached by a transformation to the verb stems immediately following them. For example, the underlying form *Past have en eat* is transformed into *had eaten*; *Past can be ing go* becomes *could be going*. The so-called future tense is analyzed as *Present* plus the modal *will*, and is not syntactically a tense parallel to *Past* and *Present* (although it seems to be a tense in some other languages). Given the naturalness of a tripartite division of time into past, present, and future, it is one of the interesting open questions whether it is simpler to treat English as having a three-way tense distinction on some "deeper" level, which is then transformationally mapped into the forms that Chomsky treated as

Barbara Hall Partee (1973) Some structural analogies between tenses and pronouns in English. *Journal of Philosophy* 70: 601–609. Reprinted by permission of The Journal of Philosophy.

underlying, or simpler to start from Chomsky's representation of the syntax and build a semantics on that. This is one of the questions I am not going to treat, although the fact that it is only the *Past* and *Present* tense morphemes that show the behavior I am about to illustrate may provide some prima facie evidence for the Chomsky analysis.

The English personal pronouns have a number of uses; I am going to discuss various uses separately for expository purposes, but I am not thereby claiming that all these uses should be analyzed as distinct or unrelated. I will try to show that there are uses of the tenses parallel to each of the uses of the pronouns, suggesting that the best representation of the English tenses should be structurally similar to the representation of pronouns (leaving open for the time being what form that representation should take).

I   Deictic pronouns and tenses

The deictic use of pronouns can be illustrated by a sentence such as (2), which may be accompanied by a gesture to point out the referent:

(2)   He shouldn't be in here.

The first- and second-person pronouns are used primarily deictically. The similarity of the deictic use of *Present* tense and the deictic use of the pronoun *I* is well known and has been captured in various systems—for example, by including both among the indices in a "point of reference" for possible-worlds semantics or by defining them as "time of utterance" and "utterer," respectively. It seems that *I* has only a deictic use; that is certainly not true of the *Present* morpheme, as will be illustrated presently.

The deictic use of the *Past* tense morpheme appears in a sentence like (3):

(3)   I didn't turn off the stove.

When uttered, for instance, halfway down the turnpike, such a sentence clearly does not mean either that there exists some time in the past at which I did not turn off the stove or that there exists no time in the past at which I turned off the stove. The sentence clearly refers to a particular time—not a particular instant, most likely, but a definite interval whose identity is generally clear from the extra-linguistic context,[3] just as the identity of the *he* in sentence (2) is clear from the context. In the case of deictic *Past* tense, there is no analog to the pointing gesture that is often used with deictic pronouns. But deictic pronouns need not be accompanied by gestures; the referent may be understood from the context without being physically present, as in (4), uttered by a man sitting alone with his head in his hands:

(4)   She left me.

The identification of the time in (3) and the woman in (4) can be made by any hearer who has the requisite knowledge of the situation plus an appreciation of the general conversational requirements of relevance.

The *Present* tense, like the pronoun *I*, clearly has a unique and unambiguous referent when used deictically. The *Past* tense often seems to be much vaguer in its reference, and is perhaps to be compared to some uses of the pronoun *they*. Compare the pronoun in (5) with the tense in (6):

(5)   They haven't installed my telephone yet.
(6)   John went to a private school.

These are not picking out particular referents in the way we generally think of deictics doing, but they are certainly not generic or anaphoric, either. 'They' in (5) seems to be referring to whoever it is that's supposed to install the telephone, and *Past* in (6) seems to refer to whenever it was that John went to school. I haven't any more to say about this nonspecific deictic use, except to point out that again the pronouns and tenses are parallel.

Interlude: A shared non-property

Before discussing anaphoric and bound-variable-like uses of pronouns and tenses, we need to consider what the analog in the tense system is to nonpronominal term phrases. Tenses, like pronouns, do not describe or name what they refer to. When a pronoun is not used deictically, it is used in connection with some full-term phrase, which may be a proper name, a definite description, or some quantified term phrase. What, if anything, plays the role of such term phrases in the tense system? The answer seems to be time adverbials. There is clearly one major nonparallelism here, in that every full clause contains a tense whether it contains a time adverbial or not, whereas a sentence containing a full noun phrase need not contain a pronoun in addition. Thus, in a sentence like (7), the tense seems to be redundant, since the time specification is provided by the time adverbial:

(7)   We climbed Mt. Baker three weeks ago.

The nearest thing to this sort of redundancy with pronouns comes in sentences like (8), which are natural in some dialects and frequently found in children's speech:

(8)   The woman in the house next door, she almost ran over me.

There are some languages which have an obligatory subject-marker (sometimes also an object-marker), virtually a pronoun, as an affix on the verb whether or not the subject (or object) is overtly expressed; these languages, if they also obligatorily include a tense in every clause, would be more parallel in their tense and pronoun systems. A language could also have more parallel tense and pronoun systems if it omitted the tense morpheme in clauses containing an explicit time adverbial, but I do not know whether there are any languages of that sort.[4]

II   Anaphoric pronouns and tenses with specific antecedents

In sentence (9), the pronoun *it* is used anaphorically to refer back to the object referred to by *the car*; whether the pronoun should here be viewed as a bound variable bound by the definite-description operator or whether it should be viewed as a "pronoun of laziness"[5] going proxy for a repetition of the same phrase, or ambiguously as either, I leave open here:

(9)   Sam took the car yesterday and Sheila took it today.

In any case, there are comparable uses of tenses, where the time is specified in one clause and the tense of a subsequent clause refers to the same time:

(10)   Sheila had a party last Friday and Sam got drunk.

The antecedent may be a time-clause, as in (11):

(11)   When Susan walked in, Peter left.

Sentence (11) presents at least two choices of analysis; to view both tenses as pronoun-like is to regard (11) as parallel to archaic forms like (12):

(12)   He who stole my cow, he will suffer the penalties.

A more natural form is (13), with no pronouns, but sentences like (13) are themselves problematical to analyze:

(13)   Whoever stole my cow will suffer the penalties.

Sentence (11) could be viewed as more like (13) than (12), with the time-clause providing a descriptive specification of the time for the main clause and both tense morphemes redundant except insofar as they indicate that the time described was in the past rather than the present or future. In either case the logical form of (11), as of both (12) and (13), would seem to be most simply represented as involving a definite-description operator connecting identical variables in the two clauses.

III   Pronouns and tenses as bound variables

Consider a sentence like (14) in contrast to a simple clause like (15):

(14)   If Susan comes in, John will leave immediately.
(15)   John will leave immediately.

In (15) if we analyze the auxiliary verb as *Present + will*, we can say that *Present* is used deictically to refer to the time of utterance, and that *immediately* interacts with *will* so that the time of John's leaving is asserted to be in the immediate future measured from the time of utterance. In (14), on the other hand, the immediate future is understood to be measured from the time of Susan's arrival. This interpretation requires that we treat the *Present* in *Present + will + leave* in (14) not as the deictic use of *Present*, but as connected to the *Present* in the *if*-clause. That occurrence of *Present* is not deictic either, and in fact has no specific reference. This kind of case, more clearly than the sort of anaphora described in the preceding section, seems to cry out for an analysis involving bound variables. As a first approximation, a representation such as (16) might do, letting φ be 'Susan come in' and ψ be 'John leave':

(16) $(\forall t)\, (\varphi\, (t) \supset \psi\, ((\text{Imm} (\text{Fut}))\, (t)))$

One deficiency of (16) is that it does not distinguish (14) from (17):

(17)   Whenever Susan comes in, John immediately leaves.

Sentence (14) suggests that a single possible future occurrence is at issue, while (16) generalizes in a way that seems more appropriate to (17). But if we want to represent (14) with a formula that begins 'if there is a time when Susan comes in, then . . .' , we are left with an unbound variable in the second clause, unless we introduce a definite description and finish with 'then John will leave in the immediate future from the time at which Susan comes in,' as in (18):

(18) $(\exists t)\, \varphi\, (t) \supset \psi\, ((\text{Imm} (\text{Fut}))\, ((\imath t)\, \varphi\, (t)))$

These two competing analyses of (14) are closely analogous to competing analyses, both widely suggested, of the pronoun usage in a sentence like (19):[6]

(19)   If one of the arrows hits the target, it's mine.

But whatever the best analysis is—and (18) certainly seems preferable to (16) for these examples—it seems clear that explicit time variables are required, rather than tense operators alone. It may be that tense operators are appropriate for tense and aspect notions, like future, progressive, and perfect, whereas variables are appropriate representations for the functions of the two tense morphemes *Past* and *Present*. But there seems to be no way for tense operators alone to capture the fact that the immediate future in (14) must be with respect to the time at which the *if*-clause event occurs.

Similar variable-binding can be seen in the following examples. The (a) examples involve tense, and the (b) examples show similar uses of pronouns:

(20)   a. When you eat Chinese food, you're always hungry an hour later.
       b. Every student spoke to the student in front of him.
(21)   a. John never answers when I call his home.
       b. No one could tell what he was being tested for.
(22)   a. Most of the time, if I write John a letter, he answers within a week.
       b. Mostly, if a man commits perjury, he has to continue committing perjury.
(23)   a. Richard always gave assignments that were due the next day.
       b. Every Englishman worships his mother.

When other elements are present in the auxiliary verb in addition to the tense morpheme, it is still only the tense morpheme that seems to behave as a bound variable, with the other elements bearing their usual relationships to whatever reference point is indicated by the tense. Thus in addition to (21a), we find examples like (21c–21e):

(21)   c. John never talks when he is eating.
       d. John never changes his mind when he has made a decision.
       e. John never drives when he has been drinking.

I do not want to try to analyze the progressive or perfect aspects here, but it seems clear that (21c), for example, can be (artificially) paraphrased by (21c') below, where the progressive in 'he is eating at *t*' bears the same relation to each time *t* that the progressive in a simple sentence such as 'He is eating' bears to the time of utterance:

(21)   c'. There is no time *t* such that John talks at *t* and John is eating at *t*.

It is my hypothesis that it is the tense morpheme in these sentences that is serving as variable quantified over by the adverbs 'never,' 'always,' et cetera. Under this hypothesis, the relation of the rest of the auxiliary to the tense is uniform for both deictic and bound variable uses of the tense.

IV   Scope matters

Sentence (24) is ambiguous:

(24)   If John had married Susan, he would have had everything he wanted.

The ambiguity hinges on the relation of 'everything he wanted' to the rest of the sentence. On one reading, the phrase 'everything he wanted' is referential; the *Past* tense refers to some actual past time (presumably some time at which he might have married Susan, though this seems to be extralinguistic interpretation of a deictic use of *Past*, and not an anaphoric connection with the tense in the *if*-clause). On the other reading, the modal construction *would have* appears to be applying to the whole clause 'he have everything he want'; the subpart 'everything he wanted' is not referential, and the *Past* tense is acting as a pro-form linking the time or times of the wanting with the time or times of the having. This interpretation could be accounted for by an analysis which posits an identical time variable in each of the subclauses: 'he t have everything he t want'; "quantifying in" the auxiliary *would have* (i.e., *Past will have* + *en*), which applies to the whole clause, is then done by substituting the full auxiliary for the first occurrence of t and its pro-form, *Past*, for the second occurrence. Such an analysis would neatly parallel the analysis of ordinary pronominalization in which a full term-phrase is substituted for one occurrence of a given variable and the appropriate pronoun for the remaining occurrences.

The ambiguity of (24) between a deictic and an anaphoric interpretation of *Past* parallels the ambiguity of virtually every sentence which contains a potentially anaphoric pronoun, since such a pronoun can just about always be interpreted deictically instead.

It is interesting that *Past* seems to be the pro-form for all the auxiliaries that contain a morphological *Past*, such as *would have*, even when the *Past* tense does not represent a past time. Correspondingly, *Present* seems to be the pro-form for all the auxiliaries containing a morphological *Present*. The following examples further illustrate this phenomenon; like (24), each of them have both an anaphoric and a deictic interpretation for the tense in question:

(25)   John will have everything he *wants*.
(26)   If you were king, you could cut off the heads of everyone who *offended* you.

In all of (24)–(26) the modal construction (*would have, will, could*) has a complex clause in its scope. The embedded clause can also contain its own modal, as in (27):

(27)   If Max had gotten in here, he would have eaten everything he could find.

In this case, the complex clause that *would have* applies to seems to be something like (28):

(28)   he eat at t everything he can find at t.

Since the pro-form for *would have* is *Past*, the *Past* tense morpheme is substituted for the t in the embedded clause, where it combines with *can* to give *could*. Thus a larger auxiliary may contain an anaphoric tense as a subpart, just as a full term-phrase like *his mother* may contain an anaphoric pronoun as a subpart. This fact is also illustrated in examples (21c)–(21e) of the preceding section.

V   Conclusion

My main hypothesis has been that there is a considerable and striking parallel in the behavior of tenses and pronouns, at least in English. The corollary seems to be that if pronouns have to be treated as variables and not as sentence operators (the latter being a view I have never heard advanced or seen any evidence for), the same must be true of tenses, though not of the other elements of the auxiliary, namely modals, perfect, and progressive. The evidence given for the main hypothesis has been informal and fragmentary, and I have not even begun to offer the explicit syntactic and semantic rules that would be necessary to turn the hypothesis into a substantive claim about the structure of English. I have suggested an approach to the treatment of tenses which seems to lead from the observed parallels, but I can't make any strong claims about it without working out a full analysis, and that remains as a future project.

Notes

Presented in an APA symposium on Logical Structure in Natural Languages, December 28, 1973; commentators, Terance Parsons and Robert C. Stalnaker; see *The Journal of Philosophy* 70: 609–610 and 610–612, respectively.

1. I will use *Past* and *Present* to refer to the English tense morphemes, and *past* and *present* to refer to times.

2. N. Chomsky, *Syntactic Structures* (The Hague: Mouton, 1957).

3. It occurs to me that it might be possible to construct a Gricean counterargument to this claim, and contend that the sentence asserts only that there is some time in the past at which I did not turn off the stove, with the narrowing down to relevant times explainable by conversational principles, particularly the principle of relevance. If such a proposal could be defended for what I am calling the deictic use of *Past*, it would remain to be seen if an analogous proposal could be made for the deictic use of third-person pronouns.

4. Some interesting suggestions about the interdependencies between tenses and time adverbials are made by Wunderlich in *Tempus und Zeitreferenz im Deutschen* (Munich: Max Hueber, 1970); his remarks concern German, but most of them apply equally to English. My remarks about the connections between time adverbials and tenses in this section and the next clearly oversimplify a number of complex issues; so whatever evidence I adduce therefrom is quite vulnerable. For some remarks on apparent disadvantages of having a tense in every clause, see W. V. O. Quine, *Word and Object* (Cambridge, Mass.: MIT Press, 1960), section 36.

5. See Peter Geach, *Reference and Generality* (Ithaca, N. Y.: Cornell, 1972b).

6. See Gilbert A. Harman, "Deep Structure as Logical Form," in Donald Davidson and Gilbert Harman, eds., *Semantics of Natural Language* (Dordrecht: D. Reidel, 1972), pp. 25–47.

26

J. A. W. (HANS) KAMP

Two Theories about Adjectives

1

I will discuss two theories about adjectives. The first theory dates from the late 1960s. It is stated in Montague (1970a) and Parsons (1968). According to this theory, the meaning of an adjective is a function which maps the meanings of noun phrases onto other such meanings; for example, the meaning of *clever* is a function which maps the meaning of *man* into that of *clever man*, that of *poodle* onto that of *clever poodle*, and so on. Predicative uses of adjectives are explained as elliptic attributive uses. Thus *This dog is clever* is analyzed as *This dog is a clever dog*—or as *This dog is a clever animal*, or perhaps as *This dog is a clever being*. Which noun phrase ought to be supplied in this reduction of predicative to attributive use is in general not completely determined by the sentence itself, and to the extent that it is not, the sentence must be regarded as ambiguous.

The main virtue of this doctrine is that it enables us to treat, within a precise semantical theory for a natural language—as, for example, that of Montague—adjectives in such a way that certain sentences which are, or might well be, false are not branded by the semantics as logically true. Examples of such sentences are:

(1)   Every alleged thief is a thief.
(2)   Every small elephant is small.
(3)   If every flea is an animal, then every big flea is a big animal.

Each of these sentences would come out logically true in Montague's model theory if it were to treat adjectives as ordinary predicates, so that the logical form of (1), for example, would be $(\forall x)(A(x) \wedge T(x) \rightarrow T(x))$.

Hans Kamp (1975) Two theories about adjectives. In E. Keenan (ed.), *Formal Semantics of Natural Language*, 123–155. Reprinted by permission of Cambridge University Press.

Moreover, the theory allows us to express in very simple mathematical terms some important semantical features which some, though not all, adjectives possess. In order to give precise formulations of such features, it is necessary to make some assumptions about the comprehensive semantical theory in which this particular doctrine about adjectives is to be embedded. These assumptions can all be found in Montague (1970a). I regard them as basically sound, but would like to point out to those who have strong qualms about possible world semantics that the distinctions drawn by the definitions below do not depend on these assumptions as such.

The assumptions are the following:

a. Each possible interpretation (for the language in question) is based upon (i) a certain non-empty set W of possible worlds (or possible situations, or possible contexts) and (ii) a set U of individuals.
b. A property relative to such an interpretation is a function which assigns to each $w \in W$ a subset of U (intuitively the collection of those individuals which satisfy the property in that particular world, or context, w).
c. The meaning of a noun phrase in such an interpretation is always a property.

Thus the meanings of adjectives in an interpretation of this kind will be functions from properties to properties.

We may call an adjective *predicative in* a given interpretation if its meaning F in that interpretation satisfies the following condition:

(4)   there is a property Q such that for each property P and each $w \in W$, $F(P)(w) = P(w) \cap Q(w)$.

Once we have singled out a given class $\mathfrak{K}$ of admissible interpretations, we can also introduce the notion of being *predicative* simpliciter: an adjective is *predicative* (with respect to the given class $\mathfrak{K}$) if and only if it is predicative in each interpretation (belonging to $\mathfrak{K}$).

Predicative adjectives behave essentially as if they were independent predicates. If, for example, *four-legged* is treated as predicative, then any sentence *If every N_1 is an N_2 then every four-legged N_1 is a four-legged N_2*, where N_1 and N_2 are arbitrary noun phrases, will be true in each admissible interpretation in all the worlds of that interpretation.

Predicative adjectives are, roughly speaking, those whose extensions are not affected by the nouns with which they are combined. Typical examples are technical and scientific adjectives, such as *endocrine*, *differentiable*, and *superconductive*.

We may call an adjective *privative in* a given interpretation if its meaning F in that interpretation satisfies the condition

(5)   for each property P and each $w \in W$, $F(P)(w) \cap P(w) = \phi$

Again, an adjective will be called *privative* if (5) holds on all admissible interpretations.

A privative adjective A is one which, when combined with a noun phrase N produces a complex noun phrase AN that is satisfied only by things which do not satisfy N. If A is a privative adjective then each sentence *No AN is an N* will be a logical truth. Adjectives that behave in this way in most contexts are, for example, *false* and *fake*. I doubt that there is any English adjective which is privative (in the precise sense here defined) in all of its possible uses.

An adjective is *affirmative in* a given interpretation if its meaning satisfies

(6)   for each P and w, $F(P)(w) \subseteq P(w)$

It is *affirmative* if (6) holds in all admissible interpretations.

Clearly all predicative adjectives are affirmative. But there are many more. In fact, the vast majority of adjectives are affirmative. Typical examples of affirmative adjectives which are not predicative are *big, round, pink, bright, sharp, sweet, heavy, clever*.

Finally, an adjective is *extensional in* a given interpretation if

(7) there is a function F' from sets of individuals to sets of individuals such that for every P and w,
$(F(P))(w) = F'(P(w))$

and *extensional* if (7) holds in all admissible interpretations.

Thus a predicative adjective is in essence an operation on extensions of properties: if two properties have the same extension in w, then the properties obtained by applying the adjective to them also have the same extension in w.

Clearly all predicative adjectives are extensional. Non-extensional adjectives are, for example, *affectionate* and *skillful*. Even if (in a given world) all and only cobblers are darts players, it may well be that not all and only the skillful cobblers are skillful darts players;[1] and even if all men were fathers the set of affectionate fathers would not necessarily coincide with the set of affectionate men.[2]

It is an interesting question whether there are any adjectives which are extensional but not predicative. It has been suggested[3] that in particular such adjectives as *small, tall, heavy,* and *hot* belong to this category. Indeed, these adjectives are evidently not predicative, whereas their extensionality follows from a certain proposal according to which they derive from their comparatives in the following way. Let A be an adjective of this kind, and let $\mathfrak{R}$ be the binary relation represented by the phrase *is more A than*. The function $\mathscr{A}$ from properties to properties which is associated with A is then characterized by

(8) for any property P and world w, $\mathscr{A}(P)(w) = \{u \in P(w')$: for most $u' \in P(w) \langle u,u' \rangle \in \mathfrak{R}(w)\}$

It will soon be evident why I have not much sympathy for analyses of positives in terms of comparatives generally. At this point, however, I only want to express some reservations which concern (8) in particular. That (8) cannot be right is brought out by the fact that it logically excludes the possibility that, for any property P, most Ps are small Ps and only a few are large Ps. Thus what we usually call a small car in England would according to (8) not be a small car; for we call most English cars small. (One might perhaps reply that this only shows that by *small car* we mean *car of a small model*. But that does not quite do. After all, it is the *individual* cars we call small.) In this case the conflict between usage and the consequences of (8) arises from the fact that cars are naturally divided into categories, and it is to these, if anything, that (8) applies.

There is yet another reason why (8) might fail for *small*. We might have a clear concept of what is the normal size of objects satisfying a certain property, even if objects of that size which have the property do not or only rarely occur. It is conceivable to me that we would then call almost all members of a species S small members of S if there was strong biological evidence that only accidental and abnormal circumstances C prevent the majority from growing into a height which most members of the species would reach under conditions we would regard as normal. Yet we might still be unwilling to call them small members of S-under-the-circumstances-C; for as objects falling under that second description they should be expected to have the size they do have. If, moreover, S and S-under-C had precisely the same extensions, the case would tend to show that *small* is not purely extensional. But that it is so difficult to come up with a concrete and convincing example of this sort is perhaps an indication that for all practical purposes *small*, and similar adjectives, are indeed extensional.

2

This theory of adjectives is of course not new. The observation that *John is a good violinist* cannot be analyzed as *John is good and a violinist* is probably too old to be traced back with precision to its origin.[4] What is perhaps new in the doctrine as I have stated it here is the emphasis on the fact that what has for a long time been observed to be a feature of certain adjectives is a common feature of them all. *All* of them are functions from noun phrases to noun phrases. Some adjectives (expressed in (4)), however, possess a certain invariance property that makes them behave as predicates, which when combined with a noun phrase give a complex equivalent in meaning to the conjunction of the predicate represented by the adjective and that represented by the noun phrase.

Even if this theory does accomplish the rather simple-minded tasks for which it was designed, one may feel dissatisfied with it for a variety of reasons. Here I will mention only one (although I believe there are other grounds for dissatisfaction as well): the theory is incapable of providing an adequate treatment for the comparative and superlative. For reasons of convenience I will concentrate on the comparative and leave the superlative aside, but the theory which will emerge from our considerations will handle the superlative as well.

From a naïve point of view, the comparative is an operation which forms out of an adjective a binary predicate. I believe that this naïve point of view is correct: that when we learn a language such as English we learn the meanings of individual adjectives and, moreover, the semantic function which this comparative-forming operation performs *in general*, so that we have no difficulty in understanding, on first hearing, the meaning of the comparative of an adjective of which we had thus far only encountered the positive. If this is so, then the meaning of an adjective must be such that the comparative can be understood as a semantic transformation of that meaning into the right binary relation.

It is quite obvious that if adjectives were ordinary predicates, no such transformation could exist. How could we possibly define the relation *x is bigger than y* in terms of nothing more than the extension of the alleged predicate *big*?

Could functions from properties to properties serve as the basis for such a transformation? This is a more problematic question. One might, for example, characterize the transformation as follows:

> For any adjective A with meaning $\mathscr{A}$ in a given interpretation, we have for any $u_1, u_2 \in U$ and $w \in W$
> (9) u_1 is more A than u_2 in w iff
>   (a) for every property P such that u_1 and u_2 both belong to $P(w)$ if u_2 belongs to $\mathscr{A}(P)(w)$, when so does u_1
>   (b) there is a property P such that $u_1, u_2 \in P(w)$, $u_1 \in \mathscr{A}(P)(w)$, and $u_2 \notin \mathscr{A}(P)(w)$.

This definition is in the right direction. But I doubt that it will do. I particular, I doubt whether (b) is a necessary condition. Take *tall*, for example. According to (9), u_1 is taller than u_2 only if there is a property P that applies to both of them and such that u_1 is a tall P while u_2 is not. But suppose that u_1 is taller than u_2 by a tiny bit. Can we then find a P which satisfies this condition? The question is not easy to answer. Let us suppose for the sake of argument that *tall* can be correctly defined by (8) as *taller than most*. Then the question depends on whether we can find a property P such that u_1 is taller than most Ps while u_2 is not. But this can only be the case if there are enough things in the extension of P which have heights intermediate between those of u_1 and u_2. And perhaps there are no such things at all. Now, in our discussion of extensional adjectives we found that (8) is probably not adequate in any case. So there may be after all a property P which satisfies the condition. In this manner we might succeed in saving (9) by imploring the assistance of some bizarre property whenever we need one. But I find this solution ad hoc and unsatisfactory. What underlies the possibility of making comparative claims is that adjectives can apply to things in various degrees. It is my strong conviction that when we learn the meaning of an adjective we learn, as part of it, to distinguish with greater or lesser precision to what degree, or extent, the adjective applies to the various entities to which it applies at all. Once we have learned this we are able to understand the comparative of the adjective without additional explanation, provided we understand the function of the comparative in general.

In order to give my view on the primacy of positive over comparative an adequate foundation, I will develop a semantical framework in which the idea of a predicate being true of an entity to a certain degree can be made coherent and precise. This specific problem is closely related to such general features of natural languages as vagueness and contextual disambiguation; indeed, I hope that the theory which I will outline will provide an adequate framework for the treatment of these problems as well.

Before stating what at this point I believe to be the most promising framework for our purpose, I first want to make some remarks on a theory of formal logic which has been often proposed just for the solution of the problems with which I want to deal, namely multi-valued, or many-valued logic.

Most systems of multi-valued logic available in the literature are systems of propositional calculus. In view of our purpose, our interest should lie with multi-valued predicate logic. But for reasons of exposition I will consider the simpler propositional logics.

Multi-valued logics differ from ordinary two-valued logic in the first place by their model theories. Indeed, many such systems are syntactically indistinguishable from standard formulations of ordinary propositional calculus; and I will consider for the time being only such systems of multi-valued logic, all of which have the same syntax, based upon an infinite set $(q_1, q_2, q_3, \ldots)$ of propositional variables. Starting with these we can recursively construct complex formulae—$\neg(\phi), \wedge(\phi, \psi), \vee(\phi, \psi), \rightarrow(\phi, \psi), \leftrightarrow(\phi, \psi)$—from already constructed formulae ϕ and ψ. (I will write $(\phi \wedge \psi)$ for $\wedge(\phi, \psi)$, etc.) Let us call this language of propositional logic L_o.

A multi-valued semantics for L_o will provide for this language a model theory based upon some set TV (of "truth values") the cardinality of which is ≥ 2. Two-valued propositional calculus emerges as a case where TV contains exactly two elements. A *model* for L_o according to such a model theory based upon TV is a function which assigns to each variable q_i an element of TV. Such a function uniquely determines the (truth) values of the complex formulae of L in virtue of another component which specifies for each t_i in TV what the value is of $\neg\phi$ given that t_i is the value of ϕ; for each t_i, t_j in TV what the value is of $(\phi \wedge \psi)$ given that ϕ has t_i and ψ has t_j; and similarly for the other connectives.

The definition of logical truth requires a third component of the theory which singles out a proper non-empty subset TV_t, of TV, the set of "designated" truth values. A formula will be regarded as *logically true* if in each model it has a value belonging to TV_t. Logical consequence can be defined in an analogous manner.

Thus we come to the following formal definition:

A *multi-valued model theory* (in short, m.m.t.) for L_o is a triple $\langle TV, TV_t, F \rangle$ where (i) TV is a set of cardinality ≥ 2; (ii) TV_t, is a proper, non-empty subset of TV; (iii) F is a function which maps each n-place connective of L_o onto an n-place function from TV into itself.

A *model for L_o relative to the m.m.t.* $\langle TV, TV_t, F \rangle$ is a function from $\{q_1, q_2, q_3, \ldots\}$ into TV.

Let $\mathcal{M} = \langle TV, TV_t, F \rangle$. The truth value of a formula ϕ of L_o in a model M relative to $\mathcal{M}$, $[\phi]_M^{\mathcal{M}}$, is defined by the clauses:
(i) $[q_i]_M = M(q_i)$;
(ii) $C(\phi_1, \ldots, \phi_n) [_M^{\mathcal{M}}] = F(C) ([\phi_1]_M^{\mathcal{M}}, \ldots, [\phi_n]_M^{\mathcal{M}})$ for any n-place connective C of L_o.
ϕ is *logically true in $\mathcal{M}$* iff $[\phi]_M^{\mathcal{M}} \in TV_t$ for all models M relative to $\mathcal{M}$.

Clearly the classical semantics for propositional calculus is the model theory $\langle\{0,1\},\{1\},F_c\rangle$ where $F_c(\neg),F_c(\wedge), \ldots , F_c(\leftrightarrow)$ are the functions defined by the usual two-valued truth tables for these connectives.

It is natural to require of a model theory for L_0 based upon a truth value set of cardinality $\geqslant 2$ that it has the feature:

(10)   there are two particular elements of TV—let us call them 0 and 1—such that (i) $1 \in TV_i$; (ii) $0 \notin TV_i$; and (iii) for each connective C, the restriction of $F(C)$ to $\{0, 1\}$ is the usual two-valued truth table for C (i.e., there are among the truth values two, which we might think of as "absolute falsehood" and "absolute truth," with respect to which the connectives behave in the ordinary classical manner).

It appears that those model theories for L_0 which have been seriously proposed in the literature do indeed satisfy (10).[5] The vast majority of these theories assume, moreover, a linear ordering of the members of TV with respect to which 0 is the smallest and 1 the largest element. The formal properties of the theory, as well as its philosophical relevance, then depend on the characterization of the functions $F(C)$. Clearly, whenever the cardinality of TV is greater than 2, there are various such functions which do not violate (i). The question is which of these "correctly capture" the function of the connectives *not, and, or,* . . . given a particular interpretation of what the truth values in TV really represent. Let us consider the case where

$$TV = \left\{0, \frac{1}{n-1}, \frac{2}{n-1}, \ldots, \frac{n-2}{n-1}, 1\right\}$$

and where these numbers represent "degrees of truth"—the higher the number the higher the degree. What function F would adequately reflect our intuitions about the semantic behavior of these connectives in this case? I think there are no such functions. The reason is that the connectives *not, and, or,* . . . are not functions of degrees of truth. This becomes evident almost immediately when one reflects upon the definition of $F(\neg)$. The natural suggestion here is that

$$F(\neg)\left(\frac{k}{n-1}\right) = 1 - \frac{k}{n-1},$$

that is, that the negation of a proposition is true exactly to the degree that that proposition itself fails to be true. And this indeed is a definition of $F(\neg)$ which is commonly accepted.

Now let us assume that n is odd so that one of the truth values is $\frac{1}{2}$. What value would $F(\wedge)$ assign to the pair of arguments $(\frac{1}{2}, \frac{1}{2})$? It is plausible that the value should be $\leqslant \frac{1}{2}$. For how could a conjunction be true to a higher degree than one of its conjuncts? But which value $\leqslant \frac{1}{2}$? $\frac{1}{2}$ seems out because if $[\phi]_M^{\mathscr{M}} = \frac{1}{2}$, then, if we accept our definition of $F(\neg)$, $[\neg\phi]_M^{\mathscr{M}} = \frac{1}{2}$. So we would have $[\phi \wedge \neg\phi]_M^{\mathscr{M}} = \frac{1}{2}$, which seems absurd. For how could a logical contradiction be true to *any* degree? However, if we stipulate that $(F(\wedge))$ $(\frac{1}{2}, \frac{1}{2}) = 0$, we are stuck with the even less desirable consequence that if $[\phi]_M^{\mathscr{M}} = \frac{1}{2}$, $[\phi \wedge \phi]_M^{\mathscr{M}} = 0$. And if we choose any number between 0 and $\frac{1}{2}$, we get the wrong values for both $\phi \wedge \neg\phi$ and $\phi \wedge \phi$.[6]

This argument indicates why we cannot represent the connectives accurately within the narrow framework of multi-valued semantics based upon linearly ordered truth-value sets. The reason can be expressed thus: the truth value of a complex formula—say $\phi \wedge \psi$—should depend not just on the truth values of the components (that is, ϕ and ψ) but also on certain aspects of these formulae which contribute to their truth values but cannot be unambiguously recaptured from them.

The possibility of treating the connectives truth-functionally in two-valued model theory (while not in model theories based on larger linearly ordered sets of truth values) is a reflection of the fact that two-element sets are the only linearly ordered truth-value sets which can be regarded as Boolean algebras in the following sense:

If we define the Boolean operations $\cap$, $\cup$, $-$ in the usual manner in terms of the ordering relation $\leqslant$ of a linearly ordered set TV (i.e., if we put $C \cap C' =_{df}$ the largest C'' under $\leqslant$ such that $C'' \leqslant C$ and $C'' \leqslant C'$; $C \cup C' =_{df}$ the smallest C'' such that $C \leqslant C''$ and $C' \leqslant C''$; and $\bar{C}$ as the largest C' such that $C \cap C' = \phi$), then, if TV consists of two elements, 0 and 1, we obtain the two-element Boolean algebra $\langle\{0,1\},\cap,\cup,-\rangle$. But as soon as TV contains more than two elements, the resulting algebra is not a Boolean algebra. In particular, the equation $C \cup \bar{C} = 1$ will no longer be satisfied by all elements C.

3

This last observation suggests in which direction a solution to our difficulty might be found: we should choose as truth-value sets not linear orderings but, rather, sets which, like the two-valued system, display the structure of the propositional calculus, namely Boolean algebras. We may then, if we want to, further "reduce" these Boolean algebras to linearly ordered systems; in this reduction, different Boolean values may be assigned the same element of the linear ordering. But this will no longer affect our semantic characterization of the connectives, as these will now be defined in the Boolean truth-value space and thus not directly on the linearly ordered, "ultimate" truth values themselves. It may now happen that even if ϕ and ψ have the same ultimate value, $\phi \cap \chi$ has a different ultimate value from that of $\psi \cap \chi$ (namely, in certain cases where the Boolean values of ϕ and ψ which reduce to the same ultimate value are nevertheless distinct).

This idea is by now quite familiar to logicians. Yet it is surprising that its use for the specific problems with which we are here concerned occurred as late as it did; for there is a branch of mathematics—probability theory—in which it has been accepted as the standard solution to what is in many ways the same problem as the one we are facing here. I am referring to the theory of probability in the definitive mathematical form that Kolmogorov (1970) gave it in the 1930s. In this theory one associates with a proposition in first instance a certain set. With this set is associated, in turn, a real number in the closed interval [0:1]. This number gives the probability of the proposition. Now while the set associated with the conjunction of two propositions is a simple function of the sets associated with the conjuncts—that is, their intersection—there is no way of telling in general the probability of the conjunction on the basis of just the probabilities of the conjuncts; and this is as it should be, for when p and q each have probability $\frac{1}{2}$, the probability of $p \wedge q$ could, intuitively, be anything between 0 and $\frac{1}{2}$.

Perhaps the main philosophical problem which this approach raises is that of giving a plausible interpretation of the sets with which propositions are associated. I will consider here only one doctrine, according to which the elements of the sets are regarded as possible worlds, or possible situations. Thus the probability of a proposition is measured in terms of the set of those possible worlds in which it is true. Seen in this light, probability theory is closely connected with the possible-world semantics for modal and other types of non-extensional logic. Both theories associate with a given sentence in any particular interpretation a set (of possible worlds, points of reference, contexts, etc.).

Of course, probability theory and intensional logic are concerned with different sorts of problems. In intensional logic we are primarily concerned with the analysis, in terms of the set of all possible "worlds" (as well as, perhaps, various structural properties of this set), of the semantical function of certain non-truth functional operators, such as *it is necessarily the case that*. In probability theory one does not consider such intensional operators, but concentrates on the probability function which associates real numbers with the sets, and investigates how the probabilities of certain complex expressions depend on the probabilities of their components—often under certain assumptions about these components, such as independence or disjointness.

There is another theory of formal semantics which fits within the general frame which we are now discussing—namely, the theory of partial interpretations and supervaluations. This theory is, in its simplest form, a generalization of ordinary two-valued model theory, which allows for the possibility that in a given interpretation for a certain formal language (say, of ordinary first-order logic with description operator) some sentences of the language are neither true nor false. Yet, in order to avoid the—from a certain standpoint undesirable—consequence that whenever p is without truth value, so are, among others, $p \wedge \neg p$ and $p \vee \neg p$, one considers the collection of all interpretations which extend the given interpretation by filling out its truth gaps in a consistent manner. If a formula comes out true in each of these completions it will be regarded as true in the interpretation even if it is not assigned a truth value directly by the (incomplete) recursive definition of truth. Similarly, it will be counted as false in the interpretation if it is false in each of its completions.

One may view this process again as one of assigning, in a given interpretation, sets to sentences: to each sentence is assigned the set of all completions in which it is true. Sentences already true in the given interpretation, and also such sentences as $p \vee \neg p$ where p itself is not assigned a truth value directly, will be assigned the set of all completions, those already false as well as sentences such as $p \wedge \neg p$ will be assigned the empty set; only sentences which neither have a truth value in virtue of the recursive truth definition nor have the form of a logical identity or contradiction may be assigned intermediate sets.

The theory, which was first introduced by Van Fraassen (1969) suggests in what way the framework under discussion might be used in an analysis of vagueness. Vagueness is one of the various reasons why certain sentences may be without truth value. Thus if we regard the world, or any specific speech situation in it, as providing an interpretation for English, what it provides is at best a *partial* interpretation.[7] For such a partial interpretation we may consider the various completions in which all instances of vagueness are resolved in one way or another. The quantity of such completions in which a certain sentence is true ought then to be in some sense a measure for the degree to which the sentence is true in the original interpretation. Such considerations would of course apply not only to adjectives but to other parts of speech as well, in particular to those grammatical categories which, like adjectives, are usually treated as 1-place predicates in simple-minded predicate-logic-symbolizations of English sentences, namely common nouns and intransitive verbs. (I will later try to say something about systematic differences between the semantic behavior of adjectives and that of these other two categories.)

These considerations naturally lead to a modification of the model theory for formal or natural languages which I will exemplify for a rather simple case: first-order predicate logic. The example will make it clear enough how one could adapt in a similar fashion more complicated model theories—such as those for intensional logics or for fragments of natural languages.

Let us consider the language L for predicate logic, the logical symbols of which are $\neg$, $\wedge$, $\exists$, and the variables v_1, v_2, v_3, . . . , and the non-logical symbols of which are the n-place predicate letters $Q_i^n (n = 1,2,3, \ldots ; i = 1,2,3, \ldots)$.

A *classical model for* L is a pair $\langle U,F \rangle$ where (i) U is a non-empty set and (ii) F assigns to each Q_i^n an n-place relation on U.

The *satisfaction value of* a formula ϕ of L *in* $M = \langle U,F \rangle$ *by* an assignment a of elements of U to the variables (in symbols $[\phi]_{M,a}$) is defined by the usual recursion:

(i) $[Q_i^n(v_{i_1} \ldots v_{i_n})]_{M,a} = 1$ iff $\langle a(v_{i_1}), \ldots, a(v_{i_n}) \rangle \in F(Q_i^n)$
(ii) $[\neg \phi]_{M,a} = 1$ iff $[\phi]_{M,a} = 0$
(iii) $[\phi \wedge \psi]_{M,a} = 1$ iff $[\phi]_{M,a} = 1$ and $[\psi]_{M,a} = 1$
(iv) $[(\exists V_i)\phi]_{M,a} = 1$ if for some $u \in U$ $[\phi]_{M,[a]_{v_i}^u} = 1$

A sentence ϕ of L is *true in M* if $[\phi]_{M,a} = 1$ for some a.

For any model M, Tr_M will be the set of sentences of L which are true in M and Fa_M, the set of sentences of L false in M.

A *partial model* for L is a pair $\langle U,F \rangle$ where (i) U is a non-empty set and (ii) F assigns to each letter Q_i^n an ordered pair $\langle F^+(Q_i^n),F^-(Q_i^n) \rangle$ of disjoint n-place-relations on U.

I will assume throughout that M is a model and is of the form $\langle U,F \rangle$.

The *satisfaction value* of a formula ϕ in M by an assignment a is now defined by:

(i)   a. $[Q_i^n(v_{j_1}, \ldots, v_{j_n})]_{M,a} = 1$ if $\langle a(v_{j_1}), \ldots, a(v_{j_n}) \rangle \in F^+(Q_i^n)$

      b. $[Q_i^n(v_{j_1}, \ldots, v_{j_n})]_{M,a} = 0$ if $\langle a(v_{j_1}), \ldots, a(v_{j_n}) \rangle \in F^-(Q_i^n)$

(ii)   a. $[\neg\phi]_{M,a} = 1$ if $[\phi]_{M,a} = 0$

      b. $[\neg\phi]_{M,a} = 0$ if $[\phi]_{M,a} = 1$

(iii)   a. $[\phi \wedge \psi]_{M,a} = 1$ if $[\phi]_{M,a} = 1$ and $[\psi]_{M,a} = 1$

      b. $[\phi \wedge \psi]_{M,a} = 0$ if $[\phi]_{M,a} = 0$ or $[\psi]_{M,a} = 0$

(iv)   a. $[(\exists v_i)\phi]_{M,a} = 1$ if for some $u \in U$ $[\phi]_{M, [a]_{v_i}^u} = 1$

      b. $[(\exists v_i)\phi]_{M,a} = 0$ if for all $u \in U$ $[\phi]_{M, [a]_{v_i}^u} = 0$

Again, a sentence ϕ is said to be *true in M* if $[\phi]_{M,a} = 1$ for some a; and ϕ is *false in M* if for some a $[\phi]_{M,a} = 0$.

Again, Tr_M is the set of true and Fa_M the set of false sentences of L in M. But now it is clearly possible that certain sentences are neither true nor false in M, so that $Tr_M \cup Fa_M$ does not coincide with the set of all sentences of L.

The partial model $M = \langle U,F \rangle$ is said to be *at least as vague as* the partial model $M' = \langle U,F' \rangle$ (in symbols: $M \subseteq M'$) if for each Q_i^n:

$$F^+(Q_i^n) \subseteq F^+(Q_i^n) \text{ and } F^-(Q_i^n) \subseteq F^-(Q_i^n)$$

(Thus $Tr_M \cup Fa_M \subseteq Tr_{M'} \cup Fa_{M'}$.)

To each classical model $\langle U,F \rangle$ for L corresponds a unique partial model: the model $\langle U,F' \rangle$ where for each (Q_i^n), $F^+(Q_i^n) = F(Q_i^n)$ and $F^-(Q_i^n) = U^n - F(Q_i^n)$. Classical models, as well as the partial models corresponding to them, will be referred to as *complete* models.

A classical model M is called a *completion* of a partial model M' if M' is at least as vague as (the partial model corresponding to) M.

4

In the theory of supervaluation one considers partial models in conjunction with *all* their completions. What I want to do here is formally almost the same, but with one crucial exception. Rather than all completions of a given partial model, we consider only a certain subset of them. In addition, we consider probability function over a field of subsets of this set of completions,[8] which contains, in particular, for each formula and assignment of elements to its free variables the set of all completions in which the former satisfies that assignment. (This condition warrants that each sentence has a measure.) The complex consisting of the partial model, the set of completions, the field over that set, and the probability function over that field I will call a *vague model*. Formally

A *vague model for L* is a quadruple $\langle M,\mathfrak{L},\mathfrak{F},p \rangle$, where
    (i) M is a partial model for L
    (ii) $\mathfrak{L}$ is a set of classical models for L which are completions of M

(iii) $\mathfrak{F}$ is a field subsets over $\mathfrak{L}$

(iv) for each $\phi \in L$ and assignment a in the universe of M, $\{M' \in \mathfrak{L}: [\phi]_{M',a} = 1\} \in \mathfrak{F}$; and

(v) p is a probability measure on $\mathfrak{F}$.[9]

Let $\mathcal{M} = \langle\langle U,F \rangle, \mathfrak{L}, \mathfrak{F}, p\rangle$ be a vague model for L. For any formula ϕ of L and assignment a of elements of U to the variables the *degree of satisfaction of* ϕ *by a in* $\mathcal{M}$, $[\phi]_{\mathcal{M}a}$, is defined as $p(\{M' \in \mathfrak{L}: [\phi]_{M,a} = 1\})$. Thus, in particular, if $\phi \in Tr_M$, then $[\phi]_{\mathcal{M}} = 1$; and if $\phi \in Fa_M$, then $[\phi]_{\mathcal{M}} = 0$.

The idea behind the notion of a vague model is this. At the present stage of its development—indeed, at any stage—language is vague. The kind of vagueness which interests us here is connected with predicates. The vagueness of a predicate may be resolved by fiat—that is, by deciding which of the objects which as yet are neither definitely inside nor definitely outside its extension are to be in and which are to be out. However, it may be that not every such decision is acceptable. For there may already be semantical principles which, though they do not determine of any one of a certain group of objects whether it belongs to the extension or not, nevertheless demand that if a certain member of the group is put into the extension, a certain other member must be put into the extension as well. Take, for example, the adjective *intelligent*. Our present criteria tell us of certain people that they definitely are intelligent, of certain others that they definitely are not, but there will be a large third category of people about whom they do not tell us either way. Now suppose that we make our standard more specific—for example, by stipulating that to have an I.Q. over a certain minimum is a necessary and sufficient criterion for being intelligent. Further, suppose that of two persons u_1 and u_2 of the third category u_1 has a higher I.Q. than u_2. Then, whatever we decide this minimum to be, our decision will put u_1 into the extension if it puts u_2 into it. Finally, let us assume for the sake of argument that any way of making the concept of intelligence precise that is compatible with what we already understand that concept to be is equivalent to the adoption of a certain minimum I.Q. Then there will be no completions in the partial model that reflect the present state of affairs and in which u_2 is put into the extension of the predicate but u_1 is not.

Formally, if Q_1^1 represents the adjective *intelligent* and the model $\langle M, \mathfrak{L}, \mathfrak{F}, p\rangle$ reflects the situation just described, and M, in particular, that which obtains before any of the possible precise definitions has been adopted, then u_1 and u_2 are both members of $U - (F^+(Q_1^1) \cup F^-(Q_1^1))$, and there is no model $M' \in \mathfrak{L}$ such that $u_2 \in F(Q_1)$ and $u_1 \notin F(Q_1)$.

My original motivation in setting up this framework was to give a uniform characterization of the operation which transforms adjectives into their comparatives. Let us see if this is now possible.

The relation x *is more A than* y (where A is any adjective) can be defined in terms of the relation x *is at least as A as* y by

(11) x is more A than y if and only if x is at least as A as y and it is not the case that y is at least as A as x.

Therefore a semantic characterization of this second relation will automatically give us one for the first as well. As there are minor but undeniable advantages in discussing the relation *at least as . . . as*, I will concentrate on that concept.

Let us assume that some of the one-place predicates of L represent adjectives, in particular Q_1^1. We add to L the operator symbol $\geqslant$. This symbol forms out of one one-place predicate Q_i^1 a two-place relation $\geqslant (Q_i^1)$. Also $\geqslant (Q_i^1)(x,y)$ should be read as x *is at least as* Q_i^1 *as* y. (What relation $\geqslant(Q_i^1)$ might represent when Q_i^1 is not an adjective is of no concern to us now.) Let L' be the language resulting from the addition of $\geqslant$ to L. Let $\mathcal{M} = \langle M, \mathfrak{L}, \mathfrak{F}, p\rangle$ be a vague model for L. In order to expand $\mathcal{M}$ to a model for L' we must determine the positive and negative extensions of the relation $\geqslant(Q_i^1)$ in M, as well as its extensions in all the members of $\mathfrak{L}$. To begin, we will consider just the positive extension in M. Two possible definitions come to mind. According to the first, an element u_1 of U stands (definitely) in the relation to u_2 if for every member M' of $\mathfrak{L}$ in which u_2 belongs to the extension of Q_i^1 u_1 belongs to that extension as well. So we get, representing the positive extension of $\geqslant (Q_i^1)$ in M as $F^+(\geqslant(Q_i^1))$,

(12) for all $u_1, u_2, \in U$, $\langle u_1, u_2 \rangle \in F^+(\geqslant (Q_i^1))$ iff $[Q_i^1 (v_1)]_{\mathscr{M}a_2} \subseteq [Q_i^1 (v_1)]_{\mathscr{M}a_1}$ (where a_1 and a_2 are any assignments with $a_1(v_1) = u_1$ and $a_2(v_1) = u_2$, respectively)

According to the second definition, u_1 stands in the relation to u_2 if the measure of the set of completions in which u_1 belongs to the extension of Q_i^1 is at least as large as that of the set of completions in which u_2 belongs to the extension. So we obtain

(13) for all $u_1, u_2 \in U$, $\langle u_1, u_2 \rangle \in F^+(\geqslant (Q_i^1))$ iff $p([Q_i^1 (v_1)]_{\mathscr{M}a_2}) \leqslant p([Q_i^1(v_1)]_{\mathscr{M}a_1})$, where a_1 and a_2 are as above

Before we consider the relative merits of these definitions, let us first remove a flaw which they share. Neither (12) nor (13) allows for the possibility that the comparative relation holds between two objects for each of which it is beyond doubt that it satisfies the positive. For if both u_1 and u_2 belong to $F^+(Q_i^1)$, then $[Q_i^1 (v_1)]_{M,a_1} = [Q_i^1 (v_1)]_{M,a_2}, = 1$, and so both (12) and (13) would exclude $\langle u_1, u_2 \rangle$ from $F^+(\geqslant(Q_i^1))$.

It seems that the only way in which we could meet this difficulty without departing too much from our present format is this: Instead of a vague model, consisting of a partial model M, a field $\mathfrak{F}$ over a set $\mathfrak{L}$ of completions of M and a probability function p over that field, we need to consider models $\mathscr{M}$, in which the set $\mathfrak{L}$ comprises besides completions of M also complete models which in certain ways conflict with M. Such models will represent (hypothetical) situations in which the standards for a predicate are set so high that certain objects which already have that predicate in M now fail to have it—or else in which the standards are set so low that objects belonging to the negative extension of the predicate in M now fall in its positive extension. This leads us to the following modification of the notion of a vague model:

A *graded model for L* is a quadruple $\langle M, \mathfrak{L}, \mathfrak{F}, p \rangle$, where
   (i) M is a partial model for L
   (ii) $\mathfrak{L}$ is a set of classical models for L with universe U
   (iii) $\mathfrak{F}$ is a field over $\mathfrak{L}$
   (iv) For each formula ϕ of L and each assignment a to elements of the universe of M,
      $\{M' \in \mathfrak{L}: [\phi]_{M',a} = 1\} \in \mathfrak{F}$
   (v) $\{M' \in \mathfrak{L}: M'$ is a completion of $M\} \in \mathfrak{F}$; and
   (vi) p is a probability function over $\mathfrak{F}$.

We may then define the degree of truth of a sentence of L just as before, except that we now consider the conditional probability of a certain set of completions of M on the set of all completions of M in $\mathfrak{L}$. On the other hand, the characterization (13) of the comparative of Q_i^1 is now no longer vulnerable to the objection which led us to the introduction of graded models.

Let us consider an example. Suppose that Q_1^1 represents the adjective *heavy*; that all other predicates represent properties of, and relations between, material objects, and (for simplicity) that Q_1^1 is the only vague predicate. Let U be the set of material objects and let $\mathscr{M} = \langle M, \mathfrak{L}, \mathfrak{F}, p \rangle$ be a graded representation (restricted to material objects) of the actual world. What should in this case $\mathfrak{L}$ and p be? As regards $\mathfrak{L}$, a simple answer seems possible in this special case: for each particular real number r there will be a member M of $\mathfrak{L}$ in which the extension of Q_1^1 consists of those objects whose weight (in grams) exceeds r.

It is not possible to say precisely what the function p should be. But this much seems beyond doubt: there should be a strictly monotonic function f from the set of all positive real numbers into the interval $[0,1]$ so that for any object u with weight r, $p([Q_1^1 (v_1)]_{\mathscr{M},a} = f(r)$ (for some a with $a(v_1) = u$). Thus, the greater u's weight, the larger the class of members of $\mathscr{L}$ in which Q_1^1 is true of u, and the greater the measure (or "intermediate truth value") of the formula $Q_1^1 (v)$ under a_1.

5

We should now compare (12) and (13). According to (12), u_1 is at least as heavy as u_2 just in case the set of models in which u_1 *is heavy* is true includes the class of those which render u_2 *is heavy* true; this will be the case if and only if u_1 has greater or equal weight. Indeed, within the context of the present example, (12) is precisely the proposal that can be found in Lewis (1970), where it is attributed to David Kaplan.

According to (13), u_1 will be at least as heavy as u_2, provided u_2 *is heavy* is true in a set of models with measure greater than or equal to that of the set of models in which u_2 *is heavy* is true. Again this will be true if and only if u_1 has greater or equal weight. Thus for this special case the two definitions are equivalent.

But this need not always be so. Suppose for example that Smith, though less quick-witted than Jones, is much better at solving mathematical problems. Is Smith cleverer than Jones? This is perhaps not clear, for we usually regard quick-wittedness and problem-solving facility as indications of cleverness, without a canon for weighing these criteria against each other when they suggest different answers. When faced with the need to decide the issue, various options may be open to us. We might decide that really only problem-solving counts, so that after all, Smith is cleverer than Jones; or we might decide on a particular method for weighing the two criteria, so that Smith's vast superiority at solving problems will warrant that in spite of Jones's slight edge in quick-wittedness Smith is cleverer than Jones; or we might decide that only quick-wittedness counts, and this time Jones will come out as the cleverer of the two.

It is not clear how the probability function of a graded model $\mathscr{M}$ representing this situation should be defined. Yet, if we assume that the third decision is less plausible than either the first or the second, then we should expect members of $\mathscr{L}$ which are compatible with that decision to have no more weight than those which are compatible with other decisions. Further, relatively few models of the first sort will be such that Jones belongs to the extension of *clever* and Smith not; for Jones is not that much quicker in conversation. But, because of the disparity in problem-solving ability, many models compatible with the first decision, as well as a good many that are compatible with the second, will have Smith in the extension of *clever* but not Jones. Given all this, we would expect the measure of the set of members of $\mathscr{L}$ in which Smith belongs to the extension to be greater than that of those members where Jones belongs to the extension. So by (13) and (11) we would have to conclude that Smith is cleverer than Jones.

But do we want to say this? I think not. Before any decision has been made it is true neither that Smith is cleverer than Jones nor that Jones is cleverer than Smith. This intuitive judgment is in agreement with (12), according to which Jones and Smith are incomparable in respect of cleverness. Indeed, it is (12) which, in my opinion, captures the comparative correctly—at least to the extent that it gives a necessary and sufficient condition for *definite* membership in the positive extension of $\geqslant (Q_1^1)$. That (13) cannot be right becomes even more evident when we realize that it implies that for any objects u_1 and u_2 and adjective A, either u_1 is at least as A as u_2 or u_2 is at least as A as u_1; and this should fail to be true in general whenever we have two, largely independent, criteria for applicability of the adjective, but no clear procedure for weighing them.

We saw that, for *heavy*, (12) and (13) are equivalent (provided p has been correctly specified). The same is true for a number of other adjectives which, like *heavy*, may be called "one-dimensional." With each such adjective is associated a unique measurable aspect. The (numerical) value of that aspect for a given object determines whether or not the adjective applies. For *heavy* the aspect is weight. Other examples are *tall* (associated with height) and *hot* (associated with temperature).

But such adjectives are rare. Even *large* is not one of them. For what precisely makes an object large? Its height? or its volume? or its surface? or a combination of some of these? Here we encounter the same phenomenon that has already been revealed by our discussion of *clever*. There is no fixed procedure for integrating the various criteria. Often it is the context of use which indicates how the criteria should be integrated or, alternatively, which of them should be taken as uniquely relevant.

This is one of the various ways in which contexts disambiguate. Formally, contextual disambiguation can be represented as a function from contexts to models less vague than the ground model. While incorporating this idea into the framework already adopted, I will at the same time eliminate a feature of vague and graded models which is unrealistic in any case but would be particularly out of place in the context-dependent models defined below: thus far I have assumed that all the members of $\mathfrak{L}$ are complete models. But this is unnatural if we want to think of these models as the results of semantical decisions that could actually be made. For most decisions will fail to render the relevant predicates completely sharp. They will only make them sharper. (Indeed, we may with Wittgenstein, doubt that we could ever make any concept completely sharp.) It therefore appears more natural to posit that the members of $\mathfrak{L}$ are partial models. It is possible, moreover, that one of these contextually determined models is less vague than another, namely, when intuitively speaking, the semantic decision reflected by the second goes in the same direction, but not as far as, that reflected by the first. Thus $\mathfrak{L}$ will be partially ordered by the relation *as vague as*.

I just suggested that a context picks from this set a particular model—which functions, so to speak, as the ground model of the graded model which represents the speech situation determined by that context. The various sharpenings acceptable from the viewpoint of that context would then be represented by those members of $\mathfrak{L}$ which are at most as vague as the new ground model. But I am not convinced that this is absolutely correct. For it could conceivably be the case that two different contexts specify for a given predicate two different criteria from the set of those which are prima facie plausible and which, though they happen to determine the same new ground model, will not permit exactly the same further sharpenings. So the context should select a certain subset of $\mathfrak{L}$ of contextually admissible further sharpenings. In addition, the context must select a subset of admissible modifications. This set we could not even hope to reconstruct from the new ground model alone.

Thus far the probability function p was defined over a class of complete models. This would now seem to be impossible as we no longer require that $\mathfrak{L}$ consists of—or even that it contains any—complete models. Yet the intuition behind the function p—which I tried to convey in the example concerning *heavy*—makes it appear unnatural to define p as a function over sets of *partial* models, especially as these sets may now be expected to contain models one of which is vaguer than the other; it is, so to speak, the number of possible *ultimate* results of repeated sharpening that p should measure, and not the number of intermediate steps that one may take on the way to these ultimate complete models.

A solution to this dilemma can be found if we assume that all individual cases of vagueness can be resolved, though not all at once, and this assumption does appear to be unexceptionable. Thus we will impose on the set $\mathfrak{L}$ the following condition:

(14)   if $\langle U, F_1 \rangle \in \mathfrak{L}$ and $\langle u_1, \ldots, u_n \rangle \in U^n - (F_1^+(Q_i^n) \cup F_1^-(Q_i^n))$, then there is a member $\langle U, F_2 \rangle$ in which Q_i^n is less vague than $\langle U, F_1 \rangle$ and such that $\langle u_1, \ldots, u_n \rangle \in F_2^+(Q_i^n) \cup F_2^-(Q_i^n)$.

Under this assumption we may construct complete models as the unions of maximal chains in $\mathfrak{L}$. Let $\mathfrak{L}$ be a set of partial models for L which all have the same universe U. Then $\mathfrak{L}$ is a *chain under the relation 'vaguer than'* if for any two of its members $\langle U, F_1 \rangle$, $\langle U, F_2 \rangle$ either

(i) for each predicate Q_j^n of L, $F_1^+(Q_j^n) \subseteq F_2^+(Q_j^n)$ and $F_1^-(Q_j^n) \subseteq F_2^-(Q_j^n)$ or

(ii) for each predicate Q_j^n of L, $F_2^+(Q_j^n) \subseteq F_1^+(Q_j^n)$ and $F_2^-(Q_j^n) \subseteq F_1^-(Q_j^n)$.

A subset $\mathfrak{L}'$ of a set $\mathfrak{L}$ of models with universe U, is a *maximal chain in* $\mathfrak{L}$ if (i) $\mathfrak{L}'$ is a chain (under the relation *vaguer than*) and (ii) for any $M' \in \mathfrak{L} - \mathfrak{L}'$, $\mathfrak{L}' \cup \{M'\}$ is not a chain. The *union of* a chain $\mathfrak{L}$ of models with universe U is the model $\langle U, F_\infty \rangle$ where for each $Q_j^n F_\infty^+(Q_j^n) =$

$$\underset{\langle U,F\rangle \in \mathfrak{L}}{\cup} F^+(Q_j^n) \text{ and } F_\infty(Q_j^n) = \underset{\langle U,F\rangle \in \mathfrak{L}}{\cup} F(Q_j^n)$$

If U is countable, then (14) entails that

(15)   The union of each maximal chain of $\mathfrak{L}$ is complete.

However, (15) does not follow automatically from (14) when U is uncountable. Since it is property (15) in which we are primarily interested in connection with the function p, I will make it, rather than (14), one of the defining conditions of graded context-dependent models.

A *graded context-dependent model for* L is a quintuple $\langle M, \mathfrak{L}, \mathfrak{C}, \mathfrak{F}, p \rangle$ where

(i) M is a partial model;

(ii) $\mathfrak{L}$ is a set of partial models with the same universe as M;

(iii) The union of each maximal chain of $\mathfrak{L}$ is complete;

(iv) $\mathfrak{C}$ is a function the range of which consists of pairs $\langle M', \mathfrak{L}' \rangle$ where (a) $M' \in \mathfrak{L}$, (b) $\mathfrak{L}' \subseteq \mathfrak{L}$, and (c) the union of each maximal chain of $\mathfrak{L}'$ is complete;

(v) $\mathfrak{F}$ is a field over the set $\bar{\mathfrak{L}}$ of unions of maximal chains of $\mathfrak{L}$;

(vi) (a) for each formula ϕ and assignment a the set of members M' of $\mathfrak{L}$ such that $[\phi]_{M',a} = 1$ belongs to $\bar{\mathfrak{L}}$; (b) $\{M' \in \bar{\mathfrak{L}}: M \subseteq M'\} \in \mathfrak{F}$; (c) for each $\langle M', \mathfrak{L}' \rangle$ in the range of $\mathfrak{C}$ if $\bar{\mathfrak{L}}'$ is the set of unions of maximal chains of $\mathfrak{L}'$, then $\{M' \in \bar{\mathfrak{L}}': M' \subseteq M''\} \in \mathfrak{F}$;

(vii) p is a probability function over $\mathfrak{F}$.

We will refer to context-dependent graded models by means of the abbreviation cgm. Henceforth $\mathcal{M}$ will always be a cgm and will always be equal to $\langle M, \mathfrak{L}, \mathfrak{C}, \mathfrak{F}, p \rangle$; M will be called the *ground model* of $\mathcal{M}$; similarly, if $\mathfrak{C}(c) = \langle M'_c, \mathfrak{L}'_c \rangle$, then M'_c is called the *ground model* (in $\mathcal{M}$) *with respect to* c.

Again we denote the set of members of $\bar{\mathfrak{L}}$ in which ϕ is true under a as $[\phi]_{\mathcal{M},a}$, where $\bar{\mathfrak{L}}$ is again the set of unions of maximal chains of $\mathfrak{L}$. Similarly, if $\mathfrak{C}(c) = \langle M_c, \mathfrak{L}_c \rangle$, $[\phi]_{\mathcal{M},c,a}$ is the set of members of $\bar{\mathfrak{L}}_c$ in which ϕ is true under a.

The domain of $\mathfrak{C}$ should be thought of as the set of contexts. Contexts may be more or less specific; correspondingly, Dom $\mathfrak{C}$ may contain elements c and c' such that $M_c \leqslant M_{c'}$ and $\mathfrak{L}_c \subseteq \mathfrak{L}_{c'}$; in this case c will be at least as specific as c'. Thus the members of Dom $\mathfrak{C}$ are partially ordered by the relation $\leqslant$, defined by: $c \leqslant c'$ iff $M_c \subseteq M_{c'}$ and $\mathfrak{L}_c \subseteq \mathfrak{L}_{c'}$. One may wonder if for every member M' of $\mathfrak{L}$ there should be a c such that M' is the ground model with respect to c. This would mean that for any possible sharpening of a predicate there is a context which indicates that the predicate should be understood in precisely *that* sharper way. I have no argument to show that this assumption is false, yet I see no gain from it; thus I prefer not to make it.

In a cgm it is possible that while the relation $\geqslant (Q^1)$ does not hold in the ground model it does hold in the ground models of certain contexts. Thus assume Q_1^1 represents the adjective *clever*; further assume that c_1 represents a context in which *clever* must be understood as '*good at solving problems*'; that c_2 represents a context in which *clever* must be understood as '*quick-witted*'; and that c_3

represents a context on which both quick-wittedness and the ability to solve problems are to be regarded as constitutive of cleverness. Then we may expect that if $a_1(v_1) = $ Smith and $a_2(v_1) = $ Jones,

(a) $[Q_1^!(v_1)]_{\mathcal{M}c_1, a_2} \subseteq [Q_1^! (v_1)]_{\mathcal{M}c_1,a_1}$; and

(b) $[Q_1^!(v_1)]_{\mathcal{M}c_2, a_1} \subseteq [Q_1^! (v_1)]_{\mathcal{M}c_2,a_2}$

while nothing, definite can be said about the relation between $[Q_1^!(v_1)]_{\mathcal{M}c_3, a}$ and $[Q_1^!(v_1)]_{\mathcal{M}c_3, a_2}$ until more is known about whether, and in what way, c_3 determines how the two criteria for *clever* are to be weighed. In order that (a) and (b) formally guarantee that in c_1 Smith is cleverer than Jones, while in c_2 Jones is cleverer than Smith, we must specify, parallel to (13)

(16) if $\mathfrak{C}(c) = \langle\langle U,F_c\rangle, \mathfrak{L}_c\rangle$ and $u_1,u_2 \in U$ then $\langle u_1,u_2\rangle \in F_c^+(\geqslant(Q_i^!))$ if and only if $[Q_i^!(v_1)]_{\mathcal{M}c, a_2} \subseteq [Q_i^! (v_1)]_{\mathcal{M}c,a_1}$.

  Since not every member of $\mathfrak{L}$ is necessarily the ground model with respect to some context, (16) may not define the positive extension of $\geqslant (Q_i^!)$ for some of these models. This is of little practical importance. If we insist on defining the extensions in these models as well, we may stipulate that for any such model $\langle U,F\rangle, \langle u_1,u_2\rangle \in F_1^+(\geqslant Q_i^!))$ if and only if for some $c, \mathfrak{C}(c) = \langle M_c, \mathfrak{L}_c\rangle$, $\langle U,F_1\rangle \in \mathfrak{L}_c, M_c \subseteq \langle U,F_1\rangle$ and $\langle u_1,u_2\rangle \in F_c^+(\geqslant(Q_i^!))$.

  What is the negative extension of $\geqslant(Q_i^!)$? It should consist in the first place of those pairs $\langle u_1,u_2\rangle$ of which it is definitely true that u_2 is more $Q_i^!$ than u_1—that is, in view of (12), those pairs for which

(17) $[Q_i^!(v_1)]_{\mathcal{M}, a_1} \subsetneq [Q_i^! (v_1)]_{\mathcal{M},a_2}$.

One might question this condition on the ground that it makes u_2 *is more* $Q_i^!$ *than* u_1 definitely true also when the difference between u_1 and u_2 is only marginal. But I do not believe that the objection is well-founded. However marginal the difference, if it is a difference in an aspect which is irrevocably bound to the predicate, so that no context can break this tie, then the relation definitely obtains irrespective of whether it is difficult, or even physically impossible, to observe this.

  This leaves us with those pairs $\langle u_1,u_2\rangle$ such that neither $[Q_i^!(v_1)]_{\mathcal{M}a_1} \subseteq [Q_i^!(v_1)]_{\mathcal{M}a_2}$ nor $[Q_i^!(v_1)]_{\mathcal{M}a_2} \subseteq [Q_i^!(v_1)]_{\mathcal{M}a_1}$. Which of these should go into $F^-(\geqslant(Q_i^!))$? I think none. As long as there are some acceptable ways of sharpening $Q_i^!$ which render u_1 at least as $Q_i^!$ as u_2, the falsehood of u_1 *is at least as* $Q_i^!$ *as* u_2 cannot be definite.

I introduced the probability function to show how the notion of "degrees of truth" can be made coherent. But so far the function has served to no good purpose. In particular it has proved useless for the characterization of the comparative: once more it turned out to be necessary to define the operation on the sets themselves rather than on the numerical values to which p reduces them.

  However, there are expressions the analysis of which does seem to require the function p. Consider *rather*. *Rather* forms adjectives out of adjectives: for example, *rather tall* out of *tall*, *rather clever* out of *clever*. When is a person rather clever? Before I can discuss the really important aspects of this question, I should first settle a minor point: *x is rather clever* sometimes seems to deny that *x* is clever, while on other occasions it appears to be entailed by the fact that *x* is clever—just as, for example, *most x are F* sometimes seems to entail *not all x are F*, while on other occasions it seems to be entailed by *all x are F*. I think that both cases, as well as a great many similar ones, ask for an explanation involving Grice's theory of implicature: *most x are F* is a consequence of *all x are F*; but when uttered by a speaker whom the hearer assumes to know whether all *x* are *F*, it will convey that not all *x* are *F*—for if all *x* were *F*, why would not the speaker have said so? Similarly, *rather clever* is weaker than *clever*. But one would use the longer phrase only if one had doubts that the shorter applies.

Thus *x is rather clever* is weaker than *x is clever*. Accordingly, x is rather clever if a certain lowering of the standards for cleverness would make x clever—that is, if the proportion of members of $\bar{\mathfrak{L}}$ in which x belongs to the extension of *clever* is large enough. Indeed, the closer x is to being truly clever, the smaller is the modification of the standards that is required, and thus the larger will be the class of those models where x is in the extension.

It should be noted that just as x may pass the test of cleverness for different reasons, so he may also pass that of being rather clever in a variety of ways. Thus it is possible that x, y, and z are all rather clever (though not unambiguously clever); x, because he is remarkably quick-witted, while hopeless at mathematical problems; y, because he is good at such problems, though slow in conversation; and z, because he has both capacities to a moderate degree. For any two of x, y, z, there will be certain modifications of standards which will warrant membership in the extension of *clever* for one but not for the other. Thus it will be true of the set of members of $\bar{\mathfrak{L}}$ in which, say, x is in the extension of clever and the set of those members of $\bar{\mathfrak{L}}$ where the extension contains, say, y, that neither will include the other. Yet they both guarantee membership in the extension of *rather clever*, essentially because they are both large enough. It is this intuition concerning the largeness of sets which p tries to capture.

Thus if *clever* is again represented by Q_1^1, then we may put:

u_1 is rather clever if and only if $[Q_1^1(v_1)]_{\mathscr{M},a_1} \geqslant p_0$ (where p_0 is some number in $(0,1)$.

Obviously p_0 should be less than $p(\{M' \in \bar{\mathfrak{L}}: M \subseteq M'\})$, but not much more can be said about it. For of course p_0 is not fixed. If that were so, *rather clever* would be a sharp predicate, which evidently it is not.

The vagueness of *rather* could be represented in the following way. We associate with each $c \in \text{Dom } \mathfrak{C}$ a pair of real numbers r_c^-, r_c^+ between 0 and 1 such that whenever $c \leqslant c'$, then $r_c^- \leqslant r_{c'}^- < r_{c'}^+ \leqslant r_c^+$. The positive and negative extensions of *rather* Q_1^1 in the ground model M_c with respect to c are then defined as the sets

$$\{u \in U: [Q_i^1(v_1)]_{\mathscr{M},c,a} > r_c^+ \cdot p(\{M \in \mathfrak{L}_c: M_c \subseteq M'\})\}$$
$$\{u \in U: [Q_i^1(v_1)]_{\mathscr{M},c,a} < r_c^- \cdot p(\{M \in \mathfrak{L}_c: M_c \subseteq M'\})\},$$

respectively; finally the intermediate value of *u is rather* Q_i^1 in the ground model is given by $p(\{M' \in \bar{\mathfrak{L}}: u$ belongs to the positive extension of *rather* Q_i^1 in $M'\})$.

There are a number of words which, like *rather*, form adjectives out of adjectives and which can be analyzed along similar lines. Another prominent example is *very*. The extension of *very* Q_i^1 is again a function of $[Q_i^1(v_1)]_{\mathscr{M},a}$. The limit which $[Q_i^1(v_1)]_{\mathscr{M},a}$ must exceed in order that $a(v_1)$ belong to the extension of *very* Q_i^1 must be larger, and not smaller, than $p(\{M' \in \mathfrak{L}; M \subseteq M'\})$.

6

For traditional logic adjectives, nouns and intransitive verbs are all of a kind—namely, one-place predicates. My second theory of adjectives tries to vindicate this view against the one expressed earlier which puts adjectives into a different category than verbs and nouns. Yet it is an undeniable fact about ordinary English that while the comparative is in general a natural operation on adjectives, similar operations on nouns are of relatively little importance, and on verbs they are virtually non-existent. This suggests a difference between adjectives on the one hand and verbs and nouns on other hand. I will leave verbs out of consideration in the following discussion, as they present problems quite different from those with which this paper is concerned. But I will try to say something about the difference between adjectives and nouns. Why is it that comparisons involving nouns are in general so much more dubious than those which involve adjectives? *This is more a table than that* sounds awkward and is perhaps never unequivocally true, except in the cases in which it is evident that this is a table and that is not (but then we can say precisely this, and thus do not need the first phrase). Yet it appears that nouns too are vague, some of them just as vague as certain adjectives. Why does not their vagueness allow for equally meaningful comparatives? To discover the reasons, it is advantageous to reconsider "one-dimensional" adjectives.

For any such adjective Q_i^1 it will be the case that, for arbitrary a_1, a_2,

(18)   either $[Q_i^1(v_1)]_{\mathscr{M},a_1} \subseteq [Q_i^1(v_1)]_{\mathscr{M},a_2}$, or $[Q_i^1(v_1)]_{\mathscr{M},a_2} \subseteq [Q_i^1(v_1)]_{\mathscr{M},a_1}$;

and this ensures that u_1 *is more* Q_i^1 *than* u_2 always has a definite truth value.

We have already seen that most adjectives do not satisfy (18) unambiguously: u_1 *is cleverer than* u_2 could remain without truth value in the ground model. Yet there should still be a fair proportion of pairs $\langle u_1, u_2 \rangle$ where u_1 and u_2 both lie in the extension gap of *clever*, but for which (18) holds (with $a_1(v_1) = u_1$ and $a_2(v_1) = u_2$). And, for the same reason, there are many contexts c in which (18) holds (with $[Q_i^1(v_1)]_{\mathscr{M},c,a_1}$ for $[Q_i^1(v_1)]_{\mathscr{M},a_i^1}$, etc.), so that in c each comparative sentence involving Q_i^1 is either definitely true or definitely false. On the other hand, if Q_i^1 is a noun, then (18) will in general be satisfied for very few pairs of objects which both fall in the extension gap of Q_i^1.

A very rough explanation for this formal distinction is the following: in order for an object to satisfy a noun, it must in general satisfy all, or a large portion, of a cluster of criteria. None of these we can promote to the sole criterion without distorting the noun's meaning beyond recognition. We cannot, therefore, compare the degrees to which two different objects satisfy the noun in terms of their degrees of satisfaction of just one of its many criteria; in order to compare them by comparing their ratings with respect to a variety of these criteria we need a method for integrating these various ratings. And such a method is in general not part of the meaning of the noun.

There is another aspect to the difference between nouns and adjectives which is related to the one discussed above, but perhaps even more important in connection with the former's resistance to comparatives. Nouns, though potentially just as vague as adjectives, tend in actual practice to behave much more like sharp predicates. Take *cat*. In principle there could be all sorts of borderline cases for this predicate, but in actual fact there, are very few at best. The same is true, be it in slightly varying degrees, of *table*, *rock* or *word*. Thus nouns often have very small, or no, extension gaps in the actual world—even if it is easy to think of possible worlds in which these gaps would be enormous. This gives an additional explanation of why comparatives involving nouns should be of relatively little use. For they are particularly important in those cases where neither of the two objects compared belongs unambiguously to the positive or to the negative extension of the predicate in question. And these cases will seldom arise when the predicate is a noun.

It is an interesting question how nouns "manage" to be as sharp as they are. The explanation must be more or less along the following lines. Even if each of the several criteria for the noun may apply to actual objects in varying degrees, these criteria tend to be, with respect to the actual world, *parallel*: an object which fails to satisfy a few of them to a reasonable degree will generally fail to score well with regard to almost all of them. Consequently, it will be recognized as either definitely inside the extension of the noun or else as definitely out. The nature of this parallelism is very much that of a physical law—it is a feature of our world, and thus in essence empirical. This is one of the ways in which the actual structure of the world shapes the conceptual frame with which we operate, and one of the reasons why it is difficult to separate the empirical from the purely conceptual.

Where the simple comparative of a predicate is non-sensical, addition of certain special expressions can restore its meaningfulness. Examples of such expressions are *in a sense, as far as function is concerned*, and *with regard to shape*.[10]

Let us consider this last phrase. How should we analyze

(19)   with regard to shape u_1 is more a table than u_2?

First we should determine the logical type of the expression *with regard to shape*. This is really a problem which does not belong in this paper. I will therefore give an answer which is convenient in connection with the issues which concern us here and does not distort them. I will treat *is more . . . than . . . with regard to shape* as an atomic—that is, not further analyzable—expression which stands for a new comparative operation, one which again forms binary relations out of predicates. This new comparative differs from the one considered thus far in the following way: the phrase *with regard to shape* places us so to speak in a context where shape is singled out as the only criterion for whatever the property is in respect of which the comparison is made. Let us suppose that there are such contexts—contexts in which those predicates to which shape is at all relevant are evaluated with respect to shape alone. Then (19) should be true in the ground model if and only if *u_1 is more a table than u_2* is true in each of these contexts.

I should like to make a brief comment at this point on the nature of contexts and the role which in my opinion they ought to play in semantic analysis of the sort of which I have tried to give instances in this paper. We could give an alternative, but evidently equivalent, account of (19) by stipulating that the phrase *with regard to shape* transforms the context in which (19) is used *into* one where shape is the only relevant issue. For our account of (19), it does not make much difference which line of explanation we choose. However, I believe that the solution to certain other semantical problems can be found only if we investigate not only the effect of the various aspects of context on the meanings of expressions used in those contexts, but also the mechanisms which *create*, or *modify*, contextual aspects. A proper understanding of these mechanisms seems essential to the analysis of more extended pieces of discourse, such as told or written stories.[11] Given that such understanding must eventually be reached in any case, an account of (19) along the lines of the second proposal may well ultimately be the more desirable. It seems, however, too early to pass judgment on this matter.

At any rate it is important to realize that contexts are made up of verbal and nonverbal elements alike. The same contextual aspect may on one occasion be manifest through the setting in which the utterance is made, while on another occasion its presence is signaled by a particular verbal expression. Exclusive preoccupation with shape, for example, can be evident to both speaker and audience either because they have been discussing shape and nothing but shape all along (think of a session about shape during a conference on industrial design); or because the previous sentence was *But let us now concentrate exclusively on shape*; or because the sentence itself contains the qualifying phrase *with regard to shape*. The three cases differ as regards the degree of permanence with which the feature in question is part of the context. In the first case, preoccupation with shape will last throughout the session and a special verbal effort would be necessary to remove it; in the third case, the modification will be in force only during the evaluation of the particular phrase to which *with regard to shape* is attached; the second case is somewhere between the two. Indeed, without further information, it is not possible to say whether the modification is valid just for the present sentence, for everything this particular speaker is going to say right now, or for the remainder of the entire discussion.

Another expression of the sort we have just been discussing is *in a sense*.[12] What is it to be clever in a sense? That depends on what are the various possible senses of the word *clever*. It will help to consider such related sentences as *Smith is clever in the sense that he is good at solving problems* or *Jones is clever in the sense of being quick-witted*. The expressions following *clever* in these two sentences have, again, the effect of transforming the context, namely into one where *clever* is given a more specific sense. The truth value of the sentence should therefore be the same as it is in any of these contexts. The contexts in question are the same as those created by antecedent specifications like *Let us understand by 'clever': 'good at solving problems'*. Each such specification will single out a set of contexts in which *clever* is understood correspondingly. Then *x is clever in a sense* is true if there is such a set of contexts such that x *is clever* is true in each of its members.

But which are the acceptable specifications of a given noun or adjective? This is a question to which no definite answer can be given; for the notion of an acceptable specification of a given concept is itself subject to just that sort of vagueness with which this paper is concerned. Clearly not every logically possible definition is acceptable; for if this were so, then all statements of the form

(20)   *x* is a ... in a sense

would be true. But what is an acceptable specification can if necessary be stretched very far indeed. That is why it is so hard to establish that a particular sentence of the form (20) is false.

I want to conclude this discussion of hedges with a few remarks on the expression *to the extent that*. Let us consider Lakoff's example:

(21)   To the extent that Austin is a linguist he is a good one.

Once more I will leave questions concerning the ultimate logical form of the expression aside. It will be adequate for our present interests if we regard *to the extent that* as a two-place sentential operator which forms out of two formulas ϕ and ψ the compound formula

(22)   to the extent that ϕ, ψ.

The semantical analysis of this connective brings into focus a problem connected with contextual disambiguation which I have so far failed to mention: to what extent does the sharpening of one predicate affect other predicates? Clearly the decisions concerning two different words cannot in all cases be independent. Sharpening of the noun *leg* will yield sharpening of the adjective *four-legged* as well. Yet there are many pairs of adjectives such that a sharpening or modification of one does not carry with it any perceptible semantic change in the other. This is true in particular of *linguist* and *good*. This is important for the following account of (21).

The truth conditions of (22) are essentially these: (22) is true (in its actual context of use *c*) if ψ is true in all contexts in which ϕ is true and which are as similar to *c* as is possible, given that they make ϕ true. In the case of (21) these contexts will be contexts in which we have modified the semantics for *linguist* in such a way that Austin is now definitely inside its extension, and have left the semantics otherwise as much the same as the modification of *linguist* permits. In particular, *good* would, it seems to me, not be affected seriously by the modification. The truth of the main clause of (21) in such a context is to be understood in the usual manner.

It is interesting to compare (21) with the slightly more complicated

(23)   To the extent that Austin and Russell are linguists, Austin is at least as good a linguist as Russell.

This sentence will be true in *c* if in every maximally similar context *c'* in which *linguist* has been modified in such a way that both Austin and Russell are in its extension, it is true that Austin is at least as good a linguist as Russell. When is it true in *c'* that Austin is at least as good a linguist as Russell? This will be the case if the pair ⟨Austin, Russell⟩ belongs to the positive extension of $\geqslant$ (good linguist) with respect to *c'*—that is, if the set of members of $\mathfrak{L}_{c'}$ in which *Austin is a good linguist* is true includes the set of those members in which *Russell is a good linguist* is true. It is important that this account will give us the intuitively correct truth conditions for (23) only if the members of $\mathfrak{L}_{c'}$ involve modifications of *good* but not of *linguist*.

It is clear from this brief discussion that a formal elaboration of such analyses within the framework provided by cgm's requires a great deal more structure on the set of contexts than I have given.

7

I have claimed that vagueness is often reduced by context. This doctrine is void, however, unless it is accompanied by a concrete analysis of those contextual factors which contribute to such reduction of vagueness and of how they succeed in doing so. To provide such an analysis is a difficult task, the completion of which will perhaps forever elude us. Yet I feel I ought to say something on this topic, more, in fact, than I actually have to offer. But let me mention at least one contextual aspect which plays a central role in almost all cases where adjectives occur in attributive position. That aspect is the noun to which the adjective is attached. In a great many cases the noun alone determines, largely or wholly, how the adjective should, in the given context, be understood. Indeed, if we assume that the noun is the *only* factor, we are back with the first theory according to which adjective meanings are functions from noun-phrase meanings to noun-phrase meanings.

But of course the noun is not always the only determining factor. *Smith is a remarkable violinist* may be true when said in comment on his after-dinner performance with the hostess at the piano, and false when exclaimed at the end of Smith's recital in the Festival Hall—even if on the second occasion Smith played a bit better than on the first.

It would be desirable to give a general account of how the meaning of the noun determines that of the adjective that combines with it. Here I will mention just one aspect of this problem. One of the main purposes of the use of an adjective in attributive position is to contribute to the delineation of the class of objects that the complex noun phrase of which it is part is designed to pick out—or, alternatively, to help determine the particular individual which is the intended referent of the description in which the adjective occurs. In order that the adjective can be of any use at all for these purposes, it should, in the presence of the noun in question, have an extension which, so to speak, cuts the extension of the noun in half—that is, if we assume for the sake of this argument that both noun and adjective (in the presence of the noun) are sharp, and that $\bar{A}$ is the extension of the adjective, and $\bar{N}$ that of the noun, then both $\bar{N} - \bar{A}$ and $\bar{N} \cap \bar{A}$ should be substantial proportions of $\bar{N}$. Thus in order to be able to use the adjective profitably in combination with an unlimited number of nouns, we should let the noun determine the criteria and/or standards for the adjective in its presence in such a way that the above condition is in general fulfilled. (The earlier proposal in (8) obviously meets this requirement.)

The distinctions between nouns and adjectives adumbrated in the previous section are of course far from absolute. *Four-legged*, for example, has virtually no extension gap, which is hardly surprising given the manner in which it is derived from the noun '*leg*'. And, indeed, it yields comparatives as infelicitous as those derived from most nouns. *This is more four-legged than that* would on most occasions sound positively non-sensical. *Blue*, though apparently not derived from a noun, also gives rise to rather strained comparatives. *This is bluer than that* is sometimes a meaningful statement, but would fail to be more often than not. So it seems that *heavy* and *four-legged* are really very far apart and that they will ultimately require analyses that are fundamentally different.

This brings us to a likely objection against the theory I have outlined. Does it not blur fundamental distinctions between different kinds of adjectives? Yes, undoubtedly it does. Still, I feel that what it reveals about adjectives in general is important. But this conviction should not bar the way to accounts that deal in detail with small provinces of the wide realm of all those concepts to which it claims to apply. It should be pointed out in this connection that the second theory itself can hardly be regarded as comprehending all adjectives. Is *alleged* a predicate, even in the most diluted sense? It seems not. Of course we can still maintain that in each particular context of use it behaves as a predicate, insofar as the accompanying (or tacitly understood) noun phrase determines to which objects in that context the adjective applies. But this is just a restatement of the first theory in slightly different terms. The original intuition which led to the second theory seems to be inapplicable to *alleged*. The same can be said to be true, to an almost equal degree, of adjectives such as *fake*, *skillful*, or *good*. Where precisely we should draw the boundaries of the class of adjectives to which the second theory applies I do not know. For example, does *skillful* belong to this class? Surely we must always ask 'skillful what?' before we can answer the question whether a certain thing or person is indeed *skillful*; this suggests that the theory is not applicable to the word *skillful*. Yet there appears to be some plausibility in the view that *having a good deal of skill* does function as a predicate—be it a highly ambiguous one as there are so many different skills. Here the question whether we face an expression that stands for a function from properties to properties or rather an ambiguous predicate which is disambiguated by accompanying expressions for properties has perhaps no definite answer. Both views appear to be equally plausible accounts of the same phenomenon. So it may be impossible to determine in a non-arbitrary manner how far the domain of our theory extends. But then it probably does not matter whether we can or not. This will certainly be unimportant once we have a complementary theory which deals specifically with such adjectives as *alleged*, *fake*, *skillful*, and *good*. It is bad to be left with a semantic phenomenon that is explained by no theory; but it does no harm to have two distinct theories which give equally adequate, albeit different, accounts of those phenomena that fall within the province of both.

8

To conclude, let me mention some of the questions which I should have liked to discuss and which I believe can be treated within the framework I have set up.

In the first place, there are intransitive verbs. I have avoided them throughout, even though they too appear to be one-place predicates and to display a good deal of vagueness. In particular, I have failed to give any account of what semantically differentiates verbs from adjectives, or, for that matter, from nouns. My excuse for this is that the proper understanding of these differences involves the consideration of tense, of the time spans during which a predicate is true of an object, and of similar issues which seem to require for their formal elaboration a framework which incorporates a good deal of tense logic.

Secondly, I have given only the scantest attention to hedges. I think that my framework is basically suitable for their analysis, although more structure on the set of contexts will be needed than I have provided.

Thirdly, I have considered only the simplest kind of comparatives. Examples of comparatives which are considerably more difficult to treat are

> Jones is more intelligent than he is kind.
> This building is higher than that is long.
> Smith is much cleverer than Jones.
> Smith is more cleverer than Jones than Jones is than Bill.

(accepting this as English).

The last two sentences in particular, present problems of a rather different kind than those I have tackled in this article. Their analysis requires more mathematical structure than has been built into the models here considered. The difference between the formal framework needed there and the one I have presented is essentially that between metric and arbitrary topological spaces. These and other problems I hope to consider in some other paper.

Notes

Since I presented the outline of this paper at the Cambridge conference, I—and, I hope, this paper—have profited from discussions with and comments by Michael Bennett, Richard Grandy, Hidé Ishiguro, David Lewis, Richmond Thomason, and, in particular George Lakoff. I was equally fortunate to hear Sally Genet's paper on comparatives at the summer meeting of the Linguistic Society of America in Ann Arbor, which proposed an approach similar to that taken here. Only after the present paper had already been given its final form did I become acquainted with Kit Fine's article "Vagueness, Truth and Logic" which expresses on the topic of vagueness—the central theme of the second part of my paper—views very similar to those which can be found here. I know that I would have been able to offer a better contribution to this volume if I had known about Fine's work earlier.

1. This example was given at the conference by Professor Lewis.

2. This example was given to me by Dr. Hidé Ishiguro of University College, London.

3. Cf. Bartsch and Vennemann (1972), part 2.

4. A clear exposition of a view about the adjective *good* which is essentially what is here proposed for adjectives in general can be found in Geach (1956). Notice, however, that not only does *good*, as Geach makes clear, fail to be a predicate; it is not even extensional (cf. *skillful*).

5. For reference, see Rescher (1969).

6. This argument is certainly not new. It can be found, for example, in Rescher (1969). Yet it seems to have failed to discourage people from trying to use multi-valued logic in contexts where the argument shows it to be inadequate.

7. Of course there are other factors whose effect is that a situation of speech will in general determine only a partial interpretation; for example, many predicates are not applicable to individuals of certain kinds—and yet not every statement which attributes a predicate to such a semantically improper object should be regarded as ill formed. Such other sources of interpretational incompleteness, however, will not concern us here.

8. A *field of subsets* of given set X (or: a *field over X*) is a set of subsets of X, such that (i) $X \in \mathfrak{F}$; (ii) $\emptyset \in \mathfrak{F}$; (iii) if $Y, Y' \in \mathfrak{F}$; then $Y \cap Y', X - Y \in \mathfrak{F}$.

A *probability function* over a field $\mathfrak{F}$ over X is a function p whose domain is $\mathfrak{F}$, whose range is included in the real interval $[0,1]$, and which has the properties: (i) $p(X) = 1$; (ii) if $Y \in \mathfrak{F}$, then $p(X - Y) = 1 - p(Y)$; and (iii) if $\mathfrak{G}$ is a countable subset of $\mathfrak{F}$ such that (a) whenever $Y, Y' \in \mathfrak{G}$ and $Y \neq Y'$, then $Y \cap Y' = \emptyset$; and (b) $\cup \mathfrak{G} \in \mathfrak{F}$; then $p(\cup \mathfrak{G}) = \Sigma_{Y \in \mathfrak{G}} p(Y)$.

9. From the mathematical point of view this notion is unproblematic only if the universe U is finite. In that case we do not really need to require that p satisfy the condition (iii) of note 1, but only the weaker condition obtained by replacing the word *countable* in (iii) by *finite*. Condition (iii) is necessary when U is denumerable; in that case, however, as well as when U is uncountable, it may happen that no intuitively correct models exist. The only way in which I can see how to cope with these cases involves non-standard analyses. I do not want to go into this here.

10. An extensive discussion of such expressions can be found in Lakoff (1972). Lakoff calls such expressions "hedges," a term I will adopt here, too.

11. Cf. Isard (1975). Others whom I know to have developed similar ideas are Thomas Ballmer of the Technische Universität, Berlin, and David Lumsden of University College, London.

12. Cf. Lewis (1970: Chapter 39 in this volume).

27

MAX J. CRESSWELL

Prepositions and Points of View

$\mathbf{T}$here are many words in our language whose meaning seems to make reference to a point of view or an hypothetical observer of the scene. I have in mind particularly such words as *come*, *go*, *left*, *right*, *behind*, and others, all of which seem to depend for their meaning of looking at things from a certain point of view. Charles Fillmore (1975) has recently shown how pervasive the use of points of view is in discourse. Indeed, his work makes the task of formalizing it look well-nigh impossible. The aim of this present paper is therefore very much more restricted, and in two ways. First I have in mind semantics conceived in the narrow sense of the contribution a word or expression makes to the truth conditions of sentences in which it occurs. Second I shall be restricting myself solely to the formal semantics of the points of view involved in some spatial senses of English prepositions. The kind of fact I wish to explain is how the truth conditions of a sentence like

(1) *Across a meadow a band is playing excerpts from* **H.M.S. Pinafore**

depend, via the meaning of *across*, on the point of view from which the band is being observed.

Obviously any study of prepositions must be restricted in some way and a restriction to their spatial uses seems natural. Luckily there is a recent study (Bennett 1975) of the spatial and temporal uses of English prepositions, and I have made extensive use of Part I of that work.[1]

The particular senses of English prepositions that I shall be discussing might be described as their "journey" senses. Following Bennett (1975, 35 f.), I shall argue that a sentence like (1) is to be understood as saying that the band is playing at the end of a hypothetical journey across a meadow from a contextually determined point.

This analysis means that the sense of *across* in which it directly modifies the journey is taken as more basic than the sense involved in (1), and in section 1 I discuss what I have perhaps con-

Max J. Cresswell (1978) Prepositions and points of view. *Linguistics and Philosophy 2:* 1–42. Reprinted by permission of Kluwer Academic Publishers.

tentiously called the basic sense of **across**. At first sight the need for a journey analysis is not obvious. I hope that enough examples involving both **across** and other prepositions will be given to make the need for the journey become plausible as the paper progresses, but perhaps we can for the moment point to the fact that (1) can be additionally modified by adverbials which seem clearly to involve properties of journeys to get sentences like

(2)   ***Two days across the desert we ran out of water.***
(3)   ***Half way across Australia by train the traveler sees no trees.***

The framework in which the semantics will be set will be that of Cresswell (1979). It will assume a formal base language of the kind called a λ-*categorial language*, together with an interpretation which provides a domain of semantic values for the expressions of each syntactic category and a procedure for determining the semantic value of all complex expressions on the basis of an assignment of values to the symbols of the language. As in Cresswell (1979), there will be some minor divergences from Cresswell (1973). The principal one is in the analysis of context. In chapter 8 of Cresswell (1973) an elaborate framework was set up in which contexts of use were construed as properties of utterances, but the only indices taken seriously here are possible worlds and time intervals. A second difference is that no attempt has been made to account for the semantics of propositional attitudes. A summary of the framework as used in this paper is provided in the appendix.

The key assumption of possible-worlds semantics is that the meaning of a sentence is the conditions under which it is true[2] or, put in another way, the set of possible worlds in which it is true. When studying tensed languages, of course we need also to speak of the times at which it is true. Thus the meaning of a sentence α will, for the purposes of this paper, be thought of, as in Cresswell (1979), as a set of pairs $\langle w, t \rangle$ where w is a possible world and t a time interval.[3] We call the set of all such pairs W, and our domain D_o (*vide* the appendix) will be the set of all subsets of W. Where $\langle w, t \rangle$ is a member of the meaning of α, according to a value assignment, we can say that α is true at $\langle w, t \rangle$ (according to that value assignment). The reason for having time intervals rather than instants is so that we can describe in a natural fashion sentences which speak about something which takes place over a (short or long) period of time. The use to which intervals can be put has been demonstrated in a number of places[4] and will also, I hope, emerge in this paper. The world member of the pair $\langle w, t \rangle$ will not play an important role in this paper but is retained so that what is said here can be integrated with the semantics of other symbols—for example, the progressive operator—and the semantics of mood, where the world index does become important.

The basic semantical idea of this paper is that the point of view involved in the spatial meaning of prepositions is often to be understood in terms of a hypothetical journey which an observer would have to make to be where the action is.

The problem for this paper is of course to put this insight into a λ-categorial framework, and so we shall begin by looking at prepositions when they are used to characterize the journeys themselves.

1   The basic use of **across**

(4)   ***Arabella walks across a meadow.***[5]

We must first put (4) into a formula of a λ-categorial language $\mathfrak{L}$, called its λ-deep structure.[6] Suppose for the moment that ***Arabella*** is in category 1—that is, it is a logically proper name—and suppose that its semantic value, V(***Arabella***), under a value assignment V to all the symbols of $\mathfrak{L}$ is simply Arabella. We suppose ***walks*** to be a one-place predicate—a symbol in category $\langle 0,1 \rangle$.

V(*walks*) will therefore be in $D_{\langle 0,1 \rangle}$; that is, in the domain of values for expressions of category $\langle 0,1 \rangle$. In fact, it will be the function ω from D_1 (the domain of values for category 1 expressions) into D_0 (the domain of values for category 0 expressions—in fact, $\mathfrak{P}W$) such that any $a \in D_1$ is in the domain of ω iff a is a physical object, and for any such a and any $\langle w,t \rangle \in W$, $\langle w,t \rangle \in \omega(a)$ iff t is an interval during which a is walking in w.[7]

A meadow is what was called in Cresswell (1973, 130) a *nominal*. It is an expression of category $\langle 0, \langle 0,1 \rangle \rangle$. Other expressions of that category are ***everyone, no one, and the present king of France***. *Meadow* is in category $\langle 0,1 \rangle$ with the semantics:

- V(***meadow***) is the function ω in $D_{\langle 0,1 \rangle}$ such that for any $a \in D_1$, a is in the domain of ω iff a is a physical object; and for any such a and any $\langle w, t \rangle \in W$, $\langle w, t \rangle \in \omega(a)$ iff a is a meadow throughout t.
- Because ***a*** forms a nominal out of a common noun, it is of category $\langle \langle 0, \langle 0,1 \rangle \rangle, \langle 0,1 \rangle \rangle$, and so ***a meadow*** is as required of category $\langle 0, \langle 0,1 \rangle \rangle$.[8]
- V (***a***) is the function ζ in $D_{\langle \langle 0, \langle 0, 1 \rangle \rangle, \langle 0,1 \rangle \rangle}$ such that where ω_1 and ω_2 are both in $D_{\langle 0,1 \rangle}$ and $\langle w,t \rangle \in W$:
- $\langle w,t \rangle \in (\zeta(\omega_2))(\omega_1)$ iff there is at least one a in D_1 in the domain of ω_1 such that $\langle w,t \rangle \in \omega_1(a)$ and $\langle w,t \rangle \in \omega_2(a)$.

The final symbol is ***across***. In a λ-categorial language a preposition is a symbol which forms a predicate modifier out of a name. It is, in other words, of category $\langle \langle \langle 0,1 \rangle, \langle 0,1 \rangle \rangle, 1 \rangle$.[9] Before we give the semantics of ***across*** we shall see how it combines with the other symbols to give a λ-deep structure for (4). In order to give this, we shall need to make use of λ-abstraction and of variables. Here $x_\sigma, y_\sigma, z_\sigma$ et cetera will stand for variables of category σ as in Cresswell (1973, 137).

The λ-deep deep structure of (4) is

(5) $\langle \langle \lambda, x_1, \langle Arabella, \langle walks, \langle across, x_1 \rangle \rangle \rangle \rangle, \langle a, meadow \rangle \rangle$.

The formation rules for λ-categorial languages ensure that (5) is a well-formed expression in category 0.[10] In considering its semantics we shall see that this is so, and how the meaning of each word contributes to the meaning of the whole.

We are now in a position to discuss the semantics of ***across***. The semantics given above for ***walk*** and ***meadow*** may have given the impression of being something of a cheat. The semantics for ***across*** will also have something of this flavor, so it may be profitable to explain why there really is no cheating.

In V(***walk***) we spoke of a time t as being an interval of walking but make no attempt to say what walking is. This is because the aim of the paper is not intended to teach people about walking. That knowledge is assumed. The aim of this paper is to show how a knowledge of what walking is is used by the speakers of a language containing the symbol ***walks***. Nor is the point of this paper to decompose ***walks*** or any other words into a number of "semantic primitives" so that its meaning can be explained. Let me try to explain this a little more specifically. Our λ-categorial language might contain, in addition to the word ***walks***, the word ***runs***. V(***runs***) would be exactly like V(***walks***) except that it would involve the notion of running at the interval t instead of walking. It is of course a fact that both running and walking involve movement. It is also a fact that those who know what running and walking are know this. One could therefore have ***runs*** and ***walks*** as complex items of which the feature MOVEMENT is a component. The point about model-theoretic semantics is that this feature of V(***walks***) and V(***runs***) need not be put into the symbols. For it is our knowledge of walking and running, represented in the structure by functions from things to world-time pairs, which enables us to see that they have this in common. To put the point in another way, if a speaker has the ability to tell whether, for any a, a is running at $\langle w,t \rangle$

and whether a is walking at $\langle w,t \rangle$ then *by that alone* he has the ability to tell that both these in-volve movement. We do not need to add any extra feature such as MOVEMENT to obtain it. It is already in the functions V(*walk*) and V(*run*). Of course, there may be many reasons, even in linguistics, for wanting to study what walking and running have in common, but they are not reasons for requiring that *walk* and *run* be further decomposed in a λ-categorial language. We shall later consider reasons for suggesting that maybe certain symbols *should* be decomposed, but they are of a rather special nature and do not depend on mere community of meaning. Simi-lar comments apply to *meadow*.

The situation with words like *across* is a little different because of their more complex syn-tactic category. It does not take too great an effort to assume that a speaker has the ability to know when an interval is, for any given person, an interval of that person's walking. Nor to as-sume that a speaker has the ability to know when an interval is an interval of walking across a meadow. But of course the ability demonstrated in a mastery of the concept of going across some-thing is a more complex one. Since *across a meadow* makes a complex predicate *walks across a meadow* out of a simpler predicate *walks*, then its value will of course be a function from $D_{\langle 0,1 \rangle}$ (the domain of predicates) into $D_{\langle 0,1 \rangle}$. It might be thought that since we are satisfied that the val-ues of predicates are functions of the kind we have just mentioned, then the problem of *across the meadow* is automatically solved, and the task of giving a semantics for *across* is one solely for word semantics and therefore of little theoretical interest. One reply to this is to assert that word semantics *does* have theoretical interest. I believe it does, if only the interest of showing that a general framework has applications. But the other, and here more important, reply is that it is only by looking at the semantics of particular modifiers that we can decide whether the kind of entities we have postulated as the semantic values of predicates really do give the modifier enough information.

This can be illustrated with an example from modal logic. Suppose that it is alleged that we have the ability to determine for a given proposition, say p, whether it is true or false. On the basis of this ability we might decide to say that the value of a sentence is its truth value. (This is done in classical propositional logic.) If we have this ability for all propositions, then we have it also for $\Box p$, the proposition that p is necessary. So if the argument of the preceding paragraph were accepted, we would have to say that the value of $\Box$ would be a function from truth values to truth values—in other words, a truth function. But of course we know that $\Box$ is not truth-functional. Given merely the truth value of p, we cannot predict the truth value of $\Box p$. The point is that our ability to determine the truth value of p depends on our knowing more about its mean-ing than its truth value. In fact, what we need to know is its truth value not merely in the actual world but in each possible world. Given that, we *can* determine the truth value of $\Box p$. In any given possible world, $\Box p$ is true, provided p is true in every possible world. Thus producing a semantics for a particular symbol told us something of the nature of the general semantic frame-work required.

The same is true of *across a meadow*. It is clear that something about the meaning of *walks* and *runs* enables us to predict the worlds and times at which a given thing walks or runs across a meadow. What is not clear is that merely knowing the worlds and times at which something walks and runs is sufficient. The only way to show that it is is to provide a semantics for *across*, even if it is a rather crude one. This explains why what looks like word semantics for particular modifiers has a rather more general significance. We shall in fact show that when W contains pairs of a world together with a time *interval* then there *is* sufficient information for *across* to operate on. In particular we shall show eventually that the point of view involved in the analysis of many prepositions does not require that the world-time pairs be augmented by the addition of an extra contextual 'index' which represents the point of view.

What function is it then which stands to *across* in the same way that walking and running stand to *walk* and *run*? I will suggest that it is the following. It is I believe based on a relation between spatial path and a spatial region. We say that the path lies acrosss the region. Maybe the region should be a physical object. Typically one thinks of something long and thin like a river and going across it as a path approaching at right angles to its sides, which begins on one side and ends on the other. Bennett (p. 85) was led to incorporate the element 'transverse' as part of its meaning, but he is concerned with giving a componential analysis of *across*. And in any case it is rather dangerous to start reading into the meaning of a word like *across* things which are at best present merely in the typical instances. Formally it will turn out most convenient to make a path p a function from moments of time so that where t is an interval and m a moment within that interval (i.e. $m \in t$), $p(m)$ is the space occupied by the path at m. This makes a path a very temporally dependent thing and perhaps it would be better to call it a journey. The time reference enables us to give it a direction, a beginning and an end, and the structure of space gives us an extent. Where p is a journey and a an object we can therefore speak of p's being *across* a in world w. We could if we liked introduce a symbol for this, say R_{across}, (p, a, w). Then we would make it clear that the task of this paper is not to define R_{across} but rather to show how the ability to recognize this relation is used by native speakers of $\mathcal{L}$ when they employ sentences containing the word *across*.

One feature of R_{across} does seem to be worth mentioning and that is that where a journey p is across a it need not follow that a larger journey p' which contains p as a part is also across a. Of course if we say simply

(6)   *Arabella went across the meadow*

we probably allow a journey of which the going across the meadow is only a part. But in a sentence like

(7)   *Arabella went across the meadow in fifteen minutes*

we do not mean that the whole journey took fifteen minutes but rather that that sub-journey which was, in the strict sense, the going across the meadow occupied (at most) fifteen minutes.

The behaviour of *and* in this connection is interesting and gives some support for the interval-based semantics suggested for it in Cresswell (1977). If we say

(8)   *Arabella went across the meadow and through the woods in fifteen minutes*

we do not mean that Arabella went across the meadow in fifteen minutes and through the woods in fifteen minutes. We mean that the whole conjunction took fifteen minutes. The semantics for *and* in Cresswell (1977) provided that $\langle \alpha, \textbf{\textit{and}}, \beta \rangle$ is true at an interval t iff t is a minimal interval which contains a subinterval at which α is true and a subinterval (not necessarily the same, or even overlapping) at which β is true. This semantics seems what is required for (8).

Given any object a and a world w and a time interval t we let $p(a,t,w)$ be a function whose domain is the set of all $m \in t$; and for any $m \in t$, $p(a,t,w)(m)$ is the space occupied by a at m in world w. (t remember is an interval and its members are therefore moments or instants of time.) Obviously $p(a,t,w)$ is a journey in the sense of the previous paragraph. And now we are ready for the semantics of *across*.

V(*across*) is the function ζ in category $\langle \langle \langle 0,1 \rangle, \langle 0,1 \rangle \rangle, 1 \rangle$ such that for any a and $b \in D_1$, a is in the domain of ζ iff it determines a spatio-temporal area.[11] For any such a and for any $\omega \in D_{\langle 0,1 \rangle}$, and $\langle w,t \rangle \in W$:

$\langle w,t \rangle \in ((\zeta(a))(\omega))(b)$ iff b is in the domain of ω and $\langle w,t \rangle \in \omega(b)$ and $R_{across}(p(b,t,w), a,w)$.

Let us now see how all this works by going through (5). The key part of the formula for the analysis of the preposition is of course the expression $\langle \textbf{\textit{walks}}, \langle \textbf{\textit{across}}, x \rangle \rangle$. Since x is a variable in category 1 then $\langle across, x \rangle$ is in category $\langle \langle 0,1 \rangle, \langle 0,1 \rangle \rangle$ and since **walks** is in category $\langle 0,1 \rangle$ then the whole expression is also of that category. We suppose that under some assignment v to the variables of $\mathfrak{L}$, x is given the value a.

Now

$V_v(\langle walks, \langle across, x \rangle \rangle)$
$= V_v(\langle across, x \rangle)(V_v(walks))$
$= (V_v(across)(v(x)))(V_v(walks))$
$= ((V(across)(a))(V(walks)))$.

By $V(across)$ this means that for any $b \in D_1$ and $\langle w,t \rangle \in W$:

$\langle w,t \rangle \in V_v(\langle walks, \langle across, x \rangle \rangle)(b)$

iff

$\langle w,t \rangle \in V(walks)(b)$ and $R_{across}(p(b,t,w), a,w)$.

And by $V(walks)$ this will be so iff b is walking throughout t in w and his route takes him across where a is in w at t. Assuming that $V(Arabella)$ is Arabella then

(9) $\langle Arabella, \langle walks, \langle across, x \rangle \rangle \rangle$

will be true at $\langle w,t \rangle$ under V_v iff Arabella walks across a in w during time t.

(10) $\langle \lambda, x, \langle Arabella, \langle walks, \langle across, x \rangle \rangle \rangle \rangle$

will then be the property of being an a of which (9) is true at $\langle w,t \rangle$ and the whole sentence (5) will say that there is something which is a meadow at $\langle w,t \rangle$ and which is an a such that Arabella walks across a at t in w. Thus (5) gives us the required meaning of (4).

2   Other uses of *across*

The last section analyzed what I would claim to be the semantically most basic use of *across*. This use makes no reference to any point of view. But of course (4) could mean something which could be more explicitly stated by

(11)   **Arabella walks across a meadow from Bill.**[12]

Even (11) is ambiguous. It could mean that Arabella's walk occupies a path across the meadow and the walk begins where Bill is; but I am more interested in the sense in which Bill is on one side of the meadow looking at Arabella walking on the other side. In other words it is Bill in this particular sentence who provides the point of view. A sentence which pretty well forces this interpretation is

(12)   **Across a river from Bill a band is playing**[13] **excerpts from Ruddigore.**

In order to analyze (12) we must give a semantics for *from*. If we follow Bennett (1975, 34) we shall want the *from* in (12) to be the same as the *from* in

(13)   **Arabella walks from a bush.**

This *from* is in category $\langle\langle\langle 0,1\rangle, \langle 0,1\rangle\rangle, 1\rangle$ and its semantics is analogous to that of *to* in Åqvist (1976).

V(*from*) is the function ζ in $D_{\langle\langle\langle 0,1\rangle,\langle 0,1\rangle\rangle,1\rangle}$ such that any $a \in D_1$ is in the domain of ζ iff a determines a spatial area and ω is in the domain of $\zeta(a)$ iff its own domain contains only entities which determine a spatial area and for any such a and ω and any b in the domain of ω and any $\langle w,t\rangle \in W$: $\langle w,t\rangle \in ((\zeta(a))(\omega))(b)$ iff $\langle w,t\rangle \in \omega$ (b) and there is an initial segment t' of t such that for any $m \in t'$, $(p(b,t,w))(m)$ overlaps $(p(a,t,w))(m)$.

In this case I have actually tried to say what the property of a journey is which makes it a journey *from* an object a. Perhaps this is too dangerous. For one thing the definition given allows the object to remain within the area of a all the time. For another it does not allow for cases where the journey begins, not actually within a but close to it, as in

(14) **Arabella walked from the post office**

where her journey may have originated just outside the post office. Perhaps we should have simply introduced an R_{from} which relates a journey and an object in a world in whatever relation speakers recognize as the 'from' relation. However it is sometimes nice to attempt a definition, even if it is only a crude counterpart of the real thing.

[Example] (13) has as its λ-deep structure

(15) $\langle\langle\lambda, x, \langle Arabella, \langle walks, \langle from, x\rangle\rangle\rangle\rangle, \langle a, bush\rangle\rangle$.

I trust that the discussion of (5) together with V(*from*) will show that (15) will be true at $\langle w,t\rangle$ iff the path taken by Arabella over t in w is taken while walking and has an initial segment overlapping with something which is a bush at $\langle w,t\rangle$.

We now can give a formalization of one of the senses of (11). Unfortunately it is not the one we want:

(16) $\langle\langle\lambda, x, \langle Arabella, \langle\langle walks, \langle across, x\rangle\rangle, \langle from, Bill\rangle\rangle\rangle\rangle, \langle a\ meadow\rangle\rangle$.

[Example] (16) gives the sense of (11) in which it is Arabella's journey that begins at Bill, whereas the point of view interpretation claims that Arabella's walking takes place in a region that is at the end of a hypothetical journey which Bill might think of making; this latter sense of (11) is roughly that there is a journey from where Bill is which goes across a meadow and which ends where Arabella is walking.

An informal paraphrase of this sense of (11) would be

(17) **Arabella walks at the end of a journey across a meadow from Bill.**

Since we get sentences like

(18) **Arabella walks from across a meadow from Bill**

which needs a paraphrase like

(19) **Arabella walks from the end of a journey across a meadow from Bill.**

it seems best to treat

(20) **the end of a journey across a meadow from Bill**

as a separate unit and therefore we need a symbol, which we shall refer to as 'G', which makes something like (20) out of the adverbial phrase

(21)   ***across a meadow from Bill.***

The choice of 'G' is prompted by Bennett's use of the word "goal" for a related though not identical purpose.

A phrase like (20) is a nominal. It cannot simply denote a particular spatial region since the occurrence in it of ***a meadow*** makes it rather like an existential quantifier. G therefore makes a nominal out of an adverbial.

It is in category $\langle\langle 0, \langle 0,1 \rangle\rangle, \langle\langle 0,1\rangle, \langle 0,1\rangle\rangle\rangle$ and is intended to pick out the "end" of a journey which has the properties represented by the adverbial. The journey of course may only be hypothetical. It may not actually occur. One way to deal with this is to treat it as a counterfactual journey. We thus go to the nearest[14] world in which such a journey actually occurs. There is however a simpler way if we look at the idea of a "basic individual" as described in Cresswell (1973, 94). If we imagine a possible world as determined by the points of space–time which are occupied by something, then a basic individual is a function ρ which associates with each possible world w a set of space-time points which represent ρ's *manifestation* in w—namely, the set of space-time points that ρ occupies in w. If ρ is an *actual* object, then we must insist, as in Cresswell (1973, 94) that the manifestation of ρ in w be points which are occupied in w, so that $\rho(w) \subseteq w$. A *hypothetical* individual is one in which this requirement need not be met.

Even if this account is not accepted and we work with an intuitive idea of an individual, hypothetical or otherwise, it must at least determine a function p which associates with each world w a set $p(w)$ of space–time points. That is what was meant by requiring that the members of the domain of V(***across***) be things that determine a spatiotemporal area. Any more stringent requirements, such as, for example, that they be physical objects, would not allow the kind of hypothetical journeys that we require for the present use of ***across***.

We also require another kind of abstract object. For we frequently want to talk simply about a certain spatiotemporal region—in this case, the region at the end of the hypothetical journey. An abstract region of space is a function p such that for any world w, $p(w)$ is a space–time region which is constant with respect to the time coordinate. In other words we need to assume the existence of "things" that exist at places where nothing in fact does. Given such "abstract" entities, then we can always be sure that for any given spatial region r and any pair $\langle w,t \rangle$ there is an "object" that occupies precisely r at $\langle w,t \rangle$. We need to use this object in the semantics for G.

V(G) is the function η in $D_{\langle\langle 0,\langle 0,1\rangle\rangle,\langle\langle 0,1\rangle,\langle 0,1\rangle\rangle\rangle}$ such that where $\zeta \in D_{\langle\langle 0,1\rangle,\langle 0,1\rangle\rangle}$ and $\omega \in D_{\langle 0,1\rangle}$ and $\langle w,t \rangle \in W$: $\langle w,t \rangle \in (\eta(\zeta))(\omega)$ iff there exist an a and a b in D_1 and an ω' in $D_{\langle 0,1\rangle}$ and a t' whose final segment lies within t, such that a is a constant function determining a region r of space and $\langle w,t \rangle \in \omega(a)$ and $\langle w,t' \rangle \in (\zeta(\omega'))(b)$ and b's position in w at the end of t' overlaps with r.

The existence of a sentence like (18) suggests that (11) should be regarded as meaning something like

(22)   ***Arabella walks at* across a meadow from Bill***

where ***at**** is a symbol like ***at***, except that it does not reach the surface. We shall be looking in section 4 at ways of dealing with symbols which do not reach the surface, so for the moment we will content ourselves with looking at (18) where there is an explicit preposition ***from*** in the place where ***at**** is in (22). The λ-deep structure of (18) is:

(23) $\langle\langle \lambda, y_1, \langle\langle \lambda, x_1, \langle$***Arabella***, $\langle$***walks***, $\langle$***from*** $x_1\rangle\rangle\rangle\rangle, \langle G, \langle \lambda, x_{\langle 0,1\rangle}, \langle\langle x_{\langle 0,1\rangle}, \langle$***across***, $y_1\rangle\rangle, \langle$***from***, ***Bill***$\rangle\rangle\rangle\rangle\rangle\rangle,$
       $\langle$***a meadow***$\rangle\rangle$.

This requires working out slowly. We have already worked on examples which show us how to evaluate

(24) $\langle Arabella, \langle walks, \langle from, x_1\rangle\rangle\rangle$

and

(25) $\langle\langle x_{\langle 0,1\rangle}, \langle across, y_1\rangle\rangle, \langle from, Bill\rangle\rangle$.

Suppose we have an assignment v to the individual variables of $\mathfrak{L}$ such that $v(x_1) = a$, $v(y_1) = c$. Consider then the ω'-variant of v, viz $(v, \omega' / x_{\langle 0,1\rangle})$.[15]

[Example] (24) will be true at $\langle w,t\rangle$ iff Arabella is walking throughout t and her walk originates in the region occupied by a. [Example] (25) will be true at $\langle w, t'\rangle$ of a b (in D_1) iff $\langle w,t'\rangle \in \omega'(b)$ and b's path over t' in w originates at Bill and lies across c.

(26) $\langle\lambda, x_{\langle 0,1\rangle}, \langle x_{\langle 0,1\rangle}, \langle across, y_1\rangle\rangle, \langle from, Bill\rangle\rangle\rangle$

is therefore the property of being an ω' of the kind satisfying (25)—that is, being true of b at $\langle w,t'\rangle$ if b's path over t' in w originates at Bill and lies across c. Thus

(27) $\langle G, \langle\lambda, x_{\langle 0,1\rangle}, \langle\langle x_{\langle 0,1\rangle}, \langle across, y_1\rangle\rangle, \langle from, Bill\rangle\rangle\rangle\rangle$

will be true of a property ω at $\langle w,t\rangle$ iff there exists an ω' in $D_{\langle 0,1\rangle}$ and a $d \in D_1$ which determines a constant spatial region r, and $\langle w,t\rangle \in \omega(d)$ and there is a b such that for some t' whose final segment lies within t, b's path in w over t' originates at Bill and lies across c.

In other words (27) is true of a property ω iff ω is in the goal area of a, possibly hypothetical, journey across c originating at Bill.

Suppose that ω is the value of

(28) $\langle\lambda, x_1, \langle Arabella, \langle walks, \langle from, x_1\rangle\rangle\rangle\rangle$.

Then $\langle w,t\rangle \in \omega(d)$ iff Arabella's walk over t in w originates from r. Thus combining (27) and (28) we have that

(29) $\langle\langle\lambda, x_1, \langle Arabella, \langle walks, \langle from, x_1\rangle\rangle\rangle\rangle,$
         $\langle G, \langle\lambda, x_{\langle 0,1\rangle}, \langle\langle x_{\langle 0,1\rangle}, \langle across, y_1\rangle\rangle, \langle from, Bill\rangle\rangle\rangle\rangle\rangle$

is true under V_v at $\langle w,t\rangle$ iff Arabella is walking throughout t and her walk originates in the region occupied at t by an object that determines a constant spatial region and whose position overlaps, at the end of the interval, with the path occupied by a (possibly abstract) object whose journey originates at Bill and lies across c. Finally to obtain (23) the nominal $\langle a\ meadow\rangle$ says that c is something which is a meadow at $\langle w,t\rangle$.

All of which says that (23) is true at $\langle w,t\rangle$ iff Arabella walks from a place that is across a meadow from Bill, which is the sense of (11) that we were trying to capture.

In this example it is the phrase $\langle from, Bill\rangle$ which provides the "point of view." But of course there need not always be one. In

(30)   *Across every river a band is playing excerpts from* **Princess Ida.**

I don't think any commitment is made to any *particular* point of view from which the relevant band is across the relevant river. In this case $V(G)$ will ensure that the claim is that from *some* point of view each band is playing across its river. (It may be of course that a particular point of view *is* intended but that it is contextually supplied. That case will be considered in section 5.)

As far as the first *from* in (23) goes, it is interesting to note that replacing it by *to* or *at* gives a slightly less natural sentence. For we do not usually say

(31)   *Arabella walks to across a meadow from Bill*

or

(32)   *Arabella walks at across a meadow from Bill.*

[Example] (31) seems just possible, but when (32) is intended, the preposition is simply omitted as in (11).

The fact that the preposition is sometimes present suggests that its omission is a feature of the surface structure, particularly if other prepositions beside *from* occur naturally in sentences like (18). Some slight evidence is given, I believe, by the existence of such sentences as

(33)   *He came via across the hill.*
(34)   *He came to behind the hill.*
(35)   *He arrived at over the hill from here but could come no further.*

I find these at least not totally unacceptable, though not everyone seems to agree.

There are a number of questions about the role of G. In the first place, since the journey whose existence is asserted by G is such an abstract thing, one wonders whether there might not be too many. Surely any region of space can be reached by a journey that goes across a meadow if we are not restricting ourselves to journeys that might actually be made? It is certainly true that a long journey may involve a sub-interval which is a going across of something, but, as mentioned in section 2, we do not need to say that the whole interval is a going across of that thing.

The fact that the journey is abstract may cause problems of a different kind. Bennett notes that while we might say

(36)   *The post office is over the hill*

we would not normally say

(37)   *The post office is through the hill*

unless there were a tunnel. Yet of course an abstract journey of the kind used in the semantics of G could certainly go through the hill. One way of dealing with this would be to require that the journey be, if not actually made in the world in question, one which is made in some world reasonably similar to the actual world. Possible worlds semantics is of course familiar with the notion of world similarity but it would be well to be sure that we need it. And in this case I believe we do not. Consider (37). By V(G) (37) will be true if (36) is. But of course (37) will be far less *appropriate* than (36). For the journey over the hill is one that can actually be made, whereas in the absence of a tunnel the journey through the hill cannot.[16] It seems quite natural to me to say, when in New Zealand,

(38)   *Spain is through the earth from here*

though I can also say

(39) *Spain is half way round the earth from here*

and in most circumstances it will be (39) which is the more appropriate. Nevertheless I do not believe that the truth conditions of the sentences are affected by this.

It is worth noting that G can operate not only on prepositional phrases but also with combinations of prepositional phrases and adverbs. Indeed, the "journey" from the point of view to the scene of action can be described in almost any amount of detail as in

(40) *Four hours from the house directly by road through the woods and diagonally for fifteen minutes across a meadow exactly halfway between two trees a band is playing excerpts from* **Patience.**

It does not seem possible to get a spatial case where G operates on an adverb alone without a prepositional phrase, but that is not surprising since it is through the prepositional phrase that reference to the specific point of view is achieved.

3   Some other prepositions

In this section some relatively informal remarks will be made about the semantics of certain other prepositions. I have tried to say something about the spatial sense of most of the prepositions considered in part I of Bennett (1975), though several prepositions will be deferred until we can discuss context-dependence. The purpose of this section is not to discuss their semantics in detail but only to try to show that there seem to be no insuperable problems in treating them in the framework we have been using. No λ-categorial formulae will be analyzed in this section.

[The words] *through*, *along*, and *around* can be conveniently considered together here because they have properties fairly similar to those of *across*. [The word] *through* conveys the idea of a path that is surrounded by the object of the preposition, and *along* involves a path that is side by side with the object. As with *across*, we shall not try to be more specific about what these relations are between paths and objects but shall assume that they are part of the conceptual competence of native speakers of English. Again by analogy with *across* we can have such sentences as

(41) *Along the river from Bill a band is playing excerpts from* **The Pirates of Penzance**

or

(42) *Through the woods from Bill a band is playing excerpts from* **Iolanthe.**

The use of G will enable these to be dealt with properly. [The word] *around* is a little more difficult. If we take the journey sense of *around* as basic, [it] would require that the path encircle the object as in

(43) *Arabella walks around a meadow.*

This would make

(44) *Around a meadow from Bill a band is playing excerpts from* **The Grand Duke**

mean, using G, that at the end of a journey encircling a meadow the band is playing. Presumably (43) must allow that the journey need not completely encircle the object, otherwise (44) would require that the band be playing back where Bill is.

The difficulty about ***around*** is that there seems to be another sense in the sentence

(45)   ***Around the city bands are playing excerpts from* The Gondoliers.**

Bennett (1975, p. 87) seems to treat this as a simple locative expression meaning something like "in the area surrounding," but I am not sure that I agree with him. ***Around*** can often refer to a journey with many curves in it, as

(46)   ***We walked around the museum***

which does not have to mean that we circumnavigated the building but can mean that we went from room to room, frequently deviating from a straight line. In the case of (45) it seems to me that we are thinking of an area which is enclosed by a possible hypothetical journey encircling the city. Exactly how these facts should be represented I am not sure, but I would not want to rule out the possibility that the basic sense of ***around*** is one which involves a journey.

There are however several prepositions whose basic sense does seem to be a locative one: ***at***, ***in***, and ***by*** in the sentence(s)

(47)   ***Arabella stands at (in, by, on) the box.***

[The word] ***at*** is the most neutral of these and claims merely that Arabella's position is in the same general area as the box; ***in*** claims that she is inside the box area, while ***by*** claims that she is in an adjacent area though not inside and ***on*** is on top of the box. A point worth noting about locative prepositions is that where an activity takes place at, in, or by something the goal area of that activity is also at, in, or by that thing. This means that G can combine with prepositions like ***from*** in sentences like

(48)   ***Arabella walks from by the box***
(49)   ***A cup fell from on the table.***

The preposition ***at***, though, usually does not reach the surface and we simply say

(50)   ***Arabella walks from the box.***

This is because ***from at*** would say no more than ***from***. When ***to*** is used in place of ***from***, it is sometimes absorbed into the preposition so that although we say

(51)   ***Arabella went to by the box.***

we say for ***in***

(52)   ***Arabella went into the box.***

Bennett describes ***via*** as the most neutral of path prepositions. A journey ***via*** something is a journey a part of which overlaps with that something. This means that the goal area of a journey via something need not be the same as the area of the thing itself. [The word] ***past*** appears to stand to ***by*** as ***via*** does to ***at***, as in

(53)   ***Past the box a band is playing excerpts from* The Yeomen of the Guard.**

[The word] *beyond* is, I think, weaker than *past* in merely relating the beginning and end of a journey saying that the end is on the other side of the object from the beginning. In this it is rather like *behind*. Bennett treats the basic sense of *behind* as a locative sense, but *behind* involves a point of view which is sometimes made explicit by a *from* phrase as in

(54) **Behind the tree across the meadow from Bill a band is playing excerpts from** Utopia Limited.[17]

If the basic sense of *behind* is the journey sense, then the sentence

(55) **Arabella walks behind a tree**

means that the end of Arabella's walk finishes at a point which is thought of as wholly or partly blocked from the view of Arabella's starting position. Given the starting position, and given the object of the preposition, the area where the journey is to finish is determined and any journey which finishes there will be a journey behind the object. This means that many extra properties of the journey which might be conveyed by additional prepositional or adverbial phrases will be irrelevant to whether it is a journey behind something. The origin of the journey is crucial, however, and so it is natural to find a *from* phrase used with *behind*. Similarly with the direction and the distance.

Extent phrases have various problems of their own. A phrase like *two inches* something appears as a nominal as in

(56) **Two inches measures a short distance**

and also as a modifier as in

(57) **The snail moved two inches.**

There is also a complicated relationship with the preposition *for*, as in

(58) **The snail moved for fifteen inches.**

The temporal sense of *for* may, in fact, be an intensional modifier in that

(59) **Arabella walked across the park for fifteen minutes**

does not seem to entail

(60) **Arabella walked across the park.**

If this last fact is right, a semantics for *for* will be needed, which is analogous to Dowty's semantics for the progressive aspect and makes essential use of the world index.

Given an appropriate semantics for the basic use of these extent sentences, we can invoke G for the semantics of other extent sentences like

(61) **Three yards behind the bush a band is playing excerpts from** Trial by Jury.

Extent sentences also link with comparative sentences involving prepositions by means of the words *far* and *further* and their like. I am not clear exactly how to treat these sentences, but I hope it is clear that an interval-based semantics enables a predicate to contain a large amount of information about the spatial path occupied by an object which satisfies the predicate in a world at that interval. Some of the ways this information can be used was shown in the analysis of *quickly* in Cresswell (1979), and it is not hard to see that it ought to be sufficient for most extent sentences.[18]

Some other prepositions, like *over* and *above*, will be treated in section 5, but I hope enough was said in this section to show that the form of the analysis of *across* is applicable to a considerably larger range of prepositions than one.

Before we can consider situations in which the point of view is determined wholly or partly by the context, we must say something about attitudes in general to the formalization of context-dependence.

4   Two kinds of context-dependence

Consider a sentence like

(62)   *I am in the bath.*

The account of meaning we have used up to now would have to say that the meaning of (62) is a set of world-time pairs. But it is obvious that the meaning of (62) cannot be just that, for the simple reason that we do not know who the *I* is. In fact, (62) will have as its value different sets of world time pairs for different *I*'s. There is of course an easy way of telling who the *I* is. In any utterance of (62) the *I* is in fact the utterer. In the earliest formal analyses of context[19] there was in addition to the world index and the time index, an utterer index so that a sentence would be assigned a set of triples $\langle w,t,u \rangle$ and (62) would be true at a triple $\langle w,t,u \rangle$ iff u is in the bath at w at t.

One objection to this approach if it is to be applied to all context-dependence is that it is not clear whether there is any natural stopping place, and so it would be nice to show that some indices are *as indices* more essential than others; without of course denying that the truth conditions of (62) are inaccessible until we know who '*I*' is. One difference between u and $\langle w,t \rangle$ is that the utterer index u used for *I* is a *non-shiftable* index, in contrast to t and w which are *shiftable*. By this is meant the following. We imagine an utterance of any sentence made by u with many occurrences of *I*, with solely the proviso that none of these occurrences are in direct quotations. That is, we imagine sentences like

(63)   *I believe that if I had ever seen a purple cow Bill would have wished that I had had a camera.*

If (63) is uttered by Arabella, the *I* is Arabella throughout.

In fact, we would get exactly the same truth conditions if we replaced the *I* by *Arabella*. To say that the index u is non-shiftable is to say that in any sentence when evaluated at $\langle w,t,u \rangle$ any word which requires the utterer index requires only the particular utterer index u. Contrast this with the time index t:

(64)   *Yesterday I walked.*

This sentence is context dependent as (63) was in terms of utterer and time, but in order to evaluate it at some $\langle w,t,u \rangle$ we must treat *yesterday* as a sentential modifier and analyze it as

(65) $\langle yesterday, \langle I, walk \rangle \rangle$.

The point is that to evaluate (65) at $\langle w,t,u \rangle$ we must look at the value of the embedded sentence

(66) $\langle I, walk \rangle$

at times *other* than t. For any sentence α

(67) $\langle yesterday, \alpha \rangle$

is true at $\langle w,t,u \rangle$ iff α is true at some $\langle w,t',u \rangle$ where t' is on the day preceding the day containing t. The index t has been replaced or has "shifted" to t' in the evaluation of the embedded sentence. An analogous thing happens in modality where we say that a thing *can* happen in world w if it *does* happen in a world w' which is, in some sense, a possible world relative to w.

This distinction may be thought to mark merely a difference in the behavior of indices. It can be seen to be a more wide-ranging difference than this, however, because it raises the question of whether the non-shiftable indices are indices at all. Part of the task of this section will be to examine alternative ways of dealing with the non-shiftable indices. Some of these ways, and indeed some of the more appealing ones, seem not naturally applicable to the shiftable indices, and so the distinction achieves a quite major theoretical status. A subsidiary question is naturally that of how many indices are shiftable. For one objection to the indexical approach has been that there is no natural end to the number of indices that may be required (Cresswell 1973, 111). If it can be shown that all but a very small number of the indices are non-shiftable and if a non-indexical treatment is used for these, then this criticism loses its force, and we may well choose to retain the indexical analysis in those cases where it is necessary. Times and worlds seem certainly necessary, and a spatial index may be needed also. A study of a wider class of adverbials than spatio-temporal ones might indicate the need for more shiftable indices, but I know of no present evidence to suggest that this must be so. In the next section certain facts will be considered which might appear to suggest the need for a shiftable point of view index, but arguments will be given to show that this is not the most profitable way of dealing with them.

The way of avoiding non-shiftable indices that I want to adopt in this paper is that developed by John Bigelow in (1975a) and (1975b), and I would like first to apply it to the non-shiftable index I in (62) and (63). Bigelow's idea is a very simple one. In essence it is that we are to take (62) and (63) not as single sentences but rather as schemata that can become sentences when certain holes are filled. When Bigelow asserts (62), we are to imagine the places when I occurs as being replaced by Bigelow and the sentence evaluated accordingly. When I utter it, the I is replaced by Cresswell. Strictly, this means that it is a different sentence when I say it. There is then a *pragmatic* rule which says that in an actual occurrence of this sentence it is the speaker who fills the I slot. Note that these sentences with their slots appropriately filled are formal entities and exist whether or not they are ever uttered. The *pragmatics* is used merely to tell the hearer *which* completed sentence to associate with the utterance he hears for the purpose of semantic evaluation.

Notice that I have spoken of Bigelow and Cresswell replacing the I. It might be thought that the *names* **Bigelow** and **Cresswell** standing for Bigelow and Cresswell are what is required. Bigelow's theory, however, is a rather ingenious one. His idea is that *things themselves* can be added to a language as their own names.[20] Formally this is done by means of a quotation-like operator as in Cresswell (1973, 104) but which can quote other things besides linguistic expressions. Thus $(qu, \text{Bigelow})$ is an expression of the language whose semantic value is Bigelow. The theory has an even wider application since, as we shall see in the next section, we can even quote the set-theoretical entities which are the meanings of expressions in λ-categorial languages. In particular, we shall have occasion to quote the kind of functions which are the meanings of adverbials and produce thereby symbols which are themselves adverbial expressions.

It should not be hard to see that Bigelow's context theory can deal with non-shiftable indices. It has the advantage of making the semantics much simpler in that the meaning of every word does not have to drag along with it the whole baggage of all the indices every time it occurs. Its disadvantage perhaps is that it leaves for the pragmatics features which seem naturally to be part of the semantics. For it seems to be part of the *meaning* of *I* that it refers to the speaker. This is surely correct, but it need not be inimical to the Bigelow approach. We merely say that on Bigelow's account the *meaning* of a word is a double thing: first it tells you, in a given situation, which formal symbol to associate with the occurrence of the word, and then it tells you how to evaluate that formal symbol. The function and argument semantics with its domains and values is a formalization of only the second of these processes, and it matters little whether we use the word "semantics" to cover it alone, or both processes. If we chose to formalize both processes, then the best way would probably be to use the notion of a context-property as expounded in chapter 8 of Cresswell (1973), though in that work context properties were introduced to deal with both shiftable and non-shiftable indices. Be that as it may, the needs of this paper can be met by taking world-time pairs as the values of sentences and treating the remaining context-dependence in the Bigelow manner.

The case for the Bigelow context theory is however different when we have shiftable indices. Let us look again at (67). On the Bigelow theory an utterance of (67) at a time t would have to be formalized as some such sentence as

(68) $\langle\langle \textbf{\textit{yesterday}}, \langle qu, t' \rangle\rangle, \alpha\rangle$

where t' is on the day preceding the day on which t is. In this sentence it is $\langle qu, t' \rangle$ which does the real semantic work. [The word] **yesterday** functions partly as a surface marker to indicate the pragmatic restrictions on allowable t's and partly as a syntactic device for converting $\langle qu, t' \rangle$ into a semantic modifier.

There are at least two difficulties with (68); first it is not clear that (67) claims that it is any *particular* t' at which α is true, merely that there be at least one occurring on the day preceding t's day; but second and more seriously, the evaluation of α itself when modified by $\langle \textbf{\textit{yesterday}}, \langle qu, t' \rangle\rangle$ still requires that we know when α is true, and so still requires the temporal index.[21]

This latter difficulty can be circumvented, but at a cost; we could construe α as a formula containing a free time variable. It is worth dwelling a bit on this solution because it will be one of the points of the analysis of point-of-view prepositions in the next section that a judicious use of variable-binding can avoid apparent counterexamples to the nonshiftability of the point of view.

As a lead-in to this, let us look at the pronoun **he**. In a sentence like

(69)   **He wants a batman outfit for Christmas**

the **he**, on the Bigelow account, would be replaced by the quotation of some particular entity (presumably a male person) according to certain pragmatic rules. But a sentence like (70) is different:

(70)   **Someone present will soon discover that he has lost a dollar.**

In this case there is no particular person who could be slotted into the **he** position, for suppose it is α; then the sentence would be

(71)   **Someone present will soon discover that α has lost a dollar.**

And this does not have the same truth conditions as (70).

The usual answer in a case like this is to say that the **he** in (70) signals a variable bound by the **someone**, and that seems a reasonably adequate solution.[22] Bigelow's problem, of course, is to reconcile the apparently two different uses of *he* in (69) and (70), and he is able to do this rather neatly. We are to think of *he* not as itself the variable, or the contextually supplied individual, but rather as a pointer to it. Thus in (69) we might have

$$\langle he, \langle qu, \text{Jeremy} \rangle \rangle$$

while in (70)

$$\langle he, x \rangle$$

he would be of semantical category $\langle 1,1 \rangle$ and would have, as semantic value, simply the identity function, so that the value of the whole expression would be the same as the value of the argument of the *he*. In the case of pronouns there is a surface signal of what is happening in that the place where it is happening is overtly marked, but it may be that sometimes variables with no surface realization can also be replaced by contextually determined entities. We shall see that it seems natural to suppose this in the case of points of view.

It would be possible to regard *I* also as in category $\langle 1,1 \rangle$. Thus an utterance by Bigelow containing the word 'I' would be represented by a formula containing the expression $\langle I, \langle qu, \text{Bigelow} \rangle \rangle$, and of course $V(\langle I, \langle qu, \text{Bigelow} \rangle \rangle) = \text{Bigelow}$. There is not quite so strong a motivation for treating *I* as in category $\langle 1,1 \rangle$ since it does not usually seem to occur with a bound variable. Nevertheless it can be so treated if uniformity is desired.[23] There is a more general reason for this kind of treatment—namely, that it distinguishes between the symbol which is the surface signal of a quotation and the quotation itself. This is important because there are many quotations which are not marked on the surface.

Is this then a plausible way of avoiding even the time index? Let me first admit that it is a *possible* way of avoiding it and many authors have.[24]

My own feeling is that there are several reasons against replacing the temporal indices by bound variables. The principal reason is that every English sentence is tensed, even sentences in which a temporal quantifier like *always* or *sometimes* appears.[25] The second is that the temporal quantifier would always bind the temporal variable, and there would only be one temporal variable.[26] The fact that every English sentence is tensed would mean that complete sentences would have to contain a free variable, rather as Montague's semantics[27] treats pronouns as variables, or else would have to have a slot filled by a Bigelow quotation. It was the practice of Cresswell (1973) not to have λ-deep structures with free variables, and I find the idea of assuming that the λ-deep structure of every English sentence must contain a Bigelow quotation somewhat unappealing.

Situations in which bound variables do seem to provide the best solution are cases where, by contrast, there are many different quantifiers and each must bind a different variable; and where further the variable, once bound, plays no role outside its quantifier. There are many situations in which quantifiers and variables seem the natural way of going about things. We shall see, in our discussion of the way the point of view enters the semantics of spatial prepositions, that the appropriate point of view can almost always be determined by either a Bigelow quotation or by a variable that is independently needed for purposes which are usually acknowledged as best treated by variable-binding. To some of this we now turn.

5   Context and prepositions

In sentence (18) a *from* phrase supplied the "point of view," but frequently a sentence like

(72)   *Arabella walks from across a meadow*

can occur where there is no point-of-view phrase. We have already seen in the discussion of (30) in section 2 that we have the formalism to represent the sense in which (72) means that the walking is from across a meadow from somewhere, but what (72) more likely means is that Arabella walks from across a meadow from some contextually supplied place. Now as we have seen in the last section one way to achieve this is by "quoting" in the Bigelow sense the place. Suppose that a is the thing from across a meadow from which Arabella is walking. What we must quote of course is not merely a but the whole function which represents 'from a'. Viz. the function ζ such that for any ω and b and $\langle w,t \rangle$ (in the appropriate domains): $\langle w,t \rangle \in (\zeta(\omega))(b)$ iff $\langle w,t \rangle \in \omega(b)$ and b's path over t in ω originates at a. We can then formalize (71) as

(73) $\langle\langle \lambda, y_1, \langle\langle \lambda, x_1, \langle \textbf{\textit{Arabella}}, \langle \textbf{\textit{walks}}, \langle \textbf{\textit{from}}, x_1 \rangle\rangle\rangle\rangle\rangle$,
       $\langle G, \langle \lambda, x_{\langle 0,1 \rangle}, \langle\langle x_{\langle 0,1 \rangle}, \langle \textbf{\textit{across}}, y_1 \rangle\rangle, \langle \textbf{\textit{qu}}, \zeta \rangle\rangle\rangle\rangle\rangle$,
       $\langle a, \textbf{\textit{meadow}} \rangle\rangle$.[28]

Sometimes the context dependence is made a little more explicit by saying something like

(74) *Arabella walks from across a meadow from here.*

This is just like (18) or (72) except for the **_from here_** part. For the purposes of this paper the surface word "here" can be treated as an ordinary adverb, but since it is context dependent it is more complicated at the λ-categorial level. It seems best to regard it as in $\langle\langle\langle 0,1 \rangle, \langle 0,1 \rangle\rangle, 1 \rangle$, viz of the same syntactic category as a preposition but with a syntactico-pragmatic restriction that the argument place be filled only with an expression which quotes a spatially constant, abstract object which occupies a region surrounding the utterer of the sentence in which it occurs.

$\quad$ V(**_here_**) would be the function ζ such that for any $a, b \in D_1$, $\omega \in D_{\langle 0,1 \rangle}$ and $\langle w,t \rangle \in W$; a is in the domain of ζ iff a determines a spatial area and b is in the domain of ω iff b determines a spatial area and $\langle w,t \rangle \in ((\zeta(a))(\omega))(b)$ iff a is spatially constant throughout $\langle w,t \rangle$ and $\langle w,t \rangle \in \omega(b)$ and b's position at some $m \in t$ overlaps with the region occupied by a at $\langle w,t \rangle$.

$\quad$ To get the required sense of (74) we must make use of G, because what "from here" says is "from a place which is a here place." Since something taking place in the goal area of something which takes place here must itself take place here, we can formalize from here as

(75) $\langle \lambda, x_{\langle 0,1 \rangle}, \langle\langle \lambda, x_1, \langle\langle \textbf{\textit{from}}, x_1 \rangle, x_{\langle 0,1 \rangle}\rangle\rangle, \langle G, \langle \textbf{\textit{here}}, \langle \textbf{\textit{qu}}, a \rangle\rangle\rangle\rangle\rangle$

I shall leave the reader to work out that this really does have the intended meaning. [Example] (74) would be formalized like (72) but with (75) in place of $\langle \textit{qu}, \zeta \rangle$.

$\quad$ One feature of the Bigelow attitude to quotation was that in the case of pronouns it integrated a bound variable approach as in (70) with a deictic approach as in (69). It is perhaps worth remarking that bound variables occur here too. In the sentences

(76) *At every village a band plays across a meadow from there*

and

(77) *At every village a band plays from across a meadow*

in both cases the point of view is not contextually supplied because it is in the scope of a quantifier.

$\quad$ [The word] *there* seems to act like *he* in sometimes signalling a bound variable and sometimes a quoted entity. [The word] *here*, on the other hand, seems analogous to *I*. Pragmatically, of course, when formalizing an utterance, *here* can only be used when it refers to an area surrounding the speaker.

In (77) although the point of view phrase is supplied by the bound variable, the *from* part[29] of it does have to be supplied by quotation. Let V(*from*) = ζ

(78) $\langle\langle$*every, village*$\rangle$, $\langle\lambda, x_1, \langle\langle$*a band*$\rangle$, $\langle\langle$*at, x_1*$\rangle$, $\langle\lambda, y_1, \langle\langle\lambda, z_1, \langle\langle\lambda, w_1, \langle\langle$*plays, $\langle$from, $w_1\rangle\rangle$, $y_1\rangle\rangle$, $y_1\rangle\rangle$,
     $\langle G, \langle\lambda, x_{\langle0,1\rangle}, \langle\langle x_{\langle0,1\rangle}, \langle$across, $z_1\rangle\rangle$, $\langle\langle qu, \zeta\rangle$, $x_1\rangle\rangle\rangle\rangle\rangle\rangle\langle$a, meadow$\rangle\rangle\rangle\rangle\rangle\rangle$

This particular use of the quotation operator may be seen as a device for preventing symbols from reaching the surface. By quoting V(*from*) (the ζ in (78)) we have the advantage of *from* in the sentence without its presence on the surface. Earlier in this paper, as in Cresswell (1973), an asterisk has been used to indicate a symbol that does not reach the surface. So we see that *from** can be defined as $\langle qu, V(from)\rangle$ and, in general, any (closed) expression α can be defined so that $\alpha^* =_{df} \langle qu, V^+(\alpha)\rangle$. Of course the * notation suppresses the dependence on V, and sometimes this dependence is crucial, but often it is not (Bigelow 1975b, 15–20). A preposition which is frequently quoted is *at*. This is presumably because it is, spatially, the most neutral of the prepositions (cf. Clark 1973).

An example involving *at** and *from** and a bound point of view is given by

(79) **At every house a band plays across a river.**

The λ-deep structure of (79) is:

(80) $\langle\langle$*every, house*$\rangle$, $\langle\lambda, w_1, \langle$*a band*$, \langle\lambda, x_1, \langle\langle\lambda, z_1, \langle\langle\langle$*at, $w_1\rangle$, $\langle\lambda, x_1, \langle\langle\lambda, y_1, \langle\langle$plays, $\langle$at*, $y_1\rangle\rangle$, $x_1\rangle\rangle$, $\langle G$,
     $\langle\lambda, x_{\langle0,1\rangle}, \langle\langle\langle$across, $z_1\rangle$, $x_{\langle0,1\rangle}\rangle$, $\langle$from*, $w_1\rangle\rangle\rangle\rangle\rangle\rangle\rangle$, $x_1\rangle\rangle$, $\langle$a, river$\rangle\rangle\rangle\rangle\rangle$.

More straightforwardly, of course, the sentence

(81) **Arabella walks across a meadow**

in the sense that her walking takes place in an area across the meadow from some contextually determined point of view can be formalized by replacing the *from* in (73) by *at**.

I would like now to turn to some examples involving **behind**. [The word] **behind** is, like **across**, in category $\langle\langle\langle 0,1\rangle, \langle 0,1\rangle\rangle, 1\rangle$ and obviously a sentence like (81) can occur with **behind** replacing **across** and the point of view determined completely by the context. However the interesting fact about **behind** is that sometimes the point of view is determined by the object of the preposition. A sentence illustrating this use is

(82) **Everyone dances behind a house.**

It is clear that in (82) the point of view which determines the appropriate area is going to vary from house to house. The point of view is not the house itself; rather, it is some point in front of the house. The situation seems to be this. An entity such as a house has what might be called a conventionally determined "front" and "back." In the case of houses, it is probably the side which first, and most naturally, presents itself to a person as he becomes acquainted with it. Be that as it may, the best formal representation seems to be a function f whose domain consists of all objects a which have a conventional front and whose range consists of hypothetical objects $f(a)$ which exist at the conventional front of a. So $f(a)$ is hypothetical in the same sense as the "journeys" of section 2 and need not actually exist in the world in question.

Formally f is the function such that for any world w and moment of time m, $(f(w))(m) = r$, where r is the region in front of a at m in w, which could be considered the "canonical viewpoint" for a. Notice that the precise nature of f has been left vague.[30] It is not the purpose of this paper to make any remarks about the principles by which canonical points of view are chosen. That is the job of a quite different area of semantics. The purpose of this paper is to show how the canonical point of view enters into a formal description of the truth-conditional semantics for sentences containing words like **behind**. (If I seem to be overstressing this point it is because I have come across people who do not appear to have appreciated the difference between these two tasks.)

The idea of a conventional front and back can be seen as part of the meaning of the surface word 'behind', although it is not involved in the semantic value of the symbol **behind** but is put in by quotation. This seems to be another example of the situation we found with I where the value of the symbol in the λ-deep structure represented only part of the meaning of the surface word.

Now let us see how (82) fares. There are, of course, several readings, depending on the relative scopes of the various nominals. We shall look at the sense which claims that for every person there is a house behind which that person dances. The other senses, though possibly interesting in themselves, throw no extra light on the point of view.

(83) $\langle$**everybody**, $\langle\lambda, x_1, \langle\langle\lambda, y_1, \langle\langle\lambda, z_1, \langle\langle$**dances**, $\langle$**at**$^*, z_1\rangle\rangle, x_1\rangle\rangle, \langle G, \langle\lambda, x_{\langle 0,1\rangle}, \langle\langle x_{\langle 0,1\rangle}, \langle$**behind**, $y_1\rangle\rangle,$
$\langle$**from**$^* \langle\langle qu, f\rangle, y_1\rangle\rangle\rangle\rangle\rangle\rangle\rangle, \langle a,$ **house**$\rangle\rangle\rangle\rangle$.

We may note in passing that there are many sentences in which the object of the preposition is also quoted. (That is why prepositions often appear to function as adverbs.) When the New Zealand farmer calls to his sheepdog

(84)   **Get in behind**

the context supplies the thing in behind which the dog is supposed to get.

The crucial point in (83) is that the quotation operator quotes the function f and gives a symbol in category $\langle 1,1\rangle$ which can operate on y_1, for each value a assigned to y_1 the expression $\langle\langle qu, f\rangle, y_1\rangle$ will have the value $f(a)$, and this is the point of view value which we are associating with each house a.

Even (82) though can, I believe, be construed with a point of view that is completely determined by context. Suppose that I am standing in the midst of a collection of houses and I can see the backs of some and the fronts of others and someone tells me that someone is dancing behind every house. It seems to me that I can interpret this sentence to mean that they are dancing behind the houses from the point of view that I occupy, and not from the conventional viewpoint of each house. To get this sense for (82) (or for some similar sentence) we would change (83) by merely replacing $\langle\langle qu, f\rangle, y_1\rangle$ by $\langle qu, a\rangle$ where a is the position of the observer being used as the point of view.

A slightly more complicated case is suggested by William James's example of the man trying to observe a squirrel on the other side of a tree trunk but failing because the man and the squirrel are both going round the tree and the squirrel is always behind the tree. Here we imagine a series of journeys, each beginning at the point the man has got to, and with reference to each new journey the squirrel is still behind the tree.

6   Over and above

There are two new theoretical problems posed by the prepositions **over** and **above** (with their converses **under** and **below**).[The word] **over** is unlike all the prepositions we have discussed so far in that its locative sense does not seem derivable from its directional sense. In the sentence

(85)   *The lamp is over the table*

we do not mean (or at least we need not mean) that the lamp is at the end of a journey over the table. Though of course that meaning is present in

(86)   *The post office is over the hill.*

On the other hand, the directional meaning does not seem easily predictable from the locative meaning. For (86) claims more than that merely the post office is at the end of a journey which passes through a position which is over the hill. (Such a journey might, e.g., return to the original place.)[31] Bennett (1974, 50) analyzes this sense of over as

[Locative [path [locative [superior of hill] place]] place],

which seems correct as far as it goes but is not finely discriminating enough for the prediction of the correct truth conditions.

One solution is to say that *over* is lexically ambiguous, though of course its two meanings are intimately related. In section 1 we noted that the semantic framework we are using enables two symbols to be very similar in meaning without this appearing in their syntactical composition. Of course when this does happen, it is very natural for these two symbols to have an identical surface realization. The two senses of *over*, if there are two, are closely enough related for them to have the same surface realization.

The other solution is to say that there is only one basic sense of *over* but that its two uses are obtained from the basic sense in a rather more complicated way than we might have thought. The difficulty with this solution is that the relation between the two does not seem expressed by symbols which are needed for purposes unconnected with the analysis of *over*. Since we are not interested in lexical decomposition, this second solution offers, at first sight at least, little advantage.

There is in any case some evidence that even the basic locative sense of *over* involves a journey, but not the kind of journey involved in (86). For in sentences like

(87)   *The lamp is two inches directly over the table from the cup*

and

(88)   *The Rembrandt is diagonally over the Reubens*

the kind of analysis given in this paper would dictate that we postulate a hypothetical journey from the cup or the Reubens to the lamp or the Rembrandt. If two journeys are involved, two series of *over* seem suggested. It may of course be that there is an analysis, more complicated and subtle than I have thought of, which will unify these senses.

The other problem with *over* is that Bennett's phrase [superior of hill] itself makes reference to a point of view—in this case, the point of view is a direction.[32] In the case of *over*, the direction might be always from the ground up, so that we can build it in to the meaning, but if H. H. Clarke[33] is to be believed the same would not be true of *above*. Clarke imagines a girl lying horizontal on the beach. We are to consider the sentence

(89)   *There's a fly two inches above your knee.*

Clarke points out that this could mean that the fly is two inches further from the ground than the knee is, or it could mean that the fly is two inches closer to her head. If Clarke is right, as seems at least plausible, then it would seem that ***above*** is after all a point-of-view preposition, since obviously the truth conditions of (89) are affected by the difference Clark notices.

The problem in formalizing the difference is to explain what is going on in the second situation. Presumably the ***above*** is used there because we think of people as typically standing upright so that their "canonical position" is one in which the two aboves coincide. (As with ***behind*** we have little to say about how a position is selected as a canonical one. Why is it, e.g., that the upright standing position is the canonical one despite the fact that we probably are sitting or lying much more of the time than we are standing?)

We have claimed that (89) is ambiguous rather than merely non-specific. To claim that it is non-specific would be to claim that (89) entails merely that the fly is above the knee according to *some* direction or other. I do no believe that this can be so. Consider

(90)   ***There is a fly two inches above everyone's knee.***

It seems to me that this could entail that all the flies were two inches above the knee measured from the ground, or two inches above the knee measured toward the head. It does *not* seem to me that (90) could be true if on some of the people the flies were two inches above the knee measured from the ground and on other people two inches above the knee measured toward the head, yet this is what it would have to mean if ***above*** meant something like "above according to some (appropriate) direction."

The question now arises of how it is that the context establishes the direction. In the case of all the other point-of-view uses of prepositions we have examined, the point of view was determined by a journey. But it seems very unlikely that the direction point of view could be established in this way. There is however some evidence that a journey is involved—namely, the phrase ***two inches*** in (89) suggests that a two-inch journey in the appropriate direction is involved. This means that we should like a basic directional sense even for ***above***. But unlike our other prepositions, even in the basic sense of ***above*** there still seems need for reference to a direction.

There seem two ways in which we can bring this direction in: either by using an index or by adding an argument place to the preposition. The discussion in section 4 provides criteria which lead, I believe, to the second of these solutions.[34] For we shall see that the point of view provided by the direction can come in either contextually or via variables which are independently needed anyway. [The word] ***above*** will therefore be in category $\langle\langle\langle\langle0,1\rangle, \langle0,1\rangle\rangle, 1\rangle, 1\rangle$. It will make an ordinary preposition out of a direction. To give its semantics we have to assume that we know when a journey from a to b is a journey whose end is higher, in a certain direction than the beginning is. Actually some care is needed here, for the basic sense of above is not that of

(91)   ***He put the lamp above the table.***

[Example] (91) says that he put the lamp in a position which is above the table. The basic sense is a journey to a point whose end is higher than its beginning.[35]

We must also assume that with at least certain objects there is associated a "natural" direction in the sense in which there is associated with people the vector which points from their feet to their head when they are stretched out. This is not quite as simple as it appears because of the possibility of movement over an interval. Suppose that instead of lying on the beach the girl is doing gymnastics. Suppose that she, somewhat miraculously, contrives to remain stretched out during the interval—that is, she does not bend at all although she turns cartwheels and swings from bars. Suppose too that the fly rather miraculously remains two inches toward her head from her knee. In order to say that the fly remains above her knee, we must suppose that the positions of the knee and the fly are understood as relative to a direction which is constant with respect to the girl although changing with respect to the wider spatial framework.

Assuming that we have got this sorted out, we shall describe the conventional direction associated with a in w over the interval t as $\uparrow(a,t,w)$.

In those cases where the direction takes the ground as its base, we simply pick some paradigmatically vertical a and quote it in the Bigelow manner: $V(\textbf{\textit{above}})$ is the function $\zeta \in D_{\langle\langle\langle\langle 0,1\rangle,\langle 0,1\rangle\rangle,1\rangle,1\rangle}$ such that for any a and $b \in D_1$, $\omega \in D_{\langle 0,1\rangle}$ and $\langle w,t\rangle \in W$: $\langle w,t\rangle \in ((\zeta(\omega))(b))(a)$ iff $\langle w,t\rangle \in \omega(b)$, and b's position is higher at the end of t than at the beginning according to $\uparrow(a,t,w)$.

To disambiguate (89) we need merely distinguish between when the direction is determined by the person in question and when it is determined completely by the context. It is worth pointing out that the direction in (89) is associated with the girl rather than her knee. If the direction were always associated with the object of the preposition (so that a would be above b by the canonical direction for a), then we could have identified the point-of-view argument with the object of the preposition. This may seem plausible in the case of the knee where the canonical direction of a person's knee might be held to be the same as the direction of the person whose knee it is. However, it is easy to get examples where it is not so. Let us imagine the girl lying on the beach with a copy of *War and Peace* on her stomach turned in such a way that the top of the book is facing toward her feet. Consider then the sentence

(92) *There is a fly two inches above* **War and Peace.**

It seems to me that the sentence should now be three-ways ambiguous, according to the direction associated with the girl or the book or if the "natural" direction takes the ground as base.

Suppose that we have a pet fly named *Fifi.* Consider the sentence

(93) *Fifi files above a book.*

We can bring out the three-way ambiguity as follows. (The sentences are a little more complicated than they might have been because of the need to use G.)

(94) $\langle\langle\lambda, y_1, \langle\langle\lambda, x^1\langle\textit{Fifi}, \langle\textit{flies}, \langle\textit{at*}, x_1\rangle\rangle\rangle\rangle, \langle G, \langle\lambda, x_{\langle 0,1\rangle}, \langle x_{\langle 0,1\rangle}, \langle\langle\textit{above}, y_1\rangle, \langle qu, a\rangle\rangle\rangle\rangle\rangle\rangle\rangle, \langle\textit{a book}\rangle\rangle.$

Where a is the paradigmatically vertical object, (94) gives the sense of (93) in which the direction is the natural one measured from the ground. Where a is the person lying on the beach, we get the reading in which the 'above' is measured toward the head. To get the third reading, we must replace $\langle qu, a\rangle$ by the bound variable y_1. This is because the third sense of (93) does not refer to any specific direction as the one determined by the book. This sense will be true provided the fly is above the book by whatever direction the book provides. This gives some support to a Bigelow analysis of the direction point of view in *above* since the variable y_1 is independently needed in the sentence in any case.

7 Sentential modifiers

All the adverbial phrases treated in this paper have been in category $\langle\langle 0,1\rangle, \langle 0,1\rangle\rangle$. But it is well known that many adverbials are sentential modifiers and must therefore be represented in a categorial language, as in category $\langle 0,0\rangle$. Many temporal adverbs—such as *yesterday*—seem to be in this category, as well as temporal prepositional phrases such as *at ten o'clock*. We can show this to be the case by noticing that a sentence like

(95) *Yesterday the president resigned*

need not, and normally does not, mean that the person who is now president resigned yesterday. It means that the person who was president yesterday resigned then. This means that the phrase *the president* has to be inside the scope of *yesterday*, and so *yesterday* must apply to the whole sentence.

The question is whether there are any sentential modifiers that involve spatial prepositions. Evidence seems difficult to come by since there are few, if any, nouns whose meaning is spatially dependent in the way a word like *president* is temporally dependent; *president* is, of course, context dependent in the sense that we have to know what the person is supposed to be president of, but that seems better handled in the Bigelow manner.

If there are genuinely spatially dependent nouns (in the sense that whether something does or does not satisfy the noun cannot be predicted on the basis of where that thing is at any given time), then there would seem to be a ground for having a spatial index, and a spatial index would seem a prerequisite for a spatially dependent sentential modifier (*vide* Cresswell 1979, section 2).

There is some slight evidence for sentential spatial modifiers from the behavior of certain quantifiers. It seems at least possible to me that in the sentence

(96)   *Behind the bushes everybody loves somebody*

the everybody means 'everybody behind the bushes'. On the other hand, (96) does not mean the same as

(97)   *Everybody behind the bushes loves somebody.*

[Example] (97) does not require that anybody's beloved be behind the bushes. This suggests that *behind the bushes* modifies the whole sentence

(98)   *Everybody loves somebody*

and is true at a given world time and place iff everybody at that place at that time in that world loves somebody at that time and place in that world. Of course, we can give *everybody* wider scope than *behind*, as in the most natural interpretation of

(99)   *Everybody loves somebody behind the bushes.*

Luckily we do not need to postulate a sentential sense of *behind* to get this reading. For the analysis of (96) will proceed along the lines of (83). By postulating an *at†* which is a symbol like *at** but in category $\langle\langle 0,0\rangle, 1\rangle$, we can obtain sentential uses for most of the prepositions we have discussed.

8   Temporal points of view

Many prepositions used in a spatial sense are also used in a temporal sense, and indeed the temporal sense often seems to have arisen fairly directly from the spatial sense.[36] An investigation of this relation within the truth-conditional framework of this paper would no doubt be interesting; it does indeed seem to pose all kinds of problems not apparent at first glance. However such an investigation is beyond our present scope and all that I intend to do in this section is to have a brief look at whether there is anything analogous in the temporal case to the spatial point of view.

The question has some interest in connection with Reichenbach's analysis of the present perfect, particularly as formalized by Lennart Åqvist and Franz Guenthner (1978). Indeed, one of the principal motivations of the present paper was to see whether the point of view postulated by Åqvist and Guenthner has any connection with the point of view involved in the spatial uses of prepositions. In fact, it would seem that it probably does not, because the spatial point of view does not seem best treated by an index. It may be, of course, that Reichenbach's point of view is not an index, either. At any rate it might be worth looking at cases in which temporal prepositions are being used in a way which suggests a point of view. The spatial point of view was analyzed in terms of a journey to the scene of the action. Now in the case of a journey through time the possibilities are much more restricted. If we ignore time travel[37] there is only one direction in which we can move through time, and between any two points there is only one route.

Prepositions like ***through*** can occur temporally as in

(100)   ***Through the night a band kept playing* My Strength and My Tower *and* Abide with Me.**

But (100) does not seem able to mean that the band was playing at the end of a temporal journey which went through the night. Some extent phrases seem to involve this, as

(101)   ***Sixty years from the flood no one remembered it***,

but even here ***after*** is more usual, and there seems no way in which the ***from*** phrase can be supplied by the context. Indeed, it does not seem that the temporal prepositions have very much use at all for the kind of point of view that is so much in evidence in their spatial counterparts. It may be that the use of an adverb like ***quickly*** in the sentence (discussed in [Cresswell 1979])

(102)   ***Quickly someone entered***

might be able to be interpreted as saying that in the goal area of a quick, temporal journey from a contextually determined point someone entered, but the detailed way in which such sentences would have to be worked out seems different enough from the spatial cases that it will probably prove wisest to study temporal modification on its own terms.

9   Appendix on λ-categorial languages

A categorial language is based on the notion of a *syntactic category*. There are two basic categories, 0 the category of *sentence* and 1 the category of *name*. Given any categories $\tau, \sigma_1, \ldots, \sigma_n$ then $\langle \tau, \sigma_1, \ldots, \sigma_n \rangle$ is also a category. (It is understood as the category of a *functor* which makes an expression of category τ out of expressions of categories $\sigma_1, \ldots, \sigma_n$, respectively.)

A λ-categorial language $\mathfrak{L}$ is specified by assigning to finitely many syntactic categories a finite set of *symbols*.[38] These can be thought of as the words of the language. This is done formally by letting F be a function from syntactic categories such that for any category σ, F_σ is the (finite) set of symbols of category σ. All variable binding is done by an *abstraction operator*, which we denote by λ. To deal with variable binding we require, for each category σ, a denumerably infinite set, X_σ of *variables of category* σ. Given F, X, and λ, we can define the set E_σ of (well-formed) expressions of category σ as the smallest set such that:

(i) $F_\sigma \subseteq E_\sigma$

(ii) If $a_1, \ldots, a_n$ are in $E_{\sigma_1}, \ldots, E_{\sigma_n}$, respectively, and $\delta \in E_{\langle \tau, \sigma_1, \ldots, \sigma_n \rangle}$, then $\langle \delta a_1, \ldots, a_n \rangle \in E_\tau$

(iii) If $x \in X_\sigma$ and $\alpha \in E_\tau$ then $\langle \lambda, x, \alpha \rangle \in E_{\langle \tau, \sigma \rangle}$.

[Statement] (i) says that every symbol of category σ is also an expression of category σ. [Statement] (ii) says that when a functor expression in category $\langle \tau, \sigma_1, \ldots, \sigma_n \rangle$ is placed before expressions in category $\sigma_1, \ldots, \sigma_n$ then it forms an expression in category τ. The best way of understanding $\langle \lambda, x, \alpha \rangle$ is to read it as 'is an x such that α'. [Statement] (iii) makes this in category $\langle \tau, \alpha \rangle$ where σ is the category of x and τ the category of α. [Statement] $\langle \lambda, x, \alpha \rangle$ is called an *abstract*.

We can associate with a λ-categorial language $\mathfrak{L}$ an *interpretation*. It is of course possible to associate many different interpretations with the same language. The model-theoretic approach to semantics is based on the idea of specifying things which are understood as the meanings of symbols of $\mathfrak{L}$ and providing rules for showing how the values of complex expressions of $\mathfrak{L}$ are determined by the values assigned to the symbols of $\mathfrak{L}$. More specifically, we want the interpretation to be set-theoretical and truth-conditional.

Each syntactic category σ has associated with it a domain D_σ, which is understood as the set of things that are appropriate values for expressions in E_σ. D_0, the values of sentences, is a set of subsets of the set W of all pairs $\langle w, t \rangle$ where w is a possible world and t an interval of time. D_1 is the set of all "things" where this includes both possible and actual things. $D_{\langle \tau, \sigma, \ldots, \sigma_n \rangle}$ is a set of total or partial functions from $D_{\sigma_1} \times \ldots \times D_{\sigma_n}$ into D_τ. Given such a system D of domains, we interpret a language by means of an assignment function V which assigns a value in D_σ to each symbol in F_σ. Where α is in F_σ, we refer to its value under V as $V(\alpha)$. Thus we speak of $\langle D, V \rangle$ as an interpretation for $\mathfrak{L}$.

In order to interpret all the expressions of the language, we have to make assigmnents to the variables as well. We distinguish between an assignment to the variables and an assignment to the constants because the expressions we shall be finally interested in will contain no free variables. Although the assignment function to the variables is important in obtaining the semantic value of an expression without free variables, it turns out that the value of such an expression is invariant under different assignments to the variables. We let v be an assignment to the variables. Where $x \in X_\sigma$, then $v(x) \in D_\sigma$. Further, where $a \in D_\sigma$, then $(v, a/x)$ is the function exactly like v except that $(v, a/x)(x) = a$.

We are now ready to show how V and v together induce a uniquely determined assignment V_v to all the expressions of $\mathfrak{L}$:

(i)   If $\alpha \in F_\sigma$ then $V_v(\alpha) = V(\alpha)$
(ii) If $x \in X_\sigma$ then $V_v(x) = v(x)$
(iii) If $\delta \in D_{\langle \tau, \sigma_1, \ldots, \sigma_n \rangle}, \alpha_1, \ldots, \alpha_n \in E_{\sigma_1}, \ldots, E_{\sigma_n}$, respectively, then $V_v(\langle \delta, \alpha_1, \ldots, \alpha_n \rangle) = (V_v(\delta)(V_v(\alpha_1), \ldots, V_v(\alpha_n))$
(iv) If $x \in X_\sigma$ and $\alpha \in E_\tau$ then $V_v(\langle \lambda, x, \alpha \rangle)$ is the function ω such that for any $a \in D_\sigma, \omega(a) = V_{(v, a/x)}(\alpha)$.

These rules are all understood, of course, under the proviso that the appropriate expressions are defined for their arguments. By allowing partial functions in D, it frequently happens that an expression is not defined. It is then said to be semantically anomalous in this interpretation. [Statement] (iii) means that the value of a functional expression is obtained by taking its value, which is a function, and letting it apply to the values of the expressions which follow it. [Statement] (iv) says that $\langle \lambda, x, \alpha \rangle$ defines a function whose value, for any a is (loosely) what you get from α by putting a in where x goes.

Given an expression α in category 0 and an interpretation $\langle D, V \rangle$ of $\mathfrak{L}$, we say that α is *true* under $\langle D, V \rangle$ in world w at time t iff $\langle w, t \rangle \in V(\alpha)$. This is why we speak of the semantics as truth-conditional.

In applying a λ-categorial language to a natural language, the idea is to get formulae that look as much like English sentences as possible. One test is to see whether representing the sentences as English words (I use boldface italic type when I can get it) produces a formula which becomes an

English sentence when the brackets, the λ's, and the variables are omitted. Of course there is still a place for transformational syntax in obtaining the surface structure, but the transformations look to be a great deal simpler than many of those who advocate a base in logic seem to require. At any rate, the material in this appendix is presented at much greater length in Cresswell (1973).

Notes

Many of the ideas developed in this paper arose as a result of conversations with Franz Guenthner, Lennart Åqvist, and Christian Rohrer while I was in Stuttgart in May and June of 1976 on a project supported by the German Science Foundation on the logic of tense and aspect. Mention should also be made of the work of Peter Lutzeier (1974) on a possible-worlds analysis of spatial propositions, although he was not concerned with quite the same range of phenomena as I am. And of course my colleagues in Wellington have also provided ideas. This paper can be considered a continuation of the study of spatio-temporal modification begun in Cresswell (1979), although I have endeavored to keep it self-contained.

1. In addition to Bennett (1975) I have consulted Hill (1968), but I would not pretend to any kind of complete study of the semantics of prepositions. I merely want to tackle a number of issues which arise when trying to put their semantics into a truth-conditional framework. Although I have used Part I of Bennett's (1975) quite extensively, I only briefly touch on the temporal sense of prepositions which he discusses in Part II, and I have nothing to say about Bennett's own semantic framework, stratificational semantics, which he uses in Part III to give his formalization of the prepositions he has described earlier.

2. This view of semantics is explicitly defended in Cresswell (1978b).

3. In dealing with ordinary language the spatio-temporal framework may not perhaps have to have all the properties ascribed to it by current physics. In addition, it may have to be relativized to an area surrounding the speaker. For instance, if someone wants to talk about the relative positions of things in an aeroplane, he is likely to ignore the fact that all these things are moving with the aeroplane. For the purpose of evaluating his sentence, we assume a spatial framework in which the aeroplane is constant. Of course, if the sentence relates something in the aeroplane to something outside it, the speaker will have to assume a wider framework, and so on until, when discussing astronomy, we may be using the whole of space as our framework.

4. Both Taylor (1974) and Dowty (1977) have used interval semantics in the analysis of the progressive form in English, and I have used it (Cresswell 1979) in the semantics of *quickly*. Some discussion of how the logical particles fare in interval semantics is found in Cresswell (1977).

5. In the semantic framework I have in mind, the present tense is taken as semantically basic (Cresswell 1973 139f.). It is therefore more convenient, when analyzing matters other than tense to take sentences which involve only the present, even thought they are sometimes a little less natural than sentences with other tenses. In examples that are not going to be formalized, the past tense is frequently used. It should be emphasized, of course, that examples involving the past tense *can* be formalized within this framework.

6. As described in the appendix to this paper (section 9).

7. Cf. Cresswell (1979). It should be clear already how important it is to have intervals as the temporal index. The importance of limiting the domains of functions like V(*walks*) is because D_1 is so big that no function can have the whole of it in its domain (Cresswell 1973, 99). This has the consequence that many expressions may end up without any value, because at some point a function is not defined for a given entity. Such sentences are called "semantically anomalous" or "semantically deviant" (Cresswell 1975b). It is a merit of the possible-worlds approach to semantics that it does not confuse semantic deviance with syntactic ill-formedness. In what follows it will frequently be left to the readers' good sense to work out how the domains of various functions should be restricted. In some cases, of course, ordinary language does not seem to have made up its mind, and so any choice will force more precision than the data will support. But that is the problem of vagueness or indeterminacy, a problem on which this paper will have nothing to say.

8. In Cresswell (1973, 135) *a* was put in category $\langle 0, \langle 0,1 \rangle, \langle 0,1 \rangle \rangle$. That category is only trivially different from $\langle \langle 0, \langle 0,1 \rangle \rangle, \langle 0,1 \rangle \rangle$, but it does mean that in Cresswell (1973) abstraction must be used to make a nominal out of *a meadow* (p. 137).

9. In Cresswell (1973, 215) a basic category 2 was suggested for common nouns but in this paper they will be put in category $\langle 0,1 \rangle$. This means that the present treatment of prepositions also accounts for

their use as adjectival phrases. Although the adjectival use of prepositions is not discussed in this paper, it does not seem to cause any difficulties for the approach adopted.

10. A liberalization of the formation rules, noted in Cresswell (1973, 78) allows us to put a functor after or between its arguments as well as before them. It is possible, by means of λ-abstraction to make *across a meadow* a constituent of a formalization of (4), *viz.*

(1) $\langle \lambda, x_{(0,1)}, \langle \lambda, y_1, \langle\langle \lambda, x_1, \langle\langle x_{(0,1)}, \langle across, x_1 \rangle\rangle, y_1 \rangle\rangle, \langle a, meadow \rangle\rangle\rangle\rangle$.

The principles of λ-conversion (Cresswell 1973, p. 88 f) will ensure that a sentence with (i) as a constituent modifying *walks* can be constructed to be equivalent in meaning to (5). The principles of λ-conversion have been criticized in Ruttenberg (1976) as being too powerful, and indeed, as noted in Cresswell (1973, 224), their use in syntax undoubtedly needs restricting. For reasons indicated in Cresswell (1976) I regard λ-conversion as about equivalent in power to unconstrained transformations. What I would hope for would be a way of turning constraints on transformations into constraints on λ-conversions. But these problems lie outside the scope of the present paper. In what follows I shall frequently produce λ-deep structures in which a certain amount of λ-conversion would be needed to make them look more like surface structure phrase markers.

11. The kinds of objects we have in mind are either physical objects or the kind of abstract objects such as the hypothetical "journeys" introduced in the next section.

12. It is interesting to note that (11) is more natural in the progressive

(i)   *Arabella is walking across a meadow from Bill.*

I think this is because we imagine ourselves starting from where Bill is and coming upon Arabella in the middle of her walk. The semantics of the progressive as offered by Dowty (1977) or Taylor (1974) could make (i) true at the moment of our arrival even if (11) were not. (The ambiguity discussed in the text is quite clear in my speech but I am told that many speakers do not recognize it.)

13. Even here, if the band is playing a march, the *across* could refer to the journey, as in

(i)   *The band played* **Colonel Bogey** *across the meadow.*

14. I have in mind theories of the counterfactual of the kind developed by Stalnaker (1968), Lewis (1973), Åqvist (1973), and others.

15. $(v, \omega'/x_{(0,1)})$ is the function exactly like v except that $(v, \omega'/x_{(0,1)})(x_{(0,1)}) = \omega'$. *Vide* 6.6 in Cresswell (1973, 85).

16. When an extent phrase is used, then the difference between *through* and *over* becomes important. Thus

(i)   *The post office is three miles over the hill*

and

(ii)   *The post office is two miles through the hill*

may both be true.

17. There is a very natural version of (55) in which the prepositional phrase is an adjectival phrase operating on *tree*. But that is not the sense here intended.

18. Bennett (1975, 42–44) treats extent sentences as a separate kind of spatial modification. He cites (p. 40)

(i)   *The mall goes from Buckingham Palace to Trafalgar Square.*

It seems to me that it is the sense of *goes* in this sentence which makes it special rather than the modifier. Other cases which deviate from the paradigm are

(ii)   *The sergeant-major shouted across the parade ground*

in the sense in which it is the sound of his voice which makes the journey, not him.

19. E.g. Montague (1974) and Lewis (1970: Chapter 11 in this volume). It is perhaps odd to speak of work as "early" when it was done around 1970, but such is the history of indexical semantics.

20. Although I believe I am giving as accurate a picture of Bigelow's context theory as required for

this paper, readers should be advised that the full treatment is more elaborate than I have suggested and they would be well advised to consult the original. It is doubtless true that calling this sort of thing "quotation" distorts the ordinary meaning of that word. Nevertheless it seems a legitimate extension.

21. Bigelow has in fact (1975b, 6) acknowledged this objection and recognizes a temporal index, although he still makes tense operators more quotational than usual.

22. *Vide* Bigelow (1975b, 2) and Cresswell (1973, 178 f.). Some linguists have been dissatisfied with the bound variable approach to pronouns, e.g. Cooper (1979) and Hausser (1976), within the framework of Montague's syntax. It is not obvious however whether their criticisms apply to λ-deep structures, nor whether their solutions are adequate. Some of what they say does seem to me formalizable in a λ-categorial language.

23. Bigelow actually has an even more complicated treatment of *I* in (1975b, 3), but his extra complexities need not detain us here. Putting *I* in category $\langle 1,1 \rangle$ enables us to deal with cases of apposition, for $\langle I, \textbf{\textit{Bigelow}} \rangle$ becomes will formed. It is not clear however that all apposition can be dealt with like this. For a discussion of the analysis of apposition in a λ-categorial language *vide* von Stechow (1974).

24. One can even avoid the world index by using variables over worlds and so do the whole formalization in an extensional language. Authors who have done this in various ways include Lewis (1968a), Tichý (1971), Rennie (1974), and Taylor (1974). Partee in (1973) feels that the analogy between tenses and pronouns is strong enough to suggest that tenses should be treated by bound variables but is by no means certain that these analogies are caused by anything more than the semantic similarities between indices and assignments to variables. Points like this are made by Parsons (1973) and Stalnaker (1973a) when commenting on Partee's paper.

25. Though as Lewis notes in (1975: Chapter 30, this volume) quantifiers like ***always*** are not just purely temporal. One of the problems to tackle in looking at a more general kind of modification than purely spatio-temporal will be to see how Lewis' unrestricted quantifiers can be formally treated in a λ-categorial language.

26. Of course if the treatment of aspect in Åqvist (1976) and Åqvist and Guenthner (1978) is correct we shall need at least two temporal indices.

27. E.g. Montague (1974, 250). Montague though, (p. 234 f.) like Lewis (1970: Chapter 11 in this volume, 175 f.) has an 'assignment co-ordinate' which makes the values of the free variables context-determined. A predicate logic without variables is set out in Hughes and Londey (1965: 167–227). It is perforce a very restricted fragment of full first-order logic.

28. $\langle qu, \zeta \rangle$ is a symbol in category $\langle \langle 0,1 \rangle, \langle 0,1 \rangle \rangle$. Since the syntactic category of the symbol does not always have to be the same as the semantic category of the quoted entity Bigelow uses a subscript on the *qu* to indicate the category of the quotation. Thus $\langle qu_{\langle\langle 0,1\rangle,\langle 0,1\rangle\rangle}, \zeta \rangle$ would be his way of writing the $\langle qu, \zeta \rangle$ which occurs in (73). Since ζ will be in D_1 as well as $D_{\langle\langle 0,1\rangle,\langle 0,1\rangle\rangle}$ (if the principle of Cresswell 1973, 99) is adhered to) $\langle qu, \zeta \rangle$ would be the symbol with ζ as its semantic value but of syntactic category 1. But although ζ does not dictate the category of $\langle qu, \zeta \rangle$ it usually strongly indicates it, at least in a sentence like (73). For this reason we shall not put subscripts on the quotation symbol.

29. The first ***from*** of course does reach the surface. Note that there is a sentence superficially like (76) in which the prepositional phrase has an explicit object *viz*:

(i)   ***A band plays across a meadow from every village.***

This sentence contains no contextually supplied material.

30. The conventionality of front and back may be illustrated by a regulation of the Horowhenua County Council that owners of beachfront properties at Waikanae Beach who wish to build a garage on the street side of their properties must obtain a certificate from the building inspector declaring that the front of their house is at the back. *Vide* also Lutzeier (1974).

31. It may be thought that this journey sense of ***over*** arose from the other sense though is now only historically related. The formalization of this kind of process is discussed in Dowty (1977). Possibly if the post office were on this side of the hill but the only road to it passed via the top, we might be inclined to say that the post office was over the hill.

32. I had originally intended calling it a vector but there seem no cases in which the magnitude as opposed to the direction is required.

33. In Clark (1973). A great deal of Clark's article is intended to show how important the spatio-temporal point of view is in language learning.

34. Decisions to complicate the syntax should not be taken lightly but in this case they are, I believe, warranted. There is probably a great deal more relativity in many words than we realize. Angelika Kratzer in (1976) and (1977), for example, has produced powerful evidence for adding a second argument place to modal operators.

35. It is possible that the reference to a direction might be involved in Taylor's problem (1974, 208 f.) of the analysis of ***downwards*** and ***sideways*** which is needed to explain how a diagonally moving ball may be moving downwards quickly but not sideways quickly. The direction tells us how to measure the amount of downward movement.

36. Within the framework adopted by Bennett (1975) the basic meaning of many prepositions is given so as to apply to both their spatial and temporal uses (p. 124f.).

37. We are right to ignore it. Even if, as David Lewis argues in (1975), time travel is logically possible the prepositions of ordinary language are severely taxed when talking about it.

38. The summary of λ-categorial languages given here does not make reference to the quotation symbol. The discussion in the text should show how it fits in, but readers who want a more formal account should consult Bigelow's treatment in (1975, pp. 6–9).

28

IRENA BELLERT

On Semantic and Distributional Properties of Sentential Adverbs

$\mathbf{I}$n this article, I will present some comments on the description of sentential adverbs proposed in the literature and will try to show that it does not satisfactorily take into account either the semantic or the surface distributional properties of adverbs. Let me first discuss the semantic aspects of the existing descriptions.

In recent linguistic literature, mention is often made of some logical forms[1] that are supposed to represent the meanings of sentences, but rarely can we find explicit statements as to what kind of logical language is presupposed. Montague's grammar is evidently one of the exceptions in this respect, but it covers only a small part of English and adverbs are not given much attention.[2] Thomason and Stalnaker (1973) have presented a semantic theory of adverbs, but they have distinguished only two classes of adverbs: sentence adverbs and predicate adverbs. Their semantics is based on intensional logic; hence, propositions are conceived of as intensions of sentences, and singulary propositional functions as intensions of predicates. All sentence adverbs denote functions taking propositions into propositions, and all predicate adverbs denote functions taking singulary propositional functions into singulary propositional functions. No other classes of adverbs have been distinguished. It is not the case, however, that all sentential adverbs can uniformly be described in such a way. I will therefore take as a starting point Jackendoff's classification of adverbs (Jackendoff 1972), which is correlated with semantic interpretation rules and which is more exhaustive (although not rigorously formalized). It seems to me that Jackendoff's principle of correlating semantic properties of adverbs with their surface distributional classes—if pushed to its logical conclusion—should allow us to arrive at a more adequate description than those to be found in the formalized proposals.

Although truth conditions are not applicable to all types of natural language sentences, they are often very helpful as a tool in semantic analysis: if there is a difference in truth conditions for some sentences, there is necessarily a difference in their semantic interpretation in the broad,

Irena Bellert (1977) On semantic and distributional properties of sentential adverbs. *Linguistic Inquiry* 8: 337–350. Reprinted by permission of MIT Press Journals.

linguistic sense of the term. Truth conditions constitute then at least a safe and useful criterion in our semantic analysis. I will try to demonstrate this point in an attempt to refine Jackendoff's classification of adverbs. Moreover, I will show that we must take into account some semantic properties other than truth conditions, which appear to be useful in describing more adequately the semantic interpretation and the respective distributional properties of adverbs—namely, the different semantic categories of the arguments the adverbs take.

Let me review the main points of Jackendoff's proposal for adverbs, in order to show that his classification into VP adverbs, subject-oriented adverbs, and speaker-oriented adverbs, and his respective projection rules P_{manner}, $P_{subject}$, and $P_{speaker}$, are not quite adequate as they stand for the reasons to be discussed. Jackendoff's claim that "a motivated separation of surface distributional classification is possible on semantic grounds," which means roughly that "knowing the meaning of an adverb is sufficient to predict in what position it can occur" (Jackendoff 1972, 67) is correct in principle, but only under the condition of further subdividing adverb classes on semantic grounds into more refined categories and further subdividing their distributional classes by taking into account other distributional properties than position alone. To summarize my claim: Jackendoff's principle is correct, but if we pursue it thoroughly, then his classification can be shown to be too broad; in addition, his surface distributional classification requires some additional features, not just the position alone, in order to be correlated with the respective semantic properties.

Jackendoff is obviously correct in rejecting the transformational derivation of adverbs. He gives enough arguments demonstrating that a transformational approach would require a large number of transformations, one for each tiny class of adverbs, each governed by an exception feature. He rightly claims that we should have gained nothing by proposing to add such power to the transformational machinery. On the contrary, we would have no explanation as to why there are any surface similarities at all among adverbs, if each small class of adverbs is inserted by a different transformation. He thus proposes to introduce adverbs into the clauses in the base component.

Let me now examine Jackendoff's classes of adverbs and the respective semantic interpretation rules one by one, first from the point of view of the contribution to, or effect on, the truth value of the sentence in which the corresponding adverbs occur, and then from the standpoint of the semantic categories of the arguments that should be assigned to sentential adverbs. (As I argued earlier, the differences in truth conditions constitute sufficient conditions for semantic differences, and as it appears, even this rudimentary semantic property helps in refining Jackendoff's classes.)

Consider first VP adverbs, for which P_{manner} is assigned as the corresponding projection rule:

(1) P_{manner}

If $\begin{Bmatrix} Adv \\ PP \end{Bmatrix}$ is dominated by VP, attach its semantic markers to the reading of the verb without

changing its functional structure.

What the rule says is that manner adverbs add something or modify the meaning of the verb. In other words, they function as predicates of predicates, and therefore they constitute part of just *one* proposition expressed by the sentence or clause in which they appear. In intensional logic they can be said to be functions taking singulary propositional functions into singulary propositional functions.

Sentences containing manner adverbs imply the corresponding sentences without adverbs; truth conditions of the latter are the necessary truth conditions of the former:

(2) John is speaking loudly. $\rightarrow$
(3) John is speaking.

If (2) is true, then (3) is necessarily true. Moreover, manner adverbs share the same semantic property: when they occur under the main stress, no matter whether the sentence is affirmative, negative, or a question, then the sentence implies (or presupposes, as some linguists would say) the corresponding affirmative sentence without the adverb:

(4) $\left[\begin{array}{l}\text{John is speaking lóudly.} \\ \text{John is not speaking lóudly.} \\ \text{Is John speaking lóudly?}\end{array}\right\} \rightarrow$ John is speaking.

As we will immediately see, this property is not shared by some other classes of adverbs.

Consider next subject-oriented adverbs, which are correlated with the interpretation rule P_{subject}:

(5) P_{subject}
If Adv_1 is a daughter of S, embed the reading of S (including any member of F to the right of Adv_1) as one argument to Adv_1, and embed the derived subject of S as the second argument to Adv_1.

Here, F designates Adv, PP, Modal, or parenthetical S.

Examples of subject-oriented adverbs are given below:

(6)
John $\left\{\begin{array}{l}\text{cleverly} \\ \text{wisely} \\ \text{carefully}\end{array}\right\}$ dropped his cup of coffee.

According to the interpretation rule P_{subject}, such an adverb functions as a predicate having two arguments; one is the derived subject of S (in this case *John*), the other one is the sentence S (without the adverb). Speaking in terms of truth conditions, we would say that the truth conditions of S (without the adverb) are the necessary truth conditions of the entire sentence, and, moreover, there are some additional truth conditions for the second proposition that John was clever (wise or careful) in what he did. In fact, we have here *two* propositions asserted in the one sentence.

Now, although we do find the corresponding negations of sentences with subject-oriented adverbs, they have different semantic properties than the negations of sentences with manner adverbs, which imply the respective affirmative sentences (cf. the examples in (4)):

(7)
John $\left\{\begin{array}{l}\text{cleverly} \\ \text{wisely} \\ \text{carefully}\end{array}\right\}$ did not drop his cup of coffee. $\rightarrow$

(8)   John did not drop his cup of coffee.

If (7) is true, then (8) (i.e., the corresponding sentence without the adverb) is necessarily true. Thus negated sentences with subject-oriented adverbs imply *negated* sentences without the adverb.

Since we have here two asserted propositions in one sentence, one of them can be negated independently of the other one. Hence we also have sentences such as (9):

(9)   John unwisely refused the offer.

Now in contradistinction to sentences with manner adverbs, we do not have the corresponding questions for sentences with subject-oriented adverbs. In the questions exemplified in (10), the adverb could have only the manner interpretation, otherwise the sentences are not well formed (or are at least anomalous):

(10)
$$\text{*Did John} \begin{Bmatrix} \text{cleverly} \\ \text{wisely} \\ \text{carefully} \end{Bmatrix} \begin{Bmatrix} \text{decide to come here?} \\ \text{drop his cup of coffee?} \\ \text{stop smoking?} \end{Bmatrix}$$

This surface distributional property of subject-oriented adverbs follows from the semantic rule, which seems to be fairly general: we cannot ask a question and *assert* a proposition in one and the same sentence (whereas we can ask a question and *imply* one, or more than one, proposition in one sentence).[3] On the other hand, manner adverbs, which are predicates of predicates, constitute part of one proposition, and thus sentences with manner adverbs do have corresponding questions. As we see, the different semantic properties of these two classes of adverbs account for, and are correlated with, the respective distributional properties of their members with regard to their occurrence in negated sentences and questions (not only with regard to their positional distribution).

The third class of adverbs, labeled by Jackendoff speaker-oriented adverbs, corresponds to the projection rule $P_{speaker}$. This class contains not only sentential adverbs with very different semantic properties but also modals and parentheticals. I will show on the example of some sentential adverbs that it is a heterogeneous class from the standpoint both of the semantic and of the surface distributional properties of its members, and hence that the projection rule $P_{speaker}$ is inadequate as it stands.

Let me first discuss frequency adverbs. Since Jackendoff's surface distributional properties are limited to position alone, he puts the adverbs *often* and *usually* in the same class as the evaluative adverbs *fortunately* and *happily* and the modal adverbs *possibly*, *probably*, et cetera, although they can clearly be shown to belong to different semantic and distributional classes. At the same time, however, the adverb *frequently* is classified as a VP adverb (p. 72), in spite of the fact that both *often* and *frequently* have not only the same semantic properties (along with *usually* and other frequency adverbs), but also the same distributional properties (not only positional), which differentiate them from the other speaker-oriented adverbs. Semantically, they can be said to contribute to the truth value of just one proposition expressed by the sentence or clause in which they appear (they do not make part of another asserted proposition as do the other speaker-oriented adverbs). Also, they behave in the same way as manner adverbs (they have the same semantic property) when occurring under the main stress in negated sentences and questions:

(11) a.
$$\begin{Bmatrix} \text{John óften comes here.} \\ \text{John does not óften come here.} \\ \text{Does John óften come here?} \end{Bmatrix} \rightarrow \text{John comes here.}$$
     b.
$$\begin{Bmatrix} \text{John has fréquently cheated.} \\ \text{John has not fréquently cheated.} \\ \text{Has John fréquently cheated?} \end{Bmatrix} \rightarrow \text{John has cheated.}$$

That is, all sentences with those adverbs under the main stress imply (or presuppose) the corresponding sentences without the adverb.

Now as regards surface distributional differences, notice that while we have no corresponding questions with the evaluative or modal adverbs (as Jackendoff himself has noticed), we do have questions with frequency adverbs, to which class *often* belongs. This fact alone makes their distributional properties different from those of other speaker-oriented adverbs. Incidentally, in Slavic languages, such as Polish or Russian, there is another distributional feature that sets frequency adverbs apart—namely, they do not cooccur with the perfective affixes of verbs. On the other hand, in English, which has no perfective markers with an analogous semantic function, there is another distributional feature characterizing the class of "punctual" adverbs, such as *immediately, suddenly,* or *at once* (notice that by positional criteria alone these adverbs belong to Jackendoff's speaker-oriented adverbs). Namely, such adverbs do not cooccur with the progressive aspect. We have no sentences such as *John was immediately sitting in his room.* These examples alone show that we should not limit a distributional analysis to positional features; rather, we must take into account the intersection of the distributional properties, position being only one of those.

Having subdivided the set of frequency adverbs, let me now discuss some subclasses of the rest of sentential adverbs labeled by Jackendoff as speaker-oriented. Although Jackendoff includes in this class what he calls neutral adverbs (which do not take the speaker as one of the arguments), there is nevertheless just one semantic interpretation rule that he correlates with this class:

(12) $P_{speaker}$
    If F_1 is a daughter of S, embed the reading of S (including any members of F to the right of F_1) as an argument to the reading of F_1.

I will try to show below that we must recognize within this class subclasses that have different semantic and distributional properties. As it stands, (12) corresponds exactly to the interpretation of sentence adverbs in Thomason and Stalnaker: such adverbs are interpreted as functions taking propositions into propositions. Let me now discuss some subclasses of this class of adverbs.

A. *Evaluative adverbs* (*luckily, fortunately, happily, surprisingly,* etc.) are—to use Kiparsky's term—factive predicates, the argument of which is the fact, event, or state of affairs denoted by the sentence in which they occur. Any sentence containing such an adverb implies the corresponding sentence without the adverb, independently of whether the sentence is a negation or not:

(13)   a. Fortunately John has come. → John has come.
       b. Fortunately John has not come. → John has not come.

The truth conditions of the sentence without the adverb are the necessary truth conditions of the entire sentence, but the adverb does not make part of just one proposition; in addition, we have here a second proposition whose predicate (the adverb) evaluates the fact, event, or state of affairs denoted by S (sentence without the adverb). Sentences with evaluative adverbs express two asserted propositions, and each of them can be negated independently. Thus we find negations as in (13), and we also have sentences with the corresponding negative adverb such as (14), in which the additional proposition evaluating the fact denoted by S is negated:

(14)   Unfortunately John has (not) come.

For semantic reasons, analogous to those discussed in the case of subject-oriented adverbs, evaluative adverbs do not occur in questions: we have here two asserted propositions, and therefore there do not exist the corresponding questions in which one proposition would be asserted and the other one questioned at the same time. Thus, (15) would make a semantically inconsistent proposition amounting to asking if John has arrived and asserting at the same time it is a surprise:[4]

(15)   *Has John surprisingly arrived?

B. *Modal adverbs* (*probably, possibly, certainly, surely, evidently*, etc.) constitute a different class. An adverb in this class is a predicate whose argument is the *truth* of the proposition expressed by the respective sentence (not the fact, event, or state of affairs denoted by the sentence in question). Every sentence containing a modal adverb can be paraphrased by a more explicit statement expressing a complex proposition, in which the adverb is clearly a predicate of the truth:

(16)
$$\text{It is} \begin{cases} \text{probably} \\ \text{possibly} \\ \text{certainly} \\ \text{evidently} \end{cases} \text{true that S.}$$

The modal adverbs have no corresponding negative adverbs that would function as sentential adverbs, nor can they be negated independently. We have no sentences such as (17), whereas we do have sentences such as those in (18) with negative evaluative adverbs, which can also be negated independently of the sentence (see also (14)):

(17)
$$\begin{bmatrix} \text{*Improbably} \\ \text{*Impossibly} \\ \text{*Uncertainly} \\ \text{*Not evidently} \\ \text{*Not probably} \end{bmatrix} \text{, John} \begin{cases} \text{has} \\ \text{will} \end{cases} \text{come.}$$

(18)
$$\begin{bmatrix} \text{Unfortunately} \\ \text{Unluckily} \\ \text{Not surprisingly} \end{bmatrix} \text{, John} \begin{cases} \text{has} \\ \text{will} \end{cases} \text{come.}$$

This follows from the semantic property of modal adverbs, not from their morphological structure (the negative morpheme involved), for we do have sentences such as (19):

(19)
$$\text{Undoubtedly John} \begin{cases} \text{has} \\ \text{will} \end{cases} \text{come.}$$

Semantically, *undoubtedly* is not a negative modal adverb, although it contains a negative morpheme. On the other hand, the modal adverb *doubtfully* is semantically a negative adverb, and therefore there are no grammatical sentences in which it occurs in the function of a sentential adverb:

(20)
$$\text{*Doubtfully John} \begin{cases} \text{has} \\ \text{will} \end{cases} \text{come.}$$

Modal sentential adverbs are predicates of the truth: they qualify the truth of the proposition expressed in the same sentence, and they do not qualify it negatively. Neither do they occur in questions:

(21)
$$\begin{cases} \text{*Has} \\ \text{*Will} \end{cases} \text{John} \begin{cases} \text{probably} \\ \text{certainly} \\ \text{evidently} \end{cases} \text{come?}$$

Again, we do not ask questions and at the same time evaluate the truth, or degree of truth, of the proposition that is being questioned. And such a restriction does not apply to the questions corresponding to sentences in (16), each of which expresses one complex proposition (cf. note 4).

However, there are adverbs that are not purely modal, such as *perhaps* and *definitely*—those have an additional meaning component that could be described by means of a corresponding meaning postulate.[5] *Perhaps* carries along an implication that gives a suggestion as to a possible answer:

(22)   Has John perhaps been here before?

(23)   Have you perhaps misunderstood the question?

Definitely carries along an implication to the effect that the matter has not been definitely settled before:

(24)   a. Has John definitely made up his mind?
       b. Have you definitely finished your work?

Neither of these adverbs is a purely modal adverb. Purely modal adverbs do not occur in questions.

There is another piece of evidence concerning distributional properties of modal adverbs, which supports my claim that they qualify the *truth* of the sentence or clause in which they appear, rather than the *fact* or *state of affairs* expressed by the sentence or clause (as in the case of evaluative adverbs). Modal adverbs occur in hypothetical *if . . . then* sentences, whereas evaluative adverbs do not. The reason is as follows. A hypothetical *if . . . then* sentence expresses counterfactual or hypothetical propositions (in the latter case, the proposition expressed by the main clause is assumed to be true only under the conditions expressed by the *if*-clause). In either case, it seems clear that the corresponding states of affairs *cannot* be qualified by a "factive" predicate, whereas the truth of any proposition, no matter whether counterfactual or hypothetical, can be qualified by a modal predicate. Hence follows the anomaly of hypothetical *if . . . then* sentences with evaluative adverbs in contradistinction to the perfect well-formedness of the same hypothetical sentences with modal adverbs:

(25)   a.

If John had not been sick, he would $\left\{\begin{array}{l}\text{probably}\\\text{certainly}\\\text{evidently}\\\text{*fortunately}\\\text{*surprisingly}\\\text{*luckily}\end{array}\right\}$ have done it.

b.

If John were sane, he would $\left\{\begin{array}{l}\text{probably}\\\text{certainly}\\\text{evidently}\\\text{*fortunately}\\\text{*surprisingly}\\\text{*luckily}\end{array}\right\}$ accept the offer.

It is interesting to notice that we find sentences with adjectives corresponding to modal adverbs, which are considered in the linguistic literature to be exact paraphrases of the respective sentences with modal adverbs:

(26)

It is $\left\{\begin{array}{l}\text{possible}\\\text{probable}\\\text{evident}\end{array}\right\}$ that John $\left\{\begin{array}{l}\text{has}\\\text{will}\end{array}\right\}$ come.

However, there are some arguments, which I spell out below, for not giving them the same semantic interpretation. My claim is that modal adverbs should be interpreted as predicates over the truth of the proposition expressed by the respective sentence, and that sentences with modal adverbs express two propositions; whereas the corresponding modal adjectives are predicates over the fact, event, or state of affairs referred to by the sentence, and sentences with modal adjectives express one complex proposition. These semantic differences account for the following distributional properties of modal adverbs and adjectives.

Sentences with modal adjectives (26) can be converted into the corresponding questions, as they express one proposition:

(27)
$$\text{Is it} \begin{bmatrix} \text{possible} \\ \text{probable} \\ \text{evident} \end{bmatrix} \text{that John} \begin{Bmatrix} \text{has} \\ \text{will} \end{Bmatrix} \text{come?}$$

The anticipatory *it* refers here to the event described by the complement sentence (the adjective is a predicate over an event rather than the truth of the proposition), and we can ask about the probability, possibility, etc. of (the occurrence of) an event without semantic incoherence. And, as it is shown in (21), this is not the case with modal adverbs: in one and the same sentence we cannot ask if S is the case and qualify the truth of S.

The modal adjectives in (26) have their corresponding negatives or can be negated independently, for we can deny the possibility, probability, et cetera of the occurrence of an event:

(28)
$$\text{It is} \begin{bmatrix} \text{impossible} \\ \text{improbable} \\ \text{not evident} \end{bmatrix} \text{that John} \begin{Bmatrix} \text{has} \\ \text{will} \end{Bmatrix} \text{come.}$$

And modal adverbs cannot be negated, as is demonstrated by the respective paraphrases of (28) shown in (17). A negative qualification of the truth of one's own assertion in one and the same sentence evidently constitutes a semantic inconsistency.

Sentences with modal adverbs can all be paraphrased into more explicit complex statements in which the adverb is clearly the predicate over the truth of the proposition expressed by the *that* clause (cf. (16)), whereas we have no such paraphrases for the corresponding sentences with modal adjectives; that is, we have no sentences in which the modal adjective would explicitly occur as the predicate over the truth of the complement sentence:

(29)
$$\text{*The truth that John} \begin{Bmatrix} \text{has} \\ \text{will} \end{Bmatrix} \text{come is} \begin{bmatrix} \text{possible} \\ \text{probable} \\ \text{evident} \end{bmatrix}.$$

The semantic difference between sentences with modal adverbs and those with modal adjectives, which express one proposition, is related to a difference in the semantic category of the argument: in the case of a modal adjective it is an event or state of affaris, an extralinguistic entity referred to by the respective proposition; in the case of a modal adverb, it is the truth of the proposition, a purely semantic concept. Hence the occurrence of a modal adverb gives rise to an additional metalinguistic proposition.

Another interesting fact noticed by Jackendoff is that some sentential adverbs do not occur with subject-auxiliary inversion. While we have sentences such as (30) and (31), we do not find the corresponding (32) and (33):

(30) John probably $\begin{Bmatrix} \text{never} \\ \text{rarely} \end{Bmatrix}$ ran so fast.

(31) John probably ran so fast that he got to Texas in ten minutes.

(32) $\begin{Bmatrix} \text{*Never} \\ \text{*Rarely} \end{Bmatrix}$ did John probably run so fast.

(33) *So fast did John probably run that he got to Texas in ten minutes.

These facts have a semantic explanation. A sentential element, taken out of its ordinary position and preposed in front of the sentence, acquires additional emphasis and scope. A modal adverb, such as *probably* in the examples above, is a predicate over the truth of the respective proposition, and as such it can apply without inconsistency to a negated sentence (*John never ran so fast*) or, more precisely, to the truth of a negated sentence. In (32), however, both the proposition and the modal adverb that qualifies its truth are in the scope of negation (the negation expressed by *never* or *rarely*), and this is a contradiction. For we cannot negate or deny a proposition and qualify its truth as probable at the same time.

Similarly, there is a semantic incoherence in (33), although the case is not as clear as with a preposed negation. A sentential element that is preposed from its ordinary position to the front of the sentence for the sake of emphasis is then no longer within the scope of the sentential adverb, which as a rule is interpreted as qualifying the truth of the entire proposition in which it occurs. The result is an effect of semantic incoherence that makes such sentences unacceptable.

The same holds true, mutatis mutandis, of evaluative adverbs. The sentences in (34) are unacceptable, while those in (35) are all right:

(34) $\begin{Bmatrix} \text{*Never} \\ \text{*Rarely} \end{Bmatrix}$ did John fortunately run so fast.

(35) John fortunately $\begin{Bmatrix} \text{never} \\ \text{rarely} \end{Bmatrix}$ ran so fast.

The evaluative adverb is a predicate over the event or state of affairs described by the entire sentence or clause in which it occurs, and we can very well evaluate an event or state of affairs described by a negative sentence as in (35). If, however, the negating element is preposed, the adverb that is interpreted as a predicate evaluating the event described by the negated sentence falls within the scope of that negation, and this makes the sentence semantically incoherent.

C. *Domain adverbs* (*logically, mathematically, morally, aesthetically*, etc.) have a semantic function analogous to that of a restrictive universal quantifier:

(36) For all x such that x is a natural number, if $x > 2$ and $x < 4$, then $x = 3$.

The proposition is asserted as true only in the domain of natural numbers. In fact, it is false, for instance, in the domain of rational numbers. This is exactly the case with sentences containing domain adverbs:

(37) Linguistically, this example is interesting.
(38) Mathematically, there is no answer to your question.
(39) Logically, John is wrong.

The speaker claims here that the proposition holds true in a given domain; he does not commit himself to the truth of the proposition in any other domain. He may very well add that his claim does not concern other domains:

(40)   Linguistically this example is interesting, but logically it is not.
(41)   Logically John is right, but morally he is wrong.

Similarly, as in the case of (36), which expresses just one proposition in logic, the entire sentence, together with its restrictive domain adverb, constitutes just one proposition. It is therefore not surprising that such sentences or clauses do have the corresponding questions; that is to say, domain adverbs occur in questions:

(42)   Is this book linguistically interesting?

(43)   Is John $\left\{ \begin{matrix} \text{logically} \\ \text{morally} \end{matrix} \right\} \left\{ \begin{matrix} \text{wrong} \\ \text{right} \end{matrix} \right\}$?

Domain adverbs have no corresponding negative sentential adverbs. In fact, it would be strange to restrict the truth of a proposition to the complement of a given domain (to all other domains but not the one referred to by the adverb). We therefore do not have sentences such as (44)–(46):

(44)   *John is immorally right.
(45)   *John is illogically wrong.
(46)   *Not logically, John is right.

D. *Conjunctive adverbs (however, nevertheless, hence, therefore, firstly, finally*, etc.) have the semantic function of sentential connectives. The truth of the sentence in which they appear depends on the truth of the preceding sentence (or sentences) in the text. For instance, the truth of (47)

(47)   Hence this statement is a theorem.

depends not only on the truth conditions of this sentence alone but also on the truth conditions of the preceding sentence or sentences, plus the truth of the causal relation between them, which is expressed by the adverb *hence*.

Some conjunctive adverbs are also "implicative" terms and carry along certain implications. *However* and *nevertheless* could, for instance, be described in terms of meaning postulates analogous to those concerning *but*. I will not go into details concerning additional meaning components of some of the adverbs discussed here, for this is a problem connected with a semantic property shared by many other lexical items and irrelevant to the argument in this article.

Conjunctive adverbs function as connectives between sentences in a text, and thus they occur not only in statements but also in questions and other performative sentences with various illocutionary functions:

(48)   Firstly I dismiss you as my secretary, and secondly I appoint you as the manager of the department.
(49)   I promise you, however, to do it in time.
(50)   I therefore apologize for my rudeness.
(51)   I order you, nevertheless, to get out of here.

E. *Pragmatic adverbs* are the only ones that are strictly speaking speaker-oriented adverbs, for one of the arguments is the speaker.[6] They can be subdivided into two classes:

    1. (*frankly, sincerely, honestly*, etc.) Adverbs in this class are predicates with two arguments: one is the speaker, the other one is the proposition (the contents of the

sentence, its intension). The speaker characterizes his attitude towards *what* he is saying.

2. (*briefly, precisely, roughly,* etc.) Adverbs in this class are also predicates with two arguments: one is the same as in (1), the speaker; the other one, however, is not the contents but the *form* of the sentence. The speaker characterizes the form, the way in which he expresses the proposition.

All pragmatic adverbs cooccur with the participle *speaking*, which is implicit in sentences containing those adverbs. That is, all sentences with pragmatic adverbs can be paraphrased by sentences in which the word *speaking* appears explicitly on the surface, immediately following the adverb. No pragmatic adverb has a corresponding negative (we do have negative adverbs of this type, but they never function as sentential adverbs), nor can it be negated directly (in contradistinction to evaluative adverbs; cf. (14)). There are no sentences such as (52)–(54):

(52)   *Dishonestly, I did it myself.

(53)   *Insincerely, I love you.

(54)   *Not briefly, John is a nice guy, a good worker and a bad dancer.

There is no semantic explanation for this fact; speakers have no means for characterizing their attitude toward the propositions they are expressing by directly negating such an adverb. Strangely enough, the same holds true of the corresponding pragmatic adverbs in several other languages, such as Polish, Russian, French, German, Spanish, and probably some others. The restriction seems to be pragmatic in nature and is based on a rather commonly accepted norm.

In distinction to the evaluative, modal, and domain adverbs, pragmatic adverbs do occur in performative sentences. This is a consequence of their being interpretable as predicates over the contents (intension) or form of the sentence in which they appear, rather than the event referred to or the truth, as in the case of evaluative and modal adverbs, respectively (where performative sentences are excluded and only statements are acceptable). Thus sentences such as (55)–(57) are possible:

(55)   Sincerely, I apologize for being so rude.

(56)   Briefly, I promise you to finish my work today.

(57)   Precisely, I order you to get out of here.

As I have tried to show in this article, one distributional property concerning the position of an adverb is not a sufficient condition for establishing one class of speaker-oriented adverbs correlated with one semantic rule of intepretation. Each of the discussed subclasses (frequency, evalautive, modal, domain, conjunctive, and pragmatic adverbs) has different surface distributional properties that are correlated with the respective different semantic properties. The surface distributional properties that differentiate these subclasses are the occurrence or nonoccurrence of adverbs in hypothetical sentences and in questions; the occurrence of the corresponding negatives; and the occurrence of adverbs in all types of performative sentences, for which the truth value is not applicable. All these properties are relevant for syntactic well-formedness of sentences. As has been shown, these properties are accounted for (explained) by the respective semantic properties of the subcategories of sentential adverbs discussed in this article. These are: the difference in the way the adverbs contribute to the truth conditions of the sentences in which they appear; the question as to whether the adverb together with the sentence in which it appears constitute one complex proposition or two propositions; and, finally, the semantic category of the arguments involved—the event or state of affairs, which is an extralinguistic entity; the truth of the proposition, which is a purely semantic concept; and the intention of a sentence or its form.

Differences in semantic categories, unimportant as they may seem to linguists, were proven at the beginning of this century to be essential for the development of logic;[7] the discovery of such differences helped logicians to solve some of the puzzling paradoxes and inconsistencies that had been detected in logical writings up to that time. As it appears, the distinctions in the semantic category of a linguistic entity, such as an argument of a sentential adverb, are also relevant to a natural language description, for they are correlated with surface syntactic differences directly related to well-formedness of sentences.

Notes

This is an extended version of a paper presented at the CLA meeting, Edmonton, 1975.

1. Statements to this effect appear in many papers on generative semantics (by Lakoff, McCawley, and others), as well as in recent papers on generative syntax. See, for instance, Dougherty (1975) or Chomsky (1974), where we find the following passage (pp. 5, 6; emphasis mine): "It seems possible to give an organized and systematic account of the syntax of the relevant expressions in terms of reasonably well-motivated principles of grammar, and the same may be true of the set of 'readings' or correlates in *some logic.*"

2. For the treatment of adverbs, see Montague (1970a).

3. For example, we can ask the question *Was it clever of John to drop his cup of coffee?*, which corresponds to the sentence *It was clever of John to drop his cup of coffee*—a sentence expressing an assertion of one complex proposition.

4. Notice that if we paraphrase a sentence with an evaluative adverb into a corresponding sentence with an evaluative adjective or participle—

$$\left(\text{It is} \begin{Bmatrix} \text{surprising} \\ \text{fortunate} \end{Bmatrix} \text{that John has come}\right),$$

we get an assertion of one complex proposition instead of two propositions asserted in one sentence. Hence it is possible to form the corresponding questions, which are semantically coherent:

$$\text{Is it} \begin{Bmatrix} \text{surprising} \\ \text{fortunate} \end{Bmatrix} \text{that John has come?}$$

5. The lexical items that carry along certain implications I have called *implicative terms* (Bellert 1970). In a number of papers I have proposed to describe lexical items in terms of sets of implicational rules that define the associated syntactic and semantic properties. See, for instance, Bellert (1972) or Bellert and Saloni (1973).

6. Otherwise every utterance can be described as a performance with the speaker (who always expresses one or another propositional attitude) as one of the arguments.

7. A solution to the famous contradiction known as the paradox of classes has been presented in the fundamental work of Whitehead and Russell (1910–1913).

29

RICHMOND H. THOMASON AND ROBERT C. STALNAKER

A Semantic Theory of Adverbs

1   Introduction

In recent years adverbial constructions have attracted the attention of many logicians, philosophers of language, and linguists. Most of this work is relevant to the content of the present article, but that of Richard Montague and his associates deserves special discussion since our formal semantic theory can be regarded as a special case of Montague's.[1]

Montague's semantics for adverbs was a component of a general program for developing a formal semiotic theory of natural languages such as English. The task of the syntactic part of the program is to develop a recursive definition of the sets of phrases of various syntactic categories of expressions (e.g., noun phrases, intransitive verb phrases, adverb phrases, sentences) of a fragment of English. The semantic part of the program furnishes an interpretation of this fragment in terms of intensional model theory, and the pragmatic part deals with the interpretation of context-dependent or "indexical" expressions such as *I*, *here*, and *now*. In Montague's linguistic writings[2] the general semiotic program is the center of attention, and detail is not lavished on specifics such as the treatment of adverbs. One function of this paper is to remedy this defect.

Also, though we accept the main features of Montague's semiotic program, we have not adopted its methodology here, but instead have followed a more conservative approach emerging from recent work in intensional logic. According to this approach, artificial logical languages are used as the objects of formal semantic theory and are linked to natural languages by an informal procedure of formalization.[3] The application of semantic theories to English is therefore indirect, rather than direct as in Montague's approach, since it is mediated by formalization.

Richmond Thomason and Robert Stalnaker (1973) A semantic theory of adverbs. *Linguistic Inquiry* 4: 195–220. Reprinted by permission of MIT Press Journals.

This makes our account of adverbs in natural language less rigorous than Montague's, but at the same time it enables us to give a freer and more open-ended discussion of semantic problems arising in connection with adverbs. By being less direct in relation to English syntax we can consider problematic and puzzling phenomena, as well as those that are more perspicuous.

2   Logical form and adverbial constructions

Adverbs are notoriously resistant to perspicuous formalization in first-order logic, which apparently requires them to be petrified components of the predicate.[4] For instance, if (1)

(1)   John walks

is formalized by Pa, where P stands for *walks* and a for *John*, then we must, it seems, formalize (2)

(2)   John walks slowly

by Qa, choosing a new predicate parameter, say Q, to stand for *walks slowly*. Perhaps this is not as bad as rendering (1) by Pa and *John doesn't walk* by Ra, but still one feels that Qa is unfaithful as a formalization of (2). The complex structure of the verb phrase *walks slowly*, with its explicit relation to the verb phrase *walks*, has been erased. Logicians, who are interested in accounting for valid inferences, may make the stronger objection that this formalization will not make (1) a logical consequence of (2). We will argue below, in section 8, that this objection is questionable. But whether or not it stands up, the need for a more faithful logical translation is clear.

An option explored by Donald Davidson is to seek a more sophisticated formalization in first-order logic itself. But Davidson's theory is explicitly narrow in its scope, adverbs such as *slowly*, *greedily*, *carefully*, and *intentionally* being excluded; and we suspect it may prove to be even more narrow than he anticipated. There remains, then, a need for a general semantic theory of adverbs. It is in response to this need that we propose to construct our extension of first-order logic. Research in other areas—for example, in the logic of tenses—has shown that it can be rewarding to build such extensions, adding new notation to the underlying formal language as it is needed to formalize a particular kind of discourse. The methodological rule governing such projects is that they must be carried out with the same degree of rigor associated with familiar logical theories. In particular, all new notation must be provided with an acceptable semantic interpretation, or model theory.[5]

We now return to (2). The obvious way to handle this sentence is simply to add a new piece of logical notation to stand for *slowly*. Then the formalization of (2) will be obtained from that of (1) by adding a new symbol, say ξ, to Pa. But how to add it? Since *slowly* modifies *walks*, not *John* or *John walks*, something like (3) seems good:

(3) ξPa

The task of formalizing (2) is then just a matter of transposing word order and replacing English with logical vocabulary. *John walks slowly* becomes *Slowly walks John*, which then becomes ξPa.

This is nice, but yet not quite right. The trouble is that it gives ξPa the same syntactic structure as $\sim Pa$, standing for the English sentence *John does not walk*. But our grammatical intuitions suggest that these should be distinguished from one another. The formula $\sim Pa$ represents the negation of a sentence formed by attaching a predicate to a subject. But ξPa is the result of modifying a predicate with an adverb, and then applying the modified predicate to a subject. So $\sim Pa$ and ξPa have the following two structures:

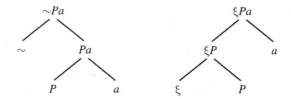

In a well-designed logical language such distinctions are built into formulas themselves. What we need, then, is something like $(\xi P)a$. This notation is more perspicuous as to syntactic structure, but is too restrictive because it provides no way of applying adverbs to complex predicates. There is no way, for instance, to formalize examples such as the following two:

(4)   With his pencil, John doodled and took notes.
(5)   John walked or was carried to the hospital.

At first glance this may not seem a serious limitation, since (4) could be simply assigned the logical form $(\xi P)a \wedge (\xi Q)a$ and (5) the form $(\xi P)a \vee (\xi Q)a$. Here the fact is exploited that (4) can be paraphrased as (6) and (5) as (7):

(6)   John doodled with his pencil and John took notes with his pencil.
(7)   John walked to the hospital or John was carried to the hospital.

Some use of paraphrase in the application of a logical calculus to English is probably inevitable, but there is a general methodological objection to this strategy. When a sentence has to be paraphrased before being analyzed, the task of interpreting natural language becomes less formal, as stress is shifted from formal semantics, where problems can be dealt with explicitly at the theoretical level, to our pretheoretic and unarticulated understanding of spoken language. Paraphrase sweeps semantic problems under the rug, and whenever we can see how to avoid using it we should do so.

In this case, however, there is a more specific objection: the paraphrases do not always work. For example, consider (8) and (9):

(8)   Reluctantly, John bought gas and had the oil changed.
(9)   John intentionally kissed Mary or kissed Susan.

Sentence (8) can be true because it was doing *both* that John disliked—say, because it cost too much—while he was not reluctant to do either separately. Similarly, John could have intentionally kissed Mary or Susan by kissing the girl in the mask, knowing that the girl in the mask was Mary or Susan. But in this case he neither intentionally kissed Mary nor intentionally kissed Susan.

The structure of (9) is something like this:

(10)

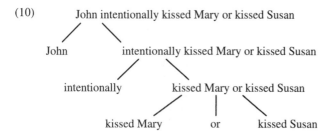

To capture this structure we need some formal way of building up complex predicates, such as *kissed Mary or kissed Susan*. Diagram (10) suggests that this predicate is obtained from *kissed Mary* and *kissed Susan* by an operation of disjunction. But in our logical language the symbol ∨, corresponding to *or*, is a *sentence connective*. It links formulas, not predicates.

It would be possible to solve this particular problem by creating another kind of disjunction acting on predicates. But there is a far more general and deeper solution. This consists in regarding the predicate *kissed Mary or kissed Susan* as derived from the sentence *He kissed Mary or he kissed Susan* by a process whereby predicates are formed from sentences. The relevant part of (10) will then appear as follows:

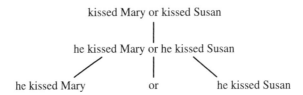

There is a familiar logical device, known as *abstraction*, which performs precisely this task. Abstraction has been used by logicians primarily in formalizing set theory (and especially in higher-order logics), but recent work suggests that it may also have a direct bearing on problems having to do with natural language.[6] Abstraction can be added to our formal language by stipulating that if A is any formula then $(\hat{x}A^x/u)$ is a predicate,[7] and that if X is a predicate and t an individual term then $X(t)$ is a formula.[8]

Abstraction yields a direct and natural formalization of sentence (9): $(\xi\hat{x}(Pxb \vee Pxc))(a)$, where ξ stands for *intentionally*, Puv for … kissed _____, a for *John*, b for *Mary*, and c for *Susan*. This formula has the following syntactic structure:

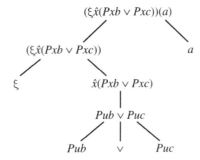

3   Scope and adverbs

The difference between (7) and (11)

(11)   John intentionally kissed Mary or John intentionally kissed Susan.

emerged in our logical language as a difference in scope, in the order in which formation rules are applied in constructing the formulas $(\xi\hat{x}(Pxb \vee Pxc))(a)$ and $(\xi\hat{x}Pxb)(a) \vee (\xi Pxc)(a)$. Such formal differences in scope frequently correspond to distinctions with which speakers of English are familiar, and which are expressed in English in a variety of ways. For example, the sentences (12) and (13) will most naturally be formalized by (14) and (15), respectively:[9]

(12)   He slowly tested all the bulbs.
(13)   He tested each bulb slowly.
(14) $(\xi\hat{x}(y)Pxy)(a)$
(15) $(y)(\xi\hat{x}Pxy)(a)$

It is important to realize that the truth conditions of (12) and (13) differ. Sentence (12) would be true if he took a long coffee break between each testing, even though he tested each single bulb quickly. His testing of all the bulbs would then be slow. The difference between (16) and (17) is represented similarly:

(16)   He slowly tested some bulbs.
(17)   He tested some bulbs slowly.

In many cases like these there seems to be no difference in meaning between the two scope readings of a single English sentence, even though the strategy of formalization predicts the existence of two such readings. An example is (18), which can be rendered as (19) or (20),

(18)   John took all his friends to the ballgame.
(19) $(x)\xi\hat{y}Pyx(a)$
(20) $(\xi\hat{y}(x)Pyx)(a)$

where ξ stands for *to the ballgame*, *Puv* for . . . *takes* _____, and, for simplicity, the quantifier ranges over John's friends. In such cases, the absence of a difference in meaning may be ascribed to particular semantic properties of the lexical items appearing in the example: in this instance, to properties of *to the ballgame*.

In other cases, different scope readings of a single sentence will correspond to significant ambiguities. An example due to Lakoff is the sentence (21):

(21)   Harry was willingly sacrificed by the tribe.

Let *Puv* stand for . . . *sacrificed* _____, *a* for *Harry*, and *b* for *the tribe*. Then the sense of (20) in which the tribe was willing appears as (22) and the sense in which Harry was willing as (23):

(22) $(\xi\hat{x}Pxa)(b)$
(23) $(\xi\hat{x}Pbx)(a)$

4   Predicate modifiers and sentence modifiers

In section 2 we took it as intuitively evident that the proper parsing of *John walks slowly* is *John (walks slowly)*, not *(John walks) slowly*. That is, we assumed that the adverb modifies the verb rather than the sentence. This may seem an innocent assumption; *slowly* is, after all, an ad-verb and not an ad-sentence. But there are many so-called adverbs, like *possibly*, *probably*, *usually*, and *unfortunately*, for which the alternative parsing seems more appropriate. The distinction between the two parsings is no mere matter of convention since it influences logical relationships among sentences containing adverbs. We will therefore try to back up our intuition with arguments and general criteria.

We shall argue that there are two kinds of adverbs in English; some modify predicates, while others modify sentences. Since a unified theory of adverbs would be simpler than ours, the burden of proof lies on us to make this claim good. We shall first give some general reasons why it is important to analyze the scope of a modifier correctly and second give some specific arguments for the claim that there are modifiers of both kinds in English. These will in turn yield criteria for classifying various adverbs either as sentence modifiers or as predicate modifiers.

It is obvious that if the scope of a modifier is analyzed as narrower than it should be, one will get a defective account of the job done by the modifier in some sentences. If, for example, negation were treated as a predicate modifier, one would have no way of representing the distinction between the two readings of (24)

(24)   Everybody didn't come,

one of which can be paraphrased by (25)

(25)   Nobody came,

and the other by (26)

(26)   Not everybody came.

In order to get the second reading, one must be able to include the subject of (24), *everybody*, within the scope of the negation, and this is possible only if negation can operate on sentences.

It is less obvious, but equally true, that if the scope of a modifier is analyzed as wider than it should be, one will get an incorrect account of the logical relationships among sentences containing the modifier and of the syntactic ambiguities in such sentences. For example, if *slowly* is a predicate modifier, then *John walks slowly* exhibits the form $X(a)$, the general form of a subject-predicate sentence. Hence, since (27) is a valid form, the inference in (28) is valid:

(27) $X(a)$
       $a = b$
       $X(b)$
(28)   John walks slowly.
       John is the mayor of New York.
       Therefore the mayor of New York walks slowly.

But if *slowly* were analyzed as a sentence modifier, then *John walks slowly* would not be an instance of $X(a)$, and so the argument would not be valid in virtue of (27). The analogous argument form for sentence modifiers, (29),

(29) $o(Fa)$
       $a = b$
       $o(Fb)$

is notoriously invalid, as is shown by examples from the philosophical literature on opacity such as the following:

(30)   Necessarily nine is odd.
       Nine is the number of the planets.
       Therefore, necessarily the number of the planets is odd.

On the relevant reading of the conclusion, it is false, even though the premises are true.[10]

We could, of course, treat adverbs like *slowly* as sentence modifiers and account for the phenomena by introducing special semantic principles, or meaning postulates, to validate inferences that seem valid for such adverbs. But as a general methodological policy it is best, all else being equal, to explain semantic relationships in terms of structure rather than in terms of the unanalyzed content of specific words. Thus the apparent validity of the substitution principle when applied to contexts containing a particular adverb will be treated as prima facie evidence that such adverbs are predicate modifiers. This evidence, together with the absence of any counterevidence, is the principal justification for treating *slowly* and other manner adverbs as predicate modifiers.

What kinds of counterevidence will show other adverbs to be sentence modifiers? We will give four semantically based criteria for identifying sentence modifiers and show why these criteria establish that a great many adverbs and adverbial phrases are in fact sentence modifiers. These criteria involve semantic notions such as scope, ambiguity, and paraphrase, and they will depend for their application on only the most general and elementary assumptions about English syntax.

First, if an adverb precipitates counterexamples to the substitution principle, this will establish it to be a sentence modifier:

CRITERION 1
Only if an adverb is a sentence modifier can it give rise to opaque contexts everywhere in a sentence in which it occurs.

Even though Richard Nixon is the President of the United States, the sentence *On a number of occasions Richard Nixon has died in office* is false, while *On a number of occasions the President of the United States has died in office* is true. This show that *on a number of occasions* modifies the sentence *The President of the United States has died in office* and not just the predicate *has died in office*. Modal adverbs like *necessarily* and *probably* and adverbs of attitude like *unfortunately* are shown by this test to be clear cases of sentence modification. Some locative adverbs like *in several restaurants* also seem to create opaque contexts. *In several restaurants, the maitre d' wears a tuxedo* may be true, even if there is no one who wears a tuxedo in several restaurants.

One must use a certain amount of care in applying this criterion. First, in order to be sure that it is the adverb being tested that is responsible for substitution failure, one should find a sentence that would have no opaque contexts if the adverb were removed. Second, in order to be sure that the adverb can give rise to opaque contexts everywhere in the sentence, one should find a sentence with all its singular terms in an opaque context created by the adverb. An adverb may give rise to opacity within a logical predicate and still be a predicate modifier.[11] For example, *John willingly trusted Harry* may be true while *John willingly trusted his worst enemy* is false (on one reading of the latter sentence), even if Harry is John's worst enemy. From this one can conclude that the object of *trusted* must be within the scope of the adverb *willingly* in those sentences, but one cannot conclude that *John* must be within its scope. And unless *John* is within its scope it is not modifying the whole sentence. Hence the example fails to show that the adverb is a sentence modifier.

If the opacity criterion fails to apply, this is no proof that the adverb is not a sentence adverb, for it is possible for an adverb to be, like negation, a referentially transparent sentence modifier. The adverb *actually* is a paradigm of a transparent sentence modifier.

The second criterion succeeds in showing negation to be a sentence modifier:

CRITERION 2
Only if an adverb is a sentence modifier can it give rise to quantifier scope ambiguities in simple universal or existential sentences.

In particular, if there can be a semantic contrast between *Q-ly someone F's* and *Someone F's Q-ly*, then *Q-ly* is a sentence modifier. So, for example, *Frequently, someone got drunk* contrasts with *Someone got drunk frequently* (on one reading of these sentences). The semantic difference can be explained only on the assumption that *frequently* is capable of modifying the sentence *Someone got drunk*, and hence is a sentence adverb.[12]

By a *simple* universal or existential sentence, we mean one containing only one quantifier and no singular terms. The claim is restricted to sentences which are simple in this sense because it is not meant to cover scope ambiguities which result from quantifiers within a logical predicate. For example, the contrast between *Sam carefully sliced all the bagels* and *Sam sliced all the bagels carefully* does not show *carefully* to be a sentence adverb. For this contrast can be explained by the difference between (31) and (32)

(31) $\xi(\hat{y}(x)Pyx)(a)$

(32) $(x)((\xi\hat{y}Pyx)(a))$

where *Puv* stands for *sliced*, *a* for *Sam*, and ξ for *carefully*. These two formalizations capture the required distinction, and in neither of them is *carefully* represented as a sentence modifier.[13]

But again, this test is not decisive. It is possible for an adverb to be a sentence adverb, and yet operate transparently through quantifiers. There is, for instance, apparently no semantic contrast between *Actually, someone got drunk*, and *Someone actually got drunk*:

CRITERION 3
If an adverb includes within its scope an adverb or adverbial phrase that has already been
  shown to be a sentence modifier, and if the whole rest of the sentence is within the scope
  of that sentence modifier, then the original adverb is also a sentence modifier.

The truth of this claim is obvious, even trivial. To apply it, it is useful to use conditional sentences, since *if* clauses are clearly shown by Criterion 1 to be sentence modifiers.[14] If a conditional sentence begins with an adverb, and if one cannot paraphrase the sentence by putting the adverb in the consequent, then there is reason to conclude that the initial adverb modifies the sentence following it.

For example, the two sentences (33) and (34) differ in meaning:

(33)   Frequently, if John walked to school Mary walked to school with him.
(34)   If John walked to school, Mary frequently walked to school with him.

On the other hand, (35) is unacceptable:

(35)   Slowly, if John walked Mary walked with him.

If one forces a reading on it, it will be the same as that given to (36):

(36)   If John walked, Mary slowly walked with him.

Locatives and temporal modifiers show themselves to be sentence modifiers by this criterion, even though many of them fail the first two tests. For example, (37) and (38) differ in meaning, as do (39) and (40):

(37)   In the morning, if John is told to walk then he walks.
(38)   If John is told to walk, then he walks in the morning.
(39)   In that restaurant, if John is asked to wear a necktie, he wears a necktie.
(40)   If John is asked to wear a necktie, he wears a necktie in that restaurant.

The fourth criterion involves paraphrase:

CRITERION 4
Only if *Q-ly* occurs as a sentence modifier can one paraphrase the sentence by deleting the adverb and prefacing the resulting sentence by *It is Q-ly true that.*

Since the form of the paraphrase is an adjectival phrase that modifies a nominalized sentence, the acceptability of the paraphrase would seem to be strong evidence that the adverb modifies a sentence.

Again, this test works well on our paradigm cases. The sentences (41) and (42) are alike in meaning:

(41)   Sam frequently sucks lemons.
(42)   It is frequently true that Sam sucks lemons.

But (43) is clearly deviant, and not an acceptable paraphrase of (44):

(43)   It is slowly true that Sam sucks lemons.
(44)   Sam slowly sucks lemons.

To take a slightly different example, although (45) is not a deviant sentence, it differs in meaning from (46):

(45)   It is happily true that Sam sucks lemons.
(46)   Sam sucks lemons happily.

According to our fourth criterion, this is evidence that *happily* is ambiguous, having one sense (roughly equivalent to *fortunately*) that is a sentence modifier and another (roughly equivalent to *gladly*) that is a predicate modifier.

Even though (47) is somewhat awkward, it is certainly grammatical and means the same thing as (48):

(47)   It is true in the morning that Mary beats her dog.
(48)   Mary beats her dog in the morning.

But like (43), (49) is deviant and does not qualify as an acceptable paraphrase of anything:

(49)   It is true with a stick that Mary beats her dog.

Locative adverbs seem to be borderline cases for this criterion. Sentence (50) is at best awkward as a paraphrase of (51):

(50)   It was true in the kitchen that Henri dropped the soufflé.
(51)   Henri dropped the soufflé in the kitchen.

But it is not as manifestly unacceptable as (52):

(52)   It was true at his assistant that Henri threw the soufflé.

And some sentences similar to (50), such as (53), seem perfectly acceptable:

(53)   It is true in several restaurants that women in trouser suits will not be admitted.

All our criteria have been presented as sufficient conditions of being a sentence modifier. Though it is strong prima facie evidence that an adverb is a predicate modifier if it fails all four tests, we have no conclusive criteria that will prove it is not a sentence modifier. Criterion 4, however, comes close to being a necessary and sufficient condition. If the operation of this criterion results in utter nonsense, such as (43), (49), and (52), we believe that this is good evidence that the adverb is a predicate modifier.

All four criteria are semantic and are justified by semantic arguments. While we feel these arguments are decisive in many cases, in others they are not entirely conclusive. It may be possible to use syntactic evidence to supplement our arguments and criteria. If syntactic features can be found that distinguish the clear cases of predicate modifiers from the clear cases of sentence modifiers (as distinguished, in part, by the above criteria), then these features might help to decide cases on which the semantic evidence is indecisive.[15]

5   Syntax of the formal language

The syntax of a formal language is specified by giving *formation rules* for generating complex members of the syntactic categories of the language from simpler members of any of these categories.[16] Given a *vocabulary* for the language, which lists the primitive expressions of each syntactic category of the language, the syntax will determine the membership of each syntactic category.

Like the formal languages discussed in Thomason (1970, ch. 9), our language will have the following syntactic categories: individual constants, individual variables, individual parameters, and formulas. In addition, there is for each n ($n \geqslant 0$) a category of n-ary predicates, for each n ($n \geqslant 0$) a category of n-ary predicate adverbs, and a category of sentence adverbs.

Many of the formation rules of the language are copied from first-order logic. If the language is to possess connectives $\vee$ and $\sim$ for disjunction and negation, and the universal quantifier (other truth-functional connectives and the existential quantifier can be defined in terms of these), then we will have the following formation rules:

(54)   If A, B are formulas then $(A \vee B)$ is a formula.
(55)   If A is a formula then $\sim(A)$ is a formula.
(56)   If A is a formula, u is an individual parameter, and x an individual variable, then $(x)A^x/u$ is a formula.[17]

A fourth formation rule serves to define the category of individual terms, whose membership consists of individual constants and individual parameters:

(57)   If t is an individual constant or an individual parameter, t is an individual term.

The formation rules having to do with predication are not to be found in the standard syntax of first-order logic, which does not deal with the abstraction operator. These rules are as follows:

(58)   If A is a formula, u is an individual parameter, and x is an individual variable, then $(\hat{x}A^x/u)$ is a singulary predicate.
(59)   If X is an n-ary predicate ($n \geqslant 1$) and $t_1, \ldots, t_n$ are individual terms, then $X(t_1, \ldots, t_n)$ is a formula.

Before adding a clause allowing predicates to be constructed by means of adverbial expressions, an analogy is needed. Consider for a moment the generalization that leads from individual constants to operators. An n-ary operator corresponds to an n-ary function on individuals; if f is a singulary operator, for instance, then $f(t)$ is an individual term if t is an individual term. More generally, if f is an n-ary operator and $t_1, \ldots, t_n$ are individual terms, then $f(t_1 \ldots t_n)$ is an individual term. Individual terms can themselves be thought of as 0-ary operators since they require no individual terms in order to produce an individual term.

We will not add operators to our formal language, but instead will perform a similar generalization on predicate adverbs. A singulary predicate adverb ξ would yield formulas of the kind $\xi(a)(\hat{x}Px)(b)$. Constructions corresponding to this formula are common enough in English; typically a singulary predicate adverb will be realized by a preposition. For instance, if Pu stands for *walks*, ξ for *to*, a for *the store*, and b for *John*, then $\xi(a)(\hat{x}Px)(b)$ will formalize the sentence *John walks to the store*.

The formation rule governing n-ary predicate adverbs ($n \geqslant 0$) is as follows:

(60)   If X is a singulary predicate, ξ an n-ary predicate adverb, and $t_1, \ldots, t_n$ individual terms, then $(\xi(t_1, \ldots, t_n)X)$ is a singulary predicate.

The last formation rule of our language deals with 0-ary sentence adverbs. As one would expect, the resembles the rule for negation:

(61)   If A is a formula and F is a sentence adverb, then F(A) is a formula.

Suppose for the moment that the vocabulary of our language is arranged so that x, y, and z are individual variables; a and b are individual constants; P is a singularly and Q a binary predicate; ξ and ζ are 0-ary predicate adverbs; η is a singulary predicate adverb; and F is a sentence adverb. Then among the formulas generated by the above syntactic rules will be the following expressions:[18]

$(\xi P)a$
F(Pa)
$(\zeta \xi P)a$
$\xi(\hat{x}Px)(a)$
$\zeta(\hat{y}\xi(\hat{x}Px)(y))(a)$
$\sim(x)(\eta x(\hat{y}Qxy)(x))$
$\eta b(\hat{x}\sim Px)(a)$
$\xi(\hat{x}(y)(\zeta(\hat{z}Qzy)(x)))(a)$
$\xi\hat{x}(Qxa \lor \eta aPx)(b)$

6   Formal semantics

In setting up our semantic theory, we will make use of possible situations.[19] We will think of *propositions* as functions from possible situations into the truth values T and F, and of *propositional functions* as functions from individuals into propositions.[20] Our present task of providing a semantic interpretation of predicate adverbs shows up clearly the advantages of this decision. The framework of possible situations makes a routine exercise of this task, and the resulting theory is at once general and explicit, applying uniformly to all predicate adverbs of English and minimizing the need for paraphrase in formalization.

Propositions are the intensions of sentences, and singulary propositional functions are the intensions of predicates. Sentence adverbs will therefore denote functions taking propositions into propositions, and predicate adverbs will denote functions taking singulary propositional functions into singulary propositional functions. For example, *walks* will have as its intension the propositional function that attaches the value T in a situation α to those and only those individuals who are walking in α. *Slowly* will denote a function applying to singulary propositional functions. When applied to the intension of *walks*, for instance, the value of this function will be the intension of *walks slowly*, which, in turn, will be the propositional function that attaches the value T in a situation α to those and only those individuals that are walking slowly in α.

This can be formulated precisely by treating the semantic interpretation of our language like that of **Q3** in Thomason (1969).[21] Suppose we are given a model structure $\langle \mathfrak{K}, \mathfrak{D} \rangle$. $\mathfrak{K}$ is the set of possible situations of the structure, and $\mathfrak{D}$ is the set of possible individuals. Let $\mathfrak{P}^0$ be the set of functions from $\mathfrak{K}$ to $\{T, F\}$. According to what we said at the beginning of this section, $\mathfrak{P}^0$ is to be thought of as the set of propositions associated with the model structure. Let $\mathfrak{P}^1$ be the set of functions from $\mathfrak{D}$ to $\mathfrak{P}^0$; $\mathfrak{P}^1$ is the set of singulary propositional functions associated with the model structure. Let $\mathfrak{A}_0^0$ be the set of functions from $\mathfrak{P}^0$ to $\mathfrak{P}^0$, and let $\mathfrak{A}_0^1$ be the set of functions from $\mathfrak{P}^1$ to $\mathfrak{P}^1$. $\mathfrak{A}_0^0$ is the set of denotations appropriate for sentence modifiers, and $\mathfrak{A}_0^1$ is the set of denotations appropriate for predicate modifiers. For $n \geqslant 1$, let $\mathfrak{A}_n^1$ be the set of functions from the Cartesian power $\mathfrak{D}^n$ to $\mathfrak{A}_0^1$. Thus, if $f \in \mathfrak{A}_n^1$ and $d_1, \ldots, d_n \in \mathfrak{D}$ then $f(d_1, \ldots, d_n)$ will be a function from $\mathfrak{P}^1$ to $\mathfrak{P}^1$.

A valuation V on a model structure $\langle \mathfrak{K}, \mathfrak{D} \rangle$ assigns values to individual constants, individual parameters, and primitive predicates, as described in Thomason (1969). If a is an individual constant, then V(a) is a function from $\mathfrak{K}$ to $\mathfrak{D}$; $V_\alpha(a)$ is V(a)(α). If u is an individual parameter, V(u) is a member of $\mathfrak{D}$. If P is a primitive singulary predicate, V(P) is a member of $\mathfrak{P}^1$. If ξ is a 0-ary predicate adverb, V(ξ) $\in \mathfrak{A}_0^1$ and, in general, if ξ is an n-ary predicate adverb, V(ξ) $\in \mathfrak{A}_n^1$. Finally, if F is a sentence adverb, then V(F) $\in \mathfrak{A}_0^0$.

This suffices to characterize the lexical aspect of valuations, which consists in the assignment of semantic values of the appropriate type to the primitive expressions of the language. To complete the semantic interpretation of the language, we lay down the following *semantic rules* showing how an arbitrary valuation V must assign values to complex expressions. In these rules, $V_\alpha(A)$ is the truth value given by V to the formula A in the situation α. And where t is a term (i.e., an individual constant or individual parameter), $V_\alpha(t)$ is the member of $\mathfrak{D}$ given by V to t in the situation α. Where X is a singulary predicate, $V_\alpha(X)$ is the member of $\mathfrak{P}^1$ given by V to X in the situation α.[22] V^d/u is the valuation like V in its assignment of values to all primitive expressions except the individual parameter u; V^d/u gives u the value d.

(62)   If X is an n-ary predicate and $t_1, \ldots, t_n$ are individual terms, then $V_\alpha(X(t_1, \ldots, t_n)) = T$ if and only if $V_\alpha(X)(\langle V_\alpha(t_1), \ldots, V_\alpha(t_n)\rangle)(\alpha) = T$.

(63) $V(\hat{x}A^x/u)$ is the function f in $\mathfrak{P}^1$ such that where $d \in \mathfrak{D}$ and $\beta \in \mathfrak{K}$, $f(d)(\beta) = T$ if and only if $V^d/u_\beta(A) = T$.

(64)   If X is a singulary predicate, ξ and n-ary predicate adverb and $t_1, \ldots, t_n$ are terms, then $V_\alpha(\xi(t_1, \ldots, t_n)X) = f(V_\alpha(X))$, where $f = V(\xi)(\langle V_\alpha(t_1), \ldots, V_\alpha(t_n)\rangle)$.

(65)   If F is a sentence adverb and A a formula, then $V_\alpha(F(A)) = V(F)(f)$, where f is the function in $\mathfrak{P}^0$ such that for all $\beta \in \mathfrak{K}$, $f(\beta) = V_\beta(A)$.

7   Some applications

The semantic theory developed in the previous section is highly abstract and leaves unexplored many questions that would have to be settled in the process of applying the theory in detail to natural languages. For example, it is not possible to specify, for any of the predicate adverbs of English we have used in our examples, the function that is to count as its intension.[23] Applications of this sort, if they are possible at all, will have to await further theoretical developments.

But if we count logical consequence as a feature of natural languages, semantic theories such as ours will be applicable at least to this feature. A relation ⊩ of logical consequence can be defined abstractly by referring to the class of all model structures and the class of all valuations on these model structures, without having to designate any particular model structure and valuation as the ones that are intended.

(66)   Let Γ be a set of formulas and A be a formula. $\Gamma \Vdash A$ if and only if for all model structures $\langle \Re, \mathfrak{D} \rangle$, all $\alpha \in \Re$ and all valuations V on $\langle \Re, \mathfrak{D} \rangle$, if $V_\alpha(B) = T$ for all $B \in \Gamma$, then $V_\alpha(A) = T$.

An inference of a conclusion A from a set Γ of premises is said to be *valid* (or, strictly speaking, to be *logically valid*) if and only if $\Gamma \Vdash A$.

We can test and explain the definitions of section 6 by showing how they account for the logical character of certain inferences. As an example, we will show why the inference (67) is logically valid while (68) is not:

(67)   Oedipus intentionally married Jocasta.
       Oedipus is the son of Laius.
       Therefore, the son of Laius intentionally married Jocasta.
(68)   Oedipus intentionally married Jocasta.
       Jocasta is Oedipus' mother.
       Therefore, Oedipus intentionally married his mother.

As a first step, note that the formalizations of (67) and (68) are (69) and (70), respectively:

(69) $\xi(\hat{x}Pxb)(a)$
       $a = a_1$
       $\xi(\hat{x}Pxb)(a_1)$
(70) $\xi(\hat{x}Pxb)(a)$
       $b = b_1$
       $\xi(\hat{x}Pxb_1)(a)$

Here *Puv* stands for . . . *married* _____, *a* for *Oedipus*, *b* for *Jocasta*, a_1 for *the son of Laius*, b_1 for *Oedipus' mother*, and ξ for *intentionally*.

Now, it follows from the definitions of section 6 that any predicate X constitutes a referentially transparent context for X in the formula $X(t)$. That is, any inference having the form (71) is valid:

(71) $X(t)$
       $s = t$
       $X(s)$

To see this, note that if $V_\alpha(X(t)) = T$ and $V_\alpha(s = t) = T$, then $V_\alpha(X)(V_\alpha(t))(\alpha) = T$, so that $V_\alpha(X(s)) = T$. Hence, as a special case of (71), the inference (69) is valid.

On the other hand, inference (70) is not valid according to our theory. This inference fails because $V_\alpha(\xi \hat{x}Pxb)$ and $V_\alpha(\xi xPxb_1)$ depend on the propositional functions $V_\alpha(\hat{x}Pxb)$ and $V_\alpha(\hat{x}Pxb_1)$. Even though $V_\alpha(b)$ may coincide with $V_\alpha(b_1)$, for some situations α, the two need not coincide for all α and, if they do not, the propositional functions can differ, and so $V_\alpha(\xi(\hat{x}Pxb)(a)$ and $V_\alpha(\xi(\hat{x}Pxb_1)(a))$ need not be the same truth value.

We noted in section 4 that the analogue of (67) fails for sentence adverbs. And according to our theory the inference (72)

(72)   Nixon never met Charles Dickens.
       Nixon is the President of the United States.
       Therefore, the President of the United States never met Charles Dickens.

though it resembles (67), is invalid because *never* is classified as a sentence adverb. The formalization of (72)—that is, (73)—

(73) $N(Pcd)$
       $c = c_1$
       $N(Pc_1d)$,

does not have the form (71), and, in fact, in $N(Pcd)$ the term c occurs within the scope of the operator N. It is a routine matter to show formally that (73) is invalid.

In making this point, however, it is important to remember that our formalized language is syntactically disambiguated, in that each grammatical expression of the language is assigned a unique syntactic structure.[24] The semantics of the language is then coordinated with the syntax in such a way that each grammatical expression is assigned a unique semantic structure. But in view of examples such as *John and Bill or Mary will go in the car* and *John met a man who kissed a woman who loved him*, English cannot be regarded as disambiguated. Thus, it may happen that one expression of English may be represented by more than one expression of our formalized language. There is much evidence to suggest that the formal operation of abstraction is hardly ever represented explicitly in English, and so is a plentiful source of such ambiguities.[25]

We may infer from this that the conclusion and first premise of (72) are ambiguous. And among the other formalizations of the inference is one that has the form (71), and so is valid.

(74) $\hat{x}N(Pxd)(c)$
       $c = c_1$
       $\hat{x}N(Pxd)(c_1)$

This reading of (72) can be captured in English by means of the locution *is true of*:

(75)   It is true of Nixon that he never met Charles Dickens.
       Nixon is the President of the United States.
       Therefore, it is true of the President of the United States that he never met Charles Dickens.

Two important conclusions can be drawn from the ambiguity of (72). First, it is an oversimplification to characterize the difference between (67) and (72) by saying that the first is valid while the second is not. More accurately, we should say that whereas (72) admits a reading on which it is invalid, (67) does not admit such a reading.[26] Second, it is possible to regard predicate modifiers in English as "special cases" of sentence modifiers, in the following sense: sentences in which a sentence modifier is used will admit a reading in which the sentence modifier is used, so to speak, as a predicate modifier. Thus, *The president frequently visits California* has a formalization (76),

(76) $(\hat{x}F(Pxb))(a)$

where F stands for *frequently*, *Puv* for *. . . visits _____*, *a* for *the president*, and *b* for *California*, as well as a formalization

(77)   F(*Pab*).

In sentence (76) the predicate is constructed by abstraction on F(*Pub*), in which F modifies the formula *Pub*. But it would be equivalent to regard this reading of *The President frequently visits California* as having the form $(\xi_F(\hat{x}Pxb))(a)$, where ξ_F is a predicate modifier derived from F and satisfying a semantic postulate to the effect that $(\xi_F(\hat{x}A^x/u))(t)$ is to be synonymous with $(\hat{x}F(A^x/u))(t)$, for all formulas *A* and terms *t*. In this way, each sentence adverb can be thought of as giving rise to a derived predicate adverb.[27]

Though this train of thought makes it possible to assimilate certain predicate adverbs to sentence adverbs, it does not make the distinction between the two types of adverbs trivial. For while a sentence adverb will also admit "de dicto" readings having the form (77), predicate adverbs will not.

Before turning to other matters we will consider one more example, due to Donald Davidson, who in Davidson (1968) points out that (78) is a correct inference:

(78)   I fly the spaceship to the morning star.
      The morning star is the evening star.
      Therefore I fly the spaceship to the evening star.

This is confirmed by our semantic theory, according to which the inference (79) is valid:

(79) $\xi a(\hat{x}Pxb)(c)$
      $a = a_1$
      $\xi a_1(\hat{x}Pxb)(c)$

On the other hand, the more complicated inference (80) must be regarded as ambiguous:

(80)   I intentionally fly the spaceship to the morning star.
      The morning star is the evening star.
      Therefore I intentionally fly the spaceship to the evening star.

On one reading it yields an invalid inference resembling (68), namely (81):

(81) $\zeta(\hat{y}\xi a(\hat{x}Pxb)(y))(c)$
      $a = a_1$
      $\zeta(\hat{y}\xi a_1(\hat{x}Pxb)(y))(c)$

Abstraction can be used in the way discussed above, however, to produce a reading of (80) that is valid:

(82) $(\hat{z}\zeta(\hat{y}\xi z(\hat{x}Pxb)(y))(c))(a)$
      $a = a_1$
      $(\hat{z}\zeta(\hat{y}\xi z(\hat{x}Pxb)(y))(c))(a_1)$

And still another reading of (80), namely (83),

(83) $\xi a(\hat{y}\zeta(\hat{x}Pxb)(y))(c)$
      $a = a_1$
      $\xi a_1(\hat{y}\zeta(\hat{x}Pxb)(y))(c)$

results from reversing the order in which the adverbs of (80) are regarded as applying. This reading of (80), in which only the flying is intentional and not its destination, is harder to associate with the English sentence. But such a reading is readily associated with slightly different examples, such as *He intentionally flew his plane within a few feet of the rooftops, over a town called Hadleyville.*

8   Adverbial constructions and validity

Logical validity is not a palpable, overt property of inferences couched in natural language. For one thing, questions of validity depend on a syntactic analysis of the language: if adverbs that are sentence modifiers are not distinguished from those that are predicate modifiers, then inference (67) must be considered invalid, since it has the same form as (72). Logical validity also depends on the extent to which the semantic theory of the language has been developed. A theory that does not treat *few* and *most* as having fixed semantic interpretations will be unable to account for the difference in logical validity between the following two inferences:

(84)   Most doctors are men.
        Most doctors are nonsmokers.
        Therefore, some men are nonsmokers.
(85)   Few doctors are women.
        Few doctors are smokers.
        Therefore, some women are smokers.

If the theory puts no restrictions whatever on the quantifiers that interpretations may assign to *few* and *most*, then an interpretation in which the customary meanings of these expressions are exchanged is not excluded. In fact, the semantic theory of logical validity will give *few* and *most* only those inferential characteristics that can be ascribed to all expressions that are construed as denoting quantifiers.[28]

Moreover, *any* syntactic-and-semantic theory of a language will determine a relation of sameness of form among inferences such that all inferences sharing the same form are alike valid or invalid. This means that imaginative talent is required in testing inferences for validity, since an inference that strikes the ear as appropriate and correct may well have the same form as one that does not. Consider, for instance, the pairs (86)–(87) and (88)–(89):

(86)   This is a tiger.
        Therefore, this is an animal.
(87)   This is a cigar.
        Therefore, this is an animal.
(88)   John realizes it is raining.
        Therefore, it is raining.
(89)   John believes it is raining.
        Therefore, it is raining.

A theory that does not distinguish between the ways in which *tiger* and *cigar*, or *knows* and *believes*, interact with interpretations cannot distinguish between the validity of (86) and (87), or that of (88) and (89).

These cautions are appropriate because many inferences in which adverbs figure seem correct but nevertheless are invalid relative to our theory. We have put no restrictions whatever on the set $\mathfrak{A}_0^1$ of functions that can be assigned to predicate adverbs. In particular, these functions need not commute with one another: where $f, g \in \mathfrak{A}_0^1$, $f(g(p))$ may differ from $g(f(p))$ for various $p \in \mathfrak{P}^1$. Consequently, it is not the case that $(\zeta \xi P)(a) \Vdash (\xi \zeta P)(a)$; therefore inferences such as (90)

(90) John carried the eggs quickly to the wrong house.
      Therefore, John quickly carried the eggs to the wrong house.

are classified as invalid, a result that clashes with the strong feeling we all have that this inference is correct. But in the absence of a theory that enables us to distinguish between *quickly* and *carefully*, we must assign (90) the same form as (91):

(91) John carried the eggs carefully to the wrong house.
      Therefore, John carefully carried the eggs to the wrong house.

This inference does not appear valid. To be fair, however, we should add that it does not appear invalid, either; the first impression it presents is one of puzzlement. But the following account of (91) explains why this should be so. In one of its senses, the premise means (92), that

(92) John was careful in his manner of carrying the eggs, but not necessarily in carrying them to the wrong house.

And in one of *its* senses, the conclusion means (93), that

(93) John was careful in carrying the eggs to the wrong house, but not necessarily careful in his manner of carrying them.

Word order in English is not in general a very reliable clue to adverbial scope; an adverb can usually be inserted in a variety of positions in a sentence without obtaining results that differ in meaning. Thus, though the word order of (91) is slightly more natural in association with the senses we chose above, the premise of (91) can mean (93) and the conclusion of (91) can mean (92). Since (93) clearly does not follow from (92), this explains why (91) should not appear valid; it has a sense in which its conclusion can be false while its premise is true. On the other hand, since (91) also has senses in which its conclusion and premise say the same thing, we can explain why it does not appear invalid.

   Notice that it is natural to explain the ambiguity of *John carefully carried the eggs to the wrong house* as one of scope.[29] On the reading associated with (92), the scope of *carefully* is *carried the eggs*; on that associated with (93), it is *carried the eggs to the wrong house*. If this is so, then commutativity must fail.

   Another principle that holds for many adverbs and at first appears plausible is that for all f, $g \in \mathfrak{A}_0^1$, $f(p_1 \wedge p_2) = f(p_1) \wedge f(p_2)$.[30] This corresponds to the joint validity of inferences such as (94) and (95).

(94) $\xi(\hat{x}Px)(a) \wedge \xi(\hat{x}Qx)(a)$
      $\xi(\hat{x}(Px \wedge Qx))(a)$
(95) $\xi(\hat{x}(Px \wedge Qx))(a)$
      $\xi(\hat{x}Px)(a) \wedge \xi(\hat{x}Qx)(a)$

But there are counterexamples to this principle, at least insofar as it implies (95): (8) is such a counterexample. It is more difficult to find evidence against (94), and it may be that this inference embodies a meaning postulate that could reasonably be imposed on all predicate adverbs of English.

Perhaps the best known and most controversial inference pattern involving adverbs is exemplified by *John walks slowly; therefore, John walks*. Formally, this is (96):

(96) $\xi(\hat{x}Px)(a)$
      Pa

This inference is endorsed in Davidson (1968), but Montague (1970a, 1972) rejects it because of examples such as *allegedly*. T. Parsons (1970), likewise rejects it because of *in a dream*. But our tests for distinguishing predicate and sentence adverbs show both *allegedly* and *in a dream* to be obvious sentence modifiers; for instance, the premises *In a dream, the President of the U.S. is Abbie Hoffman* and *The President of the U.S. is Richard Nixon* do not imply *In a dream, Richard Nixon is Abbie Hoffman*.

Once all adverbs are excluded that show themselves to be sentence adverbs according to our tests, it becomes very difficult to find counterexamples to (96). There is at least one class of such counterexamples, however, that is general enough to deserve mention. It often happens that a verb expressing the completion of some prolonged activity will take adverbs such as *halfway*, indicating that the activity is completed to a certain extent. These adverbs fail our tests for sentence modifiers and presumably are predicate adverbs. But clearly, inferences such as (97)–(99) all fail:

(97) He filled the tank halfway.
      Therefore, he filled the tank.
(98) He scaled the cliff to the first ledge.
      Therefore, he scaled the cliff.
(99) He sang the aria from the first cadenza.
      Therefore, he sang the aria.

If enough examples such as these are forthcoming, the most natural approach to (96), and the one to which we ourselves are most attracted, will be to refuse it logical validity but to establish meaning postulates that guarantee the validity of many of its instances.[31] Since they must be imposed on a piecemeal basis, meaning postulates are to be avoided. But it is difficult to see how to dispense with them entirely in any systematic account of inference.

9   Some open problems

The syntax of our artificial language permits the formation of certain expressions corresponding to nothing that can be said in English. One case of this phenomenon originates in the fact that many predicate adverbs of English can be applied sensibly only to certain kinds of predicates. The following examples illustrate cases where this restriction has been violated:

(100) John is slowly tall.
(101) John slowly ignored the music.
(102) John slowly is captain of the football team.
(103) John slowly does not walk.
(104) John slowly if he walks, walks barefoot.
(105) John slowly walks frequently.
(106) John carefully walks allegedly.

The peculiarity of these sentences need not be explained by classifying them as syntactically ill-formed. It may be, in particular, that at least some of these examples are to be regarded as resulting from the violation of selectional constraints imposed at the semantic level.[32] If this is so, then this phenomenon should be explained by setting forth various kinds of propositional functions, and regarding adverbs like *slowly* as denoting functions that apply only to certain of these kinds of propositional functions. For instance, if the propositional functions are divided into *states* on the one hand and *events or actions* on the other, then the function denoted by *slowly* will be defined only for events or actions. If the predicates *is tall, ignored the music, is the captain of the football team, does not walk,* and *if he walks, walks barefoot* are then shown to express states, this will account for the peculiarity of (100)–(105).

This, of course, is highly informal and indefinite. As it stands, our semantic theory provides us only with certain functions as the semantic values of predicates, with no means of determining which such functions are states and which are not. The distinction between propositional functions that are "negative," for instance, and those that are not cannot be made in terms of our present semantic theory. We are envisaging here an extension of the theory, not a series of definitions carried out within the theory itself.[33]

Notes

We are indebted to...

Each of the authors would like to thank the other for pointing out numerous errors in earlier drafts of this article and making many helpful suggestions; but each assures the reader that his coauthor is not responsible for any errors that remain.

We are indebted to the Council of Philosophical Studies for their sponsorship of a summer institute in the philosophy of language, where many of the ideas of this article took shape, and to George Lakoff for an extensive and provocative correspondence. This research was supported by the National Science Foundation under grant nos. GS-2517 and GS-2574.

We owe special thanks to two referees of this paper who took pains to provide us with extensive comments and criticisms. This version of the paper owes much to their care and helpfulness.

1. Of Montague's papers, Montague (1970a) devotes most attention to adverbs. See especially pp. 212–214 of this work.

2. All of these writings are listed in the bibliography. See also Montague (1974b).

3. Formalization is the procedure of translating statements of a natural language into formulas of an artificial language for the purpose of evaluating arguments using the statements, exposing ambiguities in them, or revealing their "true logical form." The procedure is informal, since the rules for carrying it out are never made fully explicit. One must use his intuitive understanding of the content and structure of the given statements. An adequate formalization must yield a formula that has the same truth conditions as the given statement, but beyond this, the standards of adequacy are unclear. All one can say is that the "relevant structure" of the given statement should be reflected in the formalized equivalent. Although this standard is unsatisfactory as an abstract account of what formalization is, in concrete cases the procedures for formalizing and evaluating formalizations are often unproblematic.

4. For discussions of the problem, see Reichenbach (1947), Davidson (1968), Clark (1970), Parsons (1970b), and Quine (1970).

5. As a branch of mathematical logic, model theory originates in the work of Tarski. Kalish (1967) contains an introduction to model theory suitable for nonspecialists.

6. We refer here to work of Barbara Partee's concerning extensions of Montague grammar [Partee 1973: chapter 25 in this volume]. Also see Thomason and Stalnaker (1968) and McCawley (1970).

7. A^x/u is the result of replacing all occurrences of the individual parameter u in the formula A by occurrences of the individual variable x; for example, Pu^x/u is Px. When the notation 'A^x/u' is used, it is presumed that u is free for x in A—that is, no occurrences of u in A are within the scope of an abstraction operator $\hat{x}$ or a quantifier (x). See Thomason (1970, 149–150, 175–180) for further discussion of the syntactic terminology used here. We will sometimes drop parentheses where doing so does not result in ambiguity, and occasionally will add them where this makes a display easier to read.

8. This introduces some of the apparatus of second-order logic, but even so our amended language remains essentially first-order. The distinctive elements of second-order logic, second-order quantification, has not been added.

9. For simplicity here, the quantifier has been taken to range over the bulbs.

10. In classical first-order logic, any sentence containing a name a is treated as having the form $X(a)$. Even though negation is a sentence operator, $\sim Pa$ is treated as an instance of the form $X(a)$, and the inference of $\sim Pb$ from $\sim Pa$ and $a = b$ is regarded as valid in virtue of the general substitution principle. Generalizing from this model, one might treat any sentence of the form $F(Pa)$ as having the form $X(a)$, and regard the counterexample as showing that the substitution principle is not valid. But this, we think, would be a mistake. The only reason that it is harmless in first-order extensional logic to treat any sentence containing a name as an instance of $X(a)$ is that, for the restricted language, A^a/u is always logically equivalent to $(\hat{x}A^x/u)(a)$, which explicitly has the form $X(a)$. But that equivalence does not hold generally, as we have argued in Thomason and Stalnaker (1968).

11. By a *logical predicate*, we mean a part of a sentence that corresponds semantically to a propositional function. From the sentence *Dick beats Hubert*, one may abstract two singularly logical predicates: *being one who beats Hubert* and *being one who is beaten by Dick*. Or, using the abstraction operator, $\hat{x}(x$ *beats Hubert*) and $\hat{x}(Dick$ *beats* $x)$.

12. There is no need to classify *frequently* as a predicate adverb, as well as a sentence adverb, in order to account for the ambiguity between *frequently someone got drunk* and *someone got drunk frequently*. These can be formalized by $F(\exists x)Px$ and $(\exists x)FPx$, respectively. In the first formula, F modifies a closed formula, $(\exists x)Px$; in the second, it modifies an expression, Px, derived by substituting the variable x for u in the open formula Pu. But in both cases F acts as a sentence adverb.

13. G. Lakoff (1970b, 233–234) uses the contrast between *Sam carefully sliced all the bagels* and *Sam sliced all the bagels carefully* to argue that manner adverbs like *carefully* must be represented as sentence operators, not as operators mapping predicates into predicates. His argument, however, fails to take account of the possibility that the contrast between the two sentences can be explained in terms of the contrast between two predicates in the way we suggest.

14. To illustrate this application of Criterion 1, suppose it is in fact true that John Connally is the man who will be elected president in 1976. On one reading of *If Daniel Berrigan will be elected president in 1976, then the man who will be elected president in 1976 will be a priest*, this sentence is true. But it does not follow that John Connally will be a priest if Daniel Berrigan will be elected president in 1976.

15. Another test for separating predicate from sentence modifiers is suggested in Geach (1970). Geach points out that *passionately and presumably* is "syntactic nonsense" and suggests that this will apply to any conjunction of a predicate with a sentence modifier. But this test is unreliable. On the one hand, there is nothing peculiar about *passionately and often*, as in *He spoke passionately and often against the bill*, or *willingly but seldom*, or *intentionally and because popular opinion was against the war*. On the other hand, *carelessly and to Mary* and *twice and if it is foggy* sound just as peculiar as *passionately and presumably*. Without refinements of the responses to evidence such as this, Geach's test does not seem workable.

16. In other words, the categories are built up by simultaneous recursion. See Montague (1970b, 377) and Montague (1970a, 202).

17. See note 7 for an explanation of this notation.

18. Some of the formulas listed do not seem to have counterparts in English. It is a commonplace feature of logicians' formal languages that they permit syntactic constructions not corresponding to ones found in natural languages, but this is not thought to reduce their logical interest or even their applicability to argumentation in natural language. Many syntactic discrepancies between English and the formal language developed in this paper could be explained by supposing that English has no syntactic mechanism capable of doing in full generality what abstraction does in logical languages.

19. Or *possible worlds*, if you prefer more familiar terminology with a more robust, metaphysical ring; or *points of reference*, if you want a more neutral term that emphasizes the abstract character of the notion. Although these terminological differences suggest different applications and philosophical interpretations, from a formal point of view they are equivalent.

20. For general discussion of this technique see Montague (1969a), Scott (1970), Lewis (1970; Chapter 11 in this volume), and Stalnaker (1970). For a methodological account, see Thomason (1972a).

21. The semantic theory of Thomason (1969) has been modified here to make our presentation more simple. We do not allow the domain to vary from situations to situations, nor do we introduce the relation between situations that are often employed in the interpretation of sentence modifiers.

22. If X is a primitive predicate or a predicate formed by means of the abstraction operator, $V_\alpha(X) = V_\beta(X)$ for all situations α and β; so, dropping the subscript, we may speak simply of $V(x)$. But this generalization fails to hold for predicates formed by means of predicate modifiers. For instance, $V_\alpha(\eta aP)$ is the result of applying the function $V_\alpha(\eta a)$ to the propositional function $V(X)$. But $V_\alpha(\eta a)$ will vary according to the denotation $V_\alpha(a)$ of a, and need not be a constant function of α. For this reason, neither need $V_\alpha(\eta aP)$ be a constant function of α.

23. All that the abstract theory tells us is that, given a model structure $\langle \mathfrak{K}, \mathfrak{D} \rangle$, the intension *walks* will be some function taking members of $\mathfrak{D}$ into functions from $\mathfrak{K}$ to $\{T,F\}$. It does not tell us how to go about characterizing particular sets of possible situations and of possible individuals, such that there will be such a function that can plausibly be called the intension of *walks*. To do this would presuppose a metaphysical theory of what is to count as possible, as well as an analysis of the conditions under which an individual can be said to walk. By saying that it is not possible to specify the intensions of certain English expressions, we mean that a theory and analysis of this kind do not at present exist.

24. See Montague (1970b) for information concerning disambiguated languages.

25. The evidence is discussed in Thomason and Stalnaker (1968), where the corresponding ambiguity is identified with the traditional distinction between *de re* and *de dicto* uses of terms.

26. According to Montague's semiotic theory, these readings would be identified with assignments of syntactic analyses to the components of the inferences, and these syntactic analyses would consist of trees showing the order in which syntactic rules have been applied in generating these sentences from basic expressions. See Montague (1970a) and (1972).

27. We cannot, however, treat predicate modifiers in general as derived in this way from sentence modifiers without imposing some semantic constraints on predicate adverbs that would not be required by a direct theory according to which predicate adverbs are not derived from sentence adverbs. To see this, consider the formulas (1) $\hat{x}(\xi(\hat{y}Pxy(b))(a)$ and (2) $\hat{y}(\xi(\hat{x}Pxy(a))(b)$. They are not logically equivalent; there are interpretations on which they express different propositions. Yet if the predicate modifier ξ were derived from a sentence modifier F in the way suggested above, then (1) would be synonymous with (1a) $\hat{x}\hat{y}FPxy(b)(a)$, and (2) would be synonymous with (2a) $\hat{y}\hat{x}FPxy(a)(b)$. The formulas (1a) and (2a) are logically equivalent, and so on any interpretations they must express the same proposition. This in itself does not show that the required semantic constraint is not a plausible one, but there is reason to think that the constraint is not satisfied by all predicate adverbs of English. For example, suppose that Puv stands for . . . *examines* _____, a for *Mary*, b for *the doctor*, and ξ for *reluctantly*. Then (2) corresponds to *The doctor reluctantly examines Mary*, and (1) to the reading of *Mary is reluctantly examined by the doctor* in which the reluctance is on Mary's part. Since we are clearly dealing here with two different propositions, *reluctantly* must not be considered to be definable by means of sentence modifiers.

28. Inadequacies such as the one exemplified by (84) and (85) can be alleviated by adding certain meaning postulates that serve to rule out unwanted interpretations, thus defining a nonlogical type of validity that renders more inferences valid. As a referee of this paper pointed out, for instance, one could introduce a meaning postulate for *most* to the effect that $P(most\ X)$ entails $P(more\ than\ half\ X)$. But though meaning postulates render a semantic theory less abstract, in no nontrivial case will they make it so concrete that there will fail to be many significantly different interpretations, each of which satisfies all the meaning postulates. And there are methodological reasons for seeking to avoid the use of meaning postulates. They detract from the coherence and systematic character of the resulting theory.

29. What is more, there seems to be no other way of explaining the ambiguity in question. For instance, it cannot be due to a lexical ambiguity in *carefully*, since *John carefully carried the eggs in his left hand to the wrong house* is three ways ambiguous. Referring the ambiguity to scope predicts this phenomenon, while lexical ambiguity is incompatible with it.

30. Here the symbol "." represents conjunction of propositional functions.

31. See Montague (1972) for examples of the use of meaning postulates.

32. Here we assume that at least some deviant sentence—for instance, *The fact that he is late regrets itself*—are to be explained in this way. For a semantic treatment of such examples, see Thomason (1972b).

33. It is at this point that research in theories such as the one we have presented begins to make contact with the work of Davidson and his associates. Davidson has restricted himself all along to adverbs that are to be conceived of as modifying actions or events, and his program has involved philosophic inquiry into the nature of these entities.

30

DAVID LEWIS

Adverbs of Quantification

Cast of characters

The adverbs I wish to consider fall into six groups of near-synonyms, as follows:

(1) Always, invariably, universally, without exception
(2) Sometimes, occasionally, [once]
(3) Never
(4) Usually, mostly, generally, almost always, with few exceptions, [ordinarily], [normally]
(5) Often, frequently, commonly
(6) Seldom, infrequently, rarely, almost never

Bracketed items differ semantically from their list-mates in ways I shall not consider here; omit them if you prefer.

First guess: Quantifiers over times?

It may seem plausible, especially if we stop with the first word on each list, that these adverbs function as quantifiers over times. That is to say that *always*, for instance, is a modifier that combines with a sentence Φ to make a sentence *Always* Φ that is true iff the modified sentence Φ is true at all times. Likewise, we might guess that *Sometimes* Φ, *Never* Φ, *Usually* Φ, *Often* Φ, and *Seldom* Φ are true, respectively, iff Φ is true at some times, none, most, many, or few. But it is easy to find various reasons why this first guess is too simple.

First, we may note that the times quantified over need not be moments of time. They can be suitable stretches of time instead. For instance,

David Lewis (1975) Adverbs of quantification. In E. Keenan (ed.), *Formal Semantics of Natural Language*, 3–15. Reprinted by permission of Cambridge University Press.

(7)   The fog usually lifts before noon here

means that the sentence modified by *usually* is true on most days, not at most moments. Indeed, what is it for that sentence to be true at a moment?

Second, we may note that the range of quantification is often restricted. For instance,

(8)   Caesar seldom awoke before dawn

is not made true by the mere fact that few of all times (past, present, or future) are times when Caesar was even alive, wherefore fewer still are times when he awoke before dawn. Rather it means that few of all the times when Caesar awoke are times before dawn; or perhaps that on few of all the days of his life did he awake before dawn.

Third, we may note that the entities we are quantifying over, unlike times,[1] may be distinct although simultaneous. For instance,

(9)   Riders on the Thirteenth Avenue line seldom find seats

may be true even though for 22 hours out of every 24—all but the two peak hours when 86% of the daily riders show up—there are plenty of seats for all.

Second guess: Quantifiers over events?

It may seem at this point that our adverbs are quantifiers, suitably restricted, over events; and that times enter the picture only because events occur at times. Thus (7) could mean that most of the daily fog-liftings occurred before noon; (8) could mean that few of Caesar's awakenings occurred before dawn; and (9) could mean that most riders on the Thirteenth Avenue line are seatless. So far, so good; but further difficulties work both against our first guess and against this alternative.

Sometimes it seems that we quantify not over single events but over enduring states of affairs. For instance,

(10)   A man who owns a donkey always beats it now and then

means that every continuing relationship between a man and his donkey is punctuated by beatings; but these continuing relationships, unlike the beatings, are not events in any commonplace sense. Note also that if *always* were a quantifier over times, the sentence would be inconsistent: it would say that the donkey-beatings are incessant and that they only happen now and then. (This sentence poses other problems that we shall consider later.)

We come last to a sweeping objection to both of our first two guesses: the adverbs of quantification may be used in speaking of abstract entities that have no location in time and do not participate in events. For instance,

(11)   A quadratic equation never has more than two solutions
(12)   A quadratic equation usually has two different solutions

mean, respectively, that no quadratic equation has more than two solutions and that most— more precisely, all but a set of measure zero under the natural measure on the set of triples of coefficients—have two different solutions. These sentences have nothing at all to do with times or events.

Or do they? This imagery comes to mind: someone is contemplating quadratic equations, one after another, drawing at random from all the quadratic equations there are. Each one takes one unit of time. In no unit of time does he contemplate a quadratic equation with more than two solutions. In most units of time he contemplates quadratic equations with two different solutions.

For all I know, such imagery may sustain the usage illustrated by (11) and (12), but it offers no hope of a serious analysis. There can be no such contemplator. To be more realistic, call a quadratic equation *simple* iff each of its coefficients could be specified somehow in less than 10,000 pages; then we may be quite sure that the only quadratic equations that are ever contemplated are simple ones. Yet

(13)   Quadratic equations are always simple

is false, and in fact they are almost never simple.

Third guess: Quantifiers over cases?

What we can say, safely and with full generality, is that our adverbs of quantification are quantifiers over cases. What holds always, sometimes, never, usually, often, or seldom is what holds in, respectively, all, some, no, most, many, or few cases.

But we have gained safety by saying next to nothing. What is a case? It seems that sometimes we have a case corresponding to each moment or stretch of time, or to each in some restricted class. But sometimes we have a case for each event of some sort; or for each continuing relationship between a man and his donkey; or for each quadratic equation; or—as in the case of this very sentence—for each sentence that contains one of our adverbs of quantification.

Unselective quantifiers

It will help if we attend to our adverbs of quantification as they can appear in a special dialect: the dialect of mathematicians, linguists, philosophers, and lawyers, in which variables are used routinely to overcome the limitations of more colloquial means of pronominalization. Taking m, n, p as variables over natural numbers, and x, y, z as variables over persons, consider:

(14)   Always, p divides the product of m and n only if some factor of p divides m and the quotient of p by that factor divides n.
(15)   Sometimes, p divides the product of m and n although p divides neither m nor n.
(16)   Sometimes it happens that x sells stolen goods to y, who sells them to z, who sells them back to x.
(17)   Usually, x reminds me of y if and only if y reminds me of x.

Here it seems that if we are quantifying over cases, then we must have a case corresponding to each admissible assignment of values to the variables that occur free in the modified sentence. Thus (14) is true iff every assignment of natural numbers as values of m, n, and p makes the open sentence after *always* true—in other words, iff all triples of natural numbers satisfy that open sentence. Likewise (15) is true iff some triple of numbers satisfies the open sentence after *sometimes*; (16) is true iff some triple of persons satisfies the open sentence after *sometimes*; and (17) is true iff most pairs of persons satisfy the open sentence after *usually*.

The ordinary logicians' quantifiers are selective: $\forall x$ or $\exists x$ binds the variable x and stops there. Any other variables y, z, ... that may occur free in its scope are left free, waiting to be bound by other quantifiers. We have the truth conditions:

(18) $\forall x \Phi$ is true, under any admissible assignment f of values to all variables free in Φ except x, iff for every admissible value of x, Φ is true under the assignment of that value to x together with the assignment f of values to the other variables free in Φ.

(19) $\exists x \Phi$ is true, under any admissible assignment f of values to all variables free in Φ except x, iff for some admissible value of x, Φ is true under the assignment of that value to x together with the assignment f of values to the other variables free in Φ.

And likewise for the quantifiers that select other variables.

It is an entirely routine matter to introduce *unselective quantifiers* $\forall$ and $\exists$ that bind all the variables in their scope indiscriminately. Without selectivity, the truth conditions are much simpler; with no variables left free, we need not relativize the truth of the quantified sentence to an assignment of values to the remaining free variables.

(20) $\forall \Phi$ is true iff Φ is true under every admissible assignment of values to all variables free in Φ.

(21) $\exists \Phi$ is true iff Φ is true under some admissible assignment of values to all variables free in Φ.

These unselective quantifiers have not deserved the attention of logicians, partly because they are unproblematic and partly because strings of ordinary, selective quantifiers can do all that they can do, and more besides. They have only the advantage of brevity. Still, brevity *is* an advantage, and it should be no surprise if unselective quantifiers are used in natural language to gain that advantage. That is what I claim; the unselective $\forall$ and $\exists$ can show up as the adverbs *always* and *sometimes*.[2] Likewise *never*, *usually*, *often*, and *seldom* can serve as the unselective analogs of the selective quantifiers *for no x*, *for most x*, *for many x*, and *for few x*.[3]

To summarize, what we have in the variable-using dialect is roughly as follows. Our adverbs are quantifiers over cases; a case may be regarded as the 'tuple of its participants; and these participants are values of the variables that occur free in the open sentence modified by the adverb. In other words, we are taking the cases to be the admissible assignments of values to these variables.

But matters are not quite that simple. In the first place, we may wish to quantify past our adverbs, as in

(22) There is a number q such that, without exception, the product of m and n divides q only if m and n both divide q.

So our adverbs of quantification are not entirely unselective: they can bind indefinitely many free variables in the modified sentence, but some variables—the ones used to quantify past the adverbs—remain unbound. In (22), m and n are bound by *without exception*; but q is immune and survives to be bound by *there is a number q such that*, a selective quantifier of larger scope.

In the second place, we cannot ignore time altogether in (16)–(17) as we can in the abstract cases (11)–(15); (16)–(17) are not confined to the present moment, but are general over time as well as over 'tuples of persons. So we must treat the modified sentence as if it contained a free time-variable: the truth of the sentence depends on a time-coordinate just as it depends on the values of the person-variables, and we must take the cases to include this time coordinate as well as a 'tuple of persons. (Indeed, we could go so far as to posit an explicit time-variable in underlying structure, in order to subsume time-dependence under dependence on values of variables.) Our first guess about the adverbs is revived as a special case: if the modified sentence has no free variables, the cases quantified over will include nothing but the time coordinate. As noted before, the appropriate time-coordinates (accompanied by 'tuples or not, as the case may be) could either be moments of time or certain stretches of time—for instance, days.

Sometimes we might prefer to treat the modified sentence as if it contained an event-variable (or even posit such a variable in underlying structure) and include an event-coordinate in the cases. The event-coordinate could replace the time-coordinate, since an event determines the time of its occurrence. If so, then our second guess also is revived as a special case: if there are no free variables, the cases might simply be events.

In the third place, not just any 'tuple of values of the free variables, plus perhaps a time- or event-coordinate, will be admissible as one of the cases quantified over. Various restrictions may be in force, either permanently or temporarily. Some standing restrictions involve the choice of variables: it is the custom in mathematics that λ is a variable that can take only limit ordinals as values (at least in a suitable context). I set up semi-permanent restrictions of this kind a few paragraphs ago by writing

(23)   Taking m, n, p as variables over natural numbers, and x, y, and z as variables over persons . . .

Other standing restrictions require the participants in a case to be suitably related. If a case is a 'tuple of persons plus a time-coordinate, we may take it generally that the persons must be alive at the time to make the case admissible. Or if a case is a 'tuple of persons plus an event-coordinate, it may be that the persons must take part in the event to make the case admissible. It may also be required that the participants in the 'tuple are all different, so that no two variables receive the same value. (I am not sure whether these restrictions are always in force, but I believe that they often are.)

Restriction by if-clauses

There are various ways to restrict the admissible cases temporarily—perhaps only for the duration of a single sentence, or perhaps through several sentences connected by anaphoric chains. If-clauses seem to be the most versatile device for imposing temporary restrictions. Consider:

(24)   Always, if x is a man, if y is a donkey, and if x owns y, x beats y now and then.

A case is here a triple: a value for x, a value for y, and a time-coordinate (longish stretches seem called for, perhaps years). The admissible cases are those that satisfy the three if-clauses. That is, they are triples of a man, a donkey, and a time such that the man owns the donkey at the time. (Our proposed standing restrictions are redundant. If the man owns the donkey at the time, then both are alive at the time; if the participants are a man and a donkey, they are different.) Then (24) is true iff the modified sentence

(25) x beats y now and then

is true in all admissible cases. Likewise for

(26)   Sometimes
(27)   Usually   } if x is a man, if y is a donkey, and if x owns y, x beats y now and then
(28)   Often
(29)   Never   } if x is a man, if y is a donkey, and if x owns y, does x beat y now and then
(30)   Seldom

The admissible cases are the triples that satisfy the if-clauses, and the sentence is true iff the modified sentence (25)—slightly transformed in the negative cases (29)–(30)—is true in some, most, many, none, or few of the admissible cases.

It may happen that every free variable of the modified sentence is restricted by an if-clause of its own, as in

(31) Usually, if x is a man, if y is a donkey, and if z is a dog, y weighs less than x but more than z.

But in general, it is best to think of the if-clauses as restricting whole cases, not particular participants therein. We may have any number of if-clauses—including zero, as in (14)–(17). A free variable of the modified sentence may appear in more than one if-clause. More than one variable may appear in the same if-clause. Or it may be that no variable appears in an if-clause; such if-clauses restrict the admissible cases by restricting their time-coordinates (or perhaps their event-coordinates), as in

(32) Often if it is raining my roof leaks

(in which the time-coordinate is all there is to the case) or

(33) Ordinarily if it is raining, if x is driving and sees y walking, and if y is x's friend, x offers y a ride.

It makes no difference if we compress several if-clauses into one by means of conjunction or relative clauses. The three if-clauses in (24) or in (26)–(30) could be replaced by any of the following:

(34) if x is a man, y is a donkey, and x owns y . . .
(35) if x is a man and y is a donkey owned by x . . .
(36) if x is a man who owns y, and y is a donkey . . .
(37) if x and y are a man and his donkey . . .

Such compression is always possible, so we would not have gone far wrong to confine our attention, for simplicity, to the case of restriction by a single if-clause.

We have a three-part construction: the adverb of quantification, the if-clauses (zero or more of them), and the modified sentence. Schematically, for the case of a single if-clause:

(38)
$$\left. \begin{array}{l} \text{Always} \\ \text{Sometimes} \\ \quad . \\ \quad . \\ \quad . \end{array} \right\} + \text{if } \Psi + \Phi$$

But could we get the same effect by first combining Ψ and Φ into a conditional sentence, and then taking this conditional sentence to be the sentence modified by the adverb? On this suggestion (38) is to be regrouped as

(39)
$$\left. \begin{array}{l} \text{Always} \\ \text{Sometimes} \\ \quad . \\ \quad . \\ \quad . \end{array} \right\} + \text{if } \Psi, \Phi$$

Sentence (39) is true iff the conditional $If \Psi, \Phi$ is true in all, some, none, most, many, or few of the admissible cases—that is, of the cases that satisfy any permanent restrictions, disregarding the temporary restrictions imposed by the if-clause. But is there any way to interpret the conditional *If* Ψ, Φ that makes (39) equivalent to (38) for all six groups of our adverbs? No; if the adverb is *always* we get the proper equivalence by interpreting it as the truth-functional conditional Ψ ⊃ Φ, whereas if the adverb is *sometimes* or *never*, that does not work, and we must instead interpret it as the conjunction Φ & Ψ. In the remaining cases, there is no natural interpretation that works. I conclude that the *if* of our restrictive if-clauses should not be regarded as a sentential connective. It has no meaning apart from the adverb it restricts. The *if* in *always if* ... , ... , *sometimes if* ... , ... , and the rest is on a par with the non-connective *and* in *between* ... *and* ... , with the non-connective *or* in *whether* ... *or* ... , or with the non-connective *if* in *the probability that* ... *if* ... It serves merely to mark an argument-place in a polyadic construction.[4]

Stylistic variation

Sentences made with the adverbs of quantification need not have the form we have considered so far: adverb + if-clauses + modified sentence. We will find it convenient, however, to take that form—somewhat arbitrarily—as canonical, and to regard other forms as if they were derived from that canonical form. Then we are done with semantics: the interpretation of a sentence in canonical form carries over to its derivatives.

The constituents of the sentence may be rearranged:

(40)   If x and y are a man and a donkey and if x owns y, x usually beats y now and then.
(41)   If x and y are a man and a donkey, usually x beats y now and then if x owns y.
(42)   If x and y are a man and a donkey, usually if x owns y, x beats y now and then.
(43)   Usually x beats y now and then, if x and y are a man and a donkey and x owns y.

All of (40)–(43), though clumsy, are intelligible and well-formed.

Our canonical restrictive if-clauses may, in suitable contexts, be replaced by when-clauses:

(44)   When m and n are positive integers, the power m^n can always be computed by successive multiplications.

Indeed, a when-clause may sound right when the corresponding if-clause would be questionable, as in a close relative of (8):

(45)   Seldom was it before dawn $\begin{Bmatrix} \text{when} \\ \text{? if} \end{Bmatrix}$ Caesar awoke.

Or we may have a where-clause or a participle construction, especially if the restrictive clause does not come at the beginning of the sentence:

(46)   The power m^n, where m and n are positive integers, can always be computed by successive multiplications.
(47)   The power m^n (m and n being positive integers) can always be computed by successive multiplications.

Always if—or is it *always when*?—may be contracted to *whenever*, a complex unselective quantifier that combines two sentences:

(48)   Whenever m and n are positive integers, the power m^n can be computed by successive multiplications.
(49)   Whenever x is a man, y is a donkey, and x owns y, x beats y now and then.
(50)   Whenever it rains, it pours.

Always may simply be omitted:

(51) (Always) When it rains, it pours.
(52) (Always) If *x* is a man, *y* is a donkey, and *x* owns *y*, *x* beats *y* now and then.
(53) When *m* and *n* are positive integers, the power m^n can (always) be computed by successive multiplications.

Thus we reconstruct the so-called generality interpretation of free variables: the variables are bound by the omitted *always*.

Our stylistic variations have so far been rather superficial. We turn next to a much more radical transformation of sentence structure—a transformation that can bring us back from the variable-using dialect to everyday language.

Displaced restrictive terms

Suppose that one of our canonical sentences has a restrictive if-clause of the form

(54) if α is τ ... ,

where α is a variable and τ is an indefinite singular term formed from a common noun (perhaps plus modifiers) by prefixing the indefinite article or *some*.

EXAMPLES
(55) if *x* is a donkey ...
(56) if *x* is an old, grey donkey ...
(57) if *x* is a donkey owned by *y* ...
(58) if *x* is some donkey that *y* owns ...
(59) if *x* is something of *y*'s ...
(60) if *x* is someone foolish ...

(Call τ, when so used, a *restrictive term*.) Then we can delete the if-clause and place the restrictive term τ in apposition to an occurrence of the variable α elsewhere in the sentence. This occurrence of α may be in the modified sentence, or in another if-clause of the form (54), or in an if-clause of some other form. Often, but not always, the first occurrence of α outside the deleted if-clause is favored. If τ is short, it may go before α; if long, it may be split and go partly before and partly after; and sometimes it may follow α parenthetically. The process of displacing restrictive terms may—but need not—be repeated until no if-clauses of the form (54) are left. For instance:

(61) Sometimes, if *x* is some man, if *y* is a donkey, and if *x* owns *y*, *x* beats *y* now and then.
⇒
Sometimes if *y* is a donkey, and if some man *x* owns *y*, *x* beats *y* now and then.
⇒
Sometimes, if some man *x* owns a donkey *y*, *x* beats *y* now and then.
(62) Often, if *x* is someone who owns *y*, and if *y* is a donkey, *x* beats *y* now and then.
⇒
Often, if *x* is someone who owns *y*, a donkey, *x* beats *y* now and then.
⇒
Often, someone *x* who owns *y*, a donkey, beats *y* now and then.

Instead of just going into apposition with an occurrence of the variable α, the restrictive term τ may replace an occurrence of α altogether. Then all other occurrences of α must be replaced as well, either by pronouns of the appropriate case and gender or by terms *that v* or *the v*, where *v* is the principal noun in the term τ. For instance:

(63)   Always, if *y* is a donkey and if *x* is a man who owns *y*, *x* beats *y* now and then.

⇒

Always, if *x* is a man who owns a donkey, *x* beats it now and then.

⇒

Always, a man who owns a donkey beats it now and then.

Now it is a small matter to move *always* and thereby derive the sentence (10) that we considered earlier. Sure enough, the canonical sentence with which the derivation (63) began has the proper meaning for (10). It is in this way that we return from the variable-using dialect to an abundance of everyday sentences.

I conclude with some further examples:

(64)   Always, if *x* is someone foolish, if *y* is some good idea, and if *x* has *y*, nobody gives *x* credit for *y*.

⇒

Always, if *y* is some good idea, and if someone foolish has *y*, nobody gives him credit for *y*.

⇒

Always, if someone foolish has some good idea, nobody gives him credit for that idea.

(65)   Often, if *y* is a donkey, if *x* is a man who owns *y*, and if *y* kicks *x*, *x* beats *y*.

⇒

Often, if *y* is a donkey, and if *y* kicks a man who owns *y*, he beats *y*.

⇒

Often, if a donkey kicks a man who owns it, he beats it.

(66)   Often, if *y* is a donkey, if *x* is a man who owns *y*, and if *y* kicks *x*, *x* beats *y*.

⇒

Often, if *x* is a man who owns a donkey, and if it kicks *x*, *x* beats it.

⇒

Often, if it kicks him, a man who owns a donkey beats it.

(67)   Usually, if *x* is a man who owns *y* and if *y* is a donkey that kicks *x*, *x* beats *y*.

⇒

Usually, if *x* is a man who owns a donkey that kicks *x*, *x* beats it.

⇒

Usually, a man who owns a donkey that kicks him beats it.

(68)   Usually, if *x* is a man who owns *y* and if *y* is a donkey that kicks *x*, *x* beats *y*.

⇒

Usually, if *y* is a donkey that kicks him, a man who owns *y* beats *y*.

⇒

Usually, a man who owns it beats a donkey that kicks him.

Notes

1. Unlike genuine moments or stretches of time, that is. But we may truly say that Miles the war hero has been wounded 100 times if he has suffered 100 woundings, even if he has been wounded at only 99 distinct moments (or stretches) of time because two of his woundings were simultaneous.

2. It is pleasing to find that Russell often explained the now-standard selective quantifiers by using an unselective adverb of quantification to modify an open sentence. For instance in *Principia 1, *9,* [White-

head and Russell 1910–1913] we find the first introduction of quantifiers in the formal development: 'We shall denote "Φx *always*" by the notation $(x).\Phi x. \ldots$ We shall denote "Φx *sometimes*" by the notation $(\exists x).\Phi x$.

3. It is customary to work with assignments of values to all variables in the language; the part of the assignment that assigns values to unemployed variables is idle but harmless. But for us this otherwise convenient practice would be more bother than it is worth. In dealing with *usually, often*, and *seldom* we must consider the fraction of value-assignments that satisfy the modified sentence. Given infinitely many variables, these fractions will be ∞/∞ (unless they are 0 or 1). We would need to factor out differences involving only the idle parts of assignments.

4. What is the price of forcing the restriction-marking *if* to be a sentential connective after all? Exorbitant: it can be done if (1) we use a third truth value, (2) we adopt a farfetched interpretation of the connective *if*, and (3) we impose an additional permanent restriction on the admissible cases. Let *If* Ψ, Φ have the same truth value as Φ if Ψ is true, and let it be third-valued if Ψ is false or third-valued. Let a case be admissible only if it makes the modified sentence either true or false, rather than third-valued. Then (39) is equivalent to (38) for all our adverbs, as desired, at least if we assume that Ψ and Φ themselves are not third-valued in any case. A treatment along similar lines of if-clauses used to restrict ordinary, selective quantifiers may be found in Belnap (1970).

31

ROLAND POSNER

Semantics and Pragmatics of Sentence Connectives in Natural Language

> When a diplomat says "yes",
> he means 'perhaps';
> when he says "perhaps",
> he means 'no';
> and when he says "no",
> he is no diplomat.
>
> When a lady says "no",
> she means 'perhaps';
> when she says "perhaps",
> she means 'yes';
> and when she says "yes",
> she is no lady.
>
> Voltaire

One need be neither a diplomat nor a lady to use the word *perhaps* to mean 'yes' one time and 'no' another. But what is the meaning of a word like *perhaps* if everyone can make it mean either 'yes' or 'no' as he pleases? Can one in any sense talk about a fixed word meaning here? But if not, what is it Voltaire is telling us when he maintains that the diplomat's uttering "yes" as well as the lady's uttering "no" *means* 'perhaps'?

What is *said* and what is *meant*, coded information and its use in communication, do not seem to coincide in all cases. But, when they don't, which content elements of an utterance should be traced back to *word meanings* and which to the specific *use of the words* in the situation in question?

In semiotic terms, I am going to deal with the delimitation of semantics and pragmatics in the description of verbal communication. In treating this problem, I shall discuss the following points:

1. Two strategies for the description of verbal communication
2. The monism of meaning

Roland Posner (1980) Semantics and pragmatics of sentence connectives in natural language. In *Speech Act Theory and Pragmatics*, 169–203. Reprinted by permission of Kluwer Academic Publishers.

1   Two strategies for the description of verbal communication

In uttering verbal expressions to achieve communicative goals, we must be able to use these expressions appropriately. But how do we proceed? Does every word have a fixed meaning that language users reproduce in their utterances? Or are there no fixed meanings but only rules of use that guide the language users in their formulations?

These questions delineate two competing strategies for the description of verbal communication. For linguists pursuing the first strategy, verbal communication can be exhaustively described by reference to word meaning, sentence meaning, and the meaning relations holding among verbal expressions.[1] Linguists pursuing the second strategy seek to avoid assuming the existence of meanings; they try to describe the same phenomena in terms of language use. Both approaches have come to develop highly elaborated and finely articulated systems of terminology:

- While proponents of the first strategy speak of meaning, semantic features and the realization of semantic features, proponents of the second talk about use, rules of use and the application of rules of use.
- While one side speaks of semantic categories, of literal versus transposed meaning, of uniqueness of meaning versus ambiguity, the other is concerned with modes of use, literal versus transposed use, consistent versus inconsistent use.
- While one side speaks of hierarchies of semantic features, involving union, intersection, and opposition of features, the other discusses hierarchies of semantic rules, involving union, intersection and opposition of rules.
- While one side speaks of presuppositions, the other talks about conditions of use; constraints on the realization of semantic features appear as constraints on the application of semantic rules; feature change appears as rule change; modifications in the meaning of a word appear as modifications in the use of that word.

These two strategies I will call *the monism of meaning* and *the monism of use*.

Comparing the two strategies in such an abstract manner might lead one to regard them as merely terminological variants of the same theory, equally applicable and equally efficient in the description of verbal communication, were it not for the fact that they involve different empirical hypotheses and apply different methods of investigation. Monists of meaning usually assume that we have direct empirical access to word meanings and that rules of word use, if such things exist, are easily derivable from word meanings. Monists of use tend to believe that only the use of a word is empirically accessible, and that the meanings of that word, if such things exist, must be derived from its use. Common to each monism, however, is the assumption that its respective approach can give a complete linguistic explanation of how language functions.

In what follows I will show that both positions fail to satisfy some rather simple theoretical and methodological requirements for the description of language. Focusing on sentence connectives, I am going to argue against monistic approaches and in favor of a theory that assigns complementary roles to the meaning and to the use of words in verbal communication.

Since the discovery of truth-tables in the logic of the late nineteenth century, many logicians have offered an explication for the so-called logical particles of natural language. Nevertheless, doubts about the adequacy of such explications have never stilled. Recently, this century-long discussion has been given a new turn by the American philosopher of language Herbert Paul Grice, whose "Logic of Conversation" indicates a new and promising direction to take in the description of sentence connectives in natural language.[2] Grice's approach has not been received without controversy, however, and the essential arguments against it must be taken into account as well. In order to show the proper role Grice's approach can play in empirical semantics, I shall begin by sketching the history of the monisms of meaning and of use, including some of their psycholinguistic ramifications.

2   The monism of meaning

At the end of the nineteenth century the conceptual semantics inherited from the Age of Enlightenment came under the influence of a newly developed empirical discipline, psychology. This interaction resulted in a linguistic conception that can be characterized as follows. To communicate is to transmit concepts, and in order to transmit concepts one must utter words whose meanings are concepts. According to Wilhelm Wundt, "every independent conceptual word . . . elicits a certain conceptual idea that is vivid to the degree to which the meaning of the word is concrete."[3] Edward Titchener taught, "The word *dog* has a meaning for us because the perception of this word elicits the idea of a dog in us."[4] While not every word is an independent conceptual word and, as such, able to transmit an idea, every word has (at least) one constant meaning which, when combined with the meanings of other words, contributes to the meaning of the expression as a whole. Thus, a speaker transmits the intended concepts by uttering the appropriate words, with which the addressee associates appropriate conceptual ideas of his own. Associations can be interpreted and tested according to the mechanism of stimulus and response. In order to find out which ideas are associated, addressees are subjected to standard tests such as drawing the associated objects or picking out their putative qualities from a list.

Unfortunately, the association experiments did not, when carried out on a large scale, confirm this theory in the expected way. The ideas elicited by a particular word differed greatly according to the context. Thus, it gradually became a commonplace of meaning-monist word semantics to claim, "The boundaries of word meaning are vague, blurred, fluid."[5] Even linguists like Karl Otto Erdmann, who took such statements as the starting-point for the introduction of new distinctions in his "Essays from the Borders of Psycholinguistics and Logic", were not able to neutralize their force.

3   The monism of use

The consequences of this failure were drawn by behaviorist psychology. If the association test does not provide reliable access to word meaning, it is useless as a linguistic method. And, if we are forced to assume that word meanings are fluid, then the concept of meaning loses its theoretical value for the description of verbal communication as well. John Watson formulated this insight most emphatically: "From the position of a behaviorist the problem of meaning is a mere abstraction."[6] And Burrhus F. Skinner laconically concurred: "The speaker does not utter any ideas or images but only words."[7]

Even Charles W. Morris prided himself on being able to do away with meanings altogether. Indeed, he thought he had renewed the connection with experimental psychology by taking dispositions into account in his semiotic program.[8] Whereas association psychologists had put word and meaning on the same level with stimulus and response and had regarded word meaning as a directly observable variable, Morris took word use to be a disposition that mediates between stimulus and response in the communication situation. Being dispositions, the rules of use cannot be directly observed but must be inferred from manifest behavior in the form of intervening variables. Thus, in the case of word use the hypothesis of direct empirical accessibility was abandoned just as it had been in the case of word meaning.[9] Not even the difficulty encountered by Erdmann disappeared for monists of use; it merely became more clearly formulated. How one and the same word can play a role in fundamentally different behavioral dispositions is a question still looking for an answer.

4   The identification of meaning and use

These empirical problems and methodological difficulties deprived the two monist positions of their initial theoretical attractiveness. To be sure, it was not only for methodological reasons that Ludwig Wittgenstein advised, "Don't ask for the meaning, ask for the use."[10] He believed that he could also give this maxim theoretical underpinnings, claiming, "For a large number of uses of the word 'meaning'—even if not for all its uses—this word can be explained thus: The meaning of a word is its use in the language."[11] But Wittgenstein failed to develop satisfactory methods for systematically collecting and describing word uses and restricted himself to analyzing examples. For this reason, he prepared the way for an elaboration of the use-monist terminology rather than for the introduction of explicit criteria justifying its application. What survived was the slogan in its truncated version: "The meaning of a word is its use." Because of the lack of guiding criteria it was no surprise that this identification of meaning to use was soon made to apply in the opposite direction. This has led to today's uncritical contamination of the terminology of meaning with the terminology of use.

Of course, even such contamination can be justified, if only in the form of an analogy: are not meaning and use just two aspects of one and the same phenomenon, like temperature and particle velocity in thermodynamics or like wave and corpuscle in quantum physics? Yet, whoever holds this view, must take into account that physics has confirmed each of the two aspects experimentally so that the coexistence of the two terminologies is justified empirically.

But, can this be said of the two aspects of language?

The lack of direct experimental evidence for the existence of meanings and of rules of use has already been pointed out. Nevertheless, it must be conceded that there are phenomena in language that are more easily describable in terms of meaning and that there are other phenomena for which a description in terms of use is more convincing. For example, consider the German color words *gelb* and *blond*. If we take these words to denote those parts of the color spectrum that are reflected by yellow and blond objects, respectively, then *gelb* and *blond* have approximately the same meaning. They are, however, used in different ways; indeed, their uses in German are mutually exclusive: *blond* generally refers to human hair; everything else reflecting the color waves in question is called *gelb* or *gelblich*. It is true, there are certain marginal uses as in *Herr Ober, bitte ein kühles Blondes!* ('Waiter, please bring me a light ale'). But even here there is no mutual substitutivity, since no one would say, *Herr Ober, bitte ein kühles Gelbes!* The words *gelb* and *blond* can therefore be said to have the same meaning but to be in *complementary distribution*.

The following example is equally instructive. When we hear little Peter say at the hairdresser's: "Mommy, look, Annie is being mowed," we smile, but we understand what he wants to say. *Mow* means the same as *cut*, but its use is restricted in such a way that human (and animal) hair is excluded.[12] What we must take into account here are the *conditions of use* that restrict the occurrence of a word beyond what its meaning would allow. In the lexicon such conditions of use normally appear as parenthetical supplements to the specification of meaning—for example, "*blond*: 'yellow (of human hair)'" and "*mow*: 'cut (of grasslike vegetation)'."

    c'. I will, but right now I'm doing something more important.

    d'. No, because I have more important things to do.

As these examples demonstrate, the utterances under (2) leave open to the addressee the possibility of understanding them not as requests but as assertions or questions and to respond to their literal meanings. Interpreted in this way, they can provide an opportunity for a discussion whether the conditions for a sensible request are satisfied at all. In using such a formulation the utterer makes it possible for his addressee to argue against making a request before such a request has in fact been uttered; he spares him an open conflict and avoids losing face himself. In short, the use of meanings like those of (2a) through (2d) to suggest a request is more polite than the use of the literal meaning of (1).

    If this explanation of the function of suggestions proves right, it gives us a strong argument for the existence of meanings: the entire explanation would collapse if meaning were reducible to use.

6   Meaning versus Suggestion

The construction of suggestions originates in the effort of the addressee to interpret the verbal behavior of his communication partner as rational behavior. If the speaker utters a sentence whose meaning, taken literally, does not contribute to the recognized purpose of communication, then the addressee asks himself if the speaker means something different from what he has said literally. He evaluates the verbal and non-verbal context of the talk-exchange, looking for supplementary information that, applied to the literal meaning, will let him infer a message conforming to the recognized purpose of communication.[16] This reasoning is a heuristic operation; it follows certain rules, but its results are not strictly deducible since it often remains unclear what the purpose of communication is and which circumstances of the context are relevant to it.

    In order to get such a reasoning process going, it is important to discover which maxim of rational behavior the utterance would have violated if it had been taken literally. Therefore, Grice has tried to supplement his principle of cooperation with a series of special maxims which are valid in particular for the exchange of information during a conversation.[17] Grice sets up these conversational maxims by facetiously employing Kant's table of categories:

(M3)   I Maxims of Quantity
               1. Make your contribution as informative as is required . . .
               2. Do not make your contribution more informative than is required . . .
        II Maxims of Quality
               1. Do not assert what you believe to be false.
               2. Do not assert that for which you lack adequate evidence.
      III Maxim of Relation
               Say only things which are relevant . . .
      IV Maxims of Manner
               1. Avoid obscurity of expression . . .
               2. Avoid ambiguity . . .
               3. Be brief (avoid unnecessary prolixity) . . .
               4. Be orderly . . .

The dots following these formulations indicate that the maxims of quantity, relation, and manner can only be understood with respect to the purpose of communication accepted for a particular stage of a conversation.

This list of maxims is neither complete nor systematically organized in a satisfying way, and the individual maxims are neither of equal importance nor completely independent from one another (e.g., compare the relationship between I/2 and III). However, these flaws do not rule out the possibility that the maxims mentioned are actually applied in the production and interpretation of conversational suggestions. Therefore, one must also take them into account when describing these processes.

How this is done may be illustrated with an example that has given logicians many headaches. A first mate does not get along well with his captain. The captain is a prohibitionist, and the mate is often drunk. Therefore the captain is looking for a pretext to have the mate fined when the ship comes to port. One day, as the captain has the watch, the mate starts bellowing out a sea chantey again. The captain can stand the mate's excesses no longer and writes in the log:

(3)   a. Today, March 23rd, the mate was drunk.

A few days later, when the mate himself has the watch, he discovers the captain's entry in the log and wonders what he can do about it without compromising himself any further. Finally, he also makes an entry in the log, which reads:

(3)   b. Today, March 26th, the captain was not drunk.

This is not an ordinary conversation, but Grice's conversational maxims are nevertheless applicable, since the institution of the log serves an accepted purpose of communication that can be realized by following the maxims.

Both entries are true statements; however, there is an important pragmatic difference between them, which is revealed by the reader's reaction. Whereas the captain's entry is interpreted and understood without hesitation, any reader who comes across the mate's entry cannot help asking, "Why is that written in here? What relevance can the statement have in a log that the captain was not drunk on a certain day?" Once the reader has established that this entry would, if taken literally, violate the maxim of relation, the next steps of his reasoning are easy. "If the writer wanted to establish communicative cooperation with the reader of the log at all, he must have considered this entry relevant himself. A log serves to register exceptional occurrences on a voyage. Evidently the writer wanted to indicate that the captain's sobriety on March 26th was exceptional. Sobriety is, of course, exceptional if one is usually drunk. Under these circumstances the writer wanted to suggest with his entry that the captain was usually drunk during the voyage." Thus the reasoning prompted by the mate's entry has, on the basis of assumptions about the purpose and context of communication, turned a trivially true statement into a false statement of a rather defamatory nature. This example shows how one can lie with true statements when the utterance of those statements violates one of Grice's conversational maxims. In our case it is the maxim of relation (III) that is involved. There are similar examples for the violation of other maxims.

What is peculiar in this defamatory suggestion is the fact that it is hardly possible to take legal action against it. When confronted with the alternative of calling the mate to account for false statements or for disorderly conduct, any court would choose the latter.

The two examples from household and sea demonstrate that the discrepancy between what an utterer formulates and what he intends to convey can be explicated on the basis of the distinction between literal meaning (which is determined grammatically) and suggested content (which is determined pragmatically). Furthermore, our analyses of these examples have shown how the utterer proceeds to produce conversational suggestions on the basis of literal meanings and how the addressee proceeds in his efforts to reconstruct these suggestions from the literal meanings.

If these analyses are not misguided, they force the linguist to postulate *duality* in the description of verbal communication. He must not only determine the literal meaning of the verbal expression uttered but must also examine how the utterer uses this meaning.

Illuminating as this conception may seem, it leads to theoretical and methodological questions that are hard to answer. How can a linguist determine which content elements of a given message must be considered as the literal meaning of the words or sentences uttered? Can we rightly claim that the sentence *Have you taken the garbage out?* is an interrogative sentence, if it can obviously be used as a request? If the negation of the word *drunk* can be used to indicate that the person in question was the opposite of sober, why do we continue connecting its affirmative with the opposite of sobriety?

One thing is certain: an undifferentiated treatment of all the uses we can find will not bring us any nearer to the literal meaning of a word or sentence. Rather, it is necessary to select from among the many uses of a word or sentence those uses in which the literal meaning does not appear to be subjected to any modifications required by specific features of the verbal or non-verbal context.

However, by being asked in this way the question is in danger of becoming circular. We are saying: (a) the meaning of a verbal expression will not be submitted to a context-dependent reinterpretation if its utterance does not violate any conversational maxims; (b) the utterance of a verbal expression does not violate a conversational maxim if it is unnecessary to reinterpret its literal meaning in a context-dependent manner. In this perspective, the literal meaning appears to be like Wittgenstein's beetle in a box: even if we assume that the beetle exists, we cannot tell how big it is.[18]

There seems to be only one way out of this dilemma, and that is the attempt to reconstruct the process of comprehension itself:

1. According to our initial assumption, the addressee proceeds from the literal meaning of an expression and, on this basis, establishes certain conversational suggestions corresponding to the particular features of the verbal and non-verbal context. A comparative analysis of the comprehension processes for all essential uses of an expression could thus furnish us with those content elements which are always involved, as against those elements that play a role only in certain classes of context. We may assume that the content elements involved in the comprehension of all the uses of an expression belong to the literal meaning of that expression; as to the other content elements, we may conclude that they are dependent on special circumstances of communication and are produced only in the process of special interpretive reasoning. This is the *postulate of variability* for suggestions.

2. Since conversational suggestions change as the situation of conversation changes, we can cancel them through the choice of certain contexts. Even simple verbal additions will do the job, and by claiming the contrary we can annul an alleged suggestion without giving rise to a contradiction. This is the Gricean *postulate of cancelability* for suggestions.[19] If, after asking one of the questions (2b) through (2d), the mother in the kitchen had added, "But I'm not requesting you to do it now," no request would have been suggested. Likewise, the mate could have avoided a defamatory use of his entry without contradicting himself, if he had supplemented (3b) by the sentence, "The captain is never drunk." Such additions cannot, however, prevent other suggestions from arising, in case the complete utterance, understood literally, still violates *some* conversational maxim.

3. Finally, one cannot avoid a conversational suggestion by simply choosing another formulation with the same literal meaning. Suggestions of the relevant sort do not result from the use of special words but rather from the specific use of meanings. Therefore a suggestion generated by a particular utterance in a given situation is

detachable from the words, but not from the literal meaning of that utterance. This is the Gricean *postulate of non-detachability* for suggestions.[20] In our examples, the mother's suggestion would not have been changed if she had said, "Has the garbage been taken out?" and the mate's suggestion would not have been changed if he had written, "Today, March 26th, the captain was sober."

Variability, cancelability and non-detachability are useful indications, but, unfortunately, they are not sufficient as criteria in determining which content elements have to be excluded from the literal meaning of an expression.[21] Nevertheless, we have to work with them, as long as there are no better analytical instruments. The imperfections of this procedure only confirm once more what meaning-monists and use-monists had to discover by experience—namely, that neither the meaning of a word nor the rules for the use of a word are directly accessible to the empirical linguist but must be inferred from manifest verbal behavior.

Now if it is theoretically certain that all verbal behavior is based upon literal meanings, as well as upon rules for the use of meanings, it becomes necessary in the course of linguistic analysis to estimate how much of the content of a given utterance may be traceable to its literal meaning and how much is to be construed as suggestion. This is a procedural problem that gains importance in view of the fact that there is hardly any word of a natural language whose uses have been exhaustively analyzed. As long as we are in the position of creating hypotheses, we can again choose between two strategies that take up the positions of the old monists in a weakened form. *Meaning-maximalists* attempt to deduce as much as possible from the literal meanings of verbal expressions and tend to assume richness and ambiguity in the meanings of words. On the other hand, *meaning-minimalists* attribute more importance to the pragmatic rules of reinterpretation as opposed to literal meanings and tend to accept only minimal meanings and unambiguous words.[22] Let us now consider the consequences of these strategies for the analysis of sentence connectives in natural language, particularly, of the word *and* in English.

7 Sentence connectives: Maximization of meaning

When the logical particle *et* (written as "&", "∧", ".") according to the various notational conventions) occurs between two propositions, it turns them into one complex proposition that is true if and only if both constituent propositions are true. This statement, which defines the connective *et* of propositional logic, also seems to apply to the word *and* as found between declarative sentences of English. What would then be easier than to assume that this definition also characterizes the meaning of this sentence connective?

However, the truth-functional definition of *and* has consequences that run counter to many uses of the word *and* in natural language. For example, it allows sentences to be connected to one another without regard to their meaning. But any speaker of English would consider the following expressions absurd and unacceptable:

(4) a. $2 \times 2 = 4$ and it is impossible to analyze further the concept of *intention*.
     b. Muller just scored a goal and eels spawn in the Sargasso Sea.

Moreover, the truth-functional definition of *and* places exactly the same condition on the two connected declarative sentences; so they should be interchangeable. But any speaker of English will interpret (5a) differently from (5b):

(5) a. Peter married Annie and Annie had a baby.
     b. Annie had a baby and Peter married Annie.

Of course, these observations are not contested by anybody. What is controversial is how they should be explained.

The meaning-maximalist draws the following conclusions: the meaning of the word *and* is richer than the meaning of the logical connective *et*; it includes not only the truth-functional feature of *conjunctivity* but also the feature of *connexity* and the feature of *successivity*. On the basis of connexity, the *and*-sentence conveys that the facts described in the second constituent sentence are part of the same situation as the facts described in the first. On the basis of successivity, it conveys that the facts described in the second constituent sentence appear at a later time than the facts described in the first.

Such an analysis of meaning, however, is liable to quite a number of objections.

1. What about the three postulates of variability, cancelability and non-detachability? It is by no means true that every use of the sentence connective *and* implies a temporal sequence between the facts described:

(6)   a. $2 \times 2 = 4$ and $\sqrt{4} = 2$.
       b. The moon revolves around the earth and the earth revolves around the sun.

This shows that successivity is variable and not fixed to the word *and*. The assumption of successivity can also easily be cancelled by an additional utterance of the right kind. Continuing with:

(7)   But I don't know in which sequence that happened.

after having said (5a), rules out the basis for the conclusion that the baby came *after* the wedding. On the other hand, one cannot get around the successivity assumption by merely reformulating the constituent sentences in such a way as to preserve their meaning. The successivity assumption is non-detachable.

These observations indicate that successivity should be regarded not as a semantic feature of the word *and*, but as a conversational suggestion. Whenever we use coordinate sentences to describe events in time, we relate the sequence of the sentences uttered to the sequence of the events they describe, even without the help of the word *and*. The utterer would violate the conversational maxim "Be orderly . . ." (IV/4), if he were not to keep the temporal sequence parallel on both levels.

However, such an objection will not deter a meaning-maximalist, since, according to him, the absence of assumptions about the sequence of the facts described in (6) should be explained in a different way. Even when we speak of *chocolate hearts*, *paper tigers*, or *roses of glass*, we do not imply that the hearts beat or that the tigers and roses are alive. Evidently, quite simple syntactic procedures like the addition of an attribute to a noun can lead to the deletion of semantic features of this noun.[23] This deletion occurs during the amalgamation of the semantic features, in order to satisfy a requirement to avoid contradiction. Let us apply this explanation to our example (6). If one had to assume both that the facts described in (6) are time-independent and that they occur one after another, a contradiction would arise. So the addressee, preferring a non-contradictory interpretation, will delete the feature of successivity in his interpretation according to the meaning-maximalists.

With this procedure we now have two proposals for grasping variable content elements. These approaches impute converse operations to the process of comprehension. According to one approach, the addressee proceeds from a literal meaning with few semantic features and reaches the required interpretation with the help of conversational maxims relying on additional information specific to the verbal and non-verbal context of utterance. According to the other approach, the addressee proceeds from a rich literal meaning and deletes, according to certain preference rules, those semantic features which would come into conflict with the verbal or non-verbal context.

What is remarkable here is that both approaches are based on a similar theoretical apparatus. As shown by the requirement to avoid contradiction, even the meaning-maximalists need additional pragmatic maxims of interpretation besides grammar and the lexicon. And if even meaning-maximalists cannot manage without pragmatic rules, then we are justified in asking why they trust this instrument so little, why they apply it only to restrict meaning and not to produce new content. One might suppose that they have become victims of hypostatizing their own concept of meaning.

2. In order to support the meaning-maximalist analysis of the word *and*, one often compares it with the word *but*.[24] *But* seems to share with *and* the semantic features of conjunctivity and connexity. Instead of successivity, it has *adversativity* as its third semantic feature. Someone who says *but* implies that the facts described in the following sentence are unexpected or contrary to the present context.[25]

However, this parallelism is misleading. In contrast to the successivity of *and* the adversativity of *but* is not cancelable. Someone who says:

(8)   a. Annie is Martha's daughter, but she is married to Peter.

and then goes on to say:

(9)   However, I don't mean to say that there is an opposition between the two facts.

will not be taken seriously, since there is then no way to explain his saying *but* in (8a).

Finally, non-detachability does not hold for adversativity. In many cases the assumption of adversativity will vanish if the *but*-sentence is reformulated in such a way that the rest of its content is preserved. Let us compare (8a) with (8b):

(8)   b. Annie is Martha's daughter and she is married to Peter.

In (8b) there is no longer any trace of unexpectedness or opposition.

Besides, whereas an *and*-sentence may or may not convey successivity, depending on the context and on the facts described in the constituent sentences, *but* without adversativity is unthinkable. In contrast to *paper tigers* and *chocolate hearts*, this semantic feature never disappears, even in the face of a possible contradiction:

(10)   (?) $2 \times 2 = 4$, but $2 \times 2 = 4$.

We will tend to simply reject an utterance like (10) as unacceptable instead of asserting that the meaning of *but* is reduced to the features of conjunctivity and connexity here.[26]

This and other observations will also make us wonder about the meaning-maximalist explication of *and*. It seems that the model of feature amalgamation in attributes and nouns is inappropriate as a model for the interpretation of sentence connectives.

3. There are, however, stronger objections to the meaning-maximalist description of utterances with *and*. Let us compare the sentences (11a) through (11g) with the versions under (11'), in which the word *and* has been replaced with a lengthier formulation and at least one possible interpretation of the respective initial sentence is preserved:

(11) a. Annie is in the kitchen and she is making doughnuts.
   b. Annie fell into a deep sleep and her facial color returned.
   c. The window was open and there was a draft.
   d. Peter married Annie and she had a baby.
   e. Paul pounded on the stone and he shattered it.
   f. Give me your picture and I'll give you mine.
   g. The number 5 is a prime number and it is divisible only by 1 and itself.

(11') a'. . . . and there . . .
   b'. . . . and during this time . . .
   c'. . . . and coming from it . . .
   d'. . . . and after that . . .
   e'. . . . and thereby . . .
   f'. If you give me your picture, I'll give you mine.
   g'. . . . and therefore . . .

The reformulations show right away that successivity need not play a role at all in *and*-sentences, even for events bound in time. The strategy of deletion of semantic features in the examples under (11) will not help, either, since *other* relations besides conjunctivity and connexity are expressed between the facts described by the constituent sentences. And those relations can in no way be acquired on the basis of successivity.

The sentences under (11) leave the meaning-maximalist no other choice but to assume that the word *and* is ambiguous. He will say: There is not only a successive *and* (as in (d)), but also a simultaneous *and* (as in (b)), a local *and* (as in (a)), a directional *and* (as in (c)), and an instrumental *and* (as in (e)), a conditional *and* (as in (f)), and an explanatory *and* (as in (g)). He will be inclined to assume that all these different *and*s share the semantic features of conjunctivity and connexity and differ only with regard to the third semantic feature.

However, even this position seems plausible only as long as no further questions are asked. To begin with, one must observe that the word *and* also occurs in the reformulations under (11'), which are supposed to make the content of the original sentences more explicit. If the word *and* on the left means the same as one of the expressions listed on the right—*and there*, *and during this time*, *and after that*—then what does the word *and* mean *in these expressions*? It is obvious that none of the seven meanings already mentioned can be considered. Now what about obtaining the meaning of this *and* by deleting the third semantic feature of one of the complete *and*s on the left? This proposal could be pursued. But from which of our seven *and*s should we proceed? From the successive or the simultaneous, the instrumental or the conditional *and*? As long as such a question cannot be answered, it would seem to be easier to postulate an eighth meaning. This one, though, would already closely approximate the truth-functional meaning of the connective of propositional logic, *et*.

4. An even stronger objection to the meaning-maximalist position can be found in the observation that the *and* in the sentences under (11) can also be omitted without involving a change of content.[27] Let us replace the *and* with a semicolon, as in the sentences under (12), or with some other punctuation mark:

(12) a. Annie is in the kitchen; she is making doughnuts.
   b. Annie fell into a deep sleep; her facial color returned.
   c. The window was open; there was a draft.
   d. Peter married Annie; she had a baby.
   e. Paul pounded on the stone; he shattered it.
   f. Give me your picture; I'll give you mine.
   g. The number 5 is a prime number; it is divisible only by 1 and by itself.

We can communicate practically the same information with (12) as with (11) or (11'). This may make us ask how the content elements explicated by the formulations of (11') are conveyed in (12). Should we say that the semicolon itself has a meaning—or rather seven different meanings? Or should we say that the meaning is somewhere in the air and that it must be read "between the lines"? If one proceeds, like a meaning-maximalist, from seven different meanings and projects them, in (11), all on the word *and*, then, to be consistent, one would have to say the same about the semicolon (and about the articulatory pause between the utterances of the constituent sentences) in (12).

The only possibility left for someone who rejects this solution is to talk about contextual determination of content elements. But he must then be ready to answer the question as to whether such a solution would not be just as appropriate for the *and*-sentences under (11).[28]

5. The conclusive argument against the meaning-maximalist analysis of the sentence connectives, however, is based on the fact that the list of sentences under (11) could be extended at will and thus give rise to a virtually infinite number of new meanings of *and*. Depending upon what the communication partners take to be the actual relationship between the facts described in the constituent sentences, one could speak about an adversative *and*, a consecutive *and*, a diagnostic *and*, and so on, as in the sentences under (13):

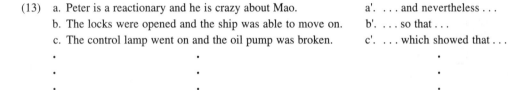

(13)   a. Peter is a reactionary and he is crazy about Mao.   a'. . . . and nevertheless . . .
       b. The locks were opened and the ship was able to move on.   b'. . . . so that . . .
       c. The control lamp went on and the oil pump was broken.   c'. . . . which showed that . . .
       .   .   .
       .   .   .
       .   .   .

In the case of ambiguous words, we can usually count the number of individual meanings on the fingers of one hand. Words with three meanings are not unusual, and one could even accept a word with twenty-seven meanings, but a word with an infinite number of meanings would be a contradiction in itself. Besides the practical difficulty that the lexicon cannot allow infinitely long entries, such a word would also raise theoretical difficulties: How could a language user learn to cope with a word of infinitely many meanings? The only solution here would be to assume a generative system of rules for the production of such an infinite number of meanings. Such a rule system cannot, by definition, be part of the lexicon but would have to be assigned either to a prelexical linguistic component or to a postgrammatical component. However, after all that has been said, it is superfluous to assume that we are dealing with an infinity of word meanings.

8   Sentence connectives: Minimization of meanings

The collapse of the meaning-maximalist position now brings us back to the beginning of the last section. So let us restrict ourselves to the content elements common to all previously mentioned uses of the word *and*: to *conjunctivity*, which requires that two sentences connected by *and* are true if and only if the entire complex sentence is true; and to *connexity*, which requires the facts described by the constituent sentences to be part of the same situation. And let us attempt to reconstruct all the supposed additional content elements on the basis of conversational maxims.

A meaning-minimalist would most probably go one step further; he would ask if conjunctivity and connexity could not be explained away in the same manner as successivity. It is easy to see how this would work in the case of connexity. The examples under (4), whose absurdity had led us to postulate such a semantic feature for *and*, do not lose any of their characteristics when one omits the *and*:

(14)   a. $2 \times 2 = 4$, it is impossible to analyze further the concept of *intention*.
      b. Müller just scored a goal, eels spawn in the Sargasso Sea.

Even when formulated asyndetically, these sentences are odd, as long as the utterer cannot rely on additional information specific to the situation of utterance that would allow the addressee to establish a connection between the facts described. This shows that the construction of a relation between the facts described by coordinate sentences is not at all specific to the use of the word *and*. It must always be possible if the addressee does not want to assume that the utterer has violated a conversational maxim. The maxims concerned here are particularly those of manner (IV, especially IV/1 "Avoid obscurity of expression . . . ," and IV/4 "Be orderly . . ."). Reasoning involving these maxims is available at any time; nothing prevents the addressee from also applying it in the event that the coordinate sentences are connected by *and*. Therefore it really is unnecessary to consider connexity to be a special semantic feature of the word *and*.

However, these considerations should not mislead us into trying to eliminate conjunctivity from the meaning of *and*. Of course, it is true that conjunctivity survives in many cases in which one omits the sentence connective *and*; that is especially so for coordinate sentences (cf. the examples under (12)). But what is interesting here is the cooccurrence of *and* with other sentence connectives in complex sentence structures. Let us consider the following conversations:

(15)   A: Annie has married, she has had a baby.
      B: ⎡That's not so. ⎤
          ⎨That's nice. ⎬
          ⎣That's too bad.⎦

      A: ⎡What's not so? ⎤
          ⎨What's nice? ⎬
          ⎣What's too bad?⎦
      B: ⎡It's not so ⎤
          ⎨It's nice ⎬ that Annie has married and that she has had a baby.
          ⎣It's too bad⎦

In B's last utterance it is not possible simply to omit the word *and* or to replace it with a semicolon. The raison d'être of this word lies in its combinatory function (not in its connecting function). In using his last utterance to elucidate the meaning of his comment "That's not so," B makes it clear that he thinks one of the constituent sentences of A's initial utterance is false, but that he does not want to specify which. It is the semantic feature of conjunctivity that enables B to do this, as can easily be seen from the following truth-table:

(M4)	p	q	$p \wedge q$	$\neg(p \wedge q)$
	T	T	T	F
	T	F	F	T
	F	T	F	T
	F	F	F	T

(The lowercase letters p and q stand for the constituent propositions; $\neg$ stands for *it's not so that . . .* ; and the capital letters T and F stand for the truth-values 'true' and 'false'. For the operators *It's nice that . . .* and *It's too bad that . . .* we arrive at analogous results.) If one claims that the formula in the righthand column of the truth-table is true, one actually leaves three possibilities for the distribution of truth-values among the constituent propositions p and q (cf. the truth-values of p and q as noted in the corresponding lines of the lefthand columns). This example shows that in certain cases we cannot do without the word *and* if we want to communicate conjunctivity: when *and* is removed, conjunctivity is also lost. This, then, is a case where conjunctivity is detachable from the meaning of the rest of the sentence.

Conjunctivity also violates the other two criteria for the occurrence of a conversational suggestion: it is neither variable nor cancelable.[29] To assert:

(16)   Peter married Annie and Annie had a baby; the complete sentence is true, but one of its constituent sentences is false.

is to contradict oneself.

Now that we have demonstrated that conjunctivity is a semantic feature of the literal meaning of *and*, we must show how it is possible to construe as conversational suggestions at least the seven other content elements discussed earlier:

Re (11a): If someone explicitly states that Annie is in the kitchen and then adds *without specifying another place* that she is making doughnuts, then he is guilty of *suppressing relevant information* if he thereby wants to convey that the doughnuts are being made outside of the kitchen. This would be a violation of maxim I/1. In order to avoid assuming such a violation, the addressee interprets the formulation of (11a) as a *suggestion of identity of place* (. . . *and there* . . .).

Re (11b): If someone explicitly states that Annie fell into a deep sleep but then adds *without specifying another time* that her facial color returned, then he is guilty of *suppressing relevant information* if he thereby wants to convey that the two events took place at a completely different time. This would again be a violation of maxim I/1. In order to avoid assuming such a violation, the addressee interprets the formulation of (11b) as a *suggestion of simultaneity* (. . . *and during this time* . . .).

Re (11c): If someone explicitly states that a window is open and then adds *without specifying another source* that there is a draft, then he is guilty of *communicating irrelevant information* if he does not want to convey that the draft is coming from that window. This would be a violation of maxim III. In order to avoid assuming such a violation, the addressee interprets the formulation of (11c) as a *suggestion of the source* of the draft (. . . *and coming from it* . . .).

Re (11d): If someone begins by reporting that a woman got married and then immediately adds *without specifying another time* that she had a baby, then he is guilty of *distortive reporting* if he thereby wants to convey that the wedding took place after the baby was born. This would be a violation of maxim IV/4. In order to avoid assuming such a violation, the addressee interprets the formulation of (11d) as a *suggestion of a temporal parallelism* between the reporting utterances and the reported events (. . . *and after that* . . .).

Re (11e): If someone explicitly reports someone's action upon a certain object and then, *without specifying another action*, reports a result of that person's acting upon that object, then he is guilty of *communicating irrelevant information*, if he does not want to convey that this result was brought about by the action mentioned. This would be a violation of maxim III. In order to avoid assuming such a violation, the addressee interprets the formulation of (11e) as a *suggestion of an instrumental relation* between the action and its result (. . . *and thereby* . . .).

Re (11f): If someone asks a favor and, in the same sentence, predicts an action of his own that can be considered as compensation for that favor, then he is guilty of *communicating irrelevant information* or of *obscure procedures of negotiation* if he does not want to make a conditional promise dependent on the accomplishment of the favor. This would be a violation of maxims III or IV, respectively. In order to avoid assuming such a violation, the addressee interprets the formulation of (11f) as a *suggestion of a conditional relation* between the two actions mentioned (*if . . .* , *then . . .*).

Re (11g): If someone uses one and the same sentence to make two statements about a number each of which implies the other, he is guilty of *prolixity* if he does not use one statement to justify or explain the other. This would be a violation of maxim IV/3. ln order to avoid assuming such a violation, the addressee interprets the formulation of (11g) as a *suggestion of an explanatory relation* between the two statements (*. . . and therefore . . .*).

These paradigms of the sources of conversational suggestions would not be complete without the following comments:

1. Conversational suggestions are dependent on the context of utterance. Any addition of a verbal utterance or of a detail of situation can direct the reasoning of the addressee in another direction. The seven paradigms should be read *with this reservation*.
2. Each reasoning process takes reference to the formulation of the sentence in question. Instead of doing this in an ad hoc way one could systematically compare the suggestion-producing qualities of sentences. On this basis, it should be possible to arrive at generalizations about the production of conversational suggestions and to approach explanatory adequacy. This can be an important methodological starting-point for progress in *descriptive stylistics*.
3. Conversational suggestions arise for the most part from specific qualities of the literal meanings conveyed. If a sentence manifests several such qualities at the same time, then several suggestions can arise. Thus

   • (11a) is interpretable not only as local, but also as simultaneous;
   • (11b) is interpretable not only as simultaneous, but also as explanatory and local;
   • (11c) is interpretable not only as directional, but also as simultaneous and explanatory;
   • (11d) is interpretable not only as successive, but also as explanatory;
   • (11e) is interpretable not only as instrumental, but also as simultaneous, explanatory, and local;
   • (11f) is interpretable not only as conditional, but also as successive.

The fact that we obtain *multiple suggestions* is a further confirmation of the meaning-minimalist approach, since it explains the vague and expressive character of the suggestive use of language. Which of the possible suggestions dominates in each case depends among other things on how the corresponding semantic dimensions are realized in the sentence in question. Thus, time plays a less significant role in (11a) than in (11b) through (11e), since (11a) is formulated in the present and not in the past tense. Place plays a more important role in (11a) than in (11b) or (11d), since (11a), in contrast to the other sentences, contains an explicit specification of place (*in the kitchen*). Abstract conceptual relationships play an exclusive role in (11g), since the facts described in both its constituent sentences are valid at any time and place.

4. From the structure and results of the reasoning processes sketched above we can conclude that the given suggestions are not to be added to the conjunctivity of *and* as semantic features of the same sort; rather, they are made possible only through the combinatory function of this word. Nor do those suggestions have the same status as connexity, since they embody rather special kinds of connection between the facts described, a connection whose existence is suggested by the contiguity of the utterances of the constituent sentences. Therefore, I propose to call them *connexity-suggestions*. With his "thesis of the dual control of linguistic structure" Charles W. Morris drew attention to this phenomenon as early as 1938, when he wrote: "From the interconnectedness of events on the one hand, and the interconnectedness of [communicative] actions on the other, signs become interconnected."[30]

The paradigms of suggestion-producing reasoning have shown the usefulness of Grice's maxims and have made it plausible that the other possible suggestions a speaker of English may intend in uttering *and*-sentences are also reconstructed pragmatically by the addressee. The truth-function defined in propositional logic has revealed itself to be the only semantic feature of the sentence connective *and* in English. And the hypothesis that other sentence connectives of natural languages also have a purely truth-functional meaning has gained in plausibility. A fresh start should be made in considering in detail whether it is possible to identify at least the literal meanings of the sentence connectives *and*, *or*, *if*, and *not* with the meanings of the connectives of propositional logic *et*, *vel*, *si*, and *non*, even if their use occasionally appears to be radically different.

At this point the meaning-minimalist position seems to have won the argument. However, this judgment may still be somewhat premature since here again things are not quite so easy. Therefore, I do not want to end this discussion without at least touching upon those difficulties.

9   The duality of semantic and pragmatic interpretation

Problems arise in the use of *and* in complex sentence structures. Let us consider the utterance of a conditional sentence that contains the word *and* in the first clause and suggests successivity:

(17)   If Annie has married and has had a baby, grandfather will be happy.

Let us assume that (17) is true. The truth-functional analysis of the word *if* indicates that, if the antecedent clause is true, the consequent clause must also be true. The truth-functional analysis of the word *and* indicates that the entire sentence is true if and only if both constituent sentences are true. Under these conditions the grandfather would have to be happy if it is true that Annie has married and if it is true that she has had a baby. But sentence (17) is not normally so interpreted. Even if (17) is true, it can also happen that the grandfather will not be happy at all, if he hears that the child came before the wedding. So the truth of the consequent clause is dependent here upon the realization not only of the literal meaning of the antecedent clause, but also of its successivity-suggestion.[31]

Thus conversational suggestions arising from constituent sentences can be crucial in the evaluation of the truth of the entire sentence. In these cases one can no longer speak of a purely truth-functional use of the sentence connectives. The choice of explanations available creates a dilemma:

- Whoever wants to save the truth-functionality of *and* by asserting that the subordinate clause of (17) is true because each of its constituent clauses is true, sacrifices the truth-functionality of *if*, since he must admit that the consequent clause can still be false.

- Whoever wants to save the truth-functionality of *if* by asserting that the consequent clause in (17) is only false if the antecedent clause is false, sacrifices the truth-functionality of *and*, since he must admit that the antecedent clause can be false even if each of its constituent sentences is true.

In view of this dilemma we are on the verge of losing our motivation for a truth-functional treatment of the sentence connectives: it would only be of theoretical importance if it could be extended to all relevant sentence connectives.

A homogeneous treatment of the sentence connectives concerned seems possible only if we weaken the thesis that in natural language the truth-value of the entire sentence is a function of the truth-value of the constituent sentences. This thesis cannot be held in the sense that in complex sentence structures the truth-value of the entire sentence is directly deducible from the truth-values of the smallest constituent sentences. Rather, after each step in the truth-functional deduction, it must be considered whether the resulting conversational suggestions alter the derived truth-value. Each deduction in the value distribution of the complex sentence on the basis of the value distributions of two constituent sentences must be open to reinterpretation according to the context in which the sentence has been uttered.[32]

This is certainly not a very elegant solution. It complicates the process of interpretation to such an extent that we might have doubts about the presuppositions of this analysis, in particular, the division of the content elements into word meaning and word use.

However, another solution is hard to find, considering the arguments against the meaning-maximalists given above. Moreover, there is a series of additional arguments that make this solution more plausible than any imaginable alternative:

1. Let us compare the following versions of sentence (17) with one another:

(18)   a. If Annie has married and has had a baby, grandfather will be happy.
      b. If Annie has married and she has had a baby, grandfather will be happy.
      c. If Annie has married and if she has had a baby, grandfather will be happy.
      d. If Annie has married and if Annie has had a baby, grandfather will be happy.

Only the subordinate clause differs each time. The number of syntactic transformations performed on the subordinate clause is greatest in (a) and is reduced progressively until (d).[33] What is significant is that in (18) the strength of the successivity-suggestion also varies. It is strongest in (a) and diminishes progressively down to (d). Obviously, the intensity of the communication of a connexity-suggestion depends on the *degree of syntactic connectedness* of the constituent sentences concerned. What we have here is a typical iconic relationship between content and syntactic form. The effect of this relationship is also noticeable, although to a lesser degree, where *and* is the only sentence connective involved:[34]

(19)   a. Annie has married and has had a child.
      b. Annie has married and she has had a child.
      c. Annie has married and Annie has had a child.
      d. Annie has married. And Annie has had a child.

2. The difference between the sentences under (19) and the sentences under (18) can be generalized in the following way: the strength of a connexity-suggestion depends on the *degree of embedding* of the clause concerned in the entire sentence. Compare (20) with (18), (21) with (20), as well as (20), (21), and (18) with (19):

(20) If grandfather finds out that Annie has married

$\left.\begin{array}{l}\text{and} \\ \text{and she} \\ \text{and that she} \\ \text{and that Annie}\end{array}\right\}$ has had a baby,

he will be happy.

(21) If grandmother finds out that Fritz has told grandfather Annie has married

$\left.\begin{array}{l}\text{and} \\ \text{and she} \\ \text{and that she} \\ \text{and that Annie}\end{array}\right\}$ has had a baby,

she will be happy.

This generalization also proves valid when we reverse the sequence of sentences connected by *and* and formulate:

(19') Annie has had a baby

$\left.\begin{array}{l}\text{and} \\ \text{and she} \\ \text{and Annie} \\ \text{. And Annie}\end{array}\right\}$ has married.

(18') If Annie has had a baby

$\left.\begin{array}{l}\text{and} \\ \text{and she} \\ \text{and if she} \\ \text{and if Annie}\end{array}\right\}$ has married, grandfather will be happy.

(20') If grandfather finds out that Annie has had a baby

$\left.\begin{array}{l}\text{and} \\ \text{and she} \\ \text{and that she} \\ \text{and that Annie}\end{array}\right\}$ has married, he will be happy.

(21') If grandmother finds out that Fritz has told grandfather that Annie has had a baby

$\left.\begin{array}{l}\text{and} \\ \text{and she} \\ \text{and that she} \\ \text{and that Annie}\end{array}\right\}$ has married, she will be happy.

In all these sentences the strength of the successivity-suggestion diminishes according to the degree of embedding, and the content of the sentence connectives *if* and *and* comes progressively closer to their truth-functional meaning. In the most expanded version of the sentences under (21), it surely is irrelevant to the grandmother's joy whether the events occurred in one sequence or another.[35]

  3. The force of embedded connexity-suggestions correlates with still other factors. Let me only mention as a last case the *meaning of the higher verb*:

(22)   If Fritz ⎡ reports to ⎤
                 ⎢ relates to ⎥
                 ⎨ communicates to ⎬ grandfather
                 ⎢ tells ⎥
                 ⎣ informs ⎦

       that Annie has had a baby and has married, grandfather will be happy.

In a "report," the sequence of the events conveyed is essential. Here, the person reporting tends to make his utterances follow the events. If he should happen to deviate from the natural sequence, he would make sure that his addressees realize that. Thus, if Fritz reports something to the grandfather and the grandfather is happy about it, the sequence of the events must undoubtedly be considered among the reasons for his being happy. In a simple transmission of information, however, the sequence of the utterances can depend on any kind of accident and does not allow any conclusion about the sequence of events. Here, then, the sequence of events will not be among the reasons for the grandfather's joy. In this way, the strength of a connexity-suggestion can be controlled by the choice of the higher verb.

These last three observations make it clear that connexity-suggestions are characterized not only by considerable variability but also by change of intensity—a property never found in literal meanings. No grammar describes cases in which the syntactic qualities of the surrounding sentence exert an influence on the semantic value of a word such that one of its semantic features is either foregrounded or suggested with varying strength or even eliminated entirely.

All this indicates then that connexity-suggestions are not lexical phenomena but have to be accounted for by pragmatics. And since that is so, there seems no way to avoid the dual procedure previously discussed for the interpretation of complex sentences. It is not without irony that pragmatic rules should play an essential role in the interpretation of expressions the analysis of which has for decades been considered the core of semantics.[36]

After this general conclusion it may be appropriate to summarize the individual results to which we were led by our discussion of the sentence connectives:

1. The delimitation of *semantics* and *pragmatics* in language description must follow the difference between *meaning* and *use* of words in verbal communication.
2. The meaning and the use of a word are not just two sides of the same thing, but have to be distinguished systematically. Speakers of a natural language master not only fixed word-meanings but also fixed rules for the use of words. Both are *empirically testable*, even if there is *no direct experimental access to them*.
3. The criteria of *variability*, *cancelability*, and *non-detachability* can help to answer the question of which content elements of a given utterance come into play through the literal meaning and which through the use of words in verbal communication.
4. On the basis of these criteria, the meaning of sentence connectives such as *and*, *or*, *if*, and *not* in natural language may be equated with the defining properties of the connectives of propositional logic *et*, *vel*, *si*, and *non*. Corresponding to the special purpose and circumstances of communication further content elements can be acquired by a sentence connective on the basis of the formulations, the meanings and the facts described in the connected sentences. These content elements occur as *conversational suggestions*—more specifically, as *connexity-suggestions*.
5. The differentiation of semantics and pragmatics in language description, and the differentiation of meaning and use in verbal communication are *theoretical* distinctions; it would be false to assume that in the actual process of comprehen-

sion one begins by applying all and only the semantic rules and then continues with the pragmatic rules. Examples with a sentence connective occurring in the scope of another sentence connective show that the meaning of a complex sentence depends not only upon the meanings of its parts, but also upon their conversational suggestions, and thus, upon their use.

6. To summarize this summary:

   a. The use of a verbal expression is partially determined by the meaning of this expression.

   b. The meaning of a complex verbal expression is determined not only by the meanings of its constituents, but also by their specific use.

In short, in verbal communication we not only make use of meanings but this use even makes sense.

Notes

For helpful comments on earlier versions of this paper, I am grateful to Jerry Edmondson, Donald Freeman, Frans Plank, and David Schwartz. I also want to express my gratitude for stimulating discussions of the material involved to students of linguistics, semiotics, and philosophy of the universities of Hamburg, Montreal, Chicago, Los Angeles, Berkeley, and Stanford. The usual disclaimers apply, of course.

1. The two *façoncs de parler* can be found in any historic-systematic presentation of linguistics, cf. Lyons (1968) and Ebneter (1973). A book exclusively applying the terminology of meaning is Schmidt (1967); presentations applying the terminology of use are Leisi (1953) and Brown (1974).

2. Cf. Grice (1968b) and Grice (1975).

3. Cf. Wundt (1904, p. 596).

4. Cf. Titchener (1912, pp. 367 ff.). See also Hörmann (1970, pp. 166 ff.).

5. Cf. Erdmann (1900; 4th edition 1925, p. 5; reprint 1966).

6. Cf. Watson (1919; 2nd edition 1924, p. 354).

7. Cf. Skinner (1937). See also Hörmann (1970, p. 165).

8. Cf. Morris (1938, pp. 43–48).

9. Cf. Kutschera (1971, 2nd edition 1975, pp. 87 f.).

10. Cf. Alston (1963, p. 84).

11. Cf. Wittgenstein (1953, I:43).

12. Cf. Leisi (1953; 4th edition 1971, pp. 73f.).

13. Cf. Kempson (1975) and Wilson (1976).

14. Cf. Grice (1968b).

15. For this example cf. Gordon and Lakoff (1971).

16. Cf. Dascal (1976, p. 23).

17. Cf. Grice (1968b), 2nd lecture.

18. Cf. Wittgenstein (1953, I:293).

19. Cf. Grice (1968b), 2nd lecture.

20. Cf. Grice (1968b), 2nd lecture.

21. For the methodological value of the three criteria, cf. Walker (1975, pp. 169 ff.).

22. Cohen (1971), who makes a similar distinction, talks about "semanticists" on the one hand and "conversationalists" on the other. However, he does not distinguish between the literal meaning (of a word or a sentence) and the lexical meaning (of a word).

23. Cf. Cohen (1971, p. 56).

24. Cf. Cohen (1971, p. 57).

25. Cf. Wilson (1976, pp. 118 ff.). See also Abraham (1975).

26. Cf. Lang (1977, pp. 230 ff.).

27. However, sentences (12d) and (12g) are ambiguous for many speakers of English. The fact described in the second sentence in (12d) need not be taken to occur later than that described in the first

sentence; it can also be taken to have been a reason for the first to occur. The fact described in the second sentence, in (12g) need not be taken to be explained by the fact described in the first sentence; it can also be given as a reason for it.

28. Naess (1961) has conducted a series of tests which show that even the decision whether the sentence connective *or* must be interpreted as an exclusive or inclusive disjunction depends on the facts described by the disjuncts involved. See also Seuren (1977, pp. 371 ff.).

29. Of course, we are dealing here only with the *and* that occurs between sentences or their transformational variants, not with the phrasal *and*, as occurring in *Peter and Annie went to Saarbrücken*. The proposed treatment can easily be applied to all cases where *and* is used to connect the propositional content of two sentences, even if these sentences are uttered with non-declarative illocutionary force. The treatment of the *and* that connects speech acts of different illocutionary force must, however, be postponed to another occasion.

30. Cf. Morris (1938, pp. 12 f.; reprint 1975).

31. Cf. Cohen (1971, pp. 58 f.). There are a number of other interpretations possible for (17). Even if the order of wedding and birth is as it should be, it is possible that the grandfather is not happy because Annie's husband was not the baby's father. On the other hand, it is conceivable that the truth of all constituent sentences still does not entail the truth of the entire sentence in its intended sense because the grandfather could be happy about something else that he has learned simultaneously. These interpretations are eliminated if we formulate (17) in a more explicit way: *If Annie has married and has had a baby, this is a reason for grandfather to be happy.*

32. Of course, the criteria of variability, cancelability, and non-detachability also apply to embedded sentences. For example, a cancelation of an embedded conversational suggestion is achieved by the following context: *If Annie has married and has had a baby, grandfather will be happy. But the sequence of these events will not leave him unaffected.*

33. The first and second versions are generated by conjunction reduction, and the second and third by pronominalization; in the underlying structures of the first three versions *if* dominates *and*, in the last *if* is dominated by *and*.

34. Cf. Freeman (1973), as opposed to Boettcher and Sitta (1972), who consider sentences like those under (19) to be different forms of realization of the same (semantic) category and the same (pragmatic) structure. Such a characterization would make it impossible to account for the semantic and pragmatic differences of these sentences.

35. Of course, these analyses should not make us blind to the fact that the sequence of the formulations can also express other aspects than the sequence of the events described. Compare *Annie now is a young mother. The fact that she has had a baby and that she has married has made grandfather very happy.* Here the sequence of the embedded clauses is rather used to foreground Annie's new role of a young mother.

36. Compare the procedures of formal logicians, who admit only a truth-functional relation between the complex sentence and its constituents and exclude all pragmatic aspects.

32

GERALD GAZDAR

A Cross-Categorial Semantics for Coordination

There have been two main motivations for the postulation of the transformation known as Co-ordination Reduction (CR).[1] One was syntactic: if, for example, passive and "post-raising" VPs were the product of transformations, then they did not exist in the base and so sentences like (1) and (2) could not involve base VP coordination but must, instead, have resulted from a transformational rule applying subsequent to passivization and raising:

(1)   John loved Mary and was given Fido by her.
(2)   Mary caught Fido and seemed to be pleased.

But if such constituents as passive VPs and "post-raising" VPs are directly generated as has been proposed by a number of linguists in the last few years (e.g., Bresnan 1978; Brame 1976, 1978; Dowty 1978; Freidin 1975; Thomason 1976), then there is no longer a syntactic motivation for CR.

The other motivation was a semantic one: since a (truth-functional) semantic theory was available (in logic) for sentential coordination, but no semantic theory had been proposed for nonsentential coordination, it seemed reasonable to reduce the latter to the former. In this note I shall show how a model-theoretic semantics can be given for *and* and *or* which entirely removes the semantic motivation for a rule of CR (or any interpretivist inverse of it).

All we need to achieve the syntactic effect of the CR transformation is the single infinite phrase structure rule schema shown in (3):[2]

(3) $\alpha \rightarrow \alpha_1 \cdots \beta \alpha_n$
where $2 \leq n$, $\beta \in \{and, or\}$, and α is any syntactic category.

Gerald Gazdar (1980) A cross-categorial semantics for coordination. *Linguistics and Philosophy* 3: 407–409. Reprinted by permission of Kluwer Academic Publishers.

Let us turn our attention now to the semantics. The only crucial assumption we need to make is that NPs denote sets or functions of some kind, rather than individuals. This assumption is independently motivated by Montague's (1974a) demonstration that it allows one to treat quantified NPs and proper names as expressions which denote the same kind of entity. The other assumptions listed below are made for expository convenience—nothing of substance hangs on them with respect to the semantics of coordination. We assume (i) that a property is a function from individuals into truth values, (ii) NPs denote functions from properties into truth values, (iii) VPs denote functions from NP denotations into truth values, (iv) sentences denote truth values, (v) all expressions of other syntactic categories denote functions of an appropriate sort as determined by assumptions (i)–(iv), and (vi) falsity (0) is identified with the empty set ($0 = \Lambda$), and truth (1) with any other set, say the set containing the empty set ($1 = \{\Lambda\}$). This last assumption, incidentally, is the opening move in von Neumann's arithmetic. We ignore matters of intensionality—again simply for convenience; nothing would be changed by, say, our taking sentence denotations to be propositions (functions from possible worlds into truth values) and altering everything else to fit. Note that $1 \cap 1 = 1$. $1 \cap 0 = 0 \cap 1 = 0 \cap 0$, and that $1 \cup 1 = 1 \cup 0 = 0 \cup 1$, $0 \cup 0 = 0$, which are, of course, isomorphic to the familiar truth tables for conjunction and disjunction in the prepositional calculus. We need to recursively define generalized intersection and union operators which will apply both to sets which are not functions, and to functions which share the same domain.

This we do as follows:

(4) $X \sqcap Y = X \cap Y$, if X and Y are not functions, otherwise $\{\langle z, x \sqcap y \rangle : (\langle z, x \rangle \in X) \ \& \ (\langle z, y \rangle \in Y)\}$

(5) $X \sqcup Y = X \cup Y$, if X and Y are not functions, otherwise $\{\langle z, x \sqcup y \rangle : (\langle z, x \rangle \in X) \ \& \ (\langle z, y \rangle \in Y)\}$

We are now in a position to give rules of semantic interpretation for coordinate constructions.[3] Let $M(\alpha)$ be the denotation of the constituent rooted in α with respect to the model M. Then for every model M, and any category α:

(6) $M\left(\left[_\alpha \alpha_1 \ldots \text{and } \alpha_n\right]\right) = \bigsqcap_{1 \leq i \leq n} M\left(\alpha_i\right)$

(7) $M\left(\left[_\alpha \alpha_1 \ldots \text{or } \alpha_n\right]\right) = \bigsqcup_{1 \leq i \leq n} M\left(\alpha_i\right)$

I shall talk about characteristic functions as if they were sets (this makes life easier). Then *John* denotes the set of all John's properties, and *Mary* denotes the set of all Mary's properties, and *run* denotes the set of all property-sets that have as a member the property of running. Given (6), *John and Mary* denotes the intersection of John's properties with Mary's properties—that is, the set consisting of exactly those properties that pertain to both John and Mary. So *John and Mary run* will come out true just in case this intersection has as a member the property of running and is thus itself a member of the set of property-sets denoted by *run*. Given (7), *run or catch Fido* denotes the union of the set of property-sets having as a member the property of running with the set of property sets having as a member the property of catching Fido. So *Mary runs or catches Fido* will come out true just in case this union has as a member the property-set denoted by *Mary*. Analogously for the coordination of other categories.

Notes

The theory proposed here was first presented as part of a talk ("Node Admissibility Conditions, Rule Schemata . . . and Coordination") given in the summer of 1978 to the Syntax Workshop at the LSA Institute at the University of Illinois, and to a seminar at the University of Texas in Austin. I am grateful to those present on both occasions for useful comments and criticism. A related semantics for *and* and *or* has been developed independently by Keenan and Faltz (1978); however, their proposals necessitate a radical revision of Montague's semantic theory which is not envisaged below.

1. I am assuming that CR, or whatever replaces it, is not to be held accountable for the phenomena associated with the rules known as "Gapping" and "Right Node Raising." For nontransformational treatments of these, see Stump (1978) and Gazdar (1979), respectively.

2. This isn't quite right since we need to ensure that the final node and the coordinating word together form a constituent (for reasons given in Ross 1967, 90–91). But that syntactic nicety is irrelevant to present concerns.

3. I'm assuming for the sake of expository convenience that surface phrase markers are directly interpreted by the semantics without the intervention of an intensional logic representation. Nothing hinges on this assumption in the present context.

33

R. E. (RAY) JENNINGS

The Meaning of Connectives

1. The puzzle about semantics

Every act of speech and every inscription is a physical intervention with physical consequences. If during a lecture I emit the stream of sounds «will-someone-please-open-a-window», that emission is a physical event. If I repeat the emission sufficiently many times, it will cause at least one medium-sized mammal to raise itself to something approaching erect stature, shuffle to the side of the room and struggle with a latch. Again, since only organisms produce language, anything that counts as language belongs to the phenomenology of biology. And even the linguistic activities of speech-generating machines, seen in the proper descriptive scale, are biological phenomena, as are the machines that generate them. It is a puzzling thing, therefore, that when we study language we should find ourselves constructing semantic theories rather than physical or more specifically biological ones. Seen in the light of my opening, admittedly banal, observation, language can be understood as a remarkably versatile switch or relay: an exercise of it is a low-energy interaction that triggers similar or larger expenditures of energy at a spatial or temporal distance. So, to put my puzzlement a different way, it is as though alien engineers, charged with acquiring an understanding of a television remote control, should content themselves with figuring out no more than which combinations of buttons produced which channels.

Now to be sure, in the sense in which those alien engineers would have failed in answering the more perplexing questions about the remote control, it is false that the totality of language engineers have neglected the corresponding questions about language. The physics, the physiology, and the neuroscience of language all have their active investigators. Progress is slow but assured. What remains a puzzle is that semantics should be thought to occupy anywhere near so large a part as it is thought to occupy of an otherwise serious explanatory enterprise. Merely to

This is an original chapter for this volume.

say that the satisfaction conditions of the string «will-someone-please-open-a-window» require that someone open a window does not explain the capacity of repeated productions of the string to move organisms about the room, and cause them to struggle with latches. The corresponding capacity of the remote control is, after all, not explained by the observations that "12" is the name of the ordinal of channel 12. Now in the case of the remote control, a plausible rejoinder is that the correlation honored in the labeling of the buttons is *conventional*. But there is no *convention*, in any ordinary understanding of the word, that correlates the phonemic string of my example with that student's fiddling with a latch or with his nearly erect stature, nor indeed with any of the particularities of opening a window on any single occasion. There is, however, one feature genuinely conventional and ordinary linguistic causality share—namely, that, unlike other physical connections, the explanation of the event lies in the history of the causal nexus itself. In broad terms, our linguistic interventions have the consequences that they do because ancestral linguistic interventions had the consequences that they did, and because of the facts of linguistic transmission.

Again, this is not to deny anything of what we ordinarily say in explanation of linguistic success: that the student heard what I said, understood it as an intentional utterance originating in a desire that a window should be opened, and so on. Nor is it to deny that the student would have given some such explanation of his having opened the window. We may say, therefore, that that explanation gives us an understanding of what has happened in the case at least to the extent that we already have an understanding of beliefs, intentions, and desires. The problem, if it is one, is that although every competent speaker of a language might confidently wield its vocabulary of belief, intention, and desire, that fact does not require any speaker to be able to say what beliefs, intentions, or desires *are*; nor have philosophers and others been notably successful in their attempts to do this. Speaking for myself, my understanding of that vocabulary consists entirely in my being able to use it in ways that do not startle my interlocutors. I suppose that the explanation for my using the vocabulary as I do is to be sought in the facts of my linguistic ancestors' uses of it and its ancestors together with the facts of linguistic transmission.

Now, so far, this is merely trite linguistics—a commonplace of our ordinary unreflective understanding of the history of language. I speak the English that I speak because it is the English I have learned and to some extent cultivated. The same can be said of my parents, and theirs before them. Yet the English of the nineteenth century is markedly different from that of the twentieth or the twenty-first, and both are just recognizably prefigured in the English of Chaucer. Facts of ancestral uses and facts of transmission would be of interest to the semanticist only if they yielded a more informative account than semantics can of a sufficiently broad range of quite specific kinds of linguistic behavior and their effects. It would seem at first blush that the level of detail required for such an explanation would be unattainable, and the facts of the case virtually inaccessible. Of course, none of this would constitute an argument against the claims of such an account were one available, only an argument against spending valuable research time in the hopes of satisfying a semanticist. But for those of us who have been dissatisfied with the offerings of the semanticists and the analysts, and who simply want an explanatory physical theory of language—a theory, that is, of the ordinary experimentally confirmable and predictive sort— there is no alternative. Semantics has not so far succeeded, and there is no reason to suppose that it can succeed. In these circumstances an explanatory theory might be all we can have. If, in addition, its offerings satisfy our cravings for understanding within some range of linguistic behaviors, it may be as much as we want. As to the question whether the accessible data are reliable grounds for such a theory, that must await the outcome. In any case, we would be doing no more than following the ordinary path of scientific investigation if we proposed an early theory that eventually gave way to a more expressive or more comprehensive one, confirmable in the measure of its greater refinement.

2   Where semantics defeats us

2.1   The Case of *or*

Since we have no difficulty in using our language—but, in certain sectors of it, have great difficulty in giving a nontrivial semantic account of it—it is a fair conclusion that our use of a language does not require us to possess a semantic theory for it. As I have already remarked, no
satisfactory semantic theory has been given for the vocabulary of folk-psychological explanation. To engage in such explanation requires nothing beyond an ordinary conversational understanding of the vocabulary. That, 1 take it, is what makes it a *folk*-theory: that one is in possession
of it in virtue of being, in the linguistic sense, one of the folk. We exercise it well or badly as we
attend to the nuances of human interaction and have bothered to master the language in which it
is described. Such a one as George Eliot wields the theory with noticeable genius, most of us
with lacklustre ease, some with clumsy and painful imprecision.

Much the same can be said of the natural language counterparts of logical connectives. It
constitutes the language of a folk-logic. The very intelligent and widely read use it well; for some
of us, the task of acquiring it is more difficult than for others; for many, its rudiments are never
reliably mastered. There is this difference, however: that the fundamentals of the theory, at least
as it applies to an artificially narrow band of uses of an artificially constricted range of the vocabulary, can be acquired with a modicum of diligence by the study of academic logic. The well-
instructed student of logic is better off than his counterpart in the philosophy of mind in that he
has a more confident mastery of the logical vocabulary of natural language. And even the mea-
gre store of connective vocabulary that logic studies can, when suitable mathematical methods
are applied, be made to give up a vast lode of abstract theory. Nothing I have to say here is intended as a diminution of the magnificent achievements of logical theorists. But the very success
of logical theory presents dangers to our understanding of natural language. An immersion in
the traditions of logic and formal semantics and a just appreciation of their successes seems to
have inspired in some recent writers what Alan Greenspan would no doubt call an irrationally
exuberant investment of effort in applying its methods to natural language. My aim in what follows is no more than a sober analysis of the state of the semantic market, in the hope that those
who have bought on metaphysical rumor can be persuaded to sell on empirical news. Fortunately
for the analyst, the delusion has had such a hypnotic grip that its tricks of fancy lie in the open,
invisible to the mesmerized, but evident to the casual inspection of any dispassionate observer.
Here I illustrate with a single example: that of English *or*.

It is a curious fact of logical history that until the advent of the truth-table, there was no
noticeable unanimity about the meaning of *or*, and much perplexity. Venn (1971[1894]) says of
the connection between *and* and *or*:

> This must rank among the many perplexities and intricacies of popular speech, but it does not
> seem at variance with the statement that regarded as mere class groupings, independent of par-
> ticular applications, '*A and B*', '*A or B*' must as a rule be considered as equivalent. (45)

Philosophers of the nineteenth century puzzled diffusely over the nature of disjunctive judgment,
but their questions were only rarely put in the form of queries about the meaning of the word *or*.
However the character of that academic discussion became noticeably more focused in the twentieth century as the advent of the truth-table re-presented the central question as that of the connection between the *or* of English on the one hand and 1110 and 0110 disjunctions on the other.
The clarity and simplicity of truth-tabular semantics mainly accounts for the simplicity and un-
clarity of logicians' opinions as to the meaning of *or*. (I say 'opinions', not 'understanding', for
they unselfconsciously use *or* in the full range of its natural roles in their texts. Expectedly, their
explicit explanations and prescriptions are usually at odds with their own practice elsewhere on

the page.¹) Nevertheless, according to the explicit accounts of the great majority of late-twentieth-century introductory logic textbooks, virtually all semantical questions about *and* and *or* can be referred to truth-tables. Moreover, truth-tables have confirmed for many textbook authors that there are two meanings of *or* in English: the meaning corresponding to the truth-conditions of 1110 disjunction ($\vee$), and that corresponding to the truth-conditions of 0110 disjunction ($\underline{\vee}$ or xor). Now we ought to have known at least since Reichenbach (1947) that there is no single piece of English connective vocabulary that corresponds to $\underline{\vee}$, and that it is extremely improbable that any natural language should have evolved such a connective. The reason is that in the general case $\underline{\vee}(a_1, \ldots, a_n)$ will be true when an odd number of its component sentences are true, and false otherwise. Thus $\underline{\vee}(a_1, a_2, a_3, a_4\, a_5)$ is true when either exactly one or exactly three or all of its component sentences are true.

There is, of course, a more fundamental reason why *or* of English cannot be identified with either the $\vee$ or the $\underline{\vee}$ of logic—namely, that $\vee$ and $\underline{\vee}$ are binary connectives. We may tolerate P $\vee$ Q $\vee$ R as an abbreviation because its syntactic ambiguity is semantically benign, but the abbreviation is nevertheless syntactically ambiguous. *He's dead or he's asleep or he's comatose* is not syntactically ambiguous. We do not regard it as an abbreviation of *Either either he's dead or he's asleep or he's comatose* or of *Either he's dead or either he's asleep or he's comatose*. Now that either of these deficiencies might escape the notice even of authors of logic texts, consciously in the grip of their subject matter ought to be expected; it merely confirms an important thesis that holds for all of us: *without conscious investigation, we can have no studied, but only a conversational, understanding of the connective vocabulary of English.* English speakers do sometimes use *or* to form sentences semantically akin to constructions with $\vee$ of formal logic. Nevertheless, the exercises of logic texts are a more reliable source of examples than speech or literary texts, where such formations represent only a very small proportion of the uses of *or*, perhaps 5 percent. Most of the other uses to which English *or* is put, both in literature and in common speech, are semantically quite remote from disjunction. So it may be entered as even more dramatic evidence of my thesis that textbook authors regularly draw on non-disjunction-like uses of *or* to illustrate the differences between what they take falsely to be the main divisions of its uses, giving nondisjunctive examples to illustrate a nonexistent contrast between 1110 and 0110 uses. Thus, for example, Patrick Suppes (1957):²

> When people use "or" in the *exclusive* sense to combine two sentences they are asserting that one of the sentences is true and the other is false. This usage is often made explicit by adding the phrase "but not both." Thus a father tells his child, "You may go to the movies or you may go to the circus this Saturday but not both." (6)

Now since the child is entitled to infer from this pronouncement that he may go to the movies this Saturday, and is likewise entitled to infer from it that he may go to the circus this weekend, the sentence could not be a disjunction of any kind, in fact must be some sort of conjunction. From a disjunction one is not entitled to infer the disjuncts. Evidently, the qualification *but not both* can be applied to non-disjunction-like sentences. We can consistently say such things as "You may go to the movies; you may go to the circus; you may not do both."

Now I stress that the point of these remarks is not to advance any positive thesis about *or* in particular or connectives in general, nor yet to impugn the authors of logic texts for inattention to detail. The whole point of the observations is to underline a fact about natural language: that a conversational knowledge of its vocabulary does not require or provide, and therefore does not guarantee, the existence of a semantic theory. There is no reason to suppose that the authors of English logic textbooks speak English worse than anyone else, and much evidence to suggest that they speak it better than many. But their ability to speak and write the language, like that of the rest of us, does not confer an explicit understanding. And they are Socratically worse off than their pre-tabular predecessors. Before the advent of truth-tables, theorists struggled without success for an understanding of the connective vocabulary of English; the effect of the tables has been that since their introduction the theorists feel no need to struggle at all.

Even Paul Grice, singular as are his contributions to our understanding of conversational uses of connectives, insisted on the sufficiency of truth-tables for the semantics of connectives. Of course, on the Gricean view, we require more than the truth-tabular semantics to explain the *uses* of *or*: for this we rely on a kind of background savvy about conversational exchanges—an acquaintance, not necessarily conscious, with conversational conventions. As Grice sees the matter, a proper understanding of the role of these conventions should forestall suggestions that the natural language correspondents of logical connective vocabulary sometimes have meanings other than those given truth-conditionally by the tables. Grice (1989) does consider one putative "strong sense" of *or*—that in which is conveyed not only that at least one of the disjuncts is true, but also that the assertion does not rest on knowledge as to which disjunct is true. This additional information conveyed is not, he says, evidence of a strong sense of *or* but, rather, of information extracted from the manner of the utterance according to some general rules that regulate conversation. That it is not a part of some strong meaning of *or* is evident from the fact of its cancelability. The reading can be coherently cancelled or forestalled by the addition of some such codicil as '. . . and of course I know which.'

Now a *for-instance* is not an argument. That there is no such strong meaning of *or* does not establish that there are no uses of *or* other than those to which the standard truth-tabular satisfaction conditions apply. In fact, the examples mistakenly given in most of the logic texts are good examples of such uses, and Suppes's illustration "You may go to the movies or you may go to the circus this Saturday . . ." is a case in point. Of course, the father could add somewhat surrealistically "but I don't know which." The effect would be to cancel the hearing according to which assent is *given* to the film-going and assent is given to the circus visit, in favor of a hearing according to which a disjunction of assents is *reported*, but according to which it is not reported which assent is actually given. In fact, we must weigh the oddness of forcing disjunctivity by the cancellation clause against the naturalness of fixing the conjunctive reading by the clause "so you decide which."

We can set beside this the fact that phrases of the same sort as "but I don't know which" can also be used with less oddity to cancel truth-tabular disjunctive readings of *or*, as in "If Elizabeth speaks to him or Margaret speaks to him, Martin will blush, but I honestly don't remember which of them has that effect on him," just as the disjunctive reading can be enforced by the clause "so you decide which to ask." These clauses and others can certainly be used to cancel readings, but they can also be used to differentiate meanings and make explicit the intended relative scopes of sentence elements.

It seems merely to be a fact of the English language that *or* can sometimes be read adsententially as *alternatively*, as in

(1)   Even once you've banished a message to your on-screen garbage, it can be pulled from the trash like a day-old sandwich. Or it can be recovered from your hard drive by someone with the know-how. (*Vancouver Sun*, 1997-02-15)

It seems a mere fact that it will sometimes bear the reading *otherwise*, as in

(2)   The indictment was wrongly drawn, or I could have flogged the man. (Hare 1991b[1946], 170)

and again, the fact that one could vex one's interlocutor by insisting in either such case that one doesn't know which is neither here nor there. If there is an argument capable of showing that cancelability proves that these are really ordinary disjunctive uses of *or*, Grice has not presented it.

There is evidence, in any case, that ought to make us suspicious of any view that would give the truth-conditions of disjunction as the central historical explanation of the uses of *or* in English—even of those uses that superficially accord with the truth-tabular account. In the first place, there are points of continuity between uses of *or* in which the equivalence to conjunction seems explainable by reference to truth-conditions of disjunction, and sentence constructions involving *or* in which truth-conditional equivalence to conjunction cannot be so explained. I refer to what could be called the *ut nunc* (or 'as things are now') character of the conjunction. Suppes's illustration is an example: 'You may φ or you may ψ' is such a conjunction. It is its *ut nunc* character that is reinforced formulaically by the addition of *but not both*. It is to be understood as saying "As things are now, you may φ; as things are now, you may ψ; but it is not guaranteed that once you do one or the other, you will still be permitted to do the other." It is a characteristic shared with some if-clause occurrences of *or*. Consider "If Elizabeth or Margaret offers a suggestion, I'll be surprised." It will be taken to be the claim that if Elizabeth offers a suggestion, I'll be surprised and if Margaret offers a suggestion, I'll be surprised, but it will not warrant the further inference that having been surprised by a suggestion from Margaret I'll be surprised again by one from Elizabeth, and that in spite of the logical truth that if the conjunction is true then the disjunction is also true.

The conjunction of conditionals is another example of *ut nunc* use. Indeed, a conditional theorist might well want the equivalence of $\alpha \vee \beta > \gamma$ with $(\alpha > \gamma) \wedge (\beta > \gamma)$ among his theorems but reject the monotonicity principle $\vdash \alpha > \beta \ \& \vdash \gamma \rightarrow \alpha \Rightarrow \vdash \gamma > \beta$. To be sure, in the formalism this can be regarded as a property of the $>$ rather than as a property of $\vee$, which retains it normal truth-condition, but there is nothing in the natural linguistic facts of the case to make us so regard its natural counterpart, and much about the behavior of *or* in other environments to make us suspect that such *if*-clause occurrences of *or* are more naturally regarded as conjunctive than as disjunctive, including uses, also *ut nunc* conjunctive, in *then*-clauses:

(3)   I will fight you here in London, or, if you are afraid of that, I will go over to France, or to America, if that will suit you better. (Trollope 1972[1864], 748)

A second linguistic fact that ought to cast suspicion upon the doctrine of the centrality of truth-tabular disjunction as the ultimate explanation for this apparent diversity is historical in character. The modern English word *or* is a contraction of *other*, and seems to be the result of a coalescence of two distinct Old English words 'oþer' meaning 'other' or 'second' (as in 'every *other* day') and 'oþþe', which we usually translate as 'or', but which seems to have a range of uses similar to that of *or* in modern English. More generally, it seems to be a fact of linguistic evolution that all functional vocabulary is descended from vocabulary that was lexical in its earlier deployments. There is simply no reason why we should expect anything but diversity from evolutionary developments, and certainly no reason to suppose, in the case of *or*, that all the inherent tendencies of such an item as 'other' toward adverbialization, then adsentential uses (*otherwise*, *alternatively*), and metalinguistic ones such that of

(4)   Sometimes, for a minute or two, he was inclined to think—or rather to say to himself, that Lucy was perhaps not worth the trouble which she threw in his way. (Trollope 1984[1861], 401)

would be absent from the development of its contracted form. One has almost to adopt a creationist's picture of language development to suppose that there would be one use of *or* in English, or of any such connective vocabulary of any natural language, and that use the one corresponding to a truth-conditionally definable item of twentieth-century invention.

That the truth-table specifically has been the instrument of seduction, there can be no doubt. There are no parallel claims in Grice's writings or in those of his followers that in the case of *since* or *so*, both logical words to be sure, the illative uses are primary and their non-illative uses derivative or the illusory products of conversational conventions. No one denies that the *since* of "I've a vehicle since I've a car" is different from the *since* of "I've been driving since I woke up," or that, moreover, if either is the more primitive, the nonlogical use is. No one denies that the *so* of "Fred is happy, so I'm happy" is different from the *so* of "Fred is happy; so Fred is a conscious being." Parallel remarks are warranted by the varieties of uses of *therefore, because, for*, and so on. Their logical uses are derivative, in ways that are not immediately clear, from their nonlogical uses. A semantic theory of the former, like a semantic theory of the latter, will not depend on truth-conditions but will, rather, outline a practice; an explanatory theory will tell us how one practice gave rise to the other, and thereby what the later practice is.

2.2   The case of *but*

It is unclear why Grice should have had such faith in the capacity of truth-tables to provide, with the help of a theory of implicatures, a sufficient semantic account of all uses of *or* in English, unless he was simply under the spell of a logico-philosophical habit of thinking of *or* rather than any other connective vocabulary of natural language as *the* reading of ∨. For if we set that habit aside, consider what parallel universal claims would be grounded by a similar fit. The sole premise vis-à-vis the vocabulary is that there is a use of it that truth-conditionally matches the table. The conclusion is that there are no uses of the vocabulary that do not. By this reasoning we could infer, for example, that the truth-table for ∨, if augmented by a theory of implicatures provides a sufficient semantic account of all of the uses of *but* in English, since the sentence "He avoids me but he wants to borrow money" on one reading has exactly the truth-conditions of the table. In fact, the case of *but* shows remarkable parallels with that of *or* since each has distinct uses that are approximately in the relationship of duality. The disjunctive use of *but*, like that of *or* is relatively rare; it more commonly found in conjunctive constructions, but as in the case of *or*, the whole story of its conjunctive uses cannot be given by a truth-tabular account. Even when we have acquired a conversationally sufficient understanding of it, we have great difficulty in explaining, even to the standards of folk-linguistic explanations what distinguishes the contexts in which it is the right connective to use.

Dictionaries resort to providing approximate synonyms that are both varied and equally difficult. The *Concise Oxford Dictionary* entry adequately illustrates those of the rest: *on the contrary, nevertheless, however, on the other hand, moreover, yet*. Paedagogical grammars classify it as adversative. Even speakers of the most exquisitely cultivated sensitivity, such as H. W. Fowler have a little difficulty: "the mere presence of the opposed facts is not enough to justify *but*; the sentences must be so expressed that the total effect of one is opposed to that of the other." That opposition is not the feature is evident from such examples as "He got here, but he got here late," and any explanation must be such as to explain the conversational inequivalence of that sentence with "He got here late, but he got here." In the end, the way to learn how to use *but* is to become immersed in the practice of its use.

Of course, such an immersion does not afford us an articulable account of what we are doing when we use it. That task, I wish to claim, must fall to an explanatory theory of connectives. Indeed, any sufficient explanatory theory must be capable of explaining satisfactorily the distinctive coordinating role of *but*. It must also yield a unified account of all the uses of *but*, including all of those exemplified by the following:

1. *But* for your help I'd be dead.
2. No one *but* his mother calls him that.
3. It never rains *but* it pours.
4. She wanted to come *but* she couldn't.

5. She was *but* fifteen years of age.
6. My, *but* that's a handsome desk!

Such a theory will also unify those Modern English uses of *but* with Old English *butan* ('outside'), as it will unify uses of *or* with Old English oþer.

3   The shape of a biological theory

3.1   The representation of meaning

If the physical significance of utterance or inscription lies in its effects, then an explanatory theory will make of a meaning an effect-type. For purposes of outline, it wouldn't matter where in the physical world those effect-types were located, but as a convenient first approximation, they can be thought of as neurophysiological and, more specifically, as types of neurophysiological effects that are accessible to the processes that give rise to speech production and other overt intervention. That restriction at least accommodates the fact that speech and inscription sometimes give rise to speech- or inscription-production, but they need not do so. It also occasions future inconvenience, since any such theory must eventually settle on a theoretical language capable of typing such neurophysiological effects in such as way as to accommodate the facts of multiple neurophysiological realization. As will become evident, ultimately such a theory must be capable of distinguishing between two kinds of differences: (a) the differences between two realizations by two different recipients of a single syntactic structure, and (b) the differences between realizations by two different such recipients when one such realization agrees with that of the producer of the string and the other does not. That is to say, it must eventually provide the means of distinguishing the class of realizations that are correct from the class of those that are in error. Certainly at this stage, we can say little or nothing about the fine structure of that language or the details of the effects. Nor do I intend any guesses as to their nature in labeling such effects *inferential effects*, a label intended here simply to locate rather than to characterize the effects in question. The biological theory to be outlined is a theory at the level of population biology, and although even at this level it applies the language of cellular biology, it applies that language to the syntax of sentences, not to the human brain.

Now the facts of linguistic transmission and change are such that the types of what I am labeling *inferential effects* must constitute *species*, where the notion of a species is that of a union of populations temporally ordered by a relation of engendering. The facts of change lend such species features that are also features of biological species. First, virtually every such species is a nonclassical set: every member of it has ancestors for which there is no principled way of deciding whether or not they are members. Second, every member of it has ancestors that are not members of it. Of course, the earliest linguistic species are temporally compressed, as are the earliest biological species, and artificially engineered species (those engendered by convention) require a different story from that of those naturally occurring, but for an explanatory theory of the connectives of English, the language of evolutionary biology is a good fit: if meanings are identified with inferential effect types, then meanings can be spoken of as evolving and historical changes in the range of uses of words as evolutionary changes. The utility of the identification must be judged when the theory has attempted some explanatory work.

3.2   The picture

Two points serve to give concreteness and a sense of scale to what must here be no more than a schematic account. They are not premises of an argument for the account, but they are part of the picture of things upon which the schema to some extent relies. The first remark is a global one:

this representation, though it is constructed for detailed and temporally local explanation, is also promising as a theoretical framework for couching an account of how human or pre-human language began. It is a fair assumption that linguistic inferential effects have ancestors that are nonlinguistic inferential effects and even earlier ancestors that are noninferential effects, such as those consisting in a tendency to detect motion and visually track moving objects. It is plausible to suppose that the earliest steps toward language involved the opportunistic exploitation of such effects.

At the other extreme of scale, the theory invites us to think of a syntactically structured string as a complex system—in fact, in much the way that a microbiologist might think of a polypeptide chain or a larger component of genetic material. The parallels, as they apply to connectives are striking, but again to be judged by the standards of explanatory usefulness rather than by competing disanalogies with the biological case. The parallels come to light only as they are revealed by the conjectured facts of linguistic evolution; they are conclusions, not premises. I register them beforehand only to give concreteness to the picture the account presents.

Biological organisms come in a great variety of shapes and sizes, from viruses to whales. The cells of medium-sized organisms also vary over a wide range of sizes. But by and large, smaller organisms are not smaller because their cells are smaller, but because they have fewer of them, and if we descend to the level of the nuclei of cells, there is remarkably little difference in nuclear size between the smallest and the largest cells of medium-sized organisms and even between the smallest and the largest organisms. It is not a coincidence that nuclei are uniformly so small: it is an essential feature of a method of chemical synthesis that depends on the coincidence of weak molecular forces and therefore on the orientation and proximity of molecules. That is the first point. The second is that the ultimate molecular components of the products of this synthesis have their informational significance not in themselves but in the combinations into which they enter—and, ultimately, in the places of those combinations in the higher-order combinations that constitute the whole. DNA has a syntax. Finally, the uncorrected reading frame errors that give rise to biological mutations are essentially syntactic in character.

The emerging linguistic parallels, which are only general in character, seem to be these: the smallest verbal components have their inferential significance only as they occur within sentences and are dependent for their inferential effects on a hierarchy of structural features of the sentence. Thus, for example, the *or* of "He is asleep or comatose" will be read disjunctively; the *or* of "He may be asleep or he may be comatose" will be read conjunctively. We do not write longer novels by writing longer sentences, but by writing more sentences within a relatively narrow range of lengths. There is some evidence that in conversation we set durational targets for the sentences we produce. There are limitations on our capacities to be reliably affected by complexities of syntax, and those limitations mainly enforce these durational restrictions. Our apprehension of syntactic structure is prosodically assisted. Thus, for example, we distinguish the two syntactic readings of "But for my son I'd stay and fight" by differences of lengthening, pitch contour, and stress. Prosodic control of syntax apprehension also enforces limitations of sentence length. Finally, mutations occur in the meanings of connective vocabulary through undetected and therefore uncorrected misapprehensions of syntax.

3.3   Compositionality

It will already have become evident from the account I am presenting that only some weakened version of the compositionality thesis will be true of natural languages. But some weak version will survive. On whatever account we give of *meaning*, the meaning of a sentence has something to do with the meanings of its component vocabulary together with its syntax, even if the connection between the two is a little murky. As I have already remarked, which meanings the elements of component vocabulary have must sometimes be gathered from an apprehension of syntax in the prosodic presentation. Consider the difference between "What is this thing called love?" and "What is *this* thing called, Love?" Sometimes, prosodic clues having been missed, the determining syntactic judgement must depend on the comparative plausibility of the alternative construals, as in "I'll have breakfast only if we are short of food." Again, I hope that I have already said enough to counter any such suggestion as that semantic problems can arise only for readings of notional vocabulary, that compositional problems arise for connective vocabulary, only through insufficiently marked syntax, that since the semantics is fixed, ambiguities must be ambiguities of scope. As we have seen, even that modest view cannot survive attention to human speech. We might read (5) as a disjunction:

(5)   It will be useful or it will be harmful.

But we would not give a disjunctive reading to (6) except under very unusual contextual pressure, and then we would be at a loss how to take the significance of the disjunction:

(6)   It could be useful or it could be harmful. (Gilbert 1976, 187)

   In fact, there is something unrealistically hypothetical and itself *ut nunc* about the usual basis for claims of compositionality. Some such principle is claimed to be required to explain our capacity to produce novel constructions in speech production and understand them in the speech of others. This may be so, but the fact is that in the course of a day's compositions, we neither produce nor process that many constructions—novel or otherwise. More important, such composition as does go on must, in fact, be a vehicle of meaning change. Else how, for example, did the word *internecine* come to have anything essentially to do with matters within a family, or *specious* anything essentially to do with spuriousness? That notional meanings undergo changes is hardly news, though the details of these changes probably deserve more philosophical study and interest than they naturally excite. Of greater significance for this study is the global fact about connective vocabulary: *All the connective vocabulary of any natural language has descended from lexical vocabulary, in most cases, from the vocabulary of temporal, spatial, and other physical relationships.*

   Thus, as we have remarked, the English *or* is a contraction of *other*, *but* descends from *butan* meaning 'outside', *if* probably from a coalescence of Old English *gif* (if) itself a descendent from the language of *doubt* and the verb *giefan* (give). Much of the vocabulary retains, in modern English, residual nonlogical physical uses (*since, then, therefore, yet, for, as*); some such as *or* have evolved a distinct morphology that masks their provenance. These facts have philosophical significance beyond the trivial remarking of etymologies. If we think that every meaning is the meaning *of* something, then we will conclude from this that at least all naturally occurring logical meanings descend from nonlogical meanings. And if I may interject a further large-scale remark: we will also conclude that human intellectual capacities that reveal themselves in propositionally expressed reasoning have their roots in the natural nonlinguistic propensities of human and pre-human organisms, and we will have some concrete clues as to how the one might have given rise to the other.

   As a topic of study, the descent of connective vocabulary from its physical forbears might be called *logicalization*, in imitation of the related topic that linguists call *grammaticalization*, the process by which lexical vocabulary acquires functional uses (as the *have* and *will* auxiliaries in English tense structure; the *-abo* and *-ibo* endings of Latin past and future verbs, and so on.) Logicalization, in being confined to connective vocabulary, is narrower in scope than grammaticalization, but it is also more protracted as a temporal development, since for much of the vocabulary, connective meanings continue to multiply, even after logicalization. Moreover, these diversities are, on the face of things, sufficiently systematic that any theory of logicalization with pretensions to completeness had better provide the means of explaining them. Now there is sufficient justification for a study of logicalization in its showing us things about our languages that we did not know. The promise that if it gets matters approximately right, its theoretical framework might shed light on the origins of language ought to earn it passive tolerance. But it will have more immediate philosophical cash value also, for if a plausible theory of logicalization individuates multiple meanings of connectives in virtue of its assigning them distinct causal histories, then the theory is an advance on the Gricean theory that connectives have only one meaning, and that the apparent diversity is attributable to conversational implicatures. It will at any rate have provided an argument where Grice has provided none.

4   Evolutionary tendencies

4.1   Usative relations

On a standard semantic account, an n-place predicate φ is interpreted as a n-ary relation, $[\varphi]$ understood extensionally as a set of ordered n-tuples. The intuitive understanding of the interpretation is that the meaning of an n place predicate, φ, is given extensionally by the set

$$\{<x_1, \ldots, x_n> \mid \varphi x_1 \ldots x_n\}$$

—that is, the set of ordered n-tuples of which it is correctly predicated. Thus, for example, a meaning of the preposition *between* is the set of triples $<x,y,z>$ of which it is true that x is between y and z. Since we are interested in the evolution of meanings, that standard semantic account will not quite do for our purpose. The representation we require is not that of a putative established meaning but that of the establishing of it. For this we must broaden our purview to include what I shall call the *usative relation*, «φ» of a predicate, φ. This «φ» includes the set of n-tuples $<x_1, \ldots, x_n>$ of items of which it has ever been claimed that $\varphi x_1 \ldots x_n$. Statistically it would make little difference if it also included the set of n-tuples of items $<x_1, \ldots, x_n>$ of which $\varphi x_1 \ldots x_n$ has been denied. And it also ought to include the set of n-tuples of items of which $\varphi x_1 \ldots x_n$ has been enjoined, and so on. Our purposes do not require a precise or even detailed definition of a usative relation, only mention of its intended role—namely, that it should be the relation that records the accumulated historical uses of the item of speech: that is to say, the set of compositions in which the predicate has played a part. In the case of *between*, it may be said, the record would not be a relation, but a hyperrelation, since it would contain n-tuples and m-tuples for $m \neq n$. In particular, it would include a set of quadruples, each of which comprises a speaker, a hearer, a lamp post, and a piece of information. Neither will it be uniformly spatial or temporal but will include a set of triples, each of which contains two alternative conditions and a choice, as in

(7)   The choice was between five hundred pounds a year . . . or penal servitude. (Trollope 1993a[1871], 181)

It will include another set of triples each containing two items and a relation, as in

(8)   . . . the difference between sinking or floating. (Engel 1990, 252)

It will also record all of the accumulated nonce uses and misuses of the vocabulary, not marking, other than statistically or incidentally, any distinctions among misrepresentations of fact, correct uses, and incomprehensible ones.

A usative relation «φ»" is the union of a temporally ordered set of relations $\{$«φ»$_t \mid t \in T\}$. Each «φ»$_t$ can be defined by «φ»$_t = \bigcup_{i \leq t}\{$«$\varphi$»$_i\}$. Hence, if $t \leq t'$, then «φ»$_t \subseteq$ «φ»$_{t'}$. This temporal monotonicity is a potent instrument of semantic innovation, since, in general, the more the *n*-tuples in the relation, the less the *n*-tuples have in common and, more particularly, the more varied the compositions experienced by any given speaker of the language of which it is an element. Again, the more varied the uses, the fewer the inferential effects that all of the experienced uses have in common and the more frequent the instances of use for which none of the subspecific inferential effects of previous spatial uses is forced or expected. Examples of vocabulary that, without having acquired logicalized meanings, have acquired nonspatial meanings partly through extensional saturation and consequent inferential dilution are *just, straight, right, flat, even*, and *downright*. But prepositions such as *but, without*, and *outside* that have now acquired logicalized meanings also have antecedently acquired nonlogical but also schematized nonspatial meanings.

The point, once appreciated, should make us skeptical of the place of metaphor in these developments. No doubt explicitly metaphorical, nonspatial extensions of physical vocabulary do occur. But we ought to resist the temptation to lay much of the generalizing work of schematization to their influence. The gradual wearing away of the capacity, independently of other cues, sometimes even with them, to occasion particularistic relational inferences can for the most part be regarded as a natural effect of ordinary nonmetaphorical use. The effect has a counterpart in the model-theoretic slogan that the wider the class of models, the fewer the valid formulae, simply because the broader the class of models, the more opportunities there are for any particular formula to be falsified. The larger the usative relation (or hyperrelation), the fewer the particularistic inferential effects supported.

What schematization amounts to in particular cases depends on the character of the ancestral vocabulary. Vocabulary that supports inferences as to spatial relationships will acquire despatialized uses in which no such inferences are supported; temporal vocabulary will acquire detemporalized uses, and so on. There is no reason to suppose, nor does my account require, that the traffic of evolution is all one way in this regard. Plenty of examples come to hand of spatial meanings with temporal ancestors or the reverse and of temporal meanings whose ancestors are inferences of relationship of manner or character. The word *as* alone furnishes sufficient examples.

4.2   Schematization and spatial and temporal examples

Much of the logical connective vocabulary of natural language is descended from ancestral vocabulary whose explication would require mention of spatial relationships, and much of that same connective vocabulary has existent homonymic cousins carrying on in much the original family business and others in related branches of trade. But at an early stage of its evolutionary development, schematized, in these cases, *despatialized* meanings must have emerged. Thus, for example, the subordinator *where* as

(9)   He was four years younger than Donovan with the same fair hair. Where Donovan's was glossy, Bennet's was coarse. (Grafton 1995, 30)

Here, though there are spatial, locational implications expressible using *where*, they are incidental to this fully logicalized use. Again, the conjunction *but* of

(10)   Mrs. Pipkin's morals were good wearing morals, but she was not strait-laced. (Trollope 1982[1875], 399),

since it takes a sentential filling, may be regarded as a logicalized use even if it is unclear which. Nevertheless, it has a distant but homographic Scottish cousin laboring as an adjective meaning *'physically outside'*, and often seen in company with *ben*, meaning 'inside':

(11)   It cannot be brought But that is not the Ben. (*OED.* BUT *s.v.*)

(12)   Gae but, and wait while I am ready. (*OED.* BUT *s.v.*)

Elsewhere, adverbial/prepositional *but* is present only in schematized nonspatial uses. Such a remark as

(13)   There is no one but the house

would seem a curious, perhaps precious, personalization, if not a selection error. The reason is that outside of the much constricted geographical regions in which *but* retains its spatial uses, the residual prepositional use is that of representing schematized relations: *categorial outsideness*:

(14)   I could see nothing but sunshine caught in leaves . . . (Cornwell 1992, 8)

or *circumstantial outsideness*:

(15)   But for the storm he would have given way. (Trollope 1982[1875], 354)

Though schematic, these are not yet logicalized uses. They do, however, take us close, since circumstances can be specified sententially or gerundially. Thus, *but*, though prepositional, could be labeled *protological* in

(16)   But for the fact that there was a storm he would have given way

as it could in

(17)   But that there was a storm he would have given way

a use that takes us to a stage only an ellipsis away from one of the completely logicalized uses such as that of

(18)   It never rains but it pours.

Were this the only logicalized use of *but*, the story could perhaps stop with that explanation. But, as we have seen, and as this sentence bears witness, it is not. It is relatively easy to see how *but* may have become logicalized as a disjunctive connective; the account of its conjunctive logical uses must await a later discussion.

More familiar than the surviving Scottish *but*, which, had its original spelling survived to justify its sense, would be spelled *by out* (as *ben* would be spelled *by in*), is the orthographically more forthright *without* of:

(19)   There is a green hill far away, Without a city wall . . .

a use corresponding to *within*. This spatial *without* has acquired—and, in turn, nearly lost—certain quasi-spatial prepositional uses

(20)   A very violent and painful heat cannot exist without [≈ outside] the mind. (Berkeley 1940[1713], 533)

that can, of course, be party to spatial metaphors:

(21)   he would be beyond the reach of law, and regarded even as without the pale of life. (Trollope 1993b[1882], 26)

This metaphorical spatiality is palpably present in

(22)   I cannot hold myself without abusing him. (Trollope 1992[1882], 134)

but is all but absent in the most usual uses of the word:

(23)   I shall always do as I like in such matters without reference to you. (Trollope 1991[1859], 499)

These are schematized, but not logicalized uses. Yet even *without* can do duty as a sentential connective:

(24)   She could not write the letter without some word of tenderness should go from her to him. (Trollope 1992[1882], 133)

or, more crudely,

(25)   He's a local lad and he won't get far without he's noticed (Hare 1991a[1938], 123),

in which some trace of the ancestral meaning is still discernible.

The curious dualization that, in the case of *but* is apparent only in its fully logicalized uses, emerges in the schematized but still protological uses of *without*. Whereas the *but* dualization has yielded an *and/or* split, the *without*-meanings, are roughly distinguishable as *and not* and *if not*. The divergence is apparent in the following two examples:

(26)   He'll die without help. (*if not*)
(27)   He'll die without fear. (*and not*)

It is worth mentioning as an aside that both *without* and *with* have protological uses, with a meaning approaching that of *because of*:

(28)   We haven't formally started to review it, but with it hitting the news . . . hopefully we'll be getting together next week and bring our findings to Caucus on Sept. 19 (*Coquitlam, Port Coquitlam, Port Moody Now*, 1994-09-03)

Like *without*, *with* has both conjunctive and conditional uses:

(29)   With frugality we'll get by. (*if*)
(30)   We'll get by with plenty to spare. (*and*)

English likewise puts *outside* to schematized, nonspatial uses, as Groucho Marx noticed:

(31)   Outside of a dog, a book is man's best friend; inside of a dog, it's too dark to read.

Compare:

(32)   His driver's license says he's Hulon Miller, Jr., but I doubt if there's anyone outside of his mother calls him Hulon. (Leonard 1992, 153)

Even *under* has found schematized uses, as

(33)   Manners were all that could be safely judged of, under a much longer knowledge than they had yet had of Mr. Churchill. (Austen 1957[1816], 129)

English also affords many examples of schematized meanings that descend from previously temporal ones. I present here only two illustrations: *yet* and *still*. Homographic descendents of *giet* find themselves employed in work, some at greater, some at less remove from the earlier meaning of *before*. Some have meant something like *in all the time before that time*:

(34)   She had no plan of revenge yet formed. (Trollope 1982[1875], i, 255)

Others mean something like *despite that circumstance*:

(35)   He need not fear the claws of an offended lioness:—and yet she was angry as a lioness who had lost her cub. (Trollope 1982[1875], 254)

Again, the obsistive *still* of

(36)   Mr. O'Callaghan was known to be condescending and mild under the influence of tea and muffins—sweetly so if the cream be plentiful and the muffins soft with butter; but still, as a man and a pastor, he was severe. (Trollope 1991[1859], 277)

is cousin to the adjective meaning *unmoving*:

(37)   Mr. Bertram sat still in his chair. (Trollope 1991[1859], 307)

and to the persistive adverb of:

(38)   He still kept rubbing his hands . . . (Trollope 1991[1859], 307).

Having illustrated developments at the earliest stages of logicalization, we move to a much later stage, without pretending that there is no more to be said of stages in between. In fact, a complete account must mention the process by which certain originally multivalent vocabulary acquires trivialized—that is, two-valued readings—and must explain how words that are originally prepositions or relative adjectives come to punctuate acts of speech. Here I offer only what I hope is sufficient evidence of the explanatory usefulness of the approach. So we move to what is perhaps the most intriguing finding of the research.

4.3   Allotropy

The label, *allotropy* is intended to suggest the physical use of the term and its cognates—that is, as denoting or pertaining to a variation in physical properties without variation of elementary matter. Diamonds and coal are allotropic forms of carbon; ozone is an allotrope of oxygen. As applied to a natural language, allotropy picks out classes of sentences that are capable of presenting themselves as of one syntactic kind to one user and of a different syntactic kind to another, while being assigned the same satisfaction-conditions by both. As a nearly trivial example, we may consider the following. A speaker says,

(39)   No trees have fallen over here

expecting the words of the sentence to be taken as having the roles that they have in "Over here no trees have fallen," and a hearer understands the sentence as "Here no trees have fallen over." They agree on the satisfaction-conditions of the sentence, but disagree on its syntax. The near-triviality of the example lies in the semantic idleness of the *over*. Of course, one might argue that the *over* of *fallen over* must therefore have a different meaning from that of the *over* of *over here*. But the effect of *over* in both constructions is at best vestigial, and the difference falls below the threshold of interest for this study. Nontrivial examples present themselves. Consider the two forms $(x)(\varphi x \to \alpha)$ and $(\exists x)\varphi x \to \alpha$, where α contains no free occurrence of x.

They are both formalizations of the schema 'If any x φ's, then α', and either represents a way of understanding the structure ot that schema. For some instances of the schema for which the different structural understandings corresponding to the two formalizations require no difference in the understandings of the satisfaction-conditions. The alternative formalizations correspond to allotropes of the schema. Notice that in one allotrope the work of *any* in the original schema is that of a long-scope universal quantifier; in the other it is that of a short-scope existential quantifier. Now for some α's, in particular, for those in which there is anaphoric reference to the whole *if*-clause, a satisfaction-conditionally significant syntactic ambiguity persists. The sentence

(40)   If any student touches my whisky, I'll know it

remains ambiguous as between (41) and (42):

(41)   If any student touches my whisky, I'll know that *some* student has touched my whisky.
(42)   If any student touches my whisky, I'll know that *that* student has touched my whisky.

Indeed, the availability of the former reading should sufficiently tarnish the sometime-expressed thesis that *any* is just a natural language long-scope universal quantifier. But, such examples aside, such conditionals are generally capable of distinct but allotropic representations of the sort given. The ambiguous anaphora of (40) confirms that neither allotrope is a uniquely correct representation and that the contrary assumption for particular cases buys no greater simplicity overall.

Negative environments also can be allotropic. Consider

(43)   I will not be brought under the power of any (I Corinthians 6:12),

which could be represented by the form $\neg(\exists x)Bx$ or by the form $(x)\neg Bx$. By contrast, interrogatives, which together with hypotheticals and negations make up all of the occurrences of *any* in the King James Version of the Bible, are nonallotropic, requiring something akin to an existential reading.

The allotropy hypothesis, as applied to the evolution of meanings, is the hypothesis that certain meanings of certain connective vocabulary are the product of a development that depends on allotropy in the sense given. In the generation of such meanings, there is a stage in which identical sequences of words, with identical or sufficiently similar satisfaction-conditions, presents one syntactic structure to one subpopulation of their users and a distinct syntactic structure to another. The evolutionary significance of allotropy is that, by using it, the earliest populations of a new meaning can be hidden and therefore protected from correction by mature populations of an older one. For convenience I shall refer to new meanings allotropically nurtured in this way as *succubinal* meanings and distinguish them by overlining. This suggests that the older, fostering meaning should be called *incubinal* and marked by underlining. Were the account to be applied directly to *any*, and were the case as simple as an examination of the King James Version of the Bible might suggest, it would regard the uses that tempt or require representation by existential quantifiers as having common ancestors with incubinal, *any*, those, such as "free choice" *any* that seem to require representation by universal quantifiers as descendents of succubinal, *any*. In fact, if some such developments account for the existential/universal dual personality of *any*, they must have occurred much earlier than in Jacobean times. The duality of use is likely inherited from *aenig*, which, in written remains, occurs predominantly in allotropic and interrogative environments earlier than the eighth century, but in its normal universal role in comparisons as well. Beowulf boasts to Unferth that he has more strength in swimming "þonne aenig oþer man" (l. 534).

It will be evident that the adjective *succubinal* refers to a stage in the generation of a new meaning. At that stage the population of users can be classified accordingly as their parsings require the incubinal or succubinal representation. So while that stage persists, there may be no generally accessible evidence that a new meaning is emerging. It is only when the new meaning is out from under the old that there can be said to be two meanings in the ordinary way of speaking—which is to say, two meanings equally available to both populations of users. The new meaning must *migrate* to nonallotropic environments in which commonly recognized satisfaction-conditions demand the formerly succubinal meaning. In the case of *any*, such an environment might be permissive or probabilistic, or the use may be triggered by adjacent vocabulary, such as

(44)   Those people probably saw things much stranger any given day of the week. (Grafton 1995, 171)

Here, perhaps, the comparative "stranger" triggers the use of *any* because comparatives normally take *any* (as *stranger than any fiction*). We will return to the matter later, but the point deserves a little flag here. The evidence suggests that adjacent vocabulary *triggers* use, rather than that conscious consideration of the *meanings* of adjacent vocabulary gives rise to deliberate deployments. As we shall see, this involuntary feature of speech-production quickly gives rise to hybridizations as vocabulary with formerly succubinal, now migratory, meanings combine with surrounding connectives as though still bearing their formerly incubinal meanings. This to the confounding of any simplehearted compositionality doctrine.

5   Mutations

Usually, we may assume, the syntax produced by a speaker is the syntax received by the hearer. Sometimes, however, this is not so. On such occasions, one of two conditions must prevail: either the error is syntactically negligible, as in (39), or it is not. If the error is not syntactically negligible, then we might suppose that one of two conditions must obtain: either the error is satisfaction-conditionally negligible, or it is not. We need not set the standards of negligibility puristically high. If a speaker says "I don't think she's there yet," and the hearer mistakenly takes this to be the claim "I think that she's not there yet," the satisfaction-conditional difference between the two, though not formally negligible, may nonetheless make no practical odds. This may sufficiently explain why the English language tolerates negation-raising verbs (though Griceans might insist on explanatory elaborations). If the difference is not satisfaction-conditionally negligible, then one of two conditions must arise: either the syntactic error is eventually corrected, or the hearer persists for a while in satisfaction-conditional error as to what was said. This, I say, is how one might have thought the cases would bifurcate.

In fact, there seems to be an intermediate case: namely that, roughly speaking, the syntactic error should be satisfaction-conditionally compensated for by a semantic one. A more precise account of what happens in the misconstrual of (39) might be made in these terms: the speaker's syntax of "fallen (over here)" is imperfectly replicated as hearer's syntax "(fallen over) here," but the error is compensated for by a semantic error in which the otiose *over* of the construction *over here* is understood as the non-otiose *over* of the construction *fallen over* (as distinct from *fallen in, fallen through*, and so on). Under certain conditions, when the syntactic error is compensated for by a novel or nonstandard semantic construal, new meanings can be introduced, which are appropriately thought of as *mutations* in something very close to the molecular biological sense of the word:

> The replacement of a codon specific for a given amino acid by another codon specific for another amino acid is called a *missense mutation*. On the other hand, the change to a codon that does not correspond to any amino acid is called a *nonsense mutation*. The existence of extensive degeneracy means that most mutations are likely to cause missense rather than nonsense. Missense mutations produce proteins changed in only one location, and so the altered proteins which they produce frequently possess some of the biological activity of the original proteins. The abnormal hemoglobins are the result of missense mutations. (Watson 1965, 374)

> Mistakes in reading the genetic code also occur in living cells. These mistakes underlie the phenomenon of suppressor genes. Their existence was for many years very puzzling and seemingly paradoxical. Numerous examples were known where the effects of harmful mutations were reversed by a second genetic change. (378)

> Those mutations which can be reversed through additional changes in the same gene often involve insertions or deletions of single nucleotides. These shift the reading frame so that all the codons following the insertion (or deletion) are completely misread. (379)

Now some of the nonsense mutations produced by such "reading frame" errors of English have been recognized as nonsense by sensitive listeners without having been diagnosed as mutations. Consider this exchange between the naive and immature Catherine and the better educated Henry Tilney (*Northanger Abbey*)

> . . . 'Have you had any letter from Bath since I saw you?'
> 'No, and I am very much surprized. Isabella promised so faithfully to write.'
> 'Promised so faithfully!—A faithful promise!—That puzzles me.—I have heard of a faithful performance. But a faithful promise—the fidelity of promising! It is power little worth knowing however, since it can deceive and pain you.' (Austen 1993[1818], 209–210)

There need be no doubt (since Henry has put his finger on it) that Austen could see how this nonsense use of *faithfully* has come into English: through some earlier misreading of the adverb as applying to the finite verb where it had applied to the succeeding infinitive. To promise *faithfully to write* makes some sort of pleonastic sense; to promise *faithfully* to write makes none. Nevertheless, the legacy of this syntactic misconstrual is the idiomatic coupling of *faithfully* and *promise* as

(45) I promise faithfully not to explore. (Milne 1980[1922], 143)

It would seem that, in the case of notional vocabulary, the distinct meaning that arises through such an error persists as an idiom only within the very restricted environment that gave rise to the error, and it does not propagate through migration to others. In this case, the reason is perhaps that *faithfully* does not seem to have any nonperplexing new meaning when attached to forms of *promise*. Something along the same lines could be said about negation-raiser verbs. Suppose the verb *think* were to acquire a distinct succubinal meaning through the construal of (46) as (47):

(46) I don't think she'll come.

(47)   I think she won't come.

The succubinal <u>t̄h̄īn̄k̄</u> would bear the relation to the standard <u>think</u> represented in the equivalence 'I <u>t̄h̄īn̄k̄</u> that α iff I do not <u>think</u> that not α'. That there is no such noncommittal meaning of *think* in English is sufficient proof that no such development has taken place. And we might suppose a priori that any such development would be unlikely. One reason might be that positive verbs of attitude are too well established in their range of uses for such a noncommittal use to persist uncorrected in negation-free environments; another is that the negation-raising reading is sufficiently robust that *I do not <u>think</u> that not-α* will be read as *I <u>think</u> that α*. Again, one might look to some such development to explain the anomalous *doubt but as*

(48)   I do not doubt but that the Viet Cong will be defeated. (Richard Nixon)

This venerable construction was already current in Jacobean English:

(49)   No doubt but ye are the people, and wisdom shall die with you. (Job 12:2)

But the anomaly is explained by the presence in English of a use of *doubt* having approximately the force of *fear* or *suspect* as in

(50)   There I found as I doubted Mr. Pembleton with my wife (Pepys 1663-5-26)
(51)   ... she could not forbear telling me how she had been used by them and her mayde, Ashwell, in the country, but I find it will be best not to examine it, for I doubt she's in fault too ... (1663-8-12)
(52)   ... he is not so displeased with me as I did doubt he is (1663-12-8)

and so on. In fact, for most of the biblical occurrences of *doubt*, there is sufficient contextual evidence, sometimes quite explicit, to support some such "middle voice" reading as *be in perplexity about* or *weigh the evidence for and against*, rather than the "active voice" reading as *think improbable*: in fact, at least seven distinct Greek verbs and nouns are translated as 'doubt' in the King James Version of the New Testament. And the preferred construction *doubt whether* is itself evidence that a distinct middle voice reading, now largely superseded, was once standard. If the *doubt but* construction is explained as an isolated survival of an earlier weak positive *doubt*, then it may be that the standard (*suspect-that-not*) use of *doubt* is the product of just the sort of mutation that stronger positive verbs of attitude so robustly resist; for the standard use approximates the use that one would predict as likely to arise, through mutation, from negated negation-raising uses of the Pepysian *doubt*. A strong verb's *modus tollens* is perhaps a weaker verb's *modus ponens*.

5.1   Metanalysis

Jespersen (1922) introduced the term *metanalysis* as a label for a phenomenon in the process of word formation:

> Each child has to find out for himself, in hearing the connected speech of other people, where one word ends and the next one begins, or what belongs to the kernel and what to the ending of a word, etc. In most cases he will arrive at the same analysis as the former generation, but now and then he will put the boundaries in another place than formerly, and the new analysis may become general. (174)

Thus we have *an umpire* from *a numpire*, *an apron* from *a naperon*, *a nickname* from *an ickname*, and so on. In such cases the mutation comes about through a misapprehension of the divisions between words. Jespersen is rather vague in the matter of how such a mutated form survives, but we can note here at least the prime condition for such a survival—that the discrepancy between speakers and audience in alternating roles should go for a time undetected, and therefore that it should make no or sufficiently little difference in the satisfaction-conditions of sentences in which the discrepancy occurs. And of course, as the difference is undetected, the metanalytic population has a chance to become established.[3]

5.2 Scope evasion

The term *metanalysis*, transposed to the level of syntactic structure, would serve equally well to label the initial stage of the development that I label *scope evasion*, for it, too, springs from a misapprehension of divisions within sentences, though at the clausal level. The more important difference is a dimensional one. For Jespersen the significance of metanalysis lies in the introduction of a new verbal expression of an existing meaning: in the course of the development *umpire* came to mean what *numpire* had meant. For us, its significance lies in the introduction of a meaning that did not previously exist. In the physicalist idiom adopted here, Jespersen's observation can be couched in semantic language as well, since, for example, *umpire* comes to have a meaning where previously it had none. But in all but one of the cases we consider, the outcome of the metanalysis is that a word that previously had *n* meanings comes to have *n + 1*. I begin with the exception.

Unless is a striking example of a connective for which the original meaning, which had a conjunctive component, has become extinct in favor of a disjunctive one, and apparently through evasion of the scope of negative sentence elements. The evidence for this lies in two features of its early development. The first is that its earliest uses are found exclusively in negative constructions; the second is that it represents the surviving coalesced core of *on [a] less [condition than that]*. Setting aside the scalar feature, the ancestral meaning of α unless β is α *with the condition that* β *unmet*, that is α *without* β—that is, α *and not* β.[4] Thus the ancestral, elementary meaning of *not . . . unless . . .* is that of not(. . . and not _____)}. The ancestral, elementary meaning of that construction, of course, gives the truth-conditional meaning of *not . . . unless* _____ in its current use, but its elementary meaning is *not*(. . .) *if not*_____. or *not*(. . .) *or* _____, the *unless* being represented by the *if not* or the *or*. The establishment of a reading in which the negative element has foreshortened scope sponsored uses in which the negative element was absent. And over that enlarged field of use we may regard *unless* as univocal, provided that the negating elements, when they occur, are always given a short-scope reading. The disjunctive reading of *unless* is sufficiently robust to withstand repositionings and the introduction of negators such as *It's not the case that*, with long scope intonationally made explicit.

It is plausible to suppose that the conditional *and* of middle and Jacobean English, the *and that*, in Shakespeare, early editors clipped to *an*, had been speciated by an earlier parallel development in which in certain constructions *not*(. . . *and* . . .). was read *not*(. . .) *and* . . . , the *and* being construed conditionally to make up the construal of the whole:

(53) Ich nolde cope me with thy catell · ne oure kirke amende,
      Ne take a meles mete of thyne · and myne herte hit wiste
      That thow were such as thow seist; · ich sholde rathere sterue. (Langland. C Passus VII. 288–290)

Compare such a construction as (54)–(56):

(54) I do not think that you should go and she stay behind.

(55)   Could he have come out and we didn't see him? (Wingfield 1995, 261)

(56)   Why am I a redhead and you have dark hair? (@discovery.ca, 1995-12-26)

Here the structure of the clause following the *and* is such as to permit a foreshortening of the scope of the negation or the modal *could* or interrogative *why* with substitution of *if* for *and*, a transformation skeletally recognizable in the *PL* equivalence: $\neg(\alpha \wedge \beta) \dashv\vdash \neg\alpha \leftarrow \beta$. It seems likely that the adversative *but* including its arrogative use (as in *not black but dark blue*) was engendered from the propositionally exceptive *but* by scope evasion. At the initial stage we would expect to find despatialized *but* in its propositionally restricted use inside the scope of a negative or modal sentence element:

(57)   He had not been long upon the scout but he heard a noise. (Defoe 1908[1722], 147)

Here what is denied is that the subject had been long on the scout without hearing a noise. If the scope of the negation is foreshortened and the sentence taken to imply absolutely that the subject had not been long upon the scout, then the sentence as a whole can have approximately the same conversational effect if it is taken, in virtue of its second clause, to imply that the subject heard a noise, and this quite independently of any understanding of the force of its *but* on this reading. Once a nonexceptive use is introduced, it can shelter beneath the exceptive use for all verbs that can be made nontrivially subject to exceptive clauses, but it must force a nonexceptive reading for verb phrases not plausibly so subject. Thus, for example, the *but* of

(58)   He wasn't given to literary exercises, but he was neat and methodical. (Snow 1974, 252)

Even without the comma, this would have no plausible exceptive reading. The foreshortened scope made explicit, the nonexceptive reading, however to be understood, persists even in the presence of preceding negations and exceptively modifiable verb phrases:

(59)   In the mystery itself there is not the slightest interest. But the mysteriousness of it is charming.
       (Trollope 1967[1867], 398)

The exceptive *but* of this development, as we have so far discussed it, is a multivalent one: the exceptive clause limits the range of some multivalent magnitude or manner of engagement of some activity. Exceptive *but* has also a bivalent use in certain conditional constructions:

(60)   I should not now have spoken to you at all, but that since we left England I have had letters from
       a sort of partner of mine (Trollope 1983[1867], i, 236)

Here a number of elements are individually significant. First, the exceptive reading is reinforced by the subordinating *that*. Second, the sentence is reliably factive at its second clause; that is, it invites (through the perfect tense of its verb) the inference that the content of the second clause is being asserted. In the presence of the second of these factors, the omission of *that* might generally prompt a nonexceptive reading, though even in the absence of *that* an exceptive reading, at least for an audience of any but recent literary experience, will be prompted by an indefinite present tense. My informal surveys of introductory logic students find very few who need not struggle to understand the central example disjunctively:

(61)   It never rains but it pours.

The puzzling character of the adversative coordinator is the product of the scope foreshortening of the negative or modal sentence element. Certainly, the effect is as in other similar developments—that the connective loses its disjunctive reading in favor of a conjunctive one—but the historical connection with the despatialized, *outside* reading of *but* is rather obscured than lost. That that connection shapes the conjunctive use of *but* is, I think, undeniable. With a properly attuned theoretical language we can account for the puzzling adsentential character of the new use. But a fine-grained account of how speech production adjusts to such new uses requires a detailed neurotheoretical understanding that we simply have not got.

Inspection reveals a similar development in the case of *for* which, from an earlier 'because' meaning,

(62)   The crew were beginning to get very much the worse for drink. (Dexter 1989, 53)

has evolved a later 'in spite of' reading:

(63)   And yet she was alert, for all the vagueness of her manner. (Potter 1986, 149)

But as a final example, I observe that *English* has a dualized *if* that seems to have come about by this process of scope evasion. The diathetic condition that rendered propositional *if* susceptible of this kind of mutation seems to have been the difficulty in English of negation placement in *if*-constructions, and possibly the obscurity of satisfaction conditions for conditionals, an obscurity inherited by their denials. In general, dualized *if* can be marked by *even*, but just as frequently it is marked only prosodically. The A *if*, we think of conveniently as the *sufficiency if*. The B *if*, we can label the *insufficiency if*. The two following examples illustrate them in that order. Contrast (64) with (65):

(64)   If he wins the lottery, he'll be MISERABLE.
       (Winning will make him miserable.)
(65)   If he wins the LOTTERY, he'll be miserable.
       (Winning won't cure his misery.)

Even in their material representation, the two are distinct, the material representative of the latter being deductively stronger than that of the former. That is: $\neg(\alpha \to \neg\beta) \vdash_{PL} \alpha \to \beta$, but $\alpha \to \beta$ $\nvdash_{PL} \neg(\alpha \to \neg\beta)$. The conjectured origin of this *if* is the misapprehended scope of a negation placed in the main clause as if in

(66)   I wouldn't do that, if the QUEEN (herself) asked me.
       (Her asking me would be insufficient.)

a short-scope sufficiency *if* with long-scope negation (*n't*) is read as a short-scope negation with long-scope *if*. The satisfaction-conditions being kept constant, the *if* must be given an insufficiency reading.

From a formal point of view, the dualized, insufficiency *if* (sometimes marked as *even if*, sometimes only prosodically) has the appearance of a sort of hybrid. The reason seems to involve the triggering phenomenon mentioned earlier. In the production of speech, the choice of conjunctive connective, whether *and* or *or* is determined by habituation rather than the anticipations of interpreted manipulation. Since sufficiency *if*-clauses with *or* are effectively conjunctive, so are those of insufficiency *if*-clauses. But since English sufficiency conditionals distribute conjunctively over a disjunctive *if*-clause, a negated conditional ought, at least by the standards of logic, to be read as a disjunction. Nevertheless, insufficiency conditionals also distribute conjunctively over disjunctive *if*-clauses. So, for example,

(67)   If the king OR the queen asked me I wouldn't do it.

will be read as

(68)   If the king asked I wouldn't, and if the queen asked I wouldn't.

but does not commit us to:

(69)   If the king AND the queen asked me I wouldn't do it

since though they might be insufficient severally, their requests might be jointly sufficient. So dualized *if* is left-downward nonmonotonic.

6   The stages of mutation

In appropriating the language of *mutation*, I claim only an abstract connection with the microbiological phenomenon. That there should be such a connection is striking only to those who have not attended to the most obvious feature of language, namely that it is a biological phenomenon transmitted through successive biological populations. The nature of specifically linguistic mutation must be a study in its own right. The following represent something like an average account of its stages, of which at least six seem to be distinguishable.

1. *Genesis.* In the case of mutation by scope evasion, the first stage in the production of a new connective meaning is the initiating scope misapprehension (by members of population B), typically involving negative and modal sentence elements (in the speech of population A), with the resulting combination of approximately correct (or at least indetectably incorrect) apprehension of satisfaction conditions on the one hand and undetected incorrect processing of syntax on the other, which forces an incorrect (or at least novel) apprehension of the use of the connective.

2. *Incubation.* The primary association intended by the label as used here is with the period during which a population of viruses establishes itself in a host organism, rather than with the hatching of a single organism from an egg. But there is a respect in which the process resembles the second: if we regard the novel reading as a *misconstrual*, then it is a misconstrual that is protected from correction by the practical overall synonymy of the proper and improper construals of the sentence as a whole. The new construal is in this way sheltered by the old one, and is conversely dependent on it, since there is no guarantee at this stage that the connective in the incorrectly apprehended use is viable in environments outside those of the highly specific kind in which it was engendered.

3. *Autonomy.* At this stage the newly engendered reading can be obtained for the connective even in the absence of a sentence element of the kind given a scope-foreshortened reading at an earlier stage. At this stage, we find occurrences of conjunctive *unless*, or suppositional *and* in the absence of negation, but otherwise in roughly the same sentence position, as,

    (70)   He shall be glad of men, and he can catch them. (Dekker 1933[1600], II, iii)

4. *Migration.* Among the early sites to which one would expect the connective in its new construal to migrate from the environment that engendered it to sites nor-

mally occupied by the connectives with which it has been newly construed as synonymous. In this stage, suppositional *and* migrates to other *if* positions, as:

(71)   Faith, and your foreman go, dame, you must take a journey to seek a new journeyman; if Roger remove, Firk follows. (Ibid.)

In such a migration, the new reading is still protected, but now by the presence of positional and modal cues which defeat a conjunctive and force a suppositional reading.

5. *Ambiguity*. When a meaning engendered by scope evasion is fully established, the reintroduction of the connective into a construction of the kind that engendered the new meaning will give rise to a semantic ambiguity, either clause of which is expressible by either of the dual readings of the connective.

6. *Marking*. In the fifth stage, the new meaning is disambiguated from the old by order or by the addition of markers generalized from particular cases or types. At this stage we find the 'in spite of' *for* at this stage marked by the addition of *all*, detached from content, and attached to the connective:

(72)   To him Zeus handed over the power, 'for all he was young and but a greedy infant' (Guthrie 1952[1935], 82)

We find universal *any* and anticipative *in case* marked by *just*:

(73)   I've never had any time for these women who go out and leave their children all day with just anyone. (Barnard 1986[1980], 18)

(74)   There was a path up to the summit he felt sure, but it might be as well to keep off it, just in case the men were looking in that direction, expecting someone else. (Barnard 1983[1977], 153)

7   The general idea

I say nothing more in defense of the evolutionary approach to the study of connectives that I have been advocating. It is essentially an Aristotelian approach, which W. K. C. Guthrie sums up pretty well:

(75)   Since motion and change are the most characteristic marks of nature, it is precisely these that have to be understood and explained—not run away from. (1981, 102)

But having said that, I must confess that the investigation of the principles of linguistic change would not be of such interest to me if it did not also dissolve puzzles about the present state of things. This, I think, this approach does accomplish: it explains both the fact and the details of the diversity of connective uses, of which I have here offered only a few examples. And where folk-semantical accounts are difficult to give, as in the case of *but*, this approach also explains the difficulty.

That, of course, speaks only to that aspect of the account that treats of the logicalization of connectives. It says nothing of that aspect of the theory with which I began—its being, as far as possible, a physical theory, rather than a semantical one. Since I seem to have made free with semantical notions such as satisfaction and satisfaction-conditions and so on throughout the exposition, it will be as well to say something about them here. I have said that acts of speech are physical interventions and that they typically have what I have called inferential effects. It should be added that, typically, acts of speech are interventions in situations in which many features of the environs have inferential effects, in which features have already had effects and in which effects of expected change are anticipated. It would, therefore, be equally correct to say that acts of speech are typically operations on effects. That is, they present dynamic modifications of the effects of other occurrences—spoken, gestural, and nonlinguistic. And it is part of the picture that parts of acts of speech are dynamic alterations and adjustments of the effects of other parts of the same acts of speech. Within that general viewpoint, we are able to hypothesize the roles of connectives understood as discriminating distinct operations on effects. Here I mention, as an illustration, only one connective, conjunctive *but*.

Conjunctive *but* is subtractive with respect to inferential effects. The effect of the *but*-clause (the subtrahend clause) of "He got here, but he got here late" to cancel or nullify or reserve some of the expected effects of what could be called the *minuend* clause. This explains the non-commutativity of such constructions—that is, why "He got here, but he got here late" is not intersubstitutable in conversation with "He got here late, but he got here." This last subtracts, by the reminder that he got here, from the effects of the utterance of "He got here late." Notice that such constructions are not compositional as that term is usually understood. The effect of the subtrahend is the subtraction of effects, but the effects to be subtracted are not determinable from the subtrahend clause independently of particularities of the minuend.

Notes

1. For example, see Jennings (1994), pp. 70–71.

2. For a more extensive sampling, see Jennings (1994).

3. Canadian English furnishes a charming example of metanalysis. The *drawing up* of a writ is constitutionally dictated preliminary to the holding of an election. The *draw up* of the formulaic announcement has been heard as 'drop', with the result that it is now standard usage to speak of the prime minister as *in course of dropping the writ* or as having *finally dropped the writ*. The absurdity of the construction is evidently sufficiently masked by the presumption of antique obscurity that attends parliamentary language generally.

4. In fact, *without* has undergone a similar mutation, except that in the case of *without* both uses survive. Compare *she'll die without medical attention* and *she'll die without betraying her friends*.

34

JAMES HIGGINBOTHAM

Interrogatives

1 Introduction

It is a pleasure to be able to present this paper as part of a volume to honor Sylvain Bromberger. My subject, interrogative sentences and the questions that they express, is one on which he has thought and written deeply and at length. I am specifically indebted to Sylvain for discussion in our seminar from some time back, and for many conversations over the years. Above all, however, I am grateful to him for his support early on of my hybrid research into language and philosophy, and I hope he may think that this work justifies it at least in part.

In this paper I advance some parts of a view of interrogative sentences and their interpretations, with reference to English examples. The details of this view depend upon assumptions about the semantics of embedded indicative sentences that I use but do not defend here. I therefore distinguish at the beginning the major theses I advance about interrogatives, which I would urge even apart from these assumptions, from others that will show up in the details of execution. The major theses are these:

1. The semantics of interrogative sentences is given by associating with them certain objects, which I will call *abstract questions*: I will say that the interrogative *expresses* an abstract question. To utter the interrogative is to ask the abstract question that it expresses.

2. Pairs of *direct* questions, as in (1), and their corresponding *indirect* questions, as in the italicized complement of (2), are related in this way: the direct question expresses what the indirect question refers to:

(1) Is it raining?
(2) John knows *whether it is raining*.

James Higginbotham (1993) Interrogatives. In Kenneth Hale and Samuel Jay Keyser (eds.), *The View from Building 20: Essays in Linguistics in Honor of Sylvain Bromberger*. Reprinted by permission of MIT Press.

3. Indirect questions are singular terms, and they occupy quantifiable places of objectual reference. Thus, for example, the argument (3) is valid:

(3)   John is certain (about) whether it is raining;
        Whether it is raining is Mary's favorite question; therefore, John is certain about (the answer to) Mary's favorite question.

4. *Elementary* abstract questions (what is expressed by simple interrogatives, or referred to by simple indirect questions) are partitions of the possible states of nature into families of mutually exclusive (and possibly jointly exhaustive) alternatives. *Complex* abstract questions (the result of quantifying into interrogatives, or conjoining them, as explained below) are constructed out of elementary ones. These form a hierarchy of orders, with abstract questions of order n being sets of sets of abstract questions of order $n - 1$.

5. Abstract questions can be constructed by generalizing along any of several different semantic dimensions and can be referred to by appropriate syntactic means even when their dimensions of generality are not domains of quantification in the indicative fragment of a language; such categories include those of predicates, quantifiers, and even parts of words. However, most abstract questions are not the reference of any interrogative sentence at all.

In sections 2–5 I present informally a number of definitions and illustrations of the point of view I advance. In section 6 I turn to a defense of theses 1 and 2. In the final section, which I have labeled an appendix because it involves more material from logic and linguistics than the others, I argue that an explanation of the licensing of negative polarity items in interrogatives can be seen to follow from the proposal I develop here and in other work.

2   Preliminary definitions and illustrations

An *abstract question*, what is expressed by an interrogative form, is not itself a linguistic form (although it is in a sense constructed from linguistic forms, in a way explained more fully below), but on the present view a nonempty *partition* Π of the possible states of nature into *cells* P_i for $i \in I$, having the property that no more than one cell corresponds to the true state of nature (i.e., the cells are mutually exclusive). If in addition at least one cell must correspond to the true state of nature, then Π is a *proper* partition (i.e., the cells are jointly exhaustive). The elements of a cell P_i can be thought of as statements, so that P_i corresponds to the true state of nature if and only if all the statements that it contains are true.

Partitions are used in probability theory, and I will freely adapt terminology from there. If Π is a partition, and S is a set of statements, let $\Pi + S$ be the result of adjoining S to each P_i. Thus, if $\Pi = \{P_i\}_{i \in I}$, then $\Pi + S = \{P'_i\}_{i \in I}$, where, for each i, $P'_i = P_i \cup S$. Since Π is a partition, so is $\Pi + S$; but Π may be proper, while $\Pi + S$ is improper.

A cell of a partition may be *satisfiable* or *unsatisfiable*. Let F be some designated unsatisfiable set, fixed throughout the discussion, for example, $F = \{p \ \& \ \neg p\}$. F is the *degenerate* set, and the improper partition $\{F\}$ is the degenerate partition. If Π is a partition, let Π^- be the result of deleting the unsatisfiable cells from Π (or $\{F\}$ if all are unsatisfiable). If S is a set of sentences, let Π/S, or the *conditionalization* of Π on S, be $(\Pi + S)^-$. Then Π/S is a partition. Also, we evidently have

$$(\Pi/S_1)/S_2 = (\Pi/S_2)/S_1 = \Pi/(S_1 \cup S_2)$$

An *answer* to a question Π is a set S of sentences that is inconsistent with one or more cells in Π. If Π is the degenerate partition $\{F\}$, then S answers Π for every S. S is a *proper* answer if it is an answer and Π/S is not $\{F\}$.

The notions introduced by the above definitions may be illustrated through a fabricated example. Let Π be a partition whose cells are statements about the possible outcomes of rolling two dice A and B, where the outcomes are distinguished according to the total shown by the dice. There are eleven cells, which will be represented by the numbers 2 through 12, each of which stands for a complex disjunctive statement giving the outcomes that would add up to those totals; thus, cell 6 is

(Die A: 1 & Die B: 5) or (Die A: 2 & Die B: 4) or . . .
. . . or (Die A: 5 & Die B: 1)

Then Π is a partition, since the outcomes are regarded as functions of A and B, and it is proper given the background information that the values of these functions are integers between 1 and 6.

The above proper partition Π is one way of construing the question expressed by (4),

(4)   What was the total of the dice?

incorporating further information about how totals in a throw of two dice may be obtained. A person who asks (4) will be said, following Belnap (1963), to have *put* the question Π.

Consider now the statements in (5) as responses to (4):

(5)   a. (The dice totaled) 12.
       b. (I don't know but) one came up 4.
       c. The sun is shining.
       d. The dice were never thrown.

In much of the literature on interrogatives, it is answers like (5a) that have been chiefly considered. Their relation to the interrogative sentence is particularly intimate: they provide *instances* of the matrix *the total of the dice was (the number)* _____, instances that are also in a sense *canonical* to the type of question asked: that is, they are *numerical* instances, rather than non-numerical instances like *the total of the dice was the number of the apostles*. Objects themselves, rather than their standard names, can also be taken as filling the blank in the matrix above. Following this course, I regard the instances arising from substitution of names as *presentations* of the instances arising from assignment of the objects themselves.

In discussions including Karttunen 1977 and Hamblin 1973, the question expressed by an interrogative was simply the totality of its instances (Hamblin) or, alternatively, the totality of its true instances (Karttunen). The totality of instances for (4), which might be indicated by abstracting over the empty matrix position as in (6),

(6) λx (the total of the dice was x)

is a natural candidate for the abstract question expressed by (4), and the question arises whether the further step to partitions does not create a needless complexity.

My belief is that the definition of answerhood requires the more complex structure. Besides canonical and noncanonical instances, there are answers that give only partial information, as illustrated by (5b). Partial answers give information by being inconsistent with some, but not with all but one, of the possibilities enumerated in the partition. Obviously, they must be distinguished from irrelevant remarks like (5c).

Not that (5c) is necessarily irrelevant. If it is known that the dice are crooked, loaded somehow to show double-six when the sun shines on them, it may be just as informative as (5a). Such knowledge, and background information more generally, is appealed to in seeing that Π really is a partition (thus, the more general notion is that of a partition *relative to* background *B*). An answer that contravenes background conditions violates the *presuppositions* of a question, in an appropriate sense of this term.[1] Technically, if X is a presupposition of Π, then every cell of Π implies X, and so if S is inconsistent with X, then S is inconsistent with every cell of Π, so that $\Pi/S = \{F\}$. The response (5d) thus violates the presupposition of (4) that the dice were thrown.

Summing up, I have suggested that simple interrogatives express partitions (relative to background assumptions), and that complete and partial answers, nonanswers, and responses that violate presuppositions can all be appropriately characterized on that assumption.

Consider now some examples or interrogatives. The partitions corresponding to yes-no questions are the simplest possible. They have two cells—one representing the affirmative, the other the negative. The elements of these cells need not be contents, in any sense over and above that of the sentences themselves, as interpreted in the indicative part of the language. Thus, for the question *Did John see Mary?* we have the partition (7):

(7)   {{*John saw Mary*} | {*John did not see Mary*}}

(I use a bar rather than a comma to separate the cells of a partition.)

For a simple *wh*-question, as in (8),

(8)   Who did John see?

I assume the logical form (9):

(9)   [WHα: person(α)]? John saw α

The cells or the partition expressed by (8) run through all the possibilities for John's seeing of persons. If in contexts there are just two persons in question—say, Fred and Mary—then a typical cell is {*John saw Fred*, $\neg$ (*John saw Mary*)}, representing the possibility that John saw Fred but not Mary.

The question (8) with its quantification restricted to persons must be distinguished from the question (10), involving unrestricted quantification:

(10)   Which things are such that John saw them and they are persons?

This can be seen by noting that (11) is a (partial) answer to (10), but is in response to (8) simply an irrelevant remark.

(11)   Fido is not a person.

It is also seen, rather more vividly, in pairs like (12)–(13):

(12)   Which men are bachelors?
(13)   Which bachelors are men?

The unrestricted question corresponding to both of these examples is (14):

(14)   Which things are both bachelors and men?

But of course (12) and (13) are very different.

The generalization that the quantifications *which N* must be understood as restricted, with the variable ranging over things that in fact satisfy *N*, is supported by examples like (15),

(15)   Which philosophers would you be annoyed if we invited?

where we never have an interpretation that would "reconstruct" the noun within the scope of the modal, giving a meaning like that of (16):

(16)   For which things x would you be annoyed if x was a philosopher and we invited x?

See Reinhart 1992 for similar examples.

Higginbotham and May (1981) showed how to characterize presuppositions of singularity, as in (17):

(17)   Which person did John see?

An utterance of (17) in virtue of its form carries the presupposition that John saw one and only one of Fred and Mary. Its partition will carry the presupposition in question by having only two cells—one affirming that John saw Mary and not Fred, and the other that John saw Fred and not Mary. The cells for affirming that John saw both and that he saw neither will not be represented. Similar remarks hold for presuppositions that are expressed by words rather than morphologically, as in (18):

(18)   Which two articles did Mary read?

Nothing prevents our asking *wh*-questions ranging over infinite domains, or domains for which we could not possibly have a singular term for every object in the range. Thus, the question expressed by (19) is perfectly in order, although we shall be powerless to give it a complete answer:

(19)   Which real numbers are transcendental?

The partition expressed by this interrogative will have cells on the order of the set of all subsets of the real numbers.

Multiple questions call for more refined partitions, as in (20):

(20)   Which people read which books?

The elements of the cells of these partitions will be sentences like "John read *War and Peace*" and their negations.[2] The account of single and multiple *wh*-questions extends to the case where the position interrogated is not in the main clause, but in one or another embedded position or positions, as in (21):

(21)   Which people did he say like to read which books?

Finally, it should be noted that many *wh*-forms incorporate prepositions or subordinating conjunctions, as *where* incorporates *at*, and is effectively equivalent to *at which place*, and *why* incorporates either *because* or *in order to*. The latter gives a simple example of interrogatives that generalize over predicate positions, so that (22), in one of its interpretations, should be taken up as in (23).

(22)   Why did John go to the refrigerator?
(23)   [WHF] ? John went to the refrigerator in order to F

Questions like (24) have long been noted ambiguous:

(24)   What did everybody say?

Intuitively, (24) asks, for each person in the range of the quantifier *everybody*, what that person said. There are some syntactic limitations on expressing questions of this form.[3] Our interest here, however, is quite general: What is the question expressed by an interrogative as in (25), where Q is a restricted quantifier, ϕ is the restriction on Q, and θ is another interrogative?

(25) $[Qv: \phi]\, \theta$

The answer is that the question should be composed of sets of questions, one set for each way in which the quantifier, construed as a function from pairs of extensions to truth values, gives the value *true*.[4] A simple example like (26) will generate the basic idea:

(26)   Where can I find two screwdrivers?

A person who asks (26) may mean to inquire what place is an x such that there are two screwdrivers at x. But she may also mean just to get hold of information that will enable her to locate two screwdrivers, and in this sense of the question it arises from the interrogative (27):

(27)   [Two x: screwdriver(x)] [What α: place(α)] x at α

The partition for the embedded interrogative

[What α: place(α)] x at α

is given by our previous semantics: 'x' is simply a free variable here. Now, the numeral *two*, construed as a restricted quantifier, is such that

Two ϕ are θ

is true if and only if at least two things satisfy both ϕ and θ. So the question expressed by (27) will be the class of all classes of partitions each of which, for at least two screwdrivers a and b as values of x (and for no other objects than screwdrivers as values of x), contains the partition for the interrogatives

[What α: place(α)] a at α
[What α: place(α)] b at α

The classes of partitions I call *blocs*, and classes of them *questions of order 1*. To *answer* a question of order 1 is to answer every question in one of its blocs. It follows that to answer (26) is to answer both the question where a is and the question where b is, for at least two screwdrivers a and b.

The above method of quantifying into questions extends to all quantifiers, since it is completely determined by their extensional meanings. A scrutiny of actual cases shows that any quantifier that is not monotone-decreasing (in the sense of Barwise and Cooper (1981: chapter

23 in this volume; see the discussion in section 5 below) can in principle get wide scope in an interrogative, including even the existential quantifier, as in one interpretation of (28):

(28)   What does somebody here think?

Intuition suggests that a speaker of (28) would expect from whoever elects to be his respondent the answer "*I* think so-and-so," and that any such answer would be sufficient for the question. The theory accords with this intuition, since the abstract question expressed by the interpretation of (28) shown in (29) consists of all nonempty sets of sets of abstract questions of the form in (30), where a is a person in the domain of quantification:

(29) $[\exists x]$ [WHα] ? x thinks α
(30)   [WHα] ? a thinks α

Truth-functional *and* and *or* are recruited for conjunction and disjunction of interrogatives, as in (31) and (32):

(31)   Will it be nice tomorrow, and will you go on a picnic if it is?
(32)   Is Mary happy or is John happy?

Their role is clarified by the analogy between connectives and quantifiers. Conjunctive interrogatives, as in (31), are obviously answered only by statements that answer both conjuncts. In the present terminology, (31) expresses a question of order 1, whose sole bloc consists of the partitions expressed by the conjuncts. Disjunctive interrogatives, as in one interpretation of (32), will have the meaning, "Choose your question, and answer it." They express questions of order 1 whose blocs consist of one or both of the partitions expressed by the disjuncts.

The more common type of disjunctive question is the *free-choice* type, exemplified by (33) in an airline setting:

(33)   Would you like coffee, tea, or milk?

My view of the role of disjunction in these cases, as explained in Higginbotham 1991a, is that they represent universal quantification into a yes-no question, as in (34):

(34) $\forall x: x = $ coffee $\vee x = $ tea $\vee x = $ milk]? you would like x

Thus, the steward who asks (33) is asking for each of coffee, tea, and milk whether you would like it (subject to the understood condition that you will have at most one of these).

Finally, multiple quantification into questions is possible and will generalize so as to produce questions of arbitrary finite order. Such questions include (35),

(35)   What did everybody say to everybody?

with both quantifiers taking wide scope.

Thus far I have considered partitions and abstract questions of higher orders with respect to domains of quantification that have not been incorporated into the abstract questions themselves. Consider (8), repeated here:

(8)   Who did John see?

The proper representation of the abstract question that it expresses must include the information that the property of having been seen by John is under consideration only for persons as values.

Let K be the class of persons, and let $\Pi = \pi(\textit{John saw } \alpha[K])$ be the partition obtained by assigning just the objects in K as values of α. If the abstract question expressed by (8) is to be distinguished from the extensionally equivalent one expressed by *Which rational animals did John see?*, then information about how the class of values is determined must be incorporated somehow.

We have already seen that domain restrictions cannot be represented by conjuncts within a question—for example, that (8) must be distinguished from *Which things are persons such that John saw them?* However, we could include in each cell of the abstract question expressed by (8) the information, about each thing in K, that it is a person. If $[person(\alpha)[K]]$ is the class of atomic sentences $person(a)$ for $a \in K$, we can propose the partition $\Pi' = \Pi + [person(\alpha)[K]]$ as answering to (8), thus distinguishing it from extensional equivalents.

However, Π' still fails to contain the information that the class K comprises *all* persons. This further information can be added where feasible, but is not finitely representable when the restriction is to an infinite class, for instance as in (36):

(36)   Which natural numbers are prime numbers?

Similarly, a set of instances constituting a complete true answer cannot always be replaced by a finite list L, together with the information that all the positive (negative) instances are to be found on L. Such is already the case for (36) since the set of prime numbers is neither finite nor cofinite.[5]

3   Indirect questions

An *indirect question* is an interrogative sentential form used as an argument. In general, I believe no distinction except a syntactic one should be made between the sentential argument S and the nominal argument *the question S*: both are singular terms. Thus, we have both (37) and (38):

(37)   I asked whether it was raining.
(38)   I asked the question whether it was raining.

Now, certain verbs that take interrogative complements cannot take nominal complements: thus, (39) is ungrammatical:

(39)   *I wondered the question whether it was raining.

Pesetsky (1982) observes, however, that this fact may be reduced to an issue of abstract Case (the verb *wonder* does not assign Case to its complement, which therefore cannot be nominal); and that the introduction of morphemes, normally prepositions, for the purpose of assigning Case gives grammatical sentences whose meaning is just that of the corresponding sentence with a sentential complement. Thus, we have both (40) and (41):

(40)   I wondered whether it was raining.
(41)   I wondered about the question whether it was raining.[6]

Inversely, the verbs that take both nominal and sentential complements can appear with Noun Phrase complements whose interpretation is that of interrogatives. These are the so-called concealed questions, exemplified by (42):

(42)   I asked the time (what the time was).

In all the above cases, in the view developed here, the complements refer to the abstract questions that they would refer to if used in isolation (with the necessary superficial syntactic adjustments). Thus, to ask whether p is to ask $\{p \mid \neg p\}$.[7]

With the epistemic verbs—and, indeed, with all verbs whose arguments are naturally taken to refer to propositions or to facts—interrogative complements are mediated by relations to answers to the abstract questions that they refer to. Thus, I assume that (43) is interpreted as in (44):

(43)   Mary knows who John saw.
(44)   Mary knows the (or an) answer to the question who John saw.

Berman (1989) has called attention to sentences with indirect questions in conjunction with quantificational adverbs, as in (45) and (46):

(45)   Mary mostly knows who John saw.
(46)   With some exceptions, Mary knows who John saw.

Examples are not limited to epistemic verbs, as (47), modeled after examples in Lahiri 1990, 1992, attests:

(47)   John and Mary mostly agree on who to invite.

I look upon these adverbs (differently from Berman) as qualifying the nature of the answers said to be known, or as in the case of (47), agreed upon; for example, (47) will be true if, out of a potential guest list of 20, John and Mary have agreed for (say) 15 on whether or not to invite them. See Lahiri 1992 for further discussion.

Finally, there are interrogative arguments to verbs that have nothing to do with acts of speech or mental states. Karttunen (1977) noted indirect questions in contexts such as (48):

(48)   What will happen depends on who is elected.

Predicates like *depend on* express relations between abstract questions, and the notion of dependence at stake, applied to (48), comes to something like: Answers to the question who is elected, together with other facts, imply answers to the question what will happen. There are many other similar locutions, such as *is influenced by*, *is relevant to*, and, of course, their negations.

It is worth observing that (48) leaves open the exact nature of the dependency, or the ways in which who is elected will influence what happens. In the parallel and simpler example (49), it may be that rising temperature causes rain or prevents it, and you may know (49) without knowing which it is:

(49)   Whether it will rain depends on whether the temperature will rise.

4   Extensions to higher types

The basic apparatus developed here can be applied to construct abstract questions with respect to expressions of any syntactic category, independently of whether they occupy quantifiable places in the indicative fragment of a language. The sense in which the variables bound by *wh*-expressions have a range then dwindles toward the substitutional. For instance, interrogatives like (50) are likely to be put forth only where a fairly narrow range of linguistic alternatives is envisaged:

(50)   What (profession) is John?

Even questions expressed with *which* are often best answered simply by filling in appropriate material in the site of syntactic movement. So for (19), repeated here, an answer might be as in (51):

(19)   Which real numbers are transcendental?
(51)   Those real numbers that are not solutions to any equation are transcendental.

Engdahl (1986) has called attention to interrogatives like (52),

(52)   Which of his poems does no poet want to read?

where, understanding the pronoun as a variable bound to *no poet*, the answer might be as in (53):

(53)   His earliest poems.

I accept Engdahl's view that these interrogatives likewise involve quantification over non-arguments, in this case over functions. Thus, their logical forms might be represented as in (54):

(54)   [Which f:$(\forall x)f(x)$ is a poem by x][For no poet y] y wants to read $f(y)$

The need for functional interpretations of this kind is not confined to questions, since it occurs also with relative clauses, and even with definite NPs, as in (55):

(55)   John made a list of the dates no man should forget.

John's list might read as follows:

   children's birthdays
   own wedding anniversary
   Independence Day
   . . . .

The list is a list of those f whose domain is the class of men and whose range is included in the class of dates $f(x)$ such that no man x should forget $f(x)$.[8]

   The recent discussion by Chierchia (1991) shows that for many purposes quantification into interrogatives can be replaced by the functional interpretation. I illustrate using the example (24), repeated here:

(24)   What did everybody say?

Suppose we understand *what* as having a functional interpretation, as in Engdahl 1986, and incorporate an appropriate description of the functions over which it ranges, as in (56):

(56)   [WHf : $(\forall x)$ x says $f(x)$] ? $(\forall y)$ y said $f(y)$

Example (56) must be allowed as possible anyway, because of possible answers to (24) such as (57):

(57)   The speech she had memorized.

But now we might regard the listiform answer (58) as simply one way of specifying a desired function f:

(58) Mary said this, and Susan that, and Margaret the other.

The representation of (24) as (59) appears then to become redundant:

(59) $(\forall y)$ [WHα] ? y said α

There are several points that would have to be clarified before (56) and (59) could be declared equivalent. As I have defined the interpretation of (59), true and complete answers to it must exhaustively specify for each person y what y said and also what y did not say. If this view is carried over to (56), then exhaustive information about the functions f would be required to answer it, and not merely the specification of some f. On the other hand, in any context in which (58) is a complete and true answer to (59), it is a complete and true answer to (56) as well.

The logical limitations of functional interpretation surface when the exported quantifier binds a variable within a larger *wh*, as in (60):

(60) Which picture of each student should we put in the yearbook?

A complete answer to (60) might be listiform, as in (61), or involve pronouns as bound variables, as in (62):

(61) (We should put) this picture of Jones, and that picture of Smith, and . . . , and that picture of Robinson.
(62) The picture in which he is wearing a hat.

From (60) we have the representation (63):

(63) [$\forall x$: student(x)] [WHα: α a picture of x] ? we should put α in the yearbook

For a functional interpretation of (60), we can no longer apply the routine exemplified in (56) but would instead have to posit something like (64):

(64) [WHf : *domain*(f) = the students & $(\forall x)f(x)$ is a picture of x] ? $(\forall y)(\forall z)$ [y is a picture of z $\rightarrow$ (we should put y in the yearbook $\leftrightarrow$ $y = f(z)$)]

There are also a number of cases where listiform answers are unavailable, which nevertheless admit functional interpretation. Among these are (65) and (66):

(65) Who did President Vest shake hands with after each student introduced him to?
(66) Which of his relatives does every student really love?

Only functional answers like *His or her mother* are appropriate for (65) and (66).[9] On the assumption that listiform answers are salient only where there is quantification into questions, these data follow from known conditions on scope of quantifiers and pronominal binding. Thus, in (65) we do not expect to be able to assign *each student* wide scope, since it is not interpretable with wide scope in (67):

(67) President Vest shook hands with his mother after each student introduced him to her.

Taken all together, then, these problems indicate that, besides functional interpretations of *wh*, genuine quantification into questions is possible in rather basic sentences of English. And in any case there is no difficulty in constructing sentences with *explicit* quantification into questions, as in (68):

(68)   I want to know for each person what that person said.

I return now to some final points about higher types for *wh*. One can sweep out positions for whole clauses (with *why*) or adverbs (with *how*) and even quantifiers, with *how many*, as in (69):

(69)   How many books have you decided to read?

Note that (69) is ambiguous, having either the interpretation indicated in (70) or that in (71):

(70)   [WH*Q*] ? You have decided to read [*Q* books]
(71)   [WH*Q*] ? [*Qx*: book(*x*)] you have decided to read *x*

All of the cases just discussed seem to fall under the theory presented here.[10]

5   The presentation of questions

The semantics of questions, as I have presented it above, abstracts completely from the ways in which the objects, or the things in ranges of higher types that are values of the interrogative variables, are given to us, or may be given to a questioner or respondent. It furthermore abstracts from the questioner's motives, if any, and other pragmatic matters. It seems to me that semantic theory, and especially the theory of truth for sentences with interrogative complements, requires this abstraction. We can raise questions that we do not know how to answer, and for which, as Bromberger (1966 and elsewhere) has pointed out, we do not even know what an answer would look like. There is, thus, no requirement in the general case that we have an effective procedure for determining whether a statement is a complete answer to a question—or, indeed, whether it is an answer at all.

The distinction between abstract questions and the ways they are presented to us is clearest when the questions are about objects, which may be given from many different perspectives. Thus, to the question *Who did John see?*, the response *John saw Bill* is, technically, not even a partial answer, since we are not given which object as value of the interrogative variable a is the reference of *Bill*.

In context, however, matters are not so bleak. We can conceive that the values of the variable are referred to by antecedently given singular terms and thus regard the response as a partial answer after all. More generally, given an abstract question $\Pi = \pi(\theta(a)[K]) + [\phi(a)[K]]$, where ϕ is the restriction on the values of a, K is the class of objects satisfying it, and $\theta(a)$ is the matrix predicate over which the partition is constructed, and given a class C of closed singular terms in 1–1 correspondence with the members of K, if $[\phi(a)[C]]$ is $\{\phi(c/a): c \in C\}$ and $\pi(\theta(a)[C])$ is the partition obtained from $\pi(\theta(a)[K])$ by replacing the objects in K by the respective terms in C that refer to them, we may define $\Pi_c = \pi(\theta(a)[C]) + [\phi(a)[C]]$ as the *presentation Π_c of Π with respect to the substitution class C*.

A presentation of an abstract question is an abstract question in its own right. In practice we are interested in presentations. If Jones asks me who is playing which position in the outfield, and I respond that the left fielder is playing left field, the right fielder is playing right field, and the center fielder is playing center field, I have understood his question all right, and feign not to understand his presentation. It should not be inferred, however, that we can take the presentations and let the questions of which they are presentations go. We can, for example, ask questions whose presentations we know we would not recognize or for which we have no particular presentations in mind. Furthermore, by relating abstract questions to their presentations, we clarify, for instance, the sense in which we say two persons may ask the same question, perhaps without realizing it.

Special attention must still be paid to questions [WHα: $\phi(\alpha)$] ? $\theta(\alpha)$ where in fact nothing satisfies ϕ at all. Their abstract questions will be $\{F\}$, and so not distinct from any number of other questions expressing $\{F\}$. Going intensional does not ameliorate the situation, since there are also restrictions $\phi(\alpha)$ that are not even possibly satisfied by anything. These cases underscore the fact that in practice the presentations are more nearly what matters to us than the questions they represent. I do not see this consequence as a difficulty of principle, but it does show that a full pragmatic theory must consider the case where, for instance, a person thinks she is asking a nondegenerate question but fails to do so.

A further pragmatic and computational issue that is clarified by the conception of abstract questions as partitions, and of partial answers as statements or sets of statements that eliminate certain of the possibilities that the cells of the partitions represent, is that of interpreting what Hintikka (1976) has called the *desideratum* of a question, or the quantity of information that is wanted by the person asking it. A simple *wh*-question such as example (8), repeated here, may be associated with different desiderata:

(8)   Who did John see?

On the view that I have defended, (8) has the logical form (9),

(9)   [WHα: person(α)] ? John saw α

and the partition it expresses runs through all the possibilities for John's seeing of persons in the domain of quantification, or at least all that are left open by the background theory.

The desideratum of (8) is, therefore, not represented in the question expressed. But desiderata can be so expressed, and among these (as Belnap and Hintikka have pointed out) the *existential*, represented by (72), and the *universal*, represented in Southern American English by (73), are quite common:

(72)   Who for example did John see?
(73)   Who-all did John see?

Question (72) asks for an example, and (73) for an exhaustive list, of persons John saw. But intermediate desiderata are possible, as in (74):

(74)   Who are two or three people John saw?

The desideratum of an abstract question may be regarded as a set of statements—namely, those that are "sufficiently informative" (even if possibly false) with respect to that abstract question. Each abstract question comes with its own *minimal desideratum*—namely, those statements that are partial answers to it. But not all partial answers meet even the existential desideratum; thus, (75) is a partial answer to (9) but would not meet the desideratum that at least one value of α be supplied that is a person John saw:

(75)   John saw Mary or Bill.

This desideratum, signaled explicitly in (72), is the class of those S implying, for some person a, *John saw c_a.* Similarly, the desideratum of (73) is

$\{S$: For all persons a, S implies *John saw c_a* or $\neg$(*John saw c_a*)$\}$

Note that (74) has a desideratum in between the universal and the existential. Desiderata may also involve substantive conditions not limited to quantity, as in (76):

(76)   What is a surprising/routine example of popular novel?

In general, a partial answer to an abstract question Ω with desideratum D is a statement in D that is a partial answer to Ω; and the ordering of desiderata by stringency corresponds to an ordering of partial answers by informativeness.

I return now to some points about quantifying into questions. First of all, with which natural-language quantifiers can one quantify in? Certainly, I think, with all of those that are not monotone-decreasing in the sense of Barwise and Cooper (1981: chapter 23 in this volume), where a quantifier Q, interpreted via a map f_Q from ordered pairs of subsets of the domain A of quantification into truth values, is monotone-decreasing if $f_Q(X,Y)$ = truth and $X' \subseteq X$ then $f_Q(X',Y)$ = truth. Examples of quantifiers not monotone-decreasing have been used in the illustrations above. Monotone-decreasing quantifiers, such as *at most two people* (77) or (at an extreme) *no one* (78), can never take wide scope:

(77)   What do at most two people have to say?
(78)   Is no one at home?

The reason is intuitively clear: it is that, when a question [WHa: $\phi(a)$] ? $\theta(x,a)$ is to be answered for at most two values of x, as in (77), or for none of them, as in (78), then it may be answered by answering for none—that is, by saying anything at all. This intuition corresponds to the feature of our construction that since there is a bloc for each set of persons consisting of at most two of them (for (77)) or none of them (for (78)), there is in each case a bloc for each set of persons consisting of none of them—that is, a bloc $\{\{F\}\}$. Answerhood then becomes degenerate. From the definition, S answers either of the questions expressed by (77) or (78) with the quantifier taking wide scope of S answers $\{F\}$, the sole question in the bloc $\{\{F\}\}$, and it answers $\{F\}$ if inconsistent with F, an unsatisfiable sentence. Then S answers F, and so answers the question, no matter what S may be.

6   Mood and reference

My discussion thus far has gone forward on the assumption that theses 1 and 2 of my introduction are correct: namely, that interrogative sentences express abstract questions, and embedded interrogatives refer to the questions that would be expressed by their direct counterparts. There are three major alternatives to these assumptions.

The first, which has been taken up in various forms, is that the interrogative, like the imperative, optative, and perhaps other moods, is constructed by attaching an indicator of mood to an indicative (moodless) core. The meaning of the mood indicator then becomes an issue, and the issue of the reference of indirect questions is left up in the air. However, the idea that the difference between *It is raining* and *Is it raining?* semantically speaking is only in their mood and not in their content is one that has enjoyed wide appeal, and I will therefore consider it in some detail.

The second alternative, elaborated especially by Jaakko Hintikka, is that all questions, whether direct or indirect, dissolve upon analysis into the more ordinary apparatus of propositional attitudes and ordinary quantifiers. On this view, not only are there no moods but also there are ultimately no quantifications like *wh* distinctive of questions. This view faces serious difficulties once we move outside direct questions and the complements to epistemic verbs and propositional attitudes, as noted by Karttunen (1977); I will therefore say no more about it here.

The third alternative, which has been prominent from time to time and is defended elegantly if briefly by Lewis (1970: chapter 11 in this volume), is that all questions are really indirect, and apparently direct questions amount to indirect questions as complements of an unexpressed performative prefix, with the meaning of "I ask" or "I ask you." To the obvious objection that it seems absurd to call interrogatives true or false, it may be responded that we do not call performatives true or false, either. However, on the view I will defend, this alternative is not so much mistaken as it is redundant: of course it is true that whoever utters an interrogative asks a question, but we do not need the higher-performative analysis to explain this.

A theory of meaning must explain why uttering an indicative sentence is saying something (not necessarily asserting it), and it must explain why uttering a *that*-clause is not saying anything but simply referring to a proposition. The explanation in truth-conditional semantics is that only sentences, or utterances of sentences, admit of truth and falsehood. That is why, in uttering a sentence, one may, in Wittgenstein's words, "make a move in the language game," and, inversely, why in uttering a *that*-clause in isolation, no move is made at all.

This explanatory charge carries over to nonindicatives. In uttering *the question whether it is raining*, one merely refers to a question, but in uttering *Is it raining?* that question is necessarily asked. But since direct questions do not appear to have truth values, the sense in which utterances of them must ask things is not apparent.

The higher-performative analysis reduces the problem of direct questions to the previous case of indicatives. Utterances of *Is it raining?* are regarded as notational variants of utterances of *I ask* (*you*) (*the question*) *whether it is raining*. Since the latter are indicatives, and say things, so do the former. The type of saying is asking, since that concept was built into the analysis.

But in fact all of this is unnecessary. Just as the semantic value of an indicative is a truth value, so the semantic value of a direct yes-no question is an unordered pair of truth values—one for each cell of its partition. Just as the semantic value of a *that*-clause is a proposition, so the semantic value of an indirect yes-no question is an unordered pair of propositions. And just as the proposition that it is raining is expressed by *It is raining*, so the pair {the proposition that it is raining, the proposition that it is not raining} is expressed by *Is it raining?* It follows immediately, first, that interrogatives cannot be called true or false; and, second, if we assume that *ask* is nothing but that variant of *say* whose proper objects are questions, that whoever utters an interrogative asks a question.

Care must be taken in not freighting up the notion of asking here with any of the motives for raising a question. English has *say* and *assert*, where to assert is to say with assertive force. The verb *ask*, however, is ambiguous. In one sense it amounts to *say*, but its objects must be questions. In another sense it involves what we might call interrogative force (and is so understood in the higher-performative analysis). One can raise questions to which one perfectly well knows the answer, or doesn't care what the answer may be, and one can also raise questions nonseriously. An actor on a stage says things without asserting them and utters questions without interrogative force. I take it that the verb *ask* may be so understood that an utterance by *a* of (79) justifies the subsequent assertion by anyone of (80):

(79)   Is dinner ready?
(80)   *a* asked whether dinner was ready.

The position I have outlined may be clarified by being expressed in an extension of the language IL of intensional logic. In that language there are sentences of the syntactic type *t* of truth values and expressions for propositions, of syntactic type (s, t), corresponding semantically to propositions—that is, sets of possible worlds. Interrogatives as I have interpreted them here would call for an extension of the type theory so that there would be a type $\{t,t\}$ of unordered pairs of type t, whose semantic interpretation would be unordered pairs of truth values, and a type $\{(s,t), (s,t)\}$ of unordered pairs of propositions. Verbs like *ask* and *wonder* would take arguments of this type. In this setting, the extension of an interrogative is a pair of truth values, and its intension a pair of propositions. Indeed, the account of interrogatives given here can be expressed in its entirety in the setting envisaged.

If we assume that the reference of indirect questions is as I have suggested, then the higher-performative analysis of direct questions becomes redundant. Whether that analysis is adopted or not, however, the semantics of interrogatives does not take us out of the truth-conditional arena. In particular, there are no moods in the semantics of questions, either because they are not represented at all or because any work they might have done is taken up by the higher performative verb. However, there is a weighty tradition of thinking of moods as semantically independent items, and I wish to turn briefly to the difficulties in making out just what this tradition has in mind.

The question we were considering was, Why can saying an interrogative sentence such as (81) constitute asking a question—namely, the question whether (82)?

(81)   Is it raining?
(82)   It is raining.

An answer that suggests itself is that the syntactic element represented in English by inversion and a characteristic intonation pattern, and in other languages by other syntactic devices, is a sign that the speaker of the sentence is performing a speech act with interrogative force, whose content is given by the clause on which the syntactic element operated. Thus, the datum (83) is an application of a rule of English:

(83)   If u is an utterance of (2), then the speaker of u asks (with interrogative force) the question whether (82).

As Davidson (1984c) points out, however, the above and kindred conceptions of mood fail to make room for nonserious uses of language. Taken quite literally, this account of mood implies that when the minister at a wedding rehearsal says (84),

(84)   Do you take this woman for your wife?

then he (or she) is asking with interrogative force whether the man addressed takes that woman for his wife. But he is not, in the desired sense, asking anything; it is only a rehearsal.

Note that the higher-performative analysis does not face counterexamples along these lines. Whether the minister is asking anything is determined by whether (85), which is what he in fact said, is true:

(85)   I ask you whether you take this woman for your wife.

But since we are only at a rehearsal, it is not true. My own view, which does not recognize a higher performative, has it that the minister in a sense asks a question, but without interrogative force.

The theory of mood developed in Davidson 1984c is specifically designed to allow for nonserious uses of language. Davidson's suggestion is that yes-no questions are a kind of portmanteau, where the indicator of mood—or, as he calls it, the mood-setter—functions as a comment on the indicative core. Thus, *Is it raining?* is understood as in (86):

(86)   It is raining. That was interrogative in force.

The minister at the wedding rehearsal says nothing with interrogative force, even though in a way he says he does.

It is obvious that Davidson's suggestion runs into difficulties with *wh*-interrogatives (as Davidson notes in 1984c, 115), although it might be suggested that the indicative core is in this case an open sentence or utterance. But does his view really explain why interrogatives cannot be assessed for their truth values? Hornsby (1986) suggests that the explanation offered—namely, that interrogatives are a portmanteau of two sentences—is rather weak; for the same problem in more detail, see Segal 1988. Hornsby herself proposes that the convention or rules of language governing interrogatives be expressed adverbially, as in (87):

(87)   By saying *Is it raining?* a speaker says interrogatively that (or: asks-whether) it is raining.

To say no more than this about interrogatives is to leave indirect questions in the lurch, as Hornsby recognizes. But her aim is to formulate a view according to which the speaker in asking a question is not, in contrast to Davidson's view, tacitly describing with words what he is doing. Still, the expression *says interrogatively* is left as an unanalyzed term of art. If it were interpreted as *says with interrogative force*, then I do not see that we would have better than Davidson's theory back again.

Now, if I am right to say that yes-no questions express partitions, unordered pairs consisting of a proposition and its negation, then we have an explanation of why yes-no questions may but need not have interrogative force that is parallel to the explanation of why indicatives may but need not have assertive force. There is no need of mood indicators at all, for the semantic work done by syntactic inversion or the abstract question morpheme formalized above by the question mark is just to convert propositions into appropriate unordered pairs. Indeed, the view that I have advocated here is partly based on the following thought: any correct account of indirect questions must assign them a reference, and that reference will have the property that, when presented via a main clause, its presentation can, but need not, constitute asking about it. If so, then we needn't suppose that an interrogative does not wear its whole logical syntax on its face.

Appendix: Licensing negative polarity

The English negative polarity items *any* and *ever* are freely licensed in interrogative environments, as in (88) and (89):

(88)   Did anybody speak?
        John wonders whether anybody spoke.
        *Anybody spoke.
(89)   Have you ever been to France?
        Whether he has ever been to France is known to the police.
        *He has ever been to France.
        *That he has ever been to France is known to the police.

In this appendix I will offer an explanation of such licensing, drawing on the discussion above and on the fuller account of English choice questions developed in Higginbotham 1991a.

Following the latter paper, I will assume without argument that English disjunction *or* is always to be construed as in construction with a possibly tacit occurrence of *either*, and that the latter is a quantifier admitting a universal interpretation. The data that support this view are exemplified by the ambiguity of modal sentences such as (90):

(90)   John will play chess or checkers.

Besides the obvious interpretation that John will play chess, or else he will play checkers, (90) also has an interpretation equivalent to *John will play chess and John will play checkers*. The second interpretation, I will assume, arises because (90) has in fact a syntactic structure as in (91),

(91)   [either]$_i$ [John will play [chess or checkers]$_i$]

and at LF a structure as in (92).

(92)   [either chess or checkers$_i$ [John will play t_i]

The prefix is a universal quantifier, so that we have in effect (93):

(93)   [$\forall x$: x = chess or x = checkers] John will play x

Proceeding now beyond my earlier discussion, I will assume that the syntax of (90) puts *either* in the Spec position of its clause, so that we have at LF (94):

(94)   [$_{CP}$ [$_{Spec}$ either chess or checkers]$_i$ [$_{C'}$ C [$_{IP}$ John will play t_i]]]

This assumption is more specific than I will actually require. What will be necessary is that there be an intervening position—here C—between the quantification and the sentence over which it quantifies, and that this position be interpreted as the "?" of the discussion above is interpreted—that is, as passing from the type of propositions to the type of partitions.

It is obvious that English *whether* is *wh + either*, as *when* is *wh + then*, *where* is *wh + there*, and so on. Suppose now that this etymological point has semantic significance, so that *whether* is interpreted as a universal quantification in [Spec, CP], hence outside the scope of "?" in C. Unlike *either*, and unlike other *wh*-words, *whether* is restricted to this syntactic position. Thus, we do not have (95), in contrast to (96) or (97):

(95)   *Who saw whether Mary or Bill?
(96)   Who saw either Mary or Bill?
(97)   Who saw who?

We may assume further that just as every occurrence of *either* must go together with an occurrence of the disjunction *or*, so must every occurrence of *whether*, the sole exception being the case where the disjunction is tacit, and over the whole indicative IP. Thus, (98) will have a structure as in (99), and (100) a structure as in (101), prior ellipsis:

(98)   whether John played chess or checkers
(99)   [$_{CP}$ [$_{Spec}$ whether]$_i$ [$_{C'}$[$_C$?] [$_{IP}$ John played [chess or checkers]$_i$]]]
(100)   whether John left (or not)
(101)   [[whether] [? [John left or John did not leave]]]

Consider now the LF representation and the accompanying semantics of (101) on the assumptions given. The representation will be (102), and its interpretation will be that of (103):

(102)   [[whether John left or John did not leave]$_i$ [? t_i]]
(103)   [$\forall p$: p = that John left or p = that John did not leave] ? p

Applying the semantics, the constituent '$?p$' expresses the partition

$$\{p \mid \neg p\}$$

with 'p' a free variable. Quantification into this position by the universal quantifier gives the question of order 1:

$$\{\{\text{John left} \mid \text{John did not leave}\}, \{\neg(\text{John left}) \mid \neg(\text{John did not leave})\}\}$$

Manifestly, the latter is equivalent, in the sense of having all the same partial and complete answers, to

$$\{\text{John left} \mid \text{John did not leave}\}$$

so that the quantification has accomplished nothing, semantically speaking.

On the assumptions stated, however, *whether*-questions in which the scope of *whether* is the whole clause all have the property at LF that the elements of the clause appear within the restriction of a universal quantification, and such appearance is known to license negative polarity items. For the licensing itself I will adopt the explanation proposed by Ladusaw (1983) and others, that negative polarity items may appear only within the scope of *downward-entailing* expressions (definitions and a theoretical discussion are provided below). It follows at once that negative polarity items are licensed within interrogatives, where the licenser is overt or tacit *whether*.

A crucial point for the above analysis of the licensing of negative polarity items in interrogatives is seen in minimal pairs such as (104)–(105) and (106)–(107):

(104)   Mary knows whether John played chess or checkers.
(105)   Mary knows whether anyone played chess or checkers.
(106)   Did John play chess or checkers?
(107)   Did anyone play chess or checkers?

Examples (104) and (106) are of course ambiguous. On the view taken here, the ambiguity derives from the possibility of construing the disjunctive constituent *chess or checkers* either with *whether*, giving the interpretation of the embedded clause as a choice question, or else with its own tacit *either* within that constituent, giving the interpretation of that clause as a yes-no question. But (105) and (107) are not ambiguous: the complement cannot be interpreted as a choice question about chess versus checkers. The explanation in terms of the analysis above is that for the choice question we have the representation (108):

(108)   [[whether chess or checkers]$_i$ [? [John/anyone played t_i]]]

But this representation fails to license the negative polarity item *anyone*. To license it, we require that the entire clause *anyone played chess or checkers* be within the scope of *whether*, as in (109):

(109)   [[whether anyone played chess or checkers (or not)$_i$ [? t_i]]

But then the disjunction of *chess or checkers* is not construed with *whether*, so that the possibility of a choice question is precluded.

The interpretation of *whether* as universal quantification is not confined to the domain of interrogatives but is corroborated by the use of *whether* analogous to a free relative pronoun, as in (110):

(110)   You'll have a good time whether you go to London or Paris.

The sentence means that you'll have a good time if you go to London and also if you go to Paris. This interpretation follows from the assignment of the LF representation (111), or, with variables explicit, (112).

(111)   [whether London or Paris]$_i$ [you'll have a good time if you go to t_i]
(112)   [$\forall x$: x = London or x = Paris] [you'll have a good time if you go to x]

When negative polarity is licensed within the scope of some other *wh*-expression than *whether*, as in (113), we assume that a tacit *whether* is present anyway, giving the LF representation (114):

(113)   Who had anything to say?
(114)   [WHα] [$\forall p$: p = that α had anything to say or p = that $\neg(\alpha$ had anything to say)] ? p

The equivalences noted above carry over to this case, so that the interpretation is not disrupted.

There are a number of further linguistic points relevant to the hypothesis presented here that I hope to expand upon in later work. To review: the hypothesis is that negative polarity items are licensed in interrogatives because the latter are governed by the disjunction-host *whether*. This word behaves like its counterpart *either* in admitting an interpretation as a universal quantification. When that quantification is over propositions, then the constituents of the interrogative clause will be within its scope and the environment will satisfy known conditions on the licensing of negative polarity in English.

I turn now to some formal points that have been so far left in abeyance. Ladusaw's notion of downward-entailingness is defined in terms of implication and thus applies in the first instance only to indicative sentences. A quantifier Q is downward-entailing (with respect to its restriction) if the schema in (115) is valid:

(115) $[Qx: F(x)]\ G(x)$
         $\dfrac{[\forall x: H(x)]\ F(x)}{[Qx: H(x)]\ G(x)}$

By analogy with the indicative case, an expression of generality Q (which may be a quantifier, *wh*, or perhaps a "mix" of the two, such as *which two*) will be said to be *downward-entailing for interrogatives* if, where $\mathfrak{Q}$ is the question expressed by the result of prefixing '$[Qx: F(x)]$' to '$?G(x)$', and $\mathfrak{Q}$' is the question expressed by the result of prefixing '$[Qx: H(x)]$' to '$?G(x)$', then we have (116):

(116)   If [$\forall x$: $H(x)$] $F(x)$, then if S is a partial (complete) answer to $\mathfrak{Q}$, then S is a partial (complete) answer to $\mathfrak{Q}$'.

In other words, speaking derivatively in terms of answers to sentences rather than to the questions they express, the schema (117) is valid:

(117) S partially (completely) answers $[Qx: F(x)]\ ?\ G(x)$
         $\dfrac{[\forall x: H(x)]\ F(x)}{S\ \text{partially (completely) answers}\ [Qx: H(x)]\ ?\ G(x)}$

We shall need the observation about quantifiers in natural language that they are all *intersective* in the sense of Higginbotham and May (1978, 1981). I construe quantifiers Q as model-theoretically interpreted by functions f_Q from ordered pairs (X, Y) of subsets of the domain of quantification A into truth values. Q is *intersective* if $f_Q(X,Y) = f_Q(X, X \cap Y)$.

From intersectivity it follows that a natural-language quantifier that is downward-entailing, or for purposes of this exposition *downward-entailing (DE) for indicatives*, is DE for interrogatives as well. For suppose that Q is DE for indicatives, and let S be a partial answer to (118):

(118) $[Qx: F(x)] ? G(x)$

Each question $\mathfrak{Q}_a$ expressed by '$?G(x)$' when a is assigned to x will be of some given order n, the same for all a. If $\bar{F}$ is the extension of 'F', then for every subset A' of $\bar{F}$ such that $f_Q(\bar{F})(A') =$ truth, there is a bloc $B_{A'}$ in the question $\mathfrak{Q}$ of order $n + 1$ expressed by (118), and $\mathfrak{Q}$ consists entirely of such blocs. Since S answers $\mathfrak{Q}$, there is a bloc B in $\mathfrak{Q}$ and a subset A' of $\bar{F}$ such that S answers $\mathfrak{Q}_a$ for every $a \in A'$. Consider the interrogative (119):

(119) $[Qx: H(x)] ? G(x)$

If $\bar{H}$ is the extension of 'H', then since Q is DE for indicatives, if $\bar{H} \subseteq \bar{F}$ then $f_Q(\bar{H})(A') =$ truth. Since Q is intersective, $f_Q(\bar{H})(\bar{H} \cap A') =$ truth. Then S answers every $\mathfrak{Q}_a$ for $a \in \bar{H} \cap A'$, and is therefore an answer to (119); and S is a complete answer if it was a complete answer to (118). So if Q is DE for indicatives and Q is intersective, then Q is DE for interrogatives. Since all natural-language Q are intersective, this completes the proof.

The converse inclusion—that if Q is DE for interrogatives it is also DE for indicatives—requires stronger assumptions than the intersectivity of Q. Following the customary terminology, say that Q is *monotone-increasing (-decreasing)* if $f_Q(X)(Y) =$ truth and $Y \subseteq Z (Z \subseteq Y)$ implies $f_Q(X)(Z) =$ truth, and *indefinite* if $f_Q(X)(Y) = f_Q(Y)(X)$, for all X, Y, and Z. All natural-language quantifiers are monotone-increasing, monotone-decreasing, or indefinite (including combinations of these). If Q is monotone-decreasing, then Q does not quantify into interrogatives, and we have seen pragmatic reasons why. For those same pragmatic reasons, we may assume that $f_Q(\phi)(Y) =$ falsehood, and, if Q is indefinite, that $f_Q(X)(\phi) =$ falsehood as well.

Suppose then that Q is not DE for indicatives, and consider a model $\mathfrak{M}$ where (120) and (121) are true and (122) is false:

(120) $[Qx: F(x)] G(x)$
(121) $[\forall x: H(x)] F(x)$
(122) $[Qx: H(x)] G(x)$

Then the extension $\bar{F}$ of 'F' is nonempty. Consider with respect to this model the interrogatives (123) and (124):

(123) $[Qx: F(x)] ? (G(x) \& H(x))$
(124) $[Qx: H(x)] ? (G(x) \& H(x))$

We are going to show that there is a true partial answer to (123) that is not a partial answer to (124), so that Q is not DE for interrogatives, either. Assume on the contrary that Q is DE for interrogatives.

Because (120) is true in $\mathfrak{M}$, the question expressed by (123) in $\mathfrak{M}$ will have a bloc for the nonempty subset $\bar{F} \cap \bar{G}$ of $\bar{F}$. Hence, if there is an object a in $\mathfrak{M}$ that lies in $\bar{F}$ and $\bar{G}$ but not in $\bar{H}$, then (125) is a true partial answer to (123) that is not a partial answer to (124):

(125) $G(a)$ & $\neg H(a)$

Hence, $\bar{F} \cap \bar{G} \subseteq \bar{H}$. Then Q cannot be indefinite; for it were, then since it follows from the truth of (121) in $\mathfrak{M}$ that $\bar{F} \cap \bar{G} = \bar{G} \cap \bar{H}$, and the truth values of (120) and (122) depend only on the respective cardinalities of $\bar{F} \cap \bar{G}$ and $\bar{G} \cap \bar{H}$, these formulas would have the same truth value in $\mathfrak{M}$, contrary to hypothesis. The only remaining possibility is that Q is monotone-increasing, but not indefinite. The blocs of the question expressed by (124) in $\mathfrak{M}$ correspond to those subsets Σ of $\bar{H}$ for which $f_Q(\bar{H}, \Sigma) = $ truth. If we could choose $\Sigma \subseteq \bar{G} \cap \bar{H}$, then since Q is monotone-increasing, (122) would be true in $\mathfrak{M}$. If there are no Σ for which $f_Q(\bar{H}, \Sigma) = $ truth, then the question expressed by (124) in $\mathfrak{M}$ is degenerate, and so has no proper partial answers. But otherwise there are elements in $\bar{G}$ that are not in $\bar{H}$; and by the previous argument (125) is then a partial answer to (123) but not to (124).

The proof above can be strengthened to show that there are complete answers to (123) that are not complete answers to (124). I omit the details here.

Notes

Most of this paper is expanded from the less technical parts of one presented at a meeting of the Ockham Society, Oxford, March 1990, Roger Teichmann commenting; at the Workshop on Logical Form, University of California, Irvine, April 1990; and at the meeting of the Association for Symbolic Logic, Carnegie-Mellon University, Pittsburgh, January 1991. Other material is new, and some of it would not have been possible without class discussion in a seminar at MIT in the spring term of 1992 taught jointly with Irene Heim. For a technical supplement on direct questions, see Higginbotham 1991b:secs. 6 and 7. I have incorporated some remarks prompted by Teichmann's comments, and discussions with a number of persons, including especially Utpal Lahiri, Gabriel Segal, and Robert Stainton, have also been very helpful.

I note here the background to this paper. My first work on the topic of interrogatives was carried out jointly with Robert May, and some was published in Higginbotham and May 1978, 1981. I presented a more extended view at the CUNY Graduate Center, New York, October 1978, and at MIT, November 1979. This work was influenced particularly by Levi (1967); May (1989) has also carried out some of the further development. Further research was done at the University of Texas at Austin in 1980 under grant BNS 76-20307 A-01 from the National Science Foundation. I am grateful to Stanley Peters for this opportunity, and to him, Hans Kamp, and Lauri Karttunen for comments and discussion. The views that I then arrived at, and presented in a seminar at MIT in 1982 together with Sylvain Bromberger, I subsequently found to overlap in part with the research report Belnap 1963, some of the material from which was published as Belnap and Steel 1976. Discussion with Belnap at a conference sponsored by the Sloan Foundation at McGill University, 1982, confirmed that the method he and Michael Bennett envisaged for adding quantification over questions was similar to mine as well. (I have noted below where I follow Belnap's terminology, but have not in general cited specific parallels to his work.) Finally, Groenendijk and Stokhof (1984, 1989) have independently arrived at a view of what simple interrogatives express that is similar to what I advance here in section I.

1. Belnap (1969) observes that interrogatives may be expected to have presuppositions even for a language whose indicatives do not.

2. The presuppositions of multiple singular *wh*-questions are examined in Barss 1990.

3. See May 1985.

4. For a different implementation of the same basic idea, see Belnap 1982, following work by Michael Bennett.

5. If the background theory is ω-incomplete, even finiteness (or emptiness) of the set of positive instances is not enough to guarantee that an answer is attainable. For example, let the background theory be Peano arithmetic, where $\mathfrak{P}$ represents provability and $g+$ is the numeral for the Gödel number of a sentence g provably equivalent to its own unprovability, and consider (i), representing the question *What is a proof of* g?

(i) $[\text{WH}\alpha]$? $\mathfrak{P}(\alpha, g+)$

In the standard model, only the cell containing '$\neg\mathfrak{P}(a+,g+)$' for each numeral $a+$ is consistent with the background theory, but the true and complete answer '$(\forall x)\,\neg\mathfrak{P}(x,g+)$' is not provable.

6. There is another, irrelevant interpretation of (41), parallel to the natural interpretation of *I wondered about school*.

7. In the interest of readability I omit extra curly brackets when no ambiguity threatens. Thus, what is displayed in the text would be fully articulated as $\{\{p\} : \{\neg p\}\}$; similarly for a number of later examples.

8. I believe that the functional interpretation also provides the proper mechanism for the examples in Geach 1969 such as (i) (p. 121):

(i)   The one woman whom every true Englishman honors above all other women is his mother.

9. Examples like (66) are due to Engdahl 1986; (65) is modeled after an example in Collins 1992.

10. See Kroch 1989, Cinque 1990, and Szabolcsi and Zwarts 1990 for a discussion of ambiguities of this type.

35

DANIEL VANDERVEKEN

Success, Satisfaction, and Truth in the Logic of Speech Acts and Formal Semantics

There has been much controversy about the role and place of speech act theory in the study of language. Following Morris (1975), *semiotics* is traditionally divided into three branches: syntax, semantics, and pragmatics. *Syntax* deals with relations that exist only between linguistic expressions (e.g., the rules of formation of sentences), *semantics* with relations that exist between linguistic expressions and their meanings (e.g., their senses or their denotations), and *pragmatics* with relations that exist between linguistic expressions and their meanings and uses in contexts of utterance. Because speakers use language to perform speech acts, most philosophers and linguists, following Carnap, have first tended to place speech act theory in pragmatics rather than in semantics.

Moreover, up to the present time, the contemporary philosophy of language has been largely divided into two trends. The *logical trend*—founded by Frege and Russell and later developed by Carnap, Montague, and others—studies how language *corresponds* to the world. It concentrates on the analysis of truth conditions of declarative sentences. The *ordinary language analysis trend*—founded by Wittgenstein and Austin and later developed by Searle and Grice—studies how and for which purposes *language is used* in discourse. It concentrates on speech acts that speakers perform by uttering all types of sentences. As Austin (1962) pointed out, by uttering sentences under appropriate conditions, speakers characteristically perform *illocutionary acts* such as assertions, promises, requests, declarations, and apologies. Moreover, when their utterances have effects on the audience, they also occasionally perform *perlocutionary acts*. For example, they can convince, influence, please, amuse, or embarrass the hearer. Like Austin and Searle, I think that the primary units of meaning in the use and comprehension of language are not propositions or isolated truth conditions but are complete illocutionary acts. By making a meaningful utterance, a speaker always attempts to perform an illocutionary act. This is part of what he means and intends to communicate to the hearer.

This is an original chapter for this volume.

In the case of a literal utterance, the speaker means to perform the illocutionary act expressed by the sentence that he uses in the context of his utterance. As Searle (1969) pointed out, most elementary illocutionary acts are of the form F(P): they consist of an *illocutionary force*[1] F with a propositional content. Austin discovered illocutionary forces by paying attention to the fact that certain sentences—for example, "I order you to come," "I swear to tell the truth"—can be used *performatively*: their literal utterances in appropriate conditions constitute the very performance of the action named by their verb. Austin called these sentences *performative sentences* in opposition to others that he called *constative sentences*. However Austin came soon to notice that all kinds of sentences whether performative or not serve to perform illocutionary acts. So the study of illocutionary acts turned out to be needed not only for the analysis of performative sentences but also for the general theory of meaning and communication. If it is not possible to express a propositional content without an illocutionary force, then most elementary sentences whose logical form is completely analyzed contain an *illocutionary force marker* in addition to a *clause* expressing a proposition. As linguists and grammarians had long acknowledged in their classification of *sentential types*, verb mood, word order, and punctuation signs are the most common features of illocutionary markers. Thus declarative sentences serve to make assertions; imperative sentences to give directives to the hearer; interrogative sentences to ask questions; and exclamatory sentences to express the speaker's attitudes.

Using logical formalisms, philosophers of the logical trend have greatly contributed to the theory of sentence meaning. They have analyzed the logical form and truth conditions of propositional contents of utterances, and they have formulated a general logic of sense and denotation. In particular, they have explicated the meanings of important words and syncategorematic expressions such as truth, modal, and temporal connectives and quantifiers, all of which serve to determine the truth conditions of propositional contents. However, because they have ignored illocutionary aspects of meaning, they have failed to analyze the meaning of expressions such as force markers and performative verbs that serve to determine the illocutionary forces of utterances.

Morris's division of semiotics was mainly programmatic. The need for a more precise characterization of the delimitations between semantics and pragmatics has become clear in recent years. New philosophical logics such as the logic of demonstratives and illocutionary logic have analyzed the logical form of expressions whose linguistic meaning is systematically related to use. First, contexts of utterance and moments of time were introduced in semantic interpretations of the logic of demonstratives and temporal logic in order to analyze the linguistic meaning of *indexical expressions* like the pronouns "I" and "you" and adverbs of time and location like "now" and "here," whose senses and denotations are systematically dependent on contextual features such as the identity of the speaker and hearer and the time and place of utterance. Since Kaplan (1978b) worked on demonstratives, the study of indexical expressions which was first assigned by Bar-Hillel (1954) and Montague (1968) to pragmatics is now commonly assigned to semantics.

Similarly, the systematic analysis by Searle and myself (1985) of English performative verbs and illocutionary force makers has shown that their meaning contributes systematically to the determination of the forces of utterances in which they occur. Thus, the identification of sentence meaning with truth conditions is now challenged in the philosophy of language. Many philosophers and linguists no longer accept the thesis that the meaning of linguistic expressions only contributes to determining the propositional content and truth conditions of utterances.

Section 1   Principles of illocutionary logic

I have formulated such principles in various papers and with Searle in *Foundations of Illocutionary Logic* (1985). I have used proof and model theory in *Meaning and Speech Acts* (1990; 1991b) in order to proceed to the formalization. As Searle and I pointed out, language use not only consists in the performance of *elementary illocutionary acts* with a force and a propositional content; it also consists in the performance of more *complex illocutionary acts* whose logical form is not reducible to that of elementary speech acts. Illocutionary denegations, conditional speech acts, and conjunctions of illocutionary acts are the three basic kinds of complex illocutionary acts. From a logical point of view, acts of *illocutionary denegations* are of the form ¬A; their linguistic aim is to make explicit the nonperformance by the speaker of an illocutionary act A. For example, a rejection is the illocutionary denegation of the acceptance of an offer. *Conditional speech acts* are of the form (P ⇒ A); their linguistic aim is to perform an illocutionary act A not categorically but on the condition that a proposition P be true. Thus, an offer is a promise that is conditional on the hearer's acceptance. Finally, *conjunctions* of illocutionary acts are of the form (A & B); their aim is to perform simultaneously two illocutionary acts A and B. For example, an alert is the conjunction of an assertion that some imminent potential danger exists and of a warning to the hearer to prepare for action against that danger. Sentences containing *illocutionary connectives* serve to perform such complex illocutionary acts. For example, "if" and the semicolon play the role of illocutionary connectives of conditional and conjunction in the two sentences "If it is difficult, help me!" and "Paul is leaving; are you going with him?"

By nature illocutionary acts are intentional actions. Speakers who perform illocutionary acts always attempt to perform these acts by making meaningful utterances. As is the case for human actions in general, attempts to perform illocutionary acts can succeed or fail. First, speakers must use appropriate sentences in order to express their attempted illocutionary act in the context of their utterance. Second, that context must be appropriate for the performance of that illocutionary act. For example, an attempt to threaten someone is not successful when the speaker speaks to the wrong person or when he is in a situation where it is obvious that he has not the least intention to do what he threatens to do. Moreover, illocutionary acts are directed at objects and states of affairs, and, even when they are successful, they can still fail to be satisfied, when the world does not fit their propositional content. Thus successful assertions can be false, successful promises can be broken, and successful requests can be refused. The *conditions of success* of an illocutionary act are the conditions that must obtain in a context of utterance in order that the speaker succeed in performing that act in that context. Thus, a condition of success of a promise is that the speaker commit himself to carrying out a future course of action. *Failure* to perform an illocutionary act is a special case of lack of performance which occurs only in contexts where the speaker makes an unsuccessful attempt to perform that illocutionary act. The *conditions of satisfaction* of an illocutionary act are the conditions that must obtain in a possible context of utterance in order that the act be satisfied in the world of that context. For example, a condition of satisfaction of a promise is that the speaker carry out in the world the promised course of action. The notion of a condition of satisfaction is a generalization of the notion of a truth condition that is necessary to cover all illocutionary forces. Just as an assertion is satisfied when it is *true*, a command is satisfied when it is *obeyed*, a promise when it is *kept*, a request when it is *granted*, and similarly for all other illocutionary forces.

According to Searle and me, one cannot understand the nature of illocutionary acts without understanding their success and satisfaction conditions. Moreover, the two types of success and satisfaction conditions of elementary illocutionary acts are not reducible to the truth conditions of their propositional contents. Consequently, the two single most important objectives of the logic of speech acts and semantics of ordinary language are to develop new theories of success and of satisfaction integrating the classical theory of truth for propositions. One reason why earlier attempts to formally analyze nondeclarative sentences and performatives have failed is that they have tended to identify illocutionary acts with their conditions of satisfaction and to reduce satisfaction to truth. However, as I have argued repeatedly, one cannot leave out the general notion of success in the analysis of the logical form of actions in general and of speech acts in particular. Moreover, as we will see later, the notion of satisfaction is richer than the notion of truth.

The fundamental philosophical concepts of success, satisfaction, and truth are logically related. On the one hand, the satisfaction of elementary illocutionary acts requires the truth of their propositional content; there is no satisfaction without correspondence. On the other hand, the successful performance of declaratory illocutionary acts brings about the truth of their propositional content; any successful declaration constitutes the performance by the speaker of the action represented by the propositional content. Searle and I have analyzed each performative utterance as being a declaration by the speaker that he performs by virtue of his utterance the illocutionary act that he represents. In this view, any successful literal utterance of a performative sentence is performative because a successful declaration makes its propositional content true, and the propositional content in this case is that the speaker performs the illocutionary act expressed by the performative verb. Thus by a successful literal utterance of "1 request your help," a speaker requests help by way of primarily declaring that he make that request. As one can expect, speakers whose utterances constitute successful, nondefective, and satisfied illocutionary acts are felicitous. So in Austin's terminology, illocutionary acts have felicity conditions. Searle and I did not analyze the logical form of propositional contents in *Foundations*. We contributed to the theory of success of illocutionary acts. Our main objective was to study *illocutionary commitment* as it is determined by types of illocutionary act. By virtue of their logical form, certain illocutionary acts *strongly commit* the speaker *to* others: it is not possible to perform them without *eo ipso* performing the others. Thus supplications and invitations contain requests. However, sometimes illocutionary commitment is weaker. The successful performance of the illocutionary act *weakly commits* the speaker to another act that he does not openly perform. For example, someone who gives an order to a hearer is committed to giving him the corresponding permission even if he does not openly give that permission. Such a weak illocutionary commitment shows itself in the fact that one cannot simultaneously give an order and denegate the permission. It is paradoxical to say "I order you and I do not permit you to go away ."

Most propositions are true or false, no matter whether or not they are expressed. All depends on whether the things are in the world as they represent them. In contrast, an illocutionary act cannot be performed unless a speaker attempts to perform it and expresses his intention in an utterance. A performed illocutionary act is always an illocutionary act that the speaker succeeds in performing. Unlike truth, success is then inseparable from thought. For that reason, the theory of success of illocutionary logic is much more effective (finite and decidable) and innate than that of truth and satisfaction. Certain illocutionary acts are *unperformable* in the sense that they cannot be performed in any possible context of utterance. We know that a priori by virtue of competence, and we never attempt to perform them. So we never speak literally when we use an *illocutionarily inconsistent* sentence like "I order and forbid you to come," which expresses a nonperformable illocution. We mean something other than what we say. However many *unsatisfiable illocutionary acts* (for example, many necessarily false assertions) are performable. So we can use with success *truth conditionally inconsistent* sentences like "Whales are fishes" expressing unsatisfiable illocutions. As Wittgenstein pointed out, meaning is well determined: "It seems clear that what we mean must always be sharp" (*Notebooks* p. 68).[2] So each speaker always knows which illocutionary act he primarily attempts to perform by his utterance. Moreover, each speaker also knows which other illocutionary acts he would perform if his utterance were successful. He knows to which illocutionary acts he is strongly committed in each context of utterance. Whenever an illocutionary force F_1 contains another force F_2 (for example, the force of prediction contains that of assertion), we know that by virtue of competence so that each speech act of the form $F_1(P)$ commits us to performing the corresponding act $F_2(P)$. Similarly, whenever we know by virtue of competence that a proposition P cannot be true unless another proposition Q is also true, illocutionary acts of the form F(P) whose force is primitive and nonexpressive strongly commit us to performing corresponding acts of the form F(Q). Thus we cannot assert a conjunction $P \wedge Q$ without asserting each conjunct P and Q. So the speaker's strong illocutionary commitments are well known and, for that reason, well founded, decidable, and finite. Here are brief explanations of the basic principles of illocutionary logic.

Components of illocutionary force

Each illocutionary force can be divided into six types of component which serve to determine the conditions of success and satisfaction of the illocutionary acts with that force. The notion of illocutionary force is too complex to be taken as a primitive notion. In illocutionary logic, it is derived from a few simpler notions. Thus, each force is divided into six types of components: an illocutionary point, a mode of achievement of illocutionary point, propositional content, preparatory conditions, sincerity conditions, and a degree of strength. Two illocutionary forces F_1 and F_2 with the same components are identical, for all illocutionary acts of the form F_1 (P) and F_2 (P) serve the same linguistic purposes in the use of language.

Illocutionary point

The principal component of each illocutionary force is its illocutionary point, for that point determines the *direction of fit* of utterances with that force. There are exactly five illocutionary points that speakers can attempt to achieve in expressing a propositional content with an illocutionary force: the *assertive, commissive, directive, declaratory*, and *expressive* points. They correspond to the four possible directions of fit that exist between words and things in language use:

> *The words-to-things direction of fit.* When the force has the words-to-things direction of fit, the illocutionary act is satisfied when its propositional content fits a state of affairs existing (in general independently) in the world. Illocutionary acts with the *assertive* point (e.g., conjectures, assertions, testimonies, and predictions) have the words-to-world direction of fit. Their point is to represent how things are. Thus, in the case of assertive utterances, the words must correspond to the objects of reference as they stand in the world.

> *The things-to-words direction of fit.* When the force has the things-to-words direction of fit, the illocutionary act is satisfied when the world is transformed to fit the propositional content. Illocutionary acts with the *commissive* or *directive* point have the things-to-words direction of fit. Their point is to have the world transformed by the future course of action of the speaker (commissives) or of the hearer (directives) in order to match the propositional content of the utterance. In this case, the things in the world have to be changed to correspond to the words uttered in the performance of the illocutionary act. Promises, threats, vows, and pledges are commissive illocutions. Requests, questions, invitations, orders, commands, and advice are directives.

> *The double direction of fit.* When the force has the double direction of fit, the illocutionary act is satisfied when the world is transformed by an action of the speaker to fit the propositional content by virtue of the fact that the speaker represents it as being so transformed. Illocutionary acts with the *declaratory* illocutionary point (e.g., resignations, definitions, condemnations, and blessings) have the double direction of fit. Their point is to get the world to match the propositional content by saying that the propositional content matches the world. In successful declarations, objects of reference are then changed to correspond to words in the very utterance of these words. As Austin pointed out, in such utterances, we do things with words.

The empty direction of fit. For some illocutionary acts, there is no question of success or failure of fit, and their propositional content is in general presupposed to be true. Such are the illocutionary acts with the *expressive* point—for example, thanks, apologies, congratulations, and boasts. They have the empty direction of fit. Their point is just to express a mental state of the speaker about the state of affairs represented by the propositional content. Thus, in expressive utterances, speakers do not attempt to establish a correspondence between words and things. They just want to manifest their feelings about the ways in which objects are in the world.

Each illocutionary point serves one linguistic purpose in relating propositions to the world, so different illocutionary points have different conditions of achievement. For that reason, the type of an illocutionary point Π is that of a function which associates with each possible context of utterance *c* and proposition P the value *success* when the speaker achieves the illocutionary point Π on proposition P in context *c*, and the value *unsuccess* otherwise.

All forces with the same illocutionary point do not play the same role in the use of language. For example, orders, commands, requests, supplications, questions, recommendations, and demands are directives to be made in different conditions.

Mode of achievement

Illocutionary points, like most purposes of our actions, can be achieved in various ways. The mode of achievement of an illocutionary force determines how its point must be achieved on the propositional content where there is a successful performance of an act with that force. For example, in a command the speaker must invoke a position of authority over the hearer, whereas in a request he must give the option of refusal to the hearer. Such modes of achievement are expressed in English by adverbs such as "please" and "whether you like it or not" in imperative sentences. From a logical point of view, the mode of achievement of a force restricts the conditions of achievement of its point by requiring certain specific means or ways of achievement. Formally, a mode of achievement μ is a restriction function which has the same type as illocutionary points.

Propositional content conditions

Many illocutionary forces impose conditions on the set of propositions that can be taken as propositional contents of acts with that force in a context of utterance. For example, the propositional content of a prediction must represent a fact which is future with respect to the moment of utterance. Such conditions are propositional content conditions. The type of a propositional content condition θ is that of a function which associates with each possible context a set of propositions. Some propositional content conditions are determined by illocutionary point. For example, all commissive illocutionary forces have as a condition that their propositional content represent a future course of action of the speaker. Other propositional content conditions are specific to certain illocutionary forces. For example, a proposal is a directive speech act with a special propositional content condition. To propose that a hearer carry out an action is to suggest that he accept doing that action. Propositional content conditions are expressed by syntactic constraints on the grammatical form of the clauses of elementary sentences. For example, the main verb of imperative sentences must be in the second person and in the future tense.

Preparatory conditions

By performing an illocutionary act, the speaker also *presupposes* that certain propositions are true in the context of the utterance. For example, a speaker who promises to do something presupposes that his future action is good for the hearer. The preparatory conditions of an illocutionary force determine which propositions the speaker would presuppose if he were performing acts with that force in a possible context of utterance. So the logical type of a preparatory condition Σ is that of a function which associates with each context c and proposition P a set of propositions. Many, but not all, preparatory conditions are determined by illocutionary point. "Yes" and "No" are often used in English to express preparatory conditions regarding the fact that the speaker gives a positive or negative answer to a previous question.

Sincerity conditions

By performing an illocutionary act, the speaker also *expresses* mental states of particular modes about the fact represented by the propositional content. For example, a speaker who makes a request expresses a desire, and a speaker who offers thanks expresses gratitude. The sincerity conditions of each illocutionary force F determine the *particular psychological modes* of the mental states that the speaker would have if he were sincerely performing an illocutionary act with *that* force. Thus, a sincerity condition is just a set of modes of propositional attitudes. Some sincerity conditions are common to all forces with the same illocutionary point. For example, each commissive force has the sincerity condition that the speaker intends to do what he commits himself to doing. But other sincerity conditions are independent of illocutionary point. For example, to agree to do something is to accept to do it with the special sincerity condition to the effect that one is in agreement with the person who has requested that action. In English, adverbs like "alas" and "O.K." express sincerity conditions. As I have pointed out (1990; 1991b), the sets of modes of achievement, propositional content, and preparatory and sincerity conditions have the formal structure of a Boolean algebra. Thus there are a neutral and an absorbent component of these types of components.[3]

Degree of strength

The mental states that enter into sincerity conditions are expressed with different degrees of strength, depending on the illocutionary force. For example, the degree of strength of the sincerity conditions of a promise is greater than that of an acceptance. A speaker who promises to do something expresses a stronger intention than a speaker who simply agrees to do it. Degree of strength is often orally expressed by intonation contour. The formal structure of the set of degrees of strength is that of an Abelian group.

The existence of preparatory and sincerity conditions is illustrated linguistically by *Moore's paradox*: it is paradoxical to attempt to perform an illocutionary act and to deny simultaneously one of these conditions. Thus utterances like "It is raining and I do not believe it" and "I promise to help you and I am absolutely unable to do it" are paradoxical and self-defeating.

Recursive definition of the set of illocutionary forces

The set of illocutionary forces of possible utterances is recursive. There are five primitive illocutionary forces. These are the simplest possible illocutionary forces: they have an illocutionary point, no special mode of achievement of that point, a neutral degree of strength, and only the propositional content and the preparatory and sincerity conditions that are determined by their point. The five primitive forces are as follows:

1. The *illocutionary force of assertion*, which is named by the performative verb "assert" and realized syntactically in the declarative sentential type
2. The *primitive commissive illocutionary force*, which is named by the performative verb "commit"

3. The *primitive directive force*, which is realized syntactically in the imperative sentential type
4. The *illocutionary force of declaration*, which is named by the performative verb "declare" and expressed in performative utterances
5. The *primitive expressive illocutionary force*, which is realized syntactically in the type of exclamatory sentences.

All other illocutionary forces are derived from the primitive forces by a finite number of applications of five simple logical operations on forces which consist in adding new components or in changing the degree of strength. Four of these operations on forces add components; they consist in *restricting the mode of achievement of the illocutionary point by imposing a new mode and in adding new propositional content or preparatory or sincerity conditions*. (From a logical point of view, these operations are Boolean operations of intersection or of union.) The fifth operation on forces consists in *increasing or decreasing the degree of strength*. (It is like addition in an Abelian group.)

Here are some examples of derived illocutionary forces:

The illocutionary force of *promise* is obtained from the primitive commissive force by imposing a special mode of achievement of the commissive point involving the undertaking of an obligation.

The illocutionary force of a *renunciation* has the special propositional content condition to the effect that it is a negative commitment. In the commissive use of renouncing, to renounce something is to commit oneself to pursue no longer certain activities.

The illocutionary force of a *pledge* is obtained from the primitive commissive force by increasing the degree of strength of the sincerity conditions.

The illocutionary force of a *threat* is obtained from the primitive commissive force by adding the preparatory condition that the future course of action represented by the propositional content is bad for the hearer.

Finally, to *consent* to do something is to accept to do it with the added sincerity condition that one is reluctant to do it.

As one can expect, it is possible to make a systematic analysis of illocutionary verbs of natural languages on the basis of this recursive definition of the set of possible forces. The same holds for force markers. Some syntactic types of sentence—for example, the declarative, imperative, and exclamatory types—express primitive forces. Others, like the conditional and interrogative types, express derived forces. For example, conditional sentences like "I could do it, if you want" and "He would like that" are used to assert with reserve and a weak degree of strength how things will be later if specified or unspecified future facts happen.

Basic definition of success

The conditions of success of elementary illocutionary acts are a function of the components of their illocutionary force and of their propositional content. Thus an illocutionary act of the form F(P) *is successfully performed* in the context of an utterance if and only if, firstly in that context, the speaker succeeds in achieving the illocutionary point of force F on proposition P with the mode of achievement of F , and P satisfies the propositional content conditions of F; secondly, the speaker succeeds in presupposing the propositions determined by the preparatory conditions of F; and, finally, he also succeeds in expressing with the degree of strength of F the mental states of the modes determined by the sincerity conditions of F about the fact represented by the propositional content P. Thus a speaker makes a promise in a context of utterance when (1) the point of his utterance is to commit himself to doing an act A (illocutionary point); (2) in his utterance, the speaker puts himself under an obligation to do act A (mode of achievement); (3) the propositional content of the utterance is that the speaker will do act A (propositional content conditions); (4) the speaker presupposes that he is capable of doing act A and that act A is in the interest of the hearer (preparatory conditions); and (5) he expresses with a strong degree of strength an intention to accomplish such an act (sincerity conditions and degree of strength).

A speaker can presuppose propositions that are false. He can also express mental states that he does not have. Consequently, successful performances of illocutionary acts may be defective. For example, a speaker can mistakenly make a promise that is not beneficial at all to the hearer. A speaker can also make an insincere promise that he does not intend to keep. In such cases, the performed promise is defective. The hearer could reply by pointing out such mistakes. From a logical point of view, an illocutionary act *is nondefectively performed* in a context of utterance when it is successfully performed and its preparatory and sincerity conditions are fulfilled in that context. Austin with his notion of felicity conditions did not distinguish clearly between utterances that are successful but defective and utterances that are not even successful. In our terminology, we can say that an illocution is *felicitous* when it is successful, nondefective, and satisfied.

Basic definition of satisfaction

The notion of a condition of satisfaction is based on the traditional correspondence theory of truth for propositions.[4] Whenever an elementary illocutionary act is satisfied in an actual context of utterance, there is a *success of fit*, or *correspondence*, between language and the world, because the propositional content of the illocutionary act corresponds to an actual fact in the world. Thus, an elementary illocutionary act of the form F(P) is satisfied in an actual context of utterance only if its propositional content P is true in that context. However, there is more to the notion of a condition of a satisfaction than the notion of truth-condition. In order that an elementary illocutionary act be satisfied, the correspondence between words and things must be established following the proper direction of fit of its illocutionary force.

When an illocutionary act has the words-to-things direction of fit, it *is satisfied* in a context of utterance when its propositional content is *true* in that context. In such a case, the success of fit between language and the world is achieved by the fact that its propositional content represents a fact which exists (in general independently) in the world. In contrast, when an illocutionary act has the things-to-words or the double direction of fit, it *is satisfied* in a context of utterance when its propositional content P is true in that context *because of* its performance. Unlike assertive utterances, commissive and directive utterances have self-referential conditions of satisfaction. An assertive speech act is true when its propositional content corresponds to an existing fact no matter how that fact came to exist. But strictly speaking, a pledge is kept or a command is obeyed only if the speaker or hearer carries out in the world a future course of action stemming from the pledge or the command. Thus truth predicates cannot be used to evaluate the satisfaction of speech acts with the world-to-words direction of fit like pledges or commands can. A pledge or a command is not true or false. A pledge is either kept or broken. Similarly, a command is either obeyed or disobeyed. It is a mistake to attempt to reduce the theory of satisfaction of illocutionary acts to the theory of truth of propositions.[5]

Success conditions of complex illocutionary acts

Any successful performance of an illocutionary act in a context somehow restricts the set of possible contexts of utterance which are illocutionarily compatible with that context. By definition two contexts are *illocutionarily compatible* when all illocutionary acts performed in one could be performed in the other. As Searle and I pointed out, this accessibility relation is Brouwerian: reflexive and anti-symmetrical. A speaker *succeeds in performing an illocutionary denegation* of the form ¬A in a context when he attempts to perform that act and A is not performed in any possible context that is illocutionarily compatible with that context. Similarly, a speaker *succeeds in performing a conditional illocutionary act* of the form P ⇒ A in a context when he attempts to perform that conditional illocutionary act and he performs illocutionary act A in all possible contexts which are illocutionarily compatible with that context where proposition P is true.

Section 2   The logical form of propositional contents

In my approach, propositions have a double nature. On the one hand, propositions are units of sense of a fundamental logical type that are expressed by sentences and have truth values. On the other hand, propositions are also the contents of conceptual thoughts such as illocutionary acts and attitudes which are representations rather than presentations of facts. As Frege already noticed, the two constitutive aspects of propositions are not logically independent. Thus, every proposition which is the sense of a sentence in a possible context of utterance is also the propositional content of the illocutionary act that the speaker would attempt to perform if he were literally using that sentence in that context. For example, the proposition which is the common sense of the sentences "John will help me" and "Please, John, help me" in a context of utterance is also the propositional content of the assertion or request that the speaker of that context would mean to make if he were using literally one of these sentences in that context.

Until now contemporary logicians have paid attention to the role that propositions play as senses of sentences rather than as contents of thought. Moreover, they have tended under the influence of Carnap to reduce propositions to their actual truth conditions in reality. Thus the type of a proposition in classical logic is that of a function from the set of possible circumstances (the term comes from Kaplan) to the set of truth values. (Circumstances can be moments of time, possible worlds, contexts, histories, etc., depending on the logic under consideration.) On this view, *strictly equivalent* propositions, which are true in the same possible circumstances are identified. However it is clear that most strictly equivalent propositions are not substituable *salva felicitate* within the scope of illocutionary forces. For example, the assertion that Paris is a city is different from the assertion that it is a city and not an irrational number, even if their contents are strictly equivalent propositions. One can make the first assertion without making the second. Illocutionary logic requires, then, a finer propositional logic.

For this purpose I have formulated in *Meaning and Speech Acts* and later essays a natural logic of propositions in terms of predication so as to take into account the fact that propositions are always in principle expressible in the performance of illocutionary acts. My propositional logic is *predicative* in the very general sense that it mainly takes into consideration the acts of predication that we make in expressing and understanding propositions. My main objective was to construct a theory of truth that would be appropriate for enriching the theory of success and satisfaction of illocutionary acts. I have analyzed the logical form of propositions on the basis of the following principles.

Structure of constituents

Propositions have a structure of constituents. As Frege, Russell, Strawson, and others pointed out, understanding a proposition consists mainly of understanding which attributes (properties or relations) certain objects of reference must possess in the world in order that this proposition be true. In expressing propositions speakers refer to objects under concepts and predicate attributes of these objects. The speakers have in mind atomic propositions whose truth in a circumstance depends on whether these objects have in that circumstance the predicated attribute. Each proposition is then composed out of atomic propositions corresponding to predications. For example, the proposition that the pope is in Rome or Venice is composed of two atomic propositions: the first predicates of him the property of being in Rome, the second the property of being in Venice. It is true if and only if at least one is true.

Senses, not objects

Propositional constituents are senses and not objects. As Frege pointed out, we cannot refer to objects without subsuming them under senses and without predicating of them attributes. Thus the formal ontology of propositional logic is realist and not nominalist. Referential and predicative expressions have a sense in addition to a possible denotation. Frege's argument against direct reference remains conclusive if one accepts that propositions are contents of thought. As Kaplan nowadays admits quite frankly, Kripke's puzzle for belief is much more a puzzle for the theory of direct reference than for propositional attitudes. From the true premise that Babylonians did not believe that Hesperus is Phosphorus, the theory of direct reference concludes that the Babylonians did not believe that Hesperus is Hesperus. Such an absurd conclusion is incompatible with the minimal rationality of competent speakers.

Finite structure

Propositions are complex senses whose structure is finite. As is well known, human beings have restricted cognitive abilities. We can only use finitely long sentences in a context of utterance. Similarly, we only can refer to a finite number of different objects and we can only predicate of them a finite number of attributes. Consequently, propositions that are the senses of sentences have a finite number of propositional constituents. Upon reflexion, this requirement of finiteness has important consequences for both illocutionary and intensional logics. A human being can only express a finite number of propositions in an act of thought. So a speaker can only perform a finite number of illocutionary acts in a possible context of use of a natural language. Furthermore, one must reject the standard objectual or substitutional analyses of quantification in propositional logic. For we do not refer to all the values that can be assigned to bound variables when we make generalizations.

Inadequacy of Carnap's explication of truth conditions

Carnap's explication of truth conditions is not adequate. It does not take into account the effective way in which we understand such conditions. To understand the truth conditions of a proposition is not to know its truth value in each possible circumstance, as most logicians tend to believe. It is, rather, to understand that it is true according to some possible truth conditions of its atomic propositions and false according to all others. We understand the proposition that whales are fishes without knowing eo ipso that it is necessarily false. It is a historical discovery that whales are mammals. In my view, to understand an elementary proposition is just to understand that it is true in a circumstance if and only if the denotations of its attribute and concepts are such that its unique atomic proposition is true in that very circumstance; it is not to know whether or not it is true in that circumstance. We often express senses without knowing their denotation in the context of utterance. We can speak of Jane's children without knowing who they are. From a cognitive point of view, atomic propositions have a lot of possible truth conditions: they can be true in all circumstances, they can be false in all circumstances, they can be false in one circumstance and true in all others, they can be false in two circumstances and true in all others, and so on. The type of possible truth conditions is that of functions from the set of all possible circumstances into the set of truth values. Among all possible truth conditions of each atomic proposition, there are, of course, its actual Carnapian truth conditions, which give as value the true in a circumstance if and only if the objects that fall under its concepts satisfy its attribute in that circumstance.

I propose to inductively analyze truth conditions by associating with each proposition (with respect to any circumstance) the unique set of possible truth conditions of its atomic propositions that are compatible with its truth in that very circumstance. As we will see, this explicates better the mechanism of truth understanding. Thus the truth of an elementary proposition in a circumstance is compatible by definition with all and only the possible truth conditions of its unique atomic proposition under which it is true in that very circumstance. As one can expect, the truth of propositional negation ¬P is compatible with all and only the possible truth conditions of its atomic propositions that are incompatible with the truth of P. And the truth of the modal proposition that "it is universally necessary that P" is compatible with all and only the possible truth conditions of its atomic propositions, which are compatible with the truth of P in all circumstances. As Wittgenstein pointed out in the *Tractatus*, there are two limit cases of truth conditions. Sometimes the truth of a proposition is compatible with all possible ways in which objects could be; in this case, it is a tautology. Sometimes it is incompatible with all of them; in this case, it is a contradiction. In my approach, *tautologies* are propositions whose truth is compatible with all the possible truth conditions of their atomic propositions, and *contradictions* are propositions whose truth is compatible with none.

Recursive definition of the set of propositions

The set of propositions is recursive. Elementary propositions are the simplest propositions. All other propositions are more complex: they are obtained by applying to simpler propositions operations that change atomic propositions or truth conditions. Truth functions are the simplest propositional operations: they only rearrange truth conditions. Thus the conjunction P ∧ Q and the disjunction P ∨ Q of two propositions P and Q have all and only the atomic propositions of P and Q. Such propositions only differ by their truth conditions. The truth of the disjunction is compatible with all the possible truth conditions of their atomic propositions, which are compatible with the truth of at least one of the two arguments P and Q. But the truth of the conjunction is only compatible with all these possible truth conditions, which are compatible with the truth of both P and Q. Unlike truth functions, quantification and modal, temporal and agentive operations on propositions change constituent atomic propositions, as well as truth conditions. Thus by way of saying that it is necessary that God does not make mistakes, we predicate of God not only the property of not making mistakes but also the modal property of infallibility—namely, that, in all possible circumstances, He does not make mistakes.

Law of propositional identity

In order to be identical, two propositions must be composed of the same atomic propositions and their truth in each circumstance must be compatible with the same possible truth conditions of their atomic propositions. This criterion of propositional identity is stronger than that of classical logics such as modal, temporal, and intensional logics and the logic of relevance. Strictly equivalent propositions composed out of different atomic propositions are no longer identified. We do not make the same predications in expressing them. Unlike Parry (1933) I do not identify all strictly equivalent propositions whose atomic propositions are the same. Such propositions whose truth is not compatible with the same possible truth conditions of their atomic propositions do indeed not have the same cognitive value. For we understand in a different way their truth conditions. For example, we can believe the necessarily false proposition that whales are fishes. But we never believe the contradiction that whales are and are not fishes. We know a priori that it is false. Notice that my criterion of propositional identity is less rigid than that of intensional isomorphism of Cresswell (1975a)'s hyperintensional logic. For all Boolean laws of idempotence, commutativity, distributivity, and associativity of truth functions remain valid laws of propositional identity.

A new concise definition of truth

In the philosophical tradition from Aristotle to Tarski true propositions correspond to reality. Objects of reference stand in certain relations in possible circumstances. Atomic propositions have then a unique truth value in each circumstance depending on the denotation of their attributes and concepts and the order of their predication. Their actual truth conditions are then well determined. However things could stand in many other relations in each circumstance. In addition to the ways in which things are, there are the possible ways in which they could be. We are not omniscient. In interpreting propositional contents of utterances we consider then a lot of possible truth conditions other than the actual truth conditions of their atomic propositions. We know a priori the actual truth conditions of few propositions. The truth of most propositions in most circumstances is compatible with many possible ways in which objects could be in them and incompatible with many others. Think about disjunctions, material implications, historic possibilities, future propositions, and so on. However, in order that a proposition P be true in a given circumstance, things must be in that circumstance as P represents them. Otherwise there would be no correspondence. Along these lines, I define truth as follows: a proposition *is true in a circumstance i*, according to an interpretation if and only if its truth in that circumstance is compatible with the actual truth conditions of all its atomic propositions in that very interpretation. One can derive from that simple definition classical laws of truth theory.

A new relation of strong implication between propositions

Human beings are not perfectionally rational. We are often inconsistent. For example, we sometimes assert propositions whose truth is impossible. Furthermore, our illocutionary commitments are not as strong as they should be from the logical point of view. Thus, we assert propositions without asserting all their logical consequences. We are not omniscient, and we even do not know all necessary truths. We therefore need in propositional logic a finer logical implication than C. I. Lewis's strict implication: a proposition *strictly implies* all others which are true in all possible circumstances where it is true. As we do not know which propositions are strictly implied by the propositional contents of our thoughts, our illocutionary and psychological commitments based on truth conditions are not explainable in terms of strict implication. Hintikka's epistemic logic according to which the set of propositional contents of our beliefs is closed under strict implication predicts far too many commitments.

Given my predicative analysis of the logical form of propositions, one can define a new relation of *strong implication* between propositions which is finer than Lewis's strict implication: a proposition P *strongly implies* another proposition Q when, first, all the atomic propositions of Q are in P and, second, the proposition P *tautologically implies* proposition Q—that is to say: all possible truth condition assignments to atomic propositions that are compatible with the truth of proposition P in a circumstance are also compatible with the truth of proposition Q in that very circumstance. Unlike strict implication, strong implication is cognitive. Whenever a proposition P strongly implies another proposition Q, we cannot express that proposition P without knowing a priori that it implies that other proposition Q. For in expressing P, we have in mind by hypothesis all atomic propositions of Q. We make all the corresponding acts of reference and predication. Furthermore, in understanding the truth conditions of proposition P, we have in mind all possible truth conditions of its atomic propositions that are compatible with its truth in any circumstance. The same possible truth conditions of atomic propositions of P which are in Q are by hypothesis compatible with the truth of proposition Q in the same circumstance. Thus we know in expressing P that 'if P then Q'.

Section 3   A new formulation of illocutionary logic

Thanks to the new predicative propositional logic, I have enriched the theory of success and satisfaction of elementary illocutionary acts. I have first formulated (1991b; 1995) an illocutionary logic incorporating the minimal predicative logic of elementary propositions and of their truth functions. Next (forthcoming a, b) I have incorporated predicative logics of quantification (1997), historic modalities, action (2003; 2004b), and time (2004a) in illocutionary logic. So we can now better explicate commissive, directive, and declaratory illocutionary forces whose propositional content, preparatory, and sincerity conditions are relative to time, action, and abilities—and thereby prove new valid laws governing the success conditions of elementary illocutionary acts having such forces. We can also develop the theory of satisfaction, thanks to the new theory of truth and derive illocutionary commitments based on strong implication. Because illocutionary acts are by nature actions, the new logic of action of illocutionary logic applies to illocutionary acts, as well as to the actions represented by their propositional content. I (1991b; 1994; forthcoming b) have adopted new principles in the formulation of illocutionary logic.

The speaker's minimal rationality

Competent speakers are minimally rational. As Greek and classic philosophers had anticipated, language is the work of reason.

First, competent speakers are *minimally consistent.* They never attempt to achieve an illocutionary point with a nonempty direction of fit on a contradictory propositional content. They know a priori that such attempts would fail. Declarative, imperative, performative sentences whose clauses express a contradiction (e.g., "Come and do not come!") are both illocutionarily and truth conditionally inconsistent. They express illocutionary acts that are both unperformable and un-satisfiable. Similarly, competent speakers never attempt to achieve an illocutionary point with the things-to-words direction of fit on a tautology. They know a priori that tautologies are true, no matter what they do and, consequently, that such attempts are pointless. So imperative and performative sentences like "Come or do not come!" and "I promise or do not promise to come" are illocutionarily inconsistent.

Second, whoever attempts to achieve an illocutionary point with a nonempty direction of fit on a proposition P also attempts to achieve that point on all other propositions Q strongly implied by P which satisfy the propositional content conditions of that point. For he knows a priori that there would not be satisfaction otherwise. Thus, by way of promising to serve red or white wine, a speaker *eo ipso* commits himself to serve wine. Such a promise, he knows, could not be kept otherwise.

Well-foundedness

Illocutionary commitment is well founded. Human agents have restricted abilities. They can only make a finite number of attempts in each circumstance. So they only attempt to achieve illocutionary points on a finite number of propositional contents in each context. And they can only succeed in carrying out a finite number of intentional (verbal and nonverbal) actions at each moment. Furthermore, they carry out all their successful actions at a moment by way of making at that moment a basic attempt that generates (causally, conventionally, or by extension) all these actions.[6] Thus speakers succeed in performing all their illocutionary acts in each context of utterance by way of attempting to perform a single primary illocutionary act in that context. In the use of language, they make that basic attempt by way of uttering a sentence. Their basic speech act is then an utterance act that generates all their successful illocutionary acts given the meaning of their words and the facts that exist in the proper circumstance of their context of utterance. In the case of a literal utterance, where speaker meaning is identical with sentence meaning, the primary illocutionary act that the speaker attempts to perform is by hypothesis the literal illocutionary act expressed by the uttered sentence.

Whenever an utterance is successful, it is in performing the primary act that he performs all others in the context of utterance. In such a case, the speaker then performs all illocutionary acts to which the primary illocutionary act strongly commits him. So if he primarily makes a testimony, then he also makes an assertion. But he can also perform other illocutionary acts—for example, a speaker who makes an assertion about the future also makes a prediction. A successful literal utterance today of the declarative sentence "It will rain tomorrow" is both an assertion and a prediction. However, the primary literal assertion does not strongly commit the speaker to the prediction, for tomorrow one can still make the same assertion by saying "It is raining today." But one cannot make the prediction any more, for tomorrow that assertion will be about the present and not the future.

Law of identity for illocutionary acts

Two types of elementary illocutionary acts are identical when they have the same propositional content and the same conditions of success. Two illocutionary denegations are identical when they are denegations of the same speech act. And two conditional speech acts are identical when their aim is to perform the same illocutionary act on the same condition.

Illocutionary acts are *natural kinds of use of language*. They serve linguistic purposes in relating propositions to the world with a direction of fit. Now different illocutionary acts should have different linguistic purposes, and different linguistic purposes should be either achievable under different conditions or directed at facts represented or obtainable under different conditions. Thus an elementary illocutionary act can be identified formally with the pair containing its propositional content and the set of possible contexts in which it is performed. And the logical type of a force F is that of a function that associates with each proposition P the pair corresponding to illocutionary act F(P). Given these remarks, there are three essential features in every illocutionary act: first, the (possibly empty) set of its antecedent propositions; second, the nonempty set of its constituent elementary illocutionary acts; and third, the set of all contexts where it is successfully performed. So, for example, each conditional speech act of the form $(P \vee Q) \Rightarrow A$ is identical with the conjunction $(P \Rightarrow A)$ & $(Q \Rightarrow A)$.

In order to formulate illocutionary logic I (1991b; 1994; forthcoming b) have used an artificial ideographical object language where the logical form of illocutionary acts is shown clearly on the surface by the grammatical form of the formulas that express them. So one can see on the surface whether one illocutionary force marker expresses a stronger force than another. And one can also determine effectively on the basis of their syntactic forms which clauses express propositions related by strong implication. The number of proper primitive notions of first-order illocutionary logic is small. Its theoretical vocabulary contains a few new logical constants and syncategorematic expressions expressing universals of language use.[7] Some of these universals are illocutionary: the five illocutionary points, the basic degree of strength, and, for each other type of force component, the neutral and absorbent components of that type and the various operations on components of illocutionary force. Other primitive notions of illocutionary logic are relative to propositions: identity, presupposition, expression of attitudes, functional application, truth functions, necessity, quantification, and the rest.

Many important notions of illocutionary and propositional logics like force, illocutionary acts, success and satisfaction conditions, performability, satisfiability, and strong and weak illocutionary commitment are derived from the few primitive notions by a series of rules of abbreviation. As one might expect, the syntactic form of a force marker is complex: it contains six constituents expressing the six different components of that force. Markers whose syntactic forms are the simplest express primitive forces: they only contain logical constants expressing an illocutionary point; the neutral mode of achievement of illocutionary point; the neutral degree of strength; and the neutral propositional content, preparatory, and sincerity conditions. Other force markers contain longer constituent expressions expressing complex propositional content, preparatory or sincerity conditions, or a greater or weaker degree of strength. Each formula expressing an elementary illocutionary act is a force marker followed by a clause.

The new illocutionary logic that I have formulated on the basis of these principles contains a unified theory of success, satisfaction, and truth. It explains why speakers are *not perfectly rational* and in which way they are always *minimally rational*. It also explains why some unsatisfiable illocutionary acts are performable and why others are unperformable but satisfiable. There are four important logical *relations of implication* between speech acts:

- Some illocutionary acts have more conditions of success than others: they *strongly commit the speaker to* these other illocutionary acts. For example, one cannot implore help and protection without making a request for help.
- Some illocutionary acts have more conditions of satisfaction than others: they cannot be satisfied unless the others are also satisfied. For example, whenever an elementary illocutionary act is satisfied, any assertion of its propositional content is *eo ipso* true.
- Some illocutionary acts have conditions of success that are stronger than the conditions of satisfaction of others: they cannot be successfully performed unless the others are satisfied. For example, by virtue of its double direction of fit, a successful declaration is *eo ipso* satisfied.
- Some speech acts have conditions of satisfaction that are stronger than the conditions of success of other speech acts: they cannot be satisfied in a context unless the others are performed in that context. For example, given the self-referential nature of the conditions of satisfaction of illocutionary acts with the things-to-words direction of fit, the satisfaction of directives and commissives requires their successful performance. Thus if a promise is kept, it has been made. Similarly, if an order is obeyed, it has been given.

Illocutionary logic can prove all the fundamental laws governing these four kinds of relations of implication between speech acts.[8]

Contrary to what was commonly believed before, the set of illocutionary acts is much more logically structured by these logical relations of implication than the set of propositions is structured by material or even strict implication. For example, given the general definition of success and the recursive definition of the set of all illocutionary forces, there are a few valid laws of comparative strength for illocutionary forces that explain strong illocutionary commitments due to force:

- First, any force F_2, which is obtained from another force F_1 by the application of an operation, is either stronger or weaker than that force. By definition, a force F_1 is *stronger than* another force F_2 when any illocutionary act of the form $F_1(P)$ strongly commits the speaker to the corresponding illocutionary act of the form $F_2(P)$. For example, the forces of a prediction and of a testimony are stronger than the force of an assertion. Conversely, a force F is *weaker than* another force F' when F' is stronger than F. All the Boolean operations (which consist in adding a new mode of achievement or a new propositional, preparatory, or sincerity condition) and the Abelian operation (which consists in increasing the degree of strength) generate stronger illocutionary forces.

- Second, the order of application of operations on forces is not important; it does not affect the success conditions.
- Third, when an illocutionary force is stronger than another force, it can always be obtained from that force by a finite number of applications of such operations.

The set of propositions is not structured so strongly by implication in standard logic. First, the applications of logical operations on propositions such as truth functions do not always generate implication. Second, the order of application of these operations is important; it often affects the truth conditions.

Furthermore, illocutionary logic has contributed to the theory of truth. It has discovered that the set of propositions is logically structured by a logical relation of strong implication much finer than all other relations of implication. Unlike strict implication, strong implication is antisymmetrical. Two propositions that strongly imply each other are identical. Unlike Parry's analytic implication, strong implication is always tautological. Natural deduction rules of elimination and introduction generate strong implication when all atomic propositions of the conclusion belong to the premises. So a conjunction $P \wedge Q$ strongly implies each conjunct P and Q. But a proposition P does not strongly imply any disjunction of the form $P \vee Q$. Strong implication is paraconsistent. A contradiction does not strongly imply all propositions. Tautologies (and contradictions) are a special kind of necessarily true (and false) propositions. Unlike other necessarily true propositions, we know a priori that tautologies are true (and that contradictions are false). Finally, strong implication is finite and decidable.

Section 4   General semantics of success and satisfaction

Contemporary logicians like Church (1951), Carnap (1956), Prior (1967), Belnap (Belnap and Perloff 1992; Belnap and Green 1994), Kripke (1963), Kaplan (1978b), and Marcus (1993) have used the resources of logical formalisms such as proof and model theory to formulate philosophical logics like modal, intensional, and temporal logic and the logic of demonstratives and agency which are important for the analysis of propositional contents. Such logicians have contributed to the theory of truth and meaning. Moreover, some like Montague (1974) and Cresswell (1973) contributed to the foundations of the formal syntax and semantics of natural languages. Thus logical formalisms, which were originally conceived by Frege, Russell, and Tarski for the sole study of formal languages, were successfully used and improved to generate and interpret important fragments of ordinary language.

Like Montague, I think that there is no important theoretical difference between formal and natural languages. Mathematical formalisms are most useful to explicate meaning and understanding. However, unlike Montague, Davidson, and many others, I do not believe that the single most important objective of semantics is to develop a recursive theory of truth. As I have explained, the primary units of meaning in the use and comprehension of language are not isolated propositions (or truth conditions) but complete illocutionary acts whose success and satisfaction conditions are not reducible to truth conditions. On my view, the primary objectives of semantics, then, are to formulate a theory of success and of satisfaction for illocutionary acts and not just to develop the theory of truth for propositions. For that purpose, formal semantics must integrate a unified illocutionary and intensional logic.

Until now, traditional formal semantics has tended to construct the linguistic competence of speakers as their ability to understand the propositional contents of utterances. For that reason, until *Meaning and Speech Acts*, most applications of formal semantics to actual natural languages have been restricted solely to the interpretation of declarative sentences. Thanks to illocutionary logic, formal semantics can now analyze other kinds of expressions like force markers and performative verbs whose meaning contributes to the determination of success and satisfaction conditions. For the first time in the history of logic, we now have formal means for interpreting without reduction all syntactic types of sentences (imperative, optative, conditional, exclamatory, and subjunctive, as well as declarative) expressing speech acts with any possible illocutionary force. In my approach, the semantic theory of truth advocated by Montague and Davidson for ordinary language is just the special subtheory for assertive speech acts of the more general theory of satisfaction for speech acts with an arbitrary illocutionary force. On my account, linguistic competence is not separable from performance, as Chomsky thinks. On the contrary, it is essentially the speaker's ability to perform and understand illocutionary acts which are meanings of utterances.

Natural languages have a vast vocabulary for specifying illocutionary act types and propositions. But they are ambiguous, and their grammatical conventions are so complicated that it is difficult to analyze directly the underlying logical form of attempted illocutionary acts.

First, *there is no one-to-one correspondence between illocutionary forces and performative verbs or force markers of natural languages*: "Illocutionary forces are, so to speak, natural kinds of use of language, but we can no more expect the vernacular expressions to correspond exactly to the natural kinds than we can expect vernacular names of plants and animals to correspond exactly to the natural kinds."[9] Thus, some possible illocutionary forces are *not actual* today in English. One can no longer repudiate one's wife and break off one's marriage by uttering words, as one could do in past civilizations in certain ways fixed by custom. Some possible illocutionary forces are actual in English but are not realized syntactically or lexicalized. For example, there is no marker in English for commissive illocutionary forces. One cannot directly commit oneself to doing something in English. One must speak nonliterally (by saying, for example, "I will do it") or performatively ("I promise to do it"). (In the first case, the speaker commits himself indirectly to an action by making a literal assertion. In the second, by making a literal declaration.) Moreover, actual forces such as "to boast" are named by speech act verbs that have no performative use. Certain forces have an implicit mode of achievement of their point. Notice also that performative verbs like "tell" and "swear" are ambiguous between different illocutionary points. One can assertively tell that something is the case, just as one can make a directive in telling someone to do something.

A second reason for distinguishing carefully between illocutionary forces, on the one hand, and performative verbs and illocutionary force markers, on the other hand, is that *natural languages are not perspicuous*. Many sentences of the same syntactic type (for example, declarative sentences like "They lost," "Frankly, they lost," "Of course, they lost," "Unfortunately, they lost," and " Alas, they lost") express illocutionary acts whose assertive forces are different. The same holds for illocutionary force markers. Sentential types like the declarative, imperative, and exclamatory types express primitive forces. But others like the conditional and interrogative types express derived forces. To ask a question is to request the hearer to perform a future speech act that would give a correct answer to that question. Many performative verbs with a superficially similar syntactic behavior (for example, "order," "forbid, " and "permit") do not name illocutionary acts with the same logical form. The verb "order" names a derived directive illocutionary force, but there is no force of forbidding. For an act of forbidding something is just an order not to do it. Furthermore, an act of granting permission is the illocutionary denegation of an act of forbidding.

As Russell and the first Wittgenstein argued, one should not trust too much the surface structure of ordinary language in order to describe its logical structure. It is better to analyze indirectly the deep structure of ordinary sentences via their translations into a logically perfect perspicuous and disambiguous formal object language. For that purpose, I have used in the formal semantics of success and satisfaction[10] the ideographic language of a higher-order unified illocutionary and intensional logic containing a revisited predicative propositional logic where strictly equivalent propositions are distinguished. All the logical constants and syncategorematic expressions of the ideographic object language of illocutionary logic express universal features of language, such as identity, success, truth, satisfaction, abstraction over contexts, functional application, and λ abstraction. Because of this, the syntactic rules of formation and abbreviation of the ideal object language, the meaning postulates governing its expressions in possible interpretations and the axioms and rules of inference of the corresponding axiomatic system make universal claims about the deep structure of language. Thanks to the new ideography, richer fragments of natural languages containing sentences of all syntactic types {both declarative and nondeclarative) can now be interpreted indirectly in logic. The first advantage of using an ideographic language is to have at one's disposal a theoretical vocabulary thanks to which any expressible illocutionary act can in principle be analyzed in a canonical way and be put into relationships with others. Another advantage is that, contrary to what is the case in ordinary language; the grammatical forms of its sentences reflect clearly on the surface the logical forms of the illocutionary acts that they express. As Montague (1970a, b, c) pointed out, by way of translating clauses of ordinary sentences into the ideal object language of intensional logic; formal semantics clarifies the logical form of propositions and proceeds to a better explication of their truth conditions. Similarly, by way of translating force markers and performative verbs into the ideographic object language of illocutionary logic, formal semantics can exhibit the logical form of illocutions and proceed to a better explication of their success and satisfaction conditions.

I have developed the foundations of a formal semantics of success and satisfaction for elementary illocutionary acts in *Meaning and Speech Acts*. The first volume, *Principles of Language Use*, introduces the theory; the second volume, *Formal Semantics of Success and Satisfaction*, uses proof and model theories to formalize the theory. I am now writing a new book, *The Logic of Discourse*, where I formulate a richer illocutionary logic capable of expressing historic modalities, time, and action and studying complex illocutionary acts like denegations and conditional speech acts and conversations with a discursive purpose such as consultations, interviews, deliberations, and eulogies. I have adopted the following principles in my formal theory of meaning.

1. *There are two types of meaning*. Most sentences contain expressions whose sense can vary in different contexts. They can serve to perform different illocutionary acts in different contexts. For example, each literal utterance of the sentence "Today it is raining" serves to assert the proposition that it is raining on the day of that utterance. So different assertions are made by uttering that sentence on different days. In my conception of semantics, the *linguistic meaning* of a sentence in a semantic interpretation is then a function from the set of possible contexts of utterance into the set of illocutionary acts. On the other hand, the *meaning of a sentence in a context* is the particular illocutionary act that it expresses in that context. (It is the value that the linguistic meaning of that sentence associates with that context.) Thus, linguistic meanings apply to *sentence types*, whereas illocutionary acts apply to *sentences in contexts or sentence tokens*.

2. *Illocutionary act types (and not tokens) are the units of sentence meaning in contexts*. The illocutionary act type expressed by a sentence in a context of utterance can be defined counterfactually as the primary illocutionary act that the speaker would mean to perform in that context if he were using that single sentence and speaking literally. Such an illocutionary act type exists even if the speaker does not use that sentence or if he uses it unsuccessfully in that context. Just as syntax and semantics are primarily concerned with the formation and interpreta-

tion of sentence types, speech act theory is primarily concerned with the analysis of illocutionary act types. Linguistic competence is *creative*. We only use and understand finitely many sentence tokens during our lifetime. However, we are able to use and understand an *infinite* set of sentences, including *new sentences*, which have never been used before. Similarly, we are able to perform and understand infinitely many illocutionary acts, including *new illocutionary acts* never performed before.

3. *Possible contexts of utterance consist of various features*. For the purposes of general semantics, a *possible context of utterance* of a semantic interpretation consists of one or several *speakers* and *hearers*, a *finite set of sentences* (uttered by the speaker(s) in that context), a *moment of time* and a *place* (which are the moment and place at which utterances are made in that context), a *history* containing moments of time before and after the moment of utterance,[11] and a *background*[12] relative to the forms of life and conversation in which are engaged protagonists of the utterance. The force and propositional content of literal illocutionary acts can depend on conversational background. Thus two utterances of the sentence "Cut the grass!" express different directives in contexts where speaker and hearer are talking of a different grass lawn. Moreover, as Searle (1980) pointed out, different denotations can correspond to the same senses in circumstances with different backgrounds. For example, in order to cut the same grass lawn, a hearer can use a lawnmower in an ordinary background where the purposes of contextual forms of life are esthetical (to make the lawn more beautiful). But he has to act differently when the purposes are to sell the lawn. (In that case he must transplant the grass.)

4. *Speaker meaning is reduced to sentence meaning*. In semantics one assumes insofar as possible that speakers speak literally and mean what they say. Thus the primary illocutionary act that the speaker means to perform in a context according to a semantic interpretation is always the conjunction of all literal illocutionary acts expressed by the sentences that he utters in that context, when all such illocutionary acts are simultaneously performable. For example, if the speaker says "Can you pass the salt?" he refers to the salt and not the sugar, and he means to ask a question about the hearer's abilities and not to indirectly request him to pass the salt. Speakers who use an illocutionarily inconsistent sentence like "I am not myself today" know by virtue of competence that it is impossible to perform the literal illocutionary act. So they do not mean what they say. They mean something else. In the present formal semantics of literal meaning, I will consider that they do not mean anything.[13]

5. *There is a double semantic indexation in the understanding of meaning*. Just as the same sentence can express different illocutionary act types in different contexts of utterance, the illocutionary act, which is the meaning of a sentence in a context, can have different success and satisfaction values in different circumstances. For example, the present utterance "I am awake right now" is a successful and true assertion about Daniel Vanderveken in the present circumstance. But that particular assertion about me is not true in other circumstances where I am sleeping. Moreover, it is not often made in the use of English. In my view, we interpret sentences and assign to them a meaning in two steps:

1. In the first step, we interpret a sentence as expressing certain *literal illocutionary acts* in various contexts of utterance. In our interpretation, we determine the nature of literal speech acts from the *linguistic meaning* of that sentence and the *relevant aspects of each context*. Sometimes, we understand the linguistic meaning of a sentence. But that sentence contains an expression such as "yesterday" or "he" whose sense is context-dependent. And we do not know the relevant feature of the context of utterance. In that case, we are not able to fully understand the illocutionary act that is the meaning of that sentence in that particular context. Expressions whose linguistic meaning is sensitive to contextual aspects of the same type (e.g., "tomorrow," "today," and "yesterday") can have the same sense

in different contexts (taking place in following days). Thus nonsynonymous sentences of ordinary language can express literally the same illocutionary act in different contexts whose contextual aspects are related in certain ways. For example, the three sentences "It will rain tomorrow," "It is raining today," and "It has rained yesterday" serve to make the same assertion whenever they are used in three days running. By virtue of linguistic competence, we are aware of such meaning similarities.

2. In the second step of our interpretation, each illocutionary act, which is the meaning of a sentence in a context, is then evaluated in its turn as having a *success* and a *satisfaction value* in various contexts of utterance. From a philosophical point of view, the success and satisfaction values of an illocutionary act in a context are dependent on particular aspects like the moment of time, history, and background that constitute the particular *circumstance* of that context. Success and satisfaction values of an illocution can then vary from one circumstance to another in an interpretation. For example, the assertion that Paul will win is true in a circumstance if and only if Paul wins in another circumstance at a posterior moment in the same history and background. As Searle (1981) pointed out, the truth value of propositions and satisfaction values of illocutionary acts are relative to the background of contexts. The same holds for success values. However, as Kaplan anticipated, these values are always the same in contexts occurring in the same circumstance.

Just as we can understand an expressed proposition without knowing whether it is true in the context of utterance, we can understand the illocutionary act that a speaker attempts to perform in a context without knowing whether or not it is successful or satisfied. We often do not know whether the relevant facts exist in the circumstance of that context.

6. *There is a general ramification of the fundamental semantic notions of analyticity, consistency, and entailment.* As I said earlier, one must distinguish the two notions of illocutionary and truth-conditional consistency in language. Similarly, one must distinguish the notions of illocutionary and truth-conditional analyticity. Some sentences—for example, Moore's paradoxical sentence "It is raining and I do not believe it"—are *analytically unsuccessful*: they can never be used literally with success. Others like "I do not exist" are *analytically insatisfied*: they can never be used literally with satisfaction. Such notions do not have the same extension. Utterances of Moore's paradoxical sentence are not analytically insatisfied.

Just as illocutionary acts are related by four different kinds of implication, sentences are related by *four different kinds of entailment* in the deep structure of language:

1. *Illocutionary entailment*: A sentence such as "I request your help" illocutionarily entails the sentence "Please, help me!": it expresses in each context of use an illocution that the speaker could not perform in that context without also performing the illocution expressed by the second sentence.

2. *Truth-conditional entailment*: A sentence like "Please, eat!" truth-conditionally entails the sentence "You are able to eat": it expresses in each context of use an illocution that could not be satisfied in that context unless the illocution expressed by the second sentence is also satisfied.

3. *Illocutionary entailment of satisfaction*: A sentence illocutionarily entails the satisfaction of another sentence when it expresses in each context an illocution whose successful performance in that context implies the satisfaction of the illocution expressed by the other sentence. For example, performative sentences illocutionarily entail their own satisfaction.

4. *Truth-conditional entailment of success*: Finally, a sentence truth conditionally entails the success of another sentence when it expresses in each context an illocution whose satisfaction in that context implies the successful performance of the illocution expressed by the second sentence. For example, imperative and performative sentences truth-conditionally entail their own success.

The four preceding relations of entailment exist between sentences when the illocutionary acts that they express in a possible context of utterance always have *in that very context* related success or satisfaction values. However illocutionary acts that are the meanings of two sentences in a given context of utterance also have success and satisfaction values in all other possible contexts. And one can quantify over all these values. So there are four strong relations of entailment of each type in the logic of language—for example, strong illocutionary and strong truth-conditional entailment. A sentence strongly illocutionarily entails (or strongly truth-conditionally entails) another sentence when it expresses in any context an illocutionary act that has the same or more success (or satisfaction) conditions than the illocutionary act expressed by the other sentence in the same context. As one can expect from Kaplan's logic of demonstratives, not all cases of illocutionary or truth-conditional entailment are strong. For example, the sentence "John asserts that he won yesterday" both illocutionarily and truth-conditionally entails (but not strongly) the sentence "John reports that he won yesterday."

Notions of illocutionary consistency, analyticity, and entailment had been completely ignored until now by formal semantics. However, as I pointed out in *Meaning and Speech Acts*, all the ramified notions that I have defined exist for all kinds of sentences (whether declarative or not) in ordinary language. And they do not coincide in extension. For example, performative sentences illocutionarily entail (but not truth-conditionally) corresponding nonperformative sentences. By assigning entire illocutionary acts as semantic values to sentences in contexts, semantics can better describe the logic of language.

On the basis of the principles that I have just explained, I have pursued Montague's program and developed in volume 2 of *Meaning and Speech Acts* a general formal semantics of success and satisfaction that is a generalization and extension of Montague's intensional logic. For my purposes, I have enriched the conceptual apparatus of intensional logic in various ways. I have used as ideal object language the ideographic object language of a higher-order illocutionary logic that contains that of intensional logic. As I said earlier, all logical constants or syncategorematic expressions express primitive notions that are *material or formal linguistic universals* relative to force or propositions. I have defined all other fundamental illocutionary and intensional notions by rules of abbreviation. I have explained how to translate the different syntactic types of declarative, conditional, imperative, performative, exclamatory, optative, subjunctive, and interrogative sentences into the ideal language. To stratify the universe of discourse, I have enriched formal ontology by admitting the new primitive type of success values in addition to those of truth values, individuals, and attributes. I have changed the definition of the logical type of propositions in the predicative way. Furthermore, I have adopted the double semantic indexation advocated above. So illocutionary acts are the meanings of sentences in contexts of interpretations. I have defined recursively truth, success, and satisfaction by induction on the length of clauses and sentences in canonical notation. And I have axiomatized all generally valid laws of my illocutionary logic. Incidentally, the axiomatic system is a conservative extension of that of Gallin for Montague's intensional logic.

Unlike Montague, who tended to consider formal semantics and universal grammar as parts of mathematics, I think—like Searle, Chomsky, and others—that philosophy, linguistics, and psychology have to take an important role in their development. Natural languages are human languages whose speakers have creative and restricted abilities. We are able to learn them and to understand rapidly the meanings of their sentences. We know by virtue of linguistic competence the logical forms of sentences whose utterances are analytically unsuccessful. We also know just by understanding them which sentences are related by illocutionary entailment. So we need a very constructive formal theory of meaning that accounts for such facts. I have formulated general semantics so as to make decidable innate notions. Here are a few important laws of the logic of language that I have stated.

There are sentences whose utterances are analytically successful and satisfied: for example, "I am speaking" and Descartes' *Cogito* "I am thinking now." But these sentences do not express necessarily and a priori true propositions. Contrary to what was commonly believed in logical positivism, the notions of analytic, a priori, and necessary truth do not coincide in extension. Kaplan (1978b) has noticed that analytically true sentences like "I am here now" are not necessarily true, and Kripke (1971) pointed out that necessarily true sentences like "Water is H_2O" are not a priori true. All their distinctions hold and can be generalized at the illocutionary level and for all types of sentences. Kaplan also discovered the existence of analytically false sentences—for example, "I do not exist"—which are, however, truth-conditionally consistent. Similarly, Moore's paradoxical sentence "It is raining today and I do not believe it" is analytically unsuccessful, but it is illocutionarily consistent. Nothing prevents my making that assertion tomorrow by saying "It was raining yesterday and I did not believe it."

Because of the minimal rationality of competent speakers, semantic paradoxes like the liar paradox do not really occur in the use of language. Contrary to what Russell and Tarski believed, natural languages are not inconsistent because they contain paradoxical sentences like "This assertion is false" and, let me add, "I will not keep this promise," "Disobey this order," et cetera. It is not necessary to prevent the formation of such sentences in logic in order to avoid paradoxes. As I have shown, one can translate without inconsistency these paradoxical sentences in the object language of general semantics. For their self-referential utterances are not both satisfied and insatisfied, as logicians wrongly believe. When their logical form is well analyzed, it appears that in order to be satisfied such utterances would have to be successful. And this is impossible given the law of minimal consistency of speakers stated above. As Prior (1971) anticipated, the liar's paradox is of the form "There exists a proposition P such that I assert P and P is not true and P is that very proposition, namely that there is a proposition P such that I assert P and P is not true." Whenever the logical form of the liar's paradox is so analyzed, one discovers that it is a false assertion that no one can make. For its propositional content is a pure contradiction incompatible with all possible truth conditions. Sentences expressing that paradox are then both illocutionarily and truth-conditionally inconsistent.

The general semantics of success and satisfaction studies inferences from a new point of view. An inference is valid whenever it is not possible for its premises to express illocutionary acts with certain success or satisfaction values unless its conclusion also expresses an illocutionary act with the same or other success or satisfaction values. So general semantics can formulate valid laws of inference for all types or sentences. It can study *practical inferences* whose conclusion has the things-to-words direction of fit, as well as *theoretical inferences* whose conclusion has the words-to-things direction of fit. Until now, contemporary logic and formal semantics have been confined to the study of the sole *assertive use* of language and to the interpretation of *declarative sentences*. They have studied the *valid forms of theoretical inferences* whose premises cannot be true unless their conclusion is also true. However, we are not able to make all such valid theoretical inferences by virtue of linguistic competence. For we understand propositions without knowing how they are related by strict implication. Moreover, there are many other kinds of inference relative to success and satisfaction conditions. From the point of view of universal grammar, the most interesting principles of valid inferences are those that speakers have necessarily internalized in learning their mother tongue. They reflect the very nature of *human reason* and constitute a decidable *natural logic* that is part of linguistic competence. The logical semantics of speech acts is able to study these principles. For example, we are all able by virtue of competence to make practical and theoretical inferences whose premises cannot be successful and satisfied unless their conclusion is also successful and satisfied. For example, when we understand the request expressed by a literal utterance of the imperative sentence "Please, come and see me tomorrow at home or in the office!" we infer automatically that the speaker also means to request "Please, come and see me tomorrow!" For we know by virtue of our competence that it is not possible to make the request expressed by the premise without making that expressed by the conclusion. And we also know by competence that it is not possible to grant the first request without also granting the second.

Here are a few characteristic laws of the semantics for speech acts.

A sentence of the form [d]f(p) strongly entails both illocutionarily and truth conditionally the shorter sentence f(p) when its complex marker [d]f contains an additional expression d naming a force component or serving to increase the degree of strength. Thus, sentences like "Come, please!" "Frankly, come!" "Come urgently!" and "O.K. come!" strongly illocutionarily and truth conditionally entail "Come!"

The interrogative type of sentence contains the imperative type. So any interrogative sentence (e.g., "Is it raining?") is synonymous with the corresponding imperative sentence ("Please, tell whether or not it is raining!").

Exclamatory sentences are the weakest type of sentences. For every successful performance of an illocutionary act is an expression of the attitudes determined by its sincerity conditions. So every elementary sentence (e.g., "Alas, he is dead") strongly illocutionary entails corresponding exclamatory sentences (e.g., "How sad that he be dead!") But the converse is not true. For there is more in the performance of an illocution with a nonempty direction of fit than a simple expression of attitudes.

Performative sentences are the strongest type of sentence. For every successful declaration is felicitous. So performative sentences like "I ask you if it is raining" strongly illocutionarily entail corresponding nonperformative sentences "Is it raining?" But the converse is not true. For we need not make a declaration in order to perform an illocutionary act. We can directly perform it. So the so-called performative hypothesis is false. Performative sentences are not synonymous with corresponding nonperformative sentences.

Every explicit performative sentence (e.g., "I hereby condemn you to death") strongly entails both illocutionarily and truth conditionally the corresponding declarative sentence ("You are condemned to death."). For any successful declaration is an assertion. But the converse is not true. So performative utterances are not assertions to the effect that the speaker performs an illocutionary act, as G. J. Warnock (1973) and others claim.

Only the rules of introduction and elimination of natural deduction whose premises contain the clauses of their conclusion generate strong illocutionary entailment between sentences whose marker expresses a nonexpressive force. Thus "Do it today or tomorrow!" illocutionarily and truth-conditionally entails "Do it!" But "Do it today!" does not illocutionarily entail "Do it today or tomorrow!" (Such laws had been formulated in an ad hoc way in *Foundations*.)

Unlike applied semantics of empirical linguistics, general semantics is above all a logico-philosophical theory of language. It deals mainly with the logical form of meanings of possible utterances of sentences of possible natural languages and only incidentally with particular actual realizations of these possibilities in living languages. Its primary objective is to articulate and exhibit the deep logical structure common to all possible natural language. As Cocchiarella (1997,

72) pointed out, my program is also an attempt to articulate what classical philosophers called a priori forms of thought: "In any case, the notion of a lingua philosophica containig both an intensional and illocutionary logic is no longer merely a program but has already in many respects been realized."

As Searle and I pointed out, illocutionary logic is transcendental in Kant's sense. Any conceptual thought is in principle expressible by means of language in the performance of an illocutionary act. Consequently, necessary and universal semantic laws determining the conditions of possibility of successful meaningful utterances reflect a priori forms of thought. It is impossible to have a thought whose expression would ever violate such laws. General semantics aims to do more than stating empirical laws governing meaning and understanding. In the tradition of transcendental philosophy, it also aims to fix limits to thought. According to Wittgenstein (1961[1922]), the logic of language fixes limits to thought indirectly by fixing limits to their expression in language. In general semantics, limits of thought show themselves in language in the fact that sentences of certain logical forms can never be used literally with success. We can of course refer to impossible thoughts, describe their forms, and even attribute them to others. But we can never really entertain these impossible thoughts in the first person, just as we cannot speak and think literally when we make analytically unsuccessful utterances. Along the same lines, the fact that sentences of certain logical forms illocutionarily entail others shows that we cannot have certain thoughts without having others. So language reflects the a priori order of thought.

Notes

1. The term of force was first used by Frege (1972; 1977).

2. See also the *Tractatus logico-philosophicus* 3.251 and section 99 of his *Philosophical Investigations*.

3. The neutral propositional content condition associates with each context of utterance the set of all propositions and the absorbent propositional content condition the empty set.

4. One can find a first formulation of the classical theory of truth by correspondence in Aristotle's Metaphysics. See also G. Frege (1977) and A. Tarski (1944).

5. Logicians and philosophers like Rescher (1966) and Belnap and Steel (1976) who have constructed earlier logics of speech acts such as the logic of commands and the logic of questions have neglected success and satisfaction in favor of truth in their analyses.

6. See Goldman (1970) for the terminology of generation of actions and my paper (Vanderveken 2004b) on the basic logic of action.

7. See Vanderveken (2001a), "Universal Grammar and Speech Act Theory."

8. See Vanderveken (1991b; volume 2 of *Meaning and Speech Acts*) and my paper (1994).

9. Searle and Vanderveken (1985), p. 179.

10. See Vanderveken 1991b.

11. Speech act theory requires a logic of branching time that is compatible with indeterminism and the liberty of human agents. In the logic of branching time, a *moment* is a possible state of the world at an instant and the temporal relation of anteriority/posteriority is partial rather than linear. On the one hand, each moment is immediately preceded by at most one moment. On the other hand, several incompatible moments might immediately follow upon a given moment. A *history* is a maxjmal chain of moments of time. See Belnap and Green (1994) and Vanderveken (2001; 2004a). Unlike Belnap, I believe that contexts of utterance occur not only at a moment but also in a history. For the utterances and illocutionary acts which are made in a context are in general part of a discourse or conversation which occur during an interval of time containing past and future moments of utterances. The discourse to which the speaker contributes by asking a question is not the same if the hearer answers one way or another. Furthermore, the interpretation of an utterance can depend on a future exchange between protagonists of the discourse. For considerations on the logical structure of discourses see Vanderveken (forthcoming a).

12. The term and notions of background are from Searle (1979; 1981).

13. It is the purpose of formal pragmatics to study nonliteral meaning. See Vanderveken (1991a) and (1997b) for considerations on nonliteral illocutionary acts.

36

DONALD DAVIDSON

The Logical Form of Action Sentences

Strange goings on! Jones did it slowly, deliberately, in the bathroom, with a knife, at midnight. What he did was butter a piece of toast. We are too familiar with the language of action to notice at first an anomaly: the "it" of "Jones did it slowly, deliberately, . . ." seems to refer to some entity, presumably an action, that is then characterized in a number of ways. Asked for the logical form of this sentence, we might volunteer something like "There is an action x such that Jones did x slowly and Jones did x deliberately and Jones did x in the bathroom, . . ." and so on. But then we need an appropriate singular term to substitute for 'x'. In fact, we know Jones buttered a piece of toast. And, allowing a little slack, we can substitute for 'x' and get "Jones buttered a piece of toast slowly and Jones buttered a piece of toast deliberately and Jones buttered a piece of toast in the bathroom . . ." and so on. The trouble is that we have nothing here we could ordinarily recognize as a singular term. Another sign that we have not caught the logical form of the sentence is that in this last version there is no implication that any *one* action was slow, deliberate, and in the bathroom, though this is clearly part of what is meant by the original.

The present paper is devoted to trying to get the logical form of simple sentences about actions straight. I would like to give an account of the logical or grammatical role of the parts or words of such sentences that is consistent with the entailment relations between such sentences and with what is known of the role of those same parts or words in other (non-action) sentences. I take this enterprise to be the same as showing how the meanings of action sentences depend on their structure. I am not concerned with the meaning analysis of logically simple expressions insofar as this goes beyond the question of logical form. Applied to the case at hand, for example, I am not concerned with the meaning of "deliberately" as opposed, perhaps, to "voluntarily"; but I am interested in the logical role of both these words.

To give another illustration of the distinction I have in mind: we need not view the difference between "Joe believes that there is life on Mars" and "Joe knows that there is life on Mars"

Donald Davidson (1966) The logical form of action sentences. In Nicholas Rescher (ed.), *The Logic of Decision and Action* (© 1966 by the University of Pittsburgh Press). Reprinted by permission of the University of Pittsburgh Press.

as a difference in logical form. That the second, but not the first, entails "There is life on Mars" is plausibly a logical truth; but it is a truth that emerges only when we consider the meaning analysis of "believes" and "knows." Admittedly, there is something arbitrary in how much of logic to pin on logical form. But limits are set if our interest is in giving a coherent and constructive account of meaning: we must uncover enough structure to make it possible to state, for an arbitrary sentence, how its meaning depends on that structure, and we must not attribute more structure than such a theory of meaning can accommodate.

Consider the sentence:

(1)   Jones buttered the toast slowly, deliberately, in the bathroom, with a knife, at midnight.

Despite the superficial grammar we cannot, I shall argue later, treat the "deliberately" on a par with the other modifying clauses. It alone imputes intention, for of course Jones may have buttered the toast slowly, in the bathroom, with a knife, at midnight, and quite unintentionally, having mistaken the toast for his hairbrush which was what he intended to butter. Let us, therefore, postpone discussion of the "deliberately" and its intentional kindred.

"Slowly," unlike the other adverbial clauses, fails to introduce a new entity (a place, an instrument, a time), and also may involve a special difficulty. For suppose we take "Jones buttered the toast slowly" as saying that Jones's buttering of the toast was slow; is it clear that we can equally well say of Jones's action, no matter how we describe it, that it was slow? A change in the example will help. Susan says, "I crossed the Channel in fifteen hours." "Good grief, that was slow." (Notice how much more naturally we say "slow" here than "slowly." But *what* was slow, what does "that" refer to? No appropriate singular term appears in "I crossed the Channel in fifteen hours.") Now Susan adds, "But I swam." "Good grief, that was fast." We do not withdraw the claim that it was a slow crossing; this is consistent with its being a fast swimming. Here we have enough to show, I think, that we cannot construe "It was a slow crossing" as "It was slow and it was a crossing" since the crossing may also be a swimming that was not slow, in which case we would have "It was slow and it was a crossing and it was a swimming and it was not slow." The problem is not peculiar to talk of actions, however. It appears equally when we try to explain the logical role of the attributive adjectives in "Grundy was a short basketball player, but a tall man," and "This is a good memento of the murder, but a poor steak knife." The problem of attributives is indeed a problem about logical form, but it may be put to one side here because it is not a problem only when the subject is action.

We have decided to ignore, for the moment at least, the first two adverbial modifiers in (1), and may now deal with the problem of the logical form of:

(2)   Jones buttered the toast in the bathroom with a knife at midnight.

Anthony Kenny, who deserves the credit for calling explicit attention to this problem,[1] points out that most philosophers today would, as a start, analyze this sentence as containing a five-place predicate with the argument places filled in the obvious ways with singular terms or bound variables. If we go on to analyze "Jones buttered the toast" as containing a two-place predicate, "Jones buttered the toast in the bathroom" as containing a three-place predicate, and so forth, we obliterate the logical relation between these sentences—namely, that (2) entails the others. Or, to put the objection another way, the original sentences contain a common syntactic element ("buttered") which we intuitively recognize as relevant to the meaning relations of the sentences. But the proposed analyses show no such common syntactic element.

Kenny rejects the suggestion that "Jones buttered the toast" be considered as elliptical for "Jones buttered the toast somewhere with something at some time," which would restore the wanted entailments, on the ground that we could never be sure how many standby positions to provide in each predicate of action. For example, couldn't we add to (2) the phrase "by holding it between the toes of his left foot"? Still, this adds a place to the predicate only if it differs in meaning from "while holding it between the toes of his left foot," and it is not quite clear that this is so. I am inclined to agree with Kenny that we cannot view verbs of action as usually containing a large number of standby positions, but I do not have what I would consider a knock-down argument. (A knock-down argument would consist in a method for increasing the number of places indefinitely.[2])

Kenny proposes that we may exhibit the logical form of (2) in somewhat the following manner:

(3)   Jones brought it about that the toast was buttered in the bathroom with a knife at midnight.

Whatever the other merits in this proposal (I shall consider some of them presently), is clear that it does not solve the problem Kenny raises. For it is, if anything, even more obscure how (3) entails "Jones brought it about that the toast was buttered" or "The toast was buttered" than how (2) entails "Jones buttered the toast." Kenny seems to have confused two different problems. One is the problem of how to represent the idea of *agency*: it is this that prompts Kenny to assign "Jones" a logically distinguished role in (3). The other is the problem of the "variable polyadicity" (as Kenny calls it) of action verbs. And it is clear that this problem is independent of the first, since it arises with respect to the sentences that replace 'p' in "x brings it about that p."

If I say I bought a house downtown that has four bedrooms, two fireplaces, and a glass chandelier in the kitchen, it's obvious that I can go on forever adding details. Yet the logical form of the sentences I use presents no problem (in this respect). It is something like "There is a house such that I bought it, it is downtown, it has four bedrooms, . . ." and so forth. We can tack on a new clause at will because the iterated relative pronoun will carry the reference back to the same entity as often as desired. (Of course we know how to state this much more precisely.) Much of our talk of action suggests the same idea: that there are such *things* as actions, and that a sentence like (2) describes the action in a number of ways. "Jones did it with a knife." "Please tell me more about it." The "it" here doesn't refer to Jones or the knife, but to what Jones did—or so it seems.

"It is in principle always open to us, along various lines, to describe or refer to 'what I did' in so many different ways," writes Austin in "A Plea for Excuses."[3] Austin is obviously leery of the apparent singular term, which he puts in scare quotes; yet the grammar of his sentence requires a singular term. Austin would have had little sympathy, I imagine, for the investigation into logical form I am undertaking here, though the demand that underlies it, for an intuitively acceptable and constructive theory of meaning, is one that begins to appear in the closing chapters of *How to Do Things with Words*. But in any case, Austin's discussion of excuses illustrates over and over the fact that our common talk and reasoning about actions is most naturally analyzed by supposing that there are such entities.

"I didn't know it was loaded" belongs to one standard pattern of excuse. I do not deny that I pointed the gun and pulled the trigger, nor that I shot the victim. My ignorance explains how it happened that I pointed the gun and pulled the trigger intentionally, but did not shoot the victim intentionally. That the bullet pierced the victim was a consequence of my pointing the gun and pulling the trigger. It is clear that these are two different events, since one began slightly after the other. But what is the relation between my pointing the gun and pulling the trigger, and my shooting the victim? The natural and, I think, correct answer is that the relation is that of identity. The logic of this sort of excuse includes, it seems, at least this much structure: I am accused of doing b, which is deplorable. I admit I did a, which is excusable. My excuse for doing b rests upon my claim that I did not know that $a = b$.

Another pattern of excuse would have me allow that I shot the victim intentionally, but in self-defense. Now the structure includes something more. I am still accused of b (my shooting the victim), which is deplorable. I admit I did c (my shooting the victim in self-defense), which is excusable. My excuse for doing b rests upon my claim that I knew or believed that $b = c$. The additional structure, not yet displayed, would reveal the following as a logical truth: $x = c \rightarrow x = b$: that is, if an action is my shooting the victim in self-defense, it is my shooting the victim.

The story can be given another twist. Again I shoot the victim, again intentionally. What I am asked to explain is my shooting of the bank president (d), for the victim was that distinguished gentleman. My excuse is that I shot the escaping murderer (e), and, surprising and unpleasant as it is, my shooting the escaping murderer and my shooting of the bank president were one and the same action ($e = d$), since the bank president and the escaping murderer were one and the same person. To justify the "since" we must presumably think of "my shooting of x" as a functional expression that names an action when the 'x' is replaced by an appropriate singular term. The relevant reasoning would then be an application of the principle $x = y \rightarrow fx = fy$.

Excuses provide endless examples of cases where we seem compelled to take talk of "alternative descriptions of the same action" seriously—that is, literally. But there are plenty of other contexts in which the same need presses. *Explaining* an action by giving an intention with which it was done provides new descriptions of the action: I am writing my name on a piece of paper with the intention of writing a check with the intention of paying my gambling debt. List all the different descriptions of my action. Here are a few for a start: I am writing my name. I am writing my name on a piece of paper. I am writing my name on a piece of paper with the intention of writing a check. I am writing a check. I am paying my gambling debt. It is hard to imagine how we can have a coherent theory of action unless we are allowed to say here: each of these sentences describes the same action. Redescription may supply the motive ("I was getting my revenge"), place the action in the context of a rule ("I am castling"), give the outcome ("I killed him"), or provide evaluation ("I did the right thing").

According to Kenny, as we just noted, action sentences have the form "Jones brought it about that p." The sentence that replaces 'p' is to be in the present tense, and it describes the result that the agent has wrought: it is a sentence "newly true of the patient."[4] Thus "The doctor removed the patient's appendix" must be rendered "The doctor brought it about that the patient has no appendix." By insisting that the sentence that replaces 'p' describe a terminal *state* rather than an *event*, it may be thought that Kenny can avoid the criticism made above that the problem of logical form of action sentences turns up within the sentence that replaces 'p': we may allow that "The patient has no appendix" presents no relevant problem. The difficulty is that neither will the analysis stand in its present form. The doctor may bring it about that the patient has no appendix by turning the patient over to another doctor who performs the operation—or by running the patient down with his Lincoln Continental. In neither case would we say the doctor removed the patient's appendix. Closer approximations to a correct analysis might be "The doctor brought it about that the doctor has removed the patient's appendix" or perhaps "The doctor brought it about that the patient has had his appendix removed by the doctor." One may still have a few doubts, I think, as to whether these sentences have the same truth conditions as "The doctor removed the patient's appendix." But in any case it is plain that in these versions, the problem of the logical form of action sentences does turn up in the sentences that replace 'p': "The patient has had his appendix removed by the doctor" or "The doctor has removed the patient's appendix" are surely no *easier* to analyze than "The doctor removed the patient's appendix." By the same token, "Cass walked to the store" can't be given as "Cass brought it about that Cass is at the store," since this drops the idea of walking. Nor is it clear that "Cass brought it about that Cass is at the store and is there through having walked" will serve; but in any case again the contained sentence is worse than what we started with.

It is not easy to decide what to do with "Smith coughed." Should we say "Smith brought it about that Smith is in a state of just having coughed"? At best this would be correct only if Smith coughed on purpose.

The difficulty in Kenny's proposal that we have been discussing may perhaps be put this way: he wants to represent every (completed) action in terms only of the agent, the notion of bringing it about that a state of affairs obtains, and the state of affairs brought about by the agent. But many action sentences yield no description of the state of affairs brought about by the action except that it *is* the state of affairs brought about by that action. A natural move, then, is to allow that the sentence that replaces '*p*' in "*x* brings it about that *p*" may (or perhaps must) describe an event.

If I am not mistaken, Chisholm has suggested an analysis that at least permits the sentence that replaces '*p*' to describe (as we are allowing ourselves to say) an event.[5] His favored locution is "*x* makes *p* happen," though he uses such variants as "*x* brings it about that *p*" or "*x* makes it true that *p*." Chisholm speaks of the entities to which the expressions that replace '*p*' refer as "states of affairs," and explicitly adds that states of affairs may be changes or events (as well as "unchanges"). An example Chisholm provides is this: if a man raises his arm, then we may say he makes it happen that his arm goes up. I do not know whether Chisholm would propose "Jones made it happen that Jones's arm went up" as an analysis of "Jones raised his arm," but I think the proposal would be wrong because although the second of these sentences does perhaps entail the first, the first does not entail the second. The point is even clearer if we take as our example "Jones batted an eyelash." In this case I think nothing will do but "Jones made it happen that Jones batted an eyelash" (or some trivial variant), and this cannot be called progress in uncovering the logical form of "Jones batted an eyelash."

There is something else that may puzzle us about Chisholm's analysis of action sentences, and it is independent of the question what sentence we substitute for '*p*'. Whatever we put for '*p*', we are to interpret it as describing some event. It is natural to say, I think, that *whole* sentences of the form "*x* makes it happen that *p*" also describe events. Should we say that these events are the *same* event, or that they are different? If they are the same event, as many people would claim (perhaps including Chisholm), then no matter what we put for '*p*', we cannot have solved the *general* problem of the logical form of sentences about actions until we have dealt with the sentences that can replace '*p*'. If they are different events, we must ask how the element of agency has been introduced into the larger sentence though it is lacking in the sentence for which '*p*' stands; for each has the agent as its subject. The answer Chisholm gives, I think, is that the special notion of making it happen that he has in mind is intentional, and thus to be distinguished from simply causing something to happen.

Suppose we want to say that Alice broke the mirror without implying that she did it intentionally. Then Chisholm's special idiom is not called for; but we could say "Alice caused it to happen that the mirror broke." Suppose we now want to add that she did it intentionally. Then the Chisholm-sentence would be: "Alice made it happen that Alice caused it to happen that the mirror broke." And now we want to know, what is the event that the whole sentence reports, and that the contained sentence does not? It is, apparently, just what used to be called an act of the will. I will not dredge up the standard objections to the view that acts of the will are special events distinct from, say, our bodily movements, and perhaps the causes of them. But even if Chisholm is willing to accept such a view, the problem of the logical form of the sentences that can replace '*p*' remains, and these describe the things people do as we describe them when we do not impute intention.

A somewhat different view has been developed with care and precision by von Wright in his book *Norm and Action*.[6] In effect, von Wright puts action sentences into the following form: "*x* brings it about that a state where *p* changes into a state where *q*." Thus the important relevant difference between von Wright's analysis and the ones we have been considering is the more complex structure of the description of the change or event the agent brings about: where Kenny and Chisholm were content to describe the result of the change, von Wright includes also a description of the initial state.

Von Wright is interested in exploring the logic of change and action and not, at least primarily, in giving the logical form of our common sentences about acts or events. For the purposes of his study, it may be very fruitful to think of events as ordered pairs of states. But I think it is also fairly obvious that this does not give us a standard way of translating or representing the form of most sentences about acts and events. If I walk from San Francisco to Pittsburgh, for example, my initial state is that I am in San Francisco and my terminal state is that I am in Pittsburgh; but the same is more pleasantly true if I fly. Of course, we may describe the terminal state as my having walked to Pittsburgh from San Francisco, but then we no longer need the separate statement of the initial state. Indeed, viewed as an analysis of ordinary sentences about actions, von Wright's proposal seems subject to all the difficulties I have already outlined plus the extra one that most action sentences do not yield a non-trivial description of the initial state (try "He circled the field," "He recited the *Odyssey*," "He flirted with Olga").

In two matters, however, it seems to me von Wright suggests important and valuable changes in the pattern of analysis we have been considering, or at least in our interpretation of it. First, he says that an action is not an event, but, rather, the bringing about of an event. I do not think this can be correct. If I fall down, this is an event whether I do it intentionally or not. If you thought my falling was an accident and later discovered I did it on purpose, you would not be tempted to withdraw your claim that you had witnessed an event. I take von Wright's refusal to call an action an event to be a reflection of the embarrassment we found follows if we say an act is an event, when agency is introduced by a phrase like "brings it about that." The solution lies, however, not in distinguishing acts from events, but in finding a different logical form for action sentences. The second important idea von Wright introduces comes in the context of his distinction between *generic* and *individual* propositions about events.[7] This distinction is not, as von Wright makes it, quite clear, for he says both: that an individual proposition differs from a generic one in having a uniquely determined truth value, while a generic proposition has a truth value only when coupled with an occasion; and that, that Brutus killed Caesar is an individual proposition while that Brutus kissed Caesar is a generic proposition, because "a person can be kissed by another on more than one occasion." In fact, the proposition that Brutus kissed Caesar seems to have a uniquely determined truth value in the same sense that the proposition that Brutus killed Caesar does. But it is, I believe, a very important observation that "Brutus kissed Caesar" does not, by virtue of its meaning alone, describe a single act.

It is easy to see that the proposals we have been considering concerning the logical form of action sentences do not yield solutions to the problems with which we began. I have already pointed out that Kenny's problem, that verbs of action apparently have "variable polyadicity," arises within the sentences that can replace '*p*' in such formulas as "*x* brought it about that *p*." An analogous remark goes for von Wright's more elaborate formula. The other main problem may be put as that of assigning a logical form to action sentences that will justify claims that two sentences describe "the same action." A study of some of the ways in which we excuse, or attempt to excuse, acts shows that we want to make inferences such as this: I flew my spaceship to the Morning Star, the Morning Star is identical with the Evening Star; so, I flew my spaceship to the Evening Star. (My leader told me not to go to the Evening Star; I headed for the Morning Star not knowing.) But suppose we translate the action sentences along the lines suggested by Kenny or Chisholm or von Wright. Then we have something like "I brought it about that my spaceship is on the Morning Star." How can we infer, given the well-known identity, "I brought it about that my spaceship is on the Evening Star"? We know that if we replace "the Morning Star" by "the Evening Star" in "My spaceship is on the Morning Star" the truth-value will not be disturbed; and so if the occurrence of this sentence in "I brought it about that my spaceship is on the Morning Star" is truth-functional, the inference is justified. But of course the occurrence can't be truth-functional: otherwise, from the fact that I brought about one actual state of affairs it would follow that I brought about every actual state of affairs. It is no good saying that after the words "bring it about that" sentences describe something *between* truth-values and propositions, say states of affairs. Such a claim must be backed by a semantic theory telling us how each sentence determines the state of affairs it does; otherwise the claim is empty.

Israel Scheffler has put forward an analysis of sentences about choice that can be applied without serious modification to sentences about intentional acts.[8] Scheffler makes no suggestion concerning action sentences that do not impute intention and so has no solution to the chief problems I am discussing. Nevertheless, his analysis has a feature I should like to mention. Scheffler would have us render "Jones intentionally buttered the toast" as "Jones made-true a that Jones-buttered-the-toast inscription." This cannot, for reasons I have urged in detail elsewhere,[9] be considered a finally satisfying form for such sentences because it contains the logically unstructured predicate "is a that Jones-buttered-the-toast inscription," and there are an infinite number of such semantical primitives in the language. But in one respect, I believe Scheffler's analysis is clearly superior to the others, for it implies that introducing the element of intentionality does not call for a reduction in the content of the sentence that expresses *what* was done intentionally. This brings out a fact otherwise suppressed: that, to use our example, "Jones" turns up twice, once inside and once outside the scope of the intentional operator. I shall return briefly to this point.

A discussion of the logical form of action sentences in ordinary language is to be found in the justly famed ch. 7 of Reichenbach's *Elements of Symbolic Logic*.[10] According to Reichenbach's doctrine, we may transform a sentence like

(4)   Amundsen flew to the North Pole

into:

(5) $(\exists x)(x$ consists in the fact that Amundsen flew to the North Pole).

The words "is an event that consists in the fact that" are to be viewed as an operator which, when prefixed to a sentence, forms a predicate of events. Reichenbach does not think of (5) as showing or revealing the logical form of (4), for he thinks (4) is unproblematic. Rather, he says (5) is logically equivalent to (4). [Example] (5) has its counterpart in a more ordinary idiom:

(6)   A flight by Amundsen to the North Pole took place.

Thus Reichenbach seems to hold that we have two ways of expressing the same idea, (4) and (6); they have quite different logical forms, but they are logically equivalent; one speaks literally of events, while the other does not. I believe this view spoils much of the merit in Reichenbach's proposal and that we must abandon the idea that (4) has an unproblematic logical form distinct from that of (5) or (6). Following Reichenbach's formula for putting any action sentence into the form of (5), we translate

(7)   Amundsen flew to the North Pole in May 1926

into:

(8) $(\exists x)(x$ consists in the fact that Amundsen flew to the North Pole in May 1926).

The fact that (8) entails (5) is no more obvious than that (7) entails (4); what was obscure remains obscure. The correct way to render (7) is:

(9) $(\exists x)(x$ consists in the fact that Amundsen flew to the North Pole and x took place in May 1926).

But (9) does not bear the simple relation to the standard way of interpreting (7) that (8) does. We do not know of any logical operation on (7) as it would usually be formalized (with a three-place predicate) that would make it logically equivalent to (9). This is why I suggest that we treat (9) alone as giving the logical form of (7). If we follow this strategy, Kenny's problem of the "variable polyadicity" of action verbs is on the way to solution; there is, of course, no variable polyadicity. The problem is solved in the natural way—by introducing events as entities about which an indefinite number of things can be said.

Reichenbach's proposal has another attractive feature: it eliminates a peculiar confusion that seemed to attach to the idea that sentences like (7) "describe an event." The difficulty was that one wavered between thinking of the sentence as describing or referring to that one flight Amundsen made in May 1926, or as describing a kind of event, or perhaps as describing (potentially?) several. As von Wright pointed out, any number of events might be described by a sentence like "Brutus kissed Caesar." This fog is dispelled in a way I find entirely persuasive by Reichenbach's proposal that ordinary action sentences have, in effect, an existential quantifier binding the action-variable. When we were tempted into thinking a sentence like (7) describes a single event we were misled: it does not describe any event at all. But if (7) is true, then there is an event that makes it true. This unrecognized element of generality in action sentences is, I think, of the utmost importance in understanding the relation between actions and desires; this, however, is a subject for another occasion.

There are two objections to Reichenbach's analysis of action sentences. The first may not be fatal. It is that as matters stand the analysis may be applied to any sentence whatsoever, whether it deals with actions, events, or anything else. Even "2 + 3 = 5" becomes "$(\exists x)(x$ consists in the fact that 2 + 3 = 5)." Why not say "2 + 3 = 5" does not show its true colors until put through the machine? For that matter, are we finished when we get to the first step? Shouldn't we go on to "$(\exists y)(y$ consists in the fact that $(\exists x)(x$ consists in the fact that 2 + 3 = 5))"? And so on. It isn't clear on what principle the decision to apply the analysis is based.

The second objection is worse. We have:

(10) $(\exists x)(x$ consists in the fact that I flew my spaceship to the Morning Star)

and

(11)   the Morning Star = the Evening Star

and we want to make the inference to

(12) $(\exists x)(x$ consists in the fact that I flew my spaceship to the Evening Star).

The likely principle to justify the inference would be:

(13) (x) $(x$ consists in the fact that $S \leftrightarrow x$ consists in the fact that S')

where 'S'' differs from 'S' only in containing in one or more places some singular term where 'S' contains another singular term that refers to the same thing. It is plausible to add that (13) holds if 'S' and 'S'' are logically equivalent. But (13) and the last assumption lead to trouble. For observing that 'S' is logically equivalent to "$\hat{y}(y = y \,\&\, S) = \hat{y}(y = y)$" we get

(14) $(x)(x$ consists in the fact that $S \leftrightarrow x$ consists in the fact that $(\hat{y}(y = y \,\&\, S) = \hat{y}(y = y)))$.

Now suppose 'R' is any sentence materially equivalent to 'S': then "$\hat{y}(y = y \,\&\, S)$" and "$\hat{y}(y = y \,\&\, R)$" will refer to the same thing. Substituting in (14) we obtain

(15) $(x)(x$ consists in the fact that $S \leftrightarrow x$ consists in the fact that $(\hat{y}(y = y \ \& \ R) = \hat{y}(y = y))$,

which leads to

(16) $(x)(x$ consists in the fact that $S \leftrightarrow x$ consists in the fact that $R)$

when we observe the logical equivalence of 'R' and "$\hat{y}(y = y \ \& \ R) = \hat{y}(y = y)$." [Example] (16) may be interpreted as saying (considering that the sole assumption is that 'R' and 'S' are materially equivalent) that all events that occur (= all events) are identical. This demonstrates, I think, that Reichenbach's analysis is radically defective.

Now I would like to put forward an analysis of action sentences that seems to me to combine most of the merits of the alternatives already discussed, and to avoid the difficulties. The basic idea is that verbs of action—verbs that say "what someone did"—should be construed as containing a place, for singular terms or variables, that they do not appear to. For example, we would normally suppose that "Shem kicked Shaun" consisted in two names and a two-place predicate. I suggest, though, that we think of "kicked" as a *three*-place predicate, and that the sentence be given in this form:

(17) $(\exists x)(\text{Kicked(Shem, Shaun, } x))$.

If we try for an English sentence that directly reflects this form, we run into difficulties. "There is an event x such that x is a kicking of Shaun by Shem" is about the best I can do, but we must remember "a kicking" is not a singular term. Given this English reading, my proposal may sound very like Reichenbach's; but of course it has quite different logical properties. The *sentence* "Shem kicked Shaun" nowhere appears inside my analytic sentence, and this makes it differ from all the theories we have considered.

The principles that license the Morning Star–Evening Star inference now make no trouble: they are the usual principles of extensionality. As a result, nothing now stands in the way of giving a standard theory of meaning for action sentences, in the form of a Tarski-type truth definition; nothing stands in the way, that is, of giving a coherent and constructive account of how the meanings (truth conditions) of these sentences depend upon their structure. To see how one of the troublesome inferences now goes through, consider (10) rewritten as

(18) $(\exists x)(\text{Flew(I, my spaceship, } x) \ \& \ \text{To(the Morning Star, } x))$.

which, along with (11), entails

(19) $(\exists x)(\text{Flew(I, my spaceship, } x) \ \& \ \text{To(the Evening Star, } x))$.

It is not necessary, in representing this argument, to separate off the To-relation; instead, we could have taken "Flew" as a four-place predicate. But that would have obscured *another* inference, namely that from (19) to

(20) $(\exists x)(\text{Flew(I, my spaceship, } x))$.

In general, we conceal logical structure when we treat prepositions as integral parts of verbs; it is a merit of the present proposal that it suggests a way of treating prepositions as contributing structure. Not only is it nice to have the inference from (19) to (20); it is also nice to be able to keep track of the common element in "fly to" and "fly away from," and this of course we cannot do if we treat these as unstructured predicates.

The problem that threatened in Reichenbach's analysis—that there seemed no clear principle on which to refrain from applying the analysis to every sentence—has a natural solution if my suggestion is accepted. Part of what we must learn when we learn the meaning of any predicate is how many places it has, and what sorts of entities the variables that hold these places range over. Some predicates have an event-place, some do not.

In general, what kinds of predicates do have event-places? Without pursuing this question very far, I think it is evident that if action predicates do, many predicates that have little relation to action do. Indeed, the problems we have been mainly concerned with are not at all unique to talk of actions: they are common to talk of events of any kind. An action of flying to the Morning Star is identical with an action of flying to the Evening Star; but equally, an eclipse of the Morning Star is an eclipse of the Evening Star. Our ordinary talk of events, of causes and effects, requires constant use of the idea of different descriptions of the same event. When it is pointed out that striking the match was not sufficient to light it, what is not sufficient is not the event, but the description of it—it was a *dry* match, and so on. And of course Kenny's problem of "variable polyadicity," though he takes it to be a mark of verbs of action, is common to all verbs that describe events.

It may now appear that the apparent success of the analysis proposed here is due to the fact that it has simply omitted what is peculiar to action sentences as contrasted with other sentences about events. But I do not think so. The concept of agency contains two elements, and when we separate them clearly, I think we shall see that the present analysis has not left anything out. The first of these two elements we try, rather feebly, to elicit by saying that the agent acts, or does something, instead of being acted upon, or having something happen to him. Or we say that the agent is active rather than passive; and perhaps try to make use of the moods of the verb as a grammatical clue. And we may try to depend upon some fixed phrase like "brings it about that" or "makes it the case that." But only a little thought will make it clear that there is no satisfactory grammatical test for verbs where we want to say there is agency. Perhaps it is a *necessary* condition of attributing agency that one argument-place in the verb is filled with a reference to the agent as a person; it will not do to refer to his body, or his members, or to anyone else. But beyond that it is hard to go. I sleep, I snore, I push buttons, I recite verses, I catch cold. Also others are insulted by me, struck by me, admired by me, and so on. No grammatical test I know of, in terms of the things we may be said to do, of active or passive mood, or of any other sort, will separate out the cases here where we want to speak of agency. Perhaps it is true that "brings it about that" guarantees agency; but as we have seen, many sentences that do attribute agency cannot be cast in this grammatical form.

I believe the correct thing to say about *this* element in the concept of agency is that it is simply introduced by certain verbs and not by others; when we understand the verb we recognize whether or not it includes the idea of an agent. Thus "I coughed" and "I insulted him" *do* impute agency to the person referred to by the first singular term; "I caught cold" and "I had my thirteenth birthday" do not. In these cases, we do seem to have the following test: we impute agency only where it makes sense to ask whether the agent acted intentionally. But there are other cases, or so it seems to me, where we impute agency only when the answer to the question whether the agent acted intentionally is "yes." If a man falls down by accident or because a truck knocks him down, we do not impute agency; but we do if he fell down on purpose.

This introduces the second element in the concept of agency, for we surely impute agency when we say or imply that the act is intentional. Instead of speaking of two elements in the concept of agency, perhaps it would be better to say there are two ways we can imply that a person acted as an agent: we may use a verb that implies it directly, or we may use a verb that is noncommittal, and add that the act was intentional. But when we take the second course, it is important not to think of the intentionality as adding an extra doing of the agent; we must not make the expression that introduces intention a verb of action. In particular, we cannot use "intentionally brings it about that" as the expression that introduces intention, for "brings it about that" is in itself a verb of action, and imputes agency, but it is neutral with respect to the question whether the action was intentional as described.

This leaves the question what logical form the expression that introduces intention should (must) have. It is obvious, I hope, that the adverbial form must be in some way deceptive; intentional actions are not a class of actions, or, to put the point a little differently, doing something intentionally is not a manner of doing it. To say someone did something intentionally is to describe the action in a way that bears a special relation to the beliefs and attitudes of the agent; and perhaps further to describe the action as having been caused by those beliefs and attitudes.[11] But of course to describe the action of the agent as having been caused in a certain way does not mean that the agent is described as performing any further action. From a logical point of view, there are thus these important conditions governing the expression that introduces intention: it must not be interpreted as a verb of action, it is intentional, and the intentionality is tied to a person. I propose, then, that we use some form of words like "It was intentional of x that p" where 'x' names the agent, and 'p' is a sentence that says the agent did something. It is useful, perhaps necessary, that the agent be named twice when we try to make logical form explicit. It is useful, because it reminds us that to describe an action as intentional is to describe the action in the light of certain attitudes and beliefs of a particular person; it may be necessary in order to illuminate what goes on in those cases in which the agent makes a mistake about who he is. It was intentional of Oedipus, and hence of the slayer of Laius, that Oedipus sought the slayer of Laius, but it was not intentional of Oedipus (the slayer of Laius) that the slayer of Laius sought the slayer of Laius.

Notes

I have profited from discussion with Daniel Dennett, Paul Grice, Sue Larson, David Pears, Merrill Provence, and David Wiggins. John Wallace and I talked on topics connected with this paper almost daily walking through the Odyssean landscape of Corfu during the spring of 1965; his contribution to the ideas expressed here is too pervasive to be disentangled. My research was supported by the National Science Foundation.

1. Anthony Kenny, *Action, Emotion, and Will* (London: Routledge and Kegan Paul, 1963), ch. 7.

2. Kenny seems to think that there is such a method, for he writes, "If we cast our net widely enough, we can make 'Brutus killed Caesar' into a sentence which describes, with a certain lack of specification, the whole history of the world." (1963, p. 160). But he does not show how to make each addition to the sentence one that irreducibly modifies the killing as opposed, say, to Brutus or Caesar, or the place or the time.

3. John Austin, "A Plea for Excuses," in *Philosophical Papers* (Oxford: Oxford University Press, 1971), p. 148.

4. Kenny, 1963, p. 181.

5. Roderick Chisholm, "The Descriptive Element in the Concept of Action," *Journal of Philosophy*, 61, no. 20 (1964a), 613–625. Also see Chisholm, "The Ethics of Requirement," *American Philosophical Quarterly*, vol. 1, no. 2 (1964b), 147–153.

6. Georg Henrik von Wright, *Norm and Action: A Logical Inquiry* (London: Routledge and Kegan Paul, 1963).

7. Ibid., p. 23.

8. Israel Scheffler, *The Anatomy of Inquiry* (New York: Knopf, 1963). See especially pp. 104–105.

9. Donald Davidson, "Theories of Meaning and Learnable Languages," in Y. Bar-Hillel (ed.), *Logic, Methodology and Philosophy of Science* (Amsterdam: North-Holland, 1965), pp. 390–391.

10. Hans Reichenbach, *Elements of Symbolic Logic* (New York: Macmillan, 1947), §48.

11. These, and other matters directly related to the present paper, are discussed in Davidson, "Actions, Reasons and Causes," *Journal of Philosophy*, vol. 60 (1963), 685–700.

CONTEXT DEPENDENCY

DAVID KAPLAN

Demonstratives

Preface

In about 1966 I wrote a paper about quantification into epistemological contexts. There are very difficult metaphysical, logical, and epistemological problems involved in providing a treatment of such idioms which does not distort our intuitions about their proper use and which is up to contemporary logical standards. I did not then, and do not now, regard the treatment I provided as fully adequate. And I became more and more intrigued with problems centering on what I would like to call the *semantics of direct reference*. By this I mean theories of meaning according to which certain singular terms refer directly without the mediation of a Fregean *Sinn* as meaning. If there are such terms, then the proposition expressed by a sentence containing such a term would involve individuals directly rather than by way of the "individual concepts" or "manners of presentation" I had been taught to expect. Let us call such putative singular terms (if there are any) *directly referential terms* and such putative propositions (if there are any) *singular propositions*. Even if English contained no singular terms whose proper semantics was one of direct reference, could we determine to introduce such terms? And even if we had no directly referential terms and introduced none, is there a need or use for singular propositions?

The feverish development of quantified modal logics, more generally, of quantified intensional logics, of the 1960s gave rise to a metaphysical and epistemological malaise regarding the problem of identifying individuals across worlds—what, in 1967, I called the problem of "Trans-World Heir Lines." This problem was really just the problem of singular propositions: those which involve individuals directly, rearing its irrepressible head in the possible-world semantics that were then (and are now) so popular.

David Kaplan (1977) "Demonstratives." In J. Almog, J. Perry, and H. Wettstein (eds.), *Themes from Kaplan*, 481–563. Reprinted by permission of David Kaplan. [eds. "Demonstratives" was copyrighted and circulated in manuscript in 1977. The bracketed comments within the printed text are the author's own, added by him to the 1989 publication. See Kaplan (1989a).]

It was not that according to those semantical theories any sentences of the languages being studied were themselves taken to express singular propositions, it was just that singular propositions seemed to be needed in the analysis of the nonsingular propositions expressed by these sentences. For example, consider $\exists x(Fx \wedge \sim \Box Fx)$. This sentence would not be taken by anyone to express a singular proposition. But in order to evaluate the truth-value of the component $\Box Fx$ (under some assignment of an individual to the variable 'x'), we must first determine whether the *proposition* expressed by its component Fx (under an assignment of an individual to the variable 'x') is a necessary proposition. So in the course of analyzing $\exists x(Fx \wedge \sim \Box Fx)$, we are required to determine the proposition associated with a formula containing a *free* variable. Now free variables under an assignment of values are paradigms of what I have been calling *directly referential* terms. In determining a semantical value for a formula containing a free variable we may be given a *value* for the variable—that is, an individual drawn from the universe over which the variable is taken to range—but nothing more. A variable's first and only meaning is its value. Therefore, if we are to associate a *proposition* (not merely a truth-value) with a formula containing a free variable (with respect to an assignment of a value to the variable), that proposition seems bound to be singular (even if valiant attempts are made to disguise this fact by using constant functions to imitate individual concepts). The point is that if the component of the proposition (or the step in the construction of the proposition) which corresponds to the singular term is determined by the individual and the individual is directly determined by the singular term—rather than the individual being determined by the component of the proposition, which is directly determined by the singular term—then we have what I call a singular proposition. [Russell's semantics was like the semantical theories for quantified intensional logics that I have described in that although no (closed) sentence of *Principia Mathematica* was taken to stand for a singular proposition, singular propositions are the essential building blocks of all propositions.]

The most important hold-out against semantical theories that required singular propositions is Alonzo Church, the great modern champion of Frege's semantical theories. Church also advocates a version of quantified intensional logic, but with a subtle difference that finesses the need for singular propositions. (In Church's logic, given a sentential formula containing free variables and given an assignment of values to the variables, no proposition is yet determined. An additional assignment of "senses" to the free variables must be made before a proposition can be associated with the formula.) It is no accident that Church rejects *direct reference* semantical theories. For if there were singular terms which referred directly, it seems likely that Frege's problem—how can $\ulcorner \alpha = \beta \urcorner$, if true, differ in meaning from $\ulcorner \alpha = \alpha \urcorner$—could be reinstated, while Frege's solution: that α and β, though referring to the same thing, do so by way of different senses, would be blocked. Also: because of the fact that the component of the proposition is being determined by the individual rather than vice versa, we have something like a violation of the famous Fregean dictum that *there is no road back* from denotation to sense [propositional component]. (Recently, I have come to think that if we countenance singular propositions, a collapse of Frege's intensional ontology into Russell's takes place.)

I can draw some little pictures (Figures 37.1 and 37.2) to give you an idea of the two kinds of semantical theories I want to contrast. (These pictures are not entirely accurate for several reasons—among them, that the contrasting pictures are meant to account for more than just singular terms and that the relation marked 'refers' may already involve a kind of Fregean sense used to fix the referent.)

I won't go into the pros and cons of these two views at this time. Suffice it to say that I had been raised on Fregean semantics and was sufficiently devout to wonder whether the kind of quantification into modal and epistemic contexts that seemed to require singular propositions really made sense. (My paper "Quantifying In" can be regarded as an attempt to *explain away* such idioms for epistemic contexts.)[1]

But there were pressures from quarters other than quantified intensional logic in favor of a semantics of direct reference. First of all there was Donnellan's fascinating paper "Reference and Definite Descriptions."[2] Then there were discussions I had had with Putnam in 1968 in which he

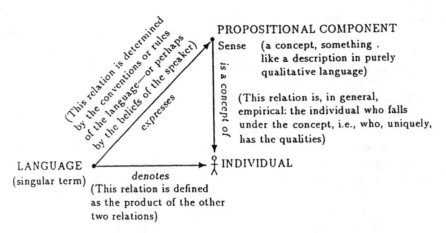

FIGURE 37.1 Fregean picture

argued, with respect to certain natural kind terms like 'tiger' and 'gold', that if their Fregean senses were the kind of thing that one grasped when one understood the terms, then such senses could not determine the extension of the terms. And finally Kripke's Princeton lectures of spring 1970, later published as *Naming and Necessity*,[3] were just beginning to leak out along with their strong attack on the Fregean theory of proper names and their support of a theory of direct reference.

As I said earlier, I was intrigued by the semantics of direct reference, so when I had a sabbatical leave for the year 1970–71, I decided to work in the area in which such a theory seemed most plausible: demonstratives. In fall 1970, I wrote, for a conference at Stanford, a paper "Dthat."[4] Using Donnellan's ideas as a starting point, I tried to develop the contrast between Fregean semantics and the semantics of direct reference, and to argue that demonstratives—although they *could* be treated on a Fregean model—were more interestingly treated on a direct reference model. Ultimately I came to the conclusion that something analogous to Donnellan's referential use of a definite description could be developed using my new demonstrative, "dthat." In the course of this paper I groped my way to a formal semantics for demonstratives rather different in conception from those that had been offered before.

In spring 1971, I gave a series of lectures at Princeton on the semantics of direct reference. By this time I had seen a transcript of *Naming and Necessity*, and I tried to relate some of my

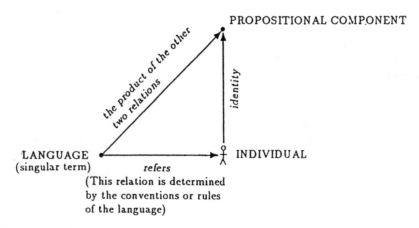

FIGURE 37.2 Direct reference picture

ideas to Kripke's.[5] I also had written out the formal semantics for my Logic of Demonstratives. That summer at the Irvine Philosophy of Language Institute I lectured again on the semantics of direct reference and repeated some of these lectures at various institutions in fall 1971. And there the matter has stood except for a bit of updating of the 1971 Logic of Demonstratives notes in 1973.

I now think that demonstratives can be treated correctly only on a direct reference model, but that my earlier lectures at Princeton and Irvine on direct reference semantics were too broad in scope, and that the most important and certainly the most convincing part of my theory is just the logic of demonstratives itself. It is based on just a few quite simple ideas, but the conceptual apparatus turns out to be surprisingly rich and interesting. At least I hope that you will find it so.

In this work I have concentrated on pedagogy. Philosophically, there is little here that goes beyond the Summer Institute Lectures, but I have tried, by limiting the scope, to present the ideas in a more compelling way. Some new material appears in the two speculative sections: XVII (Epistemological Remarks) and XX (Adding 'Says'). It is my hope that a theory of demonstratives will give us the tools to go on in a more sure-footed way to explore the *de re* propositional attitudes, as well as other semantical issues.

I Introduction

I believe my theory of demonstratives to be uncontrovertable and largely uncontroversial. This is not a tribute to the power of my theory but a concession of its obviousness. In the past, no one seems to have followed these obvious facts out to their obvious consequences. I do that. What is original with me is some terminology to help fix ideas when things get complicated. It has been fascinating to see how interesting the obvious consequences of obvious principles can be.[6]

II Demonstratives, indexicals, and pure indexicals

I tend to describe my theory as "a theory of demonstratives," but that is poor usage. It stems from the fact that I began my investigations by asking what is said when a speaker points at someone and says, "He is suspicious."[7] The word 'he', so used, is a demonstrative, and the accompanying pointing is the requisite associated demonstration. I hypothesized a certain semantical theory for such demonstratives, and then I invented a new demonstrative, 'dthat', and stipulated that its semantics be in accord with my theory. I was so delighted with this methodological sleight of hand for my demonstrative 'dthat', that when I generalized the theory to apply to words like 'I', 'now', 'here', et cetera—words which do *not* require an associated demonstration—I continued to call my theory a "theory of demonstratives" and I referred to these words as "demonstratives."

That terminological practice conflicts with what I preach, and I will try to correct it. (But I tend to backslide.)

The group of words for which I propose a semantical theory includes the pronouns 'I', 'my', 'you', 'he', 'his', 'she', 'it'; the demonstrative pronouns 'that', 'this'; the adverbs 'here', 'now', 'tomorrow', 'yesterday'; the adjectives 'actual', 'present'; and others. These words have uses other than those in which I am interested (or, perhaps, depending on how you individuate words, we should say that they have homonyms in which I am not interested). For example, the pronouns 'he' and 'his' are used not as demonstratives but as bound variables in

> For what is a man profited, if he shall gain
> the whole world, and lose his own soul?

What is common to the words or usages in which I am interested is that the referent is dependent on the context of use and that the meaning of the word provides a rule which determines the referent in terms of certain aspects of the context. The term I now favor for these words is "indexical." Other authors have used other terms; Russell used "egocentric particular," and Reichenbach used "token reflexive." I prefer "indexical" (which, I believe, is due to Peirce) because it seems less theory laden than the others, and because I regard Russell's and Reichenbach's theories as defective.

Some of the indexicals require, in order to determine their referents, an associated demonstration: typically, though not invariably, a (visual) presentation of a local object discriminated by a pointing.[8] These indexicals are the true demonstratives, and 'that' is their paradigm. The demonstra*tive* (an expression) refers to that which the demon*stration* demonstrates. I call that which is demonstrated the "demonstratum."

A demonstrative without an associated demonstration is incomplete. The linguistic rules which govern the use of the true demonstratives 'that', 'he', etc., are not sufficient to determine their referent in all contexts of use. Something else—an associated demonstration—must be provided. The linguistic rules assume that such a demonstration accompanies each (demonstrative) use of a demonstrative. An incomplete demonstrative is not *vacuous* like an improper definite description. A demonstrative *can* be vacuous in various cases. For example, when its associated demonstration has no demonstratum (a hallucination)—or the wrong kind of demonstratum (pointing to a flower and saying 'he' in the belief that one is pointing to a man disguised as a flower[9]— or too many demonstrata (pointing to two intertwined vines and saying 'that vine'). But it is clear that one can distinguish a demonstrative with a vacuous demonstration: no referent; from a demonstrative with no associated demonstration: incomplete.

All this is by way of contrasting true demonstratives with pure indexicals. For the latter, *no associated demonstration is required, and any demonstration supplied is either for emphasis or is irrelevant.*[10] Among the pure indexicals are 'I', 'now', 'here' (in one sense), 'tomorrow', and others. The linguistic rules which govern *their* use fully determine the referent for each context.[11] No supplementary actions or intentions are needed. The speaker refers to himself when he uses 'I', and no pointing to another or believing that he is another or intending to refer to another can defeat this reference.[12]

Michael Bennett has noted that some indexicals have both a pure *and* a demonstrative use. 'Here' is a pure indexical in *I am in here* and is a demonstrative in *In two weeks, I will be here* [*pointing at a city on a map*].

III Two obvious principles

So much for preliminaries. My theory is based on two obvious principles. The first has been noted in every discussion of the subject:

PRINCIPLE 1
The referent of a pure indexical depends on the context, and the referent of a demonstrative
   depends on the associated demonstration.

If you and I both say 'I' we refer to different persons. The demonstratives 'that' and 'he' can be correctly used to refer to any one of a wide variety of objects simply by adjusting the accompanying demonstration.

The second obvious principle has less often been formulated explicitly:

PRINCIPLE 2
Indexicals, pure and demonstrative alike, are directly referential.

IV   Remarks on rigid designators

In an earlier draft I adopted the terminology of Kripke, called indexicals "rigid designators," and tried to explain that my usage differed from his. I am now shying away from that terminology. But because it is so well known, I will make some comments on the notion or notions involved.

The term "rigid designator" was coined by Saul Kripke to characterize those expressions which designate the same thing in every possible world in which that thing exists and which designate nothing elsewhere. He uses it in connection with his controversial, though, I believe, correct claim that proper names, as well as many common nouns, are rigid designators. There is an unfortunate confusion in the idea that a proper name would designate nothing if the bearer of the name were not to exist.[13] Kripke himself adopts positions which seem inconsistent with this feature of rigid designators. In arguing that the object designated by a rigid designator need not exist in every possible world, he seems to assert that under certain circumstances what is expressed by 'Hitler does not exist' would have been true, and not because 'Hitler' would have designated nothing (in *that* case we might have given the sentence *no* truth-value) but because what 'Hitler' would have designated—namely, Hitler—would not have existed.[14] Furthermore, it is a striking and important feature of the possible world semantics for quantified intensional logics, which Kripke did so much to create and popularize, that variables, those paradigms of rigid designation, designate the same individual in *all* possible worlds whether the individual "exists" or not.[15]

Whatever Kripke's intentions (did he, as I suspect, misdescribe his own concept?) and whatever associations or even meaning the phrase "rigid designator" may have, I intend to use "*directly referential*" for an expression whose referent, once determined, is taken as fixed for all possible circumstances—that is, is taken as *being* the propositional component.

For me, the intuitive idea is not that of an expression which *turns out* to designate the same object in all possible circumstances, but an expression whose semantical *rules* provide *directly* that the referent in all possible circumstances is fixed to be the actual referent. In typical cases the semantical rules will do this only implicitly, by providing a way of determining the *actual* referent and no way of determining any other propositional component.[16]

We should beware of a certain confusion in interpreting the phrase 'designates the same object in all circumstances'. We do not mean that the expression *could not have been used* to designate a different object. We mean, rather, that given a *use* of the expression, we may ask of *what has been said* whether *it* would have been true or false in various counterfactual circumstances, and in such counterfactual circumstances, which are the individuals relevant to determining truth-value. Thus we must distinguish possible occasions of *use*—which I call *contexts*—from possible circumstances of *evaluation* of what was said on a given occasion of use. Possible circumstances of evaluation I call circumstances or, sometimes, just *counterfactual situations*. A directly referential term *may* designate different objects when used in different *contexts*. But when evaluating what was said in a given context, only a single object will be relevant to the evaluation in all circumstances. This sharp distinction between *contexts of use* and *circumstances of evaluation* must be kept in mind if we are to avoid a seeming conflict between Principles 1 and 2.[17] To look at the matter from another point of view, once we recognize the obviousness of both principles (I have not yet argued for Principle 2), the distinction between contexts of use and circumstances of evaluation is forced upon us.

If I may wax metaphysical in order to fix an image, let us think of the vehicles of evaluation—the what-is-said in a given context—as propositions. Don't think of propositions as sets of possible worlds but, rather, as structured entities looking something like the sentences which express them. For each occurrence of a singular term in a sentence there will be a corresponding constituent in the proposition expressed. The constituent of the proposition determines, for each circumstance of evaluation, the object relevant to evaluating the proposition in that circumstance.

In general, the constituent of the proposition will be some sort of complex, constructed from various attributes by logical composition. But in the case of a singular term which is directly referential, the constituent of the proposition is just the object itself. Thus it is that it does not just *turn out* that the constituent determines the same object in every circumstance, the constituent (corresponding to a rigid designator) just *is* the object. *There is no determining to do at all.* On this picture—and this is *really* a picture and not a theory—the definite description

(1)   The $n[(\text{Snow is slight} \wedge n^2 = 9) \vee (\sim\text{Snow is slight} \wedge 2^2 = n + 1)]$[18]

would yield a constituent which is complex although it would determine the same object in all circumstances. Thus, (1), though a rigid designator, is not directly referential from this (metaphysical) point of view. Note, however, that every proposition which contains the complex expressed by (1) is *equivalent* to some singular proposition which contains just the number three itself as constituent.[19]

The semantical feature that *I* wish to highlight in calling an expression *directly referential* is not the *fact* that it designates the same object in every circumstance, but the *way* in which it designates an object in any circumstance. Such an expression is a *device of direct reference*. This does not imply that it has no conventionally fixed semantical rules which determine its referent in each context of use; quite the opposite. There are semantical rules which determine the referent in each context of use—but that is all. *The rules do not provide a complex which together with a circumstance of evaluation yields an object. They just provide an object.*

If we keep in mind our sharp distinction between contexts of use and circumstances of evaluation, we will not be tempted to confuse a rule which assigns an object to each *context* with a "complex" which assigns an object to each *circumstance*. For example, each context has an *agent* (loosely, a speaker). Thus an appropriate designation rule for a directly referential term would be:

(2)   In each possible context of use the given term refers to the agent of the context.

But this rule could not be used to assign a relevant object to each circumstance of evaluation. Circumstances of evaluation do not, in general, have agents. Suppose I say,

(3)   I do not exist.

Under what circumstances would *what I said* be true? It would be true in circumstances in which I did not exist. Among such circumstances are those in which no one, and thus, no speakers, no agents exist. To search a circumstance of evaluation for a speaker in order to (mis)apply rule (2) would be to go off on an irrelevant chase.

Three paragraphs ago I sketched a metaphysical picture of the structure of a proposition. The picture is taken from the semantical parts of Russell's *Principles of Mathematics*.[20] Two years later, in "On Denoting,"[21] even Russell rejected that picture. But I still like it. It is not a part of my theory, but it well conveys my conception of a directly referential expression and of the semantics of direct reference. (The picture needs *some* modification in order to avoid difficulties which Russell later noted—though he attributed them to Frege's theory rather than his own earlier theory.)[22]

If we adopt a possible worlds semantics, all directly referential terms will be regarded as rigid designators in the *modified* sense of an expression which designates the same thing in *all* possible worlds (irrespective of whether the thing exists in the possible world or not).[23] However, as already noted, I do not regard all rigid designators—not even all strongly rigid designators (those that designate something that exists in all possible worlds) or all rigid designators in the modified sense— as directly referential. I believe that proper names, like variables, are directly referential. They are not, in general, strongly rigid designators, nor are they rigid designators in the original sense.[24] What is characteristic of directly referential terms is that the designatum (referent) determines the propositional component, rather than the propositional component, along with a circumstance, determining the designatum. It is for this reason that a directly referential term that designates a contingently existing object will still be a rigid designator in the modified sense. The propositional component need not choose its designatum from those offered by a passing circumstance; it has already secured its designatum before the encounter with the circumstance.

When we think in terms of possible world semantics, this fundamental distinction becomes subliminal. This is because the style of the semantical rules obscures the distinction and makes it appear that directly referential terms differ from ordinary definite descriptions only in that the propositional component in the former case must be a *constant* function of circumstances. In actual fact, the referent, in a circumstance, of a directly referential term is simply *independent* of the circumstance and is no more a function (constant or otherwise) of circumstance, than my action is a function of your desires when I decide to do it whether you like it or not. The distinction that is obscured by the style of possible world semantics is dramatized by the structured propositions picture. That is part of the reason why I like it.

Some directly referential terms, like proper names, may have no semantically relevant descriptive meaning, or at least none that is specific; that distinguishes one such term from another. Others, like the indexicals, may have a limited kind of specific descriptive meaning relevant to the features of a context of use. Still others, like 'dthat' terms (see below), may be associated with full-blown Fregean senses used to fix the referent. But in any case, the descriptive meaning of a directly referential term is no part of the propositional content.

V   Argument for principle 2: Pure indexicals

As stated earlier, I believe this principle is uncontroversial. But I had best distinguish it from similar principles which are false. I am *not* claiming, as has been claimed for proper names, that indexicals lack anything that might be called "descriptive meaning." Indexicals, in general, have a rather easily statable descriptive meaning. But it is clear that this meaning is relevant only to determining a referent in a context of use and *not* to determining a relevant individual in a circumstance of evaluation. Let us return to the example in connection with the sentence (3) and the indexical 'I'. The bizarre result of taking the descriptive meaning of the indexical to be the propositional constituent is that what I said in uttering (3) would be true in a circumstance of evaluation if and only if the speaker (assuming there is one) of the circumstance does not exist in the circumstance. Nonsense! If *that* were the correct analysis, what I said could not be true. From which it follows that *It is impossible that I do not exist.* Here is another example to show that the descriptive meaning of an indexical may be entirely *inapplicable* in the circumstance of evaluation. When I say, *I wish I were not speaking now*, the circumstances desired do not involve contexts of *use* and *agents* who are not speaking. The *actual* context of use is used to determine the relevant individual: *me*—and time: *now*—and then we query the various circumstances of evaluation with respect to *that* individual and *that* time.

Here is another example, not of the inapplicability of the descriptive meaning to circumstances but of its irrelevance. Suppose I say at t_0, "It will soon be the case that all that is now beautiful is faded." Consider what was said in the subsentence, *All that is now beautiful is faded.* I wish to evaluate that content at some near future time t_1. What is the relevant time associated with the indexical 'now'? Is it the future time t_1? No, it is t_0, of course: the time of the context of use.

See how rigidly the indexicals cling to the referent determined in the context of use:

(4)   It is possible that in Pakistan, in five years, only those who are actually here now are envied.

The point of (4) is that the circumstance, place, and time referred to by the indexicals 'actually', 'here', and 'now' are the circumstance, place, and time of the *context*, not a circumstance, place, and time determined by the modal, locational, and temporal operators within whose scope the indexicals lie.

It may be objected that this only shows that indexicals always take *primary* scope (in the sense of Russell's scope of a definite description). This objection attempts to relegate all direct reference to implicit use of the paradigm of the semantics of direct reference, the variable. Thus (4) is transformed into

> The actual circumstances, here, and now are such that it is possible that in Pakistan in five
> years only those who, in the first, are located at the second, during the third, are envied.

Although this may not be the most felicitous form of expression, its meaning and, in particular, its symbolization should be clear to those familiar with quantified intensional logics. The pronouns, 'the first', 'the second', and 'the third' are to be represented by distinct variables bound to existential quantifiers at the beginning and identified with 'the actual circumstance', 'here', and 'now', respectively:

(5) $(\exists w)(\exists p)(\exists t)[w$=the actual circumstance $\wedge$ p=*here* $\wedge$ t=*now* $\wedge$ $\lozenge$ In Pakistan In five years $\forall x(x$ is envied $\rightarrow$ x is located at p during t in $w)]$

But such transformations, when thought of as representing the claim that indexicals take primary scope, do not provide an *alternative* to Principle 2, since we may still ask of an utterance of (5) in a context c, when evaluating it with respect to an arbitrary circumstance, to what do the indexicals 'actual', 'here', and 'now' refer? The answer, as always, is: the relevant features of the context c. [In fact, although (4) is equivalent to (5), neither indexicals nor quantification across intensional operators is dispensable in favor of the other.]

Perhaps enough has been said to establish the following:

(T1)   The descriptive meaning of a pure indexical determines the referent of the indexical with respect to a context of use but is either inapplicable or irrelevant to determining a referent with respect to a circumstance of evaluation.

I hope that your intuition will agree with mine that it is for this reason that:

(T2)   When what was said in using a pure indexical in a context c is to be evaluated with respect to an arbitrary circumstance, the relevant object is always the referent of the indexical with respect to the context c.

This is just a slightly elaborated version of Principle 2.

Before turning to true demonstratives, we will adopt some terminology.

VI   Terminological remarks

Principle 1 and Principle 2 taken together imply that sentences containing pure indexicals have two kinds of meaning.

VI.1   Content and circumstance

What is said in using a given indexical in different contexts may be different. Thus if I say, today, *I was insulted yesterday*, and you utter the same words tomorrow, what is said is different. If what we say differs in truth-value, that is enough to show that we say different things. But even if the truth-values were the same, it is clear that there are possible circumstances in which what I said would be true but what you said would be false. Thus we say different things.

Let us call this first kind of meaning—what is said—*content*. The content of a sentence in a given context is what has traditionally been called a proposition. Strawson, in noting that the sentence *The present king of France is bald* could be used on different occasions to make different statements, used "statement" in a way similar to our use of *content of a sentence*. If we wish to express the same content in different contexts, we may have to change indexicals. Frege, here using 'thought' for content of a sentence, expresses the point well:

> If someone wants to say the same today as he expressed yesterday using the word 'today', he must replace this word with 'yesterday'. Although the thought is the same its verbal expression must be different so that the sense, which would otherwise be affected by the differing times of utterance, is readjusted.[25]

I take *content* as a notion applying not only to sentences taken in a context but to any meaningful part of speech taken in a context. Thus we can speak of the content of a definite description, an indexical, a predicate, et cetera. It is *contents* that are evaluated in circumstances of evaluation. If the content is a proposition (i.e., the content of a sentence taken in some context), the result of the evaluation will be a truth-value. The result of evaluating the content of a singular term at a circumstance will be an object (what I earlier called "the relevant object"). In general, the result of evaluating the content of a well-formed expression α at a circumstance will be an appropriate extension for α (i.e., for a sentence, a truth-value; for a term, an individual; for an n-place predicate, a set of n-tuples of individuals, etc.). This suggests that we can represent a content by a function from circumstances of evaluation to an appropriate extension. Carnap called such functions *intensions*.

The representation is a handy one, and I will often speak of contents in terms of it, but one should note that contents which are distinct but equivalent (i.e., share a value in all circumstances) are represented by the same intension. Among other things, this results in the loss of my distinction between terms which are devices of direct reference and descriptions which *turn out* to be rigid designators. (Recall the metaphysical paragraph of section IV.) I wanted the content of an indexical to be just the referent itself, but the intension of such a content will be a constant function. Use of representing intensions does not mean I am abandoning that idea—just ignoring it temporarily.

A *fixed content* is one represented by a constant function. All directly referential expressions (as well as all rigid designators) have a fixed content. [What I elsewhere call a *stable* content.]

Let us settle on *circumstances* for possible circumstances of evaluation. By this I mean both actual and counterfactual situations with respect to which it is appropriate to ask for the extensions of a given well-formed expression. A circumstance will usually include a possible state or history of the world, a time, and perhaps other features as well. The amount of information we require from a circumstance is linked to the degree of specificity of contents, and thus to the kinds of operators in the language.

Operators of the familiar kind treated in intensional logic (modal, temporal, etc.) operate on contents. (Since we represent contents by intensions, it is not surprising that intensional operators operate on contents.) Thus an appropriate extension for an intensional operator is a function from intensions to extensions.[26] A modal operator when applied to an intension will look at the behavior of the intension with respect to the possible state of the world feature of the circumstances of evaluation. A temporal operator will, similarly, be concerned with the time of the circumstance. If we built the time of evaluation into the contents (thus removing time from the circumstances leaving only, say, a possible world history, and making contents *specific* as to time), it would make no sense to have temporal operators. To put the point another way, if *what is said* is thought of as incorporating reference to a specific time, or state of the world, or whatever, it is otiose to ask whether what is said would have been true at another time, in another state of the world, or whatever. Temporal operators applied to eternal sentences (those whose contents incorporate a specific time of evaluation) are redundant. Any intensional operators applied to *perfect* sentences (those whose contents incorporate specific values for all features of circumstances) are redundant.[27]

What sorts of intensional operators to admit seems to me largely a matter of language engineering. It is a question of which features of what we intuitively think of as possible circumstances can be sufficiently well defined and isolated. If we wish to isolate location and regard it as a feature of possible circumstances, we can introduce locational operators: 'Two miles north it is the case that', et cetera. Such operators can be iterated and can be mixed with modal and temporal operators. However, to make such operators interesting, we must have contents which are locationally neutral. That is, it must be appropriate to ask if *what is said* would be true in Pakistan. (For example, 'It is raining' seems to be locationally as well as temporally and modally neutral.)

This functional notion of the content of a sentence in a context may not, because of the neutrality of content with respect to time and place, say, exactly correspond to the classical conception of a proposition. But the classical conception can be introduced by adding the demonstratives 'now' and 'here' to the sentence and taking the content of the result. I will continue to refer to the content of a sentence as a proposition, ignoring the classical use.

Before leaving the subject of circumstances of evaluation I should, perhaps, note that the mere attempt to show that an expression is directly referential requires that it be meaningful to ask of an individual in one circumstance whether and with what properties it exists in another circumstance. If such questions cannot be raised because they are regarded as metaphysically meaningless, the question of whether a particular expression is directly referential (or even, a rigid designator) cannot be raised. I have elsewhere referred to the view that such questions are meaningful as *haecceitism*, and I have described other metaphysical manifestations of this view.[28] I advocate this position, although I am uncomfortable with some of its seeming consequences (for example, that the world might be in a state qualitatively exactly as it is, but with a permutation of individuals).

It is hard to see how one could think about the semantics of indexicals and modality without adopting such a view.

VI.2   Character

The second kind of meaning, most prominent in the case of indexicals, is that which determines the content in varying contexts. The rule, '*I*' *refers to the speaker or writer*, is a meaning rule of the second kind. The phrase 'the speaker or writer' is not supposed to be a complete description, nor is it supposed to refer to the speaker or writer of the *word* 'I'. (There are many such.) It refers to the speaker or writer of the relevant *occurrence* of the word 'I'—that is, the agent of the context.

Unfortunately, as usually stated, these meaning rules are incomplete in that they do not explicitly specify that the indexical is directly referential, and thus do not completely determine the content in each context. I will return to this later.

Let us call the second kind of meaning, *character*. The character of an expression is set by linguistic conventions and, in turn, determines the content of the expression in every context.[29] Because character is what is set by linguistic conventions, it is natural to think of it as *meaning* in the sense of what is known by the competent language user.

Just as it was convenient to represent contents by functions from possible circumstances to extensions (Carnap's intentions), so it is convenient to represent characters by functions from possible contexts to contents. (As before we have the drawback that equivalent characters are identified.[30]) This gives us the following picture:

> Character: Contexts ⇒ Contents
> Content: Circumstances ⇒ Extensions

or, in more familiar language,

> Meaning + Context ⇒ Intension
> Intension + Possible World ⇒ Extension

Indexicals have a *context-sensitive* character. It is characteristic of an indexical that its content varies with context. Nonindexicals have a *fixed* character. The same content is invoked in all contexts. This content will typically be sensitive to circumstances—that is, the nonindexicals are typically not rigid designators but will vary in extension from circumstance to circumstance. Eternal sentences are generally good examples of expressions with a fixed character: *All persons alive in 1977 will have died by 2077* expresses the same proposition no matter when said, by whom, or under what circumstances. The truth-value of that proposition may, of course, vary with possible circumstances, but the character is fixed. Sentences with fixed character are very useful to those wishing to leave historical records.

Now that we have two kinds of meaning in addition to extension, Frege's principle of intensional interchange[31] becomes two principles:

(F1)   The character of the whole is a function of the character of the parts. That is, if two compound well-formed expressions differ only with respect to components which have the same Character, then the Character of the compounds is the same.

(F2)   The Content of the whole is a function of the Content of the parts. That is, if two compound well-formed expressions, each set in (possibly different) contexts differ only with respect to components which *when taken in their respective contexts* have the same content, then the content of the two compounds *each taken in its own context* is the same.

It is the second principle that accounts for the often noted fact that speakers in different contexts can say the same thing by switching indexicals. (And, indeed, they often *must* switch indexicals to do so.) Frege illustrated this point with respect to 'today' and 'yesterday' in "The Thought." (But note that his treatment of 'I' suggests that he does not believe that utterances of 'I' and 'you' could be similarly related!)

Earlier, in my metaphysical phase, I suggested that we should think of the content of an indexical as being just the referent itself, and I resented the fact that the representation of contents as intensions forced us to regard such contents as constant functions. A similar remark applies here. If we are not overly concerned with standardized representations (which certainly have their value for model-theoretic investigations), we might be inclined to say that the character of an indexical-free word or phrase just *is* its (constant) content.

VII   Earlier attempts: Index theory

The following picture seems to emerge. The meaning (character) of an indexical is a function from contexts to extensions (substituting for fixed contents). The meaning (content, substituting for fixed characters) of a nonindexical is a function from circumstances to extensions. From this point of view it may appear that the addition of indexicals requires no new *logic*, no sharp distinction between contexts and circumstances, just the addition of some special new *features* ("contextual" features) to the circumstances of evaluation. (For example, an *agent* to provide an interpretation for 'I'.) Thus an enlarged view of intension is derived. The intension of an expression is a function from certain factors to the extension of the expression (with respect to those factors). Originally such factors were simply possible states of the world, but as it was noticed that the so-called tense operators exhibited a structure highly analogous to that of the modal operators the factors with respect to which an extension was to be determined were enlarged to include moments of time. When it was noticed that contextual factors were required to determine the extension of sentences containing indexicals, a still more general notion was developed and called an "index." The extension of an expression was to be determined with respect to an index. The intension of an expression was that function which assigned to every index, the extension at that index:

> The above example supplies us with a statement whose truth-value is not constant but varies as a function of $i \in I$. This situation is easily appreciated in the context of time-dependent statements; that is, in the case where I represents the instant of time. Obviously the same statement can be true at one moment and false at another. For more general situations one must not think of the $i \in I$ as anything as simple as instants of time or even possible worlds. In general we will have
>
> $$i = (w, t, p, a, \ldots)$$
>
> where the index i has many *coordinates*: for example, w is a *world*, t is a *time*, $p = (x, y, z)$ is a (3–dimensional) *position* in the world, a is an *agent*, etc. All these coordinates can be varied, possibly independently, and thus affect the truth-values of statements which have indirect references to these coordinates. [From the *Advice* of a prominent logician.]

A sentence ϕ was taken to be logically true if true at every index (in every 'structure'), and $\Box\phi$ was taken to be true at a given index (in a given structure) just in case ϕ was true at every index (in that structure). Thus the familiar principle of modal generalization: if $\models \phi$, then $\models \Box\phi$, is validated.

This view, in its treatment of indexicals, was technically wrong and, more importantly, conceptually misguided.

Consider the sentence

(6)   I am here now.

It is obvious that for many choices of index—that is, for many quadruples $\langle w, x, p, t \rangle$ where w is a possible world history, x is a person, p is a place, and t is a time—(6) will be false. In fact, (6) is true only with respect to those indices $\langle w, x, p, t \rangle$ which are such that in the world history w, x is located at p at the time t. Thus (6) fares about on a par with

(7)   David Kaplan is in Portland on 26 March 1977.

[Example] (7) is empirical, and so is (6).

But here we have missed something essential to our understanding of indexicals. Intuitively, (6) is deeply, and in some sense, which we will shortly make precise, universally, true. One need only understand the meaning of (6) to know that it cannot be uttered falsely. No such guarantees apply to (7). *A Logic of Indexicals* which does not reflect this intuitive difference between (6) and (7) has bypassed something essential to the logic of indexicals.

What has gone wrong? We have ignored the special relationship between 'I', 'here', and 'now'. Here is a proposed correction. Let the class of indices be narrowed to include only the *proper* ones—namely, those $\langle w, x, p, t \rangle$ such that in the world w, x *is* located at p at the time t.

Such a move may have been intended originally since improper indices are like impossible worlds; no such contexts *could* exist, and thus there is no interest in evaluating the extensions of expressions with respect to them. Our reform has the consequence that (6) comes out, correctly, to be logically true. Now consider

(8)   □ I am here now.

Since the contained sentence (namely (6)) is true at every proper index, (8) also is true at every proper index and thus also is logically true. (As would be expected by the aforementioned principle of modal generalization.)

But (8) should not be *logically* true, since it is false. It is certainly *not* necessary that I be here now. But for several contingencies, I would be working in my garden now, or even delivering this paper in a location outside of Portland.

The difficulty here is the attempt to assimilate the role of a *context* to that of a *circumstance*. The indices $\langle w, x, p, t \rangle$ that represent contexts must be proper in order that (6) be a truth of the logic of indexicals, but the indices that represent circumstances must include improper ones in order that (8) *not* be a logical truth.

If one wishes to stay with this sort of index theory and blur the conceptual difference between context and circumstance, the minimal requirement is a system of *double* indexing—one index for context and another for circumstance. It is surprising, looking back, that we (for I was among the early index theorists) did not immediately see that double indexing was required, for in 1967, at UCLA, Hans Kamp had reported his work on 'now'[32] in which he had shown that double indexing was required to properly accommodate temporal indexicals along with the usual temporal operators. But it was *four* years before it was realized that this was a general requirement for (and, in a sense, the key to) a logic of indexicals.

However, mere double indexing, without a clear conceptual understanding of what each index stands for, is still not enough to avoid all pitfalls.

VIII   Monsters begat by elegance

My liberality with respect to operators on content—that is, intensional operators (any feature of the circumstances of evaluation that can be well defined and isolated) does not extend to operators which attempt to operate on character. Are there such operators as 'In some contexts it is true that', which when prefixed to a sentence yields a truth if and only if in some context the contained *sentence* (not the content expressed by it) expresses a content that is true in the circumstances of that context? Let us try it:

(9)   In some contexts it is true that I am not tired now.

For (9) to be true in the present context, it suffices that some agent of some context not be tired at the time of that context. [Example] (9), so interpreted, has nothing to do with me or the present moment. But this violates Principle 2! Principle 2 can also be expressed in a more theory-laden way by saying that indexicals always take primary scope. If this is true—and it is—then no operator can control the character of the indexicals within its scope, because they will simply leap out of its scope to the front of the operator. I am not saying we could not construct a language with such operators, just that English is not one.[33] And such operators *could not be added to it*.

There *is* a way to control an indexical, to keep it from taking primary scope, and even to refer it to another context (this amounts to changing its character): Use quotation marks. If we *mention* the indexical rather than *use* it, we can, of course, operate directly on it. Carnap once pointed out to me how important the difference between direct and indirect quotation is in

> Otto said "I am a fool."
> Otto said that I am a fool.

Operators like 'In some contexts it is true that', which attempt to meddle with character, I call *monsters*. I claim that none can be expressed in English (without sneaking in a quotation device). If they stay in the metalanguage and confine their attention to sentences as in *In some contexts "I am not tired now" is true*, they are rendered harmless and can even do socially useful work (as does, 'is valid' [see below]).

I have gone on at perhaps excessive length about monsters because they have recently been begat by elegance. In a specific application of the theory of indexicals there will be just certain salient features of a circumstance of evaluation. So we may represent circumstances by indexed sets of features. This is typical of the model-theoretic way, As already indicated, all the features of a circumstance will generally be required as aspects of a context, and the aspects of a context may all be features of a circumstance. If not, a little ingenuity may make it so.[34]

We could then represent contexts by the same indexed sets we use to represent circumstances, and instead of having *a logic of contexts and circumstances* we have simply *a two-dimensional logic of indexed sets*. This is algebraically very neat, and it permits a very simple and elegant description of certain important classes of characters (for example, those which are true at every pair $\langle i, i \rangle$, though the special significance of the set is somehow diminished in the abstract formulation).[35] But it also permits a simple and elegant introduction of many operators which are monsters. In abstracting from the distinct conceptual roles played by contexts of use and circumstances of evaluation, the special logic of indexicals has been obscured. Of course restrictions can be put on the two-dimensional logic to exorcise the monsters, but to do so would be to give up the mathematical advantages of that formulation.[36]

IX   Argument for principle 2: True demonstratives

I return now to the argument that all indexicals are directly referential. Suppose I point at Paul and say, *He now lives in Princeton, New Jersey*. Call *what I said*—that is, the content of my utterance, the proposition expressed—'Pat'. Is Pat true or false? True! Suppose that unbeknownst to me, Paul had moved to Santa Monica last week. Would Pat have then been true or false? False! Now, the tricky case: suppose that Paul and Charles had each disguised themselves as the other and had switched places. If that had happened, *and* I had uttered as I did, then the proposition I *would have* expressed would have been false. But in that possible context the proposition I *would have* expressed is not Pat. That is easy to see because the proposition I *would have* expressed, had I pointed to Charles instead of Paul—call this proposition 'Mike'—not only *would have* been false but actually is false. Pat, I would claim, would still be true in the circumstances of the envisaged possible context provided that Paul—in whatever costume he appeared—were still residing in Princeton.

IX.1   The arguments

I am arguing that in order to determine what the truth-value of a proposition expressed by a sentence containing a demonstrative *would be* under other possible circumstances, the relevant individual is not the individual that *would have* been demonstrated had those circumstances obtained and the demonstration been set in a context of those circumstances, but rather the individual demonstrated in the context which *did* generate the proposition being evaluated. As I have already noted, it is characteristic of sentences containing demonstratives—or, for that matter, any indexical—that they may express different propositions in different contexts. We must be wary of confusing the proposition that would have been expressed by a similar utterance in a slightly different context—say, one in which the demonstratum is changed—with the proposition that was actually expressed. If we keep this distinction in mind—that is, we distinguish Pat and Mike—we are less likely to confuse what the truth-value of the proposition *actually* expressed would have been under some possible circumstances with what the truth-value of the proposition that *would have been* expressed would have been under those circumstances.

When we consider the vast array of possible circumstances with respect to which we might inquire into the truth of a proposition expressed in some context *c* by an utterance *u*, it quickly becomes apparent that only a small fraction of these circumstances will involve an utterance of the same sentence in a similar context, and that there must be a way of evaluating the truth-value of propositions expressed using demonstratives in counterfactual circumstances in which no demonstrations are taking place and no individual has the exact characteristics exploited in the demonstration. Surely, it is irrelevant to determining whether what I said would be true or not in some counterfactual circumstance, whether Paul, or anyone for that matter, *looked* as he does now. All that would be relevant is *where he lives*. Therefore,

(T3)   the relevant features of the demonstratum *qua demonstratum* (compare, the relevant features of the x Fx *qua the x Fx*)—namely, that the speaker is pointing at it, that it has a certain appearance, is presented in a certain way—cannot be the essential characteristics used to identify the relevant individual in counterfactual situations.

These two arguments—the distinction between Pat and Mike, and consideration of counterfactual situations in which no demonstration occurs—are offered to support the view that demonstratives are devices of direct reference (rigid designators, if you will) and, by contrast, to reject a Fregean theory of demonstratives.

IX.2   The Fregean theory of demonstrations

In order to develop the latter theory, in contrast to my own, we turn first to a portion of the Fregean theory which I accept: the Fregean theory of demonstrations.

As you know, for a Fregean the paradigm of a meaningful expression is the definite description, which picks out or denotes an individual, a unique individual, satisfying a condition *s*. The individual is called the *denotation* of the definite description, and the condition *s* we may identify with the *sense* of the definite description. Since a given individual may uniquely satisfy several distinct conditions, definite descriptions with distinct senses may have the same denotation. And since some conditions may be uniquely satisfied by no individual, a definite description may have a sense but no denotation. The condition by means of which a definite description picks out its denotation is *the manner of presentation* of the denotation by the definite description.

The Fregean theory of demonstratives claims, correctly I believe, that the analogy between descriptions (short for "definite descriptions") and demonstrations is close enough to provide a sense and denotation analysis of the "meaning" of a demonstration. The denotation is the demonstratum (that which is demonstrated), and it seems quite natural to regard each demonstration as presenting its demonstratum in a particular manner, which we may regard as the sense of the demonstration. The same individual could be demonstrated by demonstrations so different in manner of presentation that it would be informative to a competent auditor-observer to be told that the demonstrata were one. For example, it might be informative to you for me to tell you that

That [pointing to Venus in the morning sky] is identical with that [pointing to Venus in the evening sky]

(I would, of course, have to speak very slowly.) The two demonstrations—call the first one 'Phos' and the second one 'Hes'—which accompanied the two occurrences of the demonstrative ex- pression 'that' have the same demonstratum but distinct manners of presentation. It is this differ- ence between the sense of Hes and the sense of Phos that accounts, the Fregean claims, for the informativeness of the assertion.

It is possible, to pursue the analogy, for a demonstration to have no demonstratum. This can arise in several ways: through hallucination, through carelessness (not noticing, in the darkened room, that the subject had jumped off the demonstration platform a few moments before the lec- ture began), through a sortal conflict (using the demonstrative phrase ⌜that F⌝, where F is a common noun phrase, while demonstrating something which is not an F), and in other ways.

Even Donnellans's important distinction between referential and attributive uses of definite descriptions seems to fit, equally comfortably, the case of demonstrations.[37]

The Fregean hypostatizes demonstrations in such a way that it is appropriate to ask of a given demonstration, say Phos, what *would* it have demonstrated under various counterfactual circum- stances? Phos and Hes might have demonstrated distinct individuals.[38]

We should not allow our enthusiasm for analogy to overwhelm judgment in this case. There are some relevant respects in which descriptions and demonstrations are disanalogous. First, as David Lewis has pointed out, demonstrations do not have a syntax, a fixed formal structure in terms of whose elements we might try to define, either directly or recursively, the notion of sense.[39] Second, to different audiences (for example, the speaker, those sitting in front of the demonstra- tion platform, and those sitting behind the demonstration platform) the same demonstration may have different senses. Or perhaps we should say that a single performance may involve distinct demonstrations from the perspective of distinct audiences. ("Exactly like proper names!" says the Fregean, "as long as the demonstratum remains the same, these fluctuations in sense are tol- erable. But they should be avoided in the system of a demonstrative science and should not ap- pear in a perfect vehicle of communication.")

IX.3   The Fregean theory of demonstratives

Let us accept, tentatively and cautiously, the Fregean theory of demonstrations, and turn now to the Fregean theory of demonstratives.[40]

According to the Fregean theory of demonstratives, an occurrence of a demonstrative ex- pression functions rather like a place-holder for the associated demonstration. The sense of a sentence containing demonstratives is to be the result of replacing each demonstrative by a con- stant whose sense is given as the sense of the associated demonstration. An important aim of the Fregean theory is, of course, to solve Frege's problem. And it does that quite neatly. You recall that the Fregean accounted for the informativeness of *That [Hes] = that [Phos]* in terms of the distinct senses of Hes and Phos. Now we see that the senses of the two occurrences of 'that' are identified with these two distinct senses so that the ultimate solution is exactly like that given by Frege originally. The sense of the left 'that' differs from the sense of the right 'that'.

IX.4   Argument against the Fregean theory of demonstratives

Let us return now to our original example: *He [Delta] now lives in Princeton, New Jersey* where 'Delta' is the name of the relevant demonstration. I assume that in the possible circumstances described earlier, Paul and Charles having disguised themselves as each other, Delta would have demonstrated Charles. Therefore, according to the Fregean theory, the proposition I just expressed,

Pat, would have been false under the counterfactual circumstances of the switch. But this, as argued earlier, is wrong. Therefore, the Fregean theory of demonstratives—though it nicely solves Frege's problem—is simply incorrect in associating propositions with utterances.

Let me recapitulate. We compared two theories as to the proposition expressed by a sentence containing a demonstrative along with an associated demonstration. Both theories allow that the demonstration can be regarded as having both a sense and a demonstratum. My theory, the direct reference theory, claims that in assessing the proposition in counterfactual circumstances it is the actual demonstratum—in the example, Paul—that is the relevant individual. The Fregean theory claims that the proposition is to be construed as if the sense of the demonstration were the sense of the demonstrative. Thus, in counterfactual situations it is the individual that *would* have been demonstrated that is the relevant individual. According to the direct reference theory, demonstratives are rigid designators. According to the Fregean theory, their denotation varies in different counterfactual circumstances as the demonstrata of the associated demonstration would vary in those circumstances.

The earlier distinction between Pat and Mike, and the discussion of counterfactual circumstances in which, as we would now put it, the demonstration would have demonstrated nothing, argue that with respect to the problem of associating propositions with utterances the direct reference theory is correct and the Fregean theory is wrong.

I have carefully avoided arguing for the direct reference theory by using modal or subjunctive sentences for fear the Fregean would claim that the peculiarity of demonstratives is not that they are rigid designators but that they always take primary scope. If I had argued only on the basis of our intuitions as to the truth-value of *If Charles and Paul had changed chairs, then he (Delta) would not now be living in Princeton*, such a scope interpretation could be claimed. But I didn't.

The perceptive Fregeans among you will have noted that I have said nothing about how Frege's problem fares under a direct reference theory of demonstratives. And indeed, if 'that' accompanied by a demonstration is a rigid designator for the demonstratum, then *that (Hes)* = *that (Phos)* looks like two rigid designators designating the same thing. Uh oh! I will return to this in my Epistemological Remarks (section XVII).

X   Fixing the reference vs. supplying a synonym[41]

The Fregean is to be forgiven. He has made a most natural mistake. Perhaps he thought as follows: If I point at someone and say 'he', that occurrence of 'he' must refer to the male at whom I am now pointing. It does! So far, so good. Therefore, the Fregean reasons, since 'he' (in its demonstrative sense) means the same as 'the male at whom I am now pointing' and since the denotation of the latter varies with circumstances, the denotation of the former must also. But this is wrong. Simply because it is a rule of the language that 'he' *refers* to the male at whom I am now pointing (or, whom I am now demonstrating, to be more general), it does not follow that any synonymy is thereby established. In fact, this is one of those cases in which—to use Kripke's excellent idiom—the rule simply tells us how to *fix the reference* but does not supply a synonym.

Consider the proposition I express with the utterance *He [Delta] is the male at whom I am now pointing*. Call that proposition 'Sean'. Now Sean is certainly true. We know from the rules of the language that any utterance of that form must express a true proposition. In fact, we would be justified in calling the *sentence, He is the male at whom I am now pointing*, almost analytic. ("Almost" because of the hypothesis that the demonstrative is *proper*—that I am pointing at a unique male—is needed.)

But is Sean necessary? Certainly not: I might have pointed at someone else.

This kind of mistake—to confuse a semantical rule which tells how to fix the reference to a directly referential term with a rule which supplies a synonym—is easy to make. Since semantics must supply a meaning in the sense of content (as I call it), for expressions, one thinks naturally that whatever way the referent of an expression is given by the semantical rules, that *way* must stand for the content of the expression. (Church [or was it Carnap?] says as much, explicitly.) This hypothesis seems especially plausible, when, as is typical of indexicals, the semantical rule which fixes the reference seems to exhaust our knowledge of the meaning of the expression.

X.1   Reichenbach on Token Reflexives

It was from such a perspective, I believe, that Reichenbach built his ingenious theory of indexicals. Reichenbach called such expressions "token-reflexive words" in accordance with his theory. He writes as follows:

> We saw that most individual-descriptions are constructed by reference to other individuals. Among these there is a class of descriptions in which the individual referred to is the act of speaking. We have special words to indicate this reference; such words are 'I', 'you', 'here', 'now', 'this'. Of the same sort are the tenses of verbs, since they determine time by reference to the time when the words are uttered. To understand the function of these words we have to make use of the distinction between *token* and *symbol*, 'token' meaning the individual sign, and 'symbol' meaning the class of similar tokens (cf. §2). Words and sentences are symbols. The words under consideration are words which refer to the corresponding token used in an individual act of speech, or writing; they may therefore be called *token-reflexive* words.
>
> It is easily seen that all these words can be defined in terms of the phrase 'this token'. The word 'I', for instance, means the same as 'the person who utters this token'; 'now' means the same as 'the time at which this token was uttered'; 'this table' means the same as 'the table pointed to by a gesture accompanying this token'. We therefore need inquire only into the meaning of the phrase 'this token'.[42]

But is it true, for example, that

(10)   'I' means the same as 'the person who utters this token'?

It is certainly true that *I am the person who utters this token*. But if (10) correctly asserted a synonymy, then it would be true that

(11)   If no one were to utter this token, I would not exist.

Beliefs such as (11) could make one a compulsive talker.

XI   The meaning of indexicals

In order to correctly and more explicitly state the semantical rule which the dictionary attempts to capture by the entry

I: the person who is speaking or writing

we would have to develop our semantical theory—the semantics of direct reference—and then state that

(D1)   'I' is an indexical, different utterances of which may have different contents.

(D3)   'I' is, in each of its utterances, directly referential.

(D2)   In each of its utterances, 'I' refers to the person who utters it.

We have seen errors in the Fregean analysis of demonstratives and in Reichenbach's analysis of indexicals, all of which stemmed from failure to realize that these words are directly referential. When we say that a word is directly referential, are we saying that its meaning *is* its reference (its only meaning is its reference, its meaning is nothing more than its reference)? Certainly not.[43] Insofar as meaning is given by the rules of a language and is what is known by competent speakers, I would be more inclined to say in the case of directly referential words and phrases that their reference is *no* part of their meaning. The meaning of the word 'I' does not change when different persons use it. The meaning of 'I' is given by the rules (D1), (D2), and (D3) above.

Meanings tell us how the content of a word or phrase is determined by the context of use. Thus the meaning of a word or phrase is what I have called its *character*. (Words and phrases with no indexical element express the same content in every context; they have a fixed character.) To supply a synonym for a word or phrase is to find another with the same *character*; finding another with the same *content* in a particular context certainly won't do. The content of 'I' used by me may be identical with the content of 'you' used by you. This doesn't make 'I' and 'you' synonyms. Frege noticed that if one wishes to say again what one said yesterday using 'today', today one must use 'yesterday'. (Incidentally the relevant passage, quoted on 758 (this volume), propounds what I take to be a direct reference theory of the indexicals 'today' and 'yesterday'.) But 'today' and 'yesterday' are not synonyms. For two words or phrases to be synonyms, they must have the same content in every context. In general, for indexicals, it is not possible to find synonyms. This is because indexicals are directly referential, and the compound phrases which can be used to give their reference ('the person who is speaking', 'the individual being demonstrated', etc.) are not.

XII   Dthat

It would be useful to have a way of converting an arbitrary singular term into one which is directly referential.

Recall that we earlier regarded demonstrations, which are required to "complete" demonstratives, as a kind of description. The demonstrative was then treated as a directly referential term whose referent was the demonstratum of the associated demonstration.

Now why not regard descriptions as a kind of demonstration, and introduce a special demonstrative which requires completion by a description and which is treated as a directly referential term whose referent is the denotation of the associated description? Why not? Why not, indeed! I have done so, and I write it thus:

dthat[α]

where α is any description, or, more generally, any singular term. 'Dthat'[44] is simply the demonstrative 'that' with the following singular term functioning as its demonstration. (Unless you hold a Fregean theory of demonstratives, in which case its meaning is as stipulated above.)

Now we can come much closer to providing genuine synonyms:

'I' means the same as 'dthat [the person who utters this token]'.

(The fact that this alleged synonymy is cast in the theory of utterances rather than occurrences introduces some subtle complications, which have been discussed by Reichenbach.)

XIII   Contexts, truth, and logical truth

I wish, in this section, to contrast an *occurrence* of a well-formed expression (my *technical* term for the combination of an expression and a context) with an *utterance* of an expression.

There are several arguments for my notion, but the main one is from Remark 1 on the Logic of Demonstratives (section XIX below): I have sometimes said that the content of a sentence in a context is, roughly, the proposition the sentence would express if uttered in that context. This description is not quite accurate on two counts. First, it is important to distinguish an *utterance* from a *sentence-in-a-context*. The former notion is from the theory of speech acts; the latter from semantics. Utterances take time, and utterances of distinct sentences cannot be simultaneous (i.e., in the same context). But in order to develop a logic of demonstratives, we must be able to evaluate several premises and a conclusion all in the same context. We do not want arguments involving indexicals to become valid simply because there is no possible context in which all the premises are uttered, and thus no possible context in which all are uttered truthfully.

Since the content of an occurrence of a sentence containing indexicals depends on the context, the notion of *truth* must be relativized to a context:

> If c is a context, then an occurrence of ϕ in c is true iff the content expressed by ϕ in this context is true when evaluated with respect to the circumstance of the context.

We see from the notion of truth that among other aspects of a context must be a possible circumstance. Every context occurs in a particular circumstance, and there are demonstratives such as 'actual' which refer to that circumstance.

If you try out the notion of truth on a few examples, you will see that it is correct. If I now utter a sentence, I will have uttered a truth just in case *what I said*, the content, is true in *these* circumstances.

As is now common for intensional logics, we provide for the notion of a *structure*, comprising a family of circumstances. Each such structure will determine a set of possible contexts. Truth in a structure, is truth in every possible context of the structure. Logical truth is truth in every structure.

XIV   Summary of findings (so far): Pure indexicals

Let me try now to summarize my findings regarding the semantics of demonstratives and other indexicals. First, let us consider the nondemonstrative indexicals such as 'I', 'here' (in its nondemonstrative sense), 'now', 'today', 'yesterday', and so on. In the case of these words, the linguistic conventions which constitute *meaning* consist of rules specifying the referent of a given *occurrence* of the word (we might say, a given token, or even utterance, of the word, if we are willing to be somewhat less abstract) in terms of various features of the context of the occurrence. Although these rules fix the referent and, in a very special sense, might be said to define the indexical, the way in which the rules are given does not provide a synonym for the indexical. The rules tell us for any possible occurrence of the indexical what the referent would be, but they do *not* constitute the content of such an occurrence. Indexicals are directly referential. The rules tell us what it is that is referred to. Thus, they *determine* the content (the propositional constituent) for a particular occurrence of an indexical. But they are not a *part* of the content (they constitute no part of the propositional constituent). In order to keep clear on a topic where ambiguities constantly threaten, I have introduced two technical terms—*content* and *character*—for the two kinds of meaning (in addition to extension) I associate with indexicals. Distinct occurrences of an indexical (in distinct contexts) may not only have distinct referents, they may have distinct meanings in the sense of *content*. If I say "I am tired today" today, and Montgomery Furth says "I am tired today" tomorrow, our utterances have different contents in that the factors which are relevant to determining the truth-value of what Furth said in both actual and counterfactual circumstances are quite different from the factors which are relevant to determining the truth-value of what I said. Our two utterances are as different in content as are the sentences "David Kaplan is tired on 26 March 1977" and "Montgomery Furth is tired on 27 March 1977." But there is another sense of meaning in which, absent lexical or syntactical ambiguities, two occurrences of the *same* word or phrase *must* mean the same. (Otherwise how could we learn and communicate with language?) This sense of meaning—which I call *character*—is what determines the content of an occurrence of a word or phrase in a given context. For indexicals, the rules of language constitute the meaning in the sense of *character*. As normally expressed, in dictionaries and the like, these rules are incomplete in that, by omitting to mention that indexicals are directly referential, they fail to specify the full content of an occurrence of an indexical.

Three important features to keep in mind about these two kinds of meaning are the following:

1. Character applies only to words and phrases as types, content to occurrences of words and phrases in contexts.
2. Occurrences of two phrases can agree in content, although the phrases differ in character, and two phrases can agree in character but differ in content in distinct contexts.
3. The relationship of character to content is something like that traditionally regarded as the relationship of sense to denotation: character is a way of presenting content.

XV   Further details: Demonstratives and demonstrations

Let me turn now to the demonstratives proper, those expressions which must be associated with a demonstration in order to determine a referent. In addition to the pure demonstratives 'that' and 'this', there are a variety of demonstratives which contain built-in sortals—'he' for 'that male', 'she' for 'that female',[45] etc.—and there are demonstrative phrases built from a pure demonstrative and a common noun phrase: 'that man drinking a martini', et cetera. Words and phrases which have demonstrative use may have other uses as well—for example, as bound variable or pronouns of laziness (anaphoric use).

I accept, tentatively and cautiously, the Fregean theory of demonstrations according to which:

1. A demonstration is a way of presenting an individual.
2. A given demonstration in certain counterfactual circumstances would have demonstrated (i.e., presented) an individual other than the individual actually demonstrated.
3. A demonstration which fails to demonstrate any individual might have demonstrated one, and a demonstration which demonstrates an individual might have demonstrated no individual at all.

So far we have asserted that it is not an essential property of a given demonstration (according to the Fregean theory) that it demonstrate a given individual, or, indeed, that it demonstrate any individual at all. It is this feature of demonstration—that demonstrations which in fact demonstrate the same individual might have demonstrated distinct individuals—which provides a solution to the demonstrative version of Frege's problem (why is an utterance of 'that [Hes] =

that [Phos]' informative?) analogous to Frege's own solution to the definite description version. There is some theoretical latitude as to how we should regard such other features of a demonstration as its place, time, and agent. Just to fix ideas, let us regard all these features as accidental. (It may be helpful to think of demonstrations as *types* and particular performances of them as their *tokens*). Then,

4. A given demonstration might have been mounted by someone other than its actual agent, and might be repeated in the same or a different place.

Although we are not now regarding the actual place and time of a demonstration as essential to it, it does seem to me to be essential to a demonstration that it present its demonstrata from some perspective—that is, as the individual that looks thusly *from here now*. On the other hand, it does not seem to me to be essential to a demonstration that it be mounted by any agent at all.[46]

We now have a kind of standard form for demonstrations:

The individual that has appearance *A* from here now

where an appearance is something like a picture with a little arrow pointing to the relevant subject. Trying to put it into words, a particular demonstration might come out like:

The brightest heavenly body now visible from here.

In this example we see the importance of perspective. The same demonstration, differently located, may present a different demonstratum (a twin, for example).

If we set a demonstration, δ, in a context, c, we determine the relevant perspective (i.e., the values of 'here' and 'now'). We also determine the demonstratum, if there is one—if, that is, in the circumstances of the context there is an individual that appears that way from the place and time of the context.[47] In setting δ and c we determine more than just the demonstratum in the possible world of the context. By fixing the perspective, we determine for each possible circumstance what, if anything, would appear like that from that perspective. This is to say, we determine a *content*. This content will not, in general, be fixed (like that determined by a rigid designator). Although it was Venus that appeared a certain way from a certain location in ancient Greece, it might have been Mars. Under certain counterfactual conditions, it *would* have been Mars that appeared just that way from just that location. Set in a different context, δ may determine a quite different content or no content at all. When I look at myself in the mirror each morning I know that I didn't look like that ten years ago—and I suspect that nobody did.

The preceding excursion into a more detailed Fregean theory of demonstrations was simply in order to establish the following structural features of demonstrations:

1. A demonstration, when set in a context (i.e., an *occurrence* of a demonstration), determines a content.
2. It is not required that an occurrence of a demonstration have a fixed content.

In view of these features, we can associate with each demonstration a *character* which represents the "meaning" or manner of presentation of the demonstration. We have now brought the semantics of demonstrations and descriptions into isomorphism.[48] Thus, I regard my 'dthat' operator as representing the general case of a demonstrative. Demonstratives are incomplete expressions which must be completed by a demonstration (type). A complete sentence (type) will include an associated demonstration (type) for each of its demonstratives. Thus each demonstrative, d, will be accompanied by a demonstration, δ, thus: $d[\delta]$. The character of a *complete* demonstrative is given by the semantical rule:

In any context c, $d[\delta]$ is a directly referential term that designates the demonstratum, if any, of
  δ in c, and that otherwise designates nothing.

Obvious adjustments are to be made to take into account any common noun phrase which accompanies or is built in to the demonstrative.

Since no immediately relevant structural differences have appeared between demonstrations and descriptions, I regard the treatment of the 'dthat' operator in the formal logic LD as accounting for the general case. It would be a simple matter to add to the syntax a category of "nonlogical demonstration constants." (Note that the indexicals of LD are all logical signs in the sense that their meaning [character] is not given by the structure but by the evaluation rules.)

XVI   Alternative treatments of demonstrations

The foregoing development of the Fregean theory of demonstrations is not inevitable. Michael Bennett has proposed that only places be demonstrata and that we require an explicit or implicit common noun phrase to accompany the demonstrative, so that *that* [*pointing at a person*] becomes *dthat* [*the person who is there* [*pointing at a place*]].

My findings do not include the claim that the—or better, a—Fregean theory of demonstrations is correct. I can provide an alternative account for those who regard demonstrations as nonrepeatable nonseparable features of contexts. The conception now under consideration is that in certain contexts the agent is demonstrating something, or more than one thing, and in others not. Thus just as we can speak of agent, time, place, and possible world history as features of a context, we may also speak of first demonstratum, second demonstratum, . . . (some of which may be null) as features of a context. We then attach subscripts to our demonstratives and regard the n-th demonstrative, when set in a context, as rigid designator of the n-th demonstratum of the context. Such a rule associates a character with each demonstrative. In providing no role for demonstrations as separable "manners of presentation," this theory eliminates the interesting distinction between demonstratives and other indexicals. We might call it the *Indexical theory of demonstratives*. (Of course, every reasonable theory of demonstratives treats them as indexicals of some kind. I regard my own theory of indexicals in general, and the nondemonstrative indexicals in particular, as essentially uncontroversial. Therefore I reserve *Indexical theory of demonstratives* for the controversial alternative to the Fregean theory of demonstrations—the Fregean theory of demonstra*tives* having been refuted.)

Let us call my theory as based on the Fregean theory of demonstrations the *Corrected Fregean theory of demonstratives*. The Fregean theory of demonstrations may be extravagant, but compared with its riches, the indexical theory is a mean thing. From a logical point of view, the riches of the Corrected Fregean theory of demonstratives are already available in connection with the demonstrative 'dthat' and its descriptive pseudodemonstrations, so a decision to enlarge the language of LD with additional demonstratives whose semantics are in accord with the Indexical theory need not be too greatly lamented.

If we consider Frege's problem, we have the two formulations:

that [Hes] = that [Phos]
$\text{that}_1 = \text{that}_2$

Both provide their sentence with an informative character. But the Fregean idea that that very demonstration might have picked out a different demonstratum seems to me to capture more of the epistemological situation than the Indexicalist's idea that in some contexts the first and second demonstrata differ.

The Corrected Fregean theory, by incorporating demonstration types in its sentence types, accounts for more differences in informativeness as differences in meaning (character). It thereby provides a nice Frege-type solution to many Frege-type problems. But it can only forestall the resort to directly epistemological issues; it cannot hold them in abeyance indefinitely. Therefore I turn to epistemological remarks.

XVII   Epistemological remarks

How do content and character serve as objects of thought?[49] Let us state, once again, Frege's problem

(FP)   How can (an occurrence of) $\ulcorner \alpha = \beta \urcorner$ (in a given context), if true, differ in cognitive significance from (an occurrence of) $\ulcorner \alpha = \alpha \urcorner$ (in the same context)?

In (FP) α, β are arbitrary singular terms. (In future formulations, I will omit the parentheticals as understood.) When α and β are demonstrative free, Frege explained the difference in terms of his notion of sense—a notion which, his writings generally suggest, should be identified with our *content*. But it is clear that Frege's problem can be reinstituted in a form in which resort to contents will not explain differences in "cognitive significance." We need only ask,

(FPD)   How can $\ulcorner$dthat[α] = dthat[β]$\urcorner$ if true, differ in cognitive significance from $\ulcorner$dthat[α] = dthat[α]$\urcorner$?

Since, as we shall show, for any term γ, $\ulcorner \gamma = \text{dthat}[\gamma] \urcorner$ is analytic, the sentence pair in (FP) will differ in cognitive significance if and only if the sentence pair in (FPD) differ similarly. [There are a few assumptions built in here, but they are O.K.] Note, however, that the *content* of $\ulcorner$dthat[α]$\urcorner$ and the *content* of $\ulcorner$dthat[β]$\urcorner$ are the same whenever $\ulcorner \alpha = \beta \urcorner$ is true. Thus the difference in cognitive significance between the sentence pair in (FPD) cannot be accounted for in terms of content.

If Frege's solution to (FP) was correct, then α and β have different contents. From this it follows that $\ulcorner$dthat[α]$\urcorner$ and $\ulcorner$dthat[β]$\urcorner$ have different characters. [It doesn't really, because of the identification of contents with intensions, but let it pass.] Is character, then, the object of thought?

If you and I both say to ourselves,

(B)   "I am getting bored"

have we thought the same thing? We could not have, because what you thought was true, while what I thought was false.

What we must do is disentangle two epistemological notions: *the objects of thought* (what Frege called "Thoughts") and the *cognitive significance of an object of thought*. As has been noted above, a character may be likened to a manner of presentation of a content. This suggests that we identify objects of thought with contents and the cognitive significance of such objects with characters.

E PRINCIPLE 1
Objects of thought (Thoughts) = Contents

E PRINCIPLE 2
Cognitive significance of a Thought = Character

According to this view, the thoughts associated with $\ulcorner$dthat$[\alpha]$ = dthat$[\beta]\urcorner$ and $\ulcorner$dthat$[\alpha]$ = dthat$[\alpha]\urcorner$ are the same, but the thought (not the denotation, mind you, but the *thought*) is *presented* differently.

It is important to see that we have not *simply* generalized Frege's theory, providing a higher order Fregean sense for each name of a regular Fregean sense.[50] In Frege's theory, a given manner of presentation presents the same object to all mankind.[51] But for us, a given manner of presentation—a character; what we both said to ourselves when we both said (B)—will, in general, present different objects (of thought) to different persons (and even different Thoughts to the same person at different times).

How then can we claim that we have captured the idea of cognitive significance? To break the link between cognitive significance and universal Fregean senses and at the same time forge the link between cognitive significance and character, we must come to see the *context-sensitivity* (dare I call it ego-orientation?) of cognitive states.

Let us try a Putnam-like experiment. We raise two identical twins, Castor and Pollux, under qualitatively identical conditions, qualitatively identical stimuli, et cetera. If necessary, we may monitor their brain states and make small corrections in their brain structures if they begin drifting apart. They respond to all cognitive stimuli in identical fashion.[52] Have we not been successful in achieving the same cognitive (i.e., psychological) state? Of course we have, what more could one ask! But wait, they believe different things. Each sincerely says, *My brother was born before I was*, and the beliefs they thereby express conflict. In this, Castor speaks the truth, while Pollux speaks falsely. This does not reflect on the identity of their cognitive states, for, as Putnam has emphasized, circumstances alone do not determine extension (here, the truth-value) from cognitive state. Insofar as distinct persons can be in the same cognitive state, Castor and Pollux are.

COROLLARY 1

> It is an almost inevitable consequence of the fact that two persons are in the *same* cognitive state, that they will *dis*agree in their attitudes toward some object of thought.

The corollary applies equally well to the same person at different times, and to the same person at the same time in different circumstances.[53] In general, the corollary applies to any individuals x, y in different contexts.

My aim was to argue that the cognitive significance of a word or phrase was to be identified with its character, the way the content is presented to us. In discussing the twins, I tried to show that persons could be in the same total cognitive state and still, as we would say, believe different things. This doesn't prove that the cognitive content of, say, a single sentence or even a word is to be identified with its character, but it strongly suggests it.

Let me try a different line of argument. We agree that a given content may be presented under various characters and that, consequently, we may hold a propositional attitude toward a given content under one character but not under another. (For example, on March 27 of this year, having lost track of the date, I may continue to hope to be finished by this March 26, without hoping to be finished by yesterday.) Now instead of arguing that character is what we would ordinarily call cognitive significance, let me just ask why we should be interested in the character under which we hold our various attitudes. Why should we be interested in that special kind of significance that is sensitive to the use of indexicals—'I', 'here', 'now', 'that', and the like? John Perry, in his stimulating and insightful paper "Frege on Demonstratives" asks and answers this question. [Perry uses 'thought' where I would use 'object of thought' or 'content' and he uses 'apprehend' for 'believe', but *note that other psychological verbs would yield analogous cases*. I have taken a few liberties in substituting my own terminology for Perry's and have added the emphasis.]

Why should we care under what character someone apprehends a thought, so long as he does? I can only sketch the barest suggestion of an answer here. *We use the manner of presentation, the character, to individuate psychological states, in explaining and predicting action.* It is the manner of presentation, the character and not the thought apprehended, that is tied to human action. When you and I have beliefs under the common character of 'A bear is about to attack me', we behave similarly. We both roll up in a ball and try to be as still as possible. Different thoughts apprehended, same character, same behavior. When you and I both apprehend that I am about to be attacked by a bear, we behave differently. I roll up in a ball, you run to get help. Same thought apprehended, different characters, different behaviors.[54]

Perry's examples can be easily multiplied. My hope to be finished by a certain time is sensitive to how the content corresponding to the time is presented, as 'yesterday' or as 'this March 26'. If I see, reflected in a window, the image of a man whose pants appear to be on fire, my behavior is sensitive to whether I think, 'His pants are on fire' or 'My pants are on fire', though the object of thought may be the same.

So long as Frege confined his attention to indexical free expressions, and given his theory of proper names, it is not surprising that he did not distinguish objects of thought (content) from cognitive significance (character), for that is the realm of *fixed* character and thus, as already remarked, there is a natural identification of character with content. Frege does, however, discuss indexicals in two places. The first passage, in which he discusses 'yesterday' and 'today', I have already discussed. Everything he says there is essentially correct. (He does not go far enough.) The second passage has provoked few endorsements and much skepticism. It too, I believe, is susceptible of an interpretation which makes it essentially correct. I quote it in full:

> Now everyone is presented to himself in a particular and primitive way, in which he is presented to no one else. So, when Dr. Lauben thinks that he has been wounded, he will probably take as a basis this primitive way in which he is presented to himself. And only Dr. Lauben himself can grasp thoughts determined in this way. But now he may want to communicate with others. He cannot communicate a thought which he alone can grasp. Therefore, if he now says 'I have been wounded', he must use the 'I' in a sense that can be grasped by others, perhaps in the sense of 'he who is speaking to you at this moment', by doing which he makes the associated conditions of his utterance serve for the expression of his thought.[55]

What is the particular and primitive way in which Dr. Lauben is presented to himself? What cognitive content presents Dr. Lauben to himself, but presents him to nobody else? Thoughts determined this way can be grasped by Dr. Lauben, but no one else can grasp *that* thought determined in *that* way. The answer, I believe, is, simply, that Dr. Lauben is presented to himself under the character of 'I'.

A sloppy thinker might succumb to the temptation to slide from an acknowledgement of the privileged perspective we each have on ourselves—only I can refer to me as 'I'—to the conclusions: first, that this perspective necessarily yields a privileged *picture* of what is seen (referred to), and second, that this picture is what is intended when one makes use of the privileged perspective (by saying 'I'). These conclusions, even if correct, are not forced upon us. The character of 'I' provides the acknowledged privileged perspective, whereas the analysis of the content of particular occurrences of 'I' provides for (and needs) no privileged pictures. There may be metaphysical, epistemological, or ethical reasons why I (so conceived) am especially *important* to myself. (Compare: why *now* is an especially important time to me. It too is presented in a particular and primitive way, and this moment cannot be presented at any other time in the same way.)[56] But the phenomenon noted by Frege—that everyone is presented to himself in a particular and primitive way—can be fully accounted for using only our semantical theory.

Furthermore, regarding the first conclusion, I sincerely doubt that there is, for each of us on each occasion of the use of 'I', a particular, primitive, and incommunicable Fregean self-concept which we tacitly express to ourselves. And regarding the second conclusion: even if Castor were sufficiently narcissistic to associate such self-concepts with his every use of 'I', his twin, Pollux, whose mental life is qualitatively identical with Castor's, would associate the *same* self-concept with *his* every (matching) use of 'I'.[57] The second conclusion would lead to the absurd result that when Castor and Pollux each say 'I', they do not thereby distinguish themselves from one another. (An even more astonishing result is possible. Suppose that due to a bit of self-deception the self-concept held in common by Castor and Pollux fits neither of them. The second conclusion then leads irresistibly to the possibility that when Castor and Pollux each say 'I' they each refer to a third party!)

The perceptive reader will have noticed that the conclusions of the sloppy thinker regarding the pure indexical 'I' are not unlike those of the Fregean regarding true demonstratives. The sloppy thinker has adopted a *demonstrative theory of indexicals*: 'I' is synonymous with 'this person' [along with an appropriate *subjective* demonstration], 'now' with 'this time', 'here' with 'this place' [each associated with some demonstration], and so on. Like the Fregean, the sloppy thinker errs in believing that the sense of the demonstration is the sense of the indexical, but the sloppy thinker commits an additional error in believing that such senses are in any way necessarily associated with uses of pure indexicals. The slide from privileged perspective to privileged picture is the sloppy thinker's original sin. Only one who is located in the exact center of the Sahara Desert is entitled to refer to that place as 'here', but aside from that, the place may present no distinguishing features.[58]

The sloppy thinker's conclusions may have another source. Failure to distinguish between the cognitive significance of a thought and the thought itself seems to have led some to believe that the elements of an object of thought must each be directly accessible to the mind. From this it follows that if a singular proposition is an object of thought, the thinker must somehow be immediately acquainted with each of the individuals involved. But, as we have seen, the situation is rather different from this. Singular propositions may be presented to us under characters which neither imply nor presuppose any special form of acquaintance with the individuals of the singular propositions. The psychological states, perhaps even the epistemological situations, of Castor and Pollux are alike, yet they assert distinct singular propositions when they each say "My brother was born before me." Had they lived at different times, they might still have been situated alike epistemologically while asserting distinct singular propositions in saying "It is quiet here now." A kidnapped heiress, locked in the trunk of a car, knowing neither the time nor where she is, may think "It is quiet here now," and the indexicals will remain directly referential.[59]

COROLLARY 2
Ignorance of the referent does not defeat the directly referential character of indexicals.

From this it follows that a special form of knowledge of an object is neither required nor presupposed in order that a person may entertain as object of thought a singular proposition involving that object.

There is nothing inaccessible to the mind about the semantics of direct reference, even when the reference is to that which we know only by description. What allows us to take various propositional attitudes towards singular propositions is not the form of our acquaintance with the objects but is, rather, our ability to manipulate the conceptual apparatus of direct reference.[60]

The foregoing remarks are aimed at refuting *Direct Acquaintance Theories of direct reference*. According to such theories, the question whether an utterance expresses a singular proposition turns, in the first instance, on the speaker's *knowledge of the referent* rather than on the *form of the reference*. If the speaker lacks the appropriate form of acquaintance with the referent, the utterance cannot express a singular proposition, and any apparently directly referring expressions used must be abbreviations or disguises for something like Fregean descriptions. Perhaps the Direct Acquaintance theorist thought that only a theory like his could permit singular propositions while still providing a solution for Frege's problem. If we could *directly* refer to a given object in nonequivalent ways (e.g., as 'dthat[Hes]' and 'dthat[Phos]'), we could not—so he thought—explain the difference in cognitive significance between the appropriate instances of $\ulcorner \alpha = \alpha \urcorner$ and $\ulcorner \alpha = \beta \urcorner$. Hence, the objects susceptible to direct reference must not permit such reference in inequivalent ways. These objects must, in a certain sense, be wholly local and completely given so that for any two *directly* coreferential terms α and β, $\ulcorner \alpha = \beta \urcorner$ will be uniformative to anyone appropriately situated, epistemologically, to be able to use these terms.[61] I hope that my discussion of the two kinds of meaning—content and character—will have shown the Direct Acquaintance Theorist that his views are not the inevitable consequence of the admission of directly referential terms. From the point of view of a lover of direct reference this is good, since the Direct Acquaintance theorist admits direct reference in a portion of language so narrow that it is used only by philosophers.[62]

I have said nothing to dispute the epistemology of the Direct Acquaintance theorist, nothing to deny that there exists his special kind of object with which one can have his special kind of acquaintance. I have only denied the relevance of these epistemological claims to the semantics of direct reference. If we sweep aside metaphysical and epistemological pseudo-explanations of what are essentially semantical phenomena, the result can only be healthy for all three disciplines.

Before going on to further examples of the tendency to confuse metaphysical and epistemological matters with phenomena of the semantics of direct reference, I want to briefly raise the problem of *cognitive dynamics*. Suppose that yesterday you said, and believed it, "It is a nice day today." What does it mean to say, today, that you have retained *that* belief? It seems unsatisfactory to just believe the same content under any old character—where is the *retention*?[63] You *can't* believe that content under the same character. Is there some obvious standard adjustment to make to the character, for example, replacing *today* with *yesterday*? If so, then a person like Rip van Winkle, who loses track of time, can't retain any such beliefs. This seems strange. Can we only *retain* beliefs presented under a fixed character? This issue has obvious and important connections with Lauben's problem in trying to communicate the thought he expresses with "I have been wounded." Under what character must his auditor believe Lauben's thought in order for Lauben's communication to have been successful? It is important to note that if Lauben said "I am wounded" in the usual meaning of 'I', there is no one else who can report what he said, using *indirect* discourse, and convey the cognitive significance (to Lauben) of what he said. This is connected with points made in section VIII, and has interesting consequences for the inevitability of so-called *de re* constructions in indirect discourse languages which contain indexicals. (I use "indirect discourse" as a general term for the analogous form of all psychological verbs.)

A prime example of the confusion of direct reference phenomena with metaphysical and epistemological ideas was first vigorously called to our attention by Saul Kripke in *Naming and Necessity*. I wish to parallel his remarks disconnecting the *a priori* and the *necessary*.

The form of *a prioricity* that I will discuss is that of logical truth (in the logic of demonstratives). We saw very early that a truth of the logic of demonstratives, like "I am here now" need not be necessary. There are many such cases of logical truths which are not necessary. If α is any singular term, then $\alpha = \text{dthat}[\alpha]$ is a logical truth. But $\square(\alpha = \text{dthat}[\alpha])$ is generally false. We can, of course, also easily produce the opposite effect: $\square(\text{dthat}[\alpha] = \text{dthat}[\beta])$ may be true, although $\text{dthat}[\alpha] = \text{dthat}[\beta]$ is not logically true, and is even logically equivalent to the contingency, $\alpha = \beta$. (I call ϕ and ψ logically equivalent when $\ulcorner \phi \leftrightarrow \psi \urcorner$ is logically true.) These cases are reminiscent of Kripke's case of the terms, 'one meter' and 'the length of bar x'. But where Kripke focuses on the special epistemological situation of one who is present at the dubbing, the descriptive meaning associated with our directly referential term dthat[α] is carried in the semantics of the language.[64]

How can something be both logically true, and thus *certain*, and *contingent* at the same time? In the case of indexicals the answer is easy to see:

COROLLARY 3

The bearers of logical truth and of contingency are different entities. It is the character (or, the sentence, if you prefer) that is logically true, producing a true content in every context. But it is the *content* (the proposition, if you will) that is contingent or necessary.

As can readily be seen, the modal logic of demonstratives is a rich and interesting thing.

It is easy to be taken in by the effortless (but fallacious) move from certainty (logical truth) to necessity. In his important article "Three Grades of Modal Involvement,"[65] Quine expresses his skepticism of the first grade of modal involvement: the sentence predicate and all it stands for, and his distaste for the second grade of modal involvement: disguising the predicate as an operator 'It is necessary that'. But he suggests that no new metaphysical undesirables are admitted until the third grade of modal involvement: quantification across the necessity operator into an open sentence.

I must protest. That first step let in some metaphysical undesirables, falsehoods. All logical truths are analytic, but they can go false when you back them up to '□'.

One other notorious example of a logical truth which is not necessary, *I exist*. One can quickly verify that in every context, this character yields a true proposition—but rarely a necessary one. It seems likely to me that it was a conflict between the feelings of contingency and of certainty associated with this sentence that has led to such painstaking examination of its "proofs." It is just a truth of logic!

Dana Scott has remedied one lacuna in this analysis. What of the premise *I think* and the connective *therefore*? His discovery was that the premise is incomplete, and that the last five words *up the logic of demonstratives* had been lost in an early manuscript version.[66]

XVIII   The formal system

Just to be sure we have not overlooked anything, here is a machine against which we can test our intuitions.

The Language LD

The *Language* LD is based on first-order predicate logic with identity and descriptions. We deviate slightly from standard formulations in using two sorts of variables, one sort for positions and a second for individuals other than positions (hereafter called simply "individuals").

Primitive symbols

PRIMITIVE SYMBOLS FOR TWO-SORTED PREDICATE LOGIC

  0. Punctuation: (,), [,]
  1. Variables:
      (i)   An infinite set of individual variables: V_i
      (ii) An infinite set of position variables: V_p
  2. Predicates:
      (i)   An infinite number of *m-n*-place predicates, for all natural numbers *m*, *n*
      (ii) The 1-0-place predicate: Exist
      (iii) The 1-1-place predicate: Located

3. Functors:
   (i) An infinite number of *m-n*-place *i*-functors (functors which form terms denoting individuals)
   (ii) An infinite number of *m-n*-place *p*-functors (functors which form terms denoting positions)
4. Sentential Connectives: $\wedge, \vee, \neg, \rightarrow, \leftrightarrow$
5. Quantifiers: $\forall, \exists$
6. Definite Description Operator: the
7. Identity: =

PRIMITIVE SYMBOLS FOR MODAL AND TENSE LOGIC

8. Modal Operators: $\square, \lozenge$
9. Tense Operators:
   (i) *F* (it will be the case that)
   (ii) *P* (it has been the case that)
   (iii) *G* (one day ago, it was the case that)

PRIMITIVE SYMBOLS FOR THE LOGIC OF DEMONSTRATIVES

10. Three 1-place sentential operators:
    (i) *N* (it is now the case that)
    (ii) *A* (it is actually the case that)
    (iii) *Y* (yesterday, it was the case that)
11. A 1-place functor: dthat
12. An individual constant (0-0-place *i*-functor): I
13. A position constant (0-0-place *p*-functor): Here

Well-formed expressions

The *well-formed expressions* are of three kinds: formulas, position terms (*p*-terms), and individual terms (*i*-terms).

1. (i) If $\alpha \in V_i$, then α is an *i*-term
   (ii) If $\alpha \in V_p$, then α is a *p*-term
2. If π is an *m-n*-place predicate, $\alpha_1, \ldots, \alpha_m$ are *i*-terms, and $\beta_1, \ldots, \beta_n$ are *p*-terms, then $\pi\alpha_1 \ldots \alpha_m\beta_1 \ldots \beta_n$ is a formula
3. (i) If η is an *m-n*-place *i*-functor, $\alpha_1, \ldots, \alpha_m, \beta_1, \ldots, \beta_n$ are as in 2, then $\eta\alpha_1 \ldots \alpha_m\beta_1 \ldots \beta_n$ is an *i*-term
   (ii) If η is an *m-n*-place *p*-functor, $\alpha_1, \ldots, \alpha_m, \beta_1, \ldots, \beta_n$ are as in 2, then $\eta\alpha_1 \ldots \alpha_m\beta_1 \ldots \beta_n$ is a *p*-term
4. If ϕ, ψ are formulas, then $(\phi \wedge \psi), (\phi \vee \psi), \neg\phi, (\phi \rightarrow \psi), (\phi \leftrightarrow \psi)$ are formulas
5. If ϕ is a formula and $\alpha \in V_i \cup V_p$, then $\forall\alpha\phi$ and $\exists\alpha\phi$ are formulas
6. If ϕ is a formula, then
   (i) if $\alpha \in V_i$, then 'the $\alpha \phi$' is an *i*-term
   (ii) if $\alpha \in V_p$, then 'the $\alpha \phi$' is a *p*-term
7. If α, β are either both *i*-terms or both *p*-terms, then $\alpha = \beta$ is a formula
8. If ϕ is a formula, then $\square\phi$ and $\lozenge\phi$ are formulas
9. If ϕ is a formula, then $F\phi, P\phi$, and $G\phi$ are formulas
10. If ϕ is a formula, then $N\phi, A\phi$, and $Y\phi$ are formulas
11. (i) If α is an *i*-term, then dthat[α] is an *i*-term
    (ii) If α is a *p*-term, then dthat[α] is a *p*-term

Semantics for LD

LD structures

DEFINITION: $\mathfrak{U}$ is an LD structure iff there are C, $\mathcal{W}$, U, $\mathcal{P}$, T, and $\mathcal{I}$ such that:

1. $\mathfrak{U} = \langle C,\ \mathcal{W},\ U,\ \mathcal{P},\ T,\ \mathcal{I} \rangle$
2. C is a nonempty set (the set of contexts; see 10 below)
3. If $c \in C$, then
    (i) $c_A \in U$ (the *agent* of c)
    (ii) $c_T \in T$ (the *time* of c)
    (iii) $c_P \in \mathcal{P}$ (the *position* of c)
    (iv) $c_W \in \mathcal{W}$ (the *world* of c)
4. $\mathcal{W}$ is a nonempty set (the set of *worlds*)
5. U is a nonempty set (the set of all *individuals*; see 9 below)
6. $\mathcal{P}$ is a nonempty set (the set of *positions*, common to all worlds)
7. T is the set of integers (thought of as the *times*, common to all worlds)
8. $\mathcal{I}$ is a function which assigns to each predicate and functor an appropriate *intension* as follows:
    (i)   If π is an *m-n*-predicate, $\mathcal{I}_\pi$ is a function such that for each $t \in T$ and $w \in \mathcal{W}$, $\mathcal{I}_\pi(t,w) \subseteq (U^m \times P^n)$
    (ii) If η is an *m-n*-place *i*-functor, $\mathcal{I}_\eta$ is a function such that for each $t \in T$ and $w \in \mathcal{W}$, $\mathcal{I}_\eta(t,w) \in (U \cup \{\dagger\})^{(U^m \times \mathcal{P}^n)}$ (Note: $\dagger$ is a completely alien entity, in neither U nor $\mathcal{P}$, which represents an 'undefined' value of the function. In a normal set theory we can take $\dagger$ to be $\{U,\mathcal{P}\}$.)
    (iii) If η is an *m-n*-place *p*-functor, $\mathcal{I}_\eta$ is a function such that for each $t \in T$ and $w \in \mathcal{W}$, $\mathcal{I}_\eta(t,w) \in (\mathcal{P} \cup \{\dagger\})^{(U^m \times \mathcal{P}^n)}$
9. $i \in U$ iff $(\exists t \in T)(\exists w \in \mathcal{W})(\langle i \rangle \in \mathcal{I}_{\text{Exist}}(t,w))$
10. If $c \in C$, then $\langle c_A,\ c_P \rangle \in \mathcal{I}_{\text{Located}}(c_T,\ c_W)$
11. If $\langle i,\ p \rangle \in \mathcal{I}_{\text{Located}}(t,w)$, then $\langle i \rangle \in \mathcal{I}_{\text{Exist}}(t,w)$

Truth and denotation in a context

We write $\vDash^{\mathfrak{U}}_{cftw} \phi$

for ϕ, when taken in the context c (under the assignment f and in the structure $\mathfrak{U}$), *is true with respect to* the time t and the world w.

We write $|a|^{\mathfrak{U}}_{cftw}$

for *The denotation of* a, when taken in the context c (under the assignment f and in the structure $\mathfrak{U}$), *with respect to* the time t and the world w.

In general we will omit the superscript '$\mathfrak{U}$', and we will assume that the structure $\mathfrak{U}$ is $\langle C,\ \mathcal{W},\ U,\ \mathcal{P},\ T,\ \mathcal{I} \rangle$.

DEFINITION: f *is an assignment* (with respect to $\langle C,\ \mathcal{W},\ U,\ \mathcal{P},\ T,\ \mathcal{I} \rangle$) iff: $\exists f_1 f_2 (f_1 \in U^{Vi}\ \&\ f_2 \in \mathcal{P}^{Vp}\ \&\ f = f_1 \cup f_2)$.

DEFINITION: $f^a_x = (f \sim \{\langle a, f(a) \rangle\}) \cup \{\langle a, x \rangle\}$ (i.e., the assignment which is just like f except that it assigns x to a).

DEFINITION: For the following recursive definition, assume that $c \in C$, f is an assignment, $t \in T$, and $w \in \mathcal{W}$:

1. If α is a variable, $|\alpha|_{cftw} = f(\alpha)$

2. $\vDash_{cftw}\pi\alpha_1 \ldots \alpha_m\beta_1 \ldots \beta_n$ iff $\langle|\alpha_1|_{cftw} \ldots |\beta_n|_{cftw}\rangle \in I_\pi(t,w)$

3. If η is neither 'I' nor 'Here' (see 12, 13 below), then

$$|\eta\alpha_1 \ldots \alpha_m\beta_1 \ldots \beta_n|_{cftw} = \begin{cases} I_\eta(t,w)\left(\langle|\alpha_1|_{cftw} \ldots |\beta_n|_{cftw}\rangle\right), \text{if none of}\,|\alpha_j|_{cftw} \ldots |\beta_k|_{cftw} \text{ are }\dagger; \\ \dagger, \text{ otherwise} \end{cases}$$

4. (i) $\vDash_{cftw}(\phi \wedge \psi)$ iff $\vDash_{cftw}\phi$ & $\vDash_{cftw}\psi$

   (ii) $\vDash_{cftw}\neg\phi$ iff $\sim \vDash_{cftw}\phi$
      etc.

5. (i) If $\alpha \in V_i$, then $\vDash_{cftw}\forall\alpha\phi$ iff $\forall i\in U_i$ $\vDash_{cf^{\alpha}_i tw}\phi$

   (ii) If $\alpha \in V_p$, then $\vDash_{cftw}\forall\alpha\phi$ iff $\forall p\in \mathcal{P}$, $\vDash_{cf^{\alpha}_p tw}\phi$

   (iii) Similarly for $\exists\alpha\phi$

6. (i) If $\alpha \in V_i$, then:

$$|\text{the }\alpha\phi|_{cftw} = \begin{cases} \text{the unique i } \in \mathcal{U} \text{ such that } \vDash_{cf^i_i tw}\phi, \text{ if there is such;} \\ \dagger, \text{ otherwise} \end{cases}$$

   (ii) Similarly for $\alpha \in V_p$

7. $\vDash_{cftw}\alpha = \beta$ iff $|\alpha_{cftw} = |\beta|_{cftw}$

8. (i) $\vDash_{cftw}\Box\phi$ iff $\forall w' \in W$, $\vDash_{cftw}\phi$

   (ii) $\vDash_{cftw}\Diamond\phi$ iff $\exists w' \in W$, $\vDash_{cftw}\phi$

9. (i) $\vDash_{cftw}F\phi$ iff $\exists t' \in T$ such that $t' > t$ and $\vDash_{cft'w}\phi$

   (ii) $\vDash_{cftw}P\phi$ iff $\exists t' \in T$ such that $t' < t$ and $\vDash_{cft'w}\phi$

   (iii) $\vDash_{cftw}G\phi$ iff $\vDash_{cf(t-1)w}\phi$

10. (i) $\vDash_{cftw}N\phi$ iff $\vDash_{cfc_Tw}\phi$

    (ii) $\vDash_{cftw}A\phi$ iff $\vDash_{cftc_w}\phi$

    (iii) $\vDash_{cftw}Y\phi$ iff $\vDash_{cf(c_T-1)w}\phi$

11. $|\text{dthat}[\alpha]|_{cftw} = |\alpha|_{cfc_Tc_W}$

12. $|\text{I}|_{cftw} = c_A$

13. $|\text{Here}|_{cftw} = c_P$

XIX Remarks on the formal system

REMARK 1: Expressions containing demonstratives will, in general, express different concepts in different contexts. We call the concept expressed in a given context the *Content* of the expression in that context. The Content of a sentence in a context is, roughly, the proposition the sentence would express if uttered in that context. This description is not quite accurate on two counts. First, it is important to distinguish an *utterance* from a *sentence-in-a-context*. The former notion is from the theory of speech acts; the latter is from semantics. Utterances take time, and utterances of distinct sentences cannot be simultaneous (i.e., in the same context). But to develop a logic of demonstratives it seems most natural to be able to evaluate several premises and a conclusion all in the same context. Thus the notion of ϕ *being true in c and* $\mathfrak{U}$ does not require an utterance of ϕ. In particular, c_A need not be uttering ϕ in c_W at c_T. Second, the truth of a proposition is not usually thought of as dependent on a time as well as a possible world. The time is thought of as fixed by the context. If ϕ is a sentence, the more usual notion of the proposition expressed by ϕ-in-c is what is here called the Content of $N\phi$ in c.

Where Γ is either a term or formula, we write: $\{\Gamma\}^{\mathfrak{U}}_{cf}$

for The Content of Γ in the context c (under the assignment f and in the structure $\mathfrak{U}$).

DEFINITION:

(i) If ϕ is a formula, $\{\phi\}^{\mathfrak{U}}_{cf}$ = that function which assigns to each $t \in T$ and $w \in W$, Truth, if $\models^{\mathfrak{U}}_{cftw}\phi$, and Falsehood otherwise.

(ii) If α is a term, $\{\alpha\}^{\mathfrak{U}}_{cf}$ = that function which assigns to each $t \in T$ and $w \in W$, $|\alpha|_{cftw}$.

REMARK 2: $\models^{\mathfrak{U}}_{cftw}\phi$ iff $\{\phi\}^{\mathfrak{U}}_{cf}(t,w)$ = Truth. Roughly speaking, the sentence ϕ taken in context c is *true with respect to t and w* iff the proposition expressed by ϕ-in-the-context-c would be true at the time t if w were the actual world. In the formal development of pages 780 and 781 it was smoother to ignore the conceptual break marked by the notion of *Content in a context* and to directly define *truth in a context with respect to a possible time and world*. The important conceptual role of the notion of Content is partially indicated by the following two definitions:

DEFINITION: ϕ *is true in the context c* (in the structure $\mathfrak{U}$) iff for every assignment f, $\{\phi\}^{\mathfrak{U}}_{cf}(c_T, c_W)$ = Truth.

DEFINITION: ϕ *is valid in LD* ($\models$) iff for every LD structure $\mathfrak{U}$, and every context c of $\mathfrak{U}$, ϕ is true in c (in $\mathfrak{U}$).

REMARK 3: $\models(\alpha = \text{dthat}[\alpha])$; $\models(\phi \leftrightarrow AN\phi)$; $\models N(\text{Located I, Here})$; $\models$ Exist I. But, $\sim\models \Box(\alpha = \text{dthat}[\alpha])$; $\sim\models \Box(\phi \leftrightarrow AN\phi)$; $\sim\models \Box N(\text{Located I, Here})$; $\sim\models \Box(\text{Exist I})$. Also, $\sim\models F(\phi \leftrightarrow AN\phi)$.

In the converse direction (where the original validity has the form $\Box\phi$, we have the usual results in view of the fact that $\models(\Box\phi \rightarrow \phi)$.

DEFINITION: If $\alpha_1, \ldots, \alpha_n$ are all the free variables of ϕ in alphabetical order then *the closure of $\phi = AN\forall\alpha_1 \ldots \forall\alpha_n\phi$.*

DEFINITION: ϕ *is closed* iff ϕ is equivalent (in the sense of Remark 12) to its closure.

REMARK 4: If ϕ is closed, then ϕ is true in c (and $\mathfrak{U}$) iff for every assignment f, time t, and world w, $\models^{\mathfrak{U}}_{cftw}\phi$.

DEFINITION: Where Γ is either a term or a formula, *the Content of Γ in the context c* (*in the structure $\mathfrak{U}$) is Stable* iff for every assignment f, $\{\Gamma\}^{\mathfrak{U}}_{cf}$ is a constant function (i.e., $\{\Gamma\}^{\mathfrak{U}}_{cf}(t,w)$ = $\{\Gamma\}^{\mathfrak{U}}_{cf}(t',w')$, for all t, t', w, and w' in $\mathfrak{U}$).

REMARK 5: Where ϕ is a formula, α is a term, and β is a variable, each of the following has a Stable Content in every context (in every structure): $AN\phi$, dthat[α], β, I, Here.

If we were to extend the notion of Content to apply to operators, we would see that all indexicals (including N, A, Y, and dthat) have a Stable Content in every context. The same is true of the familiar logical constants although it does not hold for the modal and tense operators (not, at least, according to the foregoing development).

REMARK 6: That aspect of the meaning of an expression which determines what its Content will be in each context, we call the *Character* of the expression. Although a lack of knowledge about the context (or perhaps about the structure) may cause one to mistake the Content of a given utterance, the Character of each well-formed expression is determined by rules of the language (such as rules 1–13 in the section "Truth and Denotation in a Context"), which are presumably known to all competent speakers. Our notation '$\{\phi\}^{\mathfrak{U}}_{cf}$' for the Content of an expression gives a natural notation for the Character of an expression, namely '$\{\phi\}$'.

DEFINITION: Where Γ is either a term or a formula, *the Character of Γ* is that function which assigns to each structure $\mathfrak{U}$, assignment f, and context c of $\mathfrak{U}$, $\{\Gamma\}^{\mathfrak{U}}_{cf}$.

DEFINITION: Where Γ is either a term or a formula, *the Character of* Γ *is Stable* iff for every structure $\mathfrak{U}$, and assignment f, the Character of Γ (under f in $\mathfrak{U}$) is a constant function (i.e., $\{\Gamma\}^{\mathfrak{U}}_{c'f} = \{\Gamma\}^{\mathfrak{U}}_{c'f}$, for all c, c' in $\mathfrak{U}$).

REMARK 7: A formula or term has a Stable Character iff it has the same Content in every context (for each $\mathfrak{U}$, f).

REMARK 8: A formula or term has a Stable Character iff it contains no essential occurrence of a demonstrative.

REMARK 9: The logic of demonstratives determines a sublogic of those formulas of LD which contain no demonstratives. These formulas (and their equivalents which contain inessential occurrences of demonstratives) are exactly the formulas with a Stable Character. The logic of demonstratives brings a new perspective even to formulas such as these. The sublogic of LD which concerns only formulas of Stable Character is not identical with traditional logic. Even for such formulas, the familiar Principle of Necessitation (if $\vDash \phi$, then $\vDash \Box\phi$) fails. And so does its tense logic counterpart: if $\vDash \phi$, then $\vDash (\neg P\neg\phi \wedge \neg F\neg\phi \wedge \phi)$. From the perspective of LD, validity is truth in every possible *context*. For traditional logic, validity is truth in every possible *circumstance*. Each possible context determines a possible circumstance, but it is not the case that each possible circumstance is part of a possible context. In particular, the fact that each possible context has an agent implies that any possible circumstance in which no individuals exist will not form a part of any possible context. Within LD, a possible context is represented by $\langle\mathfrak{U},c\rangle$ and a possible circumstance by $\langle\mathfrak{U},t,w\rangle$. To any $\langle\mathfrak{U},c\rangle$, there corresponds $\langle\mathfrak{U},c_{\mathrm{T}}, c_{\mathrm{W}}\rangle$. But it is not the case that to every $\langle\mathfrak{U},t, w\rangle$ there exists a context c of $\mathfrak{U}$ such that $t = c_{\mathrm{T}}$ and $w = c_{\mathrm{W}}$. The result is that in LD such sentences as '$\exists x$ Exist x' and '$\exists x\exists p$ Located x, p' are valid, although they would not be so regarded in traditional logic. At least not in the neotraditional logic that countenances empty worlds. Using the semantical developments of pages 780–781 we can define this traditional sense of validity (for formulas which do not contain demonstratives) as follows. First note that by Remark 7, if ϕ has a Stable Character,

$$\vDash^{\mathfrak{U}}_{cftw}\phi \text{ iff } \vDash^{\mathfrak{U}}_{c'ftw}\phi$$

Thus for such formulas we can define,

ϕ *is true at* t, w (*in* $\mathfrak{U}$) iff for every assignment f and every context c, $\vDash^{\mathfrak{U}}_{cftw}\phi$

The neotraditional sense of validity is now definable as follows,

$\vDash_{\mathrm{T}}\phi$ iff for all structures $\mathfrak{U}$, times t, and worlds w, ϕ is true at t, w (in $\mathfrak{U}$)

(Properly speaking, what I have called the neo-traditional sense of validity is the notion of validity now common for a quantified S5 modal tense logic with individual variables ranging over possible individuals and a predicate of existence.) Adding the subscript 'LD' for explicitness, we can now state some results:

1. If ϕ contains no demonstratives, if $\vDash_{\mathrm{T}}\phi$, then $\vDash_{\mathrm{LD}}\phi$
2. $\vDash_{\mathrm{LD}}\exists x$ Exist x, but $\sim \vDash_{\mathrm{T}}\exists x$ Exist x

Of course, '$\Box\exists x$ Exist x' is not valid even in LD. Nor are its counterparts, '$\neg F\neg\exists x$ Exist x', and '$\neg P\neg\exists x$ Exist x'.

This suggests that we can transcend the context-oriented perspective of LD by generalizing over times and worlds so as to capture those possible circumstances $\langle\mathfrak{U}, t, w\rangle$ which do not correspond to any possible contexts $\langle\mathfrak{U}, c\rangle$. We have the following result:

3. If ϕ contains no demonstratives, $\vDash_{\mathrm{T}}\phi$ iff $\vDash_{\mathrm{LD}}\Box(\neg F\neg\phi \wedge \neg P\neg\phi \wedge \phi)$.

Although our definition of the neotraditional sense of validity was motivated by consideration of demonstrative-free formulas, we could apply it also to formulas containing essential occurrences of demonstratives. To do so would nullify the most interesting features of the logic of demonstratives. But it raises the question, can we express our new sense of validity in terms of the neotraditional sense? This can be done:

4. $\vDash_{LD}\phi$ iff $\vDash_{T}AN\phi$

REMARK 10: Rigid designators (in the sense of Kripke) are terms with a Stable Content. Since Kripke does not discuss demonstratives, his examples all have, in addition, a Stable Character (by Remark 8). Kripke claims that for proper names α, β it may happen that $\alpha = \beta$, though not a priori, is nevertheless necessary. This, in spite of the fact that the names α, β may be introduced by means of descriptions α', β' for which $\alpha' = \beta'$ is not necessary. An analogous situation holds in LD. Let α', β' be definite descriptions (without free variables) such that $\alpha' = \beta'$ is not a priori, and consider the (rigid) terms dthat[α'] and dthat[β'] which are formed from them. We know that: $\vDash$ (dthat[α'] = dthat[β'] $\leftrightarrow \alpha' = \beta'$). Thus, if $\alpha' = \beta'$ is not a priori, neither is dthat[α'] = dthat[β']. But, $\vDash$ (dthat[α'] = dthat[β'] $\leftrightarrow \Box$(dthat[α'] = dthat[β'])), it may happen that dthat[α'] = dthat[β'] is necessary. The converse situation can be illustrated in LD. Since (α = dthat[α]) is valid (see Remark 3), it is surely capable of being known a priori. But if α lacks a Stable Content (in some context c), $\Box$(α = dthat[α]) will be false.

REMARK 11: Our 0-0-place i-functors are not proper names, in the sense of Kripke, since they do not have a Stable Content. But they can easily be converted by means of stabilizing influence of 'dthat'. Even dthat[α] lacks a Stable Character. The process by which such expressions are converted into expressions with a Stable Character is "dubbing"—a form of definition in which context may play an essential role. The means to deal with such context-indexed definitions is not available in our object language.

There would, of course, be no difficulty in supplementing our language with a syntactically distinctive set of 0-0-place i-functors whose semantics requires them to have both a Stable Character and a Stable Content in every context. Variables already behave this way; what is wanted is a class of constants that behave, in these respects, like variables.

The difficulty comes in expressing the definition. My thought is that when a name, like 'Bozo', is introduced by someone saying, in some context c^*, "Let's call the governor, 'Bozo'", we have a context-indexed definition of the form: $A = _{c^*} \alpha$, where A is a new constant (here, 'Bozo') and α is some term whose denotation depends on context (here, 'the governor'). The intention of such a dubbing is, presumably, to induce the semantical clause: for all c, $\{A\}^{u}_{cf} = \{\alpha\}_{c^*f}$. Such a clause gives A a Stable Character. The context-indexing is required by the fact that the Content of α (the "definiens") may vary from context to context. Thus the same semantical clause is not induced by taking either $A = \alpha$ or even $A = $ dthat[α] as an axiom.

I think it is likely that such definitions play a practically (and perhaps theoretically) indispensable role in the growth of language, allowing us to introduce a vast stock of names on the basis of a meager stock of demonstratives and some ingenuity in the staging of demonstrations.

Perhaps such introductions should not be called "definitions" at all, since they essentially enrich the expressive power of the language. What a nameless man may express by "I am hungry" may be inexpressible in remote contexts. But once he says 'Let's call me 'Bozo'," his Content is accessible to us all.

REMARK 12: The strongest form of logical equivalence between two formulas ϕ and ϕ' is sameness of Character, $\{\phi\} = \{\phi'\}$. This form of synonymy is expressible in terms of validity:

$\{\phi\} = \{\phi'\}$ iff $\vDash \Box[\neg F\neg(\phi \leftrightarrow \phi') \wedge \neg P\neg(\phi \leftrightarrow \phi') \wedge (\phi \leftrightarrow \phi')]$

[Using Remark 9 (iii) and dropping the condition, which was stated only to express the intended range of applicability of $\vDash_T$, we have: $\{\phi\} = \{\phi'\}$ iff $\vDash_T(\phi \leftrightarrow \phi')$.] Since definitions of the usual kind (as opposed to dubbings) are intended to introduce a short expression as a mere abbreviation of a longer one, the Character of the defined sign should be the same as the Character of the definiens. Thus, within LD, definitional axioms must take the unusual form indicated above.

REMARK 13: If β is a variable of the same sort as the term α but is not free in α, then $\{dthat[\alpha]\}$ = $\{$ the β $AN(\beta = \alpha)\}$. Thus for every formula ϕ, there can be constructed a formula ϕ' such that ϕ' contains no occurrence of 'dthat' and $\{\phi\} = \{\phi'\}$.

REMARK 14: Y (yesterday) and G (one day ago) superficially resemble one another in view of the fact that $\vDash (Y\phi \leftrightarrow G\phi)$. But the former is a demonstrative, whereas the latter is an iterative temporal operator. "One day ago it was the case that one day ago it was the case that John yawned" means that John yawned the day before yesterday. But "Yesterday it was the case that yesterday it was the case that John yawned" is only a stutter.

Notes on possible refinements

1. The primitive predicates and functors of first-order predicate logic are all taken to be extensional. Alternatives are possible.
2. Many conditions might be added on $\mathcal{P}$; many alternatives might be chosen for $\mathcal{T}$. If the elements of $\mathcal{T}$ do not have a natural relation to play the role of $<$, such a relation must be added to the structure.
3. When K is a set of LD formulas, $K \vDash \phi$ is easily defined in any of the usual ways.
4. Aspects of the contexts other than c_A, c_P, c_T, and c_W would be used if new demonstratives (e.g., pointings, You, etc.) were added to the language. (Note that the subscripts A, P, T, W are external parameters. They may be thought of as functions applying to contexts, with c_A being the value of A for the context c.)
5. Special continuity conditions through time might be added for the predicate 'Exist'.
6. If individuals lacking positions are admitted as agents of contexts, 3(iii) of page 780 should be weakened to: $c_P \in P \cup \{\dagger\}$. It would no longer be the case that: $\vDash$ Located I, Here. If individuals also lacking temporal location (disembodied minds?) are admitted as agents of contexts, a similar weakening is required of 3(ii). In any case it would still be true that $\vDash$ Exist I.

XX Adding 'says'

[This section is not yet written. What follows is a rough outline of what is to come.]

The point of this section is to show, in a controlled experiment, that what Quine called *the relational sense* of certain intensional operators is unavoidable, and to explore the *logical*, as opposed to epistemological, features of language which lead to this result.

I have already mentioned, in connection with Dr. Lauben, that when x says 'I have been wounded' and y wishes to report in indirect discourse exactly what x said, y has a problem. It will not do for y to say 'x said that I have been wounded'. According to our earlier remarks, it should be correct for y to report x's *content* using a character appropriate to the context of the report. For example, accusingly: 'You said that you had been wounded', or quantificationally: '$(\exists z)(F z \land x$ said that z had been wounded)' where x alone satisfied '$F z$'. I will try to show that such constructions are the inevitable result of the attempt to make (third-person) *indirect discourse* reports of the first-person *direct discourse* sayings when those sayings involve indexicals.

The situation regarding the usual epistemic verbs—'believes', 'hopes', 'knows', 'desires', 'fears', et cetera—is, I believe, essentially similar to that of 'says'. Each has, or might have, a *direct discourse* sense in which the character which stands for the cognitive significance of the thought is given (he thinks, 'My God! It is *my* pants that are on fire.') as well as an *indirect discourse* sense in which only the content need be given (he thinks that it is *his* pants that are on fire).[67] If this is correct, and if indexicals are featured in the language of thought (as suggested earlier), then any *indirect* discourse reports of someone's thought (other than first-person on-the-spot reports) must contain those features—*de re* constructions, referential occurrences, quantification in, relational senses—that have so puzzled me, and some others, since the appearance of "Quantifiers and Propositional Attitudes."[68]

What is special and different about the present approach is the attempt to use the distinction between direct and indirect discourse to match the distinction between character and content. Thus when you wonder, 'Is that me?', it is correct to report you as having wondered whether you are yourself. These transformations are traced to the indexical form of your inner direct discourse rather than to any particular referential intentions. The idea is that the full analysis of indirect discourse includes mention of the suppressed character of the direct discourse event which the indirect discourse reports, thus:

$\exists c, C$ [c is a context $\wedge$ C *is a character* $\wedge$ x is the agent of c $\wedge$ x direct-discourse-verb C at the time t of c $\wedge$ the content of C in c is that . . .]

approximates a full analysis of

x indirect-discourse-verb that . . . at t.

Rather than try to include all these semantical ideas in an object language which includes the direct discourse forms of the verbs, the object language will include, *as is usual*, only the indirect discourse forms. The information about the character of the direct discourse event will provide the metalinguistic data against which the truth of object language sentences is tested.[69]

What is not yet clear to me is whether all directly referential occurrences of terms within the scope of indirect discourse epistemic verbs are to be justified *solely* on the basis of a like (though generally distinct) term in the direct discourse event or whether in some cases the English idioms which we symbolize with quantification in (for example, "There is someone whom Holmes believes to have shot himself") involve some element of *knowing-who* or *believing-who*. To put the question another way: are all the cases that Quine describes, and others similar, which irresistibly suggest the symbolic idiom of quantification in, accounted for by the semantics of direct reference (including indexicals and possibly other expressions as well) as applied to the (putative) direct discourse events? "Quantifying In" suffers from the lack of an adequate semantics of direct reference, but its explicandum includes the epistemological idea of knowing-who, which goes beyond what can be analyzed simply in terms of direct reference. When Ingrid hears someone approaching through the fog and knows 'Someone is approaching' and even knows 'That person is approaching', is it justified to say that there is someone whom Ingrid knows to be approaching? Or must we have, in addition to the indexical 'that person', *recognition* on Ingrid's part of who it is that is approaching? My present thought is that the cases which irresistibly suggest the symbolic idiom of quantification in involve, in an ambiguous way, two elements: *direct reference* (on which we are close to getting clear, I hope) and *recognition*.[70] (The latter is my new term for knowing-(or believing)-who.) The term is chosen to reflect the idea that the individual in question is identified with respect to some prior or independent information—*re*cognition—not immediately connected with the current attribution. Of the two elements, the former is semantical; the latter, frankly epistemological. The English idiom 'There is someone such that Ingrid indirect-discourse-propositional-attitude-verb that . . . he . . .' always implies that a singular proposition is the object of Ingrid's thought (and thus that some directly referential term α occurred in her inner direct discourse) and may sometimes imply (or only suggest?) that Ingrid recognized, *who* α *is*. I offer no analysis of the latter notion.[71]

In the first paragraph, I referred to a controlled experiment. By that I mean the following. Accepting the metaphor of "inner direct discourse events" and "indirect discourse reports" in connection with the usual epistemic verbs, I want to examine the logical relations between these two. But the study is complicated by at least three factors which obscure the issues I wish to bring to light. First, there is no real syntax to the language of thought. Thus, even in the case of the simplest thoughts, the relation between the syntax of the sentential complement to the epistemic verb and the structure of the original thought is obscure. Second, in containing images, sounds, odors, et cetera, thought is richer than the language of the report. Might these perceptual elements play a role in determining logical relations? Third, thought ranges from the completely explicit (inner speech) to the entirely implicit (unconscious beliefs which explain actions) and through a variety of occurrent and dispositional forms. This makes it hard to pin down the whole direct discourse event. These three factors suggest taking as a paradigm of the relation between direct and indirect discourse—direct and indirect discourse!

Even when reporting the (outer) discourse of another, at least three obscure irrelevancies (for our purposes) remain. First, if Christopher speaks in a language different from that of the report, we have again the problem of translation (analogous to, though perhaps less severe than, that of translating the language of thought). We control this by assuming the direct discourse to be in the language of the indirect discourse report. Second, as Carnap once pointed out to me, if Christopher's discourse had the form ⌜φ ∧ ψ⌝, even the strictest court would accept as true the testimony, ⌜Christopher said that ψ ∧ φ⌝. What logical transformations on the original discourse would be allowed in the report? (If Christopher says '∃x x is round', may we report him as saying that ∃y y is round?) We control this by allowing no logical transformations (we are explicating *literal* indirect discourse). Third, if in saying 'The circle can't be squared' Christopher thought that 'can't' was synonymous with 'should not' rather than 'cannot', should he be reported as having said that the circle can't be squared? We control this by assuming that our speakers make no linguistic errors.

What then remains of the logic? Is the move from direct discourse to literal indirect discourse not simply the result of disquotation (and decapitalization) plus the addition of 'that', as in:

Christopher says 'the world is round'
∴ Christopher says that the world is round

But how then are we to report Dr. Lauben's saying, 'I have been wounded'? Certainly not as, 'Dr. Lauben says that I have been wounded'!

Even in this highly antiseptic environment, the logic of *says* should provide us with a full measure of that baffling and fascinating *de re* versus *de dicto*, notional versus relational, et cetera, behavior. And here, using the conceptual apparatus of the semantics of direct reference, we may hope to identify the source of these antics.

[I also hope to distinguish, in discussing reports of self-attribution, *x says that x is a fool*, from *x says-himself to be a fool*.]

XXI   Russell on egocentric particulars and their dispensability

In chapter VII of *Inquiry into Meaning and Truth*,[72] Russell gives a series of atrocious arguments for the conclusion that "[indexicals] are not needed in any part of the description of the world, whether physical or psychological." This is a happy no-nonsense conclusion for an argument that begins by remarking "A physicist will not say 'I saw a table', but like Neurath or Julius Caesar, 'Otto saw a table'." [Why Julius Caesar would be provoked to say 'Otto saw a table', is unexplained.]

Let us examine Russell's conclusion without prejudice to his argument. [What follows is an outline.]

In brief, there are essentially two points. First: if we have both the indexicals and an unlimited supply of unused directly referential proper names, and we can do instantaneous dubbing, then in each context c for any sentence ϕ containing indexicals we can produce a sentence ϕ^* whose character is fixed and whose content is the same as that of ϕ in c. In this sense, if you can describe it with indexicals you can describe it without.[73] There are problems: (i) things can change fast, and dubbings take time; (ii) the indexicals retain a kind of epistemic priority.

The second point is: given any *prior* collection of proper names, there will be things, times, places, et cetera, without a name. How do I say something about these unnamed entities? (E.g., how do I tell you that your pants are on fire—now? It may be that nothing in sight, including us, and no nearby time has a name.)

There are two cases. It seems most likely that without indexicals some entities cannot even be uniquely *described*. In this case we are really in trouble (unless Russell believes in the identity of indescribables—objects lacking uniquely characterizing descriptions) because without indexicals we cannot freely introduce new names. If every entity *can* be uniquely described, there is still the problem of not presenting the right content under the right character required to motivate the right action (recall the discussion on pages 774–775). The proposition expressed by 'the pants belonging to *the x F x* are on fire at *the t Gt*' is not the proposition I want to express, and certainly does not have the character I wish to convey.[74]

XXII   On proper names

Some thoughts on proper names from the perspective of the formal system are contained in Remark 11, page 784. What follows is the most hastily written section of this draft. I sketch a view that is mainly negative, without including much supporting argumentation (several of the omitted arguments seem both tedious and tendentious). My current inclination is to drop this whole section from the final draft.

A *word* is an expression along with its meaning. When two expressions have the same meaning, as with "can't" and "cannot," we call the two words *synonyms*. When two meanings have the same expression, we call the two words *homonyms*. In the latter case we also say that the expression is *ambiguous*. (Probably we would say that the *word* is ambiguous, but accept my terminology for what follows.) In a disambiguated language, semantics can associate meanings with expressions. Even in a language containing ambiguities, semantics can associate a set of meanings with an expression. But given an utterance, semantics cannot tell us what expression was uttered or what language it was uttered in. This is a presemantic task. When I utter a particular vocable, for example, the one characteristic of the first-person pronoun of English, you must decide what *word* I have spoken or, indeed, if I have spoken any word at all (it may have been a cry of anguish). In associating a word with my utterance you take account of a variety of features of the context of utterance that help to *determine* what I have said but that need not be any *part* of what I have said. My egotism, my intonation, my demeanor may all support the hypothesis that it was the first-person pronoun of English. But these aspects of personality, fluency, and mood are no part of any semantic theory of the first-person pronoun. The factors I have cited are not, of course, *criterial* for the use of the first-person pronoun. What are the criteria? What would definitively settle the question? I don't know. I think this is a very difficult question. But among the criteria there must be some that touch on the utterer's intention to use a word in conformity with the conventions of a particular linguistic community. For proper name words, in part because they are so easily introduced, this aspect of the presemantic determination is especially important.

According to the causal chain or chain of communication theory, there are two critical intentions associated with the use of the proper name word. One is the intention to use the word with the meaning given it by the person from whom you learned the word. The other is the contrary intention to create (and perhaps simultaneously use) a proper name word to refer to a given object irrespective of any prior meanings associated with the expression chosen as a vehicle. One who uses a proper name word with the first intention generally (but not always) believes that someone originated the word by using it with the second intention, and—according to the causal chain theory—intends to refer to the given object.[75]

In "Bob and Carol and Ted and Alice," appendix IX, I introduce the notion of a *dubbing* for what I took to be the standard form of introduction of a proper name word. That notion has been mistakenly taken to imply—what I deliberately sought to evoke—a formal public ceremony. What I actually had in mind was a use of a proper name word with the second intention: the intention to originate a word rather than conform to a prior usage. Thus a fleeting "Hi-ya, Beautiful" incorporates all the intentional elements required for me to say that a dubbing has taken place. I believe that my notion here is closely related to Donnellan's notion of a *referential use* of a definite description. Donnellan's distinction between referential and attributive uses of definite descriptions is easily and naturally extended to referential and attributive uses of proper names. When the intention to conform to a preestablished convention is absent we have the pure referential use. In this case, when a proper name is in question, I take it that an internal, subjective, dubbing has occurred. When a definite description is in question, again the speaker does not intend to give the expression its conventional meaning, although he may intend to *make use* of the conventional meaning in conveying who it is that is being referred to or for some other purpose associated with the act of utterance (as in "Hi-ya, Beautiful"). What is important here is that the speaker intends to be creating a meaning for the expression in question rather than following conventions. Dubbings, whether aimed at introducing a relatively permanent sense for the expression or only aimed at attaching a nonce-sense to the expression, are unconventional uses of language. Dubbings create words.

In many, perhaps most, uses of definite descriptions there is a mixture of the intention to follow convention with the intention to refer to a preconceived individual. The same mixture of 'attributive' and 'referential' intentions can occur with a proper name. If I introduce a name into your vocabulary by means of false introduction ("This is Jaakko Hintikka"—but it isn't), you are left with an undiscriminated tangle of attributive (to refer to Jaakko Hintikka) and referential (to refer to the person to whom you were introduced), intentions associated with your subsequent uses of the expression 'Jaakko Hintikka'. There are several ways in which one might attempt to account for these mixed intentions in a general theory of language. First, we might distinguish two notions: speaker's-reference and semantic-reference. The presence of an attributive intention justifies giving the expressions a conventional meaning and thus allows us to claim that preexisting *words* were used. Whereas the presence of a referential intention (not just a *belief* that the semantic referent is the given object, but an independent intention to refer to the given object) justifies the claim that the speaker is referring to the given object independent of any particular interpretation of the expressions he used as words and independent of whether the utterance has an interpretation as words. A second way of accounting for mixed intentions of this kind is to assume that one of the two intentions must be dominant. If the referential intention dominates, we regard the utterance, on the model of "Hi-ya, Beautiful," as an apt (or inept, as the case may be) introduction of a proper name word (or phrase). Thus, as essentially involving a dubbing. On this way of accounting for mixed intentions, a referential use of an expression would endow the expression with a semantic referent identical with the speaker's referent.[76]

My aim in the foregoing is to emphasize how delicate and subtle our analysis of the context of utterance must be for the presemantic purpose of determining what words, if any, were spoken. I do this to make plausible my view that—assuming the causal chain theory of reference—proper names are not indexicals. The contextual feature which consists of the causal history of a particular proper name expression in the agent's idiolect seems more naturally to be regarded as determining what word was used than as fixing the content of a single context-sensitive word. Although it is true that two utterances of 'Aristotle' in different contexts may have different contents, I am inclined to attribute this difference to the fact that distinct homonymous words were uttered, rather than a context sensitivity in the character of a single word 'Aristotle'. Unlike indexicals like 'I', proper names really are ambiguous. The causal theory of reference tells us, in terms of contextual features (including the speaker's intentions) which word is being used in a given utterance. Each such word is directly referential (thus it has a fixed content), and it also has a fixed character. Therefore, in the case of proper name words, all three kinds of meaning—referent, content, and character—collapse. In this, proper name words are unique. They have the direct reference of indexicals, but they are not context-sensitive. Proper name words are like indexicals that you can carry away from their original context without affecting their content. Because of the collapse of character, content, and referent, it is not unnatural to say of proper names that they have no meaning other than their referent.

Some may claim that they simply use 'indexical' in a wider sense than I (perhaps to mean something like 'contextual'). But we must be wary of an overbroad usage. Is every ambiguous expression an indexical because we look to utterer's intentions to disambiguate? Indeed, is every expression an indexical because it might have been a groan?

If the character and content of proper name words is as I have described it (according to the causal theory), then the informativeness of $\ulcorner \alpha = \beta \urcorner$, with α and β proper names, is not accounted for in terms of differences in either content or character. The problem is that proper names do not seem to fit into the whole semantical and epistemological scheme as I have developed it. I claimed that a competent speaker knows the character of words. This suggests (even if it does not imply) that if two proper names have the same character, the competent speaker knows that. But he doesn't. What is perhaps even more astounding is that I may introduce a new proper name word and send it on its journey. When it returns to me—perhaps slightly distorted phonologically by its trip through other dialects—I can competently take it into my vocabulary without recognizing it as the very same word! Shocking!

In earlier sections of this paper I have tried to show that many of the metaphysical and epistemological anomalies involving proper names had counterparts involving indexicals, and further that in the case of indexicals these wonders are easily explained by an obvious theory. Insofar as I am correct in regarding the anomalies as counterparts, the theory of indexicals may help to break down unwarranted resistance to the causal chain theory. It may also suggest the form of a general semantical and epistemological scheme comprehending both indexicals and proper names. This is not the place to attempt the latter task; my purpose here is simply to show that it is not trivial.[77] Those who suggest that proper names are merely one species of indexical depreciate the power and the mystery of the causal chain theory.

Notes

This paper was prepared for and read (with omissions) at a symposium on Demonstratives at the March 1977 meetings of the Pacific Division of the American Philosophical Association. The commentators were Paul Benacerraf and Charles Chastain. Much of the material, including the formal system of section XVIII, was originally presented in a series of lectures at the fabled 1971 Summer Institute in the Philosophy of Language held at the University of California, Irvine. © 1977 by David Kaplan.

1. David Kaplan, "Quantifying In," *Synthèse* 19 (1968): 178–214; reprinted in *The Philosophy of Language*, ed. A. P. Martinich (Oxford: Oxford University Press, 1985).

2. Keith Donnellan, "Reference and Definite Descriptions," *Philosophical Review* 75 (1966): 281–304; reprinted in Martinich, *Philosophy of Language*, 1985.

3. Saul Kripke, "Naming and Necessity" in *Semantics of Natural Language*, ed. G. Harman and D. Davidson (Dordrecht: Reidel, 1972); revised edition published as a separate monograph, *Naming and Necessity* (Oxford: Basil Blackwell, 1980). References are to the revised edition.

4. David Kaplan, "Dthat," in *Syntax and Semantics*, vol. 9, ed. P. Cole (New York: Academic Press, 1978); reprinted in Martinich, *Philosophy of Language*, 1985.

5. Although the central ideas of my theory had been worked out before I became familiar with *Naming and Necessity*, I have enthusiastically adopted the "analytical apparatus" and some of the terminology of that brilliant work.

6. Not everything I assert is part of my theory. At places I make judgments about the correct use of certain words, and I propose detailed analyses of certain notions. I recognize that these matters may be controversial. I do not regard them as part of the basic, obvious, theory.

7. See "Dthat," p. 320 in Martinich 1985.

8. However, a demonstration may also be opportune and require no special action on the speaker's part, as when someone shouts "Stop that man" while only one man is rushing toward the door. My notion of a demonstration is a theoretical concept. I do not, in the present work, undertake a detailed "operational" analysis of this notion, although there are scattered remarks relevant to the issue. I do consider, in section XVI below, some alternative theoretical treatments of demonstrations.

9. I am aware (1) that in some languages the so-called masculine gender pronoun may be appropriate for flowers, but it is not so in English; (2) that a background story can be provided that will make pointing at the flower a contextually appropriate, though deviant, way of referring to a man; for example, if we are talking of great hybridizers; and (3) that it is possible to treat the example as a *referential use* of the demonstrative 'he' on the model of Donnellan's referential use of a definite description (see "Reference and Definite Descriptions"). Under the referential use treatment we would assign as referent for 'he' whatever the speaker *intended* to demonstrate. I intended the example to exemplify a failed demonstration, thus a case in which the speaker, falsely believing the flower to be some man or other in disguise, but having no particular man in mind, and certainly not intending to refer to anything other than that man, says, pointing at the flower, "He has been following me around all day."

10. I have in mind such cases as pointing at oneself while saying 'I' (emphasis) or pointing at someone else while saying 'I' (irrelevance or madness or what?).

11. There are certain uses of pure indexicals that might be called "messages recorded for later broadcast," which exhibit a special uncertainty as to the referent of 'here' and 'now'. If the message "I am not here now" is recorded on a telephone answering device, it is to be assumed that the time referred to by 'now' is the time of playback rather than the time of recording, Donnellan has suggested that if there were typically a significant lag between our production of speech and its audition (for example, if sound traveled very very slowly), our language might contain two forms of 'now': one for the time of production, another for the time of audition. The indexicals 'here' and 'now' also suffer from vagueness regarding the size of the spatial and temporal neighborhoods to which they refer. These facts do not seem to me to slur the difference between demonstratives and pure indexicals.

12. Of course it is certain intentions on the part of the speaker that make a particular vocable the first-person singular pronoun rather a nickname for Irving. My semantical theory is a theory of word meaning, not speaker's meaning. It is based on linguistic rules known, explicitly or implicitly, by all competent users of the language.

13. I have discussed this and related issues in Kaplan, "Bob and Carol and Ted and Alice," in *Approaches to Natural Language*, ed. J. Hintikka et al. (Dordrecht: Reidel, 1973), especially appendix X.

14. Kripke, *Naming and Necessity*, p. 78.

15. The matter is even more complicated. There are two "definitions" of 'rigid designator' in *Naming and Necessity*, pp. 48–49. The first conforms to what seems to me to have been the intended concept—same designation in *all* possible worlds—the second, scarcely a page later, conforms to the more widely held view that a rigid designator need not designate the object, or any object, at worlds in which the object does not exist. According to this conception a designator cannot, at a given world, designate something which does not exist in that world. The introduction of the notion of a *strongly* rigid designator—a rigid designator whose designatum exists in all possible worlds—suggests that the latter idea was uppermost in

Kripke's mind. (The second definition is given, unequivocally, on page 146 of Kripke, "Identity and Necessity," in *Identity and Individuation*, ed. M. K. Munitz [New York: New York University Press, 1971].) In spite of the textual evidence, systematic considerations, including the fact that variables cannot be accounted for otherwise, leave me with the conviction that the former notion was intended.

16. Here, and in the preceding paragraph, in attempting to convey my notion of a directly referential singular term, I slide back and forth between two metaphysical pictures: that of possible worlds and that of structural propositions. It seems to me that a truly semantical idea should presuppose neither picture—and be expressible in terms of either. Kripke's discussion of rigid designators is, I believe, distorted by an excessive dependence on the possible worlds picture and the associated semantical style. For more on the relationship between the two pictures, see pages 724–725 of Kaplan, "How to Russell a Frege-Church," *Journal of Philosophy* 72 (1975): 716–729.

17. I think it likely that it was just the failure to notice this distinction that led to a failure to recognize Principle 2. Some of the history and consequences of the conflation of Context and Circumstance is discussed in section VII.

18. I would have used 'snow is white', but I wanted a contingent clause, and so many people (possibly including me) nowadays seem to have views which allow that 'snow is white' may be necessary.

19. I am ignoring propositions expressed by sentences containing epistemic operators of others for which equivalence is not a sufficient condition for interchange of operand.

20. Bertrand Russell, *The Principles of Mathematics* (London: Allen and Unwin, 1903; reprint 1936).

21. Bertrand Russell, "On Denoting," *Mind* 14 (1905): 479–493.

22. Here is a difficulty in Russell's 1903 picture that has some historical interest. Consider the proposition expressed by the sentence, 'The centre of mass of the solar system is a point'. Call the proposition, '*P*'. *P* has in its subject place a certain complex, expressed by the definite description. Call the complex, 'Plexy'. We can describe Plexy as "the complex expressed by 'the centre of mass of the solar system'." Can we produce a directly referential term which designates Plexy? Leaving aside for the moment the controversial question of whether 'Plexy' is such a term, let us imagine, as Russell believed, that we can directly refer to Plexy by affixing a kind of *meaning marks* (on the analogy of quotation marks) to the description itself. Now consider the sentence '^{m}the centre of mass of the solar system^m is a point'. Because the subject of this sentence is directly referential and refers to Plexy, the proposition the sentence expresses will have as its subject constituent Plexy itself. A moment's reflection will reveal that this proposition is simply *P* again. But this is absurd since the two sentences speak about radically different objects. (I believe the foregoing argument lies behind some of the largely incomprehensible arguments mounted by Russell against Frege in "On Denoting," though there are certainly other difficulties in that argument. It is not surprising that Russell there confused Frege's theory with his own of *Principle of Mathematics*. The first footnote of "On Denoting" asserts that the two theories are "very nearly the same.")

The solution to the difficulty is simple. Regard the 'object' places of a singular proposition as marked by some operation which cannot mark a complex. (There always will be some such operation.) For example, suppose that no complex is (represented by) a set containing a single member. Then we need only add $\{\ldots\}$ to mark the places in a singular proposition which correspond to directly referential terms. We no longer need worry about confusing a complex with a propositional constituent corresponding to a directly referring term because no complex will have the form $\{x\}$. In particular, Plexy $\neq$ {Plexy}. This technique can also be used to resolve another confusion in Russell. He argued that a sentence containing a nondenoting directly referential term (he would have called it a nondenoting "logically proper name") would be meaningless, presumably because the purported singular proposition would be incomplete. But the braces themselves can fill out the singular proposition, and if they contain nothing, no more anomalies need result than what the development of Free Logic has already inured us to.

23. This is the *first sense* of note 15.

24. This is the *second sense* of note 15.

25. From Frege, "The Thought: A Logical Inquiry," *Mind* 65 (1956): 289–311. If Frege had only supplemented these comments with the observation that indexicals are devices of direct reference, the whole theory of indexicals would have been his. But his theory of meaning blinded him to this obvious point. Frege, I believe, mixed together the two kinds of meaning in what he called *Sinn*. A *thought* is, for him, the *Sinn* of a sentence, or perhaps we should say a *complete* sentence. *Sinn* is to contain both "the manner and context of presentation [of the denotation]," according to "Über Sinn und Bedeutung" (*Zeitschrift für*

Philosophie und philosophische Kritik 100 (1892): trans. as "On Sense and Nominatum," in *Contempo-rary Readings in Logical Theory*, ed. Copi and Gould (New York: Macmillan, 1967); mistransl. as "On Sense and Meaning," in Martinich, *Philosophy of Language*, 1985). *Sinn* is first introduced to represent the cognitive significance of a sign, and thus to solve Frege's problem: how can $\ulcorner \alpha = \beta \urcorner$ if true differ in cognitive significance from $\ulcorner \alpha = \alpha \urcorner$. However, it also is taken to represent the truth-conditions or *content* (in our sense). Frege felt the pull of the two notions, which he reflects in some tortured passages about 'I' in "The Thought" (quoted below in XVII). If one says "Today is beautiful" on Tuesday and "Yesterday was beautiful" on Wednesday, one expresses the same though, according to the passage quoted. Yet one can clearly lose track of the days and not realize one is expressing the same thought. It seems then that thoughts are not appropriate bearers of cognitive significance. I return to this topic in XVII. A detailed examination of Frege on demonstratives is contained in John Perry's "Frege on Demonstratives," *Philo-sophical Review* 86 (1977): 474–497.

26. As we shall see, indexical operators such as "It is now the case that," "It is actually the case that," and "dthat" (the last takes a term rather than a sentence as argument) are also intensional operators. They differ from the familiar operators in only two ways: first, their extension (the function from intensions to extensions) depends on context; second, they are directly referential (thus they have a fixed content). I shall argue below (in section VII, "Monsters") that all operators that can be given an English reading are "at most" intensional. Note that when discussing issues in terms of the formal representations of the model-theoretic semantics, I tend to speak in terms of intensions and intensional operators rather than contents and content operators.

27. The notion of redundancy involved could be made precise. When I speak of building the time of evaluation into contents, or making contents specific as to time, or taking what is said to incorporate ref-erence to a specific time, what I have in mind is this. Given a sentence S, "I am writing," in the present context c, which of the following should we take as the content: (i) the proposition that David Kaplan is writing as of 10 A.M. on 3/26/77, or (ii) the "proposition" that David Kaplan is writing? The proposition (i) is specific as to time; the "proposition" (ii) (the scare quotes reflect my feeling that this is not the tradi-tional notion of a proposition) is neutral with respect to time. If we take the content of S in c to be (ii), we can ask whether it would be true at times other than the time of c. Thus we think of the temporally neutral "proposition" as changing its truth-value over time. Note that it is not just the noneternal sentence S that changes its truth-value over time, but the "proposition" itself. Since the sentence S contains an indexical 'I', it will express different "propositions" in different contexts. But since S contains no *temporal* indexi-cal, the time of the context will not influence the "proposition" expressed. An alternative (and more tradi-tional) view is to say that the verb tense in S involves an implicit temporal indexical, so that S is under-stood as synonymous with S': "I am writing now." If we take this point of view we will take the content of S in c to be (i). In this case *what is said* is eternal; it does not change its truth-value over time, although S will express different propositions at different times.

There are both technical and philosophical issues involved in choosing between (i) and (ii). Philosophi-cally, we may ask why the temporal indexical should be taken to be implicit (making the proposition eternal) when no modal indexical is taken to be implicit. After all, we *could* understand S as synonymous with S'': "I am actually writing now." The content of S'' in c is not only eternal, it is perfect. Its truth changes neither through time nor possibility. Is there some good philosophical reason for preferring contents which are neu-tral with respect to possibility but draw fixed values from the context for all other features of a possible cir-cumstance whether or not the sentence contains an explicit indexical? (It may be that the traditional view was abetted by one of the delightful anomalies of the logic of indexicals, namely that S, S', and S'' are all logically equivalent! See Remark 3.) Technically, we must note that intensional operators must, if they are not to be vacuous, operate on contents which are neutral with respect to the feature of circumstance the operator is interested in. Thus, for example, if we take the content of S to be (i), the application of a temporal operator to such a content would have no effect; the operator would be vacuous. Furthermore, if we do not wish the iteration of such operators to be vacuous, the content of the compound sentence containing the operator must again be neutral with respect to the relevant feature of circumstance. This is not to say that no such operator can have the effect of fixing the relevant feature and thus, in effect, rendering subsequent operations vacu-ous; indexical operators do just this. It is just that this must not be the general situation. A content must be the *kind* of entity that is subject to modification in the feature relevant to the operator. [The textual material to which this note is appended is too cryptic and should be rewritten.]

28. "How to Russell a Frege-Church," 1975. The pronunciation is "Heẋ-ee-i-tis-m." The epithet was suggested by Robert Adams. It is not an accident that it is derived from a demonstrative.

29. This does not imply that if you know the character and are in first one and then another context, you can *decide* whether the contents are the same. I may twice use "here" on separate occasions and not recognize that the place is the same, or twice hear "I" and not know if the content is the same. What I do know is this: if it was the same person speaking, then the content was the same. [More on this epistemological stuff later.]

30. I am, at this stage, deliberately ignoring Kripke's theory of proper names in order to see whether the revisions in Fregean semantical theory, which seem plainly required to accommodate indexicals (this is the "obviousness" of my theory), can throw any light on it. Here we assume that, aside from indexicals, Frege's theory is correct: roughly, that words and phrases have a kind of descriptive meaning or sense which at one and the same time constitutes their cognitive significance and their conditions of applicability. Kripke says repeatedly in *Naming and Necessity* that he is only providing a picture of how proper names refer and that he does not have an exact theory . His picture yields some startling results. In the case of indexicals we do have a rather precise theory, which avoids the difficulty of specifying a chain of communication and which yields many analogous results. In facing the vastly more difficult problems associated with a theory of reference for proper names, the theory of indexicals may prove useful: if only to show—as I believe—that proper names are not indexicals and have no meaning in the sense in which indexicals have meaning (namely a 'cognitive content' which fixes the references in all contexts). [The issues that arise, involving token reflexives, homonymous words with distinct character, and homonymous token reflexives with the same character are best saved for later—much later.]

31. See §28 of Rudolf Carnap's *Meaning and Necessity* (Chicago: University of Chicago Press, 1947; reprinted 1956).

32. Published in 1971 as Kamp, "Formal Properties of 'Now'," *Theoria* 37:227–273.

33. Thomason alleges a counterinstance: "Never put off until tomorrow what you can do today." What should one say about this?

34. Recall that in a particular formal theory the features of a circumstance must include all elements with respect to which there are content operators, and the aspects of a context must include all elements with respect to which there are indexicals. Thus, a language with both the usual modal operators '□', '◊', and an indexical modal operator 'It is actually the case that' will contain a possible world history feature in its circumstances, as well as an analogous aspect in its contexts. If a circumstance is an aspect of a context, as seems necessary for the definition of truth, then we only need worry about aspects of contexts that are not features of circumstances. The most prominent of these is the *agent* of the context, required to interpret the indexical 'I'. In order to supply a corresponding nonvacuous feature to circumstances, we must treat contents in a such a way that we can ask whether they are true for various agents. (Not *characters* mind you, but contents.) This can be done by representing the agent by a *neutral*—a term which plays the syntactical role of 'I' but gets an interpretation only with respect to a circumstance. Let a be a special variable that is not subject to quantification, and let b be a variable not in the language. Our variable α is the neutral. We wish to introduce content operators which affect the agent place and which can be iterated. Let R be a relation between individuals—for example, 'aRb' for 'b is an uncle of a'. Then we may interpret the operator $O^R\phi$ as $(\exists b)[aRb \wedge (\exists a)(b=a \wedge \phi)]$. If ϕ is 'a walks', $O^R\phi$ comes to 'an uncle of a walks'. The indexical 'I' can be represented by an operator O^I for which 'aRb' is just 'I=b'. The result should be that $O^I\phi$ is equivalent to replacing the neutral α by the indexical 'I'.

35. See, for example, Krister Segerberg, "Two-dimensional Modal Logic," *Journal of Philosophical Logic* 2 (1973): 77–96. Segerberg does metamathematical work in his article and makes no special philosophical claims about its significance. That has been done by others.

36. There is one other difficulty in identifying the class of contexts with the class of circumstances. The special relationship between the indexicals 'I', 'here', 'now' seems to require that the agent of a context be at the location of the context during the time of the context. But this restriction is not plausible for arbitrary circumstances. It appears that this approach will have difficulty in avoiding the problems of (6) and (8) (section VII).

37. I have written elsewhere, in appendices VII and VIII of "Bob and Carol and Ted and Alice," of these matters and won't pursue the topic now.

38. It could then be proposed that demonstrations be individuated by the principle: $d_1 = d_2$ if and

only if, for all appropriate circumstances c, the demonstratum of d_1 in c = the demonstratum of d_2 in c. An alternative principle of individuation is that the same demonstration is being performed in two different contexts if the standard audience can't determine, from the demonstration alone, whether the contexts are distinct or identical. This makes the individuation of demonstrations more epistemological than the metaphysical proposal above.

39. Although recent work on computer perception has attempted to identify a syntax of pictures. See P. Suppes and W. Rottmayer, "Automata," in *Handbook of Perception*, vol. 1 (New York: Academic Press, 1974).

40. The Fregean theory of demonstrations is not a part of my obvious and uncontroversial theory of indexicals. On the contrary it has the fascination of the speculative.

41. I use Kripke's terminology to expound the important distinction he introduces in *Naming and Necessity* for descriptive meaning that may be associated with a proper name. As in several other cases of such parallels between proper names and indexicals, the distinction, and its associated argument, seems more obvious when applied to indexicals.

42. H. Reichenbach, *Elements of Symbolic Logic* (New York: Macmillan, 1947), p. 284.

43. We see here a drawback to the terminology "direct reference." It suggests falsely that the reference is not mediated by a meaning, which it is. The meaning (character) is directly associated, by convention, with the word. The meaning determines the referent, and the referent determines the content. It is this to which I alluded in the parenthetical remark following the second picture (Figure 37.2). Note, however, that the kind of descriptive meaning involved in giving the character of indexicals like 'I', 'now', et cetera, is, because of the focus on context rather than circumstance, unlike that traditionally thought of as Fregean sense. It is the idea that the referent determines the content—that, contra Frege, there *is* a road back—that I wish to capture. This is the importance of Principle 2.

44. Pronunciation note on 'dthat'. The word is not pronounced dee-that or duh-that. It has only one syllable. Although articulated differently from 'that' (the tongue begins behind the teeth), the sounds are virtually indistinguishable to all but native speakers.

45. 'Male' and 'female' are here used in the grammatical sense of gender, not the biological sense.

46. If the current speculations are accepted, then in the original discussion of Pat and Mike the emphasis on the counterfactual situation in which the same agent was doing the pointing was misguided and that feature of counterfactual situations is irrelevant. It is the agent of course who focuses your attention on the relevant local individual. But that needn't be done *by* anyone; we might have a convention that whoever is appearing on the demonstration platform is the demonstratum, or the speaker might take advantage of a natural demonstration of opportunity: an explosion or a shooting star.

47. Since, as remarked earlier, the speaker and different members of the audience generally have different perspectives on the demonstration, it may appear slightly different to each of them. Thus each may take a slightly different demonstration to have been performed. Insofar as the agent and audience of a given context can differ in location, the location of a context is the location of the agent. Therefore the demonstratum of a given demonstration set in a given context will be the individual, if any, thereby demonstrated from the speaker's point of view.

48. We should not, of course, forget the many disanalogies noted earlier nor fail to note that though a description is associated with a particular character by linguistic *convention*, a demonstration is associated with *its* character by *nature*.

49. This section has benefited from the opportunity to read, and discuss with him, John Perry's 1977 paper, "Frege on Demonstratives."

50. According to Church, such higher-order Fregean senses are already called for by Frege's theory.

51. See his remarks in Frege, "On Sense and Nominatum," regarding the "common treasure of thoughts which is transmitted from generation to generation" and remarks there and in "The Thought" in connection with tensed sentences, that "Only a sentence supplemented by a time-indication and complete in every respect expresses a thought."

52. Perhaps it should be mentioned here, to forestall an objection, that neither uses a proper name for the other or for himself—only 'my brother' and 'I'—and that raising them required a lot of environmental work to maintain the necessary symmetries or, alternatively, a lot of work with the brain state machine. If proper names are present, and each uses a different name for himself (or, for the other), they will never achieve the same *total* cognitive state since one will sincerely say "I am Castor," and the other will not. They may still achieve the same cognitive state in its relevant part.

53. The corollary would also apply to the same person at the same time in the same circumstances but in different places, if such could be.

54. Perry, "Frege on Demonstratives," p. 494.

55. Frege, "The Thought: A Logical Inquiry," p. 298.

56. At other times, earlier and later, we can know it only externally, by description as it were. But now we are directly acquainted with it. (I believe I owe this point to John Perry.)

57. Unless, of course, the self-concept involved a bit of direct reference. In which case (when direct reference is admitted) there seems no need for the whole theory of Fregean self-concepts. Unless, of course, direct reference is limited to items of direct acquaintance, of which more below.

58. So far, we have limited our attention to the first three sentences of the quotation from Frege. How are we to account for the second part of Frege's remarks?

Suppose Dr. Lauben wants to communicate his thought without disturbing its cognitive content. (Think of trying to tell a color-blind person that the green light should be replaced. You would have to find another way of communicating what you wanted to get across.) He can't communicate *that* thought with *that* significance, so, he himself would have to attach a nonstandard significance to 'I'. Here is a suggestion. He points at his auditor and uses the demonstrative 'you'. If we neglect fine differences in perspective, the demonstration will have the same character for all present, and it certainly will have the same demonstratum for all present; therefore the demonstrative will have the same *character* and *content* for all present. The indexical 'now' will certainly have the same character and content for all present. Thus 'the person who is speaking to you [points] now' will have a common character and content for all those present. Unfortunately, the content is not that of 'I' as Dr. Lauben standardly uses it. He needs a demonstrative like 'dthat' to convert the description to a term with a fixed content. He chooses the demonstrative 'he', with a relative clause construction to make clear his intention. Now, if Dr. Lauben uses 'I' with the nonstandard meaning usually attached to 'he who is speaking to you [points] now' he will have found a way to communicate his original thought in a form whose cognitive significance is common to all. Very clever, Dr. Lauben.

[Perhaps it is poor pedagogy to join this fanciful interpretation of the second part of the passage with the serious interpretation of the first part.]

59. Can the heiress plead that she could not have believed a singular proposition involving the place *p* since when thinking 'here' she didn't *know* she was at *p*, that she was, in fact, unacquainted with the place *p*? No! Ignorance of the referent is no excuse.

60. This makes it sound as if an exact and conscious mastery of semantics is prerequisite to having a singular proposition as object of thought. I will try to find a better way to express the point in a succeeding draft.

61. For some consequences of this view with regard to the interpretation of demonstratives, see "Bob and Carol and Ted and Alice," appendix VII.

62. There is an obvious connection between the fix in which the Direct Acquaintance Theorist finds himself, and *Kripke's problem*: how can $\ulcorner \alpha = \beta \urcorner$ be informative if α and β differ in neither denotation nor sense (nor, as I shall suggest is the case for proper names, character)?

63. The sort of case I have in mind is this. I first think, "His pants are on fire." I later realize, "I *am* he" and thus come to think "My pants are on fire." Still later, I decide that I was wrong in thinking "I am he" and conclude "His pants were on fire." If, in fact, I am he, have I *retained* my belief that my pants are on fire simply because I believe the same content, though under a different character? (I also deny that content under the former, but for change of tense, character.) When I first thought "My pants are on fire," a certain singular proposition, call it 'Eek', was the object of thought. At the later stage, both Eek and its negation are believed by me. In this sense, I still believe what I believed before, namely Eek. But this does not capture my sense of *retaining a belief*: a sense that I associate with saying that some people have a very rigid cognitive structure, whereas others are very flexible. It is tempting to say that cognitive dynamics is concerned not with retention and change in what is believed but with retention and change in the characters under which our beliefs are held. I think that this is basically correct. But it is not obvious to me what relation between a character under which a belief is held at one time and the set of characters under which beliefs are held at a later time would constitute retaining the original belief. Where indexicals are involved, for the reasons given below, we cannot simply require that the very same character still appear at the later time. Thus the problem of cognitive dynamics can be put like this: What does it mean to say of an indi-

vidual who at one time sincerely asserted a sentence containing indexicals that at some later time he has (or has not) *changed his mind* with respect to his assertion? What sentence or sentences must he be willing to assert at the later time?

64. A case of a seemingly different kind is that of the logical equivalence between an arbitrary sentence φ and the result of prefixing either or both of the indexical operators, 'it is actually the case that' (symbolized '*A*') and 'it is now the case that' (symbolized '*N*'). The biconditional ⌜(φ ↔ *AN*φ)⌝ is logically true, but prefixing either '□' or its temporal counterpart can lead to falsehood. (This case was adverted to in note 27). It is interesting to note, in this case, that the parallel between modal and temporal modifications of sentences carries over to indexicals. The foregoing claims are verified by the formal system (section XVIII and XIX; see especially Remark 3). Note that the formal system is constructed in accordance with Carnap's proposal that the intension of an expression be that function which assigns to each circumstance, the extension of the expression with respect to that circumstance. This has commonly been thought to ensure that logically equivalent expressions have the same intension (Church's Alternative 2 among principles of individuation for the notion of sense) and that logically true sentences express the (unique) necessary proposition. Homework Problem: What went wrong here?

65. *Proceedings of the XI International Congress of Philosophy* 14:65–81; reprinted in W. V. Quine, *The Ways of Paradox* (New York: Random House, 1966) [see Quine 1953].

66. Again, it is probably a pedagogical mistake to mix this playful paragraph with the preceding serious one.

67. My notion of "indirect discourse" forms of language is linked to Frege's notion of an "ungerade" (often translated 'oblique') context. My terminology is intended to echo his.

68. Quine (1969) in his "Reply to Kaplan" in *Words and Objections*, ed. D. Davidson and J. Hintikka (Dordrecht: Reidel), raises the question—in the idiom of "Quantifiers and Propositional Attitudes" (*Journal of Philosophy* 53 (1956); reprinted in Martinich, *Philosophy of Language*, 1985)—which of the names of a thing are to count as exportable? My point here is that the indexical names must be exportable, not because of some special justification for the transformation from a *de dicto* occurrence to a *de re* occurrence, but because indexicals are devices of direct reference and have no *de dicto* occurrences. I am reminded of the zen ko-an: How do you get the goose out of the bottle? Answer: It's out!

69. If this analysis is correct, the suppressed character should wreak its mischief in cases of suspension of belief (I believe, 'that man's pants are on fire' but at the moment neither assent to nor deny 'my pants are on fire') as does its counterpart in section XI of Kaplan, "Quantifying In." T. Burge, in "Kaplan, Quine, and Suspended Belief," *Philosophical Studies* 31 (1977a): 197–203, proposes a solution to the problem of section XI which he believes is in the spirit of Quine's formulation. A similar proposal in the present context would seen starkly inappropriate. But there has been a shift in task from "Quantifying In" to the present attempt. In large part the shift is to a course outlined by Burge in the last two pages of the above-mentioned article and urged by him, in conversation, for several years. The point only began to sink in when I came on it myself from a different angle.

70. There is another form of common speech which may be thought to suggest formalization by quantification in. I call this form the *pseudo de re*. A typical example is, "John says that the lying S.O.B. who took my car is honest." It is clear that John does not say, "The lying S.O.B. who took your car is honest." Does John say δ is honest for some directly referential term δ which the reporter believes to refer to the lying S.O.B. who took his car? Not necessarily. John may say something as simple as, "The man I sent to you yesterday is honest." The reporter has simply substituted his description for John's. What justifies this shocking falsification of John's speech? Nothing! But we do it, and often recognize—or don't care—when it is being done. The form lends itself to strikingly distorted reports. As Alonzo Church has shown, in his *Introduction to Mathematical Logic* (Princeton: Princeton University Press, 1956), on page 25, when John says "Sir Walter Scott is the author of *Waverley*" use of the *pseudo de re* form (plus a quite plausible synonymy transformation) allows the report, " John says that there are twenty-nine counties in Utah"! I do not see that the existence of the *pseudo de re* form of report poses any issues of sufficient theoretical interest to make it worth pursuing.

71. There is a considerable literature on this subject, with important contributions by Hintikka, Castañeda, and others. In connection with the proposal that ⌜*a* knows who α is⌝ can be symbolized ⌜∃*x*(*a* knows that *x* = α)⌝, it should be noted that *a*'s knowledge of the logical truth ⌜dthat[α] = α⌝ leads, simply

by the semantics of direct reference, to $\ulcorner \exists x(a \text{ knows that } x = a)\urcorner$. This shows only that a *recognition* sense of knowing a singular proposition is not definable, in the obvious way, in terms of a purely *direct* reference sense of knowing a singular proposition.

72. Bertrand Russell, *Inquiry into Meaning and Truth* (London: Allen and Unwin, 1940).

73. I assume here that proper names are not indexicals. I argue the point in section XXII.

74. Some interesting arguments of a different sort for the indispensability of indexicals are given by T. Burge in "Belief De Re," *Journal of Philosophy* 74 (1977b): 338–362, and by Y. Bar-Hillel in his pioneering work, "Indexical Expressions," *Mind* 63 (1954): 689–690. In connection with the arguments of Burge and Bar-Hillel it would be interesting to check on some related empirical issues involving linguistic universals. Do all languages have a first-person singular form? Do they all have all of the standard indexicals?

75. There is disagreement as to how the given object must be given to one who introduces a proper name word with the second intention. Must he be acquainted with the object, directly acquainted, *en rapport*, perceiving it, causally connected, or what? My liberality with respect to the introduction of directly referring terms by means of 'dthat' extends to proper names, and I would allow an arbitrary definite description to *give* us the object we name: "Let's call the first child to be born in the twenty-first century 'Newman 1'." But I am aware that this is a very controversial position. Perhaps some of the sting can be removed by adopting an idea of Gilbert Harman. Normally one would not introduce a proper name or a dthat-term to correspond to each definite description one uses. But we have the means to do so if we wish. Should we do so, we are enabled to apprehend singular propositions concerning remote individuals (those formerly known only by description). Recognizing this, we refrain. What purpose—other than to confound the skeptics—is served by direct reference to whosoever may be the next president of Brazil? The introduction of a new proper name by means of a dubbing in terms of description and the active contemplation of characters involving dthat-terms—two mechanisms for providing direct reference to the denotation of an arbitrary definite description—constitute a form of cognitive restructuring; they broaden our range of thought. To take such a step is an action normally not performed at all, and rarely, if ever, done capriciously. The fact that we have the means—without special experience, knowledge, or whatever—to refer directly to the myriad individuals we can describe, does not imply that we will do so. And if we should have reason to do so, why not?

76. This is not an unnatural way to account for the use of the proper name word in the false introduction case, but it does seem a bit strange in the case of a definite description. In that case it involves hypothesizing that the speaker intended the description expression to have a meaning which made the given object its semantic referent, and only *believed* that the conventional meaning would do this, a belief that he is prepared to give up rather than acknowledge that the semantic referent of his words was not the given object. Something like this seems to happen when descriptions grow capitals, as in "The Holy Roman Empire," and in other cases as well—for example, Russell's "denoting phrases" which do not denote. But it still seems strange.

77. The issues to be resolved by "a general semantical and epistemological scheme comprehending . . . proper names" are such as these. Is the work of the causal chain theory presemantic, as I have claimed? Do proper names have a kind of meaning other than reference? Does the causal chain theory itself constitute a kind of meaning for proper names that is analogous to character for indexicals (but which, perhaps, gives all proper names the same meaning in this sense)? Are proper names words of any particular language? Is there synonymy between proper names that are expressed differently (as there is between "can't" and "cannot")? How should we describe the linguistic competence of one who does not know that Hesperus is Phosphorus? Is he guilty of linguistic error? Should we say he does not know what words he speaks? Does he know that "Hesperus" and "Phosphorus" are different words? Are they? Is it really possible, as I claim, to account for the semantics of indexicals without making use of the full conceptual resources required to account for the semantics of proper names? I raise these issues—and there are others—within the framework of a hypothetical acceptance of the causal chain theory. There are other issues, of a quite different kind, involved in trying to fill out some details of the causal chain theory itself. For example, if one who has received some particular proper name expression, say, "James," hundreds of times, uses that expression attributively as a proper name, and has in mind no particular source, how do we decide which branch to follow back? The first set of issues seems to me to be largely independent of the details of the relevant causal chains.

38

SCOTT WEINSTEIN

Truth and Demonstratives

Recently, various philosophers have argued that there is a close connection between a theory of truth for a language and a theory of meaning for that language (e.g., Davidson 1967: chapter 12 in this volume). Even if we do not wish to equate the two, I believe we must agree that a necessary component of an adequate theory of meaning is a theory of truth. We might require a complete semantical theory of a language to do many things, but it should at least give us a systematic account of the conditions under which the sentences of that language are true.

If we grant that provision of a truth definition is a condition of adequacy on a theory of meaning for some language, then we are faced with a difficulty when we embark on the project of framing semantical theories for natural languages. These languages contain what Quine has called non-eternal sentences—that is, sentences whose truth value may vary from one occasion of utterance to another. The linguistic devices which make for the non-eternality of sentences containing them are the so-called indicator words: the personal pronouns "I", "he", "she"; the demonstrative pronouns "this", "that"; tensed verbs, et cetera. The problem about sentences containing these devices is that they are, from a semantic point of view, incomplete expressions. Frege noted that "the mere wording [of a sentence containing indicator words] . . . is not the complete expression of the thought, but the knowledge of certain accompanying conditions of utterance, which are used as means of expressing the thought, are needed for its correct apprehension" (Frege 1967, 24). Consider, for example, the sentence,

(1)   I stood on that.

Let someone utter (1) and let "T" name his utterance. Then, T is true if and only if the utterer of T stands at some time prior to uttering T on the object he indicates while uttering T. The consideration of sentences containing indicator words suggests that a theory of truth for a natural language will have to treat of the conditions under which utterances and not sentences are true. In

Scott Weinstein (1974). Truth and demonstratives, *Noûs* 8: 179–184. Reprinted by permission of Blackwell Publishing.

addition, such a theory will have to give a systematic account of how the truth conditions of utterances depend upon features of the contexts in which they occur.

To illustrate how such a theory may be constructed, let us consider a simple language, L, whose only indicator word is the demonstrative pronoun "that." (Our treatment of this simple language can easily be extended to languages containing further indicator words by enriching the vocabulary of the metalanguage in order to describe other features of the context in which an utterance may occur. For example, in order to handle the first-person pronoun, we would require a relation in the metalanguage which matches an utterance with its utterer.) We specify the syntax of L as follows:

> *Terms*: the demonstrative pronoun "that" is a term; all the variables in the following infinite list are terms: "v_0", "v_1", ...
>
> *Predicates*: "is a cat" is a predicate
>
> *Atomic formulae*: if P is a predicate and t is a term, then $t \frown P$ is an atomic formula
>
> *Operations of formula formation*: if A and B are formulae and v is a variable, then "$(\frown A \frown "\lor" \frown B \frown ")$", "$\lnot" \frown "(\frown A \frown ")$", and "$\exists" \frown v \frown "(\frown A \frown ")$" are formulae.

> The set of formulae of L is the smallest set which contains all the atomic formulae and is closed under the operations of formula formation.

We want to construct a truth definition for utterances of sentences of L. Before we do so, we ought to ask what the condition of adequacy on such a definition is, so that we will know if our project succeeds. Tarski (1956) stated a condition of adequacy on truth definitions which reads as follows: an adequate definition of truth for a language L' must have as consequences all instances of the schema, $T(s) \leftrightarrow P$, where "T" is the truth predicate for L', "s" is a place holder for a structural descriptive name of some sentence of L', and "P" is a place holder for the translation of that sentence into the metalanguage—that is, the language in which the truth predicate for L' is being defined. This condition of adequacy must be modified if we are to apply it to a truth definition for utterances of the language L described above. As we have already remarked, some of the sentences of L (those which contain occurrences of the demonstrative pronoun) are incomplete expressions, and the conditions under which utterances of such sentences are true will depend on features of the contexts in which they occur. Therefore, I propose the following as a condition of adequacy on a truth definition for the language L described above: an adequate definition of truth for the language L must have as consequences all instances of the schema,

> (*DT*)   if u is an utterance of s and the referents of the demonstrative pronouns occurring in u are $w_0, \ldots, w_n$, then $T(u) \leftrightarrow P$,

where "w_0", ..., "w_n" are the first $n + 1$ variables of the metalanguage, "u" is a variable of the metalanguage distinct from each of these, "s" is a place holder for a structural descriptive name of a sentence of L, "T" is the truth predicate for utterances of sentences of L, and "P" is a placeholder for a translation into the metalanguage of the (perhaps) open sentence obtained from s by replacing the ith occurrence of the demonstrative pronoun in s by the ith variable of L and relettering the bound variables of s so as to avoid binding any of the variables introduced by the substitution. (It is understood as a convention that if a formula of L contains a free occurrence of the ith variable of L, then its translation contains a free occurrence of the ith variable of the metalanguage in the corresponding place.)

Let us now proceed to construct a definition of truth for utterances of sentences of L and to prove that it meets the condition of adequacy stated above. We give our truth theory in an informal metalanguage. In a more formal treatment our truth theory would be constructed in an extension of first-order arithmetic in which the syntactical relations we use would be represented by certain arithmetical formulae via some Gödel numbering of the symbols of L. In addition, we make implicit use of a theory of finite sequences. The structure of our truth theory is as follows. First, we define satisfaction for the eternal formulae of L—those formulae which contain no occurrences of the demonstrative pronoun, in a standard way. Then, we define truth for utterances of sentences of L in terms of the satisfaction of certain eternal formulae by specified sequences of objects. We state the axioms of our truth theory followed by an explanation of the notations that occur therein:

Axioms of the theory of satisfaction for eternal formulae of L:
   (1) x SAT "v_i is a cat" $\leftrightarrow x(i)$ is a cat.
   (2) x SAT disj$(s, s') \leftrightarrow x$ SAT $s \vee x$ SAT s'.
   (3) x SAT neg$(s) \leftrightarrow \neg x$ SAT s.
   (4) x SAT eq$(i, s) \leftrightarrow \exists x'(\forall j(j \neq i \rightarrow x'(j) = x(j)) \wedge x'$ SAT $s)$.
Additional axiom defining truth for utterances:
   (5) u UT $p \wedge x$ OC $u \wedge x$ REF $x' \rightarrow (T(u) \leftrightarrow x'$ SAT $F(p))$.

[Here] "x" and "x'" are variables ranging over finite sequences; "i" and "j" are variables ranging over natural numbers; "$x(i)$" denotes the ith term of the sequence x if i is less than the length of x; and "$x(i)$" denotes the (length of $x - 1$)-th term of x if i is greater than or equal to the length of x. (This fails to define $x(i)$ when x is the null sequence—the unique sequence whose length is 0. We don't care.) "SAT" is a relation between sequences and eternal formulae of L: its intended interpretation is the satisfaction relation for eternal formulae of L. "disj(s, s')," "neg(s)," and "eq(i,s)" denote, respectively, the disjunction of s and s', the negation of s, and the existential quantification of s with respect to the ith variable of L. [The statement] "'v_i is a cat'" denotes the formula of L which results from concatenating the ith variable of L with the predicate symbol "is a cat." [And] "u" is a variable which ranges over utterances of expressions of L (an expression of L is any finite sequence of symbols of L); "p" is a variable which ranges over eternal and non-eternal sentences, or closed formulae, of L. [Also] "u UT y" is a relation between utterances and expressions of L whose intended interpretation is: u is an utterance of y. [Then] "x OC u" is a relation between sequences and utterances whose intended interpretation is: there exists an i such that i is the number of occurrences of the demonstrative pronoun in u, and i is equal to the length of x, and for every j, if j is less than i, then $x(j)$ is the jth occurrence of the demonstrative pronoun in u. [And] "x REF x'" is a relation between sequences whose intended interpretation is: the length of x is equal to the length of x', and for every i, $x(i)$ is an utterance of the demonstrative pronoun and $x'(i)$ is the referent of $x(i)$. "$T(u)$" is a predicate of utterances whose intended interpretation is: u is true. "$F(p)$" denotes the formula of L obtained from the sentence p by substituting the ith variable of L for the ith occurrence of the demonstrative pronoun in p and, if necessary, relettering the bound variables of p in some systematic manner so as to avoid binding any of the variables introduced by the substitution.

We proceed to sketch a proof that our truth theory satisfies the condition of adequacy stated above: that it has as consequences all instances of the schema (*DT*), which, in our current notation, reads as follows:

u UT $r \wedge x$OC $u \wedge x$REF $x' \rightarrow (T(u) \leftrightarrow R(x'(0), \ldots, x'(n)))$,

where "r" stands in place of a structural descriptive name of a sentence of L, and "$R(x'(0), \ldots, x'(n))$" stands in place of the translation into the metalanguage of $F(r)$ with "$x'(i)$" substituted for all free occurrences of the ith variable of the metalanguage in the translation of $F(r)$. The proof makes use of the fact that all instances of the schema,

(*S*) x SAT $q \leftrightarrow Q(x(i_1), \ldots, x(i_n))$

(where "q" stands in place of a structural descriptive name of an *eternal formula* of L, and "$Q(x(i_1), \ldots, x(i_n))$" stands in place of the translation of that formula into the metalanguage with the indicated substitutions) are consequences of our truth theory. This is true in virtue of the standardness of our definition of satisfaction for the eternal formulae of L. The proof is completed by observing that $F(r)$ is always an eternal formula and, consequently, that for each sentence r of L, the instance of the schema (DT) for r is derivable from axiom (5) and the instance of the schema (S) for $F(r)$.

We conclude with a brief remark about some of the primitive notions of our theory. According to our theory, in order to determine the condition under which an utterance is true, we must determine what sentence it is an utterance of and what the referents of any demonstratives which occur in that utterance are. That is, we must determine whether a certain phonological and a certain semantical (or, if you prefer, pragmatical) relation hold. We have made no attempt to say anything informative about these relations in our theory.

Note

I would like to thank Professor Donald Davidson for many helpful discussions and constant encouragement without which this paper would not have been written. I am indebted to Michael Bratman for pointing out an error in an earlier version of this paper.

39

DAVID LEWIS

Scorekeeping in a Language Game

Example 1: Presupposition

At any stage in a well-run conversation, a certain amount is presupposed.[1] The parties to the conversation take it for granted; or at least they purport to, whether sincerely or just "for the sake of the argument." Presuppositions can be created or destroyed in the course of a conversation. This change is rule-governed, at least up to a point. The presuppositions at time t' depend, in a way about which at least some general principles can be laid down, on the presuppositions at an earlier time t and on the course of the conversation (and nearby events) between t and t'.

Some things that might be said require suitable presuppositions. They are acceptable if the required presuppositions are present; not otherwise. "The king of France is bald" requires the presupposition that France has one king, and one only; "Even George Lakoff could win" requires the presupposition that George is not a leading candidate; and so on.

We need not ask just what sort of unacceptability results when a required presupposition is lacking. Some say falsehood, some say lack of truth value, some just say that it's the kind of unacceptability that results when a required presupposition is lacking, and some say it might vary from case to case.

Be that as it may, it's not as easy as you might think to say something that will be unacceptable for lack of required presuppositions. Say something that requires a missing presupposition, and straightway that presupposition springs into existence, making what you said acceptable after all. (Or at least, that is what happens if your conversational partners tacitly acquiesce—if no one says "But France has *three* kings!" or "Whadda ya mean, '*even* George'?") That is why it is peculiar to say, out of the blue, "All Fred's children are asleep, and Fred has children." The first part requires and thereby creates a presupposition that Fred has children; so the second part adds nothing to what is already presupposed when it is said; so the second part has no conversational

David Lewis (1979) Scorekeeping in a language game, *Journal of Philosophical Logic* 8: 339–359. Reprinted by permission of Kluwer Academic Publishers.

point. It would not have been peculiar to say instead "Fred has children, and all Fred's children are asleep."

I said that presupposition evolves in a more or less rule-governed way during a conversation. Now we can formulate one important governing rule: call it the *rule of accommodation for presupposition*:

> If at time *t* something is said that requires presupposition *P* to be acceptable, and if *P* is not
> presupposed just before *t*, then—*ceteris paribus* and within certain limits—presupposition
> *P* comes into existence at *t*.

This rule has not yet been very well stated, nor is it the only rule governing the kinematics of presupposition. But let us bear it in mind nevertheless, and move on to other things.

Example 2: Permissibility

For some reason—coercion, deference, common purpose—two people are both willing that one of them should be under the control of the other.[2] (At least within certain limits, in a certain sphere of action, so long as certain conditions prevail.) Call one the *slave*, the other the *master*. The control is exercised verbally, as follows.

At any stage in the enslavement, there is a boundary between some courses of action for the slave that are permissible, and others that are not. The range of permissible conduct may expand or contract. The master shifts the boundary by saying things to the slave. Since the slave does his best to see to it that his course of action is a permissible one, the master can control the slave by controlling what is permissible.

Here is how the master shifts the boundary. From time to time he says to the slave that such-and-such courses of action are impermissible. Any such statement depends for its truth value on the boundary between what is permissible and what isn't. But if the master says that something is impermissible, and if that would be false if the boundary remained stationary, then straightway the boundary moves inward. The permissible range contracts so that what the master says is true after all. Thereby the master makes courses of action impermissible that used to be permissible. But from time to time also, the master relents and says to the slave that such-and-such courses of action are permissible. Or perhaps he says that some of such-and-such courses of action are permissible, but doesn't say just which ones. Then the boundary moves outward. The permissible range expands, if need be (and if possible), so that what the master says is true. Thereby the master makes courses of action permissible that used to be impermissible.

The truth of the master's statements about permissibility—one aspect of their acceptability—depends on the location of the boundary. The boundary shifts in a rule-governed way. The rule is as follows: call it the *rule of accommodation for permissibility*:

> If at time *t* something is said about permissibility by the master to the slave that requires for
> its truth the permissibility or impermissibility of certain courses of action, and if just
> before *t* the boundary is such as to make the master's statement false, then—*ceteris
> paribus* and within certain limits—the boundary shifts at *t* so as to make the master's
> statement true.

Again, this is not a very satisfactory formulation. For one thing, the limits and qualifications are left unspecified. But more important, the rule as stated does not say exactly how the boundary is to shift.

What if the master says that some of such-and-such courses of actions are permissible, when none of them were permissible before he spoke. By the rule, some of them must straightway become permissible. Some—but which ones? The ones that were closest to permissibility beforehand, perhaps. Well and good, but now we have a new problem. At every state there is not only a boundary between the permissible and the impermissible, but also a relation of comparative near-permissibility between the courses of action on the impermissible side. Not only do we need rules governing the shifting boundary, but also we need rules to govern the changing relation of comparative near-permissibility. Not only must we say how this relation evolves when the master says something about absolute permissibility, but also we must say how it evolves when he says something—as he might—about comparative near-permissibility. He might say, for instance, that the most nearly permissible courses of action in a class A are those in a subclass A'; or that some courses of action in class B are more nearly permissible than any in class C. Again, the rule is a rule of accommodation. The relation of comparative near-permissibility changes, if need be, so that what the master says to the slave is true. But again, to say that is not enough. It does not suffice to determine just what the change is.

Those were Examples 1 and 2. Examples of what? I'll say shortly; but first, a digression.

Scorekeeping in a baseball game

At any stage in a well-run baseball game, there is a septuple of numbers $\langle r_v, r_h, h, i, s, b, o \rangle$ which I shall call the *score* of that game at that stage. We recite the score as follows: the visiting team has r_v runs, the home team has r_h runs, it is the hth half (h being 1 or 2) of the ith inning; there are s strikes, b balls, and o outs. (In another terminology, the score is only the initial pair $\langle r_v, r_h \rangle$, but I need a word for the entire septuple.) A possible codification of the rules of baseball would consist of rules of four different sorts:

1. *Specifications of the kinematics of score.* Initially, the score is $\langle 0, 0, 1, 1, 0, 0, 0 \rangle$. Thereafter, if at time t the score is s, and if between time t and time t' the players behave in manner m, then at time t' the score is s', where s' is determined in a certain way by s and m.
2. *Specifications of correct play.* If at time t the score is s, and if between time t and time t' the players behave in manner m, then the players have behaved incorrectly. (Correctness depends on score: what is correct play after two strikes differs from what is correct play after three.) What is not incorrect play according to these rules is correct.
3. *Directive requiring correct play.* All players are to behave, throughout the game, in such a way that play is correct.
4. *Directives concerning score.* Players are to strive to make the score evolve in certain directions. Members of the visiting team try to make r_v large and r_h small; members of the home team try to do the opposite.

(We could dispense with rules of sorts (2) and (3) by adding an eighth component to the score which, at any stage of the game, measures the amount of incorrect play up to that stage. Specifications of correct play are then included among the specifications of the kinematics of score, and the directive requiring correct play becomes one of the directives concerning score.)

Rules of sorts (1) and (2) are sometimes called *constitutive rules.* They said to be akin to definitions, though they do not have the form of definitions. Rules of sorts (3) and (4) are called *regulative rules.* They are akin to the straightforward directives "No smoking!" or "Keep left!"

We could explain this more fully, as follows. Specifications of sorts (1) and (2) are not themselves definitions of "score" and "correct play." But they are consequences of reasonable definitions. Further, there is a systematic way to construct the definitions, given the specifications. Suppose we wish to define the *score function*: the function from game-stages to septuples of numbers that gives the score at every stage. The specifications of the kinematics of score, taken together, tell us that the score function evolves in such-and-such way. We may then simply define the score function as that function which evolves in such-and-such way. If the kinematics of score are well specified, then there is one function, and one only, that evolves in the proper way; and if so, then the score function evolves in the proper way, if and only if the suggested definition of it is correct. Once we have defined the score function, we have thereby defined the score and all its components at any stage. There are two outs at a certain stage of a game—for instance, if and only if the score function assigns to that game-stage a septuple whose seventh component is the number 2.

Turn next to the specifications of correct play. Taken together, they tell us that correct play occurs at a game-stage if and only if the players' behavior at that stage bears such-and-such relation to score at that stage. This has the form of an explicit definition of correct play in terms of current behavior. If current score has already been defined in terms of the history of the players' behavior up to now, in the way just suggested, then we have defined correct play in terms of current and previous behavior.

Once score and correct play are defined in terms of the players' behavior, then we may eliminate the defined terms in the directive requiring correct play and the directives concerning score. Thanks to the definitions constructed from the constitutive rules, the regulative rules become simply directives to strive to see to it that one's present behavior bears a certain rather complicated relation to the history of the players' behavior in previous stages of the game. A player might attempt to conform to such a directive for various reasons: contractual obligation, perhaps, or a conventional understanding with his fellow players based on their common interest in enjoying a proper game.

The rules of baseball could in principle be formulated as straightforward directives concerning behavior, without the aid of definable terms for score and its components. Or they could be formulated as explicit definitions of the score function, the components of score, and correct play, followed by directives in which the newly defined terms appear. It is easy to see why neither of these methods of formulation has found favor. The first method would pack the entire rulebook into each directive; the second would pack the entire rulebook into a single preliminary explicit definition. Understandably averse to very long sentences, we do better to proceed in our more devious way.

There is an alternative analysis—the baseball equivalent of operationalism or legal realism. Instead of appealing to constitutive rules, we might instead claim that the score is, by definition, whatever some scoreboard says it is. Which scoreboard? Various answers are defensible: maybe the visible scoreboard with its arrays of light bulbs, maybe the invisible scoreboard in the head umpire's head, maybe the many scoreboards in many heads to the extent that they agree. No matter. On any such view, the specifications of the kinematics of score have a changed status. No longer are they constitutive rules akin to definitions. Rather, they are empirical generalizations, subject to exceptions, about the ways in which the players' behavior tends to cause changes on the authoritative scoreboard. Under this analysis, it is impossible that this scoreboard fails to give the score. What is possible is that the score is in an abnormal and undesired relation to its causes, for which someone may perhaps be blamed.

I do not care to say which analysis is right for baseball as it is actually played. Perhaps the question has no determinate answer, or perhaps it has different answers for formal and informal baseball. I only wish to distinguish the two alternatives, noting that both are live options.

This ends the digression. Now I want to propose some general theses about language—theses that were exemplified by Examples 1 and 2, and that will be exemplified also by several other examples.

Conversational score

With any stage in a well-run conversation, or other process of linguistic interaction, there are associated many things analogous to the components of a baseball score. I shall therefore speak of them collectively as the *score* of that conversation at that stage. The points of analogy are as follows:

1. Like the components of a baseball score, the components of a conversational score at a given stage are abstract entities. They may not be numbers, but they are other set-theoretic constructs: sets of presupposed propositions, boundaries between permissible and impermissible courses of action, or the like.

2. What play is correct depends on the score. Sentences depend for their truth value, or for their-acceptability in other respects, on the components of conversational score at the stage of conversation when they are uttered. Not only aspects of acceptability of an uttered sentence may depend on score. So may other semantic properties that play a role in determining aspects of acceptability. For instance, the constituents of an uttered sentence—subsentences, names, predicates, et cetera—may depend on the score for their intension or extension.

3. Score evolves in a more-or-less rule-governed way. There are rules that specify the kinematics of score:

    If at time t the conversational score is s, and if between time t and time t' the course of conversation is c, then at time t' the score is s', where s' is determined in a certain way by s and c.

    Or at least:

    ... then at time t' the score is some member of the class S of possible scores, where S is determined in a certain way by s and c.

4. The conversationalists may conform to directives, or may simply desire, that they strive to steer certain components of the conversational score in certain directions. Their efforts may be cooperative, as when all participants in a discussion try to increase the amount that all of them willingly presuppose. Or there may be conflict, as when each of two debaters tries to get his opponent to grant him—to join with him in presupposing—parts of his case, and to give away parts of the contrary case.

5. To the extent that conversational score is determined, given the history of the conversation and the rules that specify its kinematics, these rules can be regarded as constitutive rules akin to definitions. Again, constitutive rules could be traded in for explicit definitions: the conversational score function could be defined as that function from conversation-stages to n-tuples of suitable entities that evolves in the specified way.

Alternatively, conversational score might be operationally defined in terms of mental scoreboards—some suitable attitudes—of the parties to the conversation. The rules specifying the kinematics of conversational score then become empirical generalizations, subject to exceptions, about the causal dependence of what the scoreboards register on the history of the conversation.

In the case of baseball score, either approach to the definition of score and the status of the rules seems satisfactory. In the case of conversational score, on the other hand, both approaches seem to meet with difficulties. If, as seems likely, the rules specifying the kinematics of conversational score are seriously incomplete, then often there may be many candidates for the score function, different but all evolving in the specified way. But also it seems difficult to say, without risk of circularity, what are the mental representations that comprise the conversationalists' scoreboards.

It may be best to adopt a third approach—a middle way, drawing on both the alternatives previously considered. Conversational score is, by definition, whatever the mental scoreboards say it is; but we refrain from trying to say just what the conversationalists' mental scoreboards are. We assume that some or other mental representations are present that play the role of a scoreboard, in the following sense: what they register depends on the history of the conversation in the way that score should according to the rules. The rules specifying the kinematics of score thereby specify the role of a scoreboard; the scoreboard is whatever best fills this role; and the score is whatever this scoreboard registers. The rules specifying the kinematics of score are to some extent constitutive, but on this third approach they enter only in a roundabout way into the definition of score. It is no harm if they underdetermine the evolution of score, and it is possible that score sometimes evolves in a way that violates the rules.

Rules of accommodation

There is one big difference between baseball score and conversational score. Suppose the batter walks to first base after only three balls. His behavior would be correct play if there were four balls rather than three. That's just too bad—his behavior does not at all make it the case that there *are* four balls and his behavior *is* correct. Baseball has no rule of accommodation to the effect that if a fourth ball is required to make correct the play that occurs, then that very fact suffices to change the score so that straightway there are four balls.

Language games are different. As I hope my examples will show, conversational score does tend to evolve in such a way as is required in order to make whatever occurs count as correct play. Granted, that is not invariable but only a tendency. Granted also, conversational score changes for other reasons as well. (As when something conspicuous happens at the scene of a conversation, and straightway it is presupposed that it happened.) Still, I suggest that many components of conversational score obey rules of accommodation, and that these rules figure prominently among the rules governing the kinematics of conversational score.

Recall our examples. Example 1: presupposition evolves according to a rule of accommodation specifying that any presuppositions that are required by what is said straightway come into existence, provided that nobody objects. Example 2: permissibility evolves according to a rule of accommodation specifying that the boundaries of the permissible range of conduct shift to make true whatever is said about them, provided that what is said is said by the master to the slave, and provided that there does exist some shift that would make what he says true. Here is a general scheme for rules of accommodation for conversational score:

> If at time t something is said that requires component s_n of conversational score to have a value in the range r if what is said is to be true, or otherwise acceptable; and if s_n does not have a value in the range r just before t; and if such-and-such further conditions hold; then at t the score-component s_n takes some value in the range r.

Once we have this scheme in mind, I think we will find many instances of it. In the rest of this paper I shall consider some further examples. I shall have little that is new to say about the individual examples. My interest is in the common pattern that they exhibit.

Example 3: Definite descriptions

It is not true that a definite description "the F" denotes x if and only if x is the one and only F in existence.[3] Neither is it true that "the F" denotes x if and only if x is the one and only F in some contextually determined domain of discourse. For consider this sentence: "The pig is grunting, but the pig with floppy ears is not grunting" (Lewis). And this: "The dog got in a fight with another dog" (McCawley). They could be true. But for them to be true, "the pig" or "the dog" must denote one of two pigs or dogs, both of which belong to the domain of discourse.

The proper treatment of descriptions must be more like this: "the F" denotes x if and only if x is the most salient F in the domain of discourse, according to some contextually determined salience ranking. The first of our two sentences means that the most salient pig is grunting but the most salient pig with floppy ears is not. The second means that the most salient dog got in a fight with some less salient dog.

(I shall pass over some complications. Never mind what happens if two F's are tied for maximum salience, or if no F is at all salient. More important, I shall ignore the possibility that something might be highly salient in one of its guises but less salient in another. Possibly we really need to appeal to a salience ranking not of individuals but rather of individuals-in-guises— that is, of individual concepts.)

There are various ways for something to gain salience. Some have to do with the course of conversation; others do not. Imagine yourself with me as I write these words. In the room is a cat, Bruce, who has been making himself very salient by dashing madly about. He is the only cat in the room, or in sight, or in earshot. I start to speak to you:

> The cat is in the carton. The cat will never meet our other cat, because our other cat lives in
> New Zealand. Our New Zealand cat lives with the Cresswells. And there he'll stay,
> because Miriam would be sad if the cat went away.

At first, "the cat" denotes Bruce, he being the most salient cat for reasons having nothing to do with the course of conversation. If I want to talk about Albert, our New Zealand cat, I have to say "our other cat" or "our New Zealand cat." But as I talk more and more about Albert, and not any more about Bruce, I raise Albert's salience by conversational means. Finally, in the last sentence of my monologue, I am in a position to say "the cat" and thereby denote not Bruce but rather the newly-most-salient cat, Albert.

The ranking of comparative salience, I take it, is another component of conversational score. Denotation of definite descriptions is score-dependent. Hence so is the truth of sentences containing such descriptions, which is one aspect of the acceptability of those sentences. Other aspects of acceptability in turn are score-dependent: non-triviality, for one, and possibility of warranted assertion, for another.

One rule, among others, that governs the kinematics of salience is a rule of accommodation. Suppose my monologue has left Albert more salient than Bruce, but the next thing I say is, "The cat is going to pounce on you!" If Albert remains most salient and "the cat" denotes the most salient cat, then what I say is patently false: Albert cannot pounce all the way from New Zealand to Princeton. What I have said requires for its acceptability that "the cat" denote Bruce, and hence that Bruce be once again more salient than Albert. If what I say requires that, then straightway it is so. By saying what I did, I have made Bruce more salient than Albert. If next I say "The cat prefers moist food," that is true if Bruce prefers moist food, even if Albert doesn't.

The same thing would have happened if instead I had said "The cat is out of the carton" or "The cat has gone upstairs." Again, what I say is unacceptable unless the salience ranking shifts so that Bruce rises above Albert, and hence so that "the cat" again denotes Bruce. The difference is in the type of unacceptability that would ensue without the shift. It is trivially true, hence not worth saying, that Albert is out of the carton. ("The carton" denotes the same carton as before; nothing has been done to raise the salience of any carton in New Zealand.) It may be true or it may be false that Albert has gone upstairs in the Cresswells' house in New Zealand. But I have no way of knowing, so I have no business saying that he has.

We can formulate a *rule of accommodation for comparative salience* more or less as follows. It is best to speak simply of unacceptability, since it may well be that the three sorts of unacceptability I have mentioned are not the only sorts that can give rise to a shift in salience:

> If at time *t* something is said that requires, if it is to be acceptable, that *x* be more salient than
> *y*; and if, just before *t*, *x* is no more salient than *y*; then—*ceteris paribus* and within certain
> limits—at *t*, *x* becomes more salient than *y*.

Although a rule of accommodation, such as this one, states that shifts of score take place when they are needed to preserve acceptability, we may note that the preservation is imperfect. It is not good conversational practice to rely too heavily on rules of accommodation. The monologue just considered illustrates this. Because "the cat" denotes first Bruce, then Albert, then Bruce again, what I say is to some extent confusing and hard to follow. But even if my monologue is not perfectly acceptable, its flaws are much less serious than the flaws that are averted by shifts of salience in accordance with our rule of accommodation. Confusing shifts of salience and reference are not as bad as falsity, trivial truth, or unwarranted assertion.

(It is worth mentioning another way to shift comparative salience by conversational means. I may say "A cat is on the lawn" under circumstances in which it is apparent to all parties to the conversation that there is some one particular cat that is responsible for the truth of what I say, and for my saying it. Perhaps I am looking out the window, and you rightly presume that I said what I did because I saw a cat; and further (since I spoke in the singular) that I saw only one. What I said was an existential quantification—hence, strictly speaking, it involves no reference to any particular cat. Nevertheless it raises the salience of the cat that made me say it. Hence, this newly-most-salient cat may be denoted by brief definite descriptions, or by pronouns, in subsequent dialogue: "No, it's on the sidewalk." "Has Bruce noticed the cat?" As illustrated, this may happen even if the speaker contradicts my initial existential statement. Thus although indefinite descriptions—that is, idioms of existential quantification—are not themselves referring expressions, they may raise the salience of particular individuals in such a way as to pave the way for referring expressions that follow.)

Example 4: Coming and going

Coming is a movement toward a point of reference.[4] Going is movement away from it. Sometimes the point of reference is fixed by the location of speaker and hearer, at the time of conversation or the time under discussion. But sometimes not. In third-person narrative, whether fact or fiction, the chosen point of reference may have nothing to do with the speaker's or the hearer's location.

One way to fix the point of reference at the beginning of a narrative, or to shift it later, is by means of a sentence that describes the direction of some movement both with respect to the point of reference and in some other way. "The beggars are coming to town" requires for its acceptability, and perhaps even for its truth, that the point of reference be in town—else the beggars' townward movement is not properly called "coming." This sentence can be used to fix or to shift the point of reference. When it is said, straightway the point of reference is in town where it is required to be. Thereafter, unless something is done to shift it elsewhere, *coming* is movement toward town and *going* is movement away. If later we are told that when the soldiers came the beggars went, we know who ended up in town and who did not.

Thus the point of reference in narrative is a component of conversational score, governed by a rule of accommodation. Note that the rule must provide for two sorts of changes. The point of reference may simply go from one place to another, as is required by the following text:

> When the beggars came to town, the rich folk went to the shore. But soon the beggars came
> after them, so they went home.

But also the point of reference is usually not fully determinate in its location. It may become
more or less determinate, as is required by the following:

> After the beggars came to town, they held a meeting. All of them came to the square.
> Afterward they went to another part of town.

The first sentence puts the point of reference in town, but not in any determinate part of town.
The second sentence increases its determinacy by putting it in the square. The initial fixing of
the point of reference is likewise an increase in determinacy: the point of reference starts out
completely indeterminate and becomes at least somewhat more definitely located.

Example 5: Vagueness

If Fred is a borderline case of baldness, the sentence "Fred is bald" may have no determinate
truth value.[5] Whether it is true depends on where you draw the line. Relative to some perfectly
reasonable ways of drawing a precise boundary between bald and not-bald, the sentence is true.
Relative to other delineations, no less reasonable, it is false. Nothing in our use of language makes
one of these delineations right and all the others wrong. We cannot pick a delineation once and
for all (not if we are interested in ordinary language), but must consider the entire range of reasonable delineations.

If a sentence is true over the entire range, true no matter how we draw the line, surely we are
entitled to treat it simply as true. But also we treat a sentence more or less as if it is simply true,
if it is true over a large enough part of the range of delineations of its vagueness. (For short: if it
is *true enough*.) If a sentence is true enough (according to our beliefs), we are willing to assert it,
assent to it without qualification, file it away among our stocks of beliefs, and so forth. Mostly
we do not get into any trouble this way. (But sometimes we do, as witness the paradoxes that
arise because truth-preserving reasoning does not always preserve the property of being true
enough.)

When is a sentence true enough? Which are the "large enough" parts of the range of delineations of its vagueness? This is itself a vague matter. More important for our present purposes,
it is something that depends on context. What is true enough on one occasion is not true enough
on another. The standards of precision in force are different from one conversation to another
and may change in the course of a single conversation. Austin's "France is hexagonal" is a
good example of a sentence that is true enough for many contexts but not true enough for many
others. Under low standards of precision, it is acceptable. Raise the standards, and it loses its
acceptability.

Taking standards of precision as a component of conversational score, we once more find a
rule of accommodation at work. One way to change the standards is to say something that would
be unacceptable if the standards remained unchanged. If you say "Italy is boot-shaped" and get
away with it, low standards are required and the standards fall if need be; thereafter, "France is
hexagonal" is true enough. But if you deny that Italy is boot-shaped, pointing out the differences,
what you have said requires high standards under which "France is hexagonal" is far from true
enough.

I take it that the rule of accommodation can go both ways. But for some reason, raising of
standards goes more smoothly than lowering. If the standards have been high, and something is
said that is true enough only under lowered standards, and nobody objects, then indeed the standards are shifted down. But what is said, although true enough under the lowered standards, may

still seem imperfectly acceptable. Raising of standards, on the other hand, manages to seem commendable even when we know that it interferes with our conversational purpose. Because of this asymmetry, a player of language games who is so inclined may get away with it if he tries to raise the standards of precision as high as possible—so high, perhaps, that no material object whatever is hexagonal.

Peter Unger has argued that hardly anything is flat. Take something you claim is flat; he will find something else and get you to agree that it is even flatter. You think the pavement is flat—but how can you deny that your desk is flatter? But "flat" is an *absolute term*: it is inconsistent to say that something is flatter than something that is flat. Having agreed that your desk is flatter than the pavement, you must concede that the pavement is not flat after all. Perhaps you now claim that your desk is flat; but doubtless Unger can think of something that you will agree is even flatter than your desk. And so it goes.

Some might dispute Unger's premise that "flat" is an absolute term, but on that score it seems to me that Unger is right. What he says is inconsistent does indeed sound that way. I take this to mean that on no delineation of the correlative vagueness of "flatter" and "flat" is it true that something is flatter than something that is flat.

The right response to Unger, I suggest, is that he is changing the score on you. When he says that the desk is flatter than the pavement, what he says is acceptable only under raised standards of precision. Under the original standards the bumps on the pavement were too small to be relevant either to the question whether the pavement is flat or to the question whether the pavement is flatter than the desk. Since what he says requires raised standards, the standards accommodatingly rise. Then it is no longer true enough that the pavement is flat. That does not alter the fact that it *was* true enough *in its original context*. "The desk is flatter than the pavement" said under raised standards does not contradict "The pavement is flat" said under unraised standards, any more than "It is morning" said in the morning contradicts "It is afternoon" said in the afternoon. Nor has Unger shown in any way that the new context is more legitimate than the old one. He can indeed create an unusual context in which hardly anything can acceptably be called "flat," but he has not thereby cast any discredit on the more usual contexts in which lower standards of precision are in force.

In parallel fashion Unger observes, I think correctly, that "certain" is an absolute term; from this he argues that hardly ever is anyone certain of anything. A parallel response is in order. Indeed, the rule of accommodation permits Unger to create a context in which all that he says is true, but that does not show that there is anything whatever wrong with the claims to certainty that we make in more ordinary contexts. It is no fault in a context that we can move out of it.

Example 6: Relative modality

The "can" and "must" of ordinary language do not often express absolute ("logical" or "metaphysical") possibility.[6] Usually they express various relative modalities. Not all the possibilities there are enter into consideration. If we ignore those possibilities that violate laws of nature, we get the physical modalities; if we ignore those that are known not to obtain, we get the epistemic modalities; if we ignore those that ought not to obtain—doubtless including actuality—we get the deontic modalities; and so on. That suggests that "can" and "must" are ambiguous. But on that hypothesis, as Kratzer has convincingly argued, the alleged senses are altogether too numerous. We do better to think of our modal verbs as unambiguous but relative. Sometimes the relativity is made explicit. Modifying phrases like "in view of what is known" or "in view of what custom requires" may be present to indicate just which possibilities should be ignored.

But sometimes no such phrase is present. Then context must be our guide. The boundary between the relevant possibilities and the ignored ones (formally, the accessibility relation) is a component of conversational score, which enters into the truth conditions of sentences with "can" or "must" or other modal verbs. It may change in the course of conversation. A modifying phrase "in view of such-and-such" does not only affect the sentence in which it appears but also remains in force until further notice to govern the interpretation of modal verbs in subsequent sentences.

This boundary may also shift in accordance with a rule of accommodation. Suppose I am talking with some elected official about the ways he might deal with an embarrassment. So far, we have been ignoring those possibilities that would be political suicide for him. He says: "You see, I must either destroy the evidence or else claim that I did it to stop Communism. What else can I do?" I rudely reply: "There is one other possibility—you can put the public interest first for once!" That would be false if the boundary between relevant and ignored possibilities remained stationary. But it is not false in its context, for hitherto ignored possibilities come into consideration and make it true. And the boundary, once shifted outward, stays shifted. If he protests "I can't do that," he is mistaken.

Take another example. The commonsensical epistemologist says: "I *know* the cat is in the carton—there he is before my eyes—I just *can't* be wrong about that!" The skeptic replies: "You might be the victim of a deceiving demon." Thereby he brings into consideration possibilities hitherto ignored, else what he says would be false. The boundary shifts outward so that what he says is true. Once the boundary is shifted, the commonsensical epistemologist must concede defeat. And yet he was not in any way wrong when he laid claim to infallible knowledge. What he said was true with respect to the score as it then was.

We get the impression that the skeptic, or the rude critic of the elected official, has the last word. Again this is because the rule of accommodation is not fully reversible. For some reason, I know not what, the boundary readily shifts outward if what is said requires it, but does not so readily shift inward if what is said requires that. Because of this asymmetry, we may think that what is true with respect to the outward-shifted boundary must be somehow more true than what is true with respect to the original boundary. I see no reason to respect this impression. Let us hope, by all means, that the advance toward truth is irreversible. That is no reason to think that just any change that resists reversal is an advance toward truth.

Example 7: Performatives

Suppose we are unpersuaded by Austin's contention that explicit performatives have no truth value.[7] Suppose also that we wish to respect the seeming parallelism of form between a performative like "I hereby name this ship the *Generalissimo Stalin*" and such non-performative statements as "Fred thereby named that ship the *President Nixon*." Then we shall find it natural to treat the performative, like the non-performative, as a sentence with truth conditions. It is true, on a given occasion of its utterance, if and only if the speaker brings it about, by means of that very utterance, that the indicated ship begins to bear the name "Generalissimo Stalin." If the circumstances are felicitous, then the speaker does indeed bring it about, by means of his utterance, that the ship begins to bear the name. The performative sentence is therefore true on any occasion of its felicitous utterance. In Lemmon's phrase, it is a sentence verifiable by its (felicitous) use.

When the ship gets its name and the performative is verified by its use, what happens may be described as a change in conversational score governed by a rule of accommodation. The relevant component of score is the relation that pairs ships with their names. The rule of accommodation is roughly as follows:

> If at time t something is said that requires for its truth that ship s bear name n; and if s does not bear n just before t; and if the form and circumstances of what is said satisfy certain conditions of felicity; then s begins at t to bear n.

Our performative sentence does indeed require for its truth that the indicated ship bear the name "Generalissimo Stalin " at the time of utterance. Therefore, when the sentence is felicitously uttered, straightway the ship bears the name.

The sentence has other necessary conditions of truth: the ship must not have borne the name beforehand, the speaker must bring it about that the ship begins to bear the name, and he must bring it about by uttering the sentence. On any felicitous occasion of utterance, these further conditions take care of themselves. Our rule of accommodation is enough to explain why the sentence is verified by its felicitous use, despite the fact that the rule deals only with part of what it takes to make the sentence true.

A similar treatment could be given of many other performatives. In some cases the proposal may seem surprising. "With this ring I thee wed" is verified by its felicitous use, since the marriage relation is a component of conversational score governed by a rule of accommodation. Is marriage then a *linguistic* phenomenon? Of course not, but that was not implied. The lesson of performatives, on any theory, is that use of language blends into other social practices. We should not assume that a change of conversational score has its impact only within, or by way of, the realm of language. Indeed, we have already seen another counterexample: the case of permissibility, considered as Example 2.

Example 8: Planning

Suppose that you and I are making a plan—let us say, a plan to steal some plutonium from a reprocessing plant and make a bomb of it. As we talk, our plan evolves. Mostly it grows more and more complete. Sometimes, however, parts that had been definite are revised, or at least opened for reconsideration.

Much as some things said in ordinary conversation require suitable presuppositions, so some things we say in the course of our planning require, for their acceptability, that the plan contain suitable provisions. If I say "Then you drive the getaway car up to the side gate," that is acceptable only if the plan includes provision for a getaway car. That might or might not have been part of the plan already. If not, it may become part of the plan just because it is required by what I said. (As usual the process is defeasible. You can keep the getaway car out of the plan, for the time being at least, by saying "Wouldn't we do better with mopeds?") The plan is a component of conversational score. The rules governing its evolution parallel the rules governing the kinematics of presupposition, and they include a rule of accommodation.

So good is the parallel between plan and presupposition that we might well ask if our plan simply *is* part of what we presuppose. Call it that if you like, but there is a distinction to be made. We might take for granted, or purport to take for granted, that our plan will be carried out. Then we would both plan and presuppose that we are going to steal the plutonium. But we might not. We might be making our plan not in order to carry it out but, rather, in order to show that the plant needs better security. Then plan and presupposition might well conflict. We plan to steal the plutonium, all the while presupposing that we will not. And indeed our planning may be interspersed with commentary that requires presuppositions contradicting the plan: "Then I'll shoot the guard (I'm glad I won't really do that) while you smash the floodlights." Unless we distinguish plan from presupposition (or distinguish two levels of presupposition), we must think of presuppositions as constantly disappearing and reappearing throughout such a conversation.

The distinction between plan and presupposition is not the distinction between what we purport to take for granted and what we really do. While planning that we will steal the plutonium and presupposing that we will not, we might take for granted neither that we will nor that we won't. Each of us might secretly hope to recruit the other to the terrorist cause and carry out the plan after all.

One and the same sentence may require, and if need be create, both provisions of the plan and presuppositions. "Then you drive the getaway car up to the side gate" requires both a getaway car and a side gate. The car is planned for. The gate is more likely presupposed.

Notes

I am doubly grateful to Robert Stalnaker: first, for his treatment of presupposition, here summarized as Example 1, which I have taken as the prototype for parallel treatments of other topics; and second, for valuable comments on a previous version of this paper. I am also much indebted to Stephen Isard, who discusses many of the phenomena that I consider here in his "Changing the Context" in Edward L. Keenan, ed., *Formal Semantics of Natural Language* (Cambridge University Press, 1975). Proposals along somewhat the same lines as mine are to be found in Thomas T. Ballmer, "Einführung und Kontrolle von Diskurswelten," in Dieter Wunderlich. ed., *Linguistische Pragmatik* (Athenäum-Verlag, 1972), and Ballmer, *Logical Grammar: With Special Consideration of Topics in Context Change* (North-Holland, 1978).

An early version of this paper was presented to the Vacation School in Logic at Victoria University of Wellington in August 1976; I thank the New Zealand–United States Educational Foundation for research support on that occasion. The paper also was presented at a workshop on pragmatics and conditionals at the University of Western Ontario in May 1978, and at a colloquium on semantics at Konstanz University in September 1978.

1. This treatment of presupposition is taken from two papers of Robert Stalnaker: "Presupposition," *Journal of Philosophical Logic* 2 (1973b), 447–457, and "Pragmatic Presuppositions," in Milton K. Munitz and Peter K. Unger, eds., *Semantics and Philosophy* (New York University Press, 1974).

2. This treatment of permissibility is discussed more fully in Lewis, "A Problem about Permission," in R. Hilpinen, I. Miiniluoto, M. B. Provence, and E. Saarinen, eds., *Essays in Honour of Jaakko Hintikka* (Reidel, 1979b).

3. Definite descriptions governed by salience are discussed in Lewis, *Counterfactuals* (Blackwell, 1973), pp. 111–117; and in James McCawley, "Presupposition and Discourse Structure," in David Dinneen and Choon-Kyu Oh, eds., *Syntax and Semantics*, Vol. 11 (Academic Press, 1979). A similar treatment of demonstratives is found in Isard 1975.

Manfred Pinkal, "How to Refer with Vague Descriptions" (presented at the Konstanz colloquium on semantics, September 1978) notes a further complication: if some highly salient things are borderline cases of *F*-hood, degree of *F*-hood and salience may trade off. See Pinkal, "How to Refer with Vague Descriptors," in R. Bäskerle, U. Egli, and A. von Stechow, eds., *Semantics from Different Points of View* (Berlin: Springer-Verlag, 1979), 32–50.

Indefinite descriptions that pave the way for referring expressions are discussed in Charles Chastain, "Reference and Context," *Minnesota Studies in the Philosophy of Science* 7 (1975), 194–269, and in Saul Kripke, "Speaker's Reference and Semantic Reference," *Midwest Studies in Philosophy* 2 (1977), 255–276.

4. See Charles Fillmore, "How to Know Whether You're Coming or Going," in Karl Hyldgaard-Jensen, eds., *Linguistik 1971* (Athenäum-Verlag, 1972), and "Pragmatics and the Description of Discourse," in Siegfried J. Schmidt, ed., *Pragmatik/Pragmatics II* (Wilhelm Fink Verlag, 1976).

5. See the treatment of vagueness in Lewis, "General Semantics," *Synthèse* 22 (1970), 18–67. For arguments that hardly anything is flat or certain, see Peter Unger, *Ignorance* (Oxford University Press, 1975), pp. 65–68. For another example of accommodating shifts in resolution of vagueness, see the discussion of backtracking counterfactuals in Lewis, "Counterfactual Dependence and Time's Arrow," *Noûs* 13 (1979a), 455–476.

6. See Angelika Kratzer, "What 'Must' and 'Can' Must and Can Mean," *Linguistics and Philosophy* 1 (1977), 337–355. The accessibility semantics considered here is equivalent to a slightly restricted form of Kratzer's semantics for relative modality.

Knowledge and irrelevant possibilities of error are discussed in Alvin I. Goldman, "Discrimination and Perceptual Knowledge," *Journal of Philosophy* 73 (1976), 771–791.

7. See J. L. Austin, "Performative Utterances," in his *Philosophical Papers* (Oxford University Press, 1961) for the original discussion of performatives. For treatments along the lines here preferred, see E. J. Lemmon, "On Sentences Verifiable by Their Use," *Analysis* 22 (1962), 86–89; Ingemar Hedenius, 'Performatives', *Theoria* 29 (1963), 1–22; and Lennart Åqvist, *Performatives and Verifiability by the Use of Language* (Uppsala University, 1972). Isard (1985) suggests as I do that performative utterances are akin to other utterances that "change the context."

40

ROBYN CARSTON

Explicature and Semantics

1 The territory

A standard view of the semantics of natural language sentences or utterances is that a sentence has a particular logical structure and is assigned truth-conditional content on the basis of that structure. Such a semantics is assumed to be able to capture the logical properties of sentences, including necessary truth, contradiction, and valid inference; our knowledge of these properties is taken to be part of our semantic competence as native speakers of the language. The following examples pose a problem for this view:

(1)   a. If it's raining, we can't play tennis.
      b. It's raining.
      c. We can't play tennis.

(2)   a. If John stopped his car in an illegal position and Bill ran into John, then John is liable for damages.
      b. Bill ran into John and John stopped his car in an illegal position.
      c. John is liable for damages.

The first example seems to be a valid argument, and the second seems to be plainly invalid.[1] However, the validity of (1) depends on requirements that do not seem to be encoded in the sentences used: that the time and place of the raining mentioned in (b) is the same as that of the envisaged tennis-playing mentioned in (c). If, in a telephone conversation between my mother in New Zealand and me in London, she utters (b), I will not draw the conclusion in (c), although I believe what she says and I believe the first conditional premise. Similarly, the invalidity of (2) depends on the assumption that there is a cause-consequence relation between the events de-

This essay was written in 1999 and first appeared in 2000 in *UCL Working Papers in Linguistics* 12: 1–44. References have been updated for this volume.

scribed by the conjuncts of the "and"-conjunctions, though few truth-conditionalists would want to ascribe that property (or the property of temporal sequence) to the semantics of "and" (or to anything else in the sentence), there being good reasons to maintain a unitary truth-functional analysis of the connective.

What is clear here is that our validity judgments depend on more than the lexical content and syntactic structure of the sentences used—that is, on more than the meaning provided by the linguistic system alone; the further content is recovered not from linguistic decoding but by some other process that is able to take account of extralinguistic context. So the propositional forms in these arguments are hybrids, made up of linguistically encoded material and contextually supplied material. The proposition expressed by (1b) in a particular context might be as in (3a), and that expressed by (2b) might be as in (3b) (both being but rough indications, using the inadequate resources of natural language boosted by a few reasonably transparent makeshift indicators):

(3)   a. It's raining in Christchurch, New Zealand, at t_x.
       b. [Bill$_i$ ran into John$_j$ at t_x]$_P$ & [as a result of P, John$_j$ stopped at t_{x+y} in an illegal position].

Examples of this sort have received a range of treatments in the existing literature of semantics and pragmatics, and two of these treatments are discussed in this chapter. The more linguistically oriented explanation is that there are hidden indexicals in the logical form of the sentences employed, so in (1b) there is a phonetically and graphologically unrealized element marking the place for a location constituent. If this is extended to the second example, then, as well as each of the conjoined sentences having a variable indicating the requirement of a temporal specification, there must be a variable indicating a relation between the conjuncts. On some formal semantic accounts, these are linked in a stipulatory fashion to contextual indices—for instance, to a location index and a temporal index—which are among the set of indices that comprise a formally conceived context. A more psychologically oriented semantics would accept that there is some pragmatic inferential process involved in finding the value of the hidden element in the context. But the crucial point of this sort of explanation is that the recovery of contextual material is dictated by the linguistic system in pretty much the same way as it is in the case of overt indexicals, such as those in (4), to which a contextual value has to be given before a complete proposition is recovered and before the sentence can be fully employed in truth-preserving inference:

(4)   She put it there.

On the alternative, more pragmatically oriented, approach, there is no level of linguistic representation of the sentences used in examples (1) and (2) in which there are variables (or silent indexicals or empty constituent slots) which indicate that contextual values must be assigned in order to determine the full truth-conditional content. The contextually supplied constituents are often termed *unarticulated* constituents, where "unarticulated" is to be understood not in the weak sense of a linguistic entity that is present but not phonologically realized, but, rather, in the strong sense that there is no linguistic entity here at all, these constituents being supplied on wholly pragmatic grounds. An adequate account of how these meaning constituents become part of the proposition expressed by the utterance, and so affect its truth conditions, is formulated entirely in terms of pragmatic mechanisms that not only effect their recovery but also motivate it. The cognitive pragmatic theory of Dan Sperber and Deirdre Wilson, developed within their wider relevance-theoretic framework, is geared toward doing this sort of work. That is, as well as accounting for the process of supplying contextual values to indexicals, a process known as *saturation*, it aims to account for the process of recovering unarticulated constituents, a process known as *free* enrichment, where what the process is "free" from is linguistic control; obviously, it is tightly constrained by the pragmatic principles involved.

The term *explicature* arose within relevance theory, as a partner to the more familiar *implicature*. Although it is related to the Gricean notion of "what is said," it also departs significantly from it. While the Gricean notion is often thought of as a semantic construct, explicature plainly is not. It belongs to a theory of communication and interpretation, and it is distinguished from most uses of the term "what is said," in that it involves a considerable component of pragmatically derived meaning, in addition to linguistically encoded meaning. A key feature in the derivation of an explicature is that it may require "free" enrichment: that is, the incorporation of conceptual material that is wholly pragmatically inferred, on the basis of considerations of rational communicative behavior, as these are conceived of on the relevance-theoretic account of human cognitive functioning. A further unorthodox characteristic of an explicature, at least in recent manifestations, is that some of its conceptual constituents may be rather different from the concepts encoded by the lexical items in the corresponding position in the logical structure of the sentence that was uttered. The idea here is that the concepts encoded by the language system are but a small subset of the repertoire of concepts that the human mind can manipulate and that can be communicated. Lexically encoded meaning often serves as just a clue or pointer to the concept the speaker has in mind, but the relevance-based comprehension strategy is such that an addressee is usually able to figure out from the lexical concept and other contextual clues what the intended concept is. It should be evident, then, that on this picture there may often be a considerable gap between the logical form encoded by the linguistic expression used and the explicature recovered by the addressee, although the logical form provides an essential framework for the processes of pragmatic construction.

This is mainly an expository essay. I will present the semantic-pragmatic hybrid that is "explicature," outline the motivation for singling it out as a natural class of phenomena, look briefly at some of the ways in which it departs from more semantically oriented notions of "what is said," and consider some of the objections that the concept might prompt, or already has prompted, from semantic quarters. There is also a more argumentative side to the essay, concerned with making a case for two hypotheses. The first is that the pragmatic principle(s) that guide an addressee in his derivation of conversational implicatures (the quintessential pragmatic phenomenon) are equally responsible for those aspects of the proposition expressed by an utterance (usually an explicature) which are contributed by context. This applies to the recovery of unarticulated constituents and to the construction of ad hoc concepts, both of which are controversial as features of truth-conditional content. But it also applies to the process of determining which among several perceptually identical linguistic entities the speaker has employed (that is, disambiguation) and to the task of finding the referents of indexical and other referring expressions, both of which are universally agreed to be essential in identifying the truth-conditional content. The second argumentative strain is concerned to establish that free enrichment remains a live option, despite recent arguments from some semanticists that if a contextual element enters into truth conditions (that is, if some pragmatic process affects truth conditions) that element must have been provided for by a variable or indexical in logical form.

In section 2, I outline the cognitive psychological approach of relevance theory, within which explicature is taken to be a natural class of interpretive entity. In section 3, I define the concept of explicature a little more carefully and discuss its relationship with the proposition expressed by (or the propositional form of) the utterance. The various pragmatic tasks that may be involved in cases of explicature derivation are surveyed and exemplified in section 4, and it is here that the contentious issues mentioned above are aired: whether the same or different pragmatic mechanisms are responsible for explicature and implicature, and whether or not there is free enrichment. I sum up in the final brief section 5.

2   Relevance-theoretic pragmatics

2.1   Cognitive underpinnings

Relevance theory is a cognitive theory resting on some general assumptions about the mind that are familiar from the work of Noam Chomsky and Jerry Fodor. The mind, or at least those aspects of it relevant to current concerns, processes information in the form of representations by performing certain sorts of computations on those representations. Its architecture is to some significant extent modular, in the sense that it comprises domain-specific subsystems which are largely autonomous from other mental systems. Peripheral perceptual systems are the best candidates for mental modules (Fodor 1983), but recent work in evolutionary psychology makes it look increasingly plausible that many of the more central conceptual systems of the mind are also modular (for discussion, see Sperber 1994b). The language input system (or parser) is almost certainly modular. It is, in effect, a perceptual system that maps an acoustic phonetic input onto whatever linguistic entities can have that particular phonetic form. It is a fairly rigid system that ignores all extralinguistic considerations and quickly delivers material in a format that the system(s) responsible for utterance interpretation can use in arriving at a hypothesis about the intended meaning.

The cognitive account of utterance understanding makes a fundamental distinction between two types of processes: the decoding processes of the language system and the pragmatic inferential processes. This processing distinction is closely allied to the way in which the distinction between semantics and pragmatics is understood in the theory. "Semantics" here is a matter of linguistically encoded meaning, entirely context-free and context-invariant; "pragmatics" is a matter of the recovery of the speaker's meaning, a thoroughly context-sensitive affair. Conceived of in this way, the semantic is simply one source of evidence (albeit a very rich one) for the pragmatic system to use in its bid to arrive at an interpretation of the utterance stimulus. This is not a representational distinction since there are no pragmatic *representations* but merely pragmatic *processes* in deriving meaning representations. However, the representation(s) output by the linguistic processor, which are schematic structured strings of concepts with both logical and causal properties, are sometimes called "semantic" representation(s), or logical form(s).[2] These are not "really" semantic in the sense (of David Lewis and other philosophers) that they make claims about an extralinguistic reality: rather, they are those formal, syntactic (generally subpropositional) representations that are in the appropriate format for integration with representations from other information sources. The result of these integration processes may be fully propositional representations that do represent possible states of affairs and so can be evaluated against an external reality for truth or falsity. A final caveat about these "semantic" representations: they are not recovered as a whole and then worked on by the pragmatic inferential system; rather, the mechanisms here (the parser and the pragmatic system) are performing on-line, millisecond by millisecond, so that very often pragmatics is making a hypothesis about an intended word sense, or an indexical referent, or even an implicature, before the entire acoustic stimulus has been processed by the linguistic system.

An obvious question at this point is how the pragmatic system fits into the overall architecture of the mind. To move toward an answer to this, we need to take a step back from language and communication and consider another, apparently quite distinct, cognitive system, that known as *theory of mind*, or "mind-reading." This is the system responsible for the irresistible tendency we humans seem to have to interpret each other's behavior in terms of the beliefs, desires, and intentions that we take to underlie it (for discussion, see Sperber 1994a). Consider coming upon the following scene, for instance: a man is lowering himself, head and arms first, down into a hole in the ground while another man holds onto his legs. Very few observers will represent this scene to themselves as I have just described it and leave it at that; most of us will try to find some plausible beliefs, desires, or intentions that we can attribute to these two men, some set of mental states which will explain their behavior. For instance, we may attribute to both men a belief that there is something worth retrieving down in that hole, to the first man an intention to retrieve it, to the second man a belief that the first may fall into the hole and hurt himself if his legs aren't held, et cetera.

The system that attributes mental states like beliefs and intentions to others has many of the standard properties of an evolved cognitive module: it is domain-specific, fast, and automatic (we can't help but make these attributions), and it apparently follows a fixed, idiosyncratic, and universal pattern of development and is subject to specific breakdown (see Baron-Cohen 1995; Scholl and Leslie 1999). The sort of representation it deals in is metarepresentational—that is, it represents the content of another representation, which is attributed to someone, and this can be iterated to several successive levels of embedding. For instance, I may attribute to you the intention to get Mary to believe that Bob wants to meet her, which is a third-order metarepresentation. The special logical properties of such representations are well known from work on the semantics of propositional attitudes; correspondingly, the theory of mind system must have its own computational properties, distinct in crucial ways from those of first-level (factual) representations. From an evolutionary point of view, the selective advantage that this capacity gives a creature is evident: it makes it possible to predict the behavior of others and so plan one's own behavior accordingly, whether the concern is self-protection, competition, exploitation, or cooperation. Moreover, it enables a particular kind of communication—namely, ostensive communication— which is of central social importance.

Continuing the scenario: suppose the second man, who is holding the legs of the first, swivels his eyes leftward in our direction and starts to jerk his head quite violently from left to right. It is likely that we'll take him to be communicating something to us, that we'll take the head movement to be not some involuntary tic he developed upon seeing us but, rather, a movement designed to make it evident to us that he wants our attention and has something to tell us. We might even hazard a guess at (infer) what the intended message is, something like "I want you to help me" perhaps. Note that this is achieved *without any element of encoding* whatsoever; the same type of head movement would be interpreted in quite different ways in different situations. Ostensive behavior of this sort involves a communicative intention—that is, a higher-order informative intention to make manifest a lower-order informative intention to make certain assumptions manifest. In other words, a speaker's meaning is a set of assumptions (with attitudes attached) that the addressee is overtly intended to recover. When the communication is verbal, accessing its linguistic meaning is a preliminary stage, a means to the end of discovering the speaker's meaning; it provides very helpful evidence, though it usually falls far short of encoding speaker meaning, not just in the case of implicated assumptions but also in many aspects of the proposition explicitly expressed (explicature). So understanding utterances (and other ostensive acts) requires the forming of a higher-order metarepresentation of a representation attributed to the speaker (the speaker's own representation being itself a metarepresentational intention).[3]

Sperber (2000) argues in favor of a comprehension module whose domain is utterances and other ostensive stimuli. This is a metarepresentational module and may be a submodule of the theory of mind (or "metapsychological") system, to which it is clearly intimately related. The main argument for its modular status hinges on the fact that the comprehension process requires a particular pattern of inference that distinguishes it from the inferential processes involved in interpreting nonostensive behavior. Someone observing the activities of the two men described above can impute to them certain intentions on the basis of an observed desirable outcome of their behavior (e.g., the retrieval of a diamond ring). But in interpreting an instance of ostensive behavior, the desirable effect (which is that the addressee grasp the communicator's meaning) cannot be achieved without the addressee's prior recognition of the communicator's intention to achieve that effect. That is, the standard pattern of inference—from behavior to identification of desirable outcome and then to intention—is not available to the ostension understanding system. Relevance theory makes a specific proposal about the particular computational strategy employed by the comprehension module. I turn to that in the next section.

2.2   Relevance and utterance understanding

Relevance is defined as a property of inputs to cognitive processes (whether perceptual or higher-level conceptual); it is a positive function of cognitive effects and a negative function of the processing effort expended in deriving those effects. Cognitive effects (or contextual effects) include the strengthening of existing assumptions of the system, by providing further evidence for them, the elimination of assumptions that appear to be false, in the light of the new evidence, and the derivation of new assumptions through the interaction of the new information with existing assumptions. A basic principle of the framework is the "cognitive principle of relevance" according to which the human cognitive system as a whole is oriented toward the maximization of relevance. That is, in effect, the various subsystems conspire in a bid to achieve the greatest number of cognitive effects for the least processing effort overall. The perceptual input systems have evolved in such a way that they generally respond automatically to stimuli which are very likely to have cognitive effects, quickly converting their sensory impact into the sort of representational formats that are appropriate inputs to the conceptual inferential systems; these systems then integrate them, as efficiently as possible, with some accessible subset of existing representations to achieve as many cognitive effects as possible. For fuller exposition, see Sperber and Wilson (1986; 1995, 261–266).

What distinguishes ostensive behavior (including verbal utterances) from nonostensive behavior (and, all the more so, from events that do not involve volitional behavior at all) is that it raises an expectation of a particular level of relevance in the relevance-seeking cognitive system of the addressee. A speaker (or more generally, an ostensive communicator) overtly requests an expenditure of mental effort from an addressee (an outlay of attentional and inferential resources), and that licenses an expectation of a worthwhile yield of cognitive effects and no gratuitous expenditure of effort. This is captured by the "communicative principle of relevance": every act of ostension communicates a presumption of its own optimal relevance; that is, a presumption that it will be at least relevant enough to warrant the addressee's attention and, moreover, as relevant as is compatible with the communicator's competence and goals. The specific procedure employed by the comprehension system, on the basis of the presumption of optimal relevance, is given in (5):

(5)   Check interpretive hypotheses in order of their accessibility—that is, follow a path of least effort until an interpretation that satisfies the expectation of relevance is found; then stop.[4]

The least effort strategy follows from the presumption of optimal relevance in that the speaker is expected to have found an utterance for the communication of her thoughts, which minimizes the hearer's effort (within the parameters set by the speaker's own abilities and goals/preferences). The justification for the addressee's stopping processing as soon as an interpretation satisfies his expectation of relevance follows similarly, in that any other interpretation that might also achieve the requisite level of effects will be less accessible and so incur greater processing costs.

The operation of this procedure, peculiar to the processing of ostensive behavior, provides a solution to the apparent problem, mentioned in the previous section, that the intended effect (the grasping of the communicator's meaning) depends on a prior recognition of the communicator's intention. Processing by the addressee's pragmatic system employing the strategy in (5) is automatically triggered by an ostensive stimulus, irrespective of the actual intentions of the producer of the stimulus, and this strategy provides a reliable, though by no means foolproof, means of inferring a speaker's meaning. As a patently nondemonstrative inference process, it sometimes fails and doesn't come up with the intended meaning. And when it is successful, what is achieved is seldom a perfect replication in the hearer's mind of the very assumptions the speaker intended to communicate. An utterance, like any ostensive stimulus, usually licenses not one particular interpretation but any one of a number of interpretations with very similar import; provided the addressee recovers one of these, comprehension is successful: that is, it is good enough.

As Stanley and Szabo put it (with some skepticism):

> Sperber & Wilson's (1986) theory describes a *general strategy* exploited by language users to discover which features of the context are relevant for the resolution of ambiguity and semantic incompleteness. . . . [They] attempt to provide a very bold solution to the foundational problem of context dependence, since they argue that *the same process* underlies phenomena as distinct as the resolution of ambiguity and contextual supplementation of semantically incomplete information. (2000, 224 n.7; my emphasis)

In fact, this considerably understates the generality of the picture, since the very same strategy is employed in the derivation of implicatures as well—that is, those communicated assumptions that, as is generally agreed, lie right outside the truth-conditional content of the utterance. Some demonstration of the strategy at work is given in section 4, where it is also shown that the derivation of implicatures and of what Stanley and Szabo, quoted above, call "contextual supplementation [of logical form]" (explicature derivation) may occur together in a process of what Sperber and Wilson (1998) call "mutual parallel adjustment," a process that is only possible if the full range of pragmatic tasks falls under the same interpretive strategy or principle.

A further question of a cognitive architectural sort concerns the extent to which, within the class of ostensive stimuli, linguistic ones are special. Certainly, they are special in that there is a distinct and quite elaborate linguistic decoding system; that's not being questioned here. Rather, the issue is whether they are further interpreted by a pragmatic system dedicated to them alone (a "linguistic" pragmatic system) or whether they are just one of a range of types of ostensive stimuli all processed by one and the same comprehension module. Stanley (2000) favors the former view, according to which there are two quite distinct types of communicative acts: genuine linguistic speech acts, whose semantic and pragmatic properties fall within linguistic theory; and nonlinguistic ostensive acts, such as tapping someone on the shoulder or catching someone's eye and making a gesture, whose interpretive properties fall within a general theory of human reasoning.[5] The relevance-theoretic view, in contrast, picks out a natural class of environmental phenomena—namely, ostensive stimuli—and the same comprehension strategy is taken to click into action in response to these stimuli, whether linguistic or not. However, it would not be incompatible with this account to posit a submodule, within the inferential comprehension module, that has some additional special properties pertaining just to acts of *linguistic* ostension. The account would be much less amenable, though, to there being two wholly distinct and unrelated systems, each with its own interpretive principles, which appears to be Stanley's view.

A few considerations support the idea of a single pragmatic system at work in the interpretation of all acts of ostensive communication, but they are far from definitive. One is the generally agreed point that intended contextual assumptions and implications (implicatures) can result from either linguistic or nonlinguistic ostension. Stanley might respond to this that the system dedicated to linguistic interpretation is confined to the derivation of the proposition expressed (and its illocutionary force), which is then submitted to the wider inferential system for implicature derivation. However, as just mentioned, it looks very much as if the pragmatic principle(s) responsible for fixing values of indexicals and other contextual elements of the proposition expressed are the same as those involved in the derivation of implicatures. Stanley and Szabo (2000,

236) themselves allow this, when they refer in passing to the probable involvement of Gricean machinery in determining what is said. This makes the positing of two distinct pragmatic systems (which would be operating according to identical principles) seem at best otiose. Finally, there is the rather underexplored fact that most verbal utterances are a complex of linguistic, paralinguistic, facial, and vocal gestures, which appear to function as a single signal receiving a unified interpretation (see Clark 1996).

Next I look more closely at the concept of explicature, before investigating in some detail the different sorts of pragmatic tasks involved in its derivation.

3   Explicit communication

There are two types of communicated assumptions on the relevance-theoretic account: explicatures and implicatures. An *explicature* is a propositional form communicated by an utterance and is pragmatically constructed on the basis of the propositional schema or template (logical form) that the utterance encodes; its content, therefore, is an amalgam of linguistically decoded material and pragmatically inferred material. An *implicature* is any other propositional form communicated by an utterance; its content consists of wholly pragmatically inferred matter (see Sperber and Wilson 1986, 182). So the explicature/implicature distinction is a derivational distinction, and, by definition, it arises only for verbal (or, more generally, code-based) ostensive communication.

Recalling the examples in the first section, an utterance of (6a), in an appropriate context, can express the proposition in (6b), which, if ostensively communicated, is an explicature; the same goes for the propositional form in (7b) expressed by an utterance of (7a):

(6)   a. It's raining.
      b. *It's raining in Christchurch, New Zealand, at time t_x.*
(7)   a. Bill ran into John, and John stopped his car in an illegal position.
      b. *[Bill$_i$ ran into John$_j$ at t_x]$_P$ & [as a result of P, John$_j$ stopped at t_{x+y} in an illegal position].*

There are several points to note here.

First, since the content of explicatures is derived from the two distinct processes of decoding and pragmatic inference, different token explicatures that have the same propositional content may vary with regard to the relative contributions made by each of these processes. That is, they may vary in degree of explicitness:

(8)   a. Mary Jones put the book by Chomsky on the table in the downstairs sitting-room.
      b. Mary put the book on the table.
      c. She put it there.
      d. On the table.

All of these could be used in different contexts to communicate explicitly one and the same propositional form. Clearly (8c) and (8d) leave a great deal more to pragmatic inference than does (8b), which, in turn, is less explicit than (8a). It follows from the relevance-driven pragmatics outlined in the previous section that the linguistically encoded element of an utterance should not generally be geared toward achieving as high a degree of explicitness as possible, but that the speaker, taking account of the addressee's immediately accessible assumptions and the inferences he can readily draw, should encode just what is necessary to ensure that the inference process arrives as effortlessly as possible at the intended meaning. A speaker who fails to heed this, or gets it wrong, may cause her hearer unnecessary processing effort (for instance, pointless decoding of concepts that are already activated or highly accessible to him) and runs the risk of not being understood, or at the least, of being found irritating or patronizing. So, in many contexts, an utterance of the highly indexical sentence in (8c), or of the subsentential expression in (8d), will be more appropriate than either of the more elaborated ones.[6]

Second, the explicature/implicature distinction applies only to *ostensively communicated* assumptions: that is, to those that the speaker has made evident she intends the hearer to pick up. Of course, an utterance will transmit much information that does not fall within the definition of ostensive communication—some falling under other types of intentions the speaker may have, some lying right outside any intentions she may have (see Wilson and Sperber 1993). This opens up the possibility of a difference between the proposition expressed by the speaker and her explicature(s): the proposition expressed may or may not be communicated; only when it is communicated is it an explicature of the utterance. This distinction is important in the context of certain nonliteral uses, such as irony, where the proposition expressed is not endorsed by the speaker and so does not fall within her communicative intention. It also arises for nondeclarative utterances, such as imperatives, as will be demonstrated shortly.

Third, on the basis of what has been said so far, it looks as if an utterance has a single explicature, the proposition it expresses when that is communicated (endorsed) by the speaker. But, in fact, Sperber and Wilson's idea is that utterances typically have several explicatures. The logical form may be embedded in a range of different sorts of higher-level schemas, including speech-act and propositional-attitude descriptions. For instance, Mary's reply to Bill's question in (9) might have the explicatures given in (10):

(9)   a. Bill: Did your son visit you over the weekend?
      b. Mary (happily): He did.
(10) a. Mary's son visited her over the weekend.
      b. Mary says that her son visited her over the weekend.
      c. Mary believes that her son visited her over the weekend.
      d. Mary is happy that her son visited her over the weekend.

The hearer may actually represent only some subset of these (though the speaker has made manifest her intention to make the others manifest as well). In a situation in which, for instance, Bill knows that Mary has been worrying about a growing rift between her son and herself, he may represent just the base-level explicature in (10a) and the higher-level explicature in (10d). These are the explicitly communicated assumptions most likely to give rise to cognitive effects (that is, to be relevant) in that context. In a different sort of example, a higher-level explicature describing the speaker's belief might be the major contributor to the relevance of the utterance—for instance, in a context in which this representation could overturn or modify the hearer's existing representation of the speaker's beliefs.

On the relevance-theoretic account, an utterance of a sentence in the imperative mood communicates an explicature that describes a certain state of affairs as desirable to some degree (to either speaker or hearer, an indeterminacy that has to be pragmatically resolved) and as achievable. For example, in an appropriate context, an utterance of (11a) could communicate the higher-level explicatures in (11b) and (11c):

(11) a. Buy some milk.
      b. It is desirable to the speaker (and achievable) that the hearer buy some milk.
      c. The speaker requests the hearer to buy some milk.

As on certain speech-act accounts, the idea here is that the proposition expressed is the same as that expressed by the corresponding declarative; here it would be "the hearer buy(s) some milk."

This is clearly not an explicature of the imperative utterance, however; what is explicitly communicated by the utterance of (11a) is the higher-level representations. (For a fuller account of imperatives and other nondeclaratives, see Wilson and Sperber 1988.)

The distinction between higher-level explicatures and the explicated propositional form of the utterance is interesting from another point of view, too. Several classes of sentential adverbial have been analyzed by theorists as not being part of the propositional form of the utterance:

(12)   a. Frankly, I'm unimpressed.
       b. Confidentially, she won't pass the exam.
       c. Happily, Mary's son visited her this weekend.
       d. Unfortunately, I missed the train.

"Frankly" and "confidentially" are illocutionary adverbials, and "happily" and "unfortunately" are attitudinal adverbials. It seems that they do not contribute to the truth-conditional content of these utterances, yet they each encode a concept that must feature in some representation derived by the hearer. Where, then, do these elements make their contribution? There is a neat answer to this in the system Sperber and Wilson have developed: they contribute to a higher-level explicature. This is most easily seen in the case of the illocutionary adverbials, which slot straightforwardly into the role of modifier of a speech-act verb in the higher-level speech-act description:

(13)   a. I tell you frankly that I'm unimpressed.
       b. I inform you confidentially that she won't pass the exam.

While there is a range of interesting issues that could be pursued around this notion of higher-level explicature, I intend to focus in the rest of this essay on the first-level explicature, whose content is that of the proposition expressed by the utterance.[7]

Finally, although "explicature" is a term specific to relevance theory, the phenomenon it picks out, at least at the first level, bears strong resemblances to that denoted by terms used in other frameworks, such as "what is said" as used by Recanati (1989; 1993), "impliciture" as used by Bach (1994), and the "pragmatic view" of "context-sensitive saying" defended by Travis (1985; 1997). They all subscribe to the notion of "free" enrichment, as discussed earlier, and so endorse a level of communicated assumptions that are neither entirely controlled by linguistic semantics (logical form) nor merely conversational implicatures; Recanati and Travis share with relevance theorists the view that this linguistic/pragmatic hybrid is what constitutes the truth-conditional content of the utterance.[8]

4   Pragmatic tasks in explicature derivation

4.1   Linguistic expression identification

One of the tasks a hearer carries out in understanding an utterance and which must, therefore, be accounted for by a pragmatic theory, is the identification of the linguistic expressions employed by the speaker. This is better known as *disambiguation*, though that term can be somewhat misleading. An utterance is ambiguous in the same way that any perceptual signal may be ambiguous until it is contextualized, but from the statement that the utterance must be disambiguated it should not be inferred that such linguistic entities as lexical items and syntactic structures are ambiguous. This would not be right: there are (at least) *two* lexical items that happen to have the phonological form /ring/; this form maps onto two unrelated concepts: a circle and a certain quality of sound. Similarly, there are *two* sentences that happen to have the surface arrangement of forms "visiting children can be tiring."[9]

According to Perry (1998) and Stanley and Szabo (2000), the role of context in the identification of the linguistic expression used is presemantic (or grammatical). This description reflects the fact that ambiguity is a nonissue for a static semantic theory of the standard truth-conditional sort,[10] a theory that assigns truth conditions to the antecedently distinguished sentences of the language and truth-conditional contributions to the antecedently distinguished lexical items, no matter what chance coincidences of form there might be. So the two sentences that would be heard as 'Tom gave Pat a ring' are each assigned a distinct set of truth conditions along the following lines (abstracting away from various factors, including tense):

(14)   a. An utterance of the sentence 'Tom gave Pat a ring$_X$' is true just in case Tom telephoned Pat.

         b. An utterance of the sentence 'Tom gave Pat a ring$_Y$' is true just in case Tom gave to Pat a circle of such and such a sort.

Grice (1975) mentioned the necessity of disambiguation in order to identify "what is said" in the case of an utterance of 'he is in the grip of a vice,' but he did not seem to conceive of his pragmatic machinery (the conversational maxims) being involved in this process. Their role seems to have been confined to the derivation of conversational implicatures, the disambiguation process lying outside the issues that occupied him (primarily a concern to maintain as lean and logical a semantics as possible, by relegating the derivation of richer related meanings to the operation of conversational principles). He did not envisage any role for conversational maxims at all in determining or identifying "what is said"; indeed, this was the point of the distinction between saying and implicating, since the statement made or the proposition expressed—the minimal truth-conditional content of the utterance—was to be distinguished from those aspects of utterance meaning that were a function of such considerations as its appropriateness, informativeness, and relevance in a particular context (considerations that are irrelevant to its truth-evaluability). The move to a cognitive pragmatic theory, whose goal is to explain how utterances are understood, brings a change in outlook, since some or other part of that theory must provide an account of *how* an addressee figures out which of two perceptually identical linguistic expressions is intended. In the absence of any evidence to the contrary, the simplest assumption is that whatever principle(s) are responsible for working out the conversational implicatures are also responsible for working out which expression has been uttered. (I return to this issue of the role of pragmatic principles in determining aspects of the proposition expressed in the next section.)

In these cases of homophony (or homography), what is it that the language module delivers to the pragmatic system (the comprehension module)? Its output might consist of all the homophonous linguistic elements, so that the pragmatic task is simply one of choosing among them. Alternatively, the language system might have internal mechanisms of a blind/dumb sort that plump for one of the candidates on some basis or other. In the case of homophonous lexical items, the basis might be degree of activation (determined by a range of factors including frequency of occurrence); in the case of homophonous syntactic structures, it might be some measure of structural economy. If preliminary choices are made by the parser, these may be confirmed or rejected at the next phase when context and relevance-based inference enter the picture. If, instead, there is either exhaustive accessing of encoded meanings, or two or more meanings are equally accessible, they are processed in parallel until one of them yields enough effects to satisfy the expectation of relevance, so that the others are dropped.

Here's a sketch of a relevance-driven account of a simple case of disambiguation. Suppose the situation is one in which a family has come to a riverside and the mother, observing her children excited at the possibility of hiring a canoe to paddle down the river, realizes that they used up all their cash on lunch. She says to her partner:

(15)   If the kids want to go on the river, I'll have to nip to the bank.

The focus here is, of course, the homophone /bank/. Suppose that both of the lexical items that have this form are activated, so the concepts encoded by both are delivered by the parser to the comprehension module, as alternative possibilities for the one position in the proposition expressed by the utterance. A choice will be made quite rapidly in favor of the financial institution sense, since accessible contextual assumptions include the following: they are currently standing on a riverbank (so that deriving cognitive effects from "nip to the riverbank" would be extremely difficult), the children want to hire a canoe, in order to hire a canoe they need cash, and cash can be got from a financial bank. However, it might be that the close proximity in the utterance of the form /river/ to the form /bank/ increases the accessibility of the "riverbank" lexical item via some sort of spreading activation through a lexical network internal to the language processor. If so, then that may be the meaning initially accessed and checked for relevance; it would be rejected as not meeting the expected level of relevance (having few, if any, cognitive effects) and the next most accessible hypothesis (presumably that involving the financial bank meaning) would be tried and accepted.

4.2   Reference assignment and other saturation processes

The issue of indexical reference is considered central to semantic concerns in a way that the (accidental) formal coincidences just discussed are not. Both Perry (1998) and Stanley and Szabo (2000) talk of the role of context here as "semantic." They mean by this that the extralinguistic contextual contribution of a value to an indexical affects the truth conditions of the utterance: one and the same indexical sentence might be deemed true if uttered in one context and false if uttered in another. Taxonomies of indexical elements are often drawn up with different types distinguished by the sort of context (narrow/semantic or wide/pragmatic) they depend on and by whether or not their designation is "automatic" or depends in part on the intention of the speaker (see, for example, Bach 1997 and Perry 1998). I focus here on those demonstratives and pronouns that would be generally agreed to require both a wide notion of context (that is, one that goes well beyond merely specifying the speaker, time, and location of the utterance) and a consideration of speaker intention, since these most clearly require a fully pragmatic inferential process to determine their value.

Two simple examples are given in (16) and (17), together with one popular account (employing the conditional T-sentence schema) of how they are to be dealt with in a truth-conditional semantics for natural language sentences:

(16)   a. She is lazy.
       b. If x is referred to by "she" in the course of an utterance of (16a) and x is female, then that utterance is true just in case lazy(x).
(17)   a. That is green.
       b. If x is referred to by "that" in the course of an utterance of (17a), then that utterance is true just in case green(x).

The T-sentence (given in the consequent) is made conditional on the fixing of certain types of contextual parameters enumerated in the antecedent; these parameters are, of course, entirely abstracted from the specifics of particular contexts. Higginbotham (1988, 40) expresses the hope that this approach promotes semantic theory "without leading into the morass of communicative context." The information that may be brought to bear from general knowledge, or from immediate perception, in the interpretation of a particular utterance of a natural language sentence has no bearing whatsoever on its semantics.

But what is it that the parser delivers up to the comprehension module in cases such as (16a) and (17a)? It is not, presumably, a statement such as (16b) or (17b) but a logical form (a template for building a propositional form) indicating that a value is to be contextually filled, a value that is minimally constrained by the encoded linguistic meaning of the demonstrative or pronoun (incorporating features such as singular/plural, male/female, proximate/distal, perhaps). What guides these processes of value assignment? The Gricean position again seems to be that this is achieved without any intervention from conversational maxims, whose role in interpretation is to make assessments of, and adjustments for, informativeness, truthfulness, relevance, and so on, once "what is said" has been identified. This is a view that prevails among semanticists with a stake in isolating a minimally truth-evaluable proposition expressed by an utterance. Even the recent quite cognitively oriented truth-conditional approach of Segal (1994) and Larson and Segal (1995) makes the following divisions among performance systems: "The cognitive systems will include at least (a) a parser (b) a system that identifies the referents of indexicals and assigns them to the relevant parts of the sentence (c) a pragmatics system" (Segal 1994, 112 n.3). Note the distinction between (b) and (c), which parallels Grice's distinction between the contextual identification of referents and intended senses of ambiguous forms on the one hand and the work of the conversational maxims on the other.

Some other philosophers, however, made the point early on that the maxims, or at least the cooperative principle, must be involved in these processes; for instance:

> In ordinary cases of ambiguity we rely on that principle [the cooperative principle] to determine which sense is intended; if I say "The bank is mossy" I can usually rely on the accepted purpose of the talk-exchange to disambiguate my remark. . . . The Co-operative Principle often helps to determine to what item a speaker is referring when he uses a proper name or a definite description. . . . It is the Co-operative Principle which enables the speaker to convey that the Tom he is talking about is the Tom we have both left, and that by "the candle on the dresser" he means the one we can both see and not some other candle on a dresser in Timbuctoo. (Walker 1975, 156–157)

Similarly, Katz (1972, 449) discusses a case of reference assignment involving Grice's first maxim of quantity and concludes: "Since identification of the referent . . . can depend on maxims . . . and on the pattern of argument for implicatures, determining what is said depends on the principles for working out what is implicated." While Stalnaker suggested in his early work, along with most formally oriented semanticists, that context alone can determine disambiguation, more recently he says, "the Gricean principles and maxims clearly play a role in resolving ambiguity and fixing contextual parameters as well as in generating conversational implicatures" (1989, 9). This has been the prevailing assumption within relevance theory since its inception: "hearers invariably ascribe sense and reference to utterances (within the limits allowed by the grammar) in such a way as to preserve their assumption that the conversational maxims have been observed" (Wilson and Sperber 1981, 157).

This sort of contextual supplying of a value that is overtly marked as required by the linguistic form used is known as a process of *saturation* (see Recanati 1993). A popular view among those semanticists who take the logical form of a sentence (relativized to a context) to be the object of (truth-conditional) semantic interpretation is that all and any pragmatic contributions to the proposition expressed by an utterance (as opposed to what the speaker meant) are cases of saturation. In other words, they adhere to the following principle:[11]

> *Linguistic Direction Principle:* A pragmatically determined aspect of meaning is part of what is said if and only if its contextual determination is triggered by the grammar—that is, if and only if the sentence itself sets up a slot to be contextually filled.

The overt indexical cases, as discussed, perceptibly set up a slot to be contextually filled, but it follows from this principle that a great many slots are not marked by such audible or visible material: that is, there are cases of hidden indexicals/variables or implicit arguments. The following are plausible cases involving saturation of a linguistically present but imperceptible constituent, such that the contextually supplied value answers the bracketed question:

(18)   a. Paracetamol is better. [than what?]
      b. It's the same. [as what?]
      c. He is too young. [for what?]
      d. It's hot enough. [for what?]
      e. The winners each get £1,000. [winners of what?]
      f. I like Sally's shoes. [shoes in what relation to Sally?]

These are all, arguably, semantically incomplete (subpropositional) until the constituent is contextually supplied. In each case, there's a lexical item which, as a matter of its meaning requires completion: *better*, *same*, *too x*, *x enough*, *winner*, genitive marker. However, even if all of these contributions to the proposition expressed (explicature) do involve hidden elements in logical form, there is a range of other cases for which this is quite implausible and a wholly pragmatic account in terms of free enrichment is preferable. At least, that is the claim of the next two sections.

4.3   "Free" enrichment

In many instances, it seems that the pragmatic contribution to the proposition expressed by an utterance goes well beyond ensuring minimal propositionality. Consider the following:

(19)   a. It'll take time for your knee to heal.
      b. Ralph drinks.
      c. Emily has a temperature.
      d. He's a person with a brain.
      e. Something has happened.

Given reference fixing, these examples are semantically complete but, without further pragmatic adjustment, they are banal obvious truths (any process takes place over a span of time; all human beings take in liquid, have some body temperature or other, and have a brain as part of their physical makeup; etc.). In virtually no instance would a speaker of these sentences intend to express that uninformative, irrelevant proposition; rather, she would intend an enriched or elaborated proposition that is relevant—that is, which interacts fruitfully with the addressee's accessible contextual assumptions. The relevance-theoretic position is that it is these enriched propositions (developments of logical form) that are communicated as explicatures—for instance, *it'll take quite a long time for your knee to heal, Ralph drinks alcohol (habitually)*—and that the uninformative minimal propositions play no role in the process of utterance understanding, which is geared to the recovery of the propositional forms (and attitudes) communicated by the utterance. As the obligatory output of linguistic processing, logical forms play an important part in directing the interpretation process; together with the presumption of relevance and accessible contextual assumptions, they provide all the evidence necessary to recover the speaker's meaning. There is no intermediate level of minimal propositionality or "what is said" (the product of decoded content, disambiguation, and indexical fixing).

     This sort of linguistically unmandated (free) enrichment, arguably, applies to a much wider range of cases than these banal truisms. The following examples are taken variously from papers by Bach, Carston, Recanati, and Sperber and Wilson:

(20)   a. Jack and Jill went up the hill [*together*].

    b. Sue got a Ph.D. and [*then*] became a lecturer.

    c. Mary left Paul, and [*as a consequence*] he became clinically depressed.

    d. She took out her gun, went into the garden, and killed her father [*with the gun, in the garden*].

    e. I'll give you £10 if [*and only if*] you mow the lawn.

    f. John has [*exactly*] four children.

    g. Louise has always been a great lecturer [*since she's been a lecturer*].

    h. There were [*approximately*] 50 people in the queue.

Without the bracketed material, each of these is, arguably, fully propositional (truth-evaluable) and is not an obvious truth, but in a great many contexts it is the enriched propositional form that is communicated and is taken by addressees to be the content of what is asserted—that is, the basis on which the speaker is judged to have or have not spoken truly. Without these developments of the logical form (in addition to disambiguation and saturation), in most contexts the interpretation of the utterance would not satisfy the presumption of optimal relevance. The relevance-theoretic position is that these are cases of free enrichment, mandated entirely by pragmatic requirements rather than by any linguistic constituent present in the logical form.

    Another set of data for which the free enrichment case has been made are certain subsentential utterances. Rob Stainton (1994, 1997a, 1998) has argued that we can make assertions with isolated words or phrases—that is, with words or phrases that are not embedded in a sentential structure. Of course, many apparently subsentential utterances turn out to be cases of syntactic ellipsis, so that although phonologically nonsentential, they are, in fact, syntactically fully sentential. The following are such cases:

(21) A: Who ate the cake?
        B: Sue.
(22) A: Mary will come to the party.
        B: Bill won't.

    It seems clear enough that B's utterance in (21) is an ellipsed version of "Sue ate the cake" and in (22) of "Bill won't come to the party." So, in these cases, arguably, the logical form of the utterance is fully sentential, with a bunch of empty syntactic categories in the phonologically unrealized positions, and recovery of the missing material is a grammatical matter.[12] However, Stainton presents a range of cases that do not seem to be elliptical:

(23) Michael's dad. [uttered while indicating to the addressee a man who has just come into the room]
(24) Only 22,000 miles. Like new. [uttered by a used car salesman]
(25) Great haircut. [uttered upon encountering a friend one hasn't seen for a while]
(26) Water. [uttered by a desperately thirsty man staggering toward a water vendor]

These have the following characteristics: they are (or, at least, can be) discourse-initial utterances, which is not a possibility for elliptical cases; there may be a degree of indeterminacy about the propositional content of the assertion, which is, again, not a property of ellipses; and they are bona fide assertions, as evidenced by the possibility of telling a lie with them (consider this possibility, in particular, in the case of the car salesman in (24)). One might even be inclined to judge the following a valid argument; if so, one is building in the appropriate constituent concerning the particular car:

(27) Only 22,000 miles.
       [If] only 22,000 miles, [then] a good buy.
       ———————————————————————————
       A good buy.

The significance of this, again, is that it shows that grammatical reconstruction processes, disambiguation, and supplying values to referring expressions are not sufficient to derive the proposition expressed in these cases; rather, a purely pragmatic process of recovering conceptual material is required. The minimal linguistic form chosen by the speaker provides all the evidence necessary for the addressee to infer the speaker's informative intention and causes him no gratuitous processing effort. Stainton (1994) gives a relevance-theoretic pragmatic account of the interpretation of an example like (23), according to which a speaker who utters "Michael's dad," is employing a noun phrase that occurs without any further linguistic structure (specifying slots to be contextually filled) and is thereby asserting the proposition *The man near the door is Michael's dad*. Any more elaborate linguistic representation, with empty category slots, would, in fact, require more effort from the addressee, and would yield no more cognitive effects, than the phrasal utterance.[13]

4.4   Free enrichment or hidden structure plus saturation?

In this section, I return to the issue of the free enrichment of fully sentential examples, in the context of a discussion of a current view that there is no such thing, that, in fact, all truth-conditional elements supplied by context are linguistically indicated by indexical elements in the logical form of the utterance: that is, they are all cases of pragmatic saturation.

Stanley (2000) makes the most sustained case to date against free enrichment and in favor of the position that "all truth-conditional effects of extra-linguistic context can be traced to logical form." Whenever a semantic value is contextually fixed, it is marked out in the logical form by an indexical (in the broad sense of "indexical")—that is, by a pure indexical, or a demonstrative pronoun, or a variable (a covert indexical); the structure is there in all instances, waiting to be filled. He targets, in particular, cases of alleged nonsentential utterances, such as those just discussed, and cases of alleged unarticulated constituents. I concentrate on the latter here.

The procedure in his most developed argument against the unarticulated constituent cases is as follows: (a) he takes a simple case which has been argued to involve the pragmatic addition of a constituent not marked out in logical form by any hidden element; (b) he embeds it in a larger structure which contains an explicit quantifier and in which the constituent in question can be understood as being bound by that quantifier; (c) he then shows that an account on which that constituent is wholly absent from the logical form is unable to predict this bound-variable interpretation, while an account on which a variable occurs in the appropriate position in logical form predicts both that interpretation (in which it is bound by the quantifier), as well as the deictic interpretation (in which the variable is free). Here's the line of argument applied to Perry's example, which is repeated in (28). First the simple sentence is embedded in a (universally) quantified sentence as in (29):

(28)   It's raining.
(29)   Every time John lights a cigarette, it rains.

There are two (at least) interpretations for (29):

(30)   For every time t at which John lights a cigarette, it rains at t at the location l in which John lights a cigarette at t.
(31)   For every time t at which John lights a cigarette, it rains at t at some location l which is salient in the context of utterance.

While the unarticulated constituent analysis can account for (31), in which a single constant location constituent is recovered from context, it cannot account for the interpretation in (30) (which, incidentally, is the preferred interpretation here), because the truth conditions it gives for the sentence in (28), assuming a temporal variable, are as follows:

(32)   An utterance of 'it is raining (t)' is true in a context c iff it is raining at t and at l, where l is the contextually salient location in c.

An account that posits a location variable (in addition to an assumed temporal variable) in the logical form can account for both readings; on reading (30), the variable l is bound by the quantifier; on reading (31), the variable is free and takes as its value the most contextually salient location. Therefore, the unarticulated constituent (free enrichment) analysis is inadequate and there must be a location variable in the logical form of (29) and, to be consistent, also in the logical form of the simple (28).

This line of argument is repeated for sentences containing degree adjectives like "small," "fast," and "old," whose truth-conditional effect involves an implicit comparison class, as in (33), for sentences containing quantifiers whose truth conditions depend on an implicit domain restriction, as in (34), and for sentences containing relational expressions, such as "home," "enemy," and "local," whose truth-conditional effect depends on what they are related to ("home of x," "local to y," etc.). In each of the following, (c) and (d) are the two readings of the quantified sentence (b):

(33)   a. Freddy is small.
        b. Most species have members that are small.
        c. Most species S have members that are small for S. [bound variable reading]
        d. Most species S have members whose size is below s, where s is the standard made salient by the utterance context. [free variable reading]
(34)   a. Every bottle is green.
        b. In most rooms in John's house, he keeps every bottle on the top shelf.
        c. In most rooms r in John's house, he keeps every bottle in r on the top shelf. [bound variable reading, which is the natural interpretation]
        d. In most rooms in John's house, he keeps every bottle in the contextually salient domain on the top shelf. [free variable reading, which is absurd]
(35)   a. Sue visited a local bar.
        b. Everyone visited a local bar.
        c. Everyone x visited a bar local to x. [bound variable reading]
        d. Everyone visited a bar local to some contextually salient entity. [free variable reading]

The crucial final step of the argument in each case is to point out that the free enrichment account, on which the constituent in question is not present in any covert form in any linguistic representation, can account only for the free variable reading in each instance—that is, the interpretation on which the logical form is supplemented by a representation of a contextually salient entity. Let's consider how convincing this step is. Focusing again on the example in (29), although a variable is required in the operator-bound interpretation, given in (30), there is no need for a variable on the other reading, given in (31), or for the interpretation of the simple unquantified sentence in (28), so we could say that while it is present in the one sort of case, it is absent from the others. This might seem to amount to an ambiguity account, whereby, for instance, the linguistic form "rains" encodes both "RAINS" *tout court* and "RAINS AT L," which would certainly be an unattractive prospect. But it is not the only way of understanding the proposal: the variable could come into being pragmatically in the case where the intended interpretation is the bound variable one. Stanley, however, claims that this is not possible:

It is easy to see how an object or a property could be provided by pragmatic mechanisms; it need only be made salient in the context either by the speaker's intentions, or contextual clues, depending upon one's account of salience. However, denotations of bound variables are odd, theoretically complex entities. It is difficult, if not impossible, to see how, on any account of salience, such an entity could be salient in a context. Certainly, neither it, nor instances of it, could be perceptually present in the context. It is equally difficult to see how speaker intention could determine reference to such an entity.

An entity such as a denotation of a bound variable is a theoretical posit, part of the machinery of a particularly complex semantic theory. It is not something about which we have beliefs or intentions. They are therefore not supplied by pragmatic mechanisms. (2000, 414)

The truth of these claims is essential to the case against the free enrichment possibility, but it rests on certain assumptions about the nature of contexts and pragmatic processes, with which one could take issue. Stanley takes a very extensionalist view of context, as consisting of perceptible objects and properties, while the operative notion of context within an on-line cognitive account of utterance understanding is of a set of mentally represented assumptions, some of which are representations of immediately perceptible environmental features, but most of which are either retrieved from memory or constructed on the basis of stored assumption schemas (see Sperber and Wilson 1986, ch. 3). On this sort of approach, these mental representations provide the material required by both linguistically indicated and pragmatically motivated contextual additions to the logical form. It is an open question at present just what these conceptual ("language of thought") representations consist of, but it should not be ruled out a priori that there are assumptions (and assumptions schemas) whose mental representation involves variables bound by quantifiers, and that these can be accessed by addressees in the process of interpreting utterances—in particular, utterances containing explicit quantifiers.

Much of our general, as opposed to particular, knowledge might well be realized as representations that quantify over instances. A plausible case in the current context is our knowledge of the way in which times and places pair up when a certain type of event (such as "raining") occurs: for each time at which it rains there is a place at which it rains; for each place at which it rains there is a time at which it rains. These could provide the basis for an inference from an appropriate temporal binding to a locational binding, as in the case of (29), or vice versa, as in an interpretation of "Every*where* John lights a cigarette, it rains." While the *denotation* of a bound variable may never be a salient entity, as Stanley claims, a (bound) variable itself may be highly accessible if it occurs as an element in a highly accessible assumption. In fact, a quantifier-binding interpretation of an utterance may be recoverable in the absence not only of a linguistically given indexical or variable but also of any linguistically encoded quantifier that might prompt the recovery of a variable. Consider the following example:

(36)   *Context:* Several crates of bottles are delivered to a large house, each designated for a different room in the house. It is the maid's job to unload the bottles and stack them in the right rooms. As she sets about her task, her employer says to her: "On the top shelf, please. I don't want the children getting at them."

The first utterance here is subsentential (a bare prepositional phrase); it contains no quantifier and no indexical, yet the proposition the employer expresses with it in this context involves quantifier-variable binding:

(37)   For each room r [for each bottle b designated for r [put b on the top shelf in r]]

If this is right, the entire binding structure is recovered by a process of free pragmatic enrichment.

The existence of a bound variable interpretation for an utterance is not, therefore, a sufficient condition for the presence of a variable in the logical form of the linguistic expression uttered. Nor is it a necessary condition, as is shown by the case of the genitive, which is usually taken to be a paradigm case involving a variable requiring contextual saturation (see, for instance, Recanati 1989). The standard analysis of "Sally's shoes" is "the shoes that are in some relation x to Sally" (where this relation could be contextually instantiated as shoes "bought by Sally," "worn by Sally," "chosen by Sally," "made by Sally," "painted by Sally," etc.). The procedure of embedding a possessive noun phrase in the scope of a quantifier does not result in a bound variable interpretation:

(38)   At all the school dances, the boys admired Sally's shoes.

There is no reading on which the interpretation of the phrase "Sally's shoes" varies with the values introduced by the quantifier expression "all the school dances."

These rather programmatic remarks have been primarily directed at example (28), the place constituent case. As regards the others that Stanley considers, it may be that some of them do have a covert indexical or variable in logical form. The strongest support for a covert indexical account would come from syntactic evidence showing an alleged covert indexical behaving syntactically like an overt indexical. This sort of evidence exists for the relational terms (e.g., "local," "friend," "enemy," "home"), which show the same "weak crossover" properties as overt indexical elements such as pronouns (see Stanley 2000, 423). Another kind of argument sometimes appealed to is that of "conceptual necessity." For instance, in these relational examples, it seems that the concept encoded by the particular lexical item requires, as a matter of conceptual necessity, that it be related to another entity: something does not have the property of being local unless it is in the appropriate relation *to some other entity*, a person who is not a friend *of someone* is simply not a friend, and so on. In fact, however, it is not obvious that, from this observation, it follows that some covert element must signal this entity in some level of linguistic representation; it may be pragmatics alone that answers to conceptual necessity, while linguistic representation is highly schematic and underdetermining. In any case, there are still many kinds of example for which an unarticulated constituent (free enrichment) account is at least a serious possibility, and some for which a hidden variable account doesn't seem possible.

Consider the case of quantifier domain restriction, where, for instance, an utterance of the sentence in (39a) may be understood as expressing the proposition in (39c). Stanley and Szabo (2000) make the case for a domain variable being present in the logical form of (39a), roughly as shown in (39b); this mandates the contextual recovery of the relevant restriction on the class of bottles:

(39)   a. Every bottle is green.
　　　 b. Every [bottle, x] is green.
　　　 c. Every bottle in this crate is green.

Bach (2000) launches a battery of arguments against this "semantic" approach and argues instead for a "free enrichment" pragmatic account.

First, he points out the widespread redundancy and unnecessary syntactic complexity that follows from the assumption of a hidden indexical in quantifier phrases. Many instances of quantifiers in subject position, such as those in (40a) and (40b), seem to be naturally understood without any domain restriction. More compellingly, for predicative uses of indefinite descriptions, such as those in (40c) and (40d), recovery of the proposition expressed *never* requires a domain restriction:

(40)   a. All men are mortal.
     b. Hardly any food is blue.
     c. That is a bottle.
     d. Pat is a woman.

Second, according to the hidden indexical approach, linguistic mandating of a contextual domain restriction occurs no matter how detailed the overtly given descriptive encoding of the domain may be. So even an utterance of (41c) calls for an obligatory contextual contribution to specify the relevant domain further:

(41)   a. Most of the [retired people, x] were Republicans.
     b. Most of the [retired people in Arkansas, x] were Republicans.
     c. Most of the [retired people in Arkansas who voted for Dole in 1996, x] were Republicans.

I note in this regard that for the other kinds of cases Stanley discusses, there is *either* an overt (phonologically realized) element *or* a hidden element; so, for instance, while there is a location variable in the sentence in (42a), there isn't one in the sentences in (42b)–(42c):

(42)   a. It's raining (1).
     b. It's raining there.
     c. It's raining in London.

The problem with the assumption of a quantifier domain variable is that the only lexical item it can plausibly originate from is the determiner itself ("every," "most of the," "a," etc.), but these elements must be complemented syntactically, and there is no limit on the complexity of their complements. Consequently, there is no cutoff point at which the alleged variable can be said to be fully replaced by overt linguistic material.[14] In the face of this, a reasonable conclusion is that there is no linguistically given domain variable in any instance, the intended domain being determined by pragmatic considerations interacting with the overtly given descriptive material.

Bach also addresses Stanley's central argument, according to which embedding in the scope of a quantifier phrase results in a reading on which the domain variable is bound by the higher quantifier, as in the examples in (43):

(43)   a. In most rooms in John's house, he keeps every bottle on the top shelf.
     b. In most rooms in John's house, the personality of the designer is evident.
     c. In most houses that John rents out, every car passing can be heard.

He claims that the natural understanding in such cases is not, in fact, a genuine "reading of the sentence" (that is, not "what is said") but is, rather, a proposition that the sentence can be used to convey (an "impliciture" in his terms; an "explicature" in mine). He develops an analysis according to which there is no quantifier domain variable in logical form, and such contextually recovered domain restrictions as those shown in italics in (44) are entirely pragmatically motivated:

(44)   a. In most rooms in John's house, he keeps every bottle [*in that room*] on the top shelf.
     b. In most rooms in John's house, the personality of the designer [*of that room*] is evident.
     c. In most houses that John rents out, every car passing [*outside that house*] can be heard.

For the full details of his pragmatic account, see Bach (2000, 277–282).

Quite generally, it looks as if we're in for a long haul, since it seems that decisions on this hidden variable issue can only be reached on a case-by-case basis.[15] In this respect, recall the set of examples in (20) in the previous section, a few of which are repeated here in (45):

(45)   a. Jack and Jill went up the hill [*together*].

      b. Mary left Paul, and [*as a consequence*] he became clinically depressed

      c. She took out the gun, she went into the garden, and she killed her father [*with the gun*] [*in the garden*].

It should be noted that an important background assumption here is that the pragmatically recovered italicized elements are taken to contribute to the proposition expressed by the utterance (the "explicature") rather than as giving rise to an implicature. An implicature account would entail denying the effect of the bracketed elements on the truth-conditional content of the utterance, which seems indefensible in these cases (recall the role of the causal relation in the invalid argument in (2)). Returning now to the issue of the source of these constituents, it is extremely difficult to see how one might argue for a hidden variable (or implicit argument) prompting their contextual recovery, or why one would want to. In (45a), unlike the relational cases (e.g. "local," "distant," "lover," etc.), there does not seem to be any lexical item carrying a variable for which "together" could be the contextual value; rather, it arises from relevance-driven inference based on general knowledge about groups of people climbing hills and is, no doubt, much encouraged by the NP-coordination (as opposed to S-coordination). Nor does this constituent appear to be able to enter into a binding relation with a quantifier; there are only two values it could take, "together" and "separately," and they do not seem to vary with different hill-climbings even when those hill-climbings are bound by a quantifier: for example, "On all the Ramblers' excursions, Jack and Jill went up a hill." The same points apply to the causal, instrumental, and locative constituents in (45b) and (45c). Furthermore, the recovered constituents in (45c) are generally entirely optional: being told that a person has killed her father *tout court* is quite relevant enough in many contexts.[16] (In the next section, on ad hoc concept construction, a different account of the instrumental case will be considered, one that does not involve a distinct constituent at all, whether by variable instantiation or free enrichment.)

Leaving aside now the variable-binding argument, I shall finish this section with a more general argument against the idea of hidden constituents, taking some observations from Wilson and Sperber (2000) as a starting point. They consider the following exchange between Alan and his neighbor Jill who has just called by:

(46)   Alan: Do you want to join us for supper?
       Jill: No thanks. I've eaten.

The sentence "I've eaten" uttered by Jill is understood by Alan as expressing a proposition that includes an object of eating and a temporal specification, both of which are pragmatically inferred. The result is represented roughly in (47):

(47)   Jill has eaten supper this evening.

On a hidden indexical view, the logical form of the sentence she uttered would contain two variables, one for the object and one for the temporal span:

(48)   I have eaten (x) at (t).

Note that quite general and routine processes of reasoning will also supply these constituents: if someone has eaten, she has eaten something; if someone has eaten (something), she has eaten at some time. Be that as it may, Wilson and Sperber go on to point out that in other situations the proposition expressed by a speaker who utters "I've eaten," or its negation, might involve a specification of the place of eating, the manner of eating, and perhaps others. Their examples:

(49)   I've often been to their parties, but I've never eaten anything [*there*].
(50)   I must wash my hands: I've eaten [*using my hands (rather than, say, being spoon-fed)*].

They comment on this:

> More and more hidden constituents could be postulated, so that every sentence would come with a host of hidden constituents, ready for all kinds of ordinary or extraordinary pragmatic circumstances. . . . We see this as a *reductio* argument that goes all the way to challenging what we accepted earlier for the sake of argument: that the use of the perfect carries with it a hidden constituent denoting a given time span. There is no need to postulate such a hidden constituent: the same [entirely pragmatic] process that explains how "eating" is narrowed down to "eating supper" also explains how the time span indicated by the perfect is narrowed down to the evening of utterance. (Wilson and Sperber 2000: 238)

They go on to describe the postulation of hidden constituents as an ad hoc process that is designed to limit as much as possible the gap between sentence meaning and proposition explicitly expressed, and they argue that, although it is at odds with certain theoretical positions on semantics, there is strong evidence of considerable slack, and, given the relevance-theoretic view of pragmatic processing, this is entirely to be expected.

I think this *reductio* argument can be carried a step further. If we assume for the moment that logical forms do come with numerous hidden indexicals, it seems that many of these do not receive any contextual value on particular occasions of use. For instance, the logical form of the sentence "I've eaten" might contain four hidden constituents or variables:

(51)   I've eaten [x] [in manner y] [at location l] [within time span t]

But in the exchange between Alan and Jill in (46), neither the manner nor the location is of any relevance at all and would not receive any specific contextual value, despite the fact that (allegedly) they are both there in the logical form that calls for contextual specification. Of course, the hidden indexical theorist might opt for a nonspecific default value for these indexicals:

(52)   I've eaten supper in some manner at some location this evening.

But this doesn't seem to be the propositional content Alan recovers from Jill's utterance; if a sentence that actually encoded these "some" elements, and so corresponded more directly with the alleged default-valued proposition, were in fact uttered, it would not have the same meaning as Jill's utterance of "I've eaten."

More important, Stanley's idea is that the hidden elements are comparable to pronouns, which may be either free (and so given a contextual value) or bound by some operator in the sentence uttered. However, when a pronoun is free it *must* be given a contextual value if the utterance is to be understood and a fully propositional content recovered. Someone who can, for whatever reason, only find a contextual value for "she" when interpreting an utterance of (53), and so fills the other indexical slots with nonspecific default values, won't have grasped the proposition expressed:

(53)   She put it there.
(54)   Lisa$_i$ put something somewhere.

Another way out might be to propose that the linguistic form "I have eaten" (and innumerable others) has a variety of logical forms, each with an array of variables, differing in number and type (including one with none), marking possible contextual completions. In the case of a sentence that has four possible variables for different constituents, this results in sixteen logical forms to cover the range of cases.[17]

Whichever way you look at it, the covert indexical approach seems to require an unwelcome proliferation of entities, whether of logical forms or default values for variables. One of the nice features of the free enrichment account is that it is not straitjacketed in this way; by definition, only the relevant constituents are recovered.[18]

4.5   Ad hoc concept construction

The examples in the previous two sections can be viewed as cases of conceptual expansion—that is, of the pragmatic addition of conceptual material: for example, "it's raining *in Christchurch*." In other cases, it seems better to construe what is going on as pragmatic adjustment of a lexical concept in the logical form, so that the concept understood as communicated by the particular lexical item is different from, and replaces, the concept it encodes; it is narrower, looser, or some combination of the two, so that its denotation merely overlaps with the denotation of the lexical concept from which it was derived. Here's an attested example:

(55)   Kato (stating of O. J. Simpson, at his trial):
       He was upset, but he wasn't upset.
       (= He was [upset*], but he wasn't [upset**].)

As far as its linguistically supplied information goes, this is a contradiction, a fact that presumably must be captured somewhere within a semantic theory for natural language. But it was not intended as, nor understood as, a contradiction. The two instances of the word "upset" were interpreted as communicating two different concepts of upsetness (as indicated by the asterisks), at least one, but most likely both, involving a pragmatic narrowing of the encoded lexical concept UPSET; the second of the two concepts carries certain implications (e.g., that he was in a murderous state of mind) that the first one does not, implications whose applicability to Simpson, Kato wants to deny. The proposition explicitly expressed here is true just in case O. J. Simpson had one sort of property at the time in question but lacked another, related but stronger, property.

There are a vast number of other cases where any one of a wide range of related concepts might be communicated by a single lexical item; for instance, think of all the different kinds, degrees, and qualities of feeling that can be communicated by "tired," "anxious," "frightened," "depressed," "well," "happy," "satisfied," "sweet," and so on. Consider the following exchange:

(56)   A: Do you want to go to the party?
       B: I'm tired.

Many of us are tired to some degree or other most of the time; what B communicates by the predicate "tired" in this context is something much more specific, something roughly paraphraseable as "tired to an extent that makes going to the party undesirable to B." Just how narrowed down this ad hoc concept of tiredness is will depend on other contextually available information, perhaps concerning B's general energy levels, her liking for parties, and so on. The prospects for finding another lexical item or phrase that fully encodes the concept of tiredness communicated here, and still others that encode the innumerable other concepts of tiredness that may be communicated by the use of this word in other contexts, look dim. Instead, the lexicalized general concept gives access to an indefinite number of more specific concepts, recoverable in particular contexts by relevance-driven pragmatic inference.

In their discussion of this example, Sperber and Wilson (1998) make an interesting proposal about how the explicature of such an example is derived: by a process of parallel mutual adjustment with the implicature(s) of the utterance. According to the relevance-theoretic comprehension strategy, the addressee takes the conceptual schema (logical form) delivered by linguistic decoding and, following a path of least effort, he enriches it at the explicit level and derives other assumptions at the implicit level, until the resulting interpretation meets his expectation of relevance. In the exchange in (56), A's question has made it plain what he is expecting by way of a relevant response from B (a "yes" or "no" answer), which is not given directly by B's utterance but is implicated by it. However, for the inferential process that results in this (negative) implicature to be warranted (that is, to be sound), the premises, which crucially include the explicature, must involve a particular concept [tired*], which is an enrichment of the concept encoded by the lexical item "tired." In short, the inference looks as follows:

(57)   B is [tired*].
       If B is [tired*], she doesn't want to go to the party.
       ‾‾‾
       B doesn't want to go to the party.

This is (part of) the end product of the interpretation process; as set out here, it masks the significant point that, as an on-line process carried out over time, the pragmatic enrichment of the explicature may have occurred subsequent to the accessing of the implicated conclusion, though final acceptance of the implicature depends on the inferential warrant provided by the enriched explicature. As Sperber and Wilson (1998, 194) put it: "The process is one of parallel adjustment: expectations of relevance warrant the derivation of specific implicatures, for which the explicit content must be adequately enriched." This process would apply equally to example (55), though it would take a bit more scene setting: the intended implicature, evident on the basis of earlier exchanges in the trial, is that Simpson was not in a murdering frame of mind on the night in question; making this a sound inference requires appropriate enrichments of the concept encoded by "upset."[19]

The examples considered so far all involve a narrowing or strengthening of the encoded concept, but others seem to require some degree of widening or loosening (as well as narrowing):

(58)   a. Ugh, this custard is *raw*. [uttered by someone who has seen the custard being stirred over a
          flame]
       b. You get *continuous* classics on Classic FM. [uttered by radio announcer]
       c. Young Billy is a *soldier*.
       d. Jane is a *bulldozer*.
       e. The *wilting violet* has finally left. [referring to a woman who has just left the room]

Consider the use of "continuous" in (58b). In fact, the radio station concerned runs long sequences of advertisements between its sets of classical musical excerpts, and it punctuates each set with the disk jockey giving details about the musicians and the recording, as well as his own opinions about the music. However, the utterance is true on a certain loosening of the concept CONTINUOUS; Classic FM is the one radio station on which the music played is confined to classical (again, given an appropriately pragmatically adjusted concept of "classical"), so that a (very rough) paraphrase of the proposition expressed is:

(59) [Musical] classics are played in all the music-playing slots on Classic FM.

In each of these examples, a logical or defining property of the lexical concept is dropped: UN-COOKED in the case of "raw," UNINTERRUPTED in the case of "continuous," MEMBER OF THE MILITARY in the case of "soldier," MACHINERY in the case of "bulldozer," PLANT in the case of "wilting violet." For instance, the proposition explicitly communicated by (58a) is true just in case the custard in question is [raw*], where [raw*] entails an unacceptable degree of undercookedness but does not entail uncookedness. More detailed discussion of the pragmatic process of concept construction is given in Carston (1997), Sperber and Wilson (1998), Breheny (1999), and Wilson and Sperber (2000).

The idea that explicature derivation may involve ad hoc concept construction is of more recent vintage than the idea of free enrichment of logical form as it was discussed in the previous sections. Once this relatively new conception is in place, an interesting possibility, suggested to me by Richard Breheny, opens up: that the pragmatic processes of developing the logical form into an explicated propositional form are exhausted by saturation and ad hoc concept construction. In other words, there may be no free enrichment, at least not of the sort that bothers the hidden indexicalists, the sort that involves the addition of a conceptual constituent to logical form and so a structural change between logical form and propositional form. With this possibility discounted, a transparent (isomorphic) structural relationship between the two can be preserved, in accordance with a particular strict version of the principle of compositionality favored by many formal semanticists. However, ad hoc concept formation is something of a wild beast from the point of view of a semanticist, since it gives considerable power to the pragmatic system in deriving the content (if not the structure) of the proposition expressed. It introduces an element of context sensitivity for every predicate in the language, so that applying the conditional T-sentence format to a simple sentence like (60a) gives something like (60b), or, even less revealingly, (60c):

(60) a. Mary is tired.
  b. If the property [tired#] is referred to by "tired" in an utterance of (a), then that utterance is true iff tired#(Mary). (where [tired#] can be any of a range of different enrichments of the concept encoded by "tired")
  c. If a property F is referred to by "tired" in the course of an utterance of (a), then that utterance is true iff F(Mary).

I suspect that many natural language semanticists would not be comfortable with formulations of this sort which do not capture lexical meaning, which is, arguably, a fundamental component of semantic knowledge.

Anyway, it is not yet clear that the idea is feasible. Can all the cases of unarticulated constituents discussed in section 4.3 (see examples (19) and (20)) be absorbed by the ad hoc concept machinery? There are promising candidates, such as the inferred instrumental or manner constituents: different manners of killing (with a knife, by poisoning, etc.), for instance, and different ways of cutting (with a knife, with scissors, with a lawn-mower, etc.) are plausible cases of narrowing the general lexical concept down to a more specific subtype. Similar comments apply to the strengthening of certain encoded scalar concepts (e.g., "if" to "if and only if," "four" to "exactly four") and to the loosening of certain encodings of a very precise or idealized sort (e.g., "hexagonal" to "roughly hexagonal," "flat" to "more or less flat"). But, intuitively, at least, the unarticulated location constituents are much less amenable; the particularity of "kill x in a garden" or "cut x at grandmother's house" does not seem to be the stuff of stable atomic concepts, and, in the case of the cause-consequence constituent recovered in example (2), and in many other examples of "and"-conjunction, there doesn't appear to be any lexically given concept on the basis of which it could have been constructed. Obviously, this is an issue that needs a great deal more consideration, but, as things currently stand, it seems that there are four different sorts of pragmatic task involved in explicature derivation: disambiguation, saturation, free constituent enrichment, and ad hoc concept construction.

5   Semantics, context, and communication

An explicature has two essential properties: it is an assumption communicated by an utterance, and it has a propositional form pragmatically developed out of a logical form of the utterance. As the last section should have made evident, it is a very different sort of entity from any of the semantically oriented concepts of "what is said" (or "proposition assigned to a sentence"), although both figure on the one side of a distinction with implicatures. What is said by an utterance is usually characterized as (context-invariant) decoded linguistic meaning together with those contextually given values for indexicals that can be supplied without any consideration of speaker intentions or intervention of pragmatic principles. I can see no role for this concept in a theory of utterance interpretation. The job of the pragmatic inferential system is to deliver the communicated assumptions (explicatures and implicatures); the information available to it includes, crucially, the logical form of the linguistic expression employed. There is no other intermediate isolable "semantic" portion, or level, of information that enters into the inferential process. For further discussion of this point, see Carston (2004).

According to the hidden indexicalist view scouted above, semantics is concerned with the interpretation of the logical form of a sentence relative to its context of utterance. This coincides with a concern to characterize the semantics of sentences in truth-conditional terms, given the correctness of the claim that any contribution of context to truth conditions is traceable to some element in the logical form of the utterance. One way of doing this is through the conditional T-sentence approach illustrated above, which packs all contextual variables into the antecedent and makes the truth statement conditional on their being given a particular value.[20] For instance:

(61)   a. It is raining (t) (l).
       b. If t refers to time T_i and l refers to location L_j in the course of an utterance of (a), then (a) is true just in case it is raining in L_j at T_i.

A free enrichment account of this and other examples, which I have been advocating, shoves a wedge into the picture: there is no variable in the logical form to which an abstract value can be given in the antecedent of the conditional form, so that an element of the truth conditions cannot be captured in the truth statement in the consequent. Consider again the "and"-conjunction case we began with:

(62)   Bill ran into John, and John stopped his car in an illegal position.

The truth conditions of each of the conjuncts may be given individually, and the truth-conditional effect of the lexical item "and" (a truth-functional contribution) can be stated. However, the cause-consequence relation, which contributes to the truth conditions of this sentence/utterance (recall the invalid argument in example (2)), would not be captured by composing these three sets of truth conditions together, or by any other means, except an arbitrary stipulation that there is a relational variable in the logical form of conjunctive sentences. The same goes for all the other cases of free enrichment. If we also bring into the account the context-sensitivity of predicates, as discussed in the preceding section, and try to incorporate that in the antecedent too (recall example (60)), we seem to be heading fast in the direction of vacuity of the following sort:[21]

(63)   If the proposition P is expressed by an utterance of sentence S, then S is true iff P.

The issues for the advocate of a truth-conditional semantic interpretation of logical forms are how much context dependence (linguistic underdeterminacy) can be, and should be, accommodated; how is the line to be drawn in a nonarbitrary way; and to what extent are native speaker intuitions about truth conditions to be observed?

An alternative would be to abandon the idea that all elements of truth-conditional content are either determined by or, at least, traceable to some constituent in logical form (linguistic meaning), and to relocate truth-conditional semantics, so that it is determinate propositional forms of the internal mental representation system that are to be semantically interpreted (that is, related to the conditions for their truth). On such a conception, the so-called semantic output of the linguistic system (logical form(s)) is simply the result of a partial mapping onto that internal (conceptual) representation system, which is the real object of semantic evaluation.

Finally, when we draw back from the specific issue of indexical saturation versus free pragmatic enrichment and pan across the different theoretical positions supporting each stance, we see two quite different pictures: the one starts from a broad cognitive perspective and takes as its main focus ostensive communicative acts, it is concerned with processes and mechanisms, and it uses a range of psychological arguments, including evolutionary considerations; the other is focused specifically on the nature of "genuine linguistic speech acts," their syntax, logic and semantics, it is philosophically based, and it is not constrained by processing considerations. They look like two different species of endeavor, but, in the long run, they will have to mesh with each other, and at least one of them will have to give up its view on the way in which the context-sensitivity of the proposition expressed by a linguistic utterance is realized in the human cognitive system.

Notes

My thanks to Richard Breheny, Annabel Cormack, Rob Stainton, Deirdre Wilson, and Vladimir Žegarac for very helpful conversations on issues addressed in this chapter. The work was supported by a research fellowship from the Leverhulme Trust (RF&G/1/9900510).

1. The first example will be recognizable as an adaptation of one made famous by Perry (1986b); the second is taken from Breheny (1999).

2. There is a confusingly large array of ways in which the semantics/pragmatics distinction has been drawn in different frameworks depending on their aims. For discussion of some of these, see Bach (1997), Carston (1999), and Stanley (2000).

3. Wilson (2000) provides an illuminating exposition of how psychological research on the theory of mind capacity and work within the broadly Gricean inferential pragmatic tradition interrelate, and how both of these bear on more general metarepresentational abilities.

4. There are more and less sophisticated versions of the strategy, depending on the different sorts of expectations of relevance the addressee has: from a naive expectation of actual optimal relevance to an expectation that allows for variations in both the ability and the willingness of the speaker to be relevant. The naive expectation employed by young children develops progressively into the more knowing expectations, though adults may vary their expectations across speakers and situations. For detailed discussion, see Sperber (1994a).

5. Stanley includes in this class of nonlinguistic ostensive communicative acts some that happen to involve language. He places strong requirements on the class of genuine linguistic speech acts, which are the concern of linguistic theories: they must be grammatical, and they must have determinate propositional content and illocutionary force. An example of a language-involving communicative act that is allegedly not properly linguistic is mentioned in section 4.3 (note 13), where subsentential utterances are briefly discussed.

6. Elsewhere (see Carston 1998, 2002) I have discussed in detail the "linguistic underdeterminacy" thesis—that is, the position that the linguistic form employed by a speaker inevitably underdetermines the proposition she explicitly expresses. I have tried to make a case for the view that this is not just a matter of processing convenience (saving of speaker or hearer effort) but is, in fact, an essential property of natural language sentences, which do not encode full propositions but merely schemas for the construction of (truth-evaluable) propositional forms.

7. For a more detailed analysis of the concept of explicature, see Carston (2002, ch. 2), where certain issues raised by the original definition (Sperber and Wilson 1986, 182) are discussed, and a revision is suggested and motivated.

8. In Carston (1998, ch. 3) and (2002), I argue in detail against there being any role in an account of linguistic communication for a notion of "what is said" additional to, and intermediate between, the decoded logical form of the utterance and the explicature (or Bach's "impliciture" or Recanati's pragmatically enriched "what is said"). This includes the original Gricean notion, which allows for just those essential contextual adjustments (standardly, disambiguation and reference fixing) which will ensure a minimally truth-evaluable proposition as what is said, and Bach's (1994) even more pared down conception, according to which what is said must correspond, constituent for constituent, with the linguistic expression used, so that what is said may be just a propositional radical—hence, not truth-evaluable.

9. In fact, it is not perfectly clear that "linguistic expression identification" should be equated with "disambiguation." Ultimately, the relationship depends on what sort of an entity a linguistic expression is—that is, whether it is (a) a complex of constitutive representations (phonological, syntactic, semantic), or (b) an externalizable representational vehicle that represents a constituent of thought (a concept), or (c) an entirely internal logico-conceptual entity that may be represented by some conventional representational system (effectively the reverse of (b)), or some other possibility. For interesting discussion of this issue, see Burton-Roberts (1994).

10. It is an issue for discourse-oriented, "dynamic" approaches to semantics, in which the domain of truth-conditional semantics is not natural language sentences but discourse representation structures (DRSs) which, like relevance-theoretic propositional forms, are an amalgam of linguistically and pragmatically supplied information. So an ambiguous form like "ring" has to be disambiguated before the DRS to which it contributes can be assigned a truth-conditional semantics. For useful discussion of discourse representation theory and semantics, see Spencer-Smith (1987); for an account of disambiguation in this sort of framework, see Asher and Lascarides (1995).

11. This is one of several "minimalist" principles that are employed by semanticists who want to minimise the role of pragmatics in determining the proposition expressed by an utterance. For discussion, see Carston (1988) and Recanati (1993).

12. As Deirdre Wilson has pointed out in discussion, this is probably too strong, since some cases of VP ellipsis are pragmatically controlled. Consider the following exchange, in which the content of the VPs has to be recovered from extralinguistic context:

(i)   [B holds out a packet of cigarettes]
       A: Should I?
       or: I shouldn't.
       B: Do.

Even when there is a linguistic antecedent, recovery of a constituent may require a fair measure of reconstruction, which may not be entirely a matter of the grammar. The obvious cases are pronoun alternations (you/me) and polarity switches (anything/something), but there are also more striking instances:

(ii)   ($_S$ She didn't say yes) and ($_S$ she didn't say no), but I did [= ($_{VP}$ say (yes or no))]

This involves some reanalysis, including a de Morgan conversion from "and" to "or." As Wilson says, this looks like a case of pragmatic reconstruction rather than a mechanical grammatical process; she suggests that in this case (and numerous others) pragmatic inference is used to yield a linguistic object as output, the grammatical constraint being simply "supply a VP."

13. Stanley (2000) disputes the position that there are nonsentential assertions; he argues that many cases, such as (23), are really elliptical and so, underlyingly, have a full sentential structure, and others, like (26), are not genuine linguistic speech acts at all, but fall in with taps on the shoulder, winks and other

bodily gestures of a communicative sort, all of which are to be studied within a nonlinguistic theory of general human reasoning. Stainton (2004) takes issue with Stanley and defends the existence of nonsentential assertion.

14. In fact, after assessing a range of possibilities for the location of the domain variable, Stanley and Szabo (2000) conclude that it accompanies the descriptive noun in the quantifier phrase (as suggested by the representations in (39b) and (41)), rather than the determiner/quantifier. They take the strong and quite counterintuitive stance that "common nouns such as 'bottle' *always* occur with a domain index" (2000: 258; my emphasis).

15. The degree adjectives might seem like another promising case for a hidden variable in logical form; the variable, indicating the requirement of a comparison class, could feature in the lexical entries for the particular adjectives ("small," "old," "rich," "fast," etc.). In fact, Heim and Kratzer (1998), employing a type-driven semantic framework, give an unarticulated constituent account of the implicit comparison class of these adjectives, but they do not address the issue of the bound variable readings, which lies outside the concerns of their textbook. For further discussion of the semantics of degree adjectives, see Breheny (1999), whose own account involves pragmatic concept construction, as discussed in section 4.5 of this paper.

16. Using the formal model of utterance interpretation developed by Kempson, Meyer-Viol, and Gabbay (2000), Marten (2002) gives an account of VP interpretation, according to which verbal sub-categorization is intrinsically underspecified and optional VP constituents (adjuncts), such as the locational and instrumental cases just discussed, are pragmatically inferred on-line during the process of syntactic structure-building.

17. There seems to be an obvious application of some modified version of Occam's Razor here. Note that a cognitively realistic pragmatics does not necessarily favor wholesale use of the Gricean version of MOR, which seems to amount to the following: for any element of meaning, if you can show how it *could* be derived pragmatically, then assume that it *is* derived pragmatically. Nevertheless, virtually any economy criterion, however hedged, is, I think, going to weigh against assuming sixteen logical forms, hence sixteen distinct sentences, each with the surface form "I've eaten."

18. See Recanati (2002) for a detailed discussion of the unarticulated constituents issue and a compelling defense of a pragmatic (free enrichment) account, albeit one that is construed in directly truth-conditional terms as distinct from the (mental) representational approach taken here.

19. This process of parallel adjustment of explicature and implicature should not be thought of as only applying to cases of ad hoc concept construction. Wilson and Sperber (2000) provide several detailed derivations of interpretations involving this process, including some cases that are better construed as involving pragmatic recovery of unarticulated constituents, such as the example of "I've eaten," discussed in section 4.4.

20. I am not attributing this particular approach to Stanley; I don't know whether he would approve it or not. I choose it as the most promising way I know of to give a truth-conditional account of natural language, which both handles the context sensitivity of the proposition expressed and is revealing of the meaning encoded in natural language expressions.

21. Recanati (2001) presses this point still further in his account of the radical and generalized underdeterminacy of truth conditions, given what Searle (1983) calls the "Background"—that is, a set of common practices and basic assumptions that are seldom represented but which are crucial ingredients of the truth conditions of the vast majority of utterances.

41

ROBERT J. STAINTON

Quantifier Phrases, Meaningfulness "in Isolation," and Ellipsis

1   Introduction

Semanticists and philosophers of language have traditionally divided expressions into two classes: those that do, and those that do not, have meaning "in isolation." Among expressions which are commonly said to *lack* meaning in isolation are particles in natural language (e.g., 'up' in 'shoot up', 'on' in 'catch on', etc.) and the logical vocabulary of both natural and artificial languages (e.g., the sentential connectives 'and', 'if', etc.). Assuming one can sort out what "having meaning in isolation" amounts to, the question arises: which expression types fall into which category? In particular, and this is the central question of the paper:

(1)   *The Question*: Do quantifier phrases have meaning in isolation?

Here's how I plan to address this question. First, I want to get a fix on what "having meaning in isolation" amounts to. After that, I will argue that quantifier phrases—for example, 'some woman' and 'eight cats'—*do* belong in the class of expressions which have meaning in isolation. The central argument for this claim: quantifier phrases can be used and understood outside the context of any sentence. (For example, a man may approach an apple cart and say nothing more than 'Six large apples', thereby requesting six large apples.) But, I aim to show, expressions which lack meaning in isolation cannot be so used. So quantifier phrases have meaning in isolation.

Having said a little about what the Question means, and having argued for an affirmative answer to it, I will consider a possible response to my argument. That response, which has great initial appeal, goes like this: though quantifier phrases *appear* to be used and understood in isolation, this is actually a matter of *ellipsis*. In the end, as I'll explain, I don't think an appeal to ellipsis can really support a negative answer to the Question. So my positive answer stands.

Robert J. Stainton (1998) Quantifier phrases, meaningfulness "in isolation," and ellipsis. *Linguistics and Philosophy* 21: 311–340. Reprinted by permission of Kluwer Academic Publishers.

That's the game plan. Before continuing, I want to emphasize as strongly as I can that this paper is not intended as an exercise in the history of philosophy. Specifically, it is not an attempted explication of, and subsequent attack upon, any theses proposed by Bertrand Russell. It is true that, in trying to get a grip on what "meaning in isolation" amounts to, I will appeal to some of Russell's (1905, 1911, 1919) ideas. But, in the end, nothing I say hangs on whether, for example, the notion of "having meaning in isolation" I arrive at really derives from Russell. Or again, in arguing for a positive answer to the Question, I make no claim to have refuted any doctrine held by Russell. Our very different purposes, and our divergent use of terms, makes it hard for me to know whether my result conflicts with Russell's views. (Anyone who does know is cordially asked to pass the word along.)

2   Meaningful in isolation: A case study

The basic problem with explicating the notion "meaningfulness in isolation" is this: what counts as "meaningful in isolation" greatly depends upon what meanings are. So, to move ahead on the Question, I need to figure out what meanings are. Obvious problem: there is, to put it mildly, rather substantial disagreement about what meanings are. Some philosophers think meanings are senses; others think they are Ideas; while still others take them to be (non-conceptualized) objects in the external world. Because of this, rather than trying to provide a general account of meaningfulness in isolation, I will try to illustrate, rather than define, the term 'meaningful in isolation'. If my discussion is sufficiently illuminating, its lessons can be applied to various theories of meaning, thereby yielding a notion of "meaningfulness in isolation" for diverse meaning-theories.

As my illustration, I choose Russell's direct reference theory, essentially because it involves a clearcut distinction between expressions which are, and are not, meaningful in isolation. Roughly speaking—and recalling that this isn't exegesis—meanings for Russell are external entities. To borrow a happy phrase from Sainsbury (1979), they are *meaning-relata*. These external entities come in two flavors: names refer to *particulars*, while predicates refer to *universals*. Crucially, at least so far as sub-sentential expressions go, these alternatives are meant to be exhaustive.

Given that there are, for Russell, only two kinds of meaning-relata, and that these correspond exclusively to names and predicates, it might seem that all other sub-sentential expressions should be meaningless. But, of course, it would be absurd to say that every other linguistic item is *gibberish*. The solution, however, is not far to seek. One need only draw a three-way distinction between (a) expressions which have meaning "in the primary way" (in Russell's case, by having a meaning-relatum), (b) expressions which have meaning in some "non-primary" way, and (c) expressions which lack meaning altogether. We may then say that an expression has meaning in isolation only if it gets its meaning in the primary way. Any expression which lacks meaning altogether, or affects the meaning of whole sentences, but not in the primary way, has no meaning in isolation.

Next step: what is it to have meaning in the "non-primary" way? It is, I take it, a matter of making a meaning-difference to whole sentences—though not by the standard means. Applied to Russell's case, then, an expression has meaning in the "non-primary" way if it affects the meaning of whole sentences but does not have a meaning-relatum. (Put otherwise: though the word/phrase alters the meaning of a sentence *S*, it does not contribute a *constituent* to the proposition expressed by *S*.)

3   The Russellian approach and quantifier phrases

To sum up the previous section: putting aside truly meaningless words and phrases (e.g., 'madatrauts'), an expression is *not* meaningful in isolation if, instead of being paired with a meaning in the usual way, one must give a rule for generating the meaning of *whole sentences*, within which the expression occurs. (As I said, what "pair with a meaning in the usual way" comes to depends very much on what you take meanings to be—e.g., external objects, modes of presentation of objects, Ideas, or what have you.) With this in mind, I now return to (1):

(1)   *The Question*: Do quantifier phrases have meaning in isolation?

In Russell's case, (1) has a reasonably straightforward answer. Quantifier phrases are neither names nor predicates, and only names and predicates have meaning-relata. Hence, quantifier phrases are not meaningful in isolation. Instead, their meaning must be specified by giving a general rule—which determines what sentences containing them mean. An example: to give the meaning of 'Every cat', one could provide a rule like:

(2)   'Every cat' combines with ⌜is G⌝ to yield a sentence; that sentence is true if and only if, for every x, if x is a cat, then x is G.

(Abstracting away from the restrictive predicate 'cat', one could give a meaning-contribution rule for ⌜Every F⌝. That rule might be:

(3)   ⌜Every F⌝ combines with a predicate ⌜is G⌝ to yield a sentence; that sentence is true if and only if, for every x, if x is F, then x is G.

Generalizing still further, the approach as a whole may be captured by the following, where **Q** is any quantifier word, and the ellipses are completed by the rule appropriate to the particular quantifier word:

(4)   *The Not-Meaningful in Isolation Approach*: ⌜**Q** F⌝ combines with a predicate ⌜is G⌝ to yield a sentence; that sentence is true if and only if . . .

Adopting the above as the semantic axiom for quantifier phrases amounts to giving a negative answer to (1). For, what (4) provides for each quantifier phrase is a method for calculating the meaning of whole sentences containing quantifier phrases, rather than giving a meaning-relatum for them. What I now want to ask is whether this is the right approach. My conclusion will be that, whatever its merits vis-à-vis artificial languages, as a perfectly general approach to quantifier phrases in natural language, (4) does not work. The reason is, (4) is only operative *when there is a predicate* ⌜is G⌝ for the quantifier phrase ⌜**Q** F⌝ to combine with. Lacking such a predicate, the rule simply does not apply. But, as a matter of empirical fact, quantifier phrases can be used and understood in the absence of any such "second predicate." Or so I'll suggest.

4   The problem: Unembedded quantifier phrases

I pause to emphasize: about quantifier phrases outside sentences, (4) says nothing whatever. Given this, rule (4), at least as it stands, can (at best) capture the semantic contribution of quantifier phrases as they occur in sentences. This wouldn't be a problem, but for the fact that quantifier phrases can be used and understood in isolation.

Time to introduce some data.[1] Suppose I'm at a linguistics meeting, talking with Andy Brook. There are some empty seats around a table. I point at one and say, 'An editor of *Natural Language Semantics*'; I then indicate another empty seat and say, 'Anyone from *Pragmatics and Cognition*'. Upon hearing these words, Andy forms the belief that the unoccupied seats are reserved for an editor of *Natural Language Semantics*, and for some representative of *Pragmatics and Cognition*, respectively. Another detail. The seats I pointed to are actually reserved for Emmon Bach and M. A. K. Halliday; and, as a matter of fact, they are not involved with these journals. I want to stress two things about this imagined situation. Point one: since, in the imagined situation, the seat I indicated first is not reserved for an editor of *Natural Language Semantics*, and since the second seat is not set aside for someone from *Pragmatics and Cognition*, I spoke falsely in uttering (5) and (6), below. I made a false statement.

(5)   An editor of *Natural Language Semantics*
(6)   Anyone from *Pragmatics and Cognition*

Point two. What I uttered, in the described situation, were two quantifier phrases. Neither time did I utter a sentence. (You might be tempted to say: "This *isn't* really a use of an unembedded quantifier phrase; it's a use of an elliptical sentence—in particular, an elliptical sentence which *contains* a quantifier phrase." I'll address this shortly.)

To repeat: the no-meaning-in-isolation approach—schematized in (4)—at best says nothing whatever about the unembedded use of (5), (6), and related cases; at worst, it says that a meaningful utterance of (5) or (6) on its own is impossible. The reason, as I said, is that (4) applies only where there is a "second predicate" available to combine with the quantifier phrase. But, crucially, when an *unembedded* quantifier phrase is used, no such predicate appears.

What to do? The obvious solution is to make quantifier phrases meaningful in isolation. This is what I propose. Importantly, however, I want to reject one means of doing this: assimilating quantifier phrases to the category of names, thereby pairing them with *individuals*. The problem with this, as Russell rightly stressed, is that logical puzzles, and bizarre ontological commitments, would thereby arise.[2] Nor is it plausible that quantifier phrases have ("ordinary," i.e., first-order) universals as their meaning-relata. So, if quantifier phrases are to be meaningful in isolation, what's needed is a third kind of meaning-relata. So be it.

5   The fix: Generalized quantifiers

Plausible assumption, part one: quantifier phrases can be used and understood in isolation. Plausible assumption, part two: the no-meaning-in-isolation approach, suggested by (4), does not predict that quantifier phrases can be used and understood in isolation. In which case, an alternative to (4) is called for. Here it is, in a nutshell: quantifier phrases, whether within a sentence or unembedded, correspond to generalized quantifiers.[3]

A generalized quantifier, for the purposes of this paper, will be a function from sets to propositions. (See Lewis 1972, Montague 1974, and Barwise and Cooper 1981 (Chapter 23 in this volume) for early work.) Two things deserve to be stressed about my usage. First, a generalized quantifier, as I use the term, is not a kind of expression: though *quantifier phrases* are linguistic items, *generalized quantifiers* are not; they're functions. Second, I'm treating generalized quantifiers in the Russellian spirit: not as functions from sets to *truth values*, but as functions from sets to *propositions*. (The reason? I want to be able to distinguish 'a king of France', 'a unicorn', and similar unsatisfied quantifier phrases from one another.)

The generalized quantifier corresponding to 'some nitwits', for example, is that function f from sets to propositions such that, for any set S, $f(S)$ is a true proposition iff the intersection of the set of nitwits with S is non-empty. And the generalized quantifier corresponding to 'every toadstool' is that function g from sets to propositions such that, for any set S, $g(S)$ is a truth iff the set of toadstools is contained in S. Applied to a sentential example, sentence (7) is true iff the intersection of the nitwits with the smokers is non-empty—that is, iff something is both a nitwit and a smoker; and sentence (8) is true iff the set of toadstools is contained in the set of broken things:

(7)   Some nitwits smoke.
(8)   Every toadstool is broken.

Having the notion of a generalized quantifier at hand, I can now lay out an alternative to (4):

(9)   *The Meaningful in Isolation Approach*: $\ulcorner Q\ F \urcorner$ denotes the function f from sets G to propositions such that $f(G)$ is a true proposition if and only if . . .

Notice: because quantifier phrases do not, on this approach, denote individuals, the afore-mentioned logical puzzles and weird ontology are avoided; nevertheless, it's worth stressing, because quantifier phrases *are* assigned meaning-relata by (9), they are *meaningful* in isolation. That is, returning to my earlier terminology, they are assigned their meanings "in the primary way." Hence, on this approach, the answer to (1) is: Yes, quantifier phrases are meaningful in isolation. This is in stark contrast with (4). Finally, since this formulation applies with equal naturalness both to quantifier phrases within sentences *and* to unembedded quantifier phrases, it is *superior* to (4): the advantage of this revised formulation, from the point of view of the use and comprehension of unembedded quantifier phrases is that it assigns meaning-relata to quantifier phrases whether or not they occur in sentences. To take an example, $\ulcorner$Every $F\urcorner$ denotes a function from sets to propositions: one which outputs a true proposition when and only when the input set contains the set F.

6   Ellipsis and other manoeuvres

I want now to consider two suggestions for defending (4), the "not meaningful in isolation" alternative, while accounting for the use of unembedded quantifier phrases. As will emerge, neither suggestion is satisfactory.

The "no meaning" gambit

Here's an initially plausible way of saving the not meaningful in isolation approach; I call it the "no meaning" gambit. Recall the crucial example: saying 'An editor of *Natural Language Semantics*' causes Andy to believe that the indicated seat is reserved for an editor of *NLS*. That this kind of thing can and does occur is indisputable. But, someone might say, this doesn't show that the sounds produced have any kind of semantic content at all, let alone meanings "in isolation." For, it is undeniable that many non-linguistic stimuli can be used to induce beliefs—without having meaning in isolation.[4] To take an obvious case, I may brandish an umbrella, in Anita's direction, thereby inducing in her the belief that it is raining outside. But "umbrella brandishings" have no semantics.

Indeed, to develop the example a bit, even supposing that I, the speaker, induce the belief that a certain chair is set aside for an editor of *NLS* by getting Andy to recognize my intention to induce said belief, and so on in familiar Gricean fashion, this *still* doesn't show that 'An editor of *Natural Language Semantics*' has semantic content. For, once again, many kinds of stimuli have *nonnatural meaning* while nevertheless lacking a semantic value.

If the objection worked, there would indeed be no need for a meaning-in-isolation for quantifier phrases. To see the failings of the "no meaning" gambit, however, it's enough to reflect upon the differences between sentence-based communication on the one hand, and non-linguistic communication on the other; and to ask, of the use of unembedded quantifier phrases, which it resembles.

Sentences can be used to communicate thoughts which are (a) of unlimited complexity and (b) systematically similar/different; what's more, the nature of the thought communicated is (c) comparatively independent of context. Consider just a few examples:

(10)   Particle accelerators often cost more than 14 million American dollars each.
(11)   Particle accelerators often cost less than 12 million American dollars each.
(12)   Digital clocks seldom cost more than thirty dollars and fifty-five cents a piece, in Canadian currency.

The thoughts one would communicate with (10) through (12) are undeniably complex and sophisticated. And more complex thoughts still can be communicated, by adding further qualifier words, or by conjoining these with other sentences, or what-have-you. These examples illustrate that there is no upper bound to the length and complexity of the thoughts one can convey using sentences. Notice also the relatively subtle and systematic similarities and differences between the thought one would typically communicate with (10) as compared to (11). The differences arise from the replacement of 'more' by 'less' and '14' by '12'; the similarities from holding the remainder constant. Finally, (10) can be used in many different circumstances to communicate essentially the same thought: the precise nature of the communicated thought may well change, but there will nevertheless remain something importantly constant across contexts.

In contrast, non-linguistic communication is comparatively simple, coarse-grained, unsystematic, and context bound. For instance, to communicate something as complex and subtle as the thoughts which (10) or (12) encode, without using language, would be no mean feat. Of course one can, by stocking one's tongue out, express disapproval; one can even be rather more specific than that. Similarly for umbrella brandishing. But, in general, there's a pretty low threshold to the complexity, precision, and so on of what one can communicate, without using sentence-like symbols.

Now, *why* does sentence-based communication exhibit these three crucial features? Essentially because sentences have semantic content, and that content is determined recursively and compositionally: the meaning of a whole sentence is a function of what its parts mean and how those parts are put together; and the rules for "putting the parts together" can apply repeatedly, thereby creating an unlimited number of meaningful sentences. In contrast, gestures and other non-linguistic stimuli, *even if* they have conventional content, do not have that content determined by a lexicon and a combinatorix.

Having noted this contrast between communication with and without compositional symbols, consider communication with unembedded quantifier phrases. For example, ask yourself what Andy would have understood, at the linguistics meeting, had I said each of the following—letting all else remain fixed:

(13)   A representative of the Uruguayan Linguistics Association
(14)   A representative of the Uruguayan Philological Society
(15)   The man who coined the phrase 'theta-role'
(16)   The woman who coined the phrase 'semantic competence'
(17)   Someone that you'll really want to meet
(18)   A student of Chomsky's that you'll really want to meet

What immediately stands out is: (a) the complexity of the thoughts communicated, (b) the subtle and systematic differences between them, and (c) the limited degree of contextual influence. (I.e., in each case, I tell Andy who will occupy the chair. As before, the chair must be contextually supplied. But practically everything else comes from the phrase uttered.) Indeed, it seems on reflection that the thoughts are, to all intents and purposes, as complex, productive, systematic, subtle, and (roughly) as context-independent as the thoughts communicable via sentences. Let me now suggest why this is: unembedded quantifier phrases, like sentences, have semantic content—which is determined recursively as a function of part meanings—and structure. In which case, it will not do to say that quantifier phrases are *wholly* meaningless.

It's also worth noting, by the way, that unembedded quantifier phrases exhibit such semantic features as ambiguity, anomaly, logical relations, and so on. And that, to understand utterances of such phrases, one must know the language in which they are uttered. Here again, this is nothing at all like umbrella brandishing.

One might reasonably reply that, while unembedded quantifier phrases must be treated as *linguistically meaningful* stimuli, no less than full sentences, it doesn't follow that they need to be assigned *meanings in isolation*. There is, as I said, an intermediate option between being meaningless and being meaningful in the primary way. Surely, it might be said, quantifier phrases are meaningful precisely in this intermediate sense: to use slightly different terminology, they have no semantic values—instead, there are syncategorematic rules for how quantifier phrases affect sentence meanings. Thus, this reply might go, in saying an unembedded quantifier phrase ('Three philosophers', for example) the speaker does produce a truly contentful linguistic stimulus. But there's no need to have an account of the *meaning-relatum* of said unembedded quantifier phrase, because it has none.

This line of response raises an obvious question: how can such phrases be *understood* in isolation, if they have no meaning in isolation? Here's a possible answer: the hearer, making use of the context, comes up with some predicate. He then combines this predicate with the heard quantifier phrase, to form a sentence. Only then does he use (4) to interpret the resulting sentence. Outcome? Quantifier phrases are used and understood in isolation, but this in no way impugns the not meaningful in isolation approach, because quantifier phrases, so used, don't need meaning-relata.

My reply. To say that the hearer "comes up with a predicate" merely re-labels the problem of how not-meaningful-in-isolation expressions manage to get interpreted; it does not solve it. Specifically, it remains a mystery how the right predicate is found: the hearer, in his search for the right predicate, cannot rely on the *meaning* of the unembedded quantifier phrase since, by hypothesis, it doesn't come into play until *after* the missing predicate has been found. But, if the quantifier phrase offers *no semantic clue* about where in the context to search, there are going to be far too many "salient predicates" to choose from. Arriving at an interpretation of the speaker would end up being a fabulous stroke of luck. It's just not credible that interpretation works like this. Pretty clearly, the quantifier phrase's content must play a central part in the search for the "right predicate." In which case, the bare phrase cannot be assigned its meaning merely in terms of (4).

Second defense: Ellipsis

In the foregoing, it was granted that a bare quantifier phrase can be used, but proposed that this didn't entail that the thing used had meaning in isolation. This approach to defending (4) having failed, another suggests itself: deny that what gets used really is a bare quantifier phrase at all. Here's the idea. When someone says 'An editor of *Natural Language Semantics*', what they produce isn't an indefinite description in isolation; rather, what they produce is an elliptical sentence. This is a natural thought. It's a plausible thought. And it's a thought which might well save (4)—after all, if quantifier phrases *aren't* actually used outside sentences, why make one's theory account for such usage? The thing is, this natural, plausible thought is also (arguably) a *false* thought. I can't go into the evidence in any detail here. But, simply by way of motivating my positive answer to the Question, let me at least sketch a couple of the considerations which mitigate against defending (4), repeated below, by appeal to ellipsis:[5]

(4)   *The Not-Meaningful in Isolation Approach*: $\ulcorner$**Q** $F\urcorner$ combines with a predicate $\ulcorner$is $G\urcorner$ to yield a sentence; that sentence is true if and only if . . .

I'll start by laying out a very general account of what ellipsis amounts to. That the following proposal is terrifically general should forestall the hope that my arguments against ellipsis work only for a particular, parochial theory of ellipsis. Crucially, this general account of ellipsis will be such that *if* all apparent uses of unembedded quantifier phrases really are uses of elliptical sentences, *then* something like (4) may still work. Having suggested what ellipsis amounts to, I'll then give several arguments designed to show that this is not what occurs when speakers (appear to) utter unembedded quantifier phrases. I conclude that (4) cannot be defended in this way and is not the correct account of the semantics of quantifier phrases; and that, indeed, quantifier phrases have meaning in isolation.

Before continuing, however, I want to warn against assuming an ordinary, commonsense notion of ellipsis—according to which, whenever someone leaves something unsaid, they are speaking elliptically. In *this* sense of ellipsis, the use of bare phrases obviously *is* elliptical: the speaker communicates more than what her words mean. But appeal to ellipsis in this weak sense won't rescue (4), since an ellipsis defense of (4) requires that the *expression uttered* be sentential. And this is not established by pointing out that *the speaker* left certain information unspoken.

In particular, so far as I can see, a speaker may convey a proposition without uttering a sentence. (Compare one of Grice's 1975: 52) cases: A professor writes, in a letter of reference, 'Mr. X's command of English is excellent, and his attendance at tutorials has been regular'. Here, the proposition communicated is something like *Mr. X is a crappy philosophy student*, but this in no way shows that *these words* were produced by the speaker.) So the mere fact that a proposition is communicated does not establish that the speaker produced any kind of sentence.

In sum, there's a sense of "elliptical" in which a use of a bare phrase would be elliptical; but it's not a sense which is especially relevant to the issue at hand. For the issue at hand is, what *expression* did the speaker produce—an unembedded quantifier phrase, or a sentence? If the answer is, "A quantifier phrase," then (4) needs patching.

That being said, what is ellipsis—in the sense in which it would preserve (4)? Preliminary remark: linguistic items, both tokens and types, fall into different classes; in particular, some are syntactically sentential, while others are syntactically lexical or phrasal. Roughly speaking, a linguistic representation is syntactically sentential if and only if it is headed by an inflectional element at the appropriate level of representation—where inflectional elements include modals, tense, and verb-subject agreement. (For further discussion, see Chomsky 1981, 1982, 1986a, 1986b; Haegeman 1991; and references cited there.) An expression is lexical/phrasal otherwise. Now, everyone agrees that speakers *appear to* utter unembedded quantifier phrases. For example, everyone recognizes that a man may approach an apple cart and say 'Three big red apples', or knock on a coworker's door and say 'The Leibnitz reading group'.[6] In both cases, the speaker performs a speech act: in the first case, the man request three big red apples; in the second case, he informs his colleague of an upcoming engagement. And, in both cases, the speakers appear to use an unembedded quantifier phrase, in the sense that the expressions they produce sound like phrases. To defend (4), then, its proponent might maintain that, despite the fact that certain utterances do not sound like ordinary sentences, they nevertheless are sentential in the syntactic sense.

How to do this? Here's an "ur-proposal." I will say that an expression r is *shortened* if and only if there exists another expression r' such that r' has a longer phonetic form than r, but r' has the same syntactic structure as r.[7] In a word, a linguistic expression becomes an *ordered pair* of a syntactic structure and a phonetic form. It is the syntactic structure of an expression that determines whether it is sentential or phrasal, and it is the phonetic form that determines how the expression sounds. (In which case, putting it crudely, ellipsis comes to this: a syntactic structure which is headed by INFL gets paired with an "abbreviated" phonetic form.) Given the notions of syntactically sentential expressions and shortened expressions, I can now introduce the ellipsis hypothesis:

(19)   *The Ellipsis Hypothesis*: Whenever a speaker performs a speech act by uttering an (apparently) unembedded quantifier phrase, what that speaker really utters is an elliptical sentence in the sense that her utterance is syntactically sentential, but it is shortened.

It is the "shortening," of course, that explains why the result does not "sound like" an ordinary sentence—even though the utterance is syntactically sentential. (Notice that the ellipsis hypothesis is stated in such a way as to be indifferent to how the abbreviation occurs—syntactic deletion, null elements, phonological deletion, or what-have-you.)

To take one example: a speaker who uses the sound *the head of philosophy* to communicate that the head of philosophy has arrived should be described not as uttering (20), but rather as uttering (21):[8]

(20)   ⟨[_QP The head of philosophy], *the head of philosophy*⟩
(21)   ⟨[_IP The head of philosophy has arrived], *the head of philosophy*⟩

Rule (4) would then straightforwardly apply—because the sentence ⟨[_IP The head of philosophy has arrived], *the head of philosophy*⟩ is, from the point of view of syntax/semantics, equivalent to the sentence 'The head of philosophy has ariived', and this latter sentence is easily captured by an instance of (4).

I hope it's now clear what it would amount to, to defend (4) by insisting that when a speaker appears to utter an unembedded quantifier phrase, what she really utters is an elliptical sentence. I now turn to the question of whether it's true. First problem for the ellipsis hypothesis: Witness the fact that, in the situation described above, 'The head of philosophy' are the first words uttered. This strongly suggests that the expression produced is not elliptical in the desired sense—since, insofar as linguists know anything about ellipsis, they know that a shortened phonetic form demands a *linguistic* context. With certain notable exceptions—for example, asking permission by saying 'May I?'—you cannot, without awkwardness, begin a conversation with an elliptical sentence: 'He doesn't' and 'I wonder when' sound odd as discourse onsets, even when they would be understood. (See Hankamer and Sag 1976 for the details.) But—in contrast to cases of authentic ellipsis—you *can* begin a conversation with a quantifier phrase, without (or with much less) awkwardness: recall the man whose first words to the apple vendor are 'Three big red apples'. Nor, incidentally, does the use of unembedded quantifier phrases require a "pragmatic controller," in the sense of Hankamer and Sag (1976); following Yanofsky (1978), I note that 'A tie' can be used to remind someone to wear a tie—this being necessary precisely when no tie is antecedently salient! Here again, there is an important contrast with true ellipsis, which does require such a pragmatic controller when no linguistic antecedent is available.

The above argument has the form: it doesn't quack like ellipsis, and it doesn't walk like ellipsis; so, plausibly, it isn't ellipsis. Arguments like this are not, of course, conclusive: one could, pending a finding of deep similarities, conclude that a non-waddling, non-quacking creature is a previously unfamiliar kind of duck; and one could, after sufficient investigation, conclude that the items produced in discourse initial position are a previously unfamiliar kind of syntactic ellipsis. But, that these fragments lack one of the fundamental properties of elliptical expressions is solid prima facie evidence that they are not elliptical.

And too, it would be surprising if elliptical sentences *could* be used in discourse initial position. In discourse initial position there are, of course, no *linguistic* cues in the context for going from the encountered phonetic form to the corresponding syntactic structure. This poses a problem because, as should be obvious, if the ellipsis hypothesis is correct, then a given phonetic form does not determine anything like a unique syntactic structure.

Consider an example. It would seem, given the ellipsis hypothesis, that all of (22) through (24) are expressions of English:

(22) ⟨[$_{IP}$ The famous lawyer loves Fred], *the famous lawyer*⟩
(23) ⟨[$_{IP}$ Fred loves the famous lawyer], *the famous lawyer*⟩
(24) ⟨[$_{IP}$ The famous lawyer detests Steve], *the famous lawyer*⟩

These expressions would exist, on the ellipsis hypothesis, because the phonetic form *the famous lawyer* can, given the right context, communicate any of the following propositions: THE FAMOUS LAWYER LOVES FRED; FRED LOVES THE FAMOUS LAWYER; and THE FAMOUS LAWYER DETEST STEVE. Given that utterances with the phonetic form *the famous lawyer* can convey any of these, there must be at least three linguistic representations that share this phonetic form—again, if the ellipsis hypothesis is correct.

Next step: For any given phonetic form, there are an *unlimited* number of propositions which it could encode. Therefore, by parity of reasoning, any phonetic form whatever corresponds to an unlimited number of syntactic structures.[9] Evidently, this raises a question about parsing; namely, how does the parser find the single intended syntactic structure? In the standard (i.e., non-elliptical) case, one must assume that it outputs the shortest syntactic structure consistent with the phonetic form. (Otherwise, to take an example, *Mary sleeps*, said in isolation, could get paired with, among other things, [$_{IP}$ Alex mistakenly supposes that on Friday nights Mary sleeps at her friend's house].) In the elliptical case, in contrast, linguistic clues from the context must provide the necessary evidence for getting the right, non-minimal, syntactic structure.

And this shows why *discourse initial* ellipsis would be peculiar: without linguistic clues from the context, it will typically be impossible to find the correct non-minimal syntactic structure of an elliptical utterance; but discourse initial position is precisely a case in which linguistic clues are unavailable. So, it's highly likely that elliptical sentences cannot be used in discourse initial position. The expressions in question, on the other hand, *can* be used in discourse initial position. Hence, it's plausible to suppose, said expressions are not elliptical sentences—at least not in the sense required by an ellipsis defense of (4).

Another argument against the ellipsis hypothesis: Certain constructions (e.g., VP deletion and sluicing) cannot acceptably occur if there is no prior syntactically sentential item in the discourse. This provides a sort of prima facie test for syntactically sentential linguistic items in prior discourse. And this test suggests that (apparent) unembedded quantifier phrases *aren't* underlyingly sentential: discourses containing VP deletion constructions and sluicing constructions become significantly less acceptable when (apparent) quantifier phrases are substituted for sentences. Here are examples:

VP DELETION
(25) Jason: The man from Paris is at the door.
      Mark: And Betty is too.
(26) Jason: The man from Paris
      Mark: ??And Betty is too

SLUICING
(27) Jason: The man from Paris is at the door.
      Mark: I wonder why.
(28) Jason: The man from Paris
      Mark: ??I wonder why

The sentence 'The man from Paris is at the door' differs minimally from the phrase 'The man from Paris', in the sense that both expressions can be used to communicate the proposition that the man from Paris is at the door. Yet, if one substitutes the phrase 'The man from Paris' for the full sentence, in (25) and (27), the result (given in (26) and (28), respectively) is less acceptable—even when the thought that the man from Paris is at the door is successfully communicated.

You might think, this doesn't show that 'The man from Paris' is non-sentential, because 'And Betty is too' requires a *non-elliptical* sentence as its linguistic antecedent. But this doesn't seem right. Notice, for example, that where 'The man from Paris' answers a wh-interrogative (which would plausibly make it an elliptical sentence), 'And Betty is too' becomes quite okay. Thus:

(29)   Lenny: Who's at the door?
       Jason: The man from Paris.
       Mark: And Betty is too.

(Another point. Though it's unclear why, 'And _____ is too' is sensitive to sentential antecedents in a way that other related expressions are not. That's why I use 'And Betty is too', rather than anything else.)

Though far from conclusive, these data suggest that 'The man from Paris' is not syntactically sentential; if it were, the discourses (26) and (28) as a whole should be perfectly acceptable—which they're not. A fortiori, 'The man from Paris' is not syntactically sentential *and shortened*. That is, 'The man from Paris' is not an elliptical sentence.

I repeat: the foregoing considerations are not definitive and decisive. They are not intended to be. But there is much more evidence of this kind, the total weight of which is quite convincing. In any case, my purpose in this section was merely to make it plausible that quantifier phrases—not elliptical sentences, mind you, but ordinary quantifier phrases—can be used and understood on their own, outside any sentence. Which should be enough to motivate, at least provisionally, hypothesis (9), and the consequent in-isolation meaningfulness of quantifier phrases:

(9)   *The Meaningful in Isolation Approach*: ⌜**Q** *F*⌝ denotes the function f from sets G to propositions such that $f(G)$ is a true proposition if and only if . . .

7   The pragmatics of unembedded quantifier phrases

A hypothesis about the semantics of an expression must, at the very least, be consistent with facts about how utterances of that expression are typically understood. I'll suppose it uncontroversial that unembedded quantifier phrases, when used in context, are often understood as communicating quantified *propositions*. But, if treating quantifier phrases as corresponding to generalized quantifiers is on the right track, this is not what unembedded quantifier phrases mean: semantically speaking, an unembedded quantifier phrase corresponds, by hypothesis, to a function from sets to propositions. The failure of fit between the semantics which I have proposed for unembedded quantifier phrases, and how these are understood, might be thought a problem. But, happily, pragmatics can bridge the gap. That, anyway, is what I'll argue.

This isn't the place for laying out the pragmatics of unembedded quantifier phrases in painstaking detail. (Interested readers might look at Stainton 1994, where the interpretation of *other* non-sentences is discussed at length.) So, I will simply sketch a story about how unembedded quantifier phrases can be used in communication. In order to do so, however, I will need to employ numerous ideas from Relevance Theory.

Some definitions. Let *logical forms* be expressions of mentalese. Let *assumptions* be propositional logical forms and *assumption schemas* be non-propositional logical forms. (In effect, assumptions are sentences of mentalese, while assumption schemas are mentalese predicates, names, quantifier phrases, etc.) A logical form is *manifest* to an individual at a time t only if she is capable of representing it mentally at t. But this is not sufficient for manifestness. Roughly, an assumption is manifest at t only if the person whose representation it is is capable of accepting it as true, or probably true, at t; an assumption schema is manifest to a person at t only if what it represents is perceptible at t. Let an individual's *assumption-set* be the collection of assumptions currently manifest to her. (Assumption-sets cannot, by definition, contain assumption schemas.) Finally, call an assumption A *relevant* to an individual at a time to the extent that A positively affects the individual's assumption-set, where an assumption-set is positively affected by having assumptions added to it, deleted from it, et cetera. The more positive effects, the more relevant; but also, the less processing cost (e.g., inferential labor, perceptual effort, memory strain), the more relevant.[10] (Note: I have included an appendix, at the end of the paper, which lays out some of the basic tenets of Relevance Theory; if unfamiliar with Sperber and Wilson's framework, you may want to read the appendix before going on. Specifically, technical terms such as 'manifest', 'affecting', etc. are discussed there.)

Time to put the definitions to work. To fix ideas, I'll focus on one example: Andy and I hear some loud noises. I peer through the window and utter the phrase 'Three dogs'. Assuming this phrase corresponds to a function from sets to propositions, as (9) demands, how can it be used communicatively—for example, to report that there are three dogs outside? Here is the general idea. The utterance of the quantifier phrase makes manifest a number of logical forms. In particular, the utterance makes manifest the following two items:

(30) *The presumption of optimal relevance*: that the utterance is relevant enough for it to be worth the addressee's while to process it; and that the utterance is the most relevant one available.

(31) The logical form corresponding to the quantifier phrase uttered (in the case at hand, the logical form corresponding to the English expression 'Three dogs'), where the content of this logical form is a generalized quantifier.

Here is the key claim: having this much manifest is enough for successful communication, because (30) and (31) can jointly serve as a basis for finding the assumption-set consistent with the presumption of optimal relevance—an assumption-set which contains the assumption that there are three dogs outside. And this, as you'll see, is sufficient for communicating the latter assumption.

The assumption-set, at the outset, does not contain (31) because, though it is a logical form, it is not an assumption. (Remember, assumptions are, by definition, *propositional* logical forms. [Example] (31) is nonpropositional: its meaning is a generalized quantifier, not a proposition.) However, an assumption-set can, with very little effort, be made to contain an assumption got from (31). This is easy enough, assuming some sets (or properties?) are salient. If a set s is salient in the environment, then, by the definition of manifestness, the logical form corresponding to s will be manifest; and a logical form which represents a set, when combined with (31), yields an assumption. (Compare: a quantifier phrase, when combined with a predicate, yields a sentence.) For instance, combining the logical form **be-outside** with the logical form of 'Three dogs' gives (32), which in turn λ-converts to (33):[11]

(32) $\lambda g \in \langle e,t \rangle.\lambda w.[\exists_3 x(dog(x)\ \&\ g(x))]^W$ (**be-outside**)

(33) $\lambda w.[\exists_3 x(dog(x)\ \&\ \textbf{be-outside}(x))]^W$

Assumption (33), whose meaning is the proposition that there are three dogs outside, will be *relevant enough* in certain circumstances: for instance, it will be relevant enough in a situation where the hearer wants to know the source of the observed noise. Hence an assumption-set

containing (33) satisfies the first of the presumption of optimal relevance. But—and this is crucial—**be-outside** will be manifest in a subset of these circumstances.[12] Indeed, in some cases
where (33) is relevant, **be-outside** will be the *most* manifest logical form, beyond (30) itself. In
such circumstances, the assumption-set containing (33) will be the most accessible assumption-
set: the first one the hearer considers in her interpretive task. And, as Sperber and Wilson argue,
the *most* accessible assumption-set which is relevant is the *only* assumption-set consistent with
the presumption of optimal relevance; in turn, the only assumption-set consistent with the presumption of optimal relevance is the assumption-set communicated by the speaker. This set includes (33). And thus you see how an utterance of 'Three dogs', taken as encoding a generalized
quantifier, succeeds in communicating a proposition. Presto.

Except for two worries. First worry: It might seem that an utterance of 'Three dogs' cannot
really succeed in communicating a proposition because it will never be the most relevant utterance available. Surely, one might say, a fully sentential utterance will always be more relevant,
since spelling everything out for the hearer would require less inferential work (hence less processing effort) on her part. The point is well taken. But, as I've argued in Stainton (1994), it is far
from clear that supplying more linguistic material *must* make an utterance easier to process. Quite
the contrary, where an appropriate assumption schema is already very manifest (as **be-outside** is
assumed to be in the example above), forcing the hearer to decode a predicate (e.g., [$_\Gamma$ are out-
side]), and then develop the predicate—only to arrive at an (already manifest) logical form—
would involve more effort than simply decoding the non-sentence and conjoining it with the
manifest assumption schema. Put more flat-footedly: sometimes it's more efficient to leave the
already-obvious unspoken.

What's more, a point also elaborated on in Stainton (1994), the use of a bare quantifier phrase
might have stylistic effects which make the recovered assumption-set richer than it would otherwise be. Such a use might indicate urgency, or informality, et cetera. Given this, though it remains
an open empirical question, I think it's fair to say that an utterance of an unembedded quantifier
phrase could well be the most relevant utterance available—given the right circumstances.

Second worry about this Relevance Theoretic story: I insisted that the use of unembedded
quantifier phrases was *not* a matter of ellipsis. But—you might wonder—haven't I just given an
ellipsis-based account? I don't think so. Let me tell you why.

First of all, the interpretive process, as I see it, goes like this. The hearer of an unembedded
quantifier phrase decodes the bare quantifier phrase and recovers its logical form; since logical
forms, being formulae in mentalese, determine meanings, this entails that the hearer recovers the
meaning—*before* she recovers the assumption communicated. On the ellipsis story, on the other
hand, the hearer cannot assign a meaning to the expression uttered until a whole sentence has
been recovered. (Remember, the whole point of introducing ellipsis would be to preserve the
idea that only *within sentences* are quantifier phrases meaningful.) So, to speak loosely, I'm in
disagreement with the ellipsis proponent about *the stage* at which the quantifier phrase is decoded and understood.

A closely related point: As I see it, in forming interpretive hypotheses the hearer employs
the assumption schema got from decoding—that is, the logical form of the unembedded quantifier phrase—as an important clue in finding the appropriate assumption schema to combine with
it. (In terms of the example, having the logical form of [$_{QP}$ Three dogs] already manifest will
surely make it easier to determine that **be-outside**, among all the manifest assumption schemas,
is the desired one.) Taking the ellipsis story seriously, however, the quantifier phrase itself provides no semantic clue to the interpreter—precisely because it is assumed to have no meaning in
isolation.

Which takes me to the final important difference between my account and an ellipsis story.
(I get a bit fuzzy-headed when I think about this last contrast, but I think the point is worth mak-

ing nonetheless.) In an ellipsis story, the hearer has to recover a *linguistic unit*—specifically, a natural language predicate—in order to continue the interpretive process. That is, she must recover whatever linguistic material was elided from the fully sentential source. This looks hard. The difficulty arises for two reasons. First, the quantifier phrase itself can provide no semantic help—I'll say it again: the ellipsis story is supposed to preserve the idea that quantifier phrases have no meaning in isolation. Second, generally speaking, the context won't allow the hearer to single out the sought-for linguistic item—even if she *did* receive a semantic clue from the quantifier phrase. I don't know how to elaborate this point, except metaphorically. Here it goes. To re-work a passage from Davidson (1984h: 263), a non-linguistic context is not worth a thousand words, or any other number. Natural language words are the wrong currency to exchange for a non-linguistic context. Put otherwise, there is no single, correct mapping from situations to public language descriptions of them; so the non-linguistic context cannot determine a linguistic item. In which case, there will generally be no (unique) "salient predicate" for the hearer to concatenate with the quantifier phrase. In contrast, logical forms, unlike words, are *precisely* the right "currency" to exchange for a non-linguistic context—since what is manifest is determined, in very large part, by the actual environment. Remember, anything *perceptually salient* is manifest; and what is perceptible in an environment obviously depends closely on the contents of the environment. So, whereas a non-linguistic something cannot generally be mapped onto a public language structure (elliptical or otherwise), a perceptible (but not necessarily perceived) non-linguistic something *will* always make a logical form manifest. This provides a final contrast between (a) selecting a natural language unit—got from the quantifier phrase and the context—and interpreting it (i.e., ellipsis); and (b) combining the logical form of a quantifier phrase—a mentalese expression—with another manifest logical form (anti-ellipsis). Hence, my account is not a mere variation on ellipsis.

To further bring out this contrast, it may help to introduce a view which is not my own. The ellipsis story has the uttered quantifier phrase combining with a contextually salient predicate, to form a sentence; this sentence is then interpreted using (4). An alternative anti-ellipsis story (again: not my own) has the *denotation* of the quantifier phrase—as given by (9)—combining with some contextually salient *non-linguistic entity*, to yield a proposition. This proposition is communicated by the speaker, but it is not the content of the words which the speaker uttered; for, what she uttered denotes not a proposition, but a propositional function.

Thinking about it this way, there is a clear difference between the two accounts. Crudely, one describes the process in the formal mode (the ellipsis account), while the other uses the material mode (the anti-ellipsis account). Furthermore, this picture highlights the sense in which a context can determine salient *entities* in a way that it need not determine salient *labels* for these entities.

Returning to my own view, this contrast is captured via explicit reference to mentalese versus natural language. That is, I cash "a non-linguistic entity is salient" as: "the mentalese predicate corresponding to said entity is manifest"; and I construe "the denotation of the quantifier phrase combines with this entity" as: "the mentalese assumption-schema which translates the public language quantifier phrase combines with the contextually manifest mentalese predicate."

Putting it my way, one can no longer draw the stark contrast between, roughly speaking, the formal mode approach (i.e., ellipsis) and the material mode approach (i.e., anti-ellipsis). For, seen Relevance Theoretically, *both* approaches are committed to the recovery of some kind of predicate, which is then combined with some kind of quantificational *expression*. But the contrast between a natural language predicate being salient, and being combined with a natural language quantifier phrase; and a mentalese predicate being manifest, and being concatenated with a mentalese correlate of a quantifier phrase, though subtle, is real enough. And it distinguishes my view, according to which quantifier phrases really are used in isolation, from the ellipsis view, according to which they are not so used.

8   Summary and conclusion

Time to sum up. I have suggested a positive answer to (1), repeated below:

(1)   *The Question*: Do quantifier phrases have meaning in isolation?

By asserting that quantifier phrases are meaningful in isolation, I mean that they are assigned meaning "in the primary way" (i.e., by receiving a denotation), rather than being allotted their meaning solely in terms of how they affect the meaning of sentences in which they occur. The grounds for this conclusion are, admittedly, a bit odd: quantifier phrases can be used and understood even when no *natural language predicate* is available, to combine with the quantifier phrase. Odd or not, I believe this fact about actual usage favors (9) over (4).

By way of defending my positive answer to (1), I considered and rejected two alternative views about how unembedded quantifier phrases apparently manage to be used and understood, consistent with (4). According to one view, they are *not* so used—appearances to the contrary are engendered by misconstruing elliptical sentences as truly unembedded phrases. This alternative was discarded on empirical (especially syntactic) grounds. According to a second view, quantifier phrases really are used and understood in isolation; but, so used, they exhibit no semantic content whatever. This alternative was rejected on the grounds that it failed to account for the complexity, subtlety, and relative context-independence of phrasal speech acts. Finally, I attempted to render pragmatically plausible the idea that quantifier phrases are meaningful in isolation—and that what they "mean in isolation" are generalized quantifiers. Here, I used Relevance Theory to show that assigning this kind of meaning to quantifier phrases is at least consistent with the fact that quantifier phrases are used and understood in isolation.

9 Appendix: A tutorial on relevance theory

Interpretation, as Sperber and Wilson (1987; 1995) see it, consists of two steps. On the one hand, the hearer must *decode* the linguistic signal; on the other hand, she must infer utterance meaning—on the basis of what is decoded, plus any other available evidence. Decoding furnishes only the linguistic representation of the utterance, including both its syntactic structure and its *logical form*—where the latter is the mentalese symbol that gives the meaning of the expression. (I'll abstract away from how the decoder achieves this task.)

Inference *develops* this logical form to arrive at the proposition(s) expressed. Development is almost always required because the logical form output by the decoding process will not, in general, be fully propositional—simply because, put in more familiar terms, expression meaning often falls short of a complete proposition. (Think of 'He bought that'. This expression, the type that is, does not correspond to a proposition; to get a proposition, the meaning of the expression must be supplemented by a context.) Put in Relevance Theoretic terms, the logical form of the expression uttered is ordinarily not an assumption—where, by definition, an assumption is a logical form that *does* express a proposition. So, to understand the proposition communicated, the hearer must "complete" the logical form, until he arrives at a logical form that *does* express a proposition. The question is, how does the hearer do this? To tell that tale I need to introduce still more background.

Sperber and Wilson (1995: 39) say that an assumption is manifest to an individual at a given time if and only if she is capable of representing that assumption mentally and accepting that representation as true or probably true at that time. There are several ways that an assumption may be manifest to an individual. It may be perceptible in the physical environment, it may be inferable from assumptions which are already manifest, or it may be retrievable from memory.

It is important to stress the modality at work in this definition. To be manifest, an assumption need not have been already perceived, remembered, or inferred; rather, what is required for manifestness is the mere possibility that the assumption be perceived, inferred, or remembered. Notice, too, it is not propositions or states of affairs which are manifest. Rather, assumptions— formulae of mentalese—are mamfest.

Manifestness, according to Sperber and Wilson, admits of degrees. Assumptions which are more likely to be held true are more manifest. Consider an example. It may be manifest to Watson that Holmes is holding a pipe, but more manifest to him that Holmes is speaking—because Watson is more likely to hold this latter assumption true. In all likelihood, it will be less manifest to Dr. Watson that Holmes has never been to the moon. Not because Watson harbors any doubts; only because he is unlikely to even entertain the possibility that Holmes has been to the moon. Nevertheless, Watson is capable of considering this assumption, however odd. Hence it is manifest to him, albeit very slightly.

Final bit of terminology. (Here I'm simplifying like mad.) Call an assumption *A* relevant to an individual at a time to the extent that *A* positively affects the individual's assumption-set, the individual's collection of currently manifest assumptions. (E.g., *A* may be relevant by adding new and useful assumptions to the individual's assumption-set; or by making more manifest assumptions which are already a little manifest; or by removing false assumptions from the assumption-set.) Next step: The very assumption *A* can be more or less relevant, to an individual at a time, depending on how much effort is required to process *A*. *A* has greater relevance to the extent that the processing effort it requires is small; and it has less relevance to the extent that the processing effort it demands is large. Given the notions of manifestness and relevance, I can now employ Sperber and Wilson's (1995: 270) *principle of relevance*.

(34) *Principle of Relevance*: Every communicative act communicates the presumption of its own optimal relevance.

(35) *Presumption of Optimal Relevance*:
    a. The utterance is relevant enough for it to be worth the addressee's while to process it, and
    b. The utterance is the most relevant one available.

If communication is to succeed, the speaker must communicate the presumption of optimal relevance. He must communicate (a) that he is communicating assumptions which are relevant enough, and (b) that he has chosen the most efficient means available for communicating these assumptions. Why is this so, according to Sperber and Wilson? Here's the idea. If the speaker is to succeed in communicating, he must persuade his audience to interpret his utterance. This requires convincing that audience to expend the necessary interpretive effort. Sperber and Wilson claim that speakers convince the audience by making it manifest that the speaker intends to communicate assumptions which are relevant to the audience. Sperber and Wilson are aware, of course, that speakers do not always communicate in good faith. A speaker may claim his audience's attention without having anything truly relevant to communicate. But, they maintain, unless a speaker at least pretends to be aiming for relevance, he will fail to communicate anything. It is in this sense that speakers inevitably communicate, about their very own utterances, that the latter are relevant enough.

So much for part (a) of the presumption of optimal relevance. What about part (b)? According to Sperber and Wilson, if communication is to succeed, a speaker must communicate that his utterance is the *most* relevant utterance available for communicating the set of assumptions in question—call it {I}. Why is this? Well, as they point out, the most effective signal for communicating some set of assumptions {I} is the one which makes it as easy as possible for the addressee to understand {I} (Sperber and Wilson 1995: 157). And the signal which makes it easy as possible for the addressee to understand {I} is precisely the one which requires the least processing effort. Finally, the signal which requires the least processing effort to recover {I} is the most relevant signal capable of making {I} manifest—because the most relevant signal is the one which yields the most positive changes in the interpreter's assumption-set, at the least cognitive cost. In a word, the following identities hold:

(36)   The most effective signal for communicating {I} = the signal which makes it as easy as possible for the addressee to understand {I}.

(37)   The signal which makes it as easy as possible for the addressee to understand {I} = the signal which requires the least processing effort to recover {I}.

(38)   The signal which requires the least processing effort to recover {I} = the most relevant signal for making {I} manifest.

By transitivity of identity,

(39)   The most effective signal for communicating {I} = the most relevant signal for making {I} manifest.

Now, if the speaker wishes to successfully communicate a set of assumptions {I}, she will undoubtedly select the most effective signal available for communicating {I}. And, as just explained, the most effective signal for communicating {I} is the most relevant signal for making {I} manifest. So, if the speaker wishes to successfully communicate, she will select the most relevant signal for making {I} manifest.[13]

In speaking, utterers communicate both that their utterance is relevant enough and that it is the most relevant one available. By assuming that this promise of optimal relevance was made in good faith, the hearer can eliminate very many hypotheses about what a speaker might have meant: she can reject any hypothesis which would have the speaker violating the presumption of optimal relevance. But, it might be thought, this criterion leaves a multitude of possible interpretations, all of which are consistent with the presumption of optimal relevance. If many interpretations satisfy this demand, how does the hearer select a single interpretation? In response to this question, Sperber and Wilson (1995: 167) argue that there is only ever one set of assumptions which is truly consistent with the presumption of optimal relevance: the only set {I} consistent with the presumption of optimal relevance is the *first* set of assumptions {I} which the hearer considers, and which is relevant enough.

This talk of "the first" presupposes some ordering of sets of assumptions. The ordering is in terms of *accessibility*. Sperber and Wilson (1995: 77) write that, "A more accessible assumption is one that is easier to recall." They add, "the more a representation is processed, the more accessible it becomes." It is not wholly clear what accessibility comes to, but the intuitive idea can be brought out as follows. Some assumptions are more easily brought to consciousness than others; furthermore, some assumptions can be retrieved from long-term memory with ease, while others require significant effort. Similarly, some assumptions can easily be introduced into an individual's assumption-set; other assumptions could become part of the individual's assumption-set only with a good deal of effort. Those assumptions which require less effort to become part of an individual's assumption-set at a given time are more accessible for that individual at that time.

Sperber and Wilson maintain that, in assessing interpretive hypotheses, hearers begin by testing the most accessible set of assumptions—in this sense of "accessible." If this set of assumptions is not consistent with the presumption of optimal relevance, the hearer goes to the next most accessible set and tests it. This continues until a set of assumptions is found which is consistent with the presumption of optimal relevance. The most accessible set of assumptions which is consistent with the presumption of optimal relevance is the only one consistent with the presumption of optimal relevance. And it is the set of assumptions being communicated.

Why, according to Sperber and Wilson, is the most accessible set of assumptions the only set of assumptions consistent with the presumption of optimal relevance? They write:

> An addressee . . . who wants to maximize cognitive efficiency, will test hypotheses in order of accessibility. Suppose he arrives at a hypothesis which is consistent with the principle of relevance. Should he stop there, or go on and test the next hypothesis on the grounds that it might be consistent with the principle of relevance too? It is easy to show that he should stop there. Suppose he does go on, and finds another hypothesis which verifies the first part of the presumption of relevance: the putative set {I} is relevant enough. In these circumstances, the second part of the presumption of relevance is almost invariably falsified. If it was at all possible, the communicator should have used a stimulus which would have saved the addressee the effort of first accessing two hypotheses consistent with the principle of relevance, and then having to choose between them (Sperber and Wilson 1995: 167–168).

This argument goes by rather fast, and it establishes a rather important conclusion. So let me unpack it. Sperber and Wilson want to establish the conclusion below:

> *Conclusion*: The first interpretation of an utterance u which is consistent with the presumption of optimal relevance is the only interpretation consistent with the presumption of optimal relevance. Therefore, for any u, there is only one interpretation of u consistent with the presumption of optimal relevance.

To establish this conclusion, assume that there is some utterance u which has two interpretations consistent with the presumption of optimal relevance. From this assumption, a contradiction will be derived:

> *Premise 1*: There is at least one utterance u such that u has two interpretations consistent with the presumption of optimal relevance: {I1} and {I2}.

Sperber and Wilson then observe that, "almost inevitably":[14]

> *Premise 2*: There exists some other utterance u' such that {I2} is the first interpretation of u' consistent with the presumption of optimal relevance.

They then point out that finding the first interpretation of u consistent with the presumption of optimal relevance (i.e., finding {I1}, rejecting it, and finally finding {I2}) involves more processing effort than finding the first interpretation of u' consistent with the presumption of optimal relevance (i.e., finding {I2}). In a word:

> *Premise 3*: Interpreting u as communicating {I2} requires more processing effort than interpreting u' as communicating {I2}.

Now, recall the second extent condition on relevance. An assumption is relevant to the extent that the effort required to process it is small (Sperber and Wilson 1995: 125). So, by premise 3, u' is more relevant than u—when both are taken as communicating {I2}. But then it is not true that {I2} is an interpretation of u which meets the presumption of optimal relevance, for there exists a more relevant means of communicating {I2}, viz. u'. This contradicts Premise 1.

This argument establishes that, for any utterance u, there cannot be two interpretations of u consistent with the presumption of optimal relevance. There can be only one. That one is the first interpretation that passes the test; and that single interpretation is the content of the communicative act.[15]

Notes

This paper was written during a visit to the University of Massachusetts–Amherst and revised while I visited Rutgers University. My thanks to my hosts and friends at both institutions, including especially Barbara Partee and Ernie Lepore, who invited me to their respective universities. An earlier draft was presented at McGill University. I'm grateful to everyone who attended, but must single out Stephen Neale, who happened to be at McGill that day. Unsurprisingly, Stephen made numerous, and very useful, comments. Thanks also to Andrew Botterell, Barbara Partee (again), and two anonymous *Linguistics and Philosophy* referees, for criticism/commentaries. Finally, I'm grateful to my home institution, Carleton University, for sabbatical time, and to the Social Sciences and Humanities Research Council of Canada, for financial support.

1. In case imaginary examples worry you, take a cursory glance at a speech corpus. You'll see that quantifier phrases are very frequently used and understood in isolation. Also, non-sentential expressions of *many* kinds can be used to perform speech acts: Noun Phrases, Verb Phrases, Prepositional Phrases, and so on. Indeed, Barton 1990 argues that any X^{max} can be used on its own. See Stainton (1994, 1995, 1997a, 1997b) for examples and discussion.

2. For example, what kind of particular could be denoted by 'a man'? And how can it be that 'a man is bald' is true, while 'a man is not bald' is also true? Is it, perhaps, that the bizarre individual denoted by 'a man' is both bald and not bald?

3. It's sometimes supposed that the generalized quantifier approach and the syncategorematic approach are mere notational variants of one another. If I'm right, this cannot be so—because they have distinct empirical consequences vis-à-vis the use and comprehension of unembedded quantifier phrases.

4. My thanks to an anonymous *Linguistics and Philosophy* referee for pressing me on this issue.

5. See Barton 1990, 1991; Brame 1979; Dalrymple 1991; Morgan 1989; Napoli 1982; and Yanofsky 1978 for additional arguments.

6. Here and elsewhere I assume a Russellian theory for definite descriptions, according to which they are quantificational rather than referential.

7. I leave open the question of how, precisely, the notion of length should be explicated—relying in what follows on an intuitive understanding of this notion.

8. A word about notational conventions. In what follows, I will represent the syntactic structure of utterances by a labelled bracketing. For example, suppose John utters the sentence 'Snow is white'. I use the following notation to give the syntactic structure of John's utterance: $\ulcorner_{IP}$ snow is white$\urcorner$. I use English orthography in italics to give the phonetic form of utterances. The phonetic form of John's utterance, for example, would be given by *snow is white*. To give the full linguistic representation of an utterance, I use an ordered pair of a syntactic structure and a phonetic form—in that order. Where no confusion will arise, I also use single quotes to talk about expressions—understood as complexes of syntactic structure, phonetic form, et cetera.

9. And, obviously, every phonetic form will correspond to infinitely many meanings.

10. Does the definition of manifestness mean that surprising facts can never be manifest? Well, it does mean that they can't be *very* manifest, at least until attention is drawn to them. However, this is precisely the reason why surprising facts can be very *relevant*. And what is communicated is what is most relevant, not what is most manifest. So there is certainly no reason why surprises can't be communicated.

11. Not knowing how to write in mentalese, I use the notation of intensional logic.

12. To say that **be-outside** is manifest seems to suggest that the set of things $\{x: x$ is outside$\}$ is perceptually salient. This may sound odd to some ears. Frankly, it sounds odd to mine. However, I believe the oddness derives not from the supposition that **be-outside** can be manifest, but rather from an overly simple notion of what this assumption schema might represent. Since what is crucial for my purposes is that **be-outside** should be manifest, I will simply abstract away from this issue.

13. This establishes that a speaker must choose the most relevant stimulus available—if he wishes to communicate successfully. But Sperber and Wilson make a stronger claim. They maintain that speakers inevitably *communicate* that they are using the most relevant stimulus available. Why this extra step? Sperber and Wilson (1995: 157) answer as follows:

> An addressee who doubts that the communicator has chosen the most relevant stimulus [available]—a hearer, say, who believes that he is being addressed with deliberate and unnecessary

obscurity—might doubt that genuine communication was intended, and might justifiably refuse to make the processing effort required. All of this is mutually manifest; it is therefore mutually manifest that the communicator intends it to be manifest to the addressee that she has chosen the most relevant stimulus capable of fulfilling her intentions.

That is, by communicating that she has chosen the most relevant stimulus, the speaker helps to ensure that the hearer will interpret her. For, if she fails to communicate this—if, for example, the hearer takes her to be using a less than optimally relevant stimulus—the hearer may not make the necessary interpretive effort. So, speakers not only inevitably select the most relevant stimulus available; they inevitably *communicate* that they have selected the most relevant stimulus available.

14. Sperber and Wilson (1995) include the hedge "almost invariably" because of situations in which the communicator has at his disposal a very limited range of stimuli with which to communicate. When this happens, there may be no stimulus that has {I2} as its most accessible interpretation. They maintain, however, that natural languages are not limited in this way.

15. Here's an example. Suppose Joe wishes to communicate the set of assumptions {A} by using the sentence S in circumstances C. Joe realizes that, given his audience's initial assumption-set, {A} is not very accessible in C. Indeed, let us assume that, in C, {A} is the third most accessible set of assumptions which is relevant enough to warrant processing the utterance. That is, before getting to {A}, the hearer will recover two other (more accessible) sets of assumptions, both of which are relevant enough to warrant the effort expended. Sperber and Wilson maintain that if Joe uses S in C to make {A} manifest, he will violate the second part of the presumption of optimal relevance. His utterance will not be the most relevant stimulus for making {A} manifest in C, because, "almost inevitably," there exists some sentence S' such that, given C, {A} would be the first interpretation of an utterance of S' consistent with the presumption of optimal relevance. Hence, in C, an utterance of S' is a more relevant stimulus than an utterance of S, because an utterance of S' does not require the hearer to access two prior sets of assumptions that are relevant enough.

BIBLIOGRAPHY

Abbott, J. C. (1969) *Sets, Lattices, and Boolean Algebras*. Boston: Allyn and Bacon.

Abraham, W. (1975) Some semantic properties of some conjunctions. In S. P. Corder and E. Roulet (eds.), *Some Implications of Linguistic Theory for Applied Linguistics*. Brussels: Aimav and Didler, 7–31.

Ajdukiewicz, K. (1967) Die syntakitsche Konexität. In S. McCall (ed.), *Polish Logic*. Oxford: Oxford University Press, 207–231. Part I translated as On syntactical coherence, *Review of Metaphysics* (1967) 20: 635–647. Original work published 1935.

Akmajian, A., and A. Lehrer (1976) NP-like quantifiers and the problem of determining the head of an NP. *Linguistic Analysis* 2: 395–413.

Akmajian, A., R. A. Demers, and R. M. Harnish (1984) *Linguistics: An Introduction to Language and Communication*, rev. ed. Cambridge, Mass.: MIT Press.

Allan, K. (1986) *Linguistic Meaning*, vol. 1. London: Routledge and Kegan Paul.

Allen, J. (1984) Towards a general theory of action and time. *Artificial Intelligence* 23: 123–154.

Alston, W. P. (1963) The quest for meanings. *Mind* 72: 79–87.

——— (1964) *Philosophy of Language*. Foundations of Philosophy Series. Englewood Cliffs, N.J.: Prentice Hall.

Amsler, R. A. (1989) Research toward the development of a lexical knowledge base for natural language processing. In *Proceedings of the 12th Annual International ACM SIGIR Conference on Research and Development in Information Retrieval*. Cambridge, Mass.: ACM Press, 242–249.

Anderson, S., and P. Kiparsky (eds.) (1973) *A Festschrift for Morris Halle*. New York: Holt, Rinehart and Winston.

Anick, P., and J. Pustejovsky (1990) An application of lexical semantics to knowledge acquisition from corpora. In *Proceedings, 13th International Conference on Computational Linguistics*. Helsinki: Helsinki University Press International Committee on Computational Linguistics, 2: 7–12.

Åqvist, L. (1972) *Performatives and Verifiability by the Use of Language*. Filosofiska Studier. Uppsala: Uppsala University.

——— (1973) Modal logic with subjunctive conditionals and dispositional predicates. *Journal of Philosophical Logic* 2: 1–76.

——— (1976) Formal semantics for verb tenses as analysed by Reichenbach. In T. A. van Dijk (ed.), *Pragmatics of Language and Literature*. Amsterdam: North-Holland, 229–236.

Åqvist, L., and F. Guenthner (1978) Fundamentals of a theory of verb aspect and events within the setting of an improved tense. In F. Guenthner and C. Rohrer (eds.), *Studies in Formal Semantics*. Amsterdam: North-Holland, 201–221.

Aronoff, M. (1970) *Word Formation in Generative Grammar*. Linguistic Inquiry Monograph 1. Cambridge, Mass.: MIT Press.

Asher, N., and Lascarides, A. (1995) Lexical disambiguation in a discourse context. *Journal of Semantics* 12: 69–108.

Atkins, B. T. (1987) Semantic ID tags: corpus evidence for dictionary senses. In *Proceedings, 3rd Annual Conference at University of Waterloo*. Waterloo: Center for the New OED.

Atkins, B. T., J. Kegl, and B. Levin (1988) Anatomy of a verb entry: from linguistic theory to lexicographic practice. *International Journal of Lexicography* 1: 84–126.

Atlas, J. D. (1984) Grammatical non-specification: the mistaken disjunction theory. *Linguistics and Philosophy* 7(4): 433–443.

Austen, J. (1957) *Emma*. Boston: Houghton Mifflin (Riverside Edition). Originally published 1816.

—— (1993) *Northhanger Abbey*. Ware, Hert: Wordsworth Classics). Originally published 1818.

Austin, J. L. (1961) Performative utterances. *Philosophical Papers*. Oxford: Oxford University Press, 1961.

—— (1962) *How to Do Things with Words*. Oxford: Clarendon Press.

—— (1971) A plea for excuses. *Philosophical Papers*. Oxford: Oxford University Press. Originally published 1950.

Avramides, A. (1989) *Meaning and Mind*. Cambridge, Mass.: MIT Press.

Bach, E. (1986a) Natural language metaphysics. In R. Barcan-Marcus, G. Dorn, and P. Weingartner (eds.), *Logic, Methodology, and Philosophy of Science*. Amsterdam: North-Holland, 573–595.

—— (1986b) The algebra of events. *Linguistics and Philosophy* 9: 5–16.

—— (1989) *Informal Lectures on Formal Semantics*. Albany: State University of New York Press.

—— (1994) Conversational impliciture. *Mind and Language* 9: 124–162.

—— (1997) The semantics/pragmatics distinction: what it is and why it matters. Special Issue on Pragmatics. *Linguistische Berichte* 8: 33–50. Reprinted in K. Turner (ed.), *The Semantics/Pragmatics Interface from Different Points of View,* Current Research in the Semantics-Pragmatics Interface 1. (Amsterdam: Elsevier 1999), 65–84.

—— (2000) Quantification, qualification and context: a reply to Stanley and Szabo. *Mind and Language* 15: 262–283.

Baker, C. L. (1978) *Introduction to Generative-Transformational Syntax*. Englewood Cliffs, N.J.: Prentice Hall.

—— (1989) (rev. ed. 1995) *English Syntax*. Cambridge, Mass.: MIT Press.

Ballmer, T. (1972) Einführung und Kontrolle von Diskurswelten. In D. Wunderlich (ed.), *Linguistische Pragmatik*. Frankfurt a. M.: Athenaum.

—— (1978) *Logical Grammar: With Special Considerations of Topics in Context Change*. Amsterdam: North-Holland.

Bar-Hillel, Y. (1953) A quasi-arithmetical notation for syntactic description. *Language* 29: 47–58. Reprinted in Y. Bar-Hillel (ed.), *Language and Information* (Reading, Mass.: Addison-Wesley, 1964), 61–74.

—— (1954a) Indexical expressions. *Mind* 63: 689–690.

—— (1954b) Logical syntax and semantics. *Language* 30: 230–237.

—— (ed.) (1964) *Language and Information*. Reading, Mass.: Addison-Wesley.

Bar-Hillel, Y., and E. Beth (1963) In P. A. Schilpp (ed.), *The Philosophy of Rudolph Carnap*. La Salle, Ill.: Open Court.

Barnard, R. (1983) *Death of an Old Goat*. New York: Penguin Books. Reprinted Penguin Editions. Originally published 1974.

—— (1986) *Death in a Cold Climate*. New York: Dell. Originally published 1980.

Baron-Cohen, S. (1995) *Mindblindness: An Essay on Autism and Theory of Mind*. Cambridge, Mass.: MIT Press.

Barsalou, L. W. (1983) Ad hoc categories. *Memory and Cognition* 11: 211–227.

—— (1996) Perceptual symbol systems. Unpublished manuscript, University of Chicago.

Barss, A. (1990) Optional movement, absorption, and the interpretation of WH-in-situ. Paper presented at NELS 21, Université du Québec à Montréal. Amherst, Mass.: Graduate Linguistics Society Association.

Barton, E. (1990) *Nonsentential Constituents*. Philadelphia: John Benjamins.

—— (1991) Nonsentential constituents and theories of phrase structure. In K. Leffel and D. Bouchard (eds.), *Views on Phrase Structure*. Dordrecht: Kluwer.

Bartsch, R. (1976) Syntax and semantics of relative clauses. In J. Groenendijk and M. Stokhof (eds.), *Proceedings of the Amsterdam Colloquium on Montague Grammar and Related Topics*. Amsterdam Papers in Formal Grammar I. Amsterdam: University of Amsterdam, Centrale Interfaculteit, 1–24.

—— (1979) The syntax and semantics of subordinate clause constructions and pronominal reference. In F. Heny and H. S. Schnelle (eds.), *Selections from the Third Groningen Round Table*. Syntax and Semantics 10. New York: Academic Press, 23–60.

Bartsch, R., and T. Vennemann (1972) *Semantic Structures*. Frankfurt a. M.: Athenaum.

Barwise, J. (1978) Monotone quantifiers and admissible sets. In J. E. Fenstad, R. O. Gandy, and G. E. Sacks (eds.), *Generalized Recursion Theory II*. Amsterdam: North-Holland, 1–38.

—— (1979) On branching quantifiers in English. *Journal of Philosophical Logic* 8: 47–80.

—— (1981) Scenes and other situations. *Journal of Philosophy* 78(7): 369–397.

—— (1987) Noun phrases: generalized quantifiers and anaphora. In P. Gardenfors (ed.), *Generalized Quantifiers*. Dordrecht: Reidel, 1–29.

Barwise, J., and R. Cooper (1981) Generalized quantifiers and natural language. *Linguistics and Philosophy* 4(2): 159–219. [Chapter 23 in this volume.]

Barwise, J., and J. Etchemendy (1987) *The Liar: An Essay on Truth and Circularity*. New York: Oxford University Press.

Barwise, J., and J. Perry (1981) Situations and attitudes. *Journal of Philosophy* 78: 668–691. [Chapter 15 in this volume.]

—— (1983) *Situations and Attitudes*. Cambridge, Mass.: MIT Press.

Bäuerle, R., U. Egli, and A. von Stechow (eds.) (1979) *Semantics from Different Points of View*. Berlin: Springer-Verlag.

Bäuerle, R., C. Schwarze, and A. von Stechow (eds.) (1983) *Meaning, Use, and Interpretation of Language*. Berlin: Walter de Gruyter.

Beckwith, R., C. Fellbaum, D. Gross, and G. Miller (1989) WordNet: a lexical database organized on psycholinguistic principles. In *Proceedings, 1st International Workshop on Lexical Acquisition*. Detroit: International Joint Conferences on Artificial Intelligence.

Bellert, I. (1970) *On the Logico-Semantic Structure of Utterances*. Wroclaw, Poland: Ossolineum.

—— (1972) Sets of implications as the interpretive component of a grammar. In F. Kiefer and N. Ruwet (eds.), *Generative Grammar in Europe*. Dordrecht: Reidel.

—— (1977) On semantic and distributional properties of sentential adverbs. *Linguistic Inquiry* 8: 337–350. [Chapter 28 in this volume.]

Bellert, I., and Z. Saloni (1973) On the description of lexical entries for verbs. *International Journal of Slavic Linguistics and Poetics* 16: 43–58.

Belnap, N. (1963) *An Analysis of Questions: Preliminary Report*. Technical Memorandum 7 1287 1000/00. Santa Monica, Calif.: System Development Corporation.

—— (1969) Questions: their presuppositions, and how they can fail to arise. In K. Lambert (ed.), *The Logical Way of Doing Things*. New Haven, Conn.: Yale University Press, 23–38.

—— (1970) Conditional assertion and restricted quantification. *Noûs* 4: 1–12.

—— (1982) Questions and answers in Montague grammar. In S. Peters and E. Saarinen (eds.), *Processes, Beliefs, and Questions*. Dordrecht: Reidel, 165–198.

Belnap, N., and M. Green (1994) Indeterminism and the thin red line. *Philosophical Perspectives* 8: 65–91.

Belnap, N., and M. Perloff (1992) The way of the agent. *Studia Logica* 51: 463–484.

Belnap, N., and T. Steel (1976) *The Logic of Questions and Answers*. New Haven, Conn.: Yale University Press.

Benacerraf, P. (1965) What numbers could not be. *Philosophical Review* 74: 47–73.

Bennett, D. C. (1975) *Spatial and Temporal Uses of English Prepositions: An Essay in Stratificational Semantics*. London: Longman.

Bennett, M. (1979) Mass nouns and mass terms in Montague grammar. In S. Davis and M. Mithun (eds.), *Linguistics, Philosophy and Montague Grammar*. Austin: University of Texas Press, 263–285.

Berkeley, G. (1713) *Three Dialogues between Hylas and Philonous*. Reprinted in T. V. Smith and M. Grene (eds.), *From Descartes to Kant: Readings in the Philosophy of the Renaissance and Enlightenment*. Chicago: Chicago University Press, 1940, 527–617.

Berlin, B., and P. Kay (1969) *Basic Color Terms: Their Universality and Evolution*. Berkeley: University of California Press.

Berman, S. (1989) The analysis of quantificational variability in indirect questions. Unpublished manuscript, University of Massachusetts–Amherst.

Bigelow, J. C. (1975a) Contexts and quotation I. *Linguistische Berichte* 38: 1–21.

——— (1975b) Contexts and quotation II. *Linguistische Berichte* 39: 1–21.

Black, M. (1952) *Critical Thinking: An Introduction to Logic and Scientific Method*. Englewood Cliffs, N.J.: Prentice Hall.

Blakemore, C., and G. F. Cooper (1970) Development of the brain depends on the visual environment. *Nature* 228: 447–448.

Bloom, L. (1974) Talking, understanding, and thinking. In R. L. Schiefelbusch and L. L. Lloyd (eds.), *Language Perspectives: Acquisition, Retardation, and Intervention*. Baltimore: University Park Press, 285–312.

——— (1991) Representation and expression. In N. Krasnegor, D. Rumbaugh, R. Achiefelbusch, and M. Studdert-Kennedy (eds.), *Biological and Behavioral Determinants for Language Development*. Hillsdale, N.J.: Lawrence Erlbaum Associates, 117–140.

Bloomfield, L. (1933) *Language*. New York: H. Holt.

Bobrow, D. G., and T. Winograd (1977) An overview of KRL, a knowledge representation language. *Cognitive Science* 1: 3–46.

Boettcher, W., and H. Sitta (1972) *Zusammengesetzter Satz und equivalente Strukturen*. Deutsche Grammatik III. Frankfurt a. M.: Athenaum.

Boguraev, B., and T. Briscoe (eds.) (1988) *Computational Lexicography for Natural Language Processing*. Harlow: Longman.

Boguraev, B., and J. Pustejovsky (1990) Lexical ambiguity and the role of knowledge representation in lexicon design. In *Proceeding of the 13th International Conference on Computational Linguistics*. Helsinki.

——— (eds.) (1996) *Corpus Processing for Lexical Acquisition*. Cambridge, Mass.: MIT Press.

Bolinger, D. (1965) The atomization of meaning. *Language* 41: 555–573.

——— (1967) Adjectives in English. *Lingua* 18: 1–34.

Bouton, L. (1969) Identity constraints on the do-so rule. *Papers in Linguistics* 1: 231–247.

Brachman, R. J. (1979) On the epistemological status of semantic networks. In N. Findler (ed.), *Associative Networks: Representation and Use of Knowledge by Computer*. New York: Academic Press, 3–50.

Brachman, R. J., and J. Schmolze (1985) An overview of the KL-ONE knowledge representation system. *Cognitive Science* 9: 171–216.

Brame, M. K. (1976) *Conjectures and Refutations in Syntax and Semantics*. Amsterdam: North-Holland.

——— (1978) The base hypothesis and the spelling prohibition. *Linguistic Analysis* 4: 1–30.

——— (1979) A note on COMP S grammar vs. sentence grammar. *Linguistic Analysis* 5: 383–386.

Breheny, R. (1999) Context dependence and procedural meaning: the semantics of definites. Ph.D. diss., University of London.

Bresnan, J. (1978) A realistic transformational grammar. In M. Halle, J. Bresnan, and G. A. Miller (eds.), *Linguistic Theory and Psychological Reality*. Cambridge, Mass.: MIT Press, 1–59.

——— (ed.) (1982) *The Mental Representation of Grammatical Relations*. Cambridge, Mass.: MIT Press.

Briscoe, E., A. Copestake, and B. Boguraev (1990) Enjoy the paper: lexical semantics via lexicology. In *Proceedings of the 13th International Conference on Computational Linguistics (COLING-90)*. Helsinki: Helsinki University Press International Committee on Computational Linguistics, 42–47.

Bromberger, S. (1966) Questions. *Journal of Philosophy* 63: 597–606.

Bronkhorst, J. (1998) Les éléments linguistiques porteurs de sens dans la tradition grammaticale du sanskrit. *Histoire Épistemologie Langage* 20(1): 29–38.

——— (1992) Pāṇini's view of meaning and its western counterpart. In M. Stamenov (ed.), *Current Advances in Semantic Theory*. Amsterdam Studies in the Theory and History of Linguistics Science 73. Amsterdam: John Benjamins, 455–464.

Brooke, C. F. T., and N. B. Paradise (1933) *English Drama 1580–1642*. Boston: Heath.

Brough, J. (1951) Theories of general linguistics in the Sanskrit grammarians. *Transactions of the Philological Society* 49: 27–46.

Brown, C. H. (1974) *Wittgensteinian Linguistics*. The Hague: Mouton.

Brunot, F. (1899) *Précis de grammaire historique de la langue française*. Paris: Masson.

Bunt, H. C. (1979) Ensembles and the formal semantic properties of mass terms. In F. J. Pelletier (ed.), *Mass Terms: Philosophical Problems*. Synthèse Language Library 6. Dordrecht: Reidel, 249–278.

———— (1981) The formal semantics of mass terms. Ph.D. diss., University of Amsterdam.

———— (1985) *Mass Terms and Model-Theoretical Semantics*. Cambridge Studies in Linguistics 42. Cambridge: Cambridge University Press.

Burge, T. (1971) Truth and some referential devices. Ph.D. diss., Princeton University.

———— (1973) Reference and proper names. *Journal of Philosophy* 70: 425–439. [Chapter 20 in this volume.]

———— (1977a) Kaplan, Quine, and suspended belief. *Philosophical Studies* 31: 197–203.

———— (1977b) Belief *De Re. Journal of Philosophy* 74: 338–362.

———— (1979) Individualism and the mental. *Midwest Studies in Philosophy* 4: 73–121.

———— (1982) Other bodies. In A. Woodfield (ed.), *Thought and Object: Essays on Intentionality*. Oxford: Oxford University Press, 97–120.

Burton-Roberts, N. (1994) Ambiguity, sentence, and utterance: a representational approach. *Transactions of the Philological Society* 92: 179–212.

Cardelli, L., and P. Wegner (1985) On understanding types, data abstraction, and polymorphism. *ACM Computing Surveys* 17(4): 471–522.

Carlson, G. (1977a) Reference to kinds in English. Ph.D. diss., University of Massachusetts–Amherst.

———— (1977b) A unified analysis of the English bare plural. *Linguistics and Philosophy* 1: 413–457.

———— (1980) *Reference to Kinds in English*. New York: Garland. Reprint with revisions of Carlson (1977a).

Carlson, G., H. Kyburg, and R. Loui (eds.) (1989) *Defeasible Reasoning and Knowledge Representation*. Studies in Cognitive Systems 5. Dordrecht: Reidel.

Carlson, L. (1980) Plural quantification. Unpublished manuscript, MIT.

Carnap, R. (1937) *The Logical Syntax of Language*. London: Routledge and Kegan Paul. Originally published 1934.

———— (1944) *Introduction to Semantics*. Cambridge, Mass.: Harvard University Press.

———— (1955) Meaning and synonymy in natural languages. *Philosophical Studies* 7: 33–47.

———— (1956) *Meaning and Necessity*. Chicago: University of Chicago Press. Originally published 1947.

———— (1958) *Introduction to Symbolic Logic*. New York: Dover.

———— (1963) Replies and Systematic Expositions. In P. Schlipp (ed.), *The Philosophy of Rudolf Carnap*. La Salle, Ill.: Open Court, 859–1016.

Carston, R. (1988) Implicature, explicature and truth—theoretic semantics. In R. Kempson (ed.), *Mental Representations: The Interface between Language and Reality*. Cambridge: Cambridge University Press, 155–181. Reprinted in S. Davis (ed.), *Pragmatics: A Reader* (Oxford: Oxford University Press, 1991), 33–51.

———— (1997) Enrichment and loosening: complementary processes in deriving the proposition expressed? *Linguistische Berichte* 8: 103–127.

———— (1998) Pragmatics and the explicit/implicit distinction. Ph.D. diss., University of London.

———— (1999) The semantics/pragmatics distinction: a view from relevance theory. In K. Turner (ed.), *The Semantics/Pragmatics Interface from Different Points of View*. CRiSPI 1. Amsterdam: Elsevier, 85–125.

———— (2002) *Thoughts and Utterances: The Pragmatics of Explicit Communication*. Oxford: Blackwell.

———— (2004) Relevance theory and the saying/implicating distinction. In L. Horn and G. Ward (eds.), *The Handbook of Pragmatics*. Oxford: Blackwell, 633–656.

Cartwright, H. (1975a) Some remarks about mass nouns and plurality. *Synthèse* 31: 395–410. Reprinted in F. J. Pelletier (ed.), *Mass Terms: Philosophical Problems*. Synthèse Language Library 6 (Dordrecht: Reidel, 1979), 15–30.

———— (1975b) Amounts and measures of amounts. *Noûs* 9: 143–163. Reprinted in F. J. Pelletier (ed.), *Mass Terms: Philosophical Problems*. Synthèse Language Library 6 (Dordrecht: Reidel, 1979), 179–198.

Castañeda, H.-N. (1989) *Thinking, Language, and Experience*. Minneapolis: University of Minnesota Press.

Catlin, J.-C., and J. Catlin (1972) Intentionality: a source of ambiguity in English? *Linguistic Inquiry* 3: 504–508.

Chao, Y. R. (1968) *Language and Symbolic Systems*. Cambridge: Cambridge University Press.

Charniak, E., and R. Goldman (1988) A logic for semantic interpretation. In *Proceedings of the 26th Annual Meeting of the Association for Computational Linguistics*. Buffalo, N.Y.: Association for Computational Linguistics.

Chastain, C. (1975) *Reference and Context*. Minnesota Studies in the Philosophy of Science 7. Minneapolis: University of Minnesota Press, 194–269.

Cheng, C. Y. (1973) Response to Moravscik. In J. Hintikka, J. M. E. Moravcsk, and P. Suppes (eds.), *Approaches to Natural Language: Proceedings of the 1970 Stanford Workshop on Grammar*. Dordrecht: Reidel, 286–288.

Chierchia, G. (1988) Dynamic generalized quantifiers and donkey anaphora. In M. Krifka (ed.), *Genericity in Natural Language*. Tübingen: Seminar für Natürlich-Sprachliche Systeme, University of Tübingen, 53–89.

——— (1989) Structured meanings, thematic roles, and control. In G. Chierchia, B. Partee, and R. Turner (eds.), *Properties Types, and Meaning*, vol. 2. Dordrecht: Kluwer, 131–166.

——— (1990) Anaphora and dynamic logic. In J. Groenendijk, M. Stokhof, G. Chierchia, and P. Dekker (eds.), *Quantifiers and Anaphora II*. Edinburgh: Centre for Cognitive Science.

——— (1991) Functional WH and weak crossover. In *Proceedings of the Tenth West Coast Conference on Formal Linguistics*. Stanford, Calif.: Stanford University, Stanford Linguistics Association, 75–91.

Chierchia G., B. Partee, and R. Turner (eds.) (1989) *Properties, Types, and Meaning*, vol. 2. Dordrecht: Kluwer.

Chihara, C. (1975) Davidson's extensional theory of meaning. *Philosophical Studies* 28: 1–15.

Chisholm, R. (1964a) The descriptive element in the concept of action. *Journal of Philosophy* 61, no. 20: 613–625.

——— (1964b) The ethics of requirement. *American Philosophical Quarterly* 1, no. 2: 147–153.

Chomsky, N. (1955) *The Logical Structure of Linguistic Theory*. Unpublished manuscript. Published as Chomsky (1975).

——— (1957) *Syntactic Structures*. The Hague: Mouton.

——— (1963) Formal properties of grammars. In R. D. Luce, R. Bush, and E. Galanter (eds), *Handbook of Mathematical Psychology*. New York: Wiley, 2:323–418.

——— (1965) *Aspects of the Theory of Syntax*. Cambridge, Mass.: MIT Press.

——— (1966) Topics in the theory of generative grammar. In T. A. Sebeok (ed.), *Current Trends in Linguistics,* vol. 3. The Hague: Mouton..

——— (1967) Recent contributions to the theory of innate ideas. *Synthèse* 17: 2–11.

——— (1973) Conditions on transformations. In S. Anderson and P. Kiparsky (eds.), *A Festschrift for Morris Halle*. New York: Holt, Rinehart and Winston.

——— (1974) Questions of form and interpretation. *Montreal Working Papers in Linguistics* 3: 1–42.

——— (1975) *The Logical Structure of Linguistic Theory*. Chicago: University of Chicago Press.

——— (1976a) *Reflections on Language*. London: Temple Smith/New York: Pantheon.

——— (1976b) Conditions on rules of grammar. *Linguistic Analysis* 2: 303–351.

——— (1977a) *Essays on Form and Interpretation*. New York: North-Holland.

——— (1977b) On *Wh*-movement. In P. W. Culicover, T. Wasow, and A. Akmajian (eds.), *Formal Syntax*. New York: Academic Press, 71–132.

——— (1979) Pisa workshop lectures. Transcribed by Jean-Yves Pollock and Hans Obenauer. Later published as Chomsky (1981).

——— (1980) On Binding. *Linguistic Inquiry* 11: 1–46.

——— (1981) *Lectures of Government and Binding: The Pisa Lectures*. Dordrecht: Foris. 2nd ed. (rev.) (1982). 7th ed. (Berlin: Mouton de Gruyer, 1993).

——— (1982) *Some Concepts and Consequences of the Theory of Government and Binding*. Cambridge, Mass.: MIT Press.

——— (1986a) *Barriers*. Cambridge, Mass.: MIT Press.

——— (1986b) *Knowledge of Language: Its Nature, Origin and Use*. New York: Praeger.

——— (1993) *Language and Thought*. Wakefield, R.I.: Moyer Bell.

—— (2000) *New Horizons in the Study of Language and Mind*. Cambridge: Cambridge University Press.

Chomsky, N., and M. Halle (1968) *The Sound Pattern of English*. New York: Harper and Row.

Church, A. (1941) *The Calculi of Lamda Conversion*. Princeton, N.J.: Princeton University Press.

—— (1951) A formulation of the logic of sense and denotation. In P. Henle, H. M. Kallen, and S. K. Langer (eds.), *Structure, Method and Meaning: Essays in Honor of H. M. Sheffer*. New York: Liberal Arts Press, 3–24.

—— (1956) *Introduction to Mathematical Logic*. Princeton, N.J.: Princeton University Press.

Cinque, G. (1990) *Types of Ā-Dependencies*. Cambridge, Mass: MIT Press.

Clark, H. (1973) Space, time, semantics and the child. In Y. T. Moore (ed.), *Cognitive Development: The Acquisition of Language*. New York: Academic Press, 27–63.

—— (1976) *Semantics and Comprehension*. The Hague: Mouton.

—— (1996) *Using Language*. Cambridge: Cambridge University Press.

Clark, H., and E. Clark (1979) When nouns surface as verbs. *Language* 55: 767–811.

Clark, H., and R. J. Gerrig (1983) Understanding old words with new meanings. *Journal of Verbal Learning and Verbal Behavior* 22: 591–608.

Clark, R. (1970) Concerning the logic of predicate modifiers. *Noûs* 4: 311–335.

Cocchiarella, N. (1997) Formally oriented work in the philosophy of language. In J. Canfield (ed.), *Philosophy of Meaning, Knowledge and Value in the 20th Century*. New York: Routledge, 39–75.

Cohen, J. L. (1971) Some remarks on Grice's views about the logical particles of natural language. In Y. Bar Hillel (ed.), *Pragmatics of Natural Languages*. Dordrecht: Reidel, 50–68.

Collins, A., and M. Quillian (1969) Retrieval time from semantic memory. *Journal of Verbal Learning and Verbal Behavior* 9: 240–247.

Collins, C. (1992) A note on quantifying into questions and functional readings. Unpublished manuscript, MIT.

Cooper, R. H. (1975) Montague's semantic theory and transformational syntax. Ph.D. diss., University of Massachusetts–Amherst.

—— (1978) *A Fragment of English with Questions and Relative Clauses*. Madison: University of Wisconsin.

—— (1979) The interpretation of pronouns. In F. Heny and H. S. Schnelle (eds.), *Selections from the Third Groningen Round Table*. Syntax and Semantics 10. New York: Academic Press, 61–92.

—— (1983) *Quantification and Syntactic Theory*. Dordrecht: Reidel, 61–92.

Cooper, R., and T. Parsons (1976) Montague grammar, generative semantics and interpretative semantics. In B. H. Partee (ed.), *Montague Grammar*. New York: Academic Press.

Copestake, A., and T. Briscoe (1991) Lexical operations in a unification-based framework. In J. Pustejovsky and S. Bergler (eds.), *Lexical Semantics and Knowledge Representation*. First SIGLEX Workshop. Berkeley, Calif.: Springer, 101–119.

—— (1995) Semi-productive polysemy and sense extension. *Journal of Semantics* 12: 15–67.

Copi, I. (1982) *Introduction to Logic*. 6th ed. New York: Macmillan. Originally published 1953.

Cornwell, P. D. (1992) *All That Remains*. New York: Avon.

Coulson, S. (1995) Analogic and metaphoric mapping in blended spaces. *Center for Research in Language Newsletter* 9(1): 2–12.

—— (1997) Semantic leaps: frame-shifting and conceptual blending. Ph.D. diss., University of California–San Diego.

Creelman, M. B. (1966) *The Experimental Investigation of Meaning: A Review of the Literature*. New York: Springer.

Cresswell, M. J. (1973) *Logic and Languages*. London: Methuen.

—— (1975a) Hyperintensional logic. *Studia Logica* 34: 25–38.

—— (1975b) Semantic deviance. *Linguistische Berichte* 35: 1–19.

—— (1976) Categorical languages. Paper presented at the Conference on the History of Logic, Cracow, Poland.

—— (1977) Interval semantics and logical words. *On the Logical Analysis of Tense and Aspect*. Tübingen: Günter Narr.

—— (1978a) Prepositions and points of view. *Linguistics and Philosophy* 2: 1–42. [Chapter 27 in this volume.]

——— (1978b) Semantic competence. In M. Guenthner-Reutter and F. Guenthner (eds.), *Meaning and Translation: Philosophical and Linguistic Approaches*. London: Duckworth, 9–43.

——— (1979) Adverbs of space and time. In F. Guenthner and S. J. Schmidt (eds.), *Formal Semantics and Pragmatics for Natural Language*. Dordrecht: Reidel, 171–200.

——— (1988) *Semantical Essays: Possible Worlds and Their Rivals*. Studies in Linguistics and Philosophy 36. Dordrecht: Kluwer.

Croft, W. (1991) *Categories and Relations in Syntax: The Clause-Level Organization of Information*. Chicago: University of Chicago Press.

Cruse, D. A. (1972) A note on English causatives. *Linguistic Inquiry* 3: 520–528.

——— (1986) *Lexical Semantics*. Cambridge: Cambridge University Press.

Culicover, P. W., T. Wasow, and A. Akmajian (eds.) (1977) *Formal Syntax*. New York: Academic Press.

Curtiss, S. (1989) The independence and task specificity of language. In A. Bornstein and J. Bruner (eds.), *Interaction in Human Development*. Hillsdale, N.J.: Lawrence Erlbaum, 105–137.

Cutrer, M. (1994) *Time and Tense in Narratives and Everyday Language*. Ph.D. diss., University of California–San Diego.

Dalrymple, M. (1991) Against reconstruction in ellipsis. Unpublished manuscript, Center for the Study of Language and Information, Stanford University.

Dascal, M. (1976) Conversational relevance. Working paper for the Colloquium on Meaning and Use, Jerusalem, Israel.

Davidson, D. (1963) Actions, reasons and causes. *Journal of Philosophy* 60: 685–700.

——— (1965) Theories of meaning and learnable languages. In Y. Bar-Hillel (ed.), *Logic, Methodology, and the Philosophy of Science*. Amsterdam: North-Holland, 383–394.

——— (1967) Truth and meaning. *Synthèse* 17: 304–323. [Chapter 12 in this volume.]

——— (1968) The logical form of action sentences. In N. Rescher (ed.), *The Logic of Decision and Action*. Pittsburgh: University of Pittsburgh Press, 81–95. [Chapter 36 in this volume.]

——— (1970) Semantics for natural language. In B. Visentini et al. (eds.), *Linguaggi nella società e nella tecnica*. Milan: Edizioni de Communità, 177–188.

——— (1984a) Belief and the basis of meaning. In *Inquiries in Truth and Interpretation*. Oxford: Oxford University Press. Originally published 1974, 141–154.

——— (1984b) Introduction to *Inquiries in Truth and Interpretation*. Oxford: Oxford University Press, xii–xx.

——— (1984c) Moods and performances. In *Inquiries into Truth and Interpretation*. Oxford: Oxford University Press. First published in A. Margalit (ed.), *Meaning and Use* (Dordrecht: Reidel, 1979), 109–121.

——— (1984d) On saying that. In *Inquiries in Truth and Interpretation*. Oxford: Oxford University Press. Originally published in *Synthèse* 19 (1968–1969): 130–146.

——— (1984e) Radical interpretation. In *Inquiries in Truth and Interpretation*. Oxford: Oxford University Press. Originally published in *Dialectica* 27 (1973): 313–328.

——— (1984f) Reply to Foster. In *Inquiries in Truth and Interpretation*. Oxford: Oxford University Press, 171–179.

——— (1984g) Truth and meaning. In *Inquiries in Truth and Interpretation*. Oxford: Oxford University Press. Originally published 1967, 17–36.

——— (1984h) What metaphors mean. In *Inquiries into Truth and Interpretation*. Oxford: Oxford University Press, 245–264. Originally published in *Critical Inquiry* 5: 31–47.

——— (1986) A nice derangement of epitaphs. In E. Lepore (ed.), *Truth and Interpretation: Perspectives on the Philosophy of Donald Davidson*. Oxford: Basil Blackwell, 156–174. First published in R. Grandy and R. Warner (eds.), *Philosophical Grounds of Rationality* (Oxford: Oxford University Press, 1986), 157–174.

——— (1999a) A reply to Kirk Ludwig. In U. M. Żegliń (ed.), *Donald Davidson, Truth, Meaning, and Knowledge*. New York: Routledge, 46–47.

——— (1999b) A reply to Gabriel Segal. In U. M. Żegliń (ed.), *Donald Davidson, Truth, Meaning, and Knowledge*. New York: Routledge, 57–58.

——— (1999c) General Comments. In U. M. Żegliń (ed.), *Donald Davidson, Truth, Meaning, and Knowledge*. New York: Routledge, 157–160.

Davidson, D., and G. Harman (eds.) (1972) *Semantics of Natural Language*. Dordrecht: Reidel.

Davis, S. (1994) The Grice program and expression meaning. *Philosophical Studies* 75: 293–299.

———— (2002) 'This' and 'that' and *de re* belief. Unpublished manuscript.

Davis, S., and M. Mithun (eds.) (1979) *Linguistics, Philosophy and Montague Grammar*. Austin: University of Texas Press.

Declerck, R. (1979) Aspect and the bounded/unbounded (Telic/Atelic) distinction. *Linguistics* 17: 761–794.

Defoe, D. (1722) *A Journal of the Plague Year*. London: Dent Dutton. (Everyman Edition, 1908.)

Dekker, P. (1990) Dynamic interpretation, flexibility, and monotonicity. In M. Stokhof and L. Torenvliet (eds.), *Proceedings of the Seventh Amsterdam Colloquium*. Amsterdam: ITLI.

Dekker, T. (1933) The shoemaker's holiday. In T. Brooke and N. B. Paradise (eds.), *English Drama, 1580–1642*. Boston: D.C. Heath, 263–293. First published in 1600.

De Morgan, A. (1862) On the syllogism no. IV and on the logic of relations. *Transactions of the Cambridge Philosophical Society* 8: 379–408.

Dennett, D. C. (1987) *The Intentional Stance*. Cambridge, Mass.: MIT Press.

Deshpande, M. (1980) Evolution of syntactic theory in Sanskrit grammar: syntax of the Sanskrit infinitive -tumUN. Ann Arbor, Mich.: Karoma Publishers.

Dever, J. (1999) Compositionality as methodology. *Linguistics and Philosophy* 22: 311–326.

Devitt, M. (1996) Coming to our Senses: A Naturalistic Program for Semantic Localism. Cambridge: Cambridge University Press.

Devitt, M., and K. Sterelny (1989) *Language and Reality: An Introduction to the Philosophy of Language*. Cambridge, Mass.: MIT Press.

Dexter, C. (1989) *The Wench Is Dead*. London: Macmillan.

Dinsmore, J. (1991) *Partitioned Representations*. Dordrecht: Kluwer.

Di Sciullo, A. M., and E. Williams (1987) *On the Definition of Word*. Linguistic Inquiry Monographs 14. Cambridge, Mass.: MIT Press.

Dixon, R. M. W. (1991) *A New Approach to English Grammar on Semantic Principles*. Oxford: Oxford University Press.

Dodgson, C. L. (1905) *Through the Looking Glass*. New York: Stokes. Originally published 1871.

Doiz-Bienzobas, A. (1995) The preterite and the imperfect in Spanish: past situation vs. past viewpoint. Ph.D. diss., University of California–San Diego.

Donnellan, K. S. (1966) Reference and definite descriptions. *Philosophical Review* 75(3): 281–304. Reprinted in A. P. Martinich (ed.), *The Philosophy of Language* (Oxford: Oxford University Press, 1985), 236–248.

———— (1970) Proper names and identifying descriptions. *Synthèse* 21(3/4): 335–358.

Dougherty, R. C. (1975) A post-aspects linguistic theory: traces, semantics and logical forms. Paper presented at the Canadian Linguistics Association meeting, Edmonton.

Douglas, M. (ed.) (1973) *Rules and Meanings: The Anthropology of Everyday Knowledge*. Harmondsworth: Penguin.

Dowty, D. R. (1975) Toward a semantic theory of word formation in Montague grammar. *Texas Linguistic Forum* 2: 69–96.

———— (1977) Toward a semantic analysis of verb aspect and the English "imperfective" progressive. *Linguistics and Philosophy* 1: 45–77.

———— (1978) Governed transformations as lexical rules in a Montague grammar. *Linguistic Inquiry* 9: 393–426.

———— (1979) *Word Meaning and Montague Grammar*. Dordrecht: Reidel.

———— (1985) On some recent analyses of control. *Linguistics and Philosophy* 8: 1–41.

———— (1989) On the semantic content of the notion "thematic role." In G. Chierchia, B. Partee, and R. Turner (eds.), *Properties, Types, and Meaning*, vol. 2. Dordrecht: Kluwer.

———— (1991) Thematic proto-roles and argument selection. *Language* 67: 547–619.

Dowty, D. R., P. Stanley, and R. E. Wall (1981) *Introduction to Montague: Semantics*. Synthèse Language Library 11. Dordrecht: Reidel.

Dretske, F. (1981) *Knowledge and the Flow of Information*. Cambridge, Mass.: MIT Press.

DuCrot, O. (1972) *Dire et ne pas dire*. Paris: Hermann.

————— (1973) *La Preuve et le dire*. Paris: Maison Mame.

Dummett, M. (1973) *Frege: Philosophy of Language*. London: Duckworth.

————— (1981) *Frege: Philosophy of Language* (2nd ed.). Cambridge, Mass.: Harvard University Press.

Ebneter, T. (1973) *Strukturalismus und Transformationalismus: Einführung in Schulen und Methoden*. Munich: List.

Elugardo, R., and R. Stainton (2001) Logical form and the vernacular. *Mind and Language*. 16(4): 393–424.

————— (forthcoming). Shorthand, Syntactic Ellipsis, and the Pragmatic Determinants of What Is Said: Critical Reflections on Stanley's 'Context and Logical Form.' *Mind and Language*.

Elman, J. L., E. A. Bates, M. H. Johnson, A. Karmiloff-Smith, D. Parisi, and K. Plunkett (1996) Rethinking innateness. *A Connectionist Perspective on Innateness*. Cambridge, Mass.: MIT Press.

Elliott, D. E. (1974) Towards a grammar of exclamations. *Foundations of Language* 11: 231–246.

Engdahl, E. (1986) *Constituent Questions*. Dordrecht: Reidel.

Engel, Howard (1990) *Dead and Buried*. Toronto: Penguin.

Erdmann, K. O. (1900) *Die Bedeutung des Wortes: Aufsätze aus dem Grenzgebiet der Sprachpsychologie und Logik*. Leipzig: Avenarius Reprint of 4th ed. [1925] Darmstadt: Wissenschaftliche Buchgesellschaft 1966). Original work published 1900 (Leipzig: Avenarius).

Esfeld, M. (1999) Holism in philosophy of mind and philosophy of physics. Habilitationsschrift, University of Konstanz.

Evans, G. (1977) Pronouns, quantifiers and relative clauses I and II. *Canadian Journal of Philosophy* 7: 467–536, 777–797.

————— (1980) Pronouns. *Linguistic Inquiry* 11: 337–362. [Chapter 21 in this volume.]

Evans, R., and G. Gazdar (1989) Inference in DATR. In *Proceedings, Fourth European Association for Computational Linguistics Conference*. Manchester, England: Association for Computational Linguistics, 66–71.

————— (1990) *The DATR Papers: February 1990*. Cognitive Science Research Paper 139. Brighton, England: School of Cognitive and Computing Science, University of Sussex.

Fass, D. (1988) *Collative Semantics: A Semantics for Natural Language Processing*. MCCS-99–118. Las Cruces: New Mexico State University, Computing Research Laboratory.

Fauconnier, G. (1984) *Mental Spaces: Aspects of Meaning Construction in Natural Language*. Cambridge, Mass.: MIT Press.

————— (1985) *Mental Spaces*. Cambridge, Mass.: MIT Press.

————— (1994) *Mental Spaces*, rev. ed. New York: Cambridge University Press.

————— (1997) *Mapping in Thought and Language*. Cambridge: Cambridge University Press.

————— (1998) Mental spaces, language modalities, and conceptual integration. In M. Tomasello (ed.), *The New Psychology of Language*. New York: Lawrence Erlbaum, 251–277. [Chapter 17 in this volume.]

Fauconnier, G., and E. Sweetser (1996) *Spaces, Worlds, and Grammar*. Chicago: University of Chicago Press.

Fauconnier, G., and M. Turner (1994) *Conceptual Projection and Middle Spaces*. Tech. Rep. No. 9401. San Diego: University of California, Department of Cognitive Science.

————— (1996) Blending as a central process of Grammar. In A. Goldberg (ed.), *Conceptual Structure, Discourse, and Language*. Stanford: Center for the Study of Language and Information Publications, 113–130.

————— (1998a) Conceptual integration networks. *Cognitive Science*, 22: 133–187.

————— (1998b) Making sense. Unpublished ms.

Fenstad, J. E. (1978) Models for natural language. In J. Hintikka, I. Niiniluoto, and E. Saarinen (eds.), *Essays on Mathematical and Philosophical Logic*. Dordrecht: Reidel.

Field, H. (1977) Logic, meaning and conceptual role. *Journal of Philosophy* 69: 347–409.

————— (1978) Mental representation. *Erkenntnis* 13: 9–61.

Fiengo, R. (1980) *Surface Structure*. Cambridge, Mass.: Harvard University Press.

Fiengo, R., and J. Higginbotham (1979) Opacity in NP. *Linguistic Analysis* 7: 395–421.

Fiengo, R., and H. Lasnik (1973) The logical structure of reciprocal sentences in English. *Foundations on Language* 9: 447–468.

Fillmore, C. (1968) The case for case. In E. Bach and R. Harms (eds.), *Universals in Linguistic Theory*. New York: Holt, Rinehart and Winston.

——— (1972) How to know whether you're coming or going. In K. Hyldgaard-Jensen (ed.), *Linguistik 1971*. Frankfurt a. M.: Athenaum, 369–379.

——— (1976) Pragmatics and the description of discourse. In S. J. Schmidt (ed.), *Pragmatik/Pragmatics II*. Munich: Wilhelm Fink.

——— (1982) Towards a descriptive framework for spatial deixis. In R. Jarvella and W. Klein (eds.), *Speech, Place, and Action*. New York: Wiley, 31–59.

——— (1985) Construction grammar. Unpublished manuscript.

——— (1997) *Santa Cruz Lectures on Deixis, 1971*. Lecture Notes no. 65. Stanford, Calif.: Center for the Study of Language and Information.

Flickinger, D., C. Pollard, and T. Wasow (1985) Structure-sharing in lexical representation. In *Proceedings: 23rd Annual Meeting of the Association for Computational Linguistics*. Chicago, Ill.: Association for Computational Linguistics, 262–276.

Fodor, J. A. (1970) Three reasons for not deriving "kill" from "cause to die." *Linguistic Inquiry* 1: 429–438.

——— (1975) *The Language of Thought*. New York: Thomas Crowell.

——— (1980) Methodological solipsism considered as a research strategy in cognitive psychology. *Behavioral and Brain Sciences* 3: 63–73.

——— (1981) The present state of the innateness controversy. In *Representations: Philosophical Essays in the Foundations of Cognitive Science*. Cambridge, Mass.: MIT Press, 257–316.

——— (1983) *The Modularity of Mind*. Cambridge, Mass.: MIT Press.

——— (1987) *Psychosemantics*. Cambridge, Mass.: MIT Press.

——— (1994) *The Elm and the Expert, Mentalese and Its Semantics: The 1993 Jean Nicod Lectures*. Cambridge, Mass.: MIT Press.

——— (1998) *Concepts*. Oxford: Oxford University Press.

Fodor, J. A., and E. Lepore (1992) *Holism: A Shopper's Guide*. Oxford: Blackwell.

——— (1998) The emptiness of the lexicon: reflections on James Pustejovsky's *The Generative Lexicon*. *Linguistic Inquiry* 29: 269–288.

Fodor, J. A., and Z. Pylyshyn (1988) Connectionism and cognitive architecture: a critical analysis. *Cognition* 28: 3–71.

Fodor, J. A., T. G. Bever, and M. Garett (1974) *The Psychology of Language*. New York: McGraw-Hill.

Fodor, J. A., M. Garrett, E. C. T. Walker, and C. H. Parkes (1980) Against definitions. *Cognition* 8: 263–367.

Fodor, J. D. (1977) *Theories of Meaning in Generative Grammar*. New York: Crowell.

Fodor, J. D., and I. Sag (1982) Referential and quantificational indefinites. *Linguistics and Philosophy* 5: 335–398.

Fodor, J. D., J. A. Fodor, and M. Garrett (1975) The psychological unreality of semantic representations. *Linguistic Inquiry* 6: 515–532.

Follett, W. (1966) *Modern American Usage: A Guide*. New York: Hill and Wang.

Foster, J. A. (1976) Meaning and truth theory. In G. Evans and J. McDowell (eds.), *Truth and Meaning*. Oxford: Oxford University Press, 1–32.

Fowler, H. W. (1937) *Modern English Usage*. Oxford: Clarendon Press.

Freed, A. F. (1979) *The Semantics of English Aspectual Complementation*. Dordrecht: Reidel.

Freeman, D. (1973) Keats's "To Autumn." Poetry as pattern and process. *Language and Style* 11: 3–17.

Freeman, M. (1997) Grounded spaces: deictic self anaphors in the poetry of Emily Dickinson. *Language and Literature* 6(1): 7–28.

Frege, G. (1950) *Die Grundlagen der Arithmetik* [*Foundations of Arithmetic*]. Transl. J. Austin. New York: Bantam Books. Original work published 1884.

——— (1956) The thought: a logical inquiry. *Mind* 65: 289–311.

——— (1963) Compound thoughts. Transl. R. Stoothoff. *Mind* 72: 1–17. Original work published 1923.

——— (1967) The thought: a logical inquiry. Transl. A. M. and M. Quinton. In P. F. Strawson (ed.), *Philosophical Logic*. London: Oxford University Press, 17–38.

——— (1975) On sense and reference. In D. Davidson and G. Harman (eds.), *The Logic of Grammar*. Encino, Calif.: Dickenson. Original work published 1892 as Über Sinn und Bedeutung, *Zeitschrift für Philosophie und philosophische Kritik* 100; transl. as "On Sense and Nominatum" in Copi and

Gould (eds.), *Contemporary Readings in Logical Theory* (New York: Macmillan, 1967); mistransl. as "On Sense and Meaning" in A. P. Martinich (ed.), *The Philosophy of Language* (Oxford: Oxford University Press, 1985), 200–212. Also published in P. Geach and M. Black (eds. and transl.), *Translations from the Philosophical Writings of Gottlob Frege*, 3rd ed. (Totowa: Barnes and Noble, 1988), 56–78.

———— (1977) *Logical Investigations*. New Haven: Yale University Press.

Freidin, R. (1975) The analysis of passives. *Language* 51: 384–405.

Fridman-Mintz, B., and S. Liddell (1998) Sequencing mental spaces in an ASL narrative. In J. P. Koenig (ed.), *Discourse and Cognition: Bridging the Gap*. Stanford, Calif.: Center for the Study of Language and Information, 255–268.

Frisby, John (1980) *Seeing*. Oxford: Oxford University Press.

Gabbay, D., and G. Franz (eds.) (1989) *Handbook of Philosophical Logic*. Vol. 4: *Topics in the Philosophy of Language*. Dordrecht: Reidel.

———— (1978) *Formal Pragmatics for Natural Language*. London: Academic Press.

———— (1979) English as a context-free language. Unpublished manuscript, University of Sussex.

Gamut, L. T. F. (1991) *Logic, Language, and Meaning*. Chicago: University of Chicago Press.

Gazdar, G. (1978) *Formal Pragmatics for Natural Language*. London: Academic Press.

———— (1979) English as a context-free language. Unpublished ms., University of Sussex.

———— (1980) A cross-categorial semantics for coordination. *Linguistics and Philosophy* 3: 407–409. [Chapter 32 in this volume.]

Gazdar, G., E. Klein, G. Pullum, and I. Sag (1985) *Generalized Phrase Structure Grammar*. Cambridge, Mass.: Harvard University Press.

Geach, P. (1956) Good and evil. *Analysis* 17: 33–42. Reprinted in P. R. Foot (ed.), *Theories of Ethics* (Oxford: Oxford University Press, 1967), 64–73.

———— (1962) *Reference and Generality*. Ithaca, N.Y.: Cornell University Press.

———— (1969) Quine's syntactical insights. *Synthèse* 19: 118–129. Reprinted in P. Geach, *Logic Matters* (Oxford: Basil Blackwell, 1972), 115–127.

———— (1970) A program of syntax. *Synthèse* 22: 3–17.

———— (1972a) *Logic Matters*. Oxford: Blackwell.

———— (1972b) *Reference and Generality*. Ithaca, N.Y.: Cornell University Press.

Gilbert, Michael (1976) *The Night of the Twelfth*. London: Arrow. Reprinted New York: Mysterious Press Books, 1988.

Gillon, B. S. (1987) The readings of plural noun phrases in English. *Linguistics and Philosophy* 10: 199–220.

———— (1989) Bare plurals as plural indefinite noun phrases. In G. Carlson, H. Kyburg, and R. Loui (eds.), *Defeasible Reasoning and Knowledge Representation*. Studies in Cognitive Systems 5. Dordrecht: Reidel.

———— (1990a) Plural noun phrases and their readings: a reply to Lasersohn. *Linguistics and Philosophy* 13: 477–485.

———— (1990b) Ambiguity, generality, and indeterminacy tests and definitions. *Synthèse* 85(3): 391–416.

———— (1992) Towards a common semantics for English count and mass nouns. *Linguistics and Philosophy* 15: 597–639. [Chapter 19 in this volume.]

———— (2001) Bhartdrharis rule for unexpressed karakas: the problem of control in classical Sanskrit. In M. Deshpande (ed.), *Indian Linguistic Studies: Festschrift in Honour of George Cardona*. Delhi: Motilal Banarsidass, 93–111.

Gjelsvik, O. (1994) Davidson's use of truth in accounting for meaning. In G. Preyer, F. Siebelt, and A. Ulfig (eds.), *Language, Mind, and Epistemology: On Donald Davidson's Philosophy*. Dordrecht: Kluwer, 21–43.

Gloy, K. (1975) *Sprachnormen I: Linguistische und soziologische Analysen*. Stuttgart: Frommann-Holzboog.

Gloy, K., and G. Presch (eds.) (1976) *Sprachnormen III: Kommunikations Orientierte Linguistik—Sprachdidaktik*. Stuttgart: Frommann-Holzboog.

Goguen, J. A. (1969) The logic of inexact concepts. *Synthèse* 19: 325–373.

Goldman, A. I. (1970) *A Theory of Human Action*. Princeton, N.J.: Princeton University Press.

———— (1976) Discrimination and perceptual knowledge. *Journal of Philosophy* 73: 771–791.

Goodman, N. (1951) *The Structure of Appearance*. Dordrecht: Reidel.

Goodwin W. W. (1930) *Greek Grammar*. Boston: Ginn.

Gordon, D., and G. Lakoff (1971) Conversational postulates. In *Papers from the Seventh Regional Meeting of the Chicago Linguistic Society*. Chicago: Chicago Linguistic Society.

Grafton, Sue (1995) *"L" Is for Lawless*. New York: Henry Holt.

———— (1996) *"M" Is for Malice*. Markham: Henry Holt.

Grandy, R. (1990) Understanding and compositionality. *Philosophical Perspectives* 4: 557–572.

Grice, H. P. (1957) Meaning. *Philosophical Review* 66: 377–388.

———— (1968a) Utterer's meaning, sentence-meaning, and word-meaning. *Foundations of Language* 4: 1–18.

———— (1968b) *The Logic of Conversation*. Working Paper. Berkeley: University of California.

———— (1969) Vacuous names. In D. Davidson and J. Hintikka (eds.), *Words and Objections*. Dordrecht: Reidel, 118–145.

———— (1971) Meaning. In D. Steinberg and L. Jacobovits (eds.), *Semantics: An Interdisciplinary Reader in Philosophy, Linguistics, and Psychology*. Cambridge: Cambridge University Press, 53–59.

———— (1975) Logic and conversation. In P. Cole and J. Morgan (eds.), *Speech Acts*. Syntax and Semantics 3. New York: Academic Press, 41–58. Reprinted in H. P. Grice, *Studies in the Way of Words* (Cambridge, Mass.: Harvard University Press, 1989), 22–40.

———— (1989) *Studies in the Way of Words*. Cambridge, Mass.: Harvard University Press.

Grimm, H., and M. Wintermantel (1975) *Zur Entwicklung von Bedeutungen: Forschungsberichte zur Sprachentwicklung II*. Weinheim: Beltz.

Grinder, J., and P. Postal (1971) Missing antecedents. *Linguistic Inquiry* 2(3): 269–312.

Grimshaw, J. (1979) Complement selection and the lexicon. *Linguistic Inquiry* 10: 279–326.

———— (1990) *Argument Structure*. Cambridge, Mass.: MIT Press.

Groenendijk, J., and M. Stokhof (eds.) (1976) *Proceedings of the Amsterdam Colloquium on Montague Grammar and Related Topics*. Amsterdam Papers in Formal Grammar 1. Amsterdam: University of Amsterdam, Centrale Interfaculteit.

———— (1984) Studies on the semantics of questions and the pragmatics of answers. Ph.D. diss., University of Amsterdam.

———— (1988) Context and information in dynamic semantics. In B. Elsendoorn and H. Bouma (eds.), *Working Models of Human Perception*. New York: Academic Press, 457–488.

———— (1989) Type-shifting rules and the semantics of interrogatives. In G. Chierchia et al. (eds.), *Properties, Types, and Meaning*. Vol. 2: *Semantic Issues*. Dordrecht: Kluwer, 21–68.

———— (1990) Dynamic Montague grammar. In L. Kálmán et al. (eds.), *Proceedings of the Second Symposium on Logic and Language*. Budapest: Akadémiai Kaidó, 3–48.

———— (1991) Dynamic predicate logic. *Linguistics and Philosophy* 14(1): 39–100. [Chapter 14 in this volume.]

Groenendijk, J., T. Janssen, and M. Stokhof (eds.) (1981) *Formal Methods in the Study of Language*. Amsterdam: Mathematical Center. Reprinted in Groenendijk et al. (eds.), *Truth, Interpretation and Information* (Dordrecht: Foris, 1984), 1–41.

———— (1984) *Truth, Interpretation and Information*. Dordrecht: Foris.

Grosz, B. J., C. L. Sidner, and M. E. Pollack (1989) Discourse. In M. Posner (ed.), *Foundations of Cognitive Science*. Cambridge, Mass.: MIT Press, 437–468.

Gruber, J. (1965) *Studies in Lexical Relations*. Ph.D. diss., MIT. Reprinted by Bloomington, IN: Indiana University Linguistics Club. Reprinted in *Lexical Structures in Syntax and Semantics* (Amsterdam: North-Holland, 1976), 1–210.

———— (1976) *Lexical Structures in Syntax and Semantics*. Amsterdam: North-Holland.

Guéron, J. (1978) On the C-Command criterion for coreference. Unpublished manuscript.

Guthrie, W. K. C. (1935) *Orpheus and Greek Religion*. Rev. ed. New York: Norton, 1952.

———— (1981) *Aristotle: An Encounter*. Cambridge: Cambridge University Press.

Haack, R. J. (1978) Davidson on learnable languages. *Mind* 87: 230–249.

Haegeman, L. (1991) *Introduction to Government and Binding Theory*. Oxford: Blackwell.

Hailperin, T. (1957) A theory of restricted quantification I, II. *Journal of Symbolic Logic* 22: 19–25, 113–129. Corrections in 25: 54–56.

Hale, K., and S. J. Keyser (1986) *Some Transitivity Alternations in English*. Lexicon Project Working Papers 7. Cambridge, Mass.: MIT, Center for Cognitive Science.

————— (1987) *A View from the Middle*. Lexicon Project Working Papers 10. Cambridge, Mass.: MIT, Center for Cognitive Science.

Halle, M., J. Bresnan, and G. A. Miller (eds.) (1978) *Linguistic Theory and Psychological Reality*. Cambridge, Mass.: MIT Press.

Hamblin, C. (1973) Questions in Montague English. *Foundations of Language* 10: 41–53. Reprinted in B. Partee (ed.), *Montague Grammar* (New York: Academic Press, 1976), 247–259.

Hankamer, J., and I. Sag (1976) Deep and surface anaphora. *Linguistic Inquiry* 7: 391–426.

Hare, C. (1951) *Methods in Structural Linguistics*. Chicago: University of Chicago Press.

————— (1991a) *Death Is No Sportsman*. New York: Harper Perennial. Originally published 1938.

————— (1991b) *With a Bare Bodkin*. New York: Harper Perennial. Originally published 1946.

Harel, D. (1984) Dynamic logic. In D. Gabbay and F. Guenthner (eds.), *Handbook of Philosophical Logic*, vol. 2. Dordrecht: Reidel.

Harman, G. A. (1972) Deep structure as logical form. In D. Davidson and G. Harman (eds.), *Semantics of Natural Language*. Dordrecht: Reidel, 25–47.

Harris, Z. (1946) From morpheme to utterance. *Language* 22: 161–183.

Haugeland, J. (1987) *Artificial Intelligence: The Very Idea*. Cambridge, Mass.: MIT Press.

Hausser, R. R. (1974) Quantification in extended Montague grammar. Ph.D. diss., University of Texas–Austin.

————— (1976) Problems of pronominalization. Paper presented at the Third Groningen Round Table. Reprinted in F. Heny and H. S. Schnelle (eds.), *Selections from the Third Groningen Round Table*, Syntax and Semantics 10 (New York: Academic Press, 1979).

————— (1979) How do pronouns denote? In F. Heny and H. S. Schnelle (eds.), *Selections from the Third Groningen Round Table*. Syntax and Semantics 10. New York: Academic Press.

Hayes, P. (1979) Native physics manifesto. In D. Mitchie (ed.), *Expert Systems in the Micro-Electronic Age*. Edinburgh: Edinburgh University Press.

Hedenius, I. (1963) Performatives. *Theoria* 29: 1–22.

Heim, I. (1982) The semantics of definite and indefinite noun phrases. Ph.D. diss., University of Massachusetts–Amherst.

————— (1983) File change semantics and the familiarity theory of definiteness. In R. Bäuerle, C. Schwarze, and A. von Stechow (eds.), *Meaning, Use and Interpretation of Language*. Berlin: de Gruyter.

————— (1990) E-type pronouns and donkey anaphora. *Linguistics and Philosophy* 13(2): 137–177.

Heim, I., and A. Kratzer (1998) *Semantics in Generative Grammar*. Oxford: Blackwell.

Heim, I., H. Lasnik, and R. May (1988) Reciprocity and plurality. *Linguistic Inquiry* 22: 63–102.

Hendrix, G. (1975) Partitioned networks for the mathematical modeling of natural language semantics. Ph.D. diss., University of Texas–Austin.

Henkin, L., J. D. Monk, and A. Tarski (1971) *Cylindric Algebras*. Studies in Logic and the Foundations of Mathematics 64. Amsterdam: North-Holland.

Heny, F., and H. S. Schnelle (eds.) (1979) *Selections from the Third Groningen Round Table*. Syntax and Semantics 10. New York: Academic Press.

Heringer, H. J. (ed.) (1974) *Der Regelbegriff in der Praktischen Semantik*. Frankfurt a. M.: Suhrkamp.

Herskovits, A. (1986) *Language and Spatial Cognition*. New York: Cambridge University Press.

Higginbotham, J. (1979) Pronouns and bound variables. In E. Battistella (ed.), *Proceedings of the Ninth Annual Meeting of the North Eastern Linguistic Society*. New York: CUNY Forum. Reprinted in *Linguistic Inquiry* 11: 679–708. [Chapter 22 in this volume.]

————— (1980) Anaphora and GB: some preliminary remarks. In J. T. Jensen (ed.), *Proceedings of NELS 10*. Amherst, Mass.: Graduate Linguistics Society Association, 223–236.

————— (1981) Reciprocal interpretation. *Linguistic Research* 3: 97–117.

————— (1983) LF, binding and nominals. *Linguistic Inquiry* 14: 395–420.

————— (1985) On semantics. *Linguistic Inquiry* 16: 547–593.

————— (1987) On semantics. In E. Lepore (ed.), *New Directions in Semantics*. London: Academic Press, 1–54.

————— (1988) Contexts, models, and meanings: a note on the data of semantics. In R. Kempson (ed.),

Mental Representations: The Interface between Language and Reality. Cambridge: Cambridge University Press, 29–48.

———— (1989) Elucidations of meaning. *Linguistics and Philosophy* 12: 465–517.

———— (1991a) Either/or. In T. Sherer (ed.), *Proceedings of North Eastern Linguistic Society 21.* Amherst, Mass: Graduate Linguistics Society Association, 143–155.

———— (1991b) Interrogatives I. *MIT Working Papers in Linguistics* 15: 47–76.

———— (1993) Interrogatives. In K. Hale and S. J. Keyser (eds.), *The View from Building 20: Essays in Linguistics in Honor of Sylvain Bromberger.* Cambridge, Mass.: MIT Press, 195–227. [Chapter 34 in this volume.]

Higginbotham, J., and R. May (1978) A general theory of crossing coreference. *CUNY Forum: Proceedings of NELS 9.* Amherst, Mass.: Graduate Linguistics Society Association, 328–336.

———— (1981) Crossing, pragmatics, markedness. In A. Belletti, L. Brandi, and L. Rizzi, eds., *Theory of Markedness in Generative Grammar: Proceedings of the Third GLOW Colloquium.* Pisa: Annali della Scuola Normale Superiore, Classe de Lettere e Filosofia, 423–444.

———— (1981) Questions, quantifiers, and crossing. *Linguistic Review* 1: 41–80.

Hill, L. A. (1968) *Prepositions and Adverbial Particles.* Oxford: Oxford University Press.

Hinrichs, E. (1985) A compositional semantics for actionsarten and NP reference in English. Ph.D. diss., Ohio State University.

Hintikka, J. (1969) *Models for Modalities.* Dordrecht: Reidel.

———— (1976) *The Semantics of Questions and the Questions of Semantics.* Acta Philosophica Fennica vol. 28 no. 4. Amsterdam: North-Holland.

Hintikka, J., and L. Carlsson (1978) Conditionals, generic quantifiers and subgames. In E. Saarinen (ed.), *Game Theoretical Semantics.* Dordrecht: Reidel, 179–214.

Hintikka, J., J. Moravscik, and P. Suppes (eds.) (1973) *Approaches to Natural Language.* Dordrecht: Reidel.

Hirst, G. (1987) *Semantic Interpretation and the Resolution of Ambiguity.* Cambridge: Cambridge University Press.

Hobbs, J. (1982) Towards an understanding of coherence in discourse. In W. Lehnert and M. Ringle (eds.), *Strategies for Natural Language Processing.* Hillsdale, N.J.: Lawrence Erlbaum Associates, 223–224.

———— (1987) World knowledge and word meaning. In *Proceedings, Theoretical Issues in Natural Language Processing 3.* Las Cruces, N.M.: New Mexico State University, 20–27.

Hobbs, J., W. Croft, T. Davis, D. Edwards, and K. Law (1987a) Commonsense metaphysics and lexical semantics. *Computational Linguistics* 13: 241–250.

———— (1987b) The TACITUS commonsense knowledge base. Unpublished manuscript, SRI International, Artificial Intelligence Center.

Hobbs, J., M. Stickel, P. Martin, and D. Edwards (1988) Interpretation as abduction. In *Proceedings, 26th Annual Meeting of the Association for Computational Linguistics.* Buffalo, N.Y.: State University of New York–Buffalo.

Hockett, C. (1954) Two models of grammatical description. *Word* 10(2–3): 210–234.

Hodges, W. (1998) Compositionality is not the problem. *Logic and Logical Philosophy* 6: 7–33.

———— (2001) Formal features of compositionality. *Journal of Logic, Language and Information* 10: 7–28.

Hoeksema, J. (1983) Plurality and conjunction. In A. ter Meulen (ed.), *Studies in Modeltheoretic Semantics.* Groningen-Amsterdam Studies in Semantics 1. Dordrecht: Foris, 63–84.

Holder, B. (1997) Blending and your ATM. Unpublished manuscript, University of California–San Diego.

Hörmann, H. (1970) *Psycholinguistics: An Introduction to Research and Theory.* Transl. H. H. Stern. Berlin and New York: Springer Verlag. Original work published *Psychologie der Sprache* (Berlin: Springer, 1967).

Horn, L. (1976) *On the Semantic Properties of Logical Operators in English.* Bloomington: Indiana University Linguistics Club.

———— (1983) In defense of privative ambiguity. *Proceedings of the Berkeley Linguistic Society* 9: 141–156.

———— (1989) *A Natural History of Negation.* Chicago: University of Chicago Press.

Horwich, P. (1998) *Meaning.* Oxford: Clarendon Press.

Hornsby, J. (1986) A note on non-indicatives. *Mind* 95: 92–99.

Hospers, J. (1953) *An Introduction to Philosophical Analysis.* Englewood Cliffs, N. J.: Prentice Hall. 2nd ed. 1967.

Hughes, G. E., and D. G. Londey (1965) *The Elements of Formal Logic*. London: Methuen.

Hutchins, E. (1995) *Cognition in the Wild*. Cambridge, Mass.: MIT Press.

Huumo, T. (1996) A scoping hierarchy of locatives. *Cognitive Linguistics* 7(3): 265–299.

Ingria, R., and J. Pustejovsky (1990) Active objects in syntax, semantics, and parsing. In C. Tenny (ed.), *The MIT Parsing Volume, 1989–1990*. Cambridge, Mass.: MIT Center for Cognitive Science.

Isard, S. (1975) Changing the context. In E. L. Keenan (ed.), *Formal Semantics of Natural Language*. Cambridge: Cambridge University Press.

Isenberg, H. (1971) Überlegungen zur Texttheorie. In J. Ihwe (ed.), *Literaturwissenschaft und Linguistik*, vol. 1. Frankfurt a. M.: Athenaum.

Jackendoff, R. (1972) *Semantic Interpretation in Generative Grammar*. Cambridge, Mass.: MIT Press.

—— (1976) Towards an explanatory semantic representation. *Linguistic* 7: 89–150.

—— (1977) *X Syntax: A Study of Phrase Structure*. Linguistic Inquiry Monograph 2. Cambridge, Mass.: MIT Press.

—— (1983) *Semantic and Cognition*. Cambridge, Mass.: MIT Press.

—— (1985) Multiple subcategorization and the Θ-criterion: the case of climb. *Natural Language and Linguistic Theory* 3: 271–295.

—— (1987) *Consciousness and the Computational Mind*. Cambridge, Mass.: MIT Press.

—— (1989). What is a concept, that a person may grasp it? *Mind and Language* 4(1–2): 68–102. [Chapter 16 in this volume.]

—— (1990) *Semantic Structures*. Cambridge, Mass.: MIT Press.

—— (1991) Part and boundaries. *Cognition* 41: 9–45.

—— (1996) Semantics and cognition. In S. Lappin (ed.), *The Handbook of Contemporary Semantic Theory*. Oxford: Blackwell, 539–560.

—— (1997) *The Architecture of the Language Faculty*. Cambridge, Mass.: MIT Press.

Janssen, T. (1983) Foundations and applications of Montague grammar. Ph.D. diss., University of Amsterdam.

—— (1986) *Foundations and Applications of Montague Grammar*. Amsterdam: Centrum voor Wiskunde en Informatica.

—— (1997) Compositionality. In J. van Benthem and A. ter Meulen (eds.), *Handbook of Logic and Linguistics*. Amsterdam: Elsevier, 417–474.

—— (2001) Frege, contextuality and compositionality. *Journal of Logic, Language and Information* 10: 115–136.

Jenkins, L. (1975) *The English Existential*. Tübingen: Max Niemeyer.

Jennings, R. E. (1994) *The Genealogy of Disjunction*. New York: Oxford University Press.

Jespersen, O. (1909) *A Modern English Grammar on Historical Principles*, vol. 7. London: Allen and Unwin.

—— (1922) *Language: Its Nature, Development and Origin*. London: Allen and Unwin.

—— (1924) *The Philosophy of Grammar*. London: Allen and Unwin/New York: Holt.

Johnson-Laird, P. N. (1989) Mental models. In M. Posner (ed.), *Foundations of Cognitive Science*. Cambridge, Mass.: MIT Press, 469–500.

Kadmon, N. (1987) On unique and non-unique reference and asymmetric quantification. Ph.D. diss., University of Massachusetts–Amherst.

Kalish, D. (1967) Semantics. In P. Edwards (ed.), *The Encyclopedia of Philosophy*. New York: Macmillan, 7: 348–358.

Kamp, H. (1971) Formal properties of 'now.' *Theoria* 37: 227–273.

—— (1975) Two theories about adjectives. In E. Keenan (ed.), *Formal Semantics of Natural Language*. Cambridge: Cambridge University Press, 123–155. [Chapter 26 in this volume.]

—— (1981) A theory of truth and semantic representation. In J. Groenendijk, T. Janssen, and M. Stokhof (eds.), *Formal Methods in the Study of Language*. Amsterdam: Mathematical Centre, 277–322. [Chapter 13 in this volume.] Reprinted in J. Groenendijk, T. Janssen, and M. Stokhof (eds.), *Truth, Interpretation and Information* (Dordrecht: Foris, 1984), 1–41.

—— (1983) Situations in discourse without time or questions. Unpublished manuscript.

—— (1990) Response to Groenendijk and Stockhof. Unpublished manuscript, University of Stuttgart.

Kamp, H., and U. Reyle (1993) *From Discourse to Logic: Introduction to Model Theoretic Semantics of*

Natural Language, Formal Logic, and Discourse Representation Theory. Studies in Linguistics and Philosophy 42. Dordrecht: Kluwer.

Kaplan, D. (1964) *Foundations of Intensional Logic*. Ph.D. diss. Ann Arbor, Mich.: University Microfilms.

—— (1966) Rescher's plurality-quantification and generalized plurality quantification, Abstracts. *Journal of Symbolic Logic* 31: 153–154.

—— (1969) Quantifying in. In D. Davidson and J. Hintikka (eds.), *Words and Objections: Essays on the Work of W. V. Quine*. Dordrecht: Reidel, 206–242. Originally published in *Synthèse* 19 (1991): 178–214. Also reprinted in A. P. Martinich (ed.), *The Philosophy of Language* (Oxford: Oxford University Press, 1985), 349–369.

—— (1972) What is Russell's theory of descriptions? In D. Pears. (ed.), *Bertrand Russell: A Collection of Critical Essays*. New York: Anchor Books, 227–255.

—— (1973) Bob and Carol and Ted and Alice. In J. Hintikka, J. Moravscik, and P. Suppes (eds.), *Approaches to Natural Language*. Dordrecht: Reidel.

—— (1975) How to Russell a Frege-Church. *Journal of Philosophy* 72: 716–729.

—— (1977) Demonstratives. Unpublished manuscript. Published as Kaplan (1989b).

—— (1978a) Dthat. *Syntax and Semantics* 9: 221–243. Reprinted in A. P. Martinich (ed.), *The Philosophy of Language* (Oxford: Oxford University Press, 1985), 315–328.

—— (1978b) On the logic of demonstratives. *Journal of Philosophical Logic* 8: 81–98.

—— (1989a) Afterthoughts. In J. Almog, J. Perry, and H. Wettstein (eds.), *Themes from Kaplan*. Oxford: Oxford University Press.

—— (1989b) Demonstratives. In J. Almog, J. Perry and H. Wettstein (eds.), *Themes from Kaplan*. Oxford: Oxford University Press, 481–563. [Chapter 37 in this volume.]

Kasher, A. (1974) Mood implicatures: a logical way of doing generative pragmatics. *Theoretical Linguistics* 1: 6–38.

Karttunen, L. (1969) Pronouns and variables. In R. I. Binnick, A. Davison, G. Green, and J. Morgan (eds.), *Papers from the Fifth Regional Meeting of the Chicago Linguistic Society*. Chicago: University of Chicago, 108–115.

—— (1971) Implicative verbs. *Language* 47: 340–358.

—— (1974) Presupposition and linguistic context. *Theoretical Linguistics* 1: 181–193.

—— (1976) Discourse reference. In J. D. McCawley (ed.), *Notes from the Linguistic Underground*. Syntax and Semantics 7. New York: Academic Press, 363–385.

—— (1977) The syntax and semantics of questions. *Linguistics and Philosophy* 1: 3–44.

Katz, J. J. (1972) *Semantic Theory*. New York: Harper and Row.

—— (1977) *Propositional Structure and Illocutionary Force: A Study of the Contribution of Sentence Meaning to Speech Acts*. Language and Thought Series. New York: Thomas Crowell.

—— (1981) *Language and Other Abstract Objects*. Oxford: Basil Blackwell.

Katz, J. J., and J. Fodor (1963) The structure of a semantic theory. *Language* 39: 170–210.

Katz, J. J., and E. Martin (1967) The synonymy of actives and passives. *Philosophical Review* 76: 476–491.

Katz, J. J., and P. Postal (1964) *An Integrated Theory of Linguistics Descriptions*. Cambridge, Mass.: MIT Press.

Kazmi, A., and F. J. Pelletier (1998) Is compositionality formally vacuous? *Linguistics and Philosophy* 21: 629–633.

Keenan, E. (1969) A logical base for English. Ph.D. diss., University of Pennsylvania.

Keenan, E., and L. M. Faltz (1978) Logical types for natural language. *UCLA Occasional Papers in Linguistics,* 3. Los Angeles: University of California–Los Angeles.

—— (1985) *Boolean Semantics for Natural Language*. Dordrecht: Reidel.

Keenan, E., and J. Stavi (1986) A semantic characterization of natural language determiners. *Linguistics and Philosophy* 9: 253–326.

Keisler, H. J. (1969) Logic with the quantifier: 'There exist uncountably many.' *Annals of Mathematical Logic* 1: 1–93.

Kempson, R. M. (1975) *Presupposition and the Delimitation of Semantics*. Cambridge: Cambridge University Press.

—— (1977) *Semantic Theory*. Cambridge: Cambridge University Press.

Kempson, R. M., W. Meyer-Viol, and D. Gabbay (2000) *Dynamic Syntax: The Flow of Language Understanding*. Oxford: Blackwell.

Kenny, A. (1963) *Action, Emotion, and Will*. London: Routledge and Kegan Paul.

Klaeber, F. (ed.) (1922) *Beowulf and the Fight at Finnsburg*. 3d ed. Boston: D.C. Heath.

Kleene, S. C. (1952) *Introduction to Metamathematics*. Amsterdam: North-Holland.

Klein, E., and I. Sag (1985) Type-driven translation. *Linguistics and Philosophy* 8: 163–202.

Kolmogorov, A. (1970) *Foundations of the Theory of Measurement*. New York: Chelsea.

Kooij, Jan G. (1971) *Ambiguity in Natural Language: An Investigation of Certain Problems in its Linguistic Description*. Amsterdam: North-Holland.

Kratzer, A. H. E. S. (1976) Was "können" und "müssen" bedeuten können müssen. *Linguistische Berichte* 42: 1–28.

——— (1977) What "must" and "can" must and can mean. *Linguistics and Philosophy* 1: 337–355.

——— (1979) Conditional necessity and possibility. In R. Bauerle, U. Egli, and A. von Stechow (eds.), *Semantics from Different Points of View*. Berlin: Springer-Verlag, 117–147.

Krifka, M. (1987) *Nominal Reference and Temporal Constitution: Towards a Semantics of Quantity*. FNS-Bericht 17. Tübingen: University of Tübingen.

Kripke, S. (1963) Semantical considerations on model logic. *Acta Philosphica Fennica* 16: 83–94.

——— (1971) Identity and necessity. In M. K. Munitz (ed.), *Identity and Individuation*. New York: New York University Press, 135–164.

——— (1972) *Naming and necessity*. In G. Harman and D. Davidson (eds.), *Semantics of Natural Languages*. Dordrecht: Reidel, 253–355.

——— (1977) Speaker's reference and semantic reference. *Midwest Studies in Philosophy* 2: 255–276.

——— (1980) *Naming and Necessity*. rev. ed. Cambridge, Mass.: Harvard University Press. Original work published 1940.

Kroch, A. (1989) "Long" WH-movement and referentiality. Unpublished manuscript, University of Pennsylvania.

Kutschera, F. von (1975) *Sprachphilosophie*. 2nd ed. Munich: Fink. Originally published 1971.

——— (1975) Conventions of language and intensional semantics. *Theoretical Linguistics,* 2: 255–83.

Ladusaw, W. (1979) *Polarity Sensitivity as Inherent Scope Relations*. Unpublished Ph.D. diss., University of Texas-Austin.

——— (1983) Logical form and conditions on grammaticality. *Linguistics and Philosophy*, 6: 373–92.

Lahiri, U. (1990) Questions, answers, and selections. Unpublished manuscript, MIT.

——— (1992) Embedded interrogatives and the predicates that embed them. Ph.D. diss., MIT.

Lakoff, G. (1968) *Pronouns and Reference*. Bloomington: Indiana University Linguistics Club.

——— (1970a) *Irregularity in Syntax*. New York: Holt, Rinehart and Winston.

——— (1970b) Linguistics and natural logic. *Synthèse* 22: 151–271.

——— (1970c) On generative semantics. In D. Steinberg and L. Jakobovits (eds.), *Semantics: An Interdisciplinary Reader in Philosophy, Linguistics, and Psychology*. Cambridge: Cambridge University Press, 232–296.

——— (1970d) A note on vagueness and ambiguity. *Linguistic Inquiry* 1(3):357–359.

——— (1972) *Hedges: A Study in Meaning Criteria and the Logic of Fuzzy Concepts*. Chicago: Chicago Linguistic Society.

——— (1987) *Women, Fire, and Dangerous Things*. Chicago: University of Chicago Press.

Lakoff, G., and M. Johnson (1980) *Metaphors We Live By*. Chicago: University of Chicago Press.

Lakoff, G., and R. Nunez. (1998) The metaphorical structure of mathematics: sketching out cognitive foundations for a mind-based mathematics. In L. English (ed.), *Mathematical Reasoning: Analogies, Metaphors, and Images*. Mahwah, N.J.: Lawrence Erlbaum Associates, 21–92.

Lambek, J. (1958) The mathematics of sentence structure. *American Mathematical Monthly* 65: 154–170. Reprinted in Buszkowski, Wojciech et al. (eds.) *Categorial Grammar* (Amsterdam: John Benjamins, 1988), 57–84.

Lambert, K. (ed.) (1969) *The Logical way of Doing Things*. New Haven, Conn.: Yale University Press.

Landau, B., and L. Gleitman (1985) *Language and Experience: Evidence from the Blind Child*. Cambridge, Mass.: Harvard University Press.

Landman, F. (1989a) Groups I. *Linguistics and Philosophy* 12: 559–606.

———— (1989b) Groups II. *Linguistics and Philosophy* 12: 723–744.

Landman, F., and F. Veltman (eds.) (1984) *Varieties of Formal Semantics*. Groningen-Amsterdam Studies in Semantics 3. Dordrecht: Foris.

Lane, H. (1977) *The Wild Boy Aveyron*. London: Allen and Unwin.

Lang, E. (1977) *Semantik der Koordinativen Verknupfung*. Studia Grammatica 14. Berlin: Akademic-Verlag.

Langacker, R. (1986) *Foundations of Cognitive Grammar*, vol. 1. Stanford, Calif.: Stanford University Press.

Langendoen, D. T. (1978) The logic of reciprocity. *Linguistic Inquiry* 9: 177–197.

Larson, R., and P. Ludlow (1993) Interpreted logical forms. *Synthèse* 95: 305–356.

Larson, R., and G. Segal (1995) *Knowledge of Meaning: An Introduction to Semantic Theory*. Cambridge, Mass.: MIT Press.

Lasersohn, P. (1990) On the readings of plural noun phrases. *Linguistic Inquiry* 20: 130–133.

Lasnik, H. (1976) Remarks on conference. *Linguistic Analysis* 2: 1–32.

Leech, G. (1974) *Semantics*. Harmondsworth: Penguin.

Lehrer, A., and K. Lehrer (eds.) (1970) *Theory of Meaning*. Englewood Cliffs, N.J.: Prentice Hall.

Leisi, E. (1953) *Der Wortinhalt: Seine Struktur im Deutschen und Englischen*. 4th ed. (Heidelberg: Quelle and Meyer, 1971).

Lemmon, E. J. (1962) On sentences verifiable by their use. *Analysis* 22: 86–89.

Leonard, E. (1992) *Rum Punch*. New York: Dell.

Lepore, E. (ed.) (1987) *New Directions in Semantics*. London: Academic Press.

Lepore, E., and K. Ludwig (2002) What is logical form? In G. Preyer and G. Peter (eds.), *Logical Form and Language*. Oxford: Oxford University Press, 54–90.

Lerdahl, F., and R. Jackendoff (1983) *A Generative Theory of Tonal Music*. Cambridge, Mass.: MIT Press.

Levi, I. (1967) *Gambling with Truth*. New York: Knopf.

Levi, J. N. (1978) *The Syntax and Semantics of Complex Nominals*. New York: Academic Press.

Levin, B. (ed.) (1985) *Lexical Semantics in Review*. Lexicon Project Working Papers 1. Cambridge, Mass.: MIT.

———— (1993) *English Verb Classes and Alternations: A Preliminary Investigation*. Chicago: University of Chicago Press.

Levin, B., and M. Rappaport (1986) The formation of adjectival passives. *Linguistic Inquiry* 17: 623–663.

———— (1988) On the nature of unaccusativity. *Proceedings, North Eastern Linguistic Society 1988*. Amherst: Mass.: Graduate Linguistics Society Association.

———— (1995) *Unaccusitivity: At the Syntax-Lexical Interface*. Cambridge, Mass.: MIT Press.

Levin, B., and T. R. Rappaport (1988) Lexical subordination. *Proceedings of Chicago Linguistics Society* 24: 275–289.

Levinson, S. C. (1983) *Pragmatics*. Cambridge: Cambridge University Press.

Lewis, C. I. (1944) The modes of meaning. *Philosophical and Phenomenological Research*. 4: 236–249.

Lewis, D. K. (1968a) Counterpart theory and quantified modal logic. *Journal of Philosophy* 65: 113–126.

———— (1968b) *Languages and Language*. Minnesota Studies in the Philosophy of Science. Minneapolis: Minnesota University Press.

———— (1969) *Convention: A Philosophical Study*. Cambridge, Mass.: Harvard University Press.

———— (1970) General semantics. *Synthèse* 22: 18–67. Reprinted in G. Harman and D. Davidson (eds.), *Semantics of Natural Language* (Dordrecht: Reidel, 1972), 169–218. [Chapter 11 in this volume.] Reprinted in B. Partee (ed.), *Montague Grammar* (New York: Academic Press, 1976), 1–50.

———— (1972) The paradoxes of time travel. *American Philosophical Quarterly* 13: 145–152.

———— (1973) *Counterfactuals*. Oxford: Blackwell.

———— (1975) Adverbs of quantification. In E. Keenan (ed.), *Formal Semantics of Natural Language*. Cambridge: Cambridge University Press, 3–15. [Chapter 30 in this volume.]

———— (1979a) Counterfactual dependence and time's arrow. *Noûs* 13: 455–476.

———— (1979b) A problem about permission. In R. Hilpinen, I. Miiniluoto, M. B. Provence, and E. Saarinen (eds.), *Essays in Honor of Jaakko Hintikka*. Dordrecht: Reidel, 163–179.

———— (1979c) Scorekeeping in a language game. *Journal of Philosophical Logic* 8: 339–359. [Chapter 39 in this volume.]

Liddell, S. K. (1995) Real, surrogate and token space: grammatical consequences in ASL. In K. Emmorey and J. Reilly (eds.), *Language, Gesture, and Space*. Hillsdale, N.J.: Lawrence Erlbaum Associates, 19–41.

―――― (1996) Spatial representations in discourse: comparing spoken and signed language. *Lingua* 98: 145–167.

Lieber, R. (1992) *Deconstructing Morphology: Word Formation in Syntactic Theory.* Chicago: University of Chicago Press.

Lindstrom, P. (1966) First-order logic and generalized quantifiers. *Theoria* 32: 187–195.

Link, G. (1983) The logical analysis of plurals and mass terms: A lattice-theoretic approach. In R. Bäuerle, C. Shwartze, and A. von Stechow (eds.), *Meaning Use, and Interpretation of Language.* Berlin: Walter de Gruyer, 302–323.

―――― (1984) Hydras: on the logic of relative constructions with multiple heads. In F. Landman and F. Veltman (eds.), *Varieties of Formal Semantics.* Dordrecht: Foris, 245–258.

―――― (1991) Plural. In A. van Stechow and D. Wunderlich (eds.), *Semantics: An International Handbook of Contemporary Research.* Berlin: de Gruyter, 418–440.

Linsky, Leonard (ed.) (1952) *Semantics and the Philosophy of Language.* Urbana: University of Illinois Press.

Lloyd, G. E. R. (1968) *Aristotle: The Growth and Structure of His Thought.* Cambridge: Cambridge University Press.

Loar, B. (1976) Two theories of meaning. In G. Evans and J. McDowell (eds.), *Truth and Meaning.* Oxford: Oxford University Press, 138–161.

Lobel, A. (1981) *Uncle Elephant.* New York: Harper and Row.

Lonning, J. T. (1987) Mass terms and quantification. *Linguistics and Philosophy* 10: 1–52.

Lorenzer, A. (1970) *Sprachzerstorung und Rekonstruktion: Vorarbeiten zu einer Metatheorie der Psychoanalyse.* Frankfurt a. M.: Suhrkamp.

Luce, R. D., R. Bush, and E. Galanter (eds.) (1963) *Handbook of Mathematical Psychology.* New York: Wiley.

Lutzeier, P. R. (1974) Der "Aspekt" Weit als Einstieg zu einem nützlichen Kontextbegriff für eine natürliche Sprache. Ph.D. diss., University of Stuttgart.

Lycan, W. G. (1984) *Logical Form in Natural Language.* Cambridge, Mass.: MIT Press.

Lyons, J. (1966) Towards a "notional" theory of the "parts of speech." *Journal of Linguistics* 2: 209–236.

―――― (1968) *Introduction to Theoretical Linguistics.* Cambridge: Cambridge University Press.

―――― (1977) *Semantics.* 2 vols. Cambridge: Cambridge University Press.

―――― (1995) *Linguistic Semantics: An Introduction.* Cambridge: Cambridge University Press.

Mandelblit, N. (1997) Creativity and schematicity in grammar and translation: the cognitive mechanisms of blending. Ph,D. diss., University of California–San Diego.

Mandelblit, N., and O. Zachar (1998) The notion of unit and its development in cognitive science. *Cognitive Science* 22(2): 229–268.

Mandler, J. (1997) Representation. In D. Kuhn and R. Siegler (eds.), *Handbook of Child Psychology.* Vol. 2: *Cognition, Perception, and Language.* New York: Wiley, 255–308.

Marcus, R. B. (1993) *Modalities.* Oxford: Oxford University Press.

Margalit, Avishai (1983) A review of Scheffler (1979). *Journal of Philosophy* 80(2): 129–137.

Marr, D. (1982) *Vision.* San Francisco: Freeman.

Marr, D., and L. Vaina (1982) Representation and recognition of the movements of shapes. In *Proceedings of the Royal Society of London* Series B 214: 501–524.

Marten, L. (2002) *At the Syntax-Pragmatics Interface: Verbal Underspecification and Concept Formation in Dynamic Syntax.* Oxford: Oxford University Press.

Martinich, A. P. (ed.) (1985) *The Philosophy of Language.* Oxford: Oxford University Press.

Mates, B. (1952) Synonymity. In L. Linsky (ed.), *Semantics and the Philosophy of Language.* Urbana: University of Illinois Press. Originally published in *University of California Publications in Philosophy* 25 (Berkeley: University of California Press, 1950): 201–226.

―――― (1968) Leibniz on possible worlds. In B. van Rootselaar and J. F. Staal (eds.), *Logic, Methodology, and Philosophy of Science III.* Amsterdam: North-Holland, 507–530.

Matthews, R. J. (1986) Learnability of semantic theory. In E. Lepore (ed.), *Truth and Interpretation.* New York: Basil Blackwell, 49–59.

May, R. (1977) The grammar of quantification. Ph.D. diss., MIT.

—— (1979) Must COMP-to-COMP movement be stipulated? *Linguistic Inquiry* 10: 719–725.

—— (1981) Movement and binding. *Linguistic Inquiry* 12: 215–243.

—— (1985) *Logical Form: Its Structure and Derivation.* Cambridge, Mass.: MIT Press.

—— (1989) Interpreting logical form. *Linguistics and Philosophy* 12: 387–435.

Mayer, V. (1997) *Semantischer Holismus: Eine Einführung.* Berlin: Akademie-Verlag.

McCawley, J. (1968a) Concerning the base component of a transformational grammar. *Foundations of Language.* 4: 243–269.

—— (1968b) Lexical insertion in a transformational grammar without deep structure. In B. Darden, C. J. N. Bailey, and A. Davison (eds.), *Papers from the Fourth Meeting of the Chicago Linguistic Society.* Chicago: Department of Linguistics, University of Chicago, 71–80.

—— (1969) Semantic representation. Paper presented to a symposium on Cognitive Studies and Artificial Intelligence Research, University of Chicago Center for Continuing Education.

—— (1970) Where do noun phrases come from? In R. Jacobs and P. Rosenbaum (eds.), *Readings in Transformational Grammar.* Waltham, Mass: Ginn, 166–183.

—— (ed.) (1976) *Notes from the Linguistic Underground.* Syntax and Semantics 7. New York: Academic Press.

—— (1979) Presupposition and discourse structure. In C. Oh. and D. A. Dineen (eds.), *Presupposition.* Syntax and Semantics 11. New York: Academic Press, 371–388.

—— (1982) Parentheticals and discontinuous constituent structure. *Linguistic Inquiry* 13: 91–106.

—— (1993) *Everything That Linguists Have Always Wanted to Know about Logic but Were Ashamed to Ask.* Chicago: University of Chicago Press.

McDowell, J. (1998) Meaning, communication and knowledge. In J. McDowell, *Meaning, Knowledge and Reality.* Cambridge, Mass.: Harvard University Press, 29–50.

McKeon, R. (1941) *The Basic Works of Aristotle.* New York: Random House.

Mejias-Bikandi, E. (1993) Syntax, discourse, and acts of mind: a study of the indicative/subjunctive in Spanish. Ph.D. diss., University of California–San Diego.

—— (1996) Space accessibility and mood in Spanish. In G. Fauconnier and E. Sweetser (eds.), *Spaces, Worlds, and Grammar.* Chicago: University of Chicago Press.

Mel'cuk, I. (1988) *Dependency Syntax.* Albany, N.Y.: SUNY Press.

Michalski, R. S. (1983) A theory and methodology of inductive learning. In R. S. Michalski, J. Carbonell, and T. Mitchell (eds.), *Machine Learning: An Artificial Intelligence Approach.* Palo Alto, Calif.: Tioga, 83–134.

Mill, J. S. (1974) *A System of Logic, Ratiocinative and Inductive, Being a Connected View of the Principles of Evidence and the Methods of Scientific Investigation.* 8th ed. In Ernest Nagel (ed.), *John Stuart Mills Philosophy of Scientific Methods.* New York: Hafner Press. Original work published 1843.

Miller, G. (1985) Dictionaries of the mind. In *Proceedings, 23rd Annual Meeting of the Association for Computational Linguistics.* Morristown, N. J.: Association for Computational Linguistics, 305–314.

Miller, G., and C. Fellbaum (1991) Semantic networks of English. *Cognition* 41: 47–81.

Miller, G., and P. Johnson-Laird (1976) *Language and Perception.* Cambridge, Mass.: Harvard University Press.

Millikan, Ruth (1984) *Language, Thought and Other Biological Categories.* Cambridge, Mass.: MIT Press.

Milne, A. A. (1980) *The Red House Mystery.* New York: Dell Publishing. Originally published 1922.

Milner, J. C. (1979) Cyclicité successive du mouvement de *qu.* Unpublished manuscript.

Milsark, G. (1977) Toward an explanation of certain peculiarities of the existential construction in English. *Linguistic Analysis* 3(1): 1–30.

Moens, M., and M. Steedman (1988) Temporal ontology and temporal reference. *Computational Linguistics* 14(2): 15–28.

Montague, R. (1960) Logical necessity, physical necessity, ethics, and quantifiers. *Inquiry* 3: 259–269.

—— (1968) Pragmatics. In R. Klibansky (ed.), *Contemporary Philosophy / La philosophie contemporaine.* Florence: Nuova Italia Editrice, 102–122.

—— (1969a) On the nature of certain philosophical entities. *Monist* 53: 159–194.

—— (1969b) Intensional logic and some of its connections with ordinary language. Talk delivered to the Southern California Logic Colloquium, Los Angeles.

────── (1970a) English as a formal language. In B. Visentini et al., *Linguaggi nella società e nella tecnica*. Milan: Edizioni di Communità. Reprinted in R. H. Thomason (ed.), *Formal Philosophy: Selected Papers of Richard Montague* (New Haven, Conn.: Yale University Press, 1974), 188–221.

────── (1970b) Universal grammar. *Theoria* 36: 373–378. Reprinted in R. H. Thomason (ed.), *Formal Philosophy: Selected Papers of Richard Montague* (New Haven, Conn.: Yale University Press, 1974), 222–246.

────── (1970c) Pragmatics and intensional logic. *Synthèse* 22: 68–94.

────── (1972) The proper treatment of quantification in ordinary English. In J. Moravcsik and P. Suppes (eds.), *Proceedings of the Stanford Workshop on Grammar and Syntax of Natural Languages*. Stanford, Calif.: Stanford University Press, 221–242.

────── (1974a) The proper treatment of quantification in ordinary English. In R. H. Thomason (ed.), *Formal Philosophy: Selected Papers of Richard Montague*. New Haven, Conn.: Yale University Press, 247–270.

────── (1974b) *Formal Philosophy: Selected Papers of Richard Montague*. Ed. R. H. Thomason. New Haven, Conn.: Yale University Press.

Mooij, J. J. A. (1976) *A Study of Metaphor: On the Nature of Metaphorical Expressions, with Special Reference to Their Reference*. Amsterdam: North-Holland.

Moravcsik, J. M. (1975) Aitia as generative factor in Aristotle's philosophy. *Dialogue* 14: 622–636.

Morgan, J. L. (1989) *Sentence Fragments Revisited*. Papers from the Parasession on Language in Context 25. Chicago: Chicago Linguistics Society, 228–241.

Morris, C. W. (1938) *Foundations of the Theory of Signs*. Chicago: Chicago University Press.

Mostowski, A. (1957) On a generalization of quantifiers. *Fundamenta Mathematicae* 44: 12–36.

Mourelatos, A. (1981) Events, processes, and states. In P. J. Tedeschi and A. Zaenen (eds.), *Tense and Aspect*. Syntax and Semantics 14. New York: Academic Press.

Mushin, I. (1998) Viewpoint shifts in narrative. In J. P. Koenig (ed.), *Discourse and Cognition: Bridging the Gap*. Stanford: Center for the Study of Language and Information.

Naess, A. (1961) A study of "or." *Synthèse* 13: 49–60.

Napoli, D. J. (1982) Initial material deletion in English. *Glossa* 16: 85–111.

Neale, S. (1990) *Descriptions*. Cambridge, Mass.: MIT Press.

Nida, Eugene A. (1949) *Morphology: The Descriptive Analysis of Words*. Ann Arbor: University of Michigan Press.

Nunberg, G. (1978) *The Pragmatics of Reference*. Bloomington: Indiana University Linguistics Club.

Nunberg, G. D., and A. Zaenen (1992) Systematic polysemy in lexicology and lexicography. *Proceedings of Euralex 92*. Tampere, Finland: University of Tampere.

Oakley, T. (1995) Presence: the conceptual basis of rhetorical effect. Ph.D. diss., University of Maryland.

Parry, W. T. (1933) Ein Axiomsystem fur eine neue Art von Implikation (analytische Implikation). *Ergebnisse eines Mathematisches Colloquiums* 4: 5–6.

Parsons, K. P. (1973) Ambiguity and the truth definition. *Noûs* 7(4): 379–394.

Parsons, T. (1968) A semantics for English. Unpublished manuscript.

────── (1970a) An analysis of mass terms and amount terms. *Foundations of Language* 6; 362–388. Reprinted in F. J. Pelletier (ed.), *Mass Terms: Some Philosophical Problems*. Synthèse Language Library 6. (Dordrecht: Reidel, 1979), 167–172.

────── (1970b) Some problems concerning the logic of grammatical modifiers. *Synthèse* 21: 320–334.

────── (1973) Tense operators versus quantifiers. (Abstract) *Journal of Philosophy* 70: 609–610.

────── (1980) *Nonexistent Objects*. New Haven, Conn.: Yale University Press.

Partee, B. (1973) Some structural analogies between tenses and pronouns in English. *Journal of Philosophy* 70(18): 601–609. [Chapter 25 in this volume.]

────── (1975a) Montague grammar and transformational grammar. *Linguistic Inquiry* 6: 203–300.

────── (1975b) Deletion and variable binding. In E. L. Keenan (ed.), *Formal Semantics of Natural Language*. London: Cambridge University Press, 16–34.

────── (1978) Bound variables and other anaphors. Unpublished manuscript.

────── (1980) Semantics—mathematics or psychology? In R. Bäuerle, U. Egli, and A. von Stechow (eds.), *Semantics from Different Points of View*. Berlin: Springer-Verlag, 1–14.

────── (1984) Compositionality. In F. Landman and F. Veltman (eds.), *Varieties of Formal Semantics*. Dordrecht: Foris, 281–312.

———— (1986) Noun phrase interpretation and type-shifting principles. In J. Groenendijk, D. de Jongh, and M. Stokhof (eds.), *Studies in Discourse Representation Theory and the Theory of Generalized Quantifiers*. Dordrecht, Foris, 115–143.

———— (1992) Syntactic categories and semantic types. In M. Rosner and R. Johnson (eds.), *Computational Linguistics and Formal Semantics*. Cambridge: Cambridge University Press, 97–126.

Partee, B. and M. Rooth (1983) Generalized conjunction and type ambiguity. In R. Bauerle, C. Schwarze, and A. von Stechow (eds.), *Meaning, Use, and Interpretation of Language*. Berlin: de Gruyter, 361–383.

Partee, B., A. ter Meulen, and R. E. Wall (1990) *Mathematical Methods in Linguistics*. Dordrecht: Kluwer.

Passonneau, R. J. (1988) A computational model of the semantics of tense and aspect. *Computational Linguistics* 14(2): 44–60.

Peacocke, C. (1979) Game-theoretic semantics, quantifiers and truth: comments on Professor Hintikka's paper. In E. Saarinen (ed.), *Game-Theoretical Semantics*. Dordrecht: Reidel, 119–134.

Peirce, C. S. (1901) Vague. In J. M. Baldwin (ed.), *Dictionary of Philosophy and Psychology,* 2 vols. New York: Macmillan, 2:748.

Pelletier, F. J. (1974) On some proposals for the semantics of mass terms. *Journal of Philosophical Logic* 3: 87–108.

———— (1975) Non-singular reference: some preliminaries. *Philosophia* 5: 451–65. Reprinted in F. J. Pelletier (ed.), *Mass Terms: Some Philosophical Problems* (Dordrecht: Reidel, 1979), 1–14.

———— (ed.) (1979) *Mass Terms: Some Philosophical Problems*. Synthèse Language Library 6. Dordrecht: Reidel.

———— (1994a) On an argument against semantic compositionality. In D. Prawitz and D. Westerståhl (eds.), *Logic and Philosophy of Science in Uppsala*. Dordrecht: Kluwer, 599–610.

———— (1994b) Semantic compositionality: the argument from synonymy. In R. Casati, B. Smith, and G. White (eds.), *Philosophy and the Cognitive Sciences*. Vienna: Hölder-Pichler-Tempsky, 311–317.

———— (1994c). The principle of semantic compositionality. *Topoi* 13: 11–24. [Chapter 9 in this volume.]

———— (2000) Semantic compositionality: free algebras and the argument from ambiguity. In M. Feller, S. Kaufmann, and M. Pauly (eds.), *Formalizing the Dynamics of Information*. Stanford, Calif.: Center for the Study of Language and Information Publications, 207–218.

———— (2001) Did Frege believe Frege's Principle? *Journal of Logic, Language and Information* 10: 87–114.

Pelletier, F. J., and L. Schubert (1989) Mass expressions. In D. Gabbay and F. Guenthner (eds.), *Handbook of Philosophical Logic*, vol. 2. Dordrecht: Reidel, 328–349.

Perry, J. (1977) Frege on demonstratives. *Philosophical Review* 86: 474–497.

———— (1979) The problem of the essential indexical. *Noûs* 13: 3–21.

———— (1986a) Perception, action and the structure of believing. In R. Grandy and R. Warner (eds.), *Philosophical Grounds of Rationality: Intentions, Categories, Ends*. New York: Oxford University Press, 333–362.

———— (1986b) Thought without representation. *Aristotelian Society Supplementary* 60: 137–151.

———— (1998) Indexicals, contexts and unarticulated constituents. In A. Aliseda, R. van Glabbeek, and D. Westerståhl (eds.), *Computing Natural Language*. Stanford, Calif.: Center for the Study of Language and Information Publications, 1–11.

Perry, J., and J. Barwise (1981) Semantic innocence and uncompromising situations. *Midwest Studies in Philosophy* 6: 387–403.

Pesetsky, D. (1982) Paths and categories. Ph.D. diss., MIT.

Peters, S. P., and R. W. Ritchie (1969) *On the Generative Power of Transformational Grammars*. Technical Report in Computer Science. Seattle: University of Washington.

Pinkal, M. (1979) How to refer with vague descriptions. In R. Bäuerle, U. Egli, and A. von Stechow (eds.), *Semantics from Different Points of View*. Berlin: Springer-Verlag, 32–50.

———— (1983) Semantics of precization. In T. Ballmer and M. Pinkal (eds.), *Approaching Vagueness*. North-Holland Linguistic Series 51. Amsterdam: North-Holland, 13–57.

Pinker, S. (1989) *The Acquisition of Argument Structure*. Cambridge, Mass.: MIT Press.

Platzack, C. (1979) *The Semantic Interpretation of Aspect and Aktionsarten*. Dordrecht: Foris.

Posner, R. (1972a) *Theorie des Kommentierens: Eine Grundlagenstudie zur Semantik und Pragmatik*. Frankfurt a. M.: Athenaum.

——— (1972b) Commenting: a diagnostic procedure for semantico-pragmatic sentence representations. *Poetics* 5: 67–88.

——— (1972c) Zur systematischen Mehrdeutigkeit deutscher Lexeme. *Linguistik und Didaktik* 12: 268–276.

——— (1980) Semantics and pragmatics of sentence connectives in natural language. *Speech Act Theory and Pragmatics*, 169–203. [Chapter 31 in this volume.]

Postal, P. (1970) On the surface verb "remind." *Linguistic Inquiry* 1: 37–120.

Potter, D. (1986) *Ticket to Ride*. New York: Random House.

Poulin, C. (1996) Manipulation of discourse spaces in ASL. In A. Goldberg (ed.), *Conceptual Structure, Discourse, and Language*. Stanford, Calif.: Center for the Study of Language and Information Publications, 421–434.

Prior A. N. (1967) *Past, Present, Future*. Oxford: Clarendon.

Presch, G., and K. Gloy (eds.) (1976) *Sprachnormen II: Theoretische Begrundungen ausserschulische Sprachnormenpraxis*. Stuttgart: Formann-Holzboog.

Pustejovsky, J. (1988) The geometry of events. In C. Tenny (ed.), *Studies in Generative Approaches to Aspect*. Lexicon Project Working Papers 24. Cambridge, Mass.: MIT.

——— (1989a) Type coercion and selection. Paper presented at West Coast Conference on Formal Linguistics, Vancouver, Canada.

——— (1989b) Issues in computational lexical semantics. In *Proceedings, Fourth European ACL Conference*. Manchester, England: n.p.

——— (1991a) The generative lexicon. *Computational Linguistics* 17: 409–441. [Chapter 18 in this volume.]

——— (1991b) The syntax of event structure. *Cognition* 41: 47–81.

——— (1993) Type coercion and lexical selection. In J. Pustejovsky (ed.), *Semantics and the Lexicon*. Dordrecht: Kluwer.

——— (1995a) Principles versus criteria: on Randall's catapult hypodissertation. In J. Weissenborn, H. Goodluck, and T. Roeper (eds.), *Theoretical Issues in Language Acquisition*. Dordrecht: Kluwer.

——— (1995b) *The Generative Lexicon: A Theory of Computational Lexical Semantics*. Cambridge, Mass.: MIT Press.

——— (1998) Generativity and explanation in semantics: a reply to Fodor and Lepore. *Linguistic Inquiry* 29: 289–311.

Pustejovsky, J., and P. Anick (1988) On the semantic interpretation of nominals. In *Proceedings of the XIIth International Conference on Computational Linguistics*. Budapest: John von Neumann Society for Computing Sciences.

Pustejovsky, J., and S. Bergler (eds.) (1991) *Lexical Semantics and Commonsense Reasoning*. Berlin: Springer-Verlag.

Pustejovsky, J., and B. Boguraev (1991) Lexical knowledge representation and natural language processing. *IBM Journal of Research and Development* 45: 4.

Putnam, Hilary (1967) The "innateness hypothesis" and explanatory models in linguistics. *Synthèse* 17: 12–22.

——— (1986) Meaning holism. In E. Hahn and P. A. Schlipp (eds.), *The Philosophy of W. V. Quine*. La Salle, Ill.: Open Court, 405–426.

——— (1988) *Representation and Reality*. Cambridge, Mass.: MIT Press.

——— (1996) The meaning of meaning. In A. Pessin and S Goldberg (eds.), *The Twin Earth Chronicles*. Armonk, N.Y.: M. E. Sharpe, 3–52. Originally published 1975.

Quillian, M. R. (1968) Semantic memory. In M. Minsky (ed.), *Semantic Information Processing*. Cambridge, Mass.: MIT Press, 216–217.

Quine, W. V. O. (1936) Truth by convention. In O. H. Lee (ed.), *Philosophical Essays for A. N. Whitehead*. New York: Longmans, 70–99. Reprinted in W. V. O. Quine, *The Ways of Paradox and Other Essays*. (New York: Random House, 1966), 70–99.

——— (1950) *Methods of Logic*. New York: Holt. 3rd ed., 1972.

——— (1953a) On What There Is. In *From a Logical Point of View*. New York: Harper and Row. Originally published 1948.

——— (1953b) Two dogmas of empiricism. In *From a Logical Point of View*. New York: Harper and Row, 20–46. First published in *Philosophical Review* (1951) 60: 20–43.

——— (1953) Three grades of model involvement. In *Proceedings of the XIth International Congress of Philosophy* 14. Amsterdam: North-Holland, 65-8. Reprinted in W. V. O. Quine, *The Ways of Paradox and Other Essays*. (New York: Random House, 1966), 156–174.

——— (1956) Quantifiers and propositional attitudes. *Journal of Philosophy* 53: 177–187. Reprinted in W. V. O. Quine, *The Ways of Paradox and Other Essays*. (New York: Random House, 1966), 183–194. Also in A. P. Martinich *The Philosophy of Language* (Oxford: Oxford University Press, 1985), 332–338.

——— (1960) *Word and Object*. Cambridge, Mass.: MIT Press.

——— (1966) *The Ways of Paradox and Other Essays*. New York: Random House.

——— (1969) Reply to Kaplan. In D. Davidson et al. (eds.), *Words and Objections*. Dordrecht: Reidel, 342.

——— (1970) *Philosophy of Logic*. Englewood Cliffs, N.J.: Prentice Hall.

Quirk, R., S. Greenbaum, G. Leech, and J. Svartik (1985) *A Comprehensive Grammar of the English Language*. London: Longmans.

Ramberg, Bjørn (1989) *Donald Davidson's Philosophy of Language*. Oxford: Blackwell.

Raz, J. (1975) *Practical Reason and Norms*. London: Hutchinson.

Recanati, F. (1989) The pragmatics of what is said. *Mind and Language* 4: 29-5–329. Reprinted in S. Davis. (ed.), *Pragmatics: A Reader* (Oxford: Oxford University Press, 1991), 97–120.

——— (1993) *Direct Reference: From Language to Thought*. Oxford: Blackwell.

——— (2001) Déstabiliser le sens. *Revue Internationale de Philosophie* 2: 217.

——— (2002) Unarticulated constituents. *Linguistics and Philosophy* 25: 299–345.

Reichenbach, H. (1947) *Elements of Symbolic Logic*. New York: Macmillan. [§ 51 Chapter 24 in this volume.]

——— (1979) Syntactic domains for semantic rules. In F. Guenther and S. J. Schmidt (eds.), *Formal Semantics and Pragmatics for Natural Language*. Dordrecht: Reidel.

Reimer, M. (1991) Demonstratives, demonstrations, and demonstrata. *Philosophical Studies* 62[2]: 187–202.

——— (1992) Three views of demonstrative reference. *Synthèse* 93(3): 373–402.

Reinhart, T. (1979) Syntactic domains for semantic rules. In F. Guenther and S. J. Schmidt (eds.), *Formal Semantics and Pragmatics for Natural Languages*. Dordrecht: Reidel, 107–130.

——— (1992) Interpreting *WH*-in-situ. Unpublished manuscript, Tel Aviv University.

Rennie, M. K. (1962) Plurality quantification. Abstract. *Journal of Symbolic Logic* 27: 373–374.

——— (1974) *Some Uses of Type Theory in the Analysis of Language*. Monograph Series No. 1. Canberra: Department of Philosophy, Research School of Social Sciences, Australian National University.

Rescher, N. (1962) Plurality quantification. Abstract. *Journal of Symbolic Logic* 27: 373–374.

——— (1966) *The Logic of Commands*. Monographs in Modern Logic. New York: Routledge and Kegan Paul.

——— (1969) *Many-Valued Logic*. New York: McGraw-Hill.

Richards, D. A. J. (1971) *A Theory of Reasons for Action*. Oxford: Clarendon.

Riegel, M., J.-C. Pellat, and R. Rioul (1994) *Grammaire méthodique du français*. Paris: Presses Universitaires de France.

Robert, A. (1998) Blending and other conceptual operations in the interpretation mathematical proofs. In J. P. Koenig (ed.), *Discourse and Cognition: Bridging the Gap*. Stanford, Calif.: Center for the Study of Language and Information, 337–350.

Roberts, C. (1987) Modal subordination, anaphora, and distributivity. Ph.D. diss., University of Massachusetts–Amherst.

——— (1989) Modal subordination and pronominal anaphora in discourse. *Linguistics and Philosophy* 12: 683–723.

Roberts, L. (1984) Ambiguity vs. generality: removal of a logical confusion. *Canadian Journal of Philosophy* 14(2): 295–313.

Roberts, R. B., and I. Goldstein (1977) *The FRL Manual*. Technical Report AI Memo 409. Cambridge, Mass.: MIT, Artificial Intelligence Laboratory.

Roeper, P. (1983) Semantics for mass terms with quantifiers. *Noûs* 22: 251–265.

Rollin, B. E. (1976) *Natural and Conventional Meaning: An Examination of the Distinction*. The Hague: Mouton.

Rooth, M. (1987) Noun phrase interpretation in Montague grammar, file change semantics, and situation semantics. In P. Gardenfors (ed.), *Generalized Quantifiers*. Dordrecht: Reidel.

Rosch, E. (1978) Principles of categorization. In E. Rosch and B. Lloyd (eds.), *Cognition and Categorization*. Hillsdale, N.J.: Lawrence Erlbaum Associates, 27–48.

Ross, J. R. (1967) Constraints on variables in syntax. Ph.D. diss., MIT.

——— (1970) On declarative sentences. In R. Jacobs and P. Rosenbaum (eds.), *Readings in English Transformational Grammar*. Boston: Blaisdell, 222–272.

Rosser, B. (1953) *Logic for Mathematicians*. New York: McGraw-Hill.

Rubba, J. (1996) Alternate grounds in the interpretation of deictic expressions. In G. Fauconnier and E. Sweetser (eds.), *Spaces, Worlds, and Grammar*. Chicago: University of Chicago Press, 227–261.

Russell, B. (1905) On denoting. *Mind* 14: 479–493.

——— (1911) Knowledge by acquaintance and by description. *Proceedings of the Aristotelian Society* 11: 108–128.

——— (1919) *Introduction to Mathematical Philosophy*. London: Allen and Unwin.

——— (1936) *The Principles of Mathematics*. 2nd ed. London: Allen and Unwin. Originally published 1903.

——— (1940) *Inquiry into Meaning and Truth*. London: Allen and Unwin.

——— (1956a) On denoting. In R. C. Marsh (ed.), *Logic and Knowledge*. London: Allen and Unwin, 39–56. Originally published 1905.

——— (1956b) The philosophy of logical atomism. In R. C. Marsh (ed.), *Logic and Knowledge*. London: Allen and Unwin, 175–282. Originally published 1918.

Ruttenberg, J. (1976) Some difficulties with Cresswell's semantics and the method of shallow structure. In J. T. Stillings (ed.), *Occasional Papers 2*. Amherst: University of Massachusetts.

Ryle, G. (1949) *The Concept of Mind*. London: Hutchinson.

Sadock, J. M. (1974) *Toward a Linguistic Theory of Speech Acts*. New York: Seminar Press.

Sainsbury, R. M. (1979) *Russell*. London: Routledge and Kegan Paul.

Salmon, N. (1991) *Frege's Puzzle*. Cambridge, Mass.: MIT Press.

Sanders, J., and G. Redeker (1996) Perspective and the representation of speech and thought in narrative discourse. In G. Fauconnier and E. Sweetser (eds.), *Spaces, Worlds, and Grammar*. Chicago: University of Chicago Press, 290–317.

Scha, R. J. H. (1983) *Logical Foundations for Question Answering*. MS 12.331. Eindhoven, Netherlands: Phillips Research Laboratories.

Schank, R. C. (1972) Conceptual dependency: a theory of natural language understanding. *Cognitive Psychology* 3: 552–631.

——— (1975) *Conceptual Information Processing*. Amsterdam: North-Holland.

Scheffler, Israel (1963) *The Anatomy of Inquiry*. New York: Knopf.

——— (1979) *Beyond the Letter: A Philosophical Inquiry into Ambiguity, Vagueness, and Metaphor in Language*. London: Routledge and Kegan Paul.

Schiffer, Stephen (1972) *Meaning*. Oxford: Oxford University Press.

Schmerling, S. F. (1975) Asymmetric conjunction and rules of conversation. In P. Cole and J. L. Morgan (eds.), *Speech Acts*. Syntax and Semantics 3. New York: Academic Press, 211–232.

Schmidt, W. (1967) *Lexikalische und aktuelle Bedeutung: Ein Beitrag zur Theorie der Wortbedeutung*. Berlin: Akademie-Verlag.

Scholl, B., and A. Leslie (1999) Modularity, development and "theory of mind." *Mind and Language* 14: 131–153.

Schubert, L. K., and F. J. Pelletier (1982) From English to logic: context-free computation of "conventional" logic translations. *Journal of Computational Linguistics* 8: 27–44.

——— (1987) Problems in the representation of the logical form of generics, plurals, and mass nouns. In E. Lepore (ed.), *New Directions in Semantics*. London: Academic Press, 1987, 387–453.

——— (1989) Generally speaking, or, using discourse representation theory to interpret genetics. In G. Chierchia, B. H. Partee, and R. Turner (eds.), *Properties, Types and Meaning*, vol. 2. Dordrecht: Kluwer, 193–268.

Scott, D. (1970) Advice on modal logic. In K. Lambert (ed.), *Philosophical Problems in Logic*. Dordrecht: Reidel, 143–173.

Searle J. R. (1958), Proper Names. *Mind* 67: 166–173;

—— (1969) *Speech Act: An Essay in the Philosophy of Language*. Cambridge: Cambridge University Press.

—— (1979) *Expression and Meaning*. Cambridge: Cambridge University Press.

—— (1981) The background of meaning. In J. R. Searle, F. Kiefer, and M. Bierwisch (eds.), *Speech Act Theory and Pragmatics*. Dordrecht: Reidel, 221–232.

—— (1983) *Intentionality*. Cambridge: Cambridge University Press.

Searle, J. R., and D. Vanderveken (1985) *Foundations of Illocutionary Logic*. Cambridge: Cambridge University Press.

Segal, G. (1988) In the mood for a semantic theory. Unpublished manuscript, King's College London.

—— (1994) Priorities in the philosophy of thought. *Aristotelian Society Supplementary* 68: 107–130.

Segerberg, K. (1973) Two-dimensional modal logic. *Journal of Philosophical Logic* 2: 77–96.

Selkirk, E. O. (1977) Some remarks on noun phrase structure. In P. W. Culicover, T. Wasow, and A. Akmajian (eds.), *Formal Syntax*. New York: Academic Press, 285–316.

—— (1982) *The Syntax of Words*. Cambridge, Mass.: MIT Press.

—— (1984) *Phonology and Syntax: The Relation between Sound and Structure*. Cambridge, Mass.: MIT Press.

Seuren, P. (1977) *Zwischen Sprache und Denken: Ein Beitrag zur empirischen Begrundung der Semantik*. Wiesbaden: Athenaion.

—— (1986) *Discourse Semantics*. Oxford: Blackwell.

Sgro, J. (1977) Completeness theorems for topological models. *Annals of Mathematical Logic* 11: 173–193.

Shastri, L., and D. Grannes (1996) A connectionist treatment of negation and inconsistency. In G. Cottrell (ed.), *Proceedings of the 18th Annual Conference of the Cognitive Science Society*. Mahwah, N.J.: Lawrence Erlbaum Associates.

Sher, Gila (1991) *Bounds of Logic: A Generalized Viewpoint*. Cambridge: MIT Press.

Simons, P. M. (1982a) Number and manifolds. In B. Smith, *Parts and Moments: Studies in Logic and Formal Ontology*. Munich: Philosophia Analytica, 160–169.

—— (1982b) Plural reference and set theory. In B. Smith (ed.), *Parts and Moments: Studies in Logic and Formal Ontology*. Munich: Philosophia Analytica, 199–256.

—— (1987) *Parts: A Study in Ontology*. Oxford: Oxford University Press.

Skeat, W. W. (1886) *The Vision of William Concerning Piers the Plowman*. In *Three Parallel Texts, Together with Richard the Redeless* by William Langland. 2 vols. Oxford: Clarendon.

Skinner, B. F. (1937) The distribution of associated words. *Psychological Record* 1: 71–76.

—— (1957) *Verbal Behavior*. New York: Appleton Century Crofts.

Sloat, C. (1969) Proper nouns in English. *Language* 45: 26–30.

Slobin, D. I. (1971) *Psycholinguistics*. Glenview, Ill.: Scott, Foresman.

Smith, B. (ed.) (1982) *Parts and Moments: Studies in Logic and Formal Ontology*. Munich: Philosophia Analytica.

—— (1987) Philosophy 266: representation, formality, and the foundations of computation. Unpublished manuscript, Stanford University.

Smith, T. V., and M. Grene (1940) *From Descartes to Kant: Readings in the Philosophy of the Renaissance and Enlightenment*. Chicago: University of Chicago Press.

Smolka, G. (1988) *A Feature Logic with Subsorts*. Wissenschaftliches Zentrum der IBM Deutschland. LILOG-Report 33. Stuttgart: Deutschland GmbH.

Snow, C. P. (1974) *In Their Wisdom*. Harmondsworth: Penguin.

Spencer-Smith, R. (1987) Survey: semantics and discourse representation. *Mind and Language* 2: 1–26.

Sperber, D. (1994a) Understanding verbal understanding. In J. Khalfa (ed.), *What Is Intelligence?* Cambridge: Cambridge University Press, 179–198.

—— (1994b) The modularity of thought and the epidemiology of representations. In L. Hirschfeld and S. Gelman (eds.), *Mapping the Mind: Domain Specificity in Cognition and Culture*. Cambridge: Cambridge University Press, 39–67.

—— (2000) Metarepresentations in an evolutionary perspective. In D. Sperber (ed.), *Metarepresentations*. New York: Oxford University Press, 117–137.

Sperber, D., and D. Wilson (1986) *Relevance: Communication and Cognition*. Oxford: Blackwell. 2nd ed., 1995.

—— (1987) Précis of relevance. *The Behavioral and Brain Sciences* 10: 697–710.

—— (1998) The mapping between the public and the private lexicon. In P. Carruthers and J. Boucher (eds.), *Language and Thought: Interdisciplinary Themes*. Cambridge: Cambridge University Press, 184–200.

Staal, J. F. (1965a) Context-sensitive rules in Pāṇini. *Foundations of Language* 1: 63–72. Reprinted in Staal (ed.), *Universals: Studies in Indian Logic and Linguistics* (Chicago: University of Chicago Press, 1988), 171–180.

—— (1965b) Reification, quotation and nominalization. In A. Tymieniecka (ed.), *Contributions to Logic and Methodology in Honor of J. M. Bochenski*. Amsterdam: North-Holland, 151–187.

—— (ed) (1988) *Universals: Studies in Indian Logic and Linguistics*. Chicago: University of Chicago Press.

Stainton, R. (1994) Using non-sentences: an application of relevance theory. *Pragmatics and Cognition* 2: 269–284.

—— (1995) Non-sentential assertions and semantic ellipsis. *Linguistics and Philosophy* 18: 281–296.

—— (1997a) Utterance meaning and syntactic ellipsis. *Pragmatics and Cognition* 5: 51–78.

—— (1997b) What assertion is not. *Philosophical Studies* 85: 57–73.

—— (1996) *Philosophical Perspectives on Language*. Peterborough, Ont.: Broadview Press.

—— (1998) Quantifier phrases, meaningfulness "in isolation," and ellipsis. *Linguistics and Philosophy* 21: 311–340. [Chapter 41 in this volume.]

—— (2004) In defense of non-sentential assertions. In Z. G. Szabo (ed.), *Semantics vs. Pragmatics*. Oxford: Oxford University Press.

Stalnaker, R. C. (1968) A theory of conditionals. In N. Rescher (ed.), *Studies in Logical Theory*. Oxford: Blackwell, 98–112.

—— (1970) Pragmatics. *Synthèse* 22: 272–289.

—— (1973a) Tenses and pronouns. *Journal of Philosophy* 70: 610–612.

—— (1973b) Presuppositions. *Journal of Philosophical Logic* 2: 447–457.

—— (1974) Pragmatic presupposition. In M. K. Munitz and P. K. Unger (eds.), *Semantics and Philosophy*. New York: New York University Press, 141–177.

—— (1984) *Inquiry*. Cambridge, Mass.: MIT Press.

—— (1989) On Grandy on Grice on language. MIT abstract, *Journal of Philosophy* 86: 526–527.

Stanley, J. (2000) Context and logical form. *Linguistics and Philosophy* 23: 391–433.

Stanley, J., and Szabo, Z. (2000) On quantifier domain restriction. *Mind and Language* 15: 219–261.

Stenius, E. (1967) Mood and language-games. *Synthèse* 17: 254–274.

Stenning, K. (1978) Anaphora as an approach to pragmatics. In M. Halle, J. Bresnan, and G. A. Miller (eds.), *Linguistic Theory and Psychological Reality*. Cambridge, Mass.: MIT Press, 162–200.

Stevenson, C. L. (1957) On what is a poem. *Philosophical Review* 66: 329–362.

Stokhof, M., and L. Torenvliet (eds.) (1990) *Proceedings of the Seventh Amsterdam Colloquium*. Amsterdam: University of Amsterdam, Institute for Language, Logic, and Information.

Strawson, P. F. (1950) On referring. *Mind* 59: 320–344.

—— (1959) *Individuals*. New York: Doubleday.

Stump, G. T. (1978) Interpretive gapping in Montague grammar. *Chicago Linguistics Society* 14: 472–481.

—— (1981) Frequency adjectives. *Linguistics and Philosophy* 4: 221–258.

Suppes, P. (1957) *Introduction to Logic*. Princeton, N.J.: Princeton University Press.

Suppes, P., and W. Rottmayer (1974) Automata. In E. C. Carterette and M. P. Friedman (eds.), *Handbook of Perception*, vol. 1. New York: Academic Press, 335–362.

Sweetser, E. (1996) Mental spaces and the grammar of conditional constructions. In G. Fauconnier and E. Sweetser (eds.), *Spaces, Worlds, and Grammar*. Chicago: University of Chicago Press, 318–333.

Szabolcsi, A., and F. Zwarts (1990) Semantic properties of composed functions and the distribution of WH-phrases. In M. Stokhof and L. Torenvliet (eds.), *Proceedings of the Seventh Amsterdam Colloquium*. Amsterdam: University of Amsterdam, Institute for Language, Logic, and Information, 529–554.

Talmy, L. (1975) Semantics and syntax of motion. In J. P. Kimball (ed.), *Syntax and Semantics*. Syntax and Semantics 4. New York: Academic Press.

—— (1978) The relation of grammar to cognition: a synopsis. In D. Waltz (ed.), *Theoretical Issues in Natural Language Processing*. Urbana-Champaign, Ill.: Association for Computational Linguistics.

—— (1983) How language structures space. In H. Pick and L. Acredolo (eds.), *Spatial Orientation: Theory, Research, and Application*. New York: Plenum, 225–282.

—— (1985) Lexicalization patterns: semantic structure in lexical forms. In T. Shopen (ed.), *Language Typology and Syntactic Description*. Cambridge: Cambridge University Press, 57–149.

—— (1988) Force-dynamics in language and thought. *Cognitive Science* 12: 49–100.

Tarski, A. (1944) The semantic conception of truth and the foundations of semantics. *Philosophy and Phenomenological Research* 4: 346–376.

—— (1956) The concept of truth in formalized languages. In J. H. Woodger (ed. and trans.) *Logic, Semantics, Metamathematics*. Oxford: Oxford University Press, 152–278 . Original work published 1936.

Taylor, B. (1974) The semantics of adverbs. D. Phil. diss., University of Oxford.

Tenny, C. (1987) Grammaticalizing aspect and affectedness. Ph.D. diss., MIT.

—— (1989) *The Aspectual Interface Hypodissertation*. Lexicon Project Working Papers 31. Cambridge, Mass.: MIT.

ter Meulen, A. (1981) An intensional logic for mass terms. *Philosophical Studies* 40: 105–125.

—— (ed.) (1983) *Studies in Model Theoretic Semantics*. Groningen-Amsterdam Studies in Semantics 1. Dordrecht: Foris.

Thomason, R. (1969) Modal logic and metaphysics. In K. Lambert (ed.), *The Logical Way of Doing Things*. New Haven, Conn.: Yale University Press, 119–146.

—— (1970) *Symbolic Logic: An Introduction*. New York: Macmillan.

—— (1972a) Philosophy and formal semantics. In H. Leblanc (ed.), *Truth, Syntax, and Modality*. Amsterdam: North-Holland, 294–307.

—— (1972b) A semantic theory of sortal incorrectness. *Journal of Philosophical Logic* 1: 209–258.

—— (ed.) (1974) *Formal Philosophy: Selected Papers of Richard Montague*. New Haven, Conn.: Yale University Press.

—— (1976) Some extensions of Montague grammar. In B. H. Partee (ed.), *Montague Grammar*. New York: Academic Press, 77–118.

Thomason, R., and R. Stalnaker (1968) Modality and reference. *Noûs* 2: 359–372.

—— (1973) A semantic theory of adverbs. *Linguistic Inquiry* 4: 195–220. [Chapter 29 in this volume.]

Tichý, P. (1971) An approach to intensional analysis. *Noûs* 5: 273–297.

Titchener, E. B. (1912) *Lehrbuch der Psychologie: Part 2*. Leipzig: Barth.

Touretzky, D. S. (1986) *The Mathematics of Inheritance Systems*. Los Altos, Calif.: Morgan Kaufmann.

Travis, C. (1975) *Saying and Understanding: A Generative Theory of Illocutions*. Oxford: Basil Blackwell.

—— (1985) On what is strictly speaking true. *Canadian Journal of Philosophy* 15: 187–229.

—— (1986) *Meaning and Interpretation*. Oxford: Blackwell.

—— (1997) Pragmatics. In B. Hale and C. Wright (eds.), *A Companion to the Philosophy of Language*. Oxford: Blackwell, 87–107.

Trollope, A. (1967) *The Last Chronicle of Barset*. Harmondsworth: Penguin. Originally published 1867.

—— (1972) *Can You Forgive Her?* Harmondsworth: Penguin. Originally published 1864.

—— (1982) *The Way We Live Now*. Oxford: Oxford University Press (World's Classics). Originally published 1875.

—— (1983) *The Prime Minister*. Oxford: Oxford University Press (World's Classics). Originally published 1876.

—— (1984) *Framley Parsonage*. Harmondsworth: Penguin. Originally published 1861.

—— (1991) *The Bertrams*. Oxford: Oxford University Press (World's Classics). Originally published 1859.

—— (1992) *Kept in the Dark*. Oxford: Oxford University Press (World's Classics). Originally published 1882.

—— (1993a) *Sir Harry Hotspur of Humblethwaite* Harmondsworth: Penguin. Originally published 1871.

—— (1993b) *The Fixed Period*. Oxford: Oxford University Press (World's Classics). Originally published 1882.

Turner, M. (1996) *The Literary Mind*. New York: Oxford University Press.

Turner, M., and G. Fauconnier (1995) Conceptual integration and formal expression. *Journal of Metaphor and Symbolic Activity* 10(3): 183–204.

—— (1998) Conceptual integration in counterfactuals. In J. P. Koenig (ed.), *Discourse and Cognition: Bridging the Gap*. Stanford, Calif.: Center for the Study of Language and Information, 269–284.

Turner, R. (1981) Counterfactuals without possible worlds. *Journal of Philosophical Logic* 10: 453–494.

Ulmann, G. (1975) *Sprache und Wahrnehmung: Verfestigen und Aufbrechen von Anschauungen durch Worter*. Frankfurt a. M.: Campus Verlag.

Unger, P. K. (1975) *Ignorance*. Oxford: Oxford University Press.

van Benthem, J. (1984) The logic of semantics. In F. Landman and F. Veltman (eds.), *Varieties of Formal Semantics*. Dordrecht: Foris, 55–80.

van den Berg, M. (1990) A dynamic predicate logic for plurals. In M. Stokhof and L. Torenvliet (eds.), *Proceedings of the Seventh Amsterdam Colloquium*. Amsterdam: ITLI.

Vanderveken, Daniel (1983) A model-theoretical semantics for illocutionary forces. *Logique et Analyse* 26: 103–104.

—— (1990) *Meaning and Speech Acts*. Vol. 1: *Principles of Language Use*. Cambridge: Cambridge University Press.

—— (1991a) Non literal speech acts and conversational maxims. In E. Lepore and R. Van Gulick (eds.), *John Searle and His Critics*. Oxford: Blackwell, 371–384.

—— (1991b) *Meaning and Speech Acts*. Vol. 2: *Formal Semantics of Success and Satisfaction*. Cambridge: Cambridge University Press.

—— (1994) A complete formulation of a simple logic of elementary illocutionary acts. In S. L. Tsohatsidis (ed.), *Foundations of Speech Act Theory*. New York: Routledge, 99–131.

—— (1995) A new formulation of the logic of propositions. In M. Marion and R. Cohen (eds.), *Quebec Studies in the Philosophy of Science*. Part 1: *Logic, Mathematics and Physics and History of Science*. Boston Studies in the Philosophy of Science vol. 177. Dordrecht: Kluwer, 95–106.

—— (1997a) Quantification and the logic of generalized propositions. In C. Martinez, U. Rivas, and L. Villegas (eds.), *Truth in Perspective: Recent Issues on Logic, Representation and Ontology*. Averbury Series in Philosophy. Brookfield, Vt.: Ashgate, 137–158.

—— (1997b) Formal pragmatics of non literal meaning. *Linguistische Berichte* 8: 324–341.

—— (1999) *The Basic Logic of Action*. Cahiers d'Epistémiologie 9907. Montreal: Université du Québec.

—— (2001a) Universal grammar and speech act theory. In D. Vanderveken and S. Kubo (eds.), *Essays in Speech Act Theory*. Amsterdam: John Benjamins, 25–62.

—— (2001b) Illocutionary logic and discourse typology. *Revue internationale de philosophie* 55: 243–256.

—— (2001c) *Attempt and Action Generation towards the Foundations of the Logic of Action*. Montreal: Cahiers d'Epistémiologie, Université du Québec à Montréal.

—— (2004a) Formal Ontology, Propositional Identity and Truth. In D. Vanderveken (ed.), *Logic, Thought and Action*. Dordrecht: Kluwer.

—— (2004b) Attempt, Success and Action Generation. In D. Vanderveken (ed.), *Logic, Thought and Action*. Dordrecht: Kluwer.

—— (forthcoming a) Modality in the logic of propositions. In F. Lepage and E. Thijsse (eds.), *Partial, Dynamic and Epistemic Logics*. Dordrecht: Kluwer.

—— (forthcoming b) *Meaning, Action and Dialogue*. Cambridge: Cambridge University Press.

—— (forthcoming c) *Propositions, Truth and Thought*. Dordrecht: Kluwer.

Van Dijk, T. E. (ed.) (1976), *Pragmatics of Language and Literature*. Amsterdam: North-Holland.

Van Fraassen, B. (1969) Presuppositions, supervaluations and free logic. In K. Lambert (ed.), *The Logical Way of Doing Things*. New Haven, Conn.: Yale University Press, 67–92.

Van Hock, K. (1996) Conceptual locations for reference in American sign language. In G. Fauconnier and E. Sweetser (eds.), *Spaces, Worlds, and Grammar*. Chicago: University of Chicago Press, 334–350.

Veltman, F. (1976) Prejudices, presuppositions, and the theory of conditionals. In J. Groenendijk and M. Stokhof (eds.), *Proceedings of the Amsterdam Colloquium on Montague Grammar and Related Topics*. Amsterdam Papers in Formal Grammar 1. Amsterdam: University of Amsterdam, Centrale Interfaculteit.

Vendler, Z. (1957) Verbs and times. *Philosophical Review* 56: 143–160.

———— (1967a) *Linguistics and Philosophy*. Ithaca, N.Y.: Cornell University Press.

———— (1967b) Singular terms. *Linguistics and Philosophy*. Ithaca, N.Y.: Cornell University Press.

Venn, John (1971) *Symbolic Logic*. 2nd ed. Bronx, N.Y.: Chelsea. Originally published 1894.

Verkuyl, H. (1972) *On the Compositional Nature of the Aspects*. Dordrecht: Reidel.

Vermazen, Bruce (1967) Review of J. J. Katz and P. Postal, *An Integrated Theory of Linguistic Descriptions*, and J. J. Katz, *Philosophy of Language*. *Synthèse* 17: 350–365.

Verma, M. K., and K. P. Mohanan (1991) *Experiencer Subjects in South Asian Language*. Chicago: University of Chicago Press.

Visentini, B. et al. (eds) (1970) *Linguaggi nella società e nella tecnica*. Milan: Edizioni de Communità.

von Stechow, A. (1974). ∈-λ-kontextfreie Sprachen: ein Beitrag zu einer natürlich formalen Semantik. *Linguistische Berichte* 34: 1–33.

von Stechow, A., and D. Wunderlich (eds.) (1991) *Semantics: An International Handbook of Contemporary Research*. Berlin: de Gruyter.

von Wright, G. H. (1963) *Norm and Action: A Logical Inquiry*. London: Routledge and Kegan Paul.

Waismann, F. (1945) Verifiability. *Proceedings of the Aristotelian Society* 19(suppl.): 119–150. Reprinted in A. Flew (ed), *Logic and Language* (*first series*) (Oxford: Basil Blackwell, 1951), 117–144.

Walker, D., A. Zampolli, and N. Calzolari (eds.) (1995) *Automating the Lexicon*. New York: Oxford University Press.

Walker, R. C. S. (1975) Conversational implicatures. In S. Blackburn (ed.), *Meaning, Reference, and Necessity*. Cambridge: Cambridge University Press, 133–181.

Wallace, J. (1965) Sortal predicates and quantification. *Journal of Philosophy* 62: 8–13.

Warnock, G. J. (1973) Some types of performative utterance. In I. Berlin (ed.), *Essays on J. L. Austin*. Oxford: Clarendon, 69–89.

Watson, J. (1924) *Psychology from the Standpoint of a Behaviorist*. 2nd ed. Philadelphia: Lippincott. Originally published 1919.

Watson, J. D. (1965) *Molecular Biology of the Gene*. New York: W. A. Benjamin.

Webber, A. (1978) *A Formal Approach to Discourse Anaphora*. Report 3761. Boston: Bolt, Beranek, and Clewman.

Weinreich, U. (1966) Explorations in semantic theory. In T. Sebeok (ed.), *Current Trends in Linguistics*, vol. 3. The Hague: Mouton.

———— (1972) *Explorations in Semantic Theory*. The Hague: Mouton.

Weinstein, S. (1974) Truth and demonstratives. *Noûs* 8: 179–184. [Chapter 38 in this volume.]

Wells, R. S. (1947) Immediate constituents. *Language* 23: 81–117.

Werning, M. (2003) Compositionality, context, categories and the indeterminacy of translation. *Erkenntnis* 60: 145–178.

Wertheimer, M. (1923) Laws of organization in perceptual forms. In W. D. Ellis (ed.), *A Source Book of Gestalt Psychology*. London: Routledge and Kegan Paul, 71–88.

Westerståhl, D. (1989) Quantifiers in formal and natural languages. In D. Gabbay and F. Guenthner (eds.), *Handbook of Philosophical Logic* vol. 4. Dordrecht: Kluwer, 1–132.

———— (1998) On mathematical proofs of the vacuity of compositionality. *Linguistics and Philosophy* 21: 635–643.

———— (2001) Quantifiers. In L. Goble (ed.), *The Blackwell Guide to Philosophical Logic*. Oxford: Blackwell, 437–460.

Wheatley, H, B. (ed.) (1942) *The Diary of Samuel Pepys*. 2 vols. New York: Heritage Press. Originally published 1893.

White, Alan R. (1958) Synonymous expressions. *Philosophical Quarterly* 8: 193–207.

Whitehead, A. N., and B. Russel (1910) *Principia Mathematica*. Cambridge: Cambridge University Press.

Wierzbicka, A. (1988) *The Semantics of Grammar*. Amsterdam: John Benjamins.

Wiggins, David (1997) Meaning and truth conditions: from Frege's grand design to Davidson's. In B. Hale and C. Wright (eds.), *A Companion to the Philosophy of Language*. Oxford: Blackwell, 3–28.

Wilensky, R. (1991) Extending the lexicon by exploiting subregularities. Report UCB/CSD 91/618. Computer Science Department, University of California-Berkeley.

Wilks, Y. (1975a) A preferential pattern seeking semantics for natural language inference. *Artificial Intelligence* 6: 53–74.

———— (1975b) An intelligent analyser and understander for English. *Communications of the ACM* 18: 264–274.

Wilks, Y., D. C. Fass, M. Guo, J. McDonald, T. Plate, and B. Slator (1988) A tractable machine dictionary as a resource for computational semantics. In B. Boguraev and T. Briscoe (eds.), *Computational Lexicography for Natural Language Processing*. Harlow, Essex: Longman.

Williams. E. (1981) Argument structure and morphology. *Linguistic Review* 1: 81–114.

Wilson, D. (1976) *Presuppositions and Non-truth-conditional Semantics*. London: Academic Press.

———— (2000) Metarepresentation in linguistic communication. In D. Sperber (ed.), *Metarepresentations*. New York: Oxford University Press, 411–448.

Wilson, D., and D. Sperber (1981) On Grice's theory of conversation. In P. Werth (ed.), *Conversation and Discourse*. London: Croom Helm, 155–178.

———— (1988) Mood and the analysis of non-declarative sentences. In J. Dancy, J. Moravcsik, and C. Taylor (eds.), *Human Agency: Language, Duty and Value*. Stanford, Calif.: Stanford University Press, 229–324.

———— (1993) Linguistic form and relevance. *Lingua* 90: 1–25.

———— (2000) Truthfulness and relevance. *UCL Working Papers in Linguistics* 12: 215–254. Reprinted in *Mind* 111: 583–632.

Wilson, R. J. (1979) *Introduction to Graph Theory*, 2nd ed. London: Longmans. Originally published 1972.

Wingfield, R. D. (1995) *Hard Frost*. New York: Bantam.

Wittgenstein, L. (1953) *Philosophical Investigations*. Oxford: Basil Blackwell.

———— (1961) *Tractatus logico-philosophicus*. London: Routledge and Kegan Paul.

Wunderlich, D. (1970) *Tempus und Zeitreferenz im Deutschen*. Munich: Max Hueber.

Wundt, W. (1904–1923) *Völkerpsychologie: Eine Untersuchung der Entweklungsgasetze von Sprache, Mythus und Sitte*. 10 vols. Leipzig: w. Engelmann.

Yanofsky, N. (1978) NP utterances. *Papers from the Regional Meeting, Chicago Linguistics Society* 14: 491–502.

Zadrozny, V. (1992) On compositional semantics. Paper presented at COLING-92, Nantes, France.

———— (1994) From compositional to systematic semantics. *Linguistics and Philosophy* 17: 329–342.

Zaefferer, D. (1987) *Bare Plurals, Naked Relatives, and Their Kin*. Stanford, Calif.: Center for the Study of Language and Information, 87–112.

Zbikowski, L. (1997) Conceptual blending and song. Unpublished manuscript, University of Chicago.

Zeevat, H. (1989) A compositional approach to discourse representation theory. *Linguistics and Philosophy* 12: 95–131.

Ziff, P. (1966) The non-synonymy of active and passive sentences. *Philosophical Review* 75: 226–232.

Zwicky, A. M., and J. M. Sadock (1975) Ambiguity tests and how to fail them. *Syntax and Semantics*. Syntax and Semantics 4. *1–36*.

———— (1987) A non-test for ambiguity. *Canadian Journal of Philosophy* 17: 185–187.

INDEX

-er, ambiguity of, 164
-un, ambiguity of, 164
a few, 524, 525
Abelian group, 716
above, 576
  ambiguity of, 582–585
Abraham, W., 657
absolute term, 812
acceptability judgement, 13,
  449–450, 514, 803, 807,
  809, 813
access principle (conceptual
  semantics), 348–349
accessibility, 719, 862
accommodation, 803–816
  of presupposition, 804, 808
  rules of, 804, 808, 808, 810,
    811, 813
acquisition, of concept (*see*
  concept acquisition)
  of language (*see* language
    acquisition)
across, 334, 564–573
action (ontology), 738
action sentence, 738, 740, 741,
  744
  logical form (logical
    formula), 735–745
action verb, 737, 740, 743, 744,
  745

activity scheduling, 334
Adams, Robert, 794
adicity, 37
adjective, 46, 261, 541–562
  affirmative, 542
  attributive, 230–231, 541,
    560
  cardinal numeral (*see* cardinal
    numeral)
  categorial grammar, 197
  comparative, 544, 550, 551,
    556, 557
  demonstrative (*see*
    demonstrative adjective)
  English, 372
  extensional, 543
  gradable, 339, 845
  modal, 600
  non-extensional, 543
  predicative, 541, 542
  privative, 542
adverb, 139, 563, 576, 577,
  593–604, 605–625
  attitudinal, 826
  categorial grammar, 198
  conjunctive, 602
  distribution, 594, 596, 597,
    599, 600, 603
  illocutionary, 826
  modal, 611

  of domain, 601–602
  of evaluation, 597, 601
  of frequency, 596
  of manner, 594
  of modality, 598–601
  pragmatic, 602–603
  scope, 606–609, 611–612
  semantics (*see* adverbial
    logic)
  sentential, 593, 597, 609–
    614, 826
  speaker-oriented, 594, 596,
    597
  subject-oriented, 594, 595
  verb phrasal, 593, 609–614
adverbial logic, entailment,
  617–620, 620–622
  formation rules, 614–615
  model, 615–616
adverbial modification, 736–
  745
adversativity, 647
agency (ontology), 740, 744,
  745
agent (ontology), 739
agentive role, 377, 383, 386
aggregate, 337, 405, 407, 411,
  413, 414, 416, 418, 421
aggregation, 335, 407, 408, 409,
  411, 412, 414, 416, 421